OXFORD MEDICAL PUBLICATIONS

Oxford textbook of public health

Editors

Walter W. Holland, MD, FRCGP, FRCP, FFCM

Professor of Clinical Epidemiology and Social Medicine,
Department of Community Medicine, and Honorary Director,
Social Medicine and Health Services Research Unit,
St. Thomas's Hospital Medical School (United Medical Schools),
London SE1 7EH, England.

Roger Detels, MD, MS

Professor of Epidemiology and Dean,
School of Public Health, Center for Health Sciences,
University of California, Los Angeles, CA 90024, USA.

George Knox, MD, BS, FRCP, FFCM

Professor of Social Medicine, Department of Social Medicine,
Health Services Research Centre,
University of Birmingham Medical School,
Edgbaston, Birmingham B15 2TG, England.

Ellie Breeze, MSc

Research Assistant, Department of Community Medicine,
St. Thomas's Hospital Medical School,
(United Medical Schools), London SE1 7EH, England.

Oxford textbook of public health

VOLUME 4

Specific applications

Edited by

Walter W. Holland, Roger Detels, and
George Knox
with the assistance of
Ellie Breeze

OXFORD NEW YORK TORONTO

OXFORD UNIVERSITY PRESS

1985

Oxford University Press, Walton Street, Oxford OX2 6DP

Oxford New York Toronto
Delhi Bombay Calcutta Madras Karachi
Kuala Lumpur Singapore Hong Kong Tokyo
Nairobi Dar es Salaam Cape Town
Melbourne Auckland

and associated companies in
Beirut Berlin Mexico City Nicosia

Oxford is a trade mark of Oxford University Press

British Library Cataloguing in Publication Data
Oxford textbook of public health.—(Oxford
medical publications)
Vol 4: Specific applications
1. Public health
I. Holland, Walter W.   II. Detels, Roger
III. Knox, George
614   RA425
ISBN 0-19-261449-5

Library of Congress Cataloging in Publication Data
(Revised for volume 4)
Main entry under title:
Oxford textbook of public health.
(Oxford medical publications)
Bibliography: p.
Includes index.
Contents: v. 1. History, determinants, scope, and
strategies —   — v. 4. Specific applications.
1. Public health—Collected works. I. Holland,
Walter W. II. Series. [DNLM: 1. Public Health.
WA 100 098]
RA425.09 1984   362.1   84-14717
ISBN 0-19-261449-5

Typeset by Cotswold Typesetting, Cheltenham
Printed in Great Britain by Thomson Litho Ltd, East Kilbride, Scotland

Preface

It is not an easy task to follow in the footsteps of such a renowned editor as Professor Hobson. We were, however, very honoured when, on the retirement of Professor Hobson, the Oxford University Press approached us about taking up the challenge of revising Hobson's *Theory and practice of public health*. Since this work first appeared in February 1961 Professor Hobson was responsible for taking it through no less than five editions. Many eminent public health academics and practitioners have contributed to this book and it has been recognized as a standard textbook on the subject. Sadly, Professor Hobson died after a long illness at the end of November 1982. After an early training in public health starting as a medical officer of health and then as a specialist in hygiene and epidemiology in the army, he went on to be a lecturer in social medicine at Sheffield University, becoming professor in 1949. From 1957 until his retirement, he served in a variety of posts at the WHO, where his major responsibilities were always concerned with education and training. His interest in this and in the international aspects of health were well exemplified by the first edition of *Theory and practice of public health*. One of the major strengths of the book has been its international nature and its link to the WHO.

On accepting the daunting task of revising this major work our first step was to look dispassionately at its role within public health, a field which has evolved and changed greatly over the last 25 years. We decided that although this book is held in great esteem in the western world it was appropriate now to introduce major revisions and thus, increase its relevance to the problems facing us as we approach the twenty-first century. A particularly important advance has been the recognition in recent years that the problems in public health facing developing countries are quite different to those facing the developed world. The interests of WHO, quite correctly, have been focused on developing countries. We consider that this book should concentrate on presenting a comprehensive view of public health as it relates to developed countries. (Perhaps there is a place now for a comparable textbook concerned specifically with developing countries.) This is not to say however, that the content will not prove relevant and of interest to the student of public health from a developing country.

The *Oxford textbook of public health* attempts to portray the philosophy and underlying principles of the practice of public health. The methods used for the investigation and the solution of public health problems are described and examples given of how these methods are applied in practice. It is aimed primarily at postgraduate students and practitioners of public health but most clinicians and others concerned with public health issues will find some chapters relevant to their concerns. It is intended to be a comprehensive textbook present in the library of every institution concerned with the health sciences. The term 'public' is used quite deliberately to portray the field. Public health is concerned with defining the problems facing communities in the prevention of illness and thus studies of disease aetiology and promotion of health. It covers the investigation, promotion, and evaluation of optimal health services to communities and is concerned with the wider aspects of health within the general context of health and the environment. Other terms in common use, such as community medicine, preventive medicine, social medicine, and population medicine have acquired different meaning according to the country or setting. This gives rise to confusion and we have avoided their use since this book is directed to a worldwide audience. Public health, we believe, is more evocative of the basic philosophy which underlies this book.

The first volume aims to lead the reader through the historical determinants of health to the overall scope and strategies of public health. Volume 2 is concerned with the process of public health promotion and Volume 3 with the investigative methods used in public health.

The final volume of this series attempts to pull together all the threads of the earlier volumes which have considered the theory, policies, strategies and research methodologies that form the basis of public health endeavour. Specific diseases and the needs of specific groups within a community have been touched on in greater or lesser detail, in earlier volumes. Here, the major disease groups, systems of the body, and special care groups are treated systematically to review the public health issues they raise, and the extent to which the methodologies described earlier have been applied to their control and prevention.

The volume is divided into three sections, the first of which is concerned with the application of public health methods to specific disease processes including acute infectious episodes, diseases related to nutrition, trauma, developmental defects, degenerative neurological diseases, psychiatric conditions, and neoplasms. Each chapter attempts to review the public health impact of the diseases in question, including their epidemiology and the contribution of public health measures. Of particular emphasis is the potential for prevention that enquiry into the aetiology has revealed, and the role of public health interventions in implementing programmes of prevention.

Leading on from specific disease states, the next section looks at the role of public health in relation to the various systems of the body. The intention is not to provide an exhaustive description of the conditions affecting each system, but to discuss the facets of the system where public health investigation has had (or indeed in some cases has failed to make) a major contribution. It will be evident to the reader that the extent to which the public-health approach has contributed to research and strategies to prevent and treat conditions affecting the various systems of the body varies tremendously. The cardiovascular system and the respiratory system provide classical examples of the application of the public health approach to a health problem. Extensive epidemiological research has clarified the causation of these conditions and public health measures form the basic framework for implementing control measures. Investigations of gastrointestinal diseases, metabolic and endocrine disorders, and conditions affecting the genito-urinary system have on the other hand, relied more on clinical than public health orientated research. The chapters dealing with these systems however describe the epidemiological work that has been carried out and its relevance to clinical practice. The chapter on the genito-urinary system, for example, illustrates the value of national and international comparative studies in informing policy decision makers of different management practices and outcomes. The problems presented by the investigation of musculo-skeletal and dental conditions are clearly demonstrated in this section of Volume 4.

The final section of this volume treats the unique problems and health service needs of special client groups. Again, this is not intended to be comprehensive or exhaustive, the emphasis being placed on demonstrating the application of public health approaches to a variety of different problems. These include investigations to identify the needs of special client groups and the extent to which these needs are satisfied, and the application of public health measures to solving the problems of these groups.

The chapter on acute emergencies is an excellent example of the ways in which epidemiological investigation can be applied to surgical conditions, providing evidence from which conclusions can be drawn about the most appropriate form of treatment. The chapter on adolescence demonstrates the relavence of a multidisciplinary approach to health problems, and the difficulties of tackling some of the problems experienced by adolescents in the changing society around us. The discussion of handicap – both physical and mental – illustrates the application of epidemiological and public health methodology to both the prevention as well as the development of care policies for specific groups of individuals.

Health care policy decision-making is fraught with difficulties as is illustrated by the chapter on maternity care, theoretically the simplest of examples, but one which demonstrates the complexity of the issues involved. The chapter on the special needs of the elderly also shows how complicated the problems facing modern public health are. In outlining the difficulties faced by the unemployed and disadvantaged Illsley demonstrates the way the social scientist approaches a public health problem.

This volume should give the reader some idea of the vast scope of public health, the range of fields and problems for which public health has a major contribution to make, and the multidisciplinary nature of much of the work. It attempts to review how we can approach and develop a methodology for the investigation, prevention, and control of the major public health problems in our society at this time.

The development of public health policy is dependent upon a series of scientific methods, and we do not attempt in this book to cover all the methods and their applications. However, it is to be hoped that those examples that have been chosen will illustrate to the reader the way in which particular problems can be approached. Each chapter includes a comprehensive list of further reading which should equip the reader with the means of obtaining a deeper knowledge should he or she wish to pursue any theme further.

This is the first of what we hope will be many editions. As each chapter was submitted to the editors we have attempted to identify gaps and areas of overlap. There is no doubt, however, that some remain. It is only through feedback from readers that we will be able to adapt, modify, and improve further editions. If the book is successful it will be entirely due to the effort of the contributors who undertook with great patience a tremendous amount of work. They were bombarded with instructions, advice, reminders, and modifications and we would like to express our thanks and extend our apologies to all of them. Our gratitude also goes to our secretaries and assistants who coped so admirably with the enormous task of compiling this work. We hope that it will be widely read by all those concerned with the formulation and execution of public health policy and that it will provide a suitable framework for devising approaches to some of the problems challenging public health today.

W.W.H.
R.D.
G.K.

Contents

Contributors

Eva Alberman
   Professor of Clinical Epidemiology, The London and St Bartholomew's Hospital Medical College, Turner Street, London E1 2AD, England.

John A.D. Anderson, MA, MD, DPH, FFCM, FRCGP
   Professor of Community Medicine, Unversity of London, United Medical and Dental Schools of Guy's and St Thomas' Hospitals, Guy's Campus, and Honorary Consultant Rehabilitation and Occupational Medicine, Guy's Hospital, London SE1 9RT, England.

Elizabeth M. Badley, DPhil, MSc
   Deputy Director, Arthritis and Rheumatism Council Epidemiology Research Unit, University of Manchester Medical School, England.

Dean Baker, MD
   Assistant Professor of Public Health, School of Public Health, Division of Epidemiology, CHS 71-269, University of California, Los Angeles, CA 90024, USA.

Ian A. Baker, MB, BS, MRCP, MSc(Soc. Med.)
   Specialist in Community Medicine, Bristol and Weston Health Authority, Mannlife House, 10 Marlborough Street, Bristol BS1 3NP, England.

John S. Bryden, MSc, MBChB, FFCM, MBCS
   Senior Epidemiologist, Institute of Neurological Sciences, Glasgow G51 4TF, Scotland.

Sabri Challah, MA, MB, BChir
   Lecturer, Department of Community Medicine, St Thomas's Hospital Medical School, United Medical and Dental Schools, London SE1 7EH, England.

J.R.T. Colley, MD, BSc, FFCM
   Professor of Community Medicine and Director, MRC National Survey of Health and Development, University of Bristol, Department of Epidemiology and Community Medicine, Canynge Hall, Whiteladies Road, Bristol BS8 2PR, England.

J. Mark Elwood, DSc, MD, SM, FRCP(C), DCH, MFCM
   Professor and Head, Department of Community Health, University of Nottingham, Queen's Medical Centre, Nottingham NG7 2UH, England.

Bruce L. Evatt, MD
   Director, Division of Host Factors, Center of Infectious Diseases, Centers for Disease Control (United States Public Health Service), Atlanta, GA 30333, USA.

John R. Froines, PhD
   Associate Professor of Public Health, School of Public Health, Division of Environmental and Occupational Health Science, CHS 56-071, University of California, Los Angeles, CA 90024, USA.

Tom Fryers, MB, ChB, DRCOG, DPH, MD, PhD, FFCM
   Specialist in Community Medicine, North West Regional Health Authority, Director, Psychiatric and Mental Handicap Registers, Salford, and Senior Lecturer in Community Medicine, Department of Community Medicine, University of Manchester Stopford Building, Oxford Road, Manchester M13 9PT, England.

N.S. Galbraith, MB, FRCP, FFCM, DPH
   Director, Communicable Disease Surveillance Centre, London and Honorary Senior Lecturer in Community Medicine, London School of Hygiene and Tropical Medicine, London WC1, England.

John C. Greene, DMD, MPD
   Dean, School of Dentistry, University of California, San Francisco, CA 94143, USA.

Clark W. Heath, Jr., MD
   Professor of Community Health, Department of Community Health, Emory University School of Medicine, 1518 Clifton Road, NE, Atlanta, GA 30322, USA.

Basil S. Hetzel, MD
   Chief, Division of Human Nutrition, Commonwealth Scientific and Industrial Research Organisation, Kintore Avenue, Adelaide, SA 5000, Australia.

Raymond Illsley, PhD
   Professor of Medical Sociology, University of Aberdeen, and, until recently, Director, MRC Sociology Research Unit, Westburn Road, Aberdeen AB9 2ZE, Scotland.

Bryan Jennett, MD, FRCS
   Professor of Neurosurgery, Institute of Neurological Sciences, University of Glasgow, Glasgow G51 4TF, Scotland.

Robert L. Kane, MD
   Professor, UCLA School of Medicine and UCLA School of Public Health, and Senior Researcher, The Rand Corporation, 1700 Main Street, Santa Monica, CA 90406, USA.

H. Keen, MD, FRCP
   Professor of Human Metabolism, Guy's Hospital Medical School, and Director, Unit for Metabolic Medicine, and Diabetic Clinic Physician, Guy's Hospital, London SE1 9RT, England.

John F. Kurtzke, MD, FACP
   Professor and Vice Chairman, Department of Neurology and Professor, Department of Community and Family Medicine, Georgetown University School of Medicine, Washington DC, and Chief Neurology Service and Chief Neuroepidemiology Research Program, Veterans Administration Medical Center, Washington DC and

Consultant in Neurology to Surgeon General of the Navy and the USNH Bethesda MD (Rear Admiral, Medical Corps US Naval Reserve).

M.J.S. Langman, BSc, MD, FRCP

Professor of Therapeutics and Honorary Consultant Physician, University Hospital Department of Therapeutics, Queens Medical Centre, Nottingham NG7 2UH, England.

Barry Lewis, MD, PhD, FRCP, FRCPath

Professor and Head, Department of Chemical Pathology and Metabolic Disorders, St Thomas's Hospital Medical School, and Honorary Consultant, St Thomas' Hospital, London SE1 7EH, England.

R.F.A. Logan, BSc, MBChB, MSc, MRCP

Senior Lecturer in Clinical Epidemiology and Honorary Consultant Physician, University Hospital, Department of Community Medicine, University of Nottingham Medical School, Queen's Medical Centre, Nottingham NG7 2UH, England.

Richard J. Madeley, MB, BS, MSc, MFCM

Senior Lecturer, Department of Community Health, University of Nottingham Medical School, Queen's Medical Centre, Nottingham NG7 2UH, England.

Ken Mullen, MA

Research Officer, MRC Medical Sociology Unit, Westburn Road, Aberdeen AB9 2ZE, Scotland.

Robert I. Pfeffer, MD

Associate Professor, Department of Neurology, University of California, Irvine, CA 92668, USA.

Leon S. Robertson, PhD

Research Scientist, Department of Epidemiology and Public Health, Yale University Medical School, 60 College Street, New Haven, CT 06510, USA.

Geoffrey Rose, DM, DSc, FRCP, FFCM

Professor of Epidemiology, London School of Hygiene and Tropical Medicine, London and Physician, St Mary's Hospital, London, England.

Rodolfo Saracci, MD, FACE

Chief, Unit of Analytical Epidemiology, International Agency for Research on Cancer, 150 Cours Albert Thomas, 69372 Lyon Cedex 08, France.

Michael Shepherd, MD, FRCP, FRCPsych, DPM

Professor of Epidemiological Psychiatry, Institute of Psychiatry, University of London, De Crespigny Park, London SE5 8AF, England.

R.F. Spicer

Medical Director, London Youth Advisory Centre, 29 Prince of Wales Road, London NW5 3LG, England.

Anthony J. Wing, MA, MD, FRCP

Consultant Nephrologist, St Thomas' Hospital, and Chairman, EDTA Registry, St Thomas' Hospital, London SE1 7EH, England.

Philip H.N. Wood, MB, FRCP, FFCM

Director, Arthritis and Rheumatism Council Epidemiology Research Unit, and Professor of Community Medicine, University of Manchester and Honorary Specialist in Community Medicine, North Western Regional Health Authority, England.

Samuel J. Wycoff, DMD, MPH

Chairman, Department of Dental Public Health, University of California, San Francisco School of Dentistry, San Francisco, CA 94143, USA.

Abbreviations

ACCN	Administrative Co-ordinating Committee on Nutrition	DRO	Disablement Resettlement Officer
		EAD	Entry into active duty
ACGIH	American Conference of Governmental Industrial Hygienists	EASD	European Association for the Study of Diabetes
ADL	Activities of daily living	EBV	Epstein–Barr virus
AFP	Alpha-fetoprotein	ECHO virus	Enteric cytopathic human orphan virus
AGN	Advisory Group on Nutrition	EDTA	European Dialysis and Transplant Association
AH	Alkylosing hyperostosis		
AHA	Area Health Authority	EEC	European Economic Community
AL	Acute leukaemia	ERC	Employment Rehabilitation Centre
ALS	Amyotrophic lateral sclerosis	ESD	Employment Services Division of the Manpower Services Commission
ANSI	American National Standards Institute		
APF	Acidulated phosphate fluoride	ESRD	End-stage renal failure
APHA	American Public Health Association	ESRF	End-stage renal failure
ARF	Acute renal failure	FAO	Food and Agriculture Organization
AS	Alkylosing spondylitis	FAS	Fetal alcohol syndrome
BCME	bis-chloromethylether	FEP	Free erythrocyte protoporphyrin
BDA	British Diabetic Association	FEV	Forced expiratory volume
BL	Burkitt's lymphoma	FEV_1	Forced expiratory volume in one second
BMG	Benign monoclonal gammopathy	FVC	Forced vital capacity
BMI	Body mass index	Gaw	Airways conductance
BP	Blood pressure	GDM	Gestational diabetes mellitus
BT	Brain tumour	GHS	General Household Survey
CAT	Computer-assisted tomography	GNP	Gross national product
CDH	Congenital dislocation of the hip	GOA	Generalized osteoarthritis
CDSC	Communicable Disease Surveillance Centre	GP	General practitioner
CGL	Chronic granulocytic leukaemia	G6PD	Glucose-6-phosphate dehydrogenase
CHD	Coronary heart disease	GPMU	General Practitioner Maternity Unit
CHO	Cholesterol	HBsAg	Hepatitus B virus antigen
CLL	Chronic lymphocytic leukaemia	HBV	Hepatitus B virus
CNS	Central nervous system	HC	Huntingdon's chorea
CNSLD	Chronic non-specific lung disease	HD	Hodgkin's disease
CRF	Chronic renal failure	HDFP	Hypertension Detection and Follow up Program
CSF	Cerebrospinal fluid		
CSO	Central Office of Statistics	HDN	Haemolytic disease of the newborn
CV	Closing volume	HIP	Health Insurance Plan of Greater New York
DBPC	Dibromo-3-chloropropane	HIPE	Hospital In-patient Enquiry
DD	Disc degeneration	HLD	Hepatolenticular disease
DHHS	Department of Health and Human Services	IARC	International Agency for Research into Cancer
DHSS	Department of Health and Social Security		
DISH	Diffuse idiopathic skeletal hypertosis	ICD	International Classification of Diseases
DM	Diabetes mellitus	ICIDH	International Classification of Impairments, Disabilities, and Handicaps
DMFT	Decayed, missing, and filled permanent teeth		
DNA	Deoxyribonucleic acid	IDD	Iodine deficiency disorder

IDDM	Insulin-dependent diabetes melitus		PCB	Polychlorinated biphenyl
IFAD	International Fund for Agricultural Development		PCV	Packed cell volume
			PDA	Patent ductus arteriosis
Ig	Immunoglobulin		PEFR	Peak expiratory flow rate
IGT	Impaired glucose tolerance		PEM	Protein energy malnutrition
IM	Infectious mononucleosis		PHLS	Public Health Laboratory Service
IQ	Intelligence quotient		PID	Pelvic inflammatory disease
ITP	Idiopathic thrombocytopenic purpura		PK	Pyruvate kinase
IUGR	Intra-uterine growth retardation		PMP	Polymalgia rheumatica
JCA	Juvenile chronic arthritis		PNH	Paoxysmal nocturnal haemoglobinuria
LBW	Low birthweight		PRD	Primary renal disease
LD	Lymphocyte-defined		RA	Rheumatoid arthritis
LSD	Lysergic acid		RAW	Airway resistance
LYAC	London Youth Advisory Centre		RCP	Royal College of Physicians
MAFF	Ministry of Agriculture, Food, and Fisheries		Rh	Rhesus
MD	Muscular dystrophy		RHD	Rheumatic heart disease
MG	Myasthenia gravis		RNA	Ribonucleic acid
MM	Multiple myeloma		SBA	Spina bifida aperta
MMEF	Maximum expiratory flow rate		SDAT	Senile dementia of the Alzheimer type
MND	Motor neuron disease		SGaw	Specific airways conductance
MOEM	Medical Officer of Environmental Health		SHE	Sentinel health events
MRC	Medical Research Council		SHHD	Scottish Home and Health Department
MRP	Medical removal protection		SLE	Systemic lupus erythematosus
MS	Multiple sclerosis		SMR	Standardized mortality ratio
MSC	Manpower Services Commission		SRaw	Specific airways resistance
MV	Metatarsus varus		SS	Systemic sclerosis
NAYPCAS	National Association of Young People's Counselling and Advisory Service		SUA	Serum uric acid
			2,4,5,T	2,4,5-trichlorophenoxyacetic acid
NCEN	National Council on Egg Nutrition		TCDD	Tetrachlorodibenzodioxin
NCHS	National Center for Health Statistics		TCV	Talipes calcaneovalgus
NDDG	National Diabetes Data Group		TEV	Talipes equinovarus
NFPA	National Fire Protection Association		TLV	Threshold limit value
NHL	Non-Hodgkin's lymphoma		TOPS	Training Opportunities Scheme
NHLBI	National Heart, Lung and Blood Institute		TSD	Training Services Division of the Manpower Services Commission
NHLI	National Heart and Lung Institute			
NHS	National Health Service		TSH	Thyroid stimulating hormone
NIDDM	Non-insulin dependent diabetes mellitus		UGDP	University Group Diabetes Programme
NIH	National Institutes of Health		UK	United Kingdom
NIOSH	National Institute for Occupational Safety and Health		UN	United Nations
			UNDP	United Nations Development Program
NOHS	National Occupational Hazard Survey		UNICEF	United Nations Children's Fund
NPC	Nasopharyngial carcinoma		UNRRA	United Nations Relief and Rehabilitation Administration
NTD	Neural-tube defect			
OA	Osteoarthrosis		UTI	Urinary tract infection
OGTT	Oral glucose tolerance test		US	United States
OHE	Office of Health Economics		UV	Ultraviolet radiation
OPCS	Office of Population Censuses and Surveys		VDT	Visual (or video) display terminal
OSHA	Occupational Safety and Health Authority		WHO	World Health Organization

Disease processes

1 The application of epidemiological methods in the investigation and control of an acute episode of infection

N. S. Galbraith

INTRODUCTION

> *The most terrible outbreak of cholera which ever occurred in this Kingdom, is probably that which took place in Broad Street, Golden Square, and the adjoining streets, a few weeks ago. Within two hundred and fifty yards of the spot where Cambridge Street joins Broad Street, there were upwards of five hundred fatal attacks of cholera in ten days* (Snow 1855).

In this outbreak of cholera near Golden Square in 1854, John Snow established the method of epidemiological investigation of an acute episode of infection and applied the method to disease control. The purpose of this chapter is to describe this method and its use in the investigation and control of episodes of acute infectious disease and of toxic conditions epidemiologically resembling acute infections. A general account of infectious disease control is given in Volume 2, Chapter 2 and for descriptions of specific infections readers are referred to Mandell *et al.* (1979), Benenson (1980), Christie (1980), Emond *et al.* (1982) and Wilson and Miles (1984).

Definitions

An 'acute episode' may comprise a group of cases, a single case, or a carrier of a pathogenic organism. The word 'epidemic' is often used, and is defined as 'the occurrence in a community or a region of cases of an illness clearly in excess of expectancy' (Benenson 1980); however, this word is probably best avoided because it lacks a precise scientific definition and because it is misleading to the public, to whom it suggests the large-scale plagues of the past. 'Outbreak' is an alternative, but this word is best restricted to mean two or more related cases or infections and, therefore, excludes a single case or carrier. In this chapter 'outbreak' is used specifically with this meaning and 'acute episode' is used generally.

Systematic investigation

The investigation of an acute episode of disease requires a systematic approach (Barker and Rose 1976). It comprises seven main activities: (i) preliminary enquiry; (ii) identification of cases; (iii) collection of data; (iv) analysis of data; (v) control; (vi) communication; and (vii) further epidemiological and laboratory studies.

It is not always necessary to follow this sequence; the order will depend on the circumstances of the acute episode under investigation, and often several of them will be undertaken at the same time. In the Golden Square outbreak of cholera, for example, Snow was sufficiently convinced by his preliminary enquiry of the association of the disease with water from the Broad Street pump that he acted immediately to control the episode by requesting the removal of the pump handle. He then followed this with a more detailed investigation to confirm his findings and undertook an incidence study in South London to demonstrate the association of cholera with sewage polluted water. Modern acute disease control remains based on Snow's methods, the main purpose being the early detection of disease, rapid investigation and timely application of control measures to prevent further cases.

Surveillance

The detection of acute episodes of disease in the past relied mainly on the appearance of groups of cases associated in time or place as in the Golden Square cholera outbreak. But with the establishment of universal death registration in the UK in 1837 it became possible to search actively for such case clusters and other variations in the patterns of disease. William Farr, the first compiler of abstracts (medical statistician) at the General Registry Office in London, founded modern surveillance (Langmuir 1976) which has been defined as 'the continued watchfulness over the distribution and trends of incidence through the systematic collection, consolidation and evaluation of morbidity and mortality reports and other relevant data' (Langmuir 1963).

The method of surveillance comprises four main activities.

First, the collection of data, which may either be accomplished by routine reporting or by special surveys designed for surveillance; second, the analysis of these data to produce statistics; third, the interpretation of the statistics to provide information; and fourth, the dissemination of the information to all who require it so that whenever necessary swift action may be taken to investigate and control disease. This method of surveillance has been applied particularly in the field of infectious disease (Galbraith 1982) but the same techniques can be applied also to non-infectious diseases in which the causative agent gives rise to disease within a short period of time. In these conditions, such as acute poisoning and acute drug-induced disease, it may be possible by early detection and investigation to identify and remove the agent and thus prevent further cases, in the same way as in acute infectious disease.

Surveillance of infectious diseases and other acute diseases in large populations, nationally and internationally, has assumed greater importance in recent years because of the increased movement of people, foodstuffs, and materials throughout the world. Indeed, sometimes surveillance is the only means of detecting an outbreak of disease when the victims have travelled during the incubation or latent period from the common place where they acquired the disease to many different destinations, or when the vehicle of the disease is geographically widely distributed. This change in the epidemiology of disease has become increasingly apparent since the late 1950s and has led many countries to establish national surveillance centres. In England and Wales a laboratory associated centre, the Communicable Disease Surveillance Centre, was set up in 1977 (Galbraith and Young 1980), and many of the examples used in the description of the investigation and control of an acute episode of disease which follows are derived from the experience of epidemiologists working from this Centre.

THE PRELIMINARY ENQUIRY

> On proceeding to the spot, I found that nearly
> all the deaths had taken place within a short
> distance of the pump (Snow 1855).

Thus did John Snow describe the beginning of his preliminary enquiry into the Golden Square outbreak. The purposes of the preliminary enquiry are (i) to confirm that the reported episode of disease exists and there is indeed a problem requiring investigation; (ii) to confirm the diagnosis of the disease; (iii) to formulate tentative hypotheses of the source and of the spread of the disease; and (iv) to initiate immediate control measures if necessary.

Confirming the problem

A reported episode of disease may not be real and may arise for several reasons. The data may be misinterpreted. The reported episode may be due to increased clinical detection of the disease following the introduction of new diagnostic techniques, or because a new treatment has become available and it is therefore more important to recognize the disease, or because a clinician in the area has a special interest in the

condition. New and improved laboratory tests or a special laboratory interest in a disease may also increase detection. False-positive results of special investigations, such as laboratory tests or radiological studies, may present as an outbreak of disease. Changes in population size and structure, and improved reporting procedures can all result in an apparent increase in incidence of disease.

'Legionitis'

The misinterpretation of data by newsmen caused a spurious outbreak of legionnaires' disease – 'legionitis' – amongst British tourists in Spain in March 1981 (Communicable Disease Report 1981). Three deaths in tourists, one of whom had legionnaires' disease, came to the notice of the local press and it was assumed that because they had all stayed at the same hotel, an outbreak of this disease had taken place. The British press and media reacted to reports from their Spanish colleagues with stories of the outbreak under headlines such as *'Virus Kills Tourists'*, and correspondents vied with each other to obtain new 'angles' on the episode and to interview doctors who were considered to be controlling the outbreak. The public were alarmed and the medical services inundated with enquiries about the 'Benidorm epidemic'. Fortunately, however, the episode came to an end after about four days, when journalists had visited the hotel and discovered for themselves that the three deaths were unrelated and that a problem did not exist. They then realized that 'legionitis' was a disease of communication potentiated by newsmen and not a communicable disease.

Pseudobacteraemia

Contaminated blood culture bottles in a hospital in Essex gave rise to another spurious outbreak of disease (Willson *et al.* 1981). Between early 1980 and March/April 1981 positive blood cultures, mainly of *Klebsiella aerogenes*, increased from 0.5 per cent to 6.5 per cent. The preliminary enquiry showed that the laboratory results were incompatible with the clinical findings. Subsequent detailed investigation demonstrated contamination of citrate bottles used for the collection of blood for the determination of the erythrocyte sedimentation rate. The organism probably was spread from these bottles to the blood culture bottles in the nozzle of the syringe, because it was the practice to fill the citrate bottles first after bleeding the patient and then to fill the blood culture bottles from the same syringe.

Meningitis and population change

A study of cases of meningitis admitted to hospital in Motherwell, Scotland, showed a steep rise in the number of cases of aseptic meningitis in the late 1950s, which then continued at about double the level previously experienced (Sharp and Dewar 1973). However, this increase was probably not due to increased incidence but to changes in the population served and to new virological techniques. In 1950 two infectious disease hospitals combined and the catchment population increased; new housing in the area attracted young families and led to a greater proportion of children and young adults in the population, age groups in which aseptic meningitis is common. New virological techniques enabled the causative viruses to be identified, creating more interest and making possible the distinction of many types of aseptic meningitis from non-paralytic poliomyelitis, under which diagnosis they may have previously been recorded.

Confirming the diagnosis

The clinical diagnosis may often be easily established by the study of several case histories of affected persons. Sometimes a knowledge of previous events in the locality is helpful, for example, the prevalence of disease and immunization uptake. Occasionally a previously unrecognized disease is encountered and then it is necessary to define carefully the new clinical entity for epidemiological study. Laboratory tests are essential to confirm the diagnosis in many infections but epidemiological investigation should usually begin on clinical diagnosis and should not await the laboratory results. In some diseases laboratory tests are the only means of identifying cases and may indeed be the means of bringing to light an outbreak of disease in the first place.

Unrecognized yersiniosis

A continuing outbreak of abdominal pain and diarrhoea in boys in a boarding school in 1980 remained undiagnosed until detailed clinical histories and appropriate laboratory investigations were carried out (Bartlett *et al.* 1983, personal communication). The predominance of abdominal pain and the finding of mesenteric adenitis at laparotomy on one child suggested yersiniosis, and this was subsequently confirmed by isolation of *Yersinia enterocolitica* from affected pupils. Recognition of the disease permitted further epidemiological and laboratory study which indicated person-to-person spread of the infection between the children, probably originally introduced into the school from an animal source on the school farm.

Misdiagnosed food poisoning

An explosive outbreak of 'food poisoning' was reported at an open-air jazz band festival in Nottingham in 1980 (Bebbington *et al.* 1980). The first child collapsed at about 10.30 a.m. and in the following 2.5 hours the local emergency services were overwhelmed by over 400 cases which were taken to hospital. The initial diagnosis of acute chemical food poisoning was rejected after a study of a few case histories; the main clinical feature was syncope – vomiting and diarrhoea were absent. Subsequent investigation led to the definition of the disease as 'epidemic syncope' associated with the excitement and tension of the festival and the hot, humid weather conditions that were prevailing.

Precise laboratory diagnosis

A geographically widespread outbreak of salmonellosis associated with calf meat in the south of England in 1958, was recognized only by the precise laboratory identification of the pathogen, *Salmonella typhimurium* phage-type 20a (Anderson *et al.* 1961). Cases infected with this organism comprised about 17 per cent of all *S. typhimurium* infections in a population of over 17 million persons. Without this precise laboratory diagnosis the outbreak would not have been recognized, epidemiological study would have been impossible, and the source of the outbreak, a calf-collecting centre, would not have been discovered.

Taking immediate control measures

It is often necessary to take immediate control measures based on the tentative hypotheses of the source and the method of spread of the infection. If the preliminary enquiry suggests a common source outbreak due to food, milk, or water, it may be possible to stop the distribution of the material or to render it safe; samples should always be taken for subsequent laboratory investigation to confirm that the material was indeed contaminated. In serious person-to-person infections, such as diphtheria, hepatitis B, or poliomyelitis, as soon as the diagnosis is suspected it is necessary to identify persons who may have been the source of infection so that they may be isolated if appropriate, and to identify those who may have been exposed to infection so that they can be traced and given protection or treatment by vaccines or chemotherapy.

A contaminated milk supply

An outbreak of 77 cases of *S. heidelberg* infection took place in Cirencester in November 1961 (Knox *et al.* 1963). Pre-

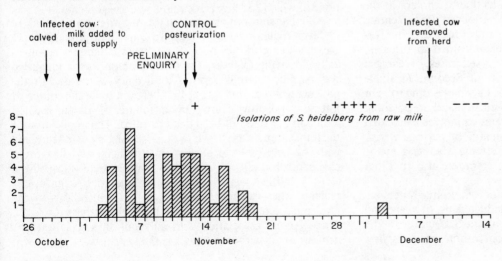

Fig. 1.1. Outbreak control after preliminary enquiry. A milk-borne outbreak of *Salmonella heidelberg* infection. (Adapted from Knox *et al.* (1963).)

liminary enquiry on 13 November of the first few cases reported suggested that raw milk from a local farm was the common factor, and so on the same evening the supply was pasteurized. Subsequent investigation showed that the 77 cases were in 56 households, 53 of which had been supplied with the contaminated milk. The outbreak declined rapidly after pasteurization, only one case being reported more than six days after distribution of the raw milk was stopped (Fig. 1.1).

Anthrax emergency

A single case of pulmonary anthrax was reported in West Ham, London, in 1965 in a 54-year-old man who had died suddenly (Enticknap *et al.* 1968). Immediate preliminary enquiry at his home and workplace revealed no association with animals or animal products except bone charcoal; his job was to empty sacks of coarse granular bone charcoal into a grinding machine to convert it into charcoal powder. The sacks he emptied were second-hand jute sacks from India and had been previously used to import the dried bones from which the charcoal was made. A tentative hypothesis that these sacks were the vehicle of infection enabled their rapid withdrawal from use, and the protection with penicillin of other operatives at the charcoal-grinding factory who had possibly been exposed to risk. Laboratory investigations confirmed the hypothesis and epidemiological enquiry demonstrated the chain of infection from sun-dried bones in India to the West Ham charcoal factory worker via the contaminated second-hand sacks.

IDENTIFICATION OF CASES

> *I requested permission, therefore, to take a list, at the General Register Office, of the deaths from cholera, registered during the week ending 2nd September . . .* (Snow 1855).

The cases first identified in an acute episode of disease often comprise only a small proportion of all the cases in the episode and are unlikely to be a representative sample. Snow appreciated this and asked the Registrar General to provide him with a list of all registered deaths due to cholera in the Golden Square area for study. Investigations of the presenting cases alone may be misleading and control measures ineffective for three reasons. First, in person-to-person diseases, such as diphtheria, there may be missed cases or carriers responsible for spreading the infection. Second, in single source outbreaks the presenting cases may have come to light because of a chance association with a place or potential vehicle of infection. Third, attack rates cannot be calculated because of the absence of a denominator of persons at risk and therefore, it is impossible to determine whether a factor common to the cases, is or is not common also to those apparently at risk but not affected.

The search for additional cases, for symptomless persons and for persons at risk may be conducted by (i) reviewing mortality and morbidity data (see Volume 3, Chapters 1–4); (ii) reviewing lay records such as school or hotel registers, lists of residents in institutions, payrolls and other occupational records, nominal rolls of travellers, and lists of persons attending functions associated with the episode; (iii) household enquiry; (iv) special appeal in the medical or lay press and through the media; and (v) screening by clinical examination or by laboratory or other tests.

A search for diphtheria contacts

A case of diphtheria was reported in a four-year-old child living in an hotel for homeless families in Hackney, London in 1975 (Chattophadhyay *et al.* 1977). The search for source contacts and persons exposed to risk in London, using hotel and school registers, and local household enquiry, detected 222 children and 60 adults. Clinical examination and nose and throat swabs identified four children with diphtheria, who were siblings of the index case, and two other children who were carriers; they were isolated and treated. The remaining contacts were protected by appropriate immunization and chemotherapy. The family of the index case had resided in Birmingham until moving to Hackney four days before the onset of symptoms; household enquiries and screening of neighbours in Birmingham led to the discovery of two carriers of the same organism who had recently arrived from Bangladesh. They were considered to be the probable source of the outbreak. Without the detailed and painstaking search for cases, carriers and persons exposed to risk, it is unlikely that the outbreak would have been so successfully contained.

Spurious associations in single source outbreaks

In April 1979, four of 58 persons taking part in a golfing tournament in the Midlands developed pneumonia in the week after the event; serological tests confirmed the diagnosis of legionnaires' disease in two of them and were suggestive in a third (Tobin *et al.* 1981). At first, the golf club was considered to be the likely source of infection but later the association with golfing was shown to be spurious by two means. First, detailed case histories showed that all four cases of pneumonia had stayed at the same hotel and of 26 golfers who stayed elsewhere none were affected, a small but statistically significant difference. Second, a search for cases using the hotel register identified a further four cases of pneumonia, none of which had any association with the golf club.

A similar spurious association was shown in an outbreak of Q fever (Salmon *et al.* 1982). In June and July 1981, 11 patients living in Newport, Wales were diagnosed serologically as having Q fever; the only common factor identified was pasteurized milk from a local dairy where one of the patients worked; this was at first believed to be the source of infection possibly caused by a failure of pasteurization, although this had not been demonstrated. The implication of the milk supply was shown to be false, first by case searching with the help of local general practitioners, and then by a case-control study. In this study the characteristics of the cases identified were compared with a control group of patients who were investigated for 'viral' infections in the local microbiological laboratory but did not have Q fever. There was no association with milk but an association was demonstrated with one area on the outskirts of the town, where infection was thought to have occurred from contaminated straw and dust scattered in the streets from passing farm vehicles.

The need for denominator data

The need for the collection of denominator data from persons apparently exposed to the risk of infection but not affected was demonstrated in an investigation of an outbreak of gastroenteritis in a London office canteen (O'Mahony *et al.* 1983*a*). Food histories from 142 affected persons and 77 who were not affected enabled the calculation of food-specific attack rates which identified the meal involved and showed an incubation period of 30–36 hours, consistent with a diagnosis of viral gastroenteritis. Furthermore, analysis of the food-specific attack rates implicated fruit juice as the most likely vehicle of infection; this had been prepared by one of the catering staff shortly after the onset of diarrhoea and vomiting and before she reported sick. Laboratory studies were negative, but the epidemiological findings made possible by the collection of denominator data, indicated that the outbreak was probably viral gastroenteritis caused by the sick foodhandler.

COLLECTION OF DATA

With regard to the deaths occurring in the locality belonging to the pump, there were sixty-one instances in which I was informed that the deceased persons used to drink the pump-water from Broad Street . . .

(Snow 1855).

A clear case definition is an essential prerequisite to epidemiological investigations. Having defined the disease, existing records, such as hospital, general practitioner, and laboratory reports and notifications are valuable means of identifying cases, but their use for the collection of data is limited because they rarely quickly provide a sufficiently accurate epidemiological description of the disease to be useful in formulating control measures. In most episodes a special enquiry is necessary, similar to that carried out by John Snow in Broad Street and the surrounding area.

The aim of the enquiry will usually be to collect data from those affected and those at risk but not affected, and will include: name, date of birth or age, sex, address, occupation, recent travel, immunization history, date of onset of symptoms, and a description of the illness and the names and addresses of the medical attendants. Other details will depend on the factors brought to light by the preliminary enquiry, for example, if it is likely that the disease was foodborne then detailed food histories will be required or if a person-to-person spread disease is probable then lists of possible source contacts and persons exposed to risk will be necessary.

The data should be collected on a carefully designed standard form of questionnaire, constructed on the findings of the preliminary enquiry, to ensure accurate and comparable records of all persons included in the enquiry and to facilitate manual analysis or coding for computer analysis (Bennett and Ritchie 1975). Whenever possible the questionnaire should be

tested rapidly in a few cases and in a few unaffected persons apparently exposed to risk; it will be appreciated that in an acute episode of disease there is insufficient time to evaluate fully a questionnaire before use.

Administration of the questionnaire will often be by direct face-to-face interview by a single investigator or a group of investigators previously given guidance on the completion of the form. This structured interview may be followed by informal questionning or an unstructured interview, which is sometimes valuable in detecting hitherto unsuspected factors common to the cases. Interview by telephone may be useful in obtaining data quickly and obviating the need to travel long distances to conduct a house-to-house enquiry. These methods of direct administration of a questionnaire are appropriate when detailed information is required or when the source of infection has not been identified, and are usually limited to a small number of cases. When numbers are large and the enquiry is straightforward a self-administered questionnaire is often more effective, although this is always liable to bias if there are many non-responders (Bennett and Ritchie 1975).

Hepatitis B: a clue from existing records

An outbreak of hepatitis B in Kent in 1978, associated with tattooing, was initially suspected because the first two cases notified as 'infective jaundice' were in young adult males who had been tattooed (Limentani *et al.* 1979). Although the routine notification records thus provided an early clue to the aetiology and spread of the infection, subsequent case searching and epidemiological and laboratory investigations were necessary to confirm the diagnosis and substantiate the association with tattooing. Altogether 34 cases of hepatitis B were identified, 31 of which had been tattooed by the same tattoo artist within six months before onset of symptoms; the other three cases were secondary cases. The first case in the outbreak became jaundiced two weeks after tattooing and was probably infectious during the incubation period and the likely source of the outbreak; spread to subsequent clients in the tattoo parlour probably took place because of defects in hygiene of the tattooing procedure. Local control measures included the provision of a guide to hygienic tattooing to improve hygiene and prevent the spread of blood-borne disease. The outbreak was followed by national advice on hygiene (Noah 1983) and by legislation to improve the methods of tattooing.

Paratyphoid: investigation by direct enquiry

A detailed questionnaire directly administered to a few cases was successful in locating the place of infection of 13 cases of paratyphoid B fever in England in September 1980 (*British Medical Journal* 1981). The 13 cases resided in eight different health districts but were all infected with organisms of the same phage-type, *S. paratyphi B* 3a var 4. This type, unusual in Britain but common in Spain and Portugal, suggested an outbreak in returning holiday-makers. This was confirmed by telephone interviews but subsequent face-to-face interviews were necessary to find the common factor; 12 of the 13 affected persons recalled visiting the same beach bar restaurant in a small village in the Algarve, Portugal within a period of five days in August. Unfortunately, local investigations by the Portuguese health authorities failed to identify the precise source of infection and further cases in holiday-makers returning from the same village were reported in 1981 and 1982.

Ornithosis: investigation by postal questionnaire

A report of a single case of ornithosis in a veterinary surgeon, who had attended a course at poultry-processing plants in East Anglia, was followed by a telephone survey of course members (Palmer *et al.* 1981*a*). Several reported respiratory illness. A subsequent postal questionnaire achieved a 96 per cent response rate. The veterinary surgeons had come to the course from many different parts of the country, so that the investigation by telephone and postal enquiry was quicker and less costly than a directly administered questionnaire. Altogether, 15 of 46 veterinary surgeons had clinical or laboratory confirmed ornithosis; analysis of attack rates by the plants they visited and their contact with different processes indicated that handling feathers and the examination of the defeathering machine in one particular duck plant was probably the source of infection.

ANALYSIS OF DATA

Time: *The greatest number of attacks in any one day occurred on the 1st September, immediately after the outbreak commenced.*

Place: *... it will be observed that the deaths either very much diminished, or ceased altogether, at every point where it becomes decidedly nearer to send to another pump than to the one in Broad Street.*

Persons: *... most conclusive of all ... the following death ... At West End, on 2nd September, the widow of a percussion cap maker, aged 59 years, ... A cart went from Broad Street to West End every day, and it was the custom to take out a large bottle of the water from the pump in Broad Street, as she preferred it* (Snow 1855).

The data should be analysed within these three classical epidemiological parameters to determine the mode of spread and source of the infection and to discover persons who may have been exposed to risk. A graph of the cases, an epidemic curve, should be drawn as soon as possible. This may suggest a

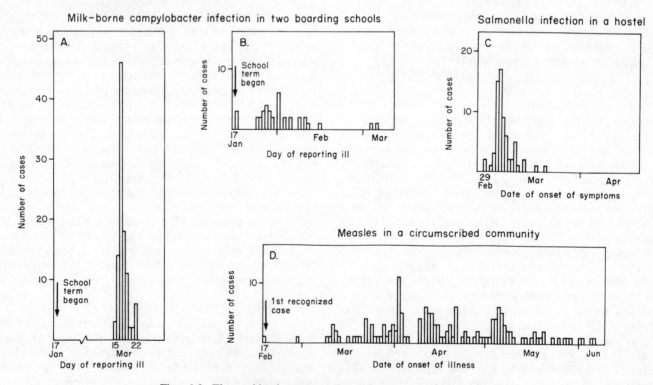

Fig. 1.2. The epidemic curve. A. Point source – milk-borne campylobacter infection in a boarding school. B. Continuing point source – milk-borne infection in a boarding school. C. Point source and person-to-person spread – *Salmonella* infection in a hostel. D. Person-to-person spread – measles in a circumscribed community. (Adapted from: A and B – Wilson *et al.* (1983, personal communications); C – Palmer *et al.* (1981*b*); D – Knightley and Mayon-White (1982).)

single point source or person-to-person spread of the disease, may show a cyclical or seasonal pattern indicative of particular infections or may show a time relationship with exposure to a suspected source. The geographical distribution of cases may also be helpful in demonstrating an association with a suspected source. Sometimes a case or cases which do not follow the general time or geographical distribution provide valuable evidence of the source of the disease, as did the lady from West End, Hampstead described by Snow.

Variations in trends in a disease in time, place, or persons may not be due to alteration in incidence but to changes in the denominator population. The size and structure of the population may change, the methods of diagnosis and effectiveness of detection may vary in time, between different places and in different age, sex, ethnic, or occupational groups. For this reason, attack rates should be calculated by time, place, and persons to confirm suspected associations.

Time

A common agent or point source outbreak usually shows an abrupt rise in the number of cases in a short period of time followed by a slower decline, as in the Golden Square outbreak of cholera. Sometimes, however, this classical picture is not seen because the point source continues over a period of time or is followed by person-to-person spread of the disease. In a propagated or person-to-person spread disease the epidemic curve rises more slowly and again falls slowly, sometimes with peaks at intervals of the incubation period.

Milk-borne Campylobacter infection in two schools

In the Winter term of 1982 two outbreaks were reported in boarding schools in the South of England (Wilson et al. 1983, personal communication). In the first of these (Fig. 1.2,A) 102 of 780 boys were admitted to the sanatorium with gastro-intestinal illness, 46 of them on one day; this explosive outbreak was probably due to post-pasteurization contamination of the milk supply on one particular day. The other outbreak was also milk-borne (Fig. 1.2, B), but in this school the milk supply was not pasteurized and the raw-milk source acted over a longer period; 35 of 370 boys were admitted to the sanatorium over the first six weeks of the term.

Salmonella infection in a hostel

In March 1980 an outbreak of gastroenteritis caused by S. typhimurium phage-type 10 affected 66 students and one member of staff in a University hall of residence in Bristol (Palmer et al. 1981b). The main wave of the outbreak was due to the consumption of contaminated meat pie but subsequent cases were due to person-to-person spread, prolonging the decline in the epidemic curve (Fig. 1.2, C).

Measles in a rural community

An outbreak affecting 151 persons in a circumscribed rural community in Oxfordshire between February and June 1981 showed a smooth epidemic curve (Fig. 1.2, D) but with distinct peaks at one, two, three, and four incubation period intervals after the first case (Knightley and Mayon-White 1982). In larger community outbreaks of person-to-person spread diseases the epidemic curve is usually smoother and the peaks at the generation time of new cases less obvious.

Cyclical and seasonal variations

The regular cyclical and seasonal patterns of some infections enables the prediction of outbreaks and the early recognition of the causative pathogen. This is particularly so in respiratory infections (Fig. 1.3); for example, respiratory syncytial virus causing bronchiolitis in infants but respiratory infections at other ages, shows a regular pattern of winter outbreaks with a peak in February or March. In contrast, the parainfluenza viruses causing croup in young children and upper respiratory infections in older children and adults, show different patterns; types 1 and 2 cause outbreaks regularly every other year with peaks in the late autumn but type 3 causes summer outbreaks every year with a peak in June or July. The pattern of Mycoplasma pneumoniae infection is less regular with outbreaks every three to four years reaching their peak about the turn of the year. Whooping cough due to Bordetella pertussis has a similar pattern with outbreaks about every four years and with a peak in the autumn; the size of these outbreaks increased in England and Wales after a decline in immunization uptake from 80 to about 30 per cent of infants in the mid-1970s.

Legionnaires' disease in a hospital

The relationship in time between a cluster of cases of legionnaires' disease and the bringing into operation of a cooling tower in a general hospital suggested that aerosol drifting from this tower might be the mode of spread of infection (Fig. 1.4). This cooling tower was part of the air conditioning system which had been brought into use in April 1980 because of the exceptionally warm weather (Fisher-Hoch et al. 1981). Extensive retrospective and prospective case-searching identified 12 cases, 11 of which were probably infected in the hospital. In four of these cases symptoms developed soon after the cooling tower was switched on and all were in wards close to the tower; subsequently, Legionella pneumophila was recovered from water in the tower. However, some cases occurred before the tower was switched on and others after it was cleaned and chlorinated and it appeared likely that these cases were infected from the plumbing system which was also found to be contaminated. Thus, there was a continuing outbreak associated with the plumbing system, superimposed upon which was the cluster of cases associated with the cooling tower, which brought the episode to notice.

Apparent outbreak of tuberculosis

Notifications of respiratory tuberculosis in Newham, London nearly doubled between 1970 and 1974 and those of non-respiratory tuberculosis more than trebled. The total population had declined and the calculation of notification rates confirmed the increased incidence. However, when the notification certificates were analysed by ethnic origin, determined by the name of the case, it was discovered that the increase could be accounted for by an increase in notifications of residents of Asian origin. There had been an influx of Asians from East Africa during the early 1970s and although their

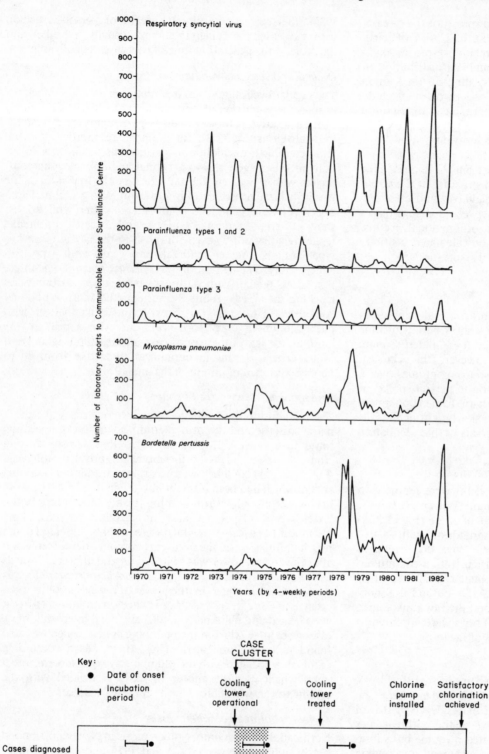

Fig. 1.3. Seasonal and cyclical changes. The regular pattern of some respiratory infections – England and Wales, 1970–82. (Source: Laboratory reports to CDSC.)

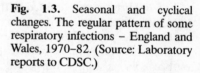

Fig. 1.4. Case cluster suggesting source of infection. Legionnaires' disease – Kingston Hospital 1979–81. (Adapted from: Fisher-Hoch *et al.* (1981).)

numbers were small relative to the total population, their incidence of tuberculosis was very high and increased substantially the overall number of notifications of the disease (Fellner and Hall 1976). Thus, there was no outbreak of tuberculosis, but a new problem of high incidence of the disease in a small immigrant population, against which special control measures were subsequently directed.

Place

The geographical distribution of disease may provide evidence of its source or method of spread, as it did in Snow's investigation of cholera near Golden Square. A detailed map of the area affected in an acute episode is therefore essential to the epidemiologist, on which can be plotted the cases as they are identified.

Salmonellosis due to chocolate

An outbreak of *S. napoli* infection was detected in Britain in 1982 by the routine surveillance of laboratory reports of isolations of salmonellas. Epidemiological investigation quickly identified two types of small chocolate-coated bars, imported from Italy, as the vehicle of infection (Gill *et al.* 1983). Between April and June the isolates of *S. napoli* were reported mainly from south-east England, but this geographical distribution changed in July when isolates were also reported from the Midlands (Fig. 1.5). This change mirrored an alteration in the distribution of the chocolate-covered bars, and the association with these products was finally confirmed by the isolation of *S. napoli* from nearly half of the bars examined. The chocolate bars were quickly withdrawn from the market and a public warning was issued in the third week of July; the outbreak ceased, and no cases were reported with dates of onset of symptoms after the end of July.

Water-borne Campylobacter infection

Mapping cases of campylobacter enteritis in a school outbreak in Essex in 1981 showed an association between the disease and the water supply (Palmer *et al.* 1983). Attack rates were higher in pupils in residential houses supplied with water from a private bore hole and lowest in those living in houses supplied by mains water alone. The bore hole water was stored in an open holding tank in the roof of the main school building; isolates of the same serotype of *Campylobacter* sp were obtained from the water and from pupils. It was thought that the water had become contaminated by faecal material from birds or bats inhabiting the loft.

Jaundice due to contaminated bread

In an outbreak of jaundice in Essex in 1965, all but one of the cases were reported in and around the towns of Epping and Ongar. This single case, the wife of a medical student at Epping hospital, was one of the initial cases in the outbreak, but she lived about 20 miles away in north-west London and had never visited Epping. It was at first assumed that the disease was infectious and that she had acquired it from her husband, but when it was realized that this was unlikely it was appreciated that she had another association with Epping; she had shared some brown wholemeal bread which her husband had purchased in the town. Subsequent investigation confirmed that this was the common factor in the outbreak and had been accidentally contaminated with a chemical hardener for epoxy resin, 4, 4'-diaminodiphenylmethane, the cause of the disease. The chemical had spilled in the delivery van carrying flour to the bakery and contaminated the flour from which the wholemeal bread was made (Kopelman *et al.* 1966).

Persons

Analysis of the data by 'persons' includes analysis by age, sex, occupation, social class, and ethnic group together with any other characteristics the preliminary enquiry indicates might be relevant; for example, food histories in food-borne

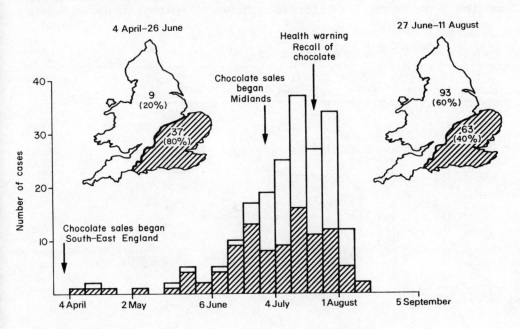

Fig. 1.5. Geographical distribution of food-borne disease. An outbreak of *Salmonella napoli* infection due to chocolate. (Adapted from Gill *et al.* (1983).)

disease, history of travel, leisure activities, and medical or nursing care.

Age distribution

A study of the age distribution of cases in a large outbreak of respiratory disease in Spain in 1981, which was originally attributed to *M. pneumoniae* infection, led to the implication of chemically contaminated 'olive oil'. It was noted that the cases were in persons over six months of age, the age of weaning; a single bottle-fed baby provided the clue, because on questioning the mother said she added 'olive oil' to the milk believing it to be good for health. She had obtained the oil at a bargain price from a street vendor. A study of the diets of hospitalized children showed that this cheap 'olive oil' was a common factor (Tabuenca 1981) and this was subsequently confirmed by case-control studies. The oil had been adulterated with denatured rape seed oil and sold fraudulently by door-to-door salesmen.

Food-borne outbreaks of infection due to milk, ice-cream, and confectionary characteristically affect children rather than adults. In a milk-borne outbreak of *S. heidelberg* infection (Fig. 1.1), 70 per cent of those affected were under 10 years of age (Knox *et al.* 1963) and in an outbreak of *S. napoli* infection due to chocolate (Fig. 1.5) over half the cases were in children (Gill *et al.* 1983). In contrast, an outbreak of *S. oranienburg* infection in Norway in 1981 and 1982 affected adults, 83 per cent of 121 cases were aged 25 years or more, suggesting a food vehicle restricted to adults. This proved to be home-cured meats, the organism originating from contaminated black pepper used as one of the ingredients (Food-borne Disease Surveillance 1982).

Food histories

In outbreaks of food-borne disease it is usually necessary to calculate food specific attack rates for each food eaten in order to identify the vehicle of infection (Committee on Communicable Diseases Affecting Man 1976). In an outbreak of hepatitis A following a dinner in London in 1980 one of the waiters, who became ill at the same time as the guests,

claimed that the only item of food he had consumed at the dinner was raspberry parfait. Food-specific attack rates were not significant for any foods but considered together with the waiters story they suggested that raspberry parfait was a possible vehicle of infection (Table 1.1). However, no other evidence was obtained to implicate this item and no further action was taken until another outbreak occurred after a party about a month later. Food-specific attack rates in this second outbreak identified raspberry ice-cream as the most likely vehicle of infection (Table 1.1) and investigation of the raspberries began. In both these outbreaks and in another family outbreak it was found that frozen raspberries had been supplied by the same firm, strongly suggesting that they could indeed have been the vehicle of infection (Noah *et al.* 1983, personal communication). However, examination of raspberries from the same batches failed to demonstrate faecal contamination, and a study of the production, harvesting, packing, storage, and distribution of the raspberries did not reveal how they could have been heavily contaminated with human faeces, urine, or sewage. Manual weighing of the frozen raspberries before packing may have provided an opportunity for minimal faecal contamination.

In outbreaks of food-borne disease not associated with a particular meal or meals but which may be associated with a widely distributed product, specific food histories for each meal possibly involved are of limited value and data on foods consumed or food preferences provide more useful information. This is especially so when there is an interval of several weeks between eating the contaminated food and the interview, as may occur in long incubation period diseases such as typhoid fever and hepatitis A.

In salmonellosis the final vehicle of infection may be different from the main vehicle of spread because of cross-contamination in the kitchens of the affected households or catering establishments. Therefore, in the investigation of widespread incidents due to the same organism questioning should include not only the food consumed by cases but also the foodstuffs brought into the household in the two or three weeks preceding the onset of symptoms of the index case and

Table 1.1. *Hepatitis A: two outbreaks in London in 1980. Food-specific attack rates*

Food	Ate food Total	Number and % ill		Did not eat Total	Number and % ill		P
Dinner							
Soup	141	51	36.2	1	1	100.0	0.366
Duck	141	52	36.9	2	0	–	0.403
Peas	139	51	36.7	4	1	25.0	0.538
Potatoes	135	49	36.3	8	3	37.5	0.609
Raspberry parfait	136	51	37.5	6	1	16.7	0.284
Lovingcup	136	49	36.0	7	3	42.9	0.500
Party							
Potato salad	26	12	46.2	12	5	41.7	0.529
Fish	33	17	51.5	11	2	18.2	0.054
Mayonnaise	14	9	64.3	27	8	29.6	0.036
Raspberry, fresh	22	12	54.5	18	5	27.8	0.083
Raspberry ice-cream	29	18	62.1	13	0	–	0.001
Green salad	29	10	34.5	7	5	71.4	0.089

P is the probability that illness is independent of the food eaten.

the origin of these foodstuffs. Using this technique in the investigation of apparently unrelated widespread incidents of *S. saint-paul* infection in the south of England in 1959, 15 of 48 incidents were shown to be associated with meat products from two abattoirs, in both of which animal infection was demonstrated (Galbraith *et al.* 1961).

Nationality, ethnic origin, and religion

Nationality, ethnic origin, and religion are sometimes important in determining the source and spread of an acute episode of disease. In an outbreak of *Brucella melitensis* infection in London in 1965, the observation that the initial two cases were in persons of Italian origin led to a case-finding search in other Italian families in the neighbourhood (Galbraith *et al.* 1969). Seven cases were identified and eventually Pecorino cheese purchased in a village market in Italy was implicated as the vehicle of infection. This was sheep's cheese made from unpasteurized milk in an area of the country where *Br. melitensis* infection in sheep was known to be widespread.

In another episode the ethnic group provided a clue to the origin of an outbreak of lead poisoning (Warley *et al.* 1979). A three-year-old Indian child was admitted to hospital in London with encephalopathy and the mother and one sibling were found also to have high blood lead levels. There was no obvious source of the lead, but eventually it was discovered that lead sulphide containing eye shadow, used by Indian women for cosmetic reasons and their children for 'health purposes', was the cause of the intoxication. Action followed locally and nationally to direct attention to the hazard and to withdraw the material from the market.

An outbreak of 110 cases of poliomyelitis in the Netherlands in 1978 was confined to members of several closely associated religious sects, none of whom had been immunized because of religious objections (Bijkerk *et al.* 1979). The absence of cases in the remainder of the community in which there were seven times the number of unimmunized persons was probably because the religious sects isolated themselves and formed a small homogeneous susceptible population in which poliovirus could readily spread.

Occupation and leisure

Occupation and leisure activities may be associated with acute episodes of disease. In 1980 the death of a 55-year-old man

from leptospirosis led to the recognition of the disease as a new occupational hazard of fish farming (Robertson *et al.* 1981). Case searching on the farm where the man worked brought to light a small outbreak associated with rat infestation of the premises and subsequently, a national serological survey to determine the prevalence of infection showed the disease to be an important although uncommon hazard of fish farming.

Another previously unrecognized occupational hazard was discovered by an investigation of two apparently unrelated cases of ornithosis in Norwich in 1980; one was a poultry meat inspector in a duck-processing plant and the other a housewife who had eviscerated ducks from this plant in her home (Andrews *et al.* 1981). Case-searching by examination of laboratory records identified five more cases in persons who had had contact with ducks. A subsequent serological survey in the duck industry showed an association between infection and working in duck plants, with the highest risk in workers eviscerating ducks. The overall attack rate in duck workers was 9 per cent, but 18 per cent in those eviscerating ducks.

An outbreak of 568 cases of jaundice was associated with the sport of cross-country running (track-finding) in Sweden between 1957 and 1963, and was shown to be due to hepatitis B transmitted by inoculation of virus into scratches and wounds on the legs sustained from thorns on bushes along the route during running; this was attributed mainly to the use of communal unhygienic washing facilities (Ringertz 1971). The outbreak was readily controlled by first prohibiting competitions and then by preventive measures that included the provision of protective clothing and improved hygiene of the washing facilities (Fig. 1.6).

Association with hospital

Surveillance systems for the detection and monitoring of hospital acquired infections are effective in discovering acute episodes of infection clearly associated with hospitalization (Lowbury *et al.* 1981). However, when the infection is associated with several widely scattered hospitals or when the incubation period is long so that symptoms manifest themselves after discharge, the link with hospitalization may not be apparent and may escape detection unless this possibility is borne in mind in investigating episodes of unknown origin.

Between February 1974 and August 1975 an increased

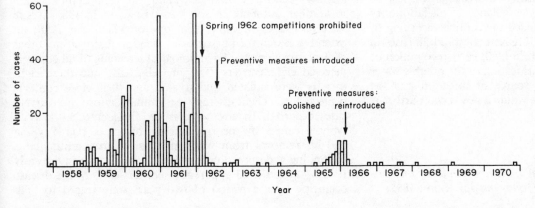

Fig. 1.6. Control of percutaneous spread. Hepatitis B in track finders. (Adapted from Ringertz (1971).)

number of isolations of two unusual *Salmonella* serotypes *S. eimsbuettel* and *S. schwarzengrund* were reported from various parts of the country (Rowe and Hall 1975). The cause of the increase was not apparent until it was noted that two cases in two separate locations were both children receiving treatment for fibrocystic disease. Subsequent study showed that 16 cases of *S. schwarzengrund* infection and 15 of *S. eimsbuettel* infection were in children receiving pancreatin in different hospitals and both salmonellas were isolated from different batches of pancreatin distributed by the same manufacturer. Although this outbreak was identified and control measures introduced it might have been discovered more quickly if the association of the cases with hospitals had been appreciated earlier.

An outbreak of seven cases of hepatitis B in London in 1978 was detected and an association with hospitalization recognized because a general practitioner noted that two cases in his practice had had gynaecological operations at the same hospital some months previously (Report 1980). A surgeon in the gynaecological team was found to be a hepatitis B surface antigen and e-antigen carrier. Detailed case searching by questionnaire to the general practitioners of over 1000 patients operated on by the team identified one additional case. Subsequently, a case-control study confirmed the association of the eight cases with the carrier surgeon.

Travel and infection

Between 1945 and 1980, the number of passengers carried on scheduled international air services increase over 70-fold, the number of passengers passing through Heathrow and other airports serving London each year increased from less than 100 000 to over 40 million; the number of visits abroad by UK residents increased from 8.5 million in 1970 to 11.5 million in 1980. These travel statistics emphasize the necessity to record travel history in the investigation of episodes of infectious disease (Bruce-Chwatt 1977).

Travellers in many countries were affected in a water-borne outbreak of typhoid fever which occurred in the Swiss holiday resort of Zermatt in 1963. Altogether 437 cases were identified and linked by phage typing of the organism, most of them in Switzerland, France, Germany, the UK, and the US (Bernard 1965). In another outbreak amongst travellers, affecting holiday-makers returning from Spain to Scotland in 1973, there were 164 cases and three deaths from respiratory illness (Reid *et al.* 1978), which was subsequently shown to be due to legionnaires' disease. Further outbreaks of this disease were identified by continuous surveillance of all laboratory reported infections, which included the routine recording of travel history. One of these outbreaks comprised 28 cases in widely scattered parts of the UK in 1980; early recognition of the outbreak enabled swift identification of the potable water at one hotel in Spain as the source of infection and the application of control measures within a few days (Bartlett *et al.* 1983).

CONTROL

> *. . . In consequence of what I said, the handle of the pump was removed on the following day* (Snow 1855).

Snow acted on the findings of his preliminary enquiry into the cholera near Golden Square and successfully interrupted the spread of the disease by persuading the parish authority to remove the handle of the Broad Street pump. Modern control measures in an acute episode may be directed against the spread of infection in a similar way, but they may also be directed against the source of infection, and measures to protect persons exposed to the risk of infection may be taken. Sometimes a single measure is effective, such as removal of contaminated food or water, but on other occasions it will be necessary to undertake several measures at the same time; for example, controlling the source of infection by isolating a carrier of diphtheria and protecting persons exposed to the risk of infection by immunization and chemotherapy. Whatever methods of control are adopted in a particular episode, they should be followed by continuing surveillance to monitor their effect.

Source

There are three sources of infection: (i) human cases or carriers; (ii) animals with or without symptoms; (iii) the environment.

Control of human cases and carriers

Infections derived from a human source can be controlled by physical isolation of the case or carrier and, if necessary, treatment until they are free from infection, provided that the cases and carriers are easily identified and carrier rates are low. For example, it is possible to control diphtheria and typhoid fever in this way because cases can be recognized clinically and confirmed by laboratory tests and because carrier rates are low and the carriers can be readily detected microbiologically. In contrast, meningococcal infection is not susceptible to control by isolation because pharyngeal carrier rates in excess of 20 per cent in the population are common in outbreaks and it is impracticable to detect and isolate all of them. The method of physical isolation used depends upon the mode of spread and severity of the disease (Bagshawe *et al.* 1978); for example, negative pressure plastic isolators are used in Britain for the African viral haemorrhagic fevers, room isolation for diphtheria, and special precautions in the disposal of secretions and excretions (isolation by 'barrier nursing') in typhoid fever.

The efficacy of isolation in the control of diphtheria has already been mentioned (p. 6) and was again demonstrated in another outbreak in south-east England in 1982. There were two cases of diphtheria, one of which was fatal; an extensive search for missed cases failed to discover any other clinical infections but bacteriological screening of all contacts detected eight carriers. The surviving case and these eight carriers were isolated and treated and their close contacts protected by chemotherapy or immunization; no further cases occurred. In another episode, the identification of a typhoid carrier by the epidemiological use of phage typing and his removal from work in a dairy farm terminated a continuing widespread outbreak of typhoid fever in the early 1940s. Altogether 23 apparently sporadic cases of the disease occurring over a period of two years were traced to milk contaminated by the carrier on a farm 100 miles distant from the outbreak. No further cases occurred after the carrier was forbidden from participating in the production, distribution, or storage of milk (Bradley 1943).

Isolation of human sources of infection may also be achieved in some diseases by 'ring immunization', that is, by encircling the case or carrier with a barrier of immune persons through whom the infection is unable to spread. This method was used for many years in the control of outbreaks of smallpox in Britain (DHSS 1975) and when applied world-wide led to the eradication of the disease (Henderson 1972). In an outbreak of poliomyelitis due to type 1 virus, in Hull in 1961, mass immunization with type 2 oral poliovaccine was used to block the spread of infection of the heterotypic virus by viral interference, effectively isolating persons infected with wild virus (Ministry of Health 1963). Similarly, trivalent oral poliovaccine was successful in limiting an outbreak of poliomyeliltis in Blackburn in 1965 (Moss *et al.* 1968) and more recently has been used in the control of outbreaks of other enterovirus infections in neonatal units (Tobin, in press).

One of the most successful examples of disease prevention by controlling the human source of infection was the virtual elimination of congenital syphilis in Britain in the 1950s. During and after the Second World War new cases of congenital syphilis increased to nearly 400 per year; antenatal serological screening for syphilis and penicillin treatment of infected mothers-to-be was introduced in the late 1940s and by the end of the 1950s new cases had declined about 20-fold to less than 20 per year (Fig. 1.7).

Eradication of animal source

Acute episodes of zoonotic infections in which spread of infection takes place by the air-borne route can usually be controlled effectively by the removal of the animal source; for example, an outbreak of seven cases of psittacosis associated with a pet shop in the west of England ceased when the birds in the shop were isolated and treated and the premises disinfected (*British Medical Journal* 1976). However, when the spread of infection is by food or milk, for example in salmonellosis (Knox *et al.* 1963; Gill *et al.* 1983), the acute episode is more readily controlled by withdrawal of the con-taminated foodstuff or pasteurization of milk; although, in the long-term control of food-borne and milk-borne zoonotic disease, eradication of the animal source plays a very impor-tant role (Bell and Palmer 1983).

Environmental control

Two newly described infections, legionnaires' disease and primary amoebic meningoencephalitis, have environmental sources and cause acute episodes of disease which can some-times be controlled by environmental measures. An outbreak of 12 cases of legionnaires' disease in a district general hospital in 1980 (Fig. 1.4) was controlled by chlorination of cooling tower water and the plumbing system (Fisher-Hoch *et al.* 1981). A single death due to primary amoebic meningo-encephalitis of an 11-year-old girl in Bath in 1978 led to the discovery of contamination of the public swimming bath water with the causative organism, *Naegleria fowleri,* which had been derived from local natural warm springs (Cain *et al.* 1981). Elimination of this water source and increased chlorination of the municipal supply to the baths prevented further cases.

In other infections there may be environmental reservoirs of infection although these may not be the original source. For example, dust may be an environmental reservoir of salmonellas, the original source of which is the intestinal contents of animals; a continuing outbreak of *S. typhimurium* infection in a school in Essex in 1965 was associated with contamination of dust and was controlled by treatment of the premises with formaldehyde vapour (Robertson 1972). In another salmonella outbreak, due to *S. virchow* affecting two hospitals in Essex and extending over five years between 1974 and 1978, recognition of persistent

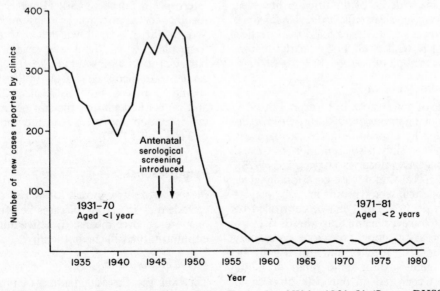

Fig. 1.7. Control of human source. Early congenital syphilis – England and Wales 1931–81. (Source: DHSS return SHB60.)

environmental contamination of ward mop buckets, bedpan washers, and dust enabled effective control measures to be introduced (Dowsett 1982, personal communication).

Other Gram-negative organisms such as *Pseudomonas* sp, *Klebsiella* sp, *Enterobacter* sp, and *Serratia* sp persist in warm moist conditions in the hospital environment and may contaminate sinks and basins, disinfectant fluids, humidifiers, and other equipment, and give rise to outbreaks of infection particularly in intensive care units. Control measures directed against such reservoirs of these organisms may terminate an outbreak and ensure continuing freedom from infection (Lowbury *et al.* 1981). For example, an outbreak of 14 cases of eye infection in premature babies in a special care baby unit, due to *Ps. aeruginosa,* was traced to contaminated resuscitation apparatus and was controlled by disinfection of the apparatus (Drewett *et al.* 1972). In another episode due to a previously undescribed organism, *Ps. thomasii*, 40 hospital patients acquired infections. These were traced to contaminated distilled water manufactured in the hospital pharmacy and widely used throughout the hospital in humidifiers of mechanical ventilators and in a rapid-cooling autoclave. Control measures were then introduced, including improved bacteriological surveillance of humidifiers and the cooling water in the rapid cooling autoclave (Phillips *et al.* 1972).

Spread

The mode of spread of infections can be classified into five main categories: (i) food, milk or water; (ii) direct or indirect contact; (iii) percutaneous, including insect-borne; (iv) air-borne; (v) transplacental.

Measures to interrupt the first four of these modes of spread may be used in the control of an acute episode of infection.

Control of food, milk, and water-borne disease

John Snow demonstrated control by interrupting the spread of water-borne disease, although in the Golden Square cholera outbreak he was not convinced that his action caused the subsequent decline in incidence of the disease; however, the two modern examples given here, milk-borne *S. heidelberg* infection (Fig. 1.1) (Knox *et al.* 1963) and *S. napoli* infection due to chocolate (Fig. 1.5) (Gill *et al.* 1983) clearly demonstrate the efficacy of this method of control.

Control of direct and indirect contact

An outbreak of 76 cases of gonorrhoea in Liverpool in 1976, due to β-lactamase producing strains of *Neisseria gonorrhoeae* appeared to be controlled by vigorous contact tracing, early effective treatment, and possibly also limitation of sexual contact by the patients whilst infectious (Arya *et al.* 1978). Direct spread of streptococcal skin disease occasionally gives rise to outbreaks of pyoderma, seen typically in rugby players ('scrumpox') (Glezen *et al.* 1972), and can be controlled by avoiding such contact. However, acute episodes of streptococcal and staphylococcal infection are more commonly spread indirectly by hands or fomites and can usually be controlled by strict hand-washing and other hygienic measures. Such action terminated an outbreak of over 40 cases of conjunctivitis due to adenovirus type 8 in Bristol in

1971. Initially, the infection was spread within an eye hospital by the hands of the staff and by ophthalmic instruments, and later involved several family contacts and patients in two hospitals for mentally subnormal patients. The control measures included vigorous hand-washing by staff after examining all patients and severe limitation of tonometry (Barnard *et al.* 1973). Many gastrointestinal infections are spread by indirect contact by the faecal–oral route and similar hygienic measures are effective in their control; for example, an outbreak of dysentery due to *Shigella sonnei* in a primary school of 192 children in Worcester in 1965 was cut short by the introduction of a strict regimen of supervised hand-washing and rinsing in disinfectant and by frequent disinfection of lavatory seats, door handles, and wash basin taps (Beer *et al.* 1966).

Control of percutaneous spread

In outbreaks of insect-borne diseases spread percutaneously by the bite of the insect, such as malaria, yellow fever and typhus, control includes destruction of the vector insect, protective clothing, and insect repellants. Hepatitis B, which is spread by the percutaneous route, can be controlled by measures to prevent contamination of broken skin or mucous membrane by the blood of a case or carrier; in an outbreak of 11 cases in the renal dialysis unit of a London hospital in 1969, screening of staff and patients, isolation of carriers, and hygienic measures prevented further cases (Knight *et al.* 1970). An even more striking example of the control of hepatitis B by interruption of the mode of spread was the introduction of protective clothing and hygienic washing facilities in the Swedish track-finders outbreak in the early 1960s (Fig. 1.6). When these measures were inadvertently relaxed the outbreak recurred and was again controlled by their re-introduction (Ringertz 1971).

Control of air-borne spread

Acute episodes of disease spread by droplets or by droplet nuclei are not usually controlled effectively by attempting to interrupt air-borne spread. However, in a classical study of meningococcal infection amongst military recruits in the First World War, it was shown that outbreaks of meningitis only took place when there was severe overcrowding in their barrack rooms with less than 1.5 ft between beds. Pharyngeal carrier rates increased sharply in these conditions to between 20 and 70 per cent but were reduced to well below 20 per cent and cases of meningitis did not occur when the bed spacing was increased above 1.5 ft to the normal peace-time spacing of 3 ft (Glover 1920).

Persons at risk

Persons possibly exposed to the risk of infection in an acute episode may in certain diseases be offered protection by one or more of three means: (i) active immunization; (ii) passive immunization; (iii) chemotherapy.

Active immunization

This was the classical method of protection of contacts of smallpox; vaccination was necessary as soon as possible after exposure, at most within three days, but, if after this period, concurrent human anti-vaccinial immunoglobulin was given (DHSS 1975). Similarly, live measles vaccine is now recommended for use within 72 hours of exposure in closed communities such as schools or hospital wards (Benenson 1980).

Passive immunization

Three types of immunological agent are available, human normal immunoglobulin derived from pooled donor blood, human specific immunoglobulin derived from blood of selected donors with high antibody titres, and antitoxins prepared in animals. Normal human immunoglobulin is used in the post-exposure prophylaxis of measles in debilitated or immunocompromised children as an alternative to active immunization. It is also used for protection against hepatitis A in institutional or household outbreaks or following possible exposure to infection from a foodhandler. Human specific immunoglobulins are used for the protection against chickenpox of neonates and immunocompromised persons; for post-exposure prophylaxis against hepatitis B following accidental inoculation of blood from a case or carrier; for protection against rabies following a bite or scratch from a possibly rabid animal; and for tetanus prophylaxis in the wounded. Antitoxins prepared in animals are used in the protection of contacts exposed to diphtheria, for protection of persons suspected of eating food contaminated with the toxin of *Clostridium botulinum*, and in tetanus prophylaxis (Emond *et al.* 1982).

Chemotherapy

Close contacts of cases of meningococcal meningitis, such as household contacts, should be offered prophylactic chemotherapy – sulphadiazine if the organism is sulphonamide sensitive or rifampicin if it is not. In the control of diphtheria, unimmunized close contacts should be similarly offered chemotherapy, with either penicillin or erythromycin. Chemoprophylaxis may also be used for family contacts of cholera, for child household contacts of leprosy, for contacts of plague, and for persons who have been exposed to serious risk of scrub typhus (Benenson 1980; Emond *et al.* 1982).

Surveillance

An essential part of control of an acute episode of disease is to monitor the effect of the control measures introduced. This may comprise national population surveillance, local population surveillance, or individual surveillance. For example, national surveillance of congenital syphilis has been maintained since the introduction of antenatal screening (Fig. 1.7), and similar national surveillance of brucellosis following progress in eradication of the disease in cattle has shown a continuing decline of human infection (*British Medical Journal* 1980). Local surveillance after the hospital outbreak of legionnaires' disease described earlier (Fig. 1.4) was maintained by a continuing study of all cases of pneumonia in the hospital and by routine sampling of the implicated water systems (Fisher-Hoch *et al.* 1981). Individual surveillance of infected persons, either cases or carriers, should continue until they no longer pose a risk to other individuals; this is easily achieved in acute infections but in persistent infections it may be more difficult. An outbreak of tooth-socket tuberculosis due to direct implantation of the organism by an infectious dental surgeon took place because individual surveillance of the dentist, a known 'recovered' case of tuberculosis had failed (Smith *et al.* 1982).

COMMUNICATION

*I had an interview with the Board of Guardians of
St. James's parish, . . .
The present edition contains . . . much new matter,
the greater part of which is derived from my own recent
enquiries. 11 December 1854* (Snow 1855).

Just as Snow presented his initial findings quickly to the local Board of Guardians a week after the onset of the outbreak and completed his final report three months later, so the modern investigator should produce a brief immediate report preferably within 48 hours of the preliminary enquiry and a final report, in a form suitable for publication, at the end of the investigation; interim reports may also be necessary in a detailed or prolonged investigation. These reports should normally be sent to all the appropriate local and national authorities and to the individuals concerned. Information given to the local press and media early in the episode will often prove helpful in promoting good relations with them and the public, and in enlisting their assistance in the investigation and in control measures should this be required.

Because the provision of accurate and timely information is often of major importance in an acute episode of disease, it is helpful to maintain a check list of authorities and persons to be informed to ensure that communications do not fail in an emergency. An example of such a list prepared for England and Wales is given in Table 1.2.

Communication in a diphtheria outbreak

In order to manage an outbreak of five cases of diphtheria in London in 1975 (p. 6) a control team was created (Chattophadhyay *et al.* 1977). This comprised the Medical Officer for Environmental Health, an environmental health officer, a nursing officer, and an administrator who met daily during the outbreak, and the local authority press officer, infectious disease physician, and microbiologist who frequently joined in discussions. The team ensured that all general practitioners, hospital casualty departments, and microbiologists were sent an immediate written report on the outbreak and that details were also sent to the medical officers for environmental health of neighbouring districts. An early press statement was issued through the local press officer, in collaboration with the Department of Health and Social Security Press Office, and this was followed by subsequent progress reports. The Chief Education Officer was informed and a letter sent to all local head teachers, and formal reports were made to the Local Authority and Health Authority. Communication nationally was first by telephone and then by the written immediate and final reports, and the final report subsequently appeared in the medical press (Chattophadhyay *et al.* 1977).

Table 1.2. *Communication in an acute episode of disease: check list of individuals and authorities who may need to be informed in England and Wales*

Local	National
1. Disease control personnel Medical Officer for Environmental Health (MOEH) District Medical Officer (if not MOEH) Hospital Control of Infection Officer and Infection Control Nursing Officer Chief Environmental Health Officer Divisional Veterinary Officer Employment Medical Advisory Service District Medical Officers of neighbouring Districts	**1. Public Health Laboratory Service (PHLS) Communicable Disease Surveillance Centre** Nationally responsible, on behalf of Department of Health and Social Security (DHSS) and Welsh Office for disease control, for assistance and co-ordination of local investigations and control measures
2. Medical services staff General practitioners Accident, emergency, and casualty department staff Hospital clinical consultants Hospital and public health laboratory microbiologists District Nursing Officer	**2. DHSS Communicable Disease Division** Responsible for national policy, for international communication and and for providing information to national press and media through DHSS Press Office
3. Staff of other services Local authority and health authority press officers Education officer and head teachers Social Services	**3. Ministry of Agriculture, Fisheries and Food** Responsible for state veterinary services
4. Authorities and administrative staff District Health Authority, Chairman and District Administrator Family Practitioner Committee, Chairman and Secretary Regional Health Authority, Regional Medical Officer District and County Council, Chief Executives	**4. Health and Safety Executive, Employment Medical Advisory Service** Responsible for health and safety at work

FURTHER EPIDEMIOLOGICAL AND LABORATORY STUDIES

> *No fewer than three hundred thousand people . . . were divided into two groups . . . one group being supplied with water containing the sewage of London . . . the other group having water quite free from such impurity* (Snow 1855).

Thus John Snow described the longitudinal study of cholera in the areas of South London supplied with water by two companies, the Southwark and Vauxhall company drawing its supply from the Thames at Battersea and the Lambeth company drawing its supply at Thames Ditton, above the sewage discharges of London. His study confirmed the association of cholera with sewage-polluted water. Similarly, more detailed epidemiological or microbiological studies may be necessary in a modern acute episode of disease to extend the investigations or to confirm the findings. The epidemiological methods for these studies have been described in detail in Volume 3.

Case-control studies

These are often used to confirm a hypothesis in an acute episode of disease, because they can be carried out quickly, easily and cheaply; indeed, they are often undertaken as part of the initial investigation, as has already been discussed. They are, however, particularly liable to bias in the selection of cases and of controls and the results must, therefore, be interpreted carefully in the light of other evidence available. In many investigations detailed case-control studies follow the initial enquiry. For example, during 1980 and 1981 in England and Wales notifications of infective jaundice increased, mainly due to an increase in hepatitis A infection. Field investigation of sporadic cases and several small outbreaks suggested an association with the consumption of cockles and a case-control study confirmed this preliminary finding (O'Mahony *et al.* 1983*b*). This study included all cases of notified infective jaundice in 18 districts between 1 November 1980 and 30 April 1981. Controls were selected from the families of these cases and also from neighbours. Both cases and controls were interviewed by investigators using a standard form of questionnaire. Altogether 314 cases, 280 family controls, and 263 neighbour controls were interviewed. The results showed a statistically significant association between infective jaundice and the consumption of several different types of shellfish. But further analysis showed that the real association was with cockle consumption and that the apparent association also with other shellfish could be explained by the tendency of cockle eaters to eat these other types of shellfish as well. Investigation of the cockle producers showed that the cockles dredged from a sewage-polluted estuary were probably inadequately cooked. Subsequently, action was taken to improve their processing. (See Volume 3, Chapter 8 for detailed account of case-control studies.)

Incidence and longitudinal studies

Assessment of the incidence of infectious diseases is often based on routinely collected data, such as notifications and laboratory reports, and less commonly on incidence or longitudinal studies. Although these routine data are valuable in measuring the incidence of diseases which are fully reported and in detecting disease trends, they may be misleading if used to assess the incidence of most diseases because of under reporting. Nevertheless, they are often used for this purpose in infectious diseases probably because of the wealth of these data that are available in this field. This appears to have resulted in the neglect of more scientific studies of incidence and the factors influencing the incidence of infection. However, some important studies have been carried out, for example a longitudinal study of hepatitis B in 20 dialysis units (Polakoff 1981), which followed outbreaks of hepatitis B in these units in the 1960s (Knight *et al.* 1970), was designed to measure the incidence of the disease and to monitor the effect of control measures. Between 1968 and 1969, at the beginning of the study, the incidence rose to 5.3 per cent in patients and 1.3 per cent in staff; subsequently, after control measures were introduced in 1970, the incidence declined reaching 0.2 per cent in patients and nil in staff by 1975. Another incidence study, of *Campylobacter enteritis* in general practice in Epsom, Surrey between 1978 and 1981, showed a higher proportion of cases of enteritis due to this cause than had previously been found (Kendall and Tanner 1982). Furthermore, the highest incidence rates were in children from birth to four years of age and lowest rates in school-aged children and adults, information which was not obtainable from the routine laboratory reporting system. (For details of methodology see Volume 3, Chapter 6.)

Studies of prevalence

Prevalence studies are less often used in infectious than in chronic disease because most infectious diseases are of short duration and such studies are time consuming and therefore not suitable in an acute episode when quick confirmation of the preliminary findings is sought. Nevertheless, prevalence studies are valuable in chronic infections, and may when repeated at intervals be useful in maintaining surveillance of acute infections. In some circumstances repeated prevalence surveys may be a more effective and cheaper method of surveillance than the use of continuously collected routine data.

A classical prevalence study of tuberculosis in South Wales (Cochrane *et al.* 1952) was undertaken in 1950–51 to detect and measure infectious tuberculosis; a control programme was then introduced and its effects monitored by further surveys. In another study, designed to measure the effect of the introduction of oral poliovaccine into the routine childhood immunization schedule on enterovirus infection in the child population, regular weekly prevalence surveys of enterovirus excretion in random samples of children under five years of age were carried out for 12 months (Galbraith 1965). A more recent prevalence study was undertaken to measure hospital infection in England and Wales because there were no routinely available national data for surveillance; this showed an overall infection rate of 19.1 per cent in 18 163 patients, about half of the infections being acquired in hospital (Report 1981). It seems likely that similar prevalence surveys carried out periodically may provide the best and most effective means of continuing national surveillance of hospital infection. (These studies are discussed in detail in Volume 3, Chapter 5.)

Intervention and experimental studies

Randomized controlled trials of prophylactic agents in infectious disease control became established in the early 1950s (Cockburn 1957) and their value in the assessment of clinical care was subsequently stressed (Cochrane 1972). However, in other areas of infectious disease control, measures introduced are mainly empirical and have not been subjected to scientific assessment.

An acute episode of a single case of paralytic poliomyelitis, due to type 2 poliovirus, in an unimmunized 12-year-old child in Newham, London in 1969 led to an assessment of the immunity of children of this age and subsequently to a controlled trial of simultaneous administration of oral poliovaccine and BCG vaccine. Of 247 children whose sera were examined, most of whom had been immunized in the 1950s with inactivated poliovaccine, 13 per cent had polio antibody titres of less than 1/8 to type 1 virus, 2 per cent to type 2, and 5 per cent to type 3 (Galbraith and Fernandes 1969). The subsequent vaccine trial showed that oral poliovaccine and BCG vaccine and indeed, also diphtheria–tetanus vaccine were effective and safe when administered simultaneously to children aged 13–14 years (Galbraith *et al.* 1971). Routine simultaneous BCG and polio vaccination was then introduced to improve the immunity of teenaged children. (See Volume 3, Chapter 7 for general discussion of these studies.)

Microbiological studies

Following an acute episode of infection it may be necessary to undertake environmental studies to further elucidate the cause. For example, an outbreak of *S. saint-paul* infection in Sussex, England in 1960 was traced to contaminated cooked meats from a local butcher's shop (Galbraith *et al.* 1962), but subsequent laboratory studies extending over nearly six months revealed that the ultimate source of the infection was probably contaminated animal feeding stuffs. In another laboratory investigation, which followed the appearance of outbreaks of *Bacillus cereus* food poisoning associated with rice in England and Wales in the early 1970s, it was shown that the spores survived cooking and germinated at optimum temperatures of between 30°C and 37°C. As a result preventive measures were recommended; rice should be kept hot (over 63°C) after cooking until consumption or cooled quickly and refrigerated (Gilbert *et al.* 1974).

CONCLUSION

> *The measures which are required for the*
> *prevention of cholera, and all diseases*
> *communicated in the same way as cholera,*
> *are of a very simple kind. They may be*
> *divided into those which may be carried out*
> *in the presence of an epidemic, and those*
> *which, as they require time, should be taken*
> *beforehand* (Snow 1855).

Snow ends his book with these words and an enumeration of the measures necessary for the prevention of cholera in an epidemic. This chapter has described the application of the epidemiological methods which he pioneered, to the investigation and control of modern acute episodes of disease with recent examples derived mainly from the experience of epidemiologists in England and Wales. The prime purpose of this application of epidemiology is to identify acute episodes of disease quickly, so that early investigation can lead to control measures to prevent further cases. The investigation must therefore be undertaken swiftly, meticulously, and in a methodical way so that control measures, usually of 'a very simple kind', as Snow says, can be applied effectively. Errors or delays in the investigation, or failures in communication of information, may lead to ineffective control measures or delay in their introduction and the occurrence of further cases of the disease.

REFERENCES

Anderson, E.S., Galbraith, N.S., and Taylor, C.E.D. (1961). An outbreak of human infection due to *Salmonella typhimurium* phage-type 20a associated with infection in calves. *Lancet* i, 854.

Andrews, B.E., Major, R., and Palmer, S.R. (1981). Ornithosis in poultry workers. *Lancet* i, 632.

Arya, O.P., Rees, E., Percival, A., Alergant, C.D., Annels, E.H., and Turner, G.C. (1978). Epidemiology and treatment of gonorrhoea caused by penicillinase-producing strains in Liverpool. *Br. J. Vener. Dis.* **54**, 28.

Barker, D.J.P. and Rose, G. (1976). *Epidemiology in medical practice.* Churchill Livingstone, London.

Barnard, D.L., Hart, J.C.D., Marmion, V.J., and Clarke, S.K.R. (1973). Outbreak in Bristol of conjunctivitis caused by adenovirus type 8, and its epidemiology and control. *Br. Med. J.* **ii**, 165.

Bagshawe, K.D., Blowers, R., and Lidwell, O.M. (1978). Isolating patients in hospital to control infection. *Br. Med. J.* **ii**, 609, 684, 744, 808, 879.

Bartlett, C.L.R., Swann, R.A., Casal, J., Canado Royo, L., and Taylor, A.G. (1984). Recurrent Legionnaires' disease from a hotel water system. Proceedings of the Second International Symposium on Legionella. Atlanta, USA. American Society for Microbiology, Washington, USA.

Bebbington, E., Hopton, C., Lockett, H.I., and Madeley, R.J. (1980). Epidemic syncope in jazz bands – logistic aspects of an investigation. *Community Med.* **2**, 302.

Beer, B., O'Donnell, G.M., and Henderson, R.J. (1966). A school outbreak of sonne dysentery controlled by hygienic measures. *Mon. Bull. Min. Health Lab. Serv.* **25**, 36.

Bell, J.C. and Palmer, S.R. (1983). Control of zoonoses in Britain: past, present and future. *Br. Med. J.* **287**, 591.

Benenson, A.S. (ed.) (1980). *Control of communicable diseases in man,* 13th edn. American Public Health Association, Washington, DC.

Bennett, A.E. and Ritchie, K. (1975). *Questionnaires in medicine.* Oxford University Press, London.

Bernard, R.P. (1965). The Zermatt typhoid outbreak in 1963. *J. Hyg., Cambridge* **63**, 537.

Bijkerk, H., Draaisma, F.J., van der Gugten, A.C., and van Os, M. (1979). De poliomyelitis-epidemie in 1978. *Nederlands Tydschrift voor Geneeskunde* **123**, 1700.

Bradley, W.H. (1943). An endemiological study of *Bact. Typhosum* Type D4. *Br. Med. J.* **i**, 438.

British Medical Journal (1976). Epidemiology. Outbreak of psittacosis. *Br. Med. J.* **ii**, 1017.

British Medical Journal (1980). Epidemiology. Human and bovine brucellosis in Britain. *Br. Med. J.* **i**, 1458.

British Medical Journal (1981). Epidemiology. Salmonella paratyphi B: Portugal. *Br. Med. J.* **283**, 69.

Bruce-Chwatt, L.J. (1977). Jet-borne pestilences: today and tomorrow. *Health Hyg.* **1**, 61.

Cain, A.R.R., Wiley, P.F., Brownell, B., and Warhurst, D.C. (1981). Primary amoebic meningoencephalitis. *Arch. Dis. Child.* **56**, 140.

Chattophadhyay, B., Fellner, I.W., Mollison, M.D., Nicol, W., and Williams, G.R. (1977). Diphtheria in London and Birmingham, 1975, *Public Health* **91**, 169.

Christie, A.B. (1980). *Infectious diseases: epidemiology and clinical practice,* 3rd edn. Churchill Livingstone, London.

Cochrane, A.L. (1972). *Effectiveness and efficiency: random reflections on health services.* Nuffield Provincial Hospitals Trust, London.

Cochrane, A.L., Cox, J.G., and Jarman, T.F. (1952). Pulmonary tuberculosis in the Rhondda Fach: an interim report of a survey of a mining community. *Br. Med. J.* **ii**, 843.

Cockburn, W.C. (1957). Field trials in the evaluation of vaccines. *Am. J. Public Health* **47**, 819.

Committee on Communicable Diseases Affecting Man (1976). *Procedures to investigate foodborne illness,* 3rd edn. International Association of Milk, Food and Environmental Sanitarians, Iowa.

Communicable Disease Report (1981). 'Legionitis'. *Community Med.* **3**, 261.

Department of Health and Social Security (1975). *Memorandum on the control of outbreaks of smallpox.* HMSO, London.

Drewett, S.E., Payne, D.J.H., Tuke, W., and Verdon, P.E. (1972). Eradication of *Pseudomonas aeroginosa* infection from a special-care nursery. *Lancet* i, 946.

Emond, R.T.D., Bradley, J.M., and Galbraith, N.S. (1982). *Infection.* Grant McIntyre, Aylesbury.

Enticknap, J.B., Galbraith, N.S., Tomlinson, A.J.H., and Elias-Jones, T.F. (1968). Pulmonary anthrax caused by contaminated sacks. *Br. J. Ind. Med.* **25**, 72.

Fellner, I.W. and Hall, C.J. (1976). Tuberculosis in East London: an analysis of notifications 1970–1974 in the City and East London Area Health Authority (Teaching). *Public Health* **90**, 157.

Fisher-Hoch, S.P., Bartlett, C.L.R., Tobin, J.O'H. *et al.* (1981). Investigation and control of an outbreak of legionnaires' disease in a district general hospital. *Lancet* i, 932.

Food-borne disease surveillance (1982). Outbreak of *Salmonella oranienburg* infection. *Weekly Epidemiol. Rec.* **57**, 329.

Galbraith, N.S., Archer, J.F., and Tee, G.H. (1961). *Salmonella saint-paul* infection in England and Wales in 1959. *J. Hyg., Cambridge* **59**, 133.

Galbraith, N.S., Mawson, K.N., Maton, G.E., and Stone, D.M. (1962). An outbreak of human salmonellosis due to *Salmonella saint-paul* associated with infection in poultry. *Mon. Bull. Min. Health Lab. Serv.* **21**, 209.

Galbraith, N.S. (1965). A survey of enteroviruses and adenoviruses in the faeces of normal children aged 0–4 years. *J. Hyg., Cambridge* **63**, 441.

Galbraith, N.S. (1982). Communicable disease surveillance. In: Smith, A. (ed.) *Recent advances in community medicine* No. 2, p. 127. Churchill Livingstone, London.

Galbraith, N.S. and Fernandes, R. (1969). Polioantibody titres in children aged 7–15 years in London. *Lancet* **ii**, 792.

Galbraith, N.S. and Young, S.E.J. (1980). Communicable disease control: the development of a laboratory associated epidemiological service in England and Wales. *Community Med.* **2**, 135.

Galbraith, N.S., Crosby, G., Barnes, J.M., and Fernandes, R. (1971). Simultaneous immunization with BCG, diphtheria, tetanus, and oral poliomyelitis vaccines in children aged 13–14. *Br. Med. J.* **ii**, 193.

Galbraith, N.S., Ross, M.S., De Mowbray, R.R., and Payne, D.J.H. (1969). Outbreak of *Brucella melitensis* type 2 infection in London. *Br. Med. J.* **i**, 612.

Gilbert, R.J., Stringer, M.F., and Peace, T.C. (1974). The survival and growth of *Bacillus cereus* in boiled and fried rice in relation to outbreaks of food poisoning. *J. Hyg., Cambridge* **73**, 433.

Gill, O.N., Sockett, P.N., Bartlett, C.L.R. *et al.* (1983). An outbreak of *Salmonella napoli* infection caused by contaminated chocolate bars. *Lancet* **i**, 574.

Glezen, W.P., De Walt, J.L., Lindsay, R.L., and Dillon, H.C. (1972). Epidemic pyoderma caused by nephritogenic streptococci in college athletes. *Lancet* **i**, 301.

Glover, J.A. (1920). Observations of the meningococcus carrier rate, and their application to the prevention of cerebrospinal fever. In: *Cerebrospinal fever.* Medical Research Council Special Report Series No. 50. HMSO, London.

Henderson, D.A. (1972). Epidemiology in the global eradication of smallpox. *Int. J. Epidemiol.* **1**, 25.

Kendall, E.J.C. and Tanner, E.I. (1982). Campylobacter enteritis in general practice. *J. Hyg., Cambridge* **88**, 155.

Knight, A.H., Fox, R.A., Baillod, R.A., Niazi, S.P., Sherlock, S., and Moorhead, J.F. (1970). Hepatitis-associated antigen and antibody in haemodialysis patients and staff. *Br. Med. J.* **iii**, 603.

Knightley, M.J. and Mayon-White, R.T. (1982). A measles epidemic in a circumscribed community. *J. R. Coll. Gen. Pract.* **32**, 675.

Knox, W.A., Galbraith, N.S., Lewis, M.J., Hickie, G.C., and Johnston, H.H. (1963). A milk-borne outbreak of food poisoning due to *Salmonella heidelberg. J. Hyg., Cambridge* **61**, 175.

Kopelman, H., Robertson, M.H., Sanders, P.G., and Ash, I. (1966). The Epping jaundice. *Br. Med. J.* **i**, 514.

Langmuir, A.D. (1963). The surveillance of communicable diseases of national importance. *New Engl. J. Med.* **268**, 182.

Langmuir, A.D. (1976). William Farr: founder of modern concepts of surveillance. *Int. J. Epidemiol.* **5**, 13.

Limentani, A.E., Elliot, L.M., Noah, N.D., and Lamborn, J.K. (1979). An outbreak of hepatitis B from tattooing. *Lancet* **ii**, 86.

Lowbury, E.J.L., Ayliffe, G.A.J., Geddes, A.M., and Williams, J.D. eds. (1981). *Control of hospital infection: a practical handbook,* 2nd edn. Chapman and Hall, London.

Mandell, G.L., Douglas, R.G., and Bennett, J.E. (1979). *Principles and practice of infectious diseases.* Wiley, New York.

Ministry of Health (1963). *Report on the outbreak of poliomyelitis during 1961 in Kingston-Upon-Hull and the East Riding of Yorkshire.* Reports on Public Health and Medical Subjects No. 107. HMSO, London.

Moss, P.D., Durge, N.G., Robertson, L., and Cowburn, G.R. (1968). The Blackburn poliomyelitis epidemic. *Lancet* **ii**, 555.

Noah, N.D. (1983). *A guide to hygienic skin piercing.* Communicable Disease Surveillance Centre, PHLS, London.

O'Mahony, M.C., Clark, P.L.S., Noah, N.D., and Tillett, H.E. (1983*a*). An outbreak of gastroenteritis of unknown aetiology. *Community Med.* **5**, 54.

O'Mahony, M.C., Gooch, C.D., Smyth, D.A., Thrussell, A.J., Bartlett, C.L.R., and Noah, N.D. (1983*b*). Epidemic hepatitis A from cockles. *Lancet* **i**, 518.

Palmer, S.R., Andrews, B.E., and Major, R. (1981*a*). A common-source outbreak of ornithosis in veterinary surgeons. *Lancet* **ii**, 798.

Palmer, S.R., Jephcott, A.E., Rowland, A.J., and Sylvester, D.G.H. (1981*b*). Person-to-person spread of *Salmonella typhimurium* phage type 10 after a common-source outbreak. *Lancet* **i**, 881.

Palmer, S.R., Gully, P.R., White, J.M. *et al.* (1983). Water-borne outbreak of campylobacter gastroenteritis. *Lancet* **i**, 287.

Phillips, I., Eykyn, S., and Laker, M. (1972). Outbreak of hospital infection caused by contaminated autoclaved fluids. *Lancet* **i**, 1258.

Polakoff, S. (1981). Hepatitis in dialysis units in the United Kingdom: a Pulbic Health Laboratory Service survey. *J. Hyg., Cambridge* **87**, 443.

Reid, D., Grist, N.R., and Nájera, R. (1978). Illness associated with 'package tours', a combined Spanish–Scottish Study. *Bull. WHO,* **56**, 117.

Report (1980). Acute hepatitis B associated with gynaecological surgery. *Lancet* **i**, 1.

Report (1981). Report on the National Survey of Infection in Hospitals, 1980. *J. Hosp. Infect.* **2**, Suppl.

Ringertz, O. (1971). Serum hepatitis in Swedish track-finders. *Scnd. J. Infect. Dis.* Suppl. 2.

Robertson, M.H. (1972). Survival of *S. typhimurium* in floor dust – a possible reservoir of infection in institutions. *Public Health* **87**, 39.

Robertson, M.H., Clarke, I.R., Coghlan, J.D., and Gill, O.N. (1981). Leptospirosis in trout farmers. *Lancet* **ii**, 626.

Rowe, B. and Hall, M.L.M. (1975). Salmonella contamination of therapeutic pancreatic preparation. *Br. Med. J.* **iv**, 51.

Salmon, M.M., Howells, B., Glencross, E.J.G., Evans, A.D., and Palmer, S.R. (1982). Q fever in an urban area. *Lancet* **i**, 1002.

Sharp, J.C.M. and Dewar, R.S. (1973). An analysis of meningitis cases admitted to Strathclyde Hospital, Motherwell 1949–71. *Health Bull.* **31**, 189.

Smith, W.H.R., Davies, D., Mason, K.D., and Onions, J.P. (1982). Intraoral and pulmonary tuberculosis following dental treatment. *Lancet* **i**, 842.

Snow, J. (1855). *On the mode of communication of cholera.* Churchill, London.

Tabuenca, J.M. (1981). Toxic-allergic syndrome caused by ingestion of rapeseed oil denatured with aniline. *Lancet* **ii**, 567.

Tobin, J.O'H, Bartlett, C.L.R., Waitkins, S.A. *et al.* (1981). Legionnaires' disease: further evidence to implicate water storage and distribution systems as sources. *Br. Med. J.* **282**, 573.

Tobin, J.O'H. Paper, XIV Annual Symp., I.C.N.A., Lancaster 1983. (In press.)

Warley, M.A., Blackledge, P., and O'Gorman, P. (1968). Lead poisoning from eye cosmetic. *Br. Med. J.* **i**, 117.

Willson, P.A., Petts, D.N., and Baker, S.L. (1981). An outbreak of pseudobacteraemia. *Br. Med. J.* **283**, 866.

Wilson, G.S., Miles, A., and Parker, M.T. *Topley and Wilson's Principles of bacteriology, virology and immunity,* 7th edn. Edward Arnold, London. (In press.)

2 The control of diseases related to nutrition

Basil S. Hetzel

INTRODUCTION

As already indicated in Chapter 4 of Volume 1, food and nutrition are major factors in disease causation in both developing and developed countries. The disease processes are different in the two settings—but methods for their control are similar.

The major nutritional disease processes at this time in developing countries are protein energy malnutrition (PEM), xerophthalmia due to vitamin A deficiency, nutritional anaemia due mainly to iron deficiency, and endemic goitre and endemic cretinism due to iodine deficiency (Beaton and Bengoa 1976). Other nutritional disorders that have been significant problems in the past such as beri beri due to thiamine deficiency, pellagra due to niacin deficiency, and rickets and scurvy due to vitamin D and vitamin C deficiency, respectively, no longer occur commonly enough to warrant categorization as public health problems.

The great reduction in the prevalence of this latter group is due to successful preventive measures. This has depended on a combination of factors—the necessary definition of the specific deficiency by a combination of clinical, epidemiological, and biochemical research and then suitable measures for its control. In the case of thiamine and niacin deficiency, diversification of food supply has been important in correcting the vitamin deficiencies. By contrast, pellagra is still to be seen in remote agricultural communities, for example in Sinjiang in China, in association with a strong dependence on maize as the major food source. The notorious susceptibility of ships' crews to scurvy in the eighteenth and nineteenth centuries has long since been overcome by suitable diet diversification with citrus juices. Rickets still occurs in special ecological situations such as in Asian migrants to the UK who continue a similar diet but no longer experience the benefit of so much sunlight to increase body stores of vitamin D. Beri beri is now seen mainly in alcoholics in developed countries— where the diet has become imbalanced by excessive alcohol intake rather than polished rice.

In developed countries, food, drink, and nutrition are important determinants of health along with other features of life-style such as cigarette smoking and physical activity. Diet is one major factor in the aetiology of the most common causes of death in developed countries, for example, in Australia—coronary heart disease (30 per cent of deaths), cancer (20 per cent), and cerebrovascular disease (14 per cent) (Hetzel 1980) (see further Chapter 4, Volume 1). Alcohol consumption is a major factor in liver disease (1 per cent) and in traffic accidents (4 per cent).

Recognition of the significance of diet for public health in developed countries is relatively recent and still not free of controversy. However, governments of many developed nations are now much more oriented towards prevention. Partly, this is for economic reasons in the hope that health costs may be reduced. They are, therefore, ready to consider the possibilities of dietary modification as an instrument of public health in relation to the diseases of the majority and not only those of special groups such as women and children, racial minorities, and those suffering from poverty who have been the main object of nutrition programmes in the past.

In this chapter, which is concerned with public health methods, we shall begin by considering the basic problem of the nutritional assessment of populations and then go on to consider methods of control separately for developing and developed countries.

ASSESSMENT OF NUTRITIONAL STATUS OF POPULATIONS

The first step in the control of nutritional disorders is the assessment and diagnosis, through community assessment, of nutritional status. A variety of approaches are used, as indicated in Table 2.1. The standard monograph on the subject with particular reference to developing countries is that of Jellife (1966), published by the WHO.

Epidemiological data on health and disease

The first category of data required is epidemiological information on health and disease.

In developing countries this includes data on the incidence and prevalence of the primary nutritional disorders of PEM, xerophthalmia, anaemia, goitre, and cretinism, and data on mortality in younger age groups, such as, infant mortality (deaths in the first year of life per 1000 live births) and infant mortality in the 1–5-year age group, both of which are greatly influenced by nutritional status. The infant mortality rate is particularly sensitive to nutrition levels—in Europe and North America this rate is 1 per 1000

Table 2.1. *Assessment of nutritional status of a community for public health programmes*

1. Epidemiological data on health and disease

MORTALITY DATA

General:	Infant mortality rate	(Age 0–1 year)
	Toddler mortality rate	(Age 1–4 years)
	Perinatal mortality rate	(Age 0–1 month and stillbirths per 1000 live births)
Special:	Crude mortality (famine)	
Developing countries	Infectious diseases in infancy	
Developed countries	Coronary heart disease mortality	
	Specific cancer mortality	
	Cirrhosis of liver	
	Traffic crashes	

MORBIDITY DATA

Developing countries	Prevalence of protein energy malnutrition
	Prevalence of xerophthalmia
	Prevalence of iron-deficiency anaemia
	Prevalence of goitre and cretinism
Developed countries	Prevalence of coronary heart disease admissions to hospital
	Traffic crash admissions

2. Clinical data

Developing countries	Clinical evidence of major primary nutritional disorders (see further Table 2.2)
Developed countries	Clinical evidence of coronary heart disease and various forms of cancer

3. Antropometric data

	Height
	Weight
	Indices—quetelet
	Skinfolds

4. Laboratory assessment

	Measurements of blood and urine constituents (see further Table 2.3)

5. Dietary assessment

	National statistics of consumption
	Special surveys—family, individual
	Food frequency studies

6. Ecological factors

	Family size, occupation etc.

Table 2.2. *Signs used in nutrition surveys in developing countries*

Hair
  Lack of lustre
  Thinness and sparseness
  Straightness (in Negroes)
  Dyspigmentation
  Flat sign
  Easy pluckability
Face
  Diffuse depigmentation
  Nasolabial dyssebacea
  Moon-face
Eyes
  Pale conjunctiva
  Bitot's spots
  conjunctival xerosis
  Corneal xerosis
  Keratomalacia
  Angular palpebritis
Lips
  Angular stomatitis
  Angular scars
  Cheilosis
Tongue
  Abnormally smooth or red
  Oedema
  Atropic papillae
Teeth
  Mottle enamel
Gums
  Spongy, bleeding gums
Glands
  Thyroid enlargement
  Parotic enlargement
Skin
  Xerosis
  Follicular hyperkeratosis
  Petechiae
  Pellagours dermatosis
  Flaky-paint dermatosis
  Scrotal and vulval dermatitis
Nails
  Koilonychia
Subcutaneous tissue
  Oedema
  Amount of subcutaneous fat
Skeletal system
  Craniotabes
  Frontal and parietal bossing
  Epiphyseal enlargement (tender or painless)
  Beading of ribs
  Persistently open anterior fontanelle
  Deformities of thorax
Muscles and nervous system
  Muscle wasting
  Motor weakness
  Sensory loss
  Loss of ankle and knee jerks
  Loss of position sense
  Loss of vibration sense
  Calf tenderness
Gastrointestinal
  Hepatomegaly
Cardiovascular
  Cardiac enlargement
  Tachycardia
Psychological
  Listlessness and apathy
  Mental confusion

Source: Modified from Jelliffe (1966) and Davidson *et al.* (1979).

---

while in many developing countries the figure is over 20. Although death certificates record gastroenteritis and respiratory infection as the cause of death, malnutrition is a major contributor (Behar 1974).

In developed countries, the occurrence of the 'diseases of affluence', as indicated by morbidity and mortality data, is of basic importance. Recent declines in coronary heart disease mortality in the US and Australia since 1968 following earlier steady rises from 1950 have raised important questions about nutrition and public health (Havlik and Feinlieb 1978; Dwyer and Hetzel 1980).

Clinical evidence on disease states

Clinical information regarding the disorders that have been under scrutiny at the population level provides important confirmation of diagnoses. In developing countries, both the clinical signs of nutritional disorders, and those of other diseases, especially infections, should be included. Table 2.2 presents a selection of clinical signs that are relevant to nutritional status.

Anthropometry

In developing countries special attention is given to the monitoring of growth and development of children by the use of anthropometric methods—measurement of height and weight. Various standards are available including the Harvard (Stuart and Stevenson 1954), which has been most widely used, those of Tanner *et al.* (1966), Tanner and Whitehouse (1975), and those more recently published by the National Centre for Health Statistics in the US (Hamill *et al.* 1979) (Fig. 2.1). At the recent XII International Nutrition Congress in San Diego, it was generally agreed that the latter standards which have been endorsed by WHO were the best available and were recommended for international use. In fact the differences between the three sets of standards is small. Undernutrition is considered to begin at 80 per cent of the standard's 50th percentile or median. There is no agreement so far on where overweight or obesity starts for children.

Various indices have been developed of which the most reliable is the Body Mass Index (BMI), also known as Quetelet's index (weight/height^2, where weight is measured in kilograms and height in metres). Such an index is also used as an indication of overweight and obesity in adults and children in developed countries. In adults a figure of 10 or more is suggested as the marker for overweight and 20 or more for obesity. Available data indicate an increase in mortality with a BMI in excess of 25 in the adult male and of 28 in the adult female (Bray 1976; DHSS and MRC 1976).

There has been some recent discussion as to whether national standards are more appropriate than an international standard. Tanner and Goldstein (1980) have advocated different standards for developing countries. But the major influence in weights and heights of children aged under five years is environmental and not ethnic or genetic (Habicht *et al.* 1974), and pre-school children in privileged groups in many developing countries compare well with those of developed countries. Waterlow (1980) supports this view and suggests that the international standards be used for the determination of suitable cut-offs as data become available regarding relation to mortality.

There has been a notable increase in height since the Second World War in a number of countries due to improved nutrition including Japan and the United Kingdom. Figure 2.2 shows the increase in height in schoolchildren aged 5–12 years in England between 1938 and 1981 (Rona, personal communication).

Measurement of skinfolds in four different positions (triceps, biceps, subscapular, and suprailiac) with specially designed callipers provides a valuable estimate of body fat. Subcutaneous fat comprises between 25 and 50 per cent of total body fat stores, the percentage varying with sex and age as well as between individuals (Durnin and Womersley 1974). There is more subcutaneous fat in females and the young and subcutaneous fat stores decrease with age. The advantage of this technique is that both limb and trunk subcutaneous fat are measured. Skinfold measurements can be carried out quickly and are now used widely. Strict adherence to consistent procedure is essential to reduce variability between observers and in repeated observations by the same observer. It is recommended that all measurements are made to the left side of the body (Durnin 1967; Tanner and Whitehouse 1975). The method is particularly valuable for the measurement of the progress of children, whether undernourished or overnourished.*

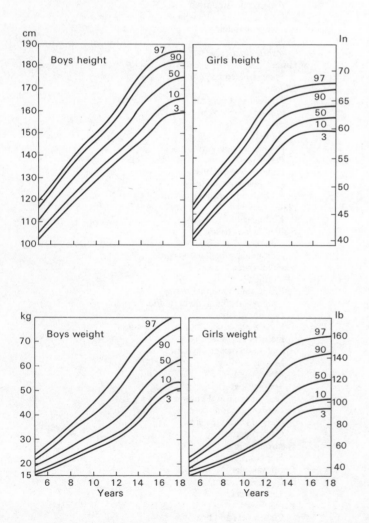

Fig. 2.1. Standard heights and weights of boys and girls 5–19 years old. (Source: Hamill *et al.* (1979).)

Laboratory assessment

Important information can be collected from laboratory examinations as in the case of serum iron, retinol and caro-

*The skinfolds are measured by picking up with the left hand a fold of skin and subcutaneous tissue, initially placed between thumb and forefinger 2 cm apart on the skin, and pinching it away from underlying muscle. The jaws of the instrument are applied 1 cm from the point at which the skinfold has been grasped, and the right hand is allowed to relax entirely its grip so that the calliper can exert its full pressure. The left hand maintains the pinch throughout the measurement. The reading should be taken one second after the callipers are applied (Jelliffe 1966).

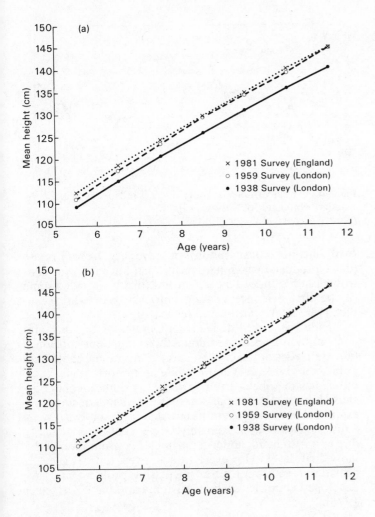

Fig. 2.2. Mean height of primary schoolchildren in England from 1938.

●————● 1938 London (Menzies 1940)
o-----------o 1959 London (Scott 1961)
x··············x 1981 England (National Study of Health and Growth— R. Rona, personal communication.)

Table 2.3. *Biochemical methods for assessing nutritional status*

Nutrient	Principal methods	
	Indicating reduced intake	Indicating impaired function (IF) or cell depletion (CD)
Iron	Plasma iron and total iron binding capacity	Haemoglobin, packed cell volume (PCV)
Calcium	Plasma calcium	Urine calcium
Iodine	Urinary (stable) iodine	Plasma thyroxine (T_4 and T_3) and thyroid stimulating hormone (TSH)
Protein	Urinary N	Plasma albumin (IF)
Zinc	Plasma zinc Hair zinc	
Fat	Serum cholesterol	Serum lipoproteins
Vitamin A	Plasma retinol Plasma carotene	
Thiamin	Urinary thiamin	RBC transketolase and TPP effect (IF)
Riboflavin	Urinary riboflavin	RBC glutathione reductase and FAD effect (IF)
Nicotinamide	Urinary N'-methylnico-tinamide and 2-pyridone	
Pyridoxine	Urinary 4-pyridoxic acid	RBC glutamic oxalacetic transaminase and PP effect (IF)
Folic acid	Plasma folate (*Lactobacillus casei*)	RBC folate (CD) Haemoglobin, PCV and smear (IF)
Vitamin B_{12}	Plasma vitamin B_{12} (*Euglena gracilis*)	Haemoglobin, PCV and smear (IF)
Ascorbic acid	Plasma ascorbic acid	Leucocyte ascorbic acid (CD)
Vitamin D	Plasma 2,5-dihydroxy-cholecalciferol	Plasma alkaline phosphatase (IF)
Vitamin E	Plasma tocopherol	RBC haemolysis with H_2O_2 *in vitro*
Vitamin K		Plasma prothrombin (IF)
Sodium	Urinary sodium	Plasma sodium
Potassium	Urinary potassium	Plasma potassium

Source: Modified from Davidson *et al.* (1979).

tene, and urinary iodine and nitrogen in developing countries, or serum cholesterol and other lipid fractions in developed countries. Determination of serum cholesterol and other lipid fractions is now the subject of international standardization through the Lipid Research Clinics Program 1974 which has become the WHO Reference Center for Lipid Determination at the Chronic Diseases Center, Atlanta, Georgia. Table 2.3 lists laboratory methods currently in use.

The combination of clinical and laboratory data provides information on 'risk factors'. In the case of coronary heart disease, records of weight and height, blood pressure, and serum lipids together with data on activity and cigarette smoking, provide basic information relevant to the future occurrence of coronary heart disease both in the individual and the community.

Diet

Information regarding the diet of a community can be derived from several sources including national statistics of apparent consumption of food and dietary surveys of whole populations or special subgroups. Recent reviews by Marr (1971) and Keys (1979) provide a more detailed discussion of dietary survey methods.

National statistics of apparent consumption of food

These data are based on 'disappearance' statistics for foodstuffs moving into the market place. Not all food that is purchased is consumed. Some is stored, preserved, given to domestic animals, or wasted. Some foods are especially likely to be wasted, for example, oils in bulk cooking (e.g. for potato chips or in takeaway stores). Allowances are made for preservation as in canning or jam making but practices have changed without reappraisal.

The basic data available are for agricultural production, and imports and exports of food. A calculation of apparent consumption can be made by deducting from the sum of production, imports, and opening stocks, the sum of exports, ships stores, non-food usage, wastage, usage for processed foods, and closing stocks. Estimates of these various components can be made only roughly and with even more uncertainty in the absence of household survey data derived from special surveys or from censuses.

In theory, individual daily consumption of food can be calculated by dividing the difference by the total population. In spite of their limitations these data are used extensively in the usual absence of any other evidence regarding individual food consumption that might be derived from a national survey (see below).

The Food Agriculture Organization (FAO) publishes annual tabulations of these data intended to describe food available for purchase at shop level (FAO 1980). Wastage will still occur after purchase but critical assessment of the figure does provide useful information related to the nutritional status of many countries. However, such tabulations are no stronger than the particular national data collections, and these must vary widely in their reliability.

Determinations can be made of the consumption of nutrients (carbohydrate, fat, protein) by use of tables of food composition, available in some countries such as the UK (Paul *et al.* 1978). They tend to be out of date in relation to the rapidly changing nature of foods consumed (e.g. convenience or 'fast' foods), but none the less such tables provide essential information for the calculation of nutrient intake. A list of national food tables from 72 countries has been published by FAO (1975).

Time trends of food and nutrient consumption can provide useful indicators for further investigation. Large fluctuations may occur in relation to economic factors, war, or famine. Examples are the fall in alcohol consumption in Australia and the UK associated with the Great Depression of the early 1930s (Fig. 2.3) and the fall in consumption of dairy products in Norway during the German occupation (Fig. 2.4). Such spontaneous fluctuations can provide opportunities to identify related fluctuations in the incidence of diseases such as upper gastrointestinal cancer

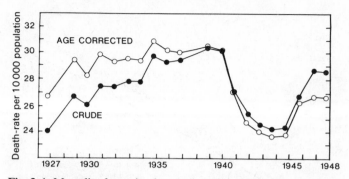

Fig. 2.4. Mortality from circulatory diseases in Norway in 1927–48. Standard population of Norway in 1940. (Source: Strom and Jensen (1951).)

(with alcohol consumption) or coronary heart disease (dairy products) which may provide an indication for control measures. Indeed the data from Norway provided some of the first evidence relating coronary heart disease to dietary fat intake (Strom and Jensen 1951).

Alcohol is a well-defined component of the diet and consumption is estimated annually as apparent consumption derived from excise returns. International tables are published (Table 2.4) and provide an important guide for public health policy (Bruun *et al.* 1975). Some alcohol purchased is stored. Comparison between daily consumption estimated from excise returns and that from surveys reveals a discrepancy of approximately 50 per cent—this is mainly due to a systematic under-reporting of consumption at the individual level. However, trends over time (Fig. 2.3) provide an indication of an increasing problem in many developed countries such as Australia and the UK (Hetzel 1978*a*).

Dietary surveys

Surveys designed to determine food consumption at the family or individual level are very important in relation to the assessment of nutritional status. However, few national

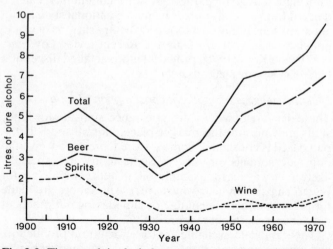

Fig. 2.3. Time trends in alcohol consumption in Australia (1900–75). (Source: Commonwealth of Australia, Department of Health (1978).)

Table 2.4. *Rank of countries based on per caput consumption of total absolute alcohol; 1975*

		Litres			Litres
1.	France	16.90	16.	Rumania	7.87
2.	Portugal	15.15	17.	Netherlands	7.78
3.	Italy	14.12	18.	United States	7.58
4.	Spain	13.65	19.	New Zealand	7.49
5.	Luxembourg	11.72	20.	Ireland	6.66
6.	West Germany	11.69	21.	Poland	6.61
7.	Austria	11.16	22.	England	6.58
8.	Hungary	11.11	23.	Finland	6.57
9.	Switzerland	10.73	24.	Sweden	6.18
10.	Australia	10.03	25.	Japan	5.91
11.	Belgium	9.77	26.	Bulgaria	5.14
12.	Czechoslovakia	9.66	27.	Norway	4.23
13.	Canada	8.25	28.	Iceland	3.79
14.	Yugoslavia	8.03	29.	Israel	1.77
15.	Denmark	7.95			

Source: Dutch Distillers Association or brewers' associations in the various countries. From Director-General of Health (1978–9).

surveys have been conducted, mainly because of the cost involved.

A recent example is the *Ten state survey* in the US, which was authorized in 1967 to determine the prevalence of malnutrition and related health problems among low-income populations in the US. Some 40 000 individuals were examined in 10 states, with careful weighing of the sample to include age, low ethnic groups believed to be at higher risk of malnutrition. Few clinical signs of malnutrition were found, there were numerous children and adolescents who were underweight and many adults who were obese. Low haemoglobin levels were found associated with low dietary and plasma iron, and low plasma vitamin A levels in Spanish Americans. Results are available in five books published by the US Department of Health, Education and Welfare (1972).

A similar study in Canada, *Nutrition Canada*, was reported in 1973 by the Department of National Health and Welfare. A total sample of 19 000 people was studied. Iron deficiency was the commonest form of malnutrition, low folate reserves were found with some cases of goitre and scurvy in Eskimos; obesity and elevated plasma cholesterol was common. It might be concluded that these results do not justify the expense involved.

In the UK, the National Household Food Consumption and Expenditure Survey records food consumption in large numbers of homes but is not designed to detect malnutrition. Special surveys of the very young and the elderly have been carried out by the Department of Health and Social Security (DHSS) but little evidence of malnutrition found. Such findings may not apply in the future with increasing economic pressure and unemployment.

In planning such surveys, great care must be given to problems of definition and sampling procedures. Discussion with a statistician is required but some knowledge of statistics is essential in order to establish a proper dialogue. Sampling needs to take into account, differences at the individual level (sex, age, and ethnic group), geographical variations, and factors changing with time that may influence food intake. The major objective is not to overlook known factors that could affect interpretation of the findings. These matters have been reviewed by Abramson (1979).

Special national surveys recently undertaken in Australia and the US have been concerned with risk factors for ischaemic heart disease. The information collected includes clinical anthropometric data, blood chemistry, dietary behaviour, alcohol usage, smoking habits, and physical activity. It is proposed that these surveys be conducted every three years in order to monitor trends that would indicate the need for public health measures.

The measurement of usual dietary intake

The limitations of apparent consumption data for the calculation of daily individual intake have already been pointed out. In general in developed countries energy consumption has been overestimated by 30 per cent (UK and USA) when comparison has been made with household consumption figures (MAFF and HANES Surveys, in US DHEW (1979)).

However, there are considerable difficulties in the measurement of usual dietary intake (Marr 1971). Four basic methods have been suggested: (i) diet records of food eaten in the present; (ii) dietary recall of actual foods eaten during a specified (usually short) time period in the past; (iii) diet histories; and (iv) food frequency questionnaires. Each of these methods has its advantages and disadvantages (Marr 1971). Baghurst and Record (1983) recommend a food frequency questionnaire as an appropriate and economic method for studies of individual diets in large groups.

Self-completed questionnaires and interviews are used to assess the frequency of consumption of a specified range of food and drinks, and can provide quantitative data. The food frequency score for individual items can be multiplied by the nutrient composition after adjustments for cooking practices and portion size deviations using tables of food composition (Paul *et al.* 1978). The values for individual food items are then calculated, added up, and adjusted to give the mean daily nutrient intake for, if necessary, over 40 nutrients (Baghurst and Record 1983). Data on one year repeatability of this procedure in a group of 40–70-year-old men and women is shown in Table 2.5. Results obtained in a series of Australian subgroups are shown in Table 2.6. There is a surprising consistency in the findings on dietary intake from the various groups.

Computer facilities allow the calculation of nutrient intake per day, frequency of consumption of particular foods, or the contribution of particular foods to nutrient intake. This method is not applicable to children under the age of 10–11 years because of their inability accurately to assess the time periods involved. Careful analysis of the influence of interpersonal and behavioural factors arising from the use of particular words and phrases in responding to questionnaires has recently been made (Worsley 1981).

Table 2.5. *One year repeatability data for nutrient intake as measured by a semi-quantitative frequency method in a group of 40–70-year-old men and women*

Nutrient	Test	Retest	Nutrient	Test	Retest
Energy*	8013	7850	Retinol*	376	360
Protein*	70.9	73.0	β-Carotein*	5263	5055
Complex CHO*	96.0	90.0	Thiamine	1.13	1.16
Simple CHO*	121	118	Riboflavin	1.76	1.77
Fat*	82.8	81.8	Vitamin B$_{12}$	6.21	5.25
Saturate fat*	34.5	34.2	Calcium	858	884
Polyunsaturated			Iron	10.8	10.8
fat†	10.9	10.0	Sodium	1999	1951
Monosaturated					
fat*	27.8	27.9	*% energy form*		
Cholesterol*	311	309	Protein*	14.8	15.5
Alcohol*	9.7	10.0	Complex CHO‡	18.7	18.0
Fibre*	20.3	19.4	Simple CHO*	24.4	24.1
Vitamin C	140	163	Fat*	38.5	38.5

Significance for individual correlation: *=0.00001; †=0.00003; ‡=0.00006; (others not calculated).

Source: Baghurst and Baghurst (1981).

Table 2.6. *Energy derived from the major nutrients in the diet of selected Australian subpopulations*

	Subjects											
	Adolescents		University students		Service recruits	Semi-rural population			Urban populations (Adelaide)			
	Male	Female	Male	Female	Male	Male	Female	Female	Male	Female	Male	Female
Age mean and (range)	14 (14–15)		18 (17–31)		23 (17–44)	39 (17–76)		25 (18–29)	41 (30–49)		63 (50–70)	
Number	77	69	247	97	883	89	87	43	23	79	162	105
% Energy derived from*												
Protein	14.2	15.1	14.6	15.3	17.2	15.3	17.1	16.8	14.0	16.3	15.1	15.8
Carbohydrate	44.4	43.1	42.1	42.7	37.8	41.5	42.6	46.7	40.9	43.5	41.6	44.2
(a) Complex	14.9	14.4	15.5	14.4	14.7	16.1	17.4	18.2	20.2	18.7	18.1	18.2
(b) Simple	29.5	28.7	26.6	28.2	23.1	25.4	25.2	28.5	20.7	24.8	23.5	26.0
Fat†	39.6	39.5	40.6	39.3	39.9	36.9	38.2	35.5	36.3	37.4	38.4	37.8
(a) Saturate fatty acids	16.9	17.3	18.6	18.3	17.4	15.8	17.0	16.1	16.4	16.9	15.9	15.6
(b) Polyunsaturated fatty acids	5.5	5.7	8.4	6.9	6.4	4.9	4.8	4.4	4.6	4.2	4.8	4.9
(c) Monounsaturated fatty acids	14.3	14.4	11.3	11.9	13.8	13.8	14.8	12.2	13.0	13.2	13.4	13.0
Alcohol	1.1	0.5	1.3	0.9	4.3	6.3	2.1	2.1	3.4	2.6	4.9	2.3

*Per cent energy was derived from the absolute intake figures—using conversion factors recommended by the Committee on Metrication in the Nutritional Sciences of the Royal Society—17 kj/g for protein; 37 kj/g for fat; 16 kj/g for carbohydrate, and 29 kj/g for alcohol.

†Total fat also includes non-fatty acid components.

Source: Baghurst and Record (1983).

Ecological factors

Malnutrition is an end result of many overlapping and inter-acting factors in the physical and social environment including socio-economic and cultural influences, patterns of food production and distribution, cooking practices, education, and housing. Such factors must be considered if a successful nutrition intervention programme is to be mounted. More details are given by Jelliffe (1966) and are summarized in Table 2.7.

The relation of nutritional assessment to the programme

The purpose of the assessment of nutritional status is to develop a programme that meets the needs defined by that assessment. The needs vary greatly between different countries and different regions.

In the following two sections, various types of programmes, meeting different nutritional needs, are discussed for developing and developed countries. The impact of these programmes, once they have been implemented, must be determined by a further assessment of nutritional status to show how far nutritional needs have been met. Assessment, therefore, is an integral part of any programme and is a necessary reference point in its evolution over a number of years. The political and legislative dimensions of this evolution are discussed below.

THE PREVENTION AND CONTROL OF NUTRITIONAL DISORDERS IN DEVELOPING COUNTRIES

The nutritional problems that face developing countries today are similar to those of developed countries in the nineteenth century. These problems may diminish with economic development as has occurred in western coun-

Table 2.7. *Ecological factors to be noted relevant to nutritional assessment*

Home

Family size:	number, relationships, ages, sex, interval between children
Occupations:	primary, secondary
Education:	adult literacy, presence of books and newspapers, children at school
House:	type and construction (roof, walls, floor), number of rooms
Economic:	furniture, clothes, radio, transport (bicycle, wagon, motor scooter, car)
Kitchen:	stove, fuel, cooking utensils, dishes in preparation
Feeding pattern:	meals seen, foods not used, breast-feeding, modern 'prestige' foods
Food storage:	size, contents, pest-proofing
Water supply:	type, distance, purity
Latrine:	type, state

Cultivation site

Land:	area, utilization with different crops (including cash crops)
Farming methods:	tilling procedure, irrigation
Livestock and fishing:	number of beasts and poultry, fish pond

Markets and shops

Food and weaning equipment	availability and prices of foods (especially protein foods for children), advertising, availability of bottles and nipples

Source: Jelliffe (1966).

tries. However, no rapid economic solutions for the developing countries can be expected so that their nutritional problems will persist for some time to come.

Some progress has, however, been made—beri beri, pellagra, and scurvy have virtually disappeared. The four major conditions remaining, protein energy malnutrition (PEM), xerophthalmia, iron-deficiency anaemia, and endemic goitre and cretinism, have now been given priority by the WHO (Beaton and Bengoa 1976). The special public health problems presented by these four conditions are discussed below. The problem of iodine deficiency illustrates the difficulties of control and the application of available technology in developing countries.

Protein–energy malnutrition

This condition denotes a range of disorders. Marasmus, due to inadequate intake of energy and protein, and kwashiorkor, in which protein intake is inadequate but energy intake sufficient, represent the extremes of a spectrum of conditions which includes all gradations and also infections and other deficiencies of vitamins and minerals (De Maeyer 1976).

Protein–energy malnutrition is a major problem in children under the age of five years. Marasmus is a condition of low body weight for age with loss of subcutaneous fat and gross muscle wasting. The severity of the disorder is classified according to the system suggested by Gomez (1979).

First degree —75–90 per cent expected weight for age and sex.
Second degree—60–75 per cent expected weight for age and sex (moderate form).
Third degree —60 per cent of expected weight for age and sex, with all children presenting with oedema (severe form).

Marasmus is more common in towns while kwashiorkor, characterized by low body weight for age with oedema, occurs more often in rural areas. Marasmus occurs in a setting of a rapid succession of pregnancies and early weaning followed by artificial feeding with very diluted milk. Repeated infections occur with further loss of intake of food. Kwashiorkor occurs in a similar situation with a greater incidence at the times where there is a shortage of food.

In rural areas, protein is often reserved for adult men, so that there is an inadequate intake for the normal growth of children. The estimated prevalence of PEM over the period of 1963–73 derived from a series of 25 community surveys is shown in Table 2.8. It is of interest that PEM is now claimed to have been eradicated in China (Chen Xue-cun, personal communication 1981). By contrast PEM has been estimated to affect 5–70 per cent of children in other developing countries so that about 500 million children now alive

will suffer from the disease (Bengoa and Donoso 1974). This figure has not gone without challenge, however. It is based on calculations of food available for consumption, but this makes no allowance for locally produced food, so that more conservative estimates of less than 100 million have been made. Nevertheless the figures are substantial enough!

In one study in Latin America and the Carribean Islands among 7318 deaths in children aged 1–4 years, malnutrition was found to be the underlying cause of death in 9 per cent (range 0–18.4 per cent) of cases and an associated cause in 48.4 per cent (range 0–61.0 per cent). This is believed to be the usual situation in other countries (Puffer and Serrano 1973).

The effect of PEM in childhood on brain development has been much investigated and discussed (Cravioto et al. 1974). The importance of the associated social environment of the child is now recognized and confirmed by studies in rats. Malnourished rats have better mental function in the presence of supporting older rats.

There is often an association between a poor social environment and PEM such that the child's mental development is retarded for both reasons. On the other hand, successful physical care with strong encouragement can lead to virtually a normal catchup in development. In the severe Dutch famine between December 1944 and April 1945 which caused protein and energy deprivation to many infants during their last few months in utero and the early months after birth, no subsequent effect on mental development could be demonstrated at the age of 19 years (Stein et al. 1972).

Xerophthalmia

This condition in its mild form affects only the conjunctiva, but when it spreads to the cornea there is likely to be a corneal ulceration and permanent defect in vision. In severe cases there is softening of the cornea (keratomalacia) which is frequently associated with PEM. A full account of the problem is given in a WHO (1982) technical monograph.

Up to 250 000 young children become blind each year due to xerophthalmia. It is a major problem in Indonesia, Bangladesh, Southern India, Sri Lanka, Afghanistan, and Nepal, but has disappeared from Japan and China. Occasional cases are seen throughout the Middle East, in Latin America, and in Africa.

Table 2.8. *Range and median of prevalence of protein malnutrition in community surveys*

Area	No. of surveys	No. of children examined (1000s)	Severe forms		Moderate forms	
			Range (%)	Median (%)	Range (%)	Median (%)
Latin America	11	109	0.5– 6.3	1.6	3.5–32.0	18.9
Africa	7	25	1.7– 9.8	4.4	5.4–44.9	26.5
Asia	7	39	1.1–20.0	3.2	16.0–46.4	31.2
Total	25	173	0.5–20.0	2.6	3.5–46.4	18.9

Source: De Maeyer (1976).

The condition occurs when the diet does not contain whole milk and butter and only limited amounts of fresh vegetables and fruit. It is rare in breast-fed infants.

Prevention starts with pregnancy when a generous intake of green leafy vegetables will ensure stores of retinol in the fetal liver. This should be continued through lactation. When the condition is of sufficient prevalence, single large oral doses of 60 mg (200 000 i.u.) of retinol in oil should be given to all children as a prophylactic measure and repeated at six-monthly intervals. Large-scale trials have been initiated without adverse effects in India, Bangladesh, Indonesia, and the Philippines. In Guatemala fortification of table sugar has been used with success.

Iron-deficiency anaemia

Iron-deficiency anaemia results from a discrepancy between the amount of iron absorbed and the amount lost from the body. Reduced absorption of iron can come from a low dietary level, poor biological availability, or both. Increased losses occur due to menstruation or to parasitic infestation and during periods of rapid growth the need for iron is increased. Young infants aged 6–18 months and women during pregnancy and menstruation have a greater than average need for iron absorption.

Iron in the predominantly vegetarian diets characteristic of the tropics has a low bioavailability. This means that an excessive quantity of food has to be consumed to provide enough iron although contamination during cooking is an important additional source (Layrisse *et al.* 1976).

The parasites associated with blood loss from the gut include hookworm, necator, and trichuris. Hookworm infestations are estimated to affect 600 million people living in Central and South America, Africa, Asia, and Oceania. Isotopic studies have shown that a single *Ancylostoma duodenale* sucks about 0.20 ml per day, so that infestations of 1000 eggs per gramme of faeces (a moderate clinical level) causes a daily faecal blood loss of 4 ml.

A haemoglobin level of 10–11 g/100 ml has been defined as early anaemia and a level below 10 g/100 ml as marked anaemia (Layrisse *et al.* 1976).

Iron-deficiency anaemia has been estimated to affect 10–15 per cent of menstruating women in temperate zones and 20–30 per cent of pregnant women. In infants the frequency of anaemia may be as high as 40 per cent in the first year of life. In tropical areas, prevalences of between 20 and 40 per cent have been observed in men with much higher prevalences in women.

Prevention can be achieved by increasing dietary intake and reducing losses due to parasitic infestation. Neither of these are achieved easily, and in such situations enrichment of food with iron has been recommended. Wheat flour and infant foods have been used but so far have not been convincingly established to be effective. Vulnerable segments of the population should be covered by iron supplementation and a WHO Expert Group (1972) has recommended levels of 120–140 mg iron per day for pregnant women where less than 10 per cent of energy comes from animal foods. In

children, in areas with high prevalence, 30 mg per day has been recommended throughout the school year.

Iodine-deficiency disorders

The term iodine-deficiency disorders (IDD) has been introduced in order to denote the spectrum of disorders which are caused by iodine deficiency (Hetzel 1983; *Lancet* 1983*a, b*). These include stillbirths, abortions, and congenital anomalies; endemic cretinism, characterized most commonly by mental deficiency, deaf mutism, and spastic diplegia and lesser degrees of neurological defect related to fetal iodine deficiency; and impaired mental function in children and adults with goitre associated with subnormal concentrations of circulating thyroxine.

Endemic goitre is a public health problem when enlargement of the thyroid gland is observed in 5 per cent of adolescent girls aged 12–14 years (Stanbury *et al.* 1974). The condition is due primarily to dietary iodine deficiency with an intake below 50 µg per day which compares with a normal level of 100–150 µg per day. It can be effectively prevented by iodine supplementation.

Endemic cretinism is epidemiologically associated with endemic goitre. It occurs with more severe iodine deficiency, that is, intakes usually below 25 µg per day. It is characterized by mental deficiency, deaf mutism, and spastic diplegia in its fully developed form (Querido *et al.* 1974) (Fig. 2.5). The causal relationship of iodine deficiency to endemic cretinism was demonstrated in a controlled trial with iodized oil in the Western Highlands of New Guinea over the period 1966–72. In this trial, alternate families were given injections of iodized oil and saline. Follow-up over the next five years revealed disappearance of cretinism in the progeny of mothers injected with iodized oil and its continued appearance in the progeny of the mothers who had received a saline injection (Fig. 2.6). With one apparent exception, cretinism was observed only in infants whose mothers had received an injection of iodized oil after pregnancy had begun. If the injection was given before pregnancy complete prevention could be achieved (Pharoah *et al.* 1971).

This finding, which has been confirmed by other uncontrolled trials of iodized oil in South America and Africa, settled the controversy regarding the primary cause of the condition. Its apparent spontaneous disappearance in parts of southern Europe in the first half of the nineteenth century, which had raised considerable doubts as to whether it was indeed related to iodine deficiency, can be attributed to diversification of the diet as a result of social and economical development.

More recently, brain retardation has been demonstrated in the fetal lamb following administration of a severely iodine-deficient diet (mainly composed of maize) to the ewe before and during pregnancy (Potter *et al.* 1982).

These conditions occur in mountainous areas all over the world (Alps, Andes, and the Himalayas) including the many mountain ranges of China. It also occurs in plains in North China, India, Africa, Europe, and North America. The

Fig. 2.5. A cretin from Sinjiang, China, who is also deaf mute, on the left, and on the right the barefoot doctor of her village. Both are about 30 years of age. (Courtesy of Dr Ma Tai, Tianjin, People's Republic of China.)

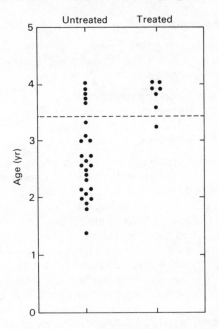

Fig. 2.6. Ages of cretins born since September 1966 in a controlled trial of the use of iodized oil injection in prevention of endemic cretinism in the Jimi River District of New Guinea. The absence of younger cretins from the treated group is clearly shown.
(Reproduced from Pharoah *et al.* (1971) by permission.)

common feature is soil low in iodine which results from leaching due to high rainfall or glaciation. Goitre persists if the population continues to eat locally produced food which is characteristic of subsistence agriculture as in China and India. Over the past 30 years moderate iodine deficiency has been corrected spontaneously by diversification of the food supply in many parts of the world. However, goitre and cretinism still persist in many areas, especially in Asia where many millions are still affected and iodine supplementation is necessary to prevent the condition.

The social impact of iodine deficiency arises not so much from goitre as from the effects on the central nervous system (Hetzel 1983). The fully developed condition of endemic cretinism is accompanied by lesser degrees of co-ordination defects in apparently healthy members of the iodine-deficient population. Children in Central Java were demonstrated to start walking at an earlier age following iodization (Dulberg *et al.* 1982). Co-ordination defects were observed in the controlled trial in the apparently normal children of iodine-deficient mothers in New Guinea but not

in those whose mothers had received iodized oil (Connolly *et al.* 1979). More recently, improved mental function has been shown in goitrous school children in Bolivia two years after oral administration of iodized oil (Bautista *et al.* 1982).

All these recent findings justify a much more aggressive approach with iodization programmes than in the past. As already pointed out (Hetzel 1983), it has been suggested that the term 'Iodine-deficiency disorders' (IDD) replace that of 'goitre' to denote the variety of conditions due to iodine deficiency. This will assist in promulgation of a broader view of the problem and will be followed by the establishment of more active programmes than in the past (*Lancet* 1983*b*).

Epidemiological assessment of iodine deficiency
Epidemiological assessment of iodine deficiency is necessary before initiating an iodization programme. It includes the following aspects:

1. Prevalence of goitre.
2. Prevalence of cretinism.
3. Assessment of iodine nutrition, usually by measurement of urinary iodine excretion.
4. Measurement of thyroid function, by determination of serum levels of thyroxine (T_4) and pituitary thyrotropic hormone (TSH).
5. Data on food production and food habits relevant to the feasibility of the different methods for iodine supplementation.

Prevalence of goitre

The prevalence of goitre is usually determined with reference to the classification of Perez et al. (1960) which grades goitre into four categories:

Grade 0: Subjects without a goitre.
Grade I: Subjects with a palpable goitre.
Grade II: Subjects with a visible goitre.
Grade III: Subjects with a very large goitre.

Minor modifications have been made to this classification since 1960 and are fully described elsewhere (Thilly et al. 1980). Goitre (Grade I) is said to occur when the thyroid gland is enlarged so that the lateral lobes are more voluminous than the last phalanx of the thumb. Two subgrades, Ia and Ib, are often used depending on whether the palpable gland is or is not visible with the neck in extension. Nodularity of the goitre is also recorded as an indication of long duration. Nodules are usually found in adults and elderly subjects but in severe endemias may be seen in pre-adolescents.

The reproducibility of determinations of goitre prevalence has been examined (Thilly et al. 1980). In general, rates of visible goitre (Grade II) are usually reproducible but there is some variation with determination of Grade I goitres. With high rates, values are usually within 3–5 per cent. Systematic non-random observer variation can be noted and allowed for in the final calculations. Comparisons between goitre rates in endemias determined by the same observers, with or without iodization, control for these errors.

Prevalence of cretinism

Recently agreement was reached on a definition of endemic cretinism comprising the following three major features (Querido et al. 1974):

1. *Epidemiology*. It is associated with endemic goitre and severe iodine deficiency.
2. *Clinical manifestations*. These comprise mental deficiency, together with either: (i) a predominant neurological syndrome consisting of defects of hearing and speech, and with characteristic disorders of stance and gait of varying degree; or (ii) predominant hypothyroidism and stunted growth. Although in some regions one of the two types may predominate, in other areas a mixture of the two syndromes will occur.
3. *Prevention*. In areas where adequate correction of iodine deficiency has been achieved, endemic cretinism has been prevented.

Cretinism is usually recorded with reference to the clinical features—mental deficiency, deafness with or without deaf mutism, and ataxia due to a spastic diplegia. With the exception of Zaïre in Africa, clinical hypothyroidism with or without dwarfism is a much less common feature of the disease.

It is essential to establish criteria for cretinism in any survey and to recognize that cretins will not appear in the usual line up of schoolchildren for determination of goitre prevalence. They are not at school and may be secreted by their families.

More recently, assessment of co-ordination (Connolly et al. 1979; Pharoah et al. 1982) has been carried out by the use of special tests involving bimanual dexterity (threading of beads or putting pegs into a peg board). Walking age has also been determined retrospectively in Indonesia and found to be reduced by iodization (Dulberg et al. 1982). These assessments have disclosed a wider prevalence of neurological defects in iodine-deficient populations than that due to cretinism.

The intelligence quota (IQ) may also be used to assess more accurately mental function. But there are major difficulties, due to cultural and educational factors, in using the usual tests (Stanford Binet or Bender Tests) in populations in developing countries due for example to variations in verbal proficiency. In developing countries, cultural factors may even influence the results of non-verbal tests of co-ordination as in the case of screwing a bolt (Connolly et al. 1979). This was a very difficult task for New Guinea children whatever their iodine nutritional status and such a test is not appropriate as a discriminating measure.

The bias of differences in culture and educational status in the performance of IQ tests cannot be controlled in simple surveys or descriptive studies (Bleichrodt et al. 1980). This requires randomized controlled trials as in the case of Papua New Guinea (Pharoah et al. 1971; Connolly et al. 1979). Recently a randomized controlled trial of the effect on IQ (Stanford Binet and Bender Tests) of oral iodized oil administration to goitrous school children in Bolivia was reported. This study showed some improvement, particularly in girls, but there was iodine contamination of the control group (Bautista et al. 1982). Such a study needs to be repeated in several endemic areas.

Assessment of iodine nutrition

The most convenient assessment of iodine nutrition is by measurement of urinary iodine excretion. A 24-hour sample can be collected, but this is often very difficult to conduct in developing countries. Much more convenient is measurement of iodine excretion in casual samples; coincident measurement of creatinine excretion enables expression of iodine excretion as microgram per gram of creatinine. Determination of such levels in 30 subjects provides a good measure of iodine nutrition by reference to observations elsewhere (Follis 1964). Follis (1964) suggested an arbitrary classification into five groups of increasing severity of iodine deficiency in terms of increments of 25 µg iodine per gram creatinine (Thilly et al. 1980).

It has been suggested (Querido et al. 1974) that goitre endemias may be classified into three groups depending on the level of urinary iodine excretion.

Grade I Goitre endemias with an average iodine excretion of more than 50 µg/g creatinine. At this level, thyroid hormone supply, adequate for normal mental and physical development can be anticipated.

Grade II Goitre endemias with an average urinary iodine

excretion of between 25 and 50 µg/g creatinine. In these circumstances adequate thyroid hormone formation may be impaired. This group is at risk for hypothyroidism but not for overt cretinism.

Grade III Goitre endemias with an average urinary iodine excretion below 25 µg/g creatinine. Endemic cretinism is a serious risk in such a population.

Observations on urine iodine excretion can be supplemented by data on iodine levels in water—usually below 1 µg per litre in endemic areas—or in soil.

Urine iodine measurements should be used as the first reference point in assessing iodine nutrition and the effects of iodization programmes. The data provides direct evidence which is essential for the rapid assessment of an iodine-deficiency problem. Monitoring is now being carried out with initial reference to urine iodine excretion. Supporting epidemiological data on other manifestations of IDD can then be sought in the light of determination of iodine excretion levels (*Lancet* 1983*b*).

Measurement of thyroid function

Circulating thyroid hormones thyroxine (T_4) and pituitary thyrotropic hormone (TSH) can now be measured on blood spots dried on filter paper. This method has permitted the development of routine neonatal screening for hypothyroidism (Dussault *et al.* 1975) in western countries. The same technology can be used to screen populations at risk of iodine deficiency with a likely reduction in circulatory T_4 and elevated levels of TSH. The spot sample on the filter paper is the equivalent of about 1.5 µl of serum. Satisfactory correlations with normally secured samples of serum T_4 have been obtained. A similar technique has been developed for the measurement of TSH in the equivalent of 3 µl of serum (Larsen *et al.* 1980). Samples can be held for six months without loss.

This is a considerable advance and is of great value for epidemiological assessment. Particular attention can be given to screening the neonate in iodine-deficient regions. There is evidence of reductions in the level of thyroid hormones in up to 10 per cent of infants born in iodine-deficient areas (Ermans *et al.* 1980). This compares with 1 in 3000–4000 in iodine-sufficient areas in developed countries (Ermans *et al.* 1980).

Determination of T_4 and TSH is carried out by immunoassay which can be automated. Suitable equipment is generally available in clinical hospital laboratories in developed countries. However, many laboratories in developing countries do not as yet possess such instruments as autogamma counters. The availability of such technology should be regarded as a high priority in developing countries with major iodine deficiency problems because of the importance of restoration of lowered levels of thyroid hormones for normal postnatal brain development.

Data on food production and food habits

Such data are relevant to the development of iodization programmes. In China strong preference for rock salt from the desert in Sinjiang and Inner Mongolia has led to the use of iodized oil injections in these endemias (Ma Tai *et al.*

1982). In Thailand the use of alternative condiments such as soya sauce and fish sauce has been successful in pilot studies (Romsai Suwanik *et al.* 1982).

The technology of iodization

Iodized salt

Many methods have been used to increase iodine intake including addition of iodine as iodide or iodate to various foods such as bread, water, and milk. In Mexico, for example, iodide has been added to sweets. However, the addition of iodine to salt is by far the most widely used and simplest method available. Unlike various foods and water, the intake of salt as a condiment tends to be more constant from day to day. However, the problem remains of acceptability to non-salt-eating populations or populations (as in Thailand and China) who prefer their own non-iodine-containing salt. A greater problem is ensuring the production of iodized salt of adequate quality in sufficient amounts for large iodine-deficient populations, as in Indonesia. Cost is also a problem whether or not it is provided by governments.

Recommended levels of iodization vary in different countries. In India 1 part per 40 000 has been recommended, and in Finland 1 part per 25 000 was required for effective control of goitre. On the assumption of an intake of 5 g of salt per day, a level of 1 part per 100 000 would provide 50 µg. If the salt intake is lower than this, as it often is in populations in developing countries, a higher level of supplementation is required. In general a level of intake of 100 µg per day can be regarded as adequate for the prevention of goitre and cretinism.

The addition of iodide (or iodate) to salt in a factory requires subsequent checking under storage conditions in the moist tropics. The feasibility of salt iodization for the moist tropics has been established in Northern India by Sooch and Ramalingaswami (1965) who showed that iodate was superior to iodide under these conditions.

Iodized oil by injection

The value of iodized oil injection in the prevention of endemic goitre and endemic cretinism was first established in New Guinea with controlled trials involving the use of saline injection as a control (McCullagh 1963; Pharoah *et al.* 1971). Experience in South America (Kevany *et al.* 1968) and Africa (Thilly *et al.* 1977) has confirmed the value of the measure and the quantitative correction of severe iodine deficiency by a single intramuscular injection 2–4 ml has been demonstrated (Buttfield and Hetzel 1967; Thilly *et al.* 1977) (Table 2.9).

The injection of iodized oil can be administered through local health services, where they exist, or by special teams. In New Guinea (Hetzel 1974) the injection of a population in excess of 100 000 was carried out by public health teams along with the injection of triple antigen (immunization procedure). Iodized oil is singularly appropriate for the isolated village community so characteristic of mountainous endemic goitre areas. It has been used in pilot studies in the Himalayan Regions of Pakistan (Chapman *et al.* 1972) and Nepal (Ibbertson *et al.* 1972).

Table 2.9. *The effect of iodized oil on thyroid function in New Guinea subjects**

Group	Urinary iodine (µg/24 h)	^{131}I uptake (% at 24 h)	Serum PBI (µg/100 ml)	T$_3$ resin uptake (% of normal)
Untreated	11.5±12.4 (91)	70±19 (181)	4.1±2.1 (204)	91±12.1 (195)
Treated 18 months and 3 years before	67±83 (47)	33±20 (94)	8.0±2.0 (79)	97±14.8 (77)
Treated 3 months before	258±109 (8)	6.0±3 (20)	44.7±18.4 (20)	110±15.5 (20)
Treated 18 months before	119±114 (18)	31±20 (51)	8.2±2.6 (27)	97±15.8 (27)
Treated 3 years before	35±25 (28)	37±19 (43)	7.8±1.6 (52)	97±14.7 (50)
Treated 4½ years before	23±21 (11)	44±18 (67)	6.4±2.4 (43)	99±16.0 (43)
Australian normal range	70–140	16–40	3.6–7.2	70–110

*Statistical analysis showed highly significant differences between the treated and untreated groups in urinary iodine, ^{131}I uptake and serum PBI ($p < 0.001$). There was no significant difference in the ^{131}I uptake or serum PBI between subjects treated three years before. The figures given are for the mean ± the standard deviation, with the number of subjects tested shown in parentheses.
Source: Buttfield and Hetzel (1967).

In a suitable area the oil should be administered to all females up to the age 40 years and all males up to the age of 20 years. A recommended dosage schedule is shown in Table 2.10. A repeat of the injection would be required in 3–5 years depending on the dose given and the age. In children the need is greater than in adults and the recommended dose should be repeated in three years if severe iodine-deficiency persists.

Table 2.10. *Recommended dosages of ethiodized oil containing 37 per cent iodine**

Age	Iodine (mg)	Dose (ml)
0–6 months	95.0–180.0	0.2–0.4
6–12 months	142.5–285.0	0.3–0.6
6 months–6 years	232.5–465.0	0.5–1.0
6–45 years	475.0–950.0	1.0–2.0

*The dosage should be reduced to 0.2 ml for all persons with nodular goitres or presenting single thyroid nodules without goitre.
Source: Stanbury *et al.* (1974).

Iodized oil by mouth
The administration of a single oral dose of iodized oil for 1–2 years proved effective in South America (Watanabe *et al.* 1974) and more recently in Burma (Kyme-Thein *et al.* 1979). This method is being further investigated in view of the saving of the considerable cost of injection which consumes more than half the total cost of such a programme. For example the cost of plastic syringes and needles for 10 000 people was estimated to be US$9177 at 1974 prices out of a total budget of $13 000 (Stanbury *et al.* 1974). However, these costs are now much less.

Water iodization
Reduction in goitre rate from 61 to 30 per cent with 79 per cent of goitres showing visible reduction has been demon-

strated following water iodization in Sarawak (Maberly *et al.* 1981). Significant rises in serum T$_4$ and falls in TSH were also shown. Urinary iodine excretions were variable due to intermittent obstruction of the iodinator but eventually the levels indicated iodine repletion. Similar results have been obtained in preliminary studies in Thailand by Suwanik *et al.* (1982).

This method is appropriate at village level if a specific source of drinking water can be identified—otherwise there is a heavy cost since less than 1 per cent of a general water supply is used for drinking purposes. The antiseptic benefit is also significant with this method.

Other methods
In Bangkok, Suwanik *et al.* (1982) have developed iodized fish sauce and iodized soya sauce as additional iodized condiments. These sauces are also being used for iron supplementation (Suwanik *et al.* 1982).

Hazards of iodization
A mild increase in incidence of thyrotoxicosis has now been described following iodized salt programmes in Europe and South America and following the introduction of iodized bread in Holland and Tasmania (Connolly *et al.* 1970; Stewart *et al.* 1971; Stanbury *et al.* 1974). A few cases have been noted following iodized oil administration in South America. No cases have yet been described in New Guinea, India, or Zaïre. This is probably due to the scattered nature of the population into small villages and limited opportunities for observation (Stewart *et al.* 1971; Larsen *et al.* 1980). The condition is largely confined to those over 40 years of age—a smaller proportion of the population in developing countries than in developed countries (Stewart *et al.* 1971; Larsen *et al.* 1980). For this reason iodized oil should preferably not be given to those aged over 40 years. However, if thyrotoxicosis develops it can be readily treated by medical management with radioiodine or antithyroid drugs.

The risk of iodism or iodide goitre seems to be very small.

An increase in lymphocytic thyroiditis (Hashimoto's disease) has been claimed following iodization but this is still disputed (Stanbury *et al.* 1974).

Implementation and surveillance

It is apparent from a recent review of goitre control programmes (Thilly and Hetzel 1980) that availability of technology does not alone determine whether an iodization programme will be successful. In Finland, a public information campaign was necessary to promote the distribution of iodized salt (Lamberg *et al.* 1970). While such measures are needed in other countries with continuing endemias, many are at a stage of economic and social development which constitutes a formidable obstacle to such programmes.

In Central and South America other factors are in operation (Schaefer 1974). These include: lack of political pressures from the isolated rural areas where the problems of endemic goitre and endemic cretinism are most evident—this applies particularly to countries such as Bolivia, Peru, and Ecuador—and problems in the production of iodized salt—including production costs and enforcement of legislation in countries where there is a large number of salt-producing plants.

In Indonesia, China and India, iodized salt production is a major problem. However, in other countries of the Western Pacific Region such as Laos, Kampuchea, and Vietnam with continuing endemias in their extensive hilly and mountainous areas, neither legislation or a programme exists.

In Africa there are special problems in countries like Zaïre with virtually no basic health services in large areas. Iodization programmes can be greatly helped by the existence of basic health services, particularly in the use of iodized oil, but only if the necessary education and information is disseminated efficiently through such channels (Hetzel 1978*b*).

Reference has been made to a number of factors such as politics, information and education, and legislation, in relation to the implementation of goitre control programmes. Elsewhere it has been suggested that a social process model, as shown diagrammatically in Fig. 2.7, may be helpful in linking together these factors (Thilly and Hetzel 1980).

The social process begins with the collection of epidemiological data on the prevalence of goitre and cretinism (1). These are then analysed (2), with a view to dissemination in mass media (3) and the planning of an iodization programme (4). After a period of discussion in the mass media, in the public health department, and with politicians, 'ground swell' is demonstrated for a plan which usually requires legislative measures which necessitates political agreement (5). Political agreement is essential before implementation (6) can occur. Implementation of the programme is followed by evaluation (7) with the collection of further survey data on the prevalence of goitre and cretinism which hopefully will demonstrate its reduction. These data should then be fed back to the community to demonstrate the benefits of the programme and the need for its continuity.

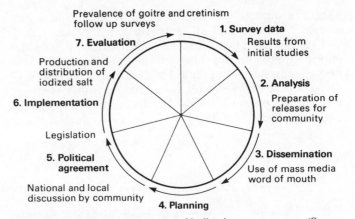

Fig. 2.7. Model of social process of iodization programme. (Source: Thilly and Hetzel (1980).)

On the other hand, demonstrable failure of the programme leads to investigation of the reasons of which the public can then be informed leading to further discussion of appropriate measures for overcoming the obstacles. The process involves a continuous feedback to the community which ensures continuity of interest and support.

Indonesia

The application of this model to the iodization programme in Indonesia has been described by Djokomoeljanto *et al.* (1982). The social process began with an extensive study of the problem of endemic cretinism in Central Java. This led to a briefing of politicians and in due course to the implementation of a major iodization programme in Indonesia which was authorized by the Second Pelita for 1974–78.

The plan followed that recommended by Stanbury *et al.* (1974). A detailed map of the distribution of goitre in Indonesia was developed and seven hyperendemic areas designated. Some 1 036 828 injections of iodized oil were given between 1974 and 1978 together with the production and distribution of up to 20 000 tons of iodized salt per year. The injections were given in the seven previously designated hyperendemic areas. In every village with a cretin, the whole population under 40 years of age was injected. Appropriate training programmes for necessary paramedical personnel were undertaken and by 1982, 1594 had been trained.

An evaluation of the programme in Central Java was recently reported by Dulberg *et al.* (1982). Determination of urine iodine excretion revealed a normal range compared to the low levels observed in 1972 prior to iodization (Fig. 2.8). Disappearance of cretinism in children under the age of 7 years (i.e. born since 1974) was demonstrated in contrast to a 7 per cent incidence in children in the age range 7–16 years. Finally a significant reduction in the age at which children began to walk was shown following iodization, as reported by mothers interviewed by young Indonesian women in their own language.

This year, the political process has gone further with legislation now passed prohibiting the consumption of non-iodized salt. The decree has now been signed by the three

Ministers directly involved (Health, Welfare, and Commerce). The aim is total prevention in the near future.

The success of the Indonesian programme provides important lessons for other developing countries. One major factor has been political recognition of the effects of severe iodine deficiency on the central nervous system—in essence the concept of IDD rather than goitre (Hetzel 1983; Djokomoeljanto *et al.* 1983).

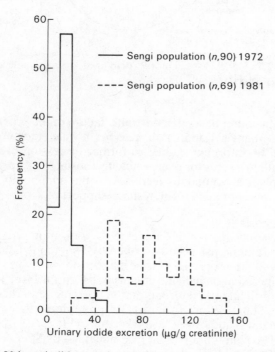

Fig. 2.8. Urinary iodide excretion (µg/g creatinine) in 1972 before the iodization programme in Sengi Central Java (which began in 1974) and after the iodization programme in 1981.

India

A recent report from India indicates a continuing major problem with iodine deficiency (Pandav and Kochupillai 1982). Only 15 per cent or less of the known endemic areas have been covered by iodization. Endemic goitre and endemic cretinism are widely distributed on the Indian subcontinent with an intense endemic running along the southern slopes, foothills, and adjacent plains of the Himalayas extending over 2400 km from Kashmir in the West to the Naga Hills in the East.

About 120 million people live in the known endemic goitre regions of whom about 40 million have been estimated to be suffering from goitre. However, other pockets of endemic goitre are constantly being discovered and the total population affected is nearer 300 million with over 60 million suffering from goitre.

A major pilot study designed to determine the effectiveness of iodized salt in the Indian endemic was carried out between 1956 and 1962 (Sooch *et al.* 1973) in the Kangra Valley (Himachal pradesh). The study area was divided into three zones, A, B, and C. After a baseline survey in 1956, the salt distributed to zones A and C was fortified with potassium iodide and potassium iodate respectively while zone B was supplied with unfortified salt. The salt fortification was such as to supply approximately 200 µg of iodine per caput per day. In 1962, six years of iodization, a striking decrease in the prevalence of goitre was observable in zones A (from 38 to 19 per cent) and C (from 38 to 15 per cent) when compared to uniodized zone B (from 38 to 40 per cent). Six years later a systematic survey of goitre prevalence showed further reduction in the prevalence rates for zone A and zone C (8.5 and 9.1 per cent respectively). In 1972, spot checks on goitre prevalence in the iodized areas by an independent group of physicians showed negligible prevalence of goitre among schoolchildren and ^{131}I uptake and urinary excretion of iodide had become normal (Table 2.11).

Table 2.11. *Effect of iodized salt on goitre rate (%) in Kangra Valley, India*

Zone	1956	1962	1968
A	38	19	8.5
B	38	40	—
C	38	15	9.1

Source: Sooch *et al.* (1973).
Zone A – iodized salt   Zone B – no fortification
Zone C – iodated salt

Encouraged by this prospective study, the Government of India between 1962 and 1965 installed a total of 12 iodization plants in different parts of the country, with the financial assistance of UNICEF. The concentration of iodate in salt is standardized at 25 p.p.m. In 10 g of salt, the iodate supplement at this concentration amounts to 250 µg which is equivalent to 150 µg of iodine. In India, the average daily consumption of salt per head is 10–15 g (Gopalan *et al.* 1978), which would give 225 µg of iodine per day. This prescribes for the daily requirement of iodine suggested by a WHO seminar on goitre control held in 1967.

However, the actual availability of salt in India is only 15 per cent of the total requirement for the known endemic regions of the country. As there are several bottlenecks in the existing organization for the implementation of the prophylactic programme, even the available quantity of iodized salt is not effectively utilized. Meanwhile, more and more areas are being demonstrated to have endemic goitre. Pandav and Kochupillai (1982) concluded by saying: 'It is, therefore, no exaggeration to say that the prophylactic measure so far adopted against the problem of endemic goitre is negligible, when compared to the real magnitude of the problem.

China

A recent report (Ma Tai *et al.* 1982) has described the massive problem of endemic goitre and cretinism in China.

Ever since the establishment of the People's Republic of

China in 1949, the Chinese government and its Ministry of Health have given full attention to the use of iodized salt for goitre prevention. It is a co-operative enterprise under the direction of the Chinese Central Government, involving members of the Ministry of Health, Ministry of Chemical Industry, and Ministry of Commerce, with the National Co-operative Head Office as executive committee. With the help of technical health experts, satisfactory results have been achieved with the close collaboration of the above-mentioned ministries and provincial governments.

Up to the end of 1979, in the 16 provinces and autonomous regions in greater North China, including north-eastern as well as north-western provinces, iodized salt has been supplied free of additional cost to 70 per cent of the areas where goitre is known to be endemic. The number of goitre patients decreased from 15 million in 1973 to 7.5 million in 1979. No new cases have been discovered in 20 per cent of these areas, and the disease has come under control in several provinces. For example, Shaanxi Province used to be a heavily endemic area, where there were 576 000 goitre patients in 1972. The number decreased to 158 000 in 1979 as a result of persistent use of iodized salt during these years. Also a salt-iodization programme has been carried out regularly in Hebei Province, where there were 1 560 000 goitre patients in 1972. By 1979, the number had dropped to 390 000.

In addition to iodized salt prophylaxis, iodized oil has been used in some areas of China. People living in the Tarim Basin of Sinjiang Autonomous Region and Nei-Monggol (Inner Mongolia) Autonomous Region can get raw rock salt at no cost from the numerous salt deposits in the desert and the ordinary salt iodization programme is not applicable there. Under such circumstances, iodized oil injection is the method of choice. In China, instead of the more expensive ethiodol, iodized walnut oil or iodized soya bean oil has been used for intramuscular injection and has given satisfactory results without significant unfavourable side effects. Oral administration of iodized oil is also under trial. Since the eleventh Session of the Communist Party Congress in 1978, following the Cultural Revolution (1966–76), there has been a major effort to institute massive iodization programmes. In Sinjiang since 1978, some 707 000 subjects in the age range of 7–45 years have been injected with iodized oil. A further 300 000–400 000 were injected in 1983 and work has begun with oral oil. A similar major programme has been initiated in Inner Mongolia.

The injections are given by barefoot doctors and China has a very appropriate infrastructure for public health measures such as mass injections of iodized oil. This contrasts with the lack of infrastructure in other South-east Asian countries (Hetzel 1978b). The Chinese take seriously the impairment of the achievement of genetic potential that iodine deficiency causes, particularly through effects on the brain, and hence give a high priority to iodization programmes.

At the recent 4th Asian Congress of Nutrition, the following recommendations were made by an international symposium on the 'Control of Iodine Deficiency in Asia' to the various international agencies concerned with the problem (WHO, UNICEF, IUNS), various national aid bodies, and national governments (Lancet 1983b):

1. The iodine-deficiency problem should in future be designated as iodine-deficiency disorders (IDD) and the term 'goitre' be discontinued as it no longer reflects the state of existing knowledge.

2. Reliable estimates indicate that 400 million people in Asia are currently suffering from iodine deficiency.

3. The major effect of iodine deficiency is on the brain. This includes the fetal and neonatal brain, as well as mental function in childhood and adult life.

4. Correction of iodine deficiency by the use of iodized salt or iodized oil has been shown to prevent the mental deficiency that might otherwise occur.

5. The eradication of iodine deficiency with prevention of mental deficiency is feasible and effective at modest cost in comparison to the cost of the disability.

6. The serious effects of iodine deficiency on human potential have now been adequately demonstrated. The constraints placed on iodine-deficient communities are such as to seriously limit their social life and development. The eradication of iodine deficiency in Asia has become mandatory.

7. Iodized oil (by injection or by mouth) offers an effective emergency method for the correction of severe iodine deficiency until iodized salt can be distributed. Such a measure can be carried out through the primary health care system.

8. Iodization programmes with iodized salt and/or iodized oil should be monitored by determinations of urine iodine in regional laboratories. Those could be in India (which might also serve Sri Lanka, Nepal, Bhutan, and Bangladesh), Burma, Thailand, Indonesia, China, and Pakistan. These could be supported by WHO and UNICEF.

9. We urge international agencies and national governments in the region to reappraise existing programmes with the aim of eradication of iodine deficiency in Asia in the next ten years. We offer our expertise and knowledge to national Governments and the international agencies with responsibility for this problem.

10. We strongly recommend regular meetings in the Asian region to evaluate programmes and monitor progress in the eradication of iodine deficiency.

11. The eradication of iodine deficiency could be a major component of Health for All by the Year 2000 in the Asian region.

It is appropriate to conclude this section with a quotation from an address by Dr Hafdan Mahler, Director-General of WHO entitled 'Blueprint for health for all' (Mahler 1977):

Nutrition activities—a cornerstone of primary health care.
Malnutrition is probably the single most important health problem in developing countries. The national and international health sectors must now come to grips with their responsibilities in nutrition, identify their proper political needs, define realistic policies and strategies, generate appropriate technologies, and formulate applicable programmes. If we do not succeed in making effective and realistic nutritional activities a cornerstone of primary health care, we are

hardly worth our salt as health managers. Once more we seem to have the knowledge but neither the political will nor the social imagination to apply it.

THE ROLE OF DIET AND NUTRITION IN THE PREVENTION AND CONTROL OF THE MAJOR HEALTH PROBLEMS OF DEVELOPED COUNTRIES

The diseases of overnutrition

The major health problems of developed countries in the second half of the twentieth century have changed completely from those so obvious at the beginning of the century. Chronic non-infectious diseases—coronary heart disease, stroke and accidents—have now displaced acute infectious diseases (particularly respiratory and gastrointestinal) as the major problems (Fig. 2.9).

Diet and nutrition are significant factors in all these conditions if we include alcohol consumption as part of the diet. These factors, together with cigarette smoking, comprise the important identified features of life-style in developed countries which are related to health and are generally considered to have been significant influences in relation to increases in incidence of these diseases that have occurred particularly over the period 1950–75—a time of unprecedented affluence in the western world. These diseases are in fact often called the 'diseases of affluence'. They have also become evident in affluent minorities living in developing countries such as India, Indonesia, and Japan.

Detailed reviews of the available evidence linking coronary heart disease to diet are provided elsewhere (Chapters 8 and 16). The relation of diet to other diseases is discussed in Volume 1, Chapter 4. Table 2.12 provides a brief summary of the findings on cardiovascular diseases and cancer at the present time. The available evidence is by no means complete—much research remains to be done—but is probably sufficient to provide a basis for public health action designed to prevent and control these disorders.

In general this evidence arises from three major approaches; the epidemiological, the clinical, and the experimental. Detailed reviews are provided in the subsequent sections in this volume concerned with particular systems of the body.

The relationship of coronary heart disease with diet continues to be the subject of much controversy. Current epidemiological evidence has been regarded as strong enough to justify advice to the community at large, by 92 per cent of a group of 211 nutritional scientists from 22 different countries doing research on atherosclerosis and lipids from both medical and experimental points of view (Norum 1978). While controversy continues, most scientists feel that the stage has been reached when some dietary advice is warranted, especially for prevention directed to younger age groups.

Less data are available on the relation between diet, nutrition, and cancer. However, in the case of the gastrointestinal cancer, including both the upper and the lower tracts, an increasing body of evidence indicates the impor-

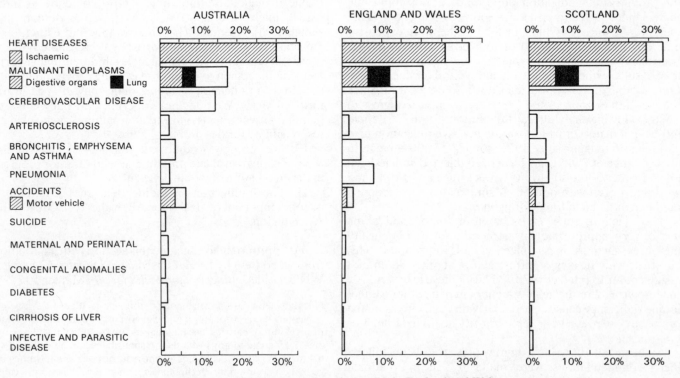

Fig. 2.9. Profile of major causes of mortality in England and Wales, Australia and Scotland. (Source: Hetzel and Selwood (1977).)

Table 2.12. *Summary of current information on the role of diet, alcohol, and smoking in the aetiology of major cardiovascular diseases and cancers*

Disease	Evidence of causal association	
	Generally accepted	Suggestive
Ischaemic heart disease	Excess caloric intake High intake of saturated fats Cigarette smoking	Moderate intake of alcohol (especially wine) may reduce risk
Hypertension and related diseases (including 'stroke')	High salt intake Excess caloric intake	Alcohol
Liver cirrhosis	Alcohol (especially spirits and wine)	
Cancer of mouth, pharynx, oesophagus	Alcohol (especially spirits and wine)	
Cancer of larynx	Alcohol (especially spirits) Cigarette smoking	
Cancer of lung	Cigarette smoking	Vitamin A deficiency
Cancer of bladder	Cigarette smoking	
Cancer of colon	High fat intake	Low dietary fibre intake High meat intake Low green and yellow vegetable intake
Cancer of rectum		As for colon High beer intake
Cancer of pancreas		High alcohol intake Cigarette smoking High fat, low fibre intake

Source: Armstrong and McMichael (1981).

tance of dietary factors (Table 2.12) (Doll 1979; Armstrong *et al.* 1982). A prospective study designed to determine the benefit of supplementary vitamin A intake in the prevention of cancer has now begun in the US following an extensive examination of the evidence (Peto *et al.* 1981).

In relation to diabetes, the role of refined carbohydrate is strongly suggested by international studies including particularly the findings on Pacific Island populations already cited in Volume 1, Chapter 4.

In the case of cerebrovascular disease, the higher prevalence in Japan is associated with a high prevalence of hypertension and a high salt intake (20–30 g/day). In New Guinea and the Pacific Islands a low salt intake is associated with low blood pressure.

Alcohol consumption is also a major factor in the prevalence of hypertension in industrialized countries, in traffic crashes (4 per cent of deaths in Australia), and in cirrhosis of the liver (1 per cent of deaths in Australia) (Hetzel 1981).

The development of dietary guidelines

This evidence provides an adequate basis for a public health strategy directed to a change in diet in industrialized countries. As already pointed out (Volume 1, Chapter 4) there is nothing 'divinely ordained' about the western diet which has only assumed its present form in this century due to great increases in agricultural production (particularly related to meat) and to the development of the modern food-proces-

sing industry. The merits of the present-day diet have now been widely questioned in relation to the major contemporary health problems (Hegsted 1978; Hetzel 1981).

In the last 12 years no less than 37 committees in different countries have recommended dietary guidelines most often related to coronary heart disease (Truswell 1981). However, since 1975, government committees in nine countries have made very similar recommendations (Table 2.13) concerning the diet in relation to all the major health problems, not just those of coronary heart disease.

In general a reduction in total fat is recommended, coupled with an increase in polyunsaturated fat in a number of instances. A reduction of fat to 35 per cent of total energy is often specified, of which about one-third should be saturated (12 per cent), one-third monounsaturated, and one-third polyunsaturated. This gives a ratio of polyunsaturated to saturated fat of 1.0.

The dietary goals advocated by the US Senate Select Committee on Nutrition and Human Needs (1977) have received considerable adverse criticism (Harper 1978; National Academy of Sciences 1980). The Senate Committe recommendations included a reduction of fat intake to 30 per cent of total dietary energy and reduction in salt intake to less than 5 g/day. Such changes are substantial and not readily achieved (Fig. 2.10).

There is a division of opinion regarding the guidelines among leading figures in nutrition and clinical medicine including cardiology, public health, and epidemiology (*Nutrition Today* 1977). Clinicians, including cardiologists, were usually against the idea of dietary guidelines while those in public health and epidemiology were generally in favour. These differences reflect the contrast between the clinical and public health views of the evidence (Hegsted 1978; Blackburn 1979).

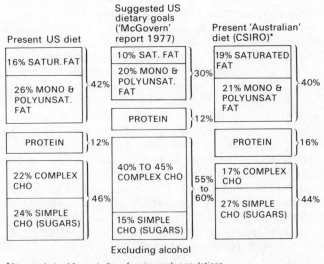

Excluding alcohol

* Figures derived from studies of various sub-populations

Fig. 2.10. A comparison of the diet recommended under the US Dietary Goals with the present US diet and the median values obtained for various Australian subpopulations. Figures are derived from various subpopulations (see Table 2.6) and excludes alcohol. (Source: Baghurst and Record (1983).)

Table 2.13. *Summary of national recommendations on dietary guidelines*

	Reduce obesity	Increase exercise	Reduce total fat	Increase polyunsaturated fat	Reduce cholesterol	Reduce sugar	Increase starch and/or fibre	Reduce salt	Moderate alcohol	Encourage breast-feeding
Swedish Medical Expert Group (1975)	Yes	Yes	Yes	Yes	Not stated	Yes	More bread, potatoes, fruit, and vegetables	Not stated	Not stated	Not stated
Norway, Ministry of Agriculture (1976)	Yes	Yes	Yes	Yes	Not stated	Yes	More fibre, bread, potatoes, fruits, and vegetables	Not stated	Not stated	Not stated
Canada, Department of Health and Welfare, 2nd edition (1977)	Yes	Yes	Yes	Yes	Not stated	Yes	More fruits, vegetables, and wholegrains	Yes	Not stated	Not stated
US Senate Select Committee, 2nd edition (1977)	Yes	Yes	Yes	Yes	Yes	Yes	Increase fruits, vegetables, and wholegrains	Yes	Implied	Not stated
Irish Agricultural Institute Health Advisory Committee (1977)	Yes	Yes	Yes—in order to reduce obesity	Yes	No	Yes	More fibre particularly from fruits and vegetables	Not stated	Not stated	Not stated
France, Ministry of Health, Family and Social Security (1978)	Yes	Yes	Yes	Not stated	Not stated	Yes	More bread and raw vegetables and fruits	Yes	Yes	Not stated
UK Department of Health and Social Security (1978)	Yes	Little mention	Yes	No	No	Yes	Yes	Yes	Yes	Yes
Australia, Department of Health (1979)	Yes	No attention	Yes	No	Yes	Yes	Yes	Yes	Yes	Yes

Source: Modified from the British Nutrition Foundation (1982).

However, these guidelines were adopted by the US government in a joint publication entitled *Nutrition and your health, dietary guidelines for Americans* in 1980 by the Department of Health, Education and Welfare and the US Department of Agriculture giving advice on the seven goals and how to achieve them (Table 2.14).

Later in 1980, the Food and Nutrition Board of the National Academy of Sciences published a Report entitled *Towards healthful diets*. Its summary dismissal of the evidence relating diet and coronary heart disease and a general very critical attitude to the dietary guidelines reflected the absence of epidemiologists, and indeed clinicians, on the Board. The lack of attention to major areas of clinical nutrition like alcohol consumption reflected the lack of experience and knowledge in this important area on the part of the members of the Food and Nutrition Board. The report was attacked in the press, conflict of interest was alleged, and subsequent Congressional hearings in June 1980 provided further major media coverage of the issues.

In the US, Blackburn (1979) has discussed the 'cholesterol-raising social forces which lead to mass hypercholesterolemia'. These include individual behaviour—'individuals and whole cultures appear to evolve from a wide austerity, punctuated by occasional orgies and traditional feasts to a continually soft self-indulgence with rare antifeasts of denial'; and public attitudes that make 'a modified (prudent) diet antithetical to the American way of life and a denial of deserved pleasures'. Agro-economic forces, such as the production, marketing, availability, and cost of foods, are also involved. One example is the remarkable

Table 2.14. *Practical guidelines for a sound diet*

Choose a nutritious diet
Eat a variety of foods—and include more fruit and vegetables. Frequently include dark green vegetables. Use more grain products, especially whole grains

Control your weight
Cut back on fats, sugars, and alcohol. Reduce the size of servings. Increase physical activity

Eat less fat
Select lean meats, trim off visible fat. Limit the amount of butter or margarine on vegetables and bread. Use low-fat and skimmed milk. Moderate the amount of organ meats (e.g. liver, kidneys) and egg yolks. Eat fewer rich desserts

Eat less sugar
Avoid or reduce sweet foods, such as sweets and soft drinks. Reduce the sugar in recipes. Use more fresh fruit instead of canned fruits

Eat more breads and cereals
Provide more vegetables and fruit. Include potatoes, corn, and peas more often. Emphasize whole grain cereal products (bran, rice, oatmeal, whole wheat cereals and breads)

Drink less alcohol
Drink alcohol less frequently, and not more than two standard size drinks per day. (Standard size drink=10 oz beer, 4 oz wine, 2 oz fortified wine, 1 oz spirits). Drink with smaller sips each time. Reserve drinking for special occasions, and keep it to one time in the day

Use less salt
Use few salty processed foods. Use little added salt, and use more fresh and frozen vegetables in preference to canned or seasoned vegetables, which have salt added. Limit your intake of salt snack foods, such as chips, pretzels and crackers. Use sauces and condiments sparingly

Source: Modified from US Department of Agriculture (1981).

increase in the availability of beef. Excellent grain crops result in surpluses which it becomes economic to feed to cattle. Physical confinement in the feed lot increases the productivity of acceptable beef with much higher content of intramuscular fat. Such beef is regarded as a 'higher' grade. Similarly with milk the grading is based on the titratable butter fat content. Breeding has been designed to increase the fat rather than protein content of milk. The sytems of quality control enforced by the US Department of Agriculture and the Food and Drug Administration are concerned with safety, spoilage, and appearance but not with nutritional considerations. The grading systems based on fat content need to change to meet more optimal requirements for human nutrition.

Food labelling and advertising add to the 'cholesterol-raising social forces'. Advertisements by the National Council on Egg Nutrition (NCEN) have promoted egg consumption by use of the motif 'Sexy Egg' and the advertisement, 'cholesterol mystery' was planned to sow confusion about this issue. A Federal Trade Practices injunction to 'cease and desist' was followed by harassment of the scientists involved with subpoenas and threats of subpoenas which also involved the American Heart Association (Blackburn 1979). The NCEN was finally reproved for advertising which was calculated to mislead. As pointed out by Blackburn, this is an example of an industry acting improperly in defence of its economic interests. Another social force was the influence of the 'agricultural establishment'— farm organizations, large farm and food companies, Congress Committees, the Department of Agriculture, and the land grant colleges.

The absence of national nutrition goals and policy in the US also contributes to the social forces elevating cholesterol. The White House Conference Report (1970) stated the issue clearly:

We recommend that the presently diffused federal machine for dealing in a piecemeal way with food and nutrition as they relate to health be administered hereafter as a total system under clear policy guidance, accountability, program management, and independent mechanisms for evaluation. Balkanization of responsibilities and activities constitute a serious impediment to a concerted attack on hunger and malnutrition.

In 1975 a penetrating series of questions were posed by Dr Theodore Cooper to the National Academy of Science:

What are the advantages and maximum health benefits of cereal grain—over animal products—as a dominant source of protein and calories in the human diet? What are the implications of efforts to grass feed rather than grain feed cattle for human consumption? What is the time frame for shifting to predominantly grass-fed cattle in this country; what would be the environmental impact and socioeconomic consequences of such a change? Is there a potential role for the Federal Government for providing incentive to facilitate a major switch in the way in which we allocate grain and raise livestock? What are the mechanisms for change and by what methods can we supplement improved educational activities to produce desired alterations in the diet and eating habits of Americans?

Blackburn (1979) goes on to consider cholesterol-lessening forces. There has been a 5–10 per cent fall in serum cholesterol in the US in the past 15 years (National Center for Health and Statistics 1977), and a tendency for younger age groups to adopt a more vegetarian style of diet. The meat industry is conducting research aimed at reducing the fat content of hogs and the Department of Agriculture grading of meat has been changed in favour of lower fat content by a lower level of marbling. Some modification of advertising practices is also beginning to occur in favour of public health. There is a significant increase in the use of vegetable oils and this has been suggested as a factor in the decline in mortality from coronary heart disease in the US (Dwyer and Hetzel 1980).

Economic considerations

The food industries are a major economical, social, and political structure in developed countries. In Britain in 1980, households spent £23 230 million, or some 19 per cent of total household expenditure, on food and a further £10 200 million on alcoholic drinks (CSO 1981). In addition, £3600 million was spent on meals outside the home; of the total of £23 230 million spent on food, some £16 750 million was spent on processed food of which £14 350 million can be attributed to foods processed in the UK and £2400 million to imported processed food (Central Statistics Office 1981).

In 1980 agriculture in the UK produced £8886 million worth of food, and the processed food industry produced £19 980 million worth of products. The liquor industry produced a gross output of £5800 million (Central Statistics Office 1981). The food production industries in Britain provide employment for over two million with a further 0.5 million are employed in the catering industries.

Agriculture in the UK is now controlled by policies developed under the Treaty of Rome (1957). The Common Agricultural Policy states that there must be European Community preference, common financing, and free trade within the European Community which necessitates the fixing of common prices. These constraints, designed to maintain existing markets and continuity of production, are significant conservative influences against changes in the pattern of food production. The 'Butter Mountain' is a vivid demonstration of the problem! Good nutrition in the light of recent scientific evidence is not an objective of the Common Agricultural Policy.

The Food Processing Industry is the largest purchaser of agricultural and fishery products. In Britain as much as 16 per cent of gross manufacturing output is produced by the food and drink industry. The major reason for such an industry is to provide an adequate and varied supply to the large urban populations. Changes in composition of foods such as reduced sugar and fat content require time and a large investment. In general, profits from the food industry have been low in recent years—usually less than 3 per cent after allowance is made for inflation (British Nutrition Foundation 1982).

However, changes in the composition of processed foods are occurring, brought about by consumer demand. In the UK there are 56 million people buying in 20.4 million households (CSO 1982). There is a limit to the expenditure on food imposed by other demands and price is an important determinant on choice of food. The composition of food is regulated by Food Laws—in Britain the Food and Drugs Act 1955 with nearly 100 sets of subordinate regulations governing the composition and labelling of food and food hygiene. Since Britain joined the EEC these regulations have been and are continually reviewed to bring them into line with those of the EEC. Minimum concentrations are legally specified as for example in the case of sugar in soft drinks or jam and fat in cheeses, cream, ice-cream, chocolate, butter, and margarine. Reductions in the amounts of sugar and fat in these items in response to recommended guidelines would infringe the law. At present such products would have to be marketed under new names such as 'reduced fat spread'. However, changes are occurring—new regulations have been recently made regarding reduced-sugar jams and margarine (MAFF 1981).

Political considerations

The question of dietary guidelines raises major economic and political issues. In the end these can only be resolved in the electorate by a better educated community—as in the nineteenth century the sanitary revolution was brought about by a combination of medical insight with political support when it became apparent that the public health was involved.

In the latter half of the twentieth century, diet has become a major public health and political issue. The relation between scientific knowledge and public health action requires much more consideration than it has so far received (Hetzel and Selwood 1977). A model (Hetzel 1980) has been proposed which attempts to describe this social process (Fig. 2.11).

The model, similar to that described earlier (Fig. 2.7), is based on a proper dissemination of health data to the community. These data have to be suitably analysed and

presented, using mass media which requires special expertise. Such presentation leads to discussion in the community at large which establishes a 'ground swell' in favour of social and possible political changes. This ground swell will be based on a community consensus which eventually convinces the politicians of the need for change. Suitable measures are incorporated in political platforms and policy statements which can become the subject of legislation. Legislation, hopefully bi-partisan, is then passed by Parliament and duly implemented. In due course the effects have to be evaluated with the collection of more data and these data provide the basis for further dissemination leading to further discussion, political action, and further legislation to correct demonstrated deficiencies from the previous measures.

This social process has been proceeding in Australia and other developed countries in the last decade in relation to smoking (for example, the abolition of television advertisements and the banning of smoking in public transport), and in relation to road safety (compulsory seatbelts and blood alcohol testing). It is now being initiated in relation to food and nutrition guidelines.

Some objection to interference with personal freedom has been ventilated from time to time in the last decade, but in general, reason has prevailed with a recognition that in the end, economic as well as humanitarian considerations are very important. The costs of injury, illness and death are not borne by the individual concerned but by the taxpayer. This produces economic pressure which is in many ways more powerful than purely humanitarian considerations in the saving of lives.

Nutrition education

Progress in the control of the diseases of overnutrition, as mentioned earlier, requires a better educated electorate in developed countries. Various strategies for nutrition education are available and are gradually being developed in different countries. Some of these will be briefly considered below.

Community education

While interest in nutrition is increasing in many developed countries, there is also much ignorance, misinformation, and confusion arising from the great diversity of sources giving advice. These include cooks and chefs, promoters of health foods, promotors of special products from primary industry or from the food-processing industry, health enthusiasts and entrepreneurs, scientists, and other academics who are often not qualified to speak on human nutrition issues.

It is in this environment of cacophony of different voices that rational nutrition education has to proceed! To meet this challenge national nutrition foundations have been established in a number of countries including the US, Australia, and in a number of western European countries including the UK, Holland, Sweden, Switzerland, and Italy. In Britain and Australia the foundations give priority to the

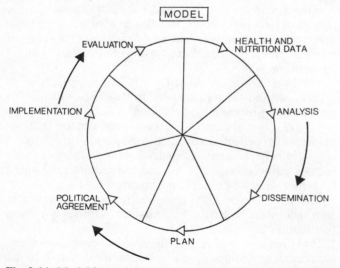

Fig. 2.11. Model for social process for improvement in nutrition and health.

education of the community through maintaining a presence in the media—and making available suitable nutrition information sources to journalists. Appearance of nutritionists on radio talk-back programmes is often sought and in Australia, taped messages on nutrition topics are prepared for telephone transmission every two weeks. In the city of Melbourne (population three million) some 200 calls are made for such information every week.

The foundations also give attention to the important area of nutrition education of professionals—including medical graduates, nurses, pharmacists, and schoolteachers who have important opportunities through their daily work.

Financial support for such foundations has been mainly derived from the food industry and the pharmaceutical industry. This raises the danger of conflict in interest between the foundation and its financial supporters, but in general this appears not to have been a major problem.

Schools

There is general agreement on the need for more nutrition and health education in both primary and secondary schools. However, there is no generally agreed plan about achieving this. Existing programmes in home economics in many countries do not keep up-to-date with recent developments in relation to dietary guidelines. Most such education is more concerned with the prevention of undernutrition than the prevention of overnutrition.

Recent new initiatives in Australia associated with the development of daily physical activity programmes (Dwyer et al. 1983) have raised new possibilities in the primary school environment. Current studies in Australia reveal the considerable interest of 10-year-old children in their bodies which is heightened by participating in the daily physical activity programme. They have acquired knowledge of elementary anatomy and physiology and through this some understanding of health. A special manual (the Body owner's manual) has been prepared for both students and teachers, and makes extensive use of cartoons and families of characters who represent different points of view and different life-styles. Attempts to encourage self-monitoring by the children themselves, by taking pulse rates, timing their runs, and monitoring their diet have been associated with significant loss of body fat as measured by skinfolds (Dwyer et al. 1983).

Children appear resistant to an initial approach through health education which lacks cogency for them. It is suggested that a much greater effort be made to consolidate knowledge of anatomy and physiology during the primary school period so that when children move to the secondary school they will be better able to maintain a healthy life-style with adequate exercise and properly balanced diet. Good health needs to become part of their acceptable body image.

There is evidence of a considerable impact of this primary school programme on parents through their children. In this way an opportunity exists for a significant impact on the whole community. The opportunities offered by the education system in developed countries should be taken much more seriously than in the past by public health authorities.

General

Other models for nutrition education arise from the workplace and special community health education programmes. A number of examples can be cited in relation to coronary heart disease prevention programmes. These include the North Karelia programme in Finland (Puska et al. 1979), and the Standford Heart Disease Prevention Programme in the US (Farquhar et al. 1977) which aim to reach the community, and the European collaborative study involving occupational interventions in England, Belgium, Italy, and Poland (Lancet 1982).

There is now some evidence that such community programmes are more effective than the traditional clinical models for health and nutrition education in relation to coronary heart disease (WHO 1982).

THE ROLE OF THE INTERNATIONAL AGENCIES

The major international agencies concerned with nutrition belong to the UN System. They include the World Health Organization (WHO), the Food and Agriculture Organization (FAO) and the United Nations Children's Fund (UNICEF). These agencies have played a major role in international nutrition since their foundation in the late 1940s (FAO in 1945, WHO in 1948, and UNICEF replacing UNRRA in 1947).

More recently these agencies have been joined by the World Bank, the UN Development Programme (UNDP) and the International Fund for Agricultural Development (IFAD), national overseas funds from various contributing countries, and private foundations such as the Ford Foundation and the Rockefeller Foundation.

These bodies meet each year in order to co-ordinate their efforts in the Administrative Co-ordinating Committee on Nutrition (ACGN) which has an expert Advisory Group in Nutrition (AGN) acting for it. These meetings are concerned with international nutrition policy and the assessment of the effectiveness of international nutrition programmes in developing countries. Substantial revenues are available, but effective interventions are not easily achieved. There has been a recognition that some problems such as xerophthalmia and cretinism have relatively simple solutions with suitable available technology in contrast to protein energy malnutrition where there is no simple solution. The former group can and should be eradicated just as smallpox has been eradicated.

The communique of the World Food Council (FAO 1977) estimated that to achieve and maintain an annual 4 per cent rate of growth of food production in developing countries required 8.3 thousand million dollars of international aid annually. This should be used to supply 'fertilisers, pesticides, high yield varieties of seeds, which are pest and disease resistant, improved breeds of livestock, credit to small farmers, irrigation equipment, and selective and appropriate implements for mechanisation'.

However, experience has shown that such measures do not necessarily improve food supply and the nutrition of the majority of the people. Such investment tends to benefit the bigger landowners, the importers and merchants, and even government officials rather than peasant communities. Special efforts are now being made by FAO to develop programmes for small farmers so that they can compete more successfully (in groups) for the resources that are available.

These international agencies have to work with and through national governments. They can and do advise on what needs to be done and can and do provide money, although, conflicts inevitably arise on priorities. None the less progress has been made over the past 30 years and the role of the international agencies has been most important and creditable.

CONCLUSION

The striking feature of nutrition and public health is the gap between knowledge and its application. In developing countries this is vividly demonstrated by the continuing occurrence of avoidable illness such as xerophthalmia due to vitamin A deficiency and cretinism due to iodine deficiency. In the developed countries the persistence of the diseases of affluence reflect a lack of adequate application of available knowledge due to social and economical factors. This also applies to developing countries—the technology is available, but the political will is lacking.

Progress is, however, being made and there is room for cautious optimism about the future. In developing countries there has been much progress, for example, in the People's Republic of China with the control of protein energy malnutrition and xerophthalmia, and the increasing control of goitre and cretinism. In some developed countries the decline in mortality due to coronary heart disease is partly due to changes in nutrition. More attention needs to be given to the definition of the factors including social and economical ones which have played a part in these advances. Such definition will accelerate further progress. In the end, the relation of food and nutrition to health is a political question which requires political answers.

REFERENCES

Abramson, J.H. (1979). *Survey methods in communicy medicine*, 2nd edn. Churchill Livingstone, Edinburgh.

Armstrong, B.K. and McMichael, A.J. (1981). Overnutrition. In *Changing disease patterns and human behaviour* (eds. N.F. Stanley and R.A. Joske) p. 492. Academic Press, London.

Armstrong, B.K., McMichael, A.J., and MacLennan, R. (In press). Diet. In *Cancer epidemiology and prevention* (eds. D. Schottenfeld and J.F. Fraumeni). Saunders, Philadelphia.

Baghurst, K.I. and Baghurst, P.A. (1981). The measurement of usual dietary intake in individuals and groups. *Trans. Menzies Found.* **3**, 139.

Baghurst, K.I. and Record, S. (1983). Intake and sources of selected Australian subpopulations of dietary constituents implicated in the etiology of chronic diseases. *J. Food Nutr.* **40**, 1.

Bautista, A., Baker, P.A., Dunn, J.T., Sanchez, M., and Kaiser, D.L. (1982). The effects of oral iodized oil on intelligence, thyroid status, and somatic growth in school-age children from an area of endemic goitre. *Am. J. Clin. Nutr.* **35**, 127.

Beaton, G.H. and Bengoa, J.M. (1976). Nutrition and health in perspective: An introduction. In *Nutrition in preventive medicine* (eds. G.H. Beaton and J.M. Bengoa) p. 13. WHO, Geneva.

Behar, M. (1974). A deadly combination. *World Health* Feb/March, 29.

Bengoa, J.M. and Donoso, G. (1974). Prevalence of protein-calorie malnutrition, 1963 to 1973. *PAG Bull.* **4**, 24.

Blackburn, H. (1979). Diet and mass hyperlipidemia: a public health view. In *Nutrition, lipids and coronary heart disease* (eds. R. Levy, B. Rifkind, B. Dennis, and N. Ernst) p. 309. Raven Press, New York.

Bleichrodt, N., Dreuth, P.J.D., and Querido, A. (1980). Effects of iodine deficiency on mental and psychomotor abilities. *Am. J. Phys. Anthropol.* **53**, 55.

Bray, G.A. (1976). *The obese patient*. In *Major problems in internal medicine* series (ed. L.H. Smith, Jr). Saunders, Philadelphia.

British Nutrition Foundation (1982). *Implementation of dietary guidelines obstacles and opportunities* (ed. M.R. Turner and J. Bray). Monograph Series BNF, London.

Bruun, K., Edwards, G., Lumio, M. *et al.* (1975). *Alcohol control policies in public health perspective*. The Finnish Foundation for Alcohol Studies, Vol. 25. Forssa, Finland.

Buttfield, H. and Hetzel, B.S. (1967). Endemic goitre in East New Guinea with special reference to the use of iodized oil in prophylaxis and treatment. *WHO Bull.* **36**, 243.

Central Statistical Office (1981). *National income and expenditure.* HMSO, London.

Central Statistical Office (1982). *National income and expenditure.* HMSO, London.

Chapman, J.A., Grant, I.S., Taylor, G., Mahmud, K., Mulk, S.U., and Shahid, M.A. (1972). Endemic goitre in the Gilgit Agency, West Pakistan. With an appendix on dermatoglyphics and taste-testing. *Phil. Trans. R. Soc. Lond (B)* **263**, 459.

Commonwealth of Australia Department of Health (1978). *Alcohol in Australia—a summary of related statistics.* Central Statistical Unit, Canberra.

Connolly, K.J., Pharoah, P.O.D., and Hetzel, B.S. (1979). Fetal iodine deficiency and motor performance during childhood. *Lancet* **ii**, 1149.

Cravioto, J., Haembusons, C., and Vahlqvist, B. (1974). *Early malnutrition and mental development.* Swedish Nutrition Foundation, Stockholm.

Davidson, S., Passmore, R., Brock, J.F., and Truswell, A.S. (1979). *Human nutrition and dietetics,* 7th edn. Churchill Livingstone, Edinburgh.

DeMaeyer, E.M. (1976). Protein-energy malnutrition. In *Nutrition in preventive medicine* (eds. G.H. Beaton and J.M. Bengoa) p. 23. WHO, Geneva.

Department of National Health and Welfare, Canada (1974). *Nutrition Canada 1973.* Information Canada, Ottawa.

DHSS and MRC (1976). *Research on obesity—a report* (ed. W.P.T. James). HMSO, London.

Director-General of Health (1978–9). *Annual report,* Canberra.

Djokomoeljanto, R., Tarwotjo, Ig., and Maspaitella, F. (1983). Goiter control program in Indonesia. In *Current problems in thyroid research* (eds. N. Ui, K. Torizuka, S. Nagataki, and K. Miyai) p. 403. AOTA, Tokyo.

Doll, R. (1979). Nutrition and cancer: a review. *Nutr. Cancer* **1**, 35.

Dulberg, E., Widjaja, K., Djokomoeljanto, R., Hetzel, B.S., and Belmont, L. (1983). Evaluation of the iodisation program in Central Java with reference to the prevention of endemic cretinism and motor coordination defects. In *Current problems in thyroid research* (eds. N. Ui, K. Torizuka, S. Nagataki, and K. Miyai) p. 394. AOTA, Toykyo.

Durnin, J.V.G.A. and Rahaman, M.M. (1967). The assessment of the amount of fat in the human body from skinfold thickness. *Br. J. Nutr.* **21**, 681.

Durnin, J.V.G.A. and Womersley (1974). Body fat assessed from total body density and its estimation from skinfold thickness: measurements on 481 men and women aged from 16 to 72 years. *Br. J. Nutr.* **32**, 77.

Dwyer, T. and Hetzel, B.S. (1980). A comparison of trends of coronary heart disease mortality in Australia, USA and England and Wales with reference to three major risk factors—hypertension, cigarette smoking and diet. *Int. J. Epidemiol.* **9**, 65.

Dwyer, T., Coonan, W.E., Leitch, D.R., Hetzel, B.S., and Baghurst, P.A. (1983). An investigation of the effects of daily physical activity on the health of primary school students in South Australia. *Int. J. Epidemiol.* **12**, 308.

Ermans, A.M., Bourdoux, P., Lagasse, R., Delange, F., and Thilly, C.M. (1980). Congenital hypothyroidism in developing countries. In *Neonatal thyroid screening* (ed. G.N. Burrow) p. 61. Raven Press, New York.

Farquhar, J.W., Wood, P.D., Breitrose, H. *et al.* (1977). Community education for cardiovascular health. *Lancet* **i**, 1192.

Follis, R.H. (1964). Recent studies on iodine malnutrition and endemic goiter. *Med. Clin. N. Am.* **48**, 1919.

FAO (1975). *Food composition tables. Nutrition Information Documents* Series No. 1. FAO, Rome.

FAO (1977). Manila communique of World Food Council. *Food Nutr.* **3**, 22.

FAO of the United Nations (1980). *Food balance sheets 1975–77. Average and per caput food supplies 1961–65. Average 1967 to 1977.* FAO, Rome.

FAO and WHO (1966). Joint FAO/WHO Technical meeting of planning and evaluation of applied nutrition programs. Tech. Rep. Ser. Wld. Hlth. Org. No. 340: FAO Nutr. Mtg. Rep. Ser. no. 39.

Gomez, F., Ramos-Galvan, R., Cravioto, J., and S. Frenk (1979). Prevention and treatment of chronic severe infantile malnutrition (kwashiorkor). *NY Acad. Sci. Ann.* **69**, 969.

Gopalan, C., Ram Sastri, B.V., and Balasubramanian, S.B. (1978). *Nutritive value of Indian foods.* National Institute of Nutrition, Indian Council of Medical Research Hyderabad and Card Box Company Hyderabad.

Habicht, J.P., Mantorell, R., Yarbrough, C., Malina, R.M., and Klein, R.E. (1974). Height and weight standards for pre-school children. How relevant are ethnic differences in growth potential? *Lancet,* **i**, 611.

Hamill, P.V.V., Drizd, T.A., Johnson, C.L., Reed, R.B., Roche, A.F., and Moore, W.M. (1979). Physical growth: National Center for Health Statistics percentiles. *Am. J. Clin. Nutr.* **32**, 607.

Harper, A.E. (1978). Dietary goals: a skeptical view. *Am. J. Clin. Nutr.* **31**, 310.

Havlik, R.J. and Feinlieb, M. (1978). *Proceedings of the Conference on the Decline in Coronary Heart Disease Mortality.* US Department of Health, Education and Welfare, Public Health Service, National Institute of Health Publication No. 761610, Bethesda.

Hegsted, D.M. (1978). Dietary goals: a progressive view. *Am. J. Clin. Nutr.* **31**, 1504.

Hetzel, B.S. (1974). The epidemiology, pathogenesis and control of endemic goitre and cretinism in New Guinea. *New Zealand Med. J.* **80**, 482.

Hetzel, B.S. (1978a). The implications of increasing alcohol consumption in Australia—a new definition of the alcohol problem. *Community Health Stud.* **2**, 81.

Hetzel, B.S. (ed.) (1978b). *Basic health care for developing countries—an epidemiological perspective.* Oxford University Press.

Hetzel, B.S. (1980). *Health and Australian society,* 3rd edn, Penguin, Ringwood, Victoria.

Hetzel, B.S. (1981). Dietary differences and disease. *Med. J. Aust.* **1**, 113.

Hetzel, B.S. (1983). Iodine deficiency disorders (I.D.D.) and their eradication. *Lancet* **ii**, 1126.

Hetzel, B.S. and Selwood, T.S. (1977). The improvement of health. In *Epidemiology and health* (eds. W.W. Holland and S. Gilderdale) p. 29. Kimpton, London.

Ibbertson, H.K., Tait, J.M., Pearl, M., Lim, T., McKinnon, J.R., and

Gill, M.B. (1972). Himalayan cretinism. In *Human development and the thyroid gland. Relation to endemic cretinism* (eds. J.B. Stanbury and R.L. Kroc) p. 51. Plenum Press, New York.

Jelliffe, D.B. (1966). *The assessment of the nutritional status of the community.* World Health Organization, Geneva.

Kevany, J., Fierro-Benitez, R., Pretell, E.A., and Stanbury, J.B. (1968). Prophylaxis and treatment of endemic goiter with iodized oil in rural Ecuador and Peru. *Am. J. Clin Nutr.* **22**, 1597.

Keys, A. (1979). Dietary survey methods. In *Nutrition lipids and coronary heart disease* (ed. R. Levy, B. Rifkind, B. Dennis, and N. Ernst) p. 1. Raven Press, New York.

Kywe-Thein, T.-T.-O., Khin-Maung-Niang, W.J., and Buttfield, I.H. (1978). A study of the effect of intramuscular and oral iodised poppy seed oil in the treatment of iodine deficiency. In *Current thyroid problems in Southeast Asia and Oceania* (eds. B.S. Hetzel, M.L. Wellby, and R. Hoschl) p. 78. AOTA, Singapore.

Lamberg, B.A., Haikonen, M., Hintze, G., Honkapohja, H., Hiltunen, R., and Pulli, K. (1970). Regression of endemic goitre and of changes in iodine metabolism during 10–15 years in the east of Finland. The role of iodine metabolism during 10–15 years in the east of Finland. The role of iodine prophylaxis. *Hormones* **1**, 80.

Lancet (1982). Trials of coronary heart disease prevention. (Editorial.) *Lancet* **ii**, 803.

Lancet (1983a). From endemic goitre to iodine deficiency disorders. (Editorial.) *Lancet* **ii**, 1121.

Lancet (1983b). Control of iodine deficiency in Asia. Resolutions from international symposium on the control of iodine deficiency in Asia, 4th Asian Congress of Nutrition, Bangkok. *Lancet* **ii**, 1244.

Larsen, P.R., Silva, J.E., Hetzel, B.S., and McMichael, A.J. (1980). Monitoring prophylactic programs: general considerations. In *Endemic goitre and endemic cretinism* (eds. J.B. Stanbury and B.S. Hetzel) p. 551. Wiley, New York.

Layrisse, M., Roche, M., and Baker, S.J. (1976). Nutritional anaemias. In *Nutrition in preventive medicine* (ed. G.H. Beaton and J.M. Bengoa) p. 55. World Health Organization, Geneva.

Lipid Research Clinic's Program (1974). *Manual of laboratory operations. Vol. 1 Lipid and lipoprotein analysis.* Department of Health, Education and Welfare, National Institute of Health Publication 75–628, Bethesda.

Ma Tai, Lu TiZhang, Tan Yubin, Chen Bingzhong, and Zhu Xianyi (H.I. Chu) (1982). The present status of endemic goitre and endemic cretinism in China. *Food Nutr. Bull.* **4**, 13.

Maberly, G.F., Eastman, C.J., and Corcoran, J.M. (1981). Effect of iodination of a village water-supply on goitre size and thyroid function. *Lancet* **ii**, 1270.

McCullagh, S.F. (1963). The Huon Peninsula Endemic I. The effectiveness of an intramuscular depot of iodised oil in the control of endemic goitre. *Med. J. Aust.* **1**, 767.

Mahler, H. (1977). Health for all. *WHO Chron.* **31**, 491.

Marr, J.W. (1971). Individual dietary surveys: purposes and methods. In *World review of nutrition and dietetics* Vol. 13. (ed. G.H. Bourne) p. 105. Karger, Basel.

Metropolitan Life Insurance Company (1959). New weight standards for men and women. *Stat. Bull. Metropolitan Life Insurance Co.* **40**, 1.

Ministry of Agriculture, Fisheries and Food (1981). *Food Standards Committee Report on Margarine and Other Table Spreads. FSC/ Report 74.* HMSO, London.

National Academy of Sciencies and National Research Council Food and Nutrition Board (1980). *Toward healthful diets* NAS, Washington DC.

National Center for Health Statistics (1977). A comparison of levels of serum cholesterol of adults 18–74 years of age in the United States in 1960–62 and 1971–74. *US Department of Health, Education and Welfare.* Washington, DC.

Norum, K.R. (1978). Some present concepts concerning diet and prevention of coronary heart disease. *Nutr. Metab.* **22**, 1.

Nutrition Today (1977). (Editorial.) **12**, No. 6, November/December.

Pandav, C.S. and Kochupillai, N. (1982). Endemic goitre in India: prevalence, etiology, attendant disabilities and control measures. *Indian J. Pediatr.* **50**, 259.

Paul, A., Southgate, D., McCance, R.A., and Widdowson, E. (eds.) (1978). *The composition of food.* HMSO, London.

Perez, C., Scrimshaw, N.S., and Munoz, J.A. (1960). Technique of endemic goitre surveys. In *Endemic goitre* p. 369. World Health Monograph. Series No. 44. WHO, Geneva.

Peto, R., Doll, R., Buckley, J.D., and Sporn, M.B. (1981). Can dietary beta carotene materially reduce human cancer rates? *Nature, Lond.* **290**, 201.

Pharoah, P.O.D., Buttfield, I.H., and Hetzel, B.S. (1971). Neurological damage to the fetus resulting from severe iodine deficiency during pregnancy. *Lancet* **i**, 308.

Potter, B.J., Mano, M.T., Belling, G.B. *et al.* (1982). Retarded fetal brain development resulting from severe dietary iodine deficiency in sheep. *Neuropathol. Appl. Neurobiol.* **8**, 803.

Puffer, R.C. and Serrano, C.V. (1973). *Patterns of mortality in childhood.* Pan American Health Organization (PAHO Scientific Publication No. 262). Washington, DC.

Puska, P., Tuomilehto, J., Salonen, J. *et al.* (1979). Changes in coronary risk factors during comprehensive five-year community programme to control cardiovascular disease (North Karelia project). *Br. Med. J.* **ii**, 1173.

Querido, A., Delange, F., Dunn, J.T. *et al.* (1974). Definitions of endemic goiter and cretinism, classification of goiter size and severity of endemias, and survey techniques. In *Endemic goiter and cretinism: continuing threats to world health* (eds. J.T. Dunn and G.A. Medeiros-Neto) p. 267. Pan American Health Organization. Scientific Publication No. 292, Washington, DC.

Romsai Suwanik *et al.* (1982). The R&D Group, Iodine, Iron, and Water Project, Siriraj Hospital, Mahidol University, Bangkok.

Schaefer, A.E. (1974). Status of salt iodization in PAHO Member Countries. In *Endemic goitre and cretinism: continuing threats to world health.* (eds. J.T. Dunn and G.A. Medeiros-Neto) p. 242. Pan American Health Organization, Scientific publication No. 292. Washington DC.

Sooch, S.A. and Ramalingaswami, V. (1965). Preliminary report of an experiment in the Kangra Valley for the prevention of Mimalayan endemic goitre with iodized salt. *Bull. WHO* **32**, 299.

Sooch, S.S., and Deo, M.G., Karmarkar, M.G., Kochupillai, N., Ramachandran, K., and Ramalingaswami, V. (1973). Prevention of endemic goitre with iodized salt. *Bull. WHO* **49**, 307.

Stanbury, J.B., Ermans, A.M., Hetzel, B.S., Pretell, E.A., and Querido, A. (1974). Endemic goiter and cretinism: public health significance and prevention. *WHO Chron.* **28**, 220.

Stein, Z., Susser, M., Saenger, G., and Marolla, F. (1972). Nutrition and mental performance. Prenatal exposure to the Dutch famine of 1944–45 seems not related to mental performance at age 19. *Science* **178**, 708.

Stewart, J.C., Vidor, G.I., Buttfield, I.H., and Hetzel, B.S. (1971). Epidemic thyrotoxicosis in Northern Tasmania: studies of clinical features and iodine nutrition. *Aust. N.Z. J. Med.* **3**, 203.

Strom, A. and Jensen, R.A. (1951). Mortality from circulatory diseases in Norway 1940–1945. *Lancet*, **i**, 126.

Stuart, H.C. and Stevenson, S.A. (1954). Tables of norms for use as reference standards in the evaluation of body measurements. In *Textbook of pediatrics,* 6th edn (ed. W.E. Nelson) p. 52. Saunders, Philadelphia.

Tanner, J.M. (1976). Population differences in body size, shape and growth rate. A 1976 view. *Arch. Dis. Child.* **51**, 1.

Tanner, J. M. and Goldstein (1980). Child growth standards. (Letter.) *Lancet* **ii**, 35.

Tanner, J.M. and Whitehouse, R.H. (1975). Revised standards for triceps subscapular skinfolds in British children. *Arch. Dis. Child.* **50**, 142.

Tanner, J.M., Whitehouse, R.H., and Takaishi, M. (1966). Standards from birth to maturity for height, weight, height velocity and weight velocity for British children 1965. *Arch. Dis. Child* **41**, 454.

Thilly, C.H. and Hetzel, B.S. (1980). An assessment of prophylactic programs: social, political, cultural, and economic issues. In *Endemic goitre and endemic cretinism* (eds. J.B. Stanbury and B.S. Hetzel) p. 475. Wiley, New York.

Thilly, C.H., Delange, F., and Stanbury, J.B. (1980). Epidemiologic surveys in endemic goiter and cretinism. In *Endemic goiter and endemic cretinism* (eds. J.B. Stanbury and B.S. Hetzel) p. 159. Wiley, New York.

Thilly, C.H., Delange, F., Ramioul, L., Lagasse, R., Luvivila, K., Ermans, A.A. (1977). Strategy of goiter and cretinism control in Central Africa. *Int. J. Epidemiol.* **6**, 43.

Treaty of Rome (1957). *Treaty establishing the European Economic Community.* 25 March 1957, Rome.

Truswell, A.S. (1981). *Diet and coronary heart disease—how much more evidence do we need?* British Nutrition Foundation Bulletin No. 32, London.

US Department of Agriculture and Department of Health, Education and Welfare (1980). *Nutrition and your health—dietary guidelines for Americans.* USDA, DHEW, Washington, DC.

US Department of Agriculture Science and Education Administration (1981). *Ideas for better eating, menus and recipes to make use of the dietary guidelines.* USDA, DHEW, Washington, DC.

US Department of Health, Education and Welfare (1972). *Ten state survey.* US DHEW, Washington, DC.

US Department of Health, Education and Welfare (1979). Fats, cholesterol and sodium intakes in the diets of persons 1–74 years: United States. *Vital and Health Statistics of the National Centre for Health Statistics, Advance Data Series,* No. 54. DHEW, Hyattsville, Md.

US Senate Select Committee on Nutrition and Human Needs (1977). *Dietary goals for the United States.* US GPO, Washington, DC.

Watanabe, T., Moran, D., El Tamer, E. *et al.* (1974). Iodized oil in the prophylaxis of endemic goiter in Argentina. In *Endemic goiter and cretinism: continuing threats to world health* (eds. J.T. Dunn and G.A. Medeiros-Neto) Pan American Health Organization, Scientific publication No. 292, p. 231, Washington, DC.

Waterlow, J. (1980). Child growth standards. *Lancet* **i**, 717.

White House Conference on Food, Nutrition and Health (1970). Final Report. The White House, Washington, DC.

World Health Organization (1978). Declaration of Alma Ata. *WHO Chron.* **32**, 428.

WHO (1972). *Report of WHO Group of Experts on Nutritional Anaemias.* WHO Technical Report Series, No. 503, Geneva.

WHO (1982). *Control of vitamin A deficiency and xerophthalmia. Report of a Joint WHO/UNICEF/USAID/Helen Keller International/ IVACG Meeting.* WHO Technical Report Series, No. 672, Geneva.

WHO (1982). *Prevention of coronary heart disease.* WHO Technical Report Series, No. 678, Geneva.

Worsley, A.W. (1981). Psychometric aspects of language dependent techniques in dietary assessment. *Trans. Menzies Foundation* **3**, 161.

FURTHER READING

Abramson, J.H. (1979). *Survey methods in community medicine.* Churchill Livingstone, Edinburgh.

Beaton, G.H. and Bengoa, J.M. (eds.) (1976). *Nutrition in preventive medicine: the major deficiency syndromes, epidemiology, and approaches to control.* World Health Organization, Geneva.

Davidson, S., Passmore, R., Brock, J.F., and Truswell, A.S. (1979). *Human nutrition and dietetics,* 7th edn. Churchill Livingstone, Edinburgh.

Stanbury, J.B. and Hetzel, B.S. (eds.) (1980). *Endemic goiter and endemic cretinism.* Wiley, New York.

3 Developmental defects

J. Mark Elwood and Richard J. Madeley

INTRODUCTION: OUTCOMES OF PREGNANCY

This chapter deals with continuous and discrete departures from normality in terms of pregnancy outcome: that is, babies born too soon, born too small, or born with a structural abnormality. These are the aspects of developmental defects which are best understood and of greatest importance for public health. We have not attempted here to fully deal with the title. A full consideration would include events shortly after conception including early fetal losses, about which there is little definite knowledge which can be applied practically, and also consideration of abnormalities arising or becoming apparent after the neonatal period, which might, if generously defined, include most of medicine.

LOW BIRTHWEIGHT

The concept of the low birthweight (LBW) baby, defined as one weighing less than 2500 g, has received a great deal of attention in recent years. It can be regarded as a failure of development, since it is a circumstance strongly correlated with a high rate both of perinatal and infant mortality and of childhood handicaps (Table 3.1).

Global prevalence of low birthweight and sources of data

In most developed countries reliable data are collected routinely as part of national registration systems. Such systems do not exist in some poorer countries where the prevalence of low birthweight is higher. In these circumstances, special surveys have to be undertaken to determine the prevalence. Often these are based in a particular health facility, for example, a hospital or group of health centres. Total population studies in developing countries are difficult to undertake but are essential to establish true patterns of low birthweight.

It has been estimated by the World Health Organization (1980) that of 122 million live births in the world in 1979, approximately 20.6 million (that is, 17 per cent of the total), had a birthweight of 2500 g or less. Of these, over 19 million were born in developing countries, with Bangladesh, India, and Pakistan between them accounting for over 10 million. In some parts of Asia the proportion of LBW babies is as high as 50 per cent whereas in some parts of Europe it is less than 5 per cent. Nearly three-quarters of the world's LBW babies are born in Asia, though the rates vary from high in the countries mentioned above to rates comparable with those in Europe, in some countries in East Asia such as Japan. The mean birthweight for Asia is 2900 g.

In Africa, LBW rates vary from 10 to 20 per cent and the percentage seems to be fairly constant between regions. Countries in northern Africa tend to have lower rates. The mean birthweight is of the order of 3000 g. In Latin America, the prevalence of low birthweight has been estimated at around 11 per cent, although the WHO feels that this may be something of an underestimation. The mean birthweight is calculated at being around 3100 g. Rates in Europe vary from 4 per cent in Scandinavia and the Netherlands, to 12 per cent in southern Europe. The mean birthweight is around 3200 g as it is in North America, where the LBW rate is fairly constant at around 7 per cent. The degree to which these differences are environmental or genetic has been the subject of extensive discussion. Migrant studies show that much of the difference between developing and more developed countries is environmental, but that immigrants from the Indian subcontinent to richer countries tend to have smaller babies than the indigenous population for at least two generations.

Table 3.1. *Mortality rates by birthweight – England and Wales 1979*

Rate	All weights	<2500 g	<1500 g	1500–1999 g	2000–2499 g	2500–2999 g	3000–3499 g	3500–3999 g	4000 g and over
Stillbirth*	7.9	76.0	269.4	102.1	27.1	5.9	2.3	1.5	2.3
Perinatal mortality*	14.1	141.1	565.1	168.8	42.5	9.5	4.1	2.6	3.8
Neonatal mortality†	7.7	80.4	455.4	83.7	19.3	5.0	2.5	1.7	2.2
Post-neonatal mortality†	4.4	14.6	30.6	19.9	10.7	5.5	3.6	2.9	2.6
Infant mortality†	12.2	95.0	485.9	103.5	30.0	10.5	6.2	4.6	4.8

*Stillbirth and perinatal mortality rates are measured per 1000 total births.
†Neonatal, post-neonatal, and infant mortality rates are measured per 1000 live births.
Source: OPCS (1982).

Problems of definition: 'premature' or 'low birthweight'

The concept includes two different abnormalities of intra-uterine growth. These are: (i) the premature birth of an infant who is of normal birthweight for that period of gestation; and (ii) the birth of an infant of low birthweight for that gestation.

This has led to some confusion over nomenclature. In 1948 the WHO recommended that babies with a birthweight of 2500 g or less should be called 'premature'. This led to considerable practical problems for doctors and midwives, as they frequently had to use the label 'premature' when the pregnancy was full-term, a clearly unsatisfactory state of affairs. In 1961 the WHO altered the definition in an attempt to overcome this problem, and suggested that the same group of babies should be described as 'of low birthweight'. This was an important development, focusing on a characteristic which could be reliably measured. A further change in the definition took place in 1976, when the 29th World Health Assembly recommended a definition of 'a birthweight less than 2500 g', that is, up to and including 2499 g. This recommendation has been incorporated into the Ninth International Classification of Disease, which was implemented in 1979. This has had the effect of causing an apparent marginal reduction in the prevalence of low birthweight, for example, in England and Wales in 1980 by 0.35 per cent, which represents that percentage of live births weighing exactly 2500 g.

It is important to distinguish between the two different types of LBW babies because the implications for prognosis and the development of services are rather different. In general, babies who are LBW and full-term have a worse prognosis including problems in later development and handicap than those of normal weight for their gestational age (Neligan *et al.* 1976). Therefore, it is important, if possible, to distinguish in each case whether an infant of 2500 g or less was born prematurely or not. This may not be easy, as the true gestational age is always in some degree unreliable, and may even be completely unknown.

An important milestone was the publication in 1963 of percentile charts relating birthweight to gestational age (Lubchenco *et al.* 1963a). This made it possible to standardize crude birthweight data for gestational age, acknowledging the difficulties in measuring the latter.

In developed countries, most babies of low birthweight are of 37 weeks gestation or less. This is typified by the data from Sweden shown in Table 3.2 where 67 per cent of babies of low birthweight fall into this category. For developing countries there seems to be a considerable difference in this proportion.

Table 3.2. *Distribution of births by length of gestation and birthweight: percentage of total number of births, Sweden, 1978*

Weeks of gestation	Birthweight		Total
	Below 2500 g	2500 g and above	
37	2.9	7.2	10.1
38 and above	1.4	88.5	89.9
Total	4.3	95.7	100.0

Source: *Statistika Meddelanden HS 1981:2 Medical Birth Registrations 1977 and 1978*. National Central Bureau of Statistics, Stockholm.

According to WHO figures (1980), the proportion of LBW infants who are of 37 or less weeks gestation varies from 66 per cent in Kenya (that is, not much different from Sweden) to 44 per cent in Tanzania. Both these figures are obtained from studies based on hospital statistics, rather than on a complete birth population and so should be regarded with some caution.

The proportion of LBW babies who are premature seems to be much lower in Asia. Data from India, including community surveys show that approximately 25 per cent of LBW babies fall into this category. The data from Indonesia and Malaysia follow a similar pattern, as do those from Sri Lanka, where overall mortality rates are much lower.

In Latin America there is much variation, ranging from 17 per cent of LBW babies in Guatemala being premature to 62 per cent in Cuba. The size of the difference casts some doubt on the validity of the data.

Such figures have to be treated with a certain amount of caution, because of: (i) the difficulties in accurately measuring gestational age; and (ii) differences in the population under review (for example, total population, hospital, other health facility). However, it does seem the case that countries with low perinatal mortality rates and high per caput incomes have a higher proportion of their LBW babies in the 'premature' category than do those of poorer countries with higher perinatal mortality rates. Within industrial countries, regions with a higher than average prevalence of low birthweight owe their position to the birth of more full-term low birthweight infants.

In what situations is a baby more likely to be of low birthweight?

In developed countries the following factors are likely to be associated with low birthweight, though it is always worthwhile to check individual factors in individual countries where such data are available.

Multiple pregnancy

In England and Wales in 1980, 52 per cent of multiple live births weighed under 2500 g, compared with six per cent of singleton live births.

Age of mother

A mother who is, from an obstetric point of view, very young or very old is more likely to give birth to a LBW baby. In England and Wales in 1980, mothers aged below 20 years had a prevalence of low birthweight of 9.3 per cent compared with 6.7 per cent for all ages. The age-groups 20–24 years (7.2 per cent) and 35 and over (7.3 per cent) also had an above average prevalence.

Parity

First and fourth or higher order children are likelier to be of low birthweight. In England and Wales in 1980, 7.5 per cent of liveborn legitimate first babies were of low birthweight, compared with 6.3 per cent of all liveborn legitimate babies; 6.6 per cent of babies which were the fourth or higher order were of low birthweight.

Social circumstances

There is a tendency for the less well off groups in a society to have a higher prevalence of LBW babies. This has been demonstrated in all industrial countries where such studies have been undertaken, including statistically significant differences in Sweden (National Central Bureau of Statistics, Stockholm 1981), the country with the lowest prevalence of LBW births and the lowest perinatal mortality rate in the world.

Race

This factor is highly specific to particular countries – for example, blacks in the US, and Indians in the UK, have high rates of LBW babies.

Height of mother

Smaller mothers tend to have lighter babies and a higher prevalence of LBW births. This is an effect of socio-economic factors and tends to diminish in importance as a society becomes more affluent.

Obstetric conditions in the mother

The presence of hypertensive disorders of pregnancy in the mother is associated with lowered placental and birthweights.

Congenital abnormalities

Babies with severe malformations tend to be of low birthweight.

Legal status of infant

The importance of this factor is as a measurement of other social factors, for example, age of mother, poverty, and degree of personal isolation. It tends to be culture specific.

These factors are often correlated with each other. For example in England and Wales, most illegitimate births are first births to single parents aged less than 24 years, often in disadvantaged social circumstances. However, they also exert an independent effect in most countries.

Environmental causes of low birthweight

Nutrition

Babies born at times of food shortage in a society are much more likely to be of low birthweight. This is well demonstrated by European data from the 1939–45 war and its aftermath. The general food intake of the whole of Europe was reduced, and in addition there were situations where famine conditions existed. The most dramatic data are those relating to the siege of Leningrad by the German forces in 1942 (Table 3.3).

A less extreme but still very serious famine occurred in parts of the Netherlands during the winter of 1944–45 (Smith 1947). In babies born to women who were in their third trimester of pregnancy during the months of the famine, there was a fall in average birthweight of over 300 g to a figure of almost 3000 g (Stein 1975). The average birthweight before and after the famine was around 3350 g.

The data from Leningrad and the Netherlands have led to

Table 3.3. *Birthweight distributions of babies born in Leningrad during the first half of 1942, compared with England and Wales 1979*

Birthweight	Number	Percentage Leningrad* 1942	Percentage England and Wales† 1979
3000 g and over	69	18.8%	72.9%
2500–2999 g	118	32.1%	20.2%
< 2500 g	181	49.1%	6.9%

Source: *Antonov, A. (1947); †OPCS (1979).

considerable discussion about the relationship between diet and birthweight under normal conditions. It is generally thought that maternal malnutrition has to be extremely severe as in Leningrad or the Netherlands or parts of the developing world, before the birthweight of the baby is affected.

Cigarette smoking

A major survey has demonstrated an association between low birthweight and smoking cigarettes (Butler and Alberman 1969). This association remains when other factors such as maternal age, parity, height, and social class have been controlled. The prevalence of LBW babies born to mothers who smoked was 9.2 per cent of live births compared to 5.4 per cent of non-smoking mothers (Butler *et al.* 1972). This study showed that the babies of the women who smoke during pregnancy were on average 200 g lighter than those of non-smoking mothers. There was no significant difference between the two groups in the period of gestation. If, however, a woman gives up smoking before the fourth month of pregnancy, her chances of giving birth to a baby of normal birthweight improve. The effect of cigarette smoking is greatest in the fourth to the ninth month of pregnancy.

Perinatal deaths are 30 per cent more frequent in the babies of mothers who smoke after the fourth month of pregnancy. This risk is particularly great where other factors associated with an increased prevalence of low birthweight and an increased perinatal mortality rate already exist, for example, high parity or extremes of maternal age (Butler and Alberman 1969).

Alcohol

Reliable data on the consumption of alcohol by individuals are notoriously difficult to obtain. Therefore, the few studies that have been attempted of the relationship between alcohol intake and birthweight, need to be interpreted with caution (Ouellette *et al.* 1977; Berkowitz 1981). The results indicate that a moderate intake of alcohol is not associated with any change in birthweight, but that heavy drinking causes a fall in average birthweight.

Trends over time

Except at times of unusual famine such as those described in Leningrad and parts of the Netherlands the prevalence of low birthweight in industrialized countries has been remarkably constant. For example, in England and Wales between 1953 and 1980 the prevalence of LBW babies lay invariably between 6.4 per cent and 7 per cent (Alberman 1977; DHSS 1982), despite a significant improvement in the standard of living of all sections of the community.

Data for the US over the same period show that there has been little change in low birthweight prevalence over the period as a whole. However, there was an increase in prevalence in blacks which started in the 1950s and began to fall back again from the mid-1960s (Chase 1977). Several possible reasons have been put forward for these puzzling trends but no concensus has emerged. Data on trends in the third world are not usually readily available, except as a result of special studies.

Birthweight specific perinatal mortality rates

Because of the close relationship demonstrated in Table 3.1 between perinatal mortality and low birthweight, crude perinatal mortality rates should never be used as a measure of evaluation of obstetric services. It is necessary to look at the perinatal mortality rate in each birthweight category.

For example, in 1978, the crude perinatal mortality rate in Sweden was 8.9 per 1000 live births against 15.1 per 1000 in England and Wales. An analysis of perinatal mortality rates in each specific birthweight category, however, reveals only slightly higher figures in England and Wales (Table 3.4). Most of the apparently large difference between the two countries is thus explained by the more favourable birthweight distribution in Sweden. Similar standardizations need to be carried out when comparing data from different hospitals or regions of a country.

Table 3.4. *Birthweight specific perinatal mortality rates – Sweden, and England and Wales, 1978*

Birthweight category (g)	Per cent in each category Sweden	Percent in each category E and W	Perinatal mortality rate Sweden	Perinatal mortality rate E and W
≤ 1499	0.62	1.02	461.1	568
1500–1999	0.92	1.34	146.2	175
2000–2499	2.76	4.68	50.1	43
2500–2999	11.40	20.20	11.3	11
3000–3499	33.57	39.40	3.4	4
3500–3999	34.21	25.97	1.7	3
4000 ≥	16.52	7.39	1.7	4
Total (all birthweights)	100.00	100.00	8.9	15.1
Standardized for birthweight*			13.2	15.1

*Standardization by direct method, to the distribution of the England and Wales births, using the data shown. Standardization based on narrower birthweight categories would reduce the difference in standardized rates even further.

Clinical significance of low birthweight

The high perinatal mortality rate in LBW babies has led to the development of special care facilities, including incubators, special baby care units, and intensive care units. The development of this technology has been a source of controversy. While it is accepted that these techniques have been successful in lowering perinatal mortality rates, the question of whether or not this success has led to the survival of an increased number of handicapped babies remains highly controversial. The earlier phase of clinical intervention did cause some increase in handicapped survivors (Drillien 1958; Lubchenco *et al.* 1963*b*). The argument now concerns what has happened since the early 1960s and the implication of this for the further development of policy (*British Medical Journal* 1980; *Lancet* 1980). Most writers avoid committing themselves, and rightly point to the profound lack of information. Pharoah and Alberman (1981) in a review of mortality of low birthweight infants in England and Wales between 1953 and 1979 state that 'the special and intensive baby care units introduced since about 1961 are exerting an appreciable effect on mortality. There is a serious lack of representative data on rates of handicap in survivors'. Stanley and Atkinson (1981) in an analysis of cerebral palsy in low birthweight babies born in Western Australia between 1966–75, state that they can find no evidence of a lowering in the rate of cerebral palsy. On the other hand, Stewart *et al.* (1981) of University College Hospital, London, who are pioneers in this field, published a review of 22 papers, all from developed countries, and conclude that although until 1960 there was evidence of significant handicap in many survivors of low birthweight, since then 'the level of major handicap in very low birthweight babies (under 1500 g) has remained constant at 6 to 8 per cent'. Doubt has been expressed about this paper by Chalmers and Mutch (1981) of the National Perinatology Epidemiology Unit, Oxford, who state using the same data and papers as Stewart *et al.*, that 'what remains unclear is whether that number of severely handicapped children is increasing or decreasing'. Clearly, the subject has some way to go before resolution. For a more detailed review, the reader is referred to the bibliography at the end of the chapter.

Can low birthweight be prevented?

The fact that, as stated, the prevalence of low birthweight has been constant in most industrialized countries suggests that 'prevention', meaning in this case a reduction in the prevalence, is not a simple proposition. This is particularly the case in developed countries, where most low birthweight is of the 'genuine prematurity', rather than the 'small for dates' type.

While treatment, with drugs, bed rest, and various types of surgical intervention may have some effect in preventing the onset of premature labour in individual cases it seems to have had little effect on figures for populations as a whole.

As for the factors affecting the 'small for dates' aspect of low birthweight, it seems that an improvement in the general standard of living, and maternal nutrition in particular, offers the best hope of reducing the prevalence. This is implied by the fact that the percentage of low birthweight due to the 'small for dates' category is lower in wealthier countries, and also by the known consequences of famines described earlier. On the other hand, in developed countries, it seems that a famine has to exist before birthweight is significantly affected. This implies that a lesser variation in nutrition is not a significant factor in the occurrence of low birthweight in these countries.

Other possible methods for reducing the prevalence in developed countries would seem to include the following:

1. Planning of pregnancy to reduce the number of births in particular age groups – for example, under 20 years, especially if the mother is also in poor social circumstances.

2. Detection and treatment of hypertensive disorders of pregnancy. This means an effective antenatal service, so that the mothers themselves and staff understand the significance of the condition and how to recognize and treat it.

3. Cessation of smoking in pregnancy especially after the first trimester.

CONGENITAL ABNORMALITIES

Currently in developed societies about 2 per cent of babies are born with major congenital abnormalities, and a further 4 per cent have some minor abnormality. Congenital anomalies now account for between 20 and 30 per cent of mortality in early life, that is stillbirths plus infant deaths. At the beginning of the twentieth century, only some 2 per cent of early mortality was due to congenital anomalies. Since then there have been dramatic declines in infant deaths and stillbirths, due more to improvements in social circumstances than to specific medical advances. The true frequency of congenital defects has remained steady or decreased slightly over this time period.

The number of congenital abnormalities which have been described is immense, and perhaps there is no limit to the number of rare even unique abnormalities or syndromes which will be described in the future. Most of these are either of unknown aetiology, or are extremely rare, genetically based conditions. The latter are of great importance to the clinical geneticist and the genetic counsellor. In terms of more general issues of public health, the rest of this chapter will concentrate on the common congenital disorders. The approach taken is firstly to describe some of the main features of specific anatomical defects, and then to review the evidence concerning the risks related to specific exposures. This approach must lead to some repetition but is inevitable as much important work on specific exposures cannot at this point be related to specific defects.

It seems likely that a large proportion, perhaps the majority, of conceptions are normally lost. Amongst known pregnancies, spontaneous abortion rates are 15 to 25 per cent, but a greater number of fetuses may be lost before pregnancy is diagnosed. Miller *et al.* (1980) used regular urinary β-chorionic gonadotrophin levels to diagnose pregnancies earlier, and reported a spontaneous abortion rate of 40 per cent.

Spontaneous abortion is a natural method of elimination of defective fetuses; over 60 per cent of early abortuses show chromosomal abnormalities, including many types never or very rarely encountered in stillbirths or livebirths. The birth of an abnormal infant can be regarded as a failure of this natural screening process, so it is possible that any 'causal' factor which increases the prevalence at birth of an abnormality may do so by decreasing the spontaneous abortion rate relative to that of unaffected pregnancies; this theoretical mechanism has, however, not been shown to explain any major observations in the epidemiology of birth defects in human populations.

Progress in understanding congenital abnormalities

The historical development of both concepts and practical measures concerning congenital defects falls into four phases. In the earliest phase, from pre-history to the end of the nineteenth century, most congenital defects were regarded wholly or partially as the results of supernatural intervention, and were often interpreted as an indication of divine wrath or a warning directed against the parents or against society in general; the term monster was previously used to include all types of congenital defect, and is derived from the Latin verb *moneo*, meaning to warn. In many cultures the belief was widely held that union between members of different species could produce monstrous offspring, this being linked with the mythical beasts of Greek mythology such as the Centaur, or the Hindu belief in transmigration of the soul from man to animal or vice versa at death.

In medieval Christian societies fears of supernatural anger at the community frequently led to both abnormal infants and their mothers being put to death. Particularly unusual circumstances were regarded as portents of major events; the birth of twin sisters conjoined at the shoulders and hips in the village of Biddenden in Kent, England, in AD 1100 was linked to the death by accident or assassination of King William of England later the same year.

The similarities in appearance between malformed infants and real and imaginary animals led to the wide acceptance of maternal impression as a cause; pregnant women were advised not to look at monkeys for fear of producing similar monstrous infants (anencephalics, perhaps?), while the Spartans ordered pregnant women to look at statues of Castor and Pollox so that their children might be healthy and strong at birth. The concept of maternal impression persists in many third world societies today.

Mechanical explanations were also widespread; Hippocrates suggested narrowness of the womb and Aristotle excessive pressure as causes of abnormalities. These ideas were maintained up to the nineteenth century, and it is currently accepted that abnormal fetal positioning or aberrant tissue bands may be related to certain defects, particularly postural deformities.

In many cultures malformed or inferior infants were killed, as were normal and particularly female children in times of hardship. The infanticide policies of the Spartans, who threw rejected offspring into a deep chasm on Mount Taygetus, and of the Romans who drowned unwanted infants in the River Tiber, are well documented. Infanticide was also widely practised in Christian societies and is directly indicated by large excesses of male children in parish records of medieval England.

The social attitude to abnormal children was most frequently cruel exclusion from normal life, but with the growth of cities came an opportunity for exploitation, and, for example, by the end of the seventeenth century London was a centre for exhibiting every variety of unusual human form, displayed like circus animals. For malformed people with adequate intelligence, displaying their uniqueness at least provided an alternative to poverty and a work-house existence. The original Siamese conjoined twins, two brothers who were born some 60 miles from Bangkok in 1811, made an adequate living through exhibitions and fairs, and settled in the US where they were married at the age of 44 to two sisters; both produced large families. Charles Stratton, a well formed dwarf who came from Bridgeport, Connecticut, became famous as General Tom Thumb. He was 25 inches tall, and his fame can be judged by the fact that his tour of Scotland and Ireland in 1846 is reputed to have grossed £150 000.

The second phase of development was introduced by the publication in 1859 of Darwin's *The origin of species*. This led to renewed interest in congenital malformations, now studied in terms of their biological importance as examples of natural variation, rather than just as curiosities. Darwin appreciated the effects of selective forces in producing changes over many generations without consideration of how this occurred; the model was that offspring were a blended mixture of the parents' characteristics. Mendel's contribution was to show that inheritance could occur in discrete units. The gap between the publication of his work in 1865 and its rediscovery in 1900 was followed closely by the demonstration of the first recessive inborn error of metabolism, alkaptonuria, by Garrod and Bateson in 1901, and the proposal that genetic material was carried on chromosomes, made by Sutton and Boveri in 1903. In the interim, Galton had described the 'regression' phenomenon, showing that the heights of children were intermediate between those of the parents and the population average. Thus the foundations of both discrete and continuous genetic variation were laid down by the early twentieth century.

The rapid development and seemingly unlimited potential of this new science of genetics, in contrast to scanty contributions from other approaches, naturally led to its over-interpretation. Many authorities believed that almost all human characteristics including intelligence and appropriate moral attitudes were genetically controlled, and thus that appropriate breeding practices were the way to improve human conditions. Galton and his follower R. A. Fisher were among many who advocated eugenic policies; Fisher proposed economic incentives in proportion to income to encourage the more intelligent and successful members of society to have larger families. A more serious consequence of this thinking was the advocacy of compulsory sterilization for mentally and physically handicapped people, which was practised in Nazi Germany.

The teratogenic effect of X-rays was shown by Müller in the 1920s and in 1930 the American veterinarian, Haye, showed that sows deficient in vitamin A bore piglets without eyes; thus the way was opened to the consideration that specific environmental factors were causes of congenital defects. This represents the third phase of development. At around the same time, a specific preventive measure for a common congenital defect was being successfully applied, namely the use of iodized salt to prevent endemic cretinism. The era from the 1930s to the present has seen great advances in experimental work on the influence of specific chemical substances and physical exposures in causing congenital defects.

In 1941 the Australian ophthalmologist Gregg demonstrated by careful clinical observation a relationship between maternal exposure to rubella in pregnancy and congenital cataract, which led soon to the recognition of the full rubella syndrome. This represented the first demonstration of a specific cause of a major human congenital defect, apart from the cretinism relationship. Since then, experimental and human observational work have gone hand in hand. Experimental work demonstrating that cortisone could easily produce congenital defects in animals, particularly oral clefts, indicated clearly its unsuitability for use in pregnant women, yet in contrast the teratogenic effects of thalidomide were only found by direct observations of humans and could not be reproduced in the most commonly used laboratory species.

Since the 1940s advances in genetics, experimental teratology, and epidemiology have been complementary, and at the same time dramatic decreases in other major causes of infant death have made congenital abnormalities a relatively more important clinical problem, leading to major improvements in therapy. While many new single gene or chromosomal abnormalities have been described, the more relevant genetic advance in terms of understanding the most common defects has been the development of the concept of multifactorial inheritance, by Fraser, Carter, and others, and with it the balanced understanding that most common congenital defects are probably due to a combination of genetic and environmental factors. In the 1960s the mechanism (nondisjunction) by which an extra chromosome occurs in Down's syndrome was clarified, and also the mechanism underlying haemolytic disease of the newborn, due to maternal–fetal blood incompatibility in terms of the Rhesus antigen, was discovered by Clarke, which led rapidly to a preventive intervention.

The fourth phase of the story comes towards the end of the 1970s with the change in social ethics supporting the use of induced abortion as a legally and ethically accepted procedure. This, linked with the development of methods to analyse amniotic fluid to diagnose a large number of abnormalities prenatally, opened the way to procedures for induced selective abortion. Studies of spontaneous abortuses demonstrated that a very high proportion of early abortuses have severe abnormalities, and that babies who are born with severe abnormalities can be regarded as failures of the natural screening procedure by which abnormal fetuses are usually rejected early. The development of induced abortion means that current questions of 'prevention', defining the term strictly as a reduction in prevalence at birth, are not only medical and scientific, but very much ethical and legal. Similar issues are raised by the success of treatment for severely damaged or very small liveborn infants; as we now have the potential to keep many such infants alive we have also the ethical problem of whether this is in their interests or in the interests of society. At the same time public knowledge and interest in the primary prevention of congenital defects has increased, and difficult public policy issues have arisen concerning known human teratogens and the much greater number of substances which show mutagenic activity on short-term *in vitro* tests and therefore may be teratogenic to humans.

In the foreseeable future, progress in the area of understanding and correcting or preventing congenital defects will remain an ethical, legal, and social issue as well as a medical and scientific one. It is likely that there will be great advances in our ability to detect defects early, and also in our ability to institute programmes so that respective parents would know the sex of their conceived fetus which raises a separate set of social problems. The current rapid advances in our understanding of genetic mechanisms, and our ability to change these by genetic engineering may lead to the ability to compensate for a specific genetic defect, or to alter the inheritable genetic material to prevent the defect being passed on.

Chromosomal abnormalities and Down's syndrome

The commoner abnormalities are listed in Table 3.5. All the autosomal trisomies show increasing frequency with maternal age. The frequencies at birth reflect the effects of fetal losses; over half of early spontaneous abortuses have chromosomal abnormalities, and of these 45,X (Turner's syndrome) and several trisomies which are never or very rarely seen in livebirths, including trisomies 16, 22, 14, and 15 are relatively common in early abortuses. Probably some 75 per cent of trisomy 21 (Down's syndrome) fetuses are aborted. An association of XYY genotype with aggressive psychopathic, or criminal behaviour has been reported. As well as these disorders involving missing or extra chromosomes many syndromes due to abnormalities of structure of chromosomes have been described. These are relatively rare; the commonest is the *cri-du-chat* syndrome due to deletion of part of chromosome five.

Table 3.5. *The commoner chromosomal abnormalities*

Autosomal trisomies	Prevalence per 1000 live births
21 (Down's syndrome)	1.0
13 (Patau's syndrome)	0.1
18 (Edward's syndrome)	0.1
Gonosomal	
XXY (Klinefelter's syndrome)	0.5 (male)
XYY	0.5 (male)
XXX	0.5 (female)
XO (Turner's syndrome)	0.1 (female)

Down's syndrome is diagnosed clinically shortly after birth, the chief features being the characteristic oval face with a flat occiput, epicanthic folds, Brushfield spots on the iris, abnormal palmar creases, and hypotonia. Nearly half of Down's syndrome children have a cardiac defect at birth, most commonly a septal defect or Fallot's tetralogy. They have a substantially increased risk of leukaemia. The prevalence at birth is around one per thousand live births in Europe and North America at present, and is similar in boys and in girls, but boys have a better survival in early childhood, resulting in a male excess in institutional statistics. The syndrome is the result of extra genetic material from chromosome 21. About 92 per cent of affected individuals have a 47 XY chromosome configuration, which is produced by fusion of a normal gamete with one carrying both parental 21 chromosomes after failure of these to be separated at meiosis (non-disjunction). In 5 per cent

it is due to a translocation, where the extra genetic material from chromosome 21 is carried most commonly on a chromosome of the D group (13, 14, or 15) or on another G group chromosome (21 or 22). In about 3 per cent it is due to a mosaic syndrome where not all cells show the trisomy; the physical and intellectual abnormalities tend to be less extreme in these individuals. Translocation or mosaic situations are relatively commoner in younger mothers, but even in these they account for less than 10 per cent of affected infants. Chromosome analyses are needed only occasionally for diagnosis but will identify translocation or mosaic states. While in the majority of cases of translocations, the parents' chromosomes are normal, in others one of the parents carries the translocation. The recurrence risks of translocation Down's syndrome are about 5 per cent if the mother has a D/G or 21/22 translocation, and 10 to 15 per cent if the father has either of these, but are close to 100 per cent if either parent has a 21/21 translocation.

Prevalence at birth shows a striking increase with maternal age (Table 3.6). This can be adequately modelled by a constant plus exponential function, where:

$$\text{risk} = a + \exp(b + cx)$$

where x is maternal age and a, b, and c are constants (Lamson and Hook 1980). This can be interpreted biologically as the sum of an age-independent process (translocations and mosaics) and a process exponentially related to maternal age (non-disjunction). More complex age models suggested earlier were derived to explain apparent departures from the simple exponential model at advanced ages, but these were largely due to the use of broad age groups and are not seen if single year-of-age specific rates are examined. Although special staining techniques have shown that the extra chromosome is paternal in 20 to 30 per cent of cases, there appears to be no independent effect on risk of paternal age, and maternal parity has a weak inverse association with risk (high parity – lower risk) at a given maternal age. Prevalence rates at birth had dropped by 30 per cent in the US in the 1970s (Table 3.7). This is due primarily to the trend in the general population towards younger maternal ages, due mainly to voluntary family size limitation, with small contributions in later years from elective abortion and from amniocenteses. So at present only 20 per cent of Down's syndrome babies are born to mothers over age 35 years; widespread use of amniocentesis and abortion in older mothers is only likely to reduce the frequency in future years by 10 to 20 per cent.

We understand the mechanism but not the causes of the syndrome. The exponential relationship of non-disjunction to maternal age suggests cumulative ovarian damage, and would be consistent with, for example, a chronic viral infection. Reported prevalence rates at birth are similar in most populations. Short-term secular trends, seasonal trends, and space-time clusters have all been reported, but not consistently enough to suggest specific aetiological factors. Suggestions of an association with prenatal radiation exposure have been made, and increases in age-specific rates in recent years have been reported although these probably are due to more complete ascertainment.

No primary prevention method can be suggested, but

Table 3.6. *Down's syndrome: estimated prevalence rates at birth by single year of maternal age, Ohio, United States, 1970–79*

Maternal age (years)	Prevalence at birth expressed as:	
	odds	rate/1000 births*
≤ 14	1/1382	0.72
15	1/1379	0.73
16	1/1374	0.73
17	1/1368	0.73
18	1/1359	0.74
19	1/1348	0.74
20	1/1334	0.75
21	1/1316	0.76
22	1/1292	0.77
23	1/1261	0.79
24	1/1223	0.82
25	1/1175	0.85
26	1/1117	0.90
27	1/1048	0.95
28	1/968	1.03
29	1/879	1.14
30	1/782	1.28
31	1/683	1.46
32	1/584	1.71
33	1/489	2.04
34	1/402	2.49
35	1/325	3.08
36	1/259	3.86
37	1/204	4.90
38	1/159	6.29
39	1/123	8.13
40	1/94	10.6
41	1/72	13.9
42	1/55	18.2
43	1/41	24.4
44	1/31	32.3
45	1/24	41.7
46	1/18	55.6
47	1/13	76.9
48	1/10	100.0
≥ 49	1/8	125.0

*The rates are based on birth certificate data, corrected for completeness of reporting and for cases diagnosed at amniocentesis, then smoothed by fitting a constant plus exponential model.
Source: Huether *et al.* (1981).

Table 3.7. *Decline in prevalence at birth of Down's syndrome from 1960 to 1978, United States.*

	Down's syndrome births		Proportion of births to women ≥ 35 years	
Year	Number	Rate/1000 births	All births	Down's syndrome
1960	5741	1.33	10.9	43.8
1965	4790	1.27	9.8	43.2
1970	4036	1.08	6.3	32.0
1975	3112	0.99	4.6	23.7
1978	3291	0.99	4.5	21.2

Source: Adams *et al.* (1981).

prenatal diagnosis by examination of cultured fetal cells obtained by amniocentesis is reliable. The policy of antenatal diagnosis most generally proposed is that women over 35 years should be offered amniocentesis. Currently it is clear that only a minority of mothers receive this service, because they are unaware of it, do not request it, or it is not available.

Even in the US facilities are inadequate to provide diagnostic services to all women over 35 years old, and in most other countries are even more limited. For example, in Washington State, US, in 1977 only 12 per cent of pregnancies to mothers over 35 years old had amniocentesis; elective abortion for 'social' reasons in older mothers has had a much larger effect than has the amniocentesis programme in avoiding births of infants with Down's syndrome (Luthy *et al.* 1980). Amniocentesis should be offered if the parents have been shown to be carriers of a translocation. The frequency of Down's syndrome and other chromosomal abnormalities is higher in amniocentesis studies than in live births, either due to selection factors or to there normally being an appreciable fetal mortality in later pregnancy.

Neural-tube defects

The spinal cord develops from the neural tube, which in turn is formed from the neural plate, which folds dorsally and fuses, the fusion commencing in the mid-dorsal region and extending cranially and caudally. This process is normally complete by 26 to 27 days' gestation.

Failure of fusion at the cranial end prevents development of the forebrain, and as a consequence the skull does not develop, yielding anencephalus. This gross abnormality is incompatible with life, and the great majority of infants are stillborn; although the proportion stillborn varies markedly between different countries and over time, because of differences in certification practices rather than for any biological reason. Because of its ease of recognition and total fatality, anencephalus is useful for epidemiological study, and is the only major common congenital defect for which mortality data give an adequately accurate estimate of prevalence at birth.

Failure of fusion caudally produces spina bifida, which varies considerably in severity. Meningocoeles, where the spinal cord is normal and a meningeal sac containing only cerebrospinal fluid protrudes through a dorsal defect in the spinal column, have a relatively good prognosis. Lower limb neurological problems and associated hydrocephalus are uncommon, although bladder disfunction and minor lower limb problems may arise. Careful follow-up is necessary as fresh neurological problems may develop as the child grows. More commonly, some neural tissue is present in the sac, yielding a myelomeningocoele. The prognosis depends on the extent of neurological damage, which if severe will involve both motor and sensory loss distal to the lesion, affecting usually the lower limbs, lower trunk, and bladder and bowel enervation.

In the majority of cases of severe spina bifida there is an associated hydrocephalus. Immediate treatment involves avoiding dehydration of the exposed tissue and infection. Long-term management consists of compensating for the neurological deficiences, and attention must be paid to orthopaedic problems, urinary tract difficulties, pressure sores, burns due to loss of skin sensation, control of hydrocephalus by cerebrospinal fluid shunts, and the problems of mental handicap. The decisions of how much surgical intervention is justifiable on individual cases involves medical, ethical, and legal problems and has been discussed by Illingworth (1974) and by Elwood and Elwood (1980). In a British series of 201 children with spina bifida treated aggressively from the first day of life, assessment at 2–4 years showed that 64 per cent were alive, and of these 36 per cent had severe physical handicap and mental retardation, 45 per cent had severe physical handicap without retardation, and the remaining 19 per cent mild or moderate physical handicap (Lorber 1971).

A dorsal deficiency of the spinal column without neurological involvement is known as spina bifida occulta, which is usually asymptomatic and may be associated with a hairy patch or birth mark on the back. Prevalence estimates are unavailable, but it may be present in a substantial proportion of the population. Other neural-tube defects include more severe spinal and cranial defects including craniorachischisis where the entire spinal cord is open, and less severe defects, including cranial meningocoele, encephalocoele, and hydroencephalocoele.

The most striking epidemiological features of these conditions are their marked variation in time and space, which allied to the fact that in the western developed countries they are the most common fatal congenital abnormality, has made them the object of many epidemiological studies, which have been summarized by Elwood and Elwood (1980). They show great geographical variation (Table 3.8). The defects are commonest in the Caucasian racial groups, with anencephalus and spina bifida being of similar frequency. Within the UK, the prevalence at birth of the two conditions varies from over eight per thousand births in Belfast to around three per thousand in London; the high

Table 3.8. *The geographical variation in prevalence at birth of anencephalus and spina bifida*

| | Rates per 1000 total births | |
	Anencephalus	Spina bifida
Europe		
UK		
Birmingham	2.4	1.0
Liverpool	3.4	1.1
London	1.4	1.5
South Wales	3.1	3.9
Glasgow	2.8	2.8
Northern Ireland	3.1	3.3
Finland	0.3	0.4
Sweden	0.4	0.7
Budapest	1.1	1.6
North America		
British Columbia	0.6	0.9
Manitoba	0.9	1.3
Quebec	1.6	1.9
New York State	0.6	0.7
Iowa	0.6	1.0
Asia		
Japan	0.4	0.1
Taiwan	1.2	0.2
Singapore	0.7	0.1
Bombay	1.9	1.1

Source: Elwood and Elwood (1980).

rates occur in Ireland, Wales, southern Scotland, and northwest England, with a decrease as one moves towards the southeast. Information is much more sparse for the rest of Europe, but appears to show a fall from the British rates as one moves eastwards, and also very low rates of one per thousand or less in Scandinavia. Data available for the whole of Canada show a threefold decrease from rates of around four per thousand in eastern Canada to rates of 1.5 per thousand in the west, and various reports from areas of the US suggest a similar trend there. Both in the UK and in Canada, it has been shown that the geographical variation in neural-tube defects is not seen in any other major type of congenital defect.

Rates in non-Caucasian racial groups, including the Jewish and black populations in the US, are generally lower than in Caucasians, and rates of spina bifida are extremely low in the Orient, being around 0.1 per thousand in studies from Japan, Taiwan, and Singapore. The prevalence at birth of anencephalus in these countries is considerably higher, around 0.5 per thousand. The oriental countries are thus characterized by a much lower ratio of spina bifida to anencephalus than is seen in western countries.

Migrant studies of Caucasian populations, such as Irish populations who migrate to the US, show changes in rates to those of the host country over two to three generations (Naggan and MacMahon 1967). However, rates in black populations and in Indian and Pakistani populations in Britain do not show any marked change on migration (Leck 1969).

Another unusual feature of the disease is the female predominance. About two-thirds of anencephalic births are female and there is a tendency for the proportion which are female to be highest in the countries where the prevalence at birth is highest. Spina bifida shows a less marked female predominance, with about 60 per cent of affected infants being female. The sex distribution of spina bifida infants in oriental countries appears similar to that figure, while for anencephalus female predominance does not appear and there is an approximately equal distribution. Studies of the sex distribution in relation to secular trends in the prevalence at birth are inconsistent, but several suggest a tendency for the female preponderance to be most marked at the peaks of prevalence rates. Both this and the geographical association suggest that the chief lability in time and space of neural-tube defect rates is in the anencephalus rate in female births.

Apart from the differences in sex distribution, and in the relative frequencies in oriental countries, the descriptive features of spina bifida and of anencephalus appear to be very similar.

The conditions show very marked secular trends. A most striking epidemic occurred in the northeast US during the 1930s (Fig. 3.1), where rates for anencephalus and spina bifida combined reached six per thousand during 1930–34, compared to two per thousand both in hospital data from around the turn of the century and in reliable population based data since the 1960s (MacMahon and Yen 1971). The marked decrease in rates from 1930 to the present has been seen in adjacent areas, but there is no indication of a trend in western Canada, where the rates are low but stable. European trends have been less dramatic although in Britain there is a current trend for rates to decrease, and it has been suggested that there was a peak in Europe seen in the 1930s at the same time as that noted in the US. In Ireland, prevalence rates at birth showed a rise from the beginning of the century to the 1970s. Short-term fluctuations have been described frequently. A seasonal trend has also been noted, with higher rates in babies conceived in the spring and born in the winter. This also is inconsistent, and for example in Canada was quite marked in the 1950s and early 1960s, but disappeared later.

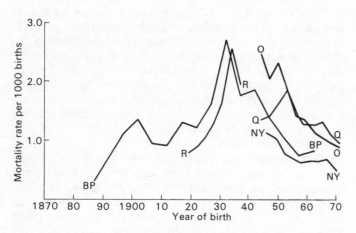

Fig. 3.1. Secular trends in prevalence at birth or mortality from anencephalus in north-east America: Boston and Providence (B P), Rochester, New York State (R), Upper New York State (NY), Ontario (O) and Quebec (Q). Spina bifida shows similar trends. (Source: Elwood and Elwood (1980), p. 111.)

A considerable amount of literature concerns the relationship of neural-tube defect prevalence at birth to maternal age and reproductive history. If account is taken of maternal age and year-of-birth effects, or studies are done within sibships, there appears to be a trend towards lower prevalence rates at birth with increasing parity, and little effect of maternal age apart from this. Canadian studies have shown increaes in risk associated with previous stillbirths, spontaneous abortions, or previous infant deaths, which provides an explanation for the commonly seen U-shaped relationship with age and parity seen in crude data without further analysis. In Canadian data, this is due to the low rates associated with high parity being compensated by increased risks associated with prior abnormal reproductive histories (Elwood *et al.* 1978). Explanations of these relationships have yet to be proposed.

Many studies show higher rates of anencephalus and spina bifida in the lower socio-economic classes, estimated by occupation or property values. A two- to threefold gradient from professional to unskilled occupational groups is seen in most, but not all, British data, and similar trends have been seen in Boston, Montreal, and Taiwan. No such gradient is seen in Israel.

Much of the literature shows risks to siblings of around 5 per cent (Carter and Evans 1973), but more recent data from North America shows sibling risks of 2 per cent (McBride 1977; Janerich and Piper 1978), and these differences are consistent with the differences in prevalence rates at birth in the different societies. The familial aggregation fits the criteria of the multifactorial inheritance model with the risk to siblings being approximately equal to the square root of the prevalence rate at birth in the population, the risk being increased after a second affected baby to about twice that after a first and the risks to more distant family members decreasing steadily. Although consistent with multifactorial inheritance, this type of familial aggregation could also be explained by an environmental agent, and several hypotheses of a totally environmental mechanism have been suggested. However, if all the available data on twins are considered together it becomes clear that the concordance rate of the defect in like sex twin pairs is much higher than that in unlike sex twin pairs, which in turn is consistent with the full sibling risk, and this provides strong evidence for an independent genetic factor. Elwood and Elwood (1980) summarized all data available at that time, which gave concordance rates of 7.6 per cent in like sex twin pairs and 2.8 per cent in unlike sex pairs: the estimated concordance rates for dizygotic and monozygotic twin pairs are therefore 2.8 per cent and 11.3 per cent. Because of the odd sex distribution, several complex genetic models involving sex linkage have been proposed, but none has been widely supported.

Although there is a great deal of descriptive information available, few large and careful analytical studies of spina bifida or anencephalus have been done, with the result that there have been a large number of aetiological hypotheses proposed, none of which to date has been shown to satisfactorily explain the major features of the condition. The rapid variation in prevalence rates with time, season, social class, and geography could suggest an infectious aetiology, and the defects can be produced in animals by infection with several viruses (Sever 1975). The effects of less common viral infections in humans including the possibility of a latent virus infection require further study. Several complex analyses of the relationships of prevalence rates of birth to calendar time, maternal age, and maternal year of birth have suggested that the disease may be related to events occurring in the mother's own childhood or at puberty, and hypotheses based on dietary or infectious actions at those times have been suggested (Emanuel and Sever 1973; Baird 1974; Janerich 1974). A further set of hypotheses concern the relationship between the affected pregnancy and earlier pregnancies, involving tissue interactions between the developing fetus and cell rest material persisting from earlier pregnancies, but these require further evaluation (Gardiner *et al.* 1978).

The geographical variation in the UK results in an association between areas of high prevalence and areas with soft water supplies, but more detailed geographical and case-control studies have not supported an association with any major element in water supplies.

Amongst the leading contenders for some years have been dietary hypotheses. Several retrospective case-control studies have suggested that mothers of affected infants have a less balanced or generally inferior diet to those of controls (Richards 1969). In 1972, the hypothesis was put forward that the defects might be due to potato blight (Renwick 1972), as the general geographical variation and the social class variation seemed to be explicable in terms of consumption of poor quality potatoes, but case-control studies and careful secular comparisons in areas of epidemic potato blight did not confirm this. A suggestion of a link with vitamin A deficiency has also not been confirmed.

The most exciting current hypothesis is that the defects may be due to deficiency of certain vitamins, particularly folic acid. This work has been developed over many years by Smithells and his colleagues. In a case-control study published in 1965 they suggested that mothers of infants with neural-tube defects, tested post-partum, have a deficiency of folic acid as compared to mothers of controls, and subsequently a small prospective study in which samples were taken for vitamin assay early in pregnancy also suggested lower levels in mothers of affected infants. A marginal vitamin deficiency hypothesis would be consistent with the social class gradient and perhaps the seasonal variation. Smithells and colleagues then embarked upon an experimental trial, offering a multivitamin preparation to mothers who had already had one infant affected with a neural-tube defect and therefore were at a high risk of having a second infant affected. Unfortunately, because ethical review committees would not permit it, the trial was not randomized. The results, however, show 23 recurrences in 493 births to mothers who apparently did not follow the advice, a recurrence rate of 4.7 per cent, and only three recurrences in 379 births to those who did take the vitamin supplements, a rate of 0.8 per cent (Smithells *et al.* 1980, 1981). Although the lack of randomization is a serious handicap in the interpretation of these studies, the relationship is still striking. Further results in terms of non-randomized trials will be forthcoming from this British group. Whether one should embark immediately on a randomized trial or apply the proposed therapy without such a step is a difficult ethical issue, and planning for further trials has been taking place. The question of whether such a protective effect in preventing recurrences in the small proportion of women who have already had an affected child is directly applicable to the primary prevention situation is also open to discussion.

Congenital heart disease

Congenital heart disease is one of the most common groups of congenital defects, being found in 6–8 per thousand births in most Caucasian populations. As some defects are not present at birth (a patent ductus arteriosus may be a normal finding), and others are not diagnosed until later, follow-up of a birth cohort for at least two years is necessary to give a reasonable estimate of prevalence. The most common specific lesions are ventricular septal defect (30 per cent of the total), patent ductus arteriosus (PDA) (10 per cent), and, each accounting for about 5 per cent, aortic stenosis, atrial septal defect, aortic coarctation, Fallot's tetralogy, pulmonary stenosis, and transposition of the great vessels.

Patent ductus arteriosis is the best understood of these, and shows several associations which are related to low oxygen tension before, during, or after birth. The prevalence of a patent ductus arteriosus in newborns decreases with increasing gestation, and is found in over a third of newborns under 1500 g. A persistent patent ductus is more common in infants with a history of prematurity, respiratory distress syndrome, or neonatal hypoxia, and the prevalence of a patent ductus in children increases with altitude of residence, being 30 times higher at 4500 metres than at sea level (Peñaloza *et al.* 1964). These findings complement the experimental observations that the ductus dilates with a lower blood oxygen tension. Two-thirds of children with a PDA are girls. The defect is a well recognized part of the rubella syndrome although this now accounts for only a few cases. The empiric recurrence risk of a congenital heart defect is about three times the population risk, suggesting a polygenic inheritance or common environmental factors. Cardiac defects are multiple in 10–15 per cent of individuals, and in a similar proportion there is a major abnormality of another system. Cardiac defects, usually septal defects or Fallot's tetralogy, are increased in infants with Down's syndrome, and also in other trisomies, Turner's syndrome, and *cri-du-chat* syndrome. Aortic stenosis, coarctation, and transposition show male excesses, and many defects show an increase in prevalence with increasing maternal age which is only partially explained by the relationship with Down's syndrome. Monozygotic twins are more liable to congenital heart disease, perhaps because of a placental anastamosis. A number of reports, including one large prospective study, suggest a twofold increase in congenital heart disease in mothers exposed to female hormones antenatally (Heinonen *et al.* 1977). The increase was not specific to any one type of defect. Reported rates of ventricular septal defect in the US steadily increased through the 1970s, and in Atlanta the increase was seen also in defects remaining open at one year of age, suggested the trend is not simply due to increased reporting of small defects (Layde 1980). Seasonal trends in various cardiac defects have been reported as have increases in prevalence at high maternal ages, but results have been inconsistent (Leck 1977).

Oral clefts

Epidemiological and genetic studies show that cleft lip alone and cleft lip combined with cleft palate can be regarded as one entity, with prevalence rates of around one per thousand live births (range 0.6–1.4) in Caucasian populations, with 60–80 per cent of affected babies being boys. The prevalence at birth is higher (around 1.7 per 1000) in oriental races and also in North American Indians and Eskimos, and is lower in blacks, around 0.4 per thousand. In boys, lip clefts on the right side appear more common than those on the left, but there seems little difference in girls. Caucasian parents of affected children tend to have flatter facial features than average and this suggests that the variability between ethnic groups may be related to their facial characteristics.

Cleft lip/palate has been extensively studied both in

animals and man. Of all common human defects, it most clearly fits the multifactorial genetic model. Compared to the population prevalence rate of one per thousand, first-degree relatives of affected children have occurrence rates of 30–50 per thousand, which is also the recurrence risk for subsequent pregnancies to the same mother. Second-degree relatives show rates of seven per thousand, third-degree relatives of 2–3 per thousand. The risk to a further sibling where there are already two affected infants is around 10 per cent. The risk to relatives increases with the severity of the malformation, from around 25 per thousand where the index patient has a unilateral cleft lip, to 60 per thousand where the index patient has bilateral cleft lip/palate. It would be expected that the risk to relatives would be higher if the affected child is a girl, and there are indications, if not proof, that that occurs.

Cleft palate alone is less common in Caucasians, at a prevalence of 0.5 per thousand births, and 60 per cent of cases are in girls. This frequency is similar in Japanese, American Indian, and black populations, although the frequency is high in native Hawaiians.

The first experimental demonstration that a drug could be teratogenic was the production of cleft palate in pregnant mice after injections of cortisone, shown in 1950. The same dose of cortisone given at the same time to different genetic strains of mice produced dramatic differences in the incidence of the defect, giving the first experimental demonstration of a genetic difference in susceptibility to a teratogen. Subsequent experimental work suggested that the difference was due to the strains with greater susceptibility having a later date of closure of the opposing folds which form the palate. Apart from cortisone, there is good evidence that cleft lip and palate in humans can be caused by anti-epileptic drugs particularly diphenylhydantoin. The risk is about three times normal and it appears that this is due to the drug exposure rather than the underlying epilepsy. There have been suggestions of relationships with other drugs, including aspirin and diazepam (valium), but these are based on small retrospective studies and cannot be taken as definitive.

In Australia, the US, and Britain, prevalence rates at birth of cleft lip/palate have decreased over the last two decades. Short-term increases, seasonal variations, and time-space clustering have been inconsistently reported. The prevalence at birth increases with maternal age, particularly at ages over 30 years. However, if infants with multiple defects, including trisomies, are excluded, the evidence for a maternal age effect on cleft lip/palate alone becomes much weaker, and some studies suggest it may be due to an association with the father's age. Maternal parity appears to have no effect. Epidemiological data on cleft palate alone are more limited, but also suggest an increase with maternal age, both for cleft palate alone and in association with defects of other systems.

In terms of prevention, genetic counselling may be given to the parents of affected children, and to parents who are themselves or have close relatives who are affected. Fairly accurate estimations of risk can be given. Such counselling is advisory rather than specifically aimed at prevention, as the condition is not life-threatening and satisfactory therapeutic results can be obtained in most cases. An important aspect of counselling is to separate defects occurring alone from defects which may be part of more serious syndromes, with specific genetic patterns: this applies to about 3 per cent of oral clefts. The condition is not serious enough to warrant antenatal diagnostic measures, although it has been detected by fetoscopy, and by ultrasound.

Pyloric stenosis

Classically this presents a few weeks after birth when the child develops projectile vomiting. The cause is hyperplasia of the circular muscle around the pylorus. It is diagnosed in 2–4 births per thousand in Britain and northern Europe, although mild cases may not come to attention. The reported frequencies in other parts of Europe and among Caucasians in the US are lower, and in blacks the frequency is below one per thousand. There is a striking male excess, with 75–80 per cent of affected babies being boys. The frequency in first-degree relatives is markedly higher if the index patient is female, as would be expected on a polygenic inheritance pattern. For first-degree relatives the risks vary from 10 to 50 times the population rate, for second-degree relatives they are about five times, and for third-degree about twice the population risk.

There has been a moderate decline in frequency of the condition over the last 20 years. The condition is markedly more common in first than in later births, although this is not found in all studies, and the time of onset is usually later in first births. In Britain there appears to be a higher rate in infants of blood groups O and B, and this may be mediated by a reduced absorption rate of fat from the intestine, related to delayed pyloric emptying. The clinical occurrence of the condition and the timing of its onset may relate to post-natal feeding practices. A study 30 years ago noted that babies born in hospital and fed every three hours tended to develop symptoms earlier than those born at home and fed less frequently or less regularly.

The overstimulation of the pyloric muscle may be due to gastrin. Infants born to women who themselves had infantile pyloric stenosis have a very high prevalence of disease (130 per thousand), which may be due to excess gastrin derived both from the infant and from placental transfer. However, excess plasma gastrin levels have not been demonstrated.

Congenital dislocation of the hip

In the absence of neonatal testing, which is discussed below, congenital dislocation of the hip (CDH) was recognized in 0.6–1.3 per 1000 births in surveys in Britain and the US. It results in walking difficulties, leg shortening, and hip osteoarthritis. The suggested mechanism of the dislocation relates to both a shallow acetabular socket, and a high degree of laxity of the ligaments and connective tissues round the joint. This 'late' disease is much commoner where infants are customarily kept with legs extended and adducted as in some Lapp and North American Indian societies, and less common where infants' hips are kept in flexion and abduction, as in many Chinese and African societies. The prevalence at birth in Caucasian populations is higher in first births and in winter births; the majority of cases are unilateral, usually left sided. Over 80 per cent are girls, giving rates of CDH of 1.0–2.2 per 1000 female and 0.2–0.5 per 1000 male births. It is much commoner after a breech delivery, and affected breech births show a less extreme sex distribution. An excess risk of neonatally diagnosed CDH has been found after amniocentesis (Medical Research Council 1978). There is a strong, presumably polygenic, familial tendency. British studies suggest risks of seven and 50 per 1000 to brothers or sisters, respectively, of affected girls, and 40 and 70 per 1000 to brothers or sisters of affected boys.

A test of hip stability in neonates was described by Ortolani in 1937, and made popular after modification by Barlow in 1962. As reviewed by Parkin (1981), the use of this test in screening newborns has resulted in positive results in 5–30 per 1000 births, with most reports being around 10 per 1000. Comparing these rates to rates of late disease suggests 90 per cent of infants with positive tests will resolve spontaneously. This low predictive value will not be a problem if infants are re-examined over 2–3 weeks before treatment; Barlow reported that 88 per cent resolved in two months, and he treated only the rest. However, treatment practices vary greatly. Centres conducting screening report rates of late or missed CDH which range from very low (0.07 per 1000) to rates approaching those seen without screening (0.6–0.8 per 1000 after 3–5 months of age). The latter results suggest that the test may miss a substantial number of affected infants, and rescreening of all infants at six months of age has been suggested. The various reports of CDH incidence after screening vary greatly in the definition and timing of diagnosis, and no one study has been large or rigorous enough to be authoritative. Parkin found no evidence that centres with high positivity rates on neonatal screening had low rates of late CDH.

Positional foot deformities

The most important of these is talipes equinovarus (TEV), a fixed inversion and plantar flexion of the foot. Prevalence estimates are inconsistent due to different criteria used; the prevalence of severe deformity requiring treatment is around 1–1.5 per 1000 live births, while total frequencies including the 'positional' defects which disappear spontaneously are reported as 2–4 per 1000 in Caucasians. Of the more severe cases, about 60 per cent respond to manipulation; night splinting up to five years of age is successful in most of the rest, with corrective bone surgery as a last resort. Frequencies are only half as high in Oriental peoples, but may be six times as high in Polynesians. Male excesses, up to 3:1 apply to the more severe disease; milder cases show a female excess. About half the cases are bilateral. The risk of non-postural disease in first-degree relatives is about 3 per cent in British studies, and the familial data are consistent with a polygenic inheritance. The main aetiological hypothesis is mechanical compression, and associations with obstetric complications such as

oligohydramnios and breech delivery, and with clinical evidence of generalized laxity of connective tissues have been reported. An excess of severe TEV was associated with amniocentesis in the British multicentre study of amniocentesis (Medical Research Council 1978). There is evidence of a moderately increased risk in births to older mothers, first births, and in births in winter or spring, and in twins.

Talipes calcaneovalgus (TCV) and metatarsus varus (MV) each occur in about one per 1000 of Caucasian births, but can usually be treated by manipulation alone. Both show a female excess, and associations with primiparity and prolonged gestation have been noted. These defects may resemble the milder forms of TEV in being caused by compression and/or joint laxity.

Hypospadias

In this condition, the urethra opens proximal to the normal position on the ventral aspect of the penis. It occurs in some two per 1000 male births in Britain, but higher rates have been found in the US and in Israel. Ten per cent of brothers of index cases are affected, compared to 2 per cent of second-degree relatives, consistent with polygenic inheritance. It has been reported to be more common in twins.

Cystic fibrosis

Occurring in about one in 2000 births in Europe and North America, cystic fibrosis is the commonest severe autosomal recessive condition. One person in 22 carries the abnormal gene. The prognosis for survival has increased greatly in recent years due to successful treatment of meconium ileus, malabsorption, and recurrent lung infections, and immunization against viral infections; *Pseudomonas* infections remain a great threat and survivors may develop cirrhosis and diabetes. Genetic counselling is essential; antenatal diagnosis is not yet available as a routine test. In some countries, neonatal screening using a test for increased protein in meconium is being used but the validity of the test is not very high and the advantage of earlier diagnosis as yet unknown.

Cerebral palsy

Cerebral palsy is a major cause of crippling handicap in children, occurring in around two per 1000 births, although accurate prevalence figures are impossible to obtain due to problems of classification and diagnosis. The common element in the condition is a permanent non-progressive brain lesion. The postulated causes are multiple, including hypoxia, hypoglycaemia, and trauma before or during birth, and structural abnormalities such as cysts, fusion defects, and aplasias. Most cases (around 70 per cent), are spastic, and a minority show dyskinesia, choreoathetosis, or ataxia. About 60 per cent have mental handicap, and epilepsy, visual impairment, squint, and speech disorders are common.

ENVIRONMENTAL CAUSES OF CONGENITAL ABNORMALITIES

Infections

Special fetal hazards following transplacental infection are well documented for rubella, cytomegalovirus, herpes simplex, the varicella-herpes zoster virus, toxoplasmosis, *Treponema pallidum,* syphilis, and gonorrhoea. Although many reports have linked influenza to congenital defects, there is no conclusive evidence of risk, and in general the larger studies using prospective methods or examining trends during epidemics show no association. The situation is similar in regard to mumps, and to ECHO and Coxsackie virus infections.

Radiation

Heavy exposure to ionizing radiation, as in mothers exposed to the atomic bomb attacks in Japan, has produced fetal death and microcephaly; human and animal work suggests these effects will be produced by doses of 10 rads to pre-implantation embryos or even higher doses at later stages. There is no other human evidence of relationships to specific defects. Radiation exposure does, however, increase the risk of leukaemia in childhood, even at dosages of around 2 rads in the first trimester. An extensive diagnostic investigation, such as a contrast enema with fluoroscopy, could give up to 2 rads of radiation dose; more usual investigations such as pelvimetry, spinal X-rays, or pyelograms give fetal doses of less than 0.5 rads (Pizzarello 1980).

Alcohol

The spectrum of effects of alcohol on reproduction is similar to that of other damaging agents: alcohol may reduce fertility, increase fetal losses, retard growth, produce a specific 'fetal alcohol syndrome', and may increase other physical or intellectual defects (Pratt 1977). The fetal alcohol syndrome (FAS) has been noted in about 1.7 per 1000 births in France and Sweden, and may occur in 2–30 per cent of infants born to consumers of more than 50 g/day of alcohol. The syndrome comprises mental deficiency, microcephaly, reduced weight and length, irritability, and a characteristic facies, accompanied by an increased frequency of cardiac, skeletal, and urogenital defects. Similar syndromes are seen in infants born to mothers with phenylketonuria or epilepsy who have been treated by hydantoins. The FAS appears to require very heavy alcohol consumption. The effects of lesser consumption are much more difficult to document and specific abnormalities have not been demonstrated; however, an effect on intellectual potential or behaviour has been suggested by some and is impossible to exclude.

The growth-retardation effect can be reduced by avoiding heavy alcohol consumption during the pregnancy, so this is advisable. The FAS must be produced early in pregnancy, however, and attempts at primary prevention must therefore be directed at all young adult women.

Diabetes

Many studies show increases in total congenital anomalies of up to four times normal in overtly diabetic women. Multiple malformations may be particularly increased, but otherwise the associations seem non-specific, with most common anomalies being reported as increased. The mechanism of these increases has not been elucidated; it does not seem to be due to insulin or other drugs, and the effect of the degree of control of the diabetic state is unclear (Dignan 1981).

Smoking

Although the relationship of smoking to low birthweight is well documented, there is no firm evidence of a relationship with any specific congenital defect. Several studies have reported increased risks of various defects in births to smokers, but the relationships seen are not consistent and the studies have problems in information bias and in distinguishing smoking from other correlated factors. Several prospective studies have shown no associations, including one of 67 609 pregnancies in south Wales (Evans *et al.* 1979).

Anticonvulsants

Studies of mothers with epilepsy show an approximate doubling of the frequency of major congenital defects and this seems wholly explained by a threefold excess in women treated with anticonvulsants, usually phenytoin, phenobarbitone, or primidone (Smithells 1976; Annegers *et al.* 1978). Most studies, being on relatively small numbers of women, can assess only total abnormality rates, but the major specific associations appear to be with cleft lip and palate (12 times excess) and cardiac lesions (three times). Increases in digital hypoplasia, in diaphragmatic and inguinal herniae, and in duplication of the ureter have also been reported. A 'fetal hydantoin syndrome' comprising growth retardation, mental retardation, craniofacial abnormalities, and nail and digital hypoplasia has been described. The mechanism may be via folate antagonism – phenytoin appears to be the strongest folate antagonist and, of the commonly used drugs, to carry the greatest risk. Trimethadione may be similarly dangerous. Little information on newer drugs is available. The issue of whether the risks are due to the epilepsy per se is still open, and some evidence suggests that good control of the disease leads to reduced risks of malformation. Studies of the risks associated with paternal epilepsy have shown no excess of abnormalities. Epilepsy tends to worsen during pregnancy, so drug reduction or withdrawal is inadvisable; folate supplementation seems a wise course, although evidence of its benefit has yet to come, and for women who may become pregnant in the future, drugs other than phenytoin or trimethadione should be used if possible.

Hormonal agents

Androgenic hormones may produce virilization of female fetuses; this occurred where androgens were used to treat breast cancer in the mother, and with the use of synthetic progestins to treat threatened abortion. Diethyl stilboesterol, also used for threatened abortion, has led to vaginal clear cell adenocarcinoma arising in young women who had been exposed to the drug prenatally when it was given to their mothers in the first 18 weeks of pregnancy. The risk of the otherwise virtually unknown condition is around one per 1000 exposed women. However, there is no clear evidence for a direct teratogenic effect of hormonal drugs used at normal doses (Wilson and Brent 1981).

Oestrogen-progesterone tablets were used extensively for the diagnosis of pregnancy, but are no longer permitted in most countries. Synthetic progestogens are still available for the treatment of threatened abortion, although there is no firm evidence that they are effective. Thus although much of the available data relate to these exposures, the only common situation now is that of accidental exposure to oral contraceptives in pregnancy, or the possible risk to pregnancies conceived shortly after discontinuation of oral contraceptives. Many of the available studies are either too small to detect a moderate risk, or are based on retrospective designs with insufficient attention to the problem of biased recall. Such retrospective case-control studies have shown associations of hormonal exposure with congenital heart disease, limb-reduction defects, and several other defects, but several similar studies show no increases. Prospective studies are more reliable but have to be very large to yield useful information. In a study of over 11 000 pregnancies in Jerusalem there was a 26 per cent higher rate of major malformations in the 432 infants born after hormonal exposure (Harlap et al. 1975). In over 50 000 pregnancies studied in the US, there were 1042 infants exposed to hormones who had a 2.3-fold increase in cardiovascular malformations (Heinonen et al. 1977). Prospective studies of pregnancies following the use of oral contraceptives show a slightly reduced chance of a normal livebirth, but no definite evidence of an increase in congenital abnormalities; however, Alberman et al. (1980) noted a 60 per cent increase in cardiac defects, although this was not statistically significant and not controlled for other factors. Deformed infants have been born after large doses of oestrogens or oral contraceptives have been used in an attempt at abortion.

Anaesthetic agents

Several studies from 1967 reported increased rates of spontaneous abortion in women working in operating rooms, and as a result the American Society of Anaesthesiologists (1974) studied reproductive outcomes in 49 585 operating room personnel. This showed increased rates of spontaneous abortion and of total anomalies, and suggested in addition an increased risk to the offspring of male anaesthetists. The retrospective nature of the surveys and the non-specificity of the results, together with the inability to indicate one precise component of the operating room environment as the causal agent make interpretation difficult.

Other drugs

Maternal exposure to warfarin, for anticoagulation, in the first trimester is linked to a syndrome of nasal hypoplasia and stippled epiphyses (chrondrodysplasia punctata). Although only a few cases have been reported, the specificity of the link suggests a causal relationship; the same syndrome can be caused by a rare dominant mutant gene. Exposure later in pregnancy may be associated with mental retardation and nervous system abnormalities. Heparin is thus the anticoagulant of choice in pregnancy: it does not cross the placenta.

Lithium, used in psychiatric treatment, has been implicated in several cases of Ebstein's anomaly of the tricuspid valve. Heroin has been associated with low birthweight and microcephaly. A few studies have looked at mothers exposed to methadone, amphetamines, LSD, marijuana, tricylic antidepressants, and minor tranquillizers. In total there is little evidence of any specific risks, but the effects of these and other drugs cannot be taken as fully explored. Aminopterin and methotrexate are unlikely to be used in pregnancy as their associations with skull and bone deformities and cleft palate are well recognized. Iodides can cause goitre, and tetracyclines cause tooth discoloration.

Environmental chemical exposures

Exposure to substantial doses of methyl mercury causes cerebral palsy and mental retardation, and has occurred following industrial pollution of water in Japan – Minamata disease – and after contamination of grain in Iraq. Methyl mercury crosses the placenta easily, and severely affected babies have been born to asymptomatic mothers.

Other environmental chemical exposures with at least suggestive evidence of risk include polychlorinated biphenyls (PCBs), dioxins, and lead (Sullivan and Barlow 1979). Exposure to PCBs, again in Japan, has been reported to lead to low birthweight. High bone and placental lead levels have been found in stillbirths and neonatal deaths.

Very little work has been done on linking reproductive outcome to the occupation and therefore to possible chemical exposures of the mother, or of the father, and undoubtably this deserves high priority in the future.

Nutritional deficiencies

The effects of malnutrition in contributing to low birthweight and to reproductive losses are discussed under these sections. While frank malnutrition clearly has severe effects, there is no human evidence that marginal deficiencies of nutrition are detrimental, or that deficiencies or excesses of a specific dietary component have led to specific abnormalities. The effects of iodine deficiency in producing cretinism is the only example of a specific nutritional cause of a major specific developmental defect. In spite of the lack of firm evidence many lay and professional people feel strongly that suboptimal nutrition may be a major cause of low birth-weight and physical and mental handicap. The arguments are usually based on extrapolation from the known human effects of severe malnutrition on birthweight, and from the results from animal work, and the mechanism suggested is often that minor degrees of suboptimal nutrition may make the fetus less able to withstand noxious effects of other genetic or environmental factors. To test these hypotheses requires much more extensive and rigorous human studies than have been done, plus the use of suitable animal models involving many species and degrees of nutritional impairment and other exposures which are closer to those experienced by mothers than have usually been the case. The recent results pertaining to neural-tube defects and vitamin supplementation are a further indication that such research should have a high priority.

PREVENTION OF CONGENITAL ABNORMALITIES

Four avenues of intervention are possible. Primary prevention, that is prevention of the occurrence of the congenital defect, requires action to be taken before the conception or in very early pregnancy. Prenatal diagnosis and selective abortion, or in rare situations prenatal treatment, may be possible. Specific screening programmes may be appropriate for neonates or at various times in childhood. Finally, the availability of competent medical care allied to an appreciation of normal and abnormal development on the part of parents and health professionals is still the major mode of intervention.

Primary prevention, with examples of successes

Primary prevention may be achieved by identifying and removing or overcoming causal factors, by identification and counselling of parents whose offspring are at high risk, and by social pressures against consanguineous unions. Genetic counselling has as its primary aim the explanation to parents of both the risks and the implications of congenital defects in future offspring, giving them options including voluntary avoidance of pregnancy, sterilization, adoption, artificial insemination from an anonymous donor, and pre- or perinatal diagnosis. While of immense value to affected parents its potential in reducing congenital defects on a community basis is slight, apart from the impact of the knowledge of higher risks to older mothers. For example, prenatal diagnosis and abortion of all neural-tube defects occurring to parents identified on the basis of a previously affected child will reduce the number of affected infants by less than 5 per cent, and if all unions between carriers of a common recessive condition such as fibrocystic disease were avoided it would take about 500

years (18 generations) to half the occurrence rate of the condition.

Several examples of successful primary prevention can be given. Endemic goitre and cretinism was a widespread and common disease in the nineteenth century and contributed greatly to mental deficiency. Its disappearance in developed countries could be credited to the understanding of the mechanisms involved and the development of a specific preventive measure, namely iodine supplementation, usually through salt. However, as is the situation when we look at dramatic declines in infectious diseases such as tuberculosis, the picture is not quite that simple, and the prevalence at birth of this condition was declining long before specific interventions were introduced in the 1930s. The decline was probably due to the increase in communications and therefore in the quantity and variety of foodstuffs, and the use of saltpetre fertilizers and feeding supplements such as cod liver oil.

The empirical clinical observations showing the link between rubella and various congenital defects led eventually to the development of rubella vaccination. The use of this vaccine either for adolescent girls, or for all young children, is discussed elsewhere, and congenital abnormalities caused by rubella have been greatly reduced, although they have not been eliminated because of practical difficulties in ensuring total coverage by vaccination.

A further dramatic success is the prevention of haemolytic disease of the newborn due to Rhesus incompatibility, by the use of anti-Rhesus antibody to ensure that Rhesus-positive fetal blood cells transferring to the maternal circulation can be rapidly destroyed without precipitating a major immunological reaction. This dramatically successful preventive measure is unusual in medicine as the action stems from precise understanding of the mechanism behind the disease rather than being suggested only by empirical observations. Deaths from Rhesus haemolytic disease had been declining for many years before the introduction of the use of anti-D in 1968, due to improved treatment of the condition and because women were having smaller families; this decline was greatly accelerated by the introduction of the prophylaxis, although deaths still occur.

Many of the other 'success' stories represent the withdrawal of noxious influences introduced as medical advances. Many pregnant women were exposed to large doses of X-rays for various therapeutic reasons in the early part of the century, resulting in intra-uterine and postnatal growth retardation, microphthalmia, and microcephaly, and this led to strict control over the use of X-rays on pregnant patients. Much more recently, in the 1960s the relationship between low-dose X-rays in the antenatal period and the subsequent development of leukaemia was demonstrated, and has led to further stringency, although undoubtedly some malignant disease is still being produced by medical use of X-rays in pregnancy.

The most tragically dramatic of these stories is that of thalidomide, a drug specifically used in pregnancy to control morning sickness, which we now know is a very potent teratogen producing severe abnormalities particularly phocomelia from even low-dose exposure early in pregnancy. The recognition of this defect had to come from the demonstration that the numbers of babies with these specific defects was increasing, and was related to sales of thalidomide seven or so months earlier. Undoubtedly the epidemic could have been recognized earlier if there had been a system of monitoring populations continuously for severe defects. As a response to the thalidomide epidemic, many countries have set up such monitoring systems, which however have not as yet recognized a similar problem. The thalidomide epidemic also gave rise to stringent animal testing regulations on drugs, although it is doubtful whether the systems being currently used in many countries would have indicated the potential damage; although thalidomide is highly teratogenic to chimpanzees and to humans, it is only very mildly so to mice, rats and rabbits which are much more commonly used in animal testing.

We do not of course know of all the relationships which we may have missed. Many chemicals, drugs, physical agents, and excesses or deficiencies of nutrients have been shown to cause abnormalities in animal models, but as the relevance of the data to man is unclear preventive actions have not been taken. On the observational side, it is very difficult to detect a moderate increase in a common abnormality which might be due to a relatively common exposure, and as has been discussed alcohol, drugs and perhaps suboptimal nutrition may be amongst the contributors to congenital abnormalities in our society.

Prenatal diagnosis of high-risk pregnancies

A large and quickly increasing number of congenital defects can be diagnosed prenatally after amniocentesis. This is usually performed at 15–16 weeks' gestation, after an ultrasound examination to locate the placenta, assess gestational age, and to exclude gross defects and multiple pregnancy. Five to ten millilitres of amniotic fluid are aspirated, containing cells from the fetal skin and amnion. The sex of the fetus can be determined by chromatin studies, and the alpha-fetoprotein concentration in the amniotic fluid can be measured. The cells are cultured for 10–14 days and then used for chromosome studies and biochemical tests for conditions where an enzyme defect exists in epithelial cells. The risks of amniocentesis have been assessed in a British study of 2428 subjects and matched controls (Medical Research Council 1978). There is a risk of Rhesus sensitization in Rh-negative mothers with Rh-positive fetuses, so such mothers should receive anti-D serum. The risk of spontaneous abortion was 1 per cent, and another 0.5 per cent excess mortality was found due to neonatal respiratory distress. A further 1.0–1.5 per cent of neonates have non-fatal respiratory distress or orthopaedic deformities, including talipes equinovarus and hip dislocation attributable to the amniocentesis. The study also found an excess of antepartum haemorrhage, but no mechanism for this is apparent and the result may be coincidental. Techniques are now available to detect by amniocentesis all chromosomal abnormalities, some 200 X-linked conditions, and 100 biochemical abnormalities, although these represent only 5 per cent of the 3000 or so known monogenic disorders (Milunsky 1981). In addition, fetoscopy and fetal blood sampling allow detection of sickle-cell anaemia and thalassaemia, as well as rare disorders. The indications for amniocentesis are a previous child with a chromosomal abnormality, evidence that the parents are carriers of chromosomal or biochemical abnormalities, or that

the mother carries an X-linked condition, and the general one of advanced maternal age, defined variously with limits of between 30 and 40 years depending on attitudes, economics, and facilities. Tay–Sachs disease is sufficiently common in Ashkenazi Jews that population screening for heterozygotes has been offered, followed by counselling and prenatal diagnosis of the homozygotic state. Sickle-cell anaemia and thalassaemia can also be diagnosed in heterozygotes, but prenatal screening tests are not simple enough for widespread use.

Population screening for neural-tube defects

In 1972, Brock and Sutcliffe showed that the amniotic fluid of pregnancies with anencephalus and spina bifida showed very high levels of alpha-fetoprotein (AFP). This alpha-globulin is synthesized in the yolk sac and fetal liver, and the concentrations in the fetal serum, which are closely mimicked by those in the amniotic fluid, peak at around 3 mg/ml at 14 weeks of gestation, then progressively fall to between 10 and 80 μg/ml at birth. From the amniotic fluid, AFP crosses the placenta into the maternal blood stream, and maternal serum levels become slightly raised by 14 weeks of gestation, then rising progressively to reach a maximum at about 30 weeks of gestation, where the levels are about 50 times that of the non-pregnant state, in the order of 30 ng/ml. Examination of AFP levels in amniotic fluid therefore became quickly established as a method of diagnosing neural-tube defects in women who had a clear indication that the test should be done, that is a previously affected child, or an otherwise strong family history. Such situations include only 5 per cent of neural-tube defects in the UK. The concept of population screening depends on the ability to detect the much lower levels in maternal serum.

The distinction between open and closed lesions becomes critical in assessing screening. Anencephalus involves exposure of much neural tissue and is therefore usually associated with very high levels of serum and amniotic serum AFP. Spina bifida lesions with complete skin closure frequently show no increase over normal concentrations. Some 80 per cent of spina bifida lesions have some exposure of neural tissue, and represent the infants who are likely to survive and be handicapped, and are therefore the appropriate targets for pre-natal screening and induced abortion. As anencephalus is always fatal, the effectiveness of screening should be measured primarily by its effect on the prevalence at birth of spina bifida, particularly open spina bifida, although the fact that that test cannot efficiently detect closed spina bifida lesions, some of which are associated with considerable morbidity, must be regarded as a limitation.

Most of the studies of population screening for neural-tube defects have been carried out in the UK, and have been reviewed by Wald and Cuckle (1980). Much of the evidence comes from the UK Collaborative Alpha-Fetoprotein Study which reported maternal serum data in 301 affected pregnancies and over 18 000 unaffected pregnancies, from 19 centres (UK Collaborative Study 1977). Individuals included in this study were those who did have a serum AFP measurement at an appropriate time in pregnancy, and whose outcome was known. The conclusions were that a gestational age of 16–18 weeks was the best time to perform the first estimation of maternal serum AFP, and at this time 75 per cent of pregnancies with open spina bifida have levels above the 97th percentile, as will about 85 per cent of pregnancies with anencephalus. It is much easier for an individual laboratory to establish a stable median value than a percentile distribution on a normal range, so the UK study considers cut-off levels in terms of ratios of the test value to the median for that particular laboratory and at that gestational time. A cut-off point of 2.5 times the median has frequently been suggested as an appropriate one, and at this level 88 per cent of anencephalus pregnancies, 79 per cent of open spina bifida pregnancies, and 3.3 per cent of unaffected pregnancies will have AFP levels above this point (Table 3.9). The risk for an individual mother of having a fetus with open spina bifida at a given AFP concentration has been estimated and is shown in Table 3.10.

Table 3.9. *Percentage of singleton pregnancies with maternal serum AFP levels at 16–18 weeks of gestation equal to or greater than specified multiples of the normal median (MoM)*

Pregnancy	Percentage ≥ cut-off level (MoM)				
	2.0	2.5	3.0	3.5	4.0
Anencephalus	90	88	84	82	76
Spina bifida	91	79	70	64	45
Unaffected	7.2	3.3	1.4	0.6	0.3

Source: UK Collaborative Study (1977).

Table 3.10. *Proportion of singleton pregnancies having open spina bifida for given levels of maternal serum AFP**

Serum AFP level	Multiples of normal median				
	2.0	2.5	3.0	3.5	4.0
Equal to specified MoM	0.2	0.7	1.6	3.6	7.2
Equal to or greater than specified MoM	2.2	4.4	8.9	16.5	26.6

*Assuming prevalence of open spina bifida of 2 per 1000 births.
Source: Wald and Cuckle (1980) and based on data from UK Collaborative Study.

To interpret a maternal serum AFP level, the estimation of gestational age is critical, and in three British population-based programmes, 20–40 per cent of women with serum AFP levels regarded initially as being raised were subsequently regarded as normal after the revision of gestational age. This is best done by ultrasound examination, which is also necessary to exclude multiple pregnancy, which results in increased AFP concentrations. Most anencephalic fetuses can be detected by ultrasound. Thus women who have an elevated maternal serum AFP level, not explained by multiple pregnancy, anencephalus detected by ultrasound, or another clear explanation, should proceed to have an amniocentesis. An elevated amniotic fluid AFP level at amniocentesis is virtually diagnostic, with very few false-positives, because the difference between NTD and unaffected pregnancies in amniotic fluid AFP levels is greater than with maternal serum AFP. The separation between abnormal and normal pregnancies decreases with gestational age, however, so higher cut-off points are recommended at longer gestations – 2.5 times median at 13–15 weeks to 4.0 times median at 22 to 24 weeks. With such cut-off points, 98 per cent of anencephalus and of open spina bifida lesions will be detected, with only 0.8 per cent of unaffected pregnancies giving false-positive tests (UK Collaborative Study 1979).

High AFP levels may be associated with other severe congenital anomalies including exophthalmos, congenital nephrosis, and Turner's syndrome. The level of AFP in amniotic fluid and in the preceding serum estimate are largely independent, so that if the amniotic fluid AFP level is equivocal, the presence of a previously high serum level may be a useful indicator for intervention.

The question of whether it is wise to repeat a maternal serum AFP estimation has received much attention. A repeat test using the same cut-off level is simply equivalent to making the cut-off point on a test more stringent, and in general the value of doing a repeat test is not great, except in cases where the first sample cannot be used, for example because of blood-staining. However, repeating the amniotic fluid estimation in borderline cases may be quite beneficial.

Elevated maternal serum AFP levels have also been seen in pregnancies ending in spontaneous abortion, in association with fetal–maternal haemorrhage, and in association with low birth weight and toxaemia in pregnancy. Pregnancies with high maternal serum AFP levels but without a neural-tube defect have about a one in seven chance of resulting in a low birthweight infant. Thus mothers with high AFP levels in the absence of neural-tube defects or another clear explanation should be regarded as at high risk.

Several other tests for neural-tube defects have been developed, and of these, measurement of acetylcholinesterase in amniotic fluid may be a useful supplement to AFP estimation (Smith *et al.* 1979). Ultrasound techniques are improving rapidly, and may play an increasing role in screening, both independently and in conjunction with other tests.

The risks of amniocentesis have been discussed above, and appear relatively small, given that the probability of a major defect being present if maternal serum estimations with accurate gestational data are elevated is very high – considerably greater for example than the risk of Down's syndrome in mothers in their late 30s.

So there is strong evidence that reasonably accurate antenatal diagnosis of open neural-tube defects can be achieved. The assessment of the broader question of the risks and benefits, and the basic decision about desirability, involves several other factors. First, introduction of the system will not ensure complete coverage. The British experience is that 70–80 per cent of patients will accept screening. The main loss is those 15–20 per cent who have their first antenatal visit too late for screening. Women in the lower socio-economic groups tend to come late for antenatal care and these women have a higher risk of being affected. A few mothers refuse the test, or are not offered it because of administrative error, or have their first antenatal visit too early and do not return at the right time for the test. However, even these estimates are based on the experience of urban communities served by major teaching centres, and it seems likely that the uptake would be considerably lower for a service introduced on a wide scale, unless considerable efforts were made to prevent these difficulties.

Secondly, introducing the service on a wide scale seems likely to result in more errors than have been seen in the studies based on major centres. There are many administrative pitfalls in terms of laboratory errors, failure to communicate the results promptly, and a particular source of concern is the accurate estimation of gestational age, which requires considerable care, skill, and experience in the use of ultrasound. The third issue is that the overall effectiveness of the programme, whether measured in human terms, that is comparing the number of severely defective fetuses which are correctly diagnosed and aborted with the number which are missed and the number of unaffected fetuses which are mistakenly aborted, or whether in financial cost-benefit terms, will depend critically on the prevalence at birth of the condition in the population. Britain has one of the highest rates of these defects in the world, and therefore the overall effectiveness of the programme will be lower elsewhere. Projections from the British experience based on a prevalence rate at birth of four per 1000, suggest that a programme will detect 153 open spina bifida lesions per 100 000 pregnancies, at a cost of four normal babies deliberately aborted, and between 10 and 31 infants accidentally lost as a result of the ill

effects of amniocentesis – the variability in this measure reflecting how difficult it is to estimate this effect. Forty-seven spina bifida infants would not be detected, and the programme would also detect 171 out of 200 anencephalic fetuses (Fig. 3.2). The ratio of fetuses with open spina bifida detected to those lost will therefore range from 11:1, down to 4:1. If the prevalence at birth is only half as high, representing rates typical of much of North America, in theory the proportion of open spina bifidas detected will not change, so that the number detected will be half, and the losses will be similar.

Financial cost-benefit studies have been done in the UK and suggest that the cost per open spina bifida infant detected by the programme is around £2200 (Wald et al. 1979). The financial consequences of severe open spina bifida are so enormous, because of much hospitalization, major surgery, special education, and family costs, that screening at the UK prevalence rates is likely to be cost-beneficial. That is also likely to apply even at considerably lower prevalence rates such as those in the west of North America, although it might become dubious at the very low rates of prevalence in Scandinavia or Asian countries.

A British governmental committee studied the question of whether routine screening should be introduced, with inconclusive findings (Working Group on the Screening for Neural-Tube Defects 1979; Harris 1980). They accepted that the system was likely to have fairly high efficiency, but felt that difficulties in assessing the risks of amniocentesis, the

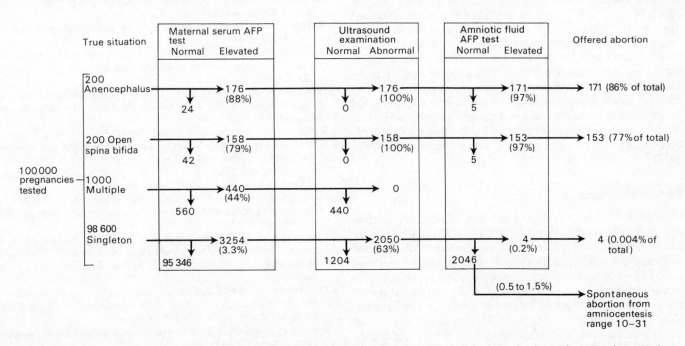

Fig. 3.2. Predicted results of applying AFP screening to 100 000 pregnancies, based on UK Collaborative Study results, assuming prevalence rates for anencephalus and for open spina bifida of (each) two per 1000 and cut-off points for serum AFP of 2.5 × normal median, amniotic fluid AFP of 3 × normal median. (Adapted from Wald and Cuckle (1980).) Notes: (1) Closed spina bifida not shown; (2) Generalization to a population requires consideration of the proportion of mothers who are not tested at an appropriate time.

variability of results from smaller laboratories, problems in making available counselling services, laboratory resources, and good ultrasound services, the considerable ethical issues, and variations in the prevalence at birth of defects between areas and over time made a clear conclusion difficult to reach. There is still (in 1984) no clear national policy in Britain concerning screening, and the extent to which it is practised or promoted varies greatly between different districts in the country. The ethical issues and the attendant legal issues are further difficulties. It has been shown that only a very small proportion of mothers feel that they would be totally against abortion under the circumstances of having virtually certain knowledge that their child was abnormal, but most authorities accept that the rights of this small minority must be protected. A particularly difficult question is whether screening should be done as a routine on all mothers, with only the minimum of information, or whether a full explanation of the programme and the action to be considered if the tests are positive, has to be given to each mother to allow her to opt positively into the programme, is a difficult one. The practical difficulties of this type of informed consent are very considerable, even though lip service is routinely paid by both the medical and legal professions to the concept that all diagnostic tests and other interventions are done after informed consent. It has been argued that the situation is really little different to performing routine tests for syphilis or rubella immune status in pregnancy, which are usually done without much explanation.

Population screening for neural-tube defects is more complex in countries with less structured medical care systems. The difficulties involved in the US have been addressed by an obstetric–paediatric task force (American Medical Association 1982). In the US, few large programmes have been developed both for this reason and because of legal and financial considerations. For example, there is no need to do karyotyping for chromosomal analysis on all amniotic fluid samples unless there is another indication, such as high maternal age, but in the US this expensive service may be given or at least offered in all cases for medico-legal reasons. A report of screening in 17 000 pregnancies in New York shows detection and abortion of 18 out of 22 neural-tube defects, but what proportion of eligible pregnancies these represent is unknown (Macri and Weiss 1982).

Postnatal screening

Careful physical examination of neonates by a doctor is routine or even legally required in many countries, and usually includes use of the Ortolani–Barlow test for hip instability, as discussed previously. A blood test for phenylketonuria is almost always done in developed countries, and often galactosaemia, maple syrup urine disease, haemocystinuria, and hypothyroidism are tested for; and serum bilirubin levels are measured. Biochemical tests done after milk feeding is introduced can assess galactose and amino-acid disorders. A very large range of biochemical disorders can be assessed by blood tests, and some populations especially in the US are extensively tested. Achieving prompt diagnosis of disorders becoming apparent later, including developmental and learning defects, is more

difficult. Special attention has often been paid to babies identified as being at 'high risk' on the basis of social and maternal factors, but the predictive value of such risk models in birth populations other than those from which they were developed is not very high.

REFERENCES

Adams, M.M., Erickson, J.D., Layde, P.M., and Oakley, G.P. (1981). Down's syndrome: recent trends in the United States. *JAMA* 246 (7), 758.

Alberman, E.D. (1977). Sociobiologic factors and birth weight in Great Britain. In *Epidemiology of prematurity*, (eds. D.M. Reed and F.J. Stanley) p. 145. Urban and Schwarzenberg, Baltimore.

Alberman, E., Pharoah, P., Chamberlain, G., Roman, E., and Evans, S. (1980). Outcome of pregnancies following the use of oral contraceptives. *Int. J. Epidemiol.* 9 (3), 207.

American Medical Association Council on Scientific Affairs (1982). Maternal serum alpha fetoprotein monitoring (1982). *JAMA* 247 (10), 1478.

American Society of Anesthesiologists (1974). Occupational disease among operating room personnel. A national study. *Anaesthesiology* 41, 321.

Annegers, J.F., Hauser, W.A., Elveback, L.R., Anderson, V.E., and Kurland, L.T. (1978). Congenital malformations and seizure disorders in the offspring of parents with epilepsy. *Int. J. Epidemiol.* 7 (3), 241.

Antonov, A. (1947). Children born during the seige of Leningrad in 1942. *J. Pediatr.* 30, 250.

Baird, D. (1974). Epidemiology of congenital malformations of the central nervous system in (a) Aberdeen and (b) Scotland. *J. Biosoc. Sci.* 6, 113.

Berkowitz, G.S. (1981). An epidemiologic study of preterm delivery. *Am. J. Epidemiol.* 113, 81.

British Medical Journal (1980). Quality not quantity in babies. *Br. Med. J.* i, 347.

Brock, D.J.H. and Sutcliffe, R.G. (1972). Alpha-fetoprotein in the antenatal diagnosis of anencephaly and spina bifida. *Lancet* ii, 197.

Butler, N.R. and Alberman, E.D. (1969). *Perinatal problems. The second report of the 1958 British Perinatal Mortality Survey.* Livingstone, Edinburgh.

Butler, N.R., Goldstein, H., and Ross, E.M. (1972). Cigarette smoking in pregnancy: its influence on birth weight and perinatal mortality. *Br. Med. J.* ii, 127.

Carter, C.O. and Evans, K. (1973). Spina bifida and anencephalus in Greater London. *J. Med. Genet.* 10, 209.

Chalmers, I. and Mutch, L. (1981). Are current trends in perinatal practice associated with an increase or a decrease in handicapping conditions? *Lancet* i, 1415.

Chase, H.C. (1977). Time trends in low birth weight in the United States 1950–74. In *The epidemiology of prematurity* (eds. D.M. Reed and F.J. Stanley) p. 17. Urban and Schwarzenberg, Baltimore.

Department of Health and Social Security (1982). *On the state of the public health for the year 1980. Annual report of the Chief Medical Officer.* p. 78. HMSO, London.

Dignan, P.St.J. (1981). Teratogenic risk and counselling in diabetes. *Clin. Obstet. Gynecol.* 24 (1), 149.

Drillien, C.M. (1958). Growth and development in a group of children of very low birth weight. *Arch. Dis. Child.* 33, 10.

Elwood, J.M. and Elwood, J.H. (1980). *Epidemiology of anencephalus and spina bifida.* Oxford University Press.

Elwood, J.M., Raman, S., and Mousseau, G. (1978). Reproductive history in mothers of anencephalics. *J. Chronic Dis.* **31**, 473.

Emanuel, I., and Sever, L.E. (1973). Questions concerning the possible association of potatoes and neural-tube defects, and an alternative hypothesis relating to maternal growth and development. *Teratology* **8**, 825.

Evans, D.R., Newcombe, R.G., and Campbell, H. (1979). Maternal smoking habits and congenital malformations: a population study. *Br. Med. J.* **ii**, 171.

Gardiner, A., Clarke, C., Cowen, J., Finn, R., and McKendrick, O.M. (1978). Spontaneous abortion and fetal abnormality in subsequent pregnancy. *Br. Med. J.* **ii**, 1016.

Harlap, S., Prywes, R., and Davies, A.M. (1975). Birth defects and oestrogens and progesterones in pregnancy. *Lancet* **i**, 682.

Harris, R. (1980). Maternal serum alpha fetoprotein in pregnancy and the prevention of birth defects. *Br. Med. J.* **ii**, 1199.

Heinonen, O.P., Slone, D., Monson, R.R., Hook, E.B., and Shapiro, S. (1977). Cardiovascular birth defects and antenatal exposure to female sex hormones. *New Engl. J. Med.* **296** (2), 67.

Heuther, C.A., Gummere, G.R., Hook, E.B., *et al.* (1981). Down's syndrome percentage reporting on birth certificates and single year maternal age risk rates for Ohio 70–79 comparison with upstate New York data. *Am. J. Public Health* **71** (12), 1367.

Illingworth, R.S. (1974). Some ethical problems in paediatrics. In *Modern trends in paediatrics,* Vol. 4 (ed. J. Apley) p. 329. Butterworths, London.

Janerich, D.T. (1974). Endocrine dysfunction and anencephaly and spina bifida: an epidemiologic hypothesis. *Am. J. Epidemiol.* **99**, 1.

Janerich, D.T. and Piper, J. (1978). Shifting genetic patterns in anencephaly and spina bifida. *J. Med. Genet.* **15**, 101.

Lamson, S.H. and Hook, E.B. (1980). A simple function for maternal age specific rates of Down's syndrome in the 20- to 49-year age range and its biological implications. *Am. J. Hum. Genet.* **32**, 743.

The Lancet (1980). The fate of the baby under 1501g at birth. *Lancet* **i**, 461.

Layde, P.M., Erickson, J.D., Dooley, K., and Edmonds, L.D. (1980). Is there an epidemic of ventricular septal defects in the USA? *Lancet* **i**, 407.

Leck, I. (1969). Ethnic differences in the incidence of malformations following migration. *Br. J. Prev. Soc. Med.* **23**, 166.

Leck, I. (1977). Correlations of malformation frequency with environmental and genetic attributes in man. In *Handbook of teratology,* Vol. 3 (ed. J.G. Wilson and F.C. Fraser) p. 243. Plenum, New York.

Lorber, J. (1971). Results of treatment of myelomeningocele. An analysis of 524 unselected cases with special reference to possible selection for treatment. *Dev. Med. Child. Neurol.* **13**, 279.

Lorber, J. (1972). Spina bifida cystica. Results of treatment of 270 consecutive cases with criteria for selection for the future. *Arch. Dis. Child.* **47**, 854.

Lubchenco, L.O., Hansman, C., Dressler, M. and Boyd, E. (1963a). Interuterine growth as estimated from live-born birth weight data at 24–42 weeks of gestation. *Pediatrics* **32**, 793.

Lubchenco, L.O., Horner, F.A., Reed, L.H. *et al.* (1963b). Sequelae of premature birth: evaluation of infants of low birth weight at ten years of age. *Am. J. Dis. Child.* **106**, 101.

Luthy, D.A., Emanuel, I., Hoehn, H., Hall, J.G., and Powers, E.K. (1980). Prenatal genetic diagnosis and elective abortion in women over 35: utilization and relative impact on the birth prevalence of Down's syndrome in Washington State. *Am. J. Med. Gen.* **7**, 375.

McBride, M.L. (1979). Sib risks of anencephaly and spina bifida in British Columbia. *Am. J. Med. Genet.* **3**, 377.

MacMahon, B. and Yen, S. (1971). Unrecognised epidemic of anencephaly and spina bifida. *Lancet* **i**, 31.

Macri, J.N. and Weiss, R.R. (1982). Prenatal serum alpha-fetoprotein screening for neural tube defects. *Obstet. Gynecol.* **59** (5), 633.

Medical Research Council (1978). An assessment of the hazards of amniocentesis. Report of the MRC Working Party on Amniocentesis. *Br. J. Obstet. Gynaecol.* **85**, Suppl. 2.

Miller, J.F., Williamson, E., Glue, J.; Gordon, Y.B., Grudzinskas, J.G., and Sykes, A. (1980). Fetal loss after implantation. A prospective study. *Lancet* **ii**, 554.

Milunsky, A. (1981). Prenatal diagnosis of genetic disorders. (Editorial.) *Am. J. Med.* **70** (i), 7.

Naggan, L. and MacMahon, B. (1967). Ethnic differences in the prevalence of anencephaly and spina bifida in Boston, Massachusetts. *New Engl. J. Med.* **227**, 1119.

National Central Bureau of Statistics Stockholm (1981). *1981:2 Medical Birth Registration 1977–78.*

Neligan, G.A., Scott, D.M., Kolvin, I., and Garside, R. (1976). *Born too soon or born too small?* Spastics International Medical Publications, London and William Heinemann, Philadelphia.

OPCS (1982). Infant mortality 1979.

OPCS (1982). *OPCS Monitors, Series DH3. 82/2.* HMSO, London.

Ouellette, E.M., Rosett, H.L., Rosman, N.P., and Weiner, L. (1977). Adverse effects on offspring of maternal alcohol abuse during pregnancy. *New Engl. J. Med.* **297**, 528.

Parkin, D.M. (1981). How successful is screening for congenital disease of the hip? *Am. J. Public Health* **71** (2), 1378.

Peñaloza, D., Arias-Stella, J., Sime, F., Recavarren, S., and Marticorena, E. (1964). The heart and pulmonary circulation in children at high altitudes. *Pediatrics* **34**, 568.

Pharoah, P.O.D. and Alberman, E.D. (1981). Mortality of low birth weight infants in England and Wales 1953 to 1979. *Arch. Dis. Child.* **56**, 86.

Pizzarello, D.J. (1980). Teratogenic effects of ionizing radiations and ultrasound. In *Perinatal medicine today.* p. 67. Alan R. Liss, New York.

Pratt, O.E. (1982). Alcohol and the developing fetus. *Br. Med. Bull.* **38** (i), 48.

Renwick, J.H. (1972). Hypothesis – anencephaly and spina bifida are usually preventable by avoidance of a specific but unidentified substance present in certain potato tubers. *Br. J. Prev. Soc. Med.* **26**, 67.

Richards, I.D.G. (1969). Congenital malformations and environmental influences in pregnancy. *Br. J. Prev. Soc. Med.* **25**, 59.

Sever, J.L. (1975). Infectious agents as teratogens. In *Methods for detection of environmental agents that produce congenital defects* (eds. T.H. Shepard, J.R. Miller, and M. Marios) p. 221. North-Holland, Amsterdam.

Smith, A.D., Wald, N.J., Cuckle, H.S., Stirrat, G.M., Bobrow, M., and Lagercrantz, H. (1979). Amniotic fluid acetylcholinesterase as a possible diagnostic test for neural tube defects in early pregnancy. *Lancet* **i**, 685.

Smith, C.A. (1947). Effects of maternal under-nutrition upon the newborn infant in Holland 1944–45. *J. Pediatr.* **30**, 229.

Smithells, R.W. (1976). Environmental teratogens of man. *Br. Med. Bull.* **12** (1), 27.

Smithells, R.W., Sheppard, S., Schorah, C.J., *et al.* (1980). Possible prevention of neural tube defects by periconceptional vitamin supplementation. *Lancet* **i**, 339.

Smithells, R.W., Sheppard, S., Schorah, C.J., *et al.* (1981). Apparent prevention of neural tube defects by periconceptional vitamin supplementation. *Arch. Dis. Child.* **56**, 911.

Stanley, F.J. and Atkinson, S. (1981). Impact of neonatal intensive care on cerebral palsy in infants of low birth weight. *Lancet* **ii**, 1162.

Stein, Z. (1975). *Famine and human development*. Oxford University Press.

Stewart, A., Reynolds, E.O.R., and Lipscomb, A.P. (1981). Outcome for infants of very low birth weight: survey of world literature. *Lancet* **i,** 1038.

Sullivan, F.M. and Barlow, S.M. (1979). Congenital malformations and other reproductive hazards from environmental chemicals. *Proc. R. Soc. B* **205,** 91.

UK Collaborative Study (1977). Alpha-fetoprotein in relation to neural tube defects: maternal serum alpha-fetoprotein measurement in antenatal screening for anencephaly and spina bifida in early pregnancy. *Lancet* **i,** 1323.

UK Collaborative Study (1979). Alpha-fetoprotein in relation to neural tube defects, second report: amniotic fluid alpha-fetoprotein measurement in antenatal diagnosis of anencephaly and open spina bifida in early pregnancy. *Lancet* **ii,** 651.

Wald, N.J. and Cuckle, H.S. (1980). Alpha fetoprotein in the antenatal diagnosis of open neural tube defects. *Br. J. Hosp. Med.* **23,** 473.

Wald, N.J., Cuckle, H.S., Boreham, J., *et al.* (1979). Antenatal screening in Oxford for fetal neural tube defects. *Br. J. Obstet. Gynaecol.* **86,** 91.

Wilson, J.G. and Brent, R.L. (1981). Are female sex hormones teratogenic? *Am. J. Obstet. Gynecol.* **141,** 567.

Working Group on the Screening for Neural Tube Defects (1979). *Report.* Department of Health and Social Security, London.

World Health Organization (1980). The incidence of low birth weight a critical review of available information. *World Health Stat. Q.* **33** (3), 197.

4 Trauma*

Leon S. Robertson

INTRODUCTION

Trauma has received increased attention in recent years as a public health problem for which solutions are possible. Although trauma usually ranks third as a cause of total deaths in the industrialized countries, prior to the usual retirement age of 65 years it is the most common cause of death (Haddon and Baker 1981). In the US, the median age at death is 27 years for motor vehicle injuries, 53 years for other unintentional injuries, 32 years for homicide and 50 years for suicide. In contrast, the median age at death for cardiovascular diseases is 76 years and for cancers, 68 years.

This chapter reviews important causes of trauma and public health strategies to reduce incidence and severity. About half of traumatic death and permanent disability (particularly spinal cord damage) results from motor vehicle injuries (Kraus *et al.* 1975). For this reason and because the literature is more complete on such injuries than for other types of trauma, a large proportion of the material in this chapter is drawn from that literature. Estimates of the costs to society of motor vehicle injuries alone in 1975 in the US were $14.4 billion, compared to $13.7 billion for coronary heart disease and $23.1 billion for cancers (Hartunian *et al.* 1981).

CAUSATION

The traditional neglect of injuries as a public health problem is attributable in part to the notion that they are a consequence of luck or 'acts of God'. The fact that infectious diseases were also once thought of in the same way indicates how shortsighted such a view can be. Like infectious diseases, trauma is the result of a noxious agent, usually conveyed to a host, at intolerable concentrations, by a vehicle or vector (Haddon 1980).

Trauma is caused by energy in its various forms – mechanical, thermal, electrical, ionizing – at concentrations beyond the resilience of the human body (Gibson 1961). Expressions of trauma include fractures, lacerations, burns, etc. Lack of oxidation, an energy transfer necessary for life, is the agent for drowning, chokings, and other forms of asphyxiation, including those initiated by mechanical energy and combustion. The properties of the agents are, for the most part, well understood. The knowledge essential to the control of mechanical energy, for example, was revealed by Sir Isaac Newton in the *Principia* nearly 300 years ago.

The vehicles and vectors of trauma are evident in the everyday environment. Motor vehicles and their drivers are vehicles and vectors, respectively, of the most common cause of severe trauma. The driver may also be the host, but quite often the host is a passenger, pedestrian, or other road users. Guns and elevated heights are also common vehicles of injury by mechanical energy.

Actions aimed at preventing injury have been patchy and inconsistent from one agent to another. The hazard of electrical energy was recognized from the outset and the means of insulating people from it were included in the development of its use. The precautions associated with atomic energy are even more elaborate. In contrast, the slaughter and maiming associated with motor vehicles were considered by public officials and most of the scientific community as mainly a behavioural problem until recent years.

Human limits

Emphasis on changing behaviour usually ignores the limits of individuals to constantly monitor and respond to the multiple sources of hazardous energy in the environment; for example, human reaction time and common motor vehicle speeds. In laboratory experiments, well-rested and sober drivers require up to two seconds to respond to stimuli such as sounds and red lights, and about 50 per cent require 0.9 or more seconds to react (Johansson and Rumar 1971). At a moderate speed of 30 miles per hour (48 kilometres per hour), a vehicle is driven at 44 feet (13.4 metres) per second. In the 0.9 or more seconds that is required for half the drivers to react to an emergency, the brakes would not be applied or the steering altered for about 40 feet (12.2 metres). A child darting into the street within that distance, for example, would inevitably be struck.

Driving at slower speeds reduces the number of inevitable casualties but speed perception is itself problematic. Under a variety of experimental conditions, persons travelling in cars, when asked to estimate their speed without seeing a speedometer, underestimated the speed by an average of 25 per cent at speeds less than 30 miles per hour. More than a third of the experiment's participants were in error by 50 per cent or more, as often as not on the low side (Evans 1970). No one can consistently monitor a speedometer, as they are currently

*Preparation of this chapter was supported by a grant from the Henry J. Kaiser Family Foundation to Yale University. Neither the Foundation nor the University is responsible for the author's viewpoint and conclusions.

designed, and the tendency to misjudge speed reduces the ability to take appropriate action in emergencies.

The phenomenon of adaptation resulting in misjudgement of speed has also been demonstrated experimentally. In cars in which the experimenter but not the driver could see the speedometer, drivers were instructed to retain a constant 70 miles per hour (113 kilometres per hour) for varying periods of time and then slow to 40 miles per hour (65 kilometres per hour). The actual speeds that the drivers thought to be 40 miles per hour were 44.5 after 5 seconds at 70, 50.5 after 20 miles driven at 70, and 53.4 after an additional 20 miles at 70 miles per hour. Such overestimates would result in longer than expected stopping distance should the driver have to stop (Schmidt and Tiffin 1969). Drivers have also been found to underestimate the distance required to pass a forward vehicle on a simulated two-lane road (Gordon and Mast 1970). The average underestimation was 78 per cent at 50 miles per hour (81 kilometres per hour).

The size of other vehicles in the environment is also apparently related to judgement of their speeds or their being seen at all. The patterns of collisions of motorcycles and cars are indicative of the problem. A survey in the US revealed that about 4 per cent of car–motorcycle collisions occur when a motorcyclist turns left into the path of an approaching car but 39 per cent of such collisions involve a car turning left in the path of a motorcyclist approaching from the opposite direction (Griffin 1974). Motorcycle organizations, paranoid about the disproportionate involvement of motorcycles in severe crashes, claim that this is the 'fault' of car drivers. Of course, some drivers are not as alert as they could be, but there is likely a more fundamental limit to the ability of drivers to perceive and estimate the speeds of smaller vehicles. Their only 'fault' may be that they are human. Since the fatality rate of motorcyclists in crashes where no other vehicles are involved is higher than that of the total rates of most cars and trucks, the excessive involvement of motorcyclists cannot be attributed entirely to the actions of car and truck drivers. Investigation is needed to determine the extent to which normal limits in perceptual, motor and judgemental abilities result in other trauma such as that in the work environment, drownings, fires, etc. The disproportionately high injury rates due to asphyxiations, falls, and burns in the very young and the elderly are undoubtedly related to such limitations. Current evidence is sufficient to conclude that exclusive emphasis on efforts at altering behaviour is substantially misguided.

Factors and phases

The combination of factors that contribute to trauma and determine its outcome has been conceived by Haddon (1972). The Haddon Matrix (Fig. 4.1) recognizes that human, vehicle, and environmental factors play roles before, during, and after, a trauma event and influence the ultimate result. The factors in the matrix can be elaborated into separate categories such as human abilities and limitations, injury-enhancing versus protective characteristics of vehicles, and physical, socio-cultural, and economic aspects of the environment. The combinations in each cell of the matrix suggests the areas in

	Human	Vehicle	Environment
Pre-event	1	5	9
During event	2	6	10
Post-event	3	7	11
Results	4	8	12

Fig. 4.1. The Haddon factor-phase matrix.

which research is needed, the alternatives for amelioration, and bases for resource allocation.

To illustrate its use, some of the applications to motor vehicle injuries are summarized. In the human–pre-event cell (numbered 1 in Fig. 4.1), the impairment of drivers' abilities by alcohol use would be prominent, along with the normal human limitations mentioned previously. About half of fatally injured drivers have blood alcohol concentrations of 0.10 per cent by weight or more compared to less than 5 per cent of drivers stopped and examined at the same time of day, day of week, and moving in the same direction as those who died (McCarroll and Haddon 1962).

Human factors during the event (cell 2) would include the human tolerance to crash forces. DeHaven's (1942) classic study of people who survived falls of up to 150 feet found that no injury occurred in cases where the object struck absorbed substantial energy often in only a few inches of space. Stapp (1957) demonstrated that the human body could tolerate rapid deceleration up to 35 times gravity with no injury and 45 times gravity with little injury if the load were distributed over sufficient body surface – in this case three-inch-wide nylon webbed harnesses over the shoulders and legs of volunteers in decelerated rocket sleds.

Type and extent of human damage in the post-event phase (cell 3), such as haemorrhage or multiple trauma, are important factors in eventual outcome. Baker (1974) and colleagues developed an Injury Severity Score based on severity of trauma in separate body regions that is strongly predictive of mortality. The results–human grouping (cell 4) would include the total human injury and disability evolving from the interaction of the factors.

Prominent among pre-event–vehicle factors (cell 5) would be defects in essential equipment such as brakes and tyres. The energy-absorbing capability of components peripheral to the passenger compartment as well as those that would be struck by moving bodies in the passenger compartment would be listed in the vehicle–event cell (number 6). Fundamental is the space needed for deceleration in a crash. Vehicles with wheelbases less than 100 inches (2.54 metres) have twice the fatalities to occupants per number of vehicles registered as those with 120-inch (3.05 metres) or longer wheelbases

(Robertson and Baker 1976). Wheelbase is distance from front to rear axle.

Fuel leakage that could result in a conflagration after an otherwise minor crash would be listed in the vehicle post-event phase (cell 7). In front-to-rear crash tests of six, 1973 model cars at speeds of 36–40 miles per hour, fuel spilled from ruptured gas tanks in every case and a spontaneous post-crash fire occurred in one of the cars. The fire filled the passenger compartment of the struck car almost instantaneously (Kelley 1973). The vehicle–result combination (cell 8) includes the enormous cost of vehicle repairs that occur from even minor crashes.

Environmental factors before the event (cell 9) include physical features of the road such as low coefficients of friction that increase crash incidence. Also, the socio-cultural factors that contribute to greater economic subsidies to use of motor vehicles than to alternative forms of transportation such as trains would be included. In the US the deaths per passenger mile travelled in automobiles is 20 times that in trains or commercially scheduled airplanes (Federal Aviation Administration 1977). During the event, the most prominent environmental factor (cell 10) would be unyielding roadside objects such as trees, utility poles, and bridge abutments placed a few inches or feet from the roadside (Kelly 1972). In the US, about 17 000 deaths per year – one-third of the motor vehicle toll – occurred in such crashes in recent years.

After a crash, the promptness and competence of the emergency medical system is an important environmental factor (cell 11). The societal results (cell 12) include the measurable economic costs in funerals, medical costs, and foregone income to families of the injured (Hartunian *et al.* 1981).

INTERVENTION STRATEGIES

Intervention to reduce the incidence, severity, and eventual result of injury can be concentrated on a wide variety of factors and phases of the problem. Exclusive attention to 'accident prevention' is irrational, particularly in view of the limited ability of human beings to anticipate and react to hazardous conditions.

Haddon (1970, 1975, 1980) devised a systematic view of the strategies available for intervention. Here his ten strategies are reviewed with examples of applications suggested for motor vehicle injuries. The reader interested in burns, drownings, asphyxiation or falls may find it useful to apply the factors–phases matrix and the ten strategies as an exercise before consulting other works where they have been used (Haddon 1973; Dietz and Baker 1974; Feck *et al.* 1977; Baker and Dietz 1979; Robertson 1981*a*). These tools may also be applied to biological hazards as well as to chemical and physical hazards (Haddon 1980).

1. *Prevent the creation of the hazard.* Motor vehicle travel would not be a hazard had these vehicles never been manufactured. Weaning society away from them now would be difficult but the diminishing supply of cheap fuel may produce that result. Prohibiting the manufacture or the use of

especially hazardous vehicles such as minibikes, motorcycles, and the Jeep C15 would be effective far disproportionately to the inconvenience of their unavailability.

2. *Reduce the extent of the hazard.* The kinetic energy in motor vehicle crashes would be diminished by decreasing the mass of a vehicle or decreasing the speed at which they travel. Lave (1981), among others, has incorrectly characterized decreased crash protection as a trade-off for increased fuel economy. Making vehicles lighter through reducing their size has had this effect. However, physics has predicted and the development of experimental 'research safety vehicles' (DiNapoli *et al.* 1977) has demonstrated that it is possible to increase crash protection *and* fuel economy by using lightweight, energy-absorbing materials in vehicle construction (O'Neill *et al.* 1974). Vehicles capable of high speeds are also less fuel efficient and generate disproportionately more potentially damaging kinetic energy. Allowing manufacturers to produce vehicles capable of speeds twice the maximum legal limits is one of society's more ludicrous follies.

3. *Prevent the release of an extant hazard.* Examples are, increased skid resistance of road surfaces, improved visibility of vehicles and road signs, more easy handling and braking characteristics of vehicles, improved driver knowledge and skills, and prohibited use of vehicles by higher risk drivers. While driver-based measures are theoretically manipulable, the limits in human abilities and the transient variation in human responses to particular stimuli make training or screening drivers a problematic strategy.

4. *Modify the rate of spatial distribution of release of the hazard from its source.* Use of child restraints and seat belts that increase the uniformity of deceleration of occupants within vehicles is an important illustration. Failure to use child restraints and belts, even where required by law, diminishes the effectiveness of this strategy.

5. *Separate the hazard and that which is to be protected in time or space.* The obvious fact that pedestrians and bicyclists would not be struck by motor vehicles if their paths did not intersect is largely ignored in the lack of over- and underpasses, or pedestrian paths and bikeways removed from roads. Vehicle crashes would be less severe if vehicles of widely varying masses were assigned to different paths, or use of roads were allocated to vehicles of different mass at different times. Another important example is the removal of trees and utility poles from the roadsides where they are commonly struck.

6. *Protect the susceptible host by a material barrier.* The use of more energy-absorbing material in the exterior components of 'research safety vehicles' has already been mentioned. Inside the vehicle, cushions that inflate automatically when sensors detect crash forces have been developed and tested in use successfully (Mohan *et al.* 1976) for a decade but have been withheld by manufacturers from mass production. These so-called air bags spread the load over larger surfaces of the bodies moving forward in frontal crashes than do seat belts. Other successful applications of this strategy, far less than universally used, are crash helmets for motorcyclists and bicyclists, material in the median of roadways that prevents vehicles from crossing into the pathway of others and that absorbs energy or guides the vehicle to a

controlled stop, and energy-absorbing materials in front of rigid objects along the roadsides such as lamp- or signposts and bridge abutments (Kelley 1972).

7. *Change the basic qualities of hazards.* In motor vehicles, hard surfaces, pointed knobs and sheet metal, and sharp-edges are unnecessary and can be eliminated. These include not only those on the interior that are struck by moving occupants in crashes but also those on the exterior that increase the severity of impact to pedestrians and bicyclists (Ashton 1982). Objects often struck by vehicles, such as utility-, light-, and signposts, can be made to sever at impacts that result in energy exchanges at greater than injurious concentrations.

8. *Make that to be protected more resistant to damage from the hazard.* Our ability to modify human structure is limited by complexity of the human organism, although treatment of diseases that lower the threshold of injury to the organism by mechanical energy, such as haemophilia and osteoporosis, may lower susceptibility somewhat. Strengthening the fuel tanks and other containers of hazardous cargo in transport is also an example of this strategy.

9. *Rapid response to counter it when damage has begun.* Training the population in stopping haemorrhage and recognizing potential spinal cord injury so as not to exacerbate the damage by avoidable movement of the injured person is important. Emergency roadside telephones and well placed and trained professionals ready to respond quickly can make a difference in outcome.

10. *Stabilization, repair, and rehabilitation to limit the damage to survivors.* Superficial scars and bone destruction can be repaired in surgery. Provision of prosthetic devices for amputees and especially designed wheelchairs, beds, and equipment used in work and other activities allows the more severely injured to live somewhat more normal lives than they would without these aids.

IMPLEMENTATION

Clearly, the continued death and disability from trauma is not for lack of understanding the basic science of the sources of energy involved or lack of intervention strategies available to eliminate or ameliorate the vast majority of cases. The failure to use this knowledge has serious health consequences particularly for the young in modern societies. Increasing knowledge of the successes and failures in attempts to implement certain strategies has revealed several principles that could be followed to sort out the approaches that are likely to be effective.

Broadly conceived, three approaches are available to implementing public health policy: (i) persuasion of individuals to change their behaviour in relation to hazards; (ii) legal or administrative requirements that individuals avoid hazards or take protective action; and (iii) regulation of the production, distribution, or modification of potentially hazardous agents and vehicles before they are used by individuals (Robertson 1975a).

Examples of the first are education for drivers, swimmers, or skiers, television advertisement urging motorcycle helmet or seat belt use, rehabilitation programmes for persons convicted of drunk driving, and the like. Laws directed at individuals include prohibitions against driving with blood alcohol above certain concentrations and at speeds above certain limits, and required use of motorcycle helmets or seat belts in some jurisdictions. Classic illustrations of the regulation of hazards to protect people, irrespective of their behaviour, include treatment of milk and water to remove or kill harmful agents before they reach the consumer. In the injury area, requirements for shielded electrical cables where electricity is to be used and energy-absorbing steering assembly installation during the manufacture of automobiles in some countries are good examples.

PERSUASION

Education

Scientific investigation suggests that persuasion should be a last resort rather than the primary approach. Formal education in schools has been found harmful in the case of driving because of its secondary effect on licensure of teenaged drivers. Studies that claimed lower crashes associated with such courses were discredited by the finding that those who selected to take the course were better students who drove less. It was the selective entry of students into the course, not driver education, that resulted in the difference (Conger *et al.* 1966; McGuire and Kersh 1969).

In Britain, the first controlled experiment, in which the experimenters rather than parents or students selected those to receive training, found no difference in crashes per miles driven between those formally trained and those trained by parents or others. The total crashes per person were higher in the formally trained group, however, because more of them began driving earlier as a result of the course (Shaoul 1975). A subsequent US experiment, in which students who intended to be licensed were assigned to an especially designed curriculum, the usual curriculum, or a control group without formal training, found no difference in subsequent crash rates among the three groups (Ray *et al.* 1982). In the case of a British experiment that assigned persons to a course in motorcyclist education and a control group, crashes per licensed driver were higher in the formally trained group than in the control group, apparently because the training increased confidence without reducing risk (Raymond and Tatum 1977).

The increased rate of licensure and the accompanying higher crash rates associated with driver education found in the British experiment has been replicated in two US studies. Comparison of 27 states found no correlation between fatal crashes per licensed 16–17-year-old drivers and the proportion who had high-school driver education. The proportion of licensed drivers in that age group, however, increased to about eight for every 10 students who took the course and the proportion who were licensed drivers was strongly correlated to the fatal crash involvement of 16–17-year-olds. The effect is specific to that age group and driver education did not effect licensure or fatal crash involvement of those 18 or older (Robertson and Zador 1978). In a US state that eliminated funding for high school driver education, three of four drivers that were expected to be licensed at age 16 or 17 years after taking the high-school course waited until they were 18 years or older when the course was no longer available. Comparison of school districts that retained and dropped the course found a commensurate decline in severe crashes associated with the reduced licensure (Robertson 1980). Since 16–17-year-old drivers kill two other people for each one of them who dies in vehicle crashes, the risk extends to everyone in the community, not just the driver and his or her family.

Although older drivers would be licensed irrespective of training, there is no evidence that training makes them better drivers. Persons trained in commercial driver training schools (Jones 1973) or on especially designed training tracks (Council et al. 1975) have no better subsequent crash records per licensed driver than those trained in high school. Claims of effectiveness of the 'defensive driving' course are flawed by numerous potential biases (O'Neill 1974). A well designed study of use of the 'defensive driving' course, conducted in New Zealand, found no effect on drivers convicted of particular offences. An experimental group given the course and a control group who received the usual court treatment had similar crash records subsequently (Hill and Jamieson 1978).

An 'alcohol safety action project' in Nassau County, New York had similar results. In this project a sample of drivers convicted of driving while impaired by alcohol were assigned to a rehabilitation–education programme rather than the usual court procedure that often included suspension of licensure to drive. Subsequent crash records of the supposedly rehabilitated group were higher than in the control group that was treated in the traditional way (Preusser et al. 1976). Studies in Texas and Wisconsin where drivers convicted of a variety of violations were assigned to training or counselling programmes and compared to drivers with similar records but who were not trained or counselled have found little or no difference in subsequent crash records (Edwards and Ellis 1976; Fuchs 1980).

Special caution should be taken in attempts to educate children. Interpretation of language, gestures, directions, and symbols by children may be substantially different than that intended by the educator. Research on the street-crossing drill suggests such a misinterpretation. The drill includes the phrase 'look to the left, look to the right'. The children perceived 'left' and 'right' as static states of the environment rather than positional directions from the child's perspective. Comparison of children who were shown a film to teach the drill and a control group that did not see it revealed an increased static perception among the children who saw the film – the opposite of the educators' intent (Pease and Preston 1967).

Clinical counselling

Clinically based attempts to educate parents and children regarding hazards have mixed results. In a prepaid medical plan serving an upper middle-class clientele, parents who brought children for non-serious medical visits were assigned to experimental and control groups. The parents in the experimental group were counselled by a health educator regarding household hazards to children and were given a booklet suggesting ten actions to reduce hazards in the home. A follow-up phone call was also made to discuss what actions had been taken. The control group was not interviewed regarding hazards until a subsequent unannounced visit to the home in both experimental and control groups. No difference in the numbers of hazards observed during this visit was found between experimental and control groups (Derschewitz and Williamson 1977).

Attempts to increase use of infant and child restraints while travelling in motor vehicles have significant but temporary results. In a maternity hospital, mothers were assigned to a variety of experimental conditions and a control group. Mothers given literature alone or literature in combination with a discussion by a health educator, especially trained in persuasive techniques, were no more likely than other mothers to be using restraints, when arriving at the hospital for follow-up visits. Another experimental group given free infant carriers along with literature made slightly more use of them 2–4 months later, but even in this group, with no cost involved, more than 70 per cent were not using the restraints (Riesinger and Williams 1978). Another programme in which parents were given free restraints and the nurse placed the infant in the restraint for the ride home, resulted in 66 per cent use on the trip home but only 28 per cent in a follow-up visit (Christopherson 1982).

Personal counselling about the importance of restraint use, and how to use it correctly, by a paediatrician who also gave the parent a prescription for a restraint, had a short-term effect on use. Compared to a control group that did not receive counselling, the experimental group had 23 per cent greater use in one month, 73 per cent in two months, but only 9 and 12 per cent greater use above the control group at 4 and 15 month follow-up visits (Riesinger et al. 1981). Personal counselling by paediatricians has had an effect on childhood falls (Kravits 1973) and purchase of smoke detectors for the home (Miller et al. 1982).

Two principles emerge from these studies. First, counselling by physicians is more often effective than by health educators, probably because the physicians have more of an aura of authority and expertise. Secondly, it is easier to influence the individual when he or she must take only a single or infrequent action than when the action must occur often with accompanying inconvenience, discomfort, and costs (Robertson 1975a; Baker 1980a). Even in those cases where counselling has some effect, there is no guarantee that the quality and enthusiasm of the counselling in the original experiments can be disseminated among large numbers of counsellors.

Mass media

The major means of mass persuasion in modern society are the mass media. But the effects of commercial advertising are less dramatic than advertising agencies would have us think. Campaigns for specific products are considered successful if they change a market for the product by a few percentage points. Public service advertising directed toward injury control is seldom evaluated experimentally on a small scale before being put into general use. The few available experiments raise doubts that it is useful.

A series of radio and television messages urging seat belt

use was used in two of three communities with similar demographic characteristics – intensively in one community and moderately in the second. Observed seat belt use was similar before and after the campaign in all three communities. (Fleischer 1972).

Televison advertisement based on research comparing belt users with non-users, were shown on one cable of a dual cable television system designed for test marketing of commercial products. The campaign was the equivalent of a new product campaign that would have cost $7 million in 1972 if conducted nationally. The advertisements were shown in prime viewing time and were directed at specific audiences, in contrast to the usual haphazard placement of public service advertising. Comparison of belt use by drivers from households on the experimental and control cables found no difference before, during, or after the nine-month campaign (Robertson et al. 1974).

In Canada, the Ontario Department of Transport developed a multimedia advertising campaign directed at seat belt use and attempted to persuade radio, television, and newspaper outlets, as well as safety councils, businesses, schools, and police departments, to use the materials. A follow-up study indicated only intermittent, unsystematic use of the materials by these organizations. Claimed belt use by drivers in collissions – as reported to the police – was unchanged by the campaign (Safety and Environmental Studies Section 1970). A similar community-wide effort to reduce burn injuries found few changes in behaviour and no evidence of an effect on the burn injury rate (McLoughlin et al. 1982).

Behaviour modification

The modification of behaviour by manipulation of rewards and punishments in laboratories has been demonstrated by psychologists for decades. Use of the principles of conditioning in the community or society to alter health-related behaviours is another matter. Results of a few such attempts to curb injuries have ranged from substantial success to failure and a rebellious public.

In the US, the federal agency responsible for regulation of vehicle safety allowed manufacturers to substitute a buzzer and lighted reminder to use seat belts as an alternative to automatic crash protection in cars manufactured from January 1972 through the 1973 model year. If a certain weight was detected in the driver or front outboard passenger seats, the buzzer sounded continuously until the belts were extended from their stowed positions. Many people reacted by permanently knotting the belts in an extended position and thus making them unusable. Observations of belt use in ten cities within six months of the buzzer's introduction revealed no significant difference in belt use of drivers in cars of the 1972 model year with and without buzzers (Robertson and Haddon 1974).

In 1974 model cars, the government allowed a system called the interlock which prevented the car from starting when belts were either not extended or connected. In these cars seat belt use increased to nearly 60 per cent in the first few months of their introduction (Robertson 1975b). Complaints to legislators about failure of cars to start when cargo

other than passengers was placed in the seats, as well as ideological objection to government imposition of the rule, resulted in prohibition of the use of interlocks. By the late 1970s, belt use was reduced to about 15 per cent in interlock-equipped cars (Phillips 1980).

Rewards, for example a prize if observed using seat belts, has increased seat belt use in small-scale experiments (Elman and Killebrew 1978). But, this is much less effective among blue collar workers (Geller 1982). Implementing reward systems on a mass scale for a variety of behaviours would be costly to sustain and has the potential for corruption.

In industrial settings, feedback of information about potential injury has an effect on subsequent behaviour. Experimental groups given audiometric examinations before and after work in a noisy environment and shown the result in reduced hearing increased their use of earplugs up to 90 per cent, five months after the experiment compared to only 10 per cent of a control group (Zohar et al. 1980). Grinding machines designed to spray water in a pattern similar to that which could occur with metal particles were used in training and resulted in greater care in the use of the machines (Rubinsky and Smith 1973). Identification of hazardous acts in a bakery and posting of counts of the numbers of such acts, observed intermittently, resulted in reduced numbers of the acts during the periods that they were posted. In subsequent periods without the posting, the number of hazardous acts returned to the frequency observed before the experiment (Komaki et al. 1978).

Changing perception

A promising approach to behaviour change is the enhancement of the environment to increase the individual's perception of hazard. Optical illusions such as an exponentially decreasing pattern of stripes painted across the road (Denton 1980) or a herringbone pattern (Shinar et al. 1980) cause drivers of certain types of vehicles to decrease their speed in approaches to bends and roundabouts. Increases in lighting of roadways also reduces night-time collisions (Box 1971). Reflectors in the roadway on or near curves greater than six degrees in one study resulted in an average 20 per cent reduction in single vehicle crashes at night (Wright et al. 1982). Front-to-rear collisions can be reduced by 50 per cent if an additional brake light is placed just below the rear window in the centre of the vehicle (Reilly et al. 1980). Despite this evidence, vehicle manufacturers have not responded with vehicles so equipped.

LAWS DIRECTED AT INDIVIDUALS

Deterrence

Another strategy to reduce injuries is to prohibit hazardous behaviours by law and administrative rules and require the use of protective equipment. Laws to deter behaviours that are difficult to observe, such as alcohol-impaired driving, are infrequently enforced. Driving while intoxicated or with greater than specified amounts of alcohol in blood, known to impair performance, has been proscribed in most countries but actual arrests and convictions for the offence are rare. Comparison of arrest rates with sample surveys of blood alcohol suggests the probablity of arrest in the US is about 1 in 2000 (National Highway Traffic Safety Administration 1974).

Highly publicized 'crackdowns' on drinking and driving result in a temporary perception of increased risk of arrest, but the effect is lost as the publicity abates. The 1967 British Road Safety Act initially created that impression and fatalities declined by about 25 per cent in the first year of the law. When drivers learned that the actual probability of arrest had changed little, the death rate returned to the level that would have been expected without the law (Ross 1973). Experience in other countries has been similar though usually with less publicity and less effect (Ross 1982).

The threat of severe penalties, such as jail sentences for drunk driving in the Scandinavian countries, has had no discernible effect on death rates coincident with their adoption (Ross 1975). Visitors to those countries believe that there is an effect when they attend gatherings where someone abstains from alcohol use and drives the others to their destinations. Most such groups probably consist of light drinkers that would not consume the amounts necessary for significant impairment whatever the law.

There is substantial evidence that probability of arrest is more important than severity of punishment in deterrence of illegal behaviours. For a variety of felonies, the incidence rate is uncorrelated to the arrest rate if the arrest rate is below 30 per cent of reported incidence. As the arrest rate increases above that level, the incidence declines (Tittle and Rowe 1974). In the case of alcohol-related driving, the highest arrest rate reported is 1 in 200 (Beitel et al. 1975), a far cry from 30 per cent.

One alcohol-related legal action that has had a sustained effect on motor vehicle fatalities is the legal minimum age for purchasing alcohol. In the 1970s several US states and Canadian provinces reduced the legal age of purchase. Comparison of states and provinces that reduced the age with similar jurisdictions that did not do so during the same period indicated an increase in fatal crashes involving those in relevant age groups and a 'trickle down' effect increasing the involvement of those younger as well (Williams et al. 1975). When this policy was fully or partially reversed in several states, the fatal crash involvement of drivers in age groups no longer legally allowed to purchase alcohol declined, particularly in night-time and single vehicle crashes in which alcohol is most often involved (Williams et al. 1981).

One likely reason for the greater effectiveness of these laws, compared to those prohibiting drunk driving, is that they are directed at the seller rather than the consumer. When enforcement of law can be augmented by persons other than police agencies in the community, the law is likely to be more effective. Another example is the legal minimum driving age. While the police have difficulty in identifying the precise age of vehicle drivers without stopping each one for identification by licensure, most parents are unlikely to allow use of family car by a youngster less than the legal driving age and rental car companies will not rent to persons without a licence (Robertson 1981b).

In countries where ownership of handguns is severely limited, such as Britain and Japan, the fatality rate from handguns is very low (Newton and Zimring, no date). In the US, handgun control laws vary widely from one state to the next making enforcement difficult. Someone who cannot obtain a gun in one state can often easily do so in a nearby state.

Comparison of fatal injury by guns among US states with different types of laws indicates lower rates of homicide, suicide, and unintentional deaths by handguns in states that have more laws restricting their sale and use. Laws regarding dealer licensure, record keeping, and licensure to purchase handguns were found more effective than those directed at conveyance or use, as might be expected from the fact that enforcement of laws affecting dealers would be augmented by the dealers. Based on the evidence, the authors concluded that some 4200–6400 fewer deaths from firearms would have been found annually in the US during the late 1960s if all US states had adopted laws of the state with the most strict laws at that time (Geisel et al. 1969).

Change in laws for reasons other than injury control may have an impact on injury incidence and severity if the change results in altered behaviour that contributes to risk. The fuel shortage associated with the OPEC oil boycott of 1973 resulted in reduction of maximum speed limits in the US to 55 miles per hour. At the same time there was economic recession and reduced travel, making it difficult to assess the separate effects of these factors on the motor vehicle fatality rate. Deaths declined about 20 per cent from 1973 to 1974 and the best evidence suggests that speed reductions accounted for about half of the total effect (Kemper and Byington 1977). Although speeds have crept up somewhat as the fuel shortage became less acute, average speeds, and especially extremely high speeds, have remained substantially below those prevalent before the change in law.

Somewhat more speculative, but correlated in patterns that strongly suggest causation, was the impact of liberalized abortion laws on infant mortality from injuries other than vehicles. These deaths per live births declined by half as abortions increased from before to after the 1973 Supreme Court decision that negated state laws against abortion. The data suggest that abortions occur more frequently in cases where the children would subsequently be neglected or abused, in some instances contributing to their deaths (Robertson 1981c).

Required protection

Laws requiring the use of protective equipment have usually been more successful than those aimed at deterrence of behaviour that increases risk. The most likely reason is that the use of equipment such as helmets and seat belts is more easily observable and thus enforceable.

In US states with laws requiring helmet use by motorcyclists, virtually 100 per cent of motorcyclists observed on the road use helmets compared to 25–60 per cent use in states without the laws. During the period that such laws were being enacted, death rates of motorcyclists declined by 30 per cent from the year before to the year after enactment of the laws compared to no change in comparable states that did not require helmets during the same period (Robertson 1976). Despite the reduction in deaths and the fact that the majority of motorcyclists questioned in public opinion polls favoured the laws, an active lobby in about half the states persuaded legislators to repeal the helmet laws (Baker 1980b). In states that repealed the law deaths of motorcyclists increased, proportionate to the decline when the laws were originally enacted (Watson *et al.* 1980).

The required use of seat belts by vehicle occupants, with exemptions, has spread to many countries following the reported success of the law in the state of Victoria, Australia. Seat belt use rose to about 70 per cent when the law was enacted in Victoria (Andreassend 1976) and was observed at about 80 per cent in several Australian cities in subsequent years after other states adopted the law (Robertson 1978a). Comparison of fatalities in Victoria before and after introduction of the law, with those of other states that had not enacted the law revealed a 20 per cent reduction in vehicle occupant deaths in urban areas and a 10 per cent reduction in rural areas attributable to the law with no effect on other road users (Foldvary and Lane 1974).

The effect of seat belt laws on their use in other countries has been variable depending on enforcement and the number and timing of experiments. Japan requires belt use on freeways only, with no penalties for not wearing them, and has less than 2 per cent seat belt use. Ontario, Canada had an initial increase in seat belt use from 21 per cent to 70 per cent when their law was first enacted in 1976. Within two months, shoulder belt use in cars manufactured before 1974 was exempted as a result of complaints of discomfort and seat belt use in general declined to about 50 per cent (Robertson 1978b). The reductions in deaths, while important, have been less than would be expected from the known effectiveness of seat belts when worn. The apparent reason is that groups that are more likely to be involved in fatal crashes, such as teenage drivers and passengers, are less often seen using seat belts (Robertson 1978b).

As late as 1982, Britain had enacted a seat belt law, not to be enforced until 1983, and no US state had enacted a seat belt law. Laws requiring child restraint use for infants and younger children transported in certain vehicles were being enacted in the early 1980s in many US states following the lead of the state of Tennessee. That state's law resulted in increased restraint use in major cities from 8 per cent before the law to 29 per cent two years afterward (Williams and Wells 1981). The lower use of child restraints as compared to seat belts, even when required by law, apparently stems from their extra inconvenience and costs. Also, their use may be less rigorously enforced.

REGULATION OF AGENTS AND VEHICLES

Modification of the hazardous agent or vehicle to reduce its potential for harm before it reaches the general public is commonly accepted as a preventive measure against traditional public health problems. Good examples are the treatments of milk and water to kill or remove harmful biological agents before the milk or water reaches the consumer. While this principle has also been applied to electrical energy for decades, it has only recently begun to be used to reduce motor vehicle and some other injuries.

Motor vehicles

Other than state laws requiring periodic inspection of vehicles for deficient lights, brakes, etc., crash-related characteristics of motor vehicles were unregulated in the US until the mid-1960s. State laws resulted in the installation of lap seat belts as standard equipment in front outboard seats of 1964 and subsequent models. The agency that purchases vehicles for federal government use was authorized to issue standards for crash protection such as energy-absorbing steering assemblies and high penetration resistant windshields beginning in 1966 models. Manufacturers responded by installing them as standard equipment in models usually sold in large volume to the government.

In 1966, federal legislation was enacted to establish an agency to set safety standards for new vehicles manufactured for sale in the US and to begin research and development toward more effective standards. William Haddon Jr, a public health physician who had played an important role in the development of injury control concepts and research, was appointed by the President to be the first head of the agency – now called the National Highway Traffic Safety Administration. The initial standards, applicable to 1968 and subsequent models, included rules for occupant protection by energy absorption in windshields, steering assemblies, and other interior surfaces, and increased strength of doors and locks to reduce intrusion by other vehicles and ejection of occupants. Crash avoidance standards were also included in provisions for reduced glare in drivers eyes, redundant braking systems, side running lights, and the like.

Although the effectiveness of particular occupant crash-protection standards in reduced severity to occupants was well documented (Nahum and Siegel 1968; Levine and Campbell 1971), controversy over the net effect of the regulations was generated by an economist who claimed that drivers with greater personal protection provided by the occupant crash-protection standards drove more 'intensively' and killed other road users to such an extent as to offset the reductions in occupant deaths (Peltzman 1975). These conclusions were based on projected rates of aggregated data in an econometric model and were subsequently found to be in error. The model contained shifting correlations of independent variables that resulted in divergence of actual and projected death rates prior to the introduction of regulation. Motorcyclists were counted as pedestrians and no controls were included to account for the fact that motorcycle registrations were doubling every five years during the 1960s (Robertson 1977).

Definitive conclusions on the issue were reached by comparison of the extent to which regulated vehicles were involved in deaths of other road users compared to unregulated vehicles, controlling for use. Cars meeting the federal standards killed significantly fewer pedestrians, motorcyclists, and bicyclists per mile of use than did unregulated vehicles. Apparently, the crash avoidance standards reduced collisions with other road users and when all standards were combined there was a total death reduction of more than 9000 deaths per year in the mid-1970s (Robertson 1981*d*). Research on the effects of motor vehicle safety regulations in Sweden also found reductions in occupant deaths and no adverse effect on other road users (Lindgren and Stuart 1980).

The safety standards for motor vehicles in the US were intended to be performance standards, for example a requirement for maximum stopping distance for brakes under particular conditions rather than specification of the type of brakes to be used. Theoretically, performance standards are preferable, to allow innovation and increases in efficiency without altering the standard every time there is a new innovation. In practice, attempts to adopt standards beyond those initially introduced have been ensnared in controversy over the 'buzzer' and 'interlock' systems mentioned earlier and the relative merit of air cushions that inflate automatically in crashes above a certain severity and seat belts that automatically envelop the occupant when the doors are closed.

Research safety vehicles that provide survivable crash protection up to 50 miles per hour (81 kilometres per hour) in crashes into a solid barrier have been developed (DiNapoli *et al.* 1977). Their cost in mass production would be about the same as current compact cars. But no standard for such protection has been proposed. Indeed, in the early 1980s, the federal agency responsible for vehicle regulation was petitioning the highest court in the land to allow it to rescind a more modest crash protection standard that a lower court ordered reinstated.

Worker injuries

Regulations intended to reduce injuries in work environments are far more effective than previously thought. Legislation in 1970 established a federal agency, the Occupational Safety and Health Administration (OSHA), to develop standards to reduce worker exposure to hazards in the US. As in the case of motor vehicles, a set of standards that had previously been extant in a limited number of settings was initially adopted and there have been few new safety standards since.

The total reported incidence of worker injuries changed little in the 1970s and a comparison of projected versus actual trends revealed little or no correlation between changes in injuries and inspection activities of OSHA (Mendeloff 1979; Smith 1976, 1979; Viscusi 1979). These studies failed to control for changes in Worker's Compensation payments that increased injury claims during the period and hence offset the effect of regulatory measures. Further, attention was focused on inspections rather than on citations for violations. An inspection of a work place would not necessarily result in altered conditions unless there were a citation for a specific violation.

Research on disaggregated injury data for the years 1973–80 in three industrial plants, each in a separate state, found that verifiable injuries, such as fractures and lacerations, were reduced by an average of 40 per cent in the year following an OSHA citation. Claims of injuries not objectively verifiable – mainly back pain and strain – did not respond to OSHA

citations, but increased rapidly during the period in response to increases in Worker's Compensation payments, particularly in years when this advanced beyond the inflation rate. As a result, injury rates apparently rose when, in fact, OSHA citations were causing a decrease in objectively verifiable injuries. Data on OSHA citations across 20 states confirmed that this finding was generalizable. When Worker's Compensation and OSHA citations were considered in the analysis simultaneously, worker injuries declined in correlation with greater OSHA citations but advanced with increased Worker's Compensation above inflation (Robertson and Keeve 1983).

Since the effect of a citation, in the individual plants studied, did not prevail beyond the first year after the citation, there is doubt that permanent alterations in hazards have been accomplished by OSHA activities. Nevertheless, the effect of citations on injury reduction is substantial. The study also cast doubt on the use of economic incentives to reduce injuries. Despite the fact that Worker's Compensation payments had risen to $100 000 per month to workers in the plants studied by 1980, the company's preventive measures against injury were effectively mobilized only when the OSHA inspectors issued a citation. The incidence of verifiable injuries was unrelated to compensation.

Consumer products

A variety of consumer products that can cause injury are regulated in the US by the Consumer Product Safety Commission. The effect of the regulations on each product to which they have been applied has not been assessed although important gains have been documented. Children's poisonings by aspirin declined markedly after containers more difficult for children to open were required (Howes 1978). Asphyxiations of children by crib slats and mattresses were reduced in relation to regulation of crib designs (Office of Strategic Planning 1979). At the local level, rules requiring coverings over windows in multilevel buildings to prevent children from falling resulted in a reduction of 80 per cent in fatal falls (Bergner 1982).

CONCLUSION

In addition to the principles stated regarding the effects of persuasion, laws directed at individuals, and regulation of agents and vehicles, more general principles of public health must be applied if injury reduction efforts are to be promoted. Scientific expertise in the nature of agents and vehicles of injury must be conveyed to those who design and manufacture the products and processes that embody them as well as to those who have the responsibility for regulations. Schools of design, engineering, and public health give little or no attention to injuries in their curricula, and law school courses are concerned mainly with post-injury compensation. Only three or four schools or medical school departments of public health in the US have a course devoted exclusively to injury epidemiology and control.

Too often injury control programmes at the local, state, and federal levels are in the hands of usually well-meaning amateurs who understand neither the problem nor the evidence regarding the success or failure of available approaches. The result is a substantial waste of effort and resources on tried and failed efforts. The US entered the 1980s with more than 50 000 disproportionately young people dying each year in motor vehicle crashes. The federal agency responsible for vehicle safety regulation was headed by a former coal industry lobbyist with no training or experience in the field. The major efforts under way included attempts to rescind previously adopted regulations not yet in effect, and to introduce a seat belt use campaign, despite the evidence that such campaigns are fruitless.

While regulations are often delayed as the evidence of their effectiveness becomes mountainous, efforts to change behaviour are launched on a mass scale with no scientific evidence of their effectiveness. Ignored is the public health principle that programmes can do harm and should be tested, on a scale large enough to assure reliable and valid results but no larger, to minimize potential harm, before being put into general use. Putting something into complicated human minds can have unanticipated results equivalent to harmful 'side-effects' of some interventions in complicated organs and cells.

The knowledge and principles necessary to reduce injury rates to small fractions of their present levels is waiting for application. The students of public health who acquire the knowledge and gain positions in the organizations where it can be applied can anticipate rewarding careers in protecting the public's health.

REFERENCES

Andreassend, D.C. (1976). Victoria and the seat belt law. *Hum. Factors* **4**, 593.

Ashton, S.J. (1982). Vehicle designs and pedestrian injuries. In *Pedestrian injuries* (eds. A.J. Chapman, F.M. Wade, and W.C. Hoof) p. 69. Wiley, London.

Baker, S.P. (1980*a*). Prevention of childhood injuries. *Med. J. of Aust.* **1**, 466.

Baker, S.P. (1980*b*). On lobbies, liberty and the public good. *Am. J. Public Health* **70**, 573.

Baker, S.P. and Dietz, P.E. (1979). The epidemiology and prevention of injuries. In *The management of trauma*, 3rd edn (eds. G.D. Zuidema, R.B. Rutherford, and W.F. Ballinger II) p. 79. Saunders, Philadelphia, Pa.

Baker, S.P. (1974). The injury severity score: a method for describing patients with multiple injuries and evaluating emergency care. *J. Trauma* **14**, 187.

Beitel, G.A., Sharp, M.C., and Glauz, W.D. (1975). Probability of arrest while driving under the influence of alcohol. *J. Stud. Alcohol* **36**, 109.

Bergner, L. (1982). Environmental factors in injury control. In *Preventing childhood injuries* (ed. A.B. Bergman) p. 57. Ross Laboratories, Columbus, Ohio.

Box, P.C. (1971). Relationship between illumination and freeway accidents. *Illuminating Engineering* May/June, 365.

Christophersen, E.R. (1982). Behavioural approaches to auto safety education. In *Preventing childhood injuries* (ed. A.B. Bergman) p. 33. Ross Laboratories, Columbus, Ohio.

Conger, J.J., Miller, W.C., and Rainey, R.V. (1966). Effects of driver education: the role of motivation, intelligence, social class, and exposure. *Traffic Safety Res. Rev.* **10**, 67.

Council, R.M., Roper, R.B., and Sadoff, M.G. (1975). *An Evaluation of North Carolina's multi-vehicle range program in driver education.* University of North Carolina Highway Safety Research Center, Chapel Hill, NC.

DeHaven, H. (1942). Mechanical analysis of survival in falls from heights of fifty to one hundred and fifty feet. *War Med.* **2**, 586.

Denton, G.C. (1980). The influence of visual pattern on the perception of speed. *Perception* **9**, 393.

Dershewitz, R.A. and Williamson, J.R. (1977). Prevention of childhood household injuries: a controlled clinical trial. *Am. J. Public Health* **67**, 1148.

Dietz, P.E. and Baker, S.P. (1974). Drowning: epidemiology and prevention. *Am. J. Public Health* **64**, 303.

DiNapoli, N., Fitzpatrick, M., Strother, C. (1977). *Research safety vehicle phase II. Volume II; comprehensive technical results.* National Technical Information Service, Springfield, Va.

Edwards, M.L. and Ellis, N.C. (1976). An evaluation of the Texas driver improvement training program. *Hum. Factors* **18**, 327.

Elman, D. and Killebrew, T.J. (1978). Incentives and seat belts: changing a resistant behavior through extrinsic motivation. *J. Appl. Pyschol.* **8**, 72.

Evans, L. (1970). Speed estimation from a moving automobile. *Ergonomics* **13**, 219.

Feck, G.A., Baptiste, M.S., and Tate, C.L. Jr. (1977). *An epidemiologic study of burn injuries and strategies for prevention.* US Department of Health, Education and Welfare, Center for Disease Control, Atlanta, Ga.

Federal Aviation Administration (1977). *FAA statistical handbook of aviation,* p.148. US Department of Transportation, Washington, DC.

Fleischer, G.A. (1972). *An experiment in the use of broadcast media in highway safety.* University of Southern California Department of Industrial and Systems Engineering, Los Angeles, Calif.

Foldvary, L.A. and Lane, J.C. (1974). The effectiveness of compulsory wearing of seat-belts in casualty reduction. *Accident Anal. Prev.* **6**, 59.

Fuchs, C. (1980). Wisconsin driver improvement program: a treatment-control evaluation. *J. Safety Res.* **12**, 107.

Geisel, M.S., Roll, R., and Wettick, R.S. Jr. (1969). The effectiveness of state and local regulation of handguns: a statistical analysis. *Duke Law J.* **1969**, 647.

Geller, E.S. (1982). *Development of industry based strategies for motivating seat belt usage. Quarterly report for DOT Contract DTRS5681-C-0032.* Virginia Polytechnic and State University, Blacksburg, Va.

Gibson, J.J. (1961). The contribution of experimental psychology to the formulation of the problem of safety. In *Behavioral approaches to accident research.* Harper and Row, New York.

Gordon, D.A. and Mast, T.M. (1970). Drivers' judgement in overtaking and passing. *Hum. Factors* **12**, 341.

Griffin, L.I., III (1974). *Motorcycle accidents: who, when, where, and why.* University of North Carolina Highway Safety Research Center, Chapel Hill, NC.

Haddon, W. Jr. (1970). On the escape of tigers: an ecologic note. *Am. J. Public Health* **60**, 2229.

Haddon, W. Jr. (1972). A logical framework for categorizing highway safety phenomena and activity. *J. Trauma* **12**, 193.

Haddon, W. Jr. (1973). Exploring the options. In *Research directions towards the reduction of injury in the very young and very old.* National Institute of Child Health and Human Development, US Department of Health, Education, and Welfare, Washington, DC.

Haddon, W. Jr. (1975). Reducing the damage of motor vehicle use. *Technol. Rev.* **77**, 53.

Haddon, W. Jr. (1980). Advances in epidemiology of injuries as a basis for public policy. *Public Health Rep.* **95**, 411.

Haddon, W. Jr. and Baker, S.P. (1981). Injury control. In *Preventive medicine, Edition 2* (eds. D. Clark and B. MacMahon) p. 109. Little Brown, Boston, Ma.

Hartunian, N.S., Smart, C.N., and Thompson, M.S. (1981). *The incidence and economic costs of major health impairments.* Lexington Books, Lexington, Ma.

Hill, P.S. and Jamieson, B.D. (1978). Driving offenders and the defensive driving course – an archival study. *J. Psychol.* **98**, 117.

Howes, D.R. (1978). *An evaluation of the effectiveness of child-restraint packaging.* Consumer Product Safety Commission, Washington, DC.

Johansson, G. and Rumar, K. (1971). Drivers' brake reaction times. *Hum. Factors* **13**, 23.

Jones, M.H. (1973). *California training evaluation study.* California State Department of Motor Vehicles, Sacramento, CA.

Kelley, A.B. (1972). *Boobytrap* (film). Insurance Institute for Highway Safety, Washington, DC.

Kelley, A.B. (1973). *Cars that crash and burn* (film). Insurance Institute for Highway Safety, Washington, DC.

Kemper, W.J. and Byington, S.R. (1977). Safety aspects of the 55 mph speed limit. *Public Roads* **41**, 58.

Komacki, J., Barwick, K.D., and Scott, L.R. (1978). A behavioural approach to occupational safety: pinpointing and reinforcing safe performance in a food manufacturing plant. *J. Appl. Psychol.* **63**, 434.

Kraus, J.F., Franti, C.E., Riggins, R.S. (1975). Incidence of traumatic spinal cord lesions. *J. Chron. Dis.* **28**, 471.

Kravitz, H. (1973). Prevention of falls in infancy by counseling mothers. *Illinois Med. J.* **114**, 570.

Lave, L.B. (1981). Conflicting objectives in regulating the automobile. *Science* **212**, 893.

Levine, D.N. and Campbell, B.J. (1971). *Effectiveness of lap seat belts and the energy absorbing steering system in the reduction of injuries.* University of North Carolina Highway Safety Research Center, Chapel Hill, NC.

Lindgren, B. and Stuart, C. (1980). The effects of traffic safety regulation in Sweden. *J. Political Econ.* **88**, 412.

McCarroll, J.R. and Haddon, W. Jr. (1962). A controlled study of fatal automobile accidents in New York City. *J. Chronic Dis.* **15**, 811.

McGuire, F.L. and Kersh, R.C. (1969). *An evaluation of driver education.* University of California Press, Berkeley, Calif.

McLoughlin, E., Vince, C.J., Lee, A.M. (1982). Project burn prevention: outcome and implications. *Am. J. Public Health* **72**, 241.

Mendeloff, J. (1979). *Regulating safety: an economic and political analysis of occupational safety and health.* MIT Press, Cambridge, Ma.

Miller, R.E., Reisinger, K.S., Blatter, M.M. (1982). Pediatric counseling and subsequent use of smoke detectors. *Am. J. Public Health* **72**, 392.

Mohan, D., Zador, P., O'Neill, B. (1976). Air bags and lap/shoulder belts: a comparison of their effectiveness in real-world frontal crashes. In *Proceedings of the 20th Conference of the American Association for Automotive Medicine*, p. 315. Morton Grove, Il.

Nahum, A. and Siegel, A.W. (1968). *Statement before the Committee on Commerce.* US Senate, Washington, DC.

National Highway Traffic Safety Administration (1974). *Alcohol and highway safety projects: evaluation of operations.* US Department of Transportation, Washington, DC.

Newton, G.D. and Zimring, F.E. (No date). *Firearms and violence in American life: a staff report to the National Committee on the Causes and Prevention of Violence.* US Government Printing Office, Washington, DC.

O'Neill, B. (1974]. Comments on 'An evaluation of the National

Safety Council's Defensive Driving Course in Various States'. *Accident Anal. Prev.* **6**, 299.

O'Neill, B., Joksch, H., and Haddon, W. Jr (1974). Relationships between car size, car weight, and crash injuries in car-to-car crashes. In *Proceedings of the Third International Congress on Automotive Safety.* US Government Printing Office, Washington, DC.

Office of Strategic Planning (1979). *Impact of crib safety activities on unjuries and deaths associated with cribs.* Consumer Product Safety Commission, Washington, DC.

Pease, K. and Preston, B. (1967). Road safety education for young children. *Br. J. Educ. Psychol.* **37**, 305.

Peltzman, S. (1975). The effects of automobile safety regulation. *J. Political Econ.* **83**, 677.

Phillips, B.M. (1980). *Safety belt use among drivers.* National Technical Information Service, Springfield, Va.

Preusser, D.F., Ulmer, R.G., and Adams, J.R. (1976). Driver record evaluation of a drinking driver rehabilitation program. *J. Safety Res.* **8**, 98.

Ray, H.W., Weaver, J.K., Brink, J.R. *et al.* (1982). *Safe performance secondary school education curriculum.* National Highway Traffic Safety Administration, Washington, DC.

Raymond, S. and Tatum, S. (1977). *An evaluation of the RAC/ACU motor cycle training scheme—final report.* University of Salford, England.

Reilly, R.E., Kurke, D.S., and Buckenmaier, C.C. Jr (1980). *Validation of the reduction of rear-end collisions by a high-mounted auxiliary stoplamp.* National Highway Traffic Safety Administration, Washington, DC.

Riesinger, K.S. and Williams, A.F. (1978). Evaluation of programs designed to increase protection of infants in cars. *Pediatrics* **62**, 280.

Riesinger, K.S., Williams, A.F., Wells, J.A.K., *et al.* (1981). The effect of pediatricians counseling on infant restraint use. *Pediatrics* **67**, 201.

Robertson, L.S. (1975*a*). Behavioral research and strategies in public health: a demur. *Soc. Sci. Med.* **9**, 165.

Robertson, L.S. (1975*b*). Safety belt use in automobiles with starter-interlock and buzzer-light reminder systems. *Am. J. Public Health* **65**, 1319.

Robertson, L.S. (1976). An instance of effective legal regulations: motorcyclist helmet and daytime headlamp laws. *Law Soc. Rev.* **10**, 467.

Robertson, L.S. (1977). A critical analysis of Peltzman's 'The effects of automobile safety regulation'. *J. Econ. Issues* **11**, 587.

Robertson, L.S. (1978*a*). Automobile seat belt use in selected countries, states and provinces with and without laws requiring belt use. *Accident Anal. Prev.* **10**, 5.

Robertson, L.S. 61978*b*). The seat belt use law in Ontario: effects on actual use. *Can. J. Public Health* **69**, 154.

Robertson, L.S. (1980). Crash involvement of teenaged drivers when driver education is eliminated from high school. *Am. J. Public Health* **70**, 599.

Robertson, L.S. (1981*a*). Environmental hazards to children: assessment and options for amelioration. In *Better health for our children: a national strategy*, Vol. 4, US Department of Health and Human Services, Washington, DC.

Robertson, L.S. (1981*b*). Patterns of teenaged driver involvement in fatal motor vehicle crashes: implications for policy choices. *J. Health Politics Policy Law* **6**, 303.

Robertson, L.S. (1981*c*). Abortion and infant mortality before and after the 1973 Supreme Court decision on abortion. *J. Biosoc. Sci.* **13**, 275.

Robertson, L.S. (1981*d*). Automobile safety regulations and death reductions in the United States. *Am. J. Public Health* **71**, 818.

Robertson, L.S. and Baker, S.P. (1976). Motor vehicle sizes in 1440 fatal crashes. *Accident Anal. Prev.* **8**, 167.

Robertson, L.S. and Haddon, W. Jr (1974). The buzzer-light reminder system and safety belt use. *Am. J. Public Health* **64**, 814.

Robertson, L.S. and Keeve, J.P. (1983). Worker injuries: the effects of Workers' Compensation and OSHA inspections. *J. Health Politics Policy Law,* **8**, 581.

Robertson, L.S. and Zador, P.L. (1978). Driver education and fatal crash involvement of teenaged drivers. *Am. J. Public Health* **68**, 959.

Robertson, L.S., Kelley, A.B., O'Neill, B. *et al.* (1974). A controlled study of the effect of television messages on safety belt use. *Am. J. Public Health* **64**, 1071.

Ross, H.L. (1973). Law, science, and accidents: the British Road Safety Act of 1967. *J. Legal Stud.* **2**, 1.

Ross, H.L. (1975). The scandinavian myth: the effectiveness of drinking and driving legislation in Sweden and Norway. *J. Legal Stud.* **4**, 285.

Ross, H.L. (1982). *Deterring the drunk driver: legal policy and social control.* Lexington Books, Lexington, Mass.

Rubinsky, S. and Smith, N. (1973). Safety training by accident simulation. *J. Appl. Psychol.* **57**, 68.

Safety and Environmental Studies Section (1970). *The 1969 Seat Belt Campaign.* Ontario Department of Transport, Toronto.

Schmidt, F. and Tiffin, J. Jr (1969). Distortion of drivers' estimates of automobile speed as a function of speed adaptation. *J. Appl. Psychol.* **53**, 536.

Shaoul, J. (1975). *The use of accidents and traffic offenses as criteria for evaluating courses in driver education.* University of Salford, England.

Shinar, D., Rockwell, T.H., and Malecki, J.A. (1980). The effects of changes in driver perception on rural curve negotiation. *Ergonomics* **23**, 263.

Smith, R.S. (1976). *The Occupational Safety and Health Act: its goals and its achievements.* American Enterprise Institute for Public Policy Research, Washington, DC.

Smith, R.S. (1979). The impact of OSHA inspections on manufacturing injury rates. *J. Hum. Res.* **14**, 145.

Stapp, J.P. (1957). Human tolerance to deceleration. *Am. J. Surg.* **93**, 734.

Tittle, C.R. and Rowe, A.R. (1974). Certainty of arrest and crime rates: a further test of the deterrence hypothesis. *Soc. Forces* **52**, 455.

Viscusi, W.K. (1979). The impact of occupational safety and health regulation. *Bell J. Econ.* **10**, 117.

Watson, G.F., Zador, P.L., and Wilks, A. (1980). The repeal of helmet use laws and increased motorcyclist mortality in the United States, 1975–1978. *Am. J. Public Health* **70**, 579.

Williams, A.F. and Wells, J.A.K. (1981). The Tennessee child restraint law in its third year. *Am. J. Public health* **71**, 163.

Williams, A.F., Rich, R.F., Zador, P.L. *et al.* (1975). The legal minimum drinking age and fatal motor vehicle crashes. *J. Legal Stud.* **4**, 219.

Williams, A.F., Zador, P.L., Harris, S.A. *et al.* (1981). *The effect of raising the legal minimum drinking age on fatal crash involvement.* Insurance Institute for Highway Safety, Washington, DC.

Wright, P.H., Zador, P.L., Park, C.Y. *et al.* (1982). *Effect of pavement markers on nighttime crashes in Georgia.* Insurance Institute for Highway Safety, Washington, DC.

Zohar, D., Cohen, A., and Azar, N. (1980). Promoting increased use of ear protectors in noise through information feedback. *Hum. Factors* **22**, 69.

5 Degenerative neurological disease: Alzheimer's disease, senile dementia of the Alzheimer type, and related disorders

Robert I. Pfeffer

INTRODUCTION

Disorders of unknown cause and progressive course are traditionally labelled 'degenerative'. This chapter emphasizes Alzheimer's presenile dementia and senile dementia of the Alzheimer type (SDAT), by far the most prevalent degenerative diseases. Distinction between these two entities may be arbitrary and they are treated jointly, apart from explicit comparisons.

Senile dementia of the Alzheimer type may be the major public health problem of the next 50 years. It is the leading cause of late-life dementia, the chief indication for nursing home admission, a major cause of mortality and an unrecognized source of hospitalization for complications. The fiscal and social impact of epidemic SDAT will force major change and resource distribution in health care.

Despite the lack of adequate somatic therapy for SDAT, we share the view of the Royal College of Physicians Committee on Geriatrics (1981) that improved techniques for early diagnosis should be the leading research priority. Reversibility of conditions which mimic SDAT, family counselling, and in-home efforts to delay complications and costly institutionalization depend upon early diagnosis. Similarities of SDAT to normal ageing imply serious contamination of most past ageing research by unidentified early cases. Aetiologic investigations in SDAT which utilize late cases under medical care may be seriously biased by selective loss of cases, by lost clues to antecedents known only to cases, and by inability to conduct searching evaluation or establish rapport in late disease. If other toxic and infectious disorders are models, the aetiologic agent may be absent and antecedents and sequelae, confused in late disease. Diagnostic uncertainty may add to disability of patient and family, and increase the probability of complications. Knowledge of the interaction between SDAT and treatable systemic disease is essential to assess presently reversible components of morbidity and mortality.

Discussion of manifestations, differential diagnosis, and descriptive epidemiology focus upon limitations of current techniques and of past studies. Rigorous epidemiological techniques, wedded to clinical expertise should solve these problems. The sections on public health impact and proposals for the future should suggest the need for urgent thought and action. We briefly review possible aetiologic links of Alzheimer's disease with parkinsonism and Down's syndrome. Two less frequent degenerative disorders, progressive supranuclear palsy and Pick's disease, have sufficiently little public health impact that they are not considered further. Interested investigators should be familiar with progressive supranuclear palsy (Steele 1972) which resembles parkinsonism combined with dementia, and with Pick's disease (Cummings 1982), as a source of diagnostic confusion with Alzheimer's disease beginning before age 70 years.

ALZHEIMER'S DISEASE AND SDAT

Clinical characteristics

Subtle, complex, and *changing* manifestations distinguish Alzheimer's disease from the well-defined onset and clear endpoints to which epidemiologists are accustomed. There are no generally accepted, operational indicators of disease onset, severity, or duration. These landmarks are essential: (i) to compare studies of antecedents, symptoms, disability, and therapy in disparate samples; (ii) to develop a coherent natural history from scattered accounts of individual manifestations which may emerge at different disease stages; and (iii) to develop positive diagnostic criteria for early Alzheimer's disease. Most reports describe highly selected samples (Liston 1979) of severe or institutionalized cases, all under medical or psychiatric care. When care is first sought, disease is moderate to moderately severe; searching inquiry typically reveals symptoms of 3–5 years' duration.

Diagnosis depends upon a multidimensional pattern across time and functional spheres. Change in specific mental functions and behaviour can be interpreted only in the context of other, preserved abilities and disease duration. Late in the illness, distinguishing features become progressively more blurred (Sim 1979); most dementias end in mutism, immobility, rigidity, and unresponsiveness to the environment. Earlier, stage-specific contrasts between preserved and failing functions may form characteristic patterns. Thus, poor memory and minimal language dysfunction may be observed when spatial orientation and social behaviour are relatively normal. Depression often occurs when insight is relatively intact and cognitive disorder mild, but clears later. Severe depression associated with profound cognitive and social disability is evidence *against* the diagnosis of Alzheimer's disease. Disease stages described in our tentative synthesis below are defined on the functional capacity scale (Pfeffer *et al.* 1982).

In the very earliest stages, formal cognitive tests demonstrate minor deficit. More sensitive than the routine clinical mental status exam or measures of orientation (Pfeffer *et al.* 1981), such tests may identify many false-positives, most often among the anxious or depressed. Further clinical evaluation (Roth 1979; Sim 1979; Pfeffer *et al.* 1981) and social function assessment (Pfeffer *et al.* 1982) increase specificity. In 'questionable' cases, experienced clinicians observe vagueness about the past and recent health, minor word-finding problems, concreteness in proverb or similarity interpretation, and fatuous or irrelevant explanations for recent decline in activity level, range, or performance. In recounting their daily routine, 'mild' and 'moderate' cases provide little detail, list few activities, describe empty pursuits which fill their day (for example, 'Clean my apartment'). They rarely leave home. Routine tasks such as paying bills are an unending, absorbing struggle. In the absence of major depression, such responses strongly suggest dementia.

Memory disturbance or *inability to learn new material* is one of the earliest findings (Miller 1977; Sim 1979; Moreley *et al.* 1980). Faulty secondary memory is demonstrated on free recall of a verbal or visual memorandum in most 'questionable', almost all 'mild,' and all 'moderate' cases.

Language disorder is frequent (Rochford 1971; Miller and Hague 1975; Cummings 1982). An orderly decline postulated by Benson (1980) begins with difficulty providing exemplars of a category or words starting with a specific letter. Subtler decrease in fluency, detail, cogency, and word-finding characterize spontaneous speech in 'questionable', 'mild', and early 'moderate' cases. In 'moderate' and 'moderately severe' disease, word-finding problems are more frequent; substantive prose gives way to empty phrases. Decline in confrontation naming, substitution of incorrect, altered, or circumlocutory compound words, impaired comprehension, and loss of syntactical structure follow. Terminal patients use language only to signal bodily states or concrete needs (for example, 'Hungry', 'Toilet') and then lapse into mutism.

Subtle *visuospatial disorders* are not well studied (Sim 1979). A tendency to get lost in unfamiliar, then in previously familiar, surroundings affects many 'moderate' and most 'moderately severe' cases. They are near-universal in the hospital and nursing home patients termed mild or moderate by many other investigators. Inability to recognize friends or family comes still later and may be linked to delusions about the identity or nefarious purposes of the misidentified person.

Alertness is preserved until very late. The patient maintains eye contact when addressed, attempts to answer direct questions, and offers appropriate greetings or interjections. This alertness rapidly separates uncomplicated cases from drowsy, inattentive patients with toxic/metabolic encephalo-pathy or increased intracranial pressure. Accounts of 'apathy' invite confusion with altered consciousness or depressive withdrawal. The 'apathy' of some moderate and most moderately severe cases is better described as 'passivity'. They defer to others in conversation, initiate little, but attend to others' emotive tone and direct requests.

Behavioural disorder is often described (Sjögren 1950; Sim 1979) but denominators are unknown; characterization of specific disturbances, particularly 'psychosis', and disease stage is inadequate. Usually originating from mental hospitals, such accounts are not representative. Personality traits and social behaviour are relatively *preserved* until terminal stages. Humour and flashes of insight may be retained: one 87-year-old lady – unable to recall her state (place) of birth – offered 'state of confusion'. Most 'psychotic' traits clearly relate to progressive difficulty with cognitive integration of the environment, functional limitations, dependence upon others, and infantilization by others. In later stages, fluctuating paranoid thoughts with plausible referents ('I don't remember a snack last night, someone must be stealing my food'), transient dejection, impatience, or evanescent anger are frequent.

Continence, ambulation, primary sensation, motor abilities, and many aspects of self-care are preserved until quite late. Patterns of serial change in self-care are defined for mid-to-late disease by Ferm (1974).

Pathological changes

Brain atrophy is no longer considered diagnostic: it is not universal nor unique to Alzheimer's and correlates poorly with functional status after controlling for age. The chief microscopic features are neuronal loss, neurofibrillary tangles, and senile plaques. Density of tangles or plaques may separate normal from demented older adults (Blessed *et al.* 1968; Tomlinson *et al.* 1970; Tomlinson and Henderson 1976). Terry *et al.* (1981) report 26 and 22 per cent loss of neurons from frontal and temporal cortex; larger neurones are more severely depleted. Neurofibrillary tangles are basket-like skeins – the strands are composed of characteristic paired helical filaments (Wisniewski *et al.* 1976) – whose presence or absence has been used to assess the relevance of animal models and purity of subcellular fractions. The senile plaque consists of degenerated neuronal processes and amyloid, and undergoes a characteristic morphological evolution (Terry and Wisniewski 1970).

The pathological changes are widespread and symmetrical, but not uniform. Hippocampus and frontal, temporal, parietal, and occipital association cortex are involved; primary motor and sensory areas and anterior cingulate gyrus, are spared (Brun and Gustafson 1976; Tomlinson 1977). The distribution of change correlates with clinical manifestations. Subcortical structures and brainstem are relatively spared (Wilkinson and Davies 1978). Depletion of cholinergic neurones in nucleus basalis, which projects diffusely to cerebral cortex (Whitehouse *et al.* 1981, 1982*b*), may explain the widespread decline in choline acetyltransferase.

Normal ageing and Alzheimer's disease: similarities and differences

Is Alzheimer's disease an acceleration of the same processes involved in normal ageing, or a discrete, superimposed disease? In almost every sphere of comparison among normal older adults, younger adults, and Alzheimer cases, the changes in Alzheimer's are *qualitatively* similar to those of normal ageing, though more intense (Table 5.1). While most authorities consider normal ageing and Alzheimer's separable, specific, and systematic contrasts—especially over time—are sparse.

The normal elderly display mild impairment of learning and recall from secondary memory; similar but more profound changes occur in cases of SDAT. Despite past contrary assertions, memory for remote events declines in normal ageing (Squire 1974) and SDAT (Wilson *et al.* 1981).

Simple reaction time increases with age; speed declines further for tasks requiring significant cerebral processing (Birren *et al.* 1980; Cerella *et al.* 1980). In copying digit or word lists, normal aged adults are significantly slowed, but faster than cases (Birren and Botwinick 1951). The WAIS Digit Symbol and Smith Symbol Digit Tests also differentiate young from old normals (Smith 1973), and normal elderly from cases (Botwinick and Birren 1951; Pfeffer *et al.* 1981).

Visuospatial deficit has not been studied systematically in early SDAT. Most nominally visuospatial tasks studied in ageing are complex or have a major – often implicit – memory requirement. On a very simple test (Money *et al.* 1966) with little memory load, normal elderly volunteers were impaired; SDAT cases performed even more poorly (Pfeffer, unpublished).

The dominant frequency of the electroencephalogram slows with age (Wang and Busse 1974; Drechsler 1978) and declines further in late SDAT (Sim 1979). Latency of the late cortical-potential evoked by auditory stimuli increases very slowly with age; significant further prolongation occurs in SDAT (Goodin *et al.* 1978 *a*,*b*).

Gyral atrophy and/or ventricular enlargement are radiological indications of normal ageing (Barron *et al.* 1976). More severe atrophy is often seen in dementia (Merskey *et al.* 1980). After controlling for age, atrophy only weakly predicts mental function (Earnest *et al.* 1979); most current investigators accept the difficulty of distinguishing between normal ageing and SDAT on cerebral CT scans.

Loss of cerebral cortical neurones is a feature of 'normal' ageing (Brody 1955, 1976). More marked loss is found in SDAT (Terry *et al.* 1981). Neurofibrillary tangles and plaques are seen in both normals and cases (Tomlinson *et al.* 1968, 1970), as are granulovacuolar changes (Peress, *et al.* 1973; Matsuyama and Nakamura 1978). Ulrich (1982) observed tangles and/or plaques in one fourth of non-demented individuals dying between 55 and 64 years of age; in many, the changes were as severe as those usually associated with clinical dementia.

Loss of dendritic branches and spines from cortical neurones occurs in ageing, but is more pronounced in Alzheimer's disease (Scheibel 1978). Buell and Coleman (1979) compared shrunken dendritic trees from non-demented and senile elderly. In elderly normals, terminal segments of dendritic trees were longer and more numerous. Preservation of terminal branching may be the morphological substrate for the ability to learn which distinguishes the normal elderly from SDAT cases.

Cerebral choline acetyltransferase activity is markedly decreased in SDAT (Bowen *et al.* 1976; Davies and Maloney 1976; Perry *et al.* 1977*b*), but not depression or vascular dementia (Perry *et al.* 1977*b*). Enzyme loss correlates with plaque counts and cognitive dysfunction (Perry *et al.* 1978; Bowen *et al.* 1979). Sparing of muscarinic receptors (White *et al.* 1977; Perry *et al.* 1978; Bowen *et al.* 1979) and of synthetic enzymes for other neurotransmitters (Bowen *et al.* 1976, 1979; Davies and Maloney 1976; Perry *et al.* 1977*a*) implies loss of a specific neuronal population. Choline acetyltransferase activity is also decreased in normal ageing (McGeer and McGeer 1976; Perry *et al.* 1977*a*, *c*; Davies 1979), though

Table 5.1. *A comparison of normal ageing with senile dementia of Alzheimer type*

Sphere	Trait	'Normal ageing'	Alzheimer's and SDAT
Clinical	Decline in memory (recall, learning)	mild	marked
	Decline in remote memory	mild	marked late in disease
	Decline in performance speed for complex tasks	mild	marked relatively early
	Decline in visuospatial performance	mild	marked mild and late (early unknown)
Electrophysiological studies	Decline in dominant frequency electroencephalogram	mild	more marked, reliable only mid-late
	Increased latency of late event-related potentials	very slight	more marked
Radiology	Cerebral atrophy: sulcal widening ventricular enlargement (computerized tomography)	variable	variable, often more severe not usually diagnostic
Pharmacological	Decline in cerebral choline acetyl transferase activity	slight	marked
Neuropathological	Neuronal loss	moderate	more severe
	Alzheimer neurofibrillary tangles	less numerous	more abundant
	Senile plaques	less numerous	more abundant
	Granulovacuolar degeneration	less numerous	often more abundant; may be scant
	Loss dendritic spines	? less pronounced	? more pronounced
	Ability to form new connections	? retained	abnormal
	Neuronal loss nucleus basalis of Meynart	less marked	marked

Bartus *et al.* (1982) describe negative studies. Low choline acetyltransferase in two strains of aged mice (Gibson *et al.* 1981) suggests a more universal biological phenomenon.

In summary, two *qualitative* differences between normal ageing and SDAT are the ability to form new terminal dendritic branches in normal brain and neuronal loss from nucleus basalis in SDAT. Important *quantitative* differences include much more profound behavioural and cognitive changes and loss of choline acetyltransferase activity in SDAT. The apparent decline in SDAT incidence (Hagnell *et al.* 1981) and in prevalence of severe necropsy changes (Peress *et al.* 1973) in the tenth decade suggests two separate processes. Differential rates of change in cognitive function over time support the same view (Pfeffer *et al.* unpublished data).

Are Alzheimer's presenile dementia and SDAT the same disease?

The relation of Alzheimer's presenile dementia to SDAT has been uncertain since the original description (see reviews by McMenemy 1963; Lauter and Meyer 1968; Roth 1971; Constantinidis 1978). All characteristic features of the presenile dementia occur in SDAT (Lauter and Meyer 1968; Sim 1979). Some authors find these traits in similar proportions of presenile and senile cases (Pearce and Pearce 1979). Others find many SDAT cases lack the full Alzheimer syndrome (Lauter and Meyer 1968; Constantinidis 1978). Tangles and plaques occur in both disorders (McMenemy 1963; Roth 1971; Corsellis 1976). Sourander and Sjögren (1970) report *abundant* tangles in hippocampus, amygdala, and temporal neocortex, and involvement of the non-temporal (frontal and occipital) neocortex in a higher proportion of presenile cases.

Go *et al.* (1978) described two forms. In type B, late-onset restricted disease, changes were mainly in hippocampus. Type A patients had widespread senile plaques and neurofibrillary tangles in the neocortex as well as in the hippocampus; aphasia, apraxia, and agnosia were marked. Onset might be early or late. More extensive change in Type A cases was associated with longer survival, after controlling for onset age. Constantinidis (1978) proposed two forms of a single disease, with duration conditioned by heredity. Because he found greater disease duration among women and more female SDAT cases at autopsy than expected, Constantinidis suggested that the hereditary factor may be sex-specific in late onset cases. Other authors believe presenile cases are mainly inherited (Heston *et al.* 1981; Harris 1982) and SDAT is not.

A growing body of evidence suggests patients that die at an earlier age with Alzheimer's differ from those who die later. Whether this is related to longer survival with disease, a different tempo of disease, or some other biological factor is not yet clear. Post-mortem counts of nucleus locus coeruleus in Alzheimer's cases have a bimodal distribution (Anderson and Hubbard 1981; Bondareff *et al.* 1982). Patients with fewer locus coeruleus neurones died younger and were more severely demented in life (Bondareff *et al.* 1982). They also had a greater loss of neuronal markers (Anderson and Hubbard 1981) and of choline acetyltransferase (Anderson and Hubbard 1981; Perry *et al.* 1981). At post-mortem, choline acetyltransferase was shown to be lower in 'younger'

Alzheimer patients (Bowen *et al.* 1979; Davies 1979; Rossor *et al.* 1981). Ventricular dilatation was also more marked (Jacoby and Levy 1980) and cerebral atrophy more widespread (Hubbard and Anderson 1981) in patients dying before age 80 years.

The relation of other degenerative disorders to Alzheimer's disease

Mental change in *parkinsonism* may be related to varying admixtures of depression, drug-related confusion, and two types of dementia. The recent literature is reviewed by Boller *et al.* (1980) and Mayeux (1982). Dementia is far more common among parkinsonians than expected for age (Celesia and Wanamaker 1972; Loranger *et al.* 1972; Martin *et al.* 1973). Dementia prevalence increases in frequency with age (Marttila and Rinne 1976; Lieberman *et al.* 1979) and its association with severity of parkinsonism persists after controlling for age (Marttila and Rinne 1976). In most affected individuals, the dementia is clinically indistinguishable from SDAT. Characteristic Alzheimer changes are more frequent at autopsy in parkinsonians than in controls (Hakim and Mathieson 1979). Neuronal loss from nucleus basalis is also reported in the dementia of parkinsonism (Whitehouse *et al.* 1982*a*). Some parkinsonians display a separate cognitive disorder termed 'subcortical dementia' (Mayeux 1982).

Almost all individuals with *Down's syndrome* who live to age 35–40 years develop clinical and/or pathological (Haberland 1969) stigmata of Alzheimer's disease. The topography of pathological change (Ball and Nuttall 1981), cholinergic (Yates *et al.* 1980), and catechol deficiency (Mann *et al.* 1980) are similar to those in Alzheimer's, suggesting a biochemical link. The risk of Alzheimer's in relatives of Down's probands is also increased.

DIFFERENTIAL DIAGNOSIS OF ALZHEIMER'S DISEASE

Differential diagnosis of dementing illness: general concerns

More than 50 disorders produce dementia in adults (Haase 1977; Cummings *et al.* 1980). Alzheimer's disease is the leading cause of mid- and late-life dementia, 40–60 per cent of most series (Table 5.2). Cerebrovascular diseases are the second most common cause. These two, with drug toxicity, psychiatric, endocrine, nutritional, or metabolic disorders account for almost 70 per cent of hospital admissions for dementia. Table 5.2 pools diagnoses from three US veterans hospitals and three Commonwealth referral centres. Hospital series unavoidably reflect unmeasured biases: socio-economic and demographic traits of the catchment population, pre-referral screening admission criteria, and specific interests of reporting units. In our experience, alcoholism, hydrocephalus, tumour, and infection are readily separated by careful outpatient evaluation. Stroke and SDAT, singly and with chronic systemic illness, are more important in older community samples. Neoplasia, subdural haematoma, and other space-occupying lesions may also mimic Alzheimer's disease. Mental disorder in parkinsonism is discussed above.

Table 5.2. *Discharge diagnoses of 584 persons hospitalized for mid-to-late-life dementia**

Potential for amelioration of dementia	Diagnosis	Number (per cent)	Per cent by group
Minimal	Alzheimer's or primary	258 (44.2)	49.3
	Huntington's (14), Parkinson's (7), Creuzfeldt–Jakob (6), Misc. (3)	30 (5.1)	
Palliation only	Gliomata; multiple metastases	16 (2.7)	2.7
Moderate for stabilization or	Multi-infarct	74 (12.7)	23.1
improvement	Alcohol-related	48 (8.2)	
	Seq. trauma (8), infection (2), hypoxia (2), misc. (1)	13 (2.2)	
Potentially reversible, organic	Occult hydrocephalus	24 (4.1)	13.9
	Space-occupying lesions (incl. 6 subdural hematomas)	16 (2.7)	
	Metabolic, endocrine, nutritional†	14 (2.4)	
	Drug toxicity	13 (2.2)	
	Infection: lues (4), fungal meningitis (2)	6 (1.0)	
	Misc. and unknown, incl. seizures	8 (1.4)	
Not demented or uncertain		17 (2.9)	2.9
Functional psychiatric disorders		47 (8.1)	8.1
	Total	584 (99.7)	100.0

*Source of data: Marsden and Harrison (1972); Freemon (1976); Victoratos *et al.* (1977); Hutton (1980); Smith and Kiloh (1981) (cases 45 + years); Delaney (1982).
†including thyroid disease (5), hepatic failure (2), pernicious anaemia (1).

Depression in dementia and its differential diagnosis

Distinction of depression from dementia (Post 1975; Finlayson and Martin 1982) can be very difficult. Withdrawal, inactivity, and poor memory may characterize both. Energy loss due to systemic disease and frequent personal losses compound confusion in the elderly (Raskin 1979). Since depressed individuals may perform as badly as the demented on traditional psychological tests, sole reliance on scores may lead to serious diagnostic error (Sim 1979).

Depression without dementia may be diagnosed by an explicit search for past and current depression, and by adequate performance when a clinical examiner is supportive and persistent or when neuropsychological tests which require only brief attention are used. In addition, adequate history from a reliable alternate informant and patient co-operation are essential. Most depressions, including most cases misdiagnosed as dementia, are identifiable by these techniques. Far less frequently, depression with profound impairment of cognitive function – 'depressive pseudo-dementia' – may be indistinguishable initially from organic brain disease (Hemsi *et al.* 1968; Post 1975). Pseudodementia is diagnosed by history, by lack of deterioration over time, and by improvement with therapy (Post 1975; Sternberg and Jarvik 1976). *Depression* may be *misdiagnosed in demented patients*. Apathy and psychomotor retardation or restlessness are frequent with frontal lobe involvement (Hecaen and Albert 1975; Blumer and Benson 1975). In mid to late SDAT, many patients display evanescent but recurrent dysphoria, brooding, irritability, or despair which have an odd 'shallow' quality. *Depression and dementia* may coexist. Dysphoria affects 12–15 per cent of community elderly; major depressions, 2.5–3.7 per cent (Comstock and Helsing 1976; Blazer and Williams 1980; Gurland *et al.* 1980). Concomitant depression and dementia may be a chance event (Post 1972) or a reaction to failing capacities which subsides as the dementia progresses (Kahn *et al.* 1975). Treatment of depression alone results in functional improvement (Brody *et al.* 1971, 1974; Kahn and Miller 1978; Wells 1982).

Strengths and limitations of current diagnostic techniques

No single test is diagnostic of Alzheimer's disease. Multiple, complementary techniques will *exclude* normals and most other causes of altered mental function. However, we still lack *positive* criteria based upon firm knowledge of stage-specific deficits and disease course.

Lacking examination antedating onset, the *clinical history* of disease onset and progression provides the sole *longitudinal* dimension and much of the diagnostic specificity. It is the single most important diagnostic tool because primary amentia, confusional states, pseudodementias, and most dementias differ in temporal evolution. Inadequate histories fail to distinguish between progressive and chronic stable disability. Because the patient may lack insight, history must be obtained from alternate informants who know him or her well. Informant reliability depends upon their own cognitive integrity, their willingness to co-operate, and their ability to recognize, accept, and report a change. They may fail to notice gradual change, accept it as normal for ageing, attribute it to an irrelevant problem, or to some event used as a false anchor-point in time, such as a surgical procedure. Difficulty in obtaining and interpreting history is the most common source of diagnostic error. Medical records may aid in reconstructing the chronology of *late* disease. They are of little value early: the patient does not seek care for dementia, so records focus on other complaints.

In expert hands, the *clinical mental status examination* establishes the presence of mental dysfunction. The *aetiology* must, however, be inferred from the history, physical examination, and laboratory data. During the interview, the examiner may detect rare slips and vagueness and assess patient initiative and effort. These observations increase sensitivity but are limited in reproducibility and objectivity.

Attempts to quantify elements of the clinical mental status in brief questionnaires (Kahn *et al.* 1960; Folstein and Folstein 1975; Pfeiffer 1975; Jacobs *et al.* 1977) may increase reliability, but are insensitive (Pfeffer *et al.* 1981; Pfeffer 1983). Like the clinical exam, these instruments used alone will not identify the cause of cognitive dysfunction.

Psychological measures are more sensitive and reproducible than clinical testing. New approaches are described by Miller (1977), Fuld (1978), Albert and Kaplan (1980), Cohen and Eisdorfer (1979), and Gainotti *et al.* (1980). Tests should be selected for relevance to the study population. The Mental Function Index (Pfeffer *et al.* 1981) is useful in community, clinic, and hospital settings. The Stockton Scale (Gilleard and Pattie 1977), Blessed Scale (Blessed *et al.* 1968) or Fuld's shortened version of the latter scale (Fuld *et al.* 1982) might be more suitable in nursing homes or day-care centres.

Assessment of *social function* by alternate informants confirms occurrence and time course of significant change. Reports are vulnerable to the same problems described under history above. The range of activities must also be appropriate to the sample. Activities of Daily Living scales are useful in institutions (Donaldson *et al.* 1973). Other scales (Lawton and Brody 1969; Pfeffer *et al.* 1982) are directed to retired community samples. Most available tests do not separate dementia from non-cognitive sources of disability such as arthritis. Save for the Functional Activities Questionnaire (Pfeffer *et al.* 1982), most do not allow for a task's never having been undertaken.

The past medical history, 'somatic' neurological examination and widely available, safe *laboratory studies* are relatively economical, may be standardized, and provide important evidence against common treatable disorders which may cause dementia or complicate Alzheimer's disease. Wells (1977) reviews the overall rationale for laboratory evaluation. Vitamin B$_{12}$ levels are mandatory because neurological sequelae of deficiency may long precede haematologic changes (Roos 1978). Frequent false-negative serological tests justify use of the *T. pallidum* microhaemagglutination test to exclude neurosyphilis (*British Medical Journal* 1978). More than half the reversible conditions in Delaney's (1982) series were diagnosed by CT scan. No test result is absolutely diagnostic. Apart from laboratory error, an abnormality may not be symptomatic or may not be the cause of dementia.

Ethical concerns (Roth 1979) will limit availability of cerebral *biopsy* material in SDAT. Biopsy has 2 per cent mortality and 13 per cent morbidity (Kaufman and Catalano

1979); results are negative or non-diagnostic in 40–48 per cent (Smith *et al.* 1966; Torack 1979; Kaufman and Catalano 1979). Even at autopsy, 10 per cent of apparently typical cases (Tomlinson *et al.* 1970, Sims *et al.* 1980) may not show characteristic changes.

Diagnostic validity

Reported diagnoses have been made with differing purpose and skill, and variable laboratory and neuropsychological confirmation. Differing proportions of normals and non-Alzheimer dementias alter the prior probability of correct diagnosis, as does disease stage. Few studies were explicitly designed for validation; most reported results are a by-product of routine care or laboratory research.

Pathological examination is considered the ultimate criterion of validity, but tangles and senile plaques occur in presumably normal individuals. Moreover, neurofibrillary tangles are found in many conditions apparently unrelated to Alzheimer's (Corsellis 1976; Wisniewski *et al.* 1979). Neuronal loss from nucleus basalis occurs in Pick's disease (Hilt *et al.* 1982) and dementia pugilistica (Uhl *et al.* 1982).

Techniques utilized to validate initial diagnoses have included the following:

1. *Hospitalization, laboratory study,* and *observation* confirm only 40–50 per cent of *routine* admission diagnoses (Table 5.2).

2. *Independent* neurological *review* confirmed most diagnoses of a specially trained nurse collecting data in a structured manner (Pfeffer *et al.* 1981).

3. Blessed Mental Test scores correlate highly with *plaque counts* ($r=0.60$; Tomlinson and Henderson 1976) and choline acetyltransferase activity at autopsy ($r=0.81$; Perry *et al.* 1978).

4. In two *longitudinal clinical* studies (Nott and Fleminger 1975; Ron *et al.* 1979) 30–50 per cent of persons with psychiatric discharge diagnoses of presenile dementia failed to deteriorate over time. Our community experience with three years' mean follow-up showed less than a 10 per cent error rate (Pfeffer, unpublished data).

5. Considering only *intrusions* in a verbal recall task, Fuld *et al.* (1982) correctly identified 19 of 21 *pathologically* confirmed Alzheimer cases and 11 of 17 non-Alzheimer cases.

6. The modified ischaemic score of Rosen *et al.* (1980) correctly separated all cases with SDAT alone from those with

Table 5.3. *Pathological confirmation of vascular and Alzheimer's dementia diagnoses**

| | Clinical diagnosis | | | |
| | Alzheimer's dementia | | Vascular dementia | |
Assumptions	Sensitivity	Specificity	Sensitivity	Specificity
1. None	0.69	0.78	0.57	0.82
2. Unclassifiable cases omitted†	0.72	0.78	0.60	0.80
3. Clinical dx correct: combined disease and no dementia	0.79	0.99	0.77	0.94
4. Clinical dx correct as in (3); unclassifiable cases omitted	0.82	0.93	0.80	0.96

*Data from Todorov *et al.* (1975). Clinical diagnoses of Alzheimer's senile dementia, Alzheimer's presenile dementia, and Alzheimerized senile dementia were pooled; histological subcategories were also pooled.

†No diagnosis could be made clinically in 41 cases, pathologically in 75 cases, or by either technique in seven cases.

autopsy evidence of multi-infarct dementia, occurring singly or combined with SDAT.

7. Gustafson and Nilsson's (1982) complex clinical criteria separated pathologically diagnosed cases of Alzheimer's, Pick's, and multi-infarct dementia.

Todorov *et al.* (1975) correlated clinical and pathological diagnoses in 776 individuals with only Alzheimer's disease, only vascular dementia, combined vascular and Alzheimer dementia, no dementia, or undefinable status. Their data from three Alzheimer subcategories have been combined. Using the pathological diagnosis as the criterion, Table 5.3 illustrates the sensitivity and specificity of clinical diagnoses. The effect of three modest assumptions is also indicated: (i) individuals considered clinically or anatomically unclassifiable are not *mis*diagnosed; (ii) the clinician may be as correct in designating the dominant disorder in combined Alzheimer-vascular cases (no quantitative pathological criteria are given); and (iii) the clinician may correctly recognize the absence of dementia. Accepting all three assumptions, the sensitivity and specificity of routine clinical diagnosis in one *specialist* unit are 80–90 per cent. Normals and SDAT cases were separated with similar facility in Newcastle (Tomlinson 1977).

EPIDEMIOLOGY OF ALZHEIMER'S DISEASE

Prevalence and incidence; sex and age

Incidence and prevalence estimates are dramatically affected by the intensity of case-finding and by diagnostic criteria. We believe that most 'mild' cases described in published series have disease of two to five years' duration and moderate to moderately severe disability. Our own preliminary estimate of 15 per cent SDAT prevalence (Pfeffer, unpublished data) in community elderly aged 65 years and over, including earlier cases is some 2.4 times the highest and 23.8 times the lowest prevalence estimates presented below. If these estimates are correct, comparison of descriptive studies is impossible without consensus among investigators on diagnostic criteria and definitions of disease severity and duration. Moreover, analytical studies may be seriously compromised by misclassi-

fication of early cases as normal and/or selection bias due to death or moveout of late cases.

Only data for SDAT are presented below. Because of its relative rarity, reliable data on presenile Alzheimer's disease are difficult to obtain. The cumulative conditional probability of developing either Alzheimer's or cerebrovascular dementia before age 65 years is less than 1 per cent (Hagnell *et al.* 1981).

The older literature suggests that women are more frequently affected by SDAT than men, even when age- and sex-specific rates are considered (Mortimer 1980; Brody 1982). It remains unclear whether the sex difference is related to disease susceptibility or an artefact of ascertainment. Possible causes of bias might include (i) greater survival of women after developing the disease and (ii) differential care-seeking behaviour. More men than women in the relevant age groups are married (90 per cent of men and 40 per cent of women in one retirement community – Pfeffer, unpublished data). Women accustomed by traditional values to caring for their husbands might be more accepting of disability in their spouses and less willing to seek care for them until late in the disease.

The following suggest that the sex difference may be an artefact. Sex-specific prevalence rates from community-based studies do not differ significantly; there is considerable overlap in the 95 per cent confidence intervals we calculated about published rates (Table 5.4). Series with higher prevalence rates which include milder cases show less disparity (Bergman *et al.* 1971; Kay *et al.* 1964*a*, *b*; Broe *et al.* 1976). Sex-specific incidence rates (Table 5.5) are more similar in Helgason's (1977) series, which contained mild cases than in Åkesson's (1969) which counted only persons with constant temporal and spatial disorientation.

Much more direct evidence comes from the Lundby cohort of 3563 persons followed carefully over 25 years (Hagnell *et al.* 1982; detailed data kindly shared by Professor Hagnell). The cumulative conditional probability of developing senile dementia was similar among men and women at all levels of severity (Table 5.6).

Hagnell *et al.* (1982) observed a secular decline in SDAT incidence. Through the seventh, eighth, and ninth decades, the age-standardized and sex-specific incidence and the cumulative conditional probability of developing SDAT

Table 5.4. *Prevalence of SDAT by sex and severity in community-based studies*

Reference	Location	Ages, Years	Ascertain-ment*	Severity	'Mild' cases only† M	F	All cases M	F
Åkesson (1969)	Sweden	65 +	2°	Severe only			6.3 (3.7–10.7)‡	8.5 (5.4–13.3)
Bergmann *et al.* (1971)	England	65 +	1°	Mild and severe			61.4 (39.2–95.0)	62.1 (43.6–87.8)
Bollerup (1975)	Denmark	70 only	1°	Severe only			26.3 (13.4–51.1)	0
Broe *et al.* (1976)	Scotland	65 +	1°	Mild and severe			50.3 (45.7–115.9)	63.3 (44.9–88.4)
Kay *et al.* (1964*a*, *b*)	England	65 +	1°	Mild and severe	26.1 (8.9–73.1)	30.9 (14.3–65.8)	26.1 (8.9–73.9)	51.5 (28.2–92.2)

Estimated prevalence: cases per thousand subjects, by sex

* Åkesson interviewed only possible cases identified from various agencies; other interviewed cases and non-cases.

† Frequency of mild cases provided only by Kay *et al.*

‡ Number in parentheses represent appoximate 95 per cent confidence intervals calculated from published data.

Table 5.5. *Estimated incidence of Alzheimer type senile dementia per 100 000 subjects per year*

Author	Ages	Cases	Subjects	Rates by sex M	F	Both sexes
Åkesson (1969)	60+	16	4167	81 (20–328)†	174 (65–464)	128 (56–292)*
Bergmann *et al.* (1971)	65+	17	676			838 (376–1856)*
Helgason (1977)	65+	101	33 469	314 (237–416)	319 (247–412)	302 (248–367)

*Estimated from three-year studies.
†Numbers in parentheses represent approximate 95 per cent confidence intervals.

Table 5.6. *Cumulative conditional probability of developing senile dementia before age 90 (incident cases, 1957–72)**

	Disease severity		
Sex	Severe only	Severe and moderate	Severe, moderate, and mild
Men	0.135 (10)†	0.215 (17)	0.235 (19)
Women	0.165 (15)	0.221 (20)	0.275 (24)

*Hagnell *et al.* (1982); detailed data provided by Professor Hagnell.
†Figures in parentheses represent number of cases from which rates were derived.

Table 5.7. *Effect of age on incidence of Alzheimer's disease: conditional probability of disease per 100 person-years at risk**

Age (years)	Probability	No. of cases
60–64	0.428	4
65–69	0.148	1
70–74	0.580	4
75–79	2.033	10
80–95	3.248	8

*Data from Sluss *et al.* (1979).

declined between the intervals 1947–57 and 1957–72 (for example, the cumulative probability of disease for women before 90 years fell from 0.400 to 0.275). A similar trend across several grades of SDAT severity and in the incidence of arteriosclerotic dementia suggests these findings are not artefactual, but the explanation is not immediately apparent.

Increasing age is intimately related to the incidence of Alzheimer's disease (Hagnell *et al.* 1982). The incidence is quite low below age 60–65 years and rises rapidly at 75 years (Sluss *et al.* 1979; Table 5.7). Mild histological stigmata increase in prevalence with age, to become near-universal even after exclusion of clinical cases (Matsuyama *et al.* 1966; Matsuyama and Nakamura 1978). From the fourth to the ninth decade, an increasing proportion of brains display a density of neurofibrillary change usually associated with clinical disease. From the ninth to the tenth decade, however, the proportion of individuals with abundant hippocampal neurofibrillary tangles declines (Peress *et al.* 1973; Matsuyama and Nakamura 1978). Clinical incidence of SDAT also declines slightly in the tenth decade (Hagnell *et al.* 1981, 1982). It is uncertain whether these observations imply

that SDAT is distinct from normal ageing, that the non-agenerians studied are exceptional, or that samples are too small for reliable estimates.

Mortality

It has long been known that SDAT is associated with an increase in age-specific mortality (Table 5.8). Even 'mild organic signs' (Kay 1962; Nielsen *et al.* 1977) are associated with greatly diminished survival. Of 18 persons with a clinical diagnosis of Alzheimer's presenile dementia, 14 had died within four years, two survivors deteriorated, and two were misdiagnosed originally (Lijtmaer *et al.* 1976). Severe cognitive impairment is a clear predictor of death within one year (Kaszniak *et al.* 1978).

Using very conservative assumptions which neglect mild and moderate disease, Katzman (1976) concluded that SDAT is the fourth or fifth most common cause of death in later life, though not so identified even in the extended US list of mortality causes. Reported causes of death among SDAT cases are quite similar to those in adults of similar age and sex (Kay 1962; Nielsen *et al.* 1977), save for a moderate excess in deaths attributed to pneumonia (Nielsen *et al.* 1977). Substantial increases in SDAT prevalence and a doubling of disease duration have been ascribed to better treatment of pneumonia (Gruenberg 1977).

Available studies rarely include sufficient data on referent populations to permit any standardized comparisons of mortality. Detailed data on the co-prevalence of systemic disease are not available, yet systemic disease and its treatment will alter both the observed mortality and the apparent severity of SDAT.

Duration of disease may be related to disease severity or to some combination of age-specific forces of mortality and the complications peculiar to the neurologically disabled, such as infection, inanition, and pulmonary embolism. In considering the relation between Alzheimer's presenile dementia and SDAT above, we considered preliminary evidence that younger patients have one or more indicators of more extensive disease at death, including more severe dementia, more marked decline in choline acetyltransferase activity, greater ventricular dilatation and more widespread cerebral atrophy. The presence of more severe neocortical involvement by neurofibrillary tangles was related to length of disease, but not to age of onset (Go *et al.* 1978). Whether these findings imply that two separable diseases are now classified under the Alzheimer rubric or that some, especially younger, patients survive longer to develop more extensive

Table 5.8. *Effect of selected disorders upon age-adjusted survival*

Reference	Original sample	Maximum follow-up (years)	Survival measure	Relative survival by diagnosis			
				SDAT	Mild dementia or organic signs	Arteriosclerotic dementia	Functional psychosis
Kay (1962)	Psychiatric hospital admissions	22	Years rel. to Stockholm population	0.23	0.77	0.39	0.88
Nielsen *et al.* (1977)	Community referrals	15	Years rel. to mentally normal	0.34	0.70	0.63	1.07
Roth (1955)	Psychiatric hospital admissions	0.5	No. rel. to total sample	0.64	–*	0.98	1.11
Roth (1955)	Psychiatric hospital admissions	2	No. rel. to total sample	0.45	–	0.50	1.18

*Data not provided.

changes is uncertain. Such an analysis requires data on duration of disease, coexistent systemic disease affecting mortality, similarly vigorous efforts at prolonging life in all patients and uniform clinical, neuropsychological, biochemical, and pathological criteria.

Race and geography

The data above derive from studies of white Northern Europeans. Epidemiological data are scant for most other races and regions. Both clinical (Kaneko 1975) and pathological studies (Matsuyama and Nakamura 1978) document Alzheimer's disease in Japan. Lin (1953) found very low (54/1000) SDAT prevalence in Taiwan, but relied on secondary reports in a culture with a high tolerance for frailties of the elderly. Cole (1977) confirmed the occurrence of Alzheimer's disease in autopsy studies of African blacks; prevalence and incidence are unknown. Katzman and Terry (1982; personal communication) have documented SDAT clinically and pathologically in American blacks. Age-specific prevalence in blacks and whites may be similar in a southern US community (Schoenberg 1982; personal communication).

Social factors

The role of stress, social factors, and premorbid personality in unmasking disease is reviewed by Gurland (1981). As he indicates, validity of diagnoses based on psychological testing may be influenced by educational and cultural factors. We agree with Miller (1977), Levy and Rowitz (1973), and Jarvik (1980) that socio-economic variables affect institutionalization in, but not susceptibility to, SDAT.

PATHOGENESIS OF ALZHEIMER'S DISEASE: THEORIES OF AETIOLOGY

Immunological function

Investigators have sought evidence for immune reaction to an external agent, autoimmune processes, and altered susceptibility to infection. No consistent change in serum immunoglobulins (Miller *et al.* 1981) is noted. T-lymphocytes are reduced in number (Tavolato and Argentiero 1980). Response to mitogens and delayed sensitivity are normal; suppressor activity is exaggerated (Miller *et al.* 1981). Nandy (1981) proposes brain-reactive antibodies as a cause of cerebral damage. Similar frequency of neuronal staining by antibody in Alzheimer cases and controls, and defects in older methods render this hypothesis less attractive (Watts *et al.* 1981).

Because the senile plaque contains amyloid and amyloid derives from immunoglobulins in *extra*cerebral disorders (Glenner 1981) many investigators implicate immune processes in plaque formation. Immunoglobulin has been demonstrated in plaques and cerebral amyloid angiopathy (Ishii *et al.* 1975; Ishii and Haga 1976). The relation of amyloid to disease remains unclear but has been reviewed by Glenner (1981) and co-workers (1981).

Heredity

We believe most SDAT and Alzheimer cases are sporadic. Rare, but dramatic pedigrees show autosomal dominant inheritance of presenile disease. Some investigators believe most early onset cases are hereditary (Harris 1982), but the reported frequency of multiple-case families is from 1–10 (Sim 1979; Pearce and Pearce 1979) to 40 per cent (Heston *et al.* 1981).

In Kallman's large twin series, 'senile psychosis' affected both index twin and 43 per cent of monozygous co-twins, 8 per cent of dizygous co-twins, 7 per cent of sibs, and 3 per cent of parents. The observed differences may be an artefact of more similar life-spans in monozygous co-twins (Slater and Cowie 1971). In single family studies, one pair of concordant identical twins and two discordant pairs have been reported (Table 5.9A).

Table 5.9B summarizes pedigrees with more than one affected member. These reports demonstrate familial aggregation in some *early* onset cases of Alzheimer's disease. The proportion of individuals affected, the involvement of both sexes and of consecutive generations are consistent with dominant inheritance in these families (Cook *et al.* 1979).

Increased frequency of Alzheimer's *presenile* dementia among first-degree relatives of presenile cases was consistent with simple polygenic inheritance (Whalley *et al.* 1982).

Table 5.9. Selected studies of Alzheimer heredity

A. Studies of presumably identical twins

Reference	Age onset	Histologically documented Alzheimer disease	Evidence uniovularity	Unaffected twin	Other family history
Davidson and Robertson (1955)	50	Index case only	Visual similarity	Alive and well at 73	Negative, two prior generations
Hunter et al. (1972)	50	Index case only	Finger prints, blood groups, biochemical markers	Normal psychol. tests age 64, 65.8 died 66	Adopted as infants
Sharman et al. (1979)	34	Both twins, mother 'atrophy', no histological exam	Visual similarity	Not applicable	Mother died of dementia age 39; sister unaffected

B. Family pedigree studies

Reference	Age onset	Consanguinity	Affected in proband's generation*	Sex of cases most affected generation	Generations affected/ at risk	Affected first degree reln. of mother
Lowenberg and Waggoner (1934)	31–35	Index case	4/5	1M/3F	2/2	0/4
Wheelan (1959)	43–48	2 probands	5/10	1M/4F	2/2	0/7
Feldman et al. (1963)	31–45	4 cases	7/27	7M/0F	4/4	5/8
Heston et al. (1966)	22–52	4 cases (incl. proband + one 1° rel.)	3/3	2M/1F	4/4	6/8
Landy and Bain (1970)	38–52	3 cases	3/6	2M/1F	3/3	4/8
Beighton and Lindenberg (1971)	50–54	3 cases	None at age of risk	2M/2F	2/2	No data
Cook et al. (1979) family R	40–47	Index case	19/36	8M/6F	4/4	No data
family E-W	49–58	Index case	10/16	4M/2F	2/3	No data
family K	43–51	Index case	4/7	2M/1F	3/4	No data

*For Cook et al., proportion is number affected divided by number at 50 per cent risk, assuming autosomal dominant transmission.

Heston et al. (1981) confirmed the high risk of Alzheimer's disease in first-degree relatives of probands whose disease began before age 70 years; the risk in a sibling of an early onset case who also had an affected parent approached 50 per cent.

The major evidence for SDAT inheritance is a study of spouses and relatives of index cases from two Stockholm mental hospitals (Larson et al. 1963). The condition occurred more often among first-order relatives than spouses or the general population. Methodological problems cast serious doubt upon the authors' conclusion that SDAT is inherited as an autosomal dominant trait:

1. The frequency in blood relatives was ascertained by intensive search and included many cases never hospitalized. The general population rate used for comparison was derived from mental hospital admissions for SDAT. Because many SDAT cases were *not* admitted and these were counted only in the family series, a major bias in the observed direction could be predicted.

2. Intensive field search for cases among unrelated individuals was conducted only among spouses of married probands. Because 77 per cent of probands were single, widowed, or divorced, and because not all spouses were contacted, the low rates among spouses may have resulted from a lack of information.

Cytogenetic studies in Alzheimer's disease are well summarized by White et al. (1981). Aneuploidy has been reported in familial and sporadic presenile cases by Ward et al. (1979)

but many investigators have been unable to confirm their observations.

Human HLA data are of interest not only as genetic markers, but also because haplotype may govern susceptibility to infection in animals. Two groups report no difference in HLA antigen frequency among SDAT cases and old controls (Sulkava et al. 1980; Wilcox et al. 1980). In other studies the B7 antigen occurred with increased frequency among SDAT cases (Cohen et al. 1979) and a combined group of early and late onset cases (Walford and Hodge 1980). Specific haplotypes do not segregate with dementia in multiple-case families of late (Henschke et al. 1978; Walford and Hodge 1980) or early onset (Goudsmit et al. 1981). Cohen et al. (1981) report a decrease in 'selective attention' among a subgroup of their SDAT cases who possess the HLA B7 antigen. This is the first evidence for a clinically identifiable subgroup with a biological marker.

Slow atypical viruses

No slow or conventional virus has been isolated from sporadic Alzheimer's cases. *Spongiform* encephalopathy has been transmitted to primates from two familial Alzheimer cases (Goudsmit et al. 1980). One Creutzfeldt–Jakob case is described in each of two Alzheimer pedigrees (Cook et al. 1979; Masters et al. 1979). Isolation of a filterable agent by DeBoni and Crapper (1978) has not been replicated. Interested readers are referred to reviews of 'virology' by Gibbs and Gajdusek (1978), clinical and epidemiological data

Table 5.10. *Similarities and differences in three human and one experimental condition: relation to aluminium*

Feature	Condition			
	Dialysis dementia	Alzheimer's disease	Normal ageing*	Experimental encephalopathy caused by aluminium
Impaired mentation	Yes	Yes	Minimal or prone	Yes
Neurofibrillary tangles	Yes ‡	Yes	Yes, few	Yes ‡
Paired helical filaments	Unknown	Yes	No data	*No* †
Whole brain aluminium	High	High–normal (*regional differences*)	No data	High
Aluminium, brain nuclei	*Low*	High	High	High
Aluminium, brain nuclear heterochromatin	*Low*	*High*	*High*	High
Heterochromatin, per cent	Normal	*High*	*High*	Normal

*Aged, non-demented human beings with moderate numbers of neurofibrillary tangles at necropsy.

†Differences most likely to be important are shown in italics.

‡Neurofibrillary tangles are reported in dialysis dementia by Saboraud *et al.* (1978) and in experimental encephalopathy by Crapper *et al.* (1973*a*).

by Brown (1980), Brown *et al.* (1979*a, b*) and Masters *et al.* (1979), and recent reports from Prusiner *et al.* (1982*a, b*). Spongiform encephalopathies may be a model for the pathogenesis of Alzheimer's disease. New data make the analogy less strained than it might have seemed a decade ago.

The natural reservoir of spongiform encephalopathy is most probably sheep and goat scrapie. Two human disorders are known: Kuru and Creutzfeldt–Jakob disease. Differences in progression rate, clinical and pathological features of the human disorders, and narrow host specificity have been major obstacles to any link between the spongiform encephalopathies and Alzheimer's. Variation in the clinical picture of the human diseases and pleomorphism in the laboratory disorders are now being discovered. The incubation period and, possibly, duration (Dickinson *et al.* 1979) of experimental disease depend upon inoculum size (Manuelides and Manuelides 1980; Prusiner *et al.* 1982*a*), recipient species or strain (Gibbs *et al.* 1980), and route of inoculation. The extent and distribution of pathological change also differs with recipient, agent strain, and route of inoculation (Outram *et al.* 1973; Bruce and Fraser 1975). The mouse scrapie agent elicits amyloid plaques with degenerated neurites (Wisniewski *et al.* 1981), though paired helical filaments are lacking.

If spongiform encephalopathies are a model for Alzheimer's, proof of exposure will be difficult to obtain. The incubation period of Creutzfeldt–Jakob disease may be up to 30 years (Masters *et al.* 1979); that of Kuru, more than 20 (Prusiner *et al.* 1982*a*). The agents may be so widespread and difficult to eradicate among animals that *near-universal* human disease would be predicted if all humans were susceptible and efficient transmission probable. Limited genetic susceptibility and inefficient transmission by small doses and the oral route might account for *infection* of only some individuals; moreover, the incubation period may exceed the host's life-span. If the above speculations are correct, the lack of simple methods for screening meat and eliminating the agent will pose formidable public health problems.

Aluminium

Table 5.10 contrasts normal ageing and three conditions in whose pathogenesis aluminium has been implicated: dialysis dementia, Alzheimer's disease, and an experimental encephalopathy produced by intracranial injection of aluminium salts. All are very probably quite different and unrelated; their common features confuse the casual reader. Altered mentation, shown in cats by impairment on conditioned avoidance tasks (Crapper *et al.* 1973*a*), and neurofibrillary tangles are features of all. The paired helical filaments characteristic of Alzheimer's do not occur in experimental aluminium encephalopathy (Wisniewski and Terry 1970). Whole brain aluminium is elevated in dialysis dementia (Arieff *et al.* 1979) and experimental encephalopathy. In Alzheimer's, Crapper *et al.* (1973*a*) and Trapp *et al.* (1978) report elevated brain aluminium; McDermott *et al.* (1977) found normal levels. Crapper *et al.* (1979, 1980) report distinct differences of brain nuclear aluminium, brain nuclear heterochromatin aluminium and proportion of brain nuclear heterochromatin among these conditions.

Three observations suggest aluminium may play a specific role in the development of Alzheimer's disease or may be a marker of the disorder. In both elderly normals and SDAT cases, X-ray spectrometry identifies aluminium in neurones which contain neurofibrillary tangles, but not in adjacent, normal neurones (Perl and Brody 1980). The aluminium concentration in nuclei and nuclear heterochromatin from brains with moderate numbers of neurofibrillary tangles is intermediate between high levels in SDAT cases and control levels (Crapper *et al.* 1980). Finally, cerebral cortical aluminium content shows regional variation and is higher in brain regions more affected by tangles than elsewhere (Crapper *et al.* 1973*a,b*; Crapper *et al.* 1976).

IMPLICATIONS OF ALZHEIMER'S DISEASE FOR PUBLIC HEALTH AND SOCIAL POLICY

The magnitude of the problem: quantitative dimensions

The number and the proportion of persons over 65 years in the US with SDAT is rising rapidly (Table 5.11). More importantly, the proportion of elderly over age 80 years will increase by 21 per cent between 1980 and 2000 (US Bureau of the Census 1976). Similar projections apply to most developed

Table 5.11. *The elderly in America: present and projected population in millions* *

Year	Assumptions about mortality	Age (years) 65–74	75 and older
1980	None	15.4	9.1
2000	Current rates	17.1	13.5
2000	1% decline/year	16.1	14.8
2030	Current rates	24.7	15.8

*Data source (McFarland 1978), values for ages 65–74 years obtained by subtraction.

nations. Given 5–15 per cent SDAT prevalence, two to six million Americans may be affected in 2030; the higher estimate is more probable. Any decrease in case-fatality rates will be a mixed blessing: dementia prevalence in Lundby virtually doubled between 1947 and 1957 (Gruenberg 1977).

Assuming no growth in inflation, personal health care expenditures for US elderly will rise from 34.9 billion dollars in 1976 to 77.6 billion dollars in 2030 (Pegels 1980). In 1977, 44 per cent of these funds went to hospitals, 17 per cent to physicians, and 39 per cent to all other needs including nursing homes. Given four million cases at $1800 monthly, nursing home costs in 2030 for SDAT alone will be $86.4 billion or 111 per cent of funds projected for all health needs. Even continued institutionalization of the most severely disabled will cause grave dislocations in health care and the economy or both, if no alternatives are available.

Utilization of medical resources by the demented elderly is staggering, yet most needs are *now* ill met. Of Roth's (1955) cases, 73 per cent of survivors were still in hospital at six months; 57 per cent, at two years. Geriatric home admission was 5.5 times as frequent among the demented (Kay *et al.* 1970). In Newcastle, demented individuals required 25 per cent of mental hospital and 46 per cent of geriatric ward admissions, 34 per cent of hospital bed-days and more than half the time in sheltered housing or nursing homes. Over half of nursing home residents suffer from senile dementia (Brody 1981). Half to three-quarters of people in sheltered housing (Clark *et al.* 1981; Ernst *et al.* 1977) and a similar proportion in low-income housing for the elderly (Fisch *et al.* 1968) are demented. In an out-patient geriatric service 86 per cent of registrants were cognitively impaired by insensitive criteria (Reifler *et al.* 1982). Seventy-seven per cent of clients in a local adult day-care centre suffer from SDAT and related conditions (Sands, personal communication, 1982). Only a small proportion of the needy have been identified. Helgason (1977) estimated that only 10 per cent of the patients with senile or vascular dementia sought psychiatric services.

The *direct* contribution of SDAT to service needs represents only a very small fraction of its effect. Disability due to non-compliance with medical instructions, malnutrition, and other complications is unmeasured. Sequelae of falls exemplify this very substantial hidden contribution. Nineteen per cent of UK beds used for rehabilitation from femoral fractures come from geriatric services (Lewis 1981). Twelve per cent of femoral fracture patients are overtly demented (Brocklehurst *et al.* 1978); one-fourth of Evans *et al.*'s fracture cases (1979)

came from institutions expected to have a very high SDAT prevalence.

Other dimensions of the burgeoning need: pressures on institutions and providers

Hospitals and other institutions face unprecedented quantitative and qualitative problems. Excluding intensive care, 19 per cent of community hospital patients 70 years and older are mildly, and 31 per cent moderately or severely confused (Warshaw *et al.* 1982). Restraints were used in 19 per cent; psychotropic medications in 43 per cent. Hearing was diminished in 34 per cent and vision in 40; 25 per cent had impaired speech and 21 per cent were incontinent. In homes for the aged visited by Clark *et al.* (1981), 88 per cent had a physical disability; 65 per cent had socially disturbing behaviour.

Some 13 per cent of the elderly require total care (Anderson 1981). Given 1.3 million nursing home beds in the US (Grimaldi 1982) and fewer per caput in the UK, it is evident that current beds fall short of needs for the year 2000 by at least 300 per cent.

A bed shortage in the US and restrictions on reimbursement for staff already result in reluctance of intermediate and skilled nursing facilities to accept seriously ill or disturbed patients. This seems quite reasonable considering intermediate care staffing standards: New Jersey requires 0.31–0.32 *minutes* of registered nurse time, 0.11 *minutes* of practical nurse time, and only 2.1 hours of nurse's aide time per patient daily (Grimaldi 1982). Residents in US nursing homes have an average of 2.2 chronic conditions; 58 per cent are 'senile'. Almost two-thirds require assistance with at least four activities of daily living; 26 per cent of discharges are attributable to death (Grimaldi 1982). The cost of care for the 30 per cent of US nursing home patients discharged to hospitals surely exceeds those for better hospital discharge planning, better staffing of nursing homes, and well-funded volunteer programmes. The quality and costs of nursing home care must be adversely affected by very high staff turnover – almost all nurses' aides and one-third of RN's in three months (Garibaldi *et al.* 1981).

Shrinking resources will create pressures to redistribute the workload. Thus, Kidd (1962) considered that more than a third of geriatric patients were 'misplaced', since they had mainly 'mental' problems. Otherwise unchanged patients who exhaust their skilled nursing benefits are currently transferred to a lower level of care (Brody 1981).

However helpless they may be, dementia patients in the US are in limbo. Neither nursing home nor adult day care for SDAT is a benefit of the federal Medicare programme, because considered 'custodial'. They qualify for Medicaid only if they *and* their spouse have less than $1500 savings and home and car below specified minumum values. Remaining families hesitate to exhaust respources needed for the other partner's survival. Agonizing decisions, divorce after 50 years' marriage, and occult intergenerational transfers of funds result. Sheltered housing facilities may be barred by law from accepting confused or non-ambulatory clients without special permits and, presumably, extra staff. Progressive closure of state-financed mental hospitals in US and UK eliminate this alternative.

Two-thirds of US nursing homes are proprietary (Brody 1981). *Without* meals or health care, a clean motel room in a large US city costs $1800–2000 monthly; an adequate nursing home, a similar sum. By comparison, monthly 1977 Medicaid expenditures for skilled and intermediate level care per recipient were only $323. Either investment or expectation must change dramatically to reconcile these figures.

New, ambiguous, and trying aspects of the physician's role

Lacking effective somatic therapies for SDAT, the physician is limited to psychological and environmental interventions. The most caring physician may lack time and training for such activities. Referral resources for home care are few and fragmented among many agencies, staffed by overburdened nurses, psychologists, social workers, masters-level gerontologists, and clerical personnel who frequently lack understanding of the medical issues. None of these is under the physician's direct *authority*, but all leave final *responsibility* with him or her, posing an almost insoluble administrative dilemma.

With disease progression, the patient becomes more passive; the family, more needy and demanding. They become the client. Painful conflicts face the physician whose interpretation of the patient's best interests conflicts with the family's. The chronic downhill course of SDAT provides ever less emotional reward. If physicians are to accept this burden, legal provisions for their new role (for example, release of information to family without patient permission is *theoretically* illegal) and fiscal provision for their supervisory and counselling efforts must be incorporated in health planning.

The family in SDAT: societal resource or sufferer?

Increased family support for the patient is commonly prescribed to relieve pressure on institutions. Such policy proposals ignore the terrible burden on families which already exists when the patient first reaches the institution. Patients lack insight into disruption of family routine by their illness (Reifler *et al.* 1981). Families seek care for dementias only *late* (Grad de Alarcon *et al.* 1975) – a mean of 4.5 years after onset (Helgason 1977). Of discharges to nursing homes from a geriatric unit, 70 per cent had previously been cared for at home (Eggert *et al.* 1977). Family resistance to nursing home care accounted for only 1.2 per cent of 1115 discharged from the Edinburgh geriatric unit; more than five times as often, families took frail patients back into the home against professional advice (Lowther and Williamson 1966).

Families bear an estimated 70 per cent of illness costs in funds and time. The family's critical role is illustrated by the demography of the institutionalized elderly who are predominantly older, widowed, never married, and geographically or emotionally isolated from their families (Brody 1981). Thus, there is no alternate 'home'.

When they first seek community services, hospitalization, or placement, the depleted family can 'no longer cope' (Sanford 1975). Family members suffer depression (Grad and Sainsbury 1968; Fengler and Goodrich 1979) and 'feelings of burden' (Zarit *et al.* 1980). Adverse psychological effects upon family occur in many chronic disorders (Golodetz *et al.* 1969), but may be more severe in dementia. Of 36 Philadelphia Geriatric Centre residents with a spouse living in the community, all had cerebral disorders (Brody 1981). Prolonged home care without help, respite, or guidance almost certainly increases medical care and costs for neglected and stress-related illness in families and social costs in lost family productivity, litigation for assistance, and needless redocumentation of permanent patient disability.

Because SDAT involves the brain, the patient's response is not only maladaptive, but of a type – for example, paranoia, aggression, or withdrawal – that is likely to alienate family and friends (Verwoerdt 1981). Helplessness to arrest decline in a loved one and emergence of frustrating and irritating behaviours create an explosive mix of guilt, antipathy, and bereavement without the cloture of somatic death. We annually encounter several family members who display pathological grief reactions.

Brody (1981) considers other social and demographic trends which will adversely affect the support available from families. These include the increasing proportion of women entering full-time employment, the ageing of children of the elderly – who may themselves be in their 60s – and increasing family mobility.

Social consequences of late diagnosis

Quite apart from methodological problems in making a diagnosis, late diagnosis is a result of care-seeking and care-provision attitudes. Family and patient do not recognize or do not accept SDAT, or believe decline to be the lot of the aged. They first seek care when incontinence, wandering, or gross disorders of behaviour or sleep disrupt daily routine. Society and insurance do not encourage 'routine' first contact with a physician who may recognize change from baseline and have the rapport to help. Early, physician attention may be directed elsewhere by patient and family; or, lacking a cure, he or she may hesitate to raise unpleasant issues for which aid was not sought. This delay may result in needless care for irrelevant complaints (for example, incomprehension becomes 'poor vision'). Non-compliance with needed medication or side effects of unnecessary medication may necessitate hospitalization. Once-reversible damage in hydrocephalus or endocrine–nutritional problems passes beyond help. Opportunities to establish viable helping patterns (such as medication reminders) are lost. Families are drained beyond hope of non-institutional solutions; they become so depressed, angry or guilty they cannot give or accept a clear account of the original problem.

If the patient is hospitalized, critical tests and care decisions wait for guardianship to legitimize consent or for family and patient to debate their implications. Consideration of placement and in-home alternatives face similar delay. Will intervention be meddlesome, prolong life, or alter the quality of life? Such deliberation should long precede admission and find family and physician emotionally and intellectually prepared.

Social implications of uncertain diagnosis and therapeutic limitations

Problems in diagnosis are discussed above. Negative test results do not preclude diseases not considered by the physician or those refractory to laboratory diagnosis. After the initial evaluation, the diagnosis is rarely questioned: expert and thorough evaluation will minimize human costs and prevent needless, expensive institutionalization.

Table 5.12 contrasts costs to identify and treat 12 reversible cases per 100 patients with one year's nursing home stay. The disease 'mix' is similar to that in Table 5.2. Fewer cases are considered reversible; palliable cases are ignored. We assume all treated individuals remain at home one year and require only aid from family and friends.

In the person with undoubted SDAT, all symptoms may be attributed to it. Undetected remedial problems such as congestive heart failure causing nocturnal agitation or depression causing delusions may result in premature institutional care. Also incompletely appreciated is the SDAT patient's exquisite sensitivity to decompensation by small doses of psychopharmaceuticals, any intercurrent systemic illness or side-effects of diuretics, eye drops, bladder medication, or arthritis and ulcer therapy.

Once institutionalized, the SDAT patient may regress and require far more aid than if stimulation, reorientation, bowel and dietary programmes, and physical therapy were available initially. Such preventable complications as dehydration, decubitus ulcer, contracture, and aspiration pneumonia require major expenditure in acute hospitals.

Finally, the uncertainty and limitations of conventional medicine in SDAT encourage untested, costly and ineffective therapeutic adventures. Expenditure for marginal therapies may deplete resources available for real needs.

HOW SHOULD ONE ORGANIZE CARE OF THE ELDERLY?

Table 5.13 depicts our perception of UK and US approaches to care of the elderly. Each has advantages and disadvantages. The personal comments below are chosen mainly to stimulate discussion.

Rapport with frightened, confused patients and detection of change are best achieved by one physician who has long known them. The chief need for patient satisfaction, for accurate assessment and for compliance is *time*. Neither 'system' rewards time in history taking or patient and family education, though these may be more valuable and less expensive than tests or treatments.

Establishment of geriatrics as a discipline in the UK has had uncertain benefits; there are only three to four chairs of Geriatric Medicine in the US. Most physicians have received no education in the specific needs of the elderly.

Home care services in the UK are provided by district nurse and health visitor through regional health and social service authorities. Analogous US roles are served by Visiting Nurse

Table 5.12. *Potential annual savings from screening for treatable causes of dementia*

Costs of definitive care	Costs, US $
3 subdural haematomas (3 days' hospitalization @ $300 & $2000 surgery)	$8,700
1 case B_{12} deficiency (18 injections @ $10)	$180
1 case hypothyroidism ($36 medication)	$36
1 case hydrocephalus (3 days' hospitaliz. @ $300 & $1500 surgery)	$7,400
1 meningioma (4 days' hospitaliz. @ $300 & 3 @ $500 & $3000 surgery)	$5,700
1 case treatable infection (14 days' hospitaliz. @ $300 & $1000 misc.)	$5,200
4 cases reversible drug toxicity/depression (4 days' hospitaliz. @ $300)	$4,800
Subtotal, care for 12 'reversible' cases	$27,016
Ambulatory care screening for 100 cases @ $800 (MD and laboratory)	$80,000
Total costs	$107,016
Cost of nursing home admission, 12 persons @ $1870/month	$269,280
Potential annual savings	$162,264

Table 5.13. *Contrasting emphases in organization of US and UK geriatric care, with emphasis on SDAT*

	United Kingdom	United States
Medical entry	Family practitioner	Specialist
	± Geriatrician	N/A
Funding emphasis	Chronic disease, maintenance	Acute disease, crisis intervention
Home care	Explicitly funded, regionally organized	Minimally funded, smaller autonomous units
Fiscal incentives for physicians	High volume of patients seen	Technical procedures
Financial coverage	Mainly governmental	Private, private insurance, governmental
Residential solutions	± centralization, isolation	Growing concern for shared housing
Inpatient care of most disabled	Oriented to mental hospital/psychiatric unit	More heavily oriented to acute general hospital and nursing home
Focus of home care	Medical	Medical
Organizational focus	District health authority	Mainly voluntary, private, governmental agencies

Association (voluntary charities), county funded nurses, and many other groups, reimbursed by various combinations of personal, state, federal, and private insurance funds. Social service, homemaker, and attendant assistance are less well covered and much more fragmented in the US.

Despite US efforts to encourage 'comprehensive' home care, such care is far from comprehensive. Agencies offer a narrow range of short-term services only if prescribed by a physician. They lack internal medical/psychological expertise and are seriously understaffed. Social workers are often obtained by contract, permitted only 1–2 hours to evaluate complex problems; follow-up is not covered. Arrangements to recruit and train home health aides or homemakers are not integral. Referral and billing for home meals, pharmaceuticals, catheters, sick-room supplies, and walking aids all involve separate agencies.

Restriction of long-stay mental hospital beds and general hospital bed-days are undoubtedly problems in both systems. There are no formally designated geriatric beds in the US, but the elderly occupy a disproportionate number of acute hospital beds. Since fewer than half of those needing nursing home care are so placed in the US (Pegels 1980), lower UK quotas may also be grossly inadequate.

In the US, the private sector builds, but private and public funds support, most sheltered housing. Efforts to create new levels of congregate housing offering meals, housekeepers, and an onsite nurse encounter unforeseen licensure liability and 'image' problems as well as the high cost of labour-intensive assistance to residents.

Resource allocation and referral in the UK should be more orderly. Politicization may offer the vulnerable elderly less when the sole central source falls upon hard times than a pluralistic system as in the US. The UK 'menu' of services may be more restricted and innovation, less likely; basic chronic needs are more likely to be met uniformly. Private US nursing homes have lower per-diem costs than government and non-profit homes, after controlling for quality. Government regulation may cause insufficient beds and raise costs (Grimaldi 1982). Because more resources are allocated to acute care in the US, the gravely ill elderly with treatable problems are more likely to be treated aggressively and recover; those with multisystem irreversible deficit are also more likely to languish wastefully.

A CALL TO ACTION

The unprecedented scope of social problems presented by SDAT demands a bold response. Its urgency must not bring precipitate remedies, for the need would absorb more resources than can possibly be mustered.

Applied research on efficient diagnosis, simple approaches to needs-assessment and controlled trials of psychosocial interventions for the patient and family are needed. Clear delineation of entry variables and reasonable outcomes are essential. Thus, adult day-care may not reverse SDAT or prolong life, but might prolong at-home stay, controlling for dementia severity, systemic health, and other patient and family entry characteristics. The pressure for answers should not force hasty mounting of expensive studies inadequately designed to collect data or assess outcomes. Measurement of private and societal costs must include the family. To accomplish this research without crippling basic biological endeavour, resources must be concentrated on few well-planned and funded programmes, rather than more inadequately funded studies.

Pressures to promulgate expertise and widen care must be weighed carefully. Dissemination of untested enthusiasm by inadequately trained volunteers or low-level trainees is politically attractive, can be achieved rapidly, and appears responsive to needs. Thoughtful development of medical, psychological, nursing, social work, and gerontology faculties, and of proven knowledge and skills they may spread, will better utilize scant resources.

The need for care will only increase; funds will remain inadequate. The greater age and poor health of potential clients, and growing numbers with no accessible family will blunt major gains from expansion of in-home care to all who can benefit. Nursing homes, hospitals, and day-care centres will become increasingly reliant upon unpaid volunteers and less highly trained staff. Innovative approaches to screening volunteers, then training, supervising, and integrating them with regular staff will be required.

Many conceptually simple, inexpensive therapies benefit severely affected SDAT patients, though they do not alter the underlying disease. These include behavioural approaches, staff training, and environmental modification (Brody 1981; Cruise et al. 1978; Hanley et al. 1981; Warshaw et al. 1982). Introduction of these may require added resources and staff retraining. Physicians may overlook simple actions with profound effects such as attention to hearing loss (Cooper et al. 1974) or avoidance of even small doses (Potamianos and Kellet 1982) of the many medications with anticholinergic effects (Greenblatt and Shader 1973). Only recently has family support received attention (Fuller et al. 1979; Hausman 1979; Lazarus et al. 1981).

REFERENCES

Åkesson, H.O. (1969). A population study of senile and arteriosclerotic psychoses. *Human Hered.* **19**, 546.

Albert, M.S. and Kaplan, E. (1980). Organic implications of neuropsychological deficits in the elderly. In *New directions in memory and aging: proceedings of the George Talland Memorial Conference* (eds. L.W. Poon, J.L. Fozard, L.S. Cermak, D. Arenberg and S.W. Thompson) p. 403. Erlbaum, Hillsdale, NJ.

Anderson, J.M. and Hubbard, B.M. (1981). Age-related changes in Alzheimer's disease. *Lancet* **i**, 1261.

Anderson, O.W. (1981). The social strategy of disease control: the case of senile dementia. In *Clinical aspects of Alzheimer's disease and senile dementia* (eds. N.E. Miller and G.D. Cohen) p. 333. Raven, New York.

Arieff, A.I., Cooper, J.D., Armstrong, D., and Lazarowitz, V.C. (1979). Dementia, renal failure, and brain aluminum. *Ann. Intern. Med.* **90**, 741.

Ball, M.J. and Nuttall, K. (1981). Topography of neurofibrillary tangles and granulovacuoles in hippocampi of patients with Down's syndrome: quantitative comparison with normal ageing and Alzheimer's disease. *Neuropathol. Appl. Neurobiol.* **7**, 13.

Barron, S.A., Jacobs, L., and Kinkel, W.R. (1976). Changes in size of normal lateral ventricles during aging determined by computerized tomography. *Neurology* **26**, 1011–3.

Bartus, R.T., Dean, R.L. III, Beer, B., and Lippa, A.S. (1982). The cholinergic hypothesis of geriatric memory dysfunction. *Science* **217**, 408.

Beighton, T.H. and Lindenberg, R. (1971). Alzheimer's disease in multiple members of a family. *Birth Defects* **7**, 232.

Benson, D.F. (1980). Dementia: a clinical approach. In *Roche Seminars on Aging* (eds. J.E. Birren and J.C. Beck). Hoffman-La Roche, Nutley, NJ.

Bergmann, K., Kay, D.W.K., Foster, E.M., McKechnie, A.D., and Roth, M.A. (1971). Followup study of randomly selected community residents to assess the effects of chronic brain syndrome and cerebrovascular disease. *Psychiatry Part II: Excerpta Medica Int. Congr. Series No. 274*, p. 856. Excerpta Medica, Amsterdam.

Birren, J.E. and Botwinick, J. (1951). The relationship of writing speed to age and to the senile psychoses. *J. Consult. Psychol.* **15**, 243.

Birren, J.E., Woods, A.M., and Williams, M.V. (1980). Behavioral slowing with age: causes, organization, and consequences. In *Aging in the 1980s. Psychological issues* (ed. L.W. Poon) p. 293. American Psychological Association, Washington.

Blazer, D. and Williams, C.D. (1980). Epidemiology of dysphoria and depression in an elderly population. *Am. J. Psychiatry* **137**, 439.

Blessed, G., Tomlinson, B.E., and Roth, M. (1968). The association between quantitative measures of dementia and of senile change in the cerebral grey matter of elderly subjects. *Brit. J. Psychiatry* **114**, 797.

Blumer, D. and Benson, D.F. (1975). Personality changes with frontal and temporal lobe lesions. In *Psychiatric aspects of neurologic disease* (eds. D. Blumer and D.F. Benson) p. 151. Grune and Stratton, New York.

Boller, F., Mizutani, T., Roessman, U., and Gambetti, P. (1980). Parkinson disease, dementia and Alzheimer disease: clinico-pathologic correlations. *Ann. Neurol.* **7**, 329.

Bollerup, T.R. (1975). Prevalence of mental illness among 70-year-olds domiciled in nine Copenhagen suburbs. *Acta Psychiatr. Scand.* **51**, 327.

Bondareff, W., Mountjoy, C.Q., and Roth, M. (1982). Loss of neurons of origin of the adrenergic projection to cerebral cortex (nucleus locus coeruleus) in senile dementia. *Neurology* **32**, 164.

Botwinick, J. and Birren, J.E. (1951). Differential decline in the Wechsler Bellevue subtests in the senile psychoses. *J. Gerontol.* **6**, 365.

Bowen, D.M., Smith, C.B., White, P., and Davison, A.N. (1976). Neurotransmitter-related enzymes and indices of hypoxia in senile dementia and other abiotrophies. *Brain* **99**, 459.

Bowen, D.M., Spillane, J.A., Curzon, G., *et al.* (1979). Accelerated aging or selective neuronal loss as an important cause of dementia? *Lancet* **i**, 11.

British Medical Journal (1978). Modified neurosyphilis. *Br. Med. J.* **ii**, 647.

Brocklehurst, J.C., Exton-Smith, A.N., Lempert Barber, J.M., Hunt, L., and Palmer, M.K. (1978). Fracture of the femur in old age: a two-centre study of associated clinical factors and the cause of the fall. *Age Ageing* **7**, 7–15.

Brody, E.M. (1981). The formal support network: congregate treatment settings for residents with senescent brain dysfunction. In *Clinical aspects of Alzheimer's disease and senile dementia* (eds. N.E. Miller and G.D. Cohen) p. 301. Raven, New York.

Brody, E.M., Kleban, M.H., Lawton, M.P., and Moss, J. (1974). A longitudinal look at excess disabilities in the mentally impaired aged. *J. Gerontol.* **29**, 79.

Brody, E.M., Kleban, M.H., Lawton, M.P., and Silverman, H.A. (1971). Excess disabilities of mentally impaired aged: impact of individualized treatment. *Gerontologist* **11**, 124.

Brody, H. (1955). Organization of the cerebral cortex. III. A study of aging in the cerebral cortex. *J. Comp. Neurol.* **102**, 511.

Brody, H. (1976). An examination of cerebral cortex and brainstem aging. In *Neurobiology of aging* (eds. R.D. Terry and S. Gershon) p. 177. Raven Press, New York.

Brody, J.A. (1982). An epidemiologist views senile dementia – facts and fragments. *Am. J. Epidemiol.* **115**, 155.

Broe, G.A., Akhtar, A.J., Andrews, G.R., Caird, F.I., Gilmore, J.J., and McLennan, W.J. (1976). Neurological disorders in the elderly at home. *J. Neurol. Neurosurg. Psychiatry* **39**, 362.

Brown, P. (1980). An epidemiologic critique of Creuzfeldt–Jakob disease. *Epidemiol. Rev.* **2**, 113.

Brown, P., Cathala, F., and Gajdusek, D.C. (1979*a*). Creuzfeldt–Jakob disease in France. III. Epidemiological study of 170 patients dying during the decade 1968–1977. *Ann Neurol.* **6**, 438.

Brown, P., Cathals, F., Sadowsky, D., and Gajdusek, D.C. (1979*b*): Creutzfeldt–Jacob disease in France. II. Clinical, characteristic of 124 consecutive verified cases during the decade 1968–1977. *Ann. Neurol.* **6**, 430.

Bruce, M.E. and Fraser, H. (1975). Amyloid plaques in the brains of mice infected with scrapie. Morphological variation and staining properties. *Neuropathol. Appl. Neurobiol.* **1**, 189.

Brun, A. and Gustafson, L. (1976). Distribution of cerebral degeneration in Alzheimer's disease. A clinicopathological study. *Arch. Psychiatr. Nervenkr.* **223**, 15.

Buell, S.J. and Coleman, P.D. (1979). Dendritic growth in the aged human brain and failure of growth in senile dementia. *Science* **206**, 854.

Celesia, G.G. and Wanamaker, W.M. (1972). Psychiatric disturbances in Parkinson's disease. *Dis. Nervous System* **33**, 577.

Cerella, J., Poon, L. W., and Williams, D.M. (1980). Age and the complexity hypothesis. In *Aging in the 1980s: psychological issues* (ed. L.W. Poon) p. 332. American Psychological Association, Washington, DC.

Clark, M.G., Williams, A.J., and Jones, P.A. (1981). A psychogeriatric survey of old people's homes. *Br. Med. J.* **283**, 1307.

Cohen, D. and Eisdorfer, C. (1979). Cognitive theory and the assessment of change in the elderly. In *Psychiatric symptoms and cognitive loss in the elderly. Evaluation and assessment techniques* (eds. A. Raskin and L. Jarvik) p. 273. Hemisphere, Washington.

Cohen, D., Eisdorfer, C., and Walford, R.L. (1981). Histocompatibility antigens (HLA) and patterns of cognitive loss in dementia of the Alzheimer type. *Neurobiol. Aging* **2**, 277.

Cohen, D., Zeller, E., Eisdorfer, C., and Walford, R.L. (1979). Alzheimer's disease and the main histocompatibility complex. (Abstract.) *Geronologist* **19** (Suppl.), 57.

Cole, G. (1977). Autopsy findings in mental patients. *S. Afr. Med. J.* **52**, 534.

Comstock, G.W. and Helsing, K.J. (1976). Symptoms of depression in two communities. *Psychol. Med.* **6**, 551.

Constantinidis, J. (1978). Is Alzheimer's disease a major form of senile dementia? Clinical, anatomical, and genetic data. In *Alzheimer's disease: senile dementia and related disorders* (ed. R. Katzman, R.D. Terry, and K.L. Bick) p. 15. Raven, New York.

Cook, R.R., Ward, B.E., and Austin, J.H. (1979). Studies in aging of the brain: IV. Familial Alzheimer disease: relation to transmissible dementia, aneuploidy and microtubular defects. *Neurology* **29**, 1402.

Cooper, A., Curry, A.R., Kay, D.W.K., Garside, R.F., and Roth, M. (1974). Hearing loss in paranoid and affective psychoses of the elderly. *Lancet* **ii**, 851.

Corsellis, J.A.N. (1976). Aging and the dementias. In *Greenfield's neuropathology* (ed. W. Blackwood and J.A.N. Corsellis) p. 796. Edward Arnold, London.

Crapper, D.R., Krishnan, S.S., and Dalton, A.J. (1973*a*). Brain aluminum distribution in Alzheimer's disease and experimental neurofibrillary degeneration. *Science* **180**, 511.

Crapper, D.R., Krishnan, S.S., and Dalton, A.J. (1973*b*). Brain aluminium in Alzheimer's disease and experimental neurofibrillary degeneration. *Trans. Am. Neurol. Assoc.* **98**, 17.

Crapper, D.R., Krishnan, S.S., and Quittkat, S. (1976). Aluminium neurofibrillary degeneration and Alzheimer's disease. *Brain* **99**, 67.

Crapper, D.R., Quittkat, S., and DeBoni, U. (1979). Altered chromatin conformation in Alzheimer's disease. *Brain* **102**, 483.

Crapper, D.R., Quittkat, S., Krishnan, S.S., Dalton, A.J., and De Boni, U. (1980). Intranuclear aluminum content in Alzheimer's disease, dialysis encephalopathy, and experimental aluminum encephalopathy. *Acta Neuropathol.* **50**, 19.

Cruise, J., Gledhill, F.E., and Wright, W.B. (1978). Better geriatric care: making it happen. *Health Trends* **10**, 92.

Cummings, J. (1982). Cortical dementias. In *Psychiatric aspects of Neurologic disease*, Vol. II (eds. D.F. Benson and D. Blumer) p. 93. Grune and Stratton, New York.

Cummings, J., Benson, D.F., and LoVerme, S. (1980). Reversible dementia: illustrative cases, definition and review. *JAMA* **243**, 2434.

Davidson, E.A. and Robertson, E.E. (1955). Alzheimer's disease with acne rosacea in one of identical twins. *J. Neurol. Neurosurg. Psychiatry* **18**, 72.

Davies, P. (1979). Neurotransmitter-related enzymes in senile dementia of the Alzheimer type. *Brain Res.* **171**, 319.

Davies, P. and Maloney, A.J.F. (1976). Selective loss of central cholinergic neurons in Alzheimer's disease. *Lancet* **ii**, 1403.

DeBoni, U. and Crapper, D.R. (1978). Paired helical filaments of the Alzheimer type in cultured neurones. *Nature, Lond.* **271**, 566.

Delaney, P. (1982). Dementia: the search for treatable causes. *S. Med. J.* **75**, 707.

Dickinson, A.G., Fraser, H., and Bruce, M. (1979). Animal models for the dementias. In *Alzheimer's disease: early recognition of potentially reversible deficits* (eds. A.I.M. Glen and L.J. Whalley) p. 42. Churchill Livingstone, New York.

Donaldson, S.W., Wagner, C.C., and Gresham, G.E. (1973). A unified ADL evaluation form. *Arch. Phys. Med. Rehabil.* **54**, 175.

Drechsler, F. (1978). Quantitative analysis of neurophysiologic processes of the ageing CNS. *J. Neurol.* **218**, 197.

Earnest, M.P., Heaton, R.D., Wilkinson, W.F., and Manke, W.F. (1979). Cortical atrophy, ventricular enlargement and intellectual impairment in the aged. *Neurology* **29**, 1138.

Eggert, G., Granger, C., Morris, R., and Pendleton, S. (1977). Caring for the patient with long-term disability. *Geriatrics* **32**, 102.

Ernst, P., Badash, D., Beran, B., Kosovsky, R., and Kleinhauz, M. (1977). Incidence of mental illness in the aged: unmasking the effects of a diagnosis of chronic brain syndrome. *J. Am. Geriatr. Soc.* **25**, 371.

Evans, J.G., Prudham, D., and Wandless, I. (1979). A prospective study of fractured proximal femur: incidence and outcome. *Public Health, Lond.* **93**, 235.

Feldman, R.G., Chandler, K.A., Levy, L.L., and Glaser, G.H. (1963). Familial Alzheimer's disease. *Neurology* **13**, 811.

Fengler, A.P. and Goodrich, N. (1979). Wives of elderly disabled men: the hidden patients. *Gerontologist* **19**, 175.

Ferm, L. (1974). Behavioral activities in demented geriatric patients. *Gerontol. Clin.* **16**, 185.

Finlayson, R.E. and Martin, L.M. (1982). Recognition and management of depression in the elderly. *Mayo Clin. Proc.* **57**, 115.

Fisch, M., Goldfarb, A.I., Shahinian, S.P., and Turner, H. (1968).

Chronic brain, syndrome in the community aged. *Arch. Gen. Psychiatry* **18**, 739.

Folstein, M.E. and Folstein, S.E. (1975). Mini-mental state. A practical method for grading the congnitive state of patients for the clinician. *J. Psychiatr. Res.* **12**, 189.

Fremon, F.R. (1976). Evaluation of patients with progressive intellectual deterioration. *Arch. Neurol.* **33**, 658.

Fuld, P.A. (1978). Psychological testing in the differential diagnosis of the dementias. In *Alzheimer's disease: senile dementia and related disorders* (ed. R. Katzman, R.D. Terry, and K.L. Bick) p. 185. Raven Press, New York.

Fuld, P.A., Katzman, R., Davies, P., and Terry, R.D. (1982). Intrusions as a sign of Alzheimer dementia. Chemical and pathological verification. *Ann. Neurol.* **11**, 155.

Fuller, J., Ward, E., Evans, A., Massam, K., and Gardner, A. (1979). Dementia: supportive groups for relatives. *Br. Med. J.* **i**, 1684.

Gainotti, G., Caltagirone, C., Masullo, C., and Miceli, G. (1980). Patterns of neuropsychologic impairment in various diagnostic groups of dementia. In *Aging of the brain and dementia* (eds. L. Amaducci, A.N. Davison, and P. Antuono) p. 245. Raven, New York.

Garibaldi, R.A., Brodine, S., and Matsuyama, S. (1981). Infections among patients in nursing homes: policies, prevalence and problems. *New Engl. J. Med.* **305**, 731.

Garrison, J.E. and Howe, J.A. (1976). Community intervention with the elderly: a social network approach. *J. Am. Geriatr. Soc.* **24**, 329.

Gibbs, C.J. Jr. and Gajdusek, D.C. (1978). Atypical viruses as the cause of sporadic, epidemic, and familial chronic diseases in man. Slow viruses and human diseases. In *Perspectives in viruses* (ed. M. Pollard) Vol. 10, p. 161. Raven Press, New York.

Gibbs, C.J. Jr, Gajdusek, D.C., and Amyx, H. (1980). Strain variation in the viruses of Creuzfeldt–Jakob disease and kuru. In *Slow transmissible diseases of the nervous system* (eds. S.B. Prusiner and W.J. Hadlow) Vol. 2, p. 87. Academic Press, New York.

Gibson, G.E., Peterson, C., and Jenden, D.J. (1981). Brain acetylcholine synthesis declines with senescence. *Science* **213**, 674.

Gilleard, C.J. and Pattie, A.H. (1977). The Stockton Geriatric Scale: shortened version with British normative data. *Br. J. Psychiatry* **131**, 90.

Glenner, C.G. (1981). Amyloidosis: the hereditary disorders, including Alzheimer's disease. *J. Lab. Clin. Med.* **98**, 807.

Glenner, C.G., Henry, J.H., and Fujihara, S. (1981). Congophilic angiopathy in the pathogenesis of Alzheimer's degeneration. *Ann. Pathol.* **1**, 120.

Go, R.C.P., Todorov, A.B., Elston, R.C., and Constantinidis, J. (1978). The malignancy of dementias. *Ann. Neurol.* **3**, 559.

Golodetz, A., Evans, R., Heinritz, G. and Gibson, C.D. Jr (1969). The care of chronic illness: the 'responsor' role. *Med. Care* **7**, 385.

Goodin, D.S., Squires, K.C., Henderson, B.H., and Starr, A. (1978*a*). Age-related variations in evoked potentials to auditory stimuli in normal human subjects. *Electroencephalogr. Clin. Neurophysiol.* **44**, 447.

Goodin, D. S., Squires, K. C., Henderson, B. H., and Starr, A. (1978*b*). Long-latency event-related components of the auditory evoked potential in dementia. *Brain* **101**, 635.

Goudsmit, L., White, B. J., Weitkamp, L. R., Keats, B. J. B., Morrow, C. H., and Gajdusek, D. C. (1981). Familial Alzheimer's disease in two kindreds of the same geographic and ethnic origin. *J. Neurol. Sci.* **49**, 79.

Goudsmit, L., Morrow, C. H., Asher, D. M. *et al.* (1980). Evidence for and against the transmissibility of Alzheimer disease. *Neurology* **30**, 945.

Grad, J. and Sainsbury, P. (1968). The effects that patients have on their families in a community care and a control psychiatric service – a two year follow-up. *Br. J. Psychiatry* **114**, 265.

Grad de Alarcon, J., Sainsbury, P., and Costain, W. R. (1975). Incidence of referred mental illness in Chichester and Salisbury. *Psychol. Med.* **5**, 32.

Greenblatt, D.J. and Shader, R.J. (1973). Anticholinergics. *New Engl. J. Med.* **288**, 1215.

Grimaldi, P. L. (1982). *Medical reimbursement of nursing home care.* American Enterprise Institute for Public policy Research, Washington, DC.

Gruenberg, E. M. (1977). The failures of success. *Milbank Mem. Fund Q.* **55**, 3.

Gurland, B., Dean, L., Cross, P., and Golden, R. (1980). The epidemiology of depression and dementia in the elderly: the use of multiple indicators of these conditions. In *Psychopathology in the aged* (eds. J.O. Cole, and J.E. Barrett) p. 37. Raven, New York.

Gurland, B. J. (1981). The borderlands of dementia: the influence of sociocultural characteristics on rates of dementia occurring in the senium. In *Clinical aspects of Alzheimer's disease and senile dementia* (eds. N.E. Miller and G.D. Cohen) p. 61. Raven, New York.

Gustafson, L. and Nilsson, L. (1982). Differential diagnosis of presenile dementia on clinical grounds. *Acta Psychiatr. Scand.* **65**, 194.

Haase, G. R. (1977). Diseases presenting as dementia. In *Dementia,* 2nd edn (ed. C. E. Wells) p. 27. Davis, Philadelphia.

Haberland, C. (1969). Alzheimer's disease in Down syndrome: clinical–neuropathological observations. *Acta Neurol. Belg.* **69**, 369.

Hagnell, O., Lanke, J. and Rorsman, B. (1982). *The diminishing incidence of chronic organic brain syndromes among the elderly.* Third European Symposium on Social Psychiatry, Helsinki, September 1982.

Hagnell, O., Lanke, J., Rorsman, B. and Öjesjö, L. (1981). Does the incidence of age psychosis decrease? A prospective longitudinal study of a complete population investigated during the 25-year period 1947–1972: The Lundby study. *Neuro. Psychobiol.* **7**, 201.

Hakim, A. M. and Mathieson, G. (1979). Dementia in Parkinson's disease: a neuropathologic study. *Neurology* **29**, 1209.

Hanley, I. G., McGuire, R. J., and Boyd, W. D. (1981). Reality orientation and dementia: a controlled trial of two approaches. *Br. J. Psychiatry* **138**, 10.

Harris, R. (1982). Genetics of Alzheimer's disease. *Br. Med. J.* **284**, 1065.

Hausman, C. P. (1979). Short-term counselling groups for people with elderly parents. *Gerontologist* **19**, 102.

Hecaen, H. and Albert, M. L. (1975). Disorders of mental functioning related to frontal lobe pathology. In *Psychiatric aspects of neurologic disease* (eds. D.F. Benson and D. Blumer) p. 137. Grune and Stratton, New York.

Helgason, L. (1977). Psychiatric services and mental illness in Iceland. *Acta Psychiatr. Scand.* Suppl. **269**, 1.

Hemsi, L. K., Whitehead, A., and Post, F. (1968). Cognitive functioning and cerebral arousal in elderly depressives and dements. *J. Psychosom. Res.* **12**, 145.

Henschke, P.J., Bell, D.A., and Cape, R.D.J. (1978). Alzheimer's disease and HLA. *Tissue Antigens* **12**, 132.

Heston, L.L., Lowther, D.L.W., and Leventhal, C.M. (1966). Alzheimer's disease: a family study. *Arch. Neurol.* **15**, 225.

Heston, L.L., Mastri, A.R., Anderson, V.E., and White, J. (1981). Dementia of the Alzheimer type. Clinical genetics, natural history and associated conditions. *Arch. Gen. Psychiatry* **38**, 1085.

Hilt, D.C., Uhl, G.R., Hedreen, J.C., Whitehouse, P.J., and Price, D.L. (1982). Pick disease: loss of neurons in the nucleus basalis. *Neurology* **32**, A229.

Hubbard, B.M. and Anderson, J.M. (1981). A quantitative study of cerebral atrophy in old age and senile dementia. *J. Neurol. Sci.* **50**, 135.

Hunter, R.A., Dayan, A.D., and Wilson, J. (1972). Alzheimer's disease in one monozygotic twin. *J. Neurol. Neurosurg. Psychiatry* **35**, 707.

Hutton, J.T. (1980). Results of clinical assessment for the dementia syndrome: implications for epidemiologic studies. In *The epidemiology of dementia* (eds. J.A. Mortimer and L.M. Schuman) p. 62. Oxford University Press, New York.

Ishii, T. and Haga, S. (1976). Immunoelectron microscopic location of immunoglobulins in amyloid fibrils of senile plaques. *Arch. Neuropathol.* **36**, 243.

Ishii, T., Haga, S., and Shimuzi, F. (1975). Identification of components of immunoglobulins in senile plaques by means of fluorescent antibody technique. *Acta Neuropathol.* **32**, 157.

Jacobs, J.W., Bernhard, M.R., Delgado, A., and Strain, J.J. (1977). Screening for organic mental syndromes in the medically ill. *Ann. Intern. Med.* **86**, 40.

Jacoby, J.J. and Levy, R. (1980). Computed tomography in the elderly. 2. Senile dementia: diagnosis and functional impairment. *Br. J. Psychiatry* **136**, 256.

Jarvik, L.F. (1980). Diagnosis of dementia in the elderly: a 1980 perspective. *Ann. Rev. Gerontol. Geriatr.* **1**, 180.

Kahn, R.L. and Miller, N.E. (1978). Adaptational factors in memory function in the aged. *Exp. Aging Res.* **4**, 273.

Kahn, R.L., Goldfarb, A.I., Pollack, M., and Peck, A. (1960). Brief objective measures for the determination of mental status in the aged. *Am. J. Psychiatry* **117**, 326.

Kahn, R.L., Zarit, S. H., Hilbert, N.M., and Niederehe, G. (1975). Memory complaint and impairment in the aged. The effect of depression and altered brain function. *Arch. Gen. Psychiatry* **32**, 1569.

Kaneko, Z. (1975). Care in Japan. In *Modern perspectives in the psychiatry of old age* (ed. J.G. Howells) p. 519. Brunner/Magel, New York.

Kaszniak, A.W., Fox, J., Gandell, D.L., Garron, D.C., Huckman, M.S., and Ramsey, R.G. (1978). Predictors of mortality in presenile and senile dementia. *Ann. Neurol.* **3**, 246.

Katzman, R. (1976). The prevalence and malignancy of Alzheimer disease, a major killer. *Arch. Neurol.* **33**, 217.

Kaufman, H.H. and Catalano, L.W. (1979). Diagnostic brain biopsy: a series of 50 cases and a review. *Neurosurgery* **4**, 128.

Kay, D.W.K. (1962). Outcome and cause of death in mental disorders of old age. A long-term follow-up of functional and organic psychoses. *Acta Psychiatr. Scand.* **38**, 249.

Kay, D.W.K., Beamish, P., and Roth, M. (1964*a*). Old age mental disorders in Newcastle upon Tyne. Part I: a study of prevalence. *Br. J. Psychiatry* **110**, 146.

Kay, D.W.K., Beamish, P., and Roth, M. (1964*b*). Old age mental disorders in Newcastle upon Tyne. Part II: a study of possible social and medical causes. *Br. J. Psychiatry* **110**, 668.

Kay, D.W.K., Bergmann, K., McKechnie, A.A., Foster, E.M., and Roth, M. (1970). Mental illness and hospital usage in the elderly: a random sample followed up. *Compr. Psychiatry* **11**, 26.

Kidd, C.B. (1962). Criteria for admission of the elderly to geriatric and psychiatric units. *J. Ment. Sci.* **108**, 68.

Klerman, G.L. (1962). Age and clinical depression: today's youth in the twenty-first century. *J. Gerontol.* **31**, 318–23.

Landy, P.J. and Bain, B.J. (1970). Alzheimer's disease in siblings. *Med. J. Aust.* **2**, 832.

Larson, T., Sjögren, T., and Jacobson, G. (1963). Senile dementia.

A clinical sociomedical and genetic study. *Acta Psychiatr. Scand.* Suppl. **167**.

Lauter, H. and Meyer, J.E. (1968). Clinical and nosological concepts of senile dementia. In *Senile dementia, clinical and therapeutic aspects* (eds. C.H. Muller and L. Ciompi) p. 13. Hans Huber, Bern.

Lawton, M.P. and Brody, E. (1969). Assessment of older people: self-maintaining and instrumental activities of daily living. *Gerontologist* **9**, 177.

Lazarus, L.W., Stafford, B., Cooper, K., Cohler, B., and Dysken, M. (1981). A pilot study of Alzheimer patients' relatives discussion group. *Gerontologists* **21**, 353.

Levy, L. and Rowitz, L. (1973). *The ecology of mental disorder.* Behavioral Publications, New York.

Lewis, A.F. (1981). Fracture of the neck of the femur: changing incidence. *Br. Med. J.* **283**, 1217.

Lieberman, A., Dziatolowski, M., Kupersmith, M. *et al.* (1979). Dementia in Parkinson disease. *Ann. Neurol.* **6**, 355.

Lijtmaer, H., Fuld, P.A., and Katzman, R. (1976). Prevalence and malignancy of Alzheimer disease. *Arch. Neurol.* **33**, 304.

Lin, T. (1953). A study of the incidence of mental disorder in Chinese and other cultures. *Psychiatry* **16**, 313.

Liston, E.H.Jr (1979). The clinical phenomenology of presenile dementia. A critical review of the literature. *J. Nerv. Ment. Dis.* **167**, 329.

Loranger, A.W., Goodell, H., McDowell, F.H., Lee, J.E., and Sweet, R.D. (1972). Intellectual impairment in Parkinson's syndrome. *Brain* **95**, 405.

Lowenberg, K. and Waggoner, R.W. (1934). Familial organic psychosis (Alzheimer's type). *Arch. Neurol Psychiatry* **31**, 737.

Lowther, C.P. and Williamson, J. (1966). Old people and their relatives. *Lancet* **ii**, 1459.

Mann, D.M.A., Lincoln, J., Yates, P.O., and Brennan, C.M. (1980). Monoamine metabolism in Down syndrome. *Lancet* **ii**, 1366.

Manuelidis, E.E. and Manuelidis, L. (1980). Observations on Creuzfeldt–Jakob disease propogated in small rodents. In *Slow transmissible diseases of the nervous system* (eds. S.B. Prusiner and W.J. Hadlow) Vol. 2, p. 147. Academic Press, New York.

Marsden, C.D. and Harrison, M.J.G. (1972). Outcome of investigation of patients with presenile dementia. *Br. Med. J.* **ii**, 249.

Martin, W.E., Lowenson, R.B., Resch, J.A., and Baker, A.B. (1973). Parkinson's disease: clinical analysis of 100 patients. *Neurology* **23**, 783.

Marttila, R.J. and Rinne, U.K. (1976). Dementia in Parkinson's disease. *Acta Neurol. Scand.* **54**, 431.

Masters, C.L., Harris, J.O., Gajdusek, C., Gibbs, C.J.Jr, Bernoulli, C., and Asher, D.M. (1979). Creutzfeldt–Jakob disease: patterns of worldwide occurrence and the significance of familial and sporadic clustering. *Ann. Neurol.* **5**, 177.

Matsuyama, H. and Nakamura, S. (1978). Senile changes in the brain in the Japanese: incidence of Alzheimer's neurofibrillary change and senile plaques. In *Alzheimer's disease: senile dementia and related disorders* (eds. R. Katzman, R.D. Terry, and K.L. Bick) p. 287. Raven, New York.

Matsuyama, H., Namiki, H. and Watanabe, I. (1966). Senile changes in the brain in the Japanese. Incidence of Alzheimer's neurofibrillary changes and senile plaques. In *Proceedings of the Fifth International Congress of Neuropathology* (eds. F. Luthy and A. Bischoff) p. 979. Excerpta Medica, Amsterdam.

Mayeux, R. (1982). Depression and dementia in Parkinson's disease. In *Movement disorders* (eds. C.D. Marsden and S. Fahn) p. 75. Butterworth, London.

McDermott, J.R., Smith, A.I., Iqbal, R., and Wisniewski, H.M. (1977). Aluminum and Alzheimer's disease. *Lancet* **ii**, 710.

McFarland, D.D. (1978). The aged in the 21st century: a demographer's view. In *Aging into the 21st century* (ed. L.F. Jarvik) p. 5. Gardner Press, New York.

McGeer, E. and McGeer, P.L. (1967). Neurotransmitter metabolism in the aging brain. In *Neurobiology of aging* (ed. R.D. Terry and S. Gershon) p. 389. Raven Press, New York.

McMenemy, W.H. (1963). Alzheimer's disease: problems concerning its concept and nature. *Acta Neurol. Scand.* **39**, 369.

Merskey, H., Ball, M.J., Blume, W.T. *et al.* (1980). Relationships between psychological measurements and cerebral organic changes in Alzheimer's disease. *J. Can. Sci. Neurol.* **7**, 45.

Miller, A.E., Neighbour, P.A., Katzman, R., Aronson, M., and Lipkowitz, R. (1981). Immunological studies in senile dementia of the Alzheimer type: evidence for enhanced supressor cell activity. *Ann. Neurol.* **10**, 506.

Miller, E. (1977). *Abnormal aging. The psychology of senile and presenile dementia.* John Wiley, London.

Miller, E. and Hague, F. (1975). Some statistical characteristics of speech in presenile dementia. *Psychol. Med.* **5**, 255.

Money, J., Alexander, D., and Walker, H.J.Jr (1966). A standardized road-map test of direction sense. Johns Hopkins Press, Baltimore.

Morley, G.K., Haxby, J.V., and Lundgren, S.L. (1980). Memory, aging and dementia. In *The aging nervous system* (ed. G.J. Maletta and F.J. Pisozzolo) p. 211. Praeger Scientific, New York.

Mortimer, J.A. (1980). Epidemiological aspects of Alzheimer's disease. In *The aging nervous system* (ed. G.J. Maletta and F.J. Pirozzolo) p. 307. Praeger Scientific, New York.

Nandy, K. (1981). Senile dementia: a possible immune hypothesis. In *The epidemiology of dementia* (ed. J.A. Mortimer and L.M. Schuman) p. 87. Oxford University Press, New York.

Nielsen, J., Homma, A., and Biørn-Henriksen, T. (1977). Follow-up 15 years after a geronto-psychiatric prevalence study. Conditions concerning death, cause of death, and life expectancy in relation to psychiatric diagnosis. *J. Gerontol* **32**, 554.

Nott, P.N. and Fleminger, J.J. (1975). Presenile dementia: the difficulty of early diagnosis. *Acta Psychiatr. Scand.* **51**, 210.

Outram, G.W., Fraser, H., and Wilson, D.T. (1973). Scrapie in mice. Some effects in the brain lesion profile of ME 7 agent due to genotype of donor, route of infection and genotype of recipient. *J. Comp. Pathol.* **83**, 19.

Pearce, J.M.S. and Pearce, I. (1979). The nosology of Alzheimer's disease. In *Alzheimer's disease: early recognition of potentially reversible deficits* (eds. A.I.M. Glen and L.J. Whaley) p. 93. Churchill Livingstone, Edinburgh.

Pegels, C.C. (1980). *Health care and the elderly.* Aspen, Rockville.

Peress, N.S., Kane, W.C., and Aronson, S.M. (1973). Central nervous system findings in a tenth decade autospy population. *Prog. Brain Res.* **40**, 473.

Perl, D.P. and Brody, A.R. (1980). Alzheimer's disease. X-ray spectometric evidence of aluminum accumulation in neurofibrillary tangle-bearing neurones. *Science* **208**, 297.

Perry, E.K., Gibson, P.H., Blessed, G., Perry, R.H., and Tomlinson, B.E. (1977*a*). Neurotransmitter enzyme abnormalities in senile dementia. *J. Neurol. Sci.* **34**, 247.

Perry, E.K., Perry, R.H., Blessed, G., and Tomlinson, B.E. (1977*b*). Necropsy evidence of central cholinergic deficits in dementia. *Lancet* **i**, 189.

Perry, E.K., Perry, R.H., Gibson, P.H., Blessed, G., and Tomlinson, B.E. (1977*c*). A cholinergic connection between normal aging and senile dementia in the human hippocampus. *Neurosci. Lett.* **6**, 85.

Perry, E.K., Tomlinson, B.E., Blessed, G., Bergmann, K., Gibson, P.H., and Perry, R.H. (1978). Correlations of cholinergic abnormalities with senile plaques and mental test scores in senile dementia. *Br. Med. J.* ii, 1457.

Perry, E.K., Tomlinson, B.E., Blessed, G., Perry, R.H., Cross, A.J., and Crow, T.T. (1981). Noradrenergic and cholinergic systems in senile dementia of Alzheimer type. *Lancet* ii, 149.

Pfeffer, R.I. (1983). A survey diagnostic tool for senile dementia. The first author replies. *Am. J. Epidemiol.* 117, 643.

Pfeffer, R.I., Kurosaki, T.T., Harrah, C.H.Jr, Chance, J.M., and Filos, S. (1982). Measurement of functional activities in older adults in the community. *J. Gerontol.* 37, 323.

Pfeffer, R.I., Kurosaki, T.T., Harrah, C.H.Jr, *et al.* (1981). A survey diagnostic tool for senile dementia. *Am. J. Epidemiol.* 114, 515.

Pfeiffer, E. (1975). A short portable mental status questionnaire for the assessment of organic brain deficit in elderly patients. *J. Am. Geriatr. Soc.* 23, 433–41.

Post, F. (1972). The management and nature of depressive illness in late life: a follow-through study. *Br. J. Psychiatry* 121, 393.

Post, F. (1975). Dementia, depression and pseudodementia. In *Psychiatric aspects of neurologic disease* (eds. D.J. Benson and D. Blumer) p. 99. Grune and Stratton, New York.

Potamianos, G. and Kellett, J.M. (1982). Anticholinergic drugs and memory: the effects of benzhexol in a group of geriatric patients. *Br. J. Psychiatry* 140, 470.

Prusiner, S.B., Gajdusek, D.C., and Alpers, M.O. (1982a). Kuru with incubation periods exceeding two decades. *Ann. Neurol.* 12, 1.

Prusiner, S.B., Cochran, S.P., Groth, D.F., Downey, D.E., Bowman, K.A., and Martinez, H.M. (1982b). Measurement of the scrapie agent using an incubation time assay. *Ann. Neurol.* 12, 1.

Raskin, A. (1979). Signs and symptoms of psychopathology in the elderly. In *Psychiatric symptoms and cognitive loss in the elderly. Evaluation and assessment techniques.* (eds. A. Raskin and L. Jarvik) p. 3. Hemisphere, Washington, DC.

Reifler, B.V., Cox, G.B., and Hanley, R.J. (1981). Problems of mentally ill elderly as perceived by patients, families and clinicians. *Gerontologists* 21, 165.

Reifler, B.V., Larson, E., and Hanley, R. (1982). Coexistence of cognitive impairment and depression in geriatric outpatients. *Am. J. Psychiatry* 139, 623.

Rochford, G. (1971). A study of naming errors in dysphasic and demented patients. *Neuropsychologia* 9, 437.

Ron, M.A., Toone, B.K., Garralda, M.E., and Lishman, W.A. (1979). Diagnostic accuracy in presenile dementia. *Br. J. Psychiatry* 134, 161.

Roos, D. (1978). Neurological complications in patients with impaired vitamin B12 absorption following partial gastrectomy. *Acta Neurol. Scand.* 59, 1.

Rosen, W.G., Terry, R.D., Fuld, P.A., Katzman, R., and Peck, A. (1980). Pathological verification of ischemic score in differentiation of dementias. *Ann. Neurol.* 7, 486.

Rossor, M.N., Iversen, L.L., Johnson, A.J., Mountjoy, C.Q., and Roth, M. (1981). Cholinergic deficit in frontal cerebral cortex is age dependent. *Lancet* ii, 1422.

Roth, M. (1955). The natural history of mental disorder in old age. *J. Ment. Sci.* 101, 281.

Roth, M. (1971). Classification and aetiology in mental disorders of old age. In *Recent developments in psychogeriatrics* (eds. D.W.K. Kay and A. Walk) p. 1. Headley Brothers, Ashford, Kent.

Roth, M. (1979). The early diagnosis of Alzheimer's disease–summary. In *Alzheimer's disease: early recognition of potentially reversible deficits* (eds. A.I.M. Glen and L.J. Whalley) p. 133. Churchill Livingstone, Edinburgh.

Royal College of Physicians, Committee on Geriatrics (1981). Organic mental impairment in the elderly. Implication for research, education and provision of services. *J. R. Coll. Physicians Lond.* 15, 141.

Sabouraud, O., Chatel, M., Menault, F. *et al.* (1978). L'encephalopathic myoclonique progressive des dialyses. *Rev. Neurol.* 134, 575.

Sanford, J.R.A. (1975). Tolerance of debility in elderly dependents by supporters at home: its significance for hospital practice. *Br. Med. J.* iii, 471.

Scheibel, A.B. (1978). Structural aspects of the aging brain: spine systems and the dendritic arbor. In *Alzheimer's disease: senile dementia and related disorders* (eds. R. Katzman, R.D. Terry, and K.L. Bick). p. 353. Raven, New York.

Sharman, M.J., Watt, D.C., Janota, L., and Carrasco, L.H. (1979). Alzheimer's disease in a mother and identical twin sons. *Psychol. Med.* 9, 771.

Sim, M. (1979). Early diagnosis of Alzheimer's disease. In *Alzheimer's disease: early recognition of potentially reversible deficits* (eds. A.I.M. Glen and L.J. Whalley) p. 78. Churchill Livingstone, Edinburgh.

Sims, N.R., Bowen, D.M, Smith, C.C.T. *et al.* (1980). Glucose metabolism and acetylcholine synthesis in relation to neuronal activity in Alzhiemer's disease. *Lancet* i, 333.

Sjögren, H. (1950). Twenty-four cases of Alzheimer's disease. A clinical analysis. *Acta Med. Scand.* Suppl. 246, 225.

Slater, E. and Cowie, V. (1971). *The genetics of mental disorders.* Oxford University Press, London,

Sluss, T.K., Gruenberg, E.M., and Kramer, M. (1979). The use of longitudinal studies in the investigation of risk factors on senile dementia – Alzheimer type. In *Epidemiology of dementia* (ed. J.A. Mortimer and L.M. Schuman) p. 132. Oxford, New York.

Smith, A. (1973). *Symbol digit modalities test.* Western Psychological Services, Los Angeles.

Smith, J.S. and Kiloh, L.G. (1981). The investigation of dementia: results in 200 consecutive admissions. *Lancet* i, 824.

Smith, W.T., Turner, E., and Sim, M. (1966). Cerebral biopsy in the investigation of senile dementia. II. Pathological aspects. *Br. J. Psychiat.* 112, 127.

Sourander, P. and Sjögren, H. (1970). The concept of Alzheimer's disease and its clinical implications. In *Alzheimer's disease and related conditions* (eds. G.E.W. Wolstenholme and M. O'Connor) p. 11. Churchill, London.

Squire, L.R. (1974). Remote memory as affected by aging. *Neuropsychologia* 12, 429.

Steele, J.C. (1972). Progressive supranuclear palsy. *Brain* 95, 693.

Sternberg, D.E. and Jarvik, M.E. (1976). Memory functions in depression: improvement with antidepressant medication. *Arch. Gen. Psychiatry* 33, 219.

Sulkava, R., Koskimies, S., Wikstrom, J., and Palo, J. (1980). HLA antigens in Alzheimer's disease. *Tissue Antigens* 16, 191.

Tavolato, B. and Argentiero, V. (1980). Immunological indices in presenile Alzheimer's disease. *J. Neurol. Sci.* 46, 325.

Terry, R.D. and Davies, P. (1980). Dementia of the Alzheimer type. *Ann. Rev. Neurosci.* 3, 77.

Terry, R.D. and Wisniewski, H. (1970). The ultrastructure of the neurofibrillary tangle and the senile plaque. In *Alzheimer's disease and related conditions* (eds. G.E.W. Wolstenholme and M. O'Connor) p. 45. Churchill, London.

Terry, R.D., Peck, A., DeTeresa, R., Schechter, R., and Horoupian, D.S. (1981). Some morphometric aspects of the brain in senile dementia of the Alzheimer type. *Ann. Neurol.* 10, 184.

Todorov, A.B., Go, R.C.P., Constantinidis, J., and Elston, R.C. (1975). Specificity of the clinical diagnosis of dementia. *J. Neurol. Sci.* 26, 81.

Tomlinson, B.E. (1977). The pathology of dementia. In *Dementia* (ed. C.E. Wells) p. 113. Davis, Philadelphia.

Tomlinson, B.E. and Henderson, G. (1976). Some quantitative cerebral findings in normal and demented old people. In *Neurobiology of aging* (eds. R.D. Terry and S. Gershon) p. 183. Raven Press, New York.

Tomlinson, B.E., Blessed, G., and Roth, M. (1968). Observations on the brains of non-demented old people. *J. Neurol. Sci.* **7**, 331.

Tomlinson, B.E., Blessed, G., and Roth, M. (1970). Observations on the brains of demented old people. *J. Neurol Sci.* **11**, 205.

Torack, R.M. (1979). Adult dementia: history, biopsy, pathology. *Neurosurgery* **4**, 434.

Trapp, G.A., Miner, G.D., Zimmerman, R.L., Mastri, A.R., and Heston, L.L. (1978). Aluminum levels in brain in Alzheimer's disease. *Br. Psychiatry* **13**, 709.

Uhl, G.R., McKinney, M., Hedreen, J.C. *et al.* (1982). Dementia pugilistica: loss of basal forebrain cholinergic neurons and cortical cholinergic markers. *Ann. Neurol.* **12**, 99.

Ulrich, J. (1982). Senile plaques and neurofibrillary tangles of the Alzheimer type in nondemented individuals at presenile age. *Gerontology* **28**, 86.

US Bureau of the Census. *Demographic aspects of aging and the older population in the US. Current Population Reports Special Studies.* Series P-34, No. 59. US Department of Commerce, Washington (1976).

Verwoerdt, A. (1981). Individual psychotherapy in senile dementia. In *Clinical aspects of Alzheimer's disease and senile dementia* (eds. N.E. Miller and G.D. Cohen) p. 187. Raven, New York.

Victoratos, G.C., Lenman, J.A.R., and Herzberg, L. (1977). Neurological investigation of dementia. *Br. J. Psychiatry* **130**, 131.

Walford, R.L. and Hodge, S.E. (1980). HLA distribution in Alzheimer's disease. In *Histocompatibility testing 1980,* Vol. I (ed. P.I. Terasaki) p. 727. UCLA tissue typing Laboratory, Los Angeles.

Wang, H.S. and Busse, E.W. (1974). EEG of healthy old persons. In *Reports from the Duke Longitudinal Study: normal aging II* (ed. E. Palmore), p. 126. Duke University Press, Durham.

Ward, B.E., Cook, R.H., Robinson, A., and Austin, J.H. (1979). Increased aneuploidy in Alzheimer's disease. *Am. J. Med. Genet.* **3**, 137.

Warshaw, G.A., Moore, J.T., Friedman, W. *et al.* (1982). Functional disability in the hospitalized elderly *J. Am. Med.* **248**, 847.

Watts, H., Kennedy, P.G.E., and Thomas, M. (1981). The significance of anti-neuronal antibodies in Alzheimer disease. *J. Neuroimmunol.* **1**, 107.

Wells, C.E. (1977). Diagnostic evaluation and treatment in dementia. In *Dementia* (ed. C.E. Wells), p. 247. Davis, Philadelphia.

Wells, C.E. (1982). Pseudodementia and the recognition of organicity. In *Psychiatric aspects of neurologic disease,* Vol. II (ed. D.F. Benson and D. Blumer), p. 167. Grune and Stratton, New York.

Whalley, L.J., Carothers, A.D., Collyer, S., DeMey, R., and Frackiewicz, A. (1982). A study of familial factors in Alzheimer's disease. *Br. J. Psychiatry* **140**, 249.

Wheelan, L. (1959). Familial Alzheimer's disease. *Ann. Hum. Genet.* **23**, 300.

White, B.J., Crandall, C., Goudsmit, J. *et al.* (1981). Cytogenetic studies of familial and sporadic Alzheimer disease. *Am. J. Med. Gener.* **10**, 77.

White, P., Goodhardt, M.J., Keat, J.P. *et al.* (1977). Neocortical neurons in elderly people. *Lancet* i, 668.

Whitehouse, P.J., Hedreen, J.C., White, C., DeLong, M., and Price, D.L. (1982a). Loss of neurons in the nucleus basalis in the dementia of Parkinson disease. *Neurology* **32**, A228.

Whitehouse, P.J., Price, D.L., Clark, A.W., Coyle, J.T., and DeLong, M.R. (1981). Alzheimer disease: evidence for selective loss of cholinergic neurons in the nucleus basalis. *Ann. Neurol.* **10**, 122.

WHitehouse, P.J., Price, D.L., Struble, R.G., Clark, A.W., Coyle, J.T., and DeLong, M.R. (1982b). Alzheimer's disease and senile dementia loss of neurons in the basal forebrain. *Science* **215**, 1237.

Wilcox, C.B., Caspary, E.A., and Behan, P.O. (1980). Histo-compatability antigens in Alzheimer's disease. A preliminary study. *Eur. Neurol.* **20**, 25.

Wilkinson, A. and Davies, I. (1978). The influence of age and dementia on the neurone population of the mammillary bodies. *Age Ageing* **71**, 151.

Wilson, R.S., Kaszniak, A.W., and Fox, J.H. (1981). Remote memory in senile dementia. *Cortex* **17**, 41.

Wisniewski, H. and Terry, R.D. (1970). An experimental approach to the morphogenesis of neurofibrillary degeneration and the argyrophelic plaque. In *Alzheimer's disease and related conditions* (eds. G.E.W. Wolstenholme and M. O'Connor) p. 223. Churchill, London.

Wisniewski, H., Moretz, R.C., and Lossinsky, A.S. (1981). Evidence for induction of localized amyloid deposits and neuritic plaques by an infectious agent. *Ann. Neurol.* **10**, 517.

Wisniewski, H., Narang, H.K., and Terry, R.D. (1976). Neurofibrillary tangles of paired helical filaments. *J. Neurol. Sci.* **27**, 173.

Wisniewski, K., Jervis, G.A., Moretz, R.C., and Wisniewski, H.M. (1979). Alzheimer neurofibrillary tangles in diseases other than senile and presenile dementia. *Ann. Neurol.* **5**, 288.

Yates, C.M., Simpson, J., Maloney, A.F.J., Gordon, A., and Reid, A.H. (1980). Alzheimer-like cholinergic deficiency in Down's syndrome. *Lancet* ii, 979.

Zarit, S.H., Reever, K.E., and Bach-Peterson, J. (1980). Relatives of the impaired elderly: correlates of feelings of burden. *Gerontologist* **20**, 649.

6 The application of public health methods to control: psychiatric

Michael Shepherd

INTRODUCTION

The general recognition of the interdependence of public health and psychiatry is relatively recent. The earlier public health teaching, as reflected in the content of nineteenth century textbooks, placed little emphasis on the need for an understanding of mental disease and disability, mental subnormality apart. Psychiatric opinion in the past has been equally limited; it was epitomized in the statement, publicly expressed in 1868, that 'the health problem of urgent concern to all public asylums is sewage irrigation in its many aspects'. The tenacious beliefs held by some psychiatrists in the aetiological importance of microorganisms for many mental illnesses probably represented their tribute to the successful public health campaigns against infectious diseases. Even so far-sighted an observer as Henry Maudsley was unable to see much future for the public health outlook in the sphere of mental illness (Rees 1957).

The isolation of mental hospital practice undoubtedly retarded the interest of psychiatrists in these matters, but in the early years of this century, R.G. Rows, Assistant Medical Officer and Pathologist to the Lancaster County Asylum, was so impressed by the organization and work of the German university psychiatric clinics as to comment adversely on the British asylum service (Rows 1912). He concluded that:

...the causes of insanity resemble the causes of other diseases to combat which our service of Public Health has been instituted; and that in order to achieve any good results in the treatment of mental disorder, the work must be undertaken by a service of men of high scientific training and keen enthusiasm.

Though the title of Rows' paper, 'The development of psychiatric science as a branch of public health', struck a challenging note at that time, it was only 14 years later that the president of the Royal Medico-Psychological Association declared this important body to be 'concerned with the practice of psychiatry in the broadest sense. Psychiatry and mental hygiene are to be regarded as part of the larger problem of public health' (Ward 1926).

None the less, until the outbreak of the Second World War, mental hygiene probably carried more meaning for public health workers than for psychiatrists. Since its inception in the US, the mental hygiene movement was primarily concerned with psychiatric issues in the community at large – the school, the home, and the courts – as well as with the out-patient clinic. In Britain between the Wars, much of the ground was broken by the voluntary organizations: an account of the pre-war activities of the Mental After-Care Association, the Child Guidance Council, the Central Association for Mental Welfare, and the National Council for Mental Hygiene is clearly set out in the Faversham Committee's report on the Voluntary Mental Health Services, originally published in 1939.

The Second World War exposed the neglected field of mental health to public scrutiny. In the armed forces the dimensions of psychiatric disability were soon recognized. Simultaneously, attention focused on the potential psychological dangers to the civilian population. Mackintosh (1944), provides a lucid commentary on these problems from the public health standpoint. In the military and non-military spheres alike, the need to develop effective community action as well as the more individual procedures associated with traditional psychiatric practice became apparent. The Goodenough Report (Ministry of Health and Department of Health for Scotland 1944) commented on the affiliations between public health, in its new guise of social medicine, and psychiatry. Whatever view is held of the claims of social medicine, Ryle's concept of a discipline which 'places the emphasis on man and endeavours to study him in relation to his environment' bears an obvious affinity to the expanded view of psychiatry, advanced by the Royal College of Physicians, as 'the study of human behaviour in its social setting'.

The administrative machinery of the UK National Health Service (NHS) was to lay the basis of co-operation between the psychiatric and the public health services. The links have been provided by epidemiological concepts, whose importance have been increasingly accepted by specialists in psychological medicine (Reid 1960; Cooper and Morgan 1973). Public health workers are dependent on estimates of the prevalence and distribution of mental disorder in order to assess the need for medical and paramedical care. In practice the mentally sick population can be sub-divided into those who are known to, or ascertained by, the mental health services and those who are undetected by such services, and for convenience these two groups are considered separately here.

CASES DETECTED BY THE MENTAL HEALTH SERVICES

The mental hospital is the traditional source of information concerning cases of mental disorder which declare themselves to the mental health services. The systematic collection of data on a large scale began in the US and Scandinavia during the early nineteenth century. In the UK national records of the institutional treatment of mentally sick persons have been available since 1845, but the routine collection of mental hospital statistics was not reorganized systematically until 1949, after the passage of the National Health Service Act. Since the Second World War a great quantity of material has been amassed in those countries which possess the means of collecting and analysing morbidity statistics. Most of the information collected in this way, however, is relatively crude and of primarily administrative interest. For scientific purposes the data are less satisfactory. It has been maintained that in-patient hospital statistics can illuminate the attack-rates and prevalence of schizophrenic disorder, because most patients suffering from this condition are admitted to hospital at some time during their illness. But this underestimates the many 'nosocomial' factors which influence hospital admission and figures obtained from this source should be treated with caution (Svendsen 1952; Norris 1959).

Despite these problems, mental hospital statistics can furnish useful information, especially by means of the 'trend analysis' which utilizes the routine statistics obtained over a period of time. This process is easier to apply when one institution is studied intensively. Historically, for example, Grob (1966) showed how the fluctuations in social policy, public attitudes, and psychiatric theory affected the activities of the Worcester State Hospital in Massachusetts from 1830 to 1920. More recently, such data have been used to assess the impact of a succession of new physical methods of treatment on mental hospital populations. Not long after the appearance of the new psychotropic drugs in the early 1950s, individual

workers began to employ this method in support of their claims for therapeutic action. Probably the most influential of these reports came from New York State, where the arrival of large scale chemotherapy had coincided with a sharp fall in the number of discharges (Brill and Patton 1959). Similar trends were recorded by the national mental hospital statistics of the UK and led to similar assumptions about causation. It was, however, quickly realized that any adequate explanation of crude statistics must take into account a host of non-specific factors which contribute to the ambience of hopeful enthusiasm which accompanies any novel therapeutic procedure. If such factors were to play a significant role it would follow that the impact of psychotropic drugs, as reflected by the population dynamics, would be much smaller in institutions where a high degree of patient care had already been attained.

To examine this hypothesis an intensive study was carried out of an English mental hospital. This employed a complex statistical analysis of several factors, including: the average annual numbers of patients in different diagnostic categories who were resident, admitted or discharged; the mortality rate, 'quittance rate' and 'net release rate'; and the numbers receiving various quantities of psychotropic drugs. An earlier study had provided base-line statistics relating to hospital activity in the 1930s and 1940s (Shepherd 1957). The period of intensive study covered the four years extending from 1954, the year preceding the introduction of the drugs, to 1957, by which time they were widely prescribed (Shepherd *et al.* 1961). A marked improvement, in terms of a higher discharge-rate and a shorter hospital stay, had already taken place in the mid-1940s – that is, long before the introduction of psychotropic drugs. This was probably attributable to the somatic treatments of the day allied to an unusually progressive mental health service. Between 1954 and 1958, however, there was very little change in the resident population (Fig. 6.1). The probable explanation is that before the introduction of large-scale pharmacotherapy, the hospital was functioning as part of an effective mental health service which had already taken up the therapeutic slack. Ødegaard (1964), analysed the mental hospital statistics of Norway over a similar period and

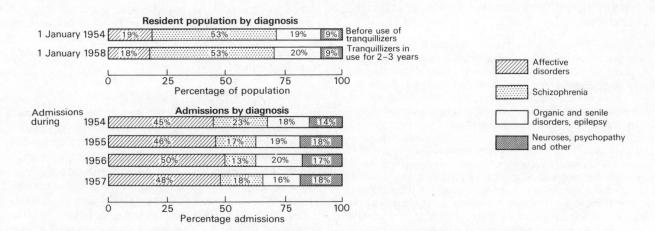

Fig. 6.1. Residents of, and admission to psychiatric hospitals before and after the introduction of tranquillizers.

in a very similar manner. His data were comparable in respect of both the relatively static picture following the introduction of psychotropic drugs and the marked change during the 1940s. Ødegaard, however, identified the general fall in unemployment in Norway as the factor which had facilitated rehabilitation. His chastening conclusion was that 'in hospitals with a favourable therapeutic situation the psychotropic drugs brought little or no improvement, or even a decrease in the rate of discharges. In hospitals with a low pre-drug discharge-rate, on the other hand, the improvement was considerable'.

Although mental hospital in-patient statistics can be used for such purposes, their potential value has been sharply limited by the increasing trend in many countries for hospitals to be functionally related to a 'catchment' area to which they provide a variety of services. In the field of psychiatry this concept has led to an extension of the mental health services to include a variety of extramural facilities, such as out-patient clinics, day hospitals, hostels, and half-way houses. This development has been accompanied by a tendency to avoid long-term institutional care. Thus, many patients who previously spent long, uninterrupted periods of time in hospitals now have their illnesses 'fragmented' into discrete episodes of contact with one or more mental health facilities. Information about these altered patterns of morbidity can be collected in a more systematic way by the use and development of psychiatric case registers, though the limitations of the case-register as an epidemiological technique must be borne in mind (Baldwin and Evans 1971).

CASES NOT DETECTED BY THE MENTAL HEALTH SERVICES

One of the most impressive contributions made by epidemiological research to public health aspects of psychiatry has been the demonstration of how relatively little mental disorder comes to the attention of the mental-health services in even highly developed countries. The early findings of Taylor and Chave (1964), who attempted to study the prevalence of mental disorder in an urban community, illustrate the patterns of morbidity in relation to medical services. They have summarized their study as follows:

Considering no single index of health to be adequate for their purpose, these investigators set out to chart mental illness in their survey population in terms of mental hospital admission, referrals to the local psychiatric out-patient clinical, general practice consultations for psychiatric symptoms and, finally, self-reported nervous complaints recorded in the course of door-to-door interviewing of a random sample of the population. The four reported complaints taken as *prima facie* evidence of psychiatric disturbance were 'nerves', depression, sleeplessness and undue irritability. Persons with one or more of these complaints who were not under medical care were regarded as at increased risk for neurotic illness and were classed as a 'sub-clinical neurosis' group. On this basis, the findings of the enquiry showed that of the adult population of Newton in 1959, 30 per 1000 were treated by general practitioners for definite psychiatric illness; 4.4 per 1000 were referred to an out-patient psychiatric clinic; 1.9 per cent were admitted as in-patients for psychiatric treatment (Taylor and Chave 1964).

The limitations of such figures are apparent: at the time little was known about the criteria for extramural case-identification, and the concept of 'sub-clinical' neurosis is very wide-ranging. None the less, the large disparity between the number of cases seen in hospital and in the community has been confirmed by other studies. This can be explained by the relatively small proportion of patients with neurotic and personality-disorder who come to the attention of the hospital-based services (Kessel and Shepherd 1962). In addition, there are many patients who suffer from psychiatric disorders primarily associated with physical disease or who exhibit prominent physical symptoms as part of their psychiatric disorder. Their principal contact with medical services is with general physicians or surgeons rather than with psychiatrists (Shepherd *et al.* 1960). The existence of this sizeable group must be recognized in any attempt to estimate the amount of undetected mental disorder.

For these reasons some importance attaches to the question of *screening* for mental disorder. Of the ten guidelines for screening proposed by Wilson and Jungner (1968), only one is wholly applicable to mental disease, namely that it is an important public health problem. Most work on psychiatric screening has been carried out indirectly as part of population studies involving case-identification. This usually must be conducted in two stages for large-scale field surveys because of the difficulty of examining large numbers of people. The first stage is a form of screening procedure which may or may not coincide with the routine work of local agencies and which, in effect, yields suspected or 'potential' cases; the second stage consists of a more intensive examination whereby such suspected cases may be verified or rejected (Cooper and Morgan 1973).

Psychiatric case-identification: Stage I

The methods which have been employed for psychiatric screening do not lend themselves readily to any simple systematic classification. Some rely upon information supplied by key informants, others make use of formal investigations or tests. Some are applicable to the general population, others only to special subcategories designated by sex, age-group, occupation, or physical health. Some are employed in the setting of medical or paramedical agencies, or of non-medical agencies such as schools or penal institutions, others are used in the wider community. Here, we need consider only the principal sources of information and the techniques which are utilized.

Sources of information

In rural areas, where both the density and the mobility of populations are low, a great deal of information can be obtained from *key informants* such as general practitioners, public health nurses, school-teachers, clergymen and the police. This method is most valuable in situations where formal testing would be difficult, and has been employed in surveys in various parts of the world (Brugger 1933; Roth and Luton 1944; Lin 1953). Key informants have proved to be reliable in surveys of the major psychoses and of mental retardation. They are, however, much less useful in detecting the milder, non-psychotic disorders with which psychiatry has come to be concerned, and in advanced industrial societies their importance is much reduced.

The general hospital is also a repository of much unrecognized psychiatric illness. Over the past forty years several surveys have confirmed the high prevalence of psychiatric disturbance among patients attending medical out-patient clinics (Davies 1964). For what is probably a complex series of reasons, general hospital out-patients constitute an important high-risk group for psychiatric screening.

The same can be said of general practice patients and, where the bulk of the population is enrolled with general practitioners, as under the British National Health Service, the registered patient-population can provide a very useful sampling frame for epidemiological inquiry. In the absence of a state health service, prepaid medical care schemes may be utilized for the same purpose, although the coverage provided by such schemes must be seriously incomplete. Estimates of psychiatric morbidity among general practice patients have varied widely, the most detailed and comprehensive survey yielding a total prevalence rate of 140 per 1000 adults at risk, or a little over one-fifth of all those who consulted during the survey years (Shepherd et al. 1981). In general, neurotic patients tend to be frequent users of medical services so that the shorter the time-span of observation, the higher the proportion of neurotic illness among those who consult. In one consecutive series of over 500 general practice attenders, for example, nearly half were diagnosed as suffering from neurotic disorders (Goldberg and Blackwell 1970).

General practitioners' lists have been used as a framework for *ad hoc* screening surveys, and the district nurse has been shown to be an effective agent for the purpose in psychogeriatrics (Harwin 1975). The systematic use of paramedical agencies may also provide a valuable screening system for some types of morbidity. A well-recognized example is the early detection of childhood disorders through routine home-visiting and testing by public health nurses. Social workers and public health nurses have also been found to be at least as effective as doctors in the detection of chronic alcoholism (Prys Williams and Glatt 1966). Social agencies concerned with delinquency, child care, and welfare of the elderly may all be viewed as potentially valuable for psychiatric screening. The school system is an important framework for surveys of mental retardation and behaviour disorders in childhood (Kushlick 1969; Shepherd et al. 1971). Industrial surveys have been used to screen working populations for neurosis and for alcoholism (Fraser 1947), and the populations of reception centres for vagrants, prisons, and detention centres are other high-risk groups (Gibbens 1963; Edwards et al. 1968).

Interviews, rating scales, and questionnaires

In recent years increasing emphasis has been laid on standardized techniques which can be applied to all persons making contact with specified agencies or to samples of the general population. These techniques consist principally in structured or semi-structured ('guided') interviews, rating scales, or self-administered tests.

In the former, a non-medical research worker interviews members of a survey sample, using a structured schedule which is afterwards scrutinized by one or more psychiatrists who then make a clinical assessment without having seen the person concerned. Although diagnosis in the accepted sense may be impossible, some discrimination between 'cases' and 'normals' can be achieved. The Midtown Manhattan and Stirling County studies which both relied heavily upon this technique, produced findings very different from those of more clinically orientated surveys (Srole et al. 1962; Leighton et al. 1963) but the validity of this kind of psychiatric interviewing is low.

The second approach depends on the administration of an instrument, the responses to which can be scored simply and, when checked against a predetermined 'cutting-score', allows the probability of classifying the respondent as a psychiatric case to be calculated. Most of the many psychological scales that are available are unsuitable for screening purposes. The self-administered quesionnaire, usually in the form of a complaint inventory, is probably the most effective form of general psychiatric screening test on the grounds of cost, feasibility, and acceptability. Despite the relatively large number of these questionnaires, very few have been employed for epidemiological inquiries. By contrast, the General Health Questionnaire is noteworthy for the care with which it has been designed and validated (Goldberg 1972). Intended to pick out non-psychotic psychiatric illness, it is applicable in clinical work, community surveys or longitudinal studies aimed at assessing clinical change. By permitting a graduated response to each item, it avoids the errors inherent in response scales, while at the same time allowing any given response to be classed as normal or morbid. The wording of the items places the emphasis throughout on current ill health rather than on personality factors.

Psychiatric case-identification: Stage II

The central importance of the interview as the criterion of diagnosis in so many psychiatric conditions carried important implications for screening procedures.

The better-known surveys of the past have mostly been restricted to the unstandardized interviewing of probable cases detected by preliminary screening. For example, Lewis (1929) examined school children who had performed poorly in group intelligence tests; Lin (1953) in Formosa interviewed persons already named by key informants, and Mayer-Gross (1948) adopted the same procedure in Scotland. Over the past decade, however, more attention has been devoted to the construction of diagnostic interviews and of standardized classifications of mental disorder.

The construction of these instruments demands careful analysis of the normal diagnostic process. For hospital patients a group of American workers have developed a 'Psychiatric Status Schedule'(Spitzer et al. 1967). In the UK a similar approach was adopted in the design of the 'Present State Examination' which calls for an essentially clinical technique (Wing et al. 1974). A standardized psychiatric interview constructed specially for community surveys is, however, more directly relevant to screening (Goldberg et al. 1970). This interview schedule, which is used in conjunction with a detailed instruction manual, allows the examiner freedom to probe as necessary to elicit the duration, frequency and severity of symptoms or morbid states. It has a number of possible applications apart from case-identification. For example, it has been employed to test for associations between clinical and social variables in controlled studies (Cooper 1972) and as a means of rating change in psychiatric state.

PSYCHIATRIC ILLNESS AND PRIMARY CARE

From the public health standpoint the approach to psychiatric illness in the past decade has been revolutionized by a growing awareness of the role of the primary-care team in identifying and treating mental disorders. The new perspective was summarized by a WHO Group in its conclusion concerning the European scene: 'The crucial question is not how the general practitioner can fit into the mental health services but rather how the psychiatrist can collaborate most effectively with the primary medical services and reinforce the effectiveness of the primary physician as a member of the mental health team' (WHO 1973). Despite the differences in their medical-care systems, the same conclusion was reached in North America (Regier 1979) and in the developing countries (Harding et al. 1980).

Much of the evidence for this change in outlook has come from the series of studies mounted by the General Practice Research Unit at the Institute of Psychiatry of London University, to investigate the nature and extent of psychiatric morbidity in general practice (Shepherd et al. 1981). The bulk of this work has focused on 'conspicuous' morbidity, defined as 'illnesses or disabilities severe enough to lead to medical consultation and conforming to recognized clinical patterns for identification by the practitioners'. In general, however, the whole range of the so-called 'minor' mental disorders have been covered by surveys at the primary-care level. Further, such surveys can be applied to one of the more intractable problems in the sphere of mental disorder – the definition of a psychiatric 'case'. For operational purposes such cases are defined as an individual whose symptoms, behaviour, distress or discomfort leads to medical consultation at which a psychiatric diagnosis is made by a qualified physician. The more important findings of the early phase of this programme of research have been summarized by Shepherd (1974):

The demographic, social and diagnostic contours of this population are quite different from those provided by hospital statistics. Corresponding discrepancies are found in respect to outcome and therapeutic responses. Thus the data show that a large proportion of psychiatric morbidity encountered in family practice is made up of chronic disorders and in a seven-year follow-up study more than half the cohort exhibited a very poor outcome in terms of recurrence or chronicity.

Emotional disorders were found to be associated with a high demand for medical care. Those patients identified as suffering from psychiatric illness attended more frequently and exhibited higher rates of general morbidity and more categories of illness per head than the remainder of patients consulting their doctors.

Since the publication of these findings, similar results have been furnished by workers as far apart as Australia (Krupinsky and Stoller 1971), Iran (Bash and Bash-Liechtl 1974), and Austria (Strotzka 1969). They raise several issues relating to (a) diagnosis and outcome; (b) the relationship between physical and emotional disorder; and (c) the links between psychiatric illness and social dysfunction. Each of these issues will be considered separately below.

Diagnosis and outcome

The broad diagnostic distribution of mental disorder encountered at the primary-care level differs from the pattern of hospital illness (Table 6.1). The bulk of disorders are classified as 'minor affective illnesses', incorporating both anxiety states and depressive reactions, which are less easy to differentiate in a general practice population than among psychiatric out-patients or in-patients. Cooper (1972), in a study of eight general practices in London, found that anxiety and depression occurred to a comparable extent in both sexes, but two-thirds of patients with depressive neuroses were women. Specific neurotic problems, such as phobias, obsessions and hypochondriasis, were found in only 2.8 per cent of cases.

Table 6.1. *Patient consulting rates per 1000 at risk for psychiatric morbidity, by sex and diagnostic group*

Diagnostic group	Male	Female	Both sexes
Psychoses	2.7	8.6	5.9
Mental subnormality	1.6	2.9	2.3
Dementia	1.2	1.6	1.4
Neuroses	55.7	116.6	88.5
Personality disorder	7.2	4.0	5.5
Formal psychiatric illness*	67.2	131.9	102.1
Psychosomatic conditions	24.5	34.5	29.9
Organic illness with psychiatric overlay	13.1	16.6	15.0
Psychosocial problems	4.6	10.0	7.5
Psychiatric-associated conditions*	38.6	57.2	48.6
Total psychiatric morbidity*	97.9	175.0	139.4
Number of patients at risk	6783	7914	14 697

*These totals cannot be obtained by adding the rates for the relevant diagnostic groups because while a patient may be included in more than one diagnostic group, he or she will be included only once in the total.

There is insufficient information about the normal course and outcome of neuroses and related non-psychotic disorders. On the basis of an extensive review, Greer and Cawley (1966) concluded that, 'it is not possible to make legitimate generalizations about the prognosis of neurotic disorders from the published data'. Longitudinal studies of psychiatric illness in general practice populations suggest that the previous duration of illness is the most important prognostic factor for neuroses and that a rough dichotomy can be established between chronic disorders of poor prognosis on the one hand and the short-term situational reactions on the other. A simple model illustrating the balance of neurotic disorders in a general practice population is shown in Fig. 6.2.

Two early studies of the natural history of minor psychiatric morbidity suggested that about half of these disorders are of brief duration (less than a year) and are probably related to environmental stresses. The other half were relatively long-standing and associated with personality disorders (Cooper *et al.* 1969; Kedward 1969). This difference appeared to be unrelated to the treatment prescribed. Murphy (1976) has further underlined the significance of personality factors in determining outcome.

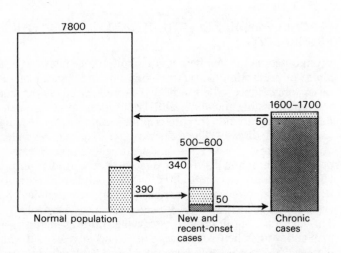

Fig. 6.2. A simple model of the changing distribution of psychiatric morbidity during one year in a standard population of 10 000.

Mann *et al.* (1981) found, in a prospective study of a representative cohort of general practice attenders with identified minor psychiatric morbidity, that at the end of twelve months half of the patients in such a cohort will be better. Detailed examination of the pattern of illness over that time period demonstrated that a third had improved within the first six months, a third pursued a variable intermittent course, and a third had chronic, persistent symptoms.

The outcome of psychiatric disorder is poorly predicted by diagnosis and clinical phenomena alone (Sims 1975; Wittenborn *et al.* 1977; Bleuler 1978; Mann *et al.* 1981). Factors that predict the duration of minor psychiatric morbidity, are the initial severity of symptoms (Huxley *et al.* 1979; Mann *et al.* 1981), and the continued presence of social stresses. Huxley *et al.* (1979) suggest that poor material conditions are important predictors of a long duration of illness, while Mann *et al.* (1981) found that stress and lack of support within the domains of social life, marriage, and family life significantly affected the outcome of minor psychological morbidity. These are all part of the social network which has been shown to play a key role in the outcome of major psychiatric illness (Vaughn and Leff 1976) and physical illness (Medalie and Gouldbourt 1976). Mann *et al.* (1981) demonstrated that personality abnormality is not associated with the final outcome at the end of twelve months, but made a marginal contribution to predicting which patients would display a chronic pattern of illness over the whole period.

The relationship between physical and emotional disorder

Patients with a psychiatric disorder not only consult more frequently and maintain higher levels of demand for medical care than average, but also present with more physical symptoms and are more often referred to medical and surgical departments. In consequence, many psychiatric illnesses appear to be misdiagnosed because of their somatic presentation. It has been argued that, while the degree of physical morbidity of the neurotic patient does not differ from that of non-psychiatric patients, the former tend to complain more and consult more frequently. Further, patients who habitually consult their doctors may well be labelled 'neurotic' whatever the true nature of their complaints.

Eastwood (1975) examined the possible correlation between physical and psychiatric morbidity as part of a health screening survey in general practice. The subjects invited to participate comprised one-half, randomly selected, of all patients aged 40–65 years registered with a large group-practice. Of a possible 2000 patients, just over two-thirds took part. Each patient underwent a battery of tests, including morphological measurements, blood pressure readings, ventilatory function tests, electrocardiogram, and a number of blood and urine tests. In addition, a questionnaire including 20 items selected from the Cornell Medical Index, was completed by each patient. Two weeks later, the patient was physically examined by the family physician who by this time had received a report of the test results. At their first attendance patients whose questionnaire scores suggested a possible psychological disturbance were given a standardized psychiatric interview; as a result, 124 (8.2 per cent) were classified as confirmed psychiatric cases. A control group, matched for age, sex, marital status, and social class, was drawn from among those patients whose questionnaire responses gave no indication of mental disturbance; any 'false negatives' were excluded at the interview stage.

The index group had a significant excess of major physical disease compared to the control group. Physical disorders appeared to 'cluster' together in some individuals, and this occurred to a significantly greater extent in the psychiatric group. Thus, 17 per cent of the psychiatric group had had two major and several minor physical conditions, compared with only 2.4 per cent of the controls. These findings agree with those of Hinkle and his colleagues (Hinkle and Wolff 1957), who found that adults within a variety of ethnic and socio-economic groups exhibited differences in their general susceptibility to illness of all types, so that some persons experienced a greater number of illnesses per unit time than others. On average, 25 per cent of the members of these populations had experienced 50 per cent of the episodes of illness over a 20-year period, whereas a further 25 per cent had suffered less than 10 per cent of the episodes.

As Eastwood and Trevelyan (1972) observe, the idea that individuals have a generalized psychophysical propensity to disease appears to be a valuable alternative model to that which seeks only specific single cause and effect relationships. The notion of multiple aetiology in disease and multiple responses by individuals to agents threatening his or her health reflects a greater acceptance of the realities of the ecology of ill-health.

Psychiatric illness and social dysfunction

The social component of psychiatric disorders in family practice is as important as their clinical features and it is necessary to employ a socio-medical framework to classify and describe them (Sylph *et al.* 1969; Cooper 1972; Fitzgerald 1978). One study compared the social functioning and psychiatric status of general practice patients defined as 'chronic neurotics' with those of a matched control group. A significant correlation was found between social difficulties and neurotic illness (Sylph *et al.* 1969). The neurotic patients tended to have limited or conflict-ridden relationships with neighbours, relatives, and workmates, an excess of problems with spouses and children, and a significantly less satisfactory adjustment to their life situation, as measured by ratings of satisfaction and dissatisfaction with several important aspects such as housing, occupation, and social role. The extensive sociological literature testifying to a positive association between certain global variables, such as social class, and mental illness, has been ably summarized by Dohrenwend and Dohrenwend (1974). Brown *et al.* (1975) have suggested that the experience of depression may be associated with major stressful life occurrences. Cooper and Sylph (1973) have shown that new cases of neurotic illness in general practice are distinguished from controls by a marked excess of life events immediately preceding the onset of illness. The findings of these British studies broadly agree with those on the social role-performance of depressed women reported by Weissman and Myers (1978) in America. Though an association between social status and the prevalence of psychiatric disturbance has often been reported, little has been established about aetiology (Henderson *et al.* 1981) or its significance for social class differences. In a random sample of women living in south London, a large class difference in the prevalence of depression was observed, particularly among women with young children at home (Brown *et al.* 1975). Severe life-events and major long-term difficulties occurring in the year prior to onset appeared to play a general aetiological role. However, although these aetiological agents were more common among working-class women, they only explained a small part of the social class difference. It was argued that the difference is

essentially due not to the greater frequency of events and difficulties, but to the much greater likelihood of working-class women breaking down once these have occurred. This greater vulnerability, it was claimed, is related to four specific social factors – the existence of an intimate confiding relationship, the number of children under the age of 14 years living at home, the loss of a mother before the age of 11 years, and whether or not the woman was employed before onset. Why other factors tend to be protective, however, remains unclear.

PSYCHOLOGICAL ASPECTS OF DISEASE PREVENTION PROGRAMMES

From outcome of treatment it is a small step to interventions aimed at prevention. This covers not only the obvious therapeutic importance of physical and non-physical factors but also the possible mental health implications of the much-debated programmes for prescriptive community screening for physical disease. The possible effects on the so-called quality of life of the detection and treatment of asymptomatic or pre-symptomatic disease have recently been studied in the UK by the large-scale clinical trial of the treatment of patients with mild to moderate hypertension conducted under the aegis of the British Medical Research Council (Mann 1977). The aim of the inquiry was to assess whether drug-therapy for men and women between the ages of 35 and 64 years and with diastolic blood-pressures between 90 and 109 mm Hg can reduce mortality or morbidity from the sequelae of hypertension, especially fatal and non-fatal strokes. During the pilot phase of this inquiry it became apparent that it would be necessary to study the possibly deleterious impact on asymptomatic subjects of: (i) their becoming aware of their raised blood-pressure: (ii) their being recruited into a long-term pattern of clinic-attendance; and (iii) their receiving medication over a period of months or years.

The design of the study is depicted in Fig. 6.3. Essentially, the subjects were asked to attend a screening centre for blood pressure (BP) measurements. Subjects with diastolic pressure above 90 mm Hg were asked to attend again. On the second screening occasion, should the pressure not have settled, the subject was considered for inclusion in the trial. If, at a third visit when a medical examination was carried out and the blood pressure elevation confirmed, there were no reasons for exclusion from the trial and the general practitioner had given

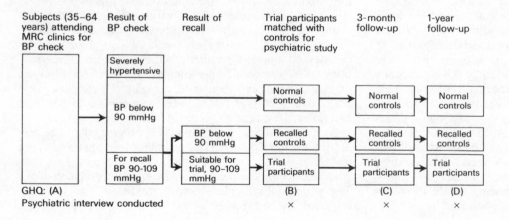

Fig. 6.3. Design of the MRC clinical trial of the treatment of patients with mild to moderate hypertension.

permission, the subject was invited to participate in the trial. Those who consented were randomly allocated to either a pharmacologically active treatment or a placebo regimen. Participants were unaware of which regimen had been prescribed.

For five years after entry into the trial, the subjects were followed up at the clinic and the health of those on active and placebo tablets were compared over this period. With regard to their mental health, all subjects attending the blood-pressure clinics were first asked to complete the general health questionnaire (GHQ) before examination. Each individual entering the trial was matched by age, sex, area of residence, and response to the questionnaire with two control subjects: one of these was randomly selected by computer from screened subjects with a normal blood pressure, the other from subjects whose pressure was initially raised but had fallen on recall. On entry into the trial each subject and the two controls were given the questionnaire for a second time, and again after three and twelve months. Comparison of the changes from first to second response between the normal control group and those recalled allowed an assessment of the effect of informing people of their raised pressure. Comparison of the responses between the recalled control group and the trial participants enabled the effect of recruitment into the trial to be assessed. Comparison of the responses of the trial group and the control groups after three and twelve months made it possible to assess the effect of participating in the trial over time. Since both the psychiatrist and the subject were ignorant of the prescribed regimen the study also incorporated a double blind investigation into the psychological side-effects of some antihypertensive agents. To provide more detailed psychiatric information, those subjects who responded positively at the outset of the follow-up were assessed clinically by means of a standardized psychiatric interview, as were those patients whose response became positive three months and a year after the follow-up. The information obtained from these interviews enabled the trial participants to be compared with the control groups in respect of both the progress of psychiatric cases diagnosed at outset and the incidence of new psychiatric episodes during the follow-up.

A comparison between trial participants and controls can therefore be made in terms of both the distribution of questionnaire response and of diagnosed psychiatric cases among the groups. There was no evidence from any of these measures to suggest that participation in the study impaired the psychological well-being of the participants. But perhaps the most important aspect of the model resides in its potential application to other physical disorders and their treatment.

ENVIRONMENTAL HAZARDS TO PSYCHOLOGICAL WELL-BEING

Finally, in a textbook of public health, it is legitimate to enquire how far epidemiological studies of mental disorder may contribute towards the formulation of a health policy which takes due account of the psychosocial aspects of morbidity. In his discussion of the role of epidemiology in this sphere Terris (1981) emphasized the need for a triple

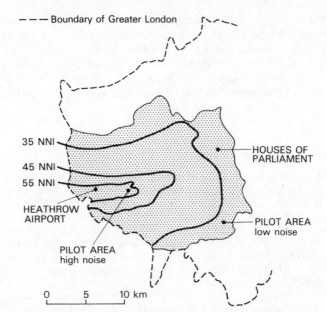

Fig. 6.4. West London 1977 survey of psychiatric morbidity.

approach based on screening, health education and control of the environment. While the growing emphasis on primary care would help initiate action towards the first two of these objectives, the case for environmental control remains *sub-judice*. Control measures for infectious diseases are well established and are also being adopted to tackle such major issues as lead pollution, accident prevention, smoking, and other disorders related to life-style. So far, however, relatively little direct action has been taken to avoid the risks of mental disease.

Aircraft noise, is one of the few environmental *noxae* to have been subjected to intensive study in relation to mental disorder (Tarnopolsky and Morton-Williams 1980). By subdividing an area of London in proximity to Heathrow Airport by noise-levels it was possible to survey some 6000 people exposed to various levels of noise (Fig. 6.4). Noise was found to be associated not with overt mental disorder but with so-called 'annoyance', a state of subjective discomfort associated with such symptoms as nervousness, headaches, insomnia, tiredness, and irritability. To establish the causal links between 'annoyance' and mental disorder it also proved necessary to take account of noise-sensitivity, a psycho-physiological factor which varies markedly between members of the general population. Mental disorder was shown to be related to predisposition and reactivity as well as to direct causation, depending less on the intensity of any single factor than on the confluence of noxious factors on 'vulnerable' or 'high-risk' members of the population. If the quality of life becomes unbearable there is a transition from annoyance and dissatisfaction to dysthymic states and then to a frankly psychiatric symptom-pattern.

As a pointer to future policy mention may be made of the recent decision by the US Appeals Court that electricity can no longer be generated by the reactor at the Three Mile Island Site in Pennsylvania until it has been shown that the mental health of the population will not suffer as a consequence

(*Nature* 1982). The implications of this decision for social policy may be profound, not least because it signifies an awareness of the impact of an environmental pollutant on psychological well-being. As such it underlines the practical as well as the theoretical significance of the epidemiological approach to mental disorders, and the need for empirical studies of the environment and its hazards.

REFERENCES

Baldwin, J.A. and Evans, J.H. (1971). The psychiatric case register. In *Aspects of the epidemiology of mental illness* (ed. J.A. Baldwin) International Psychiatry Clinics 8 (3). Little Brown, Edinburgh.

Bash, K.W. and Bash-Liechtl, J. (1974). Studies on the epidemiology of neuropsychiatric disorders among the city of Shiraz, Iran, *Soc. Psychiatry,* 9, 163.

Bleuler, M. (1978). The *schizophrenic disorders* (translated by S.M. Clemens). Yale University Press, New Haven.

Brill, H. and Patton, R.E. (1959). Analysis of population reduction in New York State mental hospitals in the first four years of large-scale therapy with psychotropic drugs. *Am. J. Psychiatry,* 116,495.

Brown, G.W., Bhrolcháin, M., and Harris, T. (1975). Social class and psychiatric disturbance among women in an urban population. *Sociology* 9, 225.

Brugger, C. (1933). Psychiatrische Ergebnisse einer medizinischen, anthropologischen und soziologischen Bevölkerungs-untersuchung. *Z. Neurol.* 146, 489.

Cooper, B. (1972). Clinical and social aspects of chronic neurosis. *Proc. R. Soc. Med.* 65, 509.

Cooper, B. and Morgan, H.G. (1973). *Epidemiological psychiatry.* Thomas, Springfield, Ill.

Cooper, B. and Sylph, J. (1973). Life events and the onset of neurotic illness: an investigation in general practice. *Psychol. Med.* 3, 421.

Cooper, B., Fry, J. and Kalton, G.W. (1969). A longitudinal study of psychiatric morbidity in a general practice population. *Br. J. Prev. Soc. Med.* 23, 210.

Davies, B. (1964). Psychiatric illness at general hospital clinics. *Postgrad. Med. J.* 40, 15.

Dohrenwend, B.S. and Dohrenwend, B.P. (1974). *Stressful life events: their nature and effects.* Wiley, New York.

Eastwood, M.R. (1975). *The relation between physical and mental illness.* Clarke Institute of Psychiatry Monograph No. 4. University of Toronto Press.

Eastwood, M.R. and Trevelyan, M.H. (1972). Relationships between physical and psychiatric disorder. *Psychol. Med.* 2, 363.

Edwards, G., Williamson, V., Hawker, A., Hensman, C., and Postoyan, S. (1968). Census of a reception-centre. *Br. J. Psychiatry* 114, 1031.

Faversham Committee (1939). *The voluntary mental health services.* The Faversham Committee, London.

Fitzgerald, R. (1978). The classification and recording of social problems. *Soc. Sci. Med.* 12, 255.

Fraser, T.R.C. (1974). *The incidence of neurosis amongst factory workers.* MRC Industrial Health Research Board, Report No. 90. HMSO, London.

Gibbens, T.C.N. (1963). *Psychiatric studies of borstal lads.* Oxford University Press, London.

Goldberg, D.P. (1972). The detection of psychiatric illness by questionnaire. Oxford University Press, London.

Goldberg, D.P. and Blackwell, B. (1970). Psychiatric illness in general practice: a detailed study using a new method of case-identification. *Br. Med. J.* ii, 439.

Goldberg, D.P., Copper, B., Eastwood, M.R., Kenward, H.B., and Shepherd, M. (1970). A standardized psychiatric interview for use in community surveys. *Br. J. Prev. Soc. Med.* 24, 18.

Greer, H.S. and Cawley, R.H. (1966). *Some observations on the natural history of neurotic illness.* Australian Medical Association, Mervyn Archdall Medical Monograph No. 3. Australian Medical Company, Glebe, NSW.

Grob, G. (1966). *The state and the mentally ill.* University of Carolina Press, Chapel Hill.

Harding, T.W., De Arango, M.V., Baltazar, J., *et al.* (1980). Mental disorders in primary health care: a study of their frequency and diagnosis in four developing countries. *Psychol. Med.* 10, 231.

Harwin, B. (1975). Psychogeriatric screening. In *Screening in general practice,* 2nd edn. Oxford Univeristy Press.

Henderson, S., Byrne, D.G., and Duncan-Jones, P. (1981). *Neurosis and the social environment.* Academic Press, Sydney.

Hinkle, L.E. and Wolff, H.G. (1957). The nature of man's adaption to his total environment and the relation of this to illness. *Arch. Intern. Med.* 99, 442.

Huxley, P.J., Goldberg, D.P., Maguire, G.P., and Kincey, V.A. (1979). Predictions of the course of minor psychiatric disorders. *Br. J. Psychiatry* 135, 535.

Kedward, H.B. (1969). The outcome of neurotic illness in the community. *Soc. Psychiatry* 4, 1.

Kessel, W.I.N. and Shepherd, M. (1962). Neurosis in hospital and general practice. *J. Ment. Sci.* 108, 159.

Krupinski, J. and Stoller, A. (eds.) (1971). *The health of a metropolis.* Heinemann Educational, Australia.

Kushlick, A. (1966). A community service for the mentally subnormal. *Soc. Psychiatry* 1, 73.

Leighton, D.C., Harding, J.S., Macklin, D.B., MacMillan, A.M., and Leighton, A.H. (1963). *The character of danger. Psychiatric symptoms in selected communities. The Stirling Country Study of Psychiatric Disorder and Socio-cultural Environment, Vol. III.* Basic Books, New York.

Lewis, E.O. (1929). *Report on the investigation into the incidence of mental deficiency in six areas, 1925–27. Board of Education and Board of Control Mental Deficiency Committee Report, pt. 4.* HMSO, London.

Lin, T-Y. (1953). A study of the incidence of mental disorder in Chinese and other cultures. *Psychiatry* 16, 313.

Mackintosh, J.M. (1944). *The war and mental health in England.* The Commonwealth Fund, New York.

Mann, A.H. (1977). The psychological effect of a screening programme and clinical trial for hypertension upon the participants. *Psychol. Med.* 7, 431.

Mann, A.H., Jenkins, R., and Belsey, E. (1981). The twelve-month outcome of patients with neurotic illness in general practice. *Psychol. Med.* 11, 535.

Mayer-Gross, W. (1948). Mental health survey in a rural area. *Eugen. Rev.* 40, 140.

Medalie, J.H. and Goldbourt, U. (1967). Angina pectoris among 10,000 men. II. Psychological and other risk factors as evidence by a multitude analysis of a five year incidence study. *Am. J. Med.* 60, 910.

Ministry of Health and Department of Health for Scotland (1944). *Report of the Interdepartmental Committee on Medical Schools.* HMSO, London.

Murphy, H.B.M. (1967). Which neuroses need specialist care? *Can. Med. Assoc. J.* 115, 540.

Nature (1982). Can change damage your mental health? (Editorial.) *Nature, Lond.* 295, 177.

Norris, V. (1959). *Mental illness in London.* Chapman and Hall, London.

Ødegaard, Ø. (1964). Pattern of discharge from Norwegian psychiatric hospitals before and after the introduction of psychotropic drugs. *Am. J. Psychiatry* **120**, 772.

Prys Williams, G. and Glatt, M.M. (1966). The incidence of (long-standing) alcoholism in England and Wales. *Br. J. Addiction* **61**, 257.

Rees, J.R. (1957). Psychiatry and public health. *J. Ment. Sci.* **103**, 314.

Regier, D. (1979). The nature and scope of mental health problems in primary care: variability and methodology. In, *Mental health services in general health care.* National Academy of Sciences, Washington, DC.

Reid, D.D. (1960). *Epidemiological methods in the study of mental disorders. Public health papers No. 2.* WHO, Geneva.

Roth, W.F. and Luton, F.H. (1942). The mental health programme in Tennessee, *Am. J. Psychiatry* **99**, 662.

Rows, R.G. (1912). The development of psychiatric science as a branch of public health. *J. Ment. Sci.* **58**, 25.

Shepherd, M. (1957). *A study of the major psychoses in an English county.* Chapman and Hall, London.

Shepherd, M. (1974). General practice, mental illness and the British National Health Service. *Am. J. Public Health* **64**, 230.

Shepherd, M., Davies, B., and Culpan, R.H. (1960). Psychiatric illness in the general hospital. *Acta Psychiatr. Neurol. Scand.* **35**, 518.

Shepherd, M., Goodman, N., and Watt, D.C. (1961). The application of hospital statistics in the evaluation of pharmacotherapy in a psychiatric population. *Compr. Psychiatry* **2**, 11.

Shepherd, M., Oppenheim, A.N., and Mitchell, S. (1971). *Childhood behaviour and mental health.* English Universities Press, London.

Shepherd, M., Cooper, B., Brown, A.C., and Kalton, G.W. (1981). *Psychiatric illness in general practice,* 2nd edn. Oxford University Press.

Sims, A. (1975). Factors predictive of outcome in neurosis. *Br. J. Psychiatry* **133**, 299.

Spitzer, R.L., Endicott, J., and Fleiss, J.L. (1967). Instruments and recording forms of evaluation of psychiatric status and history. Rationale, method of development and description. *Compr. Psychiatry* **8**, 321.

Srole, L., Langer, T.S., Michael, S.T., Opler, M., and Rennie, T.A.C. (1962). *Mental health in the metropolis: the mid-town Manhattan study,* Vol. I. McGraw Hill, New York.

Strotzka, H. (1969). *Kleinburg.* Österreichischer Bundesverlag, Vienna.

Svendsen, B.B. (1952). Psychiatric morbidity among civilians in wartime. *Acta Jutlandica* **24**, Suppl. A.

Sylph, J., Kedward, H.B., and Eastwood, M.R. (1969). Chronic neurotic patients in general practice: a pilot study. *J. R. Coll. Gen. Pract.* **17**, 162.

Tarnopolsky, A. and Morton-Williams, J. (1980). *Aircraft noise and prevalence of psychiatric disorders.* Social and Community Planning Research, London.

Taylor, S. and Chave, S. (1964). *Mental health and environment.* Harrap, London.

Terris, M. (1981). Epidemiology as a guide to health policy. *World Health Forum* **2**, 551.

Vaughn, C.E. and Leff, J.P. (1976). The influence of family and social factors on the course of psychiatric illness; a comparison of schizophrenic and depressed neurotic patients. *Br. J. Psychiatry* **129**, 125.

Ward, J.R. (1926). The clinical study of mental disorders. *J. Ment. Sci.* **LXXII**, 1.

Weissman, M.M. and Myers, J.K. (1978). Rates and risks of depressive disorders in a US suburban community. *Acta Psychiatr. Scand.* **57**, 219.

Wilson, J.M.G. and Jungner, G. (1968). *The principles and practice of screening for disease. Public Health Papers, No. 34.* WHO, Geneva.

Wing, J.K., Cooper, J.E., and Sartorius, N. (1974). *The description and classification of psychiatric symptoms: an instrument manual for the PSE and Catego System.* Cambridge University Press, London.

Wittenborn, R., McDonald, D.C., and Maurer, H.S. (1977). Persisting symptoms in schizophrenia predicted by background factors. *Arch. Gen. Psychiatry* **34**, 1057.

World Health Organization (1973). *Report of working group: psychiatry and primary medical care.* WHO, Copenhagen.

7 Neoplasms

Rodolfo Saracci

PUBLIC HEALTH AND ECONOMIC IMPACT OF NEOPLASMS

Incidence of malignant neoplasms – world-wide and in economically developed countries

Neoplasms include a family of diseases, several hundred of which can be distinguished in man by different localization, morphology, functional and clinical behaviour, and response to treatment. Whether considered from the aetiological and biological, clinical, or public health viewpoint, it is the malignant and invasive varieties of these diseases (malignant neoplasms or malignant tumours or malignancies) which are of dominant importance. Malignant neoplasms have in common certain broad qualitative attributes:

(a) *Cell neoplasia, anaplasia, and heterotopia,* namely new and progressive growth, often infiltrative and destructive; structural differences (tissue, cell, and nuclei atypism and polymorphism) between the normal and the new growth; and migration and colonization (metastatization) of cells to different sites via blood and lymph vessel penetration.

(b) *The carcinogenic process,* namely the way(s) in which a normal cell is transformed into a malignant cell. The carcinogenic process is still incompletely understood, and certain features potentially relevant to prevention will be touched upon in a later section.

The latest version (ninth) of the WHO International Classification of Diseases (ICD) (1977) incorporates a morphologically oriented system of classification of neoplasms (ICD for Oncology), that includes 71 major categories. Ten categories are histologically defined (leukaemias, lymphomas, and melanomas), seven are categories for malignancies whose origins are unknown or uncertain, and 54 correspond to major localizations or sites (if one goes down to minor sites, 304 are listed). Forty-eight of such sites are included because of neoplasms of epithelial origin arising in them, and six because of neoplasms of non-epithelial origin. In fact, 85 per cent or more (Cutler and Young 1975; Peto 1979) of malignant neoplasms derive from epithelial tissues and this provides some justification for using the terms 'malignant neoplasms' and 'cancers' interchangeably (the latter, strictly speaking, applies only to epithelial neoplasms).

Cancers represent a public health problem of major dimensions in economically developed countries, and an emerging problem in economically developing countries, at least to the extent that the still dramatic losses of lives in the first five years after birth (one out of five newborns, totalling world-wide some 40 000 deaths each day) are reduced (WHO 1982). Malignant neoplasms, on the other hand, are diseases of adulthood and old age, half of all cases occurring after the age of 65 years. As a group they rank among the first three causes of death in all countries for which data are available (WHO 1982).

Recently an estimate of the overall cancer burden, that is, of the number of new cases of cancer occurring in one year in the world, has been produced (Parkin *et al.* in press). The estimate is based on data from cancer registries supplemented by other sources such as mortality and selected hospital (particularly pathology) statistics. In this connection it is worth mentioning that data of sufficiently good quality on new cases of cancers (incidence data) were available in the 1970s for 78 populations in 28 countries; less than 5 per cent of the total world population being covered by cancer registration. Mortality data for cancers, as well as for other causes of death, were available in the WHO mortality data bank for about 36 per cent of the whole world population. These percentages of coverage were subject to wide variations, from less than 1 per cent for incidence and 10 per cent for mortality in Africa and Asia to 10–20 per cent for incidence and 80–100 per cent for mortality in Europe, North America, and Oceania (Muir and Nectoux 1982).

The estimates of the overall world-wide cancer burden are presented in Table 7.1, which shows the numbers of new cases for 10 common sites. Certain sites of cancer that are of prominent importance in some areas (for example, bladder, prostate, corpus uteri, and ovary cancer in a number of developed countries) have not been included as they are of lesser importance when looked at on the world scale. The picture is cross-sectional and existing trends may in the near future change it to some extent. For instance, with the general tendency for stomach cancer incidence to regress and for lung cancer incidence to continue to rise in many countries the relative position of these two cancers (for both sexes combined) are likely to be reversed, with lung cancer going to the top. In females, breast cancer is already number one, and with cervix cancer decreasing in many populations its prominence is bound to become even more accentuated. It can be roughly estimated that if all other sites of cancer (except, for the reasons stated below, nonmelanotic skin cancers) are added to the 10 common sites included in Table 7.1, a total of some six million new cancers per year is

Table 7.1. *Rank order and estimated number of cases (in thousands) of ten common cancers (1975)*

Rank	Males		Females		Both sexes	
	Site	Cases	Site	Cases	Site	Cases
1	Lung	458	Breast	497	Stomach	698
2	Stomach	439	Cervix	422	Lung	588
3	Mouth-pharynx	254	Stomach	259	Breast	497
4	Colon-rectum	246	Colon-rectum	242	Colon-rectum	488
5	Oesophagus	208	Lung	130	Cervix	422
6	Liver	183	Mouth-pharynx	122	Mouth-pharynx	376
7	Lymphatic tissue	129	Oesophagus	108	Oesophagus	316
8	Leukaemia	88	Lymphatic tissue	89	Liver	257
9	–		Liver	74	Lymphatic tissue	218
10	–		Leukaemia	67	Leukaemia	155
Total:		2005		2010		4015

Modified from Parkin *et al.* (in press).

reached, namely an average of 16 000 to 17 000 per day, most of which (two-thirds or more) will ultimately be the cause of death of the affected subject. Taking three years or slightly more as a gross mean for the survival time of unselected cancer patients (as can be inferred from figures for the Birmingham area – Waterhouse 1974), six million new cases per year implies about 20 million cancer patients (excluding non-melanotic skin cancers) currently present in the world.

A profile of the cancer burden as it occurs in developed countries is sketched in Fig. 7.1, which presents the percentage distribution of new cases of cancers at major sites in males and females as can be estimated for the US population (Silverberg and Lubera 1983). These cases add up to an overall incidence rate (1974–77, age-adjusted to the 1970 US population) of 331.5 per 100 000 person-years for all races and both sexes combined. Rates for white males and females were respectively 371.6 and 301.2 and for black males and females 454.3 and 288.7. Cumulative rates for the timespan birth to 74 years (based on Connecticut Cancer Registry data), which closely approximate the risk of getting cancer during that timespan in the absence of other causes of death, were: 33.2 per cent for all malignant neoplasms in males and 26.6 per cent in females; rates for individual major

sites ranged between less than 1.0 per cent for leukaemia to 1.5 per cent for lung cancer in females and 6.9 per cent in males, up to 7.8 per cent for breast cancer in females (Young and Pollack 1982).

All these figures exclude non-melanotic skin cancers, the registration of which is subject to wide variation in completeness, being a condition often treated in physicians' offices outside hospitals. From data of an *ad hoc* survey conducted in eight US areas in 1977–78, the incidence rates of these cancers (squamous cell plus basal cell) were 312.0 per 100 000 person-years for males and 173.7 for females among whites, and very low (3.4 for both sexes combined) among blacks (Scotto and Fraumeni 1982).

Survival of patients with malignant neoplasms

The non-melanotic skin tumours just mentioned are by far the most common cancers among whites; they are readily diagnosed, rarely metastasize, and involve a case fatality of about 1 per cent. It is thus evident that their inclusion may provide an overall unduly optimistic view of the current ability to control cancer once it has been detected. Thus, when considering overall statements on survival or 'cures' for cancer, it is essential to sort out whether non-melanotic skin cancers are, or are not, included, lest gross errors of appreciation are made. In contrast to the very low case fatality of non-melanotic skin cancers, survival for other major cancers is substantially less good, although displaying over time an overall tendency to improvement, as shown in Tables 7.2 and 7.3. These figures are derived from four US cancer registries (one including 35 hospitals in California, two hospital registries in Iowa and one population-based registry in Connecticut) (Myers and Hankey 1982). They represent survival of cancer patients at five years after initial diagnosis relative to the general population of the same race-sex-age in a given calendar year. Relative survival estimates the probability of escaping death due to causes related to the diagnosed cancer while the subject is at risk of dying of any cause. A relative survival of 100 per cent would indicate that there is no residual excess mortality due to the diagnosed cancer.

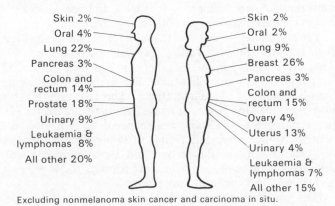

Skin 2%
Oral 4%
Lung 22%
Pancreas 3%
Colon and rectum 14%
Prostate 18%
Urinary 9%
Leukaemia & lymphomas 8%
All other 20%

Skin 2%
Oral 2%
Lung 9%
Breast 26%
Pancreas 3%
Colon and rectum 15%
Ovary 4%
Uterus 13%
Urinary 4%
Leukaemia & lymphomas 7%
All other 15%

Excluding nonmelanoma skin cancer and carcinoma in situ.

Fig. 7.1. Estimated percentage distribution of cancer incidence by site (US – 1983). (Source: Silverberg and Lubera (1983).)

Table 7.2. *Trend in survival by site for US white male cancer patients*

Site	Five-year relative survival rates (per cent)	
	1960–63	1970–73
Lip	84	87
Tongue	23	32
Salivary gland	(55)*	(53)
Mouth	42	40
Pharynx	21	27
Oesophagus	4	4
Stomach	10	12
Colon	42	47
Rectum	36	43
Liver	1	2
Gallbladder and bile duct	6	7
Pancreas	1	2
Nose, nasal cavity, and middle ear	(39)	(48)
Larynx	54	63
Lung and bronchus	7	9
Bone	31	38
Soft tissue	41	52
Melanoma of the skin	51	62
Breast	(55)	(71)
Prostate gland	50	63
Testis	63	72
Penis	(62)	(56)
Urinary bladder	53	61
Kidney	36	44
Eye	(81)	78
Brain and central nervous system	16	18
Thyroid	75	82
Hodgkin's disease	34	66
Non-Hodgkin's lymphoma	31	39
Multiple myeloma	13	20
Lymphocytic leukaemia		
Acute	4	27
Chronic	29	46
Granulocytic leukaemia		
Acute	2	3
Chronic	13	18
Monocytic leukaemia	1	3

*Rates in parentheses have standard errors between 5 and 10 per cent. For other rates the standard errors are less than 5 per cent.
Modified from Myers and Hankey (1982).

Table 7.3. *Trend in survival by site for US white female cancer patients*

Site	Five-year relative survival rates (per cent)	
	1960–63	1970–73
Lip	(88)*	Too few cases
Tongue	44	46
Salivary gland	(82)	85
Mouth	50	51
Pharynx	35	31
Oesophagus	6	4
Stomach	13	14
Colon	44	50
Rectum	41	48
Liver	3	6
Gallbladder and bile duct	9	9
Pancreas	2	2
Nose, nasal cavity, and middle ear	(44)	(50)
Larynx	(46)	56
Lung and bronchus	11	14
Bone	31	36
Soft tissue	54	54
Melanoma of the skin	68	75
Breast	63	68
Uterine cervix	58	64
Uterine corpus	73	81
Ovary	32	36
Vagina	(37)	(44)
Vulva	64	66
Urinary bladder	53	60
Kidney	39	50
Eye	74	77
Brain and central nervous system	21	22
Thyroid	87	87
Hodgkin's disease	48	69
Non-Hodgkin's lymphoma	31	43
Multiple myeloma	10	17
Lymphocytic leukaemia		
Acute	3	29
Chronic	46	59
Granulocytic leukaemia		
Acute	0	2
Chronic	11	19
Monocytic leukaemia	1	4

*Rates in parentheses have standard errors between 5 and 10 per cent. For other rates the standard errors are less than 5 per cent.
Modified from Myers and Hankey (1982).

As indicated in Table 7.2, among white males five-year survival rates for lung cancer, the most frequent cancer, increased slightly from 7 to 9 per cent. Little change occurred also for cancers of the stomach, pancreas, and brain. Other cancers, including some common ones, showed more marked improvements: prostate (the second most frequent), larynx, bladder, rectum, colon, kidney, and non-Hodgkin's lymphoma. The most substantial improvements were recorded in Hodgkin's lymphoma and lymphatic leukaemia, acute and chronic, which are comparatively less common forms of cancer.

Among white women some improvement in survival has taken place for breast cancer, the most frequent neoplasm. A slight improvement has occurred for lung cancer and stomach cancer. Larger improvements have been recorded for cancer of the cervix, ovary, colon, rectum, and bladder. Hodgkin's lymphoma and lymphatic leukaemia have undergone the same marked improvement as for males, and non-Hodgkin's lymphoma has also shown a notable improvement.

The two tables do not cover results for children (aged less than 15 years). Survival for children diagnosed during 1970–73 is better than for children diagnosed in 1960–63 for all neoplasms except retinoblastoma and brain tumours other than glioma and medulloblastoma. The most remarkable improvement took place for acute lymphatic leukaemia (20 per cent of all childhood malignancies) with a five-year relative survival moving up from 4 to 34 per cent. For glioma and neuroblastoma (the second and third most common childhood neoplasms) improvements from 48 to 58 per cent and from 17 to 38 per cent took place.

Data on survival beyond five years are less substantive, although they are becoming available for the sites with high incidence; in general, residual excess mortality due to the cancer gradually reduces with the passing of time, but persists even after 15 years from initial diagnosis.

Patient survival measures the end result of cancer treatment as administered under current conditions of practice: its usefulness lies mainly in indicating time trends in the overall management of patients. These trends, however, reflect the situation of a given area or country and cannot automatically be transferred to other areas, dependent as they are on many local factors, such as the availability of improved diagnostic, treatment, and supportive care facilities and the referral patterns of patients. Even within a country trends may differ, for instance in relation to social class, as indicated by worse survival in indigent patients, after controlling for cancer stage, care type, and other factors (Berg *et al.* 1977).

Loss of lives and economic burden

Cancer incidence and survival under current management conditions determine the mortality rates for cancers as well as its psychological, social, and economic consequences. The trends in mortality rates in the US for nine major cancer sites in each sex are displayed in Figs 7.2 and 7.3 (Silverberg and Lubera 1983). For males, there is a striking upward secular trend in lung and downward trend for stomach cancer: these are accompanied by rising rates for pancreas and, to a lesser extent, colon and rectum, while the other rates are essentially unchanged. In women there are marked downward trends for

stomach and cervical cancer, a recent upward trend in lung cancer, a rising trend in pancreas, and no appreciable changes for the other malignancies.

Complete elimination of all cancer deaths would produce a gain in life expectancy at birth of less than 2.5 years (as contrasted with a gain of some six years from elimination of coronary heart disease deaths). This gain is averaged over the whole population and appears relatively minor if compared with the gain, tenfold or more, in life expectancy which has occurred in the *past* from the control of infectious diseases. However, a better perspective of the *present* burden of cancer within developed countries may be gleaned by considering the average number of years of life lost by those people (some 20 per cent of the population) who succumb to cancer. For all malignant neoplasms taken together this loss is 16.0 years, ranging from 10.3 years lost for each death due to male genital neoplasms to 13.7 deaths due to stomach cancer, up to 20.1 years for breast, 20.8 for leukaemia, and 22.4 for cervical cancer (Hodgson and Rice 1982). These very substantial losses of years of life, when considered from the economic viewpoint, contribute to the *indirect costs* of cancer, which depend on the number, age, and sex distribution of deaths as well as on the situation of the labour market and earning opportunities. Indirect costs represent current and future outputs (computed as a stream of future earnings converted to present value by discounting) lost because of cessation or reduction of productive activities due to

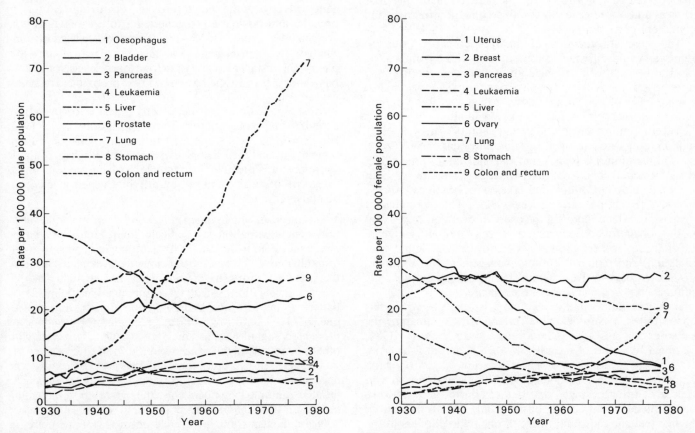

Fig. 7.2. Age-adjusted death rates for selected cancer sites – males, US, 1930–78. (Source: Silverberg and Lubera (1983).)

Fig. 7.3. Age-adjusted death rates for selected cancer sites – females, US, 1930–78. (Source: Silverberg and Lubera (1983).)

Table 7.4. *Percentage distribution of expenditure for malignant neoplasms (US – 1977)*

Site	Direct costs		Indirect costs of mortality	
	Short-stay hospital care	Physicians' services	(6% discount)	(10% discount)
Digestive organs	16.6	9.2	20.3	21.1
Respiratory organs	11.0	6.3	26.3	27.6
Skin	2.2	3.7	2.5	2.4
Breast	8.3	6.8	9.9	9.8
Female genital organs	7.2	5.9	5.7	5.7
Male genital organs	4.5	4.1	2.6	2.6
Leukaemia	2.8	1.9	5.7	4.8
All other malignant neoplasms	27.6	20.8	25.4	24.6
Benign and unspecified neoplasms	19.9	41.3	1.7	1.5
All Neoplasms	100.0	100.0	100.0	100.0

Modified from Hodgson and Rice (1982).

morbidity and mortality. *Direct costs*, on the other hand, reflect the amount and unit cost of medical care necessary for the management of cancer cases.

The percentage distribution of expenditures for the US in 1977 is shown in Table 7.4. This can be taken as only orientative for the expenditure patterns in other developed countries, as the data tend to be country specific: they depend not only (as patient survival) on the performance of the local health services, but also on the methods of financing these services and, more generally, on the economic structures and conditions of a country.

The greatest fractions of indirect costs are due to respiratory and digestive cancers, namely those contributing most to mortality. In striking contrast, a large fraction of the direct costs, particularly for physicians' services, are due to management of benign neoplasms, which contribute minimally to indirect costs because of very low fatality.

The total indirect costs in dollars amount (1977) to $18 842.1 million (computed at 6 per cent discount rate) or $14 845.6 million (assuming a 10 per cent discount rate). Total direct costs for actual cancer patient management amount to about eight billion dollars out of total expense for health care of 163 billions (Hodgson and Rice 1982). Thus, malignant neoplasms, which represent the cause of death of 20 per cent of the population, absorb some 5 per cent of total health care expenditure: other morbid conditions, less lethal but disabling, and requiring chronic management (for example, diseases of the digestive system, psychiatric disorders) absorb a proportionately larger share of the expense.

It may be added that in a country like the US, which has concentrated a considerable effort on cancer research, the expense for research (American Cancer Society 1981; National Institutes of Health 1981) can be put at 7 or 8 per cent of the health care expenses for cancer, a proportion higher than the corresponding one for medical research in general. The major single contributor to the research expenditure is the National Cancer Institute, and out of its research budget (reaching a round figure of one billion dollars in the early 1980s) some 5 per cent is devoted to epidemiological research.

AETIOLOGY AND PRIMARY PREVENTION OF MALIGNANT NEOPLASMS

The determinants of malignant neoplasms

Neoplasms, as any other normal or pathological phenomenon unfolding in living organisms, are ultimately the result of an interplay of two classes of determinants, genetical (hereditary) and environmental (exogenous). Results of genetical–environmental interplays occurring earlier in prenatal and postnatal life generate – in a way which is at present poorly understood – conditions which later on may emerge as predisposing 'host factors' to cancer development – for instance, obesity, or oestrogen levels, or even a behavioural feature such as age at first pregnancy for breast cancer.

Most human malignant neoplasms appear to occur in both heritable and non-heritable forms (Knudson *et al.* 1973; Knudson 1977). As the genetic endowment of human populations and their living environments both display ample variations, it is possible, in principle, to delineate four broad categories of cancers caused by different genetical–environmental interplays:

1. Cancers in which, independently of environmental variation, genetic variation – specifically the presence of a single autosomol dominant gene in its 'pathological' allelic variant (plus chance) determines the occurrence of cancer. These are the heritable forms of cancer. They are characterized by familial aggregation, usually an earlier age-specific incidence pattern than their non-heritable counterparts, a high frequency of bilateral involvement or of multifocal neoplasms of related organ systems, and are usually associated with other phenotypic manifestations in the form of characteristic syndromes, of variable clinical severity, preceding the appearance of the cancer(s). Examples in this category are: familial multiple polyposis coli, the typical patient having more than 100 adenomatous polyps in the colon, often before 20 years of age; familial juvenile polyposis of the colon in which benign polyps are often symptomatic in the first decade of life; familial neurofibromatosis, where multiple neuromas

occur; Peutz–Jeghers syndrome, with mucocutaneous pigmentation and hamartomatous polyps of the intestinal tract; and familial retinoblastoma, which is not accompanied by any recognizable syndrome before the tumour appears – familial cases tend to be bilateral occurring in young children who also tend to develop sarcomas, particularly after therapeutic irradiation, later in life. These heritable malignancies may represent 1–2 per cent of all neoplasms, but for certain types of tumours, like retinoblastomas, the proportion goes up to perhaps 40 per cent.

2. Cancers produced by environmental agents, independently of genetical variation – for example lung cancer due to tobacco smoking, leukaemias due to ionizing radiation, and mouth cancers due to alcohol. This category, together with the next one, covers the greatest majority of all malignant neoplasms. In fact, as knowledge accrues, a malignant neoplasm which is now regarded as due to an environmental agent may be recognized to have an important genetical determinism as well. For example, it has been suggested, but not confirmed, that possible inherited variations in enzymes involved in polycyclic hydrocarbon metabolism play a role in the aetiology of smoking-related lung cancers: should this prove to be the case it would be more appropriate to regard these cancers as belonging to the next category.

3. Cancers produced by combined environmental and genetical variations. This category includes syndromes involving, when appropriate environmental conditions occur (for example, exposure to ultraviolet light in xeroderma pigmentosum subjects), an elevated risk of specific cancers. These syndromes derive from the occurrence in the homozygous state of single autosomal (or X-linked) recessive genes. Examples are xeroderma pigmentosum, ataxia-teleangectasia, Fanconi's anaemia, Bloom's syndrome, and heritable immune deficiency disorders. Moreover, familial predisposition which may depend on combined genetical and environmental actions has been noted for common cancers such as stomach, colon, and breast cancer.

4. Cancers apparently independent of genetical and environmental variation, mainly resulting (according to hypotheses purporting that this category may include one-fourth or one-fifth of all cancers) from 'spontaneous' or 'background' somatic mutations. It is, however, unclear whether this should be a separate category or incorporated, as knowledge advances, into the other three.

As environmental (exogenous) determinants are not only of dominant importance (categories 2 and 3) but also can usually be manipulated for preventive purposes, it is on these that attention will now be focused.

Identification of environmental determinants

The identification of environmental determinants of cancer relies on two complementary approaches – the epidemiological and the experimental.

The epidemiological approach

This has produced both general and specific evidence for the role of environmental agents in cancer causation (see for instance Doll and Peto 1981 – this reference contains material relevant to every individual topic in this Section). The evidence of a more general nature derives from:

(i) The observations of large variation (often tenfold to hundredfold) of the incidence rates of most cancers in different populations, defined according to geographical area of residence (Table 7.5) or according to other characteristics such as ethnic group, religion, social class: for instance, when contrasted with other religious groups the Mormons of Utah and the Seventh-Day Adventists of California exhibit low rates for cancers of the respiratory, gastrointestinal, and genital systems. Whatever the criterion of definition of the population, every type of *common* cancer (that is, common in at least some populations) happens to be rarely found in some other population. This marked variation in rates according to different axes of exploration is unlikely to be explained chiefly by concomitant genetical variations, and points to the role of environmental determinants.

(ii) The observation of changes of incidence in migrant groups after they have moved to a new living environment. Of course, migrants are selected members of a population and they are likely to be in several aspects different from both their population of origin and from the population of the receiving countries. This demands caution when interpreting data from migrant studies, particularly when dealing with minor differences in rates. However, studies like those of Japanese migrants to Hawaii show an assimilation of their cancer incidence rates to the pattern of Caucasians, with the emergence of large differences in respect to the rates in Japan, which appears hard to explain solely on the basis of selective factors.

(iii) Changes in incidence rates in time, particularly when they take place over a few decades are incompatible with a genetical explanation, as changes in the genes of a population pool require much longer intervals. Recorded incidence rates are obviously affected by diagnostic changes and mortality rates are, in addition, affected by changes in treatment effectiveness; however, marked trends like the one for lung cancer (Fig. 7.2 and 7.3) are most likely to reflect real changes in cancer onset rates, pointing to the operation of environmental factors.

The evidence of a specific nature has been produced by analytical studies (case-control and cohort) which have shown the causal role of such agents as tobacco smoking, asbestos, and ionizing radiation (see below) in the aetiology of several malignant neoplasms. One limitation of the epidemiological approach, which may prove of critical importance in trying to detect comparatively small increases in risk, for example, from chemicals polluting the environment, is that even in the best conditions it is impossible to confidently identify by epidemiological means an increase in risk smaller than say 10 per cent (and serious problems arise in the interpretation of increases below 50 per cent) as the biases inherent in any observational study are of at least this order of magnitude. An important result of general relevance derived from epidemiological observations is that different cancers have different determinants (in many instance still unknown) and that there

Table 7.5. *Range of incidence rates for selected cancers*

Site of origin of cancer	High incidence area	Sex	Cumulative incidence,* % in high incidence area	Ratio of highest rate to lowest rate †	Low incidence area
Skin (chiefly non-melanoma)	Australia, Queensland	♂	>20	>200	India, Bombay
Oesophagus	Iran, northeast section	♂	20	300	Nigeria
Lung and bronchus	England	♂	11	35	Nigeria
Stomach	Japan	♂	11	25	Uganda
Cervix uteri	Colombia	♀	10	15	Israel: Jewish
Prostate	United States: blacks	♂	9	40	Japan
Liver	Mozambique	♂	8	100	England
Breast	Canada, British Columbia	♀	7	7	Israel: non-Jewish
Colon	United States, Connecticut	♂	3	10	Nigeria
Corpus uteri	United States, California	♀	3	30	Japan
Buccal cavity	India, Bombay	♂	2	25	Denmark
Rectum	Denmark	♂	2	20	Nigeria
Bladder	United States, Connecticut	♂	2	6	Japan
Ovary	Denmark	♀	2	6	Japan
Nasopharynx	Singapore, Chinese	♂	2	40	England
Pancreas	New Zealand, Maori	♂	2	8	India, Bombay
Larynx	Brazil, Sao Paolo	♂	2	10	Japan
Pharynx	India, Bombay	♂	2	20	Denmark
Penis	Parts of Uganda	♂	1	300	Israel: Jewish

*By age 75 years in the absence of other causes of death.
†At ages 35–64 years standardized for age to world population.
Modified from Doll and Peto (1981).

is no support for the idea that some overall determinant may regulate the all-cancers incidence. This incidence is simply the aggregate of the separate incidences of different forms of cancer, each having its own determinants. Of course, this does not exclude that a given determinant (for example, tobacco smoking) may affect more than just one cancer.

The experimental approach

The experimental approach to identification of environmental carcinogens includes at a more basic level the investigation of mechanisms of carcinogenesis, particularly of chemical carcinogenesis. A result of general relevance has been the demonstration that chemical carcinogens are usually metabolized to reactive molecules with high affinity for electron-rich molecules, like DNA, with which they form combinations ('adducts') (Miller and Miller 1977). These have been characterized in structure and properties, but the specific, critical lesions directly responsible for the carcinogen-induced malignant transformation have not yet been identified. However, recent observations (Bishop 1982; Rigby 1982) of the occurrence in normal and tumour tissues from experimental animals and humans of a limited number of DNA sequences ('oncogenes') homologous to portions of the transforming genes of oncogenic viruses (see below) have provided new hints on the possible nature of such critical lesions and have raised high hopes that some mechanisms of carcinogenesis are near to being fully understood.

At a more applied level the identification of carcinogens via the laboratory relies on two types of tests:

– *long-term (often lifetime) carcinogenicity tests* in experimental animals, most commonly rodents (mice, rats, hamsters)

– *short-term tests* assessing the effect of chemical agents on a variety of endpoints belonging to three general classes: DNA damage, mutagenicity, and chromosome damage

These tests are valuable to the extent that such effects may reflect underlying events in the carcinogenic process. Indeed, consistent positivity in tests measuring DNA damage, mutagenicity, and chromosomal damage, is usually regarded as indicating potential carcinogenicity of the tested agent. Results of laboratory tests constitute useful supporting evidence when adequate epidemiological data for the carcinogenicity of an environmental agent exists (for example, vinyl chloride) but become all the more essential when the epidemiological evidence is non-existent or inadequate in quality and/or in quantity. In the latter case, although no universally accepted criteria exist to automatically translate data from long-term animal tests or short-term tests in terms of cancer risk in humans, an evaluation of the risk can be made on a judgmental basis using *all* available scientific evidence. This policy has been applied by the International Agency for Research on Cancer (IARC) in a systematic programme of evaluation of the carcinogenic risk of chemicals to man. Between 1971 and 1981, 29 volumes presenting evaluations (and re-evaluations) for 585 chemicals, groups of chemicals, industrial processes and occupational exposures have been published and a synthesis of this ongoing programme appeared in 1982 (IARC 1982).

Established environmental determinants

For a number of physical, chemical, and biological environmental agents there is direct evidence from epidemiological studies, usually supported by experimental evidence, that they cause malignant neoplasms in humans. Among physical agents this applies to some electromagnetic radiations including part of those in the natural (solar) spectrum, ubiquitously present in the environment, as well as particulate radiations (alpha and beta particles, protons, and neutrons). According to their biological effects, which in turn depend on their energetic level, these radiations are distinguished as non-ionizing (ultraviolet radiations) and ionizing (the more energetic radiations, including particules as well as the shortest wavelengths of the electromagnetic spectrum, namely X-rays and gamma rays).

Ultraviolet radiations (Lee 1982; Scotto et al. 1982)

The ultraviolet (UV) band covers the wavelengths from 400 nm, where the visible spectrum starts, to about 100 nm, where X-rays begin. This band is subdivided into three parts (UV-A, UV-B, UV-C), based on photobiological effects. Wavelengths of the UV-A band, in the 400–320 nm range, are capable, provided they reach the skin in sufficiently large doses, of producing tanning and skin pigmentation. They were regarded as essentially harmless for the skin, though the point appears not finally settled, while they have been associated with the development of cataracts in humans. UV-B, in the 320–290 nm range, are responsible for vitamin D synthesis, delayed erythema (skin burn), and skin 'ageing', and can cause DNA lesions: it is this part of the UV spectrum which is related to skin cancer occurrence. Only a small portion of UV-B reaches the earth, the greatest fractions (as well as the totality of UV-C, with wavelength below 290–280 nm and germicidal action on unicellular organisms, and of X- and gamma rays) being absorbed by the upper stratosphere. The available epidemiological evidence indicates that UV-B include the aetiological agent of the greatest majority (80 per cent or more, particularly among white-skinned people) of basal cell epithelioma of face and neck, of squamous cell epitheliomas of the exposed surfaces, and of lip cancers. It has been estimated that a 1 per cent decrease in the upper stratosphere ozone (O_3), which forms the UV filtering layer (the reduction could derive from pollution by supersonic aircraft exhausts and chlorofluorocarbons aerosol spray propellants) would result in a 4 per cent increase in non-melanotic skin cancers.

The relation between UV radiation and melanoma is less clearly established, particularly as far as the quantitative aspect goes. The incidence of melanomas in different parts of the world correlates fairly closely with the flux of UV-B. Also, patients with xeroderma pigmentosum who are unable to repair the specific damage in their DNA (formation of bonds between adjacent bases in DNA) induced by UV-B, experience a gross excess of melanomas. On the other hand, the distribution of melanomas on the surface of the body does not correspond to the degree of exposure; and the recent increase in melanoma rates noted in most countries (in which a diagnostic component may play a part) is not limited to melanomas arising in those parts of the body exposed to light.

Ionizing radiation (Boice and Land 1982)

In ordinary present-day circumstances there are three main sources of exposure to ionizing radiations: *background*, due to cosmic rays (whose flux varies by altitude), terrestrial radiation, and radioactive elements internally deposited in the body – the total annual whole-body dose received from background at sea level being of about 100 millirem; *medical exposures*, largely due to diagnostic X-ray procedures, amounting to a dose of about 75 millirem; and exposures from *occupations*, *nuclear power*, and *fallout* from nuclear weapons testing, amounting to a dose of about eight millirem.

A body of epidemiological investigations carried out on subjects exposed because of war or accidents (atomic bomb, fallout from weapons tests), because of occupation (radiologists, uranium miners, luminous dial painters), or because of medical needs (patients irradiated for diagnostic or therapeutic purposes) has demonstrated the increase of cancers arising from ionizing radiations. The bone marrow is affected, with the appearance of leukaemias (acute and chronic myeloid), but probably all other sites can be affected, given appropriate conditions. As in chemical carcinogenesis, in radiation carcinogenesis the response depends on the type and dose of the radiation as well as on the tissue involved. Sometimes the reason for a tissue being involved is obvious: ingested radium or radioactive strontium tend to produce bone cancers because they are deposited in bone; radioactive iodine tends to produce cancer of the thyroid. However, in many cases the reason is not yet understood. Also, there is still discussion on whether alpha-particles, protons, and neutrons, which have much more localized effects than X- and gamma rays, have also a higher carcinogenic effectiveness. And there is persisting debate regarding the exact shape of the dose–response relationship at low dose, although for the practical purpose of cancer prevention a simple linear relationship with no threshold may be assumed. On this basis, and using the estimate of 250 cases of cancers induced per million person-years per rem, one can derive that ionizing radiations are responsible for 3 per cent or less of the total malignant neoplasms occurring annually in a developed country such as the US.

Tobacco smoking (US DHHS 1982)

Tobacco smoking has been shown in a large number of epidemiological studies – both case-control and cohort – to be causally associated with cancers at several sites, and with other adverse health effects as well. Tobacco smoke has been shown also to cause cancer in experimental animals. Results from the US Veterans prospective study (Rogot and Murray 1980) are presented in Table 7.6 – similar findings have been reported from other prospective studies. The neoplasms individually shown in the table are those for which the role of smoking has been most consistently identified.

Table 7.6 refers to only cigarette smokers. While there is little if any difference in risk between cigarette and pipe/cigar smokers in respect to cancers of the mouth and pharynx, larynx, and oesophagus, pipe/cigar smokers experience lesser increase in risk than cigarette smokers for cancers of lung, bladder, and pancreas. An aspect that has recently attracted attention is the possibility that 'passive smoking' (inhalation of air contaminated by other people smoking) may entail an increased risk of lung cancer. Mainstream

Table 7.6. *Mortality for selected cancers in the US veterans prospective study*

Certified cause of death	Deaths by mid-1970 of men who in the 1950s were current smokers of cigarettes only			
	No. of deaths observed	No. expected from corresponding non-smoker experience	Difference between observed and expected	Ratio of observed and expected
Cancer				
Lung	2 609	231	2 378	11.3
Mouth, pharynx, larynx, or oesophagus	452	65	387	7.0
Bladder	326	151	175	2.2
Pancreas	459	256	203	1.8
Kidney	175	124	51	1.4
All other cancers	3 660	2 796	864	1.3
TOTAL, all cancers	7 681	3 623	4 058	2.1
Other causes				
Respiratory disease	2 107	488	1 619	4.3
Cardiovascular disease	21 413	13 572	7 841	1.6
Other certified causes	3 721	2 564	1 157	1.5
Cause not available	1 221	610	611	2.0
TOTAL, all causes	36 143	20 857	15 286	1.7

Data from Rogot and Murray (1980).

Table 7.7. *Observed and expected deaths from lung cancer in non-smoking women with smoking husbands*

	Observed	Expected	Difference	Ratio	χ^2
Japan (Hirayama)	142	85.8	+ 56.2	1.7	36.81
US (Garfinkel)	88	75.3	+ 12.7	1.2	2.14*
Greece (Trichopoulos *et al.*)	29	12.1	+ 16.9	2.4	23.60
Total	259	173.2	+ 85.8	1.5	42.50

*Not significant.
Modified from Hirayama (1981).

smoke (smoke actively inhaled) and sidestream smoke (smoke released in the ambient air from cigarettes between active puffs) have similar chemical composition. This, together with the fact that in numerous studies of cigarette smokers an apparently linear dose–response relationship with no threshold has been observed, suggests that even low-level exposure to passive smoking in indoor environments may increase the risk of lung cancer. The results of the three studies (Garfinkel 1981; Hirayama 1981; Trichopoulos *et al.* 1981) hitherto available on this subject are shown in Table 7.7. Although this evidence is not sufficient to establish a role of passive and involuntary smoking in lung cancer causation in non-smokers, it confirms suspicions about a possible important public health problem.

On a less negative note it is possible, on the basis of data which have started to accrue, that today's low-tar cigarette may in the long run prove less harmful. The clear decline (Doll 1983) in lung cancer mortality in England and Wales (Table 7.8), occurring despite the relatively small change in the national consumption of cigarettes, suggests that the switch to modern cigarettes containing less tar and nicotine may have had an effect.

Whatever the trends, and their interpretation, tobacco-related cancers (that is, those individually shown in Table 7.6) represent some 30 per cent of all cancers in a developed

Table 7.8. *Trends in male mortality from respiratory cancers (excluding larynx) in England and Wales*

Age (years)	Annual death rate per 1 000 000 men	
	Born circa 1910* Observed 1940–60	Born 1930–50 † Observed 1980
30–34	40	13
35–39	98	45
40–44	253	134
45–49	597	378

*High tar intake throughout smoking history.
†High tar intake only in first decade or so of smoking history only in men aged 45–49 years.
From Doll and Peto (1981).

country. (It can be added that in certain regions of India, Thailand, and localized areas of the USSR, chewing of betel nuts and leaves, alone or in combination with tobacco and other ingredients, is associated with increased risk of mouth, pharynx, and oesophageal cancers.)

Alcohol (Tuyns 1982)

A number of epidemiological investigations have shown that alcohol (alcoholic drinks) is responsible for the occurrence of cancers of the mouth, pharynx, larynx, and oesophagus. They also indicate that, in doses capable of causing cirrhosis of the liver, it can increase the risk of liver cancer. The key variable appears to be the quantity of alcohol (ethanol), although some inconclusive evidence points to the fact that the risk may be higher when alcohol is consumed in spirits or, particularly for oesophageal cancer as it occurs in areas of north-west France, in apple-based alcoholic drinks. Whether ethanol is carcinogenic *per se* (it is not in animal experiments) or by facilitating, for example, as a carrier, contact between carcinogenic chemicals and cells of the mucosae, is an unsettled point. Often the habits of tobacco smoking and alcohol drinking go together: it has been shown in some studies that alcohol and tobacco combine their actions in a more than additive way to produce cancers of the mouth, pharynx, larynx, and oesophagus. On the whole, alcohol can be estimated to be responsible for some 3 per cent of all cancers in a developed country.

Other chemicals (IARC 1982)

Table 7.9 shows the chemicals, groups of chemicals, industrial processes, and occupational exposures for which sufficient epidemiological evidence of carcinogenicity in humans had in the IARC Monographs programme been judged to exist. This is supported for all individual chemicals (with the possible exception of arsenic) by evidence of carcinogenicity in long-term animal tests, indicating the high sensitivity of animal

Table 7.9. *Established chemical carcinogens in man*

Chemicals and groups of chemicals
4-Aminobiphenyl
Analgesic mixtures containing phenacetin
Arsenic and arsenic compounds
Asbestos
Azathioprine
Benzene
Benzidine
N,N-Bis(2-chloroethyl)-2-naphthylamine (chlornaphazine)
Bis(chloromethyl)ether and technical-grade chloromethyl methyl ether
1,4-Butanediol dimethanesulphonate (Myleran)
Certain combined chemotherapy for lymphomas (including MOPP)
Chlorambucil
Chromium and certain chromium compounds
Conjugated oestrogens
Cyclophosphamide
Diethylstilboestrol
Melphalan
Methoxsalen with ultraviolet A therapy (PUVA)
Mustard gas
2-Naphthylamine
Soots, tars, and oils
Treosulphan
Vinylchloride

Industrial processes and occupational exposures
Auramine manufacture
Boot and shoe manufacture and repair (certain occupations)
Furniture manufacture
Isopropyl alcohol manufacture (strong-acid process)
Nickel refining
Rubber industry (certain occupations)
Underground haematite mining (with exposure to radon)

From IARC (1982).

tests in detecting human chemical carcinogens. Exposure to the agents listed in the table occurs because a number of them are used as drugs, mostly in cancer chemotherapy, or because they are present in the workplace; exposure at lower levels than in the workplace sometimes occurring in the general environment (for example, soot and other products of combustion of fossil fuels).

Medical exposures, including both those in the table and others at present only suspected but not confirmed as human carcinogens, may account for some 1 per cent of all cancers in a developed country (Doll and Peto 1981); direct estimate from an *ad hoc* case-control investigation on drug use put the upper confidence limit of this estimate at 2 per cent. Of this 2 per cent, half is due to drugs and the other half to diagnostic use of X-rays, as previously mentioned.

Estimates for the burden due to occupational exposures, also including established agents in Table 7.9 plus others only suspected (not in the table), vary widely (by almost two orders of magnitude, from less than 1 per cent to 20–40 per cent). This reflects the incomplete nature of the information currently available on the risk attributable to given exposures and the mostly indirect nature of the information on how many workers are in fact exposed. A recent estimate (Doll and Peto 1981), better documented than the others, put the proportion of all cancers attributable to occupation in the US at 4 per cent (with 'acceptable' limits 2–8 per cent). If this is correct then in the segments of the adult population in which these cancers almost exclusively occur (manual workers in mining, agriculture and industry, broadly taken, who number 31 millions out of a population aged 20 and over of 158 millions – International Labour Office 1982), about one in five cancers is attributable to occupation.

Biological agents (Burton 1982; Evans 1982)

Two parasites have been shown to be associated, probably causally, with cancer. In some areas of southern China and South-east Asia infestation of small intrahepatic bile ducts with *Clonorchis sinensis* or *Opistorchis viverrini,* two liver flukes acquired by eating infested intermediate hosts (certain freshwater fish and crayfish), is followed by the development of cholangio cellular carcinomas. In other areas, such as Egypt and Mozambique, bladder cancer is one of the most common cancers and there is evidence that bilharziasis due to infestation (acquired through skin contact with infected waters while at work, for example, in farmers and fishermen) with *Schistosoma haematobium* plays an aetiological role. While in non-endemic areas bladder cancers tend to be localized in the trigonal area and to be of predominantly transitional cell type, in these endemic areas a high proportion is of squamous cell type and seldom located in the trigonal area.

Viruses have for a long time been the focus of attention as possible causes for human cancers, given the numerous examples of viruses causing cancers (oncogenic viruses) in animals; this applies both to RNA viruses (Rous virus in chickens, Gross' virus of mouse leukaemia, Bittner's virus of mammary tumour in mouse) and to DNA viruses (Marek's disease virus, producing neurolymphomatosis in chickens, Lucké's herpes virus producing renal adenocarcinoma in the leopard frog). Up to now research in this area has been rewarding particularly in the use of viruses, well characterizable and amenable to refined and exact manipulation at the molecular biology level, as powerful probes to explore the mechanisms of oncogenesis. This fundamental contribution has been more successful than the straight search for viruses causing neoplasms in man.

The best evidence – epidemiological and laboratory – supporting a causal association between a virus and a cancer, is that linking the hepatitis B virus (HBV) to primary hepatocellular carcinoma. The epidemiological evidence (Evans 1982; Trichopoulos *et al.* 1982) includes: anecdotal and clinical studies; geographical studies correlating the prevalence of chronic carrier status (as assessed by the presence of the hepatitis B surface antigen – HBsAg) with incidence of hepatitis B virus; case-control studies comparing the frequency of HBsAG in primary hepatocellular carcinoma cases and controls; and cohort studies comparing the incidence of primary hepatocellular carcinoma in HBsAg-positive and HBsAg-negative cirrhotics or in HBsAg-positive and HBsAg-negative 'healthy' people. The ensemble of these studies, individually vulnerable to several biases, consistently point to a causal association between this virus and primary hepatocellular carcinoma, with elevated relative risks, of the order of 10 or more. The position of three other associations – Epstein–Barr virus with endemic (African) Burkitt's lymphoma, the same virus with nasopharyngeal carcinoma and herpes virus 2 with cervical cancer – is less firmly established (particularly as supporting data from epidemiological prospective studies is very limited or not available) and these viruses would be better placed in the next section among 'possible' (rather than 'established') environmental determinants of cancers. What is sufficiently well established epidemiologically is the causal role of sexual promiscuity (which increases the chance of passing on an agent, possibly a virus, during intercourse) for cancer of the cervix uteri.

Possible environmental determinants

In addition to the well established human carcinogens just reviewed, evidence is available pointing to a host of other environmental agents as having a possible role in the production of malignant neoplasms. The degree of confidence in identifying them as carcinogenic factors may vary from relatively high to low, near the level of a merely reasonable hypothesis. Given this open status, to examine each factor would demand a somewhat detailed analysis presenting the arguments in favour and against its role in cancer causation: and this would be more of interest as an illustration of current questions in cancer research and epidemiology than for its implications in public health terms. Therefore, only a brief review of this second group of determinants will be presented here, under two headings: chemical pollutants and diet.

Chemical pollutants (IARC 1982)

Chemical pollution from *complex mixtures* of chemicals has been the focus of epidemiological studies investigating cancer risk in relation to contamination of air, water, and food. These studies, although particularly difficult to interpret, indicate that air pollution (pollution levels have been reduced in recent years in most developed countries), alone or in conjunction with smoking, may have contributed to some 10 per cent of lung cancers in urban areas, and therefore to a few per cent of lung cancers in a country as a whole (Doll and Peto 1981; Saracci, in press). The available evidence for drinking water pollution, particularly in relation to chlorinated compounds (some of which are carcinogenic in animals), is even less clear than that for air pollution. Similarly, food pollution, intentional (from additives) or unintentional (from natural or industrial pollutants), has not been clearly associated with evidence of increased risk of cancer in man, with the exception of aflatoxin B contamination in relation to primary hepatocellular carcinoma.

Individual chemicals which may contaminate air, water, and food include established as well as suspected carcinogens. In addition to the chemicals recognized as human carcinogens (Table 7.9) there are a number of other chemicals, exposure to which mainly occurs through use as drugs or in occupational settings, that have been rated as 'probably carcinogenic to humans': IARC (1982) has reviewed these chemicals and the supporting evidence of carcinogenicity in humans and animals. The IARC (1982) also lists a large number of chemicals (147 out of a total of 585 examined) for which sufficient evidence of carcinogenicity in long-term tests in experimental animals does exist, but *no* epidemiological data are available, although human exposure is known to occur on small or, sometimes, large scale. For instance, several nitrosamines rank among the most potent carcinogens in animals, and low-level (in the p.p.m.–p.p.b. range) exposures occur through food, air, and water. Still the answer to the question of the actual risk of cancer for man remains elusive. For the practical purposes of cancer prevention it is prudent to regard these compounds (that is, those with sufficient evidence of carcinogenicity in animals and no data in man) and, *a fortiori*, those judged as probably carcinogenic to humans, as if they entailed some risk of cancer for man, and to act accordingly (see below).

Diet (National Research Council 1982)

Diet may conceivably influence the development of cancer in a variety of ways. One mechanism is through ingestion of carcinogens formed by bacterial or fungal action during the storage of food (for example, aflatoxin B produced by *Aspergillus flavus*) or through pyrolysis or caramelization processes during cooking of meat and fish. A second type of mechanism is by providing substrates for the formation of carcinogens in the body (for example, nitrites and nitrates) or by altering the concentration or duration of contact of carcinogens with cells in the large bowel, as may be derived through varying the quantity of cellulosic fibres in the faeces. Other mechanisms include induction or inhibition of enzymes which affect carcinogen metabolism (for example, aryl hydrocarbon hydroxylase) as well as prevention of formation or deactivation of shortlived carcinogenic molecular species (free radicals, antagonized by the use of antioxidants such as selenium, vitamins E and A). Finally, being overweight, which implies over-nutrition (whatever the underlying mechanisms may be), is associated with cancer of the gall-bladder and of the endometrium.

Opinion is growing among research workers that diet may be a factor in determining the occurrence of a sizeable proportion of all cancers of the stomach and large bowel, as well as of the body of the uterus, gall-bladder, and, in tropical countries, liver. Diet is also seen as possibly affecting the incidence of cancers of breast and pancreas without excluding, through the anticarcinogenic effect of various micronutrients, an effect on incidence of cancer at other sites. The fact that a number of plausible hypotheses can be formulated, and fragmentarily supported, on the role of diet in the aetiology of many cancers, while virtually none of them has yet been conclusively corroborated in man, makes epidemiological–biochemical studies of diet and cancer a high research priority.

Primary prevention: some practical points

The environmental determinants of malignant neoplasms reviewed earlier – including UV radiation, ionizing radiations, tobacco smoke, alcohol, a number of chemicals, industrial processes, and occupational exposures, certain parasites, and the hepatitits B virus – are sufficiently well established to constitute logical priorities for preventive action. Two more reasons add weight to this priority: some of the agents are responsible for sizeable proportions of the cancers occurring today, for instance, smoking among the general population and asbestos among the working population, and for most of the agents *it is in principle feasible to reduce or even to completely eliminate exposure*. If this is taken as the objective of preventive action, some practical points are helpful in guiding such action:

(a) None of the data sets allowing a *relatively* accurate definition of dose (exposure)–response relationships for cancer in man (such data are available for ionizing radiations – Boice 1982; tobacco smoking – US DHHS 1982; and, to a lesser extent, asbestos – Health and Safety Commission 1979) indicate divergence from linearity at low dose, that is, in the portions of the curves which are of key interest when exposures can be controlled to low levels but, for whatever reason, not completely avoided. Also, environmental carcinogens do not operate in a vacuum; rather, each of them can be regarded as adding an extra risk to a background risk due to all other determinants. Under these circumstances it can be shown mathematically (Crump *et al.* 1976) that if the background dose, or even a small fraction of it (Hoel 1980), and the dose of the carcinogen under consideration act additively, the dose–response curve will be in any case approximately linear at low doses (Fig. 7.4) (Tomatis *et al.* 1982). Linearity is preserved, though the slope is changed, when a second carcinogen is considered, acting jointly with the first (Gardner 1979).

Practical point no. 1. In assessing the effect of reducing exposure to carcinogens it is at present reasonable to build and use a linear dose–response relationship with no thresholds.

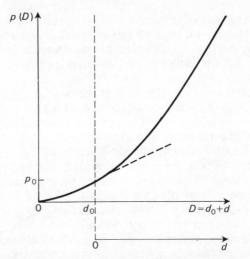

Fig. 7.4. Linearity of dose–response at low dose exposure. Excess risk over background risk (p_0) increases approximately *linearly* with the applied dose (d) of a carcinogen if background dose (d_0) acts additively with applied dose (i.e. $D = d_0 + d$). (Source: Tomatis *et al.* (1982).)

(b) In the formulation just mentioned, dose means total dose cumulated over time. This implicitly assumes that the carcinogenic effect is equally dependent on the dose rate (dose per unit of time) and on duration of exposure which, multiplied together, give total dose. However, both experimental and epidemiological data indicate that this is not the case. For lifelong exposures, for example, in regular smokers, the incidence rate (of lung cancer in smokers) depends much more strongly on duration of exposure, increasing with the fourth power of it, than on dose rate, increasing only with the first or second power of it (Peto 1977).

Practical point no. 2. For exposures in adult life, and if other biological effects (for example, genetical) can be excluded, it may be preferable to expose more people for shorter periods than less people for longer periods.

(c) Experimental and epidemiological investigations suggest that the carcinogenic process may be represented as a succession of stages, taking place in the timespan from first exposure to a carcinogenic agent to the appearance of clinical cancer (Joint IARC/IPCS/CES Working Group 1983). In its simplest form, as first brought out in mouse skin carcinogenesis experiments, the multistage process reduces to two stages: an irreversible 'initiation' stage inducing malignant cells, and a 'promotion' stage which propagates these cells into a malignant growth. A third stage of 'progression', characterized by an increased rate of growth and metastases, as well as an increase in chromosomal changes in the cell, has also been observed. Formal (statistico-mathematical) multistage models of carcinogenesis have provided a useful framework to interpret on a common basis of (postulated) mechanism both experimental and epidemiological observations. As the stages are assumed to occur in a specific sequence, some may be described as 'early' and some as 'late'. Epidemiological observations indicate that, for example, smoking has both an early stage effect, as indicated by the existence of minimum interval of several years before an increase in risk for lung cancer becomes manifest, and a late stage effect, as indicated by the decrease in elevated relative risk (in respect to non-smokers) soon after stopping smoking.

Practical point no. 3. If a carcinogen acts at a late stage, a reduction in risk will appear relatively soon after cessation of exposure while, if it acts at an early stage, no reduction at all may become apparent, even after decades.

(d) The attribution of causality to environmental agents (as done above where, for instance, smoking was said to be the cause of some 30 per cent of all cancers) is complicated by the interactive effects of several agents. This is particularly relevant when considering the relative effectiveness of removing (or reducing) exposure to one of two (or more) jointly-acting agents. To make the point clear, Table 7.10 presents the results of a large cohort study in insulator workers in the US and Canada (Hammond *et al.* 1979), classified according to their exposure to asbestos (A+ and A−) and to their smoking habits (S+ smokers, S− non-smokers). Due to the multiplicative interaction of asbestos and smoking the group exposed to both agents has the highest lung cancer rates, greatly in excess not only over those not exposed to either agent, but also over those exposed only to asbestos (the excess rate in the latter group is 47.1, while it is 590.3, that is 12.5 times greater, in the group exposed to both agents). Superficially it could be concluded that since smoking is by far the dominant factor, its removal will be correspondingly far more effective as a preventive measure than asbestos removal. However, as indicated by the figures in columns 3 and 4, this is not true. In fact, if smoking is removed the fraction, or percentage, of the excess rate removed will be $[(590.3 - 47.1)/590.3] \times 100 = 92.0$, and if asbestos is removed $[(590.3 - 111.3)/590.3] \times 100 = 81.2$. This means that smoking is more effective than asbestos removal but only $92.0/81.2 = 1.14$ times and not 12.5 times more effective as it superficially appeared. The result is not surprising if one considers that the bulk of the effect in subjects exposed to both agents is due to their positive interaction (synergism) and thus is removed whichever of the two agents is eliminated (Saracci 1981).

Practical point no. 4. Whenever a positive interaction (synergism) occurs between two (or more) hazardous exposures, there is an enlarged possibility of preventive attack; the effect of the joint exposure can be attacked in two

(or more) ways, each requiring the removal or reduction of one of the exposures; moreover, the larger the size of the interaction relative to the total effect the more these ways of attack tend to become equal in effectiveness.

(e) It has been mentioned that a number of chemicals, groups of chemicals, and industrial processes have been found, when proper account has been taken of all evidence (laboratory and epidemiological), to be 'probably' carcinogenic for man, and that a large number of other chemical agents have been demonstrated as carcinogens in animals, with no data available in humans (IARC 1982).

Practical point no. 5. These agents should be considered as if they entail a risk of cancer for humans and actions minimizing exposure accordingly taken.

(f) Exposure to carcinogens can be implemented in two major ways: by elimination of the carcinogen or its substitution with a non-carcinogen; or by impeding by various means the contact between the carcinogen and people.

Practical point no. 6. Reduction of exposure depends in each case on technical and economical considerations. As a rule, however, methods of exposure reduction which minimize the number of decisions involved are to be preferred: for instance, change to an innocuous material in preference to having each user exercise caution in using a noxious one.

EARLY DETECTION AND SECONDARY PREVENTION

Methodological issues in early detection programme evaluation

Given the limitations still constraining the primary prevention approach, early detection needs to be considered as a secondary and alternative option, based on the reasonable expectation that the earlier the diagnosis and the stage at which a malignancy is discovered the better the prognosis. Of course, this implies not only that an effective treatment for the disease exists – which is not always the case – but that what usually appears to apply at the clinical, manifest stages of the disease – namely the less advanced the cancer the better the scope for treatment and the better the prognosis – holds true also in the preclinical stages: and this also cannot be taken for granted. It is therefore useful to keep two aspects of secondary prevention separate: early detection as soon as possible after symptoms have developed, which belongs to the domain of ordinary medical care and poses problems of how to render it fully effective; and early detection in an asymptomatic ('well') population through a large-scale (mass screening) programme, to which the rest of the present discussion is devoted.

Before a screening programme can be adopted on a large scale a number of requirements need to be fulfilled over and above the fundamental one (already mentioned) that an effective treatment for the preclinical malignant lesion must be available also on a sufficient scale. These requirements have been extensively discussed in publications specifically addressing the issue of evaluating screening programmes, in particular for cancer (Cole and Morrison 1980; Miller 1982). First of all a *screening test* (that is, a relatively simple and rapid test aimed at the presumptive identification of

Table 7.10. *Percentage of excess lung cancer death rate (per 100 000 person-years) removable by elimination of smoking and asbestos*

Exposure group	Death rate (1)	Excess rate (2)	Excess rate (%) removable by elimination of:	
			Smoking (3)	Asbestos (4)
A − S −	11.3	0.0	–	–
A + S −	58.4	47.1	–	100.0
A − S +	122.6	111.3	100.0	–
A + S +	601.6	590.3	92.0	81.2

Source: Saracci (1981).

unrecognized disease) must be available that is capable of correctly identifying cases and non-cases. In other words, both sensitivity and specificity should be high, approaching 100 per cent. While high sensitivity is obviously important given that the very purpose of screening is to pick up, if possible, all cases of a cancer in its detectable preclinical phase, it is specificity that plays a dominant role in the practical utilization of the test within a defined population, that is in a *screening programme*. As the prevalence of a pre-clinical cancer to be screened in well populations is often in the range of 1 to 10 per 1000, if a test is used with a specificity of 'only' 95 per cent then 5 per cent of results will be false-positives. In other words, for every case which will turn out at the diagnostic work-up to be a true cancer (assuming 100 per cent sensitivity), there will be 5–50 cases falsely identified as such and ultimately found not to be cancers. This situation, which is likely to prove unacceptable due to too high psycho-logical and economical costs, may be obviated: (a) by increasing the test specificity, for example by developing better tests, or combination of tests, or changing the criterion of positivity of a given test to make it more stringent (this necessarily decreases sensitivity); (b) by selecting populations with relatively high prevalence of the cancer to be screened, that is, 'high risk' groups, so as to increase the number of the true positives. Whatever the group on which the programme operates, additional requirements are that the test is safe, easily and rapidly applicable, and acceptable in a broad sense to the population to be examined (for example, sigmoido-scopy may not be). It has also to be cheap, but what is or is not cheap is better evaluated within a cost-effectiveness analysis of different ways of preventing a cancer case or death, an issue not further discussed here.

If these requirements are met, still nothing is known about the possible net benefit in outcome deriving from the screening programme (in fact, screening test plus diagnostic work-up plus treatment, as applied in a given population). To evaluate benefit, several measures of outcome can be assessed. An early one, useful but not sufficient, is the distribution by stage of the detected cancer cases which, if the programme is ultimately to be beneficial, should be shifted to earlier, less invasive stages of the disease in comparison with the distribution of the cases discovered through ordinary medical care. A second measure of outcome is the survival of cases detected at screening compared with that of cases detected through ordinary medical care. This is a superficially attractive but usually equivocal criterion, to the extent that a screening may only advance the time of diagnosis (and therefore the apparent survival time), without postponing the time of death (see below, 'lead-time bias'). A final outcome (and the acid test of the programme) is the site-specific cancer mortality in the screened population compared with the site-specific cancer mortality in the unscreened population.

Correct, unbiased comparison of this outcome, and thus unbiased measure of the effect of the screening programme, can only be made within the framework of a randomized controlled trial, in which two groups of subjects are randomly allocated to the screening programme and to no screening (that is, receiving only the existing medical care system) or to two alternative screening programmes, for instance, entailing different tests or different intervals between periodical examinations.

Unfortunately, largely due to pressures to adopt on a large scale screening programmes hoped to be effective, a situation has often arisen where withholding screening to a group has been regarded as unethical, thus preventing the conduct of a proper experiment. And very few randomized trials evaluating the effectiveness of screening programmes are available. Comparisons made through non-randomized experiments (which also are infrequent for the same reason) or through observational studies of what has happened following the introduction of a screening programme in a population, are liable to distortion. Besides the sources of distortion common to all epidemiological (observational) studies, four types of biases are peculiar to comparisons of early detection pro-grammes. These biases, which should always be kept in mind, for example, when examining reports on screening program-mes, are: (a) *lead-time bias*, already alluded to – earlier detection only moves forward the time of a patient's diagnosis, without postponing the time of death: should this be the case the result would only be a longer period of morbidity for the patient; (b) *self-selection bias* – persons who elect to receive early detection may be different from those who do not: for instance, they may belong to better educated classes, be generally healthier and health conscious, and this could produce a longer survival independent of any effect of early detection; (c) *length bias* – cancers with longer preclinical phases, which may mean less biological aggres-siveness and better prognosis, are, in any case, more likely to be intercepted by a programme of periodical screening than cancers with a short preclinical phase, and a rapid, aggressive clinical course; and (d) *overdiagnosis bias* – because of criteria of positivity adopted to maximize yield of early cases, a number of lesions which in fact would never become malignant growths are included as 'cases', thus falsely improve the survival statistics.

As observational studies, however, may represent the only source of information to evaluate screening programmes, they need to be carefully considered. Among purely observational situations, one which may provide particularly useful information is that arising when a relatively small, closed population (with no migration in or out) is saturated over a short interval (a few years) with the screening programme to be evaluated. If good ordinary diagnostic and treatment services are available before, during and after the introduction of the screening, and the mortality rate from the cancer can be regarded as predictable, a clear change in mortality would represent good scientific evidence for effectiveness of the screening programme.

Early detection of cancers at individual sites

There are cancers at five sites for which the existing amount of data from screening programmes demands an evaluation in the light of the previous methodological considerations. These are cancer of the cervix uteri, breast, stomach, colon and rectum, and lung.

Cervix uteri

Some 90 per cent of cervical cancers originate in the exocervix (or *portio vaginalis*) and are squamous carcinomas. The remaining fraction includes adenocarcinomas and adenosquamous carcinomas, usually located in the endocervix (cervical canal). Early detection of cervical cancer aims at the precursor stages of these carcinomas, namely mild, moderate, or severe dysplasia, and carcinoma *in situ*. These lesions, particularly those located in the exocervix, exfoliate easily accessible cells with nuclei of abnormal size, shape, and staining properties, and this forms the basis of the screening test (Pap test). Moreover, the pre-invasive detectable period of the cancer, although not known exactly, is rarely less than five years, thus giving a good opportunity for a periodical examination to detect the pre-invasive lesion.

Soon after the initial introduction of screening, which started in the early 1950s in North America, it became apparent that women attending screening clinics were usually at lower risk of cervical cancer than non-attendees, for example, they were in the upper social classes. This would blur any comparison between screened and non-screened groups. No experimental studies, randomized or not, are available to assess the value of the screening programmes and, given the expansion of screening, they are most unlikely to ever become possible. However, the evidence from observational studies, particularly those from some of the Nordic countries, indicates the effectiveness of screening programmes in reducing mortality from cervical cancer (Day, in press). For instance, in Iceland (Johanesson *et al.* 1982) a small, closed population has been saturated (in nine years 75 per cent of women in the age group between 30 and 60 years had been screened at least once) with a screening programme which started in the mid-1960s and offered periodical examination at two to three yearly intervals. Besides a reduction in the incidence of the four most advanced stages of the disease and, later on, also of the earliest stages, 10–15 years after screening was introduced the mortality for cervical cancer had fallen by 60 per cent, while it had been rising in the preceding decade. Given the size and rapidity of this mortality trend inversion it appears reasonable to attribute at least a substantial part of the observed change to the programme.

Although the benefit of screening for cervical cancer can thus be regarded as sufficiently well-established, further information is needed on how to design maximally effective programmes at low cost. Questions like the optimum frequency of re-screening in relation to a woman's age have not yet been satisfactorily answered. Recommendations have, however, been issued on the basis of the existing evidence and Table 7.11 summarizes the recommendations of the Canadian Task Force on Screening (1976).

Breast

The evaluation of screening for breast cancer still rests heavily on the results of the one completed randomized trial carried out by the Health Insurance Plan (HIP) of Greater New York (Shapiro *et al.* 1982). This trial, which was started in the 1960s, involved a study group of 31 000 (in round figures) women aged 40–64 years, invited to be screened at yearly

Table 7.11. *Recommendations of the Canadian Task Force on Screening (1976) for cervical cancer screening*

(a) Initial smears should be obtained from all women over the age of 18 years who have had sexual intercourse

(b) If the initial smear is satisfactory and without significant atypia, a second smear should be taken within one year

(c) Provided the initial two smears and all subsequent smears are satisfactory and without significant atypia, further smears should be taken at approximately three-year intervals until the age of 35, and thereafter at five-year intervals until the age of 60

(d) Women over the age of 60 who have repeated satisfactory smears without significant atypia may be dropped from a screening programme for squamous carcinoma of the cervix

(e) Women who are not at high risk should be discouraged from having smears more frequently than is recommended above

(f) Women at continuing high risk should be screened annually. To facilitate this, provision for taking cytological smears should be made at family-planning clinics, student health clinics, youth clinics, venereal disease clinics, prenatal clinics, and medical facilities at which women are examined before admission to penal institutions

intervals for five years by mammography and clinical examination, and a non-screened control group of the same size. For the first seven years an increasing difference in mortality rates for breast cancer was observed between the screened and unscreened groups, the mortality in the former being reduced by 40 per cent, but only in women aged 50 years and above. In subsequent follow-up this reduction has been attenuated, as would be expected when a screening programme has been applied only for a limited period (in this case, five years). No statistically significant effect has been observed in women below the age of 50 years, although the sample size was relatively limited. Thus, there is a reasonable foundation, although limited to only one experimental study showing the benefit of mammography *plus* clinical examination in women aged 50 years and over, to advise screening. Various population studies, including some randomized trials (de Waard *et al.* 1978; Miller 1980; Tabar and Gad 1981; UK Trial of Early Detection of Breast Cancer Group 1981), are in progress, both to replicate (hopefully) the HIP result and to provide the information still missing on other critical issues like: assessment of the independent contribution of mammography, physical examination, and self-examination (there are virtually no solid data on this widely publicized manoeuvre); the extent to which early detection may lead to over-treatment; the benefit, if any, of screening women below the age of 50 years; and the optimal interval between re-screens.

A potential advantage of mammography is that it may detect (as areas of micro-calcification) cancers at the preinvasive stage, leading to cure; however, this may turn out to be a disadvantage if such preinvasive lesions do not in fact progress to invasive cancer and are, nevertheless, treated by mastectomy. Also, there is a small radiation risk associated with mammography; for women over 50 years screened yearly with a mammography involving the administration of one rad X-ray, the probability of getting breast cancer in the rest of their lives is increased by some 2 per cent – for example, from a probability of 6.4 per cent to 6.5 per cent

(Eddy and Shwartz 1982). Continual development of radiological techniques has, however, already succeeded in reducing the radiation dose well below one rad (to 0.1 rad or less) and might also improve the screening value in terms of specificity and sensitivity of mammography. Meanwhile, the search continues for non-radiological screening tools like new thermographic techniques (as practised in the past these have been shown to have both low sensitivity and specificity), transillumination, and ultrasound techniques.

Stomach

Cancer at this site has been steeply declining in incidence in developed countries (for reasons which remain unclear) and this may have contributed to putting it low on the scale of priorities for experimental studies evaluating screening programmes. In fact, no such studies, randomized or otherwise, are available. Observational studies are, however, available, in particular from Japan. Although stomach cancer is still the leading site for cancer in Japan, mortality rates halved between 1950 and the mid-1970s (Hirayama 1978). The results of several observational studies taken together indicate that screening using mass photofluorographic X-ray techniques has proven acceptable in the Japanese context and appears to have contributed, perhaps in the measure of 20 per cent, to the observed reduction in mortality. The evidence for this beneficial effect is, however, not as firm as 'one might have liked, or that is now being accumulated for, for example, cancer of the cervix' (Workshop discussion on screening for stomach cancer 1978).

Colon and rectum

It is very doubtful whether proctosigmoidoscopy, which has been advocated for yearly examination in all subjects above 40 years of age in some countries, is a feasible screening approach, given its low acceptability. The Guiac test to reveal occult bleeding lesions (haemoccult test) appears a feasible approach. It is usually applied in subjects kept on a meat-free, high-residue diet for at least 24 hours before the three days collection of faeces (from which six specimens are tested) is made. A recent randomized trial (Hardcastle *et al.* 1983) showed that the pathological stage distribution of cancers detected in the screened group was more favourable than in the unscreened group; one out of twelve presented lymphatic involvement in the former, while six out of ten presented lymphatic involvement or liver metastasis in the latter group. This is a promising finding, but until results of ongoing controlled trials (two of which are in progress in the US) assessing other end-points, in particular mortality, become available, no evaluation of the worth of the haemoccult test can be made.

Lung

There is no evidence of benefit of screening programmes for lung cancer (usually involving chest X-ray and/or sputum cytology) from the available observational and experimental studies, or from the one completed randomized controlled trial. The latter study (Doles *et al.* 1979) compared, at 11 years follow-up, a group including 20 per cent of subjects screened yearly versus another group including 60 per cent of subjects screened yearly, the screening consisting of chest X-ray, spirometry, and the medical questionnaire. Three major randomized studies (Levin *et al.* 1982; Martini 1982; Sanderson and Fontana 1982) are in progress in the US, comparing in male smokers above 45 years of age different schedules of administration of chest X-rays, or chest X-ray and sputum cytology. Although some results are available showing a higher proportion of resectable cancers in the groups more intensively screened, no differences in mortality have yet emerged during the limited period of observation hitherto.

Application of a large-scale screening programme to a given community will involve consideration of a number of elements, including for example, the possibility of concentrating the programme on high-risk groups (such as, families with hereditary cancers, special occupational groups), the possibility of combining screening for several sites in one programme and, needless to say, the available resources. However, one should never lose sight of the fact that consideration of these elements is only justified for programmes which have been shown to be effective in bringing about a reduction in mortality from the cancer to be screened. For the time being, such evidence is only available for the Pap test programme in respect of cancer of the cervix, and for mammography plus physical examination in women above 50 years of age for breast cancer. For communities still experiencing high rates of stomach cancer it may not be out of place to consider a screening programme by photofluorography, and embodying a component of evaluation of the effectiveness (now limited to one country – Japan) as an essential element.

CONCLUSION: PREVENTION TODAY AND TOMORROW

Today, if the objective of *complete* avoidance of the exposures already known and well established as carcinogenic in man, and for which avoidance is realistically practicable, was achieved, a considerable fraction (one-third or more) of cancers occurring in a developed country could be eliminated. Approximate contributions to this result would come from 30 per cent of cancers being prevented through avoidance of tobacco smoking, some 3 per cent through avoidance of alcoholic drinks, while avoidance of unnecessary use of hormones or X-rays, unusual exposure to sunlight, established carcinogens in the workplace, and established carcinogens in air, water, and food, would each contribute another 1 per cent or less (Doll and Peto 1981). Two per cent of cancers might be prevented by avoiding obesity, which in any case would be beneficial for health in general. A further 1 per cent or so would be gained through secondary prevention involving regular screening for cervical cancer.

An expansion of the scope for primary prevention in the foreseeable future will depend firstly and critically on our ability to firmly identify further environmental agents amenable to manipulation: this includes clarification of the role of the determinants listed earlier as 'possible', in particular the role of dietary factors. Secondly, it will depend on a better understanding of the mechanisms of action of chemical, physical, and biological carcinogens. This will, among other things, help in throwing a better light on dose–response relationships. The non-threshold linear model may not be the most appropriate for all carcinogens, particularly, for example, promoters, although for the time being there is not enough evidence to replace it with sound alternatives. Thirdly, identification of host factors which, given the present status of knowledge have been left out of this review, may contribute to identification of subjects liable to develop cancer. Fourthly, new possibilities of prevention may arise from protective actions, rather than from (or in complement to) avoidance of exposures. Retinoids have been shown in experimental systems to inhibit proliferation of initiated cancer cells (Sporn and Newton 1979), retinol (vitamin A) blood levels have been found lowered in, for example, lung cancer patients (Wald *et al.* 1980), and intervention trials are currently under way to explore the efficacy, if any, of administering Vitamin A and its precursors in the prevention of cancer occurrence or of precursor lesions. Vaccination for hepatitis B virus is now feasible (WHO Scientific Group 1983) and opens an avenue to the prevention of hepatitis B virus related primary hepatocellular carcinoma. At the same time better knowledge of the natural history of cancers including possible identification of markers of early molecular precursor lesions, and the availability of newer non-invasive diagnostic technologies, may improve the outlook for secondary prevention at different stages in the preclinical evolution of the disease.

If these developments take place successfully it may not be too rash to foresee that by the end of the century two-thirds rather than one-third of cancers in a developed country will be fully preventable.

REFERENCES

American Cancer Society (1981). *Cancer facts and figures 1982.* ACS, New York.

Berg, J.W., Ross, R., and Labourette, H.G. (1977). Economic status and survival of cancer patients. *Cancer* **39**, 467.

Bishop, J.M. (1982). Oncogenes. *Sci. Am.* **146**, 80.

Boice, J.D. and Land, C.E. (1982). Ionizing radiation. In *Cancer epidemiology and prevention* (eds. D. Schottenfeld and J.F. Fraumeni) p. 231. Saunders, Philadelphia.

Burton, G.J. (1982). Parasites. In *Cancer epidemiology and prevention* (ed D. Schottenfeld and J.F. Fraumeni) p. 408. Saunders, Philadelphia.

Canadian Task Force on Screening (1976). Cervical cancer screening programs. *Can. Med. Assoc. J.* **114**, 1003.

Cole, P. and Morrison, A.S. (1980). Basic issues in population screening for cancer. *J. Natl. Cancer Inst.* **64**, 1263.

Crump, K.S., Hoel, D.G., Langley, C.H., and Peto, R. (1976). Fundamental carcinogenic processes and their implications for low dose risk assessment. *Cancer Res.* **36**, 2973.

Cutler, S.J. and Young, J.L. (eds.) (1975). *Third national cancer survey: incidence data.* National Cancer Institute Monograph 41, Bethesda, Md.

Day, N.E. (in press). Secondary prevention of cancer of the uterine cervix. In *Cancer prevention strategies* (ed. J. Stjernswärd). World Health Organization, Geneva.

de Waard, F., Rombach, J.J., and Colette, H.J.A. (1978). The DOM project for the early diagnosis of breast cancer in the city of Utrecht. In *Screening in cancer* (ed. A.B. Miller) p. 183. UICC Technical Report No. 40. International Union Against Cancer, Geneva.

Doles, L.G., Friedman, G.D., and Cullen, M.F. (1979). Evaluating periodic multiphasic health checkups: a controlled trial. *J. Chronic Dis.* **32**, 385.

Doll, R. (1983). Prospects for prevention. *Br. Med. J.* **286**, 445.

Doll, R. and Peto, R. (1981). *The causes of cancer.* Oxford University Press.

Eddy, D.M. and Shwartz, M. (1982). Mathematical models in screening. In *Cancer epidemiology and prevention* (eds. D. Schottenfeld and J.F. Fraumeni) p. 1975. Saunders, Philadelphia.

Evans, A.S. (1982). Viruses. In *Cancer epidemiology and prevention* (eds. D. Schottenfeld and J.F. Fraumeni) p. 364. Saunders, Philadelphia.

Gardner, M.J. (1983). Effect of a second factor on a linear dose-response relationship. *J. UOEH* Suppl. 5, 183.

Garfinkel, L. (1981). Time trends in lung cancer mortality among nonsmokers and a note on passive smoking. *J. Natl. Cancer Inst.* **66**, 1061.

Hammond, E.C., Selikoff, I.J., and Seidman, H. (1979). Asbestos exposure, cigarette smoking and death rates. *Ann. N.Y. Acad. Sci.* **330**, 473.

Hardcastle, J.D., Farrends, P.A., Balfour, T.W., Chamberlain, J., Amar, S.S., and Sheldon, M.G. (1983). Controlled trial of faecal occult blood testing in the detection of colorectal cancer. *Lancet* **ii**, 1.

Health and Safety Commission's Advisory Committee (1979). *Asbestos.* HMSO, London.

Hirayama, T. (1978). Outline of stomach cancer screening in Japan. In *Screening in cancer* (ed. A.B. Miller) p. 264. UICC Technical Report No. 40, International Union Against Cancer, Geneva.

Hirayama, T. (1981). Non-smoking wives of heavy smokers have a higher risk of lung cancer. A study from Japan. *Br. Med. J.* **282**, 183.

Hodgson, T.A. and Rice, D.P. (1982). Economic impact of cancer in the United States. In *Cancer epidemiology and prevention* (eds. D. Schottenfeld and J.F. Fraumeni) p. 208. Saunders, Philadelphia.

Hoel, D.G. (1980). Incorporation of background in dose-response models. *Fed. Proc.* **39**, 73.

International Agency for Research on Cancer (1982). *Monographs on the evaluation of the carcinogenic risk of chemicals to humans* Supplement 4. IARC, Lyon.

International Labour Office (1982). *Yearbook of labour statistics 1982.* ILO, Geneva.

Johanesson, G., Geirsson, G., Day, N.E., and Tulinius, H. (1982). Screening for cancer of the uterine cervix in Iceland, 1965–1978. *Acta Obst. Gynecol. Scand.* **61**, 199.

Joint IARC/IPCS/CEC Working Group (1983). *Approaches to classifying chemical carcinogens according to mechanism of action.* IARC Internal Technical Report No. 83/001. International Agency for Research on Cancer, Lyon.

Knudson, A.G. (1977). Genetic predisposition to cancer. In *Origins of human cancer* (eds. H.H. Hiatt, J.D. Watson, and J.A. Winsten) Book A. p. 45. Cold Spring Harbor Laboratory, Cold Spring Harbor.

Knudson, A.G., Strong, L.C., and Anderson, D.E. (1973). Heredity and cancer in man. *Prog. Med. Genet.* **9**, 113.

Lee, J.A.H. (1982). Melanoma and exposure to sunlight. *Epidemiol. Rev.* **4**, 110.

Levin, M.L., Tockman, M.S., Frost, J.K., and Ball, W.C. (1982). Lung cancer mortality in males screened by chest X-ray and cytology sputum examination: a preliminary report. In *Early detection and localization of lung tumours in high risk groups* (ed. P.R. Band) p. 138. Springer, Berlin.

Martini, N. (1982). Results of the Memorial Sloan-Kettering Lung Project. In *Early detection and localization of lung tumours in high risk groups* (ed. P.R. Band) p. 174. Springer, Berlin.

Miller, A.B. (1980). National breast cancer screening study gets under way. *Can. Med. Assoc. J.* **122**, 243.

Miller, A.B. (1982). Fundamental issues in screening. In *Cancer epidemiology and prevention* (eds. D. Schottenfeld and J.F. Fraumeni) p. 1064. Saunders, Philadelphia.

Miller, J.A. and Miller, E.C. (1977). Ultimate carcinogens as reactive mutagenic electrophiles. In *Origins of human cancer* (ed. H.H. Hiatt, J.D. Watson, and J.A. Winsten) Book B, p. 605. Cold Spring Harbor Laboratory, Cold Spring Harbor.

Muir, C.S. and Nectoux, J. (1982). International patterns of cancer. In *Cancer epidemiology and prevention* (ed. D. Schottenfeld and J.F. Fraumeni) p. 119. Saunders, Philadelphia.

Myers, M.H. and Hankey, B.F. (1982). Cancer patient survival in the United States. In *Cancer epidemiology and prevention* (ed. D. Schottenfeld and J.F. Fraumeni) p. 166. Saunders, Philadelphia.

National Institutes of Health, National Cancer Program (1981). *1980 Director's report and annual plan, FX1982–1986,* p. 33. NIH Publication No. 81–2290, Chapter III. Washington, DC.

National Research Council (1982). *Diet, nutrition and cancer.* National Academy Press, Washington.

Parkin, D.M., Stjernswärd, J., and Muir, C.S. (in press). Estimates of the worldwide frequency of twelve major cancers. *WHO Bull.*

Peto, R. (1977). Epidemiology, multistage models and short-term mutagenicity tests. In *Origins of human cancer* (eds. H.H. Hiatt, J.D. Watson, and J.A. Winsten) p. 1403. Cold Spring Harbor Laboratory, Cold Spring Harbor.

Peto, R. (1979). Detection of risk of cancer to man. *Proc. R. Soc. Lond. B* **205**, 111.

Rigby, P.W.J. (1982). The oncogenic circle closes. *Nature* **297**, 451.

Rogot, E. and Murray, J.L. (1980). Smoking and causes of death in U.S. Veterans: 16 years of observation. *Public Health Rep.* **95**, 213.

Sanderson, D. and Fontana, R. (1982). Results of a major lung project: an interim report. In *Early detection and localization of lung tumours in high risk groups* (ed. P.R. Band) p. 179. Springer, Berlin.

Saracci, R. (1981). Personal-environmental interactions in occupational epidemiology. In *Occupational epidemiology* (ed. J.C. McDonald) No. 1, p. 119. Churchill Livingstone, Edinburgh.

Saracci, R. (in press). Carcinogenesis, mutagenesis and teratogenesis. In *Ambient air pollutants from industrial sources* (ed. R. Suess). WHO Regional Office for Europe, Copenhagen.

Scotto, J. and Fraumeni, J.F. (1982). Skin (other than melanoma). In *Cancer epidemiology and prevention* (eds. D. Schottenfeld and J.F. Fraumeni) p. 996. Saunders, Philadelphia.

Scotto, J., Fears, T.R., and Fraumeni, J.F. (1982). Solar radiation. In *Cancer epidemiology and prevention* (eds. D. Schottenfeld and J.F. Fraumeni) p. 254. Saunders, Philadelphia.

Shapiro, S., Venet, W., Strax, P., Venet, L., and Roeser, R. (1982). Ten to fourteen year effects of breast cancer screening on mortality. *J. Natl Cancer Inst.* **69**, 349.

Silverberg, E.S. and Lubera, J.A. (1983). A review of American Cancer Society estimates of cancer cases and deaths. *Cancer J. Clinicians* **33**, 2.

Sporn, M.B. and Newton, D.L. (1979). Chemoprevention of cancer with retinoids. *Fed. Proc.* **38**, 2528.

Tabar, L. and Gad, A. (1981). Screening for breast cancer; the Swedish trial. *Radiology* **138**, 219.

Tomatis, L., Breslow, N.E., and Bartsch, H. (1982). Experimental studies in the assessment of human risk. In *Cancer epidemiology and prevention* (eds. D. Schottenfeld and J.F. Fraumeni) p. 44. Saunders, Philadelphia.

Trichopoulos, D., Kalandidi, A., Sparros, L., and MacMahon, B. (1981). Lung cancer and passive smoking. *Int. J. Cancer* **27**, 1.

Trichopoulos, D., Kremastinou, J., and Tzonou, A. (1982). Does hepatitis B virus cause hepatocellular carcinoma? In *Host factors in human carcinogenesis* (eds. H. Bartsch and B. Armstrong) p. 317. IARC Scientific Publication No. 39. International Agency for Research on Cancer, Lyon.

Tuyns, A.J. (1982). Alcohol. In *Cancer epidemiology and prevention* (ed. D. Schottenfled and J.F. Fraumeni) p. 293. Saunders, Philadelphia.

UK Trial of Early Detection of Breast Cancer Group (1981). Trial of early detection of breast cancer: description of method. *Br. J. Cancer* **44**, 618.

US Department of Health and Human Services (1982). *The health consequences of smoking—cancer.* US Department of Health and Human Services, Public Health Service, Office on Smoking and Health, Rockville, Maryland.

Wald, N., Idle, M., Boreham, J., and Bailey, A. (1980). Low-serum-vitamin-A and subsequent risk of cancer. *Lancet* **ii**, 813.

Waterhouse, J.A.H. (1974). *Cancer handbook of epidemiology and prognosis.* Churchill Livingstone, Edinburgh.

Workshop Discussion on Screening for Stomach Cancer (1978). In *Screening in cancer* (ed. A.B. Miller) UICC Technical Report No. 40, p. 300. International Union Against Cancer, Geneva.

WHO (1977). *International classification of diseases,* 9th (1975) Revision. World Health Organization, Geneva.

WHO (1982) *Seventh general programme of work (1984–1989).* World Health Organization, Geneva.

WHO Scientific Group (1983). Prevention of primary liver cancer (World Health Organization). *Lancet* **i**, 463.

Young, J.L. and Pollack, E.S. (1982). The incidence of cancer in the United States. In *Cancer epidemiology and prevention* (eds. D. Schottenfeld and J.F. Fraumeni) p. 138. Saunders, Philadelphia.

Systems

8 Cardiovascular diseases

Geoffrey Rose

INTRODUCTION

In the nineteenth century infectious diseases dominated the public health scene, but in the twentieth century it is cardiovascular diseases which have come to overshadow all others as a cause of death. Heart attack, rather than cholera or smallpox, now makes a man's hold on life unpredictable; and, among the elderly, a stroke has come to be the most feared disability. This change has come about through the combination of a decline in major infectious diseases and an absolute as well as relative increase in the incidence rates of some major cardiovascular diseases. As with other mass diseases, each of these trends reflects changes in life-style and environment whose origins are social and economic.

The major cardiovascular diseases fall into three categories. Atherosclerotic (coronary) disease is the main cause of death; its origins are in affluence (although happily it is not its inevitable accompaniment). Strokes also kill, but their impact on public health is mainly as a cause of chronic and distressful disability; their incidence largely reflects hypertension, whose determinants partly overlap but are also in part distinct from the determinants of atherosclerosis. Thirdly, there is rheumatic heart disease, which before it kills will usually have caused long years of disability. Keeping close company with domestic overcrowding, its incidence in western countries has greatly declined; but in poorer parts of the world it continues to be the commonest form of heart disease.

Other kinds of cardiovascular disease either represent a subsidiary manifestation of a major problem (such as alcoholism) or they are not common enough to constitute a major public health problem (for example other cardiomyopathies, subarachnoid haemorrhage).

CORONARY HEART DISEASE

Manifestations

Coronary heart disease (ischaemic heart disease) is the consequence of the obstruction of coronary artery blood flow by atherosclerosis and its complications. In western countries this process begins during the second decade of life with the formation of cholesterol-rich fibro-fatty deposits under the intima of the larger arteries. It is a generalized condition, so that those in whom it is manifest in the heart are also at special risk of developing its complications in the brain

(cerebral infarction) or legs (intermittent claudication or gangrene). In the main its predisposing causes are not site-specific, except that leg disease does seem to be specially linked with smoking and with diabetes.

The most rapid progression of atherosclerosis often occurs during the third decade of life, although at that time it is silent. Subsequently the clinical effects become increasingly common. They result not just from 'furring up' of arteries but because simple plaques become complicated by haemorrhage and fissuring, which may lead to overlying thrombosis. Mass atherosclerosis is necessary for mass disease, but other factors then influence the occurrence of blood flow obstruction in individual cases. Thrombogenic factors in particular have attracted much recent attention.

The disease may affect the heart in various ways. It may lead to sudden, often instantaneous death, usually from ventricular fibrillation; and in 20 per cent of all cases this is the first recognized presentation. If successfully resuscitated these people are liable to similar recurrences. Acute ischaemia, usually associated with thrombosis, may produce a myocardial infarction, whose typical manifestations are well known but which in perhaps half the cases are so mild that the heart attack is not recognized. On other occasions no evidence of myocardial infarction appears, despite an attack of typical pain. Such patients are often admitted to hospital, but no specific diagnosis can be made. During the subsequent year their risk of death is much the same as for cases of completed infarction.

The commonest chronic effect of myocardial ischaemia is angina, which is a temporary pain or discomfort brought on by increased cardiac work. Finally, and particularly in old people, chronic ischaemia may lead to impaired pump efficiency, limited exercise tolerance, and chronic heart failure.

The population burden

Among nearly all of those countries which are wealthy enough to afford a system of vital statistics, coronary heart disease has become the leading cause of death. In western countries it is held responsible for about 30 per cent of deaths in men and 25 per cent of deaths in women. These estimates may be slightly exaggerated by the tendency of clinicians and coroners' pathologists to attribute unexplained and supposedly cardiac deaths to what is known to be so common: perhaps as many as 20 per cent of all sudden unexpected deaths are in fact due to causes other than coronary heart disease. Nevertheless coronary heart disease probably accounts for almost three-quarters of all cardiovascular deaths.

Most fatal heart attacks are in old people, the mean age of death in England and Wales being 69 years in men and 77 years in women. About one man in 11 can currently expect to have a fatal heart attack before he is 65 years old, corresponding to an annual risk of death in middle-aged men of nearly 0.5 per cent.

Age-specific case–fatality ratios are the same in the two sexes, ranging among hospital admissions from around 7 per cent under age 45 years up to 40 per cent above the age of 65 years. The average age of cases is of course much higher in women than men, partly because there are so many more old women in the population and partly because age-specific incidence rates in women correspond to those of men some 10 or 20 years younger. As a result the all-ages case–fatality ratio is much higher in women than men, emphasizing the danger of comparing the outcome of illness in different series of cases that have not been adequately matched.

In recent years data on incidence have become available from a number of community registers of all diagnosed attacks (Armstrong *et al.* 1972; Kinlen 1973; Tunstall Pedoe *et al.* 1975; WHO 1976). Incidence estimates depend greatly on the diagnostic criteria that are demanded, as well as on access to medical care. Figure 8.1 gives some representative results, in which overall 40 per cent of attacks were fatal within 28 days. About 60 per cent of all deaths occur before the arrival of the doctor.

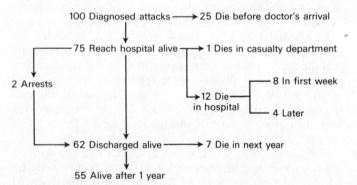

Fig. 8.1 Outcome (per cent) of acute coronary heart attacks occurring under age 65 in London. (Based on Tunstall Pedoe *et al.* (1975).)

Autopsy studies and population surveys suggest that about half of all episodes of myocardial infarction are not recognized at the time. Eventually most men in western populations will develop ischaemic myocardial scarring, and perhaps only 10 per cent will escape significant atherosclerosis. This is of central importance to preventive strategies, indicating that this is a mass disease which cannot be controlled by measures applied only to high-risk sub-groups.

Angina as it is seen in cardiac clinics is commonly either disabling, of recent onset, or a sequel of a heart attack. General practitioners, however, see many patients with mild

stable angina, who – especially if elderly – may never be referred to hospital. Still further down the severity scale, the point prevalence of angina in middle-aged men may be as much as 4 per cent, of which only a quarter may ever have been diagnosed (Reid *et al.* 1976). Transient symptoms are common, and the five-year period prevalence may be as much as 10 per cent (Rose 1968). In these milder cases, detectable by screening, there is a three- or fourfold increase in the risk of a fatal attack during the next decade; nevertheless the absolute risk is low (about 1 per cent per annum). Conclusions on prognosis and management of coronary heart disease tend to ignore the fact that any particular physician's view of the disease depends on how he comes by his cases.

Electrocardiographic signs of ischaemia have a population prevalence similar to angina. In the absence of routine examination most will go unrecognized; but again, most have a mild prognosis. The traditional view that heart attacks commonly come without warning is wrong: even a single screening examination, based on a questionnaire and technician-coded electrocardiogram, was found to predict half of all fatal attacks in the next five years (Rose *et al.* 1977). The low absolute risk, the frequency of false positives (especially in younger people), and the lack of intervention trials currently imply that screening for these early warning signs is not justifiable; but the potential is large.

Sudden death

Community registers of heart attacks have consistently demonstrated that sudden death is the central issue in the control of coronary heart disease. In about 20 per cent of all cases it is the presenting feature: these are men, previously believed healthy, who die before receiving or even calling for medical aid; for them, therapeutic advances are irrelevant.

Of all the deaths that occur within 28 days of onset of the attack, half are within the first two hours and most of these are probably within the first 15 minutes. Many patients are unable or unwilling to recognize the significance of the early symptoms, and the median delay time before seeking medical help is about three hours. Delay is no less among those who have already had one attack, nor for physician-patients, suggesting that the problem is not simply a lack of information. Attempts to educate public or patients to earlier reporting of symptoms seem not to be successful, and are anyway fraught with the risk of unprofitable anxiety and over-reacting to trivia.

The course of the attack

Figure 8.1 outlines the average course and outcome of 100 cases of heart attack in men under the age of 65 years, based on a community register in an inner city district where (in contrast with rural areas) nearly all cases are treated in hospital (Tunstall Pedoe *et al.* 1975).

In at least 60 per cent of attacks there had been some form of *prodrome*, usually new or altered chest pain or dyspnoea; in another study (Kinlen 1973) many patients were noted to have recently consulted their general practitioner, often for vaguer symptoms such as tiredness. The existence of these early warnings is tantalizing, but their predictive value is so low that they are of little practical help.

A quarter of the patients in this survey died before being seen by a doctor, constituting two-thirds of all the deaths. One per cent died in hospital before reaching the ward, maybe reflecting unnecessary delays. A further 12 per cent of all cases died in the hospital wards, and another 2 per cent were successfully resuscitated from cardiac arrest. There were thus 62 of the original 100 attacks in which the patient left hospital alive; during the next 12 months seven of them died, implying a total fatality of 45 per cent during the 12 months after an attack. Most survivors return to their original employment, but often after an unreasonable delay. The strong trend towards minimum bed rest and earlier hospital discharge has unfortunately not been accompanied by a corresponding shortening of the period of medically enforced sickness absence. In fact, the policy on rehabilitation and return to work after a heart attack can generally be just the same as after other acute illnesses. Physical work to which the patient is accustomed need not be limited unless necessitated by angina or dyspnoea.

Distribution

Geographical variation

Table 8.1, based on WHO data for 26 of the world's richer populations, shows that mortality rates vary tremendously. The pattern broadly parallels affluence and industrialization, but with some important exceptions. Japan is heavily industrialized, yet rates are low and may even be falling (perhaps reflecting a decline in salt intake and hypertension); at the other extreme North Karelia, Finland had until recently the highest rates in the world, indicating that a strenuous rural life is an insufficient protection.

International differences can be largely explained by differences in the major risk factors (pp. 136–8), but there are exceptions. For example, incidence in France is remarkably low, and that in Scotland (especially south-west Scotland) is extremely high; here the reasons are only partly apparent. A comparison of men in Edinburgh and Stockholm showed much lower levels of essential (polyunsaturated) fatty acids in the body fat of the Scotsmen, presumably reflecting a lower dietary intake (Logan et al. 1978).

Standardized measurement of atherosclerosis is difficult, and the use of autopsy material from accidental deaths implies case selection; there is, nevertheless, evidence from careful international comparisons (Strong 1972) that mortality rates are strongly correlated with differences in severity of atherosclerosis, and mass coronary disease only occurs where there is mass atherosclerosis.

Time trends

This is not a new disease. Examination of the mummified body of a Chinese princess who died 2100 years ago showed that she had died suddenly (her stomach contained a recent meal); she had severe coronary atherosclerosis. What does seem to be new is its occurrence as a mass disease.

The epidemic began at different times in different countries.

Rates started to rise in the early 1920s in the US, and in Britain a few years later. But in the Netherlands and Norway there was no major rise until 1950. In eastern Europe (Table 8.1), including the Soviet Union, the epidemic came later still and rates seem now to be rising catastrophically. Control at this stage is extraordinarily difficult, because there is such a strong popular expectation that emergence from poverty should bring a richer diet, less physical work, and more smoking. The same consequences are seen also in developing countries among professional and some urban populations; but among the rural poor – that is, the vast majority – coronary heart disease will continue for the foreseeable future to be rare.

Table 8.1. *Mortality rates in 1975 and slopes of linear trends in 1968–77; coronary heart disease (ICD 8th revision, 410–14), age-adjusted rates for men and women, 40–69 years*

Country	Deaths/100000/yr M	F	Change %/yr M	F
Finland	673	142	−1.8	−1.6
UK – Scotland	615	202	+0.1	+0.5
UK – N. Ireland	614	189	+1.3	−0.2
New Zealand	545	167	−1.2	−1.6
Australia	534	180	−2.1	−1.0
United States	528	171	−3.0	−3.6
Ireland	508	168	+2.6	−0.4
UK – England & Wales	498	138	+0.3	+1.1
Canada	473	143	−1.6	−0.9
Czechoslovakia	410	129	+0.6	0.0
Denmark	400	114	−1.7	+0.7
Norway	398	86	−1.1	−0.3
Sweden	368	102	+2.0	+1.8
Netherlands	363	87	−0.9	+0.8
Hungary	328	125	+2.6	+2.0
Fed. Rep. Germany	325	81	+0.4	+0.5
Belgium	312	84	−1.7	−1.1
Austria	308	89	+0.6	+0.3
Bulgaria	237	110	+5.6	+2.5
Poland	229	56	+6.4	+5.2
Italy	226	63	−0.1	−2.0
Switzerland	226	50	+0.2	−3.5
Yugoslavia	180	70	+6.0	+4.1
France	152	37	+1.1	−1.4
Romania	146	64	+4.3	+3.8
Japan	69	29	−2.6	−4.7

Source: WHO (1982).

In the US, where the epidemic started, it became apparent in the 1960s that a plateau had been reached. Around 1968 there began a steady decline in coronary mortality, amounting by 1980 to a 25 per cent fall. Mortality from other cardiovascular and non-cardiovascular causes has also declined (though not so rapidly) so that total mortality has fallen and 2–3 years has been added to the life expectation. Data on incidence and case fatality are inadequate, but it seems unlikely that advances in medical and surgical treatments could have accounted for more than one-fifth of the decline, and possibly much less: a major fall in incidence is assumed to have been the main factor. Substantial declines in coronary mortality are also occurring elsewhere, including Canada, Australia, Belgium, and Finland. Over the period 1978–80 rates fell also England and Wales, but it is too soon to say if the trend will be sustained.

The extension of life resulting from success in the control of coronary heart disease will impose substantial net costs, attributable to extra social security payments and care of the elderly survivors. Indeed, if American experience is any guide, cardiological activity and costs will continue to rise even though cases are diminishing fast. This should be a warning to those who seek to justify the prevention of adult diseases on economic grounds: success, far from bringing savings, will be costly.

Perhaps the most remarkable feature of the decline in coronary mortality in the US (Havlik and Feinlieb 1979) has been that it started at about the same time, and proceeded proportionately at about the same rate, at all ages, in both sexes, and in both blacks and whites. This is not a cohort pattern, but rather one suggesting that the factor or factors responsible have operated with a short latency and that the population as a whole has shared rather evenly in the altered exposure. Thus although changes in smoking, physical exercise, and medical care may have contributed, by themselves these are too selective to account for such a general benefit; the major influences seem more likely to be dietary or environmental. Over the period in question there have been substantial changes in the polyunsaturated/saturated ratio of dietary fatty acids and in alcohol intake, as well as possibly a fall in salt intake; and there is supporting evidence that blood pressure and cholesterol levels have been falling. Beyond this the explanation remains speculative: to disentangle the multifactorial determinants of a time-trend can be an impossible task (Marmot *et al.* 1981*a*).

Occupation and social class

The traditional belief that this was a disease of professional men and managers arose in part through diagnostic artefact: the same condition might be labelled 'angina' in a business man but 'degenerative heart disease' in a manual worker. If the different diagnostic categories are combined then much, but not all, of the historical social class gradient disappears.

As early as the 1960s surveys of employees of the American Bell Telephone Company (Hinkle 1973) found that coronary mortality was heavier among blue-collar than white-collar workers, and this phenomenon has since been confirmed elsewhere in North America and Europe. There is evidence in Britain of a real change in social class distribution: after about 1960 coronary mortality among upper social classes was stable (or, in the case of physicians, falling), whereas for semiskilled and unskilled men it continued to rise. As a result the disease now bears much more heavily on these lower social groups (Rose and Marmot 1981). The explanation is still largely unknown. For women in Britain the excess among lower social groups goes back longer – at least 50 years.

Men in physically active occupations tend, other things being equal, to have a lower incidence of the disease (Morris and Crawford 1958; Fox and Naughton 1972) and a lower case fatality (Shapiro *et al.* 1969). Nowadays this protective effect is weak since occupational activity is so diminished,

and it tends to be concealed by the much stronger adverse effect of low social class.

Aetiology

Coronary heart disease has stimulated more aetiological research than any other disease. This is appropriate in relation to the size of the problem and the necessity for a preventive approach. The research has been productive, and it is probable that the main determinants of population incidence are now known (WHO 1982). However, as with most diseases, much remains unknown concerning individual susceptibility: rates can be predicted much better than cases.

Familial and genetic factors

Migrants and their children tend to acquire the disease rates of their host country (Marmot *et al.* 1975), suggesting that genetic factors are not the main determinant of differences between populations. They are however important in relation to individual susceptibility, as has been confirmed by twin studies (Harvald and Hauge 1970). Genetic effects are mainly evident in younger patients and in women (Slack 1974). They do not explain all the familial tendency, since social and behavioural factors also aggregate in families.

Most, but not all, of the familial tendency is conveyed by the resemblance between relatives in such risk factors as blood pressure and lipids, and the first-degree relatives of a young patient with coronary heart disease should if possible be assessed for treatable risk factors. Genetic predisposition is not a sentence of doom, but it does indicate a particular need for timely preventive action.

Nutrition

The major causes of mass coronary heart disease must be environmental in view of the large differences between populations, the rapid changes within populations, and the experience of migrants. Nutritional factors have long been the leading suspects.

The origins of the *diet–fat theory* were from three sources: laboratory (rabbits fed on meat, milk, and eggs develop cholesterol deposits in their arteries), clinical (patients with excess serum cholesterol get more atherosclerosis), and epidemiological (Javanese eating traditionally have lower serum cholesterols than those who eat like Europeans) (Keys 1967). In 1952 Groen *et al.* showed that serum cholesterol levels were increased by saturated (mainly animal) fats, unaffected by monounsaturated fats such as olive oil, and lowered by polyunsaturated (mainly vegetable) oils. Hard margarines, though derived mainly from vegetable oils, cause hypercholesterolaemia because manufacture involves hydrogenation.

There is a generally strong correlation between the average saturated fat and cholesterol intake of a population and its mean serum cholesterol level: in a population consuming a fat-rich diet, the whole cholesterol distribution is shifted upwards. Controlled experiments confirm that changes in dietary fat lead to predictable changes in serum cholesterol levels of groups. However, the level in an individual correlates poorly with current diet, perhaps reflecting the importance of genetic factors and the problems of characterizing individuals' diet and cholesterol levels. Evidently the effect of dietary excess will be more adverse in those with a genetic predisposition, and recent work on lipoprotein transport has helped to elucidate the mechanisms (Levy 1979).

The association between serum total or low-density lipoprotein cholesterol level and coronary heart disease has been repeatedly found, in different kinds of study, to be strong, graded, and independent of other risk factors, at the level of populations (Keys 1980) as well as individuals (Kannel *et al.* 1979). The view that it is causal is moreover supported by much clinical and experimental evidence. There are no populations where coronary heart disease is a mass problem that do not have high mean levels of serum cholesterol (> 5.5 mmol/l, 210 mg/dl); and in all known populations with a low mean level (≤ 4.2 mmol/l, 160 mg/dl) there is no mass coronary heart disease. In the Seven Countries Study (Keys 1980) there was a correlation coefficient of 0.81 between mean serum cholesterol and coronary heart disease incidence. The correlation became almost perfect (0.96) when the cholesterol mean was related to the corresponding national mortality rates 15 years later, suggesting that there may be an 'incubation period of some years between exposure and maximum effect (Rose 1982).

It seems that a high average intake of saturated fat, with its accompanying upwards shift of the whole serum cholesterol distribution, is essential for the development of mass atherosclerosis and mass coronary heart disease. Many other factors may increase the incidence, or may determine which particular individuals become sick and in what manner their disease develops; but a high intake of saturated fat is uniquely important, being the one necessary factor for the occurrence of epidemic disease.

Ideally the diet–heart theory would be tested by a controlled intervention study, starting in childhood and continuing into middle age. Clearly this is impracticable. Even a short-term single-factor prevention trial, starting in middle life, proved unacceptably expensive (National Diet–Heart Study 1968). Controlled trials in older populations have strongly suggested that the incidence of coronary heart disease can be lowered by dietary change involving a reduction in saturated fat and a high intake of polyunsaturates. This certainly reduces serum cholesterol levels, but it could have other favourable effects on arterial disease and thrombosis; and in these trials there was anyway no fall in total mortality.

Reduction of serum cholesterol by the drug clofibrate similarly reduced the incidence of non-fatal heart attacks; but this time there was actually an increase in total mortality. Evidently the reduction of serum cholesterol by 'unnatural' means may have complex and disturbing results.

Multifactorial prevention trials have shown that incidence and mortality can be reduced by a combination of measures which include a reduced intake of saturated fat and anti-smoking advice (Hjermann *et al.* 1981; WHO Collaborative Group 1983).

The WHO Expert Committee on Prevention of Coronary Heart Disease (1982) 'assessed the current evidence as warranting a policy for coronary heart disease prevention that would include long-term community-wide efforts to encourage safe and palatable dietary patterns to reduce total cholesterol distributions in countries with a high incidence, and to prevent the emergence of such levels in countries not yet experiencing a large burden of coronary heart disease'.

Obesity

Fat people are more likely to suffer from coronary heart disease. In older people this effect disappears, to be replaced by a contrary trend towards higher non-cardiovascular mortality in those who are thin (Jarrett *et al.* 1982). The adverse cardiovascular effects of obesity are mediated mainly by its association with hypertension and diabetes. Its mass prevalence, reflecting the general decline in physical activity of modern populations, presumably contributes to the population burden of cardiovascular disease.

Other dietary factors

Sugar intake probably bears no direct relation to the risk of cardiovascular disease or diabetes (Working Party on the Relationship between Dietary Sugar Intake and Arterial Disease 1970). *Dietary fibre,* particularly fruit pectins, have a favourable effect on serum cholesterol levels.

Softness of water supply tends to correlate with regional cardiovascular mortality (Masironi and Shaper 1981), and artificial softening of public supplies may be followed by increased mortality (Crawford *et al.* 1971). One possible mechanism could be the leeching out of lead from domestic pipes by acidic water. It is not certain that the association is causal; but the evidence justifies great caution before deciding to soften a public water supply.

The role of *alcohol* is unclear. Alcoholics have a high risk of coronary heart disease (and also of hypertension); but moderate drinkers seem to be at lower risk than abstainers (Marmot *et al.* 1981*b*). The WHO Committee (1982) 'did not recommend the use of alcohol either as an individual or as a public health preventive measure', because its true relation to cardiovascular disease is not yet clear and because it is known to have profoundly adverse health and social consequences.

Blood pressure

Coronary heart disease is the commonest cause of death in hypertensives. The risk is related to the level, with no sign of a threshold. Most of the population attributable risk arises in those with only slight or moderate elevation (diastolic < 100 mm Hg), because of the high prevalence of such cases. Anti-hypertensive drugs, which anyway are not appropriate in very mild hypertension, are far less effective in preventing heart attacks than in preventing strokes; at present they offer little help in the control of coronary disease. In contrast, public health measures which lowered the level of blood pressure in the population as a whole might bring major benefits (Rose 1981).

Smoking

About half of the cigarette smoker's excess mortality is due to cardiovascular disease. In nearly all studies cigarette smoking has emerged as a major risk factor for coronary heart disease, with a relative risk as high as five among younger men (Doll and Peto 1977) but falling with age. In contrast, the attributable risk is high at all ages, in both men and women. The association is dose-related and independent of other predictors. Despite the paucity of experimental data or clearly identified mechanisms, it is considered to be largely (but maybe not wholly) a causal association.

Smoking interacts with other precursors of disease, so that in populations where these are common even light smoking is hazardous; but where heart disease is uncommon, the cardio-vascular effects of smoking may be undetectable.

Coronary mortality rates of ex-smokers are much lower than those of continuing smokers (Doll and Peto 1977; Rose *et al.* 1982). It seems likely that the risk is reversible, but perhaps not immediately. Cigarette smokers who change to pipes or cigars remain at risk if (as is likely) they continue to inhale.

It is not known whether the responsible noxious factor is nicotine, carbon monoxide, or some other volatile component of smoke. Some smokers who change to a low-tar/low-nicotine product maintain their nicotine intake by compensatory deeper inhalation, which could even increase their retention of gas-phase components. The public change from high- to medium-tar cigarettes has brought benefits from a reduced risk of respiratory disease; but uncertainty so far as the heart is concerned means that the overall effects on health of still further reductions are unpredictable. The continuing search for 'the safer cigarette' might be illusory.

Other behavioural factors

A *sedentary life-style* for the majority of people is a fairly recent phenomenon. One effect is often to reduce energy needs to below the level of an acceptably satisfying diet. Mass physical inactivity is thus the main determinant of mass over-weight; and hence, through secondary effects on other risk factors, it contributes importantly to the incidence of cardio-vascular diseases. Perhaps there may also be a direct protective effect of exercise, especially vigorous exercise (Morris *et al.* 1973); but this is less certain. Full-scale randomized preventive trials have not been possible.

Psychosocial stress of various kinds is common in many parts of the world where coronary heart disease is almost unknown. Clearly it is not a sufficient cause, but perhaps it might be an aggravating or precipitating cause; or in urban living there might be some specific and particularly hazardous kind of stress, related perhaps to time-pressures and com-petitiveness. Difficulties of definition, measurement, and cross-cultural comparisons have prevented any test of whether such societal characteristics are a determinant of the incidence rate of heart disease.

For the individual there is some evidence that what is called the 'Type A behaviour pattern' (hard-driving competitiveness and time-urgency) is an independent predictor of heart attacks (Rosenman *et al.* 1975). It is not clear that it is actually a cause, nor that it can be modified, nor that intervention attempts bring benefit; so it has no immediate public health application. It is nevertheless worrying that a pattern of behaviour which could be hazardous is one which is so actively promoted in modern industrial and business life.

In surveys of health knowledge among the public, 'stress' is supposed by most British men to be the main cause of heart attack. (By contrast, the role of smoking is still unfamiliar.)

This reflects a widespread discontent with the pattern of modern urban life, and perhaps also a wish to exonerate the individual from responsibility for his own health; but it is not supportable by scientific evidence. There is a danger that public and professional misconceptions in this area may divert attention from demonstrated needs in prevention.

The strategy of control

The control of this massive problem calls for multiple strategies involving diverse groups and agencies; these include the medical services, central and local government, planners of the environment, transport, and leisure, educational services (schools, health education agencies, and the news media), agriculture and the food industry, and – most important of all – an informed, responsible, and participating public.

Their activities can be considered at various levels as shown in Table 8.2.

Table 8.2. *Strategies of control*

Level	Strategy
1. Treat known cases	Therapeutics
2. Prevent recurrence and progression	Secondary prevention
3. Find and treat early/subclinical clinical disease	'Intermediate prevention'
4. Find and treat antecedent abnormality	Risk factor screening
5. Control underlying causes	Mass primary prevention
6. Prevent appearance of underlying causes	'Primordial prevention'

Each of these approaches offers to chip away a different part of the problem. Their contributions are complementary – each is necessary; they are not on the whole competing for the same resources and rivalries are misplaced. None holds the whole answer, although primary prevention comes much nearer to it than the others. Each needs medical support, but in primary prevention the medical role is subsidiary. The mobilization of this medical support requires an enlargement of the traditional view that the doctor's job is simply to treat the sick. The strategic planning and co-ordination of control measures demands a high-level review of the overall situation; at present this is lacking, and it is not clear how it should come about or what body should undertake it.

Therapeutics

The impact of advances in medical treatment has been dis-appointing, reflecting the advanced degree of myocardial and arterial damage when patients are first diagnosed. With monitoring and other intensive care it is possible to resuscitate and discharge alive some patients who suffer a cardiac arrest, chiefly those in whom it occurs during the first few hours of the attack; these successes represent perhaps 2 per cent of all admissions for heart attack. It is not clear, however, how far these expensive facilities have actually reduced the case–fatal-ity ratio (Rose 1975; Hunt *et al.* 1977).

Surgical reconstruction of coronary arteries can, at least in the best centres, improve five-year survival rates by around 10 per cent in suitable patients – an important gain, albeit expensive and applicable to only a small minority of all patients with the disease. The indications for surgery continue to enlarge. In the US there are now about 120 000 operations annually, but it is not known how many of these are for scientifically approved indications: the situation there is seriously out of hand, being influenced substantially by non-medical factors.

The argument between hospital and home care of acute heart attacks continues. From randomized controlled trials it is apparent that in many cases, particularly the uncomplicated and the elderly, the chance of survival can be just as good at home (Hill *et al.* 1978). However, social circumstances, and the added pressures on general practitioners and relatives, may often limit the choice.

The potential life-saving advantages of specialist care apply principally to the first two hours of the attack, when the risk of cardiac arrest is greatest and the results of resuscitation are best. The largest problem here is the patient's delay in calling for help, but subsequent medical delays are also important. Special coronary ambulance services have their enthusiastic supporters, the idea being to expedite the arrival of a resuscitation team. Unfortunately there are some inherent difficulties. If the journey is long, the ambulance arrives late; but if it is short, the gain to the patient is slight since he or she would anyway soon be in hospital. If the special ambulance is sent to all non-traumatic cases of 'collapse', the proportion turning out to be cardiac is likely to be unacceptably low; but if it is sent only when a doctor has verified a cardiac diagnosis then the delay is unacceptably long (Hampton *et al.* 1977). It seems then that their contribution to reducing mortality is at best small, and the cost is rather high.

In areas where there is an enthusiastic cardiologist it has been possible to teach effective resuscitation to many members of the public (for example, the Seattle 'Heart Watch' programme) or to all local ambulance crews (for example, the Brighton Ambulance Service).

Secondary prevention

Most coronary deaths occur in people who have already been identified as cases of heart disease; this indicates the large scope for secondary prevention (International Society and Federation of Cardiology 1981). Stopping smoking is of un-doubted benefit, and control of other risk factors probably brings long-term benefit; but in practice the necessary sustained advice and supervision are rarely available for either medical or surgical patients. Drug therapy is of demonstrated benefit, at least in the year or two after myocardial infarction: beta-blockers have been estimated to save one life for each 30 patient-years of treatment – a favourable cost–benefit ratio for any long-term therapy. The impact on total mortality, however, will depend on the long-term effects: a patient cannot be said to have been saved from coronary heart disease until he has died from something else.

Screening for early disease: 'intermediate prevention'

In the Whitehall Study of cardio-respiratory disease in civil servants it was found that in these middle-aged men a simple screening examination (self-adminstered chest pain questionnaire and technician-coded electrocardiogram) suggested the presence of early myocardial ischaemia in 14 per cent, among whom occurred a half of all the coronary deaths in the next five years (Rose *et al.* 1977). Preventive efforts at this stage might be considered *intermediate*, coming between true primary prevention (pre-disease) and secondary prevention (post-diagnosis). The scope is clearly large; but in this study the risk for these individuals, though high in relative terms, was low absolutely (overall, about 1–2 per cent per annum), and this implies that useful preventive measures would have to be simple, cheap, and safe. No such means have yet been demonstrated, and research in this area is much needed. Meanwhile electrocardiographic or other screening for early coronary disease cannot be justified as a service measure.

Risk factor screening

Some of the main precursors or predictors of this disease can be readily identified by screening; in particular these include family history, smoking history, blood pressure, and serum (total) cholesterol. (If these are known, measures of over-weight do not improve the prediction.) In an American study it was found that 43 per cent of cases occurred among the 20 per cent of the population with the highest multivariate risk estimate (Pooling Project Research Group 1978). Most of these cases were in individuals with simultaneous slight elev-ation of several factors, rather than those with extreme elevation of a single factor.

With regard to any one risk factor it seems that a few individuals at high-risk yield far fewer cases than the central part of the distribution, where individual risk is low but the prevalence of exposure is high. This again underlines the fact that a mass disease reflects mass exposure – a deviation of the whole risk factor distribution. The *high-risk strategy*, which concentrates preventive efforts on the fraction at highest risk, may be appropriate to those individuals and an efficient use of limited resources; but as a means of controlling coronary heart disease it is of inherently limited value (Rose 1981).

In conclusion: for each adult patient a general practitioner should note the smoking history and any strong family history of coronary heart disease, the blood pressure should be recorded, and overweight noted. Where these factors indicate special risk a serum cholesterol measurement is desirable. Appropriate preventive advice should be given (Joint Working Party, 1976).

Mass primary prevention

The high incidence of coronary heart disease is due to the upwards displacement of risk characteristics in the population as a whole, reflecting the average characteristics of modern life-style, not the deviations of a minority. Primary prevention must therefore depend on mass changes – on normalizing averages. Theoretically attractive though it might be to have everyone centred around some 'ideal' value, in practice it seems that the only way to lower the average to an acceptable level is to lower the whole distribution: individual variation is inevitable, reflecting variation both in habits and in genetic make-up.

Targets for population norms are thus defined in terms of

desirable average values of risk factors, with their corresponding behavioural norms – not in desirable individual values. Targets are of two kinds. One ('ideal') indicates the levels at which it is thought that coronary heart disease would become uncommon. The other or 'practical' target marks a distance in that direction that might be reached within a stated time period.

The principal 'ideal' targets, as set out by the WHO Expert Committee (1982), are as follows:

1. *Mean serum total cholesterol of adults < 5.17 mmol/l (200 mg/dl).* To achieve this would require reducing the mean intake of saturated fat to around 10 per cent of total energy. Some reduction in cholesterol intake might also be necessary, and a figure of 300 mg/day has been suggested; but the evidence on this point is less clear. The polyunsaturated/saturated ratio should be increased, as should the intake of complex carbohydrates and fibre. In order to achieve these targets, and also to reduce total energy intake, there should in most countries be a fall in total fat consumption to around 30 per cent of energy. All of these objectives could be achieved by the simple principle of obtaining a substantially greater proportion of energy from plant sources. Major changes are implied in national eating patterns, and in agriculture and the food industry; but there are no insuperable barriers to their achievement over a number of years.

2. *Reduction in mean salt intake in the direction of 5 g daily.* There is much to suggest that such a reduction, from the present figure of 10–12 g daily, might lower average blood pressure by several millimetres of mercury, with a consequent important fall in the incidence of cardiovascular disease. The recent experience of Belgium shows that a national reduction in salt intake is possible, and that it is not difficult for food manufacturers to follow public demand in this respect – although they are unlikely to risk leading it. (Recent success in the detection and treatment of high blood pressure has reduced the incidence of strokes but the impact on coronary heart disease is less apparent.)

3. *Cessation of cigarette smoking.* Former cigarette smokers who change to pipe or cigars should be warned that this is unsafe because of the danger of continued, usually unconscious inhalation. From the point of view of preventing cardiovascular disease no support can be given to the notion of the so-called 'safer cigarette'. Action to reduce cigarette smoking has been reviewed by various expert bodies (WHO Expert Committee 1982; Royal College of Physicians 1983).

4. *Physical activity.* This should become a normal part of daily life. It is particularly important as a means of controlling mass obesity, whose main cause is an excessively low energy expenditure. Perhaps – especially if vigorous – it may also contribute more directly to cardiac health; and it certainly improves cardio-respiratory fitness.

These changes will not come about without a major effort on the part of opinion formers, health professionals, community leaders, and local and national government. The scale of effort required is at least as great as that which in the past led to the control of other mass diseases with social and environmental origins, such as tuberculosis, typhoid, and cholera. The nature of the effort is, however, different, calling as it does for individual initiatives and choices rather than mere passive acceptance of environmental improvements. On the other hand it may be that the influence of the media in spreading information and altering public expectations is now such as to make possible what previously might have been thought unachievable.

Some of the extensive social and economic implications of a national plan for preventing coronary disease in Britain have been the subject of a recent report (Conference on Action to Prevent Coronary Heart Disease 1984).

HYPERTENSION AND CEREBROVASCULAR DISEASE

Definition

The population distribution of blood pressure is continuous: hypertension is therefore not an entity, but simply the arbitrarily-defined upper end of that distribution.

There can be various approaches to defining 'a case of hypertension'. The *statistical* definition is in terms of what is unusual for a particular age and sex: it is purely descriptive. The *clinical* approach is related to the levels at which patients are likely to show clinical effects. A *prognostic* definition would seek to identify the level above which there was a heightened risk of future complications; but in fact this proves impossible, since risk seems to be related exponentially to pressure over the whole range, with no discoverable threshold. For the physician and public health worker the most appropriate definition is likely to be *operational*, being that level above which action is preferred to inaction. This definition will take into account the clinical and prognostic criteria, but it will depend on the effectiveness and availability of treatment and of the resources to deliver it. It will be a local definition, and liable to change.

Prevalence

Table 8.3 shows typical prevalence rates for hypertension, defined at two levels: the data come from a survey of a large random sample of the US population (US National Health Survey 1977). It can be seen that 'mild' hypertension is a mass condition, affecting more than a third of elderly people. At younger ages there is a male excess, but in later life this disappears. The estimates in the table are based on single measurements. The variability of the measurement and its tendency to fall over successive examinations imply a much

Table 8.3. *Prevalence of two levels of hypertension in the population of the US (data for diastolic phase 5).*

Age (yr)	% Diastolic 90 mm +		% Diastolic 110 mm +	
	M	F	M	F
18–	9.2	3.9	0.6	0.3
25–	21.4	9.1	1.4	0.3
35–	32.8	21.9	4.2	3.0
45–	43.3	30.1	7.2	4.7
55–	42.9	41.0	5.6	5.0
65–74	39.4	38.2	4.7	5.8

lower prevalence of sustained elevation. Treatment decisions are normally based on multiple examinations, and those found eligible are likely to be less than 50 per cent of those with qualifying pressures at first screening.

In children the blood pressure distribution is normal, but as age advances there is progressive positive skewing. This is because the rate of increase of an individual's pressure correlates with the level already attained: 'to him that hath shall more be given'.

Aetiology

Research has mainly concentrated on the question of prime interest to clinicians: why do some individuals develop hypertension? In the majority of cases no explanations can be found beyond those of genetic predisposition and a contribution related to overweight. For the public health worker the more important question – and the only one that will be considered here – relates to the population as a whole, namely, what determines its average blood pressure? The difference between these two questions is illustrated by Fig. 8.2, which shows the blood pressure distributions of two populations of middle-aged men (Kenyan nomads and London civil servants). The coefficients of variation of the two distributions are similar, so that the question 'Why do some individuals have higher blood pressures than others?' is equally appropriate in either country – and might well get similar answers. But something has displaced the whole London distribution, shifting it upwards; the high prevalence of hypertension in London, and its virtual absence in Kenya, are the result of this mass effect on the average blood pressure. The prevalence of hypertension has its explanation in this mass phenomenon, not in the determinants of individual susceptibility.

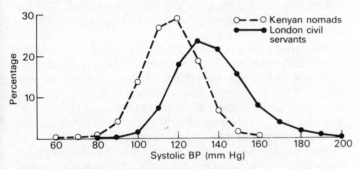

Fig. 8.2. Distributions of systolic blood pressure in a population where hypertension is absent (Kenyan nomads) and in another where it is prevalent (London). Men aged 40–59 years.

Populations with low mean pressure levels, with a correspondingly low prevalence of hypertension, are characterized by leanness, a low intake of salt, and an absence of urban stress. These three factors are not easily separated. Urbanization *per se* is perhaps the least likely to be important, since in countries where hypertension is prevalent there is not usually an urban excess.

The strongest international correlate of mean blood pressure seems to be salt intake. The available data, which are of uneven and generally poor quality, suggest that mean population diastolic pressure rises by 0.8 mm Hg per 1 g increase in salt intake (Gleibermann 1973). If the association were all causal, this would imply that a reduction of 2.5 g daily in mean salt intake (20–25 per cent of the current British level) would lower mean diastolic pressure by 2 mm Hg. This might bring benefits of the same order as all existing antihypertensive medication: thus small shifts in the whole risk distribution can bring unexpectedly large benefits to the whole population, even though they offer little to each participating individual.

The salt hypothesis requires public health evaluation in two respects: Is salt reduction feasible? Is it effective? Some community trials are in progress which should help to answer these questions.

Data on body weight suggest that in some populations the new occurrence of hypertension might be reduced by up to half through the prevention and control of overweight (Cassel 1971).

Risks of raised blood pressure

Epidemiological and life insurance studies do not identify a threshold for increased risk; every increment above the lowest carries some increase in mortality, although the rise is exponential. Table 8.4 shows the size of this excess risk for middle-aged men. Even a diastolic pressure of 95 mm Hg (phase 4, single reading), which most doctors would consider too low to treat, is associated with the death over 10 years of one man in 50; at 105 mm Hg this rises to one man in about 20. In this study a half of all the attributable deaths from coronary heart disease, and a quarter of the attributable stroke deaths, arose at diastolic pressures under 100 mm Hg. Coupled with the massive size of the hypertension problem and doubts about the effect of treatment on its main complication (coronary heart disease), this demonstrates the necessity for mass primary prevention. Screening and treatment, important though they are, offer at best an incomplete as well as a costly answer. But whereas the effectiveness of treatment is clear, the effectiveness of primary prevention has yet to be confirmed.

Table 8.4. *Excess mortality (all causes, age-adjusted) attributable to different levels of raised diastolic (phase 4) pressure. (Whitehall Study, men aged 40–64)*

Diastolic pressure (mm Hg)	Excess mortality per 100 per 10 years
< 80	(0)
80–	0.6
90–	1.6
100–	4.5
110 +	12.5

Cerebrovascular accidents

Heart attack is the commonest cause of death in hypertension, but stroke is the commonest cause of disability, as well as the second commonest cause of death. At least three-quarters of strokes in hypertensives are preventable by treatment. Other strokes, however – forming an unknown proportion of the total – are unrelated to blood pressure. Most of these other cases are presumed to be due to atherosclerosis, and so again they may be potentially preventable.

In England and Wales at the present time strokes are responsible for about 9 per cent of male deaths and 16 per cent of female deaths, the median ages at death being respectively 75 and 79 years. That is to say, this is overwhelmingly a problem of old people, especially (because there are more of them) old women. About 20 per cent of these deaths occur at home. Hospital admissions outnumber total deaths by about 40 per cent; many, of course, involve long-stay patients or subsequently call for much support in the community. Strokes – like all other mass causes of death – are concentrated in the lower social classes.

In most western countries stroke mortality has been declining for many years. In Britain the fall started around 1950, that is, well before effective antihypertensive treatment became generally available (although it has been accelerated by treatment). This suggests that blood pressure levels have been falling, and some direct evidence to this effect comes from American population surveys. Salt intake has probably fallen over this period. More recently in the US there has been an increase in the dietary intake of polyunsaturated fatty acids, and there is some evidence that this too could have a favourable effect on blood pressure.

Control measures

Primary prevention

In considering the prevention of coronary heart disease the WHO Expert Committee (1982) recommended that the balance of evidence now justifies a policy of reducing national average salt intake 'in the direction of 5 g daily', as well as an endeavour to control mass obesity. Vigorous health propaganda in Belgium appears to have had some success in reducing average salt intake and stimulating public demand for a lower salt content of manufactured foods: manufacturers have no real difficulty in responding to such a pressure, although they are unwilling to initiate it.

It has been clearly shown that individuals' salt taste threshold can be fairly rapidly changed, and a change once accepted is not difficult to sustain. There is however only a limited range of tolerance around the norm, making it difficult for an individual to deviate far from the average of his or her society or household.

Screening and treatment

It is now clear from controlled trials that the early detection and treatment of hypertension is effective in the prevention of strokes, at least in middle-aged men. In Britain, Medical Research Council trials are now in progress to identify the lower level of severity at which treatment is worthwhile, as well as the effectiveness and acceptability of treatment in the elderly. Meanwhile it is already clear that regular blood pressure measurement is desirable for all persons under the age of 65 years, with a view to treating at least those with sustained diastolic (phase 5) levels exceeding 105 mm Hg. Most of this screening and care can best be offered within general practice, provided that the necessary special organization is provided (Hart 1980). Much of the routine work of screening and surveillance can be undertaken by a trained practice nurse.

RHEUMATIC HEART DISEASE

Rheumatic fever is a sequel to infection of the throat with beta-haemolytic streptococci; any serological type can be responsible. In epidemic conditions, such as formerly occurred in institutions and army barracks, the attack rate can rise as high as 3 per cent, but in non-epidemic conditions it is very much lower (Siegel et al. 1961). Rheumatic fever occurs largely in those who develop a high antibody titre following the infection; but, for reasons that are unclear, even of such individuals only a minority become affected. In someone who has suffered one attack the risk of recurrence following further streptococcal infection may be as high as 50 per cent: hence the importance of secondary prevention.

The risk of subsequent chronic rheumatic heart disease depends on the number of attacks of rheumatic fever, which again underlines the importance of effective secondary prevention. Unfortunately, in those countries where rheumatic heart disease is still a major public health problem it is often the exception for attacks of rheumatic fever to be brought to medical attention; and even in western countries about a half of all newly-recognized patients with rheumatic heart disease do not recall any history of rheumatic fever.

The incidence and distribution of rheumatic fever and rheumatic heart disease are a simple reflection of the personal and environmental factors which promote the spread of streptococcal throat infections, with a concentration of cases in cities, slums, large families, and the winter season. This is a classical disease of poverty, with domestic overcrowding as the primary factor (Acheson 1965).

Throughout the western world the mortality and incidence of rheumatic fever have been falling throughout this century – from long before the availability of chemotherapy or antibiotics. What was once a mass disease is now a comparative rarity, new cases being mainly confined to city slums. This fall is due largely to improved housing, which has reduced the risk of multiple streptococcal infections. Streptococci, of course, are still prevalent: the great fall in the attack rate for subsequent rheumatic fever implies that the organism has lost much of its virulence. There is a parallel here with the corresponding decline in scarlet fever.

In many developing countries, and particularly in the cities, conditions remain favourable for the spread of streptococci, and rheumatic heart disease is often the commonest form of heart disease. It tends also to appear much earlier in life and to progress more rapidly than in the western world.

Control

Prevention of first attacks of rheumatic fever

The only really effective control measure is primary prevention by the eradication of bad housing. Its value has been demonstrated in western countries and also in some developing countries such as Singapore.

In theory it would be possible to prevent rheumatic fever by penicillin treatment of all streptococcal infections, but in practice the scope is limited. In countries that can afford such a policy the rheumatic fever attack rate is likely to be very low. There are no good clinical criteria for identifying which sore throats are likely to be streptococcal, so that the result of a throat swab culture ought to be known before treatment is started. Even in the winter only about 20 per cent of swabs are found to be positive, and in summer the proportion is even lower. To be effective in eradicating infection and preventing subsequent rheumatic fever, penicillin may need to be continued for 10 days, and this is not usually acceptable.

In the days of mass institutional outbreaks it was shown impressively that mass antibiotic prophylaxis given to all inmates could effectively reduce the incidence of rheumatic fever (Stollerman 1954).

Secondary prevention of rheumatic fever

Long-term penicillin therapy following all first attacks of rheumatic fever could in theory at least halve the incidence of chronic rheumatic heart disease. A twice-daily oral dose of 250 mg of phenoxymethylpenicillin is usually recommended, continued throughout childhood and (in those still at special risk) into early adult life (Wannamaker *et al.* 1964). The problems in its implementation are linked with the poverty of those who are likely to need it – their lack of long-term access to medical care and surveillance, and the fact that in poor countries the first attack itself does not usually reach medical attention.

A further strategy for limiting the progress of disease is to screen schoolchildren for evidence of rheumatic valvular lesions and to institute long-term penicillin in those found to be affected. In western countries the utility of this policy is limited by the low yield from screening. Over the period 1966–70 the US National Health Survey (1978) found a prevalence of only 1 per cent among American children aged 12–17 years; and nowadays the prevalence is presumably even lower.

REFERENCES

Acheson, R.M. (1965). The epidemiology of acute rheumatic fever. *J. Chronic Dis.* **18**, 723.

Armstrong, A., Duncan, B., Oliver, M.F. *et al.* (1972). Natural history of acute coronary heart attacks. A community study. *Br. Heart J.* **34**, 67.

Cassel, J.C. (1971). Summary of major findings of the Evans County Cardiovascular Studies. *Arch. Intern. Med.* **128**, 887.

Conference on Action to Prevent Coronary Heart Disease (1984). *Conference Proceedings.*

Crawford, M.D., Gardner, M.J., and Morris, J.N. (1971). Changes in water hardness and local death rates. *Lancet* **ii**, 327.

Doll, R. and Peto, R. (1977). Mortality among doctors in different occupations. *Br. Med. J.* **i**, 1433.

Fox, S.M. and Naughton, J.P. (1972). Physical activity and the prevention of coronary heart disease. *Prev. Med.* **1**, 92.

Gleibermann, L. (1973). Blood pressure and dietary salt in human populations. *Ecol. Food Nutr.* **2**, 143.

Groen, J., Tjiong, B.K., Kamminga, C.E., and Willebrands, A.F. (1952). The influence of nutrition, individuality and some other factors, including various forms of stress on the serum cholesterol level; an experiment of nine months duration in 60 normal human volunteers. *Voeding* **13**, 556.

Hampton, J.R., Dowling, M., and Nicholas, C. (1977). Comparison of results from a cardiac ambulance manned by medical or non-medical personnel. *Lancet* **i**, 526.

Hart, J.T. (1980). *Hypertension. Library of general practice.* Churchill Livingstone, London.

Harvald, B. and Hauge, M. (1970). Coronary occlusion in twins. *Acta Genet. Gemellol., Rome* **19**, 248.

Havlik, R.J. and Feinleib, M. (eds.) (1979). *Proceedings of the conference on the decline in coronary heart disease.* US Department of Health, Education and Welfare NIH Publication No. 79-1610. Washington, DC.

Hill, J.D., Hampton, J.R., and Mitchell, J.R.A. (1978). A randomised trial of home-versus-hospital management for patients with suspected myocardial infarction. *Lancet* **i**, 837.

Hinkle, L.E. (1973). Coronary heart disease and sudden death in actively employed American men. *Bull. NY Acad. Med.* **49**, 467.

Hjermann, I., Velve Byre, K., Holme, I., and Leren, P. (1981). Effect of diet and smoking intervention on the incidence of coronary heart disease. Report from the Oslo Study Group of a randomised trial in healthy men. *Lancet* **ii**, 1303.

Hunt, D., Sloman, G., Christie, D., and Pennington, C. (1977). Changing patterns and mortality of acute myocardial infarction in a coronary care unit. *Br. Med. J.* **i**, 795.

International Society and Federation of Cardiology (1981). Secondary prevention in survivors of myocardial infarction. *Br. Med. J.* **i**, 894.

Jarrett, R.J., Shipley, M.J., and Rose, G. (1982). Weight and mortality in the Whitehall Study. *Br. Med. J.* **ii**, 535.

Joint Working Party of the Royal College of Physicians of London and the British Cardiac Society (1976). Prevention of coronary heart disease. *J. R. Coll. Physicians, Lond.* **10**, 213.

Kannel, W.B., Castelli, W.P., and Gordon, T. (1979). Cholesterol in the prediction of atherosclerotic disease. New perspectives based on the Framingham Study. *Ann. Intern. Med.* **90**, 85.

Keys, A. (1967). Blood lipids in man – a brief review. *J. Am. Dietetic Assoc.* **51**, 508.

Keys, A. (1980). *Seven countries. A multivariate analysis of death and coronary heart disease.* Harvard University Press, London.

Kinlen, L.J. (1973). Incidence and presentation of myocardial infarction in an English community. *Br. Heart J.* **35**, 616.

Levy, R. (ed.) (1979). *Nutrition, lipids and coronary heart disease.* Raven Press, New York.

Logan, R.L., Riemersma, R.A., Thompson, M. *et al.* (1978). Risk factors for ischaemic heart disease in normal men aged 40. Edinburgh-Stockholm Study. *Lancet* **i**, 949.

Marmot, M.G., Booth, M., and Beral, V. (1981a). Changes in heart disease mortality in England and Wales and other countries. *Health Trends* **13**, 33.

Marmot, M.G., Rose, G., Shipley, M., and Thomas, B.J. (1981b). Alcohol and mortality: a U-shaped curve. *Lancet* **i**, 580.

Marmot, M.G., Syme, S.L., Kagan, A., Kato, H., Cohen, J.B., and Belsky, J. (1975). Epidemiologic studies of coronary heart disease and stroke in Japanese men living in Japan, Hawaii and California: prevalence of coronary and hypertensive heart disease and associated risk factors. *Am. J. Epidemiol.* **102**, 514.

Masironi, R. and Shaper, A.G. (1981). Epidemiological studies of health effects of water from different sources. *Ann. Rev. Nutr.* **1**, 375.

Morris, J.N. and Crawford, M.D. (1958). Coronary heart disease and physical activity of work. *Br. Med. J.* **ii**, 1485.

Morris, J.N., Chave, S.P.W., Adam, C., Sirey, C., Epstein, L., and Sheehan, D.J. (1973). Vigorous exercise in leisure time and the incidence of coronary heart disease. *Lancet* **i**, 333.

National Diet-Heart Study (1968). Final Report *Circulation* **37**, Suppl. 1, 1.

Pisa, Z. and Uemura, K. (1982). Trends of mortality from ischaemic heart disease and other cardiovascular diseases in 27 countries, 1968–77. *World Health Stat. Q.* **35**, 11.

Pooling Project Research Group (1978). Relationship of blood pressure, serum cholesterol, smoking habit, relative weight and ECG abnormalities to incidence of major coronary events. Final report of the Pooling Project. *J. Chronic Dis.* **31**, 201.

Reid, D.D., Hamilton, P.J.S., McCartney, P., Rose, G., Jarrett, R.J., and Keen, H. (1976). Smoking and other risk factors for coronary heart disease in British civil servants. *Lancet* **ii**, 979.

Rose, G. (1968). The variability of angina. Some implications for epidemiology. *Br. J. Prev. Soc. Med.* **22**, 12.

Rose, G. (1975). The contibution of intensive coronary care. *Br. J. Prev. Soc. Med.* **29**, 147.

Rose, G. (1981). Strategy of prevention: lessons learned from cardiovascular disease. *Br. Med. J.* **i**, 1847.

Rose, G. (1982). Incubation period of coronary heart disease. *Br. Med. J.* **i**, 1600.

Rose, G. and Marmot, M.G. (1981). Social class and coronary heart disease. *Br. Heart J.* **45**, 13.

Rose, G., Hamilton, P.J.S., Colwell, L., and Shipley, M.J. (1982). A randomised controlled trial of anti-smoking advice: 10-year results. *J. Epidemiol. Community Health* **36**, 102.

Rose, G., Reid, D.D., Hamilton, P.J.S., McCartney, P., Keen, H., and Jarrett, R.J. (1977). Myocardial ischaemia, risk factors and death from coronary heart disease. *Lancet* **i**, 105.

Rosenman, R.H., Brand, R.J., Jenkins, C.D., Friedman, M., Straus, R., and Wurm, M. (1975). Coronary heart disease in the Western Collaborative Study: final follow-up experience of 8.5 years. *JAMA* **233**, 872.

Royal College of Physicians (1983). *Health or smoking.* RCP, London.

Shapiro, S., Weinblatt, E., Frank, C.W., and Sager, R.V. (1969). Incidence of coronary heart disease in a population insured for medical care (HIP): myocardial infarction, angina pectoris and possible myocardial infarction. *Am. J. Public Health* **59**, Suppl. 2.

Siegel, A.C., Johnson, E.E., and Stollerman, G.H. (1961). Controlled studies on streptococcal pharyngitis in a pediatric population. I. Factors related to the attack rate of rheumatic fever. *New Engl. J. Med.* **265**, 559.

Slack, J. (1974). Genetic differences in liability to atherosclerotic heart disease. *J. R. Coll. Physicians, Lond.* **8**, 115.

Stollerman, G.H. (1954). The use of antibiotics for the prevention of rheumatic fever. *Am. J. Med.* **17**, 757.

Strong, J.P. (1972). Atherosclerosis in human populations. *Atherosclerosis* **16**, 193.

Tunstall, Pedoe, H., Clayton, D., Morris, J.N., Brigden, W., and McDonald, L. (1975). Coronary heart disease in east London. *Lancet* **ii**, 833.

US National Health Survey (1977). *Blood pressure levels of persons 6–74 years, United States, 1971–1974.* Vital and Health Statistics – Series 11 – no. 203. DHEW Publication No. (HRA) 78-1648. Washington, DC.

US National Health Survey (1978). *Cardiovascular conditions of children 6–11 years and youths 12–17 years, United States, 1963–1965 and 1966–1970.* Vital and Health Statistics – Series 11 – No. 166. DHEW Publication No. (PHS) 78-1653. Washington, DC.

Wannamaker, L.W., Denny, F.W., Diehl, A., Jawetz, E. *et al.* (1964). *Prevention of rheumatic fever.* American Heart Association, New York.

Working Party on the Relationship between Dietary Sugar Intake and Arterial Disease (1970). Dietary sugar intake in men with myocardial infarction. *Lancet* **ii**, 1265.

World Health Organization (1976). *Myocardial infarction community registers.* Public Health in Europe No. 5. WHO, Copenhagen.

WHO Expert Committee (1982). Prevention of coronary heart disease. WHO Technical Report Series No. 678. Geneva.

WHO European Collaborative Group (1983). Multifactorial trial in the prevention of coronary heart disease: 3: Incidence and mortality results. *Eur. Heart J.* **4**, 141.

9 Respiratory system

J.R.T. Colley

INTRODUCTION

This chapter will cover two major respiratory disorders, chronic bronchitis and emphysema, and asthma. Both have a world-wide distribution and make appreciable demands on health services. These disorders will be considered separately although some aspects of their definition, and methods of study in the general population, do have common features.

Chronic bronchitis and emphysema

It is worth describing the evolution of our knowledge of these chonic respiratory diseases as this will explain how their definition has changed. It also serves as a prime example of the application of epidemiology to the investigation of common, but ill-understood disease.

Clinicians have recognized chronic bronchitis at least as early as the start of the nineteenth century. Badham, published a clinical description of bronchitis in 1808. He, and others subsequently, recognized that this was a common and serious disease. It remained, however, a disease largely ignored by research workers. In 1923, Collis published a review of the mortality and morbidity data for England and Wales from bronchitis. He confirmed that it was still a major cause of death and disability and commented on the lack of interest shown in the disease. It was not until 1951 that interest grew sufficiently for the Association of Physicians of Great Britain and Ireland to hold a symposium on chronic bronchitis. In part this reflected the changing emphasis of chest physicians' work; for example, the introduction of chemotherapy for tuberculosis.

A combination of clinical studies, notably by Oswald *et al.* (1953), and a review of mortality and morbidity data by Goodman *et al.* (1953) set the scene for a major increase in research. The severe fog in London in December 1952 and the subsequent major increase in respiratory and to a lesser extent cardiovascular deaths, among those already affected by chronic respiratory and cardiovascular disease further emphasized the need for more research.

DEFINITIONS OF CHRONIC BRONCHITIS AND EMPHYSEMA

It had become apparent early on that there were no universally agreed definitions of these disorders. And Fletcher (1952) had shown that there was serious observer error in assessments using the usually accepted physical signs of emphysema. Scadding (1952) had suggested that symptoms, and specifically mucous expectoration, should be used to define chronic bronchitis. However, even questions about chest symptoms, when asked by different doctors, yielded widely different prevalence rates (Cochrane *et al.* 1951). These problems led the British Medical Research Council (MRC) to set up a committee in 1953 to advise on research into chronic bronchitis. At their first meeting they were unable to agree on the definition of chronic bronchitis. This applied particularly to the early stages of the disease, which was poorly understood (Stuart-Harris and Hanley 1957). Even in regard to the later stages there was disagreement about the relationship between emphysema and chronic bronchitis; it was assumed that emphysema was present in most patients with bronchiolar obstruction (Postgraduate Medical School 1951).

Fletcher recounts (1978) how on a visit to the US in 1957 he saw hospital patients with a diagnosis of emphysema who, had they been in England, would have been labelled as chronic bronchitics. Meneely *et al.* (1960), at the invitation of the US National Institutes of Health (NIH), visited a number of British medical schools and hospitals, to study the reasons for the reported differences in frequency of cardiopulmonary disease. They, like Fletcher, also noted wide discrepancies in terminology between American and British physicians. For example, American physicians used chronic bronchitis to mean a low-grade inflammatory process in the bronchial tree associated with persistent cough, and regarded it as mainly a nuisance, rather than, as in British eyes, a potentially serious and often progressive disease. Emphysema tended to be used by American physicians for any patient with severe pulmonary disease where evidence of chronic overdistended lungs was present, while British physicians restricted this term to a limited number of patients, and was essentially an anatomical diagnosis. These observations emphasized the crucial need to arrive at some widely agreed definition and classification of these disorders.

Reid and Rose (1964), in a more formal manner, studied death certification practices in London, Bergen, and Boston by giving physicians case histories of patients and asking them to certify cause of death using their usual conventions. Whereas British physicians tended to certify chronic bronchitis as the underlying cause of death, Norwegian and

American physicians tended instead to use the terms bronchietasis or emphysema.

It is worth making a digression at this point to discuss the accuracy of death certification, as this is relevant in discussing the definition of these disorders. Heasman (1962) described a comparison of diagnoses given on death certificates and that found by a pathologist at autopsy. Clinicians were asked to provide a 'dummy' death certificate prior to autopsy. Major differences were found between the cause of death entered on the death certificate and that found at autopsy. The clinicians appeared to grossly over-diagnose acute bronchopneumonia (by about 30 per cent of the true figure) at the expense of chronic bronchitis (Heasman and Lipworth 1966). More recently Mitchell and colleagues (1971) studied the relationship between cause of death derived from clinical evidence, and that found on subsequent autopsy for persons diagnosed as having chronic airways obstruction at two university hospitals in Denver. They concluded that chronic airways obstruction is under-diagnosed on death certificates. From these studies it is likely that mortality statistics understate the deaths from chronic bronchitis and emphysema.

Major progress occurred when, at a Ciba Guest Symposium, in 1959, proposals were agreed on the definition of chronic bronchitis, emphysema, and asthma. Chronic bronchitis was to be defined, as originally suggested by Scadding, as chronic mucous expectoration. Gough and Wentworth, in 1949, had published their technique of producing paper-thin lung slices. This had provided anatomical evidence of the basic pathology of emphysema—namely an enlargement of the air spaces beyond the terminal bronchioles. It was agreed at the symposium to use this as the basis for defining emphysema. Asthma was defined on the basis of functional reversibility to airflow obstruction. In the search for some general term to cover all three conditions the label 'chronic non-specific lung disease (CNSLD)' was suggested. To cover irreversible airflow obstruction whether due to chronic bronchitis or emphysema the term 'generalized obstructive lung disease' was proposed. The term CNSLD has not been readily accepted by British workers, in contrast to the Dutch. In part this stems from different views on the causation of these conditions. The Dutch considered that CNSLD embraced a condition with a major constitutional or hereditary basis. This underlying susceptibility, when acted upon by a variety of exogenous factors, could lead to a range of clinical manifestations (Orie and Sluiter 1961). Thus, in the Dutch view, there was a close relationship between asthma and chronic bronchitis and emphysema.

Further reports were published on the definition and classification of these diseases, notably by the World Health Organization (WHO) in 1961 and the American Thoracic Society in 1962. In 1965, the MRC's Committee published their definitions and classifications of chronic bronchitis 'for clinical and epidemiological purposes'. They recognized 'simple chronic bronchitis', 'chronic or recurrent mucopurulent bronchitis', and 'chronic obstructive bronchitis'. Implicit in all these definitions of chronic bronchitis is the notion of a single disease. While there were doubts about the interrelationships between these three components, the definitions were recognized as likely to facilitate comparison between the investigations of research workers in different units—'to clarify, not obscure, realities'.

These various attempts to produce an acceptable set of definitions and classifications gave a marked impetus to both national and international studies. However, as Fletcher (1978) notes, there is no longer the wide agreement that had been reached in the 1960s. This may be seen as almost inevitable as knowledge expands. For example, the term 'chronic obstructive bronchitis' may be too general, as it could now be used to cover peripheral airways obstruction, small airways disease, and emphysema. The current position is well described by Fletcher (1978). He particularly condemns the continuing use of 'chronic bronchitis', except to cover simple expectoration. However, while agreeing with Fletcher, in the absence of a generally acceptable substitute the term chronic bronchitis will be used here; the reader must realize this is a shorthand for what may be a group of conditions rather than a single, well-defined entity.

METHODS OF INVESTIGATION

Analysis of available statistics

Mortality, and to a lesser extent, morbidity statistics, provided the initial clues to the main associations between factors and disease. Mortality remains a potent measure of the extent of serious disease in a community. One major limitation is the lack of information on personal characteristics, for example, smoking habits, that may be relevant in the study of aetiology, and on associated factors such as childhood chest illness providing clues to natural history. However, from a public health viewpoint, morbidity may be more important, as this will provide an index of the burden of the disease upon the health services. Morbidity data, while available for restricted groups of the population, have proved insufficiently detailed to permit the investigation of the extent, or of other aetiological factors in the evolution of the disease.

It was for these reasons that population-based field surveys were undertaken. The technique needed had either to be developed *de novo* as happened with the questionnaires or mostly required adaptation of existing methods, as with some test of ventilatory function.

Questionnaires

As noted earlier, the recognition of chronic bronchitis rested substantially upon a subject's account of his symptoms, and in those with advanced disease, clinical signs. Prevalence studies that aimed to define the extent of chronic bronchitis in different populations required measurement techniques that would detect persons in the early as well as the late stages of the disease. Cochrane and co-workers (1951) using questions on cough, sputum, tightness in the chest, and dyspnoea found inter-observer differences in prevalence when studying similar groups of subjects.

It was clear from this, and other studies, that the techniques of enquiry must be standardized. Factors such as the order questions were asked, their precise wording, their location within the questionnaire, and whether administered by an interviewer or self-completed could all influence response.

In 1959, the MRC's Committee formed a sub-committee of experts, chosen for their considerable experience in the use of respiratory questionnaires in field surveys, to advise on standardized questionnaires. They produced a questionnaire that was published in 1960 (MRC 1960) with an instruction booklet. Subsequently a set of tape-recorded interviews were provided for the training and testing of interviewers. The questionnaire was revised in 1966 and again in 1976. It has gained wide acceptance and been translated into many languages. (The 1976 version is shown in the appendix to this Chapter.) In 1968 the American Thoracic Society adopted the MRC questionnaire and published instructions for its use (American Thoracic Society 1969) and this was subsequently, in 1971, modified by the National Heart and Lung Institute (NHLI) to improve its suitability for use in the US. The NHLI questionnaire, while retaining the overall structure of the MRC questionnaire, changed the wording in some questions, and added a number of new ones. For example, the questions on cough and phlegm all had minor alterations in wording.

The 1971 version of the NHLI respiratory questionnaire was produced without rigorously defined methods of administration, and there were also some doubts on comparability with the MRC questionnaire. Lebowitz and Burrows (1976) compared the MRC, NHLI, and a questionnaire of their own design (ARIZ-Q). All subjects completed the ARIZ-Q, and after an interval of up to one month completed either the MRC or the NHLI questionnaire. They found, overall, 10 per cent disagreement between questionnaires in answer to symptom questions; for factual questions such as smoking, the disagreements approached zero. Where the wording of questions between the MRC and NHLI differed, then major differences in response were found.

American and Canadian investigators co-operated in producing a specification of 'minimal' standards for respiratory symptoms questionnaires, pulmonary function tests, and chest radiographs, under the title *Epidemiology standardization project* (Ferris 1978). This booklet set out recommended respiratory disease questionnaires for use with adults and children with notes and commentary, and included a modified version of the NHLI questionnaire, referred to as the ATS-DLD-78 questionnaire.

In 1979 Comstock and colleagues (1979) published the results of a comparison between the 1975 version of the MRC questionnaire and the ATS-DLD-78 questionnaire. In a study using 946 white males, no important differences were found between the two questionnaires for the items such as cough and phlegm, that have become widely accepted in diagnosing chronic lung disease.

Thus far discussion has centred on questionnaires written in English. The MRC questionnaire had been translated into at least 12 languages at the time of the 1976 revision. Attempts to estimate any major changes in the meaning of questions as a result of translation can be judged by 'back translation' into English, and by using some objective comparison, for example, tests of ventilatory function in groups of subjects reporting symptoms, and those who do not. However, as these methods are essentially indirect attempts to validate a translation, they are not wholly satisfactory.

The EEC has developed a standardized questionnaire, primarily for use in occupational groups. Its origins were the 1962 European Coal and Steel Community questionnaire which was based upon the 1960 MRC questionnaire. The EEC questionnaire was designed from the outset to be used in the languages of the EEC member countries. A number of validation studies were carried out to test various aspects of the questionnaire (Minette 1979).

The MRC questionnaire was initially designed for use by interviewers. However, it was found suitable for self-completion by subjects, and this led to its increasing use in this form in several large-scale field surveys of chronic respiratory disease. As noted earlier the main impetus for the development of standardized questionnaires was the need to minimize observed bias in assessing respiratory symptoms. What was not investigated to any great extent was the validity of the questionnaire in terms of measuring the presence, and degree of severity of chronic respiratory disease. This is hardly surprising as there are few objective standards against which the major symptoms can be compared. The questions on phlegm have been compared with morning sputum volume and correlate well; dyspnoea has been consistently found to correlate poorly with ventilatory function. Samet (1978), has provided an extensive review of the validity and susceptibility to bias of the MRC questionnaire, and of some of the American questionnaires. He concludes, and most epidemiologists would probably agree, that as there is now a very extensive literature and experience with the MRC questionnaire, new questionnaires should be calibrated against the MRC questionnaire. This would permit valid comparisons between, for example, the prevalence of respiratory symptoms in populations studied by questionnaires other than the MRC one. Such comparisons can provide insights into whether disease frequency, severity, aetiology, and natural history differ between countries.

Tests of ventilatory function

Two reasons can be discerned for performing tests of ventilatory function. In the past their main use has been as a crude measure of the validity of answers to the respiratory questionnaire. In general, subjects without respiratory symptoms have higher levels of ventilatory function than those with symptoms; and with an increasing number of symptoms, ventilatory function shows corresponding lower levels. Such tests have tended to be almost routine in prevalence studies, particularly where the population may not have been previously investigated.

The second main use has been as a measure of the effect of a factor or factors on the respiratory tract; in other words, as an outcome measure, much in the way that respiratory symptoms have been used, and additionally providing evidence of severity of disease. An extension of this use has been where serial measurements have been made, to follow, often over several years, changes in ventilatory function. Another use has been the investigation of the effects of changing daily levels of air pollution.

There have been few long-term follow-up studies. Fletcher and co-workers (1976) conducted an eight-year follow-up of men in the early stages of chronic bronchitis. Some of these subjects had early symptoms of disease, for example, 38 per cent had persistent phlegm when recruited into the study. Onset of disease could not therefore be studied for the whole group. As the length of follow-up was relatively short for a disease of known long duration, its contribution to our knowledge of natural history is limited. Most other follow-up studies using ventilatory function have been of relatively short duration.

The laboratory techniques for measuring ventilatory function have been extensively developed in the last 20 years. The increased interest in chronic respiratory diseases in the 1950s that led to the development of respiratory questionnaires also provided a stimulus to the construction of simple, portable tests of ventilatory function that could be used in field surveys. This is not the place to describe such tests in any detail. However, extensive use has been made of instruments such as the Wright Peak Flow Meter which measures peak expiratory flow rate (PEFR) and of those that measure expired air respiratory volumes such as, in some of the early studies, the McKesson Vitalor and, more recently, the Vitalograph. These instruments measure forced expiratory volume in one second (FEV_1) and forced vital capacity (FVC). These and other tests are summarized in Table 9.1. These measurements may be criticized as being crude and non-specific in that their correlation with lung pathophysiology is incompletely understood, particularly in the early stages of disease. Their use, however, as already noted, needs to be viewed in terms of providing confirmatory evidence to support questionnaire findings, or as evidence of rate of disease progression rather than indicating the underlying pathology. The latter is better studied in respiratory laboratories. Cotes (1979) provides a very full description of techniques for measuring lung function. As

Table 9.1. *Summary of tests of lung function*

Category	Tests
I. Tests dependent on a forced expiratory manoeuvre	Peak expiratory flow rate (PEFR)
	Forced expiratory volume in one second (FEV)
	Forced vital capacity (FVC)
	The ratio FEV:FVC
II. Tests of airway resistance using a body plethysmograph	Airway resistance (Raw)
	Specific airway resistance (SRaw)
	Airway conductance (Gaw)
	Specific airway conductance (SGaw)
III. So-called tests of small airway function	Closing volume (CV)
	Frequency dependence of compliance
	Maximum expiratory flow rate at low lung volume ($MMEF_{50}$ or $MMEF_{25}$) (this also depends on a forced expiratory manoeuvre.)

Source: Holland *et al.* (1979).

with the use of questionnaires, it soon became apparent that differences between observers in the precise circumstance of ventilatory function measurments could lead to the introduction of bias. Such factors as the position of subjects, whether standing or seated, depth of inspiration, degree of force of expiration, the number of expirations made, all influenced the resulting measurements. For these reasons precise instructions on these aspects of such measurements became mandatory. In addition, where expected differences in ventilatory function between subjects of a population might be small, systematic differences between instruments could introduce major bias in comparison between such groups. This led to strenuous attempts to calibrate instruments before, during and at the end of field studies. The current position regarding tests of ventilatory function in field surveys is reviewed in Holland *et al.* (1979).

Sputum

The MRC questionnaire sought information on the presence and degree of mucous expectoration. As noted earlier there were doubts when the questionnaire was originally constructed on the validity of answers to the various questions. The questions on phlegm production were crucial in defining the presence of the disease, and led to the development of a technique for collecting sputum, measuring its volume, and grading degree of purulence (Miller and Jones 1963). The method is probably now of historical interest only, although it might be of value in validating the questions on phlegm production in populations who had not previously been investigated, or where a new translation of the questionnaire had been made.

STUDY DESIGNS

Much of the initial epidemiological investigations into chronic bronchitis used vital statistical data, particularly data on mortality. Analysis by age, sex, occupation, and geography, including international comparisons provided the background for much of the subsequent field studies.

Attention has focussed on the extent of chronic bronchitis in populuations, its aetiology and natural history. The impact of the disease for health services, in terms of provision of clinical services or preventive services have hardly been explored.

A range of study designs have been used. Comparatively little use has been made of case-control studies; and mainly to investigate the associations of personal habits such as smoking with this disease (Oswald *et al.* 1953; Fry 1954; Leese 1956). Case-control studies are unlikely to be useful in testing hypotheses about, for example, general environmental factors such as air pollution since there are serious difficulties in finding a suitable control group and in matching for confounding factors. For example, bronchitis mortality shows an urban excess, and air pollution is likewise higher in urban than rural areas. Drawing controls from urban areas would ensure similarity in a number of factors, including air pollution exposure; thus effectively invalidating the comparison. While rural controls would inevitably have lower air pollution exposure, again controls and cases would not be comparable, since there are other differences between urban and rural environment. It was to prevalence, and to longitudinal studies that investigators turned to explore this disease further.

The main expansion of epidemiological evidence both on the extent of chronic bronchitis, and its aetiology has come from prevalence studies. Point prevalence studies were appropriate as the clinical evidence clearly pointed to this being a chronic disease of long duration, and as indicated by mortality data, also a common disease. The literature contains a very large number of reports of prevalence studies, mostly conducted to study aetiology, in a variety of populations, and often defined occupational groups, in countries throughout the world (Higgins 1974).

The development of respiratory symptom questionnaires, simple tests of ventilatory function and methods of measuring and classifying sputum meant that such studies could be readily conducted, and at low cost. Such studies have shown the powerful association between cigarette smoking and chronic bronchitis and, in the UK, an association, though small, with atmospheric pollution (RCP 1977). The study of readily defined occupational groups also demonstrated associations with occupational dust exposure.

Prevalence studies, while in this instance providing evidence on associations between various factors and chronic bronchitis, do not allow estimates of risk. A number of prospective studies in the UK, US, and Canada showed a marked excess mortality from chronic bronchitis and emphysema, among cigarette smokers. The Surgeon General's report on smoking and health (US Department of Health, Education and Welfare 1964) used data from seven prospective studies to calculate risks in cigarette smokers; overall they died of chronic bronchitis and emphysema 6.1 times more frequently than non-smokers. Later prospective studies, again using mortality as the end-point, yielded similar findings.

Most of these studies were unable to furnish evidence about the natural history of the disease; its onset, progression, changing clinical features, the role of infection, and indeed whether the disease was a single entity or two largely independent diseases. Such questions could only be answered by prospective studies starting with disease-free persons, or at least with persons at an early stage of disease, who could be followed-up rigorously by serial measurements of, for example, respiratory symptoms and ventilatory function, over a sufficiently long period for changes in these to occur. Such studies require continuity in staffing and in funding; this may explain in part the relative dearth of such studies.

The study designs discussed thus far are observational in character, that is, prevalence and incidence studies, or analytical, that is, case-control studies. The evidence from these may strongly suggest that associations between a factor and chronic bronchitis are causal. One such association is that between smoking and chronic bronchitis, which is almost certainly causal. The most rigorous test for causality is to conduct an experiment; a randomized controlled trial.

For example, smokers might be randomly allocated to either give up smoking or continue. A follow-up over an appropriate period, identifying those who develop chronic bronchitis, should allow a firm statement about whether or not smoking was causally associated with the disease. However, such a study would be impractical. Compliance with allocated treatment over the duration of the study, which would need to be decades rather than years, may well be poor. Such a study would be costly and its scale, would of necessity be large. It could be argued that the data on the association with cigarette smoking obtained from observational studies, particularly when judged against Hill's criteria (1965), were more than adequate to support a causal hypothesis.

There are circumstances in which controlled trials are useful. For example, in testing the short-term effects on respiratory symptoms of changing the type of cigarette being smoked, such as from middle-tar to low-tar level. A further use would be in testing the effects of, for example, antibiotics in acute exacerbations of bronchitis, or in evaluating health education programmes, aimed at reducing cigarette smoking in persons at risk of developing chronic bronchitis or in those who have evidence of early disease.

RISK FACTORS

Table 9.2 lists some of the risk factors that observational studies have identified, with comment on their measurement.

Table 9.2. *Risk factors associated with chronic bronchitis*

Categories of risk	Examples of measurement of risk factor
Cigarette smoking	Assessed by questionnaire with confidence
Age	Directly measured
Sex	Directly measured
Air pollution	Urban vs. rural, levels of SO_2 and smoke
Atopy, allergy, or hypersensitivity	History of asthma, eczema in childhood, wheeze independent of asthma, hay fever, etc., skin reactions to allergins
Occupation	Years of dust exposure
Social class	Occupational classification, education, or income level
Alcohol	Assessed by questionnaire with little confidence
Childhood illness	History of lung trouble before age 16 years; surveillance of illness experience in children
Familial or household	Household associations
Genetic	Twin studies; measurement of a_1 antitrypsin phenotypes
Respiratory illness history	History of chest illnesses with phlegm in the previous three years

Adapted from Speizer and Tager (1979).

Cigarette smoking

The epidemiological evidence from a large number of observational studies point to cigarette smoking as being the single major factor associated with this disease. This can be seen in prevalence studies where the presence of respiratory symptoms and lower ventilatory function has been found to be higher among smokers, than non-smokers, and in prospective studies where mortality from chronic bronchitis was also higher in smokers than non-smokers (US Department of Health, Education and Welfare 1979).

The overwhelming effect of cigarette smoking has made it more difficult to study other contributory factors, such as individual susceptibility to develop the disease.

Age

Although mortality from chronic bronchitis increases with age it is unlikely that age is a risk factor independent of all others.

Sex

Mortality is almost uniformly found to be higher in males than in females. There are problems in interpreting these findings as due allowance for differences in cigarette smoking and occupational exposure between the sexes have not usually been made. It remains unclear whether there are differences in susceptibility between males and females.

Air pollution

This has already been discussed in Volume 3, Chapter 18. Childhood exposure to air pollution and relationship to adult respiratory disease is discussed later.

Atopy, allergy, and hypersensitivity

There is uncertainty as to the role of atopy in chronic bronchitis. Wheezing has been found to be a common symptom in respiratory disease surveys. While some subjects will have undoubted asthma, there remains a group in which it is not clear whether wheeze is part of the spectrum of asthma, with similar aetiological components, or a quite separate entity. It seems that in most field studies the diagnosis of asthma has relied upon a subject's memory of whether or not a doctor used this diagnostic label. This must have the effect of identifying asthmatics with moderate to severe clinical disease, while under-reporting those with less severe symptoms. There is uncertainty to what extent wheezy subjects who are not labelled as asthmatics have the same underlying mechanisms as asthmatics. Evidence, for example, from Burr and colleagues (1975) suggest that in terms of pulmonary function, these two groups may both have similarly reduced levels.

Occupation

Occupational groups have been extensively used in the study of chronic bronchitis. Partly this has been the readiness with which such populations can be defined, their accessibility, and uniformity of social, educational, and other attributes. Also there has been a need to assess the effects of exposure to dust and fumes at work. Stuart-Harris (1968) and Higgins (1974) have provided reviews of the effects of occupational exposure in relation to chronic bronchitis. In general it has proved difficult to isolate possible effects of occupational exposure from other factors. In addition, there are uncertainties in estimating work exposure to dust and fumes, and workers who remain in an industry are those likely to be more resistant to the effects of such exposure.

Social class

Consistent social class gradients in chronic bronchitis mortality have been found in the UK; rates are lowest in social class I rising to a maximum in social class V. It is not clear what are the components of social class that contribute to this gradient. Among men it was thought that occupational exposure was a major contributor to this gradient. This may well be true, but cannot explain the similar gradients seen in married women classified by their husband's social class who would not be exposed to the same extent to occupational factors. Other environmental factors must therefore play a part. Among these, differences in the rate of cigarette smoking between the social classes, family and housing circumstances, and exposure to air pollution may contribute to these gradients.

Alcohol

There is evidence from both clinical and epidemiological studies that alcohol consumption is associated with chronic bronchitis (Chomet and Gash 1967; Banner 1973; Saric *et al.* 1979; Lebowitz 1980). Animal experiments suggest that alcohol increases susceptibility to infection and that this may be mediated by disturbing ciliary function (Green and Green 1968). However, a difficulty in interpreting associations between alcohol consumption and chronic bronchitis in man is that alcohol consumption and cigarette smoking are often associated; and dissociating their indepedent effects is not simple.

Childhood experience

There have been few pointers to those who, if they smoke, are at risk of developing chronic bronchitis. Clinical observation suggested that patients with chronic bronchitis more often had a history of serious chest illness in childhood, than adults not suffering from chronic bronchitis. It was postulated that such childhood illnesses could make the respiratory tract more susceptible to the effects of cigarette smoking. There are difficulties in investigating such a hypothesis; this could be done by following a cohort of infants until they reached middle age, noting occurrence or otherwise of childhood respiratory illness and the onset of chronic bronchitis in adult life.

The nearest approach to such a study has been the follow-up of the British 1946 birth cohort. Here childhood chest illness documented at the time was linked to respiratory symptoms at age 20 and 25 years. The effects of cigarette smoking at these ages, childhood exposure to air pollution,

Table 9.3. *Adjusted prevalence rates (per cent) for cough day or night in winter, for the levels of each factor with estimates of their effects at age 25 years*

Factor and level	Adjusted prevalence rate	Effect (difference)	χ^2	Degrees of freedom	p
Air pollution					
Low	10.3	1.9	1.92	1	n.s
High	12.2				
Childhood chest illness					
None	10.0	4.7	8.47	1	$0.01 > p > 0.001$
One or more	14.7				
Occupational group					
Non-manual	9.5	2.8	3.87	1	$0.05 > p > 0.02$
Manual	12.3				
Smoking					
Never	4.9	13.8*	91.21	2	$p < 0.001$
Past	7.4				
Present	18.7				

*Difference between never smoked and present smokers.
Adapted from Kiernan *et al.* (1970).

and social class, were also assessed for their effects on adult respiratory symptoms (Colley *et al.* 1973; Kiernan *et al.* 1976). The findings at 25 years of age are given in Table 9.3 where the respiratory symptom prevalence rates have been adjusted for the effects of other factors. Not unexpectedly cigarette smoking shows the greatest effect upon respiratory symptoms, followed by childhood chest illness. This would suggest that such childhood illness may increase the susceptibility of individuals to respiratory disease in adult life.

Studies of respiratory disease in childhood point to the major effects of environmental factors in risk of disease (Colley 1976). If childhood respiratory experience is relevant for the long-term susceptibility to develop chronic bronchitis in adult life, then it is necessary to study those factors in childhood that influence risk of chest illness. The development of methods to study the epidemiology of chronic bronchitis in adults also provided the means, with suitable adaptations, to study respiratory illness in children. Questionnaires completed by parents for their children, and simple tests of ventilatory function that even quite young children can adequately perform have formed the main methods of inquiry. Mention has already been made of studies of the health effects of air pollution in children. This had led to investigation of indoor air pollution, and in particular that due to parents smoking cigarettes in the home.

Various studies into 'passive smoking' by infants suggest an important increase in risk of lower respiratory tract illness; a doubling of risk may occur in exposed infants in their first year of life (Colley *et al.* 1974). In contrast to other factors, such as social, economic, and educational factors, that influence the risk of respiratory illness in childhood, passive smoking is theoretically at least amenable to change; most of the other factors could only be changed with difficulty.

Familial and genetic factors

Similarities in respiratory disease experience between hus-

bands and wives are suggestive of some shared environmental factors, such as cigarette smoking and home environment. The only specific genetic factor to be implicated so far in this disease is alpha-antitrypsin deficiency, a rare cause of early onset, familial emphysema.

While it is likely there are other genetic factors that contribute to susceptibility to chronic bronchitis these are at present unknown.

Respiratory infection

The role of respiratory infections in the evolution of chronic bronchitis, whether they initiate the disease, or are a consequence of it, is uncertain. This will only be resolved from prospective studies that take individuals before the onset of symptoms.

NATURAL HISTORY

Much of the epidemiological evidence about aetiology has come from mortality studies and prevalence surveys. Neither of these approaches are wholly suitable for the study of natural history. This requires follow-up of persons initially free of disease and the facilities to accurately measure exposure to factors such as smoking and perform clinical measurements over the whole period of follow-up. Despite the problems, early studies resulted in various hypotheses being advanced about the evolution of chronic bronchitis. Table 9.4 shows in simplified form two major contenders, known as the 'British' and the 'Dutch' hypotheses. The 'British' hypothesis held that bronchial irritation, mainly from cigarette smoking but assisted by air pollution and respiratory infections, led to mucous hypersecretion, recurrent infection of the bronchial tree, and ultimately bronchiolar obstruction and emphysema. The 'Dutch' hypothesis suggested that an over-reactive bronchial tree led to bronchiolar muscle constriction, mucosal swelling and mucous hypersecretion. This then could progress to

Table 9.4. *Hypotheses on the aetiology of chronic bronchitis*

(a) **British**

Bronchial irritation   →   Mucous hypersecretion   →   Recurrent infection   →   Irreversible bronchiolar obstruction and emphysema

(b) **Dutch**

Mucous hypersecretion

Hypersensitive bronchial airways   ⇄   →   Irreversible bronchiolar obstruction and emphysema

Bronchial obstruction

irreversible bronchial obstruction and emphysema. There were analogies in the underlying mechanism with asthma. Both hypotheses evolved from prevalence study data or patients already suffering from the disease. Further speculation on the correctness or otherwise of these hypotheses has had to await the outcome of prospective studies.

The major prospective study that has contributed to our understanding of the early stages of this disease is that by Fletcher and co-workers (1976), referred to earlier. They followed up 792 working men, aged 30–59 years, between 1961 and 1969, measuring respiratory symptoms and ventilatory function. These authors interpret their findings to indicate that there are two main disorders involved in this disease. First, an airflow obstructive disorder that may lead to progressive disability, respiratory failure, and death. The second is more benign, a mucous hypersecretory disorder which may accompany the obstructive disorder. Recurrent chest infections may occur with the hypersecretory disorder but do not themselves cause obstructive changes. Both disorders are caused by smoking.

Their ideas on the evolution of airflow obstruction are summarized in Fig. 9.1. The decline in FEV_1 from the level at age 25 has been plotted for groups with differing smoking habits and susceptibility. Their study suggested a continuous and steady decline over an individual's life. It appeared that the non-smoker's rate of decline in FEV_1 was not sufficient for clinically significant airways obstruction to develop; and that some smokers appeared to be unaffected by their habit as their rate of decline was similar to the non-smoker. However, it is the smoke-susceptible individual who is at greatest risk. They showed a high rate of decline if

they continued to smoke and ultimately developed airways obstruction; giving up smoking resulted in a slowing of rate of decline. This is an important observation in that in terms of reducing disability and possibily death from airways obstruction it is clearly to the susceptible smoker's advantage to give up the habit, and to do this well before early evidence of airways obstruction has occurred.

This study has also thrown doubt upon the role of mucous hypersecretion and bronchial infection in the aetiology of airways obstruction. No evidence was found that these play any part in the development of airways obstruction, and thus throws doubt upon the 'British' hypothesis (Table 9.4).

The 'Dutch' hypothesis, with its stress on susceptibility, and the absence of a role for bronchial infection in the development of airways obstruction, might appear to accord more closely with the evidence from this study. It would be speculative to take discussion of natural history further. One important lesson is to realize the limitations of prevalence data in constructing hypotheses on aetiology and natural history.

THE EXTENT OF CHRONIC BRONCHITIS

As noted earlier chronic bronchitis, as it presents in clinical practice, can be a serious and apparently common disease. This is borne out by mortality statistics where it is one of the leading causes of death. For example, in the US in 1977, 44 651 deaths were ascribed to bronchitis (chronic and unqualified), emphysema, and chronic obstructive lung disease and thus accounted for about 2.5 per cent of all deaths (Table 9.5). There has been a general trend for mortality in the US to rise since the 1950s (Fig. 9.2). As will

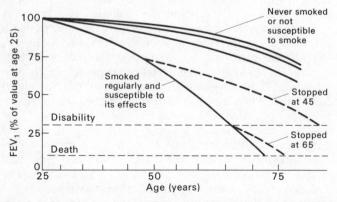

Fig. 9.1. Smoking and loss of forced expiratory volume (FEV_1). (Source: Fletcher and Peto (1977).)

Table 9.5. *Numbers of deaths from chronic respiratory diseases, United States, 1977*

Cause of death	ICDA Code*	Number of deaths
Emphysema	492	16 376
Bronchitis—chronic and unqualified	490, 491	4 313
Chronic obstructive lung disease	519.3	23 962
Subtotal	(490–492, 519.3)	(44 651)
Asthma	493	1 674

*Based on The Eighth Revision of International Classification of Diseases, adapted for use in the US.
Adapted from US DHHS (1980).

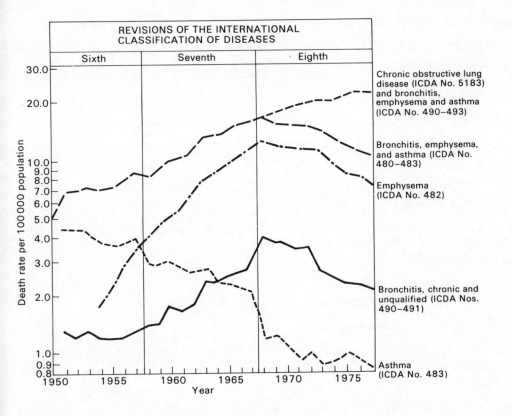

Fig. 9.2. Crude death rates from bronchitis, emphysema, asthma, and other chronic obstructive lung diseases, United States 1950–77. (Source: US DHHS (1980).)

be noted later the recent trend for mortality in England and Wales has been downward. It seems likely that these data underestimate the extent to which these diseases contribute to mortality; only underlying cause of death is presented in vital statistics, so that if these diseases are mentioned as a contributory cause they will not appear in the published data.

The extent of morbidity from these diseases is more difficult to assess. Tables 9.6 and 9.7 provide data on the prevalence of these conditions derived from sample surveys, and Tables 9.8 and 9.9, physician contacts and hospital discharges respectively. Although the prevalence of chronic bronchitis and emphysema is not high their chronic nature results in demands upon health services out of all

Table 9.6. *Prevalence (percentage) of selected chronic respiratory conditions reported in health interviews, United States, all ages 1970 and 1978*

Condition	ICDA code*	Total 1970	1978	Men 1970	1978	Women 1970	1978
Chronic bronchitis	490, 491	3.3	3.3	3.1	2.9	3.4	3.7
Emphysema	492	0.7	0.9	1.0	1.4	0.3	0.5
Asthma	493	3.0	2.8	3.2	2.8	2.9	2.8

*Based on the Eighth Revision International Classification of Diseases, adapted for use in the US.
Adapted from US DHSS (1980).

Table 9.7. *Percentages of subjects who reported selected conditions. Health and Nutrition Examination Survey. Adults 18–74 years, United States, 1971–74*

Condition	Total Ever present	Still present	Males Ever present	Still present	Females Ever present	Still present
Bronchitis/emphysema	6.3	4.1	5.5	3.9	7.0	4.3
Asthma	5.5	3.5	5.6	3.5	5.4	3.6
Chronic cough	3.1	2.5	3.6	3.0	2.6	2.0

*Based on the Eighth Revision International Classification of Diseases, adapted for use in the US.
Adapted from US DHSS (1980).

Table 9.8. *Numbers of office visits for acute and chronic diseases of the respiratory system, by diagnosis, United States, 1975–76*

Diagnosis	ICDA code*	Number of visits in thousands Principal diagnosis	Second or third listed diagnosis
Chronic diseases of the respiratory system	491–493 502–503, 507	45 602	
Chronic bronchitis	491	1646	5930
Emphysema	492	5223	4592
Asthma	493	10 591	4503
Chronic pharyngitis and nasopharyngitis	502	2486	1367
Chronic sinusitis	503	8284	4599
Hay fever	507	17 012	5919
Other acute chronic diseases	500–501 504–506, 508 510–519	9589	

*Based on the Eighth Revision International Classification of Diseases, adapted for use in the US.
Adapted from US DHSS (1980).

Table 9.9. *Numbers of hospital discharges for patients with chronic lung diseases, United States, 1977*

First-listed diagnosis	ICDA code*	Hospital discharges Number of discharges (thousands)	Length of stay in days	Number of days (thousands)
Total chronic lund diseases		1003	7.5	7536
Chronic bronchitis and emphysema	490–492	321	7.1	2266
Asthma	493	199	5.6	1106

*Based on the Eighth Revision International Classification of Diseases, adapted for use in the US.
Adapted from US DHSS (1980).

proportion to their apparent frequency. The contacts with health services represent, for office visits some 4 per cent of the total, 3 per cent of all hospital discharges, and 3 per cent of all days of hospitalization. It is not easy to estimate the precise burden these diseases place upon health services. The report of the Task Force on Epidemiology of Respiratory Diseases (US DHHS 1980) quotes a total cost to the US for the fiscal year 1975, for respiratory diseases overall, as 19.7 billion dollars. Unfortunately no estimates are available for the costs of specific respiratory diseases.

In general the measures available to define the extent of these diseases are still rather crude. There is a need at the national level to be able to monitor changes in, for example, the occurrence of these diseases, in their case-fatality, and response to changing patterns of smoking. To develop programmes for prevention information is needed on prevalence and severity that is often unavailable.

SCOPE FOR PREVENTION

Smoking

The major association of chronic bronchitis with cigarette smoking forcefully suggests that the disease would be a rarity in the absence of smoking. Thus the ultimate goal of a prevention programme would be that nobody should take up cigarette smoking; a quite unrealistic objective.

Only a proportion of cigarette smokers show progressive deterioration but knowledge of natural history is insufficient to be able to identify those individuals who are at risk of developing disabling disease. In the absence of markers of susceptibility it has been suggested that detection of the early stages of disease by screening, might offer scope for intervention. However, what to screen for is not wholly clear; whether this should be respiratory symptoms, and which ones, or some sensitive tests of early lung dysfunction. There are sufficient uncertainties on the screening tests to throw doubt upon the utility of general population screening.

There is reasonably secure evidence that ceasing to smoke does reduce the respiratory symptoms and slows the faster fall in FEV, seen in continuing smokers (Fletcher *et al.* 1976). That mortality from chronic bronchitis tends to be lower in ex-smokers than in those who continue to smoke (Doll and Hill 1964; Hammond 1966), likewise suggests that this may have prevented the development of disabling disease. Mortality rates have not remained stationary; for example, in England and Wales between 1973 and 1978 rates for bronchitis have shown a steady fall at ages under 75 years (Table 9.10). The changing patterns of cigarette smoking and reduction in particulate air pollution may have contributed to this.

Table 9.10. *Mortality from bronchitis*, England and Wales, 1973–78*

	Rates per 100 000					
	Males			Females		
	Age (years)			Age (years)		
	45–64	65–74	75+	45–64	65–74	75+
1973	70	407	1041	19	72	229
1974	62	390	981	19	69	228
1975	59	372	984	18	64	217
1976	55	348	979	18	65	229
1977	46	300	886	16	57	188
1978	47	296	908	17	58	194

*ICD 9th revision 466, 490, 491.
Source: OPCS (1980a).

Air pollution

Reductions in air pollution are thought to have had a modest effect upon the evolution of disease. Fletcher *et al.* (1976), have suggested that the falling levels of air pollution in London have caused a reduction in productive cough. Howard (1974), in a study of patients with obstructive airways disease in Sheffield over a period when air pollution levels were falling, found less productive cough and a lower rate of decline in FEV, in those exposed at the time to the lower levels of air pollution.

Respiratory infections

The effects of respiratory infection upon progression of disease is unclear, as is the value of treating such infections with broad-spectrum antibiotics. The evidence as far as it goes suggests that antibiotic treatment for up to 10 years had no influence upon the rate of decline of FEV, in patients with chronic bronchitis (Johnson *et al.* 1976).

Management of established disease

There is little or no evidence to suggest that any forms of therapy have any except minor effects upon the natural history of the established disease.

ASTHMA

Asthma, in spite of considerable clinical and epidemiological research, remains a poorly understood condition. Of the number of reasons for this, probably the main one is the lack of a wholly satisfactory definition of asthma. This influences the precision with which the condition can be identified in a population, and produces uncertainties when comparing frequency between different studies. Unlike chronic bronchitis and emphysema, mortality from asthma is very low. Thus mortality studies are unlikely to prove a potent source of clues to aetiology, although as will be seen later, mortality comparisons have provided important information about the effects of treatment.

DEFINITIONS OF ASTHMA

As noted earlier the major step in defining asthma was taken at the Ciba Guest Symposium in 1959. They considered that asthma 'refers to the condition of subjects with widespread narrowing of the bronchial airways, which changes its severity over short periods of time either spontaneously or under treatment, and is not due to cardiovascular disease'. This was followed by the American Thoracic Society (1962) whose definition was 'asthma is a disease characterized by an increased responsiveness of the trachea and bronchii to various stimuli and manifested by a widespread narrowing of the airways that changes in severity either spontaneously or as a result of therapy'.

The adoption of these definitions at least provided a starting point for studies into asthma. However, it proved difficult to translate them into definitions applicable for use in field studies. Their main drawback was that reversible airways narrowing can also occur in obstructive lung disease, and emphysema.

METHODS OF INVESTIGATION

Analysis of available statistics

Mortality

Mortality ascribed to asthma is low in comparison with that due to emphysema and bronchitis (see Fig. 9.2). Doubts about possible differences over time in the ways in which clinicians certify asthma as the underlying cause of death limit the interpretation of time trends in asthma mortality. Furthermore, systematic differences probably exist between countries in the readiness with which clinicians certify this disease. Thus, in contrast to the study of chronic bronchitis, where large international differences in mortality were thought to reflect true differences in disease frequency, with asthma less weight can be placed upon apparently different international mortality rates. This has not, however, diminished the importance of studying time trends in mortality within a country.

Some fairly general observations can be made on the epidemiology of asthma as suggested by mortality studies. Mortality is low in childhood and early adult life, and increases with age (Table 9.11). The rates tend to be higher in women than men, although this is not wholly consistent. A number of factors need to be considered in interpreting

Table 9.11. *Asthma (ICD 493) death rates per million by sex, 1978, England and Wales*

Age (years)	Male	Female	Age (years)	Male	Female
All	19	28	35–44	19	12
<1	0	0	45–54	21	29
1–4	7	4	55–64	26	50
5–14	4	3	65–74	55	70
15–24	6	8	75–84	89	95
25–34	11	8	85+	101	98

Source: OPCS (1980b).

these age trends. In middle- and old-age the clinical associations between asthma and other serious respiratory diseases, such as chronic bronchitis, may lead to an under-reporting of asthma; it may not be mentioned as the underlying cause of death. This is not likely to be a problem in childhood and early adult life. When time trends are examined, changes in the ICD classification as applied to asthma, and in the rules for certifying deaths may limit the conclusions drawn.

Some large changes, particularly increases, in asthma mortality have been observed over the last 20 or so years. This is surprising, as a number of highly effective treatments for asthma have been discovered. It might have been expected with the introduction of corticosteroids, and later the bronchodilator aerosols, that mortality from asthma would have fallen.

Smith (1966) reported an increase in the number of deaths from asthma in children over five years of age between 1961 and 1964 in England and Wales. This stimulated studies of asthma mortality by Speizer and colleagues (Speizer *et al.* 1966, 1968; Speizer and Doll 1968). They looked at asthma mortality rates in England and Wales from 1867 to 1966 (Fig. 9.3) and also from 1959 to 1964 in other countries. In Britain, Australia, and Japan, mortality rates in the early 1960s rose in the 5–34-year age group. No appreciable rise was observed in the US and other west European countries. This trend was not due to changes in diagnostic criteria used in the former three countries. Since it was thought unlikely that asthma incidence had changed, this suggested case-fatality had increased. In the absence of environmental factors that might increase asthma severity, new methods of treatment, such as corticosteroids and bronchodilator aerosols were suggested as likely causes.

In 1969, Inman and Adelstein reported that asthma mortality in England and Wales, after arising between 1961 and 1966, had shown a major fall (Fig. 9.4). They ascribed these trends to concurrent changes in the use of pressurized aero-

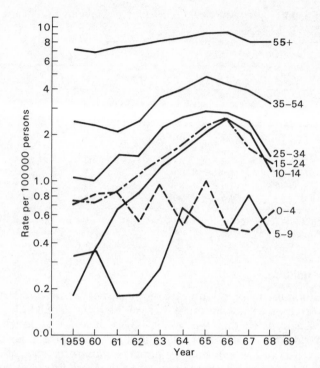

Fig. 9.4. Mortality from asthma (ICD 241) in England and Wales expressed as annual age-specific rates per 100 000 living, 1959–68. (Source: Inman and Adelstein (1969).)

sols containing sympathomimetic bronchodilators; the fall being a result of doctors becoming more aware of the dangers of these preparations as a result of the earlier publications. Stolley (1972) also concluded that the US and other countries were spared this increase in deaths either because of low overall consumption of aerosol bronchodilators, or the absence of nebulizers with highly concentrated sympathomimetics. He stressed that these preparations were unlikely to be the sole cause of the increased mortality. Jackson *et al.* (1982), reporting on asthma mortality in New Zealand, noted that while mortality in England and Wales, Australia, and New Zealand had fallen from peaks in the mid-1960s, New Zealand had experienced a major rise from 1976 (Fig. 9.5). They considered changes in management to be the most likely explanation for this rise.

Continuing observation of asthma mortality is important to detect possible further adverse effects of treatment. However, mortality can provide only limited evidence on the incidence of asthma, upon severity, and aetiology. For these reasons there has been a pressing nead to study asthma morbidity.

Morbidity

There is a relative paucity of data from routine sources on morbidity ascribed to asthma. Hospital discharge data were used by Anderson (1978) to study hospitalization of children for asthma. He demonstrated a threefold increase in admissions for asthma between 1959 and 1973 in children

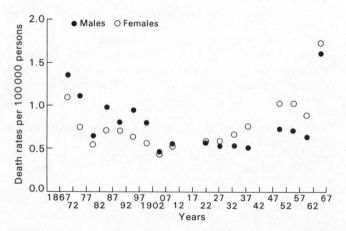

Fig. 9.3. Death rates from asthma in males and females aged 5–34 years, England and Wales, 1867–1966. (Source: Speizer and Doll (1968); data from Registrar General *Annual reports* for the years 1867–1966.)

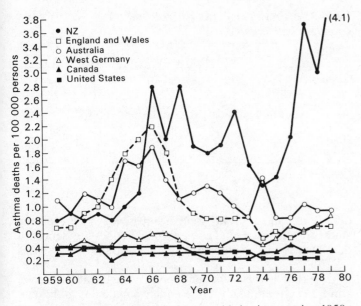

Fig. 9.5. Asthma mortality in 5–34-year-olds in six countries, 1959–79. (Source: Jackson *et al.* (1982).)

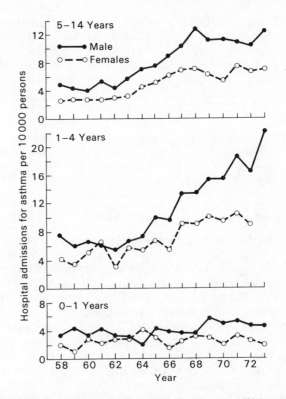

Fig. 9.6. Hospital admissions for asthma, England and Wales, 1958–73. (Source: Anderson (1978); data from Hospital Inpatient Enquiry, various years.)

under 15 years of age (Fig. 9.6). Part of the increase may have been due to a rise in re-admission rate as these data only relate to spells, not persons but Anderson concluded that these increasing rates might reflect an increase in morbidity. General practice consultation rates (Logan and Cushion 1958; Office of Population Censuses and Surveys 1974) also indicate an increase in consultation rates for children under 15 years of age over time. However, the nature of these data is inadequate to assess whether or not asthma has become more common since they might equally represent changes in asthma severity, increasing knowledge of the availability of effective treatments, and pressure extended by parents in terms of greater attendance at general practitioners and admission for hospital treatment. Resolution of these possibilities require field studies that are able to assess disease prevalence, incidence, and severity as well as the determinants of attendance at the general practitioner, referral and admission to hospital.

Evidence from hospital discharges and general practitioner consultation data for adults do not give such a clear pattern. However, clinicians working with chronic respiratory diseases in adults believe that asthma in adults has become commoner. Unfortunately, the epidemiological evidence is not yet available to allow these impressions to be investigated.

Questionnaires

Questionnaires developed to study chronic bronchitis included questions to elicit the presence of wheezing. The MRC questionnaire attempted to identify persons with attacks of wheezing, and also if associated with shortness of breath (see Appendix). The use of symptoms in epidemiological studies of asthma was necessary due to the variations between clinicians, and particularly between clinicians in

different countries, in labelling persons as asthmatic. Where questionnaires have asked about asthma, this may be limited to asthma 'diagnosed by a doctor', thereby excluding self-diagnosis, and hopefully improving the precision of the question.

Tests of ventilatory function

These have already been discussed in relation to chronic bronchitis. The main physiological change in asthma is variable air flow obstruction. Those tests listed in Table 9.1, particularly categories I and II, are appropriate for providing objective evidence of airways obstruction. A major limitation to their use is the often wide variability within subjects in the degree of airways obstruction. Thus there may be occasions when airways obstruction may not be demonstrated in a person with undoubted asthma. This can be a serious problem if ventilatory function is used in a point prevalence study to identify persons with asthma.

An important additional use of such tests has been to study the effects of challenge by histamine, the response to exercise, and the inhalation of a bronchodilator. These are not tests that can be routinely used in field studies, due to time required for their completion, and, in the case of histamine challenge, the potential risks of the procedure. In this context the ethics of performing the challenge in persons who do not require the procedure for clinical purposes need to be considered. There appear to be some asthmatics who have a variable response to histamine, and exercise; on some occasions a major increase in airways obstruction occurs, while on others there is little change. This variability limits the value of such tests, particularly in prevalence studies. The response to exercise in schoolchildren has been used successfully to discriminate between asthmatics, and those with wheeze or atopic disease, and normal children (Burr *et al.* 1974). However, in general, tests of ventilatory function in population studies of asthma do not appear to provide the clear, objective evidence of the condition that might be expected.

Atopy, allergy, and hypersensitivity

The role of atopy in chronic bronchitis has already been discussed when considering risk factors. As the evidence on the aetiology of asthma strongly suggests that allergy plays an important role, studies have often included tests aimed at seeking evidence for various allergic phenomena. These have consisted of skin tests, usually prick tests using a series of allergen extracts; for example, house dust, grass, pollens, cat fur, dog hair, various fungi, house mites, and foods. The fairly non-specific nature of the tests, and the finding that non-asthmatics can give positive prick tests has limited their usefulness in epidemiological studies.

While immunological tests have been used in the investigation and management of patients with asthma, for example total, and specific IgE antibody, their use in field studies has been minimal.

Bronchial challenge by inhalation of histamine has already been described, and the same technique can be used to test the bronchial provocation effects of allergens. Apart from skin tests, these other methods have been little used in field studies of asthma.

STUDY DESIGNS

In spite of the limitations of prevalence studies in investigating a condition as variable as asthma, these studies form the main source of our knowledge of morbidity.

Much of the emphasis has been placed on investigations into asthma prevalence in childhood. There are a number of reasons for this. Asthma is an important cause of chronic disability in childhood. Furthermore, the condition can be more readily identified in children, than in adults, since there is little confusion with other respiratory disease. Aetiological investigation is aided by the availability of parents and siblings in determining the role of familial factors, and avoids confounding factors such as occupation and smoking habits. Finally, populations of children tend to be readily defined, and during the school years, accessible for study.

Reported prevalence rates in children vary widely (Table 9.12) and this includes wide within-country variation. The absence in many of these reports of the definitions of asthma used and an explanation of what is meant by prevalence, whether point-prevalence or cumulative prevalence, makes interpretation of such differences uncertain. Gregg *et al.*

Table 9.12. *Prevalence of asthma reported in different countries (percentage)*

	Children	Adults
Scandinavia	0.8–2.0	1.1–3.8
United Kingdom	1.5–5.1	0.9–5.4
United States	0.5–6.3	0.9–6.6
Australia/New Zealand	5.4–11.4	—
India	0.2*	5.0*
Japan	0.7*	—
Barbados	1.1*	—

*Single studies.

(1977) provide a useful source and review of prevalence studies in childhood and adult asthma, as does the Report of the Task Force Epidemiology of Respiratory Diseases (1979).

Uncertainties also surround the prevalence rates found in adults. These are likely to be underestimates, as is thought to be the case for asthma mortality in adults. Among smokers, late-onset asthma may commonly be labelled chronic bronchitis. Doubts about the accuracy of these prevalence rates limit the extent to which they can be used to explore the role of environmental or constitutional factors in aetiology.

Incidence studies of asthma would be expected to overcome some of the deficiencies of prevalence studies, particularly if follow-up was long. In practice this has not been the case. Partly this has been due to the difficulties in defining the onset of asthma and in adequately describing changes in severity, but also to the need for intense surveillance of the population, to identify onset and change in severity.

As with prevalence studies, children have been the main focus of investigation. Broadly these studies have investigated the role of infections in aetiology, or have been concerned with natural history. In contrast, incidence studies in adults have largely explored the relationship between meteorological and other environmental factors, such as air pollution, and asthma.

RISK FACTORS

Familial and genetic factors

Family studies

It has been long suspected that there may be a genetic basis for asthma. Clinical observation suggests that parents with a history of asthma, are more likely to have children who develop this condition.

Leigh and Marley (1967) studied asthma and control probands on the list of two general practices in London to estimate the genetic contribution in the risk of asthma. A higher proportion of first-degree relatives of asthma probands than of control probands suffered from asthma, and this indicated a significant genetic contribution in the development of this disorder. A further study of childhood asthma and wheezy bronchitis in a general practice in

London between 1967 and 1976 likewise showed strong associations between asthma, and wheezy bronchitis, in first-degree relatives of the probands (Sibbald *et al.* 1980). These findings suggest that asthma and wheezy bronchitis share a common genetic defect.

Sex

In childhood there is a higher prevalence of asthma in boys, the ratio varying from 3.3:1 to 1.5:1; the ratio tending to be higher in younger children. There has been no ready explanation of this sex difference. However, boys show a greater susceptibility to lower respiratory tract infections than girls, suggesting some more general predisposition to respiratory tract disorders.

Asthma with onset during adult life appears to be more common in women. This may be an artefact; asthma in men, and particularly in smokers, may be labelled as chronic bronchitis, thus underestimating the true prevalence of asthma.

Age

Asthma prevalence and, to a more marked degree, mortality show an apparent trend with age. As with chronic bronchitis it is unlikely that age itself is a factor independent of others.

Atopy

The association, particularly in children, between hay fever, allergic rhinitis, eczema, and asthma has pointed to a possible atopic basis for asthma. A number of epidemiological studies have reported associations between atopic disorders and asthma. However, the inclusion of a wide range of doubtfully atopic conditions in some of these studies has tended to confuse the picture. The relevance of atopy in the aetiology of asthma is not wholly clear.

Respiratory tract infections

In childhood, respiratory infections have for long been implicated in causing exacerbations of asthma, and more recently there has been evidence of such infections initiating onset. A number of studies have reported an association of viral infections in children with wheeze bronchitis and asthma (Horn *et al.* 1975; Mitchell *et al.* 1976), and of the relationship between bronchitis and subsequent asthma (Wittig *et al.* 1959; Eisen and Bacal 1963; Pullan and Hey 1982). Respiratory syncitial virus is the main agent causing acute bronchitis in young children. Thus there is good evidence for the common respiratory viruses, and particularly respiratory syncitial virus being initiators of attacks of wheezing in young children. Gregg (1977), provides a useful review of the role of infection in asthma.

Air pollutants

A wide range of dusts and chemicals have been shown to cause bronchoconstriction in asthmatics, including exposure to high levels of sulphur dioxide.

Aspirin

Some asthmatics appear to be highly susceptible to aspirin, which causes an acute exacerbation of their asthma.

Psychological factors

Clinical observations suggest that psychological factors can have a major role in initiating asthma, and in provoking attacks. These views have proved difficult to investigate due, in part, to the absence of wholly reliable methods to measure psychological factors. Furthermore, with prevalence studies, it may be difficult to assess the extent to which a psychological disturbance preceded, or followed, asthma.

Exercise

Vigorous exercise produces an increase in airways obstruction in many asthmatics, and has been used, as noted earlier, as an additional method for identifying asthmatics.

Meteorological factors

Asthmatics exposed to low ambient temperatures often respond by an increase in airways obstruction.

The multiplicity of factors that appear to influence the severity of asthma and the great variability of their effects, has limited the extent to which epidemiological investigation can contribute to knowledge of aetiology. There are two main views on the disease: (i) a single disease with multifactorial causes and (ii) a group of closely related diseases but with different causes.

NATURAL HISTORY

Onset in childhood

There remain a number of questions on the relationship between wheezing in infancy and its relevance to the subsequent development of asthma. Williams and McNicol (1969) considered that asthma and wheezy bronchitis are manifestations of a common defect. However, others, for example, Taussig and Lebowitz (1976), found differences in lung function, and evidence of atopy between wheezy and asthmatic children. However, a study by Sibbald *et al.* (1980) into the genetic basis of asthma and wheezy bronchitis suggested that these two conditions shared a common genetic basis.

Paediatric opinion has supported the view that most asthmatic children grow out of the condition by puberty. A number of studies have reported follow-up of wheezy or asthmatic children. Some of these have studied asthmatic children who were initially seen in hospital, for example the study by Johnstone (1968). Others have been population based such as the study in Melbourne by Williams and

McNicol (1969) with follow-up to age 14 years and subsequent follow-up to age 21 years by Martin and co-workers (1980). There must be some reservations in basing knowledge of natural history on follow-up of cases attending hospital; they will tend to be children with more severe forms of the disease.

The Melbourne study provides the best evidence for the natural history of wheezing with onset in childhood. Their findings confirmed the clinical impression of improvement in late childhood and adolescence. Some 55 per cent of children whose wheeze had started before seven years of age had stopped before adolescence and were still wheeze-free at age 21 years. Nevertheless, there remained a group of children who continued to wheeze through adolescence to age 21 years, although for most of these the disease was not so troublesome.

Onset in the adult

Even less is known about the pattern of adult-onset asthma. There have been no population-based longitudinal studies comparable to the Melbourne follow-up study.

SCOPE FOR PREVENTION AND CONTROL OF ASTHMA

Our limited understanding of the aetiology of asthma provides few pointers to preventing onset of asthma. We may be better placed to prevent attacks of asthma in those who have already developed the disease. Two basic approaches are possible; first, to prevent attacks by the effective use of drugs, and secondly to control exposure to factors that may precipitate attacks.

With the introduction of drugs that are effective in controlling asthma it might be expected that asthma mortality and morbidity would fall. As we have seen earlier, mortality may actually have risen, albeit temporarily, as a result of treatment. Hospital admission rates for asthma in childhood in England and Wales rose steeply over the period 1959–73 (Anderson 1978) (Fig. 9.6) and in one region in England between 1970 and 1978 (Anderson et al. 1980). Anderson and co-workers (1983) investigated the medical care given to asthmatic children of school age in a London borough in 1969 and 1970. They concluded that there was considerable under-use of the health services, and a substantial proportion of asthmatic children were not having any drug treatment. If the findings from this study are representative of the management of asthma elsewhere, doubts must arise as to the general effectiveness of treatment. These authors drew attention to the need for better education of parents and patients, and of doctors, in management of asthma, and in the way the various services are co-ordinated. There does appear to be considerable scope for improving the overall management of asthma.

A study by the British Thoracic Association (1982) into deaths from asthma in adults in two regions in England in 1979, concluded, as did Anderson and colleagues, that under-treatment was prevalent. They likewise suggested that improved education of patient and doctors was needed.

The control of factors that can precipitate attacks may be more difficult. However, exposures to drugs, such as aspirin, and to side-stream tobacco smoke could readily be reduced. More difficult would be the reduction of risks of respiratory infections, although the production of effective vaccines against the common respiratory virus are a distinct possibility.

APPENDIX—MRC QUESTIONNAIRE ON RESPIRATORY
SYMPTOMS (MRC 1978)

Questionnaire on

CONFIDENTIAL

Respiratory Symptoms (1976)

Approved by Medical Research Council's Committee on Research into Chronic Bronchitis

Before this questionnaire is used the instruction sheet must be read

Surname

First name(s)

Address

Serial number

Sex [M=1 F=2]

	Day	Month	Year
Date of birth			

Name at birth if
different from above

Own doctor
Name   Address

Other identifying data

Civil state

Occupation

Industry

Ethnic group

Interviewer

	Day	Month	Year
Date of interview			

Use the actual wording of each question. Put 1 = Yes, 2 = No, or other codes as indicated in boxes. When in doubt record as no.

Preamble

I am going to ask you some questions, mainly about your chest. I should like you to answer **Yes** or **No** whenever possible.

Cough

1 Do you **usually** cough first thing in the morning in the winter? ☐

2 Do you **usually** cough during the day — or at night — in the winter? ☐

If Yes to 1 or 2
3 Do you cough like this on most days for as much as three months each year? ☐

Phlegm

4 Do you **usually** bring up any phlegm from your chest first thing in the morning in the winter? ☐

5 Do you **usually** bring up any phlegm from your chest during the day — or at night — in the winter? ☐

If Yes to 4 or 5
6 Do you bring up phlegm like this on most days for as much as three months each year? ☐

Periods of cough and phlegm

7a In the past three years have you had a period of (increased) cough and phlegm lasting for three weeks or more? ☐

If Yes
7b Have you more than one such period? ☐

Breathlessness

If the subject is disabled from walking by any condition other than heart or lung disease, omit question 8 and enter 1 here. ☐

8a Are you troubled by shortness of breath when hurrying on level ground or walking up a slight hill? ☐

If Yes
8b Do you get short of breath walking with other people of your own age on level ground? ☐

If Yes
8c Do you have to stop for breath when walking at your own pace on level ground? ☐

Wheezing

9a Does your chest ever sound wheezing or whistling? ☐

If Yes
9b Do you get this on most days — or nights? ☐

10a Have you ever had attacks of shortness of breath with wheezing? ☐

If Yes
10b Is/was your breathing absolutely normal between attacks? ☐

Chest illnesses

11a During the past three years have you had any chest illness which has kept you from your usual activities for as much as a week? ☐

If Yes
11b Did you bring up more phlegm than usual in any of these illnesses? ☐

If Yes
11c Have you had more than one illness like this in the past three years? ☐

Past illnesses
Have you ever had:

12a An injury or operation affecting your chest ☐

12b Heart trouble ☐

12c Bronchitis ☐

12d Pneumonia ☐

12e Pleurisy ☐

12f Pulmonary tuberculosis ☐

12g Bronchial asthma ☐

12h Other chest trouble ☐

12i Hay fever ☐

Tobacco smoking   1 = Yes, 2 = No

13a Do you smoke? ☐

If No

13b Have you ever smoked as much as one cigarette a
day (or one cigar a week or an ounce of tobacco a
month) for as long as a year? ☐

> If No to both parts of question 13, omit remaining
> questions on smoking.

14a Do (did) you inhale the smoke? ☐

If Yes

14b Would you say you inhaled the smoke
slightly = 1, moderately = 2 or deeply = 3? ☐

15 How old were you when you started smoking
regularly? ☐☐

16a Do (did) you smoke manufactured cigarettes? ☐

If Yes

16b How many do (did) you usually smoke per day
on weekdays? ☐☐

16c How many per day at weekends? ☐☐

16d Do (did) you usually smoke plain [=1]
or filter tip [=2] cigarettes? ☐

16e What brands do (did) you usually smoke? ☐☐☐

17a Do (did) you smoke hand-rolled cigarettes? ☐

If Yes

17b How much tobacco do (did) you usually
smoke per week in this way? ☐☐☐

17c Do (did) you put filters in these cigarettes? ☐

18a Do (did) you smoke a pipe? ☐

If Yes

18b How much pipe tobacco do (did) you
usually smoke per week? ☐☐☐

19a Do (did) you smoke small cigars? ☐

If Yes

19b How many of these do (did) you usually
smoke per day? ☐☐

20a Do (did) you smoke other cigars? ☐

If Yes

20b How many of these do (did) you usually
smoke per week? ☐☐

For present smokers

21a Have you been cutting down your smoking
over the past year? ☐

For ex-smokers

Month   Year

21b When did you last give up smoking? ☐☐ ☐☐

Additional observations

Ventilatory capacity

Standing height [m]

Weight [kg]

Ambient temperature [°C]

Barometric pressure [mm Hg]

Time of day [24 h]

Observer

Spirometer

Instrument number

Enter readings as made, for subsequent correction to BTPS.

If additional readings are made, enter below number 5 and delete the ones they replace.

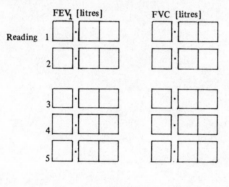

FEV$_1$ [litres]   FVC [litres]

Reading 1

2

3

4

5

Peak expiratory flow

Instrument number

If additional readings are made, enter below number 5 and delete the ones they replace

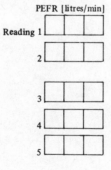

PEFR [litres/min]

Reading 1

2

3

4

5

Additional tests

Further copies of this questionnaire may be obtained from Publications Group, Medical Research Council, 20, Park Crescent, London W1N 4AL
Dd 097307 50M Forms S&K 7/76

REFERENCES

American Thoracic Society (1962). Chronic bronchitis, asthma and pulmonary emphysema: a statement by the Committee on Diagnostic Standards for Non-Tuberculous Respiratory Disease. *Am. Rev. Resp. Dis.* **85**, 762.

American Thoracic Society (1969). *Standards for epidemiologic surveys in chronic respiratory disease.* National Tuberculosis and Respiratory Disease Association, Washington, DC.

Anderson, H.R. (1978). Increase in hospitalisation for childhood asthma. *Arch. Dis. Child.* **53**, 295.

Anderson, H.R., Bailey, P., and West, S. (1980). Trends in the hospital care of acute childhood asthma 1970–8: a regional study. *Br. Med. J.* **281**, 1191.

Anderson, H.R., Bailey, A., Cooper, J.S., Palmer, J.C., and West, S. (1983). Medical care of asthma and wheezing illness in children: a community survey. *J. Epidemiol. Community Health* **37**, 180.

Badham, C. (1808). *Observations on the inflammatory affections of the mucous membrane of the bronchie.* Callow, London.

Banner, S.A. (1973). Pulmonary function in chronic alcholism. *Am. Rev. Resp. Dis.* **108**, 851.

Burr, M.L., Eldridge, B.A., and Borysiewicz, L.K. (1974). Peak expiratory flow rates before and after exercise in schoolchildren. *Arch. Dis Child.* **49**, 923.

Ciba Foundation Guest Symposium (1959). Terminology, definition and classification of chronic pulmonary emphysema and related conditions. *Thorax* **14**, 286.

Chomet, B. and Gash, B.M. (1967). Lobar pneumonia and alcholism; an analysis of thirty-seven cases. *Am. J. Med. Sci.* **253**, 300.

Cochrane, A.L., Chapman, P.J. and Oldham, P.D. (1951). Observers errors in taking medical histories. *Lancet* **i**, 1007.

Colley, J.R.T. (1976). The epidemiology of respiratory diseaes in childhood. In *Advances in paediatrics* (ed. D. Hull) p. 221. Churchill Livingston, Edinburgh.

Colley, J.R.T., Holland, W.W., and Corkhill, R.T. (1974). Influence of passive smoking and parental phlegm on pneumonia and bronchitis in early childhood. *Lancet* **ii**, 1031.

Colley, J.R.T., Douglas, J.W.B., and Reid, D.D. (1973). Respiratory disease in young adults: influence of early childhood lower respiratory tract illness, social class, air pollution and smoking. *Br. Med. J.* **iii**, 195.

Collis, E.L. (1923). The general and occupational prevalence of bronchitis and its relation to other respiratory diseases. *J. Ind. Hyg. Toxicol.* **5**, 264.

Comstock, G.W., Tockman, M.S., Helsing, K.J., and Hennesy, K.M. (1979). Standardized respiratory questionnaire: comparison of the old with the new. *Am. Rev. Resp. Dis.* **119**, 45.

Cotes, J.E. (1979). *Lung function: assessment and application in medicine,* 4th edn. Blackwell, Oxford.

Doll, R. and Hill, A.B. (1964). Mortality in relation to smoking: ten years' observations of British doctors. *Br. Med. J.* **i**, 1399.

Eisen, A.H. and Bacal, H.L. (1963). The relationship of acute bronchiolitis to bronchial asthma—a 4 to 14 year follow-up. *Pediatrics* **31**, 859.

Ferris, B.G., Higgins, I.T.T., Higgins, M.W., and Peters, J.M. (1973). *Chronic non-specific respiratory disease in Berlin,* New Hampshire, 1961 to 1967. *Am. Rev. Resp. Dis.* **107**, 110.

Ferris, B.G. (1978). Epidemiology standardization project. *Am. Rev. Resp. Dis.* **118**, 1.

Fletcher, C.M. (1952). The clinical diagnosis of pulmonary emphysema—an experimental study. *Proc. R. Soc. Med.* **45**, 577.

Fletcher, C.M. (1978). Terminology in chronic obstructive lung diseases. *J. Epidemiol. Community Health.* **32**, 282.

Fletcher, C.M. and Peto, R. (1977). The natural history of chronic airflow obstruction. *Br. Med. J.* **i**, 1645.

Fletcher, C.M., Peto, R., Tinker, C.M., and Speizer, F.S. (1976). *The natural history of chronic bronchitis and emphysema.* Oxford University Press, London.

Fry, J. (1954). Chronic bronchitis in general practice. *Br. Med. J.* **i**, 190.

Goodman, N., Lane, R.E., and Rampling, S.B. (1953). Chronic bronchitis: an introductory examination of existing data. *Br. Med. J.* **ii**, 237.

Gough, J. and Wentworth, J.E. (1960). Sections of entire organs mounted on paper. In *Recent advances in pathology,* 7th edn (ed. C.V. Harrison) p. 80. Churchill Livingston, Edinburth.

Green, L.H. and Green, G.M. (1968). Differential suppression of pulmonary antibacterial activity as the mechanism of selection of a pathogen in mixed bacterial infection of the lung. *Am. Rev. Resp. Dis.* **98**, 819.

Gregg, I. (1977). Infection (Chapter 8), Epidemiology (Chapter 1), Role of the family doctor in management (Chapter 19). In *Asthma* (ed. T.J.H. Clark and S. Godfrey) pp. 162, 214, 395. Chapman and Hall, London.

Hammond, E.C. (1966). Smoking in relation to the death rates of one million men and women. *Natl. Cancer Inst. Monog.* **19**, 127.

Heasman, M.A. (1962). *Accuracy of death certification. Proc. R. Soc. Med.* **55**, 733.

Heasman, M.A. and Lipworth, L. (1966). *Accuracy of certification of cause of death.* Studies on Medical and Population Subjects No. 20. General Register Office, HMSO, London.

Higgins, I.T.T. (1974). Epidemiology of chronic respiratory disease: a literature review. Environmental Health Effects Research Series. EPA 650/1-74-007. US Government Printing Office, Washington, DC.

Hill, A.B. (1965). The environment and disease. Association or causation? *Proc. R. Soc. Med.* **58**, 295.

Holland, W.W., Bennett, A.E., Cameron, I.R. *et al.* (1979). Health effects of particulate pollution: reappraising the evidence. *Am. J. Epidemiol.* **110,k** 527.

Horn, M.E.C., Brain, E., Gregg, I., Yealland, S.J., and Inglis, J.M. (1975). Respiratory viral infection in childhood. A survey in general practice. Roehampton, 1967–72. *J. Hyg.* **74**, 157.

Howard, P. (1974). The changing face of chronic bronchitis with airways obstruction *Br. Med. J.* **ii**, 89.

Inman, W.H.W. and Adelstein, A.M. (1969). The rise and fall of asthma mortality in England and Wales in relation to use of pressurised aerosols. *Lancet* **ii**, 279.

Jackson, R.T., Beaglehole, R., Rea, H.H. and Sutherland, D.C. (1982). Mortality from asthma: a new epidemic in New Zealand. *Br. Med. J.* **285**, 771.

Johnston, R.N., McNeill, R.S., Smith, D.H., Legge, J.S., and Fletcher, F. (1976). Chronic bronchitis—measurement and observations over 10 years. *Thorax* **31**, 25.

Johnstone, D.E. (1968). A study of the natural history of bronchial asthma in children. *Am. J. Dis. Child.* **115**, 213.

Kiernan, K.E., Colley, J.R.T., Douglas, J.W.B., and Reid, D.D. (1976). Chronic cough in young adults in relation to smoking habits, childhood, environment and chest illness. *Respiration* **33**, 236.

Lebowitz, M.D. (1980). Respiratory symptoms and disease related to alcohol consumption. *Am. Rev. Respir. Dis.* **123**, 16.

Lebowitz, M.D. and Burrows, B. (1976). Comparison of questionnaires: the BMRC and NHLI respiratory questionnaires and a new self-completion questionnaire. *J. Am. Rev. Resp. Dis.* **113**, 627.

Leese, W.L.B. (1956). An investigation into bronchitis. *Lancet* **ii**, 762.

Leigh, D. and Marley, E. (1967). *Bronchial asthma. A genetic, population and psychiatric study.* Pergamon Press, Oxford.

Logan, W.P.D. and Cushion, A.A. (1958). *Morbidity statistics from general practice Vol. 1. General.* Studies on medical and population subjects, No. 14. HMSO, London.

Martin, A.J., McLennan, L.A., Landau, L.I., and Phelan, P.D. (1980). The natural history of childhood asthma to adult life. *Br. Med. J.* **1**, 1397.

Medical Research Council (1960). Standardized questionnaire on respiratory symptoms. *Br. Med. J.* **ii**, 1665.

Medical Research Council (1965). Definition and classification of chronic bronchitis for clinical and epidemiological purposes. A report to the Medical Research Council by Their committee on the aetiology of chronic bronchitis. *Lancet* **i**, 775.

Meneely, G.R., Paul, O., Dorn, H.F., and Harrison, T.R. (1960). Cardiopulmonary semantics. *JAMA* **174**, 1628.

Miller, D.L. and Jones, R. (1963). A study of techniques for the examination of sputum in a field survey of chronic bronchitis. *Am. Rev. Resp. Dis.* **88**, 473.

Minette, A. (1979). *Epidemiology of chronic bronchitis.* Industrial health and medicine series No. 2. Commission of the European Communities, Luxembourg.

Mitchell, I., Inglis, H., and Simpson, H. (1976). Viral infection in wheezy bronchitis and asthma in children. *Arch. Dis. Child.* **51**, 707.

Mitchell, R.S., Maisel, J.C., Dart, G.A., and Silvers, G.W. (1971). The accuracy of the death certificate in reporting cause of death in adults, with special reference to chronic bronchitis and emphysema. *Am. Rev. Resp. Dis.* **104**, 844.

Office of Population Censuses and Surveys (1974). *Morbidity statistics from general practice. Second national study 1970–71.* Studies on medical and population subjects No. 26, HMSO, London.

OPCS (1980*a*). *Mortality Statistics, England and Wales 1978.* Series DH1, No. 6. HMSO, London.

OPCS (1980*b*). *Routine Mortality Statistics. Cause, 1978.* Series DH2, No. 5. HMSO, London.

Orie, N.G.M. and Sluiter, H.J. (eds.) (1961). *Bronchitis.* Royal Van Gorcum, Assen.

Orie, N.G.M., Sluiter, H.J., De Vries, K., Tammeling, G.J., and Withrop, J. (1961). The lost factor in bronchitis. In *Bronchitis* (ed. N.G.M. Orie and H.J. Sluiter) p. 57. Royal Van Gorcum, Assen.

Oswald, N.C., Harold, J.T., and Martin, W.J. (1953). Clinical pattern of chronic bronchitis. *Lancet* **ii**, 539.

Postgraduate Medical School (1951). Emphysema; clinicopathological conference No. 10. *Postgrad. Med. J.* **27**, 25.

Pullan, C.R. and Hey, E.N. (1982). Wheezing, asthma, and pulmonary dysfunction 10 years after infection with respiratory syncytial virus in infancy. *Br. Med. J.* **284**, 1665.

Royal College of Physicians (1977). *Smoking and health.* RCP, London.

Reid, D.D. and Rose, G.A. (1964). Assessing the comparability of mortality statistics. *Br. Med. J.* **ii**, 1437.

Samet, J.M. (1978). A historical and epidemiologic perspective on respiratory symptoms questionnaires. *Am. J. Epidemiol.* **108**, 435.

Saric, M., Lucic-Palaic, S., and Horton, R.J.M. (1977). Chronic non-specific lung disease and alcohol consumption. *Environ. Res.* **14**, 14.

Scadding, J.G. (1952). Introduction to symposium on chronic bronchitis. *Q.J.Med.* **21**, 460.

Sharp, J.T., Paul, O., McKean, H., and Best, W.R. (1973). A longitudinal study of bronchitic symptoms and spirometry in a middle-aged male, industrial population. *Am. Rev. Resp. Dis.* **108**, 1066.

Sibbald, B., Horn, M.E.C., and Gregg, I. (1980). A family study of the genetic basis of asthma and wheezy bronchitis. *Arch. Dis. Child.* **55**, 354.

Smith, J.M. (1966). Death from asthma. *Br. Med. J.* **i**, 1042.

Speizer, F.E. and Doll, R. (1968). A century of asthma deaths in young people. *Br. Med. J.* **iii**, 245.

Speizer, F.E. and Tager, I.B. (1979). Epidemiology of chronic mucus hypersecretion and obstructive airways disease. In *Epidemiological reviews Vol. 1* (ed. P.E. Sartwell) Johns Hopkins University Press, Baltimore.

Speizer, F.E., Doll, R., and Heaf, P. (1968). Observations on recent increase in mortality from asthma. *Br. Med. J.* **i**, 335.

Speizer, F.E., Doll, R., Heaf, P. and Strang, L.B. (1968). Investigation into use of drugs proceding death from asthma. *Dr. Med. J.* **i**, 339.

Stolley, P.D. (1972). Asthma mortality: why the United States was spared an epidemic of deaths due to asthma. *Am. Rev. Resp. Dis.* **105**, 883.

Stuart-Harris, C.H. (1968). Chronic bronchitis. *Abstr. World Med.* **42**, 649, 737.

Stuart-Harris, C.H. and Hanley, T. (1957). *Chronic bronchitis, emphysema and cor pulmonale.* Wright, Bristol.

Taussig, L. and Lebowitz, M. (1976). Cough and wheeze syndromes in children. (Abstract.) *Am. Rev. Resp. Dis.* **113, 114**, 45.

US Department of Health, Education and Welfare (1964). *Smoking and health.* US Government Printing Office, Washington, DC.

US Department of Health, Education and Welfare (1979). *The health consequences of smoking.* US Government Printing Office, Washington, DC.

US Department of Health and Human Services (1980). *Report of Task Force on Epidemiology of Respiratory Diseases. State of knowledge, problems, needs.* National Institutes of Health, Pub No. 81–2019, Washington, DC.

Williams, H.E. and McNicol, K.N. (1969). Prevalence, natural history and relationship of wheezy bronchitis and asthma in childhood. *Br. Med. J.* **iv**, 321.

Wittig, H.J., Cranford, N.J., and Glaser, J. (1959). The relationship between bronchiolitis and childhood asthma. *J. Allerg.* **30**, 19.

World Health Organization (1961). *Chronic cor-pulmonale: report of an expert committee.* Technical Report Series No. 213. WHO, Geneva.

10 Gastrointestinal disease

M.J.S. Langman and R.F.A. Logan

INTRODUCTION

This chapter considers the prospects for preventing chronic digestive disease; cancer, and infectious disease which constitutes the bulk of acute gastrointestinal disorders of which we have any understanding, are discussed elsewhere (Chapter 7 and Chapter 1 respectively). Chronic gastrointestinal illness presents peculiar problems for applying public health measures to reduce the risk of contracting disease or ameliorating its impact. Our understanding of causes is rudimentary. The scarcity of reliable comparative data makes it difficult to decide if particular illnesses present special problems in one place or seldom cause significant disability elsewhere. Furthermore, the variety and precision of diagnostic measures is changing rapidly. It would therefore be unwise to assume that illness which in the past was primarily diagnosed by radiographic means but now is being increasingly assessed by fibreoptic methods, will necessarily represent the same range and proportions of severity in both periods.

If, despite these problems, the value of public health measures in prevention is to be examined, the strengths and frailties of individual indicators of disease presence and activity should be examined. Peptic ulceration presents a paradigm of all the difficulties of assessment, and the limited means of reducing disease disability by public health measures.

PEPTIC ULCER

Disability due to gastric or duodenal ulceration presents a major health problem in western populations, where 10 per cent or more may be affected at some time in their lives. It is also a problem in many underdeveloped areas. Ulcer frequency varies greatly from time to time, and from place to place, reflecting the interplay of environmental and genetic influences – environmental factors being of critical importance.

Methods of assessment

Mortality rates

Death usually occurs from ulcer complications or as a sequel to an operation. Few die as a direct result of a peptic ulcer, but mortality rates rise steeply with advancing age. In the UK the chance of dying from peptic ulcer is several hundred-fold greater in people over 70 years of age than in those under 30

(Table 10.1). Therefore mortality statistics are most useful when assessing severe and complicated forms of peptic ulceration in the elderly. Factors which predispose to peptic ulcer differ in younger and older people. Age specific data for example indicate that whilst hospitalization rates from duodenal ulcer are falling steeply in younger people, they are rising in the elderly (Table 10.2). Individuals who die from peptic ulceration are likely to be those with severe ulcers. But the proportion of patients with severe ulcer that are certified as dying from ulcer disease may differ from time to time and from place to place. Pneumonia or pulmonary embolism in the post-operative period, for example, may be recorded as cause of death and not the ulcer disease, without which those conditions would never have supervened.

Table 10.1. *Annual death rates per 100 000 per year from peptic ulcer in England and Wales, 1973–77*

	Age (years)					
	25–34	35–44	45–54	55–64	65–74	75+
Ulcer						
Gastric	0.2	0.6	2.2	7.2	20.2	57.3
Duodenal	0.2	1.0	3.4	8.5	23.5	58.6

Source: Coggon *et al.* (1981).

Table 10.2. *Annual admission rates per 100 000 per year from duodenal ulcer in England and Wales*

	Age (years) Men		Women		Age (years) Men		Women	
	25–34	35–44	25–34	35–44	65–74	75+	65–74	75+
1958–62	19.4	27.3	2.7	3.9	44.6	45.3	6.8	10.8
1973–77	10.1	16.1	0.8	3.5	33.6	45.9	9.9	17.3
% change	−48	−41	−70	−10	−25	+1	+46	+60

Source: Coggon *et al.* (1981).

Autopsy surveys

Careful scrutiny of the stomach and duodenum at autopsy can give reliable information about the current frequency of ulcer and about past frequency as judged by stigmata of previous surgery. But it may be difficult to decide if there is duodenal or gastric scarring due to previous ulceration, and individual judgement may vary from one time or place to another. Matters are complicated in two more ways. First, the group of people in whom autopsy examination is performed do not necessarily form a reasonable sample of those dying. Secondly, the autopsy rate in many countries is falling steadily, and it would be dangerous to assume that the findings at a certain time when, say, two-thirds of all those dying in hospital were subjected to autopsy can be simply related to findings at a time when a third or less are being so examined.

Hospital admission rates

The reasons why patients with ulcer are admitted to hospital are complex. Factors influencing such a decision include the severity and duration of symptoms, the presence of complications, physician judgement or prejudice about the best means of treatment, and the range of treatments available.

Figure 10.1 shows data collected in the US in non-federal short-stay hospitals and in a hospital group covered by an insurance scheme. Data collected from the non-federal hospitals (CPHA and NCHS) show a clear fall in admission rates at a time when figures for admissions to an insurance based service (KPMCP) were not changing. These differences were largely accounted for by changes in the admission rates for uncomplicated ulcer disease, showing the dominant effect of physician opinion about management methods.

Another difficulty has arisen through the advent of new potent drug treatments. The recent fall in the general admission rate for ulcer disease in the UK has been due in part to the widespread adoption of out-patient histamine H_2

antagonist treatment. Figures obtained recently in the UK almost certainly reflect this trend (Wyllie *et al.* 1981).

Perforation rates have been commonly used as indices of ulcer frequency. This assumes that perforated ulcer forms a fixed proportion of ulcer disease and that the chances of ulcer perforation have not changed with time or since new treatments have been introduced. These assumptions may be justified, but have not been examined formally.

Sickness certificates

Observed changes in data for returns of disability may be due to alterations in fashions of labelling as much as to changes in disease patterns. The recent fall in hospital in-patient diagnoses of acute appendicitis has been nicely balanced by a rise in the numbers of cases labelled as abdominal pain of unknown origin (Fig. 10.2). Similarly a fall in the use of the label of dyspepsia has occurred at a time when labels of a psychiatric nature have been increasingly commonly used.

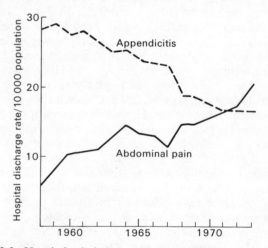

Fig. 10.2. Hospital admissions with appendicitis and abdominal pain of uncertain origin. Figures estimated from data of the Hospital In-Patient Enquiry.

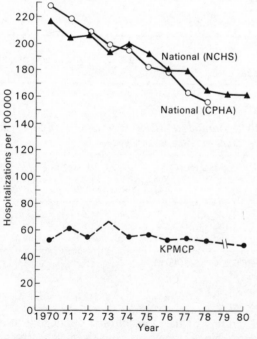

Fig. 10.1. Hospital admissions per 100000 people each year with peptic ulcer to national non-federal short-stay hospitals as measured by two different indices (NCHS and CPHA) and to an insurance-based hospital group in California (KPMCP). (Data of Kurata *et al.* (1982) reproduced by kind permission of the authors and of *Gastroenterology*).

Diagnostic rates

Very few investigators have examined the overall frequency with which diagnoses of ulcer have been made over time. It is doubtful whether any reliable data could, in fact, be obtained. The increase in the availability and sophistication of diagnostic methods militates against the possibility. The last 20 years have seen the double-contrast barium meal replace single-contrast examinations, with an attendant rise in the chance of detecting small mucosal lesions. Latterly the advent and increasing use of fibreoptic endoscopy has further complicated matters.

Reliance upon any single index of disease frequency is likely to be misleading and corroborative evidence should be sought whenever possible. Analyses of ulcer perforation rates are, however, the best single measure of changes in the general burden imposed by ulcer disease.

Measures influencing disease frequency or severity

Social factors

In the past gastric ulcer was more common in the poor than the rich, while the reverse was true of duodenal ulcer. However, the social class patterns for gastric and for duodenal ulcer are now much the same. Table 10.3 compares mortality and morbidity patterns according to social class in the UK. In general terms ulcer seems to be about twice as common in those of low social class.

Table 10.3. *Ulcer mortality* and morbidity according to social class in UK*

	Social class				
	I	II	III	IV	V
(a) Mortality 1959–63					
Gastric	46	58	94	106	109
Duodenal	70	84	113	102	136
(b) Morbidity					
Gastric					
Observed	6	11	12	13	28
Expected	2	11	30	14	7
Duodenal					
Observed	13	41	125	136	158
Expected	14	80	218	108	52

*As standardized mortality ratios.
Source: (a) Registrar General (1971); (b) Litton and Murdoch (1963).

The reasons for these patterns are not easily explained. Ulcer might be expected to cause death in those who are disadvantaged socially and hence less likely to obtain high quality medical care. However, 50 years ago higher mortality rates for duodenal ulcer were obtained in those of social class I than in those of low social class. The current common trend of morbidity and mortality patterns suggests that they are describing real differences.

Examination of occupational data does not suggest that any particular type of job is associated with liability to ulcer. Smokers are in general more prone to peptic ulceration than non-smokers, and the social class distribution of ulcer might simply reflect heavier smoking in those of lower social class. However, when social class was judged by level of educational attainment, peptic ulceration was found to be more common in smokers than non-smokers at each educational level (Table 10.4), and Massachusetts physicians who smoked were more liable to peptic ulceration than those who did not smoke (Monson and MacMahon 1969).

Table 10.4. *Smoking habits, ulcer frequency, and educational attainment in men*

	Elementary school only	High or trade school	College
Smokers [% with ulcer]	15.1	13.3	10.7
Non-smokers [% with ulcer]	7.7	6.2	6.1

Source: Friedman *et al.* (1974).

Stress

Despite many attempts to relate the development, complications, or exacerbations of ulcer to stress, no coherent body of evidence has emerged to support the concept. Polednak (1974) noted that certain somatic symptoms, notably palpitation and sleeplessness were associated with the later development of ulcer, but these were two against many, and Piper *et al.* (1978, 1981*a*), concluded that no association could be detected with stressful life events for either gastric or duodenal ulcer.

Smoking

There is clear evidence that smokers are more likely to die from peptic ulceration than non-smokers, that ulcer is likely to be found more often in smokers than non-smokers, and that duodenal ulcers are less likely to heal during histamine H_2 antagonist treatment if patients are smokers (Hammond and Horn 1958; Doll and Hill 1964; Freidman *et al.* 1974; Gugler *et al.* 1982). Examination of the smoking habits of Massachusetts physicians has suggested that those smokers who had an ulcer were likely to have smoked more heavily, and from an earlier age than those who did not have ulcers (Monson 1970).

The association of peptic ulcer with smoking is independent of other associations with coffee and cola-type soft drink consumption (Paffenbarger *et al.* 1974).

Alcohol consumption

Despite widespread belief that those who drink alcoholic beverages are more likely to develop peptic ulcers than those who do not, no confirmatory evidence has yet been obtained. Harvard and Pennsylvania students who admitted to drinking alcohol whilst undergraduates proved to be no more liable to later ulceration than those who were teetotal (Paffenbarger *et al.* 1974). Alcoholic cirrhotics have not been found to be more liable to peptic ulceration than other cirrhotics (Tabaqchali and Dawson 1964).

Drug intake

Corticosteroids, aspirin, and other non-steroidal anti-inflammatory agents have long been accepted clinically as predisposing to peptic ulceration. The general evidence is difficult to interpret.

Corticosteroids

A comprehensive review of all data collected in controlled clinical trials suggested that those randomly allocated treatment with corticosteroids were only slightly more likely to develop ulcers than those receiving placebo treatment (Conn and Blitzer 1976). Within the total group, those receiving high doses of corticosteroids may have been at increased risk, but there is insufficient data to allow reliable judgement.

Aspirin

A high frequency of gastric ulcer, particularly with perforation, was detected in middle-aged women living in New South Wales, and attribute to habitual intake of compound analgesic preparations containing aspirin, phenacetin, and caffein (Gillies and Skyring 1969). A large number of retrospective hospital based case-control studies also suggest that aspirin takers are particularly liable to suffer from haematemesis or melaena. The strength of association has been contested, mainly on the grounds that hospital controls may be inappropriate and that aspirin intake which was causal of bleeding could not be separated from intake consequential upon the presence of symptoms (Langman 1970).

Analysis of results in trials of aspirin treatment in the prevention of cardiovascular disease suggests that dyspepsia, proven ulcer, and ulcer complications are more common in takers of the active drug (Table 10.5). Comparisons of aspirin and paracetamol intake (the latter used as a drug control) have given conflicting results. In Australia, aspirin and paracetamol intake were associated with identical risks, though the latter is not believed to harm the stomach (Piper *et al.* 1981*b*). In the UK, however, upper gastrointestinal bleeding was judged to be about twice as likely to occur in habitual aspirin takers as in habitual paracetamol takers who were thought to have no increased risk (Coggon *et al.* 1982). Estimates of actual risk are difficult to make. In the Boston Collaborative Drug Enquiry heavy consumers were judged to have a risk of the order of 10 per 100000 per year (Levy 1974).

Table 10.5. *Episodes of haematemesis or melaena recorded during controlled trials of therapy for thromboembolic diseases*

	AMIS	CDPR	PARIS
Aspirin	8.2	6.2	6.4
Placebo	4.9	4.6	2.5

Figures recorded the percentage of individuals reporting such events. Each trial lasted approximately three years, and aspirin dosage was in the range 900–1000 mg daily.

AMIS – Aspirin, myocardial infarction study research group (1980).
CDPR – Coronary drug project research group (1976).
PARIS – Persantin–aspirin reinfarction study research group (1980).

Non-steroidal anti-inflammatory agents

No satisfactory analyses have been undertaken; a high frequency of perforated ulcer has been detected in indomethacin consumers, but no properly controlled data have been presented. In the UK perforated ulcer seems to have increased in frequency in elderly women, whilst it has fallen in other groups. Whether the difference is due to non-steroidal anti-inflammatory drug intake by elderly women remains a matter for speculation (Coggon *et al.* 1981).

Associated disease

There is an increased chance of having a second disease detected when already under medical surveillance for another illness. This makes it difficult to decide if a higher ulcer frequency in those with another specific illness represents a true increase or not. Problems of interpretation have been extensively discussed (Donaldson 1975; Elashoff and Grossman 1980).

Conditions claimed to be associated with increased liability to ulcer include degenerative vascular disease, chronic lung disorders, renal disease, endocrine abnormalities, joint disorders, and hepatic cirrhosis. Those associations which seem to hold good under close scrutiny include chronic renal disease when undergoing dialysis or after transplantation (possibly a drug effect), hepatic cirrhosis, and hyperparathyroidism, the latter two being less certain (Barrera 1973; Shepherd *et al.* 1973; Langman and Cooke 1976).

One intriguing suggestion has been that those with low blood pressure, but within the normal range, may be more liable to develop peptic ulcers (Medalie *et al.* 1970; Paffenbarger *et al.* 1974).

Diet

The role of nutritional factors is discussed more fully elsewhere. Despite the likelihood that dietary factors are of central significance in affecting liability to upper gastrointestinal disease, there is little supportive evidence. Those who drink coffee and cola-type soft drinks may be more liable to later ulcers, whilst milk drinkers may be relatively protected (Paffenbarger *et al.* 1974). The buffering capacities of foods vary, proteins being better buffers but more likely to stimulate gastric secretion, whilst carbohydrate foods are indifferent buffers but are less promoters of acid output. No useful data are available to show whether specific dietary items or major changes in protein, carbohydrate, or fat intake materially alter liability to peptic ulceration. An increase in dietary fibre intake has been claimed to protect against the development of ulcer. This is based upon comparative analyses of ulcer frequency in places where dietary fibre intake is thought to differ markedly. A recent controlled clinical study also suggests that relapse of duodenal ulcer is less likely to occur in those taking dietary fibre supplements (Rydning *et al.* 1982). Even if true, it is unclear whether it is the quantity or a specific quality of dietary fibre that is important.

Prospects for prevention

We remain largely ignorant of the cause of peptic ulceration, and if we were to capitalize upon current knowledge it seems unlikely that we would materially influence liability to ulcer. However, alterations in disease patterns during the last hundred years indicate that the environmental factors which predispose to ulcer have changed greatly with the almost sole occurrence of gastric ulcer before the twentieth century, and the eclipse of gastric ulcer by duodenal ulcer thereafter.

Changes have been rapid, suggesting that environmental factors may only have to act for a short time before altering disease frequency. Table 10.6 shows the rapid increase in gastric ulcer frequency as a cause of death in the elderly in the UK between 1912 and 1924. Changes may well be continuing. Although in the USA duodenal ulcer frequency, as judged by admission rates, may not be altering (Elashoff and Grossman 1981), age-specific data from the UK suggest that there has been a remarkable fall in the frequency of ulcer perforation, particularly gastric ulcer in the young (Coggon *et al.* 1981). The reasons are not understood – better treatment does not seem plausible, and genuine decrease of ulcer frequency seems likely.

Data obtained in tropical countries indicates that duodenal

Table 10.6. *Ulcer deaths in England and Wales*

Age		1912 No.	Sex ratio M:W	1924 No.	Sex ratio M:W
Under 35 years	Men	182	0.5:1.0	151	1.4:1.0
	Women	338		109	
35 or more years	Men	691	1.1:1.0	1219	2.0:1.0
	Women	635		620	

Source: Registrar General (1914, 1925).

ulcer may be common in some areas and rare in others, patterns not necessarily reflecting the impact of western cultural patterns (Tovey and Tunstall 1975), and prospects for prevention there are indifferent.

INFLAMMATORY BOWEL DISEASE

Materially the same problems exist for the examination of changes in the frequency of inflammatory bowel disease as for peptic ulceration. In addition, there are no absolute criteria by which Crohn's disease and ulcerative colitis can be separated with reliability.

Methods of assessment

Mortality rates

Measurement of death rates concentrates upon severe and complicated disease, with post-operative deaths and deaths in the elderly forming particularly important groups. Despite difficulties of interpretation it is worth noting that in the UK, death rates and hospital discharge rates for Crohn's disease have shown a similar upward trend in recent years (Miller *et al.* 1974; Langman 1979).

Hospital admission rates

In the past, most, if not all, patients with Crohn's disease were admitted to hospital at some time during the course of their illness. Whether this is still true, in a period when the range of medical treatments has increased, is unclear. By contrast, ulcerative colitis varies markedly in severity; those with disease of limited extent, who form the majority, are seldom now admitted to hospital, and disease is more likely to remain limited in extent and severity than not. Disease which was formerly managed in its acute phases in hospital may now be being increasingly treated in out-patient clinics, hence largely unchanging admission rates, which seem to prevail in the UK, do not necessarily indicate that disease frequency is unchanging.

Admission rates with Crohn's disease, and also incidence rates have risen markedly in those north-western European countries which have accumulated sets of data in the last 20 years (Fig. 10.3). The general belief is that the increases reflect true rises in disease frequency, although there can be little doubt that changing fashions in diagnostic labelling have also contributed. Crohn's colitis was a virtually undescribed entity 20 years ago, and some, if a minor part of any apparent increase in disease frequency could be due to the use of

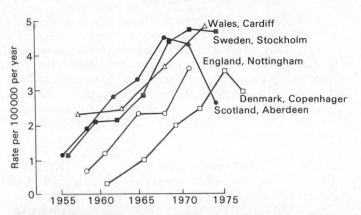

Fig. 10.3. Changes in the incidence of Crohn's disease in Europe. Figures as average rates per 100 000 population per year. Sources: Denmark data of Binder *et al.* (1982); England data of Miller *et al.* (1974); Scotland data of Kyle and Stark (1980); Sweden data of Hellers (1981); Wales data of Mayberry *et al.* (1979).

Crohn's disease than ulcerative colitis as a diagnosis. However, the rise in frequency of Crohn's disease has not been attended by a fall in the frequency of ulcerative colitis.

Factors affecting disease patterns

We are largely ignorant of the causes of chronic inflammatory bowel disease. Both Crohn's disease and ulcerative colitis seem to be associated with western cultural patterns, and their frequency contrasts with the rarity of infective dysenteric illness in those countries.

Social patterns

The trend, if any, in social class distribution of Crohn's disease and ulcerative colitis, is towards a rather greater frequency of disease in the more affluent. However, this has not been recorded consistently, and we cannot be sure that differences do not simply reflect an increased likelihood of diagnosis in those of higher social class. No specific occupational group seems to be at special risk.

Predisposing factors

Diet

No clear evidence has emerged to associate liability to ulcerative colitis with specific dietary items. A high intake of sugars, however, is associated with liability to Crohn's disease (Martini and Brandes 1976; Miller *et al.* 1976; Thornton *et al.* 1979).

Convincing evidence is hard to obtain, but increased sugar intake seems to have preceded the onset of disease symptoms, and is not explainable by altered taste sensitivity. The same pattern has not been detected for ulcerative colitis. Inevitably it has been claimed that reduced dietary fibre intake predisposes to both ulcerative colitis and Crohn's disease, but no clear support for this view has yet been obtained.

Infection

An infectious aetiology has been a favourite subject for investigation. particularly in recent years, for Crohn's disease.

A multiplicity of experimental studies has failed to yield a coherent pattern of results, and the few epidemiological investigations undertaken have yielded negative findings. If Crohn's disease or ulcerative colitis are persistent and delayed responses to infection, then we have no knowledge of what the causal agents may be. A range of 'new' pathogens, such as *Campylobacter* and clostridial infections has generated attention, but none have emerged as likely causal agents.

Smoking

It has been shown that ulcerative colitis, but not Crohn's disease, is associated with not smoking (Harries *et al.* 1982; Jick and Walker 1983). The basis for such an association is unclear and careful control for social class factors is needed before it is accepted. It is worth noting that the observed mortality of colitic patients from lung cancer is lower than the expected figure (Gyde *et al.* 1982).

Childhood influences

Crohn's disease and ulcerative colitis have their maximum impact in early adult life, and therefore causal factors must be sought in early life. The only associated factor which has so far emerged is early weaning (Hellers 1981), although the evidence is not strong. It is uncertain whether control for social factors might diminish or eliminate the association, although results obtained in this large Swedish study suggest not.

Psychological factors

No coherent body of evidence exists to support the view that liability to inflammatory bowel disease is materially influenced by psychological factors. A study conducted in Baltimore suggested that, if anything, individuals with symptoms of bowel irritability were more likely to have a background of stress (Mendeloff *et al.* 1970).

Functional abdominal symptoms

Functional bowel disease accounts for by far the largest proportion of abdominal complaints. Approximately four times as many people are investigated fruitlessly for abdominal complaints as are found to have specific causes. Matters are complicated because functional complaints tend to be vague, poorly localized, and variable in pattern. Further problems arise because enumeration of individuals with such complaints will yield figures which differ according to the availability of diagnostic facilities, the expense which attends the obtaining of those facilities, and the prevailing attitude to the use of functional diagnostic labels. Thus the fall in diagnoses of appendicitis in the UK which has been balanced by a rise in diagnoses of non-specific symptoms may reflect real trends in both, or the application of more stringent criteria for the diagnosis of appendicitis as time has passed.

The occurrence of functional upper gastrointestinal symptoms is widely attributed to excessive smoking, alcohol consumption, and irregular eating patterns, but convincing evidence to support these views is hard to obtain. By contrast, lower bowel symptoms, usually of alternating constipation and diarrhoea, and often with associated pain and radio-logically demonstrable diverticular disease, have been ascribed to fibre-deficient diets in western communities. Although formal controlled trials and within-population group evidence is relatively scanty, international comparisons strongly suggest that functional lower bowel symptoms, the occurrence of piles and possibly of lower abdominal herniae are substantially less in areas where diets are based upon unrefined carbohydrate foods. The case favouring such views is extensively discussed by Burkitt and Trowell (1975).

APPENDICITIS

Appendicectomy for acute appendicitis continues to be the commonest emergency operation in the UK and most other western countries. Provided some allowance is made for removal of normal appendices and for elective appendicectomy, disease frequency can be monitored using operation rates. Many patients (sometimes up to 50 per cent) admitted to hospital with possible acute appendicitis have functional abdominal symptoms and several studies have found that a diagnosis of acute appendicitis is confirmed in only about three-quarters of acute appendicectomies (Donnan and Lambert 1976).

Mortality rates are now less useful in disease monitoring, since current case fatality rates are 0.5 per cent in the younger age groups and rise to over 5 per cent in the over 65-year-olds. In England and Wales mortality rates have fallen steadily since reaching a peak in the 1930s and predominantly reflect improvements in medical care (Donnan and Lambert 1976).

Disease patterns

A striking feature of the epidemiology of the disease was the rapid increase in incidence in Europe and North America in the early part of this century. In England and Wales, mortality rates between 1901 and 1915 rose from 40 to 70 per million at a time when better treatment was reducing case fatality rates. This suggests a several-fold increase in incidence.

The pattern of disease in countries where appendicitis is common is fairly uniform, the peak incidence being between the ages of 5 and 25 years, with a similar rate in men and women (Table 10.7). In western countries appendicitis was initially more common in the more affluent socio-economic groups, but in the UK this gradient, as measured by mortality rates, had disappeared by 1960 (Donnan and Lambert 1976; Barker and Liggins 1981).

In contrast, Burkitt (1971) has drawn attention to the rarity of acute appendicitis among natives of rural Africa and in other rural areas of the Third World. A recent survey of 17 000

Table 10.7. *Appendicectomy rates per 100 000 in Scotland, 1975*

	All ages	Age (years) 0–4	5–14	15–24	25–44	45–64	65–74	75+
Males	184	60	377	345	132	70	58	55
Females	186	32	293	440	191	83	57	41

Source: Scottish Hospital In-Patient Statistics (1975).

16–18-year-olds in South Africa found the prevalence of appendicectomy to be 0.6 per cent in rural African, 0.7 per cent in urban African, 2.9 per cent in Indian and 10.5 per cent in white populations (Segal *et al.* 1982). In countries such as Nigeria and Kenya, where the disease is now appearing in the native population, it is first being reported in the more affluent natives of urban areas (Burkitt 1971).

Recently, in the UK, the US, and other western countries, hospital admissions for appendicitis have been declining (Table 10.8). This is due in part to changes in diagnostic coding practices, transferring appendicitis discharges to abdominal pain discharges (Fig. 10.2). Nevertheless, the decline is of the same order for both sexes of all ages, and it may be a real decline in incidence.

Table 10.8. *Appendicitis discharges per 100 000 in England and Wales*

Year	1968	1970	1972	1974	1976	1978
Males	211	197	182	170	169	144
Females	201	190	179	162	158	138

Aetiological factors

Appendicitis is thought to result from obstruction of the appendix lumen by faecoliths which may be formed more readily on a low-fibre diet (Royal College of Physicians, 1980). Surprisingly, few studies of diet in appendicits cases have been reported and, as yet, no deficit in dietary fibre intake has been proven (Cove-Smith and Langman 1975). Psychological factors have been postulated, but Creed (1981) found that threatening life-events were only more common preceding appendicectomy when the appendix removed was found to be normal.

Prospects for prevention

These rapid changes in appendicitis incidence underline the importance of environmental factors in its aetiology. While these are likely to be dietary, a simple deficit of dietary fibre or one of its components does not account for the recent decrease in incidence in many western countries.

DIVERTICULAR DISEASE OF THE COLON

In western countries colonic diverticulosis is an increasingly common condition, such that the prevalence at age 80 years is often over 50 per cent (Almy and Howell 1980). Possibly only a tenth of cases will ever develop symptoms and for the remainder the condition is no more than an anatomical curiosity. It is not possible to predict if and when diverticulosis will produce symptoms.

Most estimates of prevalence have been obtained from either autopsy data or routine barium enema examinations. Both sources have obvious limitations, and tend to over-estimate prevalence. An X-ray technique suitable for population surveys, using oral barium and a single film at 48 hours, has been described, but as yet has been used only in a few studies (Manousos *et al.* 1967; Foster *et al.* 1978).

Mortality data for diverticular disease are of limited value because case fatality rates are low, and any change is as likely to reflect improvements in medical care or differing diagnostic coding practices as changes in the disease itself. Hospital admission data are similarly difficult to interpret, particularly as the indications for admission to hospital and colectomy are ill-defined. In Scotland, depending on age, only 4–14 per cent of cases admitted to hospital, even in surgical units, have surgery performed (Chalmers *et al.* 1983).

Disease patterns

Like appendicitis, the striking feature of the epidemiology of diverticular disease is the great increase in prevalence that has taken place in western countries in the twentieth century and the continuing low prevalence in less developed countries. Between 1923 and 1963, the mortality from diverticular disease in England and Wales rose from 2 to 25 per million with a plateau during and immediately after the Second World War and food rationing (Painter and Burkitt 1971).

In countries where diverticular disease is common, the prevalence is similar in men and women, being rare before the age of 30 years and rising sharply at 60 years and over (Table 10.9). No relationship with socio-economic status has been determined.

Table 10.9. *Diverticular disease: prevalence by age in Oxford, England*

Age	45–49	50–54	55–59	60–64	65–69	70 +
Prevalence (%)	12	20	30	33	48	65

Source: Gear *et al.* (1979).

Although many of the estimates are anecdotal, diverticular disease is almost non-existent in rural Africans (Painter and Burkitt 1971). In these areas diverticulosis was detected in less than one in 1000 autopsies or barium enemas, and the agreement is so consistent that age, under-reporting or biased selection are insufficient explanations. In urban living Africans in South Africa and Kenya, diverticular disease is now being reported with increased frequency (Calder 1979; Segal and Walker 1982).

Factors influencing disease frequency

To account for the geographical distribution attention has focused mainly on dietary factors. Painter and Burkitt (1971) have suggested that diverticular disease is a disease of western civilization, related to a deficiency in dietary fibre. This hypothesis is supported by a recent study of 56 English vegetarians (mean dietary fibre intake of 41.5 g/day) whose prevalence of asymptomatic diverticular disease was 12 per cent, compared to 33 per cent in a matched control population (mean dietary fibre intake 21.4 g/day) (Gear *et al.* 1979). Two case-control studies of symptomatic diverticular disease have also found lower fibre intakes in cases than controls (Brodribb and Humphreys 1976; Segal and Walker 1982).

Other factors such as obesity, arteriosclerosis, and weakness of the colonic muscle, once considered responsible, are now regarded as secondary associations. In particular, diverticular disease has been shown to be associated with other diseases of western civilization, such as ischaemic heart disease and gallstones (Almy and Howell 1980), as well as haemorrhoids, varicose veins, and hiatal hernia.

Prospects for prevention

Although a deficiency of dietary fibre is probably not the sole aetiological factor, the evidence for its central role is stronger than for any other disease where it has been implicated. At least one randomized controlled trial has shown benefit in symptomatic diverticular disease (Brodribb and Humphreys 1976). On these grounds recommendations to increase dietary fibre intake can be supported.

COELIAC DISEASE

Unlike other chronic digestive diseases the aetiology of coeliac disease is relatively well understood, as is indicated by its alternative name of gluten-sensitive enteropathy. Dietary gluten, the protein fraction of wheat, rye, barley, and oats, is essential to the development of the disease. When gluten is eliminated from the diet the characteristic intestinal villous atrophy recovers, often completely, and the disease remits. Gluten intolerance as demonstrated by the development of villous atrophy is believed to be life-long and in most coeliacs reintroduction of gluten leads to recurrence of villous atrophy within six months.

Genetic factors predisposing to coeliac disease are well recognized. Family studies have consistently found that 10–15 per cent of first-degree relatives have villous atrophy, which is often asymptomatic (Pěna 1981). Genetic studies have shown a relative risk for HLA type B8 of between 5 and 7, and for HLA type DR3 of between 8 and 14.

However, the fact that 6 of 15 monozygotic twins reported have been discordant for coeliac disease and the variable delay in recurrence of villous atrophy after gluten reintroduction both point to the importance of other unidentified environmental factors.

Methods of assessment

The range of clinical disease is considerable and for many years coeliac disease may be asymptomatic or produce only minor symptoms. Mortality data are of little value since coeliacs have only a small increase in mortality, which is rarely due to coeliac disease itself, and post-mortem autolysis makes autopsy surveys impossible (Logan *et al.* 1982). At present no methods of diagnosis are suitable for population surveys. This means that, as for inflammatory bowel disease, data on incidence and prevalence are dependent on series of hospital diagnosed cases which are affected by varying thresholds for investigation. The steadily increasing estimates of prevalence in the UK are almost certainly a consequence of

increased use of jejunal biopsy rather than any change in incidence (Swinson and Levi 1980; Logan *et al.* 1983).

Patterns of disease

Figures for prevalence of coeliac disease in childhood have been reported from many European countries (Table 10.10). There are less data on prevalence in adult life which, in view of the low mortality, might be of the same order or greater than the prevalence in childhood. Age-specific prevalence data in adulthood are almost certainly modified by a secular effect resulting from improved ascertainment of a disease whose severity and likelihood of diagnosis varies through life (McConnell, McConnell, Spiegelhalter, and Langman, unpublished data).

Making allowance for varying ascertainment, the prevalence of symptomatic coeliac disease in northern Europe is between 100 and 200 per 100 000. There are few figures on the prevalence of coeliac disease in North America and Australasia. While it does occur in these countries, from anecdotal accounts, it is clearly less common. Coeliac disease has been found in Asians in Britain (Nelson *et al.* 1973), but has not been reported in the Mongoloid or Negroid races.

Table 10.10. *Coeliac disease prevalence**

Region	Period	No./100 000	No. of cases
Childhood			
Co. Galway, Ireland	1960–78	180	267
Graz, Austria	1969–77	203	205
Basle, Switzerland	1966–75	86	354
Malmö, Sweden	1966–75	102	34
Copenhagen, Denmark	1971–79	73	35
Derby, England	1965–72	95	24
Edinburgh, Scotland	1965–75	90	180
All ages			
Linkoping, Sweden	1980	38 (58)*	48
Edinburgh, Scotland	1979	61*	469

*Includes cases of dermatitis herpetiformis.
Source: Hallert *et al.* (1981); McConnell (1981); Logan *et al.* (1983).

Other factors affecting incidence

Recently several sources in the UK have suggested a decline in the prevalence of coeliac disease in children. The decline appears to date from the mid-1970s after a peak in prevalence that probably resulted from increasing use of jejunal biopsy in children (Fig. 10.4). Two factors that might account for this are, first, the increase in the proportion of women breast-feeding, and, secondly, the introduction of gluten-free baby foods. Both will tend to delay the introduction of dietary gluten, the time of which has been found to correlate with the age of onset in infant cases.

Prevention

If delaying the introduction of dietary gluten is beneficial, then public health measures to encourage this pattern of

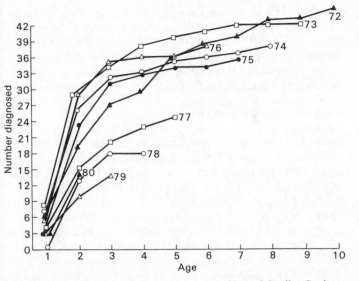

Fig. 10.4. Cumulative numbers of new members of Coeliac Society by age of onset for birth years 1972–80. Source: (unpublished data from McConnell *et al.* (1983).

infant feeding should reduce prevalence in childhood. Whether this will prevent the disease or merely postpone the onset of overt disease into adulthood remains to be determined.

PANCREATITIS

The frequency of pancreatic disease is difficult to determine. Acute illness associated with grossly raised serum amylase levels is readily detected, but lesser varieties of acute disease may have no clear markers of occurrence, and the diagnosis of chronic disease in the absence of gross pancreatic calcification is dependent upon the use of sophisticated examination procedures of doubtful sensitivity and specificity. The few sets of data available, give incidence rates for acute pancreatitis of between 5 and 12 per 100 000 per year with mortality rates of about one-tenth of these levels, and the incidence of chronic pancreatitis as approximately a third of that of acute disease. Data from non-European countries show that disease may be common in tropical areas, such as South India, where gross calcific pancreatitis is regularly seen.

Factors influencing disease frequency

Alcohol intake

In those areas where alcohol consumption is heavy, pancreatitis and also cirrhosis tend to be common. But, when clinical series from different areas are compared, the frequency with which disease is attributed to alcohol intake can vary from less than 5 per cent in the UK to almost 90 per cent in France (Howat 1963; Sarles *et al.* 1965). Sets of figures obtained in single clinical series should not necessarily be taken to apply uniformly. Differences may be partially, and sometimes largely, attributed to the source from which the patients are collected, whether charity, general or private hospitals, and to

vagaries of questioning technique. Thus in the US, less than a quarter, and almost nine-tenths of disease has been ascribed to alcohol intake.

However, in tropical areas pancreatitis occurs commonly in places where little or no alcohol is drunk.

Gallstones

These are discussed below. There is no evidence that there are any special peculiarities about gallstone disease associated with pancreatitis.

Nutrition

No specific nutritional factors have been associated with liability to pancreatitis. Claims in western countries of an association with protein or fat intake accord ill with the suggestion from tropical areas that malnutrition is of significance.

Drug-induced disease

Acute pancreatitis has been said to occur following treatment with, *inter alia*, corticosteroid drugs, analgesic agents, oral contraceptives, and diuretics. Almost all these claims rest upon anecdotal evidence, and taken overall it seems unlikely that drug-induced disease accounts for more than a very small proportion of the total.

Other factors

If there are other important environmental factors, and the general lack of aetiological information suggests that there must be, then they are unknown. It has been persistently suggested that viral infections can cause pancreatitis. Mumps virus could account for a very small proportion of cases of idiopathic, non-gallstone, non-alcoholic pancreatitis, but little is known about other possible causes.

GALLSTONES (CHOLELITHIASIS)

In western countries gallstones, like colonic diverticuloses, are extremely common, with a prevalence in the elderly approaching a third or more (Table 10.11). In common with diverticular disease, the relationship between the presence of gallstones and the development of symptoms is poorly understood. If cholecystectomy rates are any guide, then symptomatic gallstone disease is increasing in many countries. Even so, from combining prevalence data and cholecystectomy rates it is probable that over a half of gallstones never produce symptoms.

Gallstones contain varying proportions of cholesterol and bile pigments and by tradition have been classified as being

Table 10.11. *Gallstones: autopsy prevalence by age in Dundee, Scotland, 1953–73*

Age	30–39	40–49	50–59	60–69	70–79	80–89	90+
Prevalence (%)							
Men	1	4.4	6.2	9.9	15.2	17.9	24.4
Women	6	12.0	15.8	25.4	28.9	30.9	35.4

Source: Bateson and Bouchier (1975).

cholesterol, pigment, or mixed stones. In western countries the majority are mixed and by weight consist of 75 per cent or more of cholesterol. Few epidemiological studies distinguish the types and, from the evidence available, any recent increases have been in cholesterol-rich stones. Formation of cholesterol-rich stones is believed to be a four-stage process involving: (i) an individual with the genetic propensity or metabolic abnormality that allows; (ii) the production of bile saturated with cholesterol; (iii) the initiation of stone formation; and (iv) stone growth.

Methods of assessment

Surveys

Data on the prevalence of gallstones have been obtained mainly from autopsy surveys. Once formed, gallstones do not dissolve spontaneously. Besides the obvious weakness that autopsied deaths may not be a representative sample of the general population, surveys also assume consistent examination and recording of the state of the gallbladder.

As yet few population surveys have been performed, although surveys are possible using a modified oral cholecystogram. One study using this method was marred by a non-response rate of 35 per cent (Bainton *et al.* 1976). The recent introduction of ultrasound to detect gallstones should improve the acceptability of population surveys and enable confirmation of available autopsy data.

Hospital admission and operation rates

Measurement of disease using cholecystectomy rates seems logical, but the complex relationship between the presence of gallstones, the development of symptoms, and eventual cholecystectomy creates problems. In approximately a third of cases, symptoms continue after cholecystectomy, indicating that gallstones were not the cause. Hospital admission data are further complicated by the fact that several admissions may occur before cholecystectomy is performed. This was normal practice until recently. Surgeons are now advocating cholecystectomy during the first admission.

Mortality rates

Death from gallstones or their complications is now uncommon. In Dundee more patients died from postoperative complications of cholecystectomy than from the complications of untreated gallstones (Bateson and Bouchier 1975). Mortality rates are therefore of little value in assessing prevalence. Changes in mortality rates probably reflect a combination of improvements in medical care, declining case fatality, and the increasing frequency of cholecystectomy in the elderly.

Disease patterns

Geographic

According to autopsy data, there are great variations in gallstone prevalence, from high in western countries, such as the UK, US, and Scandinavia, and low in many African and Third World nations. Within each country prevalence is greatest in elderly women (over 60 years). Using this as a measure of gallstone proneness, prevalence in this age group ranges from Chile – 64 per cent, Sweden – 61 per cent, Czechoslovakia – 55 per cent, US (whites) – 41 per cent, Germany – 39 per cent, Australia – 37 per cent, Norway – 35 per cent, to England – 30 per cent (Royal College of Physicians 1980). Fewer figures are available for non-industrialized countries, but in Uganda, Ghana, and Thailand less than 5 per cent of elderly women have gallstones. Gallstone disease is a rare cause of admission to hospital in Africa, India, and Arabia (Burkitt and Tunstall 1975).

Within England and Wales, a recent autopsy survey of nine towns, selected to represent various socio-economic conditions, found a twofold variation in age- and sex-standardized prevalence of 9 to 21 per cent. Prevalence did not correlate with all-cause mortality, and negatively correlated with ischaemic heart disease, suggesting that differences related to affluence within high prevalence areas were not major determinants of disease (Barker *et al.* 1979).

Secular trends

In areas where gallstones are now common it is generally believed that prevalence has been increasing since 1900, with a very rapid increase since 1945 – in some areas doubling in a decade (Holland and Heaton 1972; Fowkes 1980). However, this increase may only reflect a more aggressive use of investigation and surgery. In an autopsy survey Bateson and Bouchier (1975) found that any rise in prevalence between 1902–09 and 1953–73 disappeared after age and sex standardization. They did find some short-term fluctuations with an almost twofold increase between 1962 and 1972.

Age, sex, and race

At most ages gallstones are approximately twice as common in women as men (Table 10.11). Prevalence increases with age and Opit and Greenhill (1974) have suggested that since the increase in prevalence with age is linear, incidence is largely independent of age, at least between the third and eighth decades.

Gallstone prevalence is strongly influenced by racial factors, presumably reflecting genetic predisposition. This is exemplified by American Pima Indian women, 70 per cent of whom have gallstones by the age of 25 years, compared to less than 10 per cent of black women of the same age. Race is also believed to account for the difference between Sweden and Norway.

Parity

The effect of fertility on gallstone formation is unclear, possibly because of the confounding role of obesity. Clinical gallbladder disease is more common in women who have been pregnant, but a clear effect from increasing parity has been difficult to demonstrate (Friedman *et al.* 1966). Using data from women in a weight reduction programme, Bernstein *et al.* (1977), have shown increasing risk of clinical gallbladder disease with increasing parity. The effect of parity was much less than that of obesity or age.

Environmental factors influencing disease frequency

Obesity

Obesity has long been recognized as a major risk factor in gallstone formation (Bennion and Grundy 1978). Depending on age, it may account for 50–80 per cent of the variation in incidence of symptomatic gallbladder disease. The same study found a relative risk for developing symptomatic disease of six for extremely obese young women, compared to those only slightly obese (Bernstein *et al.* 1977). Obesity is accompanied by highly supersaturated gallbladder bile which is believed to account for the predisposition to cholelithiasis. Obese individuals have significantly higher bile saturation than matched non-obese controls. This abnormality can be reversed by weight reduction, and recurs if weight is regained.

Diet

The role of nutritional factors is discussed more fully elsewhere. Nutritional factors are undoubtedly important in gallstone formation, if only because obesity is a consequence of 'over' nutrition. Several dietary surveys by Sarles *et al.* (1970, 1978), have suggested that an excessive dietary energy intake occurs in cholelithiasis patients compared to controls matched for age, sex, size, and physical activity. Others have disputed this finding, but this may only reflect the difficulties of dietary measurement.

Despite much work, an excess or deficiency of no single dietary component has been shown to promote gallstone formation. There is no evidence that altering dietary fat or cholesterol intake has any marked effect on the formation of gallstones. The low prevalence of gallstones in the East African Masai who take a diet rich in animal fat is in keeping with this finding (Biss *et al.* 1971).

Lack of dietary fibre has been implicated in gallstone formation. No data exists on whether a high-fibre diet taken over a long time reduces gallstone prevalence. Experimental studies have suggested that fibre can reduce cholesterol saturation of bile, but only when the bile is already highly supersaturated (Royal College of Physicians 1980).

Drugs

Some drugs have been shown to increase gallstone formation, particularly clofibrate and oestrogens, usually in the form of the oral contraceptive pill. Both act by increasing cholesterol excretion in bile. Clofibrate is no longer widely used. Several cohort studies of oral contraceptive users have found an increased risk of symptomatic gallbladder disease. Recent analyses indicate that the increased risk diminishes with duration of use, suggesting that oral contraceptive use only accelerates the presentation of the disease in those prone to develop gallstones (Royal College of General Practitioners 1982). A report that thiazide diuretic use was associated with a relative risk of acute cholecystitis of 2.0 has not been so far confirmed elsewhere (Rosenberg *et al.* 1980).

Associated diseases

As with peptic ulcer, the increased surveillance of patients with gallstones probably accounts for early claims, now discounted, that gallstones are associated with diseases such as diabetes mellitus and hyperparathyroidism. In western countries where prevalence is high, gallstones associated with cirrhosis of the liver, haemolytic disease, ileal disease, and resection and biliary tract infection make only a small contribution to overall prevalence. In Japan biliary infection with roundworms appears to have been involved in pigment stone formation in the past, but recently this has declined along with a dramatic decline in prevalence of pigment stones (Bennion and Grundy 1978).

Prospects for prevention

Cholesterol gallstone formation is strongly associated with western countries. Of the risk factors that can be modified, obesity is pre-eminent. Public health measures that reduce the prevalence of obesity might be expected to reduce gallstone formation. Although experimental studies suggest a beneficial effect from an increase in dietary fibre, at present there is insufficient evidence to support more specific dietary measures to reduce gallstone disease.

LIVER DISEASE

Throughout the world mortality from liver disease varies considerably. In countries where liver disease is common, mortality from that condition can account for up to 5 per cent of all deaths, whereas in the UK, mortality from liver disease is less than 0.5 per cent of all deaths. In the main, mortality results from (i) infective liver disease including the acute viral hepatitides; (ii) hepatocellular cancer; and (iii) cirrhosis of the liver. In African countries such as Mozambique and Uganda, and also in developed countries like Greece and Japan, mortality is predominantly the result of Hepatitis B virus infection and hepatocellular cancer. The relationship between the two conditions is discussed elsewhere, as are the other infective liver diseases (Chapters 1 and 7).

Of the other acute liver diseases, Reye's syndrome, first described in 1963, is now estimated to account for between one and two thousand cases per year in the USA (Sullivan-Bolyai and Corey 1981). The condition mainly affects children and produces an acute encephalopathy with cerebral oedema and liver failure due to hepatic steatosis. Case-control studies have shown a strong association with prior aspirin ingestion and, despite criticisms of these studies, many authorities are advising caution in the use of aspirin in children with viral illnesses (Committee on Infectious Diseases 1982).

Cirrhosis of the liver

The term 'cirrhosis' indicates an end-stage histopathological state resulting from a wide range of causes. Death usually results from liver failure often precipitated by gastrointestinal bleeding or from development of an hepatocellular carcinoma. Fewer than 15 per cent survive five years once liver failure is established, making mortality rates a reasonable measure of disease frequency. Liver failure is not an inevitable consequence of cirrhosis, as demonstrated in a recent survey when 11 per cent of cases were an incidental finding at autopsy (Saunders *et al.* 1981).

In western countries alcohol abuse is the most important cause of cirrhosis, accounting for a proportion which varies with per caput alcohol consumption. This subject is discussed fully elsewhere (Volume 3, Chapter 23).

Of the other causes of cirrhosis, a substantial number (half of non-alcoholic cirrhosis) are labelled cryptogenic and assumed to be the result of an autoimmune process such as chronic active hepatitis and primary biliary cirrhosis. Little is known of the epidemiology of any of these autoimmune chronic liver diseases which accounted for 70 per cent of non-alcoholic cirrhosis in Birmingham, UK (Saunders *et al.* 1981).

CONCLUSION

Knowledge of factors which explain the occurrence of chronic digestive disease is scanty and it is correspondingly difficult to envisage applying simple public health measures in the hope of preventing or ameliorating such disease, although the frequency of appendicitis and diverticular disease could be reduced if hypotheses postulating dietary fibre deficiency prove correct. Reduction of tobacco and alcohol consumption could also contribute significantly to reducing the burdens of peptic ulcer and of cirrhosis.

REFERENCES

Almy, T.P. and Howell, D.A. (1980). Diverticular disease of the colon. *New Engl. J. Med.* **302**, 324.

Aspirin Myocardial Infarction Study Research Group (1980). A randomized controlled trial of aspirin in persons recovered from myocardial infarction. *JAMA* **243**, 661.

Bainton, D., Davies, G.T., Evans, K.T., and Gravelle, I.H. (1976). Gallbladder disease: prevalence in a South Wales industrial town. *New Engl. J. Med.* **294**, 1147.

Barker, D.J.P., Gardner, M.J., Power, C., and Hutt, M.S.R. (1979). Prevalence of gallstones at necropsy in British towns. *Br. Med. J.* **11**, 1389.

Barker, D.J.P. and Liggins, A. (1981). Acute appendicitis in non-British towns. *Br. Med. J.* **283**, 1083.

Barreras, R.F. (1973). Calcium and gastric secretion. *Gastoenterology* **64**, 1168.

Bateson, M.C. and Bouchier, I.A.D. (1975). Prevalence of gallstones in Dundee: a necropsy study. *Br. Med. J.* **iv**, 425.

Bennion, L.J. and Grundy, S.M. (1978). Risk factors for the development of cholelithiasis in man. *New Engl. J. Med.* **299**, 1221.

Bernstein, R.A., Giefer, E.E., Vieira, J.J., Werner, L.H., and Rimm, A.A. (1977). Gallbladder disease – II. Utilisation of the Life Table Method in obtaining clinically useful information. *J. Chronic. Dis.* **30**, 529.

Binder, V., Both, H., Hansen, P.K., Hendriksen, C., Kreiner, S., and Torp-Pedersen, K. (1982). Incidence and prevalence of ulcerative colitis and Crohn's disease in the County of Copenhagen, 1962 to 1978. *Gastroenterology* **83**, 563.

Biss, K., Ho, K.-J., Mikkelson, B., Lewis, L., and Taylor, C.B. (1971). Some unique biological characteristics of the Masai of East Africa. *New Engl. J. Med.* **284**, 694.

Brodribb, A.J.M. and Humphreys, D.M. (1976). Diverticular disease: three studies. *Br. Med. J.* **i**, 424.

Burkitt, D.P. (1971). The aetiology of appendicitis. *Br. J. Surg.* **58**, 695.

Burkitt, D.P. and Trowell, H.C. (eds.) (1975). *Refined carbohydrate foods and disease*. Academic Press, London.

Burkitt, D.P. and Tunstall, M. (1975). Gallstones: geographical and chronological features. *J. Trop. Med. Hyg.* **78**, 140.

Calder, J.F. (1979). Diverticular disease of the colon in Africans. *Br. Med. J.* **i**, 1465.

Chalmers, K., Wilson, J.M.G., Smith, A.N., and Eastwood, M.A. (1983). Diverticular disease of the colon in Scottish Hospitals over a decade. *Health Bull.* **41**, 32.

Coggon, D., Lambert, P., and Langman, M.J.S. (1981). Twenty years of hospital admissions for peptic ulcer in England and Wales. *Lancet* **i**, 1302.

Coggon, D., Langman, M.J.S., and Spiegelhalter, D. (1982). Aspirin, paracetamol, and haematemesis and melaena. *Gut* **23**, 340.

Committee of Infectious Diseases, American Academy of Paediatrics (1982). Aspirin and Reye Syndrome. *Pediatrics* **69**, 810.

Conn, H.O. and Blitzer, B.L. (1976). Non-association of adrenocortocosteroid therapy and peptic ulcer. *New Engl. J. Med.* **294**, 473.

Coronary Drug Project Research Group (1976). Aspirin in coronart heart disease. *J. Chronic. Dis.* **29**, 625.

Cove-Smith, J.R. and Langman, M.J.S. (1975). Appendicitis and dietary fibre. *Gut* **16**, 409.

Creed, F. (1981). Life events and appendicectomy. *Lancet* **i**, 1381.

Doll, R. and Hill, A.B. (1964). Mortality in relation to smoking: 10 years observation of British Doctors. *Br. Med. J.* **i**, 1399; 1460.

Donaldson, R.M. (1975). Factors complicating observed associations between peptic ulcers and other diseases. *Gastroenterology* **68**, 1608.

Donnan, S.P.B. and Lambert, P.M. (1976). Appendicitis: incidence and mortality. *Popul. Trends* **5**, 26.

Elashoff, J.D. and Grossman, M.I. (1980). Trends in hospital admission and death rates for peptic ulcer in the United States from 1970 to 1978. *Gastroenterology* **78**, 280.

Foster, K.J., Holdstock, G., Whorwell, P.J., Guyer, P., and Wright, R. (1978). Prevalence of diverticular disease of the colon in patients with ischaemic heart disease. *Gut* **19**, 1054.

Fowkes, F.G.R. (1980). Cholecystectomy and surgical resources in Scotland. *Health Bull.* **38**, 126.

Friedman, G.D., Kannel, W.B., and Dawber, T.R. (1966). The epidemiology of gallbladder disease: observations on the Framingham study. *J. Chronic Dis.* **19**, 273.

Friedman, G.D., Siegelaub, A.B., and Seltzer, C.C. (1974). Cigarettes, alcohol, coffee and peptic ulcer. *New Engl. J. Med.* **290**, 469.

Gear, J.S.S., Ware, A., Fursdon, P., Mann, J.I., Nolan, D.J., Brodribb, A.J.M., and Vessey, M.P. (1979). Symptomless diverticular disease and intake of dietary fibre. *Lancet* **i**, 511.

Gillies, M.A. and Skyring, A. (1969). Gastric and duodenal ulcer. The association between aspirin ingestion, smoking and family history of ulcer. *Med. J. Aust.* **2**, 280.

Gugler, R., Rohner, H.G., and Kratochvil, P. (1982). Effect of smoking on duodenal ulcer healing with cimetidine and oxmetidine. *Gut* **23**, 866.

Gyde, S., Prior, P., Dew, M.J., Saunders, V., Waterhouse, J.A.H., and Allan, R.N. (1982). Mortality in ulcerative colitis. *Gastroenterology* **83**, 36.

Hallert, C., Gotthard, R., Norrby, K., and Walan, A. (1981). On the prevalence of adult coeliac disease in Sweden. *Scand. J. Gastroenterol.* **16**, 257.

Hammond, E.C. and Horn, D. (1958). Smoking and death rates – report on forty-four months of follow-up of 187, 783 men. I. *JAMA* **166**, 1294.

Harries, A.D., Baird, A., and Rhodes, J. (1982). Non-smoking. A feature of ulcerative colitis. *Br. Med. J.* **284**, 706.

Hellers, G. (1981). Some epidemiological aspects of Crohn's disease in Stockholm County, 1955–1979. In *Recent advances in Crohn's disease* (eds. A.S. Pena, I.T. Weterman, C.C. Booth, and W. Strober) p. 158 Martinus Nijhoff, The Hague.

Holland, C. and Heaton, K.W. (1972). Increasing frequency of gallbladder operations in the Bristol clinical area. *Br. Med. J.* iii, 627.

Howat, H.T. (1963). In Symposium of Marseilles, April 1963. Etiology and pathological anatomy of chronic pacreatitis. *Bibliotheca gastroenterologica* (Basel).

Jick, H. and Walker, A.M. (1983). Cigarette smoking and ulcerative colitis. *New Engl. J. Med.* 308, 261.

Kurata, J.H., Honda, G.D., and Frankl, H. (1982). Hospitalization and mortality rates for peptic ulcers: a comparison of a large health maintenance organisation and United States data. *Gastroenterology* 83, 1008.

Kyle, J. and Stark, J. (1980). Fall in the incidence of Crohn's disease. *Gut* 21, 340.

Langman, M.J.S. (1970). Epidemiological evidence for the association of aspirin and acute gastrointestinal bleeding. *Gut* 11, 627.

Langman, M.J.S. (1979). *The epidemiology of chronic digestive disease.* Edward Arnold, London.

Langman, M.J.S. and Cooke, A.R. (1976). Gastric and duodenal ulcer and their associated disease. *Lancet* i, 680.

Levy, M. (1974). Aspirin use in patients with major upper gastro-intestinal bleeding and peptic ulcer disease. *New Engl. J. Med.* 290, 1158.

Litton, A. and Murdoch, W.R. (1963. Peptic ulcer in South West Scotland. *Gut* 4, 360.

Logan, R.F.A., Rifkind, E.A., and Ferguson, A. (1982). Mortality in coeliac disease. *Gut* 23, A452.

Logan, R.F.A., Tucker, G., Rifkind, E.A., Heading, R.C., and Ferguson, A. (1983). Changes in clinical features of coeliac disease in adults in Edinburgh and the Lothians, 1960–79. *Br. Med. J.* i, 95.

McConnell, R.B. (ed.) (1981). *The genetics of coeliac disease.* MTP Lancaster.

Manousos, D.N., Truelove, S.C., and Lumsden, K. (1967). Transit times of food in patients with diverticulosis or irritable colon syndrome and normal subjects. *Br. Med. J.* iii, 760.

Martini, G.A. and Brandes, J.W. (1976). Increased consumption of refined carbohydrates in patients with Crohn's disease. *Klin. Wochenschr.* 54, 367.

Mayberry, J., Rhodes, J., and Hughes, L.E. (1979). Incidence of Crohn's disease in Cardiff between 1934 and 1977. *Gut* 20, 602.

Medalie, J.H., Neufeld, H.N., Goldbourt, U., Kahn, H.A., Riss, E., and Oron, D. (1970). Association between blood pressure and peptic ulcer disease. *Lancet* ii, 1225.

Mendeloff, A.I. and Dunn, J.P. (1971). *Digestive diseases.* Harvard University Press, Massachusetts.

Mendeloff, A.I., Monk, M., Siegel, C.I., and Lilienfeld, A. (1970). Illness experience and life stresses in patients with irritable colon and with ulcerative colitis. *New Engl. J. Med.* 282, 16.

Miller, B., Fervers, F., Rohbeck, R., and Strohmeyer, G. (1976). Zuckerkonsum bei patienten mit morbus Crohn. *Dtsch. Inn. Med.* 82, 922.

Miller, D.S., Keighley, A.C., and Langman, M.J.S. (1974). Changing patterns in epidemiology of Crohn's disease. *Lancet* ii, 691.

Monson, R.R. (1970). Cigarette smoking and body form in peptic ulcer. *Gastroenterology* 58, 337.

Monson, R.R. and MacMahon, B. (1969). Peptic ulcer in Massachusetts physicians. *New Engl. J. Med.* 281, 11.

Morgan, M.Y. and Sherlock, S. (1977). Sex related difference among 100 patients with alcoholic liver disease. *Br. Med. J.* i, 939.

Nelson, R., McNeish, A.S., and Anderson, C.M. (1973). Coeliac disease in the children of Asian immigrants. *Lancet* i, 348.

OPCS (1981). *Trends in morbidity, 1968–1978 applying surveillance techniques to the HIP Enquiry, England and Wales.* OPCS, London.

Opit, L.J. and Greenhill, S. (1974). Prevalence of gallstones in relation to differing treatment rates for biliary disease. *Br. J. Prev. Soc. Med.* 28, 268.

Paffenbarger, R.S., Wing, A.L., and Hyde R.T. (1974). Coffee, cigarettes and peptic ulcer. *New Engl. J. Med.* 290, 1091.

Paffenbarger, R.S., Wing, A.L., and Hyde, R.T. (1974). Chronic disease in former college students. XIII Early precursors of peptic ulcer. *Am. J. Epidemiol.* 100, 307.

Painter, N.S. and Burkitt, D.P. (1971). Diverticular disease of the colon. A deficiency disease of Western civilisation. *Br. Med. J.* ii, 450.

Pëna, A.S. (1981). Genetics of coeliac disease. In *Topics in gastro-enterology* (eds. D.P. Jewell, and E. Lee). Blackwell, Oxford.

Persantin–aspirin Reinfarction Study Research Group (1980). Persantin and aspirin in coronary heart disease. *Circulation* 62, 449.

Piper, D.W., Greig, M., Shinners, J., Thomas, J., and Crawford, J. (1978). Chronic gastric ulcer and stress. *Digestion* 18, 303.

Piper, D.W., McIntosh, J.H., Ariotti, D.E., Calgiuri, J.V., Brown, R.W., and Shy, C.M. (1981a). Life events and chronic duodenal ulcer: a case-control study. *Gut* 22, 1011.

Piper, D.W., McIntosh, J.H., Ariotti, D.E., Fenton, B.H., and MacLennan, R. (1981b). Analgesic ingestion and chronic peptic ulcer. *Gastroenterology* 80, 427.

Polednak, A.P. (1974). Some early characteristics of peptic ulcer decedents. *Gastroenterology* 67, 1094.

Register General (1971). *Decennial supplements. Occupational mortality tables for 1959–63.* HMSO, London.

Registrar General (1914 and 1925). *Statistical reviews for 1912 and 1924.* HMSO, London.

Rosenberg, L., Shapiro, S., Slone, D., Kaufman, D.W., Miettinen, O.S., and Stolley, P.D. (1980). Thiazides and acute cholecystitis. *New Engl. J. Med.* 303, 546.

Royal College of General Practitioners Oral Contraception Study (1982). Oral contraceptives and gallbladder disease. *Lancet* ii, 957.

Royal College of Physicians (1980). *Medical aspects of dietary fibre.* Pitman, London.

Rydning, A., Berstad, A., Aadland, E., and Odegaard, B. (1982). Prophylactic effect of dietary fibre in duodenal ulcer disease. *Lancet* ii, 736.

Sarles, H., Gérolami, A., and Bord, (1978). Diet and cholesterol gallstones. *Digestion* 17, 128.

Sarles, H., Hawton, J., Planche, N.E., Lafont, H., and Gérolami, A. (1970). Diet, cholesterol gallstones and composition of bile. *Am. J. Dig. Dis.* 15, 251.

Sarles, H., Sarles, J.C., Camatte, R. *et al.* (1965). Observations in 205 confirmed cases of acute pancreatitis, recurring pancreatitis and chronic pancreatitis. *Gut* 6, 545.

Saunders, J.B., Walters, J.R.F., Davies, P., and Paton, A. (1981). A 20-year prospective study of cirrhosis. *Br. Med. J.* 282, 263.

Scottish Home and Health Department (1975). *Scottish hospital in-patient statistics, 1975.* HMSO, Edinburgh.

Segal, I. and Walker, A.R.P. (1982). Diverticular disease in urban Africans in South Africa. *Digestion* 24, 42.

Shepherd, A.M.M., Stewart, W.K., and Wormsley, K.G. (1973). Peptic ulceration in chronic renal failure. *Lancet* i, 1357.

Sullivan-Bolyai, J.Z. and Corey, L. (1981). Epidemiology of Reye syndrome. *Epidemiol. Rev.* 3, 1.

Swinson, C.M. and Levi, A.J. (1980). Is coeliac disease under-diagnosed? *Br. Med. J.* **ii**, 1258.

Tabaqchali, S. and Dawson, A.M. (1964). Peptic ulcer and gastric secretion in patients with liver disease. *Gut* **5**, 417.

Thornton, J.R., Emmett, P.M., and Heaton, K.W. (1979). Diet and Crohn's disease: characteristics of the pre-illness diet. *Br. Med. J.* **ii**, 762.

Tovey, F.I. and Tunstall, M. (1975). Duodenal ulcer in black populations in Africa south of the Sahara. *Gut* **16**, 564.

Walker, A.R.P., Walker, B.F., Davenhage, A., Jones, J., Neonguione, J., and Segal, I. (1982). Appendicectomy prevalences in South African adolescents. *Digestion* **23**, 274.

Wyllie, J.H., Clark, C.G., Alexander-Williams, J. *et al.* (1981). Effect of cimetidine on surgery for duodenal ulcer. *Lancet* i, 1037.

11 The epidemiology of genito-urinary disease

Sabri Challah and Anthony J. Wing

INTRODUCTION

Topics for this chapter have been selected on the basis of their importance as public health issues and for their epidemiological interest. In particular, the question of chronic renal failure has been singled out, because of the potential expansion of high cost treatment. By 1987, it is estimated that the end-stage renal failure (ESRF) programme in the US will cost the government three billion dollars (Guttman 1979).

Venereal diseases are dealt with elsewhere (see Volume 3, Chapter 31).

MORTALITY OF GENITO-URINARY DISEASES

Death occurs from malignant disease of the urinary tract and from renal failure. In western countries genito-urinary disease is outranked only by cardiovascular, respiratory, and malignant disease as a cause of death; the most recent available WHO mortality figures are given in Table 11.1. There are marked differences in mortality between countries, and a tendency for a higher mortality in males. In the developed nations, deaths from genito-urinary disease have declined since the beginning of the twentieth century (Fig. 11.1).

The *WHO Statistics annual* lists among other genito-urinary diseases: nephritis and nephrosis, infection of the kidney, and prostatic hypertrophy. However, differences in diagnostic practice probably distort renal disease statistics more than any other group of pathologies, and may account for many of the observed differences. Even within one country, the US, an apparent decline in deaths from nephritis was largely attributable to a change in diagnostic fashion (Florey *et al.* 1971).

Genito-urinary disease is often not fatal, and even when it is, the course is prolonged. A comparison of deaths and hospital admissions is shown in Table 11.2 for nephritis and nephrosis in the UK over a five-year period.

MORBIDITY FROM GENITO-URINARY DISEASE

Morbidity from genito-urinary diseases can be studied by looking at hospital discharge data (Table 11.2) or by considering attendance at primary and referral centres for genito-urinary problems. This has been done with studies of urinary tract infection (Logan and Cushion 1958) and

Table 11.1. *Deaths from diseases of the genito-urinary system per 100 000 population. Year of report in parentheses, males and females shown separately. (WHO Statistics Annual 1975–81)*

Country	Deaths per 100 000 Males	Females
Australia (1978)	9.9	10.8
Austria (1978)	22.1	20.6
Belgium (1976)	21.2	17.7
Bulgaria (1977)	26.9	15.1
Canada (1977)	9.9	7.1
Chile (1978)	16.9	12.5
Denmark (1978)	16.9	17.3
Egypt (1977)	21.0	11.6
El Salvador (1973)	5.2	2.6
Fed. Rep. Germany (1978)	20.9	17.1
Finland (1975)	12.2	13.7
France (1976)	18.7	13.0
Greece (1978)	25.1	17.2
Hungary (1978)	33.8	25.0
Iceland (1978)	8.9	9.9
Israel (1978)	18.1	14.9
Italy (1975)	19.8	9.6
Japan (1978)	9.9	9.7
Netherlands (1978)	15.9	14.2
Poland (1978)	15.3	9.5
Portugal (1975)	18.8	11.5
Spain (1976)	19.3	13.5
Sweden (1978)	19.1	13.3
Switzerland (1978)	13.8	11.3
United Kingdom (1978)	17.5	17.9
USA (1977)	13.1	11.2
Venezuela (1978)	10.1	7.5

Table 11.2. *Death versus discharge rate for nephritis and nephrosis (ICD 580–584) per 100 000 population in England and Wales between 1974 and 1978. (Data from Office of Population Censuses and Surveys Hospital Survey and Mortality Statistics)*

Year	Discharge rate Male	Female	Death rate Male	Female
1974	24	18	6.3	5.4
1975	23	18	6.2	5.9
1976	26	18	6.7	5.9
1977	28	19	6.3	6.2
1978	30	21	7.1	6.4

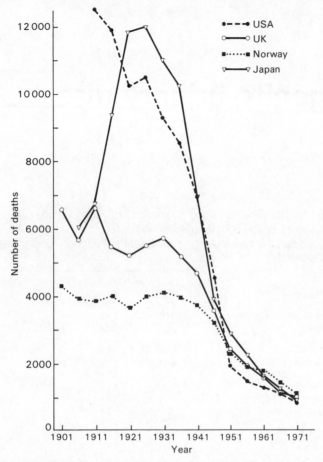

Fig. 11.1. Deaths from genito-urinary disease between 1901 and 1971 in the United States, United Kingdom, Norway, and Japan. (Data from Alderson (1981).)

chronic renal failure (Mausner *et al.* 1978). Urinary tract infection (UTI) is the commonest reason in primary medical care for the prescription of an antibiotic to an adult.

It should be remembered that much urinary and renal disease is subclinical, and may be detected at routine medical examinations and by screening programmes. Asymptomatic though significant bacteriuria, haematuria, and proteinuria are all known to occur; many cases of prostatic carcinoma are found only at autopsy, and chronic renal failure may be very advanced before it presents to a doctor.

Large-scale screening studies for urinary tract infection have been carried out (Kunin *et al.* 1960; Kass *et al.* 1965, Freedman *et al.* 1965; Meadow *et al.* 1969). These were motivated initially by concern that bacteriuria might cause severe long-term problems, but more recently, because bacteriuria may be a marker for serious urinary tract abnormalities, such as vesico-ureteric reflux in children.

The prevalence of chronic renal failure has been studied in certain populations and within defined catchment areas (Table 11.3). Data from these studies are the starting point for prediction of true need for dialysis and transplantation. All of them have flaws. None reach beyond primary referral

and into the general population. The studies of McCormick and Navarro (1973) in south-east Scotland and McGeown (1972) in Northern Ireland come closest to evaluating the prevalence of renal failure; they identified all the patients in a region who had been found to have a blood urea in excess of 100 mg per cent, whether in hospital or general practice. This is not the complete picture, and one can only speculate about the number of elderly and confused, and middle-aged and hypertensive individuals with elevated serum urea who never had a blood test. An attempt to collect and evaluate information about end-stage renal failure has been made with the establishment of the Registry of the European Dialysis and Transplant Association (EDTA). This is a registry of all patients on treatment for renal failure in 32 European countries. Its value as an epidemiological tool is blunted by the fact that it includes only the treated population, and in Europe this is as much a reflection of economical as clinical factors. However, in certain age and diagnostic categories, where referral and treatment are highly probable, it provides valuable information about the occurrence of renal failure, and the specific conditions leading to it in the population at large. Data from the Registry are quoted in many parts of this chapter.

FACTORS AFFECTING THE INCIDENCE OF GENITO-URINARY DISEASE

Genetic factors

Race

Racial comparisons are difficult in view of the inadequacy of the data on genito-urinary disease from many parts of the world, and the problem of teasing out economic and cultural influences. However, a number of disorders seem to be influenced by race: for example, there is a consistent excess of renal failure amongst blacks in the US (Table 11.4), which has been attributed to the greater frequency of hypertension amongst them compared with whites (Hypertension and Detection Follow-up Program Cooperative Group 1977). Some authors have claimed that chronic glomerulonephritis, diabetic and interstitial kidney disease, leading to renal failure, are also more common in US blacks (Rostand *et al.* 1982).

Racial differences in incidence of carcinoma of the prostate are well recognized, with particularly low rates among yellow races (Wynder *et al.* 1971). Renal carcinoma is less common in the Indian and Chinese populations of Singapore than Europeans, and less frequent in Africa than western Europe or the US (Hutt 1983). Whether any of the observed differences reflect true racial tendencies is unclear: Japanese who have migrated to the US lose some measure of protection from prostatic carcinoma (Haenszel and Kurihara 1968) and closer examination of other racial differences may show them to have a dietary or social basis.

Genetically-caused genito-urinary disease

A growing number of genito-urinary diseases are being identified as having a genetic basis with familial occurrence

Table 11.3. *The incidence and prevalence of chronic renal failure in ten studies*

Reference (date of study)	Place	Method	Incidence per 1 000 000 population	Prevalence	Criticism
Branch *et al.* (1971) (1966–68)	Glamorgan UK	Biochemical records in 400 bed hospital: Urea > 7100 mg %	39 (<60 years and suitable for dialysis)		Hospital population
McGeown (1972) (1968–70)	N. Ireland	Questionnaire to doctors: Urea >100 mg %		424 CRF*/3y 222 ESRD†/3y	
Pendreigh *et al.* (1972) (1968–69)	Scotland	Questionnaire to doctors: Urea >100 mg % and death certificate	52 (<65 years and suitable for treatment)		
McCormick *et al.* (1973) (1969)	S.E. Scotland	Questionnaire to doctors: Urea > 100 mg %		190	
Dombey *et al.* (1975) (1970, 1973–74)	Nottingham, UK	Laboratory records: Urea >100 mg %	45 (<65 years and suitable for treatment)		Hospital population
Modan *et al.* (1975) (1966)	Israel	All hospital records: Urea > 100 mg %	70		Hospital population
Mausner *et al.* (1978) (1973)	Greater Delaware Valley, US	Review patients on treatment for ESRD	46	115	Treated population, but liberal policy
Mausner *et al.* (1978) (1974)	Greater Delaware Valley, US	Review patients on treatment for ESRD	63	156	Referred population
Rostand *et al.* (1982) (1974–78)	Jefferson County Alabama, US	Review patients referred for treatment ESRD	91		Referred population
Hiatt and Friedman (1982) (1972–77)	N. California, US	Review patients referred for treatment ESRD	50		Referred population

*CRF=chronic renal failure.
†ESRD=end-stage renal disease.

Table 11.4. *Comparison of annual presentation rate per million population of blacks and whites with end-stage renal disease (ESRD) in the United States*

	Annual incidence/million population			
Reference	White Male	Female	Black Male	Female
Mausner *et al.* (1979)	57	30	245	197
Hiatt and Friedman (1982)	39.6	31.5	98.5	101.4
Rostand *et al.* (1982)	44.4		188.4	

(Perkoff 1967). They range from gross structural abnormalities to subtle defects of renal tubular function.

Familial Mediterranean fever is a condition found in Sephardic Jews, Arabs, and Armenians, and is probably transmitted as an autosomal recessive disorder (Sohar *et al.* 1961) though isolated cases without familial involvement are described. Mamou and Cattan (1952) pointed out that patients with this condition, also known as 'periodic disease', may die of uraemia, which was later shown to be due to amyloidosis (Heller *et al.* 1961). In Israel, familial Mediterranean fever accounts for 7 per cent of patients requiring treatment for end-stage renal disease (Modan *et al.* 1975).

Polycystic kidney disease accounts for about 1 in 10 of all patients treated for end-stage renal failure in Europe, the US and Australia (Wing *et al.* 1983*a*). Clinically, there are two main types, the most common, adult form, appears to be inherited as an autosomal dominant, while an autosomal recessive type occurs in infants and is associated with early death. There may be geographical differences in distribution of polycystic kidney disease with a low incidence in Japan (Wing *et al.* 1983*b*).

Alport's syndrome, familial amyloidosis, and familial Mediterranean fever appear to be uncommon in tropical countries. The haemaglobinopathies probably contribute more to morbidity and mortality from renal disease in the tropics than any other genetic disorders (Hutt 1983). Sickle-cell disease, thalassaemia, and glucose 6-phosphate dehydrogenase deficiency are widely distributed through sub-Saharan Africa and the Middle East, but to a lesser extent in black populations of the New World, where the advantage conferred by the traits in relation to malaria has lost its relevance (Alleyne *et al.* 1975).

In some tropical areas, the occurrence of acute tubular necrosis with acute infection may be related to a high incidence of glucose 6-phosphate dehydrogenase deficiency (Lwanga and Wing 1970), which is 15 per cent in parts of East Africa (Allison 1960), 20 per cent in areas of Nigeria (Gilles and Ikeme 1960) and 24.3 per cent in S. Ghana (Adu *et al.* 1960). Haemolysis due to this defect may result from treatment with antimalarials, an effect enhanced by bacterial infection (Tarlov *et al.* 1962).

Cystinosis is a lysosomal storage disease, which has an autosomal recessive inheritance. It occurs in three clinically and genetically distinct forms (Watts 1983). In the infantile or nephropathic type, renal tubular damage results in a Fanconi syndrome with progressive renal failure and death in the first decade of life. Glomerular damage develops less rapidly in the juvenile (intermediate) form of the disease, while adult or benign cystinosis is not associated with renal failure. Estimates of the incidence of infantile cystinosis vary, and are reported as 1:150 000 in Switzerland (Pfandler and Berger 1956), 1:115 000 in Denmark (Ebbesen *et al.* 1976), and 1:40 000 in parts of the UK (Bickel and Harris 1952). There also appears to be some regional variation: the incidence in Brittany is reported as 1:26 000 live births, compared to 1:326 000 in the rest of France (Bois *et al.* 1976). The clustering of cases described in French-speaking Quebec may reflect migration from Brittany and Normandy (Bois *et al.* 1976). The highest incidence of cystinosis, 1:20 000, is found in the North African Jews of Israel (Godoth *et al.* 1975).

Environmental factors

Infectious and parasitic disease

Although the importance of infectious and parasitic disease has declined dramatically in Europe and the US during the last century, it remains a major cause of genito-urinary and other diseases in tropical and underdeveloped countries.

Infectious agents may act directly on the genito-urinary system to produce damage, as in acute pyelonephritis, gonococcal urethritis, renal tuberculosis, and schistosomiasis, or indirectly through immune or other mechanisms, as in the case of glomerulonephritis, carcinoma of the bladder and penis, and renal amyloid.

Bacterial infection of the urinary tract is dealt with on p. 185; schistosomal, malarial, and streptococcal infection are discussed below.

Schistosomiasis

Schistosoma haematobium is a major cause of urinary disease in tropical countries, and in endemic areas of Africa and South America the prevalence of schistosomal infection approaches 100 per cent. Both *S. mansoni* and *S. haematobium* have been proposed as causes of immune complex glomerulonephritis (Beaufils *et al.* 1978; Andrade and Rocha 1979). Scarring of the lower urinary tract particularly when complicated by bacterial infection (as often occurs after instrumentation) accounts for most of the morbidity and mortality from schistosomal infection. *Schistosoma haematobium* infection is also implicated in the aetiology of squamous carcinoma of the bladder (Brand 1979), and this may account for the high frequency of the tumour in Africa and the Middle East compared with Europe and North America (Pugh 1959).

Malaria

Blackwater fever due to *Plasmodium falciparum* was common among early explorers of the tropics, but is rare in the indigenous adult population of holo-endemic malarious areas, providing they are undisturbed in their natural environment (Hutt 1984). Proteinuria is common in acute *P. falciparum* infection, which can produce glomerular damage (Berger *et al.* 1967; Bhamarapravati *et al.* 1973).

The association between quartan malaria and nephrotic syndrome was recognized by Hippocrates (Kibukamusoke 1973) and some authors cite *P. malariae* as the single most important identified cause of soluble complex glomerulonephritis world-wide (Kibukamousoke 1978).

Streptococcal infection

The decline in incidence of post-streptococcal acute nephritis in Europe and North America is not reflected in underdeveloped parts of the world, where it remains fairly common (Wing *et al.* 1972). It classically follows pharyngeal infection, but epidemics in Trinidad (Poon-King *et al.* 1967) and parts of the US (Dillon 1967) are reported following skin sepsis, such as impetigo or infected scabies.

The decline in western countries is probably due to improvements in nutrition and sanitation; antibiotics have played little or no part.

Climate

This is closely allied with the role of infectious and parasitic disease in the aetiology of genito-urinary disorders, but otherwise seems to have no direct role among indigenous populations.

Socio-economic factors

These have a profound influence on all diseases, and genito-urinary disorders are a particularly good example. The decline in post-streptococcal acute glomerulonephritis in the developed world is almost certainly due to improved living conditions, including the elimination of body lice and better nutrition, and antedates the introduction of antibiotics (Cameron 1979*a*). An interesting though weak association between social class and chronic renal failure was noted by McCormick (1973) in a study in south-east Scotland on the prevalence of chronic renal failure.

Diet

Over and above the general influence of nutritional status on immunocompetence and therefore susceptibility to infectious diseases, diet has been specifically implicated in a number of genito-urinary conditions.

The marked national differences in carcinoma of the prostate may in part be due to diet, and this is invoked to explain changing incidence of the tumour with migration (Franks 1972). Diet is a major factor in aetiology of urinary stones, a role which is discussed in detail in the section on urolithiasis.

Drugs and chemicals

The increased risk of bladder cancer in dye industry employees was recognized in 1895 by Rehn. Since then an increasing list of occupations, and more importantly aromatic amines, are described as being associated with the disease. Arsenic and inorganic mercurial compounds, cadmium, and lead can all produce renal damage (Harrington and Waldon 1981). Mercurial diuretics (Cameron and Trounce 1965) and mercurial skin-lightening creams used by women in Nairobi (Barr *et al.* 1972) are known to cause nephrotic syndrome.

The range of drugs with nephrotoxicity is enormous: amongst them are anti-inflammatory agents, antibiotics, diuretics, and analgesics, acting by direct toxicity or through hypersensitivity reactions.

The recognition of analgesic nephropathy is fairly recent; the earliest report came from Switzerland (Zollinger 1955) and was followed by reports from Scandinavia (Harvald 1963) and Australia (Jacobs and Morris 1962), which indicated that renal papillary necrosis associated with analgesic abuse was a frequent clinical, radiological, and *post mortem* finding in those countries. This condition is not confined to a group of nations (Sanerkin and Weaver 1964; Reynolds and Edmondson 1963), but there are dramatic geographical differences. Table 11.5 shows that renal papillary necrosis is many times more common in Australia than in the UK or the US. Comparison of registry data from Europe (Gurland *et al.* 1976) and Australia shows a tenfold difference in the number of patients with analgesic nephropathy presenting for dialysis and transplantation (Kincaid-Smith 1978). Eighteen per cent of patients in Switzerland on treatment for renal failure are said to have drug-induced nephropathy (Jacobs *et al.* 1980; Table 11.6). Even within a country, there are differences in distribution of this disease related to the rate of analgesic abuse (Kincaid-Smith 1978). Analgesic nephropathy is four times more common in women than men; the typical case is a middle-aged female who abuses analgesics for their mood-altering property (Kincaid-Smith 1969). Phenacetin was long presumed to be the agent responsible, but this has now been questioned, and aspirin put forward as an alternative (Saker and Kincaid-Smith 1969). Reduction in incidence of analgesic nephropathy is beginning to be reported following the introduction of legislation eliminating or controlling the availability of

Table 11.5. *The incidence of renal papillary necrosis per 100 autopsies in four countries. (After Kincaid-Smith (1978))*

Country	Reference	Date	Renal papillary necrosis per 100 autopsies
US	Hepinstall (1974)	1947–1961	0.20
UK	Davies *et al.* (1970)	1961–1967	0.16
Switzerland	Gloor (1978)	1938–1947	0.76
		1948–1957	1.32
		1955–1972	1.00
		1971–1976	1.10
Australia	Jacobs and Morris (1962)	1962	3.70
	Burry (1964)	1964	9.90
	Nanra *et al.* (1970) (Melbourne)	1968–1969	8.70
	Arnold *et al.* (1977)	1973–1974	21.40
	Nanra (1976) (Newcastle)	1976	20.00

Table 11.6. *Prevalence of analgesic nephropathy in patients on treatment for end-stage renal disease (ESRD) in six European countries. (From Jacobs et al. (1980))*

Country	Patients per million population	Percentage of all patients on treatment
Switzerland	44.6	18
Belgium	26.0	11
Denmark	11.5	6
Federal Republic of Germany	7.7	4
Netherlands	6.4	4
UK	1.6	1
Total registry	2.7	2

phenacetin. This represents a triumph for preventive measures—a rare achievement in genito-urinary diseases.

SPECIFIC GENITO-URINARY DISEASES

Urinary tract infection and pyelonephritis

One in every 100 general practice consultations in the UK is due to symptoms which suggest urinary tract infection (Logan and Cushion 1958), and in New Zealand, the figure is one in every 56 (Gallagher 1974). The EDTA Registry (Jacobs *et al.* 1981) shows pyelonephritis/interstitial nephritis as the second most common cause of end-stage renal failure. The problem of urinary tract infection and its sequelae is ever present, and although antibiotics may have had an impact on mortality from this condition, this is not reflected in morbidity. Symptoms of urinary tract infection are very common, and it is predominantly a disease of women, and in particular young women (OPCS 1974). A study of the symptom of dysuria in south Wales produced a prevalence of 21.8 per cent in females between the ages of 20 and 65 years, and showed the condition to be commoner in married than single subjects (Waters 1969).

Asymptomatic bacteriuria has been studied using semi-quantitative culture techniques to assess significant infection. Prevalence studies in populations in Wales, Jamaica (Kas *et al.* 1965), and Japan (Freedman *et al.* 1965) were in broad agreement: 4 per cent of females between the ages of 16 and 45 years had significant bacteriuria which rose to 10 per cent at 55–64 years, and was in excess of 15 per cent after 64 years of age. In comparison, the prevalence amongst males was 0.5 per cent. Studies on schoolchildren indicate a prevalence of asymptomatic bacteriuria among girls of between 1 and 2 per cent depending upon the age of the group (Meadow *et al.* 1969; Savage *et al.* 1969; Verrier-Jones *et al.* 1975), and in boys of 0.2 per cent or less (Kunin and Paquin 1965; Newcastle Asymptomatic Bacteriuria Research Group 1975). Series from Africa suggest great variability in the prevalence of bacteriuria (Hendricks 1980); it is reported in 25 per cent of children with kwashiorkor in Nigeria (Ransome-Kuti and Ransome-Kuti 1960) and 24 per cent of rural children in the same country (Akinkugbe *et al.* 1973).

Among pregnant women, some 20 per cent of those with bacteriuria at booking clinics develop acute pyelonephritis, a complication which can be prevented by treatment of asymptomatic infection (Kass 1960). Claims that pregnant bacteriuric women run a higher risk of pre-eclamptic toxaemia, premature birth, and fetal loss have not been substantiated (Condie *et al.* 1973). Long-term studies of the natural history of significant bacteriuria in non-pregnant women suggest that it is a benign condition provided that it is not associated with obstructive uropathy (Asscher *et al.* 1973; Waters *et al.* 1970).

Screening for significant bacteriuria is of established cost-benefit. Updating Asscher's exercise (1969), then, using dip-slide testing, at approximately 50 pence a test, the cost of bacteriuric screening for the 636 884 maternities in England and Wales in 1979 (OPCS 1981) would be £318 442. To this must be added the cost of repeat cultures in the 8 per cent with one positive culture, £25 475, and the cost of treatment of the 5 per cent with confirmed significant bacteriuria, £10 190 (a week's sulphonamide at 32 pence for each course), giving a total cost for screening and treatment of £354 107. This would prevent acute pyelonephritis in approximately 6369 women, that is, 20 per cent of the 31 844 with significant bacteriuria. If it is assumed that half of these would otherwise require hospitalization for pyelonephritis for two weeks, at £70.00 a day, the cost of treatment comes to £3 120 320. This amounts to a saving of over £2.7m per annum for prevention rather than cure. The saving is even greater if simple inspection of the urine sample by a skilled technician is the screening procedure used. In contrast, formal microscopy and culture of specimens would turn a large saving into a small loss.

Urinary tract infections in childhood have more serious consequences than in the adult. Women with scarred kidneys and bacteriuria date the onset of urinary symptoms to childhood more often than bacteriuric subjects with normal renal radiology (Asscher *et al.* 1971).

Vesico-ureteric reflux is a frequent association of chronic pyelonephritis in the adult, and is an invariable finding in children with scarred kidneys (Smellie 1967; Hodson 1969). It is the most important cause of atrophic pyelonephritis in the young (Hendren 1970) and accounts for 65 per cent of all cases of severe childhood hypertension (Still and Cottom 1967). By comparison, 27 per cent of Australian adults with malignant hypertension have reflux nephropathy or chronic pyelonephritis (Kincaid-Smith *et al.* 1958). Primary vesico-urinary reflux is usually a congenital disorder, and seems to be inherited both as an autosomal dominant of variable expression and as an autosomal recessive trait. No familial cases have been described in blacks, and reflux is less commonly found in black schoolgirls with asymptomatic urinary tract infection (Kunin 1970).

Between 15 and 60 per cent of children with asymptomatic bacteriuria have vesico-ureteric reflux (Kunin *et al.* 1960; Savage and Wilson 1973; Smellie 1967; Rolleston *et al.* 1970; Winberg *et al.* 1970) depending upon age of investigation; in 79 per cent of cases it disappears during childhood but between 8 and 13 per cent have radiological evidence of chronic pyelonephritis at diagnosis (Normand

and Smellie 1979; Kunin 1970; Shannon 1972). Chronic pyelonephritis does not inevitably follow vesico-ureteric reflux, and the severity of the defect seems to be the single most important factor in determining whether scarring occurs (Rolleston *et al.* 1970). Reflux of sterile urine alone may lead to atrophic pyelonephritis, if severe enough (Hodson 1981).

Bacteriuria remains a valuable marker for reflux, and once a diagnosis of urinary tract infection has been made unequivocally in a child or infant, investigation is mandatory. The problem is that gross intrarenal reflux probably produces damage very soon after birth, and though it would be desirable to screen all neonates for the defect this seems an impossible task. Nephrosonography is a relatively new and non-invasive technique which may provide one approach to the problem (Barnett and Morely 1972), particularly in families known to be at risk.

Until a suitable screening technique is available, the priority is to detect infants with gross vesico-ureteric reflux before renal damage has occurred. It is therefore essential to investigate all neonates, infants, or children with proven urinary tract infection, whether girls or boys. Screening of offspring or siblings of those with demonstrated reflux is a second valuable measure and might be extended to first-degree relatives of those with any renal tract anomaly (Bailey 1973). All children admitted to hospital with fever should have their urine cultured (Rolleston *et al.* 1970).

The results of controlled trials on surgical correction of vesico-ureteric reflux suggest that it offers no advantage over conservative management with antibiotics (Kincaid-Smith 1983).

Glomerulonephritis

There has been a marked decline in deaths from nephritis in developed nations over the last century, even allowing for changes in diagnostic custom and accuracy (Fig. 11.2). However, it remains the most common cause of end-stage renal failure. The situation which prevailed in Europe 100 years ago persists in the third world, particularly in Africa, where nephrotic syndrome is still strikingly common (Table 11.7). Cameron (1979*a*) has attributed this change to improved social and economic conditions in developed countries, freeing individuals from the tyranny of malnutrition and the threat of infection.

The pattern of glomerulonephritis in temperate regions has been extensively studied and is fairly well documented. Minimal change glomerulonephritis occurs in 80–90 per cent of children with nephrotic syndrome (Churg *et al.* 1970); in adults, proliferative glomerulonephritis accounts for 50 per cent of cases, while minimal change and membranous account for 30 and 12 per cent respectively (Sharpstone *et al.* 1969). The age distribution of the various histological diagnoses underlying the nephrotic syndrome are summarized in Figs. 11.3 and 11.4. Most cases must be diagnosed as idiopathic, although many causes are recognized.

This temperate pattern of glomerulonephritis is in marked contrast to the tropical and underdeveloped world;

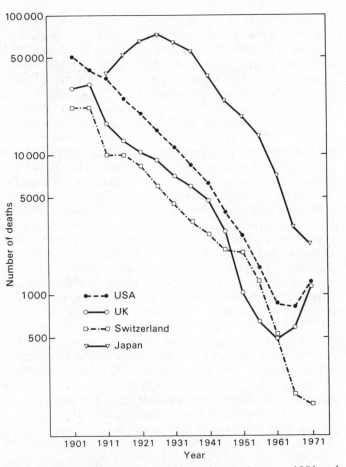

Fig. 11.2. Deaths from acute nephritis in females between 1901 and 1971 in the United States, United Kingdom, Switzerland, and Japan. (Data from Alderson (1981).)

Table 11.8 compares features of the nephrotic syndrome seen in children in tropical and temperate climates. Proliferative glomerulonephritis is the predominant histological type among both adults and children in Africa, though there are regional variations (Fig. 11.5). In South America and parts of North Africa, where schistosomal nephropathy is described, membranoproliferative disease is the most common finding (Andrade 1978). Reports from India suggest that the pattern of nephrotic syndrome seen there is similar to that in the west, with minimal change glomerulonephritis frequent among children (Srivartava *et al.* 1975).

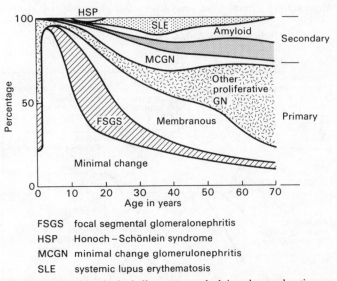

FSGS   focal segmental glomeralonephritis
HSP   Honoch – Schönlein syndrome
MCGN   minimal change glomerulonephritis
SLE   systemic lupus erythematosis

Fig. 11.3. The histological diagnoses underlying the nephrotic syndrome. (Reproduced by kind permission of Professor J.S. Cameron.)

Table 11.7. *Incidence of nephrotic syndrome (as admission rate) in different countries (1973). (Personal communication from Professor J.S. Cameron)*

			Admission rate for nephrotic syndrome	
Malaria status	Country	Area	%	Average %
Endemic malarial areas	Nigeria	Ibadan	2.40	
		Lagos	2.10	
	Uganda	Mulago	2.00	
		Fort Portal	1.80	2.60
	Yemen	Taiz	3.00	
	Papua New Guinea	Port Moresby	>4.00	
	Guyana	Mackenzie	2.80*	
Tropical, relatively non-malarial	Senegal	Dakar	0.85	
		Havare	0.70	0.40
	Zimbabwe	Bulawayo	0.15	
	Guyana	Demerara	0.05	
Temperate non-malarial	US	LA County	0.03	
		Utah	0.15	0.06
	UK	SE Thames	0.04	
	China	Human Medical College	0.02	

*0.05 *after elimination of malaria.*

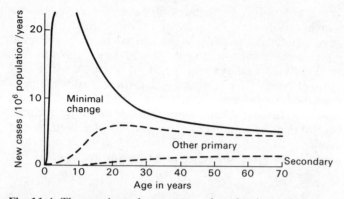

Fig. 11.4. The number of new cases of nephrotic syndrome per million population according to age in years, shown separately by underlying histological diagnosis. (Reproduced by kind permission of Professor J.S. Cameron.)

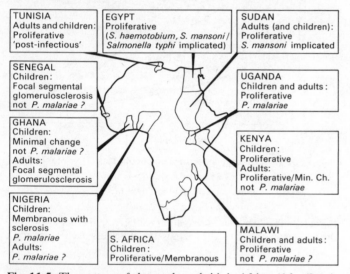

Fig. 11.5. The pattern of glomerulonephritis in Africa. (After Seggie (1982).)

In Iran, 60 per cent of glomerulonephritis is mesangiocapillary in type, while in China the pattern of histology seems similar to Europe and the US (Cameron 1983, personal communication).

Although interesting, the national differences and regional peculiarities in distribution of glomerulonephritis, of which there are many, remain largely unexplained. Cameron (1981) has suggested a model of glomerular disease in which the environment and the individual's immune system interact. In the underdeveloped world, glomerulonephritis is seen as a common outcome of widespread infection and parasitaemia in the presence of an immune system compromised by malnutrition. With the eradication of malaria, leprosy, and infectious disease in general in industrialized countries, glomerulonephritis is the outcome of an antigenic challenge in an individual with genetically impaired immune competence. The implication of this difference is that much can be done to decrease the incidence of glomerulonephritis in developing countries, by control of infection. The experience of Giglioli (1962) in Guyana is a powerful example of the way in which regulation of the environment, in this case malaria control, in an impoverished region leads to a decline in frequency of disease—nephrotic syndrome and glomerulonephritis.

Most reports of the nephrotic syndrome from tropical Africa stress the importance of *Plasmodium malariae* in its aetiology (Hendrickse and Gilles 1963; Hendrickse *et al.* 1972). In Uganda and Nigeria, this is almost certainly the case, although post-streptococcal glomerulonephritis, characterized by high mortality, seems also to be common among young adults (Wing *et al.* 1972). Hendrickse and Gilles (1963) drew attention to the strong association between malarial parasitaemia and nephrotic syndrome in Nigerian children, with *P. malariae* identified in the blood of 88 per cent of cases. A similar relationship was demonstrated for both adults and children in Uganda by Kibukamusoke *et al.* (1967). The most convincing evidence for the role of malaria in these countries is the identification of *P. malariae* antigens in the glomeruli of affected patients (Ward and Kibukamusoke 1969; Houba *et al.* 1971) by immunofluorescent microscopy and the elution of antibodies to the parasite from them (WHO 1972).

In Kenya, Senegal, the Ivory Coast, and Ghana, there is no evidence for the role of malaria in the aetiology of nephrotic syndrome (Rees *et al.* 1972; Morel-Maroger *et al.* 1975; Adu *et al.* 1981). In Nairobi, many cases were due to the use of skin-lightening creams containing mercury, which accounted for the predominance of sophisticated young African women among the patients (Barr *et al.* 1972), a problem which disappeared when the creams were banned. In Senegal, there is a remarkably high prevalence of extra-

Table 11.8. *Comparison of nephrotic syndrome in children in temperate versus tropical climates*

Factor	Temperate climate	Tropical climate
Aetiology	Majority idiopathic	In many countries malaria implicated
Sex incidence	Males predominate	Equal between sexes
Age	Peak at 2–3 years	Peak at 5 years
Presentation	Oedema	Oedema and fever
Physical findings	Oedema	Oedema, ascites, pleural effusion, and enlargement of liver and spleen
Renal biopsy	Usually minimal change	Localized focal glomerulitis with tubular changes which progresses to glomerular sclerosis
Treatment	Steroids	No specific measures
	Immunosuppressants	Control of malaria
Course and prognosis	Minimal change shows good response to treatment	In 30% of cases, renal insufficiency and hypertension develop in 3–5 years. Death may occur from intercurrent infection

membranous nephropathy amongst children (Satge *et al.* 1970) which may be due to hepatitis B antigen. Minimal-change glomerulonephritis is not an uncommon finding amongst Ghanaian children (Adu 1981), in contrast to other parts of Africa. Adu *et al.* (1981) described two cases of systemic lupus erythematosis (SLE) with nephritis in Ghana, an interesting observation in view of its rarity in tropical Africa (Greenwood 1968; Kanyerezi *et la.* 1980). This is in contrast to American blacks of West African origin in whom SLE is common (Fessel 1974).

Information from South Africa suggests that minimal-change glomerulonephritis is an infrequent cause of nephrotic syndrome among blacks of any age, but not amoung Indian children (Coovadia *et al.* 1979). The most common finding is membranous or proliferative disease, and this is also the case in Malawi (Brown *et al.* 1977) (Fig. 11.5).

Glomerulonephritis complicating hepatosplenic schistosomiasis, due to *Schistosoma mansoni*, was first described in Brazil (Andrade *et al.* 1971). The most common form of presentation is the nephrotic syndrome (Brito *et al.* 1970; Queiroz *et al.* 1973), with gradual development of hypertension. There are reports from Egypt, the Sudan, and Zimbabwe confirming cirrhosis with a variety of histoligical types of glomerulonephritis, as well as amyloidosis (Musa *et al.* 1980).

Renal disease is a feature of leprosy, especially the leprotamous type, and usually takes the form of amyloidosis or glomerulonephritis (Shwe 1972). Secondary amyloidosis is a leading cause of death in leprosy patients as a result of renal involvement (Shuttleworth and Ross 1956).

Urolithiasis

Urinary stone has existed as long as civilization. In an examination of 9000 mummies, Elliott Smith found three cases of urinary calculus. Hippocrates (470–360 BC) was a practised lithotomist, and the profusion of barber surgeons who 'cut for stone' for almost a millenium in Europe shows urolithiasis to have been a common condition. However, the bladder stones which gave them employment have now completely disappeared from the developed world.

The geography of urinary stone

There are two populations of stone (Table 11.9) which, as Andersen (1973) has pointed out, may represent only one epidemiological problem: different manifestations of the

same factors in developed and underdeveloped nations. The vesical calculus has disappeared from Europe with improved economic conditions, but is still common in developing countries lying in a broad belt from North and Central Africa to Syria, Iran, Pakistan, Burma, Thailand, and Indonesia. Within these countries, there are interesting regional variations; for example, higher rates are described in north and west India (83.6/100 000 in-patients) than south and east India (18.9/100 000 in-patients) (Andersen 1973). In Thailand, there is a marked difference between urban and rural areas (Halstead and Valyasevi 1967). Bladder calculus is not reported with great frequency in Southern Africa, South and Central America, and the Pacific Islands.

Renal stone is a disease of rich nations, and rising incidence has paralleled growth of industrialization and net domestic product (Fig. 11.6). This increase is apparent from both hospital admission records and population studies. Between 1907 and 1954, the incidence of renal stone in Finland doubled (Sallinen 1959), while in Norway between

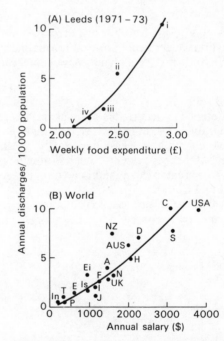

Fig. 11.6. A. The annual discharge rate from hospital per 10 000 of the population for urinary stone disease in males in Leeds according to social class between 1971 and 1973 in relation to the average weekly expenditure of food per person.

Fig. 11.6. B. The annual discharge rate from hospital per 10 000 of the population for urinary stone disease in adults in relation to the average salary in various countries of the world.

In=India   F=Finland   AUS=Australia
T=Thailand   EI=Eire   D=Denmark
P=Pakistan   UK=United Kingdom S=Sweden
E=Egypt   N=Norway   C=Canada
Is=Israel   A=Austria   USA=United States
J=Japan   NZ=New Zealand   of America
I=Italy   H=Holland
(After Robertson *et al.* (1981).)

Table 11.9. *Comparison of the features of vesical and upper urinary tract calculi*

	Vesical calculus	Upper urinary tract calculus
Distribution	Developing countries Rural areas	Developed countries Urban areas
Age incidence	Children	Adults
Sex incidence	Males predominate	Males predominate
Natural history	Do not recur	Tend to recur

1920 and 1960, there was a threefold increase (Andersen 1973). Rates of renal stone per 100 000 have been reported as 74.5 in Sweden (Hedenburg 1951), 43.1 in Mississipi and 196.5 in South Carolina (Boyce *et al.* 1956), 68 in Stornoway, Scotland (Andersen 1964), and 2500 in Jordan (Dajani *et al.* 1981). In addition to this national variation, there are regional differences: a survey of 24 hospitals in the UK showed that admission rates for urinary stone varied from 1.4 to 11.1 per 1000 total admissions (Rose and Westbury 1969).

Aetiology of urinary stone

Urolithiasis is probably a multifactorial phenomenon, and the relative importance of individual factors will vary according to context. For example, although renal stones are uncommon amongst the inhabitants of most African countries, they are common in European visitors to those countries. The same local environmental conditions operate with different effect in the native inhabitant and the visitor. The following are some of the factors implicated in the aetiology of urinary stone.

Physiology

Urolithiasis may result from inborn errors of metabolism such as cystinuria and endocrine abnormalities, such as hyperparathyroidism. Infection may have some role in stone formation.

Age and sex

The age difference in occurrence of renal and vesical calculi is shown in Table 11.9. In both, there is a male preponderance. Renal calculus is characteristically a disease of middle-age, but there is evidence that it is affecting younger individuals to a greater extent and at a younger age than 25 years ago (Fig. 11.7).

Endemic bladder stone has a peak incidence between the ages of two and four years, and 90 per cent of cases are male.

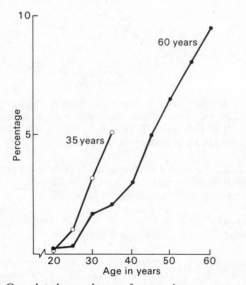

Fig. 11.7. Cumulated prevalence of stones in two age groups of unselected male stone-formers in Sweden. (After Ljunghall (1981).)

Genetic

The frequent observation of a family history of urinary calculus among stone formers (Grossman 1938; McGeown 1960; Ljunghall and Hedstrand 1975) should not too readily be taken as evidence for a genetic origin. Dietary and other factors may be responsible, and in this context, it is interesting that Halstead *et al.* (1967) have shown in Thailand that stones occur at a higher rate among family members living in the same household as the patient, than in blood relatives living separately.

Race

David Livingstone first drew attention to the rarity of renal stones in the indigenous inhabitants of Africa (Hutt 1984), and the condition is still uncommon among the black population of the continent (Esho 1978). Negroes in the US seem also to be protected (Reaser 1935), although the situation is changing (Quinland 1945; Dodson and Clark 1946). In contrast, stones are common among Arabs (Parry and Lister 1975; Husain *et al.* 1979) and Europeans living in Africa. These differences provide no evidence for racial predisposition as there are dietary and cultural factors which may account for the observation. A significant and isolated increase in the incidence of renal stone in the Ruhr (Boshamer 1961) was found to be due to a large number of cases among Turkish and south-east European immigrants to the area. These people had come from regions where the incidence of renal stone is low, suggesting increased susceptibility due to a local environmental factor. Accounts of this kind throw doubt on involvement of racial factors in urolithiasis.

Climate

The role of climate in urolithiasis is unclear. There are reports of seasonal variation in stone incidence (Leonard 1961; Bateson 1973; Robertson *et al.* 1975; Barker and Donnen 1978), and descriptions of increased incidence of renal calculi in European soldiers serving in the desert (Pierce and Bloom 1945; Boshamer 1961). However, Blalock's (1969) celebrated study of urolithiasis in the Royal Navy failed to confirm a simple correlation between stone incidence and climate. Wisniewski *et al.* (1981) showed that urinary calculus was more common in immigrants to Western Australia, who had arrived after the Second World War, than in those who had arrived earlier or than in the indigenous Aborigine population. It may be that a change in climate provokes stone formation. Increased exposure to ultraviolet light (with its effect on vitamin D metabolism) and dehydration are cited as mechanisms whereby a hot climate might predispose to the development of a renal calculus. The urinary content of important stone-forming elements has been shown to be influenced by ultraviolet light (Parry and Lister 1975; Robertson *et al.* 1975; Hallson *et al.* 1977).

Diet

This is the factor most consistently associated with urolithiasis. The WHO Regional Symposium on Vesical Calculus (1972) concluded that there is a positive correlation between endemic bladder stone disease in children and malnutrition, particularly of protein. Dietary influence on stone formation was suggested as early as 1830 by Yellowly in England (Shaw 1970), and has subsequently received support from many sources; one of the most interesting of these is a study carried out in Sicily (Andersen 1969). In a detailed review of records at the Children's Hospital in Palermo, Andersen demonstrated a strikingly consistent inverse relationship between incidence of bladder stone and intake of animal protein in the years 1928–63. There was an abrupt rise in the incidence of vesical calculi coinciding with gross protein shortage towards the end of the Second World War, which fell following the provision of a supplementary diet rich in protein by the United Nations Relief and Rehabilitation Administration (UNRRA) from 1944. The incidence of bladder stone in Palermo continued falling until 1963 when it disappeared completely. Over the same period, there has been an increase in renal calculi among adults.

In northern Thailand, differences in incidence of endemic bladder stone correspond to variation in dietary protein intake among the mothers of affected children during pregnancy and lactation (Halstead *et al.* 1968). In the communities where bladder stone is common among infants and children, gestating mothers practise food restriction in the belief that the new child will be small and parturition easier.

The rising incidence of renal stone in industrialized western countries over the last 70 or 80 years is paralleled not only by increased intake of animal protein but also more fat and refined carbohydrate and less fibre. However, of these the only one that correlates with stone formation at all demographic levels is animal protein (Andersen 1973). A unified hypothesis for the causation of vesical and renal calculi relates occurrence to the level of animal protein intake (Fig. 11.8).

Diabetic nephropathy

It has been estimated that there were 9.7 million diabetics in the US, including all those with undiagnosed glucose intolerance. Of these, six million are known (Burton and Hirschman 1980). Overall, 9 per cent of diabetic deaths are attributed to glomerulosclerosis: 6 per cent in the maturity-onset group, but as much as 48 per cent in young insulin-dependent diabetics (Burton and Hirschman 1980).

Persistent proteinuria, detectable by dip-slide testing, appears in 30–40 per cent of insulin-dependent diabetics after an average duration of 15–20 years (Deckert *et al.* 1978). This is followed by a gradual decline in glomerular filtration rate and a rise in arterial blood pressure (Morgensen 1976; Parving *et al.* 1981) which is unrelated to sugar control (Viberti *et al.* 1982) and seems to be self-perpetuating. However, control of hypertension slows the increase in albumin excretion, and in some patients the decline in glomerular filtration rate (Morgensen 1982). Haemodynamic factors seem to play a prominent role in the development of renal failure in diabetics at the stage of macroproteinuria (Hostetter *et al.* 1982; Viberti and Wiseman 1983).

As many as one in four new patients commencing treatment for end-stage renal disease in the US are diabetic

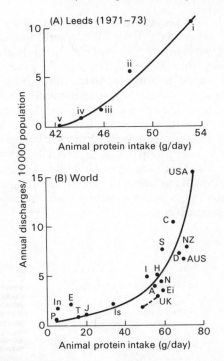

Figs.11.8A and B. The annual discharge rate from hospital for urinary stone disease in relation to animal protein consumption in each of the populations described in Figs. 11.6A and B. (After Robertson *et al.* (1981).)

(Friedman 1982). The number of diabetics with chronic renal failure treated by dialysis and transplantation in Europe passed 5000 during 1981 (Wing *et al.* 1983*b*), and of these, 2734 were still alive on therapy at the end of that year. The majority of these were in the larger European countries: the Federal Republic of Germany, France, and Italy, where diabetics accounted for 4, 3, and 3 per cent respectively, of the patients on treatment (Jacobs *et al.* 1983). Acceptance of new diabetics for treatment is increasing throughout Europe, and this trend is particularly striking in Scandinavian countries. In Sweden acceptance of diabetics per million population rose from under 3 to over 11 between 1976 and 1981.

The five years up to 1981 have witnessed a shift in the age distribution of diabetics accepted for treatment of end-stage renal failure in Europe. Whereas in 1976, it was predominantly a young diabetic population with uraemia who were being offered dialysis and transplantation, in 1981, 72 per cent of the new diabetics offered treatment were above 40 years of age. This is a reflection of changing attitudes to management of these patients together with an expansion in available facilities for treatment. The treated population mirrors more closely each year the diabetic population at large with uraemia. Analysis of the age- and sex-specific rate of acceptance of uraemic diabetics for treatment in Europe shows the Scandinavian countries to differ from their neighbours in treating more young (i.e. under 40 years of age) diabetics. The age-specific acceptance of these young patients remains high in Sweden, Finland, Denmark, and

Norway, where it ranged from 4 to 8.1 per million population in 1981, compared to 0.9 in France, and 1.6 in the Federal Republic of Germany (Jacobs *et al.* 1983). It is likely that this group suffers from Type I diabetes as they are under 40 years at the start of treatment, and the observation suggests that there may be differences in epidemiology of diabetes across Europe. Support for this suggestion comes from published international mortality data (WHO 1980, 1981) which show a higher age-specific mortality from diabetes in the 25–44-year age group in Scandinavian than other European countries. There are three plausible explanations for the observation. It may reflect a variation in the incidence of Type I diabetes, its natural history, or its management in different European countries.

Carcinoma of the prostate

There are dramatic racial and geographical differences in the incidence of carcinoma of the prostate (Fig. 11.9) which cannot be explained in terms of diagnostic practice or case finding. Studies of latent prostatic carcinoma suggest that differences may be less marked than seems at first sight (Liavag *et al.* 1972), but even when this is taken into account, the disparity remains. Mortality and morbidity data are similar.

The highest rates of prostate cancer are amongst US blacks and in particular those who live in Alameda County, California (California Department of Health 1967), in contrast to African negroes, in whom incidence is low

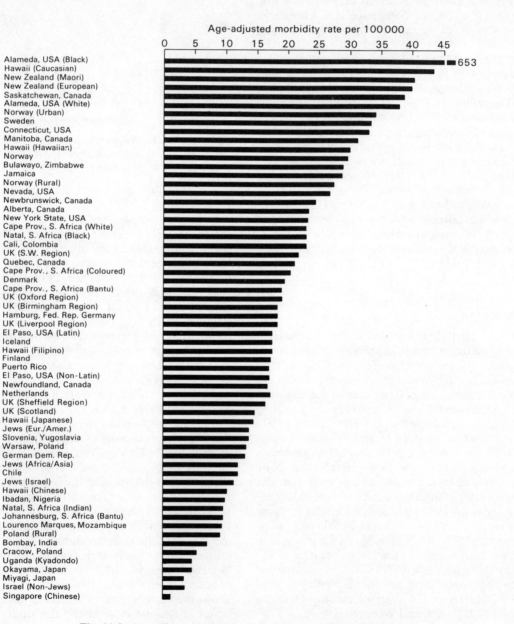

Fig. 11.9. Age-adjusted morbidity rate from carcinoma of the prostate per 100 000. (After Dhom and Hohbach (1973).)

(UICC 1966). In Europe, the disease is most common in Norway and Sweden, and in these two countries it is the leading form of malignancy in males (WHO and IARC 1976). The lowest rates are seen in orientals, in Japan, the Phillipines, Taiwan, and also non-Jews in Israel. It is said to be more common in urban than rural areas (Cancer Registry of Norway 1969), protestants than Jews, and professional than manual workers (King *et al.* 1963). There is a positive correlation between carcinoma of the prostate and female breast cancer in 24 countries (Wynder *et al.* 1967).

Regional differences are even more striking than the national ones; the age-adjusted morbidity rate for carcinoma of the prostate in Canada ranges from 17 in Newfoundland to 32 in Saskatchewan (Franks 1972).

Studies of migrant populations suggest that environmental factors may be of importance in the aetiology of prostate cancer. Haenszel and Kurihara (1968) made an extensive study of cancer incidence in Japanese in Japan, Japanese immigrants in the US (Issei), and their US-born offspring (Nissei and Sansei). There has been a rise in incidence of carcinoma of the prostate amongst Issei, but the rate does not approach that in Caucasian. The same pattern has also been shown in Polish immigrants to the US (Straszewski and Haenszel 1965). Somewhat confusingly, surveys in Hawaii show persisting and marked racial differences: rates of prostatic carcinoma are 3–4 times higher among Chinese immigrants than Caucasians or native Hawaiians.

The age-associated incidence of prostate cancer is established beyond reasonable doubt, and this holds for all countries for which statistics are available. However, no significant relationship has been found with socio-economic status, fertility, social habits, previous diseases, and weight or height (Wynder *et al.* 1971). The aetiology seems to be multifactorial with racial and environmental components. As the mean age of the male population rises, and as prostatectomy becomes a more common operation, registration rates for carcinoma of the prostate are likely to rise.

Carcinoma of the bladder

In the UK, carcinoma of the bladder is the sixth commonest cause of cancer in men after lung, stomach, prostate, colon, and rectum. In nearly every country, bladder cancer is most common among males, except in Egypt where sex incidence is equal (Table 11.10). Bladder tumours are rare in the young, but the age-specific death rate for the disease rises dramatically after the age of 45 years.

Age-standardized rates for the tumour in west European countries, Israel, Canada, and US (whites) are similar, at around 100 per million per year. Incidence in East Europe is lower, with Hungary at $30/10^6$ per year, Yugoslavia at $50/10^6$ per year, and Poland at $60/10^6$ per year. Low rates are also found in China and Japan at $50/10^6$, and India at $20/10^6$ per year (Segi and Kurihara 1972). A role for racial factor in aetiology of bladder carcinoma is substantiated by the observation that rates for the disease are twice as high in US white as black men, and 44 per cent higher in white than black women (Wynder and Goldsmith 1977), and higher for Euro-

Table 11.10. *Age-adjusted incidence rate for malignant neoplasms of the bladder by sex, per 100 000 population in 18 countries. (From Doll et al. (1970))*

Country	Incidence per 100 000		
	Male	Female	M:F ratio
England and Wales (Liverpool)	21.1	3.5	6.0
USA (Connecticut)	19.9	5.9	3.4
Israel: Jews	11.9	3.0	4.0
Scotland	11.4	3.5	3.3
Canada (Alberta)	10.9	3.6	3.0
Colombia (Cali)	10.6	3.4	3.1
S. Africa: White (Cape Province)	9.6	3.0	3.2
S. Africa: Black (Cape Province)	8.6	2.0	4.3
Puerto Rico	7.6	3.1	2.5
Finland	7.4	1.6	4.6
Norway	6.2	2.2	2.8
Israel: Non-Jews	6.1	0.2	30.5
Canada (Newfoundland)	5.7	2.5	2.3
Yugoslavia (Sloveria)	5.3	1.2	4.4
Japan (Miyagi)	4.7	1.6	2.9
Poland (Katowice)	4.6	0.9	5.1
Hungary (Vas)	2.8	0.8	3.5
India (Bombay)	2.3	0.8	2.9
New Zealand (Maori)	0.9	3.0	0.3

peans than Maoris in New Zealand, though admittedly rates are low for both (12 and $9/10^6$ per year respectively).

Bladder cancer incidence is related to social class, an association more marked in women than men (Berry 1982) and is more frequent in urban than rural areas (Wynder and Goldsmith 1977). The relationship with occupation was recognized almost a century ago and there is an ever-increasing list of jobs and aromatic amines associated with increased risk of the tumour (Tables 11.11 and 11.12).

Retrospective studies in England, Scandinavia, and America (Armstrong and Doll 1974; Stevens and Mollgarker 1979; Howe *et al.* 1980) have established that smoking carries a two- to fourfold increase in risk of bladder cancer, and there may be a dose–response relationship. There is a weak association with coffee drinking (Cole 1971).

Table 11.11. *Occupations known or suspected of being associated with bladder cancer. (After Wynder and Goldsmith (1977))*

Occupations known or suspected of being associated with bladder cancer

Chemical and dye-stuffs manufacture
Rubber and cable manufacture
Pigment and paint manufacture
Textiles, dyeing and printing
Laboratory workers
Rodent controllers
Pitch, coal, and tar workers
Leather workers
Furnace stokers
Hairdressers
Gas industry
Tailoring
Printing
Cooks and kitchen workers

Table 11.12. *Industrial aromatic amines suspected or known to induce bladder cancer in man. (After Wynder and Goldsmith (1977))*

Industrial aormatic amines suspected or known to induce bladder cancer in man

> Benzidine
> 1-Naphthylamine
> 2-Naphthylamine
> 4-Aminobiphenyl
> 4-Nitrobiphenyl
> Auramine
> Magenta
> Dianisidine
> 3.3'-Dichlorobenzene
> O-Tolidine

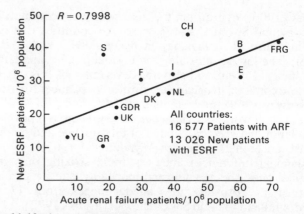

Fig. 11.10. Acute (reversible) renal failure (ARF) compared to acceptance of new end-stage renal failure (ESRF) patients in 1982 in 13 European countries treating more than 1000 ESRF patients. (B=Belgium, CH=Switzerland, D=Denmark, E=Spain, F=France, FRG=Federal Republic of Germany, GDR=German Democratic Republic, GR=Greece, I=Italy, NL=Netherlands, S=Sweden, UK=United Kingdom, YU=Yugoslavia.) (From Wing *et al.* (1983).)

A relationship between bilharzia and carcinoma of the bladder was first suggested by Ferguson in 1911, and has since received much support (Cheever 1978). In areas endemic for schistosomiasis, squamous carcinoma predominates (Lucas 1982*a*) and peak incidence of bladder tumours is at a younger age than either Europe, or comparable regions in Africa free of bilharzia (Makhyoun *et al.* 1971). Schistosomiasis may explain the equal sex incidence of bladder cancer in Egypt.

It has been suggested that secondary bacterial infection in the damaged bilharzial bladder may lead to production of nitrosamines, which then act as carcinogens (Lucas 1982*b*). Chronic bacterial cystitis associated with urethral stricture may account for the frequency of bladder cancer in parts of Africa where schistasomiasis does not occur (Owor 1975).

Acute renal failure

An epidemiological survey of acute renal failure (ARF) produced an incidence of 4.8 per 100 000 (Eliahou *et al.* 1975) with a 50 per cent higher risk in males than females. In the industrialized world, there seems to have been a change in pattern of referral for acute renal failure to dialysis centres, with a decline in the proportion of obstetric cases (Kerr *et al.* 1968; Kennedy *et al.* 1973); this may be due to improved obstetric care or fewer illegal abortions. An increase in the proportion of cases due to surgical and medical problems has occurred with an increase in median age of the patients (Cattell 1975). The number of patients treated for acute (reversible) renal failure in European countries in 1982 ranged from 10 to 70 per million population and was greatest in those countries with the highest acceptance rate for treating patients with end-stage renal failure (Fig. 11.10). Since this information was collected only from the centres reporting the treatment of end-stage renal failure, the numbers are likely to be an underestimate, for many cases of acute renal failure are treated in other units. A high proportion of these patients have multi-sytem failure and are treated in intensive care units. Although the average length of the illness is under two weeks, they utilize an area

of high technology with associated high costs and there is some suggestion (Fig. 11.10) that it is the availability of facilities and skills which determine the number of patients given dialytic therapy.

The commonest cause of acute renal failure is acute tubular necrosis, associated with ischaemia of the renal circulation. Increasing mechanization inevitably leads to a growing number of admissions for major trauma in developing countries (Hutt and Wing 1971). In a hospital study in tropical Africa (Adu 1976), massive intravascular haemolysis after a short febrile illness was the most frequent cause of acute renal failure; this presented as blackwater fever, but in only one case out of 55 was *Plasmodium falciparum* demonstrated. Classical blackwater fever with *P. falciparum* is now rare, and appears to have been a feature of malarial attacks in the partially-immune European adult.

People with glucose 6-phosphate dehydrogenase (G6PD) deficiency are particularly prone to haemolysis from infection or drug treatment, and an association between acute renal failure and G6PD deficiency has been described (Lwanga and Wing 1970). Inherited G6PD deficiency is prevalent in many parts of the world and is especially common in Caucasians of Mediterranean origin, and Sephardic and Kurdish Jews. However, renal failure complicating acute haemolysis appears to be infrequent in Mediterraneans compared with Africans (Symvoulidis *et al.* 1972).

The introduction of dialysis has made survival from acute renal failure possible but mortality remains high owing to a progressive shift in the type of patients encountered, with an increasing proportion of high-risk and elderly cases. Experience in war has shown that early and effective treatment of shock can significantly reduce the incidence of acute tubular necrosis (Whelton and Donadio 1969), and this is more pertinent in the underdeveloped world than the need for acute dialysis.

Chronic renal failure

This is a disease of middle- and old-age, with the majority of patients presenting at 40 years and above. The incidence of chronic renal failure increases progressively with age, and in most series, males predominate. The difference in age-specific incidence for males and females reflects the different proportions of underlying diseases, glomerulonephritis and hypertension in males, pyelonephritis in females.

In all series, glomerulonephritis is the leading cause of renal failure. Tables 11.13, 11.14, and 11.15 come from a variety of sources, and include data from Europe, the US, and Japan. Table 11.13 includes all patients entering the registry of the EDTA in 1976: there is a preponderance of males with glomerulonephritis. Pyelonephritis is the second most common diagnosis, and is more frequent among females, as are drug and analgesic nephropathy. The latter is second only to glomerulonephritis as a cause of end-stage renal disease in Australia (Table 11.15), and is markedly more common in Switzerland and Benelux countries than elsewhere in Europe (Table 11.14).

Many different renal diseases discussed above result in chronic renal failure. When there is mild impairment of excretory function (creatinine clearance 30–50 ml/min) it is likely to be asymptomatic and to require no therapy. As failure becomes more marked (creatinine clearance less than 20 ml/min) so dietary restriction of protein intake is required to control symptoms. Chronic renal failure is often insidiously progressive and patients may remain totally unaware of their renal disease until they reach end-stage renal failure. Thus their presentation may be sudden, producing an uraemic emergency. Following emergency treatment, usually by peritoneal dialysis, investigations are performed and frequently reveal small, contracted 'end-stage' kidneys. The antecedent disease remains a mystery and thus one in ten of end-stage renal failure patients are honestly diagnosed as 'chronic renal failure, aetiology uncertain' (Brynger *et al.* 1980).

Occult chronic renal failure may be diagnosed after a routine medical examination has revealed proteinuria or hypertension. The value of early detection rests almost entirely in the control of hypertension, although the relief of

Table 11.13. *Distribution according to primary renal disease, sex, and age (at start of treatment) of patients commencing renal replacement therapy in 1982 in European countries. (After Wing et al. (1983))*

Primary renal disease	Age and sex (%) Male			Female		
	0–15	15–55	55+	0–15	15–55	55+
Chronic renal failure, aetiology uncertain	2.8	9.7	18.2	4.2	11.0	15.5
Glomerulonephritis	18.9	40.5	20.3	33.1	27.1	11.4
Pyelonephritis/interstitial nephritis	23.8	14.1	18.9	27.1	24.2	27.6
Drug nephropathy	0.7	0.9	3.2	0	3.7	9.0
Cystic kidney disease	7.7	8.6	7.4	6.8	11.1	10.8
Hereditary renal disease	7.7	1.8	0.1	3.4	1.3	0.2
Congenital renal disease	17.5	1.3	0.2	8.5	1.9	0.4
Reno-vascular/hypertensive disease	0.7	7.9	14.7	2.5	5.0	9.4
Diabetes mellitus	0	8.7	7.3	0.8	6.7	8.7
Multi-system disease	16.1	3.1	4.4	11.0	5.1	3.9
Other renal disease	4.1	3.4	5.3	2.6	2.9	3.1
Total 100% (number)	143	4129	2688	118	2709	2185

Table 11.14. *Distribution of patients commencing renal replacement therapy per million population, in nine European countries in 1982 according to primary renal disease. (After Wing et al. (1983))*

Primary renal disease	Belgium pmp	Fed. Rep. Germany pmp	France pmp	German Dem. Rep. pmp	Italy pmp	Spain pmp	Sweden pmp	Switzerland pmp	United Kingdom pmp
Chronic renal failure, aetiology uncertain	2.6	4.6	3.7	0.8	5.2	5.7	0.7	3.2	2.1
Glomerulonephritis	7.3	9.9	6.7	8.4	6.8	6.7	9.3	9.5	4.8
Pyelonephritis/interstitial nephritis	4.9	9.0	4.3	5.1	6.4	6.0	5.4	6.6	3.0
Drug nephropathy	6.3	2.4	0.4	0.2	0.3	0.1	1.0	11.2	0.2
Cystic kidney disease	4.1	3.3	2.5	2.8	2.8	3.0	4.0	3.6	2.2
Hereditary renal disease	0.1	0.3	0.4	0.1	0.3	0.4	0.2	0.2	0.3
Congenital renal disease	0.1	0.2	0.8	0.2	0.2	0.4	0.1	0.4	0.4
Reno-vascular/hypertensive disease	2.7	2.2	4.3	0.7	3.8	2.8	5.3	2.7	2.2
Diabetes mellitus	3.2	3.9	1.9	1.3	2.0	2.1	6.8	3.3	1.3
Multi-system disease	2.0	1.1	1.2	0.4	1.1	1.0	3.4	0.8	1.2
Other renal disease	1.0	1.0	0.8	0.2	1.1	1.3	1.2	1.4	0.6

pmp=per million population.

Table 11.15. *Distribution of main primary renal diseases in Australia, Europe, Japan and the United States. Analysis of new (1979) patients in Australia, Europe and Japan; of total file for the United States where only 49 per cent had a diagnosis recorded. (PRD=primary renal disease.) (After Wing et al. (1983))*

| | Australia | Europe | Japan | US
All patients on file (only 49% had primary renal disease recorded) |
| | New patients in 1979 | | | |
	%	%	%	%
Glomerulonephritis	35	30	71	30
Pyelonephritis	7	21	3	13
Analgesic/drug nephropathy	19	3	(not coded)	1
Cystic kidney disease	9	9	2	9
Hypertension/ renovascular	5	8	4	22
Diabetic nephropathy	4	7	9	14
Other primary renal disease	21	22	11	11
Total patients	463	10 229	7523	31 276

urinary obstruction, eradication of urinary infection, or specific therapy of some multi-system disease involving the kidneys may slow or halt progressive damage. However, it has been recently claimed that reduction of protein and phosphorus intake slows the rate of progression of renal failure (Brenner 1983). This suggestion is attracting a great deal of interest because of the opportunity for extending the period of conservative management and delaying the need for dialysis and transplantation. Dietitians may therefore make a very significant contribution to reducing the costs of treating chronic renal failure, although achievements so far indicate that the gains for individual patients are often marginal.

Some geographical differences have been described in the distribution of primary renal disease causing end-stage renal failure (Wing *et al.* 1983). However, apparent differences must be interpreted in the light of different fashions in diagnosis, and some result from variation in the availability of treatment facilities. In countries with limited facilities for dialysis and transplantation, fewer old patients and patients with multi-system disease can be accepted for treatment. Selection is therefore particularly likely to exclude hypertensives and patients with diabetes as the cause of their end-stage renal failure. Table 11.14 is a further analysis of patients who commenced treatment in 1982, to show the crude acceptance rate per million population of patients in nine different European countries according to primary renal disease. There was a notably high incidence of glomerulonephritis in Italy and Spain, while pyelonephritis contributed many patients in the Federal Republic of Germany and cystic kidney disease was more frequent in northern than in southern Europe. Analgesic nephropathy was an important contributor to end-stage renal failure in

Belgium and Switzerland as was diabetes in Sweden. The total crude acceptance rate may be used as a gauge of available facilities and a low acceptance rate in the UK is associated with a low rate of treatment of diabetics with end-stage renal failure.

Excellent registry data are available for Australia and a summary of Japanese patients is also available. Unfortunately, information from the US End Stage Renal Disease Program is of poor quality. Comparison of these data (Table 11.15) must not be pressed too hard because of assumptions made in equating the different code structures. Glomerulonephritis accounted for over 70 per cent of new Japanese patients in 1979, possibly because of a lower rate of diagnosis of pyelonephritis/interstitial nephritis. Analgesic nephropathy caused 1 in 5 cases of end-stage renal failure in Australia, similar to its contribution in Belgium and Switzerland (Table 11.14), but only 1 in 100 in America and was not even included in codes for primary renal disease in Japan. Hypertension caused 22 per cent of cases of end-stage renal failure in the US due both to the older age of American patients and to the high incidence of hypertensive renovascular disease in American blacks. Diabetic nephropathy was already accounting for 14 per cent of American cases in 1979 and is now thought to cause one in every four new patients (Friedman 1982).

The data given in Tables 11.12, 11.14, 11.15 are drawn

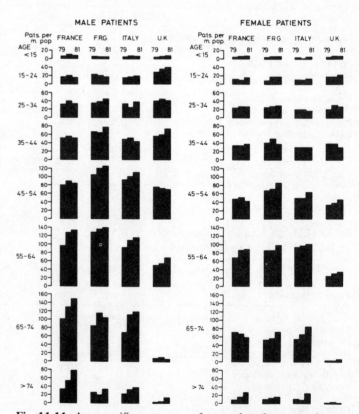

Fig. 11.11. Age-specific acceptance for renal replacement therapy per million population (pmp) in four European countries, between 1979 and 1981. Males and females shown separately. (Data by courtesy of EDTA.)

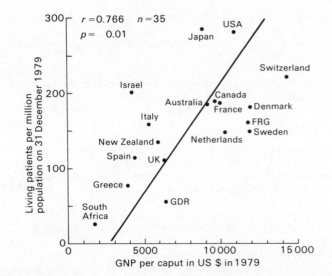

Fig. 11.12. Correlation between number of patients alive on treatment for end-stage renal failure (ESRF) and per caput gross national product (GNP). Eighteen countries are named in the figure but the regression was performed with data from 35 countries. (From Jacobs *et al.* (1981).)

from the populations treated by dialysis and transplantation. The availability of treatment varies between countries and Fig. 11.11 shows the age-specific acceptance rate for males and females in four large western European countries. World-wide, the number of patients per million population on treatment correlates with the economic productivity (GNP) expressed in US $ per caput (Fig. 11.12). The intercept of the regression line in Fig. 11.12, at US $2700 suggests that it is difficult of even inappropriate for countries with a GNP lower than this to put many patients on treatment.

Three-quarters of the world's population lives in countries with a per caput GNP of less than US $2700. Chronic renal failure is undoubtably a common cause of death in the third world. In a large *post-mortem* series from Uganda and Nigeria, 45 per cent of deaths were associated with evidence of progressive glomerulonephritis (Edington and Mainwaring 1966), an important cause of hypertension in young Ugandan adults (Hutt and Coles 1969). Unpublished observations in Kenya led to the conclusion that between 80 and 100 patients per million population died of renal failure in that country in 1978–79. None could be offered treatment. A handful of patients have been treated in the great Indian subcontinent (Chugh 1979) where perhaps 50 000 people die annually of end-stage renal failure. The high cost of renal-failure therapy cruelly exemplifies the medical component in the north–south divide (Brandt 1980).

PREVENTION IN GENITO-URINARY DISEASE

This chapter contains only a few instances of successful preventive measures in genito-urinary disease. These successes are small and isolated: the eradication of nephrotic syndrome in small group of affluent Nigerian women by withdrawal of mercurial skin-lightening creams, a reduction in incidence of analgesic nephropathy following legislation to control availability of phenacetin, and a decline in glomerulonephritis due to control of malaria in Guyana. The major impact on the incidence of genito-urinary disease, for example glomerulonephritis, has come not as a result of specific measures, but rather because of the improvement in social and economic conditions in developed countries. Viewed over a long time scale this impact has been considerable in developed countries and should now take effect in the developing nations where the greater influence of glomerulonephritis is found at present. However, this depends on political and economic developments more than on public health measures (Brandt 1980).

Screening of pregnant women for occult urinary tract infection (UTI) at the time of booking reduces the incidence of pyelitis of pregnancy which is a serious complication associated with considerable maternal morbidity and fetal loss. However, the cost–effectiveness depends on adopting the less costly methods for screening.

Screening programmes to detect occult UTI in young children have not been shown to produce cost-effective benefits. Health education might improve public awareness and lead to the selection of a subset of children amongst whom a higher yield of positive findings might be achieved.

Routine medical examinations to detect proteinuria and hypertension may be pointers to important diseases of the urinary system.

Public health measures might have an impact on the incidence of genito-urinary diseases in the following cases:

1. Control of parasitic infections in tropical countries. The association between glomerulonephritis and schistosomal and malarial infection has been discussed.

2. Diagnosis and treatment of hypertension (which may lead to chronic renal failure) with particular reference to the marked susceptibility of blacks to raised blood pressure, and the importance of blood pressure control in diabetics who become hypertensive.

3. The prompt and effective treatment of shock to reduce the incidence of acute renal failure.

4. The detection of asymptomatic urinary tract infection in high-risk young children (under five years) as a marker for vesico-ureteric reflux.

5. Genetic advice and counselling could reduce the incidence of congenital renal diseases which contribute almost one in ten patients to end-stage renal failure treatment programmes.

6. Reduction by genetic counselling or by discovery of causal factors, of insulin-dependent diabetes. Variation in geographical distribution of this disease suggests that certain populations (notably Scandinavia) are more susceptible than others.

7. Care in the prescription and use of drugs known to be nephrotoxic. Analgesic nephropathy has only been recognized in the last 20 years and is probably still under-diagnosed. For instance, in Italy the median age of patients with a diagnosis of pyelonephritis at time of commencing renal replacement therapy is 60 years, compared

to a figure for the whole of Europe close to 50 years (Wing *et al.* 1983). An explanation of this difference may be misdiagnosis of analgesic nephropathy (which has an older age distribution) as pyelonephritis.

8. Identification of other nephrotoxic substances in the environment (hydrocarbons have been implicated at an anecdotal level).

In 1972, the US government introduced legislation which rendered treatment of chronic renal failure free, a situation unique in American health care. The dramatic expansion in the end-stage renal disease programme which resulted was clearly unexpected: the government was unprepared for the revenue implications and has subsequently reviewed acceptance policy for treatment, and revised eligibility. Few individuals and no government can afford the open-ended treatment of chronic renal failure. The case for prevention is clear, with obvious medical, social, and economic benefits. It is the only rational response to the ever increasing cost of treatment of end-stage renal disease.

ACKNOWLEDGEMENTS

We would like to express our thanks to Professors M. Hutt and J.S. Cameron, and to the EDTA Registry (which is supported by governments and organizations named in its combined reports) for their help with this chapter.

REFERENCES

Abbott, G.D. (1972). Neonatal bacteriuria: a prospective study in 1460 infants. *Br. Med. J.* **i**, 267.

Adu, D., Anim-Addo, Y., Foli, A.K. *et al.* (1976). Acute renal failure in tropical Africa. *Br. Med. J.* **i**, 890.

Adu, D., Anim-Addo, Y., and Foli, A.K. (1981). The nephrotic syndrome in Ghana: clinical and pathological aspects. *Q. J. Med.* **199**, 297.

Akinkugbe, F.M., Familusi, J.B., and Akinkugbe, O.O. (1973). Urinary tract infection in infancy and early childhood. *E. Afr. Med. J.* **50**, 515.

Alderson, M. (1981). *International mortality statistics.* Macmillan, London.

Alleyne, G.A.O., Statius Van Eps, L.W., Addae, S.K. *et al.* (1975). The kidney in sickle cell anaemia. *Kidney Intl.* **7**, 371.

Allison, A.C. (1960). Glucose-6-phosphate dehydrogenase deficiency in red blood cells of East Africans. *Nature, Lond.* **186**, 531.

Andersen, D.A. (1969). Historical and geographical differences in the pattern of incidence of urinary stones considered in relation to possible aetiological factors. In *Proceedings Renal Stone Research Symposium,* Leeds 1968 (eds. A. Hodkinson and B.E.C. Nordin) p. 7. Churchill, London.

Andersen, D.A. (1973). Environmental factors in the aetiology of urolithiasis. In *Urinary calculi; proceedings of the International Symposium on Renal Stone Research.* Madrid 1972. (eds. L. Cifuentes Delatte, A. Rapado, and A.S. Hodgkinson) p. 130. Karker, Basel.

Andersen, G.S. (1964). Urinary calculus in an island community. *Br. J. Urol.* **36**, 556.

Andrade, Z.A. (1978). Schistosomal nephropathy. In *Proceedings 7th International Congress of Nephrology,* Montreal 1978 (eds. R. Barcelo,, M. Bergeron, S. Carriere *et al.*) p. 61. Karger, Basel.

Andrade, Z.A., Andrade, S.G., and Sadigursky, M. (1971). Renal changes in patients with hepatosplenic schistosomiasis. *Am. J. Trop. Med. Hygiene* **20**, 77.

Andrade, Z.A. and Rocha, H. (1979). Schistosomal glomerulopathy. *Kidney Intl.* **16**, 23.

Armstrong, B. and Doll, R. (1974). Bladder cancer mortality in England and Wales in relation to cigarette smoking and saccharine consumption. *Br. J. Prev. Soc. Med.* **28**, 233.

Arnold, L., Collins, C., and Stramer, G.A. (1977). Analgesic abuse, renal papillary necrosis and concomitant drug intake. *Aust. NZ Med. J.* **7**, 253.

Asscher, A.W. (1969). The early diagnosis of urinary tract infection, p. 23. Office of Health Economics, London.

Asscher, A.W., Chick, S., and Waters, W.E. (1971). The need for treatment. *Post-grad. Med. J.* Suppl. **47**, 28.

Asscher, A.W., Chick, S., Radford, N. *et al.* (1973). Natural history of asymptomatic bacteriuria in non-pregnant women. In *Urinary tract infection* (eds. W. Brumfitt, and A.W. Asscher) p. 51. Oxford University Press.

Bailey, R.R. (1973). The relationship of vesico-ureteric reflux to urinary tract infection and chronic pyelonephritis–reflux nephropathy. *Clin. Nephrol.* **1**, 132.

Barnett, E. and Morely, P. (1972). Diagnostic ultrasound in renal disease. *Br. Med. Bull.* **28**, 196.

Barker, E.J.B. and Donnen, S.P.B. (1978). Regional variations in the incidence of upper urinary tract stones in England and Wales. *Br. Med. J.* **i**, 67.

Barr, R.D., Rees, P.H., Cordy, P.E. *et al.* (1972). Nephrotic syndrome in adult Africans in Nairobi. *Br. Med. J.* **ii**, 131.

Bateson, E.M. (1973). Renal tract calculi and climate. *Med. J. of Aust.* **2**, 111.

Beaufils, H., Lebon, P., Auriol, M. *et al.* (1978). Glomerular lesions in patients with *Schistosoma haematobium* infection. *Trop. Geogr. Med.* **30**, 183.

Berger, M., Birch, L.M., and Conte, N.F. (1967). The nephrotic syndrome secondary to acute glomerulonephritis during falciparum malaria. *Ann. Intern. Med.* **67**, 1163.

Berry, R.J. (1982). Carcinoma of the bladder. In *Epidemiology of diseases* (eds. D.L. Miller and R.D.T. Farmer) p. 266. Blackwell, Oxford.

Bhamarapravati, N., Boonpucknavig, S., Boonpucknavig, V. *et al.* (1973). Glomerular changes in acute *Plasmodium falciparum* infection. *Arch. Pathol.* **96**, 289.

Bickel, H. and Harris, H. (1952). The genetics of Lignac–Fanconi disease. *Acta Paediatr. Scand.,* Suppl. **90**, 22.

Blalock, N.J. (1969). The pattern of urolithiasis in the Royal Navy. In *Proceedings of the renal stone research symposium, Leeds 1968).* (ed. A. Hodgkinson, and B.E.C. Nordin) p. 33. Churchill, London.

Bois, E., Feingold, J., Frenay, P. *et al.* (1976). Infantile cystinosis in France: genetics, incidence, geographic distribution. *J. Med. Genet.* **13**, 434.

Boshamer, K. (1961). The calculus areas of the world. In *Handbook of urology,* p. 34. Springer, Berlin.

Boyce, W.H., Garvey, F.K., and Strawcutter, A.G. (1956). Incidence of urinary calculi among patients in general hospitals. *JAMA* **161**, 1437.

Branch, R.A., Clark, G.W., Cochrane, A. *et al.* (1971). Incidence of uraemia and requirements for maintenance haemodialysis. *Br. Med. J.* **i**, 249.

Brand, J.G. (1979). Schistosomiasis—cancer: aetiological considerations. *Acta Trop.* **36**, 203.

Brandt, W. (1980). *North–South: a programme for survival.* Pan Books, London.

Brenner, B. (1983). Dietary protein intake and the progressive nature of kidney disease; the role of haemodynamically mediated glomerular injury in the pathogenesis of progressive glomerular sclerosis in ageing, renal ablation, and intrinsic renal disease. *New Engl. J. Med.* **307**, 652.

Brito, T., Gunji, J., Camargo, M.E. *et al.* (1970). Advanced kidney disease in patients with hepatosplenic Manson's schistosomiasis. *Rev. Inst. Med. Trop. Sao Paulo.* **12**, 225.

Brown, K.G.E., Abrahams, C., and Myers, A.M. (1977). The nephrotic syndrome in Malawian Blacks. *S. African Med. J.* **52**, 275.

Brynger, H., Brunner, F.P., Chantler, C. *et al.* (1980). Combined report on regular dialysis and transplantation in Europe X, 1979. In *Proceedings of the European Dialysis and Transplant Association* (ed. B.H.B. Robinson) Vol. 17, p. 2. Pitman, London.

Burry, A.F., De Jersey, P., and Weedon, D. (1966). Phenacetin and renal papillary necrosis. *Med. J. Aust.* **1**, 873.

Burton, B.T. and Hirschman, G.H. (1980). Diabetes in the USA: a demographic overview. In *Diabetic renal syndrome* (eds. E.A. Friedman and F.A. L'Esperance) p. 5. Grune and Stratton, New York.

California Department of Health (1967). *Incidence of cancer in Alameda County, California, 1960–1964.* California Department of Health, San Francisco.

Cameron, J.S. (1979a). The natural history of glomerulonephritis. In *Renal disease* (eds. D. Black and N.F. Jones) p. 329. Blackwell, Oxford.

Cameron, J.S. (1979b). Clinicopathological correlations in glomerular disease. In *Kidney disease* (eds. J. Churg, B.H. Spargo, F.K. Mostifi *et al.* p. 76. Williams and Wilkins, Baltimore.

Cameron, J.S. (1981). The prevention of glomerulonephritis. In *Proceedings 8th International Congress of Nephrology,* Athens 1981. (eds. W. Zurukzoglu, M. Papadimitriou, and M. Pyrpasopoulos) p. 32, Karger, Basel.

Cameron, J.S. and Trounce, J.R. (1965). Membranous glomerulonephritis and the nephrotic syndrome appearing during mersalyl therapy. *Guy's Hosp. Rep.* **114**, 101.

Cancer Registry of Norway (1969). Cancer registration in Norway. The incidence of cancer in Norway 1964–1966. Cancer Registry of Norway, Oslo.

Cattell, W.R. (1975). Acute renal failure. In *Recent advances in renal disease.* (ed. N.F. Jones) p. 1. Churchill Livingstone, London.

Cheever, A.W. (1978). Schistosomiasis and neoplasia. *J. Natl. Cancer Inst.* **61**, 13.

Chen, B.T.M., Ooi, B.-S., Tan, K.-K. *et al.* (1973). Nephrotic syndrome in Singapore. *J. Chronic Dis.* **26**, 237.

Chugh, K.S. (1979). Management of renal failure in India. Proceedings of the second meeting of the International Society for Aritificial Organs (ISAO). New York, 1979, in Singapore. *J. Chronic Dis.* **26**, 237.

Churg, J., Habib, R., and White, R.H.R. (1970). Pathology of the nephrotic syndrome in children. *Lancet* **i**, 1299.

Cole, P. (1971). Coffee drinking and cancer of the lower urinary tract. *Lancet* **i**, 1335.

Condie, A.P., Brumfitt, W., Reeves, D.S. *et al.* (1973). The effects of bacteriuria in pregnancy on foetal health. In *Urinary tract infection* (eds. W. Brumfitt and A.W. Asscher) p. 108. Oxford University Press.

Coovadia, H.M., Adhikari, M., and Morel-Maroger, L. (1979). Clinico-pathological features of the nephrotic syndrome in South African children. *Q. J. Med. NS* **48**, 77.

Dajani, A.M., Bjornesjo, K.B., and Shehabi, A.A. (1981). Urinary stone disease in Jordan. In *Urinary calculus* (eds. J.G. Brockis and B. Finlayson) p. 35. PSG, Boston.

Davies, D.J., Kennedy, A., and Roberts, C. (1970). The aetiology of renal medullary necrosis: a survey of adult cases in Liverpool. *J. Pathol.* **100**, 257.

Deckert, T., Poulsen, J.E., and Larsen, M. (1978). Prognosis of diabetics with diabetes onset before the age of thirty-one. *Diabetology* **14**, 363.

Dhom, G. and Hohbach, M. (1973). Mortality and morbidity of prostatic carcinoma. In *Current problems in the epidemiology of cancer and lymphomas* (eds. E. Grundman and H. Tulinius) p. 140. Heinemann, London.

Dillon, H.C. (1967). Pyoderma and nephritis. *Ann. Rev. Med.* **18**, 207.

Dodson, A.I. and Clark, J. (1946). Incidence of urinary calculi in the American Negro. *JAMA* **132**, 1063.

Dombey, S.L., Sagar, D., and Knapp, M.S. (1975). Chronic renal failure in Nottingham and requirements for dialysis and transplant facilities. *Br. Med. J.* **ii**, 484.

Ebbesen, F., Mygind, K., and Holck, F. (1976). Infantile nephropathic cystinosis in Denmark. *Dan. Med. Bull.* **23**, 216.

Edington, G.M. and Mainwaring, A.R. (1966). Nephropathies in West Africa. In *The kidney* (eds. F.K. Mostofi and D.E. Smith) p. 488. Williams and Wilkins, Baltimore.

Eliahou, H.E., Boichis, H., Bott-Kanner, G. *et al.* (1975). An epidemiological study of renal failure. 2. Acute renal failure. *Am. J. Epidemiol.* **101**, 281.

Esho, J.O. (1978). The rarity of urinary calculus in Nigeria. *Trop. Geogr. Med.* **30**, 477.

Ferguson, A.R. (1911). Associated bilharziasis and primary malignant disease of the urinary bladder with observations in a series of fourty cases. *J. Pathol. Bact.* **16**, 76.

Fessel, W.J. (1974). Systemic lupus erythematosus in the community. *Arch. Intern. Med.* **134**, 1027.

Florey, C. du V., Kessner, D.M., Kashgarian, M. *et al.* (1971). Mortality trends for chronic nephritis and infections of the kidney. *J. Chronic Dis.* **24**, 71.

Franks, L.M. (1972). The incidence of carcinoma of the prostate: an epidemiological survey. In *Current problems in epidemiology of cancer and lymphomas* (eds. E. Grundmann, and H. Tulinius) p. 149. Heinemann, London.

Freedman, L.R., Phair, J.P., Seki, M. *et al.* (1965). The epidemiology of urinary tract infection in Hiroshima. *Yale J. Biol. Med.* **37**, 262.

Friedman, E.A. (1982). (Editorial.) *Diabetic Nephropathy* **1**, 1.

Gadoth, N., Moses, S.W., and Boichis, H. (1975). Cystinosis in Israel. *Harefuah* **88**, 122.

Gallagher, D.J.A. (1974). Quoted by Miller, T.E. and North, J.D.K. Host response in urinary tract infections. *Kidney Int.* **5**, 179.

Giglioli, G. (1962). Malaria and renal disease with special reference to British Guiana. II. The effect of malaria eradication on the incidence of renal disease in British Guiana. *Ann. Trop. Med. Parasitol.* **56**, 225.

Gilles, H.M. and Ikeme, A.C. (1960). Haemaglobinuria among adult Nigerians due to glucose-6-phosphate dehydrogenase deficiency with drug sensitivity. *Lancet* **ii**, 889.

Gloor, F.J. (1978). Changing concepts in pathogenesis and morphology of analgesic nephropathy seen in Europe. *Kidney Int.* **13**, 27.

Greenwood, B.M. (1968). Autoimmune disease and parsitic infections in Nigerians. *Lancet* **ii**, 380.

Grossman, W. (1938). Current urinary stone wave in Central Europe. *Br. J. Urol.* **10**, 46.

Gurland, H.J., Chantler, F.P., Jacobs, C. *et al.* (1976). Combined report on regular dialysis and transplantation in Europe IV, 1975. In *Proceedings of the European Dialysis and Transplant Association* (ed. B.H.B Robinson) Vol. 3, p. 3. Pitman, London.

Guttmann, R.D. (1979). Renal transplantation. *New Engl. J. Med.* **301**, 975.

Haenszel, W. and Kurihara, M. (1968). Studies of Japanese migrants. 1. Mortality from cancer and other diseases among Japanese in the United States. *J. Natl. Cancer Inst.* **40**, 43.

Hall, P.W. and Dammin, G.J. (1978). Balkan nephropathy. *Nephron* **22**, 281.

Hall, P.W., Dimitrov, T.S., and Dinev, I. (1981). Endemic Balkan nephropathy. In *Proceedings 8th International Congress of Nephrology,*

Athens 1981 (eds. W. Zurukzoglu, M. Papadimitriou, M. Pyrpasopoulos *et al.*) p. 481. Karger, Basel.

Hallson, P.C., Kasidas, G.P., and Rose, G.A. (1977). Seasonal variations in urinary excretion of calcium and oxalate in normal subjects and in patients with idiopathic hypercalciuria. *Br. J. Urol.* **49**, 1.

Halstead, S.B. and Valyasevi, A. (1967). Studies of bladder stone disease in Thailand. III Epidemiological studies in Ubol Province. *Am. J. Clin. Nutr.* **20**, 1329.

Halstead, S.B., Valyasevi, A., and Umpaivit, P. (1968). Studies of bladder stone disease in Thailand. Dietary habits and disease prevalence. *Am. J. Clin. Nutr.* **20**, 1352.

Harrington, J.M., and Waldron, H.A. (1981). Occupation and renal disease. In *Occupational health practice*, 2nd edn (ed. R.S.F. Schilling) p. 89. Butterworth, London.

Harvald, B. (1963). Renal papillary necrosis: a clinical survey of 66 cases. *Am. J. Med.* **35**, 481.

Heale, W.F. (1971). Chronic pyelonephritis in the adult. *Aust. NZ J. Med.* **3**, 283.

Hedenberg, I. (1951). Renal and ureteric calculi: a study of the occurrence in Sweden during 1911 to 1983. *Acta Chir. Scand.* **101.** 17.

Heller, H., Sohar, E., Gafni, J. *et al.* (1961). Amyloidosis in familial Mediterranean fever: independent genetically determined character. *Arch. Intern. Med.* **107**, 539.

Hendren, W.H. (1970). A ten year experience with ureteral reimplantation in children. In *Renal infection and renal scarring* (eds. P. Kincaid-Smith and K.F. Fairley) p. 269. Mercedes Publishing Services, Melbourne.

Hendrickse, R.G. (1980). Epidemiology and prevention of kidney disease in Africa. *Trans. R. Soc. Trop. Med. Hygiene* **74**, 8.

Hendrickse, R.G. and Gilles, H.M. (1963). Nephrotic syndrome and other renal diseases in children in Western Nigeria. *E. Afr. Med. J.* **40**, 186.

Hendrickse, R.G., Adeniyi, A., Edington, G.M. *et al.* (1972). Quartan malarial nephrotic syndrome. *Lancet* **i**, 1143.

Hepinstall, R.H. (1974). *Pathology of the kidney.* Little Brown, Boston.

Hiatt, R.A. and Friedman, G.D. (1982). Characteristics of patients referred for treatment of end-stage renal disease in a defined population. *Am. J. Public Health* **72**, 829.

Hodson, C.J. (1969). The effects of disturbance of flow on the kidney. *J. Infect. Dis.* **120**, 54.

Hodson, J. (1981). Sterile reflux. In *Proceedings 8th International Congress of Nephrology*. Athens 1981 (eds. M. Zurukzoglu, M. Papadimitriou and M. Pyrpasopoulos) p. 368. Karger, Basel.

Hostetter, T.H., Rennke, H.G., and Brenner, B.M. (1982). The case for intrarenal hypertension in the initiation and progression of diabetic and other glomerulopathies. *Am. J. Med.* **72**, 375.

Houba, V., Allison, A.C., Adeniyi, A. *et al.* (1971). Immunoglobulin classes and complement in biopsies of Nigerian children with the nephrotic syndrome. *Clin. Exp. Immunol.* **8**, 761.

Howe, G.R., Burch, J.D., Miller, A.B. *et al.* (1980). Tobacco use, occupation, coffee, various nutrients, and bladder cancer. *J. Natl. Cancer Inst.* **64**, 701.

Husain, I., Badsha, S.A., Al-Ali, I.H. *et al.* (1979). A survey of urinary stones disease in Abu Dhabi. *Emirates Med. J.* **1**, Suppl. 17.

Hutt, M.S.R. (1984). The geographical pathology of genito-urinary diseases in the tropics. In *Tropical urology*. Churchill Livingstone, London.

Hutt, M.S.R. and Coles, R. (1969). Post-mortem findings in hypertensive subjects in Kampala, Uganda. *E. Afr. Med. J.* **46**, 342.

Hutt, M.S.R. and White, R.H.R. (1975). Geographical aspects of glomerulonephritis. In *Recent advances in renal disease* (ed. N.F. Jones) p. 119. Churchill Livingstone, London.

Hutt, M.S.R. and Wing, A.J. (1971). Renal failure in the tropics. *Br. Med. Bull.* **27**, 122.

Hypertension Detection and Follow-up Program Co-operative Group (1977). Blood pressure studies in 14 communities: a two-stage screen for hypertension. *JAMA* **237**, 2385.

Jacobs, C., Broyer, M., Brunner, F.P. *et al.* (1981). Combined report on regular dialysis and transplantation in Europe, XI, 1980. In *Proceedings of the European Dialysis and Transplant Association* (ed. B.H.B. Robinson) vol. 18, p. 2. Pitman, London.

Jacobs, C., Brunner, F.P., Brynger, H. *et al.* (1983). The first five thousand diabetics treated by dialysis and transplantation in Europe. *Diabetic Nephropathy* **2**, 12.

Jacobs, L.A. and Morris, J.G. (1962). Renal papillary necrosis and the abuse of phenacetin. *Med. J. Aust.* **2**, 531.

Kanyerezi, B.R., Lutalo, S.K., and Kigonya, E. (1980). Systemic lupus erythematosus: clinical presentation among Ugandan Africans. *E. Afr. Med. J.* **57**, 274.

Kass, E.H. (1960). The role of asymptomatic bacteriuria in the pathogenesis of pyelonephritis. In *Biology of pyelonephritis* (eds. E.L. Quinn and E.H. Kass) p. 399. Little Brown, Boston.

Kass, E.H., Savage, W., and Santamarina, B.A.G. (1965). The significance of bacteriuria in preventive medicine. In *Progress in pyelonephritis* (ed. E.H. Kass). Davies, Philadelphia.

Kennedy, A.C., Burton, J.A., Luke, R.G. *et al.* (1973). Factors affecting prognosis in acute renal failure. *Q. J. Med.* **42**, 73.

Kerr, D.N.S., Rabindranath, G., and Elliot, R.W. (1968). The treatment of acute renal failure. In *Fourth Symposium on Advanced Medicine* (ed. O. Wrong) p. 74. Pitman, London.

Kibukamusoke, J.W. (1973). *Nephrotic syndrome of quartan malaria.* Arnold, London.

Kibukamusoke, J.W. (1978). Quartan malaria nephropathy. In *Proceedings 7th International Congress of Nephrology* (eds. R. Barcelo, M. Bergeron, S. Carriere *et al.*) p. 69. Karger, Basel.

Kibukamusoke, J.W. and Hutt, M.S.R. (1967). Histological features of the nephrotic syndrome associated with quartan malaria. *J. Clin. Pathol.* **20**, 117.

Kibukamusoke, J.W., Hutt, M.S.R., and Wilks, N.E. (1967). The nephrotic syndrome in Uganda and its association with quartan malaria. *Q. J. Med.* **36**, 393.

Kincaid-Smith, P.S. (1969). Analgesic nephropathy. A common form of renal disease in Australia. *Med. J. Aust.* **2**, 1131.

Kincaid-Smith, P.S. (1978). Analgesic nephropathy. In *Proceedings 7th International Congress of Nephrology* (eds. R. Barcelo, M. Bergeron, S. Carriere *et al.*) p. 45. Karger, Basel.

Kincaid-Smith, P. (1983). Reflux nephropathy. *Br. Med. J.* **286**, 2002.

Kincaid-Smith, P., McMichael, J., and Murphy, E.A. (1958). The clinical course and pathology of hypertension with pailloedeam (malignant hypertension). *Q. J. Med.* **28**, 117.

King, H., Diamond, E., and Lilienfeld, A.M. (1963). Some epidemiological aspects of cancer of the prostate. *J. Chronic Dis.* **16**, 117.

Kunin, C.M. (1970). Tendency of vesico-ureteric reflux to disappear coincident with specific antimicrobial therapy. *In Renal infection and renal scarring* (eds. P. Kincaid-Smith and K.F. Fairley) p. 287. Mercedes Publishing Services, Melbourne.

Kunin, C.M., Southall, I., and Paquin, A. (1960). Epidemiology of urinary tract infection: a pilot study of 3057 school children. *New Engl. J. Med.* **263**, 817.

Kunin, C.M. and Paquin, A.J. (1965). Frequency and natural history of urinary tract infection in schoolchildren. *In Progress in pyelonephritis* (ed. E.H. Kass) p. 33. Davis, Philadelphia.

Leonard, R.H. (1961). Quantitative composition of kidney stones. *Clin. Chem.* **7**, 546.

Liavag, I., Harbitz, T.B., and Haugen, O.A. (1972). Latent carcinoma of the prostate. In *Current problems in the epidemiology of cancer and lymphomas* (eds. E. Grundmann and H. Tulinius) p. 131. Heinemann, London.

Ljunghall, S. and Hedstrand, H. (1975). Epidemiology of renal stone in a middle-aged population. *Acta Med. Scand.* **197**, 439.

Ljunghall, S., Backman, U., Danielson, B.G. *et al.* (1981). Epidemiology of renal stones in Sweden. In *Urinary calculus* (eds. J. Gwynne Brockis and B. Finlayson) p. 13. PSG, Boston.

Logan, W.P. and Cushion, A.A. (1958). *Morbidity statistics from general practice*, Vol. 1. *General studies on medical and population subjects*. No. 14. HMSO, London.

Lucas, S.B. (1982*a*). Bladder tumours in Malawi. *Br. J. Urol.* **54**, 275.

Lucas, S.B. (1982*b*). Squamous cell carcinoma of the bladder and schistosomiasis. *E. Afr. Med. J.* **59**, 345.

Lwanga, D. and Wing, A.J. (1970). Renal complications associated with typhoid fever. *E. Afr. Med. J.* **47**, 146.

McCormick, M. and Navarro, V. (1973). Prevalence of chronic renal failure and access to dialysis. *Int. J. Epidemiol.* **2**, 247.

McGeown, M.G. (1960). Heredity in renal stone disease. *Clin. Sci.* **19**, 465.

McGeown, M.G. (1972). Chronic renal failure in N. Ireland 1968–70. A prospective study. *Lancet* **i**, 307.

Makhyoun, N.A., El-Kashlan, K.M., Al-Ghorab, A. *et al.* (1971). Aetiological factors in Bilharzial bladder cancer. *J. Trop. Med. Hyg.* **74**, 73.

Mamou, H. and Cattan, R. (1952). La maladie periodique (sur 14 cas personels dont 8 compliques de nephropathies). *Sem. Hôp. Paris* **28**, 1062.

Mausner, J.S., Kapp-Clark, J., Coles, B. *et al.* (1978). An areawide survey of treated end-stage renal disease. *Am. J. Public Health* **68**, 166.

Meadow, S.R., White, R.H.R., and Johnston, N.M. (1969). Prevalence of symptomless urinary tract disease in Birmingham schoolchildren. 1. Pyuria and bacteriuria. *Br. Med. J.* **3**, 81.

Modan, B., Boichis, H., Bott-Kanner, G. *et al.* (1975). An epidemiological study of renal failure. 1. The need for maintenance dialysis. *Am. J. Epidemiol.* **101**, 276.

Morel-Maroger, L., Saimot, A.G., Sloper, J.C. *et al.* (1975). 'Tropical nephropathy' and 'tropical extramembranous glomerulonephritis' of unknown aetiology in Senegal. *Br. Med. J.* **i**, 541.

Morgensen, C.E. (1976). Progression of nephropathy in long-term diabetics with proteinuria and effects of initial antihypertensive treatment. *Scand. J. Clin. Lab. Invest.* **36**, 383.

Morgenson, C.E. (1982). Long-term antihypestensive treatment inhibiting progression of diabetic nephropathy. *Br. Med. J.* **285**, 685.

Musa, A.M., Abu-Asha, H., and Veress, B. (1980). Nephrotic syndrome in Sudanese patients with *Schistosoma mansoni* infection. *Ann. Trop. Med. Parasitol.* **74**, 615.

Nanra, R.S. (1976). Analgesic nephropathy. *Med. J. Aust.* **1**, 745.

Nanra, R.S., Hicks, J.D., McNamara, J.H. *et al.* (1970). Seasonal variation in the post-mortem incidence of renal papillary necrosis. *Med. J. Aust.* **1**, 293.

Newcastle Asymptomatic Bacteriuria Research Group (1975). Asymptomatic bacteriuria in schoolchildren in Newcastle-upon-Tyne. *Arch. Dis. Child.* **50**, 90.

Normand, C. and Smellie, J. (1979). The case for conservative management. In *Reflux nephropathy* (eds. J. Hodson and P. Kincaid-Smith) p. 281. Masson, New York.

Office of Population Censuses and Surveys (1974). *Morbidity statistics from General Practice*. Studies on medical and population subjects No. 26. HMSO, London.

Office of Population Censuses and Surveys (1974–78). *Hospital in-patient enquiry*. HMSO, London.

Office of Population Censuses and Surveys (1974–78). *Mortality statistics for England and Wales*. HMSO, London.

Office of Population Censuses and Surveys (1981). *Birth statistics*. HMSO, London.

Owor, R. (1975). Carcinoma of bladder and urethra in patients with urethral strictures. *E. Afr. Med. J.* **52**, 12.

Parry, E.S. and Lister, I.S. (1975). Sunlight and hypercalcaemia. *Lancet* **i**, 1063.

Parving, H.H., Smidt, U.M., Frisberg, B. *et al.* (1981). A prospective study of glomerular filtration rate and arterial blood-pressure in insulin-dependent diabetics with diabetic nephropathy. *Diabetologia* **20**, 457.

Pendreigh, D.M., Heasman, M.A., Howitt, L.F. *et al.* (1972). Survey of chronic renal failure in Scotland. *Lancet* **i**, 304.

Perkoff, G.T. (1967). The hereditary renal diseases. *New Engl. J. Med.* **277**, 129.

Pfandler, U. and Berger, H. (1956). Zur genetik der cystinose (Cystin-speicnerkrankheit) und ihre. Beziehungen zur cystinurie und hyperaminoacidurie. *Ann. Paediata* **187**, 1.

Pierce, L.W. and Bloom, B. (1945). Observations on urolithiasis among American troops in a desert area. *J. Urol.* **54**, 466.

Poon-King, T., Mohammed, I., Cox, R. *et al.* (1967). Recurrent epidemic nephritis in S. Trinidad. *New Engl. J. Med.* **277**, 728

Pugh, R.C.B. (1959). The pathology of bladder tumours. In *Tumours of the bladder* (ed. D.M. Wallace). Livingstone, Edinburgh.

Queiroz, F.P., Brito, E., Martinelli, R. *et al.* (1973). Nephrotic syndrome in patients with *Schistossoma mansoni* infections. *Am. J. Trop. Med. Hygiene* **22**, 622.

Quinland, W.S. (1945). Urinary lithiasis: review of 33 cases in Negroes. *J. Urol.* **53**, 791.

Ransome-Kuti, O. and Ransome-Kuti, S. (1960). Studies on the specimens of urine collected from children admitted to hospital for non-renal disease in a pediatric ward in the tropics. *W. Afr. Med. J.* **16**, 89.

Reaser, E.F. (1935). Racial incidence or urolithiasis. *J. Urol.* **34**, 148.

Rees, P.H., Barr, R.D., Cordy, P.E. *et al.* (1972). Possible role of malaria in the aetiology of the nephrotic syndrome in Nairobi. *Br. Med. J.* **ii**, 130.

Reynolds, T.B. and Edmondson, H.A. (1963). Chronic renal disease and heavy use of analgesics. *JAMA* **184**, 435.

Robertson, W.G., Peacock, M., Heyburn, P.J. *et al.* (1981). The risk of calcium stone formation in relation to affluence and dietary animal protein. In *Urinary calculus* (eds. J.G. Brockis and B. Finlayson). PSG, Boston.

Robertson, W.G., Peacock, M., Marshall, R.W. *et al.* (1975). Seasonal variations in the composition of urine in relation to calcium stone-formation. *Clin. Sci. Mole. Med.* **49**, 597.

Rolleston, G.L., Shannon, F.T., and Uttley, W.L.F. (1970). Relationship of infantile vesico-ureteric reflux to renal damage. *Br. Med. J.* **i**, 460.

Rose, G.A. and Westbury, E.J. (1969). The influence of calcium content of water, intake of vegetables and fruit and other food factors upon the incidence of renal calculi. *Urol. Res.* **3**, 61.

Rostand, S.G., Kirk, K., Rutsky, E. *et al.* (1982). Racial differences in the incidence of treatment for end-stage renal disease. *New Engl. J. Med.* **306**, 1276.

Saker, B.M. and Kincaid-Smith, P. (1969). Papillary necrosis in experimental analgesic nephropathy *Br. Med. J.* **i**, 161.

Sallinen, A. (1959). Some aspects of urolithiasis in Finland. *Acta Chir. Scand.* **118**, 479.

Sanerkin, N.G. and Weaver, C.M. (1964). Chronic phenacetin nephropathy. ('Chronic interstitial nephritis' with papillary necrosis.) *Br. J. Med. J.* **i**, 288.

Satge, P. Habib, R., Querum, C. *et al.* (1970). Particularite du syndrome nephrotique chez l'enfant au Senegal. *Ann. Pediat.* **5**, 382.

Savage, D.C.L., Wilson, M.I., Ross, E.M. *et al.* (1969). Asymptomatic bacteriuria in girl entrants to Dundee primary schools. *Br. Med. J.* **iii**, 75.

Savage, D.C.L. and Wilson, M.I. (1973). Covert bacteriuria in childhood. In *Urinary tract infection* (eds. W. Brumfitt and W.A. Asscher) p. 39. Oxford University Press.

Segi, M. and Kurihara, M. (1972). *Cancer morbidity for selected sites in 24 countries.* Report No. 6. Japan Cancer Society, Tokyo.

Seggie, J. (1982). MD Thesis, University of Birmingham.

Shannon, F.T. (1972). Urinary tract infection in infancy. *NZ Med. J.* **75**, 282.

Sharpstone, P., Ogg, C.S., and Cameron, J.S. (1969). Nephrotic syndrome due to primary renal disease in adults. I Survey of incidence in Southern England. *Br. Med. J.* **ii**, 533.

Shaw, A.B. (1970). The Norwich School of lithotomy. *Med. Hist.* **14**, 221.

Shuttleworth, J.S. and Ross, H. (1956). Secondary amyloidosis in leprosy. *Ann. Intern. Med.* **45**, 23.

Shwe, T. (1972). Immune complexes in glomeruli of patients with leprosy. *Leprosy Rev.* **42**, 282.

Smellie, J.M. (1967). Medical spects of urinary infection in children. *R. Coll. Physicians* **1**, 189.

Sohar, E., Pras, M., Heller, J. *et al.* (1961). Genetics of familial Mediterranean fever (FMF): disorder with recessive inheritance in non-Ashkenazi Jews and Armenians. *Arch. Intern. Med.* **107**, 529.

Srivartava, R.N., Mayekar, G., Anand, R. *et al.* (1975). Nephrotic syndrome in Indian children. *Arch. Dis. Child.* **50**, 626.

Staszewiski, J. and Haenszel, W. (1965). Cancer mortality among the Polish-born in the US. *J. Natl. Cancer Inst.* **35**, 291.

Stevens, R.G. and Mollgarker, S.H. (1979). Estimations of relative risk from valid data: smoking and cancers of the lung and bladder. *J. Natl. Cancer Inst.* **63**, 1351.

Still, J.L. and Cottom, D. (1967). Severe hypertension in childhood. *Arch. Dis. Child.* **42**, 34.

Symvoulidis, A., Voudiclaris, S., Mountokalakis, T. *et al.* (1972). Acute renal failure in G6PD deficiency. *Lancet* **ii**, 819.

Tarlov, A.R., Brewer, G.J., Carson, P.E. *et al.* (1962). Primaquine sensitivity glucose-6-phosphate dehydrogenase deficiency: an inborn error of metabolism of medical and biological significance. *Arch. Intern. Med.* **109**, 209.

UICC (1966). *Cancer incidence in five continents. A technical report.* Springer, Berlin.

Verrier-Jones, E.R., Meller, S.T., McLachlan, M.S.F. *et al.* (1975). Treatment of bacteriuria in schoolgirls. *Kidney Int.* **8**, Suppl. 4, S85.

Viberti, G.C., Mackintosh, D., Bilous, R.W. *et al.* (1982). Proteinuria in diabetes mellitus: role of spontaneous and experimental variation of glycaemia. *Kidney Int.* **21**, 174.

Viberti, G.C. and Wiseman, M.J. (1983). The natural history of proteinuria in insulin-dependent diabetes mellitus. *Diabetic Nephropath.* **2**, 22.

Ward, P.A. and Kibukamusoke, J.W. (1969). Evidence for soluble immune complexes in the pathogenesis of the glomerulonephritis of quartan malaria. *Lancet* **i**, 283.

Waterhouse, J.A.H. (1974). *Cancer handbook of epidemiology and prognosis.* Churchill Livingstone, London.

Waters, W.E. (1968). Trends in mortality from nephritis and infections of the kidney in England and Wales. *Lancet* **i**, 241.

Waters, W.E. (1969). Prevalence of symptoms of urinary tract infection in women. *Br. J. Prev. Soc. Med.* **23**, 263.

Waters, W.E., Elwood, P.C., Asscher, A.W. *et al.* (1970). Clinical significance of dysuria in women. *Br. Med. J.* **ii**, 754.

Watts, R.E.W. (1983). Inborn errors of amino-acid and organic acid metabolism. In *Oxford textbook of medicine* (eds. D.J. Weatherall, J.G.G. Ledingham, and D.H. Warrell) p. 89. Oxford University Press.

Whelton, A. and Donadio, J.V. (1969). Post-traumatic acute renal failure in Vietnam. A comparison with Korean ware experience. *Johns Hopkins Med. J.* **124**, 95.

WHO (1972). Memorandum. Immunopathology of nephritis in Africa. *Bull. WHO* **46**, 387.

WHO (1975–81). *World health statistics annual. Vital statistics and causes of death.* WHO, Geneva.

WHO and IARC (1976). *Cancer incidence in five continents,* Vol. III (ed. J. Waterhouse, C. Muir, P. Correa, and J. Powell) IARC, Lyon.

Winberg, J., Larsen, H., and Bergstrom, T. (1970). Comparison of the natural history of urinary infection in children with and without vesico-ureteric reflux. In *Renal infection and renal scarring* (ed. P. Kincaid-Smith, and K.F. Fairley) p. 293. Mercedes Publishing Services, Melbourne.

Wing, A.J., Hutt, M.S.R., and Kibukamusoke, J. (1972). Post streptococcal glomerulonephritis and the nephrotic syndrome in Uganda. *Trans. Soc. Trop. Med. Hygiene* **65**, 543.

Wing, A.J., Broyer, M., Brunner, F.P. *et al.* (1983). Combined report on regular dialysis and transplantation in Europe, XIII, 1982. In *Proceedings EDTA/ERA,* Vol. 20 (ed. S. Damon) p. 2. Pitman, London.

Wing, A.J., Brunner, F.P., Brynger, H.O.A. *et al.* (1983*a*). Comparative review between dialysis and transplantation. In *Replacement of renal function by dialysis, 2nd ed.* (ed. W. Drukker, F.M. Parsons, and J.F. Maher) p. 850. Martinus Nijhoff, Boston.

Wing, A.J., Brunner, F.P., Brynger, H. *et al.* (1983*b*). EDTA Registry data on dialysis and transplantation in uraemic diabetics in Europe. In *Nephrology '83* (eds. G. D'Amico and G. Colasanti) p. 73. Wichtig Editore, Milan.

Wisniewski, Z.S., Armstrong, B., and Gwynne Brockis, J. (1981). The pattern of urinary calculus disease in Western Australia. In *Urinary calculus* (ed. J. Gwynne Brockis and B. Finlayson) p. 47. PSG, Boston.

Wynder, E.L., Hyams, L., and Shigematsu, T. (1967). Correlations of international cancer death rates. *Cancer* **20**, 113.

Wynder, E.L., Mabuchi, K., and Whitmore, W.F. (1971). Epidemiology of cancer of the prostate. *Cancer* **28**, 344.

Wynder, E.L. and Goldsmith, R. (1977). The epidemiology of bladder cancer: a second look. *Cancer* **40**, 1246.

Zollinger, H.V. (1955). Chronische interstitielle nephritis bei abusus von phenacetinhaltigen analgetika (Saridon USW). *Schweiz Med. Wschr.* **85**, 746.

12 Neurological system

John F. Kurtzke

INTRODUCTION

In the US, neurology emerged as a distinct clinical specialty apart from psychiatry or internal medicine only shortly before the Second World War. Since then, however, this field has grown geometrically. This growth has also spawned a category called neuroepidemiology. There are now several volumes available on the epidemiology of neurological disease (Kurland et al. 1973b; Clifford Rose 1980; Schoenberg 1978), and it is a rare symposium or monograph on neurological illness that does not include a chapter on epidemiology. A major textbook on clinical neurology provides an overview of the subject (Kurtzke and Kurland 1973) which has now been updated (Kurtzke and Kurland 1984), and it is in large measure on this last work that the current chapter is based.

Neuroepidemiology is considered important, at least by its proponents, primarily because of the nature of clinical neurology which relies on history taking and physical examination as prerequisites for correct diagnosis. And of course diagnosis is essential to all epidemiological inquiries.

Data resources

The basic materials for epidemiological investigations are mortality data and incidence and prevalence estimates from community surveys. Mortality rates in particular are bound to the rubrics of the International Statistical Classification of Diseases, Injuries and Causes of Death, the ISC or ICD. For most neurological diseases, routine data as to specific cause of death were unavailable until 1948 with the advent of the sixth revision; they were best coded in the eighth revision (1969–1978), the ninth being, neurologically, inferior (Kurtzke 1979a).

Death rates for the conditions to be discussed have been drawn principally from several unique resources. For international comparisons, the paper of Goldberg and Kurland (1962) remains invaluable. From 33 countries, including all the continents, they were able to obtain deaths for a number of neurological disorders during the 1950s, mostly covering a five-year period. They calculated average annual mortality rates age adjusted to the 1950 US population.

The mortality data presented here are mainly those for the US. This is not merely a matter of provincialism. The national subcontinent contains almost a quarter of a billion people in over 3.6 million square miles. The populace is of varied racial, ethnic, and social composition, containing large numbers of intranational as well as international migrants. Of the 179 million resident population in 1960, 20.5 million or 11.4 per cent were non-white. Of the latter, blacks or Negroes comprised 92 per cent (18.9 million), with the remainder being Amerindian (524 000), Japanese (464 000), Chinese (237 000), Filipino (176 000), and all others (218 000). Data for all non-whites combined, then, would essentially reflect the black population.

Routine publications on cause of death have been largely limited to some basic distributions and mostly only for three-digit codes. Recognizing these limitations, the American Public Health Association sponsored a series of monographs based upon special tabulations of deaths in the US for 1959–61 versus the 1960 census population. Deaths were coded to ICD7 and rates were also age adjusted to the 1940 US population.

For 1955, mortality data for the US included an assessment of secondary causes of death (contributory causes and associated conditions) (National Center for Health Statistics 1965). This provides at least one estimate of allocation by cause when the condition is recorded on the death certificate.

For non-American mortality information especial attention will be paid to the publications of The (National) Health Service—Sundhedsstyrelsen—of Denmark. These mortality data are extensive and detailed, and as likely to be accurate as any in existence. For instance, data for Denmark include the N codes (nature of injury), as well as the E codes (external cause) for deaths from trauma.

A principal source of neurological morbidity data has been the study of the Rochester, Minnesota, and its Olmsted County population (Kurland et al. 1982a). A large number of incidence, prevalence, follow-up, and case-control studies have been accomplished for this midwestern population of (now) some 60 000 for Rochester and 90 000 for the county. Without Kurland's sustained eforts (and data), this would have been an exceedingly short chapter. The strengths of these studies include an unsurpassed level of diagnostic accuracy, virtually complete ascertainment of the affected as they have presented for medical care within the defined population, and a record compilation, storage, and retrieval system which is the envy of other centres.

PRIMARY NEOPLASMS OF THE CENTRAL NERVOUS SYSTEM

Based on experience in clinical centres, about 85 per cent of primary central nervous system (CNS) tumours are intracranial and 15 per cent intraspinal. The principal groupings for the brain are gliomas (some 40 per cent) and meningiomas (some 20 per cent). In the former, the predominant tumour is glioblastoma multiforme (Slooff *et al.* 1964). The three most common spinal cord tumours are neurofibroma, meningioma, and ependymoma, each of which occurs at a similar frequency.

Mortality data

Broadly, neoplasms of the CNS have been divided into malignant, benign, and unspecified, although in the 9th revision of ICD unspecified CNS tumours are only included as 4 digit (optional) subcodes (National Center for Health Statistics 1968; World Health Organization 1977; Kurtzke 1979*a*). Death rates for malignant brain tumour will, after childhood, essentially reflect glioblastoma multiforme. A major contributor to such deaths earlier in life is medulloblastoma. For benign tumour deaths there is no single type to which they can be equated, although meningioma provides a considerable proportion, especially with advancing age.

International death rates

Figure 12.1 summarizes the data for brain tumour death rates in 26 countries for the years 1951–58. Although rates were similar, mostly between 4 and 5 per 100 000 population, the proportions atributed to malignant, benign, and unspecified tumours varied widely. With the loss of a rubric for unspecified brain tumour in the ninth revision of ICD, comparisons such as this have become impossible and may result in misleading findings.

Age, sex, and race

The APHA monograph on cancer included brain tumour. Kurtzke and Kurland (1973) analysed the basic data from the American Public Health Association (APHA) project on cancer (Lilienfeld *et al.* 1972). Differences by sex and race were limited to the malignant group (Table 12.1), where there was an approximately twofold excess of males and of whites. By age, the death rates for all CNS neoplasms declined from birth until early adulthood and then rose steeply to a peak of some 14 per 100 000 at 60 years of age (Fig. 12.2). The greatest contribution to this curve came from malignant neoplasm (code 193), especially that of the brain (code 193.0). The other groupings varied little through adult life, though they were rarely reported for children.

The pattern of age-specific death rates was similar in whites and non-whites and for both sexes. The predominance among the white population was more marked with a maximal age-specific death rate for whites 2.5 times than for non-whites. The twofold excess in males was apparent in both racial groups.

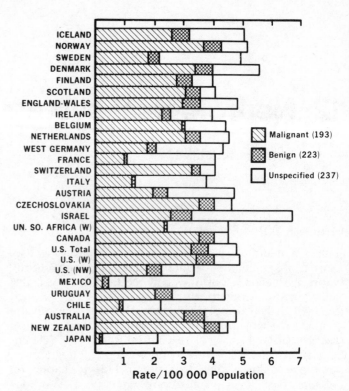

Fig. 12.1. Primary neoplasms of nervous system: average annual age-adjusted (US 1950) death rates per 100 000 population by type of tumour, selected countries, 1951–58. (Data of Goldberg and Kurland (1962).)

Table 12.1. *Primary neoplasms of the nervous system: average annual age adjusted (US 1940) death rates per 100 000 population by type (ICD 7 code), sex, and colour, United States 1959–61*

Type (ICD 7 Code)	Total			White			Non-white		
	T*	M	F	T	M	F	T	M	F
All types	4.7	5.4	4.0	4.8	5.6	4.1	3.4	3.9	3.1
Malignant (193)	3.3	4.0	2.6	3.5	4.2	2.7	1.9	2.2	1.5
Benign (223)	0.5	0.5	0.6	0.5	0.5	0.6	0.6	0.6	0.5
Unspecified (237)	0.8	0.9	0.8	0.8	0.9	0.7	1.0	1.1	1.0

*T/M/F = total/male/female.

Modified from Kurtzke and Kurland (1973).

Geography

Brain tumour death rates in US for 1959–61 were quite uniform by state, irrespective of sex, race, or whether malignant or not (Kurtzke and Kurland 1973).

Other periods in the 1950s and 1960s have also been assessed in like manner and with similar results, by state in the US and by *amt* in Denmark (Kurland *et al.* 1962; Kurtzke 1969*a*; Lilienfeld *et al.* 1972). In Denmark the slight variations seen were inconsistent over time: in the US they were highly correlated with the distribution of physicians (Kurtzke 1969*a*). The impression remains one of uniformity.

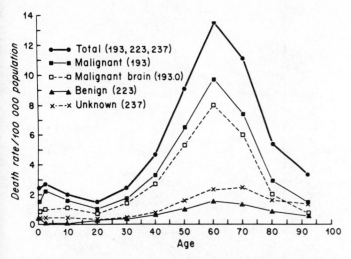

Fig. 12.2. Primary neoplasms of nervous system: average annual age-specific death rates per 100 000 population by type of tumour, United States, 1959–61. (Source: Kurtzke and Kurland (1973).)

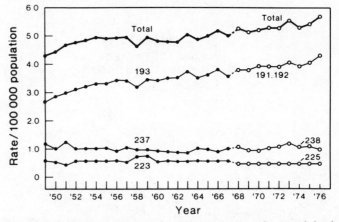

Fig. 12.3. Primary neoplasms of nervous system: crude annual death rates per 100 000 population by type of tumour: malignant (ICD6,7 code 193; ICD8 code 191 + 192); benign (codes 223; 225); unspecified (codes 237; 238), United States, 1949–76. (Source: Kurtzke and Kurland (1984).)

Time trend

In the US, between 1949 and 1976 there was a modest increase in the crude annual death rates, from approximately 4.3 per 100 000 in 1949 to 5.7 in 1976 (Fig. 12.3). The rise was attributable to the malignant tumours, whose rates rose from 2.7 to 4.3 in this interval (Kurtzke and Kurland 1984). The lack of change in the other categories suggests that this is not a result of reallocation within the brain tumour codes, and that little of the increase would likely be due to our ageing population. Much of it, however, could be the result of improved accuracy of diagnosis, with fewer glioblastomas having been called 'stroke'. Thus a true increase in these tumours remains to be proven.

Morbidity data

Incidence rates

Average annual incidence rates for primary CNS neoplasms have ranged from 6 per 100 000 population in Denmark to 16 in Rochester, Minnesota (Table 12.2). The Danish rate was an underestimate, as many benign tumours were not

recorded (Clemmesen 1965a, b, 1969). In Rochester, intracranial tumour rates were closer to 10 than 15 when neoplasms discovered at autopsy were deleted (Kurland 1958a; Percy et al. 1972; Annegers et al. 1981).

Pituitary tumour rates were between 1 and 2 per 100 000 population, and spinal cord tumours had rates of about 1. The latter approximately equally divided among neurofibroma, ependymoma, meningioma, and others in both Israel (Leibowitz et al.1971) and Rochester (Percy et al. 1972). Peripheral nerve tumours provided a rate of 1.5 per 100 000 in Israel.

Age and sex

Age specific incidence rates for CNS tumours were approximately constant from birth to age 30 years when they started to rise, at least to age 60 years (Fig. 12.4). Thereafter, they scattered widely in the several surveys.

Part of the difference is explicable by tumour-type. The configuration for Denmark is largely due to glioblastoma multiforme, which taken separately has a similar distribution to all malignant brain tumours.

Other variations shown in Fig. 12.4 are unlikely to be accounted for by histology. The steadily increasing rate for

Table 12.2. *Primary neoplasms of the central nervous system: average annual incidence rates per 100 000 population by site of tumour, selected surveys, various years, 1935–77*

Locale	(Reference)	Period	n	Pituitary	Brain only	Brain and pituitary	Spinal cord	All CNS
Denmark	(Clemmesen 1965a,b, 1969)	1943–57	(3961*)	—	4.9	—	1.3	6.2
Iceland	(Guðmundsson 1970)	1954–63	(150)	0.5	7.3	7.8	1.1	8.8
Israel	(Leibowitz et al. 1971)	1961–65	(1354)	0.6	9.1	9.7	0.9	11.3
Rochester, Minn.	(Percy et al. 1972)	1935–68	(174)	1.5	12.9	14.5	1.3	15.7
Rochester	(revised)	1935–68	(130)†	1.3	9.5	10.8	1.0	11.8
Rochester, Minn.	(Annegers et al. 1981)	1935–77	(223)	1.9	12.2	14.1	—	—
Rochester	(revised)	1935–77)	(145)†	1.6	7.6	9.2	—	—

*Benign tumours greatly underreported.
†Excluding asymptomatic cases discovered at autopsy.

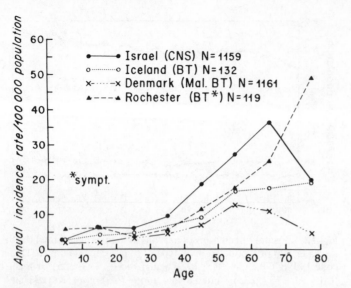

Fig. 12.4. Primary neoplasms of central nervous system: average annual age-specific incidence rates per 100 000 population by type of tumour and location of study: central nervous system, Israel (Leibowitz *et al.* 1971); brain tumour, Iceland (Guđmundsson 1970); chiefly malignant brain tumour, Denmark (Clemmesen 1965*a*, *b*, 1969); brain tumour, symptomatic only, Rochester, Minn. (Percy *et al.* 1972). (Source: Kurtzke and Kurland (1973).)

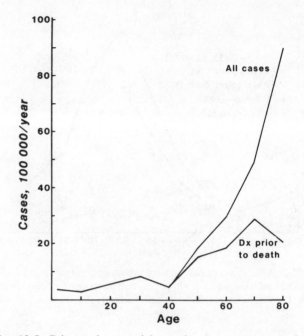

Fig. 12.5. Primary intracranial neoplasms: average annual age-specific incidence rates per 100 000 population, all cases and those diagnosed antemortem. Rochester, Minn. 1935–77. (Source: Annegers *et al.* (1981).)

Rochester was even more dramatic when tumours first diagnosed at autopsy were added (Fig. 12.5). For 1935–77, this rate then reached 90 per 100 000 for the oldest age-group, while for those diagnosed ante-mortem, the maximum rate of 30 was attained at age 70 years (Annegers *et al.* 1981; Kurland *et al.* 1982*b*). Most of the missed cases antedated the use of computerized tomography; they included two-thirds of the meningiomas and one-fifth of the gliomas—mostly glioblastoma. Annual incidence rates for all gliomas in Rochester were 5.0 per 100 000 (5.1 male and 4.8 female); for meningiomas 5.4 (4.9 male, 5.8 female). Rates limited to ante-mortem diagnosis were about 4 and 2 for gliomas and meningiomas respectively.

An overall estimate for malignant intracranial tumours may be taken as some 5 per 100 000 for annual incidence; the largest contributor will be glioblastoma multiforme. For benign tumours, a reasonable estimate is near 10 per 100 000; 5 for meningioma, and between 1 and 2 each for benign gliomas, pituitary tumours, and all others. The brain tumour incidence rates as a whole increase with age, at least through the seventh decade. Glioblastomas attain a peak in most studies somewhere near the age of 60 years, and then decline with increasing age, whereas the rate for meningiomas continues to increase with age. Some tumours, such as neuroblastoma and medulloblastoma, are age-limited to infancy, childhood, and adolescence. The incidence rate of benign astrocytoma varies little throughout life. Pituitary adenomas have been more frequent at middle-age. There seems to be a male predilection in the glioma group, especially glioblastoma, and a female preponderance for meningioma and perhaps acoustic neurinoma (Kurtzke and Kurland 1973, 1984).

Race

Mortality data in the US demonstrated a non-white deficit for malignant brain tumour but not for the other types. The available community surveys contained few, if any, blacks. Autopsy and clinical series have indicated in each a paucity of blacks with tumours—and in particular with gliomas (Earle *et al.* 1957; Froman and Lipschitz 1970; Newbill and Anderson 1944; Steiner 1954; Mosee and Barber 1970).

In Israel the age-standardized incidence rate of CNS neoplasms among residents of European birth has been estimated as 15.6 per 100 000, 13.7 for native Israelis, and 10.1 for Asians; but for Africans it was only 7.3 (Leibowitz *et al.* 1971). The differences were noted for various tumour types and sites. The authors believed the deficit was real, at least for the Africans who were mainly from North Africa. These findings suggest the possibility of 'protection' in blacks against gliomas.

Brain tumour death rates are low in Japan, but this may be due to under-reporting. Primary intracranial tumours were found in 2.2 per cent of reported autopsies in Japan; a frequency 'which is comparable with that in series outside Japan' (Araki and Matsumoto 1969). The types of tumours were similar to those in occidental clinical and autopsy series except for notably higher frequencies of pinealoma and craniopharyngioma.

Survival and prevalence

The primary factor in survivorship is the histological type of tumour. In the Rochester and Israeli series the five-year survival rates were about 60 per cent for those with clinically diagnosed meningioma and some 20 per cent for all those with gliomas. For glioblastoma multiforme, the median survival time after diagnosis was about one year in a large clinical series (Jelsma and Bucy 1969). A reasonable estimate for median survival for all benign intracranial tumours is six years (Percy *et al.* 1972; Kurtzke and Kurland 1973; Kurland *et al.* 1982*b*; Kurtzke 1982*b*).

With an incidence of 5 per 100 000 and average survival of one year, then a point prevalence rate for malignant brain tumour would also be about 5 per 100 000 population. Similarly, a likely prevalence for benign intracranial tumour would be some 60 per 100 000.

Genetic factors

The influence of heredity in brain tumours has been studied by Kurland *et al.* (1962) and Refsum and Mohr (1971). Only a few types were thought to have any genetic basis: retinoblastoma and glomus tumours. Brain tumours are part of the symptomatology of several autosomal dominant traits: Von Recklinghausen's disease, tuberous sclerosis, (some dominant) Von Hippel–Lindau disease, and (rarely dominant) Sturge–Weber syndrome.

Harvald and Hauge (1956) and Hauge and Harvald (1957) in Denmark investigated the family trees of patients with glioblastoma, astrocytoma, and medulloblastoma; they found no significant excess of deaths from any type of brain tumour among relatives of the index patients. Among their series were eight pairs of twins; and even though only two were monozygous, all were discordant for brain tumour. There was no concordance in the majority of other series of gliomas and meningiomas in twins reviewed by Kurland *et al.* (1962).

Other risk factors

In clinical folklore and sporadic case reports, a temporal association of head trauma and brain tumour has been noted. In the only cohort (prospective) study to date, Annegers *et al.* (1979) followed almost 3000 patients with head trauma in Rochester, Minnesota, for an average of ten years. The four subsequent brain tumours did not differ from the expected number, 4.1; and the severity and location of the head injuries did not influence the subsequent occurrence of brain tumours. Aronson and Aronson (1965) reported that gliomas were rare among diabetics autopsied at Kings County Hospital in Brooklyn, New York. Apparently this finding has not yet been confirmed—or refuted.

In Rochester, Minnesota, there was a striking increase in pituitary tumours diagnosed in women of childbearing age since 1970. From then to 1980 there were 17 such cases with an average annual incidence rate of 7.4 per 100 000 females aged 15–55 years. In a case-control study, no differentiating features were found; in particular, there was no evidence that the rise was associated with oral contraceptive use. The authors concluded that the apparent increase was a result of improved diagnostic methods (Annegers *et al.* 1978*a*, 1982*a*; Coulam *et al.* 1979).

CONVULSIVE DISORDERS

Classification

There is little agreement on the classification of convulsive disorders, or epilepsy, or the epilepsies. Seizure types continue to undergo redefinition (Commission on Classification in Terminology of the International League Against Epilepsy 1981). However, the four broad categories proposed by Hauser and Kurland (1975) have gained considerable acceptance for epidemiological studies: (i) epilepsy; (ii) isolated seizures; (iii) febrile convulsions; and (iv) acute symptomatic seizures. The terms seizure, fit, and convulsion are used interchangeably.

Isolated seizures are single convulsive episodes which are presumably not due to an associated cerebral insult. Obviously the time of observation (and treatment) determines their frequency *vis à vis* epilepsy. Operationally, no recurrence in two years would seem a satisfactory criterion.

Febrile convulsions are generalized seizures occurring in infants and young children during high fever but without any other presumed cause. They may be subdivided into simple and complex. Complex febrile convulsions, which carry a higher risk of subsequent epilepsy (see below), have one or more of the following characteristics: (i) prolonged seizure (more than 15 minutes in duration); (ii) focal features; (iii) postictal paralysis; or (iv) pre-existing neurological deficit— for example, cerebral palsy or mental retardation.

Symptomatic seizures are those that occur only in association with the acute effects of either structural brain insults (e.g. head trauma, CNS infection, cerebrovascular disease) or in association with acute metabolic disturbances (e.g. hypoglycaemia, or ethanol or drug withdrawal). When limited to the time of acute insult and whether then single or multiple, they are generally excluded from the category of epilepsy.

Once patients are classified as having epilepsy, they are then usually further subdivided into two groups: idiopathic or primary, and secondary. Secondary epilepsy has a presumed cause, with recurrent seizures after recovery from the acute insult. All focal or focal onset seizures are, by definition, secondary. Absence (with a French pronunciation) seizures are almost always primary or idiopathic, as are many, but not all, grand mal.

Mortality data

International death rates

Average annual age adjusted mortality rates due to epilepsy are shown in Fig. 12.6 for various countries in 1951–58. In all listed countries except Israel there was a male preponderance in the rates, averaging 1.6:1 (Kurtzke *et al.* 1973*d*). The highest rates reported were for several Central and South American countries, Portugal, and US non-whites. The lowest rates were for US whites, Sweden, Denmark, Poland, and Israel. Most other countries had an annual mortality rate around 2 per 100 000 population. It is conjectural whether higher rates reflect a lower frequency of correct diagnosis of underlying causes of secondary or symptomatic seizures, an increased incidence of epilepsy, or a higher case–fatality ratio.

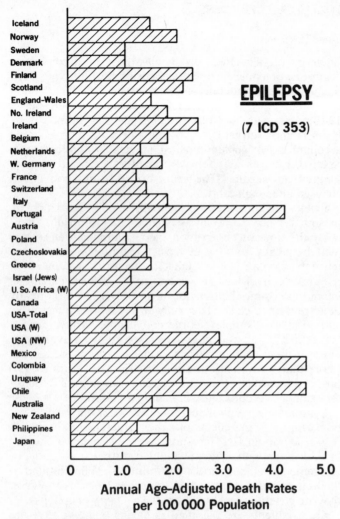

EPILEPSY

(7 ICD 353)

Fig. 12.6. Epilepsy (ICD7 code 353): average annual age-adjusted (US 1950) death rates per 100 000 population, selected countries, 1951–58. (Data of Goldberg and Kurland (1962).)

Age, sex, and race

There were nearly 6000 deaths with epilepsy as underlying cause in the US 1959–61. To assess the impact of secondary cause/associated condition attributions, data for 1955 were also reviewed.

In Fig. 12.7, the rate in 1955 for all deaths from epilepsy is the sum of those *due to* epilepsy (underlying cause) and those *with* epilepsy (contributory cause) (National Center for Health Statistics 1965). For whites, the death rates for underlying cause alone remained virtually even throughout adulthood (Fig. 12.7, right), whereas the rates for all deaths related to epilepsy showed an increase with age (Fig. 12.7, left).

The rates for non-whites differed from those of whites, with an excess among non-white males which was even greater when both underlying and contributory cause deaths were included. The male excess for both racial groups suggests either that there is less reluctance in certifying epilepsy in males, that there is a miscoding of effects of trauma and toxins, or that epilepsy is indeed more common in males. Similar possibilities exist for the white–non-white difference.

Geography

In the US, age-adjusted death rates for epilepsy among whites (national average 1.0 per 100 000) showed only minor variation between states, ranging in 1959–61 from 0.7 to 1.5 per 100 000. Rates for non-whites by state showed both a south-eastern and a midwestern concentration. Because of residence patterns of the several races, the former would be compatible with an excess rate in non-whites, and the latter would suggest the possibility of an excess in Amerindians as well. The non-white distributions were based on some 1500 deaths (as opposed to 4400 for whites) in these years (Kurtzke 1972*b*; Kurtzke *et al.* 1973*b*). If these findings are valid, they would suggest a disorder equally distributed by geography but not by race.

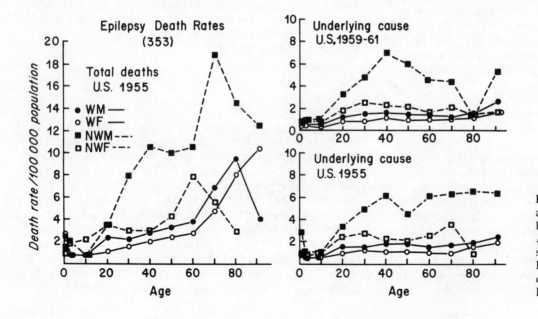

Fig. 12.7. Epilepsy: age-specific annual death rates per 100 000 population by sex and race, United States. *Left:* Total deaths (underlying and secondary causes) 1955. *Right:* Deaths due to epilepsy (underlying cause) 1955 and 1959–61. (Source: Kurtzke (1972*b*).)

Time trend

The crude annual death rate for epilepsy as underlying cause in the US has declined by more than half in the last third of the century, from about 2.0 per 100 000 population near 1940 to 0.8 in the mid-1970s. Age-adjustment altered rates very little. The degree of change seems too great to attribute to coding artefacts. The decline correlated well in time not only with better diagnosis and treatment of underlying causes of epilepsy, but also with the introduction of more effective anticonvulsant therapy. Since the greatest rate of change occurred in the 15 years after 1945, therapeutic efficacy for phenytoin and other agents introduced by 1960 would perhaps appear the more likely explanation.

Death rates have been declining in both sex and racial groups in the US and since 1968 the difference between white and non-whites has begun to lessen.

Morbidity data

Prevalence rates

Variability of survey techniques only adds to differing diagnostic criteria in complicating comparisons of population survey results. Nevertheless, epilepsy prevalence rates, mostly for socio-economically advanced regions, are provided in Table 12.3. In general, the prevalence of convulsive disorders was about 3–9 per 1000 population. Only in Bogotá, Columbia, was there a strikingly high rate, 19.5 per 1000 (Gomez *et al.* 1978). Mortality rates were also highest in Columbia and Chile in the international comparisons (Fig. 12.8). While cerebral cysticercosis is common in South America and thus a possible cause for the high rates, it is said to be rare in Columbia. Except for Bogotá and a low rate recorded in Mexico City (Olivares 1972), none of the studies suggested any major geographical or racial difference, despite the mortality data.

Penry and Rose pioneered a questionnaire technique to ascertain the prevalence of epilepsy in schoolchildren (Rose *et al.* 1973). They estimated childhood prevalence to be 5–10 per 1000 for active, recurrent, afebrile seizures. This is in accord with prevalence rates for all ages (Table 12.4). After the first decade of life, age-specific prevalence rates remained relatively constant in most series. In Rochester, this also held until age 70 years; for those age 70 and over, the prevalence was about twice that for the younger ages, but the confidence intervals were wide. An overall estimate of the point prevalence of epilepsy may be taken as about 6–7 per 1000 population.

Table 12.3. *Epilepsy: point prevalence rates per 1000 population and average annual incidence rates per 100 000 population, selected surveys, various years 1935–77*

Reference	Locale	Prevalence Year	Prevalence Rate	Incidence Period	Incidence Rate
Logan and Cushion (1958)	England and Wales*	1955	3.3	—	—
Crombie *et al.* (1960)	England and Wales*	1957	4.2	1957	63
Pond *et al.* (1960)	South-east England*	1961	6.2†	1955	70
Brewis *et al.* (1966)	Carlisle, England	1961	5.5†	1955–61	28
G. Guðmundsson (1966)	Iceland	1960	3.6	1959–64	33
G. Guðmundsson (1966)	Iceland	1960	5.6†	—	—
Henriksen and Krohn (1969)	Northern Norway	1968	3.7	—	—
DeGraaf (1974)	Northern Norway	1973	3.5	1968–72	33
Juul-Jensen (1964) and Kurtzke (1968*a*)	Jutland, Denmark	—	—	1959–61	36
Juul-Jensen and Ipsen (1975)	Aarhus, Denmark	1972	3.5	—	—
Juul-Jensen and Ipsen (1975)	Aarhus, Denmark	1972	6.9‡	1960–72	30‡
Grudzinska (1974)	Zabrza, Poland	1970	3.4	1966–70	22
Zielinski (1974)	Warsaw, Poland	1972	6.5	—	—
Beaussart *et al.* (1980)	N. Pas-de-Calais, France	1977	8.8	1963–73	43
Leibowitz and Alter (1968)	Jerusalem, Israel	1961	4.1	—	—
Bird *et al.* (1962)	Bantu miners	1961	3.7	—	—
Levy *et al.* (1964)	Semokwe, Africa	1964	7.4†	—	—
Dada (1968)	Lagos, Nigeria	1967	3.1	—	—
Lessell *et al.* (1962)	Merizo, Guam	1961	3.7	—	—
Mathai *et al.* (1968)	Other Marianas	1962	3.4	—	—
Chen *et al.* (1968)	Guam	1967	5.0	1960–66	47
Stanhope *et al.* (1972)	Guam Survey	1968	5.3	1958–67	46
Olivares (1972)	Mexico City	1971	3.5	—	—
Gomez *et al.* (1978)	Bogotá, Columbia	1974	19.5†	—	—
Kurland (1959)	Rochester, Minn.	—	—	1945–54	30
Hauser and Kurland (1975)	Rochester, Minn.	1940	3.7	1935–44	35
Hauser and Kurland (1975)	Rochester, Minn.	1950	5.3	1945–54	55
Hauser and Kurland (1975)	Rochester, Minn.	1960	6.2	1955–64	54
Annegers *et al.* (1983)	Rochester, Minn.	1974	6.5	1965–74	33

*General practice surveys.
†Includes 'inactive' cases.
‡Includes single seizures.
Modified from Kurtzke and Kurland (1984).

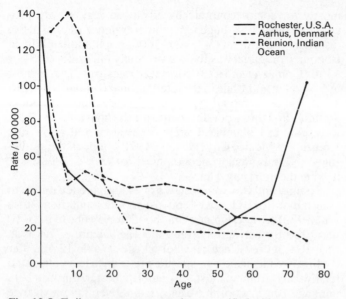

Fig. 12.8. Epilepsy: average annual age specific incidence rates per 100 000 population, Rochester, Minn.: Aarhus, Denmark; Reunion Island. (Unpublished data of Annegers *et al.* (1983).) (Source: Kurtzke and Kurland (1984).)

Table 12.4. *Outcomes of pregnancy according to maternal seizure experience and anticonvulsant treatment (Rx) during pregnancy in the Collaborative Perinatal Project. Rates per 1000 children**

	Maternal seizure group					
	Current seizures					
	In this pregnancy		Not in this pregnancy		Never seizures	
Outcome	Rx +	Rx ○	Rx +	Rx ○	Rx +†	Rx ○
Stillbirth	58	33	28	22	29	18
Head size ≦ 2SD	61	44	31	55	28	22
IQ < 70 white	44	0	0	27	21	16
IQ < 70 black	121	227	100	70	52	49
Afebrile fits	42	82	16	26	11	8
'Bad outcome' alive	152	244	89	140	85	71
'Bad outcome' +dead	257	279	150	200	150	126

*No differences between treated and not treated were statistically significant within either current seizure group.

†Phenobarbital usually for toxaemia of pregnancy.

Modified from Nelson and Elleberg (1982).

Incidence rates

Average annual incidence rates for epilepsy are summarized in Table 12.3. The rates ranged from about 20–70 per 100 000 population per year. There was a slight male excess, which averaged about 1.2:1. An expected range for annual incidence would be some 30–60 per 100 000, with a reasonable general estimate of 50. With the prevalence estimates, an average duration of active seizure disorders could then be calculated as about 13 years.

Rates by age

Age-specific incidence rates show a sharp decrease from maximal rates in infancy to adolescence, and thereafter a slower decline for new cases throughout life. In Rochester, however, the configuration was U-shaped, with a marked increase in incidence rates for those aged 75 years and over (Fig. 12.8). The curve for Aarhus was essentially the same as that previously described for Iceland; Carlisle, England; and Jutland, Denmark (Kurtzke 1972*b*). In Reunion, the rates were notably higher in childhood, but the series was small (Soulayol and Yoyer-Vidil 1974).

The increase in the rates for the elderly in Rochester, Minnesota, although based on small numbers, has been found consistently over the years. Even though this pattern is unique to Rochester, it may be real and reflect the superior case ascertainment and the unusually complete medical care available to the elderly in Rochester. But the biological significance of a U-shaped attack curve would seem quite different from that of an inverted parabola. To decide which of the two better reflects 'epilepsy' is, therefore, of clinical importance. The U-shaped curve in Rochester persisted even when only 'idiopathic' grand mal was considered.

Rates by age and type

Most clinicians have assumed that 'idiopathic' or 'primary' grand mal disappears as a new entity with increasing age, and have attributed instances of new generalized seizures in the elderly to conditions such as small strokes or cortical scars from trauma when a clearly demonstrable cause was not evident (Kurtzke 1968*a*).

Age-specific annual incidence rates according to each clinical type of seizure are available only for Rochester. Myoclonic seizures were the major type diagnosed during the first year of life; they were also common in the 1–4 year age group, but rarely occurred after five years of age. Absence (petit mal) seizures peaked in the 5–9-year age group and were rare after 20 years of age. Complex partial (psychomotor) and generalized tonic clonic (grand mal) seizures both had fairly consistent incidence rates of 5–15 per 100 000 from low maxima about age 5–9 years, up through age 70 years. After 70 years, the rates of each rose sharply. Simple partial (focal) seizures had a bimodal distribution with the highest rates for those in the first year of life and over 70 years of age. Grand mal rates included both primary and secondary seizures (Kurtzke and Kurland 1984).

Febrile seizures

The risk of a child developing febrile seizures has been estimated as 2 per cent in the US and Europe (Van den Berg and Yerushalmy 1969; Hauser and Kurland 1975; Meighan *et al.* 1976; Ross *et al.* 1980). Japan and the Mariana Islands have much higher risk or cumulative incidence rates of 7 and 11 per cent (Stanhope *et al.* 1972; Tsuboi and Endo 1977). These high rates could be due to differences in ascertainment and classification of febrile convulsions, such as inclusion of secondary seizures. As with epilepsy in general, there was a male preponderance of about 1.2:1 for febrile convulsions.

Symptomatic and single convulsions

These categories have been little used, and therefore little studied. The incidence rate of identified symptomatic seizures in Rochester, Minnesota, was 15 per 100 000 per year (Annegers *et al.* 1983). The age-specific incidence rates had the same U-shaped distribution as did epilepsy, with the highest rates occurring in the very young and the most elderly. The major causes were alcohol or drug withdrawal (21 per cent), CVA (16 per cent), trauma (16 per cent), neoplastic or cardiac (14 per cent), infection (10 per cent), metabolic (8 per cent), and eclampsia (6 per cent). For a more urbanized population, the first category (withdrawal) might be appreciably higher and the U-shape of the curve less pronounced. The incidence rate for single or isolated seizures, as defined above, was approximately 20 per 100 000 per year. Many of these patients, however, had received anticonvulsant medication from the time of the seizure.

Course and survival

There were some 450 patients with epilepsy in the Rochester cohort who had been followed for at least five years (Annegers *et al.* 1980*b*). Remission was defined as being free of seizures for any period (after onset) of at least five years, regardless of medication use. By the sixth year after initial diagnosis, 42 per cent of the patients had achieved a five-year remission status, and by the seventh year after initial diagnosis, this proportion was 51 per cent. Some 70 per cent of the rather small numbers of patients followed 15–20 years after diagnosis had attained a remission.

There was also a group of patients without medication as well as without seizures for at least five years. In fact, for some interval within the 20 years after diagnosis, 45 per cent of patients were without seizures *and* anticonvulsant medication for at least five years.

The prognosis for remission was poor for those with epilepsy related to congenital neurological defects and best in patients with generalized onset seizures and epilepsy diagnosed under 10 years of age. The chances for remission were lower and relapse higher in patients with partial complex and adult-onset seizures (Annegers *et al.* 1979*a*).

This study shows that 50 per cent of all patients with epilepsy will be seizure-free for at least five years while off medication, 20 per cent will be seizure-free with medication, and 30 per cent will continue to have seizures despite anticonvulsant use.

An analysis of causes of death among patients with a history of epilepsy was carried out for the 1935–74 cohort of patients in Rochester (Hauser *et al.* 1980). There was an excess number of deaths relating to pulmonary events, accidents, extracranial neoplasms, and non-cerebral or non-cardiac vascular disease observed, but this only bordered on statistical significance.

Genetic factors

In clinical series of patients with epilepsy, positive family histories for seizures are common. This has also been noted among patients with febrile convulsions (Kurland 1959; Frantzen *et al.* 1968), and patients with paroxysmal or temporal lobe abnormalities in the EEG (Metrakos and Metrakos 1961; Rodin and Gonzalez 1966; Frantzen *et al.* 1968). Evans (1962) found in cases of equivalent head inju-

ries that more of the patients who developed seizures reported relatives with seizures than did those whose injury was not followed by seizures. Vercelletto and Courjon (1969) noted concordance for epilepsy in 10 of 14 pairs of monozygotic twins but provided few details of their case selection methods. From the Danish twin registry, Harvald and Hauge (1966) recorded 127 sets of twins having a diagnosis of epilepsy in at least one twin. Ten of the 27 monozygotes were concordant for epilepsy, but only six of 43 same-sexed dizygotes and four of 57 opposite-sexed dizygotes were concordant. The difference between the monzygote ratio and the dizygote ratio was statistically significant.

In Rochester, the risk of seizure disorders in relatives of patients with childhood-onset epilepsy was evaluated in a study of the other descendants of the parents of the probands with epilepsy (Annegers *et al.* 1982*b*). The risk of epilepsy through to 20 years of age among the siblings and children of the probands was 4 per cent, or three times the risk in the general population. The risk of any type of seizures (including isolated seizures, febrile convulsions, and symptomatic seizures) through to age 20 years was also elevated, at 11 per cent in proband siblings and 13 per cent in children of the probands. However, the frequency of seizure disorders among nieces and nephews of probands was not greater than in the general population.

Other risk factors

Head trauma

An association between epilepsy and penetrating brain wounds has been well established in studies of the wounded of each conflict since at least the First World War. The risk of seizures after civilian head injuries, however, has been based on retrospective information from referral centres (Burkinshaw 1960; Bruce *et al.* 1978). The question was addressed in a cohort study of residents of Olmsted County identified as having had closed-head trauma with 'brain involvement' between 1935 and 1974 (Annegers *et al.* 1980*a*). There were 51 cases of post-traumatic seizures compared to an expected 14.3, representing a relative risk of 3.6. Risk was 12.7 for the first year after trauma, 4.4 for the next three years and 1.4 five or more years afterwards. Risk was strongly related to the severity of injury. Cumulative risk of seizures was 7.1 per cent by one year and 11.6 per cent by five years after severe injury. Similar frequencies were 0.7 and 1.6 per cent for moderate injury, and 0.1 and 0.6 per cent for mild injury, the last not being statistically significantly elevated. Children were less prone than adults; respective five-year figures following severe head injuries were 7.4 per cent for children and 13.3 for adults.

Febrile seizures

Estimated risks of epilepsy following febrile convulsions based on referral or clinic sources have been very variable (Livingston 1954; Nelson and Ellenberg 1976). Population-based studies, on the other hand, show more consistent results, with the occurrence of subsequent epilepsy ranging from 2.0 to 4.4 per cent by about 10 years of age (Herlitz 1941; Friderichsen and Melchoir 1954; Frantzen *et al.* 1968;

Van den Berg and Yerushalmy 1969; Nelson and Ellenberg 1976; Annegers *et al.* 1979*b*). In Rochester, the cumulative risk up to 20 years of age was 6 per cent (vs. expectation of 1 per cent), 2.5 per cent for uncomplicated, and 17 per cent for complex febrile seizures (Annegers *et al.* 1979*b*).

Childbirth and epilepsy

The risk of major congenital malformations among infants born to epileptic mothers receiving anticonvulsants has been estimated to be in the order of 6–10 per cent as opposed to an expectation of 3 per cent (Annegers *et al.* 1974).

The increased risk appeared to be specific for certain types of malfomations—cleft lip and/or cleft palate, congenital heart disease (particularly ventricular septal defects), and possibly ureter duplication. In the Mayo study, Tridione®, phenytoin, and/or phenobarbital usage appeared to be associated with these malformations, while the occurrence of seizures per se as documented during pregnancy did not seem to be related. Also, children of epileptic fathers showed neither an excess of any malformations nor the presence of those listed above (Annegers *et al.* 1979*b*).

Nelson and Ellenberg (1982) have also studied this problem with the data of the NINCDS Collaborative Perinatal Project. This was a study of the outcome of pregnancy in some 54 000 women from 12 centres throughout the US in 1959–66, with follow-up examinations of the children up to seven years of age. Of the 45 000 mothers followed, 204 had had non-eclamptic seizures during pregnancy, another 206 current seizures (within five years but not during this pregnancy), 306 remote afebrile seizure(s), and 151 only febrile fits.

Stillbirth rates were significantly elevated at 51 per 1000 births of mothers with seizures in pregnancy and 24 for those with other current seizures, as opposed to 19 per 1000 births of mothers with no history of any seizures. Similar excesses were found for children among those same three maternal groups for: (i) small head size (56, 46, and 23 per 1000 respectively); (ii) post-neonatal afebrile seizures (54, 22, 9); (iii) febrile to afebrile fits (12, 11, 1); (iv) mental retardation—IQ<70 (81, 51, 34) and IQ<50 (47, 13, 4); and (v) 'any bad outcome' including death (263, 181, 129). Cerebral palsy was insignificantly elevated (12, 11, 4).

Efforts were made to assess the influence of treatment as prescribed (Nelson and Ellenberg 1982) (Table 12.4). Of the current-seizure mothers on anticonvulsants, almost 50 per cent were taking phenytoin and phenobarbital, 30 per cent only phenytoin, and 20 per cent only phenobarbital. Small numbers had had other drugs, especially primidone. The non-seizure mothers were almost all receiving phenobarbital, many for toxaemia of pregnancy. When toxaemics were removed from this last group, only the stillbirth excess persisted as significant. None of the apparent differences by treatment were statistically significant within each seizure group, but in many cases the numbers were very small.

Most recently, valproate usage in pregnancy has come under question (*Lancet* 1982). A number of major congenital malformations have been reported among infants exposed to valproate *in utero*, including spina bifida. *The Lancet* reviewed reports from the Rhône-Alpes region of France where, of 146 cases of spina bifida aperta (SBA) in 1976–82, 10 had been born of epileptic mothers, nine of whom were receiving valproate—the only drug taken in five cases. Of some 6600 babies with other malformations there were 61 of epileptic mothers, of whom 21 were taking valproate. Expected numbers of malformations for epileptic mothers were not provided, and, conversely, the Paris-Yvelines region of France had 65 SBA births in 1980–82, none of which were associated with maternal epilepsy.

It would appear, therefore, that more data are required before deciding whether the increased frequency of adverse effects in pregnancy, including malformations, that is seen in *mothers* receiving *treatment* for *convulsive disorders* should be attributed to any one or more of these three components, each of which has multiple facets.

MULTIPLE SCLEROSIS

It has been said that to know multiple sclerosis (MS) is to know neurology—and vice versa. Its cause is unknown, treatment is inadequate, and it has an unpredictable course. Diagnosis remains a clinical decision. There are now several laboratory tests such as averaged evoked potentials, cerebrospinal fluid (CSF) gamma globulin levels, and computerized tomography, but while useful none of these is pathognomonic.

Clinicians have generally divided their cases into 'MS' and 'possible or suspected MS'. An early grouping for epidemiological purposes was that of Allison and Millar (1954); probable; early probable and latent; and possible. Some later workers have added 'definite' and 'clinically definite'; some include first bouts as 'probable MS' while others consider them 'possible'. Many recent clinical and epidemiological investigators, however, have tended to use some variant of the criteria of the Schumacher committee (Schumacher *et al.* 1965) as (clinically definite) MS, often also retaining the Allison–Millar 'probable' category.

The geographical distribution of multiple sclerosis has been a subject of extensive study (Kurland *et al.* 1965; Hyllested and Kurland 1966; Poskanzer 1967, 1968; Alter and Kurtzke 1968; Kurland 1970; Acheson 1972*a,b*, 1977; Field *et al.* 1972; Kurtzke *et al.* 1973*a*; Alter 1977; Kurtzke 1977*a,b*, 1980*a,b*, 1983*c*; Detels 1978; Kranz and Kurland 1982).

Mortality data

Deaths from MS have been coded to rubrics 345 (ICD 6 and 7) and 340 (ICD 8 and 9). For ICD 8 and 9 'other demyelinating disease' was coded 341.

International death rates

The earliest analysis of MS mortality rates from many countries was made by Limburg (1950). He found higher rates in the temperate zone than in the tropics and subtropics and an inverse relationship between the death rates and mean annual temperature. Goldberg and Kurland (1962) collated mortality data for MS from 31 countries for 1951–58. The rates ranged from well over 3 per 100 000 to almost zero. The highest rates were those for Northern Ireland, Scotland, and the Republic of Ireland. Other western European countries had rates of 2 per 100 000, except for the northernmost lands of Norway, Sweden, and Finland, and the Mediterranean countries of Greece, Italy, and Portugal. The rates for these two groupings were closer to 1 per 100 000, similar to those for Canada, Australia, New Zealand, and US whites; non-whites in the US had half the rates of whites. Lowest by far were rates from Asia, Africa, and the Caribbean.

In Iceland a low rate of 0.3 was reported, in apparent contrast to its high prevalence rates (see below). There is evidence that MS frequency may have changed in Iceland, with support for a death rate such as this in the 1950s.

Age, sex, and race

There were 4305 deaths in the US coded to MS as underlying cause in 1959–61, with 4044 among whites and 261 among non-whites. The age-adjusted annual death rate was 0.8 per 100 000. The rate for whites alone was also 0.8, with 0.7 for males and 0.9 for females; that for non-whites was 0.5 – 0.4 for males and 0.6 for females. The white:non-white ratio was 1.6:1 and the male:female ratio was 0.9:1 (Kurtzke *et al.* 1973*a*).

Figure 12.9 presents the age-specific mortality rates for US, 1959–61, by sex and race. There were few deaths below 30 years of age, and a broad maximum for whites at over 2 per 100 000 between ages 40 and 70 years. At these ages the non-white rates were half those of the whites. In contrast, in Denmark there was a clear maximum mortality rate for MS in 1963–68 at age 60 for both males and females, whether for underlying cause or for total deaths coded (Fig. 12.10) (Kurtzke 1972*a*). The underlying cause maxima were more than twice those of US whites.

The proportions of total deaths coded as underlying cause were 75 per cent in Denmark, 72 per cent in the US for 1955, and 77 per cent in Norway for 1956–60 (Kurtzke 1972*a*). For the Netherlands, in 1953–60, the proportion was 85 per cent (Kurtzke *et al.* 1973*a*).

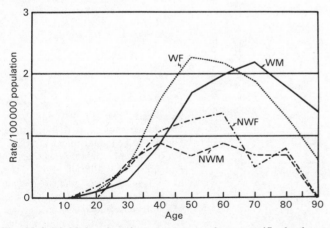

Fig. 12.9. Multiple sclerosis: average annual age-specific death rates per 100 000 population by sex and race, United States, 1959–61. (Source: Kurtzke and Kurland (1973).)

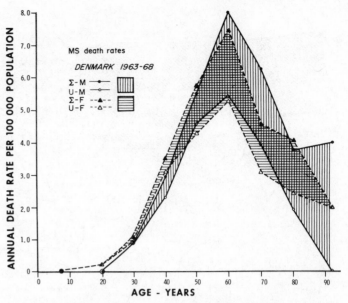

Fig. 12.10. Multiple sclerosis: average annual age-specific death rates per 100 000 population by sex and cause of death, Denmark, 1963–68; total conditions coded (upper lines) and underlying cause (lower lines). (Source: Kurtzke (1972*a*).)

Geography

Age-adjusted rates by state in the US revealed a north–south difference (Fig. 12.11). All states below the 37th parallel of latitude were low, although in the east the dividing line seemed to be at 39°, with Virginia and Maryland below the mean. The same distribution was seen for whites alone and for crude death rates by place of birth (Kurtzke *et al.* 1973*a*).

Time trend

In the US age-adjusted MS death rates for whites were 0.9 for 1949–51, 0.8 for 1959–61 and 1965–67 (Kurtzke 1972*a*; Kurtzke *et al.* 1973*a*), and 0.7 for 1974–76 (Kranz and Kurland 1982). In Canada, the age-adjusted death rates had declined from 1.3 for 1949–51 to 1.0 for 1959–61 (Kurland *et al.* 1965). The slight decrease is most likely a result of increased survival, as will be discussed below.

Morbidity data

Prevalence rates

With diseases like MS, where incidence is low (and rates often unstable), onset is difficult to establish, diagnosis is frequently made years after onset, and survival is generally prolonged, the use of prevalence rates to assess geography has become widely accepted. There are now nearly 250 prevalence surveys for MS, most of which have been performed since the Second World War (Kurtzke 1975, 1980*c*). The findings from these surveys are summarized below.

Geography: Europe

Prevalence rates for Europe and the Mediterranean basin are plotted against geographical latitude in Fig. 12.12. The rates

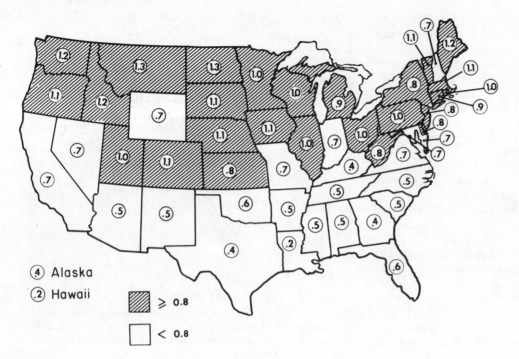

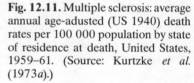

Fig. 12.11. Multiple sclerosis: average annual age-adusted (US 1940) death rates per 100 000 population by state of residence at death, United States, 1959–61. (Source: Kurtzke *et al.* (1973*a*).)

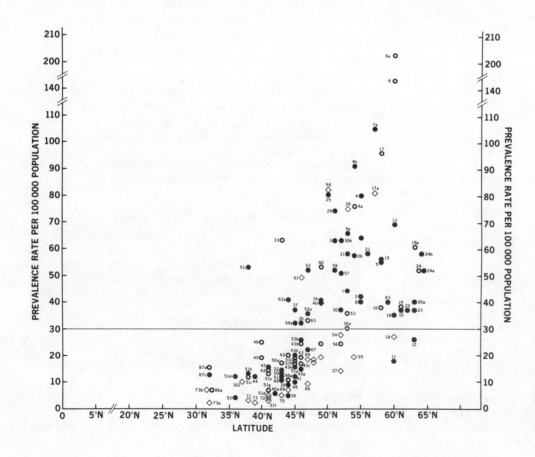

Fig. 12.12. Multiple sclerosis: prevalence rates per 100 000 population for survey sites plotted by latitude, Europe and Mediterranean area as of 1980. Numbers identify studies in Kurtzke (1975, 1980*c*). Solid circles are Class A (best) surveys, open circles Class B, open diamonds Class C (inadequate), solid diamonds Class E (estimates). Class C studies listed only if no better quality survey available for the site. (Source: Kurtzke (1980*c*).)

appear to separate into two zones or clusters, one with rates of 30 and over, considered high frequency, and the other with rates below 30 but above 4 per 100 000 population, classed as medium frequency. Using only those judged Class A studies (those with good case ascertainment and comparable methodology and diagnostic criteria), the high prevalence band as defined extended from 44 to 64° N. latitude. The prevalence survey from north-east Scotland, point 7a in Fig. 12.12 (Shepherd and Downie 1978) and the Shetland–Orkney Islands (Sutherland 1956; Allison 1963; Fog and Hyllested 1966; Poskanzer *et al.* 1980) 6 and 6a in Fig. 12.12, are of particular interest because their rates, between 100 and 300 per 100 000 population, are the highest reported to date.

The northernmost parts of Scandinavia and the Mediterranean basin comprised medium prevalence regions. Geoffrey Dean has contested the inclusion of Italy within the medium zone, first with his survey of Enna in Sicily where a rate of 53 per 100 000 was recorded (Dean *et al.* 1979). This has received considerable support, and there are now seven other recently published surveys from Italy and its islands with rates between 30 and 45 per 100 000 (Granieri and Rosati 1982). The Italian findings would seem to refute the zonal concept for MS distribution in Europe, and *a fortiori* the more widely held interpretation that there is a gradient of MS risk with geographical latitude. However, all these studies were intensive surveys of small regions, and the case-finding may thus not be comparable to other (larger) surveys. Second, the cases are so few and the confidence intervals on the rates so large that a true rate below 30 cannot be rejected. Third, they could indeed be accurate but the dividing line between 'high' and 'medium' may now be set too low. Most 'medium' rates were near 10 per 100 000 in the 1950s and 1960s; many were 20–25 in the 1970s. Perhaps 40 or so will prove to be a preferable point in the future, if this zonal concept is valid.

Clustering

In Europe there were a number of surveys of the entirety of a country at a single time, covering Norway, Denmark, Sweden, Switzerland, Northern Ireland, northern Scotland, the Netherlands, Iceland, and Finland, with repeated surveys of different generations of patients (and doctors) in Norway, Denmark, and Switzerland. While the distribution within the small area of Northern Ireland was uniform and those within the Netherlands and Iceland rather equivocal, in all other countries surveyed there were very highly significant deviations from homogeneity, and the high rate areas tended to be contiguous, forming clusters or foci. The differences in the rates between the highest and lowest regions in each land were in order of sixfold or more, and thus the variations would seem of biological as well as statistical significance (Kurtzke 1967). Not only was there clustering, but in each of the three countries resurveyed a generation apart, there was a very strong correlation between the early and the later distributions, with coefficients of correlation each of about 0.8.

When contiguous countries were considered, the high frequency MS areas in the north appeared to describe one single 'Fenno–Scandian focus' (Kurtzke 1974b) extending from the waist and south-eastern mountain plains of Norway eastward across the inland lake area of southern Sweden, then across the Bay of Bothnia to south-western Finland, and then back to Sweden in the region of Umeå on the north-eastern shore. The clustering, as well as the broader geographical distributions, would indicate that the occurrence of MS is intrinsically related to geography. If this is correct, then MS can be defined as an acquired, exogenous environmental disease.

Geography: America

On the basis of prevalence rates for MS the Americas can be divided into the same three zones: high frequency from 37 to 52°, medium frequency from 30 to 33°, and low frequency (prevalence less than 5 per 100 000) from 12 to 19° and from 63 to 67° N. latitude (Kurtzke 1975, 1980c). The best information on the nationwide distribution of MS in the US, though, arose from a study of a series of 5305 US veterans of the Second World War or the Korean War, who were adjudged by the Veterans Administration to be 'service connected' for MS. Each of the MS patients was matched to a military peer on the basis of age, date of entry into and branch of service, and survival of the war. This provided an unbiased, pre-illness case-control series of nationwide composition and unprecedented size (Kurtzke *et al.* 1979b).

Figure 12.13 shows the distribution of MS expressed as case-control ratio percentages for WW II white male veterans according to state of residence at entry into military service. From calculations described elsewhere (Bobowick *et al.* 1978), the case control ratios provided estimated prevalence rates such that regions of less than 30 per 100 000 prevalence would be those with a ratio of less than 0.75. States below the 37th parallel all fell in the medium frequency zone, and the states (and northern California) above the 37th parallel were in the high-frequency zone, except for Virginia (0.69 ratio) and Kentucky (0.60). In the east, the high-to-medium dividing line passed the 39th parallel. This distribution was therefore very similar to that for MS mortality rates (Fig. 12.11).

Geography: world-wide

Prevalence rates from other regions conform in general with the threefold division noted, and the world-wide distribution is then described within these three zones of frequency or risk in Fig. 12.14.

The high-risk zone, with prevalence rates of 30 and above per 100 000 population, include northern and central Europe into the USSR, northern US and southern Canada, New Zealand, and south-eastern Australia. These regions are bounded by areas of medium frequency, with prevalence rates currently between 5 and 29 per 100 000, consisting of the southern US, south-western Norway and northernmost Scandinavia, and probably the USSR from the Ural Mountains into Siberia as well as the Ukraine. Except for small studies in Italy with apparently high rates, the entire Mediterranean basin from Spain to Israel is also of medium prevalence. This zone also includes most of Australia, and perhaps Hawaii and the mid-portion of South America, plus one white group of South Africa. Low-frequency areas, with prevalence rates below 5 per 100 000, comprised all other known areas of Asia and Africa, Alaska and Greenland, and the Caribbean region to include Mexico and probably northern South America.

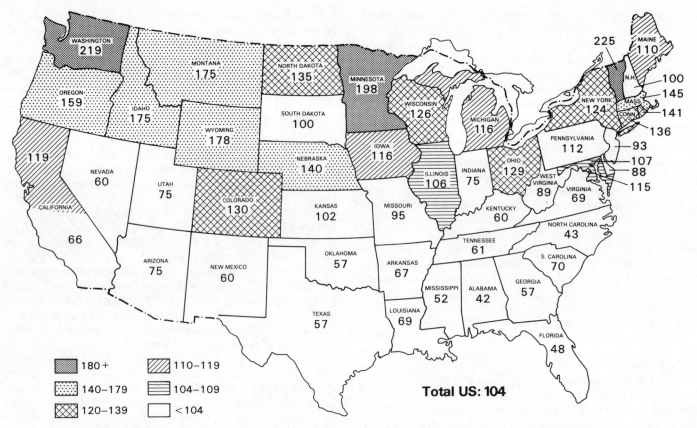

Fig. 12.13. Multiple sclerosis case-control ratio percentages for white male veterans of Second World War by state of residence at entry into service. (Modified from Kurtzke (1978*a*).)

Age, sex, and race

The majority of the more recent prevalence studies reported higher rates among females than males by a ratio of about 1.5:1. The sex difference was most marked at younger ages, with little difference beyond the age of 50 years. Age-specific prevalence rates are illustrated by the Danish nationwide survey of Hyllested (1956) (Fig. 12.15). Here the maximal rates were 179 for females and 137 for males. The findings of a nationwide survey of multiplie sclerosis in Ireland in 1971 were similar to those of the Danish study (Brady *et al.* 1977).

From the world-wide distribution of Fig. 12.14, it may be seen that all the high- and medium-risk areas were those of predominantly white populations. In the US, non-whites had this disorder recorded as a cause of death only half as often as whites. In the veteran series, blacks or Negroes had only half the risk of white males regardless of residence (Table 12.5). Note too that young white females had nearly twice the risk of MS as did the white males. The same series indicated a paucity of Orientals, Filipinos, and Amerindians, though with small numbers; an apparent deficit of Latin Americans was explicable by geography.

Prevalence estimates among native Japanese have been uniformly low (Kurtzke 1975, 1980*c*). Detels *et al.* (1972, 1974, 1977) have presented good evidence of low MS mortality rates and prevalence rates among Japanese and Japanese-Americans in California and Washington State.

Data from Hawaii (Alter *et al.* 1971) suggested low MS risk among Polynesians and Filipinos residing in the state.

Multiple sclerosis, then, is predominantly the white man's burden. However, the other racial groups still manifest the same geographical gradients as the whites, but at lower levels.

Table 12.5. *Multiple sclerosis: case/control ratios by tier of residence at entry into active duty (EAD) for the major sex and race groups, US military-veteran series*

	Tier of residence at EAD			
Sex and race	North	Middle	South	Total*
Case/control ratios				
White male	1.41	1.02	0.58	1.04
White female	2.77	1.71	0.80	1.86
Black male	0.61	0.59	0.31	0.45
Total series†	1.41	1.00	0.53	1.00
Case/control numbers				
White males	2195/1544	2059/2022	688/1161	4922/4737
White females	97/35	65/38	20/25	182/98
Black males	28/46	88/150	61/194	177/390
Total series†	2323/1647	2213/2219	762/1425	5298/5291*

*Excludes one male case and 11 male controls inducted in foreign countries.

†Includes black females and persons of other races.

Modified from Kurtzke *et al.* (1979*b*).

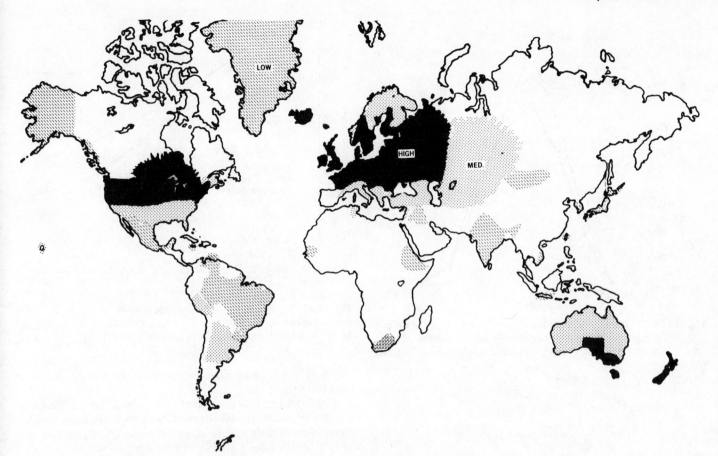

Fig. 12.14. Multiple sclerosis: world-wide distribution as of 1980 according to high (black), medium (dots), and low (diagonal dashes) zones of prevalence or frequency. Open areas are regions without data. South American frequencies are tentative. (Source: Kurtzke (1980*c*).)

Incidence rates

The annual incidence rate in high-risk MS areas at present is probably at least 3 per 100 000 population and in low-risk areas about 1 per 1 000 000 (Kurtzke 1983*c*). There was no apparent change in incidence in Winnipeg and New Orleans over several decades (Stazio *et al.* 1964, 1967), in Rochester, Minnesota, for 70 years (Kranz 1983; Percy *et al.* 1971), or in Northern Ireland for over 25 years (Millar 1972).

In the Danish study, average annual incidence rates were calculated from the incident cases 1939–45. An annual rate of 3.4 per 100 000 was found: 3.0 male and 3.7 female (Kurtzke 1968*b*, 1969*b*). Age-specific rates rose rapidly from virtually zero in childhood to a peak at about age 27 years of more than 9 per 100 000 for females and almost 7 for males (Fig. 12.16). Beyond 40 years of age there was little difference between the sexes, both of whose rates declined equally to zero by the age of 60 years.

Survival

In studies antedating the Second World War, hospital series indicated an average duration of life after onset of MS of about 10 years. The prevalence studies of the early 1950s estimated averaged survival times of at least 20 years (Kurland and Westlund 1964). Survival rates were calculated by life-table methods for the patients resident in Rochester, Minnesota (Percy *et al.* 1971), and for US Army male patients hospitalized in the Second World War (Kurtzke *et al.* 1970). Among both the Army groups and the Rochester series, the average duration of illness or median survival was estimated at some 35 years from onset (Kurtzke *et al.* 1970; Kurland and Molgaard 1981). About three-fourths of the patients had survived 20 years, and two-thirds 30 years. In the Rochester series, half the survivors were still ambulatory after 20 years of illness.

An increasing proportion of causes of death other than MS with increasing duration of illness was noted in the Army survivorship study (Fig. 12.17). Here causes were allocated by personal review of the records but a similar pattern is found in routine death data (Fig. 12.10).

Migration

Table 12.6 summarizes rates among immigrants to and from the different MS risk areas. The rates were those regardless of age at immigration and clinical onset. In broad terms, there

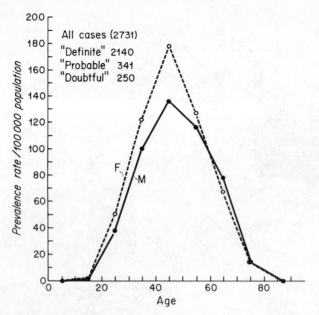

Fig. 12.15. Multiple sclerosis: age-specific prevalence rates per 100 000 population by sex and diagnosis (definite, probable, doubtful). (Data of Hyllested (1956).) (Source: Kurtzke and Kurland (1973).)

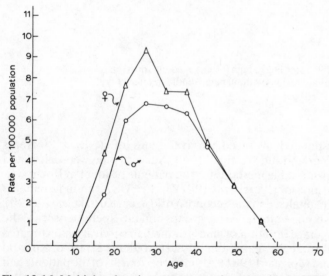

Fig. 12.16. Multiple sclerosis: average annual age-specific incidence rates per 100 000 population by sex (excludes doubtful cases). Denmark, 1939–45. MS series of Hyllested (1956).) (Source: Kurtzke (1968b).)

was tendency for immigrants to retain much of the risk of their birth place if they came from a high- or medium-risk area, but a suggestion that low-to-high migrants may have increased their risk of MS. The data should be assessed from the horizontal rows, since several figures are for different age-specific prevalence rates, others are age-adjusted, and for one set they are cumulative risk estimates. For the last, a risk calculated for Denmark has been assigned to Paris, the site of

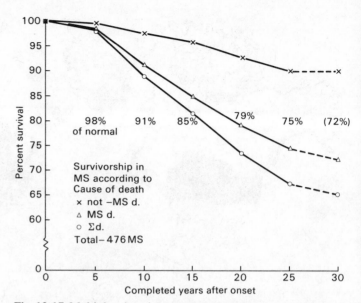

Fig. 12.17. Multiple sclerosis: percentage survival by years after onset according to cause of death (MS or not). United States Army Second World War series. (Modified from Kurtzke *et al.* (1970).)

the half-Vietnamese immigrants (Kurtzke 1978*c*; Kurtzke and Bui 1980).

If the risk of MS is defined at or near birth, or the disease is innate, then migrants from low-to-high regions would demonstrate no increase in risk. In the US, as mentioned above, death rates for MS were distributed so that states to the north of 37° N. latitude had twice the rates of those to the south (Fig. 12.11). However, when MS deaths among those who were born in the north and died in the south were compared to those who were born in the south and died in the north, the north–south difference disappeared (Fig. 12.18). The death rate for the US southern-born MS cases who had died in the north (0.68) was significantly higher than that for the southern-born who died in the south (0.46) (Kurtzke *et al.* 1971).

In Table 12.5 the residences of the US veteran case-control series were allocated within three horizontal tiers for the coterminous United States. The marginal totals of Table 12.7 provide the ratios for birthplace and for residence at service entry within the three tiers for white male US veterans of the Second World War. Migrants would be those born in one tier and who entered service from another. The major diagonal (north–south, middle–middle, south–south) gives the case-control ratios for non-migrants, and cells off this diagonal define the ratios for migrants (Kurtzke *et al.* 1979*a*).

All ratios decrease from north to south. Migrants born north and entering service from the middle tier decreased their ratio from 1.41 to 1.26; if they entered from the south the ratio was 0.70. Birth in the middle tier was marked by an increase in the MS/C ratio for northern entrants to 1.30 and a decrease to 0.72 for the southern ones. Migration after birth in the south provided ratios of 0.62 (middle) and 0.73 (north).

Other prevalence studies for migrants from high- to low-risk areas also suggest that the age of adolescence is

Table 12.6. *Multiple sclerosis prevalence rates per 100 000 population among native born and immigrants in different risk areas.*

Reference	Immigration site by its MS risk	Population group			
		Native born	Immigrants from MS-risk areas		
			High	Medium	Low
		(rate per 100 000)			
High risk					
Rischbieth (1966)	South Australia	38	37	4	—
Detels *et al.* (1978)	Washington State	—*	55*	19*	—
Kurtzke and Bui (1980)	Paris	(92)†	—	—	89†
Medium risk					
McCall *et al.* (1968, 1969)	Perth, Western Australia	14	22	—	—
McCall *et al.* (1968, 1969)	Perth, Western Australia	40‡	87‡	—	—
Sutherland *et al.* (1962)	Queensland	9	15	—	—
Saint and Sadka (1962)	Western Australia	10	31	—	—
Alter *et al.* (1962)	Israel	4	33	8	3
Leibowitz *et al.* (1972)	Israel	9§	19§		6§
Detels *et al.* (1978)	Los Angeles	—*	30*	15*	—
Low risk					
Dean (1967)	South Africa	6	48	15	—
Moffie (1966)	Netherlands Antilles	3	59	—	—

*Age-adjusted (US 1970) rates age 20+ years for cases with onset after migration; no comparable rates for native born.
†Cumulative risk: 20-year Denmark natives and 18-year half-Vietnamese immigrants to Paris.
‡Age-speecific rate, 40–49 years.
§Age-adjusted (US 1960) rates.

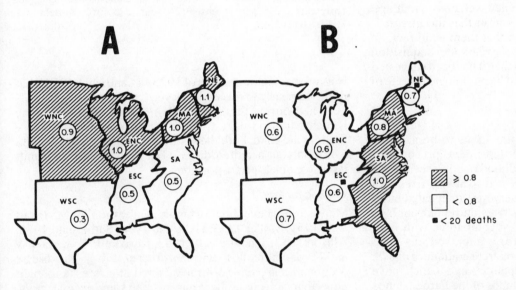

Fig. 12.18. Multiple sclerosis: average annual crude death rates per 100 000 population by residence at death within seven of the nine Census Regions, United States 1959–61. (A) Persons born in the same tier (northern or southern) as at death. (B) Persons born in tier opposite from that at death. (Modified from Kurtzke *et al.* (1971).)

Table 12.7. *Multiple sclerosis: case-control ratios for white males of Second World War by tier of residence at birth and at entry into active duty (EAD), coterminous US only, US military-veteran series*

Birth tier	EAD tier			Birth total
	North	Middle	South	
Case-control ratios				
North	1.41	1.26	0.70	1.38
Middle	1.30	1.04	0.72	1.04
South	0.73	0.62	0.56	0.57
EAD Total	1.39	1.04	0.58	1.04
Case-control numbers				
North	1611/1140	112/89	32/46	1755/1275
Middle	125/96	1544/1482	68/94	1737/1672
South	16/22	42/68	439/788	497/878
EAD Total	1752/1258	1698/1639	539/928	3989/3825

Data of Kurtzke *et al.* (1979a).

critical for risk retention: those migrating after the age of 15 years retaining the MS risk of their birthplace; those migrating before that age acquiring the lower risk of their new residence (Dean and Kurtzke 1971; Alter *et al.* 1966, 1971, 1978; Detels *et al.* 1978). Several low-to-high studies have also shown that those migrating in childhood or adolescence increase their risk of MS (Dassell 1972; Kurtzke and Bui 1980). However, there is some disagreement as to whether risk increases with migration to high-risk areas. Detels *et al.* (1972, 1978) found no significant increase in either death rates or prevalence rates for southern-born migrants to Washington State. Numbers, however, were small and a true increase cannot be ruled out. Dean *et al.* (1976, 1977) described a marked paucity of MS in England among immigrants from low-risk areas. The estimates for expected number of MS cases for such immigrants were markedly inflated, primarily because of the very rapidly expanding immigrant population during the study period and the short length of residence in the new country (Kurtzke 1976).

The veteran series provides the best evidence as to increasing MS risk by migration from low to high areas—and it also indicates that the time when such moves are critical is well before clinical onset. In the earlier Army study, similar case-control ratios were found for the same three tiers for residence at birth and at entry into the service; but the gradient had totally disappeared for residences while in military service but before clinical onset (Beebe *et al.* 1967).

Other evidence suggesting acquisition of MS between approximately ages 10–15 years, based largely on ages of maximal geographical clustering, has been presented elsewhere (Kurtzke 1965*b*, 1969*b*, 1972*c*, 1977*b*). Shapira *et al.* (1963) came to similar conclusions from the ages of common residence for sibs, both of whom had MS. All these inferences arose from surveys in high-risk areas.

While it is premature to state that risk for MS has become fixed by about 20 years of age among migrants from low to high areas, there is strong evidence that for natives of high-risk zones and for migrants from high- to low-risk zones, the risk of MS is by-and-large determined well before that age. This has also been interpreted to mean that the *disease* is acquired well before this age, and that there is, in fact, an 'incubation' or 'latency' period of some years after acquisition before clinical symptom onset. Further, it has been suggested that part of this 'latent' period could be pathologically one of active subclinical disease.

Multiple sclerosis epidemics

Multiple sclerosis appears from the above to be a place-related disorder, with risk primarily dependent upon place of residence, particularly during childhood or adolescence. As to the place itself, the risk has seemed relatively fixed. All geographical areas that have been surveyed at repeated intervals have provided stable incidence rates, and either stable or increasing prevalence rates, the last compatible with both better case-ascertainment and perhaps improved survival.

However, there have been two apparent epidemics of MS, which may have common precipitants, and which have occurred in the ethnically-similar lands of the Faroe Islands and Iceland. Up to 1977, 25 cases of MS had been identified on the Faroes among native-born resident Faroese. All but one had clinical onset of MS between 1943 and 1960; one began in 1970 (Fig. 12.19). Onset in the 24 cases of 1943–60 followed a log-normal distribution, and met all criteria for a point-source epidemic. One possible source for this epidemic was the British occupation of the Faroes for five years from April 1940 (Kurtzke and Hyllested 1979). By 1982 several further cases had been discovered, but not one case of MS has been found occurring before 1943 among native-born resident Faroese (Kurtzke and Hyllested 1982). The cumulative risk of MS for the Faroese population of 1940 was the same as the cumulative risk calculated for Danes in Denmark (Kurtzke 1983*a*).

A study of cases in Iceland between 1900 and 1975 (Kurtzke *et al.* 1982) shows a sudden increase in cases in 1945, the annual incidence rate of 3.2 per 100 000 for 1945–54

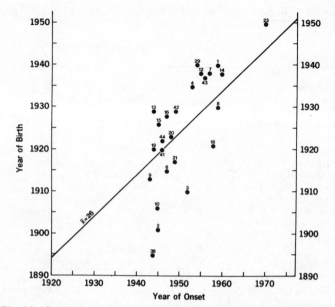

Fig. 12.19. Multiple sclerosis: cases among native-born resident Faroese by calendar year of birth vs. year of clinical onset. Diagonal represents mean age at onset (26 years). (Source: Kurtzke and Hyllested (1979).)

was twice as high as the rate of 1923–44 and since 1954 it has returned nearly to this earlier level. Iceland was also heavily occupied during the Second World War, not only by the British but also by the Canadians and Americans. If these findings are valid, both these studies would indicate that MS is not only an acquired disease but perhaps also transmittable—or at least transportable.

Genetic factors

Many studies have shown a family aggregation for MS (Pratt *et al.* 1951; Müller 1953; Hyllested 1956; Sutherland 1956; Allison 1963; Schapira *et al.* 1963; Kurtzke 1965*a*; Mackay and Myrianthopoulos 1966; Stazio *et al.* 1967). The disease occurs among siblings of the affected at a rate six to eight times that expected. There may also be some excess among their parents.

Most published twin studies on MS suffer from selection bias and retrospective ascertainment. The only one for which the *prospective* occurrence of MS within a defined cohort of twins has been assessed is that of Bobowick *et al.* (1978), utilizing the National Research Council Twin Registry. Among its 16 000 sets of white male twins, both members of whom had been in US military service during the Second World War, only 16 cases of MS in 15 pairs of twins could be identified by 1972. This number was half that expected in the general population. One of six sets of monozygous twins was concordant for MS, while none of eight dizygous pairs nor the one set of unknown zygosity was concordant.

That certain histocompatibility (HLA) antigens may be related to MS has broadened the controversy surrounding the role of genetics. In whites of northern European ancestry, there is generally an excess of HL-A3, B7, DW2, and DrW2 among MS cases. A large and contradictory literature has arisen as to shared genetic components, predominantly in the HLA series, in families of MS patients. Some studies indicated that the majority of affected siblings in multicase families shared a common haplotype, but different haplotypes have been noted in different families (Hens and Carton 1978; Visscher *et al.* 1979). However, other investigations (Eldridge *et al.* 1978; Alter and Quevedo 1979), have failed to demonstrate one parental haplotype segregating preferentially in affected siblings as compared to unaffected siblings.

Roberts *et al.* (1979*a, b*) studied family histories in cases and controls ascertained in the MS surveys of the Orkney Islands, which share with the Shetland Islands the highest rate of MS so far reported. They found that MS patients did not differ from controls in HLA patterns or in other blood groups, isoenzymes, or serum proteins, nor were they more or less inbred than controls. The only possible single-gene inheritance the authors felt at all likely was an autosomal recessive with 12 per cent penetrance. 'Much more likely is a complex aetiology, the genetic contribution being polygenic and possibly subordinate to the environmental...' (Roberts *et al.* 1979*b*).

Other risk factors

Attempts to identify factors which would explain the unique geographical distribution of MS have been numerous but unsuccessful (Acheson *et al.* 1960; Barlow 1960; Acheson 1972*a*). Dietary fat (Sutherland *et al.* 1962), trace elements, and heavy metals (Campbell *et al.* 1950; Warren *et al.* 1967; Wikstrom *et al.* 1976; Ryan *et al.* 1978) have been implicated, but are unsupported. Most case-control comparisons (Westlund and Kurland 1953; Poskanzer 1965, 1968; Antonovsky *et al.* 1967; Alter *et al.* 1968; Alter and Speer 1968; Poskanzer *et al.* 1980) have revealed no significant associations (other than the accepted geographical variations) with the exception of the finding by Poskanzer (1965, 1968) that patients had had tonsillectomy in more cases than had either their spouses or their nearest siblings. Studies in Israel suggested inverse relationships with indices of poor sanitation and a direct relationship to some features of urbanization; however, there were no strong correlations (Antonovsky *et al.* 1965, 1968). Reports implicating dog exposure have been published (Cook and Dowling 1977, 1978; Cook *et al.* 1978, 1979), but to date also remain unverified (Poskanzer *et al.* 1977; Bunnell *et al.* 1979; Kurtzke and Priester 1979; Kranz 1983).

In a recent case-control study (Kranz 1983) in Olmsted and Mower Counties, Minnesota, small family size was significantly associated with MS. Whether this reflects socio-economic status (see below) is uncertain, but urban residence and high educational achievement did have relative risk estimates greater than one. However, for prior infections, trauma, animal exposure (including dogs), prior surgery, and other illnesses, no association could be demonstrated. Bobowick *et al.* (1978) in their study of twin series reported an excess of prior 'environmental events' among affected versus unaffected twins. These 'events' included operations, trauma, and infections as the major groups, and differentiating frequencies were mostly within the 20 years

before clinical onset rather than in early childhood. Early birth order has been reported to increase MS risk (Isager *et al.* 1980); but others have found no relationship to birth order (Alperovich *et al.* 1981, Visscher *et al.* 1982).

Beebe *et al.* (1967) compared MS patients with matched controls from the earlier US Army series. Characteristics that significantly differentiated patients from controls included geographical location at birth or service entry but not during military service. There was also a strong positive correlation with urbanization of residence, high socio-economic status, and visual defects (refractive errors) at entry into service. A lower risk of MS was found among blacks—less than half the expected number.

Some laboratory correlates

A number of workers have reported elevated levels of measles antibody in the serum and spinal fluid of MS patients (Adams and Imagawa 1962; Reed *et al.* 1964; Sibley and Foley 1965; Sever and Zeman 1968). There is also some evidence that the measles serum antibodies in siblings of patients are higher than in controls (Henson *et al.* 1970; Ammitzbøll and Clausen 1972), but this has not been found consistently (Brody *et al.* 1972). There was no association with influenza or influenza vaccination, including the 'swine flu' vaccine (Sibley *et al.* 1976; Myers *et al.* 1977; Bamford *et al.* 1978; Brooks *et al.* 1983).

Various other serological alterations have been reported, but not confirmed, including elevations in antibody titers to herpesvirus, vaccinia, mumps, rickettsia, rubella, varicella-zoster, and others (Ross *et al.* 1965; Catalano 1972; Salmi *et al.* 1974; Ito *et al.* 1975; Thompson *et al.* 1975; Szekeres *et al.* 1980). This has prompted speculation that there may be nonspecific alterations in the immune system of MS patients. Apparent defects in the cellular immune response and/or abnormalities in the T-cell populations that mediate this response have been found (Nordahl and Froland 1978; Antel *et al.* 1978*a, b*; Bach *et al.* 1980; Goust *et al.* 1980; Noronha *et al.* 1980). While there has been variation in the types of defects and the consistency of the findings, there is little doubt but that immune defects are present in MS (Arnason and Waksman 1980). Whether they are of aetiological importance or the consequence of the disease process is much less clear (Symington and MacKay 1978; McFarland and McFarlin 1979; Walker and Cook 1979).

PARKINSONISM

Paralysis agitans was first described in 1817 by Sir James Parkinson, after whom the disorder is named. The parkinsonian syndrome may result from traumatic, vascular, or tumourous lesions of the brain, or from exposure to certain toxins such as carbon monoxide, manganese, and phenothiazines. It may be part of the symptomatology of widespread degenerative diseases such as Shy–Drager syndrome and progressive supranuclear palsy. Such cases, considered secondary parkinsonism, will not be discussed here. Postencephalitic parkinsonism was the early or late sequel of von Economo's type A encephalitis that followed the influenza pandemic after the First World War. Idiopathic parkinsonism or paralysis agitans is the most common form of the syndrome. Some authors add arteriosclerotic parkinsonism, but most investigators agree that arteriosclerosis in the elderly patient with parkinsonism represents a concurrent disease (Kessler 1978; Marttila and Rinne 1976).

One other illness is the parkinsonism–dementia complex. This is highly prevalent in Guam and some of the other Mariana Islands and appears to be a clinical variant of the Guam form of amyotrophic lateral sclerosis (Kurland 1965; Kurland *et al.* 1969*c*; Gibbs and Gajdusek 1972); any relationship to classical parkinsonism seems remote.

Among the reviews of the epidemiological aspects of parkinsonism are those of Hoehn (1971), Kurland (1958*b*), Kurland *et al.* (1969*b*, 1973*e*), Kessler (1973, 1978), and Williams *et al.* (1966).

Mortality data

When listed on the death certificate, parkinsonism coded as underlying cause comprised a quarter to a half of the total deaths in the US, Canada, Norway, and the Netherlands (Kurland 1958*b*; Williams *et al.* 1966). For deaths among known parkinsonian patients in Rochester, it was coded as underlying cause in one-fifth. Among such patients in Baltimore, it was listed on the death certificate as underlying cause for 10 per cent and for 28 per cent as a secondary cause (Kessler 1972).

International death rates

Age-adjusted death rates for parkinsonism in the 1950s were available for 24 countries (Goldberg and Kurland 1962). The rates ranged from 0.5 per 100 000 for Japan, Czechoslovakia, Mexico—and US non-whites, to 3.8 per 100 000 in Australia. High rates (2.5 or more) were recorded for the UK, Ireland, Belgium, Netherlands, France, and Switzerland, as well as for Israel, Uruguay, and Australia–New Zealand. Scandinavia, Canada, and US whites were intermediate.

Thus parkinsonism deaths seemed especially common in western Europe, excluding Scandinavia, and in their emigrant nations of Australia, New Zealand, and Israel. The deaths in Israel would actually have been for immigrants, considering the age at death for parkinsonism.

There was a marked white:non-white difference in the US. For every country except Iceland, the age-adjusted death rates were higher for males than for females, with an average male:female ratio of 1.4:1 (Kurland *et al.* 1973*e*).

Age, sex, and race

There were almost 8700 deaths coded to parkinsonism in the US in 1959–61. The average annual mortality rate was 1.6 per 100 000, age-adjusted to 1.2 for the 1940 US population. The crude rate was 1.8 for males and 1.5 for females. The age-adjusted rates were 1.3 for whites (1.5 male, 1.1 female); and for non-whites 0.4 (0.5 male and 0.3 female). The non-white rates were based on 235 deaths (Kurland *et al.* 1973*e*).

Of the US deaths attributed to parkinsonism in 1959–61, 84 per cent occurred in persons aged 65 years or older and 96 per cent in those aged 55 years or over. The rate was negli-

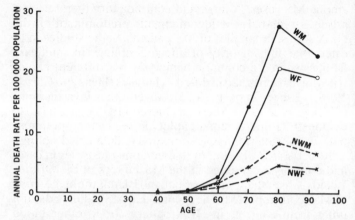

Fig. 12.20. Parkinsonism: average annual age-specific death rates per 100 000 population by sex and race. United States, 1959–61. (Modified from Kurtzke and Kurland (1984).)

gible for persons under 45 years of age, but increased sharply and steadily to a peak at 75–84 years (Fig. 12.20). The rate for males was consistently greater than that for females. The death rate for parkinsonism among US whites was about three times that of non-whites, but the moderate male preponderance persisted in each group. If deaths where Parkinson's disease is given as a secondary cause are included the total death rate then reached a maximum of some 70 per 100 000 at 80 years of age for whites, as opposed to the underlying cause rate of about 20. This configuration was found for each sex and race; in particular, the non-white deficit persisted. The underlying cause rates for 1955 were essentially the same as for 1959–61.

Geography

In the US 1959–61, age-adjusted rates by state ranged from 0.5 per 100 000 in Mississippi to 1.9 in Alaska and 1.8 in South Dakota and Vermont. Most of the states with high mortality rates were in the north-western and north central sections of the country.

Because of age and racial differences, attention was limited to the distribution for whites aged 65 years or more (Fig. 12.21). Again there was an excess in the north-west and a deficit in the south. When sex and racial groups were examined separately, the same distribution pattern was observed (Kurland *et al.* 1973*a*). The sex ratio (1.4:1 male:female) was quite uniform in each Region, the race ratio, however, which averaged 3.7:1 white:non-white, was greatest in the three south-eastern regions where blacks predominate and least (1.7 and 1.8) in the Mountain and Pacific regions with their multiracial compositions.

The geographical distribution for whites suggests a clustering of high- and of low-rate states and Regions. The international and the intranational geographical and racial distributions (though not the sex) are quite reminiscent of the distributions for MS, although in the US the north–south difference was more discrete and did not extend from coast to coast. Perhaps parkinsonism, too, is an exogenous, environmental disease?

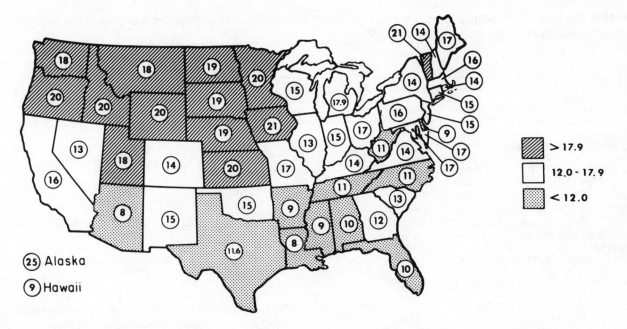

Fig. 12.21. Parkinsonism: average annual age-adjusted (US 1940) death rates per 100 000 whites age 65+ years by state of residence at death, United States, 1959–61. (Source: Kurland *et al.* (1973*e*).)

Time trends

Crude death rates for parkinsonism in the US have remained fairly stable at about 1.4 per 100 000 annually from 1949 to 1961; from 1962 through 1975, the rates fluctuated between 1.4 and 1.6 (Kurtzke and Kurland 1984). The death rates in Britain also have varied little over time (Duvoisin and Schweitzer 1966).

Morbidity data

Prevalence rates

Point-prevalence rates among whites have ranged from 0.7 to 1.8 per 1000 population (Table 12.8). The highest rates were from Rochester and Iceland. Broman's (1963) data for Göteborg, Sweden, were limited to hospitalized patients, and he believed the true rate was likely to be twice as high. In Carlisle (Brewis *et al.* 1966), criteria for diagnosis were rather strict. The low rate in Australia (Jenkins 1966) may reflect incomplete ascertainment. The rate for Sardinia when compared with those for the rest of Europe are compatible with the mortality differences. Conversely, those for Australia–New Zealand apparently do not reflect their high death rates. Based primarily on the Rochester and Iceland rates, a reasonable overall estimate for prevalence of parkinsonism would be about 2 per 1000 among white populations.

Age, sex, and race

Kessler's (1972*b*) estimated Baltimore rates—with good methodology but small numbers—were markedly low for blacks (Table 12.12), which would be in accord with the US death data. There was a modest male excess, averaging 1.2:1

in all surveys, except for that of Finland where the ratio was 0.7:1.

In the Rochester survey, parkinsonism was rarely noted before the age of 40 years, whereas 1 per cent of the population aged over 60 years was affected; among the oldest age-group the rate exceeded 2 per cent. For the other series the curves were similar, even though the absolute rates were lower.

Incidence rates

Average annual incidence rates ranged from 5 to 19 per 100 000 population (Table 12.8), with variations similar to the prevalence rates. Again, the more complete studies indicate a rate close to 20 per 100 000. This rate, with a likely prevalence near 200, would imply an average duration of illness of some 10 years. In Rochester, median survival was about 10 years from onset (Rajput *et al.* 1983). Kurland (1958*c*), had earlier calculated a cumulative risk, or 'lifetime cumulative incidence', at some 2.5 per cent.

Age and sex

By sex, there was the same modest male excess, about 1.2:1, for the incidence rates as with the prevalence rates. Fig. 12.22 presents age-specific incidence rates from the three major surveys. Those from Iceland and Rochester were very similar when the Rochester data were described according to age of onset (mean 65 years) rather than age at diagnosis (69 years). The Carlisle rates were notably lower at all ages. As mentioned above, this deficit may reflect differences in case ascertainment and diagnostic criteria.

The peak incidence rates were noted at about 75 years of age in all the major studies. Such age-specific attack rate

Table 12.8. *Parkinsonism: point prevalence rates per 1000 population and average annual incidence rates per 100 000 population, selected surveys, various years 1960–72*

Reference	Locale	Prevalence			Incidence		
		Year	*n*	Rate	Period	*n*	Rate
Broman (1963)	Göteborg, Sweden	1960	270	0.7*	1957–61	—	6*
K. R. Guðmundsson (1967)	Iceland	1963	317	1.7	1954–63	272	16
Marttila and Rinne (1967*a*)	Turku CHD, Finland	1971	484	1.2	1969	67	17
Brewis *et al.* (1966)	Carlisle, England	1961	80	1.1†	1955–61	60	12
Rosati *et al.* (1980)	Sardinia	1972	967	0.7	1961–71	796	5
Pollock and Hornabrook (1966)	Wellington, NZ	1962	131	1.1	—	—	—
Jenkins (1966)	Gippsland, Australia	1965	70	0.8	1959–64	35	7
Kessler (1972*b*)	Baltimore, Md. whites	1967–9	211	1.3‡	—	—	—
Kessler (1972*b*)	Baltimore, Md. blacks	1967–9	17	0.2‡	—	—	—
Nobrega *et al.* (1967)	Rochester, Minn.	1965	75	1.6	1935–66	191	18
Nobrega *et al.* (1967)	Rochester, Minn.	1965	75	1.8§	1935–66	191	19§
Rajput *et al.* (1983)	Rochester, Minn.	—	—	—	1967–79	120	18¶

*Hospitalized patients only.   §Age-adjusted (US 1960) rate.
†Diagnostic criteria rather strict.   ¶Age-adjusted (US 1970) rate.
‡Rates estimated from community sample.

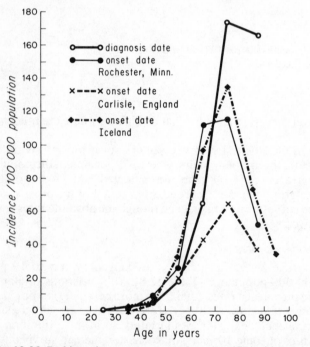

Fig. 12.22. Parkinsonism: average annual age-specific incidence rates per 100 000 population, Rochester, Minn., 1935–66; Carlisle, England. 1955–61: Iceland, 1954–63. Rochester rates for age at diagnosis as well as age at onset, others by age at onset. (Source: Kurland and Kurtzke (1972).)

curves suggest an exogenous insult affecting primarily the elderly, and further support the need to seek a cause for this illness aside from the ageing process.

Genetic factors

Although some recent studies indicated little or no familial tendency to parkinsonism (Marttila and Rinne 1976*b*), most investigators have recorded a familial aggregation of cases. In the early survey from Rochester, the history of a similar

illness in an immediate member of the family was obtained in 16 per cent of the cases of idiopathic parkinsonism (Kurland 1958*c*). Mjönes (1949) in Sweden obtained positive family histories in 41 per cent of the idiopathic and 19 per cent of the arteriosclerotic cases—as well as 42 per cent of the post-encephalitic patients. In Iceland, Kjartan Guðmundsson (1967) reported positive family histories for 20 per cent of his idiopathic and arteriosclerotic patients and for 13 per cent of the postencephalitic. Allan (1937) and Mjönes (1949) compiled striking series of pedigrees with parkinsonism in members of several generations, in a pattern compatible with autosomal dominance with incomplete penetrance. In support of this Martin *et al.* (1972) described parkinsonism as more than twice as common among siblings of index patients than among siblings of controls. The frequency in parents of index cases was three times that of the parents of controls. Similar assertions as to high familial occurrence but with a multifactorial genetic basis were made by Young *et al.* (1977) and Kondo *et al.* (1973). Myrianthopoulos *et al.* (1962) recorded an increased familial frequency among phenothiazine-induced parkinsonism patients compared to matched patient controls.

In contrast in a recent study (Ward *et al.* 1983) of 43 monozygotic and 19 dizygotic twin sets in which an index case had Parkinson's disease, only one monozygotic pair was definitely concordant for parkinsonism although four monozygotic and one dizygotic pairs were concordant when 'possible' cases were included. It was concluded that the frequency was no greater in the co-twins than expected in the general population, and that environmental agents should be regarded as major factors in the aetiology of Parkinson's disease. The data for the prior 'positive' family studies were frequently based on assertions of the patient or his family, with documentation of such cases seldom provided in the publications.

Other risk factors

More than a risk factor, a specific aetiology has been claimed for parkinsonism. As mentioned above, postencephalitic parkinsonism was an early or late result of von Economo's encephalitis. As this cohort aged, so too did the mean age at onset for new cases. The proportions such cases have contributed to all parkinsonism have dropped precipitously with time; there were none in the most recent Rochester survey (Rajput *et al.* 1983). Noting a rising mean age at onset over time for parkinsonian patients seen at the Massachusetts General Hospital, Schwab *et al.* (1956) and Poskanzer and Schwab (1963) propounded that all parkinsonism was a result of subclinical encephalitis, and thus the disease would soon disappear. There is strong evidence, discussed elsewhere (Kurtzke and Kurland 1973, 1984), that this is not the case: population-based onset ages have been constant; incidence rates have been constant through 1976; and many patients were born well after the 1920s.

Evidence has been presented that cigarette smokers are at lower risk for parkinsonism than non-smokers. This was reported from prospective mortality data for US smokers (Hammond 1966; Kahn 1966), in morbidity studies of varied composition (Nefzger *et al.* 1967, Kessler and Diamond 1971, Kessler 1972*b*, Baumann *et al.* 1980), and in the twin survey of Ward *et al.* (1983). Competing risks of death for smokers do not provide a satisfactory explanation. This point, plus the consistency of the findings despite the variety of sources and methods utilized in the studies, make it likely that this is a real association. What it means in pathogenesis, though, is unclear.

HUNTINGTON'S CHOREA

Huntington's disease, or Huntington's chorea (HC), is characterized by progressive dementia and choreoathetotic movements, *chorea* being Greek for dance.

The multivolumed report of the Commission for the Control of Huntington's Disease (Guthrie *et al.* 1977) included an extensive assessment of its epidemiology, from which a large part of this section is derived (Kurtzke *et al.* 1977). Adaptations of this material are also available (Hogg *et al.* 1979; Kurtzke 1979*b*).

Mortality data

Huntington's chorea was first coded in ICD8 within 331, hereditary diseases of the striatopallidal system, as 331.0 (hereditary chorea); dystonia musculorum deformans was 331.1, progressive familial myoclonic epilepsy 331.2, and other (athetosis, pallidal degeneration, Vogt's syndrome) 331.9. Huntington's chorea was therefore the great bulk of code 331, and thus this three-digit code could be used as an approximation for mortality data. Unfortunately, in ICD9 code 333 (other extrapyramidal disease and abnormal movement disorders) include all the 331 subcodes of ICD8 and many more, with 333.4 for HC but a minor component. Virtually all the mortality information available for HC is that specially collected for the HC Commission report (Kurtzke *et al.* 1977), though Kurland (1958*a*) had provided a mortality rate of 2 per million for Canada in 1951.

International death rates

Table 12.9 provides crude and age-adjusted (US 1950) average annual mortality rates per million population for HC. Underlying cause rates were derived from 1627 deaths (68 non-white) in the US, 83 in Sweden, 117 in Denmark, 83 in England and Wales and 99 in Japan. The rate for Chile was based on two deaths (Cruz-Coke 1976). Contributory cause rates were provided by 38 deaths in Sweden and 56 in Denmark.

Table 12.9. *Huntington's chorea (ICD8 code 331.0): average annual and age-adjusted (US 1950) death rates per million population, selected countries, various years 1951–75*

Locale	Period	Crude rate	Adjusted rate
US total	1968–74	1.14	1.15
US white	1968–74	1.25	1.22
US non-white	1968–74	0.38	0.48
Sweden	1969–74	1.71	1.38
Denmark	1951–55	1.51	1.40
Denmark	1956–60	1.46	1.30
Denmark	1961–65	1.24	1.05–
Denmark	1966–70	1.81	1.53
Denmark	1971–75	1.76	1.41
England and Wales*	1960–73	1.55	—
England and Wales†	1973–74	(2.24)	(1.78)
Japan	1969–75	0.13	0.14
Chile	1974	0.19	—

*ICD8 code 331 total.
†Estimated rates for code 331.0 from samples of deaths (likely to be overly high).
Source: Kurtzke (1979*b*).

Among whites, the crude annual death rates ranged from 1 to 2 per million, averaging about 1.6. The rates for England and Wales for HC (code 331.0) had been estimated from samples of a quarter (1973) and a half (1974) of the deaths; the rate reported of 2.2 was notably higher than the average of 1.6 for that country for the total code 331 for 1960–73, and thus may be an overestimate. For each country the age-adjusted rates were somewhat less than the crude rates.

In the US, the white:non-white ratio was 3.3:1. For Japan, death rates from HC averaged only one-tenth the occidental rates, as did that for Chile.

Age, sex, and race

Similar age distributions have been observed in most countries studied (Fig. 12.23). The curve for US whites was similar to that for Scandinavia at younger years, but seemed to peak earlier, at about age 60 years at 4 per million, and thereafter to remain appreciably below the Danish curve. The difference may be merely a reflection of the more complete reporting that one would expect from Scandinavia. Only for Sweden was there a suggestion of bimodality, probably an artefact of the small numbers.

In Denmark the underlying cause rate had a maximum of almost 6 per million at age 70; adding contributory cause deaths increased this to 8 per million, but retained the configuration. The contributory cause deaths in Sweden and Denmark raised the rates by almost a half, so that the total

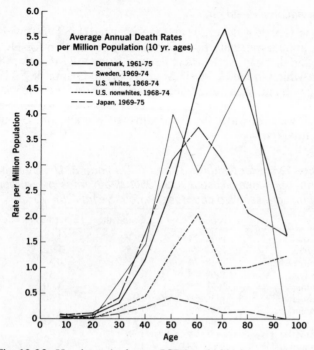

Fig. 12.23. Huntington's chorea (ICD8 code 331.0): average annual age-specific death rates per million population, Denmark, 1961–75: Sweden, 1969–74: US whites and non-whites, 1968–74; Japan, 1969–75. (Source: Kurtzke (1979b).)

death rate for persons *with* HC was about 2.4 per million population.

Geography

An analysis of the distribution by state of residence of the 1559 deaths among US whites, 1968–74, excluding data for 1972 which were incomplete (Hogg *et al.* 1979), revealed no north–south or east–west gradient. The distribution of high rate states extending from the Great Lakes region into the Plains States from Canada to Mexico, and also occupying the West Coast, bears a remote resemblance to the pattern of Scandinavian migration and settlement in the US.

Time trends

In Denmark annual HC death rates for 1951–75 fluctuated between 1 and 2 per million with no obvious trend. For England and Wales, death rates for total code 331 for 1960–73 were quite similar to the Danish HC rates. In the US, the annual rate for HC 1968–74 was virtually constant (Hogg *et al.* 1979).

Morbidity data

Prevalence rates

Prevalence surveys for HC meet with problems not encountered in many other neurological diseases. An area may have been studied because it is known or thought to have an unusually high frequency of the disorder. Cases may be ascertained by standard survey methods, *or* by seeking out families

of probands, *or* by a combination of both. Especially with proband studies, it is often difficult to decide from the publications whether residence requirements within the defined community were met, and even whether the patients were all alive at prevalence day. Conversely, standard epidemiological surveys are most often done in such small populations that the few cases obtainable provide very unstable rates. A further problem common to all studies is whether to include or exclude 'sporadic' cases; most authors accept them into their series, especially since there is a tendency for families to 'hide' positive histories of HC.

Since the aim here is to provide baseline information as to the general distribution of HC, rates recorded from 'genetic isolates' will not be considered. This refers to several studies from the UK, Switzerland, and Sweden (Kurtzke *et al.* 1977), as well as to the fascinating collection of HC in the Lake Maracaibo region of Venezuela as first reported by Negrette (1963). This last focus was summarized for the Commission Report by Myrianthopoulos (1977). The estimated prevalence of Huntington's chorea in this region was in the order of 7 per *thousand* population; in nearly one-third of the cases it was reported that *both* parents had been affected. Further information on this isolate has been published by Avila-Giron (1973).

With these points in mind, from among the 40-odd communities with prevalence-rate estimates (Kurtzke *et al.* 1977), a group of 14 recent studies which had appropriate and comparable clinical and epidemiological criteria will be discussed here (Table 12.10).

Occidental rates ranged from 27 to 70 per million population, and averaged 48 per million. Only Queensland (Wallace 1973) seemed appreciably higher than the mean and the Kassel region of Germany (Wendt and Drohm 1972) lower. Prevalence in the latter region in 1939 had been 32 (95 per cent confidence interval of 22 to 45) and Panse (1942) had recorded a rate of 32 for the Rhineland in 1933 but there were reasons for reporting low rates at those times. The 95 per cent confidence limits on the Iceland rate of 27 were 9 and 63.

For Japan, there was an extraordinarily low rate of 4 per million (95 per cent confidence interval 2–7) reported for the Aichi Prefecture (Kishimoto *et al.* 1957). Just as with the mortality data, this rate was one-tenth the prevalence for occidentals. In Taiwan, only nine cases of HC were diagnosed in seven years at the Taipei University (Hung 1977). And in Djakarta, with 5.5 million population, only two patients with the diagnosis were identified in ten years (Soemargo 1977).

Non-whites in the US also appear to have a low rate. A prevalence of 15 per million (95 per cent confidence interval of 3–44) was calculated for blacks in Michigan based on three cases of HC (Reed and Chandler 1958). Beebe, in the Commission Report (Kurtzke *et al.* 1977), determined from Veterans Administration hospital discharges 1970–76 that the relative frequency for blacks with a diagnosis of HC was 0.3 and that for whites was 1.0.

Duration

Wendt and Drohm (1972) reported from a number of large series an average duration of 14 years with a range of 12–16

Table 12.10. *Huntington's chorea: point prevalence rates per million population from surveys likely to be complete and representative of their regions, various years 1940–72*

Reference	Locale	Prevalence year	Number	Prevalence rate
Bickford and Ellison (1953)	Cornwall, England	1950	19	56
Pleydell (1954)	Northamptonshire, England	1954	17	65
Brewis *et al.* (1966)	Carlisle, England	1961	2	28
Stevens (1973)	Leeds, England	1970	133	42
K.R. Gudmundsson (1969)	Iceland	1963	5	27
Mattson (1974)	Sweden	1965	362	47
Wendt and Drohm (1972)	Kassel region, Germany	1950	34	27
Leger *et al.* (1974)	Haute-Vienne, France	1972	24	70
Cendrowski (1964)	Pruszkow, Poland	1960	2	48
Reed and Chandler (1958)	Michigan whites	1940	200	42
Kurland (1958*a*)	Rochester, Minn.	1955	2	67
Wallace (1973)	Queensland, Australia	1969	111	63
Brothers (1964)	Victoria, Australia	1963	138	46
Kishimoto *et al.* (1957)	Aichi Prefecture, Japan	1957	13	4

Modified from Kurtzke (1979*b*).

years. Durations in early studies were the same as those of more recent vintage. Cumulative frequencies for age at onset and age at death from one large series indicated that duration did not change appreciably with age at onset, reflecting only a slight decrease compatible with ageing (Kurtzke and Kurland 1973).

Incidence rates

Taking an average prevalence of 48 per million and a mean duration of 14 years, an estimated average annual incidence rate for HC among whites was calculated at 3.4 per million population (Kurtzke 1979*b*).

Rates by age

With an incidence rate available, age-specific rates can be estimated if distributions of cases by age at onset and of the ages for the population at risk are known. There is a steep rise in incidence rates during adolescence and young adulthood to reach a maximum near age 32 years of over 7 per million (Fig. 12.24). Rates then decrease with a precipitous drop after the age of 60 years to zero over the next decade.

Genetic and other factors

There is no question as to the mode of transmission of HC as an autosomal dominant trait. There is an excess of fathers affected among HC patients of young onset but attempts to identify a 'helper' or contributory gene have been unsuccessful. However, this excess might be related to a greater propensity of affected males than females to produce offspring (McCormack and Lazzarini 1982), with the resultant usual search for early symptoms in proband children providing younger onsets.

Estimates of gene frequency, mutation rates, linkage studies, survival, and other questions are discussed elsewhere (see Barbeau *et al.* 1973; Guthrie *et al.* 1977; Chase *et al.* 1979).

One point is clear, though: this is not a lethal gene. The Venezuelan focus wherein both parents were said to have been affected in one-third the cases was discussed above. One possible advantage for the gene is that in most (but not

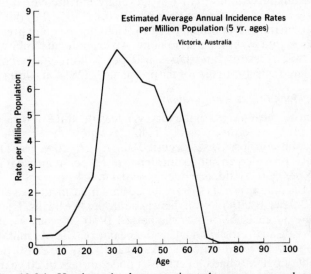

Fig. 12.24. Huntington's chorea: estimated average annual age-specific incidence rates per million population (five-year age classes), Victoria, Australia. Case material of Brothers (1964). (Source: Kurtzke (1979*b*).)

all) studies, HC patients produce more offspring than the general population, much of this occurring before disease onset. In the pre-modern era when survival averaged perhaps 35 years, a disorder beginning after this age would pose little handicap to the population, while increased fertility would be a decided asset.

WILSON'S DISEASE

Hepatolenticular degeneration or HLD, described by Wilson in 1912, is characterized by cirrhosis with neurological involvement. The disease is progressive and fatal if untreated. It is transmitted as an autosomal recessive trait (Pratt 1967), and represents an inborn metabolic error resulting in a deficiency of ceruloplasmin, a copper-binding protein.

Mortality data

Wilson's disease has been a minor fourth-digit subcode: 273.3 under 'other and unspecified congenital disorders of metabolism' (ICD8); and 275.1 under 'disorders of mineral metabolism' (ICD9). It is not surprising, therefore, that no data are available from mortality statistics. In a special survey of Canadian death certificates for 1951, Kurland (1958a) calculated a mortality rate of 0.3 per million population—considerably below the simultaneous HC rate of 2 per million.

Morbidity data

Prevalence rates

In Iceland, the three patients with this condition alive in 1963 gave a prevalence rate of 16 per million population with 95 per cent confidence limits of 3 and 37 (Guðmundsson 1969). Bachmann et al. (1979) in East Germany had discovered 123 cases of Wilson's disease between 1949 and 1977. For the 78 alive in the 1974 population of 16.9 million, the point prevalence rate was 4.6 per million. An overall rate midway between these two and thus near 10 per million could be considered a usable figure for the prevalence of Wilson's disease.

Incidence rates and duration

During the ten years of the survey of Iceland, three new cases of HLD were discovered, all siblings whose parents were second cousins. Onset occurred at ages 16–26 years. The cases provided an annual incidence of 1.8 per million with a 95 per cent confidence interval of 0.4 to 5.4.

Bachmann et al. (1979) reported an 'annual incidence rate of 2.9 per 100 000'—but this was a rate per live births. There were 32 cases born over the period 1950–54; they would provide an average annual incidence rate of 0.38 per million population (confidence interval 0.26–0.54). Over 80 per cent of patients had clinical onset under the age of 20 years.

Durations calculated from each study's rates suggests an average of some nine years in Iceland and 12 years in Germany. If we accept an overall estimate of 10 years duration, then an annual incidence rate of 1 per million population could be calculated.

HEREDITARY ATAXIAS

The hereditary ataxias are a grouping of presumably genetic affections of the nervous system characterized by dysfunction due to degenerative changes in the cerebellum and its connections. Some authors include Charcot–Marie–Tooth disease in this general category; here it is excluded. The term covers a heterogeneous group of disorders, the classification of which is complicated by existence of formes frustes and at times by the occurrence of several types of ataxia within different members of the same families (Schut 1950, 1951). Further, there has been no agreed-upon categorization. As useful as any is that of Greenfield (1954), where major types were Friedreich's spinocerebellar degeneration, Marie–Sanger cerebellar ataxia with spasticity, olivopontocerebellar degeneration, and ataxia with atrophy of Roussy–Lévy. A separate category of parenchymatous cerebellar degeneration might be added.

Mortality data

The hereditary ataxias were first coded in the eighth revision of the ICD as 332 for 'hereditary ataxia', with 332.0 as 'hereditary spinal ataxia (Friedreich's)', 332.1 as 'hereditary cerebellar ataxia (Marie's)', and 332.9 as 'other and unspecified'. In ICD9, code 334 is 'spinocerebellar disease' which excludes 'olivopontocerebellar degeneration' (code 333.0 under 'other extrapyramidal disease and abnormal movement disorders') but includes 'hereditary spastic paraplegia' (334.1) and 'primary cerebellar degeneration' (334.2)—this last whether hereditary or sporadic.

Deaths, all ages only, were available in the annual vital statistics series of the US, 1968–76, for the ICD8 codes (Table 12.11). Of the deaths, 14 per cent were coded to 'cerebellar' and but 3 per cent to 'other', the remainder falling under the code for Friedreich's. The overall annual death rate was only 0.2 per million. There was a suggestion of a moderate male excess and a marked white predominance in the Friedreich's variety (code 332.0); the white rate was three times that for the non-whites—the latter based on only 11 cases. Conversely, despite the small numbers, the rates were equivalent by sex and race for the Marie form.

Morbidity data

Prevalence rates

Table 12.12 presents prevalence rates per 100 000 population for hereditary ataxias as a group. In the cases reported from Iceland by Kjartan Guðmundsson (1969), the two patients both had the Friedreich's variety and they were siblings whose parents were first cousins. The 95 per cent confidence interval on the rate of 1 was 0.1–3.9 per 100 000.

Table 12.11. Hereditary ataxias (ICD8 code 332): average annual crude death rates per million population by type, sex, and colour, US 1968–76

Type (ICD8 code)	Number	Total	WM*	WF	NWM	NWF
Hereditary ataxia (332)	327	0.17	0.21	0.17	0.09	0.09
Hereditary spinal ataxia (332.0)	274	0.15−	0.18	0.14	0.06	0.03
Hereditary cerebellar ataxia (332.1)	43	0.02	0.02	0.02	0.03	0.05−
Other/unspecified (332.9)	10	0.01	0.00	0.01	−	0.01

*W/NW = white/non-white, M/F = male/female.
Source: Appropriate annual volumes Vital Statistics of the US, Volume II–Mortality, Part A, Tables T1–22/23.

Table 12.12. *Hereditary ataxias: point prevalence rates per 100 000 population, selected surveys, various years 1935–68*

Reference	Locale	Prevalence year	Number	Prevalence rate
Guðmundsson (1969)	Iceland	1963	2	1
Sjögren (1943)	Sweden	1935	120	2
Kreindler et al. (1964)	Romania	1962	395	2
Chen *et al.* (1968)	Guam	1966	2	5
Skre (1964)	Sogn and Fjordane, Norway	1963	23	23
Skre (1971)	Hordaland and Bergen, Norway	1968	61	31
Brewis *et al.* (1966)	Carlisle, England	1961	5*	7

*Whether hereditary not stated.
Modified from Kurtzke and Kurland (1973).

From Carlisle, England, Brewis *et al.* (1966) reported five cases of 'cerebellar ataxia' but did not state whether any or all of these were hereditary. Although in the early 10-year survey of Rochester (Kurland 1958*a*) there were no cases, the upper 95 per cent confidence limit would be 12.3 per 100 000. The 120 cases credited to Sjögren (1943) were those of the survivors among 188 patients from 118 families in Sweden that he had found over the 30 years to 1935. Sjögren estimated that he had ascertained but half of the living patients with the disease and thought the prevalence rate should be double the calculated rate of 2 per 100 000.

As may be seen, the reported rates varied widely. The rate of 23 from the isolated Norwegian county surveyed by Skre (1964) is not appropriate for application elsewhere. Refsum and Skre (1978) were unable to add additional material to that of Table 12.12. Arbitrarily, one might take a rate of some 8 per 100 000 as a reasonable base-line figure for prevalence of the hereditary ataxias. If, as seems likely from clinical experience, survival would conservatively average some 20 years after onset, this would suggest an annual incidence rate in the order of 0.4 per 100 000 population (Kurtzke 1982*b*).

MOTOR NEURON DISEASE

More than a century ago Charcot described amyotrophic lateral sclerosis as a progressive and fatal disease of the motor neuron in adults. This apparently simple delineation has, however, become more complex. When used with lower case letters, motor neuron diseases reflects three major groupings: (i) the heredofamilial spinal muscular atrophies; (ii) motor neuron disease (MND); and (iii) other and unclassified affections of the anterior horn cell without obvious cause.

Some workers also include in 'other' mnd, thus excluding from 'true' MND, that form previously called 'Guamanian amyotrophic lateral sclerosis' and now 'the Western Pacific Islands form' of ALS with its presence in others of the Mariana Islands, and in Japan and perhaps New Guinea (Kurland and Molgaard 1982; Kurtzke 1982*a*). The familial and presumably hereditary spinal muscular atrophies are disorders of infancy and childhood, with, however, some forms demonstrating onset in adolescence or young adult years—or even later.

True (upper case) motor neuron disease may itself be considered a generic term incorporating three clinical variants: (i) amyotrophic lateral sclerosis (ALS) for the combination of anterior horn cell plus pyramidal tract involvement; (ii) progressive myelopathic (spinal) muscular atrophy (PMMA) when lesions are limited to the anterior horn below the foramen magnum; and (iii) progressive bulbar palsy (PBP) for anterior horn cell lesions of the brainstem. However, to some investigators MND and ALS are equivalents.

Mortality data

In the sixth and seventh revisions of ICD, code 356 was 'motor neuron disease and muscular atrophy'. The hereditary muscular atrophies were excluded only from ICD8. In ICD9, no subcategorization of MND is possible, even at the fourth-digit level. This is especially unfortunate, since the lethality of the disorder makes mortality data uniquely important.

Of death certificates in Norway, the Netherlands, and the US which mentioned ALS or MND, 76 to 93 per cent designated it as the underlying cause (Kurland *et al.* 1973*c*).

International death rates

Age-adjusted death rates in the 1950s for MND varied mostly from 0.4 to 1.2 per 100 000 population (Goldberg and Kurland 1962). Considering the small numbers in some and vagaries of death certification in all, this was a rather uniform distribution. There was a consistent preponderance of males, averaging about 1.6:1.

More recent mortality assessment in Scotland (Holloway and Emery 1982) provided an average crude rate of 1.4 per 100 000 for 1968–77. Their data suggested a slight increase in death rates over this interval. Kondo and Tsubaki (1977) also reported similar increases in death rates from MND for 18 of the countries for 1966–71, with an overall average age-adjusted (US 1950) rate close to 1.4 per 100 000. The range was only 0.8–2.1. Higher rates would be explicable by improved accuracy of diagnosis and death certification.

Age, sex, and race

For 1959–61 in the US, there were nearly 4000 deaths coded to MND, including over 3100 for ALS alone; of the latter only 162 were for non-whites. The age-adjusted (US 1940) death rates for ALS were 0.5 per 100 000; 0.7 male and 0.4 female. The rates were identical to those for whites only, but for either blacks alone or for all non-whites the adjusted rates were 0.3 (0.4 male, 0.2 female). The American Japanese rates with but 13 deaths were 0.9 (1.4 male, 0.4 female); other races had too few deaths for assessment (Kurland *et al.* 1973*c*).

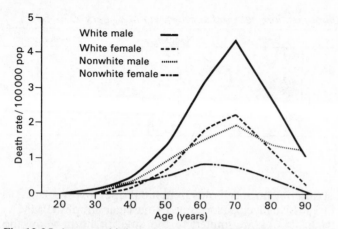

Fig. 12.25. Amyotrophic lateral sclerosis (ICD 356.1): average annual age-specific death rates per 100 000 population by sex and race, United States 1959–61. (Source: Kurland *et al.* (1973*c*).)

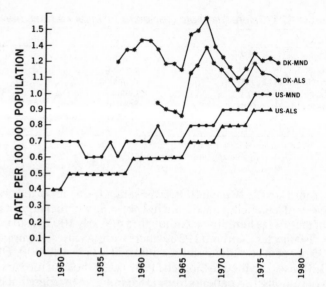

Fig. 12.26. MND and ALS: annual crude death rates per 100 000 population, United States 1949–76, Denmark (three-year-centred moving averages) 1957–77. (Source: Kurtzke (1982*a*).)

Death rates by age, sex and race for ALS (code 356.1), in the US, 1959–61, are plotted in Fig. 12.25. Of the deaths 98 per cent occurred in persons between 35 and 84 years of age, and about 75 per cent in those aged 55–84 years. Rates were highest at age 70 years and decreased sharply in the oldest age-groups. For all ALS deaths the median age was approximately 62 and the mean 61 years. Rates were notably higher in males, the sex ratio being 1.8:1. The white:non-white ratio was 1.7:1.

In Denmark 1972–77, with 427 MND and 398 ALS deaths, there was a similar configuration with the same maximum at age 70 for both sexes. The higher absolute rates in Denmark may reflect merely a higher proportion of deaths correctly allocated in that country.

Geography

There was a remarkably small spread in the death rates by state in the US in 1959–61, the range being from 0.3 per 100 000 (two states) to 1.0 (one state). Most of the southern states had rates of 0.4, but these data referred to both whites and non-whites. Within the nine Census Regions, the range for whites was only from 0.5 (five scattered regions) to 0.7 (one region). For non-whites, the three southern Regions had rates of 0.2 in two and 0.3 in the other. Their rates in the other six Regions ranged from 0.3 (one Region) to 0.5 (one Region); thus there is further support for less ALS deaths in blacks among the non-whites (Kurland *et al.* 1973*c*).

Time trends

Over nearly 30 years (Fig. 12.26), the annual crude death rate per 100 000 for MND in the US had gradually increased from about 0.7 to 1.1: ALS rates increased in parallel from 0.1 to 1.0, whereas progressive muscular atrophy (including progressive bulbar palsy) decreased from 0.2 to 0.1. Although this trend for ALS may reflect a true increase, it may simply by related to ageing of the population or to better diagnosis and reporting. That the last is more probable is suggested by the Danish death rates, which had fluctuated about 1.3 for MND and 1.1 for ALS over most of the same interval.

Morbidity data

Incidence rates

Average annual incidence rates for MND ranged from 0.4 to 1.9 per 100 000 population (Table 12.13). The only rates below 0.6 were for Eastern Bohemia at 0.5 (Kovařík 1974) and Mexico City at 0.4 (Olivares 1972). Both of these surveys may have been incomplete. In Mexico also, the study was limited to government employees and their families, which may well have provided a notable underestimate of the incidence considering the age distribution of MND. An apparent excess for Filipinos on Hawaii (Matsumoto *et al.* 1972) did not seem striking when age-adjusted rates were considered.

Surveys where it was clear the authors were speaking of classical ALS actually provided incidence rates in the same general range as MND, from 0.7 to 1.5 per 100 000 population.

Age, sex, and race

There was no significant difference among the rates for MND among the several races of Hawaii (Matsumoto *et al.* 1972; Kurtzke 1982*a*). There is a male excess with a ratio of about 1.5:1. A peak in age-specific rate was noted at age 65 years in all studies except that of Rochester. There the age-specific rate appeared to be higher for those age 75 years or more than for those aged 65–74 years (Juergens and Kurland 1980).

The essential question—which cannot be resolved—is whether incidence continues to rise with age, like a 'degenerative' or 'ageing' disease, or whether there is a maximal age at risk for those aged 55 to 75 years. All incidence and mortality data support the latter view—except for the small series from Rochester. Figure 12.27 shows that the ALS incidence curve in Rochester paralleled that for MND, and both seemed to contrast notably with the Danish death rates. Overall, the

Table 12.13. *Motor neuron disease (MND): average annual incidence rates per 100 000 population, selected surveys, various years 1925–77*

Reference	Locale	Period	Number	Incidence rate
Kurland *et al.* (1969*a*)	Rochester, Minn.	1925–64	17	1.4
Juergens and Kurland (1980)	Rochester, Minn.	1925–77	35	1.9
Zack (1977)	Lehigh County, Pa.	1968–75	31	1.5
Kristensen and Melgaard (1977)	Funen Amt, Denmark	1948–72	88	0.8
Kovařík (1974)	E. Bohemia, Czechoslovakia	1945–71	114	0.5*
Lorez (1969)	Basel, Switzerland	1951–67	89	1.4
Rosati *et al.* (1977)	Sardinia, Italy	1965–74	96	0.6
Bracco *et al.* (1979)	Florence, Italy	1967–76	83	0.7
Kahana *et al.* (1976)	Israel	1960–70	185	0.8
Olivares *et al.* (1972)	Mexico City	1962–69	16	0.4†
Matsumoto *et al.* (1972)	Hawaii			
	total	1952–68	118	1.0
	whites	1952–68	23	0.8‡
	Japanese	1952–68	31	0.9‡
	Filipino	1952–68	42	1.6‡
	others	1952–68	22	1.2‡

*Source: cases at University Clinic.
†ISSTEE government workers health programme.
‡Age-adjusted to 1960 population of Hawaii.
Modified from Kurtzke (1982*a*).

incidence rates, all ages, were quite close to one another, and estimates of about 1.5 per 100 000 for ALS and perhaps 2 per 100 000 for all MND would seem reasonable figures.

Prevalence rates

The point prevalence rates from the Occident have ranged from about 1 to 7 per 100 000 population for MND and 2 to 7 for ALS (Table 12.14). Several low rates were based on large numbers, this may merely reflect difficulties in ascertainment when large populations are surveyed.

There was considerably more variation in prevalence rates than was found for incidence rates—mostly from the same studies. For the Occident, an overall prevalence of 4–6 per 100 000 for ALS would seem reasonable; in other works an estimate of 5 per 100 000 as an expected value (modified

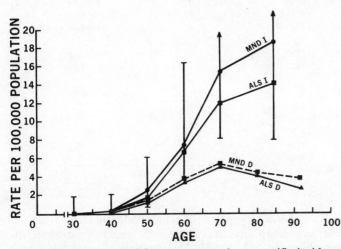

Fig. 12.27. MND and ALS: average annual age-specific incidence rates per 100 000 population with 95 per cent confidence intervals on the MND rates. Rochester, Minn., 1925–77 (Juergens and Kurland 1980); average annual age-specific death rates per 100 000 population, Denmark, 1972–77. (Source: Kurtzke (1982*a*).)

from a first estimate of 4 per 100 000) has been used. One could then use 6 per 100 000 for MND prevalence.

Rates from surveys in Japan were omitted from Table 12.14 because of the inclusion of 'Guamanian ALS' on parts of Honshu, the main island of Japan. However, in the southern island of Kyushu and on much of Honshu itself, the MND rates were quite similar to occidental experience, also ranging from 1 to 6 per 100 000 (Table 12.15).

The Kii peninsula of south-eastern Honshu has been noted since the early 1960s to contain a focus, and now a second, of a disorder that clinically and pathologically is identical with the 'Guamanian (or Marianas) form of ALS'—including the coincidence of the parkinsonism–dementia complex. Prevalence has been 100–200 per 100 000. Kurland and Molgaard (1982) have covered this topic extensively. Gajdusek (1963) and Gajdusek and Salazar (1982) have described clinical cases which they considered identical to 'Guamanian ALS' in two remote tribal groups of south-west New Guinea (Table 12.15). Rates there were even higher than in Hobara, Japan. However, because of the location, and facilities available, this diagnosis was based entirely on clinical impression, and neither laboratory nor pathological studies were feasible. With the presence of obscure myelopathies in other parts of the world as well, it may be premature to assign these cases of neurological disease to the category of MND.

Age and sex

The prevalence series of Finland (Jokelainen 1978) provided age-specific rates by sex. The configuration was similar to those for all death rates and for incidence rates (outside Rochester): a sharp peak, at age 65 years, and a notable male excess. The similarity with the other frequency measures suggests a disease of quite short average duration.

Duration

Duration of illness from eight of the community surveys of MND listed above provided an unweighted average of 36.1

Table 12.14. *Motor neuron disease (MND) and amyotrophic lateral sclerosis (ALS): point prevalence rates per 100 000 population, selected surveys outside the Orient, various years 1950–77*

Reference	Locale	Prevalence year	Number	Prevalence rate
MND				
Kurland *et al.* (1969*a*)	Rochester, Minn.	1960	2	6.7
Juergens and Kurland (1980)	Rochester, Minn.	1970–77	25	6.3*
Kristensen and Melgaard (1977)	Funen Amt, Denmark	1970	—	2.5†
Lorez(1969)	Basel, Switzerland	1967	20	6.6
Kreindler (1964)	Romania	1950–62	—	3.7‡
Rosati *et al.* (1977)	Sardinia, Italy	1971	23	1.6
Bracco *et al.* (1979)	Florence, Italy	1967–76	83	2.1§
Kahana *et al.* (1976)	Israel	1970	62	3.0‖
Olivares *et al.* (1972)	Mexico City	1970	5	0.8¶
Matsumoto *et al.* (1972)	Hawaii	1969	19	2.4
ALS				
Juergens and Kurland (1980)	Rochester, Minn.	1970–77	22	5.5*
Jokelainen (1977)	Finland	1973	168	3.6
K.R. Guðmundsson (1968)	Iceland	1963	12	6.4
Brewis *et al.* (1966)	Carlisle, England	1961	5	7.0
Cendrowski *et al.* (1970)	Poznan area, Poland	1965	56	2.2
Cendrowski *et al.* (1970)	Poznan city	1965	—	2.8

*Average point prevalence 1970–77.
†Average annual period prevalence, per authors.
‡Average point prevalence, per authors.
§Authors' estimate as 3 × incidence rate.
‖Rate age-adjusted to US 1970 population.
¶ISSTEE government workers health programme.
Modified from Kurtzke (1982*a*).

Table 12.15. *Motor neuron diseases (MND): point prevalence rates per 100 000 population, selected surveys in the Orient, various years 1958–76*

Reference	Locale	Prevalence year	Number	Prevalence rate
Japan–Honshu				
Goto *et al.* (1973)	(N) Aomori	1972	5	2.0
Goto *et al.* (1973)	(N) Hirosaki	1972	5	2.0
Otsuka (1964)	(NC) Niigata	1958	6	2.6
Sobue *et al.* (1969)	(S) Nagoya	1961	49	3.3
(S. Honshu) Kii peninsula				
Yuasa *et al.* (1976)	Osaka pref.	1973	86	1.0
Okinaka *et al.*(1962)	Wakayama	1960	8	3.3
Okinaka *et al.* (1962)	Tanabe	1960	3	5.8
Yase *et al.* (1973)	Kozagawa area	1972	6	96.9
Kimura (1965)	Kozagawa area	1961–64	8	138.3
Yase *et al.* (1973)	Hobara	1972	4	194.3
Japan–Kyushu				
Katsuki and Asaki (1961)	(N) Fukuoka	1958	9	1.5
Igata and Nagamatsu (1973)	(S) Kagoshima	1972	13	3.2
Japan–Ryukyus				
Tsubaki *et al.* (1963)	(N) Amami–Oshima	1961	1	6.5
Southwest New Guinea				
Gajdusek and Salazar (1982)	Auyu villages	1974–76	24	400
Gajdusek (1963)	(same) Auyu villages	1962	13	260
Gajdusek and Salazar (1982)	Jakai villages	1974–76	0	0*
Gajdusek (1963)	(same) Jakai villages	1962	7	280

*Upper 95 per cent confidence limit 148 per 100 000.
Modified from Kurtzke (1982*a*).

months, when calculated from the prevalence/incidence relationship. Direct estimates from five of them averaged 35.0 months (Kurtzke 1982*a*). For Rochester, Finland, and Poland together, ALS duration in like manner were also 35.2 and 36.0 months with the two methods. Longer durations (eight and seven years respectively) were cited by Kjartan Guðmundsson (1968) for the small series from Iceland and by Brewis *et al.* (1966) for the even smaller one from Carlisle, England. Durations averaging three years or so, then, do seem likely for ALS or MND as a whole.

Race

Aside from US blacks (see below), there is little evidence of racial predilection in MND. No significant variations by ethnic origin were found in the modest-sized series from Israel (Kahana *et al.* 1976). The reported excess among Hawaiian Filipinos (Matsumoto *et al.* 1972) and 'protection in Mexicans' (Olivares *et al.* 1972) have both been discussed; neither difference being convincing.

While highly significant deficits in ALS and MND death rates have been found in the US for blacks, no community-based morbidity series have been conducted to substantiate—or refute—this viewpoint. In a study of ALS death among Second World War veterans, comparing them with pre-illness military peers, a white:non-white ratio of 1.5:1 was found (Kurtzke and Beebe 1980). This was quite close to the US mortality rate ratio of 1.7:1. Among ALS cases there were 34/504 (0.067) non-whites versus 49/504 (0.097) in the controls. For blacks alone the proportions were 0.054 ALS versus 0.082 controls for a relative risk of 0.66. Both comparisons had *p* of 0.08, and thus did not attain the conventional (5 per cent) level of statistical significance. Note that non-whites of other races had a ratio near unity (0.013 case vs. 0.015 control).

Genetic factors

For the usual patient with MND there is no genetic component, but there is a subset where heredity is a factor. In about 5–10 per cent of the large series of referral patients with MND seen at the Mayo Clinic, the disease was considered familial, occurring in a pattern compatible with an autosomal dominant trait with high penetrance (Kurland and Mulder 1955; Mulder 1957). About 40 per cent of the familial cases began with symptoms in the lower extremities, notably higher than in sporadic ALS, and many of them had clinically silent involvement of spinocerebellar tracts and posterior columns (Hirano *et al.* 1967). Perhaps these latter cases are a specific variant between the hereditary ataxias and ALS, since other familial cases appeared to be pathologically identical to the sporadic cases (Lorez 1969). In the familial cases, the sex ratio was equal, contrasting with the male preponderance in the sporadic variety. The mean duration was similar to that of the sporadic cases. The mean age at onset in the familial series of Kurland and Mulder (1955) was 47 years, considerably lower than in the same clinical series of sporadic ALS. No consistent alterations of HLA patterns have been found for non-familial ALS (Kurtzke 1982*a*).

Other risk factors

An association between ALS and malignancy was noted by Norris and Engel (1965) in 10 per cent of 130 ALS patients, but the number expected for that age-group was unknown. In the earlier Rochester series of 17 patients there had been two with malignancy, treated successfully before ALS symptom-onset. Again expected numbers were not known, but a real relation between ALS and carcinoma seems remote.

There have been a number of case-control studies carried out in a search for risk factors in the development of ALS (Kurtzke 1982*a*). In the main, they have either been negative or putative findings have not been confirmed.

Perhaps the most complete retrospective case-control surveys were those of Kondo and Tsubaki (1981). Their first group (A) consisted of spouses of some 700 patients dying of MND versus those with other causes of death; the second (B) consisted of 158 MND patients and matched controls. For both groups an extensive standardized questionnaire was used. There were no consistent differences found, except for an association with mechanical injury in Group A. Similarly in Group B, the relative risk for mechanical injuries was 1.36 for the 34.7 per cent frequency among male MND vs. 21.6 per cent among male controls. For the females the relative risk was 1.54 for 23.1 per cent (case) and 9.6 per cent (control).

The US veteran series (Kurtzke and Beebe 1980) of 504 male deaths from ALS matched to military peers, showed an excess of operations before service in ALS cases (5.8 per cent vs. 2.8 per cent for controls—*p* = 0.03). Pre-service injuries were recorded for 7.5 per cent vs. 3.2 per cent (*p* < 0.01). Relative risk was 2.2 for operations, and 2.6 for injuries. Injuries of limbs were particularly predominant: 32 in ALS vs. 9 in controls. Of all hospitalizations during service, only those for accidents were in excess among ALS cases: 163 vs. 115 (*p* < 0.01). The excess was entirely for trauma, in particular fractures of which there were 40 ALS cases compared to 18 controls.

It would seem then, that trauma—and in particular major limb trauma—is in fact a risk-factor for ALS. Trauma might indeed explain the relative preponderance of males. What this means in pathogenesis, though, is conjectural. However, in the days when poliomyelitis was a major topic of investigation, there was considerable evidence that peripheral trauma predisposed to localization of the virus in the relevant anterior horn cells. Trueta (1955) demonstrated that such trauma produced a visually-evident increase in blood flow in the appropriate spinal cord segment. Thus any available noxious agent might well tend to 'settle' in such an altered environment in preference to the unaffected surround.

MYOPATHIES

Myopathies may be divided into the acquired and the inherited groups. Within the acquired category, the principal component is polymyositis. The inherited varieties are the muscular dystrophies (MD) and myotonic dystrophy or atrophy.

In classifying dystrophies, Walton (1963, 1964) proposed three major divisions: the Duchenne type, the facioscapulo-humeral type, and the limb-girdle type. Myotonic dystrophy (atrophy) is classified separately.

The Duchenne pseudohypertrophic variety is essentially limited to males, has its onset within the first four years of life, and is usually fatal before or during adolescence. It is transmitted as a sex-linked recessive trait, but perhaps half of the recognized cases are sporadic and presumably result from new mutations (Gardner-Medwin 1970). A mutation rate affecting 1 in 10 000 pregnancies has been calculated (Tyler and Stephens 1951: Gardner-Medwin 1970). A variant of the Duchenne type, but clinically similar, is the sex-linked recessive pseudohypertrophic dystrophy of Becker (1962), which has onset at a later age and benign course compatible with a normal life-span. Whether there is truly an autosomal recessive form of pseudohypertrophic dystrophy has been argued

(Pratt 1967; Gardner-Medwin 1970). However, later evidence clearly establishes this variety (Stern 1972; Ionescu and Zellweger 1974; Hazama *et al.* 1979).

The facioscapulohumeral type, which affects both sexes, has its onset in the period from late childhood well into adulthood. The pattern of transmission is usually autosomal dominant (Walton 1963), perhaps occasionally recessive (Pratt 1967). *Formes frustes* are not uncommon.

The limb-girdle type occurs in either sex and usually has its onset within the first three decades of life. Transmission is 'usually as an autosomal recessive character, but in rare instances as an autosomal dominant; many cases appear to be sporadic' (Walton 1963).

Muscular dystrophy mortality data

For the seventh revision of the ICD, code 744 was 'other diseases of muscle, tendon and fascia'. Its subcodes were 744.0 for mysthenia gravis, 744.1 for 'inborn defect of muscle', and 744.2 for 'others'. In ICD8 muscular dystrophy (330.3) was a subcode of 'hereditary neuromuscular disorders' (330), which also included Charcot–Marie–Tooth disease (330.0), hereditary spinal muscular atrophies (330.1), and amyotonia congenita (330.2). For ICD9, code 359 is 'muscular dystrophies and other myopathies' with *inter alia*, 359.1 for 'hereditary progressive muscular dystrophy' and 359.2 for 'myotonic disorders'.

In an analysis of death certificates for Canada, 1951, it was estimated that two-thirds of those listing inborn defect of muscle (ICD7 code 744.1), coded it as the underlying cause of death (Kurland 1958*a*). Nearly 80 per cent of the deaths coded to 744.1 were for MD and about 20 per cent were attributable to amyotonia congenita. Though included in the code, none of the deaths were for myotonic dystrophy.

International death rates

Average annual crude death rates have been calculated by Goldberg (1972) for 24 countries. From nine countries both code 744 and 744.1 were available (Kurland *et al.* 1973*d*, Kurtzke and Kurland 1983), while an additional 15 included only deaths coded to ICD 744. Rates for 'inborn defect of muscle', the subcode, ranged from 0.1 to 0.4 per 100 000 population (Table 12.16). Rates were only slightly more variable for 'other diseases of muscle' (Fig. 12.28). In the US there was little difference by race. The only country with appreciable numbers of deaths where the rate was overly low was Japan. The highest rate was for Norway, but this was out of line with its Scandinavian neighbours.

Age, sex, and race

In the US, 1959–61, there were some 1700 deaths coded to 'inborn defect of muscle', of which 110 were for non-whites. Crude and age-adjusted (US 1940) death rates were identical: 0.3 per 100 000 for whites (0.5 male, 0.2 female) and 0.2 for non-whites (0.3 and 0.1) (Kurland *et al.* 1973*d*).

Age-specific rates by sex in the US revealed a trimodal distribution (Fig. 12.29), with the highest rate of about 3 per 100 000 for those aged less than one year. The sharp peak at age 20 years, for males alone, doubtless represented

Table 12.16. *Myopathies: average annual crude death rates per 100 000 population for 'Other diseases of muscle' (ICD7 code 744)* and 'Inborn defect of muscle' (code 744.1), selected countries, various years, 1951–1958*

Locale	Other diseases of muscle (744)*	Inborn defect of muscle (744.1)
Canada	0.4	0.3
Iceland	0.3	0.3
Ireland	0.2	0.1
Israel	0.4	0.2
Italy	0.2	0.1
New Zealand	0.3	0.2
Norway	0.5	0.4
Sweden	0.3	0.1
United States	0.5	0.3
white	0.5	0.2
non-white	0.4	0.3

*Also includes myasthenia gravis (744.0) and 'other' (744.2).
Modified from Kurtzke and Kurland (1984).

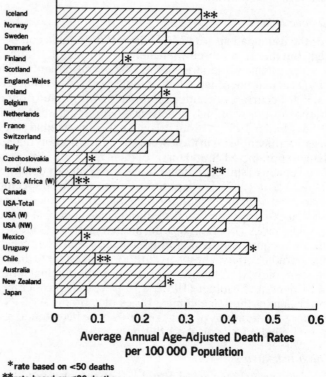

* rate based on <50 deaths
** rate based on <20 deaths

Fig. 12.28. Myopathy ('other diseases of muscle' ICD7 code 744): average annual crude death rates per 100 000 population, selected countries, 1951–58. (Unpublished data of Goldberg (1972).)

Duchenne dystrophy. The modest male peak at 80 years of age (0.6 per 100 000), if real, might reflect Becker dystrophy and/or miscoding of motor neuron disease. For most age groups, there was some degree of male excess.

Similar rates were found at non-peak ages for whites and non-whites up to 75 years of age. Among those aged less than one year, however, there was a white:non-white ratio of 2.9:0.7 and for males aged 15–24 years rates were 1.3 and

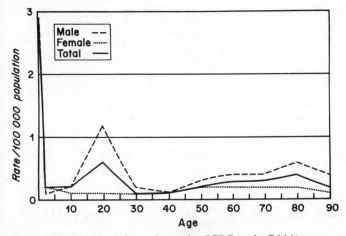

Fig. 12.29. Inborn defect of muscle (ICD7 code 744.1); average annual age-specific death rates per 100 000 population by sex, United States 1959–61. (Modified from Kurland *et al.* (1973*d*).)

0.5, for white and non-white respectively. No deaths were reported for non-whites age 75+ in this small series.

Geography

Age-adjusted death rates by Census Region of the US for these same three years were essentially identical within each sex and race, and for several different age groups as well. The white male excess was quite uniform (Kurland *et al.* 1973*d*).

Myopathies: morbidity data

Muscular dystrophy incidence rates

From several series in the US and England incidence rates per 100 000 live births for both sexes were estimated as 14 for Duchenne dystrophy, 7 for limb-girdle, and 0.4 for facio-scapulohumeral dystrophy (Morton and Chung 1959). In their own series, the Duchenne rate was 28 per 100 000 live births. Another estimate for Duchenne dystrophy in north-eastern England was 17 per 100 000 live births (Gardner-Medwin 1970). Perhaps an overall rate of 20–30

per 100 000 live births for dystrophies might be in order. For an annual birth rate approximating 2 per 100 population, this would suggest an annual incidence rate for dystrophies of about 5 per million population. An incidence of 8.6 per million was calculated for Uruguay, 1960–77, where there was an average of 24 new patients per annum (Defféminis Rospide *et al.* 1978). Their rates for Duchenne and limb-girdle variants were similar at 2.9 and 3.6 per million respectively; facioscapulohumeral rates were 1.4 per million. In other experience the Duchenne form has represented at least half of all MD and limb-girdle about one-fourth.

Muscular dystrophy prevalence rates

Prevalence rates for all ages and both sexes, have ranged from 3 to 10 per 100 000 population (Table 12.17). The unweighted average was about 6 per 100 000. The rates for Japan (Kuroiwa and Miyazaki 1966; Takeshita *et al.* 1977) were in accord with other studies, unlike the death rate given in Fig. 12.28. There was a striking variation in Israel, with a prevalence of 10.4 for non-Ashkenazi Jews and 2.2 for Ashkenazim, or Middle European Jews (Kott *et al.* 1973). However, this difference may well be the result of selection bias, since the emigration of Jews from Europe was perforce limited to the survivors of the Second World War. There was otherwise no apparent racial difference based on the rates—though blacks were not represented. A prevalence of 6–7 and an incidence of 0.5–0.8 suggests an average duration of some 8–14 years for the dystrophies as a whole.

Myotonic dystrophy

Prevalence rates for myotonic dystrophy ranged from 1 to 10 per 100 000 (Table 12.18). Perhaps 3 per 100 000 is a reasonable overall estimate. Grimm (1975) had registered over 1000 such cases from Germany at his institute in Göttingen; in 1960 almost 600 were alive, and he estimated for West Germany a prevalence of 5.5 per 100 000 population.

The rate for Guam was exceedingly high. Both the Guam and Iceland surveys were directed to neurological diseases in general, without prior suspicion that prevalence for this disorder would be discrepant. If theirs were not chance findings,

Table 12.17. *Muscular dystrophy: point prevalence rates per 100 000 population, selected surveys, various years about 1950–77*

Reference	Locale	Prevalence year	Number	Prevalence rate
Herndon (1954)	North Carolina	c1950	133	4
Kurland (1958*a*)	Rochester, Minn.	1955	2	6
Defféminis Rospide (1978)	Uruguay	c1977	200	7*
Kuroiwa and Miyazaki (1966)	Fukuoka, Japan	1961	23	4
Takeshita *et al.* (1977)	Shimane Prefecture, Japan	1975	76	10
Guðmundsson (1969)	Iceland	1963	17	9
Walton and Nattrass (1954)	northern England	c1952	84	4
Brewis *et al.* (1966)	Carlisle, England	1961	5	7
Badiu (1973)	Bucharest, Rumania	c1970	52	3*
Nigro *et al.* (1973)	Campania, Italy	1972	211	4
Danieli *et al.* (1974)	north-east Italy	c1973	334	5*
Kott *et al.* (1973)	Israel			
	Total	c1970	156	6
	Non-Ashkenazi	c1970	130	10
	Ashkenazi	c1970	26	2

*Cases from hospital or centre records only.

Table 12.18. *Myotonic dystrophy: point prevalence rates per 100 000 population, selected surveys, various years about 1952–75*

Reference	Locale	Prevalence year	Number	Prevalence rate
Kurland (1958a)	Rochester, Minn.	1955	1	3
Chen et al. (1968)	Guam	1967	29	76
Takeshita et al. (1977)	Shimane Prefecture, Japan	1975	7	1
Guðmundsson (1969)	Iceland	1963	18	10
Walton and Nattrass (1954)	northern England	c1952	15	1
Brewis et al. (1966)	Carlisle, England	1961	2	3
Grimm (1975)	Germany	1960	—	6*
Badiu (1973)	Bucharest, Rumania	c1970	49	3†
Danieli et al. (1974)	north-east Italy	c1973	32	1†

*Estimate of author.
†Cases from hospital or centre records only.

Table 12.19. *Polymyositis; average annual incidence rates per 100 000 population, selected surveys, various years 1947–76*

Reference	Locale	Period	Number	Incidence rate
Rose and Walton (1966)	Northumberland, England	1954–65	89	0.3
Benbassat et al. (1980)	Israel	1960–76	83	0.2
Pearson (1966)	Los Angeles, Calif.	—	—	0.1*
Kurland et al. (1969b)	Rochester, Minn.	1951–67	4	0.6
Medsger et al. (1970)	Shelby County, Tenn.	1947–68	61	0.5
		1963–68	34	0.8
	White male	1963–68	5	0.4
	White female	1963–68	8	0.6
	Black male	1963–68	6	1.0
	Black female	1963–68	15	1.8

*Author's estimate.

they may reflect the situation in isolated populations in which the gene for myotonic dystrophy was introduced when the population was small. Since the disorder is transmitted as an autosomal dominant trait (Thomasen 1948; Pratt 1967), inbreeding *per se* should not influence the gene frequency.

Grimm (1975) in his material had calculated an average age at onset of 37.1 years and an average age at death of 56.7 years. A duration of 20 years and a prevalence of 3 suggests an incidence of 0.1–0.2 per 100 000 population for myotonia.

For all hereditary myopathies combined, reasonable estimates may be taken as about 0.7 per 100 000 for incidence and 10 per 100 000 for prevalence, with 14 years for duration.

Polymyositis

This is an inflammatory disease of muscle, characterized by weakness, often with pain, which involves primarily the proximal muscles of the limbs. The disorder may be acute or subacute, less often chronic. Recurrences occur. Barwick and Walton (1963) had categorized the illness into: (i) idiopathic; (ii) associated with mild collagen disease; (iii) associated with severe collagen disease; and (iv) associated with malignancy. There has been a tendency to delete group (iii) when the muscle involvement is a minor part of the clinical symptomatology (Medsger et al. 1970).

Average annual incidence rates have ranged from 0.2 to 0.8 per 100 000 population (Table 12.19). Pearson's (1966) rate of 0.1 was based on his impression that most patients in Los Angeles would have attended his large clinic. A conservative overall estimate would be about 0.5 per 100 000.

In their classical paper, Medsger et al. (1970) provided annual age-specific rates (Table 12.20). For much of the interval the rates were no more than half that of the 8.4 per million for 1963–68. Thus, the true rates of Table 12.20 might be higher, but the relative values should be comparable. In whites the sex ratio was reversed from that of Table 12.19; this suggests that little difference exists between the sexes among whites. But in both tables, blacks—and particularly black females—predominated. The age-specific rates suggested bimodal peaks: a major one at age 45–64 years and a lesser one at age 5–14 years. Considering the

Table 12.20. *Polymyositis: average annual age specific incidence rates per million population by race and sex, Shelby County, Tennessee, 1947–68*

Age (years)	Total	White		Black	
		Male	Female	Male	Female
0–4	0.6	0.0	0.0	0.0	3.0
5–9	3.7	5.1	2.7	3.4	3.3
10–14	4.3	3.0	6.2	0.0	7.8
15–24	1.0	1.4	0.0	0.0	2.6
25–34	3.7	3.2	0.0	3.8	11.9
35–44	6.9	1.8	3.4	11.4	18.7
45–54	10.1	9.3	8.7	12.8	11.3
55–64	10.3	3.5	3.0	5.9	38.3
65+	5.4	4.3	2.9	0.0	11.0
Total*	5.0	3.7	2.7	4.6	10.8
Number	61	14	11	9	27

*Age-adjusted to 1960 Shelby County population.
Modified from Medsger et al. (1970).

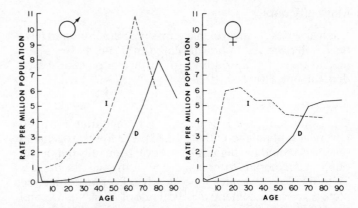

small numbers at hand, the configuration by age was similar for each sex and race.

Survivorship was also studied by Medsger *et al.* (1971). There was a rather sharp drop in the survival rate within the first two years to 72 per cent; and then a slower decline to 55 per cent survival after seven years. Median survival was probably about eight years.

MYASTHENIA GRAVIS

First described by Thomas Willis in 1672, myasthenia gravis (MG) is characterized by fatiguability and weakness of striated muscle. Recent studies (Drachman 1978) have implicated an autoimmune mechanism in its pathophysiology. Patients with myasthenia gravis have a high level of T-cell-dependent antibodies to acetylcholine receptor (Lundstrom *et al.* 1976; Richman *et al.* 1976; Newsom-Davis *et al.* 1978).

Mortality data

Since the sixth revision of ICD, myasthenia gravis (MG) has been a wandering fourth-digit subcode. As mentioned above, in ICD6 and 7 it was 744.0 under 'other diseases of muscle, tendon and fascia'. In ICD8 it was 733.0 under the same title; 'muscular atrophy, idiopathic' being 733.1. In ICD9 code 358 is 'myoneural disorders' with 358.0 as MG, and with several other subcodes as well.

International death rates

Goldberg (1972) calculated crude death rates for MG in nine western countries in the 1950s. The average annual death rate was about 1 per million population, with little variation. For Finland, 1957–66, the average annual death rate was 0.9 per million population (Hokkanen 1969).

Age, sex, and race

In the US, 1959–61, there were 675 deaths coded to MG (Kurland *et al.* 1973*a*). Of these, 567 were for whites and 108 for non-whites. The age-adjusted (US 1940) death rate was 1.2 per million, the crude rate being 1.3. Among whites the age-adjusted rate was 1.04 (0.86 male and 1.22 female). For non-whites the adjusted rates were twice as high at 2.02 (1.40 male, 2.59 female), though the non-white male rate did not differ significantly from that for white males.

The annual age-specific death rate per million population under age one year was 0.6. For ages 1–4 years it was 0.1, but it rose steadily thereafter with each succeeding age-group to peak at a maximum of 6.4 at age 75–84 years (Fig. 12.30).

The female excess persisted for each age-group up to 65 years of age. The rates for each sex converged at 65–74 years. The rate for females rose only slightly in the older age groups while in men there was a further steep rise to a peak of 7.9 at 75–84 before falling to a rate comparable to that in women in those 85 years and older (5.5 for males and 5.3 for females).

Despite small numbers among non-whites, the sex difference by age was the same as for whites, that is, a definite

Fig. 12.30. Myasthenia gravis: annual age-specific incidence (I) and death (D) rates per million population for each sex, United States. (Source: Kurtzke (1974*a*).)

female preponderance up to age 65 with a male preponderance becoming evident thereafter.

There was thus a strange discrepancy between the sexes for the racial difference. To resolve this, annual death rates were calculated by sex and race for the years 1950–72 in the US. There were 5412 deaths coded to MG: 2076 for white males, 2647 for white females, 253 for non-white males and 436 for non-white females. The average annual crude death rates were then 1.14, 1.43, 1.11, 1.81 per million respectively. Ratios on the average rates were thus: by sex, among whites 0.80 M:F and 0.61 among non-whites; by race 1.03 white:non-white for males and 0.79 for females. Age-adjustment would not seem likely to alter the findings appreciably.

Thus, from death data, there was no racial difference among males but there was among females, non-white rates being higher. Overall, for each racial group, females predominated. There is then further evidence of a possible difference in MG between the sexes, aside from the shift in the sexual preponderance from female to male death rates at age 70 years.

Geography

Data for the US, 1959–61, suggest that there is no significant regional variation. For an earlier period, 1950–54, Kurland and Alter (1961) also found a quite even distribution of the death rates by Census Region in the US. By Census Region for 1959–61, age-adjusted rates were uniform for all deaths, with an exceedingly small range of 0.7–1.3 per million. The female preponderance was consistent within each geographical area. The non-white excess was also found throughout all Regions except for the Mountain Region where there were no deaths in the small non-white population. The Regions with the greatest difference between whites and non-whites were the New England, Middle Atlantic, East North Central, and Pacific, where medical facilities in general are above average for the country; while the difference by race was less in the south where specialized medical care has been less readily available.

Morbidity data

Clinical series on myasthenia gravis are numerous and have been well reviewed by Storm-Mathisen (1966, 1976). There are, however, few morbidity series with a population-based denominator (Kurtzke 1978b).

Prevalence rates

The estimated point prevalence rates range from 5 to 100 per million population (Table 12.21). The lowest was based on one case and the highest has not yet been fully defined in published material. Without these two extremes, the range is 12 to 64. Two low rates were clearly reflections of incomplete case ascertainment: the 1950 rate of 22 in Norway and the 1968 rate of 25 in Finland. Other rates in the 20s may also reflect incomplete ascertainment in the large metropolitan areas of Leeds and Merseyside, or were countered by higher rates (Japan). A reasonable estimate of the likely prevalence of myasthenia gravis would be about 40 per million population. However, there are no prevalence estimates for blacks.

Incidence rates

The range on the incidence rates from those same surveys was much smaller than that for the prevalence rates (Table 12.21). The average annual incidence ranged from 2 to 6 per million population, with a median value of 4 per million. With this incidence rate a duration of some 10 years can be expected.

Age and sex

Osserman and Genkins (1971) described age at onset for over 1200 patients from their clinic in New York. These distributions were very similar to those found in Boston (Perlo et al. 1966), Michigan (Simpson et al. 1966), and London (Turner 1974). By adjusting the US population so that these total cases provide an incidence rate of 4.0 per million

population, one may calculate age- and sex-specific rates (Fig. 12.30).

If the age-specific incidence rates are compared with US death rates there is a curious finding (Fig. 12.30). For males, the incidence rates rose steeply to a sharp peak at age 65 years, and then declined equally sharply at older ages. About 15 to 20 years later, the death rates followed the same curve. This suggests a reasonably constant case–fatality ratio for adult-onset MG in males regardless of age at onset. The incidence rate for MG in females rose rapidly in adolescence and slowly declined thereafter. The death rates increased gradually with age. It is this combination of young onset and prolonged course which gives us the clinical impression that MG is largely a disorder of females, out of proportion even to the real difference which does exist. In the young, females predominate in incidence, mortality and prevalence. In the elderly, the male is notably more prone than the female, especially as measured by incidence.

These aspects of the incidence and mortality curves raise the possibility that MG in males is a different disease from that in females. Further, non-white females are more prone to MG than whites, but there is no obvious racial differential among men.

Genetic factors

When the available data were reviewed by Kurland and Alter (1961) there did not seem to be sufficient evidence to implicate genetic factors in MG. However, an extensive review by Herrmann (1966) indicated considerable familial aggregation. Warrier and Pillai (1967) reported an unusual family, with MG affecting one brother and sister and two children of one of their unaffected sisters.

Among their 702 patients in 683 families at a Brooklyn centre, Namba et al. (1971) stated that 27 cases, or 3.8 per cent, had occurred in 12 families. One family had four brothers affected, all with onset by two years of age. Another family had two affected brothers with onset at six

Table 12.21. *Myasthenia gravis: point prevalence and average annual incidence rates per million population, selected surveys, various years 1950–1973*

Reference	Locale	Prevalence			Incidence		
		Year	n	Rate	Period	n	Rate
Kurland and Alter (1961)	Rochester, Minn.	1954	1	33	1945–54	1	3
Kurland and Choi (1973)	Rochester, Minn.	1960	2	43	—	—	—
Alter et al. (1960)	Charleston, S.C.	1955	6	32	1946–55	9	6
Alter and Talbert (1973)	Halifax, Nova Scotia	1954	1	5	1945–54	3	2
Garland and Clark (1956)	Leeds, England	1955	13	26	—	—	—
Pennington and Wilson (1961)	Merseyside, England	1958	32	23	1948–58	33	2
Storm-Mathisen (1961, 66)	Norway	1950	70	22	1941–50	—	2
Storm-Mathisen (1976)	Norway	1960	—	43	1953–72	—	4
Storm-Mathisen (1976)	Norway	1970	—	100	—	—	—
Guðmundsson (1968)	Iceland	1963	12	64	1954–63	14	4
Hokkanen (1969)	Finland	1968	117	25	1956–65	102	2
Hokkanen (1969)	Helsinki, Finland	1968	40	42	1956–65	31	4
Hokkanen and Pirskanen (1973)	Finland	1973	199	43	1968–72	—	4
Oosterhuis (1977)	Amsterdam, Netherlands	1965	48	56	1961–65	16	4
Okinaka et al. (1966)	Niigata, Japan	1960	6	26	—	—	—
Goto et al. (1973)	Aomori, Japan	1972	9	37	—	—	—
Goto et al. (1973)	Hirosaki, Japan	1972	8	51	—	—	—

Modified from Kurtzke (1978b).

months of age. Excluding these two families, age at onset ranged from 11 to 49 years in all instances except for one brother–sister pair with onset at birth. In their review of published material, 3.4 per cent of reported patients were considered instances of familial MG.

Bundey (1972) believed that there were two forms of childhood MG, one an early onset form with symptoms under age 2 years where there is frequent occurrence of MG in other sibs. She thought this variety was likely inherited as an autosomal recessive trait. For those with onset between ages 2 and 20 years, there was less of a genetic contribution and no recognizable pattern of inheritance. In the cases with adult onset, she thought familial aggregation was uncommon.

Twins

Herman (1969) described concordance for MG in his set of monozygous twins and half of other monozygous twins reported in the literature. Namba *et al.* (1971) summarized available published information (including that reported by Herman) on 13 sets of monozygotic twins, seven dizygotic sets, and one set of undetermined zygosity, which Herman had reported as monozygous. No twins were concordant for MG among the seven dizygous sets, while six were concordant among 14 monozygous sets. Only one of the concordant twin sets was male, and in that instance, the onset was at age 15 months. Adler's (1966) concordant twins had been raised in separate foster homes since their mother had died of tuberculosis shortly after the birth of the girls.

Among the concordant monozygotic twins (Namba *et al.* 1971), onset was at birth in one pair, at age one year in another, at ages four and seven years in a third set, 16 and 18 years in a fourth, and 23 and 25 years in a fifth pair; no data were available for the pair described by Walsh/Lavin (Herman 1969). Consequently, the genetic subdivision described by Bundey (1972) according to age at onset may be premature. However, the evidence does appear stronger for some genetic influence in this disorder than seemed apparent in previous assessments.

Histocompatibility antigens

From several large series there was a moderately consistent excess of HL-A1 and HL-A8 in myasthenics vs. controls overall, but no difference for HL-A2 (Kurtzke 1978*b*). Females showed higher proportions of HL-A1 and HL-A8; however, males were in excess for HL-A2. By age at onset, with age 35 or 40 years as the dividing line, early onset MG patients showed the greater excess for the HL-A1 and HL-A8, and the late onset for HL-A2. When age and sex were considered jointly—but only for HL-A8 (Dick *et al.* 1974; Pirskanen 1976), the relationship appeared stronger for age at onset.

Kaakinen *et al.* (1975) found an excess of certain lymphocyte-defined (LD) antigens related to the serologically defined HL-A8 antigen—in particular LD_m which they thought similar to the LD8a antigen. Moller *et al.* (1976) found a greater preponderance of MG patients with HL-A8 than with LD8a, and both were higher in females than males.

Considering all these points, and if one accepts that male MG and female MG are different disorders, it would seem likely that it is in females that the disease tends to follow a genetic pattern, possibly a recessive trait (X-linked) with manifestations first appearing after menarche. Infantile MG may well, however, be a second genetic disorder, perhaps reflecting an autosomal recessive trait. Most of the MG in males could conceivably be an acquired illness wherein risk is maximal at age 65 years. Much more clinical, genetic, and epidemiological evidence is necessary, however, before these concepts could be accepted.

ACKNOWLEDGEMENTS

I am most grateful to the following for permission to reproduce figures from previous works: American Academy of Neurology, *Special Course on Neuroepidemiology*, 1974 (Fig. 12.30); American Medical Association, *Archives of Neurology*, Vol. 22, 1970 (Fig. 12.17) and Vol. 38, 1981 (Fig. 12.5); Harcourt Brace Jovanovich Publications, *Neurology*, Vol. 18, 1968 (Fig. 12.16) and Vol. 21, 1971 (Fig. 12.13); Harper & Row Publishers, Inc., Baker & Baker, *Clinical neurology*, 1973 (Figs. 12.2, 12.4, 12.9, 12.15) and *Clinical neurology*, 1984 (Figs. 12.3, 12.8, 12.20); Harvard University Press, Kurland, Kurtzke, and Goldberg, *Epidemiology of neurologic and sense organ disorders*, 1973 (Figs. 12.11, 12.21, 12.25, 12.29); Little Brown and Company, *Annals of Neurology*, Vol. 5, 1979 (Fig. 12.19); McGraw-Hill Book Co., Minckler, *Pathology of the nervous system*, 1972 (Fig. 12.22); Munksgaard Publishers, *Acta Neurologica Scandinavia* Vol. 48, 1972 (Fig. 12.10) and Vol. 62, 1980 (Figs. 12.12, 12.14); and Raven Press, *Advances in Neurology*, Vol. 19, 1978 (Fig. 12.13), Vol. 23, 1979 (Figs. 12.23, 12.24), and Vol. 36, 1982 (Figs. 12.26, 12.27).

My gratitude to the following for permission to cite their unpublished or thesis-published works and figures: J.F. Annegers, M. Alter, J.B. Barber, N.W. Choi, I.D. Goldberg, E. Hokkanen, M. Jokelainen, J.S. Kranz, C. Mosee, R. Pirskanen, A.H. Rajput, and O.R. Talbert.

My special thanks also to my many co-workers (and friends), among whom are: M. Alter, T.L. Auth, G.W. Beebe, S. Bergmann, R. Bobowick, J.A. Brody, J. Brown, Q.H. Bui, G. Dean, T. Fog, I.D. Goldberg, the late K.R. Guđmundsson, H. Hamtoft, Z. Hrubec, K. Hyllested, L.T. Kurland, Y. Kuroiwa, B. Nagler, J.E. Norman, Jr., D. Poskanzer, W.A. Priester, A.S. Rose, J.L. Sever, W.A. Sibley, and W.W. Tourtellotte.

Especially, though, I must acknowledge my debt to Gilbert Beebe and Leonard Kurland, not only for the latter's permission to adapt our recent chapter on Epidemiology of Neurologic Diseases for this present work, but also for the more than a quarter-century of training in epidemiology that the two of them have provided to me.

This work was supported in part by the Veterans Administration (Neuroepidemiology Research Program). The statements contained are my own views and do not necessarily reflect the policies or opinions of other individuals or agencies, governmental or academic.

REFERENCES

Acheson, E.D. (1972a). The epidemiology of multiple sclerosis. In *Multiple sclerosis: a reappraisal.* 2nd edn. (ed. D. McAlpine, C.E. Lumsden, and E.D. Acheson) p. 3. Livingstone, Edinburgh.

Acheson, E.D. (1972b). Migration prior to onset and the risk of multiple sclerosis: a brief review of published data. In *Multiple sclerosis. progress in research* (ed. E.J. Field, T.M. Bell, and P.R. Carnegie) p. 204. North-Holland, Amsterdam.

Acheson, E.D. (1977). Epidemiology of multiple sclerosis. *Br. Med. Bull.* **33**, 9.

Acheson, E.D., Bachrach, C.A., and Wright, F.M. (1960). Some comments on the relationship of the distribution of multiple sclerosis to latitude, solar radiation, and other variables. *Acta Psychiat. Neurol. Scand.* **35**, Suppl. 147, 132.

Adams, J.M. and Imagawa, D.T. (1962). Measles antibodies in multiple sclerosis. *Proc. Soc. Exp. Biol. Med.* **111**, 562.

Adler, E. (1966). Myasthenia gravis bei eineiigen Zwillingen. *Deutsch. Med. Wschr.* **91**, 396.

Allan, W. (1937). Inheritance of shaking palsy. *Arch. Intern. Med.* **60**, 424.

Allison, R.S. (1963). Some neurological aspects of medical geography. *Proc. R. Soc. Med.* **56**, 71.

Allison, R.S. (1969). Multiple sclerosis in Northern Ireland. Read at the meeting of the Symposium on Multiple Sclerosis sponsored by the National Multiple Sclerosis Society, New York, 24 September 1969.

Allison, R.S. and Millar, J.H.D. (1954). Prevalence of disseminated sclerosis in Northern Ireland. *Ulster Med. J.* **23**, Suppl. 2, 5.

Alperovich, A., LeCanuet, P., and Marteau, R. (1981). Birth order and risk of multiple sclerosis: are they associated and how? *Acta Neurol. Scand.* **63**, 136.

Alter, M. (1977). Clues to the cause based upon the epidemiology of multiple sclerosis. In *Multiple sclerosis; a critical conspectus* (ed. E.J. Field) p. 35. MTP, Lancaster.

Alter, M., Antonovsky, A., and Leibowitz, U. (1968). Epidemiology of multiple sclerosis in Israel, in *The epidemiology of multiple sclerosis* (ed. M. Alter and J.F. Kurtzke) p. 83. Thomas, Springfield, Ill.

Alter, M., Halpern, L., Kurland, L.T., Bornstein, B., Leibowitz, U., and Silberstein, J. (1962). Multiple sclerosis in Israel; prevalence among immigrants and native inhabitants. *Arch. Neurol.* **7**, 253.

Alter, M., Kahana, E., and Loewenson, R. (1978). Migration and risk of multiple sclerosis. *Neurology* **28**, 1089.

Alter, M. and Kurtzke, J.F. (1968). *The epidemiology of multiple sclerosis.* Thomas, Springfield, Ill.

Alter, M., Leibowitz, U., and Speer, J. (1966). Risk of multiple sclerosis related to age at immigration to Israel. *Arch. Neurol.* **15**, 234.

Alter, M., Okihiro, M., Rowley, W., and Morris, T. (1971). Multiple sclerosis among Orientals and Caucasians in Hawaii. *Neurology* **21**, 122.

Alter, M. and Quevedo, J. (1979). Genetic segregation of multiple sclerosis and histocompatibility (HLA) haplotypes. *J. Neurol.* **222**, 67.

Alter, M. and Speer, J. (1968). Clinical evaluation of possible etiology factors in multiple sclerosis. *Neurology* **18**, 109.

Alter, M., Talbert, O.R., and Kurland, L.T. (1960). Myasthenia gravis in a southern community. *Arch. Neurol.* **3**, 399.

Ammitzbøll, T. and Clausen, J. (1972). Measles antibody in serum of multiple sclerosis patients, their children, siblings and parents. *Acta Neurol. Scand.* **48**, 47.

Annegers, J.F., Coulam, C.B., and Laws, E.R., Jr (1982a). Pituitary tumors: epidemiology. In *Hormone-secreting pituitary tumors* (ed. J.R. Gibens) p. 393. Year Book Medical, Chicago.

Annegers, J.F., Hauser, W.A., and Elveback, L.R. (1979a). Remission of seizures and relapse in patients with epilepsy. *Epilepsia* **20**, 729.

Annegers, J.F., Hauser, W.A., and Kurland, L.T. (1983). Classification and measurements of the frequency of seizure disorders. *Neuroepidemiology,* in press.

Annegers, J.F., Elveback, L.R., Hauser, W.A., and Kurland, L.T. (1974). Do anticonvulsants have a teratogenic effect? *Arch. Neurol.* **31**, 364.

Annegers, J.F., Hauser, W.A., Anderson, V.E., and Kurland, L. T. (1982b). The risks of seizure disorders among relatives of patients with childhood onset epilepsy. *Neurology* **32**, 174.

Annegers, J.F., Hauser, W.A., Elveback, L.R., and Kurland, L.T. (1979b). The risk of epilepsy following febrile convulsions. *Neurology* **29**, 297.

Annegers, J.F., Hauser, W.A., Elveback, L.R., and Kurland, L.T. (1980b). Remission and relapse of seizures in epilepsy. In *Advances in epileptology: the Xth Epilepsy International Symposium* (ed. J.A. Wada and J.K. Penry) p. 143. Raven Press, New York.

Annegers, J.F., Laws, E.R., Jr, Kurland, L.T., and Grabow, J.D. (1979c). Head trauma and subsequent brain tumors. *Neurosurgery* **4**, 203.

Annegers, J.F., Schoenberg, B.S., Okazaki, H., and Kurland, L.T. (1981). Epidemiologic study of primary intracranial neoplasms: case ascertainment and incidence rates. *Arch. Neurol.* **38**, 217.

Annegers, J.F., Coulam, C.B., Abboud, C.F., Laws, E.R., Jr, and Kurland, L.T. (1978a). Pituitary adenoma in Olmsted County, Minnesota, 1935–1977: a report of an increasing incidence of diagnosis in women of childbearing age. *Mayo Clin. Proc.* **53**, 641.

Annegers, J.F., Hauser, W.A., Elveback, L.R., Anderson, V.E., and Kurland, L.T. (1978b). Congenital malformations and seizure disorders in the offspring of parents with epilepsy. *Int. J. Epidemiol.* **7**, 241.

Annegers, J.F., Grabow, J.D., Groover, R.V., Laws, E.R. Jr, Elveback, L.R., and Kurland, L.T. (1980a). Seizures after head trauma: A population study. *Neurology* **30**, 683.

Antel, J.P., Richman, D.P., Medof, M.E., and Arnason, B.G.W. (1978a). Lymphocyte function and the role of regulator cells in multiple sclerosis. *Neurology* **28**, 106.

Antel, J.P., Weinrich, M., and Arnason, B.G.W. (1978b). Mitogen responsiveness and suppressor cell function in multiple sclerosis, *Neurology* **28**, 999.

Antonovsky, A., Leibowitz, U., Medalie, J.M., Smith, H.A., Halpern, L., and Alter, M. (1967). Epidemiological study of multiple sclerosis in Israel: III. Multiple sclerosis and socio-economic status. *J. Neurol. Neurosurg. Psychiat.* **30**, 1.

Antonovsky, A., Leibowitz, U., Medalie, J.M., Smith, H.A., Halpern, L., and Alter, M. (1968). Reappraisal of possible etiologic factors in multiple sclerosis. *Am. J. Public Health* **58**, 836.

Antonovsky, A., Leibowtiz, U., Smith, H.A. *et al.* (1965). Epidemiologic study of multiple sclerosis in Israel. I. An overall review of methods and findings. *Arch. Neurol.* **13**, 183.

Araki, C. and Matsumoto, S. (1969). Statistical reevaluation of pinealoma and related tumors in Japan. *J. Neurosurg.* **30**, 146.

Arnason, B.G.W. and Waksman, B.H. (1980). Immunoregulation in multiple sclerosis. *Ann. Neurol.* **8**, 237.

Aronson, S.M. and Aronson, B.E. (1965). Central nervous system in diabetes mellitus: lowered frequency of certain intracranial neoplasms. *Arch. Neurol.* **12**, 390.

Avila-Giron, R. (1973). Medical and social aspects of Huntington's chorea in the state of Zulia, Venezuela. *Adv. Neurol.* **1**, 261.

Bach, M.-A., Phan-Dinh-Tuy, F., Tournier, E. *et al.* (1980). Deficit of suppressor T cells in active multiple sclerosis. *Lancet* **ii**, 1221.

Bachmann, H., Lossner, J., Gruss, B., and Ruchholtz, V. (1979). Die Epidemiologie der Wilsonschen Erkrankung in der DDR und die derzeitige Probematik über populationsgenetischen Bearbeitung. *Psychiat. Neurol. Med. Psychol.* **34**, 394.

Badiu, G. (1973). Genetic-epidemiological studies of muscular dystrophy on a sample of population in Romania. Part I, Incidence of disease, genetic transmission, sporadic factor, sex involvement, gene manifestations in heterozygotes, onset in muscular dystrophy. *Rev. Roum. Neurol.* **10**, 519.

Bamford, C.R., Sibley, W.A., and Laguna, J.F. (1978). Swine influenza vaccination in patients with multiple sclerosis. *Arch. Neurol.* **35**, 242.

Barbeau, A. (1979). Update on the biochemistry of Huntington's chorea. *Adv. Neurol.* **23**, 449.

Barbeau, A., Chase, T.N., and Paulson, G.W. (1973). *Huntington's chorea 1872–1972.* (*Adv. Neurol.* Vol. 1). Raven Press, New York.

Barlow, J.S. (1960). Correlation of the geographic distribution of multiple sclerosis with cosmic-ray intensities. *Acta Psychiat. Neurol. Scand.* **35**, Suppl. 147, 108.

Barwick, D.D. and Walton, J.N. (1963). Polymyositis. *Am. J. Med.* **35**, 646.

Baumann, R.J., Jameson, H.D., McKean, H.E., Haack, D.G., and Weisberg, L.M. (1980). Cigarette smoking and Parkinson disease. 1. A comparison of cases with matched neighbors. *Neurology* **30**, 839.

Beaussart, M., Faou, R., and Defaye, J. (1980). Epidémiologie de l'epilepsie dans la région du Nord Pas-de-Calais (à propos de 12.290 cas). *Lille Méd.* **25**, 183.

Becker, P.E. (1962). Two new families of benign sex-linked recessive muscular dystrophy. *Rev. Canad. Biol.* **21**, 551.

Beebe, G.W., Kurtzke, J.F., Kurland, L.T., Auth, T.L., and Nagler, B. (1967). Studies on the natural history of multiple sclerosis. 3. Epidemiologic analysis of the Army experience in World War II. *Neurology* **17**, 1.

Benbassat, J., Geffel, D., and Zlotnick, A. (1980). Epidemiology of polymyositis-dermatomyositis in Israel, 1960–76. *Isr. J. Med. Sci.* **16**, 197.

Bickford, J.A.R. and Ellison, R.M. (1953). The high incidence of Huntington's chorea in the Duchy of Cornwall. *J. Ment. Sci.* **99**, 291.

Bird, A.V., Heinz, H.J., and Klintworth, G. (1962). Convulsive disorders in Bantu mine-workers. *Epilepsia* **3**, 175.

Bobowick, A.R. and Brody, J.A. (1973). Epidemiology of motor-neuron disease. *New Eng. J. Med.* **288**, 1047.

Bobowick, A.R., Kurtzke, J.F., Brody, J.A., Hrubec, Z., and Gillespie, M. (1978). Twin study of multiple sclerosis: an epidemiologic inquiry. *Neurology* **28**, 978.

Bracco, L., Antuono, P., and Amaducci, L. (1979). Study of epidemiological and etiological factors of amyotrophic lateral sclerosis in the province of Florence, Italy. *Acta Neurol. Scand.* **60**, 112.

Brady, R., Dean, G., Secerbegovic, S., and Secerbegovic, A.M. (1977). Multiple sclerosis in the Republic of Ireland. *J. Irish Med. Assoc.* **70**, 500.

Brewis, M., Poskanzer, D.C., Rolland, C., and Miller, H. (1966). Neurological disease in an English city. *Acta Neurol. Scand.* **42**, Suppl. 24, 9.

Brody, J.A., Sever, J.L., Edgar, A., and McNew, J. (1972). Measles antibody titers of multiple sclerosis patients and their siblings. *Neurology* **22**, 492.

Broman, T. (1963). Parkinson's syndrome, prevalence and incidence in Gotenberg. *Acta Neurol. Scand.* **39**, Suppl. 4, 95.

Brooks, B.R., Jubelt, B., Herndon, R.M., O'Donnell, P., Johnson, R.T., and Noble, G.R. (1983). Safety, efficacy, seroconversion rates, antibody persistence, protection rates and disease exacerbation rates in multiple sclerosis patients following subunit influenza virus immunization—a two year study. Unpublished data.

Brothers, C.R.D. (1964). Huntington's chorea in Victoria and Tasmania. *J. Neurol. Sci.* **1**, 405.

Bruce, D.A., Schut, L., Bruno, L.A., Wood, J.H., and Sutton, L.N. (1978). Outcome following severe head injuries in children. *J. Neurosurg.* **48**, 679.

Bundey, S. (1972). A genetic study on infantile and juvenile myasthenia gravis. *J. Neurol. Neurosurg. Psychiat.* **35**, 41.

Bunnell, D.H., Visscher, B.R., and Detels, R. (1979). Multiple sclerosis and house dogs: a case-control study. *Neurology* **29**, 1027.

Burkinshaw, J. (1960). Head injuries in children: observations on their incidence and causes with an inquiry into the value of routine skull x-rays. *Arch. Dis. Child.* **35**, 205.

Campbell, A.M.G., Herdan, G., Tatlow, W.F.T., and Whittie, E.G. (1950). Lead in relation to disseminated sclerosis. *Brain* **73**, 52.

Catalano, L.W., Jr (1972). *Herpesvirus hominis* antibody in multiple sclerosis and amyotrophic lateral sclerosis. *Neurology* **22**, 473.

Cendrowski, W. (1964). Niektóre dane o geografii plasawicy dziedzicznej. [Some data on the geography of hereditary chorea.] *Neurol. Neurochir. Psychiat. Pol.* **14**, 63.

Cendrowski, W., Wender, M., and Oswianowski, M. (1970). Analyse épidémiologique de la sclérose latérale amyotrophique sur le territoire de la Grande-Pologne. *Acta Neurol. Scand.* **46**, 609.

Chase, T.N., Wexler, N.S., and Barbeau, A. (1979). *Huntington's disease* (*Adv. Neurol.* Vol. 23). Raven Press, New York.

Chen, K., Brody, J.A., and Kurland, L.T. (1968). Patterns of neurologic diseases on Guam. I. Epidemiologic aspects. *Arch. Neurol.* **19**, 573.

Clemmesen, J. (1965*a*). Statistical studies in the aetiology of malignant neoplasms. I. Review and results. *Acta Path. Microbiol. Scand.* Suppl. 174 (part 1), 1.

Clemmesen, J. (1965*b*). Statistical studies in the aetiology of malignant neoplasms. II. Basic tables: Denmark 1943–1957. *Acta Path. Microbiol. Scand.* Suppl. 174 (part 2), 1.

Clemmesen, J. (1969). Statistical studies in the aetiology of malignant neoplasms. III. Testis cancer: Basic tables, Denmark 1958–62. *Acta Path. Microbiol. Scand.* Suppl. 209, 1.

Commission on Classification in Terminology of the International League against Epilepsy (1981). Proposal for revised clinical and electroencephalographic classification of epileptic seizures. *Epilepsia* **22**, 489.

Cook, S.D. and Dowling, P.C. (1977). A possible association between house pets and multiple sclerosis. *Lancet* i, 980.

Cook, S.D. and Dowling, P.C. (1978). Multiple sclerosis and canine distemper. *Lancet* i, 605.

Cook, S.D., Dowling, P.C., Norman, J., and Jablon, S. (1979). Multiple sclerosis and canine distemper in Iceland. (Letter.) *Lancet* i, 380.

Cook, S.D., Natelson, B.H., Levin, B.E., Chavis, P.S., and Dowling, P.C. (1978). Further evidence of a possible association between house dogs and multiple sclerosis. *Ann. Neurol.* **3**, 141.

Coulam, C.B., Annegers, J.F., Abboud, C.F., Laws, E.R., Jr and Kurland, L.T. (1979). Pituitary adenoma and oral contraceptives: a case-control study. *Fertil. Steril.* **31**, 25.

Crombie, D.L., Cross, K.W., Fry, J., Pinsent, R.J.F.H., and Watts, C.A.H. (1960). A survey of the epilepsies in general practice: a report by the Research Committee of the College of General Practitioners. *Br. Med. J.* ii, 416.

Cruz-Coke, R. (1976). Personal communication of 28 December, 1976, to Kurtzke *et al.* (1977). *Report: Commission for the Control of Huntington's Disease and its Consequences,* Vol. III. Part 1. Work Group Reports. Research. DHEW Publications No. (NIH) 78–1503, US Government Printing Office, Washington, DC.

Dada, T.O. (1968). Epilepsy in Nigeria: a study of the incidence, pathogenesis, clinical patterns and socio-psychological problems of epilepsy. Thesis. Bristol, England.

Danieli, G.A., Vecchi, C., and Augelini, C. (1974). Geographic distribution of hereditary myopathies in Northwest Italy. *Soc. Biol.* **21**, 235.

Dean, G. (1967). Annual incidence, prevalence, and mortality of multiple sclerosis in white South-African-born and in white immigrants to South Africa. *Br. Med. J.* ii, 724.

Dean, G., Brady, R., McLoughlin, H., Elian, M., and Adelstein, A.M. (1977). Motor neurone disease and multiple sclerosis among immigrants to Britain. *Br. J. Prev. Soc. Med.* **31**, 141.

Dean, G., Grimaldi, G., Kelly, R., and Karhausen, L. (1979). Multiple sclerosis in southern Europe. I. Prevalence in Sicily in 1975. *J. Epidemiol. Community Health* **33**, 107.

Dean, G. and Kurtzke, J.F. (1971).On the risk of multiple sclerosis according to age at immigration to South Africa. *Br. Med. J.* **iii**, 725.

Dean, G., McLoughlin, H., Brady, R., Adelstein, A.M., and Tallett-Williams, J. (1976). Multiple sclerosis among immigrants in Greater London. *Br. Med. J.* **i**, 861.

Defféminis Rospide, H.A., Pietra, M., Vincent, O. *et al.* (1978). Estudio epidemiológico de la distrofia muscular progresiva en el Uruguay. *Acta Neurol. Latinoamer.* **24**, 115.

DeGraaf, A.S. (1974). Epidemiological aspects of epilepsy in northern Norway. *Epilepsia* **15**, 291.

DeJong, R.N. (1982). *A history of American neurology.* Raven Press, New York.

Detels, R. (1978). Epidemiology of multiple sclerosis. *Adv. Neurol.* **19**, 459.

Detels, R., Brody, J.A., and Edgar, A.H. (1972). Multiple sclerosis among American, Japanese and Chinese migrants to California and Washington. *J. Chronic Dis.* **25**, 3.

Detels, R., Visscher, B.R., Coulson, A., Malmgren, R., and Dudley, J. (1974). Multiple sclerosis in Japanese-Americans: a preliminary report. *Int. J. Epidemiol.* **3**, 341.

Detels, R., Visscher, B.R., Haile, R.W., Malmgren, R.M., Dudley, J.P., and Coulson, A.H. (1978). Multiple sclerosis and age at migration. *Am. J. Epidemiol.* **108**, 386.

Detels, R., Visscher, B.R., Malmgren, R.M., Coulson, A.H., Lucia, M.V., and Dudley, J.P. (1977). Evidence for lower susceptibility to multiple sclerosis in Japanese-Americans. *Am. J. Epidemiol.* **105**, 303.

Dick, H.M., Behan, P.O., Simpson, J.A., and Durward, W.F. (1974). The inheritance of HL-A antigens in myasthenia gravis. *J. Immunogenet.* **1**, 401.

Drachman, D.B. (1978). Myasthenia gravis, Part 1 and Part 2. *New Engl. J. Med.* **298**, 136, 186.

Duvoisin, R.C. and Schweitzer, M.D. (1966). Paralysis agitans mortality in England and Wales, 1855–1962. *Br. J. Prev. Soc. Med.* **20**, 27.

Earle, K.M., Rentschler, E.H., and Snodgrass, S.R. (1957). Primary intracranial neoplasms; prognosis and classification of 513 verified cases. *J. Neuropath. Exp. Neurol.* **16**, 321.

Eldridge, R., McFarland, H., Sever, J., Sadowsky, D., and Krebs, H. (1978). Familial multiple sclerosis: clinical, histocompatibility, and viral serological studies. *Ann. Neurol.* **3**, 72.

Evans, J.H. (1962). Post-traumatic epilepsy. *Neurology* **12**, 665.

Feltkamp, T.E.W., Van Den Berg-Loonen, P.M., Nijenhuis, L.E. *et al.* (1974). Myasthenia gravis, autoantibodies and HL-A antigens. *Br. Med. J.* **i**, 131.

Field, E.J., Bell, T.M., and Carnegie, P.R. (eds.) (1972). *Multiple sclerosis: progress in research.* North-Holland, Amsterdam.

Fog, M. and Hyllested, K. (1966). Prevalence of disseminated sclerosis in the Faroes, the Orkneys and Shetland. *Acta Neurol. Scand.* **42**, Suppl. 19, 9.

Frantzen, E., Lennox-Buchthal, M., and Nygaard, A. (1968). Longitudinal EEG and clinical study of children with febrile convulsions. *Electroenceph. Clin. Neurophysiol.* **24**, 197.

Friderischsen, C. and Melchior, J. (1954). Febrile convulsions in children, their frequency and prognosis. *Acta Paediatr.* **43**, Suppl. 100, 307.

Froman, C. and Lipschitz, R. (1970). Demography of tumors of the central nervous system among the Bantu (African) population of the Transvaal, South Africa. *J. Neurosurg.* **32**, 660.

Gajdusek, D.C. (1963). Motor neuron disease in natives of New Guinea. *New Engl. J. Med.* **268**, 474.

Gajdusek, D.C. and Salazar, A.M. (1982). Amyotrophic lateral sclerosis and parkinsonian syndromes in high incidence among the Auyu and Jakai people of West New Guinea. *Neurology* **32**, 107.

Gardner-Medwin, D. (1970). Mutation rate in Duchenne type of muscular dystrophy. *J. Med. Genet.* **7**, 334.

Garland, H. and Clark, A.N.G. (1956). Myasthenia gravis: a personal study of 60 cases. *Br. Med. J.* **i**, 1259.

Gibbs, C.J., Jr. and Gajdusek, D.C. (1972). Parkinson's disease and the ALS parkinsonian–dementia complex on Guam: a review and summary of attempts to demonstrate infectious etiology. *J. Clin. Pathol.* **6**, Suppl., 132.

Goldberg, I.D. and Kurland, L.T. (1962). Mortality in 33 countries from diseases of the nervous system. *World Neurol.* **3**, 444.

Gomez, J.G., Arciniegas, E., and Torres, J. (1978). Prevalence of epilepsy in Bogotá, Colombia. *Neurology* **28**, 90.

Goto, Y., Matsunaga, M., Narita, S., and Masuda, M. (1973). [Epidemiology of multiple sclerosis in Aomori-Ken, Japan. I. The prevalence study in Aomori and Hirosakil]. In *Special Report by MS Study Group—1972 Study Report* (ed. Y. Kuroiwa) p. 15, Health and Welfare Department of Japan, Tokyo.

Goust, J.M., Hoffman, P.M.N., Pryjma, J., Hogan, E.L., and Fudenberg, H.H. (1980). Defective immunoregulation in multiple sclerosis. *Ann. Neurol.* **8**, 526.

Granieri, E. and Rosati, G. (1982). Italy: a medium- or high-risk area for multiple sclerosis? An epidemologic study in Barbagia, Sardinia, southern Italy. *Neurology* **32**, 466.

Greenfield, J.G. (1954). *The spino-cerebellar degenerations.* Blackwell, Oxford.

Grimm, T. (1975). The age at onset and the age at death in patients with dystrophia myotonica. *J. Genet. Hum.* **23**, 301.

Grove, R.D. and Hetzel, A.M. (1968). *Vital statistics rates in the United States, 1940–1960.* PHS Publ. No. 1677.) Government Printing Office, Washington, DC.

Grudzinska, B. (1974). Epidemiologia podaczki in populacji duzezo miasta przemyshowego. Rozpowszechnienie i zachorowalnosc. [Epidemiology of epilepsy in the population of a large industrial city. Incidence and prevalence.] *Neurol. Neurochir. Polska.* **8**, 175.

Gudmundsson, G. (1966). Epilepsy in Iceland: a clinical and epidemiological investigation. *Acta Neurol. Scand.* **42**, Suppl. 25, 1.

Gudmundsson, K.R. (1967). A clinical survey of parkinsonism in Iceland. *Acta Neurol. Scand.* **43**, Suppl. 33, 1.

Gudmundsson, K.R. (1968). The prevalence of some neurological diseases in Iceland. *Acta Neurol. Scand.* **44**, 57.

Gudmundsson, K.R. (1969). The prevalence and occurrence of some rare neurological diseases in Iceland. *Acta Neurol. Scand.* **45**, 114.

Gudmundsson, K.R. (1970). A survey of tumours of the central nervous system in Iceland during the 10-year period 1954–1963. *Acta Neurol. Scand.* **46**, 538.

Guthrie, M., Wexler, M., Aronson, S.M. *et al.* (1977). *Report: Commission for the Control of Huntington's Disease and Its Consequences. Volume I: Overview, Volume II: Technical Report, Volume III, Part 1: Work Group Reports-Research, Volume III, Part 2: Work Group Reports-Social Management.* DHEW Publications Nos. (NIH) 78-1501, 1502, 1503, 1504, US Government Printing Office, Washington, DC.

Hammond, C.A. (1966). Smoking in relation to the death rates of one million men and women. In *Epidemiologic approaches to the study of cancer and other chronic diseases.* NCI Monograph No. 19, p. 127. US Government Printing Office, Washington, DC.

Harvald, B. and Hauge, M. (1956). On the heredity of glioblastoma. *J. Natl. Cancer Inst.* **17**, 289.

Harvald, B. and Hauge, M. (1965). Heredity factors elucidated by twin studies. In *Genetics and the epidemiology of chronic diseases* (ed. J.V. Neel, M.W. Shaw, and W.J. Schull) p. 66. Public Health Service Publication No. 163. US Government Printing Office, Washington, DC.

Hauge, M. and Harvald, B. (1957). Genetics in intracranial tumours. *Acta Genet. Stat. Med.* **7**, 573.

Hauser, W.A., Annegers, J.F., and Elveback, L.R. (1980). Mortality in patients with epilepsy. *Epilepsia* **21**, 399.

Hauser, W.A. and Kurland, L.T. (1975). The epidemiology of epilepsy in Rochester, Minnesota, 1935 through 1967. *Epilepsia* **16**, 1.

Hazama, R., Tsujihata, M., Mori, M., and Mori, K. (1979). Muscular dystrophy in six young girls. *Neurology* **29**, 1486.

Henriksen, G.F. and Krohn, W.H. (1969). The organization of a national system for the medical care of epileptics, abstracted. *Excerpt. Med. Int. Congr. Ser.* **193**, 5.

Hens, L. and Carton, H. (1978). HLA Determinants and familial multiple sclerosis: HLA typing of 13 families with at least two affected members. *Tiss. Antigens* **11**, 75.

Henson, T.E., Brody, J.A., Sever, J.L., Dyken, M.L., and Cannon, J. (1970). Measles antibody titers in multiple sclerosis patients, siblings and controls. *JAMA* **211**, 1985.

Herlitz, G. (1941). Studien über die sog. initialen Fieber-Krampfe bei Kindern. *Acta Paediatr. Scand.* **29**, Suppl. 1, 110.

Herman, M.N. (1969). Familial myasthenia gravis. Report of a case in identical twins and review of family aggregates. *Arch. Neurol.* **20**, 140.

Herndon, C.N. (1954). Three North Carolina surveys. *Am. J. Hum. Gen.* **6**, 65.

Herrmann, C., Jr. (1966). Myasthenia gravis occurring in families. *Neurology* **16**, 75.

Hirano, A., Kurland, L.T., and Sayre, G.P. (1967). Familial amyotrophic lateral sclerosis: A subgroup characterized by posterior and spinocerebellar tract involvement and hyaline inclusions in the anterior horn cells. *Arch. Neurol.* **16**, 232.

Hoehn, M.M. (1971). The epidemiology of parkinsonism. In *Monoamines. Noyaux gris centraux et syndrome de Parkinsonism* (ed. J. de Ajuriaguerra and G. Gautier) p. 281. George Cie, SA, Geneva.

Hogg, J.E., Massey, E.W., and Schoenberg, B.S. (1979). Mortality from Huntington's disease in the United States. *Adv. Neurol.* **23**, 27.

Hokkanen, E. (1969). Epidemiology of myasthenia gravis in Finland. *J. Neurol. Sci.* **9**, 463.

Hokkanen, E. and Pirskanen, R. (1973). Epidemiology of myasthenia gravis in Finland. Presented at the International Congress of Neurology, Barcelona, Spain, 14 September, 1973.

Holloway, S.M. and Emery, A.E.H. (1982). The epidemiology of motor neurone disease in Scotland. *Muscle Nerve* **5**, 131.

Hung, T.P. (1977). personal communication to the Commission for the Control of Huntington's Disease and Its Consequences, 24 March, 1977.

Hyllested, K. (1965). *Disseminated sclerosis in Denmark: prevalence and geographical distribution.* Jørgensen, Copenhagen.

Hyllested, K. and Kurland, L.T. (1966). Studies in multiple sclerosis: VI. Further explorations on the geographic distribution of multiple sclerosis. *Acta Neurol. Scand.* **42**, Suppl. 19, 1.

Igata, A. and Nagamatsu, K. (1973). [Epidemiological study of multiple sclerosis in Kagoshima City and Kagoshima Prefecture.] In *Special Report by MS Study Group—1972 Study Report* (ed. Y. Kuroiwa) p. 20. Health and Welfare Department of Japan, Tokyo.

Ionescu, V. and Zellweger, H. (1974). Duchenne muscular dystrophy in young girls? *Acta Neurol. Scand.* **50**, 619.

Isager, H., Anderson, E., and Hyllested, K. (1980). Risk of multiple sclerosis inversely associated with birth order position. *Acta Neurol. Scand.* **61**, 393.

Ito, M., Barron, A.L., Olszewski, W.A., and Milgrom, F. (1975). Antibody titers by mixed agglutination to varicella zoster, herpes simplex and vaccinia viruses in patients with multiple sclerosis.

Proc. Soc. Exp. Biol. Med. **149**, 835.

Jelsma, R. and Bucy, P.C. (1966). Glioblastoma multiforme: its treatment and some factors affecting survival. *Arch. Neurol.* **20**, 161.

Jenkins, A.C. (1966). Epidemiology of parkinsonism in Victoria. *Med. J. Aust.* **2**, 496.

Jokelainen, M. (1977). Amyotrophic lateral sclerosis in Finland. I. An epidemiologic study. *Acta Neurol. Scand.* **56**, 185.

Jokelainen, M. (1978). Amyotrophic lateral sclerosis in Finland. Epidemiological and clinical studies. Academic dissertation. University of Helsinki.

Juergens, S.M. and Kurland, L.T. (1980). Epidemiology. In *The diagnosis and treatment of amyotrophic lateral sclerosis* (ed. D. W. Mulder) p. 35. Houghton Mifflin, Boston.

Juergens, S.M., Kurland, L.T., Okazaki, H., and Mulder, D.W. (1980). ALS in Rochester, Minnesota, 1925–1977. *Neurology* **30**, 463.

Juul-Jensen, P. (1964). Epilepsy: a clinical and social analysis of 1,020 adult patients with epileptic seizures. *Acta Neurol. Scand.* **40**, Suppl. 5, 1.

Juul-Jensen, P. and Ipsen, J. (1975). Prevalens og incidens af epilepsi i Stor-Århus. *Ugeskr. Laeg.* **137**, 2380.

Kaakinen, A., Pirskanen, R., and Tiilikainen, A. (1975). LD antigens associated with HL-A8 and myasthenia gravis. *Tissue Antigens* **6**, 175.

Kahana, E., Alter, M., and Feldman, S. (1976). Amyotrophic lateral sclerosis: a population study. *J. Neurol.* **212**, 205.

Kahn, H.A. (1966). The Dorn study of smoking and mortality among U.S. veterans: report on eight and one-half years of observations. In *Epidemiologic approaches to the study of cancer and other chronic diseases.* NCI Monograph No. 19, p. 127. US Government Printing Office, Washington, DC.

Katsuki, S. and Araki, S. (1961). [Epidemiologic investigations and diagnostic problems of motor neuron disease.] *Psychiat. Neurol. Jap.* (Tokyo) **29**, 99.

Kessler, I.I. (1972a). Epidemiologic studies of Parkinson's disease: II. A hospital-based survey. *Am. J. Epidemiol.* **95**, 308.

Kessler, I.I. (1972b). Epidemiologic studies of Parkinson's disease: III. A community-based survey. *Am. J. Epidemiol.* **96**, 242.

Kessler, I.I. (1973). Parkinson's disease: perspectives on epidemiology and pathogenesis. *Prev. Med.* **2**, 88.

Kessler, I.I. (1978). Parkinson's disease in epidemiologic perspective. *Adv. Neurol.* **19**, 355.

Kessler, I.I. and Diamond, E.L. (1971). Epidemiologic studies of Parkinson's disease. I. Smoking and Parkinson's disease: a survey and explanatory hypothesis. *Am. J. Epidemiol.* **94**, 16.

Kimura, K. (1965). [Studies of amyotrophic lateral sclerosis in the Kozagawa district of the Kii Peninsula, Japan. (Epidemiological, genealogical and environmental studies.)] *Wakayama Med. Rep.* **9**, 177.

Kishimoto, K., Nakamura, M., and Sotokawa, Y. (1957). On population genetics of Huntington's chorea in Japan. *Ann. Rep. Res. Inst. Environ. Med.* **9**, 84.

Kondo, K. (1978). Motor neurone disease: changing population patterns and clues for etiology. *Adv. Neurol.* **19**, 509.

Kondo, K. (1979). Population dynamics of motor neuron disease. In *Amyotrophic lateral sclerosis* (ed. T. Tsubaki and Y. Toyokura) p. 61. Japan Medical Research Foundation Publ. No. 8, University Park Press, Baltimore.

Kondo, K., Kurland, L.T. , and Schull, W.J. (1973). Parkinson's disease: genetic analysis and evidence of a multifactorial etiology. *Mayo Clin. Proc.* **48**, 465.

Kondo, K. and Tsubaki, T. (1977). Changing mortality patterns of motor neuron disease in Japan. *J. Neurol. Sci.* **32**, 411.

Kondo, K. and Tsubaki, Y. (1981). Case control studies of motor neuron disease. Association with mechanical injuries. *Arch. Neurol.* **38**, 220.

Kott, E., Golan, A., Don, R., and Bornstein, B. (1973). Muscular dystrophy: the relative frequency in different ethnic groups in Israel. *Confinia Neurologica* **35**, 177.

Kovařík, J. (1974). Unsere Erfahrungen auf dem Forschungsgebiet der myatrophischen Lateralsklerose. *Sborník Vedeckých Prací Lekařské Fakulty Univ. Karlovy v Hradci Králové* **17**, 233.

Kranz, J.S. and Kurland, L.T. (1982). General overview of the epidemiology of multiple sclerosis with emphasis on the geographic pattern and long-term trends. In *Multiple sclerosis east and west* (ed. Y. Kuroiwa and L.T. Kurland) p. 3. Kyushu University Press, Kyushu Japan.

Kranz, J.S. (1983). *A multiple sclerosis case control study in Olmsted and Mower Counties, Minnesota.* Ph.D. thesis. University of Minnesota.

Kreindler, A., Ionăşescu, V., and Drincă-Ionescu, M. (1964). Repartitia bolilor neurologice eredo-familiale in Romînia: Notă preliminară. *Stud. Cercet. Neurol.* **9**, 401.

Kristensen, O. and Melgaard, B. (1977). Motor neuron disease. Prognosis and epidemiology. *Acta Neurol. Scand.* **56**, 299.

Kurland, L.T. (1957). Epidemiologic investigations of amyotrophic lateral sclerosis. III. A genetic interpretation of incidence and geographic distribution. *Proc. Staff Meet. Mayo Clin.* **32**, 449.

Kurland, L.T. (1958*a*). Descriptive epidemiology of selected neurologic and myopathic disorders with particular reference to a survey in Rochester, Minnesota. *J. Chronic Dis.* **8**, 378.

Kurland, L.T. (1958*b*). Epidemiology. incidence, geographic distribution and genetic considerations. In *Pathogenesis and treatment of parkinsonism* (ed. W.S. Fields) p. 5. Thomas, Springfield, Ill.

Kurland, L.T. (1959). The incidence and prevalence of convulsive disorders in a small urban community. *Epilepsia* **1**, 143.

Kurland, L.T. (1965). The geographic and genetic characteristics of amyotrophic lateral sclerosis and other selected chronic neurological diseases. In *Genetics and the epidemiology of chronic diseases.* (ed. J.V. Neel, M.W. Shaw, and W.J. Schull) p. 145. Public Health Service Publication No. 1163, US Government Printing Office, Washington, DC.

Kurland, L.T. (1970). The epidemiologic characteristics of multiple sclerosis. In *Handbook of clinical neurology,* Vol. 9. *Multiple sclerosis and other demyelinating diseases* (ed. P.J. Vinken and G.W. Bruyn) p. 63. North-Holland, Amsterdam.

Kurland, L.T. and Alter, M. (1961). Current status of the epidemiology and genetics of myasthenia gravis. In *Myasthenia gravis* (The 2nd International Symposium, Los Angeles, 1959) (ed. H.R. Viets) p. 307. Thomas, Springfield, Ill.

Kurland, L.T. and Kurtzke, J.F. (1972). Geographic neuropathology. In *Pathology of the nervous system,* Vol. 3 (ed. J. Minckler) p. 2803. McGraw-Hill, New York.

Kurland, L.T. and Molgaard, C.A. (1982). Guamanian ALS: hereditary or acquired? *Adv. Neurol.* **36**, 165.

Kurland, L.T. and Mulder, D.W. (1955). Epidemiologic investigations of amyotrophic lateral sclerosis: 2. Familial aggregations indicative of dominant inheritance. *Neurology* **5**, 182, 249.

Kurland, L.T. and Westlund, K.B. (1954). Epidemiologic factors in the etiology and prognosis of multiple sclerosis. *Ann. N.Y. Acad. Sci.* **58**, 682.

Kurland, L.T., Choi, N.W., and Sayre, G.P. (1969*a*). Implications of incidence and geographic patterns on the classification of amyotrophic lateral sclerosis. In *Motor neuron diseases: research on amyotrophic lateral sclerosis and related disorders* (ed. F.H. Norris, Jr and L.T. Kurland) p. 28. Grune and Stratton, New York.

Kurland, L.T., Kurtzke, J.F., and Goldberg, I.D. (1973*b*). *Epidemiology of neurologic and sense organ disorders.* Harvard University Press, Cambridge, Mass.

Kurland, L.T., Molgaard, C.A., and Schoenberg, B.S. (1982*a*). Mayo Clinic records-linkage: contributions to neuroepidemiology. *Neuroepidemiology* **1**, 102.

Kurland, L.T., Myrianthopoulos, N.C., and Lessell, S. (1962). Epidemiologic and genetic considerations of intracranial neoplasms. In *The biology and treatment of intracranial tumors* (ed. W.S. Fields, and P.C. Sharkey) p. 5. Thomas, Springfield, Ill.

Kurland, L.T., Stazio, A., and Reed, D. (1965). An appraisal of population studies of multiple sclerosis. *Ann. N.Y. Acad. Sci.* **123**, 520.

Kurland, L.T., Choi, N.W., Goldberg, I.D., and Kurtzke, J.F. (1973*a*). Myasthenia gravis. In *Epidemiology of neurologic and sense organ disorders* (ed. L.T. Kurland, J.F. Kurtzke, and I.D. Goldberg) p. 144. Harvard University Press, Cambridge, Mass.

Kurland, L.T., Hauser, W.A., Ferguson, R.H., and Holley, K.E. (1969*b*). Epidemiologic features of diffuse connective tissue disorders in Rochester, Minnesota, 1951 through 1967, with special reference to systemic lupus erythematosus. *Mayo Clin. Proc.* **44**, 649.

Kurland, L.T., Hauser, W.A., Okazaki, H., and Nobrega, F.T. (1969*c*). Epidemiologic studies of parkinsonism with special reference to the cohort hypothesis. In *Third symposium on Parkinson's disease,* p. 12. Livingstone, Edinburgh.

Kurland, L.T., Kurtzke, J.F., Goldberg, I.D., and Choi, N.W. (1973*c*). Amyotrophic lateral sclerosis and other motor neuron diseases. In *Epidemiology of neurologic and sense organ disorders* (ed. L.T. Kurland, J.F. Kurtzke, and I.D. Goldberg) p. 108. Harvard University Press, Cambridge, Mass.

Kurland, L.T., Kurtzke, J.F., Goldberg, I.D., and Choi, N.W. (1973*d*). Muscular dystrophy and other myopathies. In *Epidemiology of neurologic and sense organ disorders* (ed. L.T. Kurland, J.F. Kurtzke, and I.D. Goldberg) p. 128. Harvard University Press, Cambridge, Mass.

Kurland, L.T., Kurtzke, J.F., Goldberg, I.D., Choi, N.W., and Williams, G. (1973*e*). Parkinsonism. In *Epidemiology of neurologic and sense organ disorders* (ed. L.T. Kurland, J.F. Kurtzke, and I.D. Goldberg) p. 41. Harvard University Press, Cambridge, Mass.

Kurland, L.T., Schoenberg, B.S., Annegers, J.F., Okazaki, H., and Molgaard, C.A. (1982*b*). The incidence of primary intracranial neoplasms in Rochester, Minnesota, 1935–1977. *Ann. N.Y. Acad. Sci.* **381**, 6.

Kuroiwa, Y. and Miyazaki, T. (1966). Epidemiological study of myopathy in Japan. *Exerpta Med. Intl. Congress Series* **147**, 98.

Kurtzke, J.F. (1965*a*). Familial incidence and geography in multiple sclerosis. *Acta Neurol. Scand.* **41**, 127.

Kurtzke, J.F. (1965*b*). On the time of onset in multiple sclerosis. *Acta Neurol. Scand.* **41**, 140.

Kurtzke, J.F. (1967). Further considerations on the geographic distribution of multiple sclerosis. *Acta Neurol. Scand.* **43**, 283.

Kurtzke, J.F. (1968*a*). Some epidemiologic and clinical features of adult seizure disorders. *J., Chronic Dis.* **21**, 143.

Kurtzke, J.F. (1968*b*). Multiple sclerosis and infection from an epidemiologic aspect. *Neurology* **18** (part 2), 170.

Kurtzke, J.F. (1969*a*). Geographic pathology of brain tumors: I. Distribution of deaths from primary tumors. *Acta Neurol. Scand.* **45**, 540.

Kurtzke, J.F. (1969*b*). Some epidemiologic features compatible with an infectious origin for multiple sclerosis. *Addendum ad Int. Arch. Allergy* **36**, 59.

Kurtzke, J.F. (1970). Clinical manifestations of multiple sclerosis. In *Handbook of clinical neurology,* Vol. 9. *Multiple sclerosis and other demyelinating diseases* (ed. P.J. Vinken and G.W. Bruyn) p. 161. North-Holland, Amsterdam.

Kurtzke, J.F. (1972*a*). Multiple sclerosis death rates from underlying cause and total deaths. *Acta Neurol. Scand.* **48**, 148

Kurtzke, J.F. (1972*b*). Mortality and morbidity data in epilepsy. In *The epidemiology of epilepsy* (ed. M. Alter and W.A. Hauser) p. 21. NINDS Monograph No. 14, DHEW Publication No. (NIH)73–

390, Government Printing Office, Washington, DC.

Kurtzke, J.F. (1972c). Migration and latency in multiple sclerosis. In *Multiple sclerosis. Progress in research* (ed. E.J. Field, T.M. Bell, and P.R. Carnegie) p. 208. North-Holland, Amsterdam.

Kurtzke, J.F. (1974a). Epidemiology of myasthenia gravis. In *Neuroepidemiology: American Academy of Neurology special course* (ed. J.F. Kurtzke) p. 41. Education Marketing Corp, Minneapolis.

Kurtzke, J.F. (1974b). Further features of the Fennoscandian focus of multiple sclerosis. *Acta Neurol. Scand.* **50**, 478.

Kurtzke, J.F. (1975). A reassessment of the distribution of multiple sclerosis. Part One, Part Two. *Acta Neurol. Scand.* **51**, 110, 137.

Kurtzke, J.F. (1976). Multiple sclerosis among immigrants. *Br. Med. J.* **i**, 1527.

Kurtzke, J.F. (1977a). Geography in multiple sclerosis. *J. Neurol.* **215**, 1.

Kurtzke, J.F. (1977b). Multiple sclerosis from an epidemiological viewpoint. In *Multiple sclerosis. A critical conspectus* (ed. E.J. Field) p. 83. MTP Press, Lancaster.

Kurtzke, J.F. (1978a). Data registries on selected segments of the population: Veterans. *Adv. Neurol.* **19**, 55.

Kurtzke, J.F. (1978b). The epidemiology of myasthenia gravis. *Adv. Neurol.* **19**, 545.

Kurtzke, J.F. (1978c). The risk of multiple sclerosis in Denmark. *Acta Neurol. Scand.* **57**, 141.

Kurtzke, J.F. (1979a). ICD-9: a regression. *Am. J. Epidemiol.* **109**, 383.

Kurtzke, J.F. (1979b). Huntington's disease: mortality and morbidity data from outside the United States. *Adv. Neurol.* **23**, 13.

Kurtzke, J.F. (1980a). Epidemiologic contributions to multiple sclerosis—an overview. *Neurology* **30** (part 2), 61.

Kurtzke, J.F. (1980b). Multiple sclerosis: an overview. In *Clinical neuroepidemiology* (ed. F.C. Rose) p. 170. Pitman Medical, Tunbridge Wells.

Kurtzke, J.F. (1980c). The geographic distribution of multiple sclerosis: an update with special reference to Europe and the Mediterranean region. *Acta Neurol. Scand.* **62**, 65.

Kurtzke, J.F. (1982a). Epidemiology of amyotrophic lateral sclerosis. *Adv. Neurol.* **36**, 281.

Kurtzke, J.F. (1982b). The current neurologic burden of illness and injury in the United States. *Neurology* **32**, 1207.

Kurtzke, J.F. (1983b). Axon neuronque cano: Amyotrophic lateral sclerosis and related disorders. *Internat. Med.* **2**, 12.

Kurtzke, J.F. (1983c). Epidemiology of multiple sclerosis. In *Multiple sclerosis. Pathology, diagnosis and management* (ed. J.F. Hallpike, C.W.M. Adams, and W. W. Tourtellotte) p. 47. Chapman and Hall, London.

Kurtzke, J.F. and Beebe, G.W. (1980). Epidemiology of amyotrophic lateral sclerosis: 1. A case-control comparison based on ALS deaths. *Neurology* **30**, 453.

Kurtzke, J.F., Beebe, G.W., Nagler, B., Nefzger, M.D., Auth, T.L., and Kurland, L.T. (1970). Studies on the natural history of multiple sclerosis. V. Long-term survival in young men. *Arch. Neurol.* **22**, 215.

Kurtzke, J.F. and Bui, Q.H. (1980). Multiple sclerosis in a migrant population. 2. Half-Orientals immigrating in childhood. *Ann. Neurol.* **8**, 256.

Kurtzke, J.F. and Hyllested, K. (1979). Multiple sclerosis in the Faroe Islands: 1. Clinical and epidemiological features. *Ann. Neurol.* **5**, 6.

Kurtzke, J.F. and Hyllested, K. (1982). Multiple sclerosis on the Faroe Islands: a reassessment. *Jubilee Conference on Multiple Sclerosis Scientific Abstracts,* Copenhagen, Denmark, 6–9 June, p. 51.

Kurtzke, J.F. and Kurland, L.T. (1973). The epidemiology of neurologic disease. In *Clinical neurology,* Vol. 3 (ed. A.B. Baker and L.H. Baker) Ch. 48, p. 1. Harper and Row, Hagerstown, Md.

Kurtzke, J.F. and Kurland, L.T. (1984). The epidemiology of neurologic disease. In *Clinical neurology* (ed. A.B. Baker and L.H. Baker) Ch. 66, p. 1. Harper and Row, Philadelphia.

Kurtzke, J.F. and Priester, W.A. (1979). Dogs, distemper and multiple sclerosis in the United States. *Acta Neurol. Scand.* **60**, 312.

Kurtzke, J.F., Beebe, G.W., and Norman, J.E. Jr. (1979a). Migration and multiple sclerosis in the United States. *Neurology* **29**, 579.

Kurtzke, J.F., Beebe, G.W., and Norman, J.E. Jr. (1979b). Epidemiology of multiple sclerosis in US veterans: race, sex and geographical distribution. *Neurology* **29**, 1228.

Kurtzke, J.F., Gudmundsson, K.R., and Bergmann, S. (1982). Multiple sclerosis in Iceland: 1. Evidence of a postwar epidemic. *Neurology* **32**, 143.

Kurtzke, J.F., Kurland, L.T., and Goldberg, I.D. (1971). Mortality and migration in multiple sclerosis. *Neurology* **21**, 1186.

Kurtzke, J.F., Kurland, L.T., Goldberg, I.D., and Choi, L.T. (1973a). Multiple sclerosis. In *Epidemiology of neurologic and sense organ disorders* (ed. L.T. Kurland, J.F. Kurtzke, and I.D. Goldberg) p. 64. Harvard University Press, Cambridge, Mass.

Kurtzke, J.F., Kurland, L.T., Goldberg, I.D., Choi, N.W., and Reeder, F.A. (1973b). Convulsive disorders. In *Epidemiology of neurologic and sense organ disorders* (ed. L.T. Kurland, J.F. Kurtzke, and I.D. Goldberg) p. 15. Harvard University Press, Cambridge, Mass.

Kurtzke, J.F., Anderson, V.E., Beebe, G.W. *et al.* (1977). Report of the work group on epidemiology, biostatistics and population genetics. In *Report: Commission for the Control of Huntington's Disease and Its Consequences.* Vol. III. Part I. *Work Group Reports, Research.* DHEW Publications No. (NIH) 78-1503, p. 1–133. US Government Printing Office, Washington, DC.

Lancet (1982). Valproate and malformations. (Editorial.) *Lancet* **ii**, 1313.

Leger, J.-M., Ranouil, R., and Vallat, J.-N. (1974). [Huntington's chorea in Limousin. Statistical and clinical study.] *Rev. Méd. Limoges* **5**, 147.

Leibowitz, U. and Alter, M. (1968). Epilepsy in Jerusalem, Israel. *Epilepsia* **9**, 87.

Leibowitz, U., Kahana, E., and Alter, M. (1972). Population studies of multiple sclerosis in Israel. In *Multiple sclerosis: progress in research* (ed. E.J. Field, T.M. Bell, and P.R. Carnegie) p. 179. North-Holland, Amsterdam.

Leibowitz, U., Yablonski, M., and Alter, M. (1971). Tumors of the nervous system: incidence and population selectivity. *J. Chronic Dis.* **23**, 707.

Lessell, S., Torres, J.M., and Kurland, L.T. (1962). Seizure disorders in a Guamanian village. *Arch. Neurol.* **7**, 37.

Levy, L.F., Forbes, J.I., and Perirenyatwa, T.S. (1964). Epilepsy in Africans. *Cent. Afr. J. Med.* **10**, 241.

Lilienfeld, A.M., Levin, M.L., and Kessler, I.I. (1972). *Cancer in the United States.* Harvard University Press, Cambridge, Mass.

Limburg, C.C. (1950). The geographic distribution of multiple sclerosis and its estimated prevalence in the United States. *Proc. Assoc. Res. Nerv. Ment. Dis.* **28**, 15.

Livingstone, S. (1954). *The diagnosis and treatment of convulsive disorders in children.* Charles C. Thomas, Springfield, Ill.

Logan, W.P.D. and Cushion, A.A. (1958). *Studies on medical and population subjects, No. 14, Morbidity statistics from general practice,* Vol. 1: *General.* HMSO, London.

Lorez, A. (1969). Ein Beitrag zu Klinik und Vorkommen der amyotrophischen Lateralsklerose (isolierte und familiäre Fälle). *Schweiz. med. Wschr.* **99**, 51.

Lundstrom, J.M., Seybold, M.E., Lennon, V.A., Whittingham, S., and Duane, D.D. (1976). Antibody to acetylcholine receptor in myasthenia gravis: prevalence, clinical correlates, and diagnostic value. *Neurology* **26**, 1054.

McCall, M.G., Brereton, T. Le G., Dawson, A., Millingen, K., Sutherland, J.M., and Acheson, E.D. (1968). Frequency of multiple sclerosis in three Australian cities—Perth, Newcastle and Hobart. *J. Neurol. Neurosurg. Psychiat.* **31**, 1.

McCall, M.G., Sutherland, J.M., and Acheson, E.D. (1969). The frequency of multiple sclerosis in Western Australia. *Acta Neurol. Scand.* **45**, 151.

McCormack, M.K. and Lazzarini, A. (1982). Patterns of reproduction for people at risk for Huntington's disease. *Lancet* **ii**, 1333.

McFarland, H.F. and McFarlin, D.E. (1979). Cellular immune response to measles, mumps and vaccinia viruses in multiple sclerosis. *Ann. Neurol.* **6**, 101.

Mackay, R.P. and Myrianthopoulos, N.C. (1966). Multiple sclerosis in twins and their relatives: final report. *Arch. Neurol.* **15**, 449.

Martin, W.E., Young, W.J., and Alter, M. (1972). What is the mechanism of the genetic transmission of parkinsonism? *Neurology* **22**, 443.

Marttila, R.J. and Rinne, U.K. (1976a). Epidemiology of parkinson's disease in Finland. *Acta Neurol. Scand.* **53**, 81.

Marttila, R.J. and Rinne, U.K. (1976b). Arteriosclerosis, heredity, and some previous infections in the etiology of Parkinson's disease: a case-control study. *Clin. Neurol. Neurosurg.* **79**, 46.

Marttila, R.J. and Rinne, U.K. (1979). Changing epidemiology of Parkinson's disease: predicted effects of levodopa treatment. *Acta Neurol. Scand.* **59**, 80.

Mathai, K.V., Dunn, D.P., Kurland, L.T., and Reeder, F.A. (1968). Convulsive disorders in the Mariana Islands. *Epilepsia* **9**, 77.

Matsumoto, N., Worth, R.M., Kurland, L.T., and Okazaki, H. (1972). Epidemiologic study of amyotrophic lateral sclerosis in Hawaii: Identification of high incidence among Filipino men. *Neurology* **22**, 934.

Mattson, B. (1974). Huntington's chorea in Sweden. II. Social and clinical data. *Acta Psychiat. Scand.* **255**, Suppl., 221.

Medsger, T.A. Jr., Dawson, W.N., Jr., and Masi, A.T. (1970). The epidemiology of polymyositis. *Am. J. Med.* **48**, 715.

Medsger, T.A., Robinson, H., and Masi, T. (1971). Factors affecting survivorship in polymyositis. A life-table study of 124 patients. *Arthritis Rheumatism*, **14**, 249.

Meighan, S.S., Queener, L., and Wheitman, M. (1976). Prevalence of epilepsy in children of Multnomah County, Oregon. *Epilepsia* **17**, 245.

Metrakos, K. and Metrakos, J.D. (1961). Genetics of convulsive disorders: II. Genetic and electroencephalographic studies in centrencephalic epilepsy. *Neurology* **11**, 474.

Millar, J.H.D. (1972). Discussion on the epidemiology of MS. In *Multiple sclerosis. Progress in research* (ed. E.J. Field, T.M. Bell, and P.R. Carnegie) p. 233. North-Holland, Amsterdam.

Mjönes, H. (1949). Paralysis agitans: a clinical and genetic study. *Acta Psychiat. Neurol. Scand.* **54**, 1.

Moffie, D. (1966). De geografische verbreiding van multipele sclerose. *Nederl. T. Geneesk.* **110**, 1454.

Moller, E., Hammorstrom, L., Smith, E., and Matell, G. (1976). HL-A8 and LD-8a in patients with myasthenia gravis. *Tissue Antigens* **7**, 39.

Morton, N.E. and Chung, C.S. (1959). Formal genetics of muscular dystrophy. *Am. J. Hum. Genet.* **11**, 360.

Mosee, C. and Barber, J.B. (1970). The ethnic distribution of primary brain tumors, presented at the meeting of the Section on Neurology and Neurological Surgery, DC Medical Society, March 5, Washington, DC.

Mulder, D.W. (1957). The clinical syndrome of amyotrophic lateral sclerosis. *Proc. Staff Meet. Mayo Clin.* **32**, 427.

Müller, R. (1953). Genetic aspects of mutiple sclerosis. *Arch. Neurol. Psychiat.* **70**, 733.

Myers, L.W., Ellison, G.W., Lucia, M. *et al.* (1977). Swine influenza virus vaccination in patients with multiple sclerosis. *J. Infect. Dis.* **136**, Suppl., S546.

Myrianthopoulos, N.C., Kurland, A.A., and Kurland, L.T. (1962). Hereditary predisposition in drug induced parkinsonism. *Arch. Neurol.* **6**, 5.

Namba, T., Brunner, N.G., Brown, S.G., Muguruma, M., and Grob, D. (1971). Familial myasthenia gravis. Report of 27 patients in 12 families and review of 164 patients in 73 families. *Arch. Neurol.* **25**, 61.

National Center for Health Statistics (1968). *Vital statistics of the United States, 1955 supplement: Mortality data, multiple causes of death, estimated number of conditions coded on death certificates.* US Government Printing Office, Washington, DC.

National Center for Health Statistics (1965). *International clasification of diseases, adapted for use in the United States, eighth Revision,* Vol. 1 *Tabular list;* Vol. 2 *Alphabetical index.* PHS Publ. No. 1693. US Government Printing Office, Washington, DC.

Nefzger, M.D., Quadfasel, F.A., and Karl, V.C. (1967). A retrospective study of smoking and Parkinson's disease. *Am. J. Epidemiol.* **88**, 149.

Negrette, A. (1963). [*Huntington's chorea. (Study of one single family investigation across several generations.).*] University Zulia, Maracaibo, Talleres Graficos.

Nelson, K.B. and Ellenberg, J.H. (1976). Predictors of epilepsy in children who have experienced febrile seizures. *New Engl. J. Med.* **295**, 1029.

Nelson, K.B. and Ellenberg, J.H. (1982). Maternal seizure disorder, outcome of pregnancy, and neurologic abnormalities in the children. *Neurology* **32**, 1247.

Newbill, H.P. and Anderson, G.C. (1944). Racial and sexual incidence of primary intracranial tumors: statistical study of one hundred and thirty-three cases verified by autopsy. *Arch. Neurol. Psychiat.* **51**, 564.

Newsom-Davis, J., Pinching, A.J., Vincent, A., and Wilson, S.G. (1978). Function of circulating antibody to acetylcholine receptor in myasthenia gravis: investigation by plasma exchange. *Neurology* **28**, 266.

Nigro, G., Comi, L.I., Limongelli, F. *et al.* (1973). Studio sulla distribuzione delle distrofe muscolari progressive in Campania. *Med. Sociale*, **23**, 199.

Nobrega, F.T., Glattre, E., Kurland, L.T., and Okazaki, H. (1967). Comments on the epidemiology of Parkinsonism including prevalence and incidence statistics in Rochester, Minnesota, 1935–1966. *Excerpta Med. Int. Congr. Ser.* **175**, 474.

Nordahl, H.G. and Froland, S.S. (1978). Lymphocyte subpopulations and cellular immune reactions in vitro in patients with multiple sclerosis. *Clin. Immunol. Immunopath.* **9**, 87.

Noronha, A.B.C., Richman, D.P., and Arnason, B.G.W. (1980). Detection of in vivo stimulated cerebrospinal fluid lymphocytes by flow cytometry in patients with multiple sclerosis. *New Engl. J. Med.* **303**, 713.

Norris, F.H. Jr and Engel, W.K. (1965). Carcinomatous amyotrophic lateral sclerosis. In *The remote effects of cancer on the nervous system* (ed. W.R. Brain and F.H. Norris Jr.) p. 24. Grune and Stratton, New York.

Okinaka, S., Hirayama, K., Kusui, K., Iwahashi, Y., Katsuki, S., Kuroiwa, Y., and Araki, S. (1962). [Epidemiologic study of amyotrophic lateral sclerosis and related diseases in the Kii Peninsula.] *Clin. Neurol.* (Tokyo) **2**, 295.

Okinaka, S., Reese, H.H., Katsuki, S. *et al.* (1966). The prevalence of multiple sclerosis and other neurological diseases in Japan. *Acta Neurol. Scand.* **42**, Suppl. 19, 68.

Olivares, L. (1972). Epilepsy in Mexico: a population study. In *The epidemiology of epilepsy* (ed. M. Alter and W.A. Hauser) p. 21. NINDS Monograph No. 14, DHEW Publication No. (NIH) 73–390. US Government Printing Office, Washington, DC.

Olivares, L., San Estéban, E., and Alter, M. (1972). Mexican 'resistance' to amyotrophic lateral sclerosis. *Arch. Neurol.* **27**, 397.

Oosterhuis, H.J.G.H. (1977). Epidemiologie der myasthenie in Amsterdam. In *Myasthenia Gravis und Anderere Storungen der Neuromuskularen Synapse* (ed. G. Hertel, H.G. Mertens, K. Ricker, and K. Schimrigk) p. 103. Thieme, Stuttgart.

Osserman, K.E. and Genkins, G. (1971). Studies in myasthenia gravis: review of a twenty-year experience in over 1200 patients. *Mt. Sinai J. Med.* **38**, 497.

Otsuka, A. (1964). [Epidemiological and clinical study of several neurological and neuromuscular disorders in Niigata City]. *Adv. Neurol. Sci.* (Tokyo) **8**, 181.

Panse, F. (1942). *Die Erbchorea. Eine Klinisch-Genetische Studie.* Thieme, Leipzig.

Pearson, C.M. (1966). Polymyositis. *Ann. Rev. Med.* **17**, 63.

Pennington, G.W. and Wilson, A. (1961). Incidence of myasthenia gravis in the Merseyside conurbation. In *Myasthenia gravis* (ed. H.R. Viets) p. 337. Thomas, Springfield, Ill.

Percy, A.K., Elveback, L.R., Okazaki, H., and Kurland, L.T. (1972). Neoplasms of the nervous system: epidemiologic considerations. *Neurology* **22**, 40.

Percy, A.K., Nobrega, F.T., Okazaki, H., Glattre, E., and Kurland, L.T. (1971). Multiple sclerosis in Rochester, Minn: a 60-year appraisal. *Arch. Neurol.* **25**, 105.

Perlo, V.P., Poskanzer, D.C., Schwab, R.S., Viets, H.R., Osserman, K.E., and Genkins, G. (1966). Myasthenia gravis: evaluation of treatment in 1,355 patients. *Neurology* **16**, 431.

Pirskanen, R. (1976). Genetic associations between myasthenia gravis and the HL-A system. *J. Neurol. Neurosurg. Psychiat.* **39**, 23.

Pleydell, M.J. (1954). Huntington's chorea in Northamptonshire. *Br. Med. J.* **ii**, 1121.

Pollock, M. and Hornabrook, R.W. (1966). The prevalence, natural history and dementia of Parkinson's disease. *Brain* **89**, 429.

Pond, D.A., Bidwell, B.H., and Stein, L. (1960). A survey of epilepsy in fourteen general practices: I. Demographic and medical data. *Psychiat. Neurol. Neurochir.* **63**, 217.

Poskanzer, D.C. (1965). Tonsillectomy and multiple sclerosis. *Lancet* **ii**, 1264.

Poskanzer, D.C. (1967). Neurological disorders. In *Preventive medicine* (ed. D.W. Clark and B. MacMahon) p. 373. Little Brown, Boston.

Poskanzer, D.C. (1968). Etiology of multiple sclerosis: analogy suggesting infection in early life. In *The epidemiology of multiple sclerosis* (ed. M. Alter and J.F. Kurtzke) p. 62. Thomas, Springfield, Ill.

Poskanzer, D.C., Prenney, L.B., and Sheridan, J.L. (1977). House pets and multiple sclerosis. *Lancet* **i**, 1204.

Poskanzer, D.C., Prenney, L.B., Sheridan, J.L., and Yonkondy, J. (1980). Multiple sclerosis in the Orkney and Shetland Islands. I. Epidemiology, clinical factors and methodology. *J. Epidemiol. Community Health* **34**, 229.

Poskanzer, D.C. and Schwab, R.S. (1963). Cohort analysis of Parkinson's syndrome: evidence for a single etiology related to subclinical infection about 1920. *J. Chronic Dis.* **16**, 961.

Poskanzer, D.C., Shapira, K., and Miller, H. (1963). Multiple sclerosis and poliomyelitis. *Lancet* **ii**, 917.

Pratt, R.T.C. (1967). *The genetics of neurological disorders.* Oxford University Press, London.

Pratt, R.T.C., Compston, N.D., and McAlpine, D. (1951). The familial incidence of disseminated sclerosis and its significance. *Brain* **74**, 191.

Rajput, A.H., Offord, K., Beard, .C.M., and Kurland, L.T. (1983). Incidence and case-control study of parkinsonism in Rochester, 1967–1979. Unpublished data.

Reed, D., Sever, J., Kurtzke, J., and Kurland, L.T. (1964). Measles antibody in patients with multiple sclerosis. *Arch. Neurol.* **10**, 402.

Reed, D.M. and Brody, J.A. (1975). Amyotrophic lateral sclerosis and parkinsonism–dementia on Guam, 1945–1972. I. Descriptive epidemiology, *Am. J. Epidemiol.* **101**, 287.

Reed, T.E. and Chandler, J.H. (1958). Huntington's chorea in Michigan. 1. Demography and genetics. *Am. J. Hum. Genet.* **10**, 201.

Refsum, S. and Mohr, J. (1971). Genetic aspects of neurology. In *Clinical neurology,* 3rd edn (ed. A.B. Baker and L.H. Baker) Ch. 47, p. 1. Harper and Row, Hagerstown, Md.

Refsum, S. and Skre, H. (1978). Nosology, genetics, and epidemiology of hereditary ataxias, with particular reference to the epidemiology of these disorders in western Norway. *Adv. Neurol.* **19**, 497.

Richman, D.P., Patrick, J., and Arnason, B.G.W. (1976). Cellular immunity in myasthenia gravis: response to purified acetylcholine receptor and autologous thymocytes. *New Engl. J. Med.* **294**, 694.

Rischbieth, R.H. (1966). The prevalence of disseminated sclerosis in South Australia. *Med. J. Aust.* **1**, 774.

Roberts, D.F., Papiha, S.S., and Poskanzer, D.C. (1979a). Polymorphisms and multiple sclerosis in Orkney. *J. Epidemiol. Community Health* **33**, 236.

Roberts, D.F., Roberts, M.J., and Poskanzer, D.C. (1979b). Genetic analysis of multiple sclerosis in Orkney. *J. Epidemiol. Community Health* **33**, 229.

Rodin, E. and Gonzalez, S. (1966). Hereditary components in epileptic patients: electoencephalogram family studies. *JAMA* **198**, 221.

Rosati, G., Granieri, E., Pinna, L. *et al.* (1980). The risk of Parkinson disease in Mediterranean people. *Neurology* **30**, 250.

Rosati, G., Pinna, L., Granieri, E. *et al.* (1977). Studies on epidemiological, clinical and etiological aspects of ALS disease in Sardinia, Southern Italy. *Acta Neurol. Scand.* **55**, 231.

Rose, A.L. and Walton, J.N. (1966). Polymyositis: a survey of 89 cases with particular reference to treatment and prognosis. *Brain* **89**, 747.

Rose, F.C. (ed.) (1980). *Clinical neuroepidemiology.* Pitman Medical, London.

Rose, S.W., Penry, J.K., Markush, R.E., Radloff, L.A., and Putnam, M. (1973). Prevalence of epilepsy in children. *Epilepsia* **14**, 152.

Ross, C.A.C., Lenman, J.A.R., and Rutter, C. (1965). Infective agents and multiple sclerosis. *Br. Med. J.* **i**, 226.

Ross, E.M., Peckham, C.S., West, P.B., and Butler, N.R. (1980). Epilepsy and childhood: findings from the national child development study. *Br. Med. J.* **i**, 207.

Ryan, D.E., Holtbecher, J., and Stuart, D.C. (1978). Trace elements in scalp-hair of persons with multiple sclerosis and of normal individuals. *Clin. Chem.* **24**, 1996.

Saint, E.G. and Sadka, M. (1962). The incidence of multiple sclerosis in Western Australia. *Med. J. Aust.* **2**, 249.

Salmi, A., Panelius, M., and Vainionpaa, R. (1974). Antibodies against different viral antigens in cerebrospinal fluid of patients with multiple sclerosis and other neurologic diseases. *Acta Neurol. Scand.* **50**, 183.

Schapira, K., Poskanzer, D.C., and Miller, H. (1963). Familial and conjugal multiple sclerosis. *Brain* **86**, 315.

Schoenberg, B.S. (ed.) (1978). *Neurological epidemiology: principles and clinical applications.* (*Adv. Neurol.* Vol. 19). Raven Press, New York.

Schumacher, G.A., Beebe, G., Kibler, R.F. *et al.* (1965). Problems of experimental trials of therapy in multiple sclerosis. Report by the panel on the evaluation of experimental trials of therapy in multiple sclerosis. *Ann. N.Y. Acad. Sci.* **122**, 552.

Schut, J.W. (1950). Hereditary ataxia: clinical study through six generations. *Arch. Neurol. Psychiat.* **63**, 535.

Schut, J.W. and Haymaker, W. (1951). Hereditary ataxia: a pathologic study of five cases of common ancestry. *J. Neuropath. Clin. Neurol.* **1**, 183.

Schwab, R.S., Doshay, L.J., Garland, H., Bradshaw, P., Garvey, E., and Crawford, B. (1956). Shift to older age distribution in parkinsonism: a report on 1000 patients covering the past decade from three centers. *Neurology* **6**, 783.

Sever, J.L. and Zeman, W. (eds.) (1968). Conference on measles virus and subacute sclerosing panencephalitis. *Neurology* **18** (part 2), 1.

Shepherd, D.E. and Downie, A.W. (1978). Prevalence of multiple sclerosis in northeast Scotland. *Br. Med. J.* **ii**, 314.

Sibley, W.A., Bamford, C.R., and Laguna, J.F. (1976). Influenza vaccination in patients with multiple sclerosis. *JAMA* **236**, 1965.

Sibley, W.A. and Foley, J.M. (1965). Infection and immunization in multiple sclerosis. *Ann. N.Y. Acad. Sci.* **122**, 457.

Simpson, J.F., Westerberg, M.R., and Magee, K.R. (1966). Myasthenia gravis. An analysis of 295 cases. *Acta Neurol. Scand.* **42**, Suppl. 23, 1.

Sjögren, T. (1943). Klinische und erbbiologische Untersuchungen über die Heredoataxien. *Acta Psychiat. Neurol.* Suppl. 27, 1.

Skre, H. (1964). Heredoataxia in Western Norway: Some experiences from a preliminary investigation. *J. Genet. Hum.* **13**, 86.

Slooff, J.L., Kernohan, J.W., and MacCarty, C.S. (1964). *Primary intramedullary tumors of the spinal cord and filum terminale.* Saunders, Philadelphia.

Sobue, I., Ando, K., Iida, M., Umemura, N., and Nishigaki, K. (1969). [Epidemiologic investigations of motor neuron disease in Nagoya City.] *Adv. Neurol. Sci. (Tokyo)* **7**, 290.

Soemargo, S. (1977). Personal communication to the Commission for the Control of Huntington's Disease and its Consequences.

Soulayol, R. and Yoyer-Vidil, N. (1974). *l'Epilepsie dans la Réunion.* Doin, Paris.

Stanhope, J.M., Brody, J.A., Brink, E., and Morris, C.E. (1972). Convulsions among the Chamorro people of Guam, Mariana Islands. II. Febrile convulsions. *Am. J. Epidemiol.* **95**, 299.

Stazio, A., Kurland, L.T., Bell, L.G., Saunders, M.G., and Rogot, E. (1964). Multiple sclerosis in Winnipeg, Manitoba: methodological considerations of epidemiologic survey: ten year follow-up on a communitywide study, and population re-survey. *J. Chronic Dis.* **17**, 415.

Stazio, A., Paddison, R.M., and Kurland, L.T. (1967). Multiple sclerosis in New Orleans, Louisiana, and Winnipeg, Manitoba, Canada: follow-up of a previous survey in New Orleans, and comparison between the patient populations in the two communities. *J. Chronic Dis.* **20**, 311.

Steiner, P.E. (1954). *Cancer: race and geography: some etiological, environmental, ethnological, epidemiological, and statistical aspects of Caucasoids, Mongoloids, Negroids and Mexicans.* Williams and Wilkins, Baltimore.

Stern, L.M. (1972). Four cases of Duchenne-type muscular dystrophy in girls. *Med. J. Aust.* **2**, 1066.

Stevens, D.L. (1973). Heterozygote frequency for Huntington's chorea. *Adv. Neurol.* **1**, 191.

Storm-Mathisen, A. (1961). *Myasthenia gravis: a clinical study with special reference to prevalence and prognosis.* Almqvist and Wiksell, Stockholm.

Storm-Mathisen, A. (1966). Epidemiological and prognostic aspects of myasthenia gravis in Norway. *Ann. N.Y. Acad. Sci.* **135**, 431.

Storm-Mathisen, A. (1976). Epidemiological and prognostic aspects of myasthenia gravis in Norway. *Acta Neurol. Scand.* **54**, 120.

Sutherland, J.M. (1956). Observations on the prevalence of multiple sclerosis in northern Scotland. *Brain* **79**, 635.

Sutherland, J.M., Tyrer, J.H., and Eadie, M.J. (1962). The prevalence of multiple sclerosis in Australia. *Brain* **85**, 149.

Symington, G.R. and MacKay, I.R. (1978). Cell-mediated immunity to measles virus in multiple sclerosis: correlation with disability. *Neurology* **28**, 109.

Szekeres, J., Palffy, G.Y., and Paradi, J. (1980). Rickettsia specific antibodies in multiple sclerosis. *Lancet* **ii**, 1089.

Takeshita, K., Yoshino, K., Kitahara, T., Nakashima, T., and Kato, N. (1977). Survey of Duchenne type and congenital type of muscular dystrophy in Shimane, Japan. *Jap. J. Hum. Genet.* **22**, 43.

Thomasen, E. (1948). *Myotonia: Thomsen's disease (myotonia congenita), paramyotonia, and dystrophia myotonica: a clinical and heredobiologic investigation* (translated from Danish by F.B. Carlsen). Universitetsforlaget, Aarhus, Denmark.

Thompson, J.A., Bray, P.F., and Glascow, L.A. (1975). Multiple sclerosis and elevation of cerebrospinal fluid vaccinia virus antibody. *Neurology* **25**, 94.

Trueta, J. (1955). Physiological mechanisms involved in the localization of paralysis. *Ann. N.Y. Acad. Sci.* **61**, 883.

Tsubaki, T., Nakanishi, T., Suga, M., and Kuroiwa, Y. (1963). [Study of neurologic disorders in Amami-Oshima Island.] *Clin. Neurol. (Tokyo)* **3**, 394.

Tsuboi, T. and Endo, S. (1977). Febrile convulsions followed by nonfebrile convulsions: a clinical, electroencephalographic and follow-up study. *Neuropaediatrie* **8**, 209.

Turner, J.W.A. (1974). Myasthenia gravis. *Proc. R. Soc. Med.* **67**, 763.

Tyler, F.H. and Stephens, F.E. (1951). Studies in disorders of muscle: IV. Clinical manifestations and inheritance of childhood progressive muscular dystrophy. *Ann. Intern. Med.* **35**, 169.

Van den Berg, B.J. and Yerushalmy, J. (1969). Studies on convulsive disorders in young children: I. Incidence of febrile and non-febrile convulsions by age and other factors. *Pediatr. Res.* **3**, 298.

Vercelletto, P. and Courjon, J. (1969). Heredity and generalized epilepsy. *Epilepsia* **10**, 7.

Visscher, B.R., Detels, R., Dudley, J. *et al.* (1979). Genetic susceptibility to multiple sclerosis. *Neurology* **29**, 1354.

Visscher, B.R., Liv, K.-S., Sullivan, C.B., Valdiviezo, N.L., and Detels, R. (1962). Birth order and multiple sclerosis. *Acta Neurol. Scand.* **66**, 209.

Walker, J.E. and Cook, J.D. (1979). Lymphoblastic transformation in response to viral antigens in multiple sclerosis. *Neurology* **29**, 1341.

Wallace, D.C. (1973). Huntington's chorea in Queensland. A not uncommon disease. *Med. J. Austr.* **2**, 299.

Walton, J.N. (1963). Clinical aspects of human muscular dystrophy. In *Muscular dystrophy in man and animals* (ed. G.H. Bourne and M.N. Golarz) p. 263. Hafner, New York.

Walton, J.N. (1964). Muscular dystrophy: some recent advances in knowledge. *Br. Med. J.* **i**, 1344.

Walton, J.N. and Nattrass, F.J. (1954). On the classification, natural history and treatment of the myopathies. *Brain* **77**, 169.

Ward, C.D., Duvoisin, R.C., Ince, S.E., Nutt, J.D., Eldridge, R., and Calne, D.B. (1983). Parkinson's disease in 65 pairs of twins and in a set of quadruplets. *Neurology* **33**, 815.

Warren, H.V., Delavault, R.E., and Cross, C.H. (1967). Possible correlations between geology and some disease patterns. *Ann. N.Y. Acad. Sci.* **136**, 657.

Warrier, C.B.C. and Pillai, T.D.G. (1967). Familial myasthenia gravis. *Br. Med. J.* **iii**, 839.

Wendt, G.G. and Drohm, D. (1972). [Huntington's chorea. A population-genetic study.] In *Humangenetik: advances in human genetics.* Vol. 4, p. 1. Thieme, Stuttgart.

Westlund, K.B. and Kurland, L.T. (1953). Studies in multiple sclerosis in Winnipeg, Manitoba, and New Orleans, Louisiana: I. Prevalence: Comparison between the patient groups in Winnepeg and New Orleans. *Am. J. Hyg.* **57**, 380.

Wikstrom, J., Westermarck, T., and Palo, J. (1976). Selenium, vitamin E and copper in multiple sclerosis. *Acta Neurol. Scand.* **54**, 287.

Williams, G.R., Kurland, L.T., and Goldberg, I.D. (1966). Morbidity and mortality with parkinsonism. *J. Neurosurg.* **24**, 138.

World Health Organization (1967, 1969). *Manual of the international statistical classification of diseases, injuries and causes of death, 1965 revision,* Vol. 1, 2. World Health Organization, Geneva.

World Health Organization (1977). *Manual of the international statistical classification of diseases, injuries and causes of death, ninth revision,* Vol. 1. World Health Organization, Geneva.

Yase, Y., Matsumoto, N., Yoshimasu, F., and Handa, Y. (1973). Clinico-epidemiological studies in a new focus of motor neuron disease in Japan. *Neurol. India* Suppl. IV, 531.

Young, W.I., Martin, W.E., and Anderson, V.E. (1977). The distribution of ancestral secondary cases in Parkinson's disease. *Clin. Genet.* **11**, 189.

Yuasa, R., Hiyama, H., and Hashimoto, T. (1976). [Motor neuron disease in the Osaka prefecture, Japan.] *Clin. Neurol. (Tokyo)* **16**, 207.

Zack, M.M., Levitt, L.P., and Schoenberg, B. (1977). Motor neuron disease in Lehigh County, Pennsylvania: an epidemiologic study. *J. Chronic Dis.* **30**, 813.

Zielinski, J.J. (1974). Epileptics not on treatment. *Epilepsia* **15**, 203.

13 Haematopoietic diseases

Clark W. Heath, Jr. and Bruce L. Evatt

INTRODUCTION

Haematological diseases can be grouped under three headings: (i) disorders affecting red blood cells; (ii) disorders affecting white blood cells; and (iii) disorders affecting haemostasis and blood coagulation. In each category, illness arising primarily in blood or blood-forming organs must be differentiated from the common secondary involvement of such tissues by systemic disease originating elsewhere. The complexity of this disease spectrum is matched by the diversity of public health approaches used for its control and prevention. Strategies range from environmental control and improved nutrition to health education and health care promotion. This reflects the fact that haematological illnesses have many different causes: genetic factors, nutritional deficiencies, immune mechanisms, infectious agents, and exposure to chemical and physical agents. Since many other diseases share these same aetiologies, the impact of control measures is by no means limited to haematological illness. This chapter reviews the entire scope of haematological disorders and focuses on those diseases which are relatively common or are of particular public health interest.

DISORDERS OF RED BLOOD CELLS

Red cell disorders express themselves clinically as abnormal concentrations of red cells or abnormal levels of haemoglobin in peripheral blood; decreased values result in anaemia, increased values in polycythaemia. Anaemias pose by far the greater health problem, and as a disease grouping they may in fact represent the single most common form of human illness.

Many different causes for anaemia exist. These may be broadly characterized either as problems of inadequate red cell production or as problems of excessive red cell destruction. Since both forms of abnormality frequently occur together in the same patient, many cases of anaemia encountered in clinical practice are of mixed origin. Within each category of red cell abnormality, causes can be broadly classified in terms of inherited (genetical) or acquired (environmental) aetiology.

Inadequate red cell production

Table 13.1 provides a classification of conditions associated with decreased red cell production. These disorders can be

Table 13.1. *Conditions involving inadequate red cell production*

Deficiency of cell nutrients

Iron
Blood loss: gastrointestinal lesions, menstruation, hookworm, blood donation, etc.
Inadequate diet: relative to need
Impaired absorption: gastric resection, achlorhydria, pica, sprue

Folic acid
Inadequate diet: relative to need (infancy, pregnancy, proliferative disease)
Impaired absorption: sprue, gluten-induced enteropathy
Drugs: dilantin (?mechanism)

Vitamin B$_{12}$
Impaired absorption: pernicious anaemia (gastric atrophy and intrinsic factor deficiency), gastric resection, inherited defects, drugs
Decreased availability: intestinal loops, fish tapeworm
Inadequate diet: strict vegetarians

Other nutrients
Protein, ? trace materials

Impaired erythropoiesis

Aplastic anaemia
Chemicals: benzene, drugs
Ionizing radiation
Infection
Idiopathic

Sideroblastic anaemias
Hereditary: often pyridoxine-responsive
Acquired: drugs, alcohol, lead
Idiopathic

Porphyrias
Acquired: chemicals
Inherited

Anaemias secondary to systemic illness
Cancer (marrow infiltration), endocrine disease, renal disease, cirrhosis, chronic inflammation

divided into those in which erythropoiesis is disturbed by deficiencies in particular cell nutrients and those in which impairment comes from a variety of other causes.

Iron deficiency

By far the most common form of haematological disease in man is iron deficiency. The condition can exist without anaemia if tissue iron stores are low but not depleted, but it is usually recognized clinically only when stores are fully depleted and anaemia develops. The clinical hallmark of iron deficiency is hypochromic microcytic anaemia. When anaemia is present, haemoglobin and packed cell volume are decreased in association with cells which appear paler and smaller than normal.

Iron is an essential component both for haemoglobin, the oxygen-carrying molecule in red blood cells, and for myoglobin in muscle. The body's iron needs are provided through the diet and are governed by demands of growth and by loss of iron from bleeding and cell desquamation. Daily tissue requirements range from about 0.5 to 2.5 mg (Williams 1982), depending on age (children versus adults) and on the presence or absence of pregnancy or menstrual bleeding in women (Table 13.2). Most body iron (60–70 per cent) is contained in haemoglobin. The remainder exists in myoglobin and as stored reserves in macrophages in marrow, liver, and other tissues (Wintrobe 1981). Average reserves are two to five times greater in men than in women because of lower iron requirements in men. These larger reserves are in turn associated with lower frequency of iron-deficiency anaemia in men.

Table 13.2. *Average daily amounts of iron needed in tissue to meet normal tissue requirements associated with growth, pregnancy, and loss of iron*

Persons with different iron requirements	Required iron (mg/day)
Children	1.0–1.5
Girls age 12–15 years	1.5–2.5
Menstruating women	1.0–2.0
Pregnant women	1.5–2.5
Post-menopausal women	0.5–1.0
Men	0.5–1.0

Daily dietary requirements are estimated at about 5–10 mg in men and 7–20 mg in women (Hallberg 1982). In the presence of adequate iron stores in tissue, only about 5–10 per cent of dietary iron is absorbed; with depleted iron stores, however, efficiency of dietary absorption can increase three- to fivefold (Bezwoda *et al.* 1979). Since an 'average' diet may contain only about 5–6 mg of iron per 1000 calories, negative iron balance can easily occur, especially in women, if increased iron loss or utilization is present.

The prevalence of iron deficiency is difficult to determine with precision. Undoubtedly it varies greatly in different populations, being closely related to dietary patterns and to socio-economic levels. The fact that iron-deficiency anaemia is considerably more prevalent throughout the world than anaemias of other causes makes surveys of haemoglobin levels a crude indicator of population iron deficiency (defining anaemia as a haemoglobin level in men below 14 g/dl and in women below 12 g/dl) (Wintrobe 1981). More sensitive and meaningful, however, are measures of plasma iron and iron-binding capacity which both measure iron deficiency directly and take into account pre-anaemic states. On this basis, it appears that in developed countries iron deficiency exists in about 3 per cent of men,

20 per cent of women, and more than 50 per cent of pregnant women (Monsen *et al.* 1967; Hallberg and Nilsson 1964; Finch *et al.* 1968). Among pre-school children, particularly under the age of two years, 50 per cent or more may show iron deficiency, especially in lower social class families (Williams 1982; Bothwell and Charlton 1982). In less developed countries, where malnutrition is often commonplace, it can be assumed that significant iron deficiency is even more frequent (Bothwell *et al.* 1979).

On a world-wide basis, it is likely that a large production of iron deficiency is caused solely by insufficiency of diet, which at the same time leads to other nutritional diseases including megaloblastic anaemia due to folate deficiency. As noted above, such problems can be expected to be most frequent and severe in young children and in women, especially pregnant women.

Where diet is more adequate, it is axiomatic among clinicians to assume that iron deficiency is nearly always the result of blood loss. The most common sites for bleeding are the gastrointestinal tract (haemorrhoids, peptic ulcer, polyps, oesophageal hiatus hernia) and the uterus (menstruation). Although many other causes of bleeding could be listed, none are commonplace or of special public health significance except for hookworm disease in which worms infesting the upper small intestine can suck substantial volumes of blood from the host. Since this parasitic disease affects about 20 per cent of the world population (Layrisse and Roche 1964), particularly lower socio-economic populations in developing tropical and subtropical countries, it represents a major cause of iron deficiency and one particularly appropriate for public health control.

In addition to malnutrition and bleeding, iron deficiency can also result from various disorders involving impaired iron absorption. Such disorders include the sprue syndromes, in which atrophy of upper intestinal mucosa impairs absorption of iron as well as of other nutrients (Williams 1982), and pica (the habit of eating soil or clay) which is common in many parts of the world, especially among women and children, and which appears to involve sequestration of dietary iron by ingested clay in the gastrointestinal tract (National Academy of Sciences 1968).

Public health programmes play a vital role in prevention of iron deficiency. These include community programmes designed to guarantee adequate nutrition as well as programmes aimed at elimination of hookworm disease. Nutritional programmes should include special provision of iron supplements for young children (particularly premature infants) and for women of childbearing age with emphasis on adequate iron during pregnancy.

Folic acid deficiency

Both folic acid and vitamin B_{12} are essential for the orderly synthesis of deoxyribonucleic acid (DNA) in all tissue cells. In bone marrow, both vitamins are required for normal production and maturation of both red and white blood cells. The absence of either folate or vitamin B_{12} leads to macrocytic anaemia in which red cells in peripheral blood as well as their nucleated precursors in bone marrow are larger than normal (macrocytes and megaloblasts). Macrocytic changes can also be seen in white blood cells and in their marrow precursors (myelocytes and myeloblasts). Megaloblastic changes in marrow reflect asynchronous cell development in which haemoglobin production and iron incorporation proceed at a normal pace but nuclear maturation and DNA replication are slowed (Wintrobe 1981). When folate or vitamin B_{12} deficiency co-exists with iron deficiency (as often occurs in combined deficiency states), megaloblastic and macrocytic features may be masked, later to emerge if iron therapy is given (Williams 1982).

Folic acid is synthesized by plants and microorganisms and hence is widely available in the human diet, especially in leafy vegetables. Much of the folate available in food, however, is destroyed by prolonged cooking. The average daily adult human tissue requirement is for about 50 µg (National Academy of Sciences 1968). Needs are increased in the presence of active body growth (children and infants), in pregnancy, and under conditions of increased red cell proliferation. The recommended daily adult dietary intake is about 200 µg for pregnant women. Folate is stored primarily in the liver. Body stores are sufficient to meet body needs for two to four months in the face of dietary folate deficiency (Herbert 1962).

Prevalence of folate deficiency parallels the prevalence of malnutrition in the world and is especially common in tropical regions where diet is compromised by poverty and inadequate living conditions. As with other dietary deficiencies in such circumstances, folate deficiency particularly affects infants, young children, and pregnant women. In developed countries, the condition is much less common but occurs in particular association with pregnancy and with excessive alcoholic consumption.

The causes of folate deficiency (Table 13.1) primarily relate to dietary lack, whether arising from outright malnutrition or from relative dietary insufficiency in the face of increased tissue requirements. The latter include not only the growth requirements of pregnancy, infancy, and childhood, but various disease states involving increased cell proliferation and hence tissue folate need. Such proliferation occurs in various haemolytic conditions (such as thalassaemia and sickle-cell anaemia) in which rapid red cell destruction requires greatly increased rates of marrow cell production (Jandl and Greenberg 1959; Lindenbaum and Klipstein 1963).

Folate deficiency can also result both from impaired intestinal absorption and from the administration of certain drugs or toxins. The latter category includes certain anticonvulsant drugs such as diphenylhydantoin and phenobarbitol. The mechanism by which such medications lead to folate deficiency is unclear (Klipstein 1964). Alcohol ingestion can also lead to folate deficiency through mechanisms thought to be related to folate metabolism and storage in liver. Folate malabsorption occurs in association with sprue syndromes, both tropical sprue and gluten-induced enteropathy (non-tropical sprue or idiopathic steatorrhoea in adults and coeliac disease in children). Both conditions involve atrophic changes in upper intestinal mucosa, diffuse in the case of tropical sprue, largely jejunal in the case of gluten-induced enteropathy (Williams 1982).

This atrophic change is associated with malabsorption not only of folate but of other nutrients such as vitamin B_{12}, iron, and fats (Gardner 1958; Sheehy *et al.* 1961). Tropical sprue is relatively frequent in developing countries and may well result from the recurrent intestinal infections which are highly prevalent in such settings. Gluten-induced enteropathy is a relatively rare condition which appears to result from intestinal sensitivity to gluten, a protein component of wheat and other grains. Lymphomas arising in small intestinal lymphoid tissues are rare sequelae in this illness.

As with all nutritional diseases, public health programmes in health education and in nutritional supplementation can have an important impact on prevalence of folate deficiency. This is particularly important in developing, tropical countries and in relation to infants, children, and pregnant women. In addition, public health action directed at control of intestinal food-borne infections is probably of great importance for eventual control of tropical sprue and its associated malabsorption consequences. Finally, the association between alcohol use and folate levels suggests that public health action in controlling alcohol abuse can directly affect prevalence of folate deficient states.

Vitamin B_{12} deficiency

Vitamin B_{12}, like folic acid, is essential for proper DNA synthesis and for normal maturational division of haemopoietic cells. Deficiency in vitamin B_{12} produces marrow megaloblastosis and a macrocytic anaemia (pernicious anaemia) which haematologically is indistinguishable from macrocytic anaemia due to folate deficiency. Vitamin B_{12} deficiency in many patients, however, can also be associated with neurological abnormalities (subacute combined degeneration) which produce both sensory and motor symptoms, both from peripheral neuropathy and from degenerative lesions in lateral and posterior spinal cord tracts.

Vitamin B_{12} is synthesized by bacteria and moulds (but not by higher forms of life) and is present in foods of animal origin (meat, liver). It is absorbed in the distal ileum after forming a molecular complex with intrinsic factor, a glycoprotein produced by the gastric mucosa (Grasbeck 1969). It is present in the body in much smaller quantities than either iron or folate (about 2000–4000 µg) and only about 2–3 µg are necessary as an average daily dietary requirement (Heyssel *et al.* 1966).

The primary causes of vitamin B_{12} deficiency relate either to malabsorption or to decreased availability in the gastrointestinal tract (Williams 1982). In contrast to iron and folate deficiency, vitamin B_{12} deficiency only rarely results from dietary insufficiency, and then only in extreme situations involving very strict and long-maintained vegetarian diets (Smith 1962). The reason for this difference is the relative abundance of vitamin B_{12} in diet, its low tissue requirements, and the fact that vitamin B_{12} reserves persist in tissue for years (Grasbeck 1959).

Malabsorption of vitamin B_{12} can occur from various causes, none of them common. Most well known is an acquired deficiency in intrinsic factor production, the underlying physiological disturbance in classical Addisonian pernicious anaemia (Wintrobe 1981). This deficiency may be partly hereditary in nature and appears to result from autoimmune processes affecting the gastric mucosa. Persons with pernicious anaemia tend to be older adults who display varying degrees of gastritis, gastric mucosal atrophy, and achlorhydria. Other causes of intrinsic factor deficiency include surgical removal of gastric tissue, interference by certain drugs or chemicals (Paulson and Harvey 1954), and in rare instances, its congenital or inherited absence (Miller *et al.* 1966).

Deficiency of vitamin B_{12} may also occasionally arise because of diminished availability of the vitamin for absorption in the gastrointestinal tract despite adequate presence of intrinsic factor and sufficient diet. This situation arises when a blind loop of intestine is created surgically in which overgrowth of bacteria in the loop encourages bacterial consumption of dietary vitamin B_{12} (Cameron *et al.* 1949). Similarly, intestinal infestation with fish tapeworm, a disorder not uncommon in parts of northern Europe and America, can lead to preferential consumption of vitamin B_{12} by parasitic worms (Nyberg 1958).

Public health programmes are of importance in the control of vitamin B_{12} deficiency more through support of health care programmes which provide detection and treatment of macrocytic anaemia than through improved nutrition. Work to control parasitic infestations can also be of importance where fish tapeworms are prevalent.

Other dietary deficiencies

In addition to iron, folate and vitamin B_{12}, deficiency of dietary protein may play a general role in encouraging the development of anaemia in malnourished populations (Drenick *et al.* 1964). There is also experimental evidence in animals that deficiency in certain other vitamins and trace elements (copper, cobalt, pyridoxine, and riboflavin) may lead to anaemia, although direct evidence in humans is lacking (Williams 1982).

Aplastic anaemia

In addition to nutritional deficiencies, inadequate red cell production can result from various conditions in which haematopoiesis is either slowed (insufficient erythropoiesis) or disrupted (ineffective erythropoiesis) (Williams 1982). Aplastic anaemia, or marrow hypoplasia, in which blood cell production becomes insufficient to meet body needs, can result from exposure to numerous toxic agents and from exposure to ionizing radiation. Although such illnesses are uncommon, control of the exposures which cause them (and other illnesses at the same time) is of great public health importance. Marrow suppression can lead to pancytopenia, insufficiency of all three structural elements of blood (red cells, white cells, and platelets), or to predominant deficiency of single elements (thrombocytopenia, leukopenia, or pure red cell aplasia) (Wintrobe 1981).

The marrow suppression effects of ionizing radiation develop in a matter of weeks after exposure to relatively high single doses (several hundred rads or more) (Wald *et al.*

1962). The radiation may be from external sources (X-ray) or may be internal (ingestion of radioisotopes). Lower doses of radiation or fractionated doses received over a period of time may be associated with delayed effects such as cancer. Public health protection against radiation hazards centres on proper design and use of medical radiation technology (X-ray machines, training of technologists), on control and monitoring of radiation uses and worker exposures in industry, and on systems for sequestering nuclear wastes, guaranteeing safe transport of radioactive materials, and maintaining surveillance of possible radiation exposures from operations using nuclear power (nuclear power plants, fallout, etc.).

Chemical agents that can cause aplastic anaemia include benzene and its derivatives, and an extensive list of present and past therapeutic agents. Benzene is of particular public health importance both because of its wide and varied uses in industry, leading to frequent possibilities for occupational exposure (Elkins and Pagnatta 1956), and because it is a common ingredient used to boost fuel power in gasoline in lieu of lead additives. The antimicrobial agent chloramphenicol has been strongly linked to development of aplastic anaemia because of which its use should be greatly limited. Other marrow-toxic agents include arsenicals, quinine (with its wide application for malaria control), and certain anticonvulsants (Custer 1946; Witkind and Waid 1951; Wintrobe 1981; and Williams 1982).

Sideroblastic anaemia

Disorders grouped here as sideroblastic anaemia constitute miscellaneous disorders of red cell production that share in common the morphological feature of sideroblasts, or red cell precursors which contain perinuclear rings of deposited iron granules resulting from a relative excess of iron uptake in the presence of disordered haeme synthesis. The causes of this metabolic defect are varied, often obscure, and in some instances heritable. Familial anaemias of this sort are often responsive to treatment with pyridoxine (Horrigen and Harris 1964; MacGibbon and Mollin 1965; Kushner *et al.* 1971; Bottomley 1977). Of importance for public health is the fact that sideroblastic anaemia may result from exposure to drugs, such as isonicotinic acid hydrazide (INH) used in tuberculosis therapy (Biehl and Vilter 1954), from alcohol abuse (Eichner and Hillman 1971), and especially in relation to lead exposure (Mollin 1965) which represents a major, widespread public hazard. Lead interferes with erythropoiesis in various ways, including cell membrane injury (leading to mild haemolysis), impaired globin synthesis, and defective haeme production (Westerman *et al.* 1965; Waxman and Rabinovitz 1966). An enzymatic reflection of the latter abnormality, free erythrocyte protoporphyrin (FEP), is commonly used, together with blood lead levels, for screening exposed populations for preclinical evidence of excessive lead exposure. Clinical signs of lead poisoning can appear at blood lead levels of 80 mg/dl. Since subclinical damage can occur at lower levels, however, public health efforts must be maintained to reduce blood levels, especially in children, to below 30 mg/dl.

Porphyrias

Although not frequent or of great public health importance, the porphyrias deserve brief mention because of their occasional association (acquired porphyria cutanea tarda) with exposure to toxic organic chemicals such as polychlorinated biphenyls (PCB), hexachlorobenzene, tetrachlorodibenzodioxin (TCDD), and the pesticide, 2,4,5-trichlorophenoxyacetic acid (2,4,5-T). Misuse of such chemicals has in the past been associated with epidemic porphyria (Schmid 1960), and the potential for this to happen again obviously remains. Porphyrias arise from enzymatic disturbances in haeme synthesis, and their clinical manifestations relate to excessive accumulation of porphyrin by-products. Many such abnormalities represent inherited enzymatic defects. Chemical-induced porphyria appears to result particularly from interference with the enzyme uroporphyrinogen decarboxylase which converts uroporphyrins to coproporphyrins.

Secondary anaemias

A major source of anaemia, and one of prime importance for clinical differential diagnosis, is other systemic illness. Such secondary involvement of haematopoietic tissues is frequent and can take the form of haemolysis (excess red cell destruction) as well as inadequate or depressed marrow production. Anaemia is therefore a common feature in cases of cancer (often as the result of marrow infiltration by cancer cells), endocrine disorders, renal disease and uraemia, hepatic cirrhosis, and chronic infection and inflammation. The public health importance of these forms of anaemia rests with the control of underlying disease processes. In developing countries particularly, a substantial proportion of anaemias may reflect persistently high prevalence rates of infectious diseases.

Excessive red cell destruction

Haemolysis is the physiological process by which red blood cells are destroyed, marrow production of new red cells being balanced against removal of old red cells from the circulation. The average normal lifespan of the red cell is about 120 days (Lajtha and Oliver 1960). Since the normal bone marrow can increase its red cell production about six- to eight-fold, a decrease in red cell life span or survival to as little as 15–20 days can be accommodated by the body without development of anaemia (Wintrobe 1981; Williams 1982). Haemolytic disease, like iron deficiency, therefore, can be classified according to the presence or absence of anaemia. Haemolysis can be intravascular (occur within the blood vessel system itself) or extravascular (occur in tissues, usually through the action of tissue macrophages).

The causes of haemolysis can be divided into those which are inherited or genetically determined and those which are acquired or caused by environmental events (Table 13.3). Generally, inherited forms of haemolysis arise from abnormalities intrinsic to or present within the red cell itself (abnormalities in its membrane or its molecular constituents) while acquired forms result from conditions extrinsic to or outside the cell.

Table 13.3. *Conditions involving excessive red cell destruction*

Inherited conditions
Abnormalities of globin structure and synthesis
  Sickle-cell disease and other haemoglobinopathies
  Thalassaemia

Abnormalities of red cell membrane
  Hereditary spherocytosis
  Hereditary elliptocytosis

Abnormalities of red cell metabolism
  Anaerobic glycolysis: pyruvate kinase (PK) deficiency, etc.
  Nucleotide metabolism
  Glutathione metabolism and the pentose phosphate shunt: glucose 6-phosphate dehydrogenase (G6PD) deficiency, etc.

Acquired conditions
Immunological abnormalities
  Autoimmune haemolysis
  Haemolytic disease of the newborn (HDN): ABO incompatibility, Rh incompatibility

Environmental exposures
  Chemicals, drugs, toxins, infection, trauma, physical agents

Abnormalities of globin structure (haemoglobinopathies)

Inherited abnormalities of haemoglobin are a major source of haemolytic disease throughout the world. Haemoglobin is a combination of haeme which contains iron and of globin which is a protein consisting of two double polypeptide chains. Abnormalities in the structure or synthesis of either peptide chain can lead to decreased red cell survival through increased haemolysis. Structural globin abnormalities arise when single amino acid substitutions occur in normal chains (Williams 1982). These substitutions are genetically determined, and they form the molecular basis for identifying structural haemoglobin variants.

Although many variants have been identified, all are rare except for four: S, C, D, and E haemoglobins. Of these, S or sickle haemoglobin is by far the most widespread. It occurs across tropical sub-Sahelian Africa with prevalence rates as high as 50 per cent in certain East African tribes. It also exists in Mediterranean countries, in the Middle East, in southern India, and in the US and other western countries which contain populations of African origin (Allison 1961). Genetical studies suggest that S haemoglobin may have arisen from single gene mutations in Africa or the Middle East. It exists in either heterozygous or homozygous states. The latter is called sickle-cell anaemia and the former sickle-cell trait. Persons homozygous for the S gene exhibit frank haemolytic anaemia while heterozygous individuals develop active haemolysis under conditions of physiological stress or hypoxia (Williams 1982). About 8 per cent of American blacks carry the S gene, and the frequency of the homozygous condition (sickle-cell anaemia) is estimated at birth at about one in 600–700 blacks. In addition to enduring varying degrees of anaemia, persons with sickle-cell anaemia have increased risk for secondary illness and have a shortened life expectancy (Went and MacIver 1958; Charache and Richardson 1964). Anaemia results from splenic sequestration and destruction of red cells distorted by their structural haemoglobin abnormality into bizarre sickle-like shapes.

The perpetuation of the S variant is postulated to be the result of a balanced polymorphism whereby intense exposure to falciparum malaria in Africa may be counteracted by the relative resistance of S haemoglobin red cells to malarial parasitic infection or by the preferential destruction of such cells when parasitized. This cell-parasite interplay may have encouraged the evolutionary persistence of the S haemoglobin gene, as well as those of other genetical variants of haemoglobin structure and synthesis (thalassaemia). In support of this concept are observations showing lower rates of blood parasitization in persons with sickle trait living in regions endemic for malaria (Allison 1957).

Haemoglobin C is found principally in sharply defined regions in West Africa, Haemoglobin D in certain populations in the Indian Punjab, and haemoglobin E throughout much of South-east Asia, especially parts of Thailand and Kampuchea (Flatz 1967). Intermingling of populations gives rise to occasional cases of mixed haemoglobin variants such as so-called S-C disease and S-thalassaemia (Kaplan et al. 1951; Weatherall 1965). Public health measures to reduce health impairment by sickle-cell disease and related haemoglobinopathies is limited at present to programmes of health education and genetic counselling (Evatt et al. 1982).

Abnormalities of globin synthesis (thalassaemia)

Thalassaemia is so named because it was first described among persons from Italy and other countries bordering the Mediterranean Sea (Valentine and Neel 1944). Patients with major clinical illness and haemolytic anaemia were originally described as having thalassaemia major while their parents or other relatives in whom only morphological red cell abnormalities were found in the absence of frank illness or anaemia were said to have thalassaemia minor. Later investigations showed these disorders to involve heritable defects in the quantitative synthesis of one or the other globin polypeptide chains. This familial trait is now known to exist widely in populations from the Mediterranean basin to the Indian subcontinent and the Far East. Prevalence of all thalassaemias, whether homozygous (thalassaemia major) or heterozygous (thalassaemia minor), varies in these regions from 5 to 35 per cent. Public health control of thalassaemia, as with the haemoglobinopathies, rests at present only with health education programmes, support for health care systems, and provision of diagnostic and genetic counselling services.

Abnormalities of the red cell membrane

Aside from disorders of globin structure and synthesis, two other important forms of inherited haemolytic disease exist, those which arise from abnormalities in the red cell membrane, and those that relate to abnormalities in red cell metabolism. Membrane abnormalities include principally the disorders of hereditary spherocytosis (congenital spherocytic anaemia) and hereditary elliptocytosis (Bannerman and Renwick 1962). Both are transmitted as autosomal dominant traits. Although hereditary elliptocytosis is about twice as prevalent as spherocytosis in the general population (about 4 cases per 10 000), most affected individuals are free of clinical illness, and haemolytic diseae when it occurs is relatively mild (Geerdink et al. 1966). The more frequent and often more severe haemolysis seen in hereditary spherocytosis is dramatically responsive to splenectomy, while splenectomy has only variable success in the treatment of hereditary elliptocytosis (Lipton 1955). The fundamental membrane lesion and subsequent mechanism of haemolysis are not clearly understood in either disorder.

Morphologically, however, red cells in each disorder lose their normal biconcave shape and become spherical or oval and elliptical. This change in shape is associated with altered cell membrane permeability and with greater sequestration and destruction of cells, primarily in the spleen (Young 1955). Although the relative frequency of these haemolytic conditions make them of importance for public health, their control or prevention at present rest with adequate health education, genetic counselling, and health care provision.

Abnormalities in red cell metabolism

Three groups of inherited abnormalities in red cell metabolic enzymes are associated with haemolytic disease: those affecting enzymes involved in anaerobic glycolysis, those affecting nucleotide metabolism, and those affecting glutathione metabolism and the pentose phosphate pathway. With one exception (glucose 6-phosphate dehydrogenase or G6PD deficiency), such disorders are rare. Of those affecting enzymes in the anaerobic glycolysis pathway, pyruvate kinase (PK) deficiency has been most intensively studied. It is inherited as an autosomal recessive trait and has been described primarily in persons of northern European origin (Valentine and Tanaka 1978). Also related to abnormal red cell metabolism may be the uncommon acquired condition of paroxysmal nocturnal haemoglobinuria (PNH), in which episodic haemolysis occurs, often during sleep. The disease is thought to be caused by a somatic mutation in marrow producing an abnormal clone of intrinsically defective red cells (Wintrobe 1981).

Deficiency of G6PD exists in much the same regions and populations as thalassaemia and sickle-cell disease (populations in or derived from central Africa, the Mediterranean basin, the Middle East, India, and the Orient). As with such haemoglobin disorders, deficiency in G6PD activity is postulated to have evolved as a red cell trait which confers resistance against falciparum malaria infection (Luzzato et al. 1969). At least 100 million persons are affected with the enzyme disorder, frequencies ranging in different populations from less than 1 to over 20 per cent (Williams 1982).

Glucose 6-phosphate dehydrogenase serves both as the first step in the aerobic pentose phosphate pathway and as an essential agent for maintaining glutathione in its reduced state. The latter function prevents the oxidative denaturation of haemoglobin and thus protects the red cell's capacity to transport oxygen. Deficiency in G6PD activity reflects the presence of genetically determined mutant enzyme forms. More than 140 such variants have been described.

The genes which control their synthesis and structure are transmitted as a sex-linked recessive characteristic and are associated on the X-chromosome with genes for haemophilia A and colour blindness (Childs *et al.* 1958).

Most persons in whom G6PD deficiency exists have no clinical illness from it. In others, severe anaemia may either occur episodically or persist chronically and be lifelong (Wintrobe 1981). Haemolysis may be precipitated by exposure to particular oxidative drugs, by episodes of diabetic acidosis, by infections of different sorts, or by ingestion of the fava bean (Luisoda 1941). Haemolysis associated with the fava bean (favism) has long been recognized in Mediterranean countries where the bean is commonly consumed (Kattamis *et al.* 1969). Drugs which can induce haemolysis include various sulphur-containing medications and antimalarial compounds such as primaquine (Dern *et al.* 1955). Haemolysis occurring in the absence of drug use or of fava bean ingestion has been termed 'congenital nonspherocytic haemolytic anaemia', an entity which also encompasses haemolytic anaemias associated with other red cell enzyme defects (Beutler *et al.* 1968).

No specific public health measures are at hand to correct G6PD and related enzyme deficiencies. Their control at present is therefore a matter for health education, genetic counselling, promotion of careful medication use in susceptible patients, and prevention of infectious diseases to the extent that they may precipitate haemolytic episodes.

Immunological abnormalities

Excessive red cell destruction can arise from immunological reactions between red cells and antibodies produced against them by the host's own immune system. Such autoimmune processes occur infrequently in a variety of conditions such as cancer, viral infections, drug reactions, and immune disorders such as lupus erythematosis (Dacie 1967). Such cell–antibody interactions are often classified according to their dependence on temperature (warm and cold reactive autoantibodies) (Williams 1982).

Another form of immunological abnormality is haemolytic disease of the newborn (HDN) which results from the action of maternal antibodies against fetal red cells and which reflects genetic differences in maternal–fetal cell antigens. The illness appears with a frequency of about six cases per 1000 births, and affects approximately one in every 15 pregnancies at risk (Mallison 1972). Immune reactions occur principally in relation to the ABO and Rh red cell antigen systems. Thus the importance of HDN for public health relates to its relative frequency and to the availability of methods for treatment and prevention. Although maternal-fetal ABO incompatibility causes most cases, illness resulting from Rh incompatibility is considerably more severe. The disease in its severe form can lead to fetal death or to cerebral damage after birth from progressive hyperbilirubinaemia (kernicterus) (Van Proagh 1961). Prompt neonatal exchange transfusion can effectively prevent damage caused by bilirubin accumulation by keeping the serum bilirubin level below 15–20 mg/ml (Van Proagh 1961).

Nearly all cases of disease due to ABO incompatibility occur in infants of blood group O mothers, since only in such individuals are anti-A and anti-B isoantibodies sufficiently small (IgG as opposed to IgM) to cross the placental barrier (Abelson and Rawson 1961). Since ABO isoantibodies exist naturally and do not require prior maternal sensitization for their production, first as well as later pregnancies in Group O mothers are at risk of HDN. With Rh incompatibility, however, anti-Rh antibody production requires maternal sensitization by cross-placental passage of Rh-positive fetal red cells into the Rh-negative maternal circulation (Williams 1982). Haemolytic disease of the newborne due to Rh incompatibility occurs, therefore, with increasing frequency in second and later pregnancies. Initial sensitization and resensitization in later pregnancies is dependent on the number of fetal cells which cross-circulate. Prevention of this immune reaction rests with prophylactic passive immunization of all Rh-negative mothers with hyperimmune anti-Rh gammaglobulin given within three days following delivery of an Rh-positive infant, following miscarriage or abortion, or during pregnancy if specific evidence of fetal–maternal transfusion exists (Freda *et al.* 1963). Such immunization effectively clears the maternal circulation of Rh-positive fetal cells which might otherwise cause lasting maternal sensitization. Public health programmes concerned with maternal and child health should stress the importance of Rh-immune globulin and should promote its universal application.

Environmental exposures

Haemolysis occurs in association with a wide range of environmental exposures: infectious agents, chemical toxins, drugs, venoms, thermal injury, and ionizing radiation. Many of these exposures are discussed earlier in this chapter to the extent that they cause haemolysis by inducing enzyme deficiency (G6PD deficiency) or by stimulating anti-red cell autoantibodies. Others cause marrow hypoplasia (ionizing radiation, benzene) or disordered erythropoiesis (lead) with or without accompanying haemolysis. There remains a group of rare haemolytic conditions in which direct environmental cell injury appears to produce increased red cell destruction. This can occur in connection with many forms of infectious disease, including malaria, toxoplasmosis, clostridial sepsis, and other microbial infections (Dacie 1967). Oxidant drugs may affect red cell survival directly as well as through mechanisms of underlying enzyme deficiency (Dacie 1967), and direct red cell damage can be caused by various toxic chemicals (arsine) (Jenkins *et al.* 1965) and by venoms from the bites of certain spiders, bees, and snakes (Rubenberg *et al.* 1968). Haemolysis can also follow massive thermal burns and can occur as part of the haematological reaction to high doses of ionizing radiation (Lawrence *et al.* 1948). Public health programmes directed at infectious disease control and at safeguards against radiation and chemical exposure (especially in occupational settings) have obvious implications for prevention in this area of red cell disease.

Other red cell disorders

Two types of red cell disorders which do not involve either

haemolysis or inadequate red cell production are erythrocytosis (polycythaemia) and acute conditions in which the capacity of haemoglobin to bind oxygen is compromised. Erythrocytosis can reflect a relative increase in the red cell compartment because of acute plasma loss or can constitute an absolute increase in red cell mass. Absolute erythrocytosis is seen either with prolonged decrease in blood oxygenation leading to a compensatory proliferation of red blood cells or by uncontrolled cell proliferation as in polycythaemia rubra vera (or erythraemia), a rare condition in which idiopathic red cell proliferation is accompanied by increased numbers of granulocytes and platelets. The aetiology of polycythaemia rubra vera is probably related to that of the granulocytic leukaemias (Stohlman 1966).

Absolute erythrocytosis secondary to hypoxia results from conditions which diminish tissue oxygen supplies: various chronic pulmonary diseases, right-to-left cardiopulmonary shunts, hypoventilation, and the mere fact of living at high altitudes where atmospheric oxygen tension is reduced (Winslow 1984). None of these forms of secondary erythrocytosis occurs commonly, and none is of major public health concern, except perhaps for that related to populations living at high altitudes.

Disorders which interfere with the binding of oxygen to haemoglobin to form oxyhaemoglobin include carboxyhaemoglobinaemia, sulphaemoglobinaemia, and acquired methaemoglobinaemia, in addition to various rare inherited haemoglobin anomalies. Acquired methaemoglobinaemia results from exposure to chemicals capable of oxidizing haemoglobin from its ferrous form (oxyhaemoglobin) to its ferric form (methaemoglobin). Of particular public health interest are nitrates which may occur in high concentration in food and water. In the intestine, nitrates are reduced to nitrites which in turn can act to oxidize haemoglobin to methaemoglobin (Bodansky 1951). The resulting tissue hypoxia can be fatal, especially in infants receiving feedings mixed with well water high in nitrates (Comly 1945).

Carboxyhaemoglobin and sulphaemoglobin represent the combination of carbon monoxide and sulphur compounds with haemoglobin. Sulphaemoglobin arises from the action of various oxidative drugs (Lemberg and Legge 1949), while carboxyhaemoglobin comes largely from inhaling the partial combustion products of organic materials. Because the latter process is an ever-present hazard of industrial wastes and of inadequately ventilated internal combustion engines, it represents a particular concern for public and occupational health (Loumanmaki and Coburn 1969). Because carbon monoxide is both colourless and odourless, its effect on haemoglobin can often rise to fatal levels without warning.

DISORDERS OF HAEMOSTASIS AND BLOOD COAGULATION

The methods which the body uses to arrest bleeding have three components: the process by which blood vessels constrict and repair themselves after damage, the role of platelets in sealing endothelial breaks, and the action of

Table 13.4. *Disorders of haemostasis and blood coagulation*

Vascular abnormalities
  Allergic purpura: ?autoimmune process
  Drug-associated purpura
  Infection-associated purpura
  Hereditary haemorrhagic telangiectasia
  Scurvy: vitamin C deficiency
  Senile purpura

Platelet abnormalities
  Idiopathic or immune thrombocytopenic purpura (ITP)
  Secondary thrombocytopenic purpura: infection, drugs, chemicals, other diseases

Plasma protein abnormalities
  Factor VIII disorders
    Haemophilia A
    Von Willebrand's disease
  Factor IX deficiency: haemophilia B (Christmas disease)
  Vitamin K deficiency

plasma proteins in building fibrin clots. The major haemorrhagic disorders can be considered under three headings (Table 13.4) and can also be classified according to whether they arise from hereditary causes or reflect acquired environmental aetiology.

Vascular abnormalities

Bleeding can result from a variety of conditions which damage blood vessels and their supporting tissues. Purpura is not uncommonly associated with a wide range of infections and medications. Allergic purpura occurs probably as the result of autoimmune reactions which lead to inflammation around capillaries and small vessels. Such disease principally affects children (Sterky and Thilen 1960). At the other end of the age scale, senile purpura reflects degenerative changes in collagen and tissues supporting dermal blood vessels. In scurvy, deficiency of vitamin C leads to collagen and connective tissue degeneration, producing gingival haemorrhages as well as bleeding in muscles and subcutaneous tissues.

Vascular haemorrhage can also occur as a hereditary disorder. Hereditary haemorrhagic telangiectasia is a vascular anomaly inherited as an autosomal dominant trait and characterized by thin-walled vascular nexi which are prone to bleed with minimal trauma (Bird and Jaques 1959). Although none of these vascular purpuric diseases, acquired or inherited, is common, the occurrence of many of them can be affected by public health programmes directed at infectious disease control, full nutrition, and genetic counselling.

Platelet abnormalities

A common cause of purpura and bleeding is thrombocytopenia, whether it appears alone or in conjunction with anaemia and leukopenia (pancytopenia). Thrombocytopenia can occur either without any obvious predisposing cause (idiopathic or immune thrombocytopenic purpura or ITP) or secondary to a wide range of infections, reactions to drugs, and miscellaneous diseases. Whether the disorder is idiopathic or is secondary to a predisposing event or illness, autoimmune mechanisms are generally considered to underly the reduction in platelets. Idiopathic thrombocytopenia purpura is most commonly encountered in children and young adults.

Hereditary disorders of blood coagulation

Hereditary disorders of plasma clotting factors are relatively infrequent (perhaps one case per 10 000 persons) and as a group may be the least common of all haemorrhagic diseases. Their dramatic and recurrent clinical features, however, together with the insights they provide for understanding blood coagulation, have earned them particular scientific and public health attention. They represent a series of genetic disorders resulting in qualitative or quantitative abnormalities of individual plasma proteins which constitute the so-called clotting factors. The most frequent of these disorders are abnormalities affecting factor VIII: haemophilia A and Von Willebrand's disease.

Haemophilia A, or classical haemophilia, accounts for 80 per cent or more of disorders called haemophilia. It is inherited as a sex-linked recessive trait. Since the underlying mutation rate is relatively high, about 20–30 per cent of cases appear without a preceding family history of abnormal bleeding. Although most cases occur in males (because of its sex-linked recessive nature), female cases are seen on occasion from matings between affected males and heterozygous females, and more often in heterozygous females with unusually low levels of factor VIII resulting from early embryonic-chromosome inactivation (Graham 1968). Detection of female carriers, an important tool for genetic counselling, depends upon measuring factor VIII levels directly and by immunoassay.

Haemophilia A is characterized by repeated episodes of haemorrhage in various tissues, often after only minimal trauma. Clinical severity can differ widely among cases but is relatively consistent within families. Haemarthroses, or bleeding within joints, is the most common form of bleeding, and it can produce particularly severe discomfort and secondary disability. Other common bleeding sites are in subcutaneous, intramuscular, gastrointestinal, and genitourinary tissues. Intracranial haemorrhage is a common cause of death. Preventive treatment consists of intravenous administration of purified factor VIII concentrate at the earliest sign of bleeding. The availability of such clotting factor concentrates and their effectiveness in promptly arresting haemorrhage in patients with heritable clotting defects has led to their widespread use at home by patients themselves or their relatives. The recurring need in such patients for intravenous protein concentrates or for blood to replace haemorrhage loss is accompanied by increased risk of infusion-related illnesses (serum hepatitis, acquired immune deficiency syndrome, etc.) (Ministry of Health 1954).

Von Willebrand's disease involves a deficiency in factor VIII which is largely transmitted as an autosomal dominant trait and which affects both the coagulation capacity of factor VIII and its role in the normal functioning of platelets. The illness is perhaps as frequent as haemophilia A, but its chemical manifestations, although similar, are generally more mild (Williams 1982).

Haemophilia B, sometimes known as Christmas disease, represents deficiency of factor IX and accounts for about 10–15 per cent of all so-called haemophilias (Williams 1982). Like haemophilia A, it is inherited as a sex-linked recessive trait but not linked to the X-chromosome genes affecting factor VIII. Clinical features are similar to haemophilia A, but perhaps less severe.

Modern methods of clinical management have enabled most haemophiliacs to lead near-normal lives if they receive prompt and appropriate therapy for bleeding episodes. Such therapy, however, is expensive, and since costs are largely reimbursed through health insurance or welfare, society carries the brunt of the financial burden (National Institutes of Health 1972).

Clinical complications of haemorrhage associated with haemophilia add significantly to this cost. The most expensive problems are orthopaedic. If severe, such problems often limit the ability of patients to find productive work and therefore can lead to economic dependence on government resources. Such economic costs may greatly exceed direct clinical costs. Many disabling problems, however, can be minimized or eliminated through early treatment and by the use of co-ordinated comprehensive care facilities. Public health approaches to the management of haemophilia should promote the availability of adequate clinical resources to forestall chronic orthopaedic impairment and to provide genetic counselling, preventive dental services, and immunization against transfusion-acquired viral hepatitis.

Acquired disorders of blood coagulation

Various conditions are associated with acquired impairment of blood coagulation. Since such diseases commonly interfere with several different mechanisms of haemostasis and clotting, they can present quite complex clinical situations. This is particularly true of severe liver disease which may be associated with thrombocytopenia and platelet dysfunction as well as with impaired biosynthesis and metabolism of many proteins necessary for blood clotting (Finkbiner et al. 1959).

A second category of acquired coagulation disorder involves deficiency of vitamin K. Since prothrombin (factor II) and clotting factors VII, IX, and X all require the presence of vitamin K for their synthesis in liver, deficiency in this vitamin can cause haemorrhagic illness by various chemical routes. Deficiency may result from severe nutritional restrictions in malnourished populations, from malabsorption in various intestinal diseases (sprue, ulcerative colitis, etc.), and from the action of drugs of different sorts (Moore et al. 1956). Of particular public health concern is vitamin K deficiency in newborn infants, reflecting a relative lack of gut bacteria to synthesize the vitamin (Aballi et al. 1959). Such deficiency was once a major cause of newborn bleeding (haemorrhagic disease of the newborn), especially in premature infants. The routine administration of vitamin K at birth now prevents this disease, although it remains a public health problem in impoverished and malnourished populations.

Thrombotic disorders

Thrombotic disorders (cerebral thrombosis, coronary thrombosis, peripheral vascular disease) are at present collectively the leading cause of morbidity and mortality in developed countries. These disorders therefore are a major public concern and one to which a large share of modern medical resources are directed. The causes and pathogenetic mechanisms of thrombotic disease are still largely obscure (Mason *et al.* 1981; Williams 1982). A few primary causes of thrombosis, accounting for a small proportion of cases, have been defined: deficiencies in clotting-inhibition factors (anti-thrombin III, protein C) (Griffin *et al.* 1981), abnormal fibrinogens, low plasminogens, polycythaemia, essential thrombocytosis, and various congenital abnormalities of collagen (Harker and Ross 1979). Numerous other factors which also contribute to risk of thrombosis have been studied extensively: cigarette smoking, stress, and various aspects of diet and life-style. Current public health strategies for prevention of thrombotic disorders focus on modification of such factors primarily through techniques of health education. Hopefully, continued research regarding the causes of thrombotic disease will eventually lead to improved methods for primary disease prevention.

DISORDERS OF WHITE BLOOD CELLS

Diseases arising in white blood cells, with the exception of infectious mononucleosis, consist principally of malignant conditions: leukaemias, lymphomas, and plasma cell dyscrasias (monoclonal gammopathies). None of these diseases occurs commonly by itself, and their collective incidence in the US in 1973–77 was estimated at 25.7 cases per 100 000 population per year (Table 13.5), only about 8 per cent of total cancer incidence (Young and Pollack 1982). Despite this relatively low level of occurrence, white cell malignancies are of considerable public health importance because they continue to provide a major focus for studies of cancer causation. The clinical diagnosis of leukaemias and lymphomas requires that they be distinguished from the far more frequent changes seen in blood, marrow, and lymphoid tissue in response to infection of inflammation (leukocytosis, leukaemoid reaction, lymphadenitis).

Infectious mononucleosis

Infectious mononucleosis (IM) is an acute, self-limited illness caused by a herpes virus, the Epstein–Barr virus (EBV), which principally infects lymphocytes. Illness is characterized by fever, malaise, and pharyngitis with frequent enlargement of lymph nodes and spleen. Patients show absolute lymphocytosis with atypical lymphocyte forms in peripheral blood, a rise in antibodies reactive against heterologous (sheep) red blood cells (heterophile antibodies), and a rise in anti-EBV antibodies (Wintrobe 1981).

Infection of lymphocytes with EBV is virtually universal in all human populations, but it produces illness (IM) primarily in young, white adults (age 17–25 years), in upper socio-economic groups, and in developed countries. Illness affects both sexes equally, but women at a slightly younger age than

Table 13.5. *Relative frequencies of malignant diseases of white blood cells by sex and race, United States, 1973–77*

| White cell malignancy | Average annual age-adjusted incidence rates per 100 000 persons* | | | | |
	Total	Sex Male	Female	Race White	Black
Leukaemias	9.8	12.8	7.7	9.9	8.6
Acute leukaemias	4.4	5.3	3.7	4.5	3.2
Chronic granulocytic leukaemia	1.4	1.8	1.1	1.4	1.5
Chronic lymphocytic leukaemia	2.7	3.8	2.0	2.8	2.6
Other leukaemias	1.3	1.9	0.9	1.2	1.3
Lymphomas	12.0	14.0	10.3	12.3	7.9
Hodgkin's disease	3.0	3.5	2.4	3.1	2.0
Non-Hodgkin's lymphoma	9.0	10.4	7.9	9.3	5.8
Multiple myeloma	3.9	4.7	3.3	3.5	7.9
Total	25.7	31.5	21.3	25.7	24.4

*Age-adjusted to 1970 standard.
Source: SEER Program data, National Cancer Institute (Young and Pollack 1982).

men (Heath *et al.* 1972). This contrast between ubiquitous infection and selective illness appears to reflect the fact that EBV spreads by way of close interpersonal contact but with different clinical consequences in different settings. Under lower socio-economic living conditions (crowding, etc.), where close personal contact may be more intense early in life, nearly all persons are infected in early childhood or before puberty. Such infections are nearly always asymptomatic.

In higher socio-economic settings, however, where crowding and interpersonal contact may be less intense, infection often does not occur until after puberty. Unlike prepubertal infection, about 10 per cent of post-pubertal or adult EBV infections are accompanied by the clinical picture of IM. In adolescents or young adults, interpersonal viral spread is often associated with the mingling of oral secretions through kissing. The virus has been shown to be shed from pharyngeal lymphoid tissue as long as 18 months after primary infection. It appears to persist in lymphoid cells throughout life and can also be transmitted by blood transfusion. The latent period for development of IM after EBV infection can range from one to two months. The frequency of IM is highest in school, college, and university students, and the disease represents a major health problem for university student health departments (Brodsky and Heath 1972).

Infection with EBV seems also related to the development of at least two malignant tumours: Burkitt's lymphoma (BL) and undifferentiated nasopharyngeal carcinoma (NPC). The exact relationship of EBV infection to the pathogenesis of NPC is unclear, although both NPC and BL are regularly associated with high levels of anti-EBV antibodies. As discussed later in this chapter, BL conceivably may arise from the action of EBV in a host whose immune responses are affected by intense malarial infection. Since EBV infects primarily lymphoid cells, its relationship to lymphoid tumours and to the immunological conditions in which such tumours may arise is of great medical interest. Of possible importance in this regard is the observation that risk of Hodgkin's disease is somewhat increased in persons with a past medical history of IM (Kvale *et al.* 1979).

No public health measures have yet been developed for prevention of IM or for modification of EBV infection, although the feasibility of immunization against herpes infections is being explored (de-The 1979). Infections of EBV remain of particular public health interest both because of their widespread occurrence and because of their potential relation to the causation of different diseases.

Leukaemias

Leukaemias are characterized by the presence of malignant white cells in circulating blood. Cases are classified histopathologically by type of white cell (granulocyte, lymphocyte, monocyte, etc.) and by degree of cell maturity. Although terminology varies and many different types of leukaemia have been described, three major varieties stand out: chronic granulocytic leukaemia (CGL), chronic lymphocytic leukaemia (CLL), and the acute leukaemias (AL). In contrast to CGL and CLL where most leukaemic cells appear mature or differentiated, cells involved in AL are young or primitive (largely undifferentiated blast or stem cells), although often their cell line origin can be identified (lymphoblast, myeloblast, etc.).

Presenting clinical features can vary widely but commonly include anaemia (from various causes), thrombocytopenia, haemorrhage, lymphadenopathy, hepatomegaly, and splenomegaly. Advances in therapy have greatly improved remission rates and survival times for chronic leukaemias and for certain forms of childhood leukaemia.

Overall leukaemia incidence, like that for most cancers, increases dramatically with age. Annual rates rise from about one to two cases per 100 000 in young adults to 30 or more cases per 100 000 over age 50 years (Young and Pollack 1982). Unlike other cancers, however, leukaemia incidence displays a childhood peak in which annual incidence rises to about five cases per 100 000 between age two and four years before decreasing in later childhood. Although the cause of this childhood pattern is unclear, it may conceivably reflect particular leukaemogenic influences affecting the fetus during pregnancy.

Age patterns also vary by leukaemic cell type: CLL, like certain forms of lymphoma to which it may well be closely related, is rarely seen before age 50 years. However, CGL, although primarily an adult disease, occurs in younger adults and occasionally appears in children. At all ages, AL is the most common form of leukaemia, accounting for the great majority of childhood cases and for about half of all adult cases. Childhood AL is predominantly lymphoblastic or undifferentiated (stem cell), while granulocytic (myeloblastic) cell types predominate in adults. Leukaemias are somewhat more frequent in males than in females, particularly CLL (Table 13.5). This male predeliction may partly reflect the influence of occupational leukaemogens. Rates in whites are generally higher than those in blacks (Table 13.5), a racial difference which may be more a matter of socio-

economic differences than genetic makeup. Genetic constitution, however, may well account for the fact that CLL and related forms of lymphoma are extraordinarily rare in Oriental populations (Heath 1976).

Although leukaemia incidence, adjusted for age, has risen dramatically since the early 1900s, much of this rise may be due to improved diagnostic methods and increased clinical recognition. Some of the increase may also reflect increasing opportunity for exposure to radiation and chemicals in industrialized society. Efforts to prevent such exposures may partly account for slight declines in rates among whites in recent years. The increasing lifespan of modern populations, of course, is accompanied by increasing numbers of age dependent cancers such as leukaemias and lymphomas, despite stability or decline in age-specific rates.

Geographical differences in leukaemia incidence are not as great as those for many other cancers. Age-adjusted rates, however, do vary as much as two- to four-fold between countries (Muir and Nectoux 1982). Some of these differences may reflect variable genetic susceptibility as in the case of CLL in Orientals. Other differences may come from socioeconomic variations to the extent that these relate to opportunities for exposure to environmental leukaemogens.

Genetic factors

The aetiology of white cell malignancies, like cancers generally, involves a variety of different host and environmental factors, most of which are not yet clearly understood. Genetic constitution is one important influence. Although not a strongly familial disease, leukaemia does occasionally recur in families and there is some evidence that consanguinity may increase leukaemia risk (Heath 1976). The striking tendency for childhood leukaemia to be concordant in monozygous twins, however, may be more a reflection of shared placental circulation than genetic predisposition.

The tendency for leukaemias to occur in association with chromosome abnormalities and with certain hereditary diseases, also suggests the importance of genetic causation. Evidence includes the fact that CGL is almost always associated with an abnormal chromosome in myeloid cells (Ph[1] chromosome), that the incidence of AL is greatly increased in persons with Down's syndrome (G trisomy) and, perhaps, in other meiotic disorders, and that leukaemias occur with increased frequency in certain hereditary conditions associated with increased chromosomal fragility (Bloom syndrome, Fanconi anaemia) (Hecht and McCaw 1977). The occurrence of lymphocytic leukaemias is also increased in certain inherited immunological disorders (ataxia talangiectasia, X-linked agammaglobulinaemia) (Spector *et al.* 1978). This latter association reinforces the idea that immunological mechanisms may be important in the pathogenesis of lymphoid tumours.

Radiation

The leukaemogenic potential of ionizing radiation has been strongly demonstrated by studies of Japanese populations following the 1945 atomic bomb explosions (Beebe *et al.* 1978) and by various studies of patient groups receiving therapeutic medical radiation for different disorders (Boice and Land 1982). These studies demonstrate that leukaemia risk is directly related to radiation dose, at least for doses over 50 rem. Public health standards for radiation protection are based primarily on these data with linear extrapolation for dose–response relationships at lower doses, assuming no safe exposure threshold. Studies of populations exposed to low radiation doses (nuclear fallout, diagnostic medical radiation) generally support these assumptions but have thus far been of insufficient size or accuracy to produce definitive data (Boice and Land 1979; Lyon *et al.* 1979; Caldwell *et al.* 1980). The effects of radiation leukaemogenesis are clearly limited to CGL and AL and do not involve any greatly increased risk of CLL or related lymphomas. Latency for radiation-caused leukaemia can range from 2 to 20 years or more, depending on the nature and dose of radiation exposure.

Chemicals

Various chemicals have clear leukaemogenic potential, and it seems likely that more such leukaemogens exist than are presently recognized. Evidence comes from various occupational health studies and from observations in patients treated with various therapeutic chemicals. Workplace studies have strongly implicated benzene as a cause of leukaemia, particularly AL arising in myeloid cell lines (Rinsky *et al.* 1981). Benzene exposure is also linked to the occurrence of aplastic anaemia, a condition which may precede the development of leukaemia. Studies of mortality patterns in farmers have suggested an increased risk of leukaemia which may perhaps be related to use of agricultural chemicals (Blair and Thomas 1979). Patients treated for various cancers with alkylating agents such as melphelan and busulphan show a clear increase in risk of subsequent leukaemia (Greene *et al.* 1982). The public health implications of such data reinforce the need for close control of chemical exposures both in occupational settings and in the general environment. Benzene and related compounds are of particular importance not only because of wide industrial use but because benzene is a common ingredient in petroleum fuel.

Infection

The continuing search for cancer viruses has long focused on leukaemias and lymphomas. The viral aetiology of such tumours in animal models is well established (Heath 1975). Although recent studies have now demonstrated one such oncogenic virus in certain forms of human acute leukaemia (Gallo and Wong-Staal 1982), other evidence linking leukaemia or other cancers to infectious agents has been largely indirect and inconclusive. Despite close and frequent contacts between humans and various animal species, no cross-species transmission of known animal leukaemia or tumour viruses has been demonstrated (for example, feline and bovine leukaemia viruses). Leukaemia incidence does not appear to be increased in relation to various human viral illnesses (influenza in particular), and risk does not rise after various forms of immunization (killed polio virus vaccine, yellow fever vaccine) (Heath 1982b). Cases of leukaemia and lymphoma do occasionally occur in clusters, whether by time-space closeness or in relation to past interpersonal contacts. In general, however, such clustering does not appear to occur more frequently than chance might predict, except perhaps for acute childhood leukaemia (Heath 1982b; Smith 1982).

Lymphomas

The lymphomas are non-leukaemic white cell malignancies which arise in lymphoreticular tissues. They may best be considered under three headings: Hodgkin's disease (HD), non-Hodgkin's lymphoma (NHL), and Burkitt's lymphoma (BL).

As a group, lymphomas account for about half of all white cell malignancies (Table 13.5). Their pathogenesis, although not yet well understood, seems particularly to involve immunological factors, shaped perhaps by genetic makeup, infectious agents, and chemical exposures. Certain forms of lymphoma bear a close histopathological and clinical resemblance to lymphocytic leukaemias, especially CLL. Those similarities suggest that such disorders may represent a single disease entity or share a common aetiology (Wintrobe 1981).

Clinical features vary widely but frequently include peripheral lymphadenopathy as a presenting finding. Symptoms and clinical course are governed by the organ location of lymphomatous tumour, by extent of tumour spread, and by degree of tumour responsiveness to therapy. No direct public health measures for the control or prevention of lymphomas have yet been developed.

Hodgkin's disease

Although Hodgkin's disease (HD) accounts for only about 25 per cent of all lymphomas (Table 13.5), it has received greater research attention than other lymphomas. The disease is identified by the presence of distinctive histocytic cells (Reed–Sternberg cells) in lymphoma tissue. Four varieties of HD are currently recognized on the basis of tumour cell patterns (the 1966 Rye Classification): lymphocyte predominance, nodular sclerosis, mixed cellularity, and lymphocyte depletion. This sequence of histological diagnoses correlates generally with worsening prognosis and decreasing responsiveness to anti-tumour therapy. It replaces an earlier but less specific histological classification which differentiated HD into paragranuloma, granuloma, and sarcoma forms.

There is a distinctive age distribution for the occurrence of HD in which two incidence peaks are apparent: one in young adults (age 20–30 years), the other in older adults (over age 50 years) (Grufferman 1982). This prominent bimodal pattern is not seen in other forms of lymphoma, and it suggests that HD may consist of two quite different diseases. It has been postulated that young adult cases, in which the nodular sclerosis form of HD predominates, may represent a predominantly infectious or infection-related illness, while older cases constitute a more truly neoplastic condition. At all ages, the incidence of HD is greater in men than in women. In adults, at least, this may suggest the influence of occupational environmental exposures.

A striking feature of HD is its increased frequency in higher social class settings and the corresponding observation that childhood forms of the disease tend to be relatively more frequent in less developed countries (Correa and O'Conor 1971). In developed countries, cases are less common in blacks than in whites. These patterns suggest an infectious aetiology, for childhood and young adult cases at least, in which improved socio-economic conditions may postpone primary infection beyond childhood. This idea has led to comparisons with known infectious diseases such as poliomyelitis in which age, race, and socio-economic status all correlate with the manner in which virus spreads and disease is expressed (Gutensohn and Cole 1977).

Analytical epidemiological studies of HD suggest that genetic factors, infection, and chemical exposures may all play a role in causing the disease. It occurs with somewhat increased frequency in family settings. Studies of sibling case pairs, however, raise the possibility that such familial aggregations may be more a reflection of shared environment than inherited predisposition (Grufferman et al. 1977).

Reports of case clustering, particularly instances in which cases are linked by past interpersonal acquaintance, have suggested the existence of infectious agents which might produce illness after long and variable latency (Vianna and Polan 1973). Statistical confirmation of such clustering has not developed, however, and the search for infectious agents continues to be unfulfilled (Evans 1982). A possible association between HD and prior tonsillectomy, although confounded by relation to socio-economic status, has suggested an immunologic mechanism which might affect host susceptibility to nasopharyngeal infection (Gutensohn and Cole 1977). As mentioned previously, a possible relationship to EBV infection has been postulated on the basis of epidemiological studies which show an increase in HD risk following clinical IM (Kvale et al. 1979).

Associations between HD and chemical exposure have been suggested largely on the basis of studies in occupational groups. Although no clearcut patterns have been confirmed, risk of HD appears somewhat increased in the woodworking trades (carpentry, sawmills, etc.), among chemists, in rubber workers, and in persons exposed occupationally to benzene (Grufferman 1982). None of these associations is yet sufficient to establish firm causal relationships or to pinpoint particular toxins.

Non-Hodgkin's lymphoma

Lymphomas other than HD or BL, form a heterogeneous group of diseases which can be generally classified by histopathological appearance. In the past, three forms of NHL have been recognized: lymphosarcoma, reticulum cell sarcoma, and giant follicular lymphoma. This classification has now been replaced by one in which tumours are first characterized by whether or not normal lymph node structure is preserved (nodular and diffuse forms of NHL) and then by the cytological appearance and relative maturity or differentiation of tumour cells (lymphocytic, histiocytic, and mixed cell categories) (Greene 1982). This spectrum of diagnostic types, although only based on appearance of cells and tissues, correlates quite well with clinical prognosis:

nodular and lymphocytic forms of NHL respond more favourably to therapy than diffuse and histocytic forms. Nodular and diffuse lymphomas occur with about equal frequency. The histological subtypes most commonly encountered are nodular, poorly differentiated lymphocytic lymphoma (corresponding largely to the earlier designation of lymphosarcoma), and diffuse histiocytic lymphoma (corresponding to reticulum cell sarcoma). All forms of NHL taken together, including mycosis fungoides, a cutaneous variety of lymphoma, account for about 75 per cent of all lymphomas (Table 13.5).

Most NHL represents malignant change affecting B (bursal-equivalent) lymphocytes, cell lines which are responsible for humoral immunity (antibody production through differentiation to plasma cells). As with other forms of leukaemia and lymphoma, cases are somewhat more frequent in males and in whites (Table 13.5). Age-specific incidence rises steadily with age, but without peaks among children or young adults. Age-adjusted rates have shown some tendency to rise over the past several decades.

Various lines of epidemiological evidence suggest that immunological abnormalities play a major role in the aetiology of NHL. Cases of NHL have been seen to aggregate in families in which inherited or acquired immune deficiencies are present (Ladish et al. 1978). It also occurs at greatly increased frequency both in patients with various forms of primary immunodeficiency (Spector et al. 1978) and as a complication following therapeutic immunosuppression for organ transplantation and other purposes (Kinlen et al. 1979). Short latency for tumour development after renal transplantation (often one year or less) suggests the possibility of oncogenic virus activity aroused somehow by immunological compromise. Additional evidence for a relationship between immunological mechanisms and the development of NHL comes from the increased frequency of NHL in such disorders as rheumatoid arthritis, systemic lupus erythematosis, Sjogren's syndrome, Hashimoto's thyroiditis, gluten-sensitive enteropathy (coeliac disease), and dermatitis herpetiformis (Steinberg and Klassen 1977).

Several studies have suggested (but not proved) a role for certain drugs in NHL causation, phenytoin in particular (Li et al. 1975). Other data suggest an association with particular occupations (Greene 1982). Exposure to ionizing radiation at doses over 100 rem has been linked to slight but definite increases in NHL risk (Beebe et al. 1978). As with other forms of leukaemia and lymphoma, no clear evidence has yet implicated infectious agents in the aetiology of NHL. This possibility remains important, however, in light of the relationship of NHL to immune deficiency conditions.

Burkitt's lymphoma

This condition was first identified in 1958 and is now recognized as the most common childhood cancer both in central Africa and in lowland New Guinea (de-The 1979). Although rare elsewhere in the world, the disease is of special public health interest because of its unique clinical and epidemiological features. Studies of BL have contributed greatly to concepts of how infection and immunological responses may interact to cause cancer.

Commonly, BL presents as a jaw tumour with frequent involvement of intra-abdominal lymph nodes and other abdominal viscera. The disease may be classified histologically as an undifferentiated lymphocytic lymphoma. Unlike other lymphomas, however, cases of BL frequently show dramatic and complete response to chemotherapy.

Occurrence of BL in Africa and New Guinea is closely limited to low-lying regions where falciparum malaria is holoendemic. Cases particularly affect children 5–8 years old and are rare before the age of two years and after adolescence. Cases occur at a somewhat later age in children immigrating from non-malarious regions and in children living in regions where BL rates are relatively low (Morrow 1982). The disease affects males about twice as commonly as females, and it shows no evidence of familial or genetic predisposition. In some parts of Africa a striking degree of time-space case clustering has been described. This has not been a constant phenomenon, however, and its interpretation is not clear.

The original discovery of EBV in 1964 was made through studies of BL cells in tissue culture (Epstein *et al.* 1964). Subsequent work has shown that EBV regularly exists in BL cells, and that a cytogenetic translocation involving chromosome 14 is also consistently present (Zech *et al.* 1976). Patients with BL have much higher levels of anti-EBV antibodies than do controls, and these levels are present for months or years before BL develops (de-The *et al.* 1978).

Although the precise role of EBV in the pathogenesis of BL remains unclear, the geographical correlation with intense malarial infection strongly suggests that these two factors somehow interact. It has been proposed that this interaction may involve: (i) infection of B lymphocytes with a high dose of EBV in early childhood; (ii) intense stimulation of these lymphocytes by severe, sustained malarial infection, particularly in mid-childhood; and (iii) eventual emergence from these stimulated lymphocytes of a malignant lymphoid cell line characterized by chromosome 14 translocation (Morrow 1982). If such a sequence of events does in fact occur, future control or prevention of BL might develop either from control of malarial infection in areas where BL occurs or from modification or prevention of EBV infection, perhaps through development of an EBV vaccine.

Plasma cell dyscrasias

The plasma cell dyscrasias, alternately known as monoclonal gammopathies, are disorders marked by the overproduction of antibody or immunoglobulin proteins (IgG, IgM, IgA, IgE, etc.) or of fragments of such protein molecules, (heavy chains, light chains, Bence–Jones proteins). Immunoglobulins are secreted by plasma cells and constitute the humoral or non-cellular phase of the body's immunological defence system. Monoclonal gammopathies are so named because in any individual case only a single immunoglobulin or immuno-globulin fragment is produced. Each such gammopathy is therefore believed to arise from a single clone of cells directed at production of a single immunoglobulin protein entity.

Multiple myeloma (MM) is by far the most common clinical disorder among the monoclonal gammopathies. Individual cases of MM can be associated with overproduction of any of the immunoglobulins or immunoglobulin fragments but only rarely involves IgM. Overproduction of IgM is characteristic of a separate disorder, Waldenstrom's macroglobulinaemia. So-called heavy chain disorders are a further set of clinical entities within the spectrum of monoclonal gammopathies and are marked by over-production of heavy chain fragments associated with any of the several immunoglobulins.

The collective incidence of plasma cell dyscrasias is about four cases per 100 000 persons per year (Table 13.5) or about 15–20 per cent of all white cell malignancies. These dyscrasias exist against a backdrop of a more common condition known as benign monoclonal gammopathy (BMG) (Wintrobe 1981) which occurs with a prevalence of about 1 or 2 per cent in the general population over age 50 years, and increases in frequency with age. Cases of BMG consist of monoclonal serum protein peaks in the absence of clinical illness. Most cases appear not to predispose to the later development of plasma cell dyscrasias.

Multiple myeloma

Multiple myeloma is a lymphoproliferative malignancy which arises in B-lymphocyte clones and is expressed as malignant proliferation of plasma cells. Cases usually present clinically with bone fractures associated radiographically with characteristic 'punched out' lesions in bones. Bone marrow is infiltrated with sheets of plasma cells which often show abnormal cytological features. Plasma cell infiltration can also affect other organs, especially the kidney. Anaemia results from marrow infiltration and is a common clinical feature. Abnormal plasma cells are occasionally present in peripheral blood (plasma cell leukaemia).

The pathognomonic finding in MM is the demonstration of a monoclonal protein spike on serum or urine protein electrophoresis. The proteins most commonly involved are IgG or IgA. If the monoclonal protein or protein fragment has properties of precipitating and then redissolving with increasing temperature, it is termed a cryoglobulin or Bence–Jones protein.

Incidence of MM has increased somewhat in recent years, particularly among blacks (Blattner 1982). Its most striking epidemiological feature is the fact that its frequency among blacks is generally more than twice that among whites (McPhedran *et al.* 1972). Incidence rises steadily with age. The disease is rarely seen before age 30 years, and it affects males somewhat more often than females.

The aetiology of MM, like that of other white cell malignancies, is unknown. Epidemiological studies have suggested some tendency for cases to recur in families. Disease incidence is somewhat increased in populations heavily exposed to ionizing radiation. It also seems more frequent in farmers, a finding which may suggest a relationship to chemical exposures. Time–space clusters of cases have been described (Kyle *et al.* 1972) but are of uncertain biological significance. No methods for public health control or prevention of MM currently exist.

Macroglobulinaemia

This rare gammopathy involves proliferation of lymphocytoid plasma cells in the presence of excess production of IgM (Waldenstrom's macroglobinaemia). Clinically and histopathologically the disease seems closely related to NHL. It is differentiated from NHL by demonstration of a macroglobulin peak in serum and by clinical manifestations related to deposits of macroglobulin in tissue and to the viscosity of serum containing large amounts of macroglobulin (Wintrobe 1981). The disease is perhaps one-fourth as frequent as MM. Its age distribution is similar to that of MM, but it has not been shown to occur with increased frequency in blacks. Occasional multiple case families are recorded, and the disease has been described in relation to other conditions in which immunological abnormalities exist (Blattner *et al.* 1980).

Heavy chain disease

The heavy chain diseases are very rare disorders characterized by monoclonal peaks of the heavy chain components of immunoglobulin. To date, cases have been described involving the heavy chains of IgG (gamma chain), IgA (alpha chain), and IgM (mu chain) (Wintrobe 1981). Alpha-chain disease occurs with the greatest frequency and is of particular epidemiological interest. Most cases have been described in countries in the Middle East or near the Mediterranean Sea, giving rise to the term 'Mediterranean lymphoma'. In these settings, the disease is characterized by lymphoplasmacytic proliferation in the lymphoid tissues of the jejunum or upper small intestine. Such proliferation may progress to frank intestinal or abdominal lymphoma and in many cases is marked by monoclonal production of alpha heavy-chain fragments. This disease spectrum has recently been designated 'immunoproliferative small intestinal disease' to allow for the fact that not all cases progress to lymphoma or produce alpha-chain fragments (World Health Organization 1976). It is a disease of children and young adults and may originate from the intense immunostimulation of intestinal lymphoid tissue which undoubtedly accompanies the severe gastrointestinal infections which commonly occur among infants and young children in lower socio-economic populations in the Middle East. The same disease has been described in South Africa among mulatto, but not black, populations (Levin *et al.* 1976). This suggests that cultural transition from primitive to developed societies may play some role in this peculiar disease process. Control of the disorder seems likely to rest with prevention of intestinal infections among infants and children and improvement of general socio-economic conditions (Heath 1982*a*).

SUMMARY

Diseases arising in blood and blood-forming organs encompass disorders of red blood cells, disorders of white blood cells, and disorders of haemostasis and blood coagulation. Red cell disorders consist principally of anaemias caused either by deficiency in essential nutrients (iron, folate, vitamin B_{12}) or by excessive destruction of red cells (haemolysis) reflecting inherited abnormalities in red cell structure or metabolism or exposure to particular toxic environmental agents. Primary conditions affecting white blood cells consist mostly of white cell malignancies (leukaemias, lympomas, plasma cell disorders). Disorders of haemostasis and blood coagulation include both haemorrhagic conditions (haemophilia, thrombocytopenia) and thrombotic disease (vascular thromboses). Within this diverse spectrum of haematological illness, nutritional anaemias and thrombotic disorders occur with the greatest overall frequency and hence may be considered of greatest public health importance.

Although no specific measures are presently available for directly controlling most primary haematological conditions (prevention of Rh disease through maternal immunization is an exception), a wide range of public health activities can have substantial indirect impact. These include programmes for improving nutrition, for controlling infection, for preventing excessive environmental exposures to chemicals, radiation, and drugs, for providing health education and genetic counselling, and for promoting adequate health care systems. Improved nutrition is of foremost concern because iron and folate deficiency states are highly prevalent in developing countries, especially among pregnant women. Attention to infection control may lead to reduction in post-infectious red cell and haemostasis disorders. Particular attention to control of intestinal infections in developing countries may improve intestinal absorption of folate and other nutrients and should reduce frequency of iron deficiency associated with hookworm disease. Control of exposure to radiation and to chemicals such as benzene should eventually help reduce frequency of aplastic anaemia and certain forms of leukaemia. Other chemical exposures of concern include lead, carbon monoxide from internal combustion engines, and nitrates in drinking water, as well as improper use of medications, which may lead to various haematological reactions, and alcohol abuse, which can contribute to development of folate-deficiency anaemia. Lastly, public promotion of health education and health-care systems is important for the medical care of persons with haemophilia and for helping patients and their families understand and manage other genetically determined haematological conditions such as G6PD deficiency, thalassaemia, and haemoglobinopathies.

REFERENCES

Disorders of red blood cells

Abelson, N.M. and Rawson, A.J. (1961). Studies of blood group antibodies. *Transfusion* **1**, 116.

Allison, A.C. (1957). Malaria in carriers of sickle-cell trait and in newborn children. *Exp. Parasitol.* **6**, 418.

Allison, A.C. (1961). *Genetical variations in human populations.* Pergamon, New York.

Bannerman, R.M. and Renwick, J.H. (1962). The hereditary elliptocytoses: clinical and linkage data. *Ann. Hum. Genet.* **26**, 23.

Beutler, E., Mathai, C.K., and Smith, J.E. (1968). Biochemical variants of glucose-6-phosphate dehydrogenase giving rise to congenital nonspherocytic hemolytic disease. *Blood* **31**, 131.

Bezwoda, W.R., Bothwell, T.H., Torrance, J.D. *et al.* (1979). The relationship between marrow iron stores, plasma ferritin concentration, and iron absorption. *Scand. J. Haematol.* **22**, 113.

Biehl, J.P. and Vilter, R.W. (1954). Effects of isoniazide on pyridoxine metabolism. *JAMA* **156**, 1549.

Bodansky, O. (1951). Methemoglobinaemia and methemoglobin-producing compounds. *Pharmacol. Rev.* **3**, 144.

Bothwell, T.H., Charlton, R.W., Cook, J.D. *et al.* (1979). *Iron metabolism in man.* Blackwell, Oxford.

Bothwell, T.H. and Charlton, R.W. (1982). A general approach to the problems of iron deficiency and iron overload in the population at large. *Seminar Hematol.* **19**, 54.

Bottomley, S.S. (1977). Porphyrin and iron metabolism in sideroblastic anemia. *Seminar Hematol.* **14**, 169.

Cameron, D.G., Watson, G.M., Witts, L.J. (1949). The clinical association of macrocytic anemia with intestinal stricture and anastomosis. *Blood* **4**, 793.

Charache, S. and Richardson, S.N. (1964). Prolonged survival of a patient with sickle cell anemia. *Arch. Intern. Med.* **113**, 844.

Childs, B., Zinkham, W., Browne, E.A. *et al.* (1958). A genetic study of a defect in glutathione metabolism of the erythrocyte. *Bull. Johns Hopkins Hosp.* **102**, 21.

Comly, H.H. (1945). Cyanosis in infants caused by nitrates in well water. *JAMA* **129**, 112.

Custer, R.P. (1946). Aplastic anaemia in soldiers treated with atabrine (quinacrine). *Am. J. Med. Sci.* **212**, 211.

Dacie, J.V. (1967). *The haemolytic anaemias*, 2nd edn. Grune and Stratton, New York.

Dern, R.J., Beutler, E., and Alving, A.S. (1955). The hemolytic effect of primaquine. V. Primaquine sensitivity as a manifestation of a multiple drug sensitivity. *J. Lab. Clin. Med.* **45**, 30.

Drenick, E.J., Swendseid, M.E., Blahd, W.H., and Tuttle, S.G. (1964). Prolonged starvation as treatment for severe obesity. *JAMA* **187**, 100.

Eichner, E.R. and Hillman, R.S. (1971). The evolution of anemia in alcoholic patients. *Am. J. Med.* **50**, 218.

Elkins, H.B. and Pagnatta, L.D. (1956). Benzene content of petroleum solvents. *Arch. Ind.* **13**, 51.

Evatt, B.E., Lewis, S.M., Lothe, F., and McArthur, J.R. (1982). *Anemia: diagnostic hematology.* WHO monograph, Geneva.

Finch, C.A., Beutler, E., Brown, E.B. *et al.* (1968). Iron deficiency in the United States. *JAMA* **203**, 407.

Flatz, G. (1967). Hemoglobin E: distribution and population dynamics. *Humangenetik* **3**, 189.

Freda, V.J., Gorman, J.G., and Pollack, W. (1963). Successful prevention of sensitization to Rh with an experimental anti-Rh gamma₂ globulin preparation. *Fed. Proc.* **22**, 374.

Gardner, F.H. (1958). Tropical sprue. *New Engl. J. Med.* **158**, 791, 835.

Geerdink, R.A., Helleman, P.W., and Verloop, M.C. (1966). Hereditary elliptocytosis and hyperhaemolysis: a comparative study of 6 families with 145 patients. *Acta Med. Scand.* **179**, 715.

Grasbeck, R. (1959). Calculations on vitamin B_{12} turnover in man. *Scand. J. clin. Lab. Invest.* **11**, 250.

Grasbeck, R. (1969). Intrinsic factor and the other vitamin B_{12} transport proteins. *Progr. Hematol.* **6**, 233.

Griffin, J.H., Evatt, B.L., Zimmerman, T.S. *et al.* (1981). Deficiency of protein-C in congenital thrombotic disease. *J. Clin. Invest.* **68**, 1370.

Hallberg, L. and Nilsson, L. (1964). Constancy of individual blood loss. *Acta Obstet. Gynecol. Scand.* **43**, 352.

Hallberg, L. (1982). Iron nutrition and food iron fortification. *Seminar Hematol.* **19**, 31.

Harker, L.A. and Ross, R. (1979). Pathogenesis of arterial vascular disease. *Seminar Thromb. Haemost.* **5**, 274.

Herbert, V. (1962). Minimal daily adult folate requirement. *Arch. Intern. Med.* **110**, 649.

Heysell, R.M., Bozian, R.C., Darby, W.J., and Bell, M.C. (1966). Vitamin B_{12} turnover in man: the assimilation of vitamin B_{12} from natural foodstuff by man and estimates of minimal daily dietary requirements. *Am. J. Clin. Nutr.* **18**, 176.

Horrigan, D.L. and Harris, J.W. (1964). Pyridoxine-responsive anemia: analysis of 62 cases. In *Advances in internal medicine*, Vol. 12 (ed. W. Dock and I. Snapper) p. 103. Yearbook, Chicago.

Jandl, J.H. and Greenberg, M.S. (1959). Bone marrow failure due to relative nutritional deficiency in Cooley's hemolytic anaemia. *New Engl. J. Med.* **260**, 461.

Jenkins, G.C., Ind, J.E., Kozantzio, G., and Owen, R. (1965). Arsine poisoning. Massive haemolysis with minimal impairment of renal function. *Br. Med. J.* **ii**, 78.

Kaplan, E., Zuelzer, W.W., and Neel, J.V. (1951). A new inherited abnormality of hemoglobin and its interaction with sickle cell hemoglobin. *Blood* **6**, 1240.

Kattamis, C.A., Kyriazakow, M., and Chaidas, S. (1969). Favism. Clinical and biochemical data. *J. Med. Genet.* **6**, 34.

Klipstein, F.A. (1964). Subnormal serum folate and macrocytosis associated with anticonvulsant drug therapy. *Blood* **23**, 68.

Kushner, J.P., Lee, G.R., Wintrobe, M.M., and Cartwright, G.E. (1971). Idiopathic refractory sideroblastic anemia. Clinical and laboratory investigation of 17 patients and review of the literature. *Medicine* **50**, 139.

Lajtha, L.G. and Oliver, R. (1960). Studies on the kinetics of erythropoiesis: a model of the erythron. In *Ciba Foundation Symposium on Haemopoiesis* (eds. G.E.W. Wolstenholme and M. O'Connor) p. 289. Little Brown, Boston.

Lawrence, J.S., Dowdy, A.H., and Valentine, W.N. (1948). Effects of radiation on hemopoiesis. *Radiology* **51**, 400.

Layrisse, M. and Roche, M. (1964). The relationship between anemia and hookworm infection. *Am. J. Hygiene* **79**, 279.

Lemberg, R. and Legge, J.W. (1949). *Hematin compounds and bile pigments.* Interscience, New York.

Lindenbaum, J. and Klipstein, F.A. (1963). Folic acid deficiency in sickle cell anemia. *New Engl. J. Med.* **269**, 875.

Lipton, E.L. (1955). Elliptocytosis with hemolytic anemia: the effects of splenectomy. *Pediatrics* **15**, 67.

Loumanmaki, K. and Coburn, R.F. (1969). Effects of metabolism and distribution of carbon monoxide on blood and body stores. *Am. J. Physiol.* **217**, 354.

Luisoda, L. (1941). Favism: singular disease affecting chiefly red blood cells. *Medicine* **20**, 229.

Luzzatto, L., Usanga, E.A., and Reddy, S. (1969). Glucose-6-phosphate dehydrogenase deficient red cells: resistance to infection by malarial parasites. *Science* **164**, 839.

MacGibbon, B.H. and Mollin, D.L. (1965). Sideroblastic anaemia in man: observations on seventy cases. *Br. J. Haematol.* **11**, 59.

Mallison, B.L. (1972). *Blood transfusion in clinical medicine*, 5th edn. Blackwell, Oxford.

Mason, R.G., Mohammod, S.F., and Balis, J.U. (1981). An overview of the pathophysiology of thrombosis. In *Perspectives in hemostasis* (eds. J. Fareed, H.L. Messmore, J.W. Fenton, II, and K.M. Brinkhouse) p. 70. Pergamon Press, New York.

Miller, D.R., Bloom, G.E., Streiff, R.R. *et al.* (1966). Juvenile 'congenital' pernicious anemia: clinical and immunologic studies. *New Engl. J. Med.* **275**, 978.

Mollin, D.L. (1965). Sideroblasts and sideroblastic anaemia. *Br. J. Haematol.* **11**, 41.

Monsen, E.R., Kuhn, I.N., and Finch, C.A. (1967). Iron status of menstruating women. *Am. J. Clin. Nutr.* **20**, 842.

National Academy of Sciences, National Research Council, Food and Nutrition Board (1960). *Recommended dietary allowances*, 7th edn, 1968. NAS Publication No. 1694, Washington, DC.

Nyberg, W. (1958). Absorption and excretion of vitamin B_{12} in subjects infected with *Diphyllobothrium latum* and in non-infected subjects following oral administration of radioactive B$_{12}$. *Acta Haematol.* **19**, 90.

Paulson, M. and Harvey, J.C. (1954). Haematological alterations after total gastrectomy. Evolutionary sequences over a decade. *JAMA* **156**, 1556.

Rubenberg, M.L., Regoeczi, E., Bull, B.S. *et al.* (1968). Microangiopathic haemolytic anaemia: the experimental production of haemolysis and red cell fragmentation by defibrination in vivo. *Br. J. Haematol.* **14**, 627.

Schmid, R. (1960). Cutaneous porphyria in Turkey. *New Engl. J. Med.* **263**, 397.

Sheehy, T.W., Perez-Santiago, E., and Rubini, M.E. (1961). Tropical sprue and vitamin B$_{12}$. *New Engl. J. Med.* **265**, 1232.

Smith, A.D.M. (1962). Veganism: a clinical survey with observations of vitamin B$_{12}$ metabolism. *Br. Med. J.* **i**, 1655.

Stohlman, F., Jr. (1966). Pathogenesis of erythrocytosis. *Seminar Hematol.* **3**, 181.

Valentine, W.N., and Tanaka, K.R. (1978). Pyruvate kinase and other enzyme deficiency hereditary hemolytic anemias. In *The metabolic basis of inherited disease*, 4th edn (eds. J.B. Stanbury, J.B. Wyngaarden, and D.S. Fredrickson) p. 1416. McGraw Hill, New York.

Van Proagh, R. (1961). Diagnosis of kernicterus in the neonatal period. *Pediatrics* **28**, 870.

Wald, W., Thoma, F.E., Jr, and Brown, G., Jr (1962). Hematologic manifestations of radiation exposure in man. *Progr. Hematol.* **3**, 1.

Waxman, H.S. and Rabinowitz, M. (1966). Control of reticulocyte polyribosome content and hemoglobin synthesis by heme. *Biochem. Biophys. Acta* **129**, 369.

Weatherall, D.J. (1965). *The thalassemia syndromes.* Blackwell, Oxford.

Went, I.N. and MacIver, J.E. (1958). Sickle-cell anaemia in adults and its differentiation from sickle-cell thalassemia. *Lancet* **ii**, 824.

Westerman, M.P., Pfitzer, E.A., Ellis, L.D., and Jensen, W.N. (1965). Concentrations of lead in bone in plumbism. *New Engl. J. Med.* **173**, 1246.

Williams, W.J. (1982). *Hematology*, 3rd edn. McGraw-Hill, New York.

Winslow, R.M. (1984). High-altitude polycythemia. In *High altitude and man* (eds. J.B. West and S. Lahiri) p. 163. American Physiological Society, Bethesda, Md.

Wintrobe, M.M. (1981). *Clinical hematology*, 8th edn. Lea and Febiger, Philadelphia.

Witkind, E. and Waid, M.E. (1951). Aplasia of the bone marrow during mesantoin therapy. *JAMA* **147**, 757.

Young, L.E. (1955). Observations on inheritance and heterogeneity of chronic spherocytosis. *Trans. Assoc. Am. Physic.* **68**, 141.

Disorders of haemostasis and blood coagulation

Aballi, A.J., Lopez-Banus, V., de Lamerons, S., and Rozengvaig, S. (1959). Coagulation studies in the newborn period. III. Hemorrhagic disease of the newborn. *Am. J. Dis. Child.* **97**, 524.

Bird, R.M. and Jacques, W.E. (1959). Vascular lesion of hereditary hemorrhagic telangiectasia. *New Engl. J. Med.* **260**, 597.

Finkbiner, R.B., McGovern, J.J., Goldstein, R., and Bunker, J.P. (1959). Coagulation defections in liver disease and response to transfusion during surgery. *Am. J. Med.* **26**, 199.

Graham, J.B. (1968). von Willebrand's disease and hemophilia A. *Semin. Enfance Hemophil.* **1**, 144.

Ministry of Health (1954). Homologous serum jaundice after transfusion of whole blood, dried, small-pool plasma, dried irradiated plasma, and kaolin-treated, filtered liquid plasma. *Lancet* **i**, 1328.

Moore, M.J., Strickland, W.H., and Prichard, R.W. (1956). Sprue with bleeding from hypoprothrombinemia. **97**, 814.

National Institutes of Health (1972). Pilot study of hemophilia treatment in the United States. US Department of Health, Education and Welfare, Washington, DC.

Sterky, G. and Thilen, A. (1960). A study on the onset and prognosis of acute vascular purpura (the Schonlein–Henoch syndrome) in children. *Acta Paediatr.* **49**, 217.

Wintrobe, M.M. (1981). *Clinical hematology*, 8th edn. Lea and Febiger, Philadelphia.

Disorders of white blood cells

Beebe, G.W., Kato, H., and Land, C.E. (1978). Studies of the mortality of A-bomb survivors. 6. Mortality and radiation dose, 1950–1974. *Radiat. Res.* **75**, 138.

Blair, A. and Thomas, T.L. (1979). Leukemia among Nebraska farmers: a death certificate study. *Am. J. Epidemiol.* **110**, 264.

Blattner, W.A. (1982). Multiple myeloma and macroglobulinemia. In *Cancer epidemiology and prevention* (ed. D. Shottenfeld and J.F. Fraumeni, Jr.) p. 795. Saunders, Philadelphia.

Blattner, W.A., Garber, J., Mann, D.L. *et al.* (1980). Waldenstein's macroglobulinemia and autoimmune disease in a family. *Ann. Intern. Med.* **93**, 830.

Boice, J.D., Jr. and Land, C.E. (1979). Adult leukemia following diagnostic x-rays. *Am. J. Public Health* **69**, 137.

Boice, J.D., Jr. and Land, C.E. (1982). Ionizing radiation. In *Cancer epidemiology and prevention* (eds. D. Schottenfeld and J.F. Fraumeni) p. 231. Saunders, Philadelphia.

Brodsky, A.L. and Heath, C.W., Jr. (1972). Infectious mononucleosis: epidemiologic patterns at United States colleges and universities. *Am. J. Epidemiol.* **96**, 87.

Caldwell, G.C., Kelley, D.B., and Heath, C.W., Jr. (1980). Leukemia among participants in military maneuvers at a nuclear bomb test. *JAMA* **244**, 1575.

Correa, P. and O'Conor, G.T. (1971). Epidemiologic patterns of Hodgkin's disease. *Int. J. Cancer* **8**, 192.

de-The, G. (1979). The epidemiology of Burkitt's lymphoma: evidence for a causal association with Epstein–Barr virus. *Epidemiol. Rev.* **1**, 32.

de-The, G., Geser, A., Day, N.E. *et al.* (1978). Epidemiological envidence for causal relationship between Epstein–Barr virus and Burkitt's lymphoma from Ugandan prospective study. *Nature, Lond.* **274**, 756.

Epstein, M.A., Achong, B.G., and Barr, Y.M. (1964). Virus particles in cultured lymphoblasts from Burkitt's lymphoma. *Lancet* **i**, 702.

Evans, A.S. (1982). Viruses. In *Cancer epidemiology and prevention* (eds. D. Schottenfeld and J.F. Fraumeni, Jr.) p. 364. Saunders, Philadelphia.

Gallo, R.C. and Wong-Staal, F. (1982). Retroviruses as etiologic agents of some animal and human leukemias and lymphomas and as tools for elucidating the molecular mechanism of leukemogenesis. *Blood* **60**, 545.

Greene, M.H. (1982). Non-Hodgkin's lymphoma and mycosis fungoides. In *Cancer epidemiology and prevention* (eds. D. Schottenfeld and J.F. Fraumeni, Jr.) p. 754. Saunders, Philadelphia.

Greene, M.H., Boice, J.D., Jr., Greer, B.E. *et al.* (1982). Acute non-lymphocytic leukemia after therapy with alkylating agents for ovarian cancer. *New Engl. J. Med.* **307**, 1416.

Grufferman, S. (1982). Hodgkin's disease. In *Cancer epidemiology and prevention* (eds. D. Schottenfeld and J.F. Fraumeni, Jr.) p. 739. Saunders, Philadelphia.

Grufferman, S., Cole, P., Smith, P.G. *et al.* (1977). Hodgkin's disease in siblings. *New Engl. J. Med.* **196**, 248.

Gutensohn, N. and Cole, P. (1977). Epidemiology of Hodgkin's disease. *Int. J. Cancer* **19**, 595.

Heath, C.W., Jr. (1975). The epidemiology of leukemia. In *Cancer epidemiology and prevention*. (ed. D. Schottenfeld) p. 318. Thomas, Springfield, Ill.

Heath, C.W., Jr. (1976). Hereditary factors in leukemia and lymphomas. In *Cancer genetics* (ed. H.T. Lynch) p. 233. Thomas, Springfield, Ill.

Heath, C.W., Jr. (1982*a*). Epidemiology of gastrointestinal lymphomas. In *Epidemiology of cancer of the digestive tract* (ed. P. Correa and W. Haenszel) p. 147. Martinus Nijhoff, The Hague.

Heath, C.W., Jr. (1982*b*). In *Cancer epidemiology and prevention* (eds. D. Schottenfeld and J.F. Fraumeni, Jr.) p. 728. Saunders, Philadelphia.

Heath, C.W., Jr., Brodsky, A.L., and Potolsky, A.I. (1972). Infectious mononucleosis in a general population. *Am. J. Epidemiol.* **95**, 46.

Heath, C.W., Jr., Caldwell, G.C., and Feorino, P.C. (1975). Viruses and other microbes. In *Persons at high risk of cancer. An approach to cancer etiology and control* (ed. J.F. Fraumeni, Jr.) p. 241. Academic Press, New York.

Hecht, F. and McCaw, B.K. (1977). Chromosome instability syndromes. In *Genetics of human cancer* (eds. J.J. Mulvihill, R.W. Miller, and J.F. Fraumeni, Jr.) p. 105. Raven Press, New York.

Kinlen, L.J., Shiel, A.G.R., Peto, J. *et al.* (1979). A collaborative study of cancer in patients who have received immunosuppressive therapy. *Br. Med. J.* **ii**, 1461.

Kvale, G., Hoiby, E.A., and Pederson, E. (1979). Hodgkin's disease in patients with previous infectious mononucleosis. *Int. J. Cancer* **23**, 593.

Kyle, R.A., Finkelstein, S., Elveback, L.R. *et al.* (1972). Incidence of monoclonal proteins in a Minnesota community with a cluster of multiple myeloma. *Blood* **40**, 719.

Ladish, S., Holiman, B., Poplack, D.G. *et al.* (1978). Immunodeficiency in familial erythrophagocytic lymphohistiocytosis. *Lancet* **i**, 581.

Levin, K.J., Kahn, L.B., and Novis, B.H. (1976). Primary intestinal lymphoma of "Western" and "Mediterranean" type, alpha chain disease and massive plasma cell infiltration. A comparative study of 37 cases. *Cancer* **38**, 2511.

Li, F.P., Willard, D.R., Goodman, R. *et al.* (1975). Malignant lymphoma after diphenyl hydantoin (Dilantin) therapy. *Cancer* **36**, 1359.

Lyon, J.L., Klauber, M.R., Gardner, J.W., and Udall, K.S. (1979). Childhood leukemias associated with fallout from nuclear testing. *New Engl. J. Med.* **300**, 397.

McPhedran, P., Heath, C.W., Jr., and Garcia, J. (1972). Multiple myeloma incidence in metropolitan Atlanta, Georgia: racial and seasonal variations. *Blood* **39**, 866.

Morrow, R.H., Jr. (1982). Burkitt's lymphoma. In *Cancer epidemiology and prevention* (eds. D. Schottenfeld and J.F. Fraumeni, Jr.) p. 779. Saunders, Philadelphia.

Muir, C.S. and Nectoux, J. (1982). International patterns of cancer. In *Cancer epidemiology and prevention* (ed. D. Schottenfeld and J.F. Fraumeni, Jr.) p. 119. Saunders, Philadelphia.

Rinsky, R.A., Young, R.J., and Smith A.B. (1981). Leukemia in benzene workers. *Am. J. Ind. Med.* **2**, 217.

Smith, P.G. (1982). Spatial and temporal clustering. In *Cancer epidemiology and prevention* (eds. D. Schottenfeld and J.F. Fraumeni, Jr.) p. 391. Saunders, Philadelphia.

Spector, B.D., Perry, G.S., III, and Kersey, J.H. (1978). Genetically determined immunodeficiency diseases (GDID) and malignancy: report from the Immunodeficiency Cancer Registry. *Clin. Immunol. Immunopathol.* **11**, 12.

Steinberg, A.D. and Klassen, L.W. (1977). Role of suppressor T cells in lymphopoietic disorders. *Clin. Haematol.* **6**, 439.

Vianna, N.J. and Polan, A.K. (1973). Epidemiologic evidence for transmission of Hodgkin's disease. *New Engl. J. Med.* **10**, 499.

Wintrobe, M.M. (1981). *Clinical hematology*, 8th edn. Lea and Febiger, Philadelphia.

World Health Organization (1976). Alpha-chain disease and related small intestinal lymphoma: a memorandum. *Bull. WHO* **54**, 615.

Young, J.L., Jr., and Pollack, E.S. (1982). The incidence of cancer in the United States. In *Cancer epidemiology and prevention* (eds. D. Schottenfeld and J.F. Fraumeni, Jr.) p. 138. Saunders, Philadelphia.

Zech, L., Haglund, U., Nilsson, K. *et al.* (1976). Characteristic chromosomal abnormalities in biopsies and lymphoid cell lines from patients with Burkitt and non-Burkitt lymphomas. *Int. J. Cancer* **17**, 47.

14 Diabetes mellitus: a problem in personal and public health

H. Keen

INTRODUCTION

Diabetes affects 1–2 per cent of most ascertained populations though prevalence varies from near zero (Sagild *et al.* 1966; Mouratoff *et al.* 1969) in some, to near 50 per cent among those aged over 45 years in others (Bennett *et al.* 1976; Zimmet *et al.* 1977). In a few high-prevalence groups, for example the Amerindian Pima tribe in the US (Bennett *et al.* 1976) and the Micronesian population of the phosphate-rich Pacific Island of Nauru (Zimmett *et al.* 1977), one person in two can expect to become diabetic by late middle-age. In all populations, prevalence rises steeply with age and this must be allowed for in any comparison of rates. Rates also depend critically (and artificially) on diagnostic criteria used and this is considered in more detail below.

The clinical types of the disorder (and very probably their aetiology) differ from group to group, region to region, and race to race, though in all, the non-insulin-dependent variety exceeds the insulin-dependent, sometimes overwhelmingly. The pattern of the long-term consequences of diabetes also shows distinct variation. In the sense that comparatively large numbers of people get diabetes, that the disorder or its consequences may be preventable and that the provision of adequate medical care is costly and requires organization, diabetes can properly be considered a public health problem. It is with some of these aspects that this account concerns itself.

DIABETES MELLITUS – DEFINITION

Much of the confusion over the definition of diabetes is semantic and arises from attempts to apply arbitrary numerical values to an originally qualitatively defined phenomenon. The diagnostic term was originally a description of the distinctive clinical syndrome of thirst, polyuria, wasting, coma, and death (Keen 1983*a*). With the recognition of the role of glucose excess in urine and blood as the marker of the diabetic state and technical advances which have made it possible to transfer the detection of the biochemical abnormality from the laboratory to the population, the diagnosis has come to be defined as a 'state of chronic hyperglycaemia'. Defined in this way, the syndrome includes but almost submerges the original clinical paradigm. A wide variety of

mechanisms, virtually all involving inadequate insulin secretion or effect (Pfeifer *et al.* 1981), can give rise to chronic glucose intolerance. The clinical evolution, the severity, and form of the diabetic state may give some broad indication of the underlying pathogenic mechanisms identifiable particularly *within* ethnically relatively homogeneous population groups (Cudworth 1978; Fajans *et al.* 1978). The classical form of diabetes is easily defined, florid with symptoms and lethal if untreated. Heavy glycosuria, ketonuria, and clinical evidence of acidosis and dehydration virtually establish the diagnosis; a single measurement of the blood glucose concentration is so elevated as to offer diagnostic certainty. In most advanced societies, this clinical type of the syndrome, now known as insulin-dependent diabetes mellitus (IDDM, Type 1), represents no more than 10–20 per cent of patients recognized as diabetic (Falconer *et al.* 1971), and, in some (Shanghai Diabetes Research Group 1981), considerably fewer.

It was the inclusion of people with less severe and life-threatening symptoms but with heavy glycosuria and unequivocal hyperglycaemia which greatly swelled the numbers qualifying for diagnosis. It was the recognition that this variant of the diabetic state (non-insulin-dependent diabetes mellitus, NIDDM, Type 2) could be virtually asymptomatic but was none the less associated with long-term diabetic complications which prompted the diagnostic screening of populations in the 1950s and 1960s (West 1978*b*), aimed at establishing earlier diagnosis and effective treatment.

The results of these surveys raised new problems. Glycosuria, the traditional clinical pointer to the diabetic state, proved to be an inadequate primary screening procedure in population use; it was insufficiently specific in the young and relatively insensitive in the old (Butterfield *et al.* 1967). Increasingly, the primary screening procedure became *blood* glucose measurement, hyperglycaemia being the central diagnostic marker of diabetes and the urine test simply an index of it. When populations of blood glucose measurements, gathered from such screening exercises, were evaluated no obvious division could be distinguished in the frequency distribution between 'diabetic' and 'normal' values, a 'continuous variation' typical of most western populations (Gordon *et al.* 1964; West and Kalbfleisch 1966; Keen 1983*a*).

The application of these distributions of diagnostic

glycaemic criteria current at the time (for example, British Diabetic Association 1964) led to greatly inflated estimates of diabetes prevalence in typical western populations, totals amounting to between 10 and 20 per cent (Table 14.1), and composed largely of older people with lesser degrees of glucose intolerance. Glycaemic criteria have therefore come under intensive review in the past few years. The conclusions of the Second Report of the World Health Organization Expert Committee on Diabetes Mellitus (1980) fairly summarize the present consensus and present new recommendations for diagnosis (Table 14.2). In essence, the glycaemic requirement for diagnosis of diabetes mellitus has been considerably raised. The lesser degrees of glucose intolerance previously included as diabetes mellitus but now diagnostically disenfranchised however have not been classed as normal. They are described by the new category of 'impaired glucose tolerance' (IGT). This category, intermediate between 'normal' and 'abnormal', recognizes the 'at-risk' status of such subjects by comparison with the normoglycaemic for later deterioration to the state of diabetes mellitus (Jarrett et al. 1979; Sartor et al. 1980; Keen et al. 1981), for the development of coronary heart disease, (Jarrett et al. 1982a; Fuller et al. 1983) and for the outcome of pregnancy (Symposium on Gestational Diabetes 1980). It does, however, also register the considerable likelihood that borderline metabolic abnormality of this degree will fail to worsen or even return spontaneously to normal and that, at least over 10 years of observation, it is free of clinically significant risk for the development of the specific complications of diabetes mellitus in eye and kidney and nerve (see below). Thus, glucose tolerance joins the large group of biological variables like arterial pressure, uricaemia, cholesterolaemia, adiposity, and intelligence which show 'continuous variation' within populations and which do not lend themselves to simple dichotomy into normal and abnormal in respect of disease. This 'blurring' of diagnostic boundaries is the result

Table 14.1. *Estimates of diabetes prevalence based upon various diagnostic criteria projected onto a random sample of the population of Bedford, England 1962*

	Prevalence of diabetes with blood glucose criteria %			
Age	≥120 mg/dl 2 h after glucose	≥140 mg/dl 2 h after glucose	Peak value ≥180 mg/dl	Peak ≥180* and 2 h ≥120
20–	7.3	2.1	11.5	2.1
30–	6.4	1.1	14.9	1.1
40–	9.7	4.3	29.0	6.5
50–	15.4	6.0	48.4	14.3
60–	18.4	5.7	51.7	11.5
70+	40.2	22.0	61.0	34.1
Total	15.7	6.6	35.2	11.1

*British Diabetic Association (1964) criteria.

Estimates were based on full OGTT (50 g glucose, capillary blood, ferricyanide Autoanalyser method) after overnight fast in a randomly drawn sample of 528 Bedford citizens, stratified to give equal numbers in each age group with men and women equally represented.

Corrected for age structure of UK population, total prevalence by British Diabetic Association (BDA) criteria (column 4) would be approximately 16 per cent.

Table 14.2. *WHO criteria for diagnosis of diabetes mellitus and impaired glucose tolerance from OGTT* (expressed as venous plasma glucose)*

A. When there are symptoms and signs of diabetes a random value of ≥11.1 mmol/l (200 mg/dl) establishes diagnosis

B. When OGTT is done
Diabetes mellitus – fasting ≥7.8 mmol/l or 2 h ≥11.1 mmol/l
          (140 mg/dl)   (200 mg/dl)
Impaired glucose
tolerance – fasting <7.8 mmol/l and 2 h 7.8–11.1 mmol/l

C. O'Sullivan Criteria for Gestional Diabetes Mellitus†
Test with 100 g oral glucose, venous samples (fasting 1, 2, and 3 h)
GDM when two or more values exceed (mg/dl): fasting 105; 1 h 190; 2 h 165; 3 h 145
Suggested values for 'gestational IGT' 2 h 120–164

D. Criteria in children †
Diabetes mellitus – fasting ≥7.9 mmol/l and 2 h ≥11.1 mmol/l
          (140 mg/dl)   (200 mg/dl)
Impaired glucose tolerance – fasting <7.8 mmol/l and 2 h ≥7.8 mmol/l

---

*OGTT: Oral load 75 g glucose in 250–300 ml water (or partial starch hydrolysate preparation equivalent) for adults or 1.75 g/kg body-weight (to max of 75 g for children), taken in morning after overnight fast. Values correspond to specific enzymatic glucose assay method. NB: The performance of a GTT is rarely necessary for the clinical confirmation of diabetes. In the presence of symptoms (or sometimes even without) a single unprepared but unequivocally raised glucose concentration is adequate to establish diagnosis. Standardized tests are of value for equivocal cases, in pregnancy or as a tool in epidemiological or research studies.

† These are criteria recommended by NDDG; WHO makes no special distinction in DM and IGT criteria between pregnant and non-pregnant, adult or child. NDDG also requires elevated (≥2 h) values between 0 and 2 h. Both WHO and NDDG require confirmatory test for *clinical* diagnosis.

of the operation of many factors, environmental and genetic, which interact in complex ways to affect the resultant level of a biological quantity. In operational terms, it necessitates the creation of an 'at risk' class between the clearly normal and the clearly abnormal, a class likely to be heterogeneous in composition, to require monitoring of its evolution, and research to define recognizable subtypes and the components which determine its progression and regression.

CLASSIFICATION

A classification of diabetes and allied states of glucose intolerance, compiled by the National Diabetes Data Group (NDDG) of the US National Institutes of Health (National Diabetes Data Group 1979) (Table 14.3), reflects the current developing state of knowledge; it was accepted with reservations by the WHO Expert Committee. Its problems have been discussed elsewhere (Keen 1982) and relate in the main to the growing claim of aetiological and pathogenic factors to find a place in the classification and terminology of diabetes. However, classification remains essentially clinical, based upon clinical manifestation (for example, the major IDDM and NIDDM varieties). These clinical classes indicate but do not correspond exactly with aetiology or mechanisms. Thus, in Caucasoid societies, IDDM usually affects individuals of a particular immunogenetic constitution (HLA DR4 and/or DR3) (Nerup et al. 1982), its course is characterized by autoimmune phenomena (Bottazzo et al. 1980) and its clinical onset is usually in youth. However, the autoimmune markers

Table 14.3. *Classification of types of diabetes mellitus and related categories*

Clinical classes

Diabetes mellitus	Insulin-dependent type (IDDM, type 1)
	Non-insulin-dependent type (NIDDM, type 2)
	Other types (secondary to pancreatic, hormonal, drug-induced, insulin/receptor, genetic, and other identifiable abnormalities)
	Gestational (GDM)
Impaired glucose tolerance	Obese, non-obese, secondary, other types

Statistical risk classes

Previous abnormality of glucose tolerance (PrevAGT)

Potential abnormality of glucose tolerance (PotAGT)

Source: National Diabetics Data Group (1979).

may be associated with a prolonged non insulin-dependent or even non-diabetic phase (Irvine *et al.* 1980; Gorsuch *et al.* 1981). *Per contra*, infective, traumatic or other stresses may convert the long-standing NIDDM patient to a state of insulin dependency, usually temporarily. Types of diabetes clinically intermediate between insulin-dependent and non-dependent are not uncommon in western societies and may predominate in some developing, usually tropical (West 1978c) countries; the 'failure of fit' of the current classification in this respect has been forcefully remarked upon (Morrison 1981). Some understanding of the ambiguities and inadequacies of both diagnostic criteria and classification and, in particular, an appreciation of the heterogeneity of the diabetic syndrome are necessary to any public health approach to the overall problem of diabetes.

PREGNANCY IN DIABETICS AND GESTATIONAL DIABETES

Pregnancy in the established diabetic woman was disastrous for both mother and fetus before insulin; for many years afterwards, the fetal loss rate remained very high. It is only over the past decade with great improvement in both diabetic and obstetric care that perinatal mortality has begun to approach that of the non-diabetic (Freinkel 1980; Jovanovic *et al.* 1981). Even now, perinatal mortality is 2–3 times higher in the established diabetic woman, with fetal malformation as a major residual cause (Pedersen 1977; Gabbe 1981). In developing countries (for example Kenya – Fraser 1982) the situation remains bad though much can be done with quite simple measures.

Gestational diabetes is defined as that first diagnosed in pregnancy (Davidson and O'Sullivan 1966). It is usually asymptomatic and suspected because glycosuria is found on routine urine testing, because of a history of earlier obstetric misadventure, a previous baby of unusually high birthweight, or a strong family history of the disease. Diagnosis is usually established on the results of a formal oral glucose tolerance test (OGTT). The methodology for this and the diagnostic interpretation of the results aroused considerable contention (Jarrett 1981; Beard and Hoet 1982; Keen 1983b). At one extreme, it is argued that even the smallest departure from normal glucose tolerance must be detected and treated; the

exponents of this view usually espouse the use of the O'Sullivan OGTT and criteria (O'Sullivan and Mahan 1964). At the other extreme, it is argued that evidence for fetal hazard with lesser degrees of glucose intolerance (for example the zone defined by WHO as IGT) (WHO Expert Committee 1980) is very dubious and that reported hazards can be attributed to 'confounding' variables such as maternal age, adiposity, or multiparity, or to non-metabolic factors responsible for previous obstetric misadventures. Exponents of this view espouse the recommended WHO criteria for diabetes mellitus and IGT in the pregnant as well as in the non-pregnant state. The antidiabetic 'treatment' appropriate to these lesser degrees of glucose intolerance in pregnancy is also uncertain, practice varying from its virtual neglect to intensive application of insulin injections and diet (Roversi *et al.* 1979). There is no convincing demonstration of benefit or estimate of harm from the application of anti-diabetic treatment in this zone of glucose intolerance. The logistical implications of this debate are considerable for, depending on the diagnostic philosophy adopted, gestational diabetes mellitus occurs in as few as one per thousand or as frequently as three or four per hundred pregnancies. The cost of systematic detection and treatment in the latter case would be enormous, the yield uncertain and small at best. Much more research is necessary before any serious recommendation can be made to apply diagnostic screening and vigorous treatment for gestational diabetes mellitus on a large scale.

POPULATION SCREENING FOR DIABETES

The drive to early detection and treatment was inspired by the comparatively high frequency with which diabetes presented in middle-aged or older people as a result of its long-term complications, for example with visual disability due to diabetic retinopathy or cataract, or with chronic foot ulceration or gangrene due to vascular or neuropathic tissue damage. When automated biochemistry made possible the processing of thousands of samples for glucose measurement in the 1950s and 1960s, mass diagnostic screening drives were carried out in populations (West 1978b). Enthusiasm for this early indiscriminate approach has waned markedly over the past decade. A major reason has been the recognition of the very high frequency of lesser degrees of glucose intolerance in most westernized populations increasing in prevalence in the middle and later years of life. Though these fell within the criteria for diabetes recommended in 1964 by the British Diabetic Association (Fitzgerald and Keen 1964), there was great uncertainty about their true significance to health. As mentioned earlier, prolonged follow-up of such IGT subjects in Bedford and elsewhere showed that only a minority, 2–3 per cent per year, underwent metabolic deterioration to unequivocally diabetic levels. The rest either remitted 'spontaneously' to normal or remained glucose intolerant within the IGT limits, showing no significant development of specific diabetic complications. At least two-thirds of those diagnosed as diabetic in the population surveys of the 1960s, most of them in the later years of life, would now fall within the newly defined zone of IGT. The extent of the variation in glycaemic criteria for diagnosis among diabetes experts was very wide

(West 1975). Even for the hard core of the newly-found unequivocal diabetics, the utility and even the danger of treatment with oral anti-diabetic agents were called into question by the findings of the US University Group Diabetes Program (UGDP) (1970, 1975). One of the few adequately controlled studies comparing a group of diabetics detected by population screening with a matched group presenting by the usual clinical paths, concluded that no demonstrable advantage in respect of mortality or morbidity accrued from pre-emptive diagnosis (Panzram and Rutomann 1978). The group detected by screening even failed to show the advantage of diagnostic lead-time. A comparatively recent re-evaluation of diabetes screening, sponsored by the US Centers for Disease Control, the American Diabetes Association, and the National Institutes of Health (Herron 1979), concluded that there was no place for mass screening in asymptomatic populations with the possible exception of screening for gestational diabetes (see discussion above). However, the importance of selective, planned studies for identification of susceptible groups and for risk factors, and for the evaluation of effectiveness of preventive campaigns and for descriptive population epidemiology was fully acknowledged. Also recognized was the considerable value of regular screening activities *within* diabetic populations for the prevention, detection, and appropriate management of the delayed complications of the disease.

PREVENTION OF DIABETES

The newer knowledge of the aetiology of the different forms of the diabetic syndrome has renewed interest in the potential for prevention. For both IDDM and NIDDM the prevailing view is that diabetes often occurs in genetically predisposed persons subjected to some environmental diabetogenic 'load'. However, the nature of the genetic susceptibility differs for the major clinical types of the syndrome and so too does the environmental factor.

The strong association between obesity and the development of NIDDM has long been recognized (West 1978a) and re-emphasized by the striking coexistence of the two in the Pima and Nauruan ethnic subgroups (Bennett *et al.* 1976; Zimmet *et al.* 1977). In the former and also in European populations the interactive effect of obesity and genetics has been amply demonstrated. Baird (1972) for example showed that the rate of diabetes in the obese sibling of a lean NIDDM patient was six to seven times more than in the lean sibling of an obese proband. The often dramatic clinical response of obese diabetics to weight loss and the semi-anecdotal accounts of the rarity of new NIDDM during wartime deprivation (Himsworth 1949; Goto *et al.* 1958) lend weight to the belief that obesity control would notably reduce NIDDM incidence. It would help to motivate the target population if those genetically at risk could be more clearly identified; genetic markers of some forms of NIDDM may indeed be currently emerging (Bell *et al.* 1981). There is no direct scientific evidence of the preventive efficacy of obesity control but it makes reasonable sense to counsel leanness to family members of an NIDDM patients. Physical activity

may also affect glucose metabolism (Björtorp *et al.* 1972), and should be part of an anti-obesity regimen.

Obesity appears to play no role in IDDM pathogenesis. Although genetic susceptibility is linked with HLA status, and, within families with an IDDM member, is identified by haplo or total HLA identity with the proband (Gorsuch *et al.* 1982), the factor or factors initiating the process which culminates in B cell destruction and severe insulin deficiency remain obscure. Virus infection has been the most favoured hypothesis, operating directly by attack upon the islets of Langerhans or indirectly by initiating a B-cytotoxic sequence of autoimmune events. Coxsackie B strains have been implicated; congenital rubella is also diabetogenic (Gamble 1980). However, the evidence is certainly inadequate as yet to justify a positive protective action by such means as vaccination; and it remains entirely possible that non-infective agencies (for example food contaminants, additives, fungal toxins etc.) may be initiating factors. At present there is interest in the possibility of 'post-primary' prevention of IDDM, that is, the use of immunosuppression or modulation in genetically susceptible individuals with evidence of active anti-B cell auto-immune processes. However, the certainty that such persons will develop IDDM is low and the adverse effects of immunosuppression high so that considerable scientific advance is necessary before this approach becomes a realistic option. Attempts to provoke or prolong remission of IDDM soon after clinical onset with immunosuppression or other immuno-modulatory manoeuvres have so far had little success.

COMPLICATIONS OF DIABETES

Diabetes and the eye

Diabetic retinopathy is now the single commonest cause of visual disability and blindness in the middle years of life in most industrialized nations (Kahn and Hiller 1974; Kohner *et al.* 1982). In the UK, estimates based on blindness registration suggest that 1500 or so diabetics will be registered blind annually as a result of retinopathy (DHSS 1979). This probably represents a considerable underestimation of the true incidence of visual disability from this cause (Cullinan 1978). It also fails to distinguish between those in whom visual loss is mainly central but who have some residual 'navigational' vision, and those with global loss. In younger-onset, usually IDDM patients, proliferative retinopathy with severe retinal and vitreous haemorrhage, gliosis, fibrosis, neovascularization and retinal traction detachment is usually the cause of global blindness. In older NIDDM patients, numerically of far greater importance, diabetic maculopathy with haemorrhagic and exudative lesions and retinal oedema damaging the perifoveal region and destroying central vision is the commonest cause. In both of these categories, clinical trials in which one eye was randomly selected for treatment and the other used as control convincingly demonstrated that early detection and effective photocoagulation reduces the risk of blindness by 70–80 per cent (Chang *et al.* 1975; Diabetic Retinopathy Study Research Group 1981). The need for adequate diagnostic and therapeutic facilities is clearly apparent; some of the considerations applying on a national basis have been reviewed (Blach and Bloom 1978). The resource implications in terms of blindness prevention justify the costs of providing manpower and equipment adequate for a systematic attack upon this problem.

The development and progression of diabetic retinopathy (and other microvascular complications) is broadly related to the degree of metabolic control achieved in the diabetic (Pirart 1978), although this cannot necessarily be simply interpreted as a cause and effect relationship. Nevertheless, with the availability of new methods for obtaining much improved glycaemic control of IDDM, this has raised the important question of prevention of retinopathy by their widespread and intensive application. This is likely to be demanding and costly so that controlled clinical trials (themselves also demanding and costly) of intensified control and the evolution of retinopathy are needed and under way (Salans and Siebert 1982).

Accelerated formation of cataract is a well-recognized association of diabetes (Caird 1968); it may be the agency which brings the diabetes to diagnosis. Clinical studies and animal experiments strongly suggest that lens opacities are positively related to poorly controlled (for example, unrecognized) hyperglycaemia.

Diabetes and the kidney

The susceptibility of the diabetic to chronic kidney disease was recognized by Richard Bright, and described as a specific entity by Kimmelstiel and Wilson (1936). Diabetic nephropathy, as a cause of renal failure, was recently reviewed in relation to certain other kidney diseases by the European Dialysis and Transplant Association (EDTA) (1981). Cohort studies suggest that between one-third and one-half of youthful onset, insulin-depedent diabetics will go into end-stage renal failure (ESRF) after an average diabetes duration of 20–25 years (Marks 1965; Mogensen et al. 1981). Renal failure is anteceded and reliably predicted by an average period of seven years of clinical proteinuria. Although the duration of diabetes and the average level of prior 'diabetic control' appear to be major determinants of diabetic kidney disease (Pirart 1978), a substantial proportion of diabetics will not go into renal failure, however long their diabetes lasts (Deckert et al. 1978). Diabetic patients susceptible to end-stage renal failure may be characterized soon after diabetes onset by small but significant increase above normal of glomerular excretion of plasma albumin (and some other plasma proteins) (Viberti et al. 1982). Once glomerular filtration rate falls below normal in the diabetic, renal failure inexorably worsens with time at a rate which, though fixed for the individual patient (Mogensen 1976), varies widely between patients (Jones et al. 1979). The only intervention claimed to slow the rate of loss of renal function is meticulous reduction to normal of elevated arterial pressure (Mogensen 1982; Parving et al. 1983). Renal failure in the diabetic, often accompanied by retinopathic blindness and by other complications, has, therefore, only recently been accepted with great reluctance into dialysis and transplant programmes. Photocoagulation treatment for retinopathy and improved management and prevention of other diabetic complications have combined with the greater efficacy of renal support in ESRF to generate a rapidly increasing demand for acceptance of diabetics into renal support programmes. In the US, diabetic nephropathy accounts for about 25 per cent of patients presenting for support (Rao and Friedman 1982). There is wide variation among European countries in meeting this demand. In Finland, for example, approximately 25 per cent of kidneys offered for first renal transplant operations go to diabetics in end-stage renal failure (EDTA 1981) compared with under 5 per cent in the UK. Diabetics are accepted for home and hospital haemodialysis with similar variability, usually determined by the resources available for the support of renal failure patients generally. The very substantial rising demand has attracted the attention of health economists and patient organizations as well as diabetes and renal physicians. The unsatisfactory situation in the UK has been editorialized recently (Cameron 1983), and clearly requires review. Two major preventive research initiatives are in progress. The first seeks measures to slow the rate of decline of renal function in diabetics in whom early renal failure is already manifest. Such conservation of function could postpone and perhaps even obviate the ultimate need for dialysis and transplantation. The second seeks the primary prevention of renal failure by the application of new measures of intensified diabetic control to those patients with markers of nephropathic susceptibility (Parving et al. 1982; Viberti et al. 1982).

Arterial disease, diabetes, and glucose intolerance

Premature death and prolonged ill health due to cardiovascular disease affect the diabetic with increased frequency and impact (Garcia et al. 1974; Jarrett et al. 1982b; Pyörälä and Laakso 1983). Both of the major clinical types of diabetes manifest in excess the classical syndromes of myocardial infarction and angina pectoris, intermittent claudication and gangrene, and stroke and other cerebrovascular disease (Fuller et al. 1983). 'Atherosclerosis' or 'macrovascular disease' affects the diabetic male two to three times more than the non-diabetic and represents an even greater relative risk to the diabetic woman. However, susceptibility to arterial disease varies widely between diabetic populations (Keen and Jarrett 1979). Epidemiological studies suggest that environmental factors are, in large part, responsible for this variation, as in non-diabetics. The Japanese diabetic provides an illustrative example with relatively low frequency of coronary and peripheral vascular disease (as with non-diabetics) by comparison with US or European populations. Japanese diabetic migrants in Hawaii, however, show a rise in risk approaching that of Caucasian diabetics (Kawate et al. 1978). Whether macrovascular disease prevalence is low or high, however, the diabetic appears to be about twice as vulnerable as the non-diabetic. The mechanism of this diabetic 'amplification' of cardiovascular risk is not clear. There are many candidates, including altered plasma lipid metabolism, increased frequency of hypertension, changes in clotting factors, flow properties of blood, and platelet function (Steiner 1981). Some mechanisms may be inherent in the diabetic state itself but some enhanced atherogenesis is probably attributable to the operation of specific environmental factors. Suspicion has come to rest on the composition of the diabetic diet, in particular the high fat content characteristic of the traditional western 'diabetic diet', and of traditional western diets generally. Selective restriction of carbohydrate foods in the diabetic diet was offset by increased intake of dairy products such as eggs, butter, cheese, and cream. *Dietary recommendations for diabetics for the 1980s*, recently published by the British Diabetic Association (1983), comprehensively reviews the evidence for and against carbohydrate restriction and recommends a substantial increase (to about 50 per cent of dietary food energy) in the proportion of carbohydrate (largely unrefined) at the expense of fat in the dietary prescription. The variability in the recognition and treatment of hypertension in diabetics (and the success of the intervention) is indicated in Fig. 14.1. Clearly, there is room for improvement.

Impaired glucose tolerance and vascular disease

Degrees of glucose intolerance short of diabetes mellitus (viz. IGT, see discussion above), have also been found to be

associated with increased risk of cardiovascular disease, though this relationship may not be a universal one (Stammler and Stammler 1979). In a ten-year study (Fuller *et al.* 1983) of cause-specific deaths in a population of approximately 18 000 male Civil Servants aged 40–64 years at recruitment, the rate of deaths certified as due to CHD (ICD codes 410–414) and to stroke (ICD codes 430–438) was doubled among the men lying in the top fifth percentile of the blood glucose distribution measured two hours after a 50 g oral glucose load (Fig. 14.2). Glucose intolerance so defined appears to operate as a 'step function' in increasing risk of CHD and stroke; below a critical 'threshold' level of glucose tolerance, there is no evident relation between glycaemia and risk. Above it, the risk doubles. The threshold two hour blood glucose value is surprisingly low at 95 mg/dl – 5.4 mmol/l. No further gradient in risk of stroke with degree of two hour glycaemia was found above this level. CHD mortality rates were higher among civil servants composing a 'diabetic group' (that is 168 known to be diabetic and 56 with

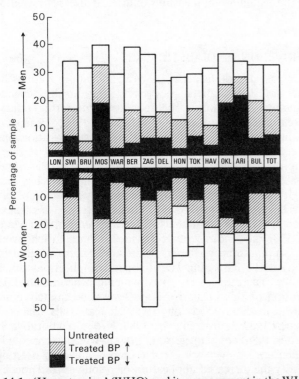

Fig. 14.1. 'Hypertension' (WHO) and its management in the WHO multinational study of diabetics. Heights of columns indicate prevalence of 'hypertension' by sex in each of 14 national/ethnic groups of diabetics. Hypertension defined as per WHO by systolic ≥160 or diastolic ≥95 or receiving antihypertensive treatment (hatched column also qualifies for hypertension by blood pressure; black segment blood pressure below 160/95). Populations of diabetics of approximately 500 from each centre, aged 35–54 years, stratified by sex and diabetes duration (see Keen and Jarrett 1979).

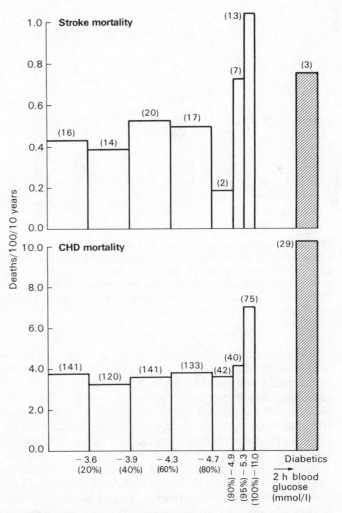

Fig. 14.2. Age-adjusted 10-year stroke and coronary heart disease mortality by two-hour blood glucose concentration. Numbers at top of columns are number of deaths. Percentages are percentile points. (Reprinted from Fuller *et al.* (1983).)

two-hour blood glucose values over 11.1 mmol/l). These numbers were comparatively small and the significance of the CHD mortality rate difference from that in the glucose intolerant is therefore uncertain. Using multiple logistic analysis, it was possible to allocate a proportion of the increased risk for CHD and stroke mortality in the glucose intolerant and diabetic subjects to known 'risk factors' for CHD mortality, such as age, arterial pressure, obesity, cigarette-smoking, plasma cholesterol concentration, and pre-existing electrocardiographic abnormalities. After age, arterial pressure was the major determinant of excess CHD and stroke death but between 60 and 75 per cent of the excess risk was unaccounted for by the risk factors examined (Fig. 14.3).

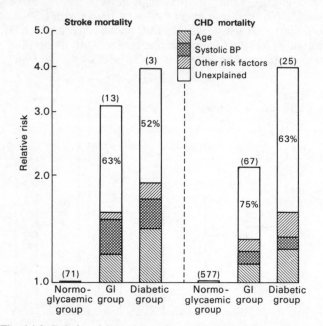

Fig. 14.3. Relative risks (odds ratios) of stroke deaths and coronary heart disease death explained by risk factors (age standarized) for (a) glucose intolerant (GI) groups and (b) diabetic group compared with normoglycaemic group. Figures at top of columns are numbers of deaths. Includes only subjects with complete information. (Reprinted from Fuller *et al.* 1983).

The nature of the 'diabetic doubling factor' remains unknown. From a purely numerical point of view, however, much could potentially be done to reduce the heavy burden of atherosclerotic disease in diabetics by reversing the 'non-diabetic' risk factors. Taking the Japanese as a low risk-factor reference point, atherosclerotic risk affects about 5 per cent of non-diabetics and 10 per cent of the diabetic population. This compares with 'westernized' rates of about 30 per cent and 60 per cent for non-diabetic and diabetic populations respectively. Reversal of 'non-diabetic' risk factors would drop rates from 60 per cent (current western diabetes mellitus risk) to 10 per cent (current Japanese diabetes mellitus risk), that is a reduction of 50 per cent of risk but of 83.3 per cent in numbers of affected diabetics. Reversal of the 'diabetic factor' only would drop rates from 60 to 30 per cent (current

western non-diabetes mellitus risk), a reduction of 30 per cent of risk but of 50 per cent in numbers. Reversal of both components of risk would drop rates from 60 to 5 per cent (current Japanese non-diabetes mellitus risk), a fall of 55 per cent of risk but 91.7 per cent in numbers. Diabetic women lose the relative advantage of non-diabetic women over men in respect of atherosclerotic disease; for them, reversal of risk factors would be numerically more impressive than in men.

It is administratively convenient but probably technically incorrect to attribute the whole of the diabetic excess of heart and limb disease to 'atherosclerosis'. The existence of specific, non-coronary diabetic cardiopathy has been largely accepted (Ledet 1979), accounting for an unknown proportion of chronic congestive heart failure and exertional angina in diabetics, particularly in long-term, insulin-treated women (Kannel *et al.* 1974). Sudden death in diabetics may be related to CHD but has also been shown to be associated with the presence of severe neuropathy. Its autonomic component may be responsible for the cardiopulmonary arrest, sometimes provoked by drugs or anaesthesia (Clarke *et al.* 1979). Neuropathy may also play an important part in the genesis of chronic foot ulceration, deep tissue destruction, and the high rate of limb amputation. The need to make suitable distinctions between primarily ischaemic and primarily neuropathic tissue damage should be borne in mind in the evaluation of measures of arterial disease prevention.

PROVISION OF DIABETIC CARE

The past decade has seen many technical innovations in the care of the diabetic (especially the insulin-dependent), including new simple methods for monitoring (and self-monitoring) blood glucose (Sönksen 1980; Peacock and Tattersall 1982), purified and modified duration insulin preparations (Watkins 1983), and pumps and devices for improved patterns of insulin administration (Pickup *et al.* 1980; Schiffrin and Belmonte 1982). The drive has increasingly been towards obtaining better glycaemic control and this has been founded on the conviction (supported by experimental evidence in animals (Engerman *et al.* 1977; Mauer *et al.* 1981) and indirect clinical evidence in man (Tchobroutsky 1978)) that improved levels of metabolic control will delay or prevent the damaging late diabetic complications discussed above. There has been no convincing experimental demonstration of this in man though several adequately designed short, medium, and long-term clinical trials (Salans and Siebert 1982; Lauritzen *et al.* 1983; Kroc Collaborative Study Group 1984) are in progress at present which may provide the much needed evidence. That evidence is needed not only to justify the increased application of resources to diabetic care but also to stiffen the resolution of patients, doctors, and nurses alike to undertake the demanding requirements of achieving and maintaining 'tight control'.

Although the long-term benefit of prevention of blindness, renal failure, neuropathy and perhaps arterial disease represent a compelling argument in favour of improved diabetic care, there are also significant short-term gains to be anticipated. For the IDDM patient, better control implies not only lessened exposure to hyperglycaemia and risk of keto-acidosis with the symptoms, the diminished vigour and impaired resistance to banal infection which goes with it, but also reduced risk of severe and unpredictable hypoglycaemia. The disruption to life and morale caused by hypoglycaemia is frequently underestimated and can often be assessed only by questioning other family members, school teachers, and employers.

Needs of the non-insulin-dependent diabetes mellitus patient

The provision of care for the NIDDM patient has special problems. Usually diagnosed much later in life than IDDM, the expected years of life are fewer and the risks of the 'long-term' complications seemingly less. This is often proffered as a reason for laxity with diabetic care. However, the risk of retinopathic blindness, cataract, ischaemic heart disease, cerebrovascular and peripheral arterial disease are all raised, evident in terms of prolonged ill health, if not premature mortality.

Chronic ulcerative, tissue-destroying lesions of the feet represent an excellent example of the importance of adequate supervision and care provision in the prevention of disease and reduction of a major personal and public health problem. Regular foot inspection with skilled chiropodial and, if necessary, orthopaedic assistance along with facilities for construction or modification of footwear can unquestionably prevent the development of chronic foot ulceration, gangrene, and amputation.

Similar regular anticipatory activity can preserve vision; the combined effects of more vigorous hypertension control, anti-smoking propaganda, and the reduction in fat intake can hardly fail, if systematically applied, to reduce athero-sclerotic disease, a major scourge for the older diabetic.

It should be noted that glycaemic correction in NIDDM, though of obvious importance, is only one element in a much more comprehensive programme of management aimed primarily at prevention and early detection of abnormality. In all of these activities the active and instructed participation of the patient to the greatest possible extent is of major importance. Further, it clearly requires a well-integrated operation of primary health care facilities (pre-primary with the patient's role) with special services of both paramedical and high-skill medical nature. 'Team-work' with a 'centre of gravity' bestriding hospital and community are major organizational needs.

Education

R.D. Lawrence wrote in his first edition of *The diabetic life* (1925) of the 'understanding of the patient whose intelligent co-operation is necessary for the best results'. This has become a central and essential requirement for the new measures of improved control and also for the effective application of many of the measures for health protection and prevention of complications now available to the diabetic. The past decade has seen a growing availability of trained staff, accommodation, equipment and, above all, formalized schemes of patient education, increasingly intelligently tailored to the social, emotional, cultural, and intellectual characteristics of the patients concerned (Graber *et al.* 1977; Gfeller and Assal 1979; EASD 1983; Assal *et al.* 1983). The importance of the well-informed, well-motivated patient in diabetes care has been recognized for decades but has been indifferently achieved. The advances in methods and understanding of diabetes management of the last decade have created new demands for patient education and there is striking growth, world-wide, in the facilities for providing this vital aspect of diabetes care. Experienced and well-organized diabetes care centres are evolving slowly and in different forms. Their information must be deliberately diffused into a wide variety of community agencies. The trained nurse, operating principally in the community but based upon the clinic or care centre maintains an important liaison between the patient, the general practitioner, and the hospital services. This liaison has been put on a more formal basis with GP-run diabetic miniclinics operating independently but with occasional personal visits from a concerned hospital consultant with special interest in diabetes as in Wolverhampton (Thorn and Russell 1973); or with a network of GP clinics linked centrally and sharing care with the hospital centre as in Poole (Hill 1976). Other variations on the general theme of providing regular systematic care for diabetics by general practitioners have been tried elsewhere (Wilkes and Lawton 1980) but have in the main been highly dependent upon the organizational drive of dedicated local physicians. There is a strong case for a formal re-evaluation of the provision of care with patient education as its central theme and with the creation of a new type of day care unit where routine treatment and systematic education can proceed side by side. A comprehensive review, edited by Assal *et al.* (1983), provides an up-to-date survey of the many initiatives, methods, and evaluatory procedures currently developing.

Employment

There is in the UK comparatively little well-documented evidence on employment prospects for diabetics (Lister 1982). It is generally accepted that all occupations are suitable for diabetics other than those in which the diabetes may create dangers for the diabetic himself or for others. Thus working at heights or with poorly protected machinery represent hazards to which the insulin-taking diabetic should not be exposed. Occupations involving control of dangerous machinery and heavy vehicles are unsuitable for diabetics. The British Diabetic Association, though firmly espousing the right of the well-controlled insulin-taking diabetic to drive a private motor car, reluctantly accepts that he should not drive a heavy goods vehicle or a public service vehicle. Piloting an aircraft is also forbidden for diabetics on insulin. The withdrawal of a vocational licence from a person who has developed diabetes and gone on to insulin can lead to serious economic hardship if a job is lost. Insurance, protection against such an unforeseen eventuality, could be provided, perhaps by the employer, perhaps by the Trade Union, and consideration of such economic protection is urged.

There remains a degree of unjustifiable prejudice against

diabetics in a number of apparently eminently suitable jobs. A number of large banks, for example, will employ diabetics only with great difficulty. In some, this is due to the fallacious belief that diabetics will draw unduly upon Superannuation and Sickness Funds. In fact, sadly, the diabetic is, on average, unlikely to survive retirement age and will often have made large contributions to the fund without surviving to draw benefit.

Despite the apparent obstacles and hindrances, a recent survey of employment among diabetics in Scotland suggested that, at a time and in an area of high unemployment, the diabetic was little if at all worse off for jobs than the non-diabetic (Hutchingson *et al.* 1983).

CONCLUSION

As with other life-long disabilities, diabetes mellitus imposes a number of obligations upon the individual and upon society. Meeting them adequately is a measure of the civilization and perhaps the prosperity of the individuals and societies concerned. However, the costs and benefits have never been fully worked out for diabetes in the UK. In approaching an evaluation one must accept the essential heterogeneity of the disease. The problems and needs of the insulin-dependent schoolchild are clearly different from those of the 30-year-old entering renal failure or losing vision and the elderly partially-sighted amputee. No single agency can satisfactorily cover all these needs. A role of the public health nexus could be to take the larger, more comprehensive view of the problems of diabetes, drawing in those agencies best fitted to deal with particular aspects and, to the extent that it is useful, providing organization to integrate the whole. The rapid accruing of new knowledge means that this would itself be an evolving process.

ACKNOWLEDGEMENTS

The contribution of many colleagues and collaborators to the work described is gratefully acknowledged and in particular to Dr R.J. Jarrett and Dr J.H. Fuller. Research Grant support from the Department of Health and Social Security for the long-term population studies and clinical trials in Bedford and Whitehall is also recognized with thanks. Other support has come from the Medical Research Council, the Wellcome Trust, and the British Diabetic Association and this is also gratefully acknowledged. Special thanks are due to our laboratory, technical and secretarial staff and particularly to the many thousands of citizens, subjects of the various studies.

REFERENCES

Assal, J.P., Berger, M., Gay, N., and Canivet, J. (1983). *Diabetes education. How to improve patient education.* Excerpta Medica, Amsterdam.

Baird, J.D. (1972). Diabetes mellitus and obesity. *Proc. Nutr. Soc.* **32**, 199.

Beard, R. and Hoet, J. (1982). Is gestational diabetes a clinical entity? *Diabetologia* **23**, 307.

Bell, G.L., Karani, J.H., and Rutter, W.J. (1981). Polymorphic DNA region adjacent to the 5 end of the human insulin gene. *Proc. Natl. Acad. Sci. USA* **78**, 5759.

Bennett, P.H., Rushforth, N.B., Miller, M., and Le Compte, P.M. (1976). Epidemiologic studies in diabetes in the Pima Indians. *Recent Prog. Horm. Res.* **32**, 333.

Björtorp, P., Fahén, M., Grimby, G., *et al.* (1972). Carbohydrate and lipid metabolism in middle-aged, physically well-trained men. *Metabolism* **21**, 1037.

Blach, R.K. and Bloom, A. (1978). Diabetic eye centres for management of diabetic eye disease. *Health Trends* **10**, 88.

Bottazzo, G.E., Dean, B.M., Gorsuch, A.N., Cudworth, A.G., and Doniach, D. (1980). Complement-fixing islet cell antibodies in type 1 diabetes; possible monitors of active beta cell damage. *Lancet* **i**, 668.

British Diabetic Society (1983). *Dietary recommendations for diabetics for the 1980s. A policy statement.* British Diabetic Association, 10 Queen Anne Street, London W1M 0BD.

Butterfield, W.J.H., Keen, H., and Whichelow, M.J. (1967). Renal glucose threshold variations with age. *Br. Med. J.* **iv**, 505.

Caird, F.I., Pirie, A., and Ramsell, T.G. (1968). *Diabetes and the eye.* Blackwell Scientific Publications, Oxford.

Cameron, J.S. (1983). The management of diabetic renal failure in the United Kingdom. *Diabetic nephropathy* **2(2)**, 1.

Chang, H., Kohner, E.M., Keen, H., Blach, R.H., and Hill, D.N. (1975). Photocoagulation in the treatment of diabetic maculopathy. *Lancet* **ii**, 1110.

Clarke, B.F., Ewing, D.J., and Campbell, I.W. (1979). Diabetic autonomic neuropathy. *Diabetologia* **17**, 195.

Cudworth, A.G. (1978). Type 1 diabetes mellitus. *Diabetologia* **14**, 281.

Cullinan, T.R. (1978). Visually disabled people at home. *Health Trends* **10**, 90.

Davidson, R. and O'Sullivan, J.G. (1966). Obstetrical hazards of gestational diabetes. *Am. J. Obstet. Gynecol.* **96**, 1144.

Deckert, T., Poulsen, J.F., and Larsen, M. (1978). Prognosis of diabetics with diabetes onset before the age of 31. *Diabetologia* **14**, 366.

DHSS (1979). *Blindness and partial sight in England 1969–76.* Report on Public Health and Medical Subjects No. 129. HMSO, London.

Diabetic Retinopathy Study Research Group (1981). Photocoagulation treatment of proliferative diabetic retinopathy. Clinical application *Ophthalmology* **88**, 583.

Engerman, R., Bloodworth, J.J., and Nelson, S. (1977). Relationship of microvascular disease in diabetes to metabolic control. *Diabetes* **26**, 760.

European Association for the Study of Diabetes (EASD) (1983). Diabetes Education Study Group, 10 Queen Anne St., London W1M 0BD.

European Dialysis and Transplantation Association (1981). *Report, 1981.* EDTA, London.

Fajans, S.S., Cloutier, M.C., and Crowther, R.L. (1978). Clinical and etiologic heterogeneity of idiopathic diabetes mellitus. *Diabetes* **27**, 1112.

Falconer, D.S., Duncan, L.J.P., and Smith, C. (1971). A statistical and genetical study of diabetes. 1 Prevalence and morbidity. *Ann. Hum. Genet.* **34**, 347.

Fitzgerald, M.G. and Keen, H. (1964). Diagnostic classification of diabetes. *Br. Med. J.* **i**, 1568.

Fraser, R.B. (1982). The fate of the pregnant diabetic in a developing country: Kenya. *Diabetologia* **22**, 21.

Freinkel, N. (1980). Of pregnancy and progeny. *Diabetes* **29**, 1023.

Fuller, J.H., Shipley, M.J., Rose, F., Jarrett, R.J., and Keen, H. (1983). Mortality from coronary heart disease and stroke in relation to degree of glycaemia: the Whitehall Study. *Br. Med. J.* **287**, 867.

Gabbe, S.G. (1981). Diabetes mellitus in pregnancy: have all the problems been solved? *Am. J. Med.* **70**, 613.

Gamble, D.R. (1980). The epidemiology of insulin dependent diabetes, with particular reference to the relationship of virus infection to its aetiology. *Epidemiol. Res.* **2**, 49.

Garcia, M.J., McNamara, P.M., Gordon, T., and Kannell, W.B. (1974). Morbidity and mortality in diabetics in the Framingham population: sixteen year follow-up study. *Diabetes* **23**, 105.

Gfeller, R. and Assal, J.P. (1979). Une expérience pilote en diabétologie clinic et en psychologie médicale: l'unité de traitement et d'enseignement pour malades diabétiques de l'hôpital Cantonal de Génève. *Med. Hyg.* **37**, 2966.

Gordon, T. *et al.* (1964). *Glucose tolerance of adults, United States 1960–62*. Vital and Health Statistics series 11, No. 2 US Government Printing Office, Washington, DC.

Gorsuch, A.N., Spencer, K.M., Lister, J. *et al.* (1981). Evidence for a long prediabetic period in type 1 (insulin-dependent) diabetes mellitus. *Lancet* **ii**, 1363.

Gorsuch, A.N., Spencer, K.M., Wolf, E., and Cudworth, A.G. (1982). HLA and family studies. In *The genetics of diabetes mellitus* (eds. J. Köbberling and R. Tattershall) p. 43. Academic Press, London and New York.

Goto, Y., Nakayama, Y., and Yagi, T. (1958). Influence of the World War II food shortage on the incidence of diabetes mellitus in Japan. *Diabetes* March/April, 133.

Graber, A.L., Christman, B.G., Alojna, M.T., and Davidson, J.K. (1977). Evaluation of diabetes education programs. *Diabetes* **26**, 61.

Herron, C.A. (1979). Screening in diabetes mellitus: report of the Atlanta Workshop. *Diabetes Care* **2**, 357.

Hill, R.D. (1976). Running a diabetic clinic. *Br. J. Hosp. Med.* **16**, 218.

Himsworth, H.P. (1949). Diet in the aetiology of human diabetes. *Proc. R. Soc. Med.* **42**, 323.

Hutchingson, S.J., Kesson, C.M., and Slater, S.D. (1983). Does diabetes affect employment prospects? *Br. Med. J.* **287**, 946.

Irvine, W.J., Gray, R.S., and Steel, J.M. (1980). Islet-cell antibody as a marker for early stage type 1 diabetes mellitus. In *Immunology of diabetes* (ed. W.J. Irvine) p. 117. Teviot Scientific Publications, Edinburgh.

Jarrett, R.J. (1981). Reflections on gestational diabetes. *Lancet* **ii**, 1220.

Jarrett, R.J., Keen, H., and Chakrabarti, R. (1982a). Arterial disease in diabetes mellitus. In *Complications of diabetes,* 2nd edn (eds. H. Keen and J. Jarrett) p. 179. Edward Arnold, London.

Jarrett, R.J., McCartney, P., and Keen, H. (1982b). The Bedford Survey: ten-year mortality rates in newly diagnosed diabetics, borderline diabetics and normoglycaemic controls and risk indices for coronary heart disease in borderline diabetics. *Diabetologia* **22**, 79.

Jarrett, R.J., Keen, H., Fuller, J.H., and McCartney, M. (1979). Worsening to diabetes in men with impaired glucose tolerance ('borderline diabetes'), *Diabetologia* **15**, 25.

Jones, R.H., Hayakawa, M., Mackay, J.D. *et al.* (1979). Progression of diabetic nephropathy. *Lancet* **i**, 1105.

Jovanovic, L., Druzin, M., and Peterson, C. (1981). Effect of euglycaemia on the outcome of pregnancy in insulin-dependent diabetic women as compared with normal control subjects. *Am. J. Med.* **71**, 921.

Kahn, H.A. and Hiller, R. (1974). Blindness caused by diabetic retinopathy. *Am. J. Ophthalmol.* **78**, 58.

Kannel, W.B., Hjortland, M., and Castelli, W.P. (1974). Role of diabetes in congestive heart failure: the Framingham Study. *Am. J. Cardiol.* **34**, 29.

Kawate, R., Miyanishi, M., Yamakido, M., and Nishimoto, Y. (1978). Preliminary studies of the prevalence and mortality of diabetes in Japanese in Japan and on the Island of Hawaii. *Adv. Metab. Dis.* **9**, 201.

Keen, H. (1982). Problems in the diagnosis of diabetes and its subtypes. In *The genetics of diabetes mellitus* (ed. J. Köbberling and R. Tattershall) p. 1. Academic Press, London.

Keen, H. (1983a). Criteria and classification of diabetes mellitus. In *Diabetes in epidemiological perspective* (eds. J.J. Mann, K. Pyörälä, and A. Teuscher) p. 167. Churchill Livingstone, Edinburgh.

Keen, H. (1983b). Glucose intolerance in pregnancy. *Diabetologia* **24**, 460.

Keen, H. and Jarrett, R.J. (1979). The WHO multinational study of vascular disease in diabetes. 2. Macrovascular disease prevalence. *Diabetes Care* **2**, 187.

Keen, H., Jarrett, R.J., and McCartney, P. (1982). The ten-year follow-up of the Bedford Survey (1962–1972): Glucose tolerance and diabetes. *Diabetologia,* **22**, 73.

Kimmelstiel, P. and Wilson, C. (1936). Intercapillary lesions in the glomeruli of the kidney. *Am. J. Pathol.* **12**, 83.

Kohner, E.M., Mcleod, D., and Marshall, J. (1982). Diabetes and the eye. In *Complications of diabetes,* 2nd edn (ed. H. Keen and J. Jarrett). Edward Arnold, London.

Kroc Collaborative Study Group (1984). Blood glucose control and the evolution of diabetic retinopathy and albuminuria: a multicentre randomized feasibility trial. *New Engl. J. Med.* in press.

Lauritzen, T., Frost-Larsen, K., Larsen, H.-W., and Deckert, T. (Steno Study Group) (1983). Effect of 1 year of near-normal blood glucose levels on retinopathy in insulin-dependent diabetics. *Lancet* **i**, 200.

Lawrence, R.D. (1925). *The diabetic life.* Churchill, London.

Ledet, T. (1979). Diabetic cardiopathy. *Diabetologia* **16**, 207.

Lister, J. (1982). The employment of diabetics. *J. Soc. Occup. Med.* **32**, 153.

Marks, H.H. (1965). Longevity and mortality of diabetics. *Am. J. Public Health* **55**, 416.

Mauer, S., Steffes, M., and Brown, D. (1981). The kidney in diabetes. *Am. J. Med.* **70**, 603.

Mogensen, C.E. (1976). Progression of nephropathy in long-term diabetes with proteinuria and effects of initial anti-hypertensive treatment. *Scand. J. Clin. Invest.* **36**, 383.

Mogensen, C.E. (1982). Long-term antihypertensive treatment inhibiting progression of diabetic nephropathy. *Br. Med. J.* **285**, 608.

Mogensen, C.E., Steffes, M.W., Deckert, T., and Sandahl Christiansen, J. (1981). The kidney in diabetes. *Acta Endocrinol.* **97** (Supp. 242), 1.

Morrison, E. (1981). Diabetes mellitus – a third syndrome. Phasic insulin dependence (PID). *Intl. Diabetes Fed. Bull.* **26**, 6.

Mouratoff, C.J., Carroll, N.V., and Scott, E.M. (1969). Diabetes mellitus in Athabaskan Indians in Alaska. *Diabetes* **18**, 29.

National Diabetes Data Group (1979). Classification and diagnosis of diabetes mellitus and other categories of glucose intolerance. *Diabetes,* **28**, 1039.

Nerup, J., Christy, M., Green, A. *et al.* (1982). HLA and insulin-dependent diabetes – population studies. In *The genetics of diabetes mellitus* (eds. J. Köbberling and R. Tattershall) p. 35. Academic Press, London.

O'Sullivan, J.B. and Mahan, C.M. (1964). Criteria for the oral glucose tolerance test in pregnancy. *Diabetes* **13**, 278.

Panzram, G. and Rutomann, B. (1978). *Schw. Med. Wchschr.* **108**, 221.

Parving, H.-H., Andersen, A.R., Smidt, U.M., and Svendsen, P.A. (1983). Early aggressive antihypertensive treatment reduces rate of decline in kidney function in diabetic nephropathy. *Lancet* **i**, 1175.

Parving, H.-H., Oxenboll, B., Svendsen, P.A. *et al.* (1982). Early detection of patients at risk of developing diabetic nephropathy. A longitudinal study of urinary albumin excretion. *Acta Endocrinol.* **100**, 550.

Peacock, I. and Tattersall, R. (1982). Methods of self monitoring of diabetic control. In *Clinics in endocrinology and metabolism,* Vol. 11, No. 2. *New aspects of diabetes* (eds. D.G. Johnston and K.G.M.M. Alberti) p. 485. Saunders, London.

Pedersen, J. (1977). *The pregnant diabetic and her newborn.* 2nd edn. Williams and Wilkins, Baltimore.

Pfeifer, M.A., Halter, J.B., and Porte, D.K. (1981). Insulin secretion in diabetes mellitus. *Am. J. Med.* **70**, 579.

Pickup, J.C., Keen, H., Viberti, G. *et al.* (1980). Continuous subcutaneous insulin infusion in the treatment of diabetes mellitus. *Diabetes Care* **3**, 200.

Pirart, J. (1978). Diabetes mellitus and its degenerative complications: a prospective study of 4400 patients observed between 1947 and 1973. *Diabetes Care* **1**, 168, 252.

Pyörälä, K. and Laakso, M. (1983). Macrovascular disease in diabetes mellitus. In *Diabetes in epidemiological perspective* (eds. J.I. Mann, K. Pyöräla, and A. Teuscher) p. 183. Churchill Livingstone, London.

Rao, T.K.S. and Friedman, E.A. (1982). Diabetic nephropathy in Brooklyn. In *Diabetic renal-retinal syndrome,* Vol. 2. *Prevention and management* (eds. E.A. Friedman and F.A. L'Esperance) p. 3. Grune and Stratton, New York.

Roversi, G.D., Garguilo, M., and Nicolini, U. (1979). A new approach to the treatment of diabetic pregnant women. *Am. J. Obstet. Gynecol.* **135**, 565.

Sagild, U., Littauer, J., Jespersen, C.S., and Andersen, S. (1966). Epidemiological studies in Greenland 1962–1964. *Acta Med. Scand.* **179**, 29.

Salans, L.B. and Siebert, C.W. (1982). National Institutes of Health (NIH) diabetes clinical trial: the relationship of blood glucose control and complications. In *Advances in diabetes epidemiology* (ed. E. Eschwege) p. 323. Elsevier Biomedical Press, Amsterdam.

Sartor, G., Schersten, B., and Carlstrom, S. (1980). Ten-year follow-up of subjects with impaired glucose tolerance. Prevention of diabetes by tolbutamide and diet regulation. *Diabetes* **29**, 41.

Schiffrin, A. and Belmonte, M. (1982). Comparison between continuous insulin infusion and multiple injections of insulin: a one year prospective study. *Diabetes* **31**, 255.

Shanghai Diabetes Research Cooperative Group (1981). A survey of diabetes mellitus among the population of Shanghai. *Chinese Med. J.* **60**, 323.

Sönksen, P.H. (1980). Home monitoring of blood glucose by diabetic patients. *Acta Endocrinol.* **94** (Suppl. 238), 145.

Stammler, R. and Stammler, J. (1979). Asymptomatic hyperglycaemia and coronary heart disease. A series of papers by the International Collaborative Group, based on studies of fifteen populations *J. Chronic Dis.* **32**, 683.

Steiner, G. (1981). Diabetes and atherosclerosis – an overview. *Diabetes* **30** (Suppl. 2), 1.

Symposium on Gestational Diabetes (1980). *Diabetes Care,* **3**, 399.

Tchobroutsky, G. (1978). Relation of diabetic control to development of microvascular complications. *Diabetologia* **15**, 143.

Thorn, P.A. and Russell, R.G. (1973). Diabetic clinics today and tomorrow, mini-clinics in general practice. *Br. Med. J.* **ii**, 534.

University Group Diabetes Program (1970). A study of the effects of hypoglycaemic agents on vascular complications in patients with adult onset diabetes: 1 Design, methods and baseline results. *Diabetes* **19** (Suppl. 2), 747.

University Group Diabetes Program (1975). A study of the effects of hypoglycaemic agents on vascular complications in patients with adult onset diabetes: 5 Evaluation of phenformin therapy. *Diabetes* **24**, (Suppl. 1), 65.

Viberti, G.C., Hill, R.D., Jarrett, R.J. *et al.* (1982). Microalbuminuria as a predictor of clinical nephropathy in insulindependent diabetes mellitus. *Lancet* **i**, 1430.

Watkins, P.J. (1983). Choice of insulin. *Br. Med. J.* **287**, 1571.

West, K.M. (1975). Substantial differences in diagnostic criteria used by diabetic experts. *Diabetes* **24**, 641.

West, K.M. (1978a). Factors associated with the occurrence of diabetes. In *Epidemiology of diabetes and its vascular lesions* (K.M. West) p. 224. Elsevier, New York.

West, K.M. (1978b). Screening, detection and diagnosis. Prevalence and incidence. In *Epidemiology of diabetes and its vascular lesions* (K.M. West) p. 41. Elsevier, New York.

West, K.M. (1978c). Special types of diabetes. In *Epidemiology of diabetes and its vascular lesions* (K.M. West) p. 321. Elsevier, New York.

West, K.M. and Kalbfleisch, J.M. (1966). Glucose tolerance, nutrition and diabetes in Uruguay, Venezuela, Malaya and East Pakistan. *Diabetes* **15**, 9.

Wilkes, E. and Lawton, E.E. (1980). The diabetic, the hospital and primary care. *J. R. Coll. Gen. Pract.* **30**, 199.

World Health Organization Expert Committee on Diabetes Mellitus (1980). Second Report. WHO Technical Report series No. 646. WHO, Geneva.

Zimmet, P., Taft, P., Guinea, A., Guthrie, W., and Thoma, K. (1977). The high prevalence of diabetes mellitus on a Central Pacific Island. *Diabetologia* **13**, 111.

15 Musculoskeletal system

Philip H.N. Wood and Elizabeth M. Badley

INTRODUCTION

Judged by the morbidity burden to which they give rise, disorders of the musculoskeletal system are cause for serious concern. However, these conditions have rarely commanded commensurate priority in either epidemiological enquiry or public health planning. Our appraisal will begin with specification of the nature of the problem, including consideration of the validity of regarding it as a single entity.

DEFINITION OF THE PROBLEM

No archetypal condition epitomizes the features of musculoskeletal disorders, partly because no single condition dominates the scene in the way that ischaemic heart disease does in the cardiovascular system. The consequences have been quite unhelpful, retarding appreciation of the scale of problems and obscuring the most appropriate strategies for their control. The very diversity of musculoskeletal structures has contributed its own complexity because no unitary end-expression of involvement is detectable, nothing that can be systematized in a concept of locomotor failure.

The musculoskeletal system

There are compelling reasons to justify regarding musculoskeletal disorders as an entity. The common factor is that the supporting or connective tissues of the body are the seat of whatever lesions occur. Clinical involvement is characterized by difficulty in moving the parts of the body, and is commonly associated with pain and stiffness and often with swelling. The interference with locomotor function is primarily mechanical.

Expert knowledge of the musculoskeletal system is shared between surgical and medical specialties, orthopaedic surgery on the one hand and rheumatology on the other. Unfortunately, diffusion of knowledge across specialty boundaries leaves something to be desired, and paediatrics and, perhaps to a lesser extent, geriatrics may not fully exploit curent awareness. There are also short-comings in primary care which have more diffuse origins, including the variable level of undergraduate rheumatological education (Wood and Badley 1980a). These contribute to a challenge from various forms of heterodox practice (osteopathy, chiropractic, etc.—Hewitt and Wood 1975), a situation that may be encouraged by the subjective nature of much rheumatism.

There are some 200 or more recognized afflictions of the musculoskeletal system and connective tissue, to which must be added tumours and the results of trauma. This range of conditions can usefully be divided into two broad groups. The first consists of primarily orthopaedic disorders and the second comprises all other conditions affecting the musculoskeletal system, which may be referred to collectively as rheumatic disorders. Fuller specification of the two groups is shown in Table 15.1. Apart from certain specific types of aetiology (tumours, congenital deformities, and injury), most musculoskeletal conditions are assigned to Chapter XIII of the *International Classification of Diseases* (ICD) (WHO 1977). Because of their diversity we have had to assume a certain level of knowledge, at least of the major conditions, and leave readers to refer to standard texts for additional information.

PRIORITY OF THE PROBLEM

A reasonable picture of the impact of musculoskeletal disorders on the health of the community can be built up by drawing on published sources of routinely collected data (Table 15.2). The three dimensions of experience relevant to the priority of the problem are mortality, morbidity, and disablement.

Measures of impact

Mortality

Conditions such as malignant neoplasms are life-threatening, and so it is possible to learn something from death statistics. Most other musculoskeletal disorders are not generally fatal, and mortality data on these tend to be dismissed. However, such information can be instructive.

Every year in Great Britain some 5500 deaths are related to the consequences of rheumatic fever, and about 1000 are attributed to rheumatoid arthritis (RA); the numbers are proportionately larger in the US. Modes of death and contributory factors can indicate ways in which the outcome might be averted—a point borne out by the fact that anti-rheumatic drugs are one of the leading causes of fatal therapeutic misadventures. There is also a potential to learn more of disease associations from such sources, especially now that multiple-cause coding is being undertaken.

Table 15.1. *The range of disorders affecting the musculo-skeletal system (identifying the relevant rubrics of the ninth revision of the International Classification of Diseases)*

ICD rubric (9th revision)	Class of musculoskeletal disorder
PRIMARILY ORTHOPAEDIC DISORDERS	
170, 171, 213–215 (chapter II)	**Neoplasms of bone and connective tissue.** These include both malignant and benign tumours of bone, articular cartilage, and connective and other soft tissue
730–739 (chapter XIII)	**Osteopathies, chondropathies, and acquired musculoskeletal deformities.** These include infections of bone, Paget's disease, osteo-chondropathies, osteoporosis, aseptic necrosis, Tietze's disease, other disorders of bone, hallux valgus, curvature of the spine, and other acquired deformities
754–756 (chapter XIV)	**Congenital anomalies of musculoskeletal system.** These consist of reduction deformities and other anomalies of the limbs (including accessory structures), osteodystrophies, and deformities (e.g. varus or valgus of feet) and other congenital anomalies of the musculoskeletal system.
810–839 (chapter XVII)	**Trauma**—fractures of limb bones, and dislocations
RHEUMATIC DISORDERS	
710–719 (chapter XIII)	**Arthropathies and related disorders.** These include diffuse diseases of connective tissue (such as systemic lupus erythematosus, polymyositis, and dermatomyositis), gout, chondrocalcinosis, rheumatoid arthritis, juvenile chronic arthritis, (osteo)arthrosis, arthritis associated with other disorders (such as infection, psoriasis, and ulcerative colitis), and internal derangement and other disorders of joints
720–724 (chapter XIII)	**Dorsopathies.** These include ankylosing spondylitis, other inflammatory spondylopathies, spondylosis, intervertebral disc prolapse and degeneration, lumbago, sciatica, and other disorders related to the neck and back
725–729 (chapter XIII)	**Rheumatism** (excluding the back). This set of rubrics includes polymyalgia rheumatica, peripheral enthesopathies (such as capsulitis, tennis elbow, and calcaneal spur), synovitis, tendinitis, bursitis, disorders of muscle, ligament, and fascia, and other disorders of soft tissue (such as myalgia and pain in a limb)
840–848 (chapter XVII)	**Sprains and strains of joints and adjacent muscles.** This category of soft-tissue injury is largely self-explanatory; it also includes the nose, jaw, thyroid cartilage, rib cage, and pelvis, as well as less definitely traumatic lesions such as sacro-iliac or lumbosacral strain
390–392 (chapter VII)	**Other relevant conditions.** Although assigned elsewhere in the ICD, certain other conditions are also commonly considered to be rheumatic and are therefore usually included in this context, the most notable of these is acute rheumatic fever

A different use for mortality data is as an independent source for comparative estimates. We used 20-year follow-ups of consecutive attenders at hospital with RA to provide a measure of the average duration of disease from onset to death. This also allowed us to determine how the disease featured on death certificates—whether it was mentioned at all and, if so, how frequently as either the underlying or a contributory cause. With duration and the bridging estimate we were then able to use the Registrar General's reported annual mortality as an incidence measure, from which to calculate prevalence. The estimate of prevalence was of the same order of magnitude as that obtained from a population prevalence survey (unpublished observations).

Morbidity

In a 14-day period 29 per cent of adults are likely to experience acheing in their limbs and joints, 21 per cent backache, and 19 per cent trouble with their feet (Dunnell and Cartwright 1972). Only a minority of these complaints are taken to a doctor, because for every 1000 persons on a general practitioner's list only 152 will consult with a rheumatic problem during a year (OPCS 1974). Table 15.2 shows further details, together with estimates of the burden of sickness incapacity for work. Statistics on the latter represent another much neglected source of information.

Three measures are illuminating. First, people often suffer from more than one type of rheumatic problem, so that these complaints account for 25 per cent of all conditions presenting for consultation to a family doctor. Secondly, prior to recent changes in the arrangements, 15–17 per cent of all sickness incapacity was attributable to disorders of the musculoskeletal system; only the combined figures for the common cold, influenza, and bronchitis attained the same order of magnitude. Finally, rheumatic disorders are the third biggest cause for referral by a general practitioner for a specialist opinion.

Disablement

Musculoskeletal disorders are much the biggest class of condition giving rise to physical impairment, being responsible for two-fifths of the total at all ages and an even larger proportion in the elderly. Among the severely disabled the contribution is slightly greater. However, although orthopaedic and rheumatic disorders cause serious difficulties in everyday activities, particularly in regard to tempo of execution, they are not as commonly totally incapacitating as neurological conditions.

Frequency estimates

Incapacity, hospitalization, and mortality in Table 15.2 relate to the most recent year for which all three were available in the UK, 1978, but the other items are older because they are derived from *ad hoc* studies. In summary, with figures in parentheses indicating musculoskeletal disorders as a proportion of the burden from all conditions:

● 9.5 million musculoskeletal episodes (9.6 per cent of the total, but 25.9 per cent of all conditions presenting) were presented to general practitioners; these involved 16.9 million consultations (10.3 per cent).

● 1.7 million spells of incapacity for work were certified (16.7 per cent), and these gave rise to 73 million days lost from work (20.5 per cent).

● 1.2 million new referrals were made for a specialist opinion in outpatients (16.0 per cent); these were associated

Table 15.2. *Measures of the frequency of experiences with musculoskeletal disorders (expressed as rates per thousand population at risk mainly for the year 1978)* *

Musculoskeletal disorders	ICD rubric (8th revision)	GP consultations (home population)		Sickness incapacity certifications (insured population)		Hospital attendances (home population)			Impaired persons (adults > 16 years of age)		Deaths (home population)
		Consultations	Episodes	Spells	Days lost	Outpatients New	Total	Admissions	All degrees	Severe and very severe	
PRIMARILY ORTHOPAEDIC DISORDERS											
Neoplasms of bone and connective tissue		5.8	2.3	0.85	94	†	†	0.33	†	†	0.02
Malignant	170, 171	3.1	0.6	†	†	†	†	0.11	†	†	0.02
Benign	213–215	2.7	1.7	†	†	†	†	0.22	†	†	0.0006
Osteopathies and related disorders		7.7	4.2	0.65	32	†	†	0.72	0.10	(0)	0.02
Osteomyelitis, periostitis	720	†	†	†	†	†	†	0.06	0.10	(0)	0.001
Paget's disease	721	†	†	†	†	†	†	0.03	†	†	0.003
Other diseases of bone	722–723	†	†	†	†	†	†	0.16	†	†	0.02
Internal derangement of joint	724	6.4	3.3	0.65	32	†	†	0.32	†	†	0.00002
Hallux valgus and varus	737	1.3	0.9	†	†	†	†	0.15	†	†	0
Musculoskeletal congenital anomalies	754–756	0.9	0.7	0.09	8	†	†	0.32	†	†	0.002
Trauma		16.9	8.0	5.37	360	†	†	3.04	2.33	0.41	0.07
Fractures	N810–N829	16.9	8.0	5.37	360	†	†	2.85	2,33	0.41	0.07
Dislocations	N830–N839	†	†	†	†	†	†	0.19	†	†	0.001
ALL ORTHOPAEDIC DISORDERS		31.3	15.2	6.96	503	22.96	90.64	4.34	(2.43)	(0.41)	0.1
RHEUMATIC DISORDERS											
Arthropathies		79.9	35.6	7.64	964	†	†	1.47	22.10	4.30	0.05
Gout	274	3.8	1.8	0.83	21	†	†	0.01	†	†	0.0007
Rheumatoid arthritis (incl. AS)	712	18.9	5.9	†	†	†	†	0.5	3.44	1.29	0.02
Spondylosis	713.1	13.7	7.6	†	†	†	†	†	†	†	0.002
Other osteoarthrosis	713 remainder	43.5	20.3	3.12	421	†	†	0.8	3.56	0.52	0.015
Other arthritis	710–715 remainder	†	†	3.70	522	†	†	0.1	15.10	2.49	0.002
Connective tissue diseases	716 and 734	†	†	†	†	†	†	0.04	†	†	0.01
Dorsopathies (excl. AS and spondylosis)		68.0	36.1	20.69	738	†	†	0.88	2.00	0.20	0.0005
Sciatica	353	3.3	1.7	2.79	115	†	†	0.06	0.34	0.01	0.00002
Lumbago	717.0	15.3	9.1	3.56	72	†	†	†	†	†	0
Displacement of intervertebral disc	725	17.5	6.4	3.79	277	†	†	0.3	1.66	0.19	0.0002
Vertebrogenic pain	723 excl. 728.9	10.9	5.4	3.54	120	†	†	0.5	†	†	0.0003
Other back pain	728.9	21.0	13.5	7.00	154	†	†	†	†	†	0
Non-articular rheumatism		60.3	40.3	13.49	301	†	†	0.63	†	†	0.0004
Frozen shoulder	717.1	3.2	1.8	†	†	†	†	†	†	†	†
Other rheumatism	717 and 718 remainder	14.3	9.9	†	†	†	†	†	†	†	0.0004
Other arthritis and rheumatism	710–718 remainder	9.2	5.9	7.01	165	†	†	0.07	†	†	0
Bursitis and synovitis	731	12.0	7.6	1.87	41	†	†	0.2	†	†	0.00002
Symptoms referred to limbs	787	21.6	15.1	4.61	95	†	†	0.4	†	†	0.00002
Affection of sacroiliac joint	726	†	†	†	†	†	†	0.001	†	†	0
Sprains and strains	N840–N848	46.6	32.5	20.45	375	†	†	0.1	0.81	0.09	0.0001
Other relevant conditions		24.0	14.6	1.94	201	†	†	1.16	3.10	0.14	0.13
Rheumatic fever and rheumatic heart disease	390–398	4.5	1.4	0.12	62	†	†	0.3	0.19	0.02	0.11
Other soft tissue disorders	730–733 remainder	†	†	†	†	†	†	0.21	†	†	0.001
Other musculoskeletal disorders	720–738 remainder	19.5	13.2	1.82	139	†	†	0.65	2.91 0.12	0.02	
ALL RHEUMATIC DISORDERS		278.8	159.1	64.21	2579	2.18	10.90	4.24	28.01¶	4.73	0.18
ALL MUSCULOSKELETAL DISORDERS		310.1	174.3	71.17	3082	25.14	101.54	8.58	30.44¶	5.14	0.3
ALL DISEASES AND CONDITIONS‡		3009.6 (671.7)	1808.6§	429.41	15 191	157.07	691.45	89.7"	77.99	12.66	11.93

*Sizes of populations for computation of national experience in Britain (England, Wales, and Scotland)—multiply rate shown by home population, 54.3×10^3; insured population, 19.5×10^3; or adult population, 40.99×10^3, as appropriate. Population <15 years, 12.74×10^3. (All population figures quoted in thousands.)

†Not separately identifiable in primary source.

‡Includes all medical and surgical conditions, shown here for purposes of comparison.

§The rate for episodes for all diseases and conditions is inflated by persons experiencing more than one episode, due to different causes; the rate in parentheses is that for patients consulting and is more useful for comparison with the individual rates shown.

"Hospital admissions for all diseases and conditions exclude maternity admissions and those to psychiatric hospitals.

¶The total of impaired persons with all rheumatic disorders is less than the sum of the individual rates because more than one disorder was present in a proportion of people.

Expanded from Wood and Badley (1985); primary sources—OPCS, 1974; Harris (1971); and Hospital In-patient Enquiry (DHSS) and Registrar General's Statistical Review of England and Wales.

with 5.0 million attendances (14.7 per cent), although only 0.5 million required admission to hospital (10.1 per cent).
● Some 15 000 deaths were attributed to musculo-skeletal disorders (2.5 per cent).
● Turning from incidence to prevalence, 1.3 million people were impaired to some degree (39.9 per cent of the physically impaired), and almost 0.25 million of these were severely or very disabled (40.6 per cent).

Of musculoskeletal disorders in primary care contacts, sickness spells, and physical impairment, the primarily orthopaedic disorders accounted for about a tenth and rheumatic disorders for the remainder. Orthopaedic conditions were less prominent in the severely disabled, contributing only 1.6 per cent. On the other hand they were more evident in time lost from work (almost one-fifth), in mortality (a third), and in admissions to hospital (just over half). In all categories fractures were the dominant condition.

One-fifth of the musculoskeletal burden in primary care and incapacity is accounted for by each of back troubles, rheumatism, and soft-tissue injury, though the two latter made less contribution to work loss (i.e. their durations tended to be shorter). Arthropathies are similarly important in primary care contacts but, because females are less adequately represented in incapacity data, these conditions are responsible for only a tenth of spells. Despite this, arthropathies account for almost a third of days lost from work due to musculoskeletal disorders. They are also responsible for three-quarters of musculoskeletal impairment and severe disability.

Dorsopathies, rheumatism, and other relevant conditions are each responsible for about a tenth of hospital admissions, and arthropathies for almost twice this proportion. Mortality experience illustrates how impressions are distorted by the severely affected unless heed is paid to relative frequencies of occurrence (Wood and Badley 1981). Of musculoskeletal deaths almost half are attributed to rheumatic fever and its sequelae, more than a quarter to fractures, and about a fifteenth to each of rheumatoid arthritis, other arthropathies, and malignant tumours of the musculoskeletal system.

The profile in other industrialized countries is not dissimilar. There is a different spectrum in developing countries, the consequences of trauma and infection playing a much larger part. The characteristics of persons affected by musculoskeletal disorders, such as sex, age, and occupation, obviously vary between the different conditions and no meaningful generalizations can be made. However, the age distribution of musculoskeletal disorders indicates that changes in demographic structure, particularly in developing countries, are likely to lead to an increase in many of the problems.

The International Classification

Anyone wishing to carry out a similar appraisal is likely to encounter problems. For instance, routine tabulations of incapacity spells in men attributable to the painful back, based on ICD 8, revealed only two-thirds of the total, the remaining third being concealed in other categories that could be retrieved only by special enquiry and effort (Benn and Wood 1975).

The first difficulty is that many sources arrange information only in terms of the abbreviated lists published at the end of Volume 1 of the ICD (Table 15.3). A number of categories enumerated in Table 15.1 are submerged in more comprehensive groupings (e.g. benign tumours of bone are lost amongst all other benign tumours). The result is that a complete profile of the burden cannot be constructed from such sources—one factor that contributes to underestimation of the problem. This difficulty has been more

Table 15.3 *Musculoskeletal disorders in the abbreviated listings suggested in the ninth revision of the International Classification of Diseases. (Some conditions are subsumed in categories in the mortality and morbidity listings that include many non-musculoskeletal disorders (e.g. malignant tumours), so that there is considerable variation in specifity in the categories included in this table)*

Basic tabulation list

11	Malignant tumours of bone, connective tissue, skin, and breast (ICD 170–175)
110	Malignant tumours of bone and articular cartilage (ICD 170)
15	Benign tumours (ICD 210–229)
25	Rheumatic fever and rheumatic heart disease (ICD 390–398)
250	Acute rheumatic fever (ICD 390–392)
251	Chronic rheumatic heart disease (ICD 393–398)
43	Diseases of musculoskeletal system and connective tissue (ICD 710–739)
430	Rheumatoid arthritis, except spine (ICD 714)
431	Other arthropathies (ICD 710–713, 715, 716)
432	Other disorders of joints (ICD 717–719)
433	Ankylosing spondylitis (ICD 720.0)
434	Other dorsopathies (ICD 720.1–724)
435	Rheumatism, excluding the back (ICD 725–729)
436	Osteomyelitis, periostitis, and other infections involving bone (ICD 730)
437	Acquired deformities of limbs (ICD 734–736)
44	Congenital anomalies (ICD 740–759)
446	Congenital dislocation of hip (ICD 754.3)
447	Other congenital anomalies of musculoskeletal system (ICD 754.0–754.2, 754.4–756)
47	Fractures (ICD 800–829)
472	Fracture of humerus, radius, and ulna (ICD 812, 813)
473	Fracture of neck of femur (ICD 820)
474	Fracture of other parts of femur (ICD 821)
475	Fracture of tibia, fibula, and ankle (ICD 823, 824)
476	Other fractures of limbs (ICD 810–811, 814–819, 825–829)
48	Dislocations, and sprains and strains (ICD 830–848)

Mortality list

250	Acute rheumatic fever (ICD 390–392)
251	Chronic rheumatic heart disease (ICD 393–398)
44	Congenital anomalies (ICD 740–759)
47	Fractures (ICD 800–829)

Morbidity list

251	Chronic rheumatic heart disease (ICD 393–398)
43	Diseases of musculoskeletal system and connective tissue (ICD 710–739)
44	Congenital anomalies (ICD 740–759)
47	Fractures (ICD 800–829)

troublesome in editions of the ICD prior to the ninth revision, in which the abbreviated tabulation listings (the A and B lists, etc.) were even less representative in their musculo-skeletal coverage.

The second difficulty is that related conditions often used to be scattered widely in different parts of earlier revisions of the ICD. Rather arbitrary guidelines were followed on where to classify conditions, influenced more by presumptions about the nature and system involvement of supposed pathologies than they were by the likely meaning of diagnostic terms inscribed on pieces of paper. For example, sciatica used to be regarded as an inflammatory disorder of the nervous system (353 in ICD 8), whereas the largely indistinguishable complaints designated as lumbago and displacement of intervertebral disc (717.0 and 725 in ICD 8) were assigned to disorders of the musculoskeletal system and connective tissue.

What prevails in the ninth revision is a more consistent adherence to two practical considerations—the greatest reliability of information, which recognizes that the accuracy of the reported location of a lesion is likely to be greater than assumptions about its pathology; and maximum correspondence between the contents of ICD chapters and the spheres of work of medical specialties, facilitating assessments of the related community burden and the extent to which services are utilized for their relief.

This has had two practical consequences. First, many symptoms and ill-defined conditions have been reassigned to the body system chapter to which they most closely relate. Can 'rheumatism' really be differentiated from 'pain in a limb'? And yet the two used to be assigned to different chapters. Secondly, the facility has been introduced to identify manifestations (asterisked categories in ICD 9) as an alternative to underlying causes; this allows arthropathies associated with maladies such as infections and metabolic disorders to be acknowledged as musculoskeletal disorders.

Sources of information

Confronted by any unfamiliar topic, the first hope of someone working in Great Britain is that the Office of Health Economics (OHE) may have produced one of their excellent booklets on the problem—which, in the case of arthritis and rheumatism, they have done (OHE 1973). Alternatively, one may approach disease-oriented voluntary agencies—for example, the Arthritis and Rheumatism Council in the UK and the Arthritis Foundation in the USA. More specialized sources fall into three classes:

● those concerned with inherited disorders of the musculoskeletal system (Wynne-Davis 1973; Carter and Fairbank 1974; Beighton 1978).
● standard works on the primarily orthopaedic disorders (e.g. Mercer and Duthie 1983) and on the rheumatic diseases (e.g. Scott, in press).
● monographs synthesizing experience in the USA (Kelsey et al. 1978) and in the UK (Wood 1977), and those surveying rheumatological epidemiology (Bennett and Wood 1968), including descriptions of the work and experience of the pioneers in the USA (Cobb 1971) and in the UK (Lawrence 1977).

The principal sources of routine data are shown in Table 15.4. For specific medical topics the clinical and epidemiological literature is obviously important as well. An important routine source not identified is notification procedures, which are relevant only to diseases reported for other reasons; for example rheumatological complications may be associated with rubella, and were formerly encountered occasionally with smallpox vaccination.

Measures of morbidity derived from service contacts tend to be insufficiently precise for aetiological enquiries. Nevertheless these data have considerable value, influencing health service planning and focusing the attention of the community on the relative importance of particular health

Table 15.4. *Principal sources used to build up a profile of morbidity and mortality from musculoskeletal disorders (the emphasis being mainly on British sources)*

Routine

Sickness incapacity and injury benefit certifications (from DHSS—Department of Health and Social Security, in UK, and from Social Security Administration in US)

Insurance data (e.g. from publications of Metropolitan Life Insurance Company, such as their *Statistical bulletin*)

Out-patient statistics and hospital bed availability (from forms SH 3, summaries available from DHSS)

In-patient statistics from hospital activity analysis (HAA) and the hospital in-patient enquiry (HIPE, from OPCS—Office of Population Censuses and Surveys) in the UK, which includes details of surgical operations, and from Commission on Professional and Hospital Activities in the US

Mortality from publications by the Registrar General in the UK and by the National Center for Vital and Health Statistics in the US

Personpower, appliances, prescriptions, and local authority provisions (from DHSS)

General classes register of handicapped persons (from municipal authorities in UK, and from DHSS)

Register of disabled persons (from Department of Employment)

Annual reports, such as those of the Chief Medical Officer at DHSS, the Chief Inspector of Factories, and the Department of Education and Science

Occasional

Frequency of symptoms in the community (e.g. Dunnell and Cartwright 1972)

Health interview and examination surveys (the rainbow-coloured booklets from the US National Center for Vital and Health Statistics; the British General Household Survey is less useful for specific health-related questions)

General practice experience (the national morbidity surveys, from the Royal College of General Practitioners and OPCS); works on common diseases (Fry 1974) may also be helpful

Adverse effects of drugs (from the Committee on Safety of Medicines in UK, and the Food and Drug Administration in US)

Disablement (government social survey in UK, Harris (1971), and Social Security Administration in US, e.g. Haber (1971), together with derivative work—e.g. Badley et al. (1978)

Reports from local authorities and other agencies

Outlines

Much of the above data is often summarized in British series such as *Population trends, Social trends, Abstracts of statistics,* and *Health trends;* additional detail is often available on request problems. Moreover, identification of geographical differences in such data can pose questions of deeper significance. As regards the consequences of disease, trial introduction of a supplement to the ICD, the *International classification of impairments, disabilities, and handicaps* (ICIDH) (WHO 1980), may enhance availability of routine information relevant to these concerns and contribute to establishment of outcome measures and other methods necessary for evaluation.

There are usually delays before routine information becomes generally available. However, although trends may be detected, the magnitude of fluctuation between adjacent years is commonly small. There might appear to be a credibility problem, but in practice far too much is made of whether information is 'up-to-date'. Too often the fact that data are not the most recent is used as a pretext for neglecting or ignoring what lessons could be learned.

Views on the use of rough data (Blackett 1962) merit repetition: 'No pregnant problem should be left unattempted for lack of exact numerical data, for often it is found on doing the analysis that some significant conclusions recommending concrete action can be drawn even with very rough data'. The availability of useful information could certainly be improved, and epidemiologists and other public health professionals could be much more effective in the way they marshal and present their evidence. Nevertheless, a wealth of data do exist that could inform our appraisal of health problems; unfortunately it is largely untouched by human thought.

Ascertainment of the afflicted

For specific enquiries it is necessary to have some means of identifying cases in the community. Ascertainment depends on how conditions are conceived of, how they express themselves, and what methods may be appropriate to their recognition.

Disease concepts

Concepts such as rheumatoid arthritis (RA) are well established, and have provided a valuable means for recognizing similarity in clinical problems. However, community studies rely on strict definition, and even RA presents nosological uncertainties akin to those encountered with many other less well-characterized rheumatic complaints. The difficulty is that most of these conditions lack a hallmark—some uniquely defining property by which to identify affected individuals, such as a typical derangement or lesion or the presence of a specified microbial agent. Even if some highly characteristic attribute is acknowledged, it can rarely serve for definition because of the likelihood of its occurrence with other complaints as well.

Rheumatological epidemiologists were among the first to recognize the need for criteria (Ropes *et al.* 1957), and these have been drawn up for identification of RA and a number of other rheumatic disorders. Such approaches have promoted standardization in the process of diagnosis and in the consistency of clinical reports, but their value in community

studies has been notably less. The approach has generally been based on modal profiles, the characteristics of so-called 'typical' cases. Discrimination in preselected individuals, such as those attending a clinic, is likely to differ from performance in population samples.

The critical difficulty relates to what criterion or combination of criteria is necessary and sufficient to justify a diagnostic assignment. There is a variable overlap in features such as is represented by a Venn diagram (Fig. 15.1) (Kellgren 1968). Thus there may be discordance between illness and disease, such as symptoms occurring without pathology or abnormal tests being found when illness is not present, as well as between clinical and epidemiological distributions of the associated features (Wood 1970). From what has been said earlier, about the absence of a hallmark, it will be realized that to decide what is necessary and sufficient to permit diagnostic conclusions can raise difficulties that are conceptual as well as practical.

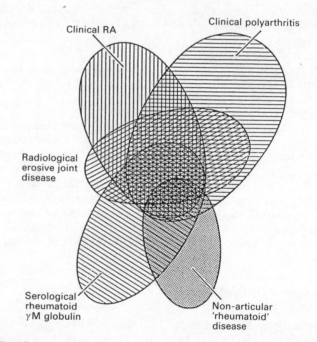

Fig. 15.1. Venn diagram to illustrate relationships between the distributions of different characteristics of rheumatoid arthritis. (Source: Kellgren (1968).)

Disease expression

Few rheumatic disorders are associated with well-defined events. Thus onsets are often not clear, frequently tending to be insidious and gradual; gout and the hexenschuss or witch's blow, a type of sudden acute back pain, are notable exceptions in this regard. Terminations are similarly non-universal; the conditions are rarely fatal and recovery is variable, residual impairment and disability often lasting until death. When the latter does occur it is usually attributable to unrelated causes. Intermediate events, such as consultation, initiation of treatment, and hospitalization, are also relatively unhelpful because they are commonly 'contaminated' by less biomedical influences.

Direct study of disease incidence is therefore rarely possible. Instead, incidence often has to be inferred from the differences between two prevalence estimates made at different points in time. Some of the problems associated with this method have been noted by Wood and Badley (1985). The other important implication is that, when well-defined events are not encountered, evaluation of outcome becomes correspondingly more difficult. The obvious exception to these general cautions is provided by the primarily orthopaedic disorders which, apart from the osteopathies and related conditions, should be more amenable to conventional direct studies of incidence.

Rheumatic disorders express themselves in uncertain and ill-defined ways. A spectrum of manifestations may arise from a number of causes, and to some degree they are experienced by everyone. This is compounded by variability in threshold because features are subjective, like pain, or non-specific, such as swelling. A number of joints may be affected, which creates additional problems in pattern recognition. With such diversity in localization, failure to develop a concept of locomotor failure analogous to that invoked with the heart, lungs, and kidney, is therefore not surprising. However, observation of the individual moving his body and its parts serves to screen for most musculoskeletal disorders.

The other difficulty in identifying disease states stems from the variable course of rheumatic disorders. Some conditions, such as gout, are episodic or recurrent, whereas others tend to fluctuate, with a pattern of remissions and exacerbations such as is encountered with rheumatoid arthritis. This means that a clear distinction has to be made between prevalence estimates based on respondents in episode at the time of study and those based on all persons who have ever experienced the condition. The implications of all these limitations are that prevalence estimates are subject to variability.

Survey methodology

Uncertainty about onset and variability of threshold confound retrospective ascertainment, and also make durations difficult to estimate. The process is further influenced by variability in recall, and by discordance in perception and understanding of symptom significance between respondent and observer. Survey conditions call for instant assessment, denying one the confirmation afforded by unfolding disease patterns. As a result, ascertainment or assignment generally tend to have unsatisfactory accuracy and sensitivity, especially with recent, mild, or atypical disease. This particular difficulty may be diminished when the disorder is long-standing or serious, or if permanent changes take a characteristic form.

The relative infrequency of many of the more serious musculoskeletal disorders commands the study of large samples. It is necessary to cover a diversity of subjective experiences and sites of involvement, which means the data base has to be fairly extensive. This large number of variables inevitably complicates data management and analysis.

Thus the efficiency and cost-effectiveness of surveys is relatively low, and this can be overcome only partially by studying more than one condition at a time. These difficulties notwithstanding, a considerable amount has been learned about the occurrence of musculoskeletal disorders in the community. However, more sophisticated interpretation founders on other problems, but these will be considered after a discussion of what is known about some of the individually more important conditions.

Individual conditions

Constraints on space compel us to be both terse and highly selective in commenting on musculoskeletal disorders individually. Estimates of prevalence and incidence in Great Britain are shown in Table 15.5. Readers wishing to pursue further detail and identify sources are referred to a fairly exhaustive review of the epidemiology of rheumatic disorders that has recently been completed (Wood and Badley 1985).

Rheumatoid arthritis

The standard diagnostic criteria (Bennett and Wood 1968) have largely stood the test of time. Prevalence increases fairly markedly with age, although a two- or threefold excess mortality is observed on long-term follow-up. The prevalence of RA in the first-degree relatives of affected persons is of the order of 4 per cent, and the heritability of liability is between 50 and 60 per cent. There is a link between RA and the leucocyte antigen HLA DR4/Dw4.

Prevalence appears to be low in Africa, Polynesia, Puerto Rico, and much of Asia. The criteria give rise to difficulty in tropical countries where frequencies of rheumatoid factor and erosive changes are raised by infections and trauma respectively. Prevalence in members of the same tribe in Africa is increased when they migrate from a rural to an urban environment. Anecdotal evidence suggests that joints stressed at work may become more severely damaged by RA, but overall no link with occupation has been detected.

Juvenile chronic arthritis

The term juvenile chronic arthritis (JCA) is a generic descriptor which identifies a heterogeneous collection of conditions; unfortunately these are often referred to as juvenile RA in the US. The identity of subtypes is reinforced by similar patterns of affection within some families, and first-degree relatives of affected children show clinical ankylosing spondylitis (AS) in just over 1 per cent, sacroiliitis in 9 per cent, and polyarthritis in 5 per cent. Criteria have been developed, but the frequency of the JCA variants has not been estimated satisfactorily.

The earliest reported onset is within the first year of life so that prenatal and postnatal experiences perhaps have equal likelihood of being relevant to causation. Mortality is increased, but after the age of 15 years less than 10 per cent of affected children are likely to be handicapped. Associated amyloidosis is encountered more frequently in Europe than in North America.

Table 15.5. *Summary of reported frequency estimates for various musculoskeletal disorders in Great Britain**

Disorder	Prevalence (per thousand)	Annual incidence (per thousand)
Inflammatory arthropathies	>22	>0.7
Rheumatoid arthritis (definite disease)	10.0	>0.2
Juvenile chronic arthritis (in children <15 years)	0.6	0.06
Ankylosing spondylitis	1.5	0.07
Enteropathic arthropathy	0.02	†
Reiter's disease	†	0.01
Psoriatic arthropathy	1.0	†
Gout	<3.0	0.3
Chondrocalcinosis (on radiographic evidence)	6.0	†
Septic arthritis	†	†
Connective tissue diseases	>0.2	(>0.01)
Systemic lupus erythematosus	0.04	†
Systemic sclerosis	(0.02)	(0.002)
Polymyositis and dermatomyositis	(0.04)	(0.004)
Sjøgren's disease	†	†
Polyarteritis nodosa	(0.06)	(0.007)
Arthrosis and dorsopathies (estimates for components not exclusive)	†	†
Peripheral joints (on radiographic evidence)	110	†
Spondylosis (on radiographic evidence)	450	†
Other back troubles (lifetime incidence 60%)	†	†
Soft-tissue syndromes	†	†
Polymyalgia rheumatica	>0.4	0.03
Occupational disorders	†	†
Other non-articular rheumatism	(25)	†
Other musculoskeletal disorders	†	†
Inherited conditions	†	†
Rheumatic fever	†	†
Bone disorders	(>30)	†
Dupuytren's contracture	(2.0)	†

*In the adult population (except where otherwise noted); the main value of the figures is to indicate relative frequencies of occurrence, as the precision of the estimates varies—less confidence can be placed in the accuracy of figures shown in parentheses.

†No satisfactory estimate.

Adapted from Wood and Badley (1985).

Ankylosing spondylitis

A monograph on the disease is a useful source for reference (Moll 1980). Criteria have not proved to be very satisfactory. An almost twofold increase in mortality over a period of 13 years has been observed, even in patients not submitted to radiotherapy, but long-term functional outlook is otherwise good. The condition can be identified in up to 4 per cent of the first-degree relatives of spondylitic probands, and the heritability of liability is 70 per cent. The frequency of HLA-B27 is increased in spondylitics and their families. Discordance for AS in B-27-positive monozygotic twins suggests an environmental factor is also important.

Ankylosing spondylitis predominantly affects men in their twenties, often those of athletic inclination. There have been no consistent suggestions of influences attributable to social status or occupation. Of external agents the role of enterobacteria has attracted much attention, although the topic is still controversial. Amerindians living near the west coast of Canada manifest AS some 10 times more often than Caucasoids. The frequency of AS in American blacks is about four times less than the rate in Caucasoids, and the disease also appears to be rare in Africa and relatively so in Japan.

Other spondylarthropathies

A number of rather similar conditions occur and have been studied extensively by Wright and Moll (1976). All show familial aggregation, and are associated with an increased frequency of the B27 antigen—9 per cent in the general population; 92 and 53 per cent respectively in AS and enteropathic arthropathy; and 71 and 30 per cent respectively in Reiter's disease and psoriatic arthropathy.

A preliminary evaluation of criteria for Reiter's disease has been undertaken. In many parts of Europe onset is usually preceded by dysentery, while in the UK and North America most cases occur following extramarital sexual intercourse. The condition appears to be less common in coloured patients, and it accounts for the majority of cases of arthritis in young males in Papua.

Criteria for psoriatic arthropathy have been suggested. Little has been established about environmental determinants. Apart from the deforming arthritis, overall impact on the individual generally tends to be less than that related to other major rheumatic disorders.

Crystal arthropathies

Recent work on criteria for gout has been directed at diagnosis in clinical contexts. Prevalence tends to be underestimated, and incidence overestimated. Elevated serum uric acid (SUA) levels are a risk factor. Overall there is a six- to sevenfold male preponderance. Prevalence has increased since the Second World War, to which thiazide diuretics have contributed. Prevalence in first-degree relatives is 6 per cent, and the heritability of liability is of the order of 80 per cent. However, there is an appreciable correlation in SUA between spouses.

High frequencies of gout are observed on the periphery of the Pacific Ocean, in Polynesians, Micronesians, and Filipinos. Migrant studies have indicated that the key to this experience appears to be a blend of nature and nurture. Apart from exposure to lead, no links with occupation have been identified. A high standard of living and postulated stress act as precipitators of gout, and the overall influence of culture and life-style is indicated by the very low prevalence of gout under primitive conditions, compared with experience in urbanized Africans.

Another form of arthritis is associated with pyrophosphate crystals in the joints. Chondrocalcinosis is commoner in the elderly, and 5 per cent of the adult population probably have knee joint deposits at the time of death. Kindreds in various countries show apparent dominant transmission, but it seems likely these relatively isolated occurrences represent a different form of the condition and familial occurrence in representative communities has yet to be studied.

Other inflammatory arthropathies

At least three classes of musculoskeletal response to micro-organisms have been identified. In addition to the classical septic arthritis, there is postinfective arthropathy and a 'reactive' arthropathy. Lyme disease in the north-eastern US is of topical interest. A tick bite is followed 3–20 days later by erythema chronicum migrans and about four weeks after that by a pauciarticular arthropathy, often recurrent. A spirochaete has recently been isolated from a small proportion of sufferers. Suggestive cases have been reported from Europe.

A wide variety of other joint disorders associated with inflammatory processes has been described, including conditions such as Behçet's disease and hypogammaglobulinaemia (Wood and Badley 1985).

Systemic lupus erythematosus

Much work has been done on criteria, and a screening strategy for population studies has been put forward recently. A realistic estimate of prevalence in relatives is of the order of 0.1 per cent. However, familial aggregation of various phenomena is also seen in spouses and household contacts, indicating that extraneous (environmental) factors are also important. It appears that races originating from eastern Asia and the Pacific region are at some fourfold greater risk. In Africa, SLE and autoimmune phenomena appear to be less common, but American Negroes suffer from the disease at least three times as frequently as neighbouring Caucasoids.

Between 3 and 12 per cent of all cases of SLE in New York City follow ingestion of medication. Ultraviolet light is a well-established trigger factor. A viral aetiology for SLE has long been favoured, and family studies have often appeared to reinforce these views; however, this has not yet been substantiated.

Other connective tissue diseases

A standardized approach to diagnostic criteria for systemic sclerosis (SS) has been adopted recently. The condition shows a threefold female preponderance, a sevenfold increase in incidence over 20 years has been noted, and vertical transmission in families has been described. Like other connective tissue diseases, SS may be less common in New Zealand, but geographical variation is not apparent in the US.

The other connective tissue diseases include polymyositis, dermatomyositis, mixed connective tissue disease, Sjøgren's disease, and polyarteritis nodosa. The epidemiology of these conditions is discussed in detail elsewhere (Wood and Badley 1985).

'Degenerative' conditions

Most clinicians differentiate between the inflammatory arthropathies and so-called mechanical or degenerative disorders. Arthrosis and back troubles together account for

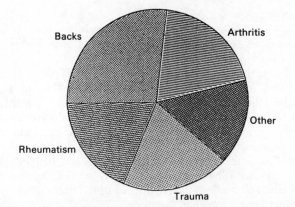

Fig. 15.2. Crude case mix in patients with rheumatic problems presenting to a general practitioner. (Derived from the Second National Morbidity Study—OPCS (1974).)

at least a third of all rheumatic suffering (Fig. 15.2). Most of our knowledge is based on structural changes seen on radiographs. Although associated complaint rates generally increase with the severity of these changes, the discordance or 'false-positive' rates indicate how incomplete an explanation is provided by such shadowy evidence. Standards for interpretation of radiographs are available (Atlas 1963), but a sustained approach to construction of diagnostic criteria has been undertaken only recently, and that was confined to arthrosis of the knee joint. A complementary approach is to concentrate on perceived health problems (Hunt *et al.* 1981).

Arthrosis of peripheral joints

Arthrosis (osteoarthrosis or OA) may be subdivided according to whether it is localized to a single site, which appears to be much commoner than polyarticular involvement. The prevalence of all forms of arthrosis increases with age, and frequency appears to be fairly similar in the two sexes. The detailed work of Lawrence (1977) has included all the more important individual joints. The knee is the most commonly involved major joint, but the hip is the most disabling site. Predisposing factors to the latter include congenital dislocation of the hip, Leg–Calvé–Perthes disease, slipped epiphysis, trauma, and polyarthritis; it has been estimated that some 40 per cent of cases can be attributed to these underlying causes.

Inherited factors contribute to properties such as the geometry of joints, but observed ethnic differences have been attributed more to patterns of use than to genetic influences. Trauma is important in some forms of arthrosis. Although rheumatoid arthritis is commonly regarded as the most disabling form of arthropathy, the very much higher prevalence of arthrosis puts this apparently less disabling condition number one in the league table of physical causes of severe disablement, and by a long lead (Badley *et al.* 1978*b*). Interference with sexual activity is also an important problem.

Polyarticular arthrosis

Polyarticular involvement is occasionally related to familial chondrodysplasia. More often multiple joints are affected without evidence of underlying developmental defects. There is an association with Heberden's nodes, but a non-nodal form also exists.

The term generalized osteoarthrosis (GOA) is best reserved for the primary nodal disorder (Kellgren and Moore 1952). Individuals may well complain of symptoms related to only a single joint, but radiographic investigation reveals the typical pattern. Population surveys indicate a prevalence of up to 15 per cent in women aged 45 years and over, but almost a third of those affected had never experienced pain. What we now identify as GOA was first described as menopausal arthritis but the menopause does not seem to be a critical factor.

Spondylosis

Spondylosis is a generic descriptor for 'degenerative' processes in the spine, be these in the apophyseal joints or related to intervertebral discs. Disc degeneration (DD) is the disorder for which the term is often used as a synonym. Standards for radiographic gradings have been developed, although intraobserver variation is still a problem. Symptoms usually arise from an articular segment that is vulnerable to instability because of DD, but the presence of osteophytes indicates that stabilization has probably begun to occur. This contrast provides an explanation for the fall-off in incidence of many back complaints with age (Fig. 15.3), despite the fact that X-ray abnormalities tend to show a sustained increase in extent and severity.

Work on DD has been reviewed by Lawrence (1977). Prevalence increases with age, and after 60 years it is rare to find a completely normal spine. Familial aggregation occurs, and both concordance in twins and relative freedom from cervical spondylosis in other families have been recorded. Variations in DD are most likely to represent differential stress related to habitual patterns of use, rather than ethnic or geographical differences. Only infrequently are antecedent causes identifiable, such as adolescent kyphosis, scoliosis, tuberculous infection, spondylolysis or spondylolisthesis, spinal osteochondrosis, and ochronosis. Heavy manual work encourages multiple DD. However, sedentary workers exhibit similar frequencies of involvement of the cervical spine, but the severity of changes is only minimal.

Other anatomical abnormalities

Ankylosing hyperostosis (AH) is often referred to as Forestier's disease, or diffuse idiopathic skeletal hyperostosis (DISH). The condition is distinct from spondylosis—it occurs later in life and is unrelated to strenuous work—and its frequency is 6–10 times less. Lawrence (1977) quotes prevalence ratios of 14 per cent in men and 5 per cent in women over the age of 34 years, but these estimates are higher than those observed in other experience.

Developmental anomalies such as spina bifida occulta and transitional vertebra are probably commoner than has been realized. However, the evidence does not support the view that these anomalies have a meaningful relation to back complaints. The same also appears to be true of spondylo-lysis and spondylolisthesis. On currently inadequate knowledge, pre-employment screening by radiographs is probably an unwarrantable infringement of individual liberty.

The situation is even less satisfactory in regard to scoliosis. Lateral spinal curvature can be identified in 15 per cent of schoolchildren, but in two-fifths it is related to pelvic tilt due to inequality in leg lengths rather than primary abnormality of the spine itself. The greater the curvature the more likely the problem represents a true idiopathic scoliosis, which has an overall frequency of 0.2 per cent; this occurs more frequently in girls, is associated with a median sagittal asymmetry, and tends to be progressive. The remaining children have spinal scoliosis, which probably represents irrelevant coronal asymmetry in normal healthy children.

Spinal stenosis describes a disproportion between the sizes of the spinal canal and associated tunnels and foramina on the one hand and of the nervous structures disposed within them on the other. The result can be compression of the latter, and interference with the blood supply. A variety of lesions may give rise to the condition. Pulsed-echo ultrasound has been used to study particular groups, but unselected population samples have not been investigated.

Disc prolapse

Much of the literature on back complaints is confused by references to prolapse of the intervertebral discs. Although these structures undoubtedly may prolapse, herniate, or in other ways be displaced, the difficulty lies in establishing both when this may have happened and whether it is clinically significant. In particular, narrowing of the disc space on its own has never been established a having a relationship to symptoms. The result is loose usage of the term, disc prolapse, by both practitioners and the public.

We are not satisfied that reports supposedly concerned with epidemiological aspects of disc prolapse in fact contribute any enlightenment on this condition. We prefer to acknowledge the uncertainties and consider all that has been so ascribed in the more general context of non-specific back pain. The relationship between disc prolapse and DD has also not been adequately elucidated, so that one is often compelled to resort to generic designation of disc lesions. In fact much of the evidence would suggest that DD is of much more general importance than uncomplicated prolapse. However, readers wishing to pursue a specific focus on disc prolapse despite these caveats may consult a recent review (Kelsey and White 1980).

Back pain

The evidence has been reviewed by Wood and Badley (1980b). Estimates of prevalence for what is usually a relatively short-lived but very common complaint are not particularly enlightening. More graphic is the appreciation Hult (1954) developed in his pioneer work—that 60 per cent of men up to age 69 years had at some time suffered symptoms related to the lower back, and that the proportion increased to 80 per cent when attention was focused on those involved in physically demanding occupations. Lumbar disorders outnumber cervical by a factor of 2:1.

Figure 15.3 depicts the crude age pattern observed in consultations with general practitioners, which reflects the maximal burden of complaints in the middle years of life. Translated into lifetime experience, symptoms are usually first experienced in the earlier part of adulthood. Surgical treatment is most commonly undertaken for those aged 35–45 years, but durations of incapacity tend to increase progressively with age. The longer the incapacity the less is the likelihood of a return to gainful employment, and chronic backache is an important cause of premature retirement.

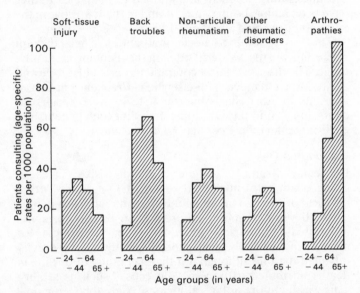

Fig. 15.3. Age-specific incidence rates for categories of rheumatic disorders in general practice. (Derived from OPCS (1974).)

Sickness absence because of back troubles has increased over time, but this is unlikely to reflect a real increase in occurrence. Geographical comparisons are difficult because cultural influences on expression of discomfort tend to vary *parris passu*. The relationship between back pain and bodily activity, especially as determined at the workplace, has been studied extensively. Campaigns of instruction in manual handling and lifting derive from such observations, although satisfactory evidence on the protective effect of these initiatives is not available.

How is one to seek enlightenment from this welter of information? A recurring theme is the notion that back pain is an epiphenomenon of cultural evolution of the human species. However, there is no agreement on what characteristic of this process might be implicated. It is likely that the complaint represents the resultant of a complex interplay of factors (Wood 1980).

Polymyalgia rheumatica

Diagnostic criteria for polymyalgia rheumatica (PMR) have only recently been submitted to rigorous testing. A relation-ship to temporal arteritis exists but has not been adequately quantified. The best population estimate relates to the latter, and is shown in Table 15.5. Prevalence is markedly influenced by age, being 0.03 per cent in the sixties and rising to 0.8 per cent in the over eighties. The condition is probably under-recorded, so that realistic estimates may well be somewhat higher. Age-specific incidence rates are some three times greater in women. Familial aggregation has been described; some mother–daughter pairs have become affected within a year of each other and conjugal affection has been reported, which might favour a common extraneous precipitant, but other relatives have developed PMR in the absence of evidence of space–time interaction.

The geography of the disorder is indicated only indirectly by the origin of published papers, predominantly from Scandinavia, the UK, and northern cities in the US. Polymyalgia rheumatica has been reported in American blacks, although the impression persists that it is rare in British immigrants originating from the Indian subcontinent. The biggest hazard of both PMR and temporal arteritis is blindness, though the risk has not been adequately quantified.

Occupational disorders

Lawrence (1977) has reviewed a series of specific occupations. Occupation plays an essential part in certain industrial diseases affecting the musculoskeletal system, including Caplan's syndrome, aseptic necrosis of the femoral head in caisson disease, and industrial injury prescribed diseases 32, beat knee, 33, beat elbow, and 34, synovitis of the wrist. With most other conditions one is confronted at most with an apparent increase in risk in certain industries, without being certain whether there is an absolute increase or just that the rate of developing the disorder is accelerated. The concept of high-risk groups may seem attractive, but our earlier remarks on pre-employment medical examinations are relevant in this context.

Theoretically, at least, it should be possible to devise methods of working that could prevent these problems. Colloquial names suggest aspects of aetiology (Wood *et al.* 1979), and the manner of use or over-use of parts of the body appears to play an important part in pathogenesis. This view encompasses soft-tissue injury, in the form of sprains and strains; the role of pressure in bursitis; and the contribution of repetitive movement to the development of tenosynovitis. Ages at presentation to primary care show a fall-off at older ages (Fig. 15.3). Sufferers are in considerable hazard of repeated attacks, as indicated by recrudescence rates for the prescribed diseases—12 per cent for beat knee, 7 per cent for beat elbow, and 6 per cent for tenosynovitis of the wrist.

Non-articular rheumatism

Dixon (1979) has described soft-tissue rheumatism as 'the great outback of rheumatology, a vast frontier land, ill-defined and little explored, its features poorly categorized'. Development of the unifying concept of the enthesopathies marks some progress in this area. Lawrence (1977) has reviewed the occurrence of pain in various parts of the body. A population survey in Sweden showed a prevalence of all forms of soft-tissue rheumatism of 1.6 per cent in men and 3.6 per cent in women.

The painful shoulder ranks after the painful knee in frequency of presentation. Probably the best-documented, though ill-understood, problem is the so-called frozen shoulder or adhesive capsulitis. Peak incidence is between 50 and 70 years, and the condition is encountered slightly more commonly in women than men. The left (non-dominant) shoulder is more frequently involved. Immobility and trauma appear to be important and, in principle at least, the condition should be preventable in many circumstances.

Inherited conditions

Most congenital anomalies remain obscure. General disorders whose occurrence conforms to the simple Mendelian laws of inheritance are encountered infrequently, and the best reference sources are McKusick (1972), Wynne-Davies (1973), Carter and Fairbank (1974), and Beighton (1978).

Joint mobility has been studied in various groups. Hypermobility of individual joints is a continuously distributed attribute (Wood 1971), which suggests that it may be benign and not a systemic connective tissue disorder. Familial joint laxity may well be transmitted as a dominant character, but its manifestation is very dependent on age. The resultant general hypermobility is a well-recognized cause of rheumatic complaints.

Congenital dislocation of the hip (CDH) has a complex inheritance; what might be regarded as risk factors include first-born children, older than average fathers, breech presentation, a significant lack of menstrual problems in the mother, and maternal upper respiratory infection during pregnancy. A recent report that neonatal screening appears to have failed to make a substantial impact on morbidity from CDH naturally gives rise to concern, and questions have to be raised about the efficacy of the treatment used.

Rheumatic fever

There has been a dramatic reduction in the frequency and severity of rheumatic fever and its sequelae, so that today these conditions are numerically infrequent in most developed countries. The situation is very different in much of Asia and Africa, where poverty, slums, crowding, very poor housing, and grossly inadequate health services are all relevant. In India there has been no change in the prevalence of rheumatic heart disease (RHD) since the Second World War, whilst in Thailand RHD accounts for a steady third of cardiovascular admissions. The modified Duckett Jones criteria for diagnosis have been evaluated mainly in individuals of European origin, and their applicability in other parts of the world is less because at least two of the major criteria, chorea and polyarthritis, are not encountered so frequently.

European mortality statistics have tended to show high death rates in the oldest age groups, which is at variance with common experience. Our own studies of this anomalous mortality showed that the problem was erroneously inflated by coding rules in earlier revisions of the ICD. For example, pericarditis not otherwise qualified would be assigned to acute rheumatic fever even when it was recorded in older persons in the presence of uraemia or lung cancer. The problem can be avoided if attention is confined to those aged 15–24 years (Strasser 1976). In countries such as France and the US mortality in these young adults was 0.4 per 100 000, whereas in some southern and eastern European countries it was almost 10 times higher.

Paget's disease of bone

Less than 0.1 per cent of hospital discharges and of deaths of persons over the age of 45 years are assigned to Paget's disease. On the other hand necropsy studies reveal a frequency of 3–4 per cent, and in radiographic surveys the prevalence is as high as 6 per cent. Prevalence increases with age, and is more frequent in men than women. Death rates have been falling, both in the UK and in the US, those in the latter country being about one-fifth of those in Britain.

There is a south to north gradient in England, with clustering on the western side of the Pennine mountain range. The disease is fairly common in parts of Europe and Australasia and much rarer elsewhere. Frequency in British migrants to Australia is intermediate between local residents and that in the UK, indicating that both genetic and environmental influences may be important.

Osteoporosis

Between 1950 and 1970, there was a progressive increase in crude death rates attributed to the ICD category 'other diseases of bone'. The apparent epidemic affected people aged 80 years or more, suffering from osteoporosis and associated pathological fractures. After adjustment for increase in the elderly population, the change almost exactly reflected the rate although not the magnitude of decline in deaths attributed to non-specific causes such as senility. This was therefore not a real increase, probably being only part of a more general tendency to use terms of greater specificity for death entries. Whether postmenopausal oestrogens prevent osteoporosis remains controversial.

Dupuytren's contracture

The general concept of the fibromatoses links together various conditions, such as Garrod's pads and nodular or plantar fasciitis, which exhibit certain common features (Mackenzie 1970). The most frequent expression is contracture of palmar fascia, associated with the name Dupuytren. Early (1962) reported prevalence as being 3.9 per cent in men and 0.5 per cent in women in Leigh, with a steep age gradient. Manual occupations do not appear to influence development of the condition. Frequency in Scandinavia is probably higher, but the condition is said to be rare in races with darker skin pigmentation. Family studies have suggested transmission as a Mendelian dominant, although other interpretations of the evidence are possible.

Bone tumours

Primary malignancies of bone occur mainly in young adults, whereas secondary tumours develop mostly in older people (governed by the age of occurrence of neoplasms with a predilection to metastasize to bone). Older data on primary bone tumours tended to distort their age distribution because reports of epithelial origin (i.e. carcinoma with spread to adjacent bone, such as in the paranasal sinuses, but which was not clearly identified as involving bone only secondarily) were not taken into account in the process of coding to ICD categories. Malignant neoplasms of other musculoskeletal elements are uncommon, but they also tend to arise most often in the first half of life.

Other orthopaedic disorders

Major long-standing orthopaedic conditions, notably bone and joint infections, such as osteomyelitis and tuberculosis, and the skeletal consequences of poliomyelitis, have virtually disappeared from developed countries. In developing countries there is still a lot of headway to be made in the control of these problems. This development has had considerable implications for health care organization. In particular, surgeons have been freed from straightening children so that they have been able to turn their energies to other things. This has led to development of artificial replacements for joints, the insertion of which has now come to take up a large part of surgeons' time (Wood 1976a); the subject has been considered in some detail by Laing and Taylor (1982).

The very disposition of the locomotor apparatus determines preferential exposure of structures to injury. Brief mention has been made of soft-tissue trauma, and major points about fractures are better considered under the epidemiology of accidents. However, it is worth noting that fracture proneness in elderly women has too readily been attributed to hormonal changes (Wood and Badley 1983). A textbook of orthopaedics should be consulted for points about other disorders.

Interpretation

Problems in disease ascertainment make it difficult to come to many firm conclusions about changes over time. Change in demographic structure has been the most important influence. Since most musculoskeletal disorders tend to be commoner in older people (Wood and Badley 1983) and the size of the population at risk has increased, these conditions are now a major cause of morbidity. Other aspects of change, including the expectations of the public and the responses of health care facilities, have been described elsewhere (Wood et al. 1980).

Known hazards

Wood (in press) has reviewed conditions known to influence the occurrence of musculoskeletal disorders (Table 15.6). Certain very general conclusions can be drawn, as follows:

1. With a few notable exceptions, such as caisson disease, musculoskeletal disorders are only rarely the primary manifestation of environmental hazard.

2. Diverse environmental exposures may nevertheless affect parts of the locomotor apparatus, and these include skeletal fluorosis, saturnine gout, and various industrial intoxicants such as polyvinyl chloride and many other compounds; in seeking the effects of hazards the most important target to be considered is bone.

3. There is a variety of well-recognized occupational disorders, including different forms of bursitis, vibration-induced white finger, and chronic crepitant synovitis (e.g. of the wrist); leisure pursuits add to the range, notably with enthesopathies such as tennis elbow.

4. Although encountered relatively infrequently in industrialized countries, the role of microbial agents is diverse when global experience is assimilated; noteworthy are the relationship between the streptococcus and acute rheumatic fever, various forms of viral polyarthritis, such as in association with rubella or through the medium of an insect vector, and the recent concept of 'reactive' arthropathies.

Apart from specific hazards, there is little to be said about other influences that are particular to the musculoskeletal system.

Age and genetics

There is a dynamic interrelationship between understanding of nosology and aetiology but, sadly, causal models for most rheumatic disorders are obscure. Most rheumatic disorders occur mainly from middle-age onwards. As disease onset is too late for selection pressures to have operated, this would suggest that genetic components of aetiology may be relatively large. Age distributions also give rise to difficulties in interpretation. For example, arthrotic changes show an association with increasing age. Are the joint changes an integral part of ageing? If so, surely they should be consistent and universal? If not a feature of the ageing process, does the association reflect a relatively nonspecific concomitant of age, such as greater exposure to wear, or is it the consequence of a more specific nonuniversal pathological process which is itself commoner in those of greater age? Osteophytosis is probably a nonspecific accompaniment, whereas arthrosis is likely to be a disease (Wood 1976b).

Another aspect of age relates to latency, the interval between operation of putative causes and manifestation of the condition to which these may give rise. Latency has not been determined but the characteristics of many rheumatic disorders, especially the more chronic ones, suggest that it is likely to be both long and variable. Comparative studies, both between and within groups, including families and twins, may be confounded not only by the variation in latency and the time scale this covers, but also by premature mortality within this span.

The role of genetic factors is to determine susceptibility or diathesis, rather than disease occurrence. There are few indicators or markers of inherited predisposition, so that interpretation of familial aggregation is largely speculative. However, much excitement has resulted from identification of the human leucocyte system of isoantigens. The most notable association is between HLA-B27 and ankylosing spondylitis (AS), although impressive but lesser frequencies

Table 15.6. *Musculoskeletal effects of environmental influences* *

Environmental component	Specific factor influencing health	Musculoskeletal manifestations
(a) Involuntary		
Geography		
Parts of Africa	Arbovirus (V: mosquito)	Polyarthritis associated with chikungunya and o'nyong nyong
Australia	Arbovirus (Ross river)	Epidemic Australian polyarthritis
New England	Spirochaete	Lyme arthritis (V: black-legged tick, *Ixodes dammini*)
Tropical countries	Mycobacterium	Acute polyarthritis associated with leprosy; also neuropathic arthropathy
	Treponeme	Periostitis, osteitis, and rarely arthritis in yaws
	Filaria (V: mosquito)	Chylous arthritis (of knee) associated with elephantiasis
West and East Africa	Microfilaria (V: buffalo gnat)	Arthritis (usually knee or hip) associated with onchocerciasis
Bantu	?	Ulcero-osteolytic neuropathy giving rise to neuropathic (Charcot) arthropathy
Atmosphere		
Droplets	Viral and bacterial	E.g. Polyarthritis in association with mumps, rubella, and meningococcal infection (haemorrhagic arthritis)
Spores	Fungi	Migratory pauciarticular involvement, or erythema multiforme or nodosum, or bone and joint involvement when disseminated, with coccidiomycosis, histoplasmosis, and other mycoses
?Spore	?Fungi (cereal grains)	Degenerative arthropathy associated with Kaschin–Beck disease
Dust	?	Caplan's syndrome (rheumatoid arthritis with pulmonary nodules) in coal and iron workers
Ionizing radiation†	Bone-seeking isotopes	Bone necrosis and sarcoma of bone with strontium
Sound	Ultrasonics	Bone necrosis
Electricity	Electric shock	Trauma leading to cervical disc degeneration
Barometric pressure	Gas embolism	Aseptic necrosis (particularly of head of humerus and femur) in caisson disease and related conditions
	Weightlessness	Bone changes (prevented by exercise)
Climate		
Sunlight	Ultraviolet irradiation	Activates lysosomal enzymes; may precipitate systemic lupus erythematosus (SLE)—?due to immunogenicity of UV-irradiated DNA
Ambient temperature	Thermal sensitivity	Raynaud syndrome (including cryoprecipitates); also pain perception heightened in cold exacerbating rheumatic symptoms
Weather change	Unknown but heterogeneous	Exacerbation of certain rheumatic symptoms
Water and soil		
Minerals	Fluoride	Skeletal fluorosis (also influenced by tea and wine drinking)
	Iron	Siderosis in Bantu progressing to spinal osteoporosis and destructive lesions, and arthropathy, especially of hands
	Lead	Saturnine gout associated with lead poisoning and renal failure
Contamination	Bacteria (especially *Salmonella*)	Specific arthritis (i.e. organism in joint) or postinfective and reactive arthropathies
Infestation	Nematode (in infected flea)	Mon-articular arthritis (usually knee) associated with dracontiasis
Effluents	Arsenic	Pulmonary osteoarthropathy
	Cadmium	Secondary osteomalacia resulting from renal damage, leading to weakness
	Phosphorus	Bone necrosis (phossy jaw)
(b) Individual		
Ingestion		
Dietary deficiency	Vitamin C	Arthritis and tender bone ends associated with scurvy
	Vitamin D	Painful bone lesions adjacent to joints and osteogenic synovitis in rickets (similar problems in hyperparathyroidism and osteomalacia)
Dietary excess	Hypervitaminosis D	Localized osteoporosis or cf. hyperparathyroidism (osteogenic synovitis, pyrophosphate arthropathy due to hyercalcaemia, or secondary gout)
	'Good' living	Increased frequency of gout since Second World War
Contamination	Trichinosis	Muscle pains in trichiniasis
Drugs (iatrogenic)	(Diverse)	Various musculoskeletal disorders*, notably thiazide-induced gout and drug-induced SLE
Occupation		
Support	Pressure	Bursitis (e.g. beat knee and beat elbow in miners) and beat hand
Vibration	Any vibration	Raynaud phenomenon (vibration-induced white finger)
	With piston hammering	Carpal decalcification (small areas—? with any heavy manual work), or occasionally soft-tissue injury in hand (chronic bursitis, muscle atrophy, or Dupuytren's contracture), or arthrosis (esp. elbow)
Overuse	Repetitive movement	Chronic crepitant synovitis (especially of wrist) and occupational cramp
	Trauma	Occupational arthropathy leading to traumatic arthrosis (e.g. gamekeeper's thumb, porter's neck, cotton worker's fingers, spine in miners and dockers, etc.)
Exposure to artiodactylate ungulates (cattle and goats)	*Brucella* spp.	Arthralgia, arthritis, spondylitis, and spinal calcification and ossification associated with brucellosis

Table 15.6. *(continued)*

Environmental component	Specific factor influencing health	Musculoskeletal manifestations
Industrial intoxicants	Polyvinyl chloride	Osteolysis
	Asbestos	Hypertrophic pulmonary osteoarthropathy with pleural mesothelioma
	Radioactive isotopes	Bone-seeking isotopes causing necrosis and sarcoma of bone, and (with wax substances carrying isotopes) epithelioma of paranasal sinuses—as in dial painters (radium—also sometimes ingested therapeutically), and with uranium, thorium, plutonium, yttrium, and strontium
Cultural		
Civilization	(?)	Increased frequency of rheumatoid arthritis in transition from bush to township
	(?)	Increased prevalence of back pain (epiphenomenon of man's cultural evolution)
Culture	Infectious agents	Obligatory treating of the sick at home (e.g. Philippines) increases risk of transmission of organisms responsible for bone and joint tuberculosis and rheumatic fever
	'Strain'	Home care of the sick may involve 'back strain' with heavy lifting
Poverty	Host resistance	Rheumatic fever
Posture	Neurovascular disturbance (stasis)	Swelling and discomfort of traveller's ankle
	?	Exacerbation of complaints like back pain (e.g. soft mattress or habitual bending)
Hygiene	Cervical cord or root compression	Flexion and hyperextension of rheumatoid neck in barber's and dentist's chairs
Pets	*Pasteurella* spp.	Occasional septic arthritis or osteomyelitis following bite from pet
Attitudes	Pain tolerance	Complaint rate for any rheumatic condition
Alienation	Psychogenic	Many rheumatic complaints an acceptable cover for frustration, etc.
Behaviour and life style		
Sport	Repetitive	Enthesopathies (tennis or golfer's elbows) and other specific syndromes (e.g. carpal tunnel)
	Trauma	Various musculoskeletal injuries including stress fractures, those resembling occupational conditions in leading to traumatic arthrosis (e.g. bowler's foot, wicket-keeper's hand, and yoga wrist)
Sexual exposure	Infection	Reiter's disease
Drug addiction	Infection	Septic arthritis
Alcoholism	Liver damage	Dupuytren's contracture and hepatic arthropathy

*A simple reference source is Huskisson and Hart (1975); V=vector.

†Indirect radiation, by contamination of water and grass and thus also of animal sources of human food, leading to internal radiation—effects of external radiation, such as leukaemia, not considered.

of this antigen are observed in other types of spondyl-arthropathy. The temptation to exploit B27 as a hallmark has led to attempts at disease redefinition (Metzger *et al.* 1974) and to inflationary estimates of the prevalence of AS (Calin and Fries 1975), but experience has not vindicated these indulgences (Hollingsworth *et al.* 1983).

The recorded associations of gene products with other rheumatic disorders are less impressive. Phenomena such as linkage disequilibrium are commonly invoked to account for incompatibilities in data, in a manner reminiscent of the way the concept of incomplete penetrance has been used before. However, it is likely that disease susceptibility is determined by more than one gene, so that we are probably perceiving only a very incomplete picture. Confounding variables notwithstanding, further study of these markers, prospectively and in regard to ethnic variation, should nevertheless sharpen the possibilities for identifying non-genetic determinants of disease.

Obstacles to understanding

Our present knowledge of such determinants is shaky. A major reason for this is that many supposed contributory factors tend to be ubiquitous. For example, the occurrence of influences such as trauma, occupation, or climate appear to be too universal to account for prevalences less than

unity. However, if presently concealed subpopulations of susceptibles could be identified, then the role of these and other determinants might become more evident. On a note of caution, though, it has to be recognized that quasi-unifactorial models of aetiology have serious limitations (Wood 1985), and that the origins of ill-health are wider than is often realized (Wood and Badley 1984).

The difficulties are increased when account is taken of the likelihood of heterogeneity. The observation of indistinguishable results from distinct causes is obviously germane in any target tissue with a limited response variation. Thus pathological similarities and the notion of arthrosis as a general phenomenon could be concealing diverse aetiologies (Wood 1976b). Equally, our concepts may be confounded because of failure to differentiate between clinical entities, such as is now known to have been the case with juvenile chronic arthritis (Ansell and Wood 1976) and which may also be relevant to diseases like RA. Finally, there is the conundrum of overlap between different rheumatic disorders, such as the various clinical associations with inflammatory spondylopathies and the merging of features between different connective tissue diseases.

In order to pursue questions that are important clinically, the epidemiologist has to depend on the concepts and assignment techniques transmitted to him—even if, in the process, he modifies them. The net result of all the difficulties noted has been to introduce considerable uncertainty into the process of ascertainment, and thus to inhibit epidemiologists.

It is therefore not surprising that a number of other consequences have stemmed from the present state of understanding, especially from over-reliance on clinical syndromes reassuringly designated by specific diagnostic terms. First, there has been general neglect of symptomatic conditions for which acceptable clinical concepts have not been developed, such as back pain and non-articular (soft-tissue) rheumatism. Secondly, the discordance between clinical and epidemiological pictures of disease should have raised fundamental questions about the significance of individual features, but these have been pursued to only a very limited extent. Thirdly, examination for disease heterogeneity and the delineation of syndromes has been subject to only limited exploitation. Fourthly, concentration on clinical perspectives has diverted attention from more community-oriented aspects, and yet these alternative features might permit case ascertainment by different means. Finally, confining study to a biomedical model of illness has led to neglect of the study of remediable consequences (Wood and Badley 1978).

However, options are still open for a range of useful work. At this juncture it may be helpful to indicate important principles. Both experience and the preceding discussion suggest that hypothesis testing is scarcely within our reach at the present time. The goal therefore has to be hypothesis generation, with an underlying need for general models or conceptual frameworks. As we are probably in danger of being blinded by current views that have proved unrewarding, the remedy is to return to the foundation of scientific enquiry, observation. Unfortunately the refinement of many research technologies has accustomed support agencies to sophisticated study designs. As a result there has been a disturbing tendency towards pejorative dismissal of descriptive projects. Nevertheless, it would appear that unbiased observational studies are sorely needed.

CONTROL OF THE PROBLEM

The potential for control of many musculoskeletal disorders is certainly not being fully exploited at the present. An illustrative selection of appropriate measures at different levels is shown in Table 15.7. On the basis of this schematic presentation it is possible to identify a major reason for current shortcomings. At both primary and tertiary levels, the greatest contribution could be anticipated not from technical health-related procedures applied to individuals, nor from changes in personal life-style, but from social policy initiatives mainly in areas not directly connected to health care such as employment, housing, and transport. At the primary level the greatest feasible inroads into the current toll of musculoskeletal suffering on a global scale could be anticipated from prevention of acute rheumatic fever and other infections, improvements in diet, reduction of accidents, and development of less injurious methods of working.

Table 15.7. *Examples of control measures for musculoskeletal disorders*

Primary control (to prevent)

(i) Health promotion	Immunization (cf. infectious diseases noted in Table 15.5)
(a) Disease oriented	Adequate diet (especially in elderly, and by means such as availability of small portions for purchase, pricing, meals on wheels, luncheon clubs, etc.) to avoid occurrence of metabolic bone disorders such as osteoporosis and osteomalacia
	Physical activity to maintain integrity of musculoskeletal system (including protective effect against trauma to joints and other structures); also includes posture (less height loss in long-serving veterans)
(b) Handicap oriented (enablement)	Urban design (especially in regard to isolation); education, employment, and recreational opportunities; transport policies; availability of energy (influence of ambient temperature on pain tolerance); social attitudes; welfare provisions (including pensions)
(ii) Hazard containment	
(a) Collective	Measures to control hazards identified in Table 15.6. (especially occupational exposures), and to prevent or reduce the impact of trauma (including highway control, pedestrianization, domestic illumination, etc.)
(b) Individual	Prophylaxis (e.g. penicillin for rheumatic fever)

Secondary control (to arrest)

(i) Reaction (identification of damage)	
(a) Prompt response	Automobile seatbelts, emergency (rescue) services, decompression (for caisson disease)
(b) Screening	Early detection and treatment (including anticipatory care of the elderly)—e.g. congenital dislocation of hip, rheumatic fever, and polymyalgia rheumatica and associated cranial arteritis—to avoid hazard of blindness in absence of treatment)
(ii) Stabilization (countering damage)	
(a) Cure	Gout (by control of uric acid metabolism and excretion); antibiotics (for infectious conditions); treatment of fractures
(b) Mitigation	Optimum treatment to avoid impairment and disability by arrest of disease progression (e.g. rheumatoid arthritis, systemic lupus, erythematosus, etc.)—by drugs and other measures (e.g. splinting to avoid deformities), and including balance between primary, secondary, and tertiary care

Tertiary control (to repair or ameliorate—control of disablement)

(i) Restoration (control of disability—WHO's second-level disability prevention)	
(a) Reconstruction	Total hip replacement
(b) Rehabilitation	Remedial services, provision of aids
(ii) Maintenance (control of handicap—WHO's third-level disability prevention)	
(a) Continuing care	Monitoring for deterioration; terminal care
(b) Enablement	Extension of opportunities, including vocational resettlement
(c) Support	Welfare provisions; assistance; aid to family

Derived from Wood (1983).

The lack of suitable means for the early detection of most rheumatic disorders is not of great moment at the present time because of limitations in therapeutic potential to arrest disease progression; congenital dislocation of the hip is a notable exception. However, effective secondary control of gout is now possible, and the same applies to polymyalgia rheumatica (with the dividend of avoiding the hazard of blindness).

Two other interesting possibilities exist. The first is that, despite the high frequency of adverse effects from antirheumatic drugs, earlier and more aggressive intervention with so-called disease-modifying drugs (e.g. penicillamine) in rheumatoid arthritis may have potential at least to delay joint destruction and deformity. If this possibility were taken up on a large scale it would have considerable repercussions on, among other things, the need for laboratory facilities for monitoring.

Effective treatment by local steroid injection is available for many forms of soft-tissue rheumatism, and yet this therapy is not widely exploited in primary care; needlessly prolonged morbidity results. This epitomizes a more general challenge for the organization of health care, devolution of a large part of routine long-term management of chronic conditions to general practitioners, and the liberation of time for specialists to undertake the expanded educational role that such a change would necessitate. The status of the principal rheumatic disorders in regard to devolution of care has been summarized (Wood and Badley 1976).

Of particular relevance to considerations just discussed is neglect of remediable consequences of musculoskeletal disorders in the form of impairments, disabilities, and handicaps, over which there are grounds for serious concern. A considerable proportion of people who are disabled to some extent by one of these conditions are not seen regularly by specialists, nor are they in frequent contact with their general practitioners. It is, therefore, scarcely surprising that unmet needs and missed opportunities for amelioration are encountered fairly frequently (Thompson et al. 1974). In fact, the problem is more diffuse, affecting most classes of people with disabilities and concerning all aspects of rehabilitation. Specifically rheumatological aspects have been considered elsewhere (de Blécourt et al. 1981), as have less specialized guidelines for regional planning of rehabilitation services (Wood and Hold 1980).

Lack of understanding of these conditions inhibits effective control initiatives. Developments may be anticipated in various basic science fields, but there is also scope for epidemiological involvement. We have indicated problems with the nosology of musculoskeletal disorders. The basis for improving this state of affairs will be by systematic recording and interpretation of clinical and other features in quantitative as well as qualitative terms, so as to document patterns of natural history and outcome.

Some efforts have been made in this direction, but the uniform clinical data bases currently employed are probably insufficiently problem-oriented for resolution of existing quandaries. There is a role for epidemiologists to stimulate the interest and co-operation of clinicians in such research. Utilization of existing data sources for research and planning also needs to be increased.

CONCLUSION

We have tried to present an appraisal of the problem posed by musculoskeletal disorders, together with an indication of how such an exercise in community diagnosis may be carried out. The problem emerges as a major and yet neglected cause of morbidity and disablement, though the mortality associated with most of the conditions included in this category is small. The principal options for control of the problem have been reviewed, and we suggest that three areas deserve particular attention: (i) the important contribution that could be made by social policy initiatives in areas other than health care; (ii) the potential for more appropriate deployment of many available technologies for intervention (which also has implications for professional education); (iii) and the need for investment in research to enhance our understanding of the various conditions, so as to improve the basis for developing control measures.

Difficulties that need to be confronted when undertaking such enquiries have been discussed, from which we draw two optimistic conclusions. First, and despite the difficulty of scientific enquiry when faced with heterogeneity, a frequently chronic course, and the subjective nature of a large part of the experiences, it is possible to make significant, if humble, headway in seeking further understanding of musculoskeletal disorders. Secondly, that such apparently less sophisticated approaches have a much wider relevance in the context of chronic illnesses of other types.

REFERENCES

Ansell, B.M. and Wood, P.H.N. (1976). Prognosis in juvenile chronic polyarthritis. In *Rheumatic disorders in childhood. Clinics in rheumatic diseases*, Vol. 2 (ed. B.M. Ansell) p. 397. Saunders, London.

Atlas of Standard Radiographs of Arthritis (1963) *The epidemiology of chronic rheumatism*, Vol. 2. Blackwell, Oxford.

Badley, E.M., Thompson, R.P., and Wood, P.H.N. (1978). The prevalence and severity of major disabling conditions—a reappraisal of the Government Social Survey of the Handicapped and Impaired in Great Britain. *Int. J. Epidemiol.* 7, 145.

Beighton, P. (1978). *Inherited disorders of the skeleton.* Churchill Livingstone, Edinburgh.

Benn, R.T. and Wood, P.H.N. (1975). Pain in the back; an attempt to estimate the size of the problem. *Rheumatol. Rehabil.* **14,** 121.

Bennett, P.H. and Wood, P.H.N. (eds.) (1968). *Population studies of the rheumatic diseases.* International congress series No. 148. Excerpta Medica, Amsterdam.

Blackett, P.M.S. (1962). Operational research, 1948. In *Studies of war, nuclear and conventional*, p. 185. Oliver and Boyd, Edinburgh.

Calin, A. and Fries, J.F. (1975). Striking prevalence of ankylosing spondylitis in 'healthy' W27-positive males and females: a controlled study. *New Engl. J. Med.* **293,** 835.

Carter, C.O. and Fairbank, T.J. (1974). *The genetics of locomotor disorders.* Oxford University Press, London.

Cobb, S. (1971). *The frequency of the rheumatic diseases.* American Public Health Association statistics monograph. Harvard University Press, Cambridge, Mass.

de Blécourt, J.J., Wood, P.H.N., and Badley, E.M. (1981). Aims of rehabilitation for rheumatic patients. In *Rehabilitation in the rheumatic diseases. Clinics in rheumatic diseases,* Vol. 7 (ed. D. Woolf) p. 291. Saunders, London.

Dixon, A.St.J. (1979). Soft tissue rheumatism: concept and classification. In *Soft tissue rheumatism. Clinics in rheumatic diseases,* Vol. 5 (ed. A.St.J. Dixon) p. 739. Saunders, London.

Dunnell, K. and Cartwright, A. (1972). *Medicine takers, prescribers and hoarders,* chapter 2. Routledge and Kegan Paul, London.

Early, P.F. (1962). Population studies in Dupuytren's contracture. *J. Bone Joint Surg.* **44B**, 602.

Fry, J. (1974). *Common diseases—their nature, incidence and care.* MTP, Lancaster.

Harris, A.I. (1971). *Handicapped and impaired in Great Britain, part 1.* OPCS, Social Survey Division. HMSO, London.

Hewitt, D. and Wood, P.H.N. (1975). Heterodox practitioners and the availability of specialist advice. *Rheumatol. Rehabil.* **14**, 191.

Hollingsworth, P.M., Cheah, P.S., Dawkins, R.L., Owen, E.T., Calin, A., and Wood, P.H.N. (1983). Observer variation in grading sacro-iliac radiographs in HLA B27 positive individuals. *J. Rheumatol.* **10**, 247.

Hult, L. (1954). The Munkfors investigation. *Acta Orthopaed. Scand.* Suppl. 16.

Hunt, S.M., McKenna, S.P., and Williams, J. (1981). Reliability of a population survey tool for measuring perceived health problems: a study of patients with osteoarthrosis. *J. Epidemiol. Community Health* **35**, 297.

Huskisson, E.C. and Hart, F.D. (1975). *Joint disease: all the arthro-pathics,* 2nd edn. Wright, Bristol.

Kellgren, J.H. (1968). Epidemiology of rheumatoid arthritis. In *Rheumatic diseases* (ed. J.J.R. Duthie and W.R.M. Alexander). University Press, Edinburgh.

Kellgren, J.H. and Moore, R. (1952). Generalized osteoarthritis and Heberden's nodes. *Br. Med. J.* **i**, 181.

Kelsey, J.L. and White, A.A. (1980). Epidemiology and impact of low-back pain. *Spine* **5**, 133.

Kelsey, J.L., Pastides, H., and Bisbee, G.E. (1978). *Musculo-skeletal disorders; their frequency of occurrence and their impact on the population of the United States.* Prodist Division, Neale Watson Academic Publications, New York.

Laing, W. and Taylor, D. (1982). *Hip replacement and the NHS.* Papers on current health problems No. 71. Office of Health Economics, London.

Lawrence, J.S. (1977). *Rheumatism in populations.* Heinemann, London.

Mackenzie, D.H. (1970). *The differential diagnosis of fibroblastic disorders.* Ch. 9, p. 67. Blackwell, Oxford.

McKusick, V. (1972). *Heritable disorders of connective tissue,* 4th edn. Mosby, Saint Louis.

Mercer, W. and Duthie, R.B. (1983). *Orthopaedic surgery,* 8th edn. Edward Arnold, London.

Metzger, A.L., Morris, R.J., and Bluestone, R. (1974). Biologic significance of HL-A W27 in rheumatic disease (editorial). *J. Rheumatol.* **1**, 247.

Moll, J.M.H. (ed.) (1980). *Ankylosing spondylitis.* Churchill Livingstone, Edinburgh.

Office of Health Economics (OHE) (1973). *Rheumatism and arthritis in Britain.* Paper No. 45. Office of Health Economics, London.

Office of Population Censuses and Surveys (OPCS) (1974). *Morbidity statistics from general practice, second national study 1970–1971.* Royal College of General Practitioners, OPCS, and Department of Health and Social Security. Studies on Medical and Population Subjects No. 26. HMSO, London.

Ropes, M.W., Bennett, G.A., Cobb, S., Jacox, R., and Jessar, R.A. (1956). Proposed diagnostic criteria for rheumatoid arthritis. *Bull. Rheum. Dis.* **7**, 121. See also *Annals of the Rheumatic Diseases* **16**, 118 (1957).

Scott, J.T. (ed.) (in press). *Copeman's textbook of the rheumatic diseases,* 6th edn. Churchill Livingstone, Edinburgh.

Strasser, T. (1976). Rheumatic fever and rheumatic heart disease in the 1970s. *Pub. Health Rev.* **5**, 207.

Thompson, M., Anderson, M., and Wood, P.H.N. (1974). Locomotor disability: a study of need in an urban community. *Br. J. Soc. Prev. Med.* **28**, 70.

Wood, P.H.N. (1970). Epidemiology of rheumatic disorders: problems in classification. *Proc. R. Soc. Med.* **63**, 189.

Wood, P.H.N. (1971). Is hypermobility a discrete entity? *Proc. R. Soc. Med.* **64**, 690.

Wood, P.H.N. (1976a). Arthritis calling for surgical treatment—aetiology and epidemiology. *Proc. R. Soc. London* B **192**, 131.

Wood, P.H.N. (1976b). Osteoarthrosis in the community. In *Osteo-arthrosis. Clinics in rheumatic diseases,* Vol. 2 (ed. V. Wright) p. 495. Saunders, London.

Wood, P.H.N. (ed.) (1977). *The challenge of arthritis and rheuma-tism—a report on problems and progress in health care for rheumatic disorders.* British League against Rheumatism, London.

Wood, P.H.N. (1980). Understanding back pain. In *The lumbar spine and back pain,* 2nd edn (ed. M.I.V. Jayson) p. 1. Pitman Medical, Tunbridge Wells.

Wood, P.H.N. (1983). Prospects for control. In *Disability prevention, the global challenge.* (ed. J. Wilson) p. 87. Leeds Castle Foundation. Oxford University Press, Oxford.

Wood, P.H.N. (1985). The basis of rheumatological practice. In *Copeman's textbook of the rheumatic diseases.* 6th edn. (ed. J.T. Scott) Chapter 2. Churchill Livingstone, Edinburgh.

Wood, P.H.N. (In press). Musculoskeletal effects of environmental influences. *Ann. Rheum. Dis.*

Wood, P.H.N. and Badley, E.M. (1976). *Options in the delivery of medical care* (the Brindle Lodge report). Report of a working conference sponsored by DHSS. Arthritis and Rheumatism Council, London. (Also reproduced in Wood, 1977.)

Wood, P.H.N. and Badley, E.M. (1978). An epidemiological appraisal of disablement. In *Recent advances in community medicine* (ed. A.E Bennett) p. 149. Churchill Livingstone, London.

Wood, P.H.N. and Badley, E.M. (eds.) (1980a). *People with arthritis deserve well-trained doctors.* Report on a workshop on under-graduate education in rheumatology. Arthritis and Rheumatism Council, London.

Wood, P.H.N. and Badley, E.M. (1980b). Epidemiology of back pain. In *The lumbar spine and back pain,* 2nd edn (ed. M.I.V. Jayson) p. 29. Pitman Medical, Tunbridge Wells.

Wood, P.H.N. and Badley, E.M. (1981). *People with disabilities—toward acquiring information which reflects more sensitively their problems and needs.* Monograph No. 12. World Rehabilitation Fund, New York.

Wood, P.H.N. and Badley, E.M. (1983). An epidemiological appraisal of bone and joint disease in the elderly. In *Bone and joint disease in the elderly* (ed. V. Wright) p. 1. Churchill Livingstone, Edinburgh.

Wood, P.H.N. and Badley, E.M. (1984) The origins of ill health. In *Recent advances in community medicine.* No. 3 (ed. A. Smith) p. 11. Churchill Livingstone, Edinburgh.

Wood, P.H.N. and Badley, E.M. (1985). Epidemiology of individual rheumatic diseases. In *Copeman's textbook of the rheumatic diseases,* 6th edn (ed. J.T. Scott). Churchill Livingstone, Edinburgh.

Wood, P.H.N. and Holt, P.J.L. (1980). The development of strategic guidelines for regional planning of rehabilitation services. *Int. Rehabil. Med.* **2**, 143.

Wood, P.H.N., Bury, M.R., and Badley, E.M. (1980) Other waters flow—an examination of the contemporary approach to care for rheumatic patients. In *Topical reviews of rheumatic disorders,* Vol. 1

(ed. A.G.S. Hill) p. 1. Wright, Bristol.

Wood, P.H.N., Sturrock, A.W., and Badley, E.M. (1979). Soft tissue rheumatism in the community. In *Soft tissue rheumatism. Clinics in rheumatic diseases,* Vol. 5 (ed. A.St.J. Dixon) p. 743. Saunders, London.

World Health Organization (WHO) (1977). International statistical classification of diseases, injuries and causes of death (ICD), 9th revn. WHO, Geneva.

World Health Organization (WHO) (1980). *International classification of impairments, disabilities, and handicaps (ICIDH).* WHO, Geneva.

Wright, V. and Moll, J.M.H. (1976). *Seronegative polyarthritis.* North-Holland, Amsterdam.

Wynne-Davies, R. (1973). *Heritable disorders in orthopaedic practice.* Blackwell, Oxford.

16 Environment, metabolic systems, and public health

Barry Lewis

INTRODUCTION

This chapter is concerned with the triangular relationship between environmental variables, metabolism, and chronic disease. It is possible to recognize environmental factors that are linked to ill health by identified metabolic mechanisms, where the evidence for a causal sequence is sufficiently rigorous to justify intervention. More often the available evidence is insufficient. Those areas which are relevant to the current practice of preventive medicine are discussed in terms of the social engineering required; other environmental factors are reviewed in the context of the need for specific research. In each instance the five limbs of cohesive clinical research require comment: namely epidemiology, clinical observations, experimental work in animal models, the availability of evidence of plausible mechanisms, and controlled clinical trials.

NUTRITION

Fats

In addition to the evidence from many disciplines relating the quantity and nature of dietary fats to coronary heart disease, there is a growing body of information concerning fat intake as a determinant of risk of some forms of cancer; indications of a link between venous thrombosis and fat consumption are also worthy of mention. The latter, less familiar relationships will be discussed first.

Fat consumption and cancer

Mortality rates from most forms of cancer display considerable diversity in different countries. Incidence ratios include a 35-fold difference between England and Nigeria for lung cancer, a tenfold difference between highest and lowest rates of colon cancer, and a fourfold difference for gastric cancer (Doll and Peto 1981). While such observations do not in isolation distinguish between genetic susceptibility and environmental causes, the latter interpretation is inescapable since it has been observed that mortality rates in migrating populations change within one or two generations from those of the country of origin to those of the host country (Doll *et al.* 1966: Haenszel and Kurihara 1968). The most striking examples have been recorded among persons of Japanese stock migrating to Hawaii and California. Within one generation colon cancer mortality has risen steeply from the low rates of Japan towards the high rates of the US; by the second generation breast cancer shows a comparable increase while gastric cancer mortality has fallen towards US levels. Many risk factors for breast cancer that have been examined cannot, alone or together, account for this increase; examples are parity and age at first pregnancy (Wynder and Gori 1977).

Consequently much interest has been centred on nutritional changes associated with migration. Among these is an increase in availability of dietary fat. In Japan this was 26 g/day in 1961 while American figures, declining slightly since 1970, are now 152 g/day. Among the cancers showing a cross-cultural correlation between mortality rates and availability of dietary fat for consumption are those of the colon ($r=0.85$ in men) and breast ($r=0.89$) (Armstrong and Doll 1975; Carroll 1980). Similar trends have been reported for cancers of the uterus, ovary, and pancreas, and for leukaemia. Stomach cancer is a special case, the negative correlation being largely due to high Japanese mortality rates.

Within Japan itself there has been a clearly rising secular trend in age-standardized rates of colon and breast cancers and of all cancers, also for leukaemia during the post-war period, during which fat consumption has increased strikingly (Fig. 16.1) (Japanese Ministry of Health 1982).

Some case-control studies have indicated a higher fat intake in patients with breast cancer (Miller 1977) but there have also been negative reports.

A finding of potential theoretical and clinical importance is that the case fatality of postmenopausal breast cancer as well as the overall mortality from the disease is higher in the US than in Japan (Morrison *et al.* 1977). Not only the prevalence of breast cancer but also its natural history are influenced by environmental factors.

None of these findings specify fat intake uniquely as a determinant of cancer rates. Numerous cultural changes accompany population migration, and as many have attended the westernization of the Japanese way of life. The impressive feature of the fat–cancer association is its congruence with the findings in experimental carcinogenesis in rodents.

Several relatively organ-specific carcinogens have been employed in nutritional experiments. Dimethylhydrazine and methylnitrosourea are inducers of carcinomas and benign

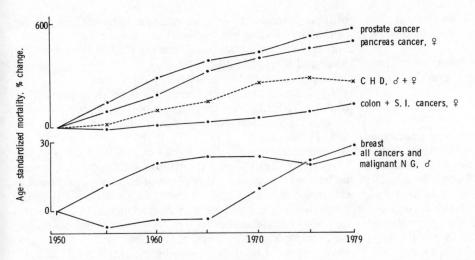

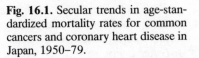

Fig. 16.1. Secular trends in age-standardized mortality rates for common cancers and coronary heart disease in Japan, 1950–79.

tumours in the colon of the rat. The tumour yield in rats is 2–4 fold greater when the diet provides some 40 per cent of energy from fat when fat comprises 20 per cent of dietary energy, or when fed rat chow (Reddy *et al.* 1976; Weisburger *et al.* 1977). The time relationships indicate that the dietary effect is one of promotion, not induction (Bull *et al.* 1979). Similarly, dimethylbenzanthracene induces breast tumours in rats, the yield of tumours being increased by a high intake of fat (Hopkins and Carroll 1979). A dose–response relationship with fat consumption is demonstrable in these fat–carcinogen interactions.

In view of the differential effects of saturated, mono-unsaturated, and polyunsaturated fatty acids (exemplified respectively by beef fat and butter, olive oil, and corn oil and fatty fish) on lipid metabolism and coronary heart disease risk, there has been interest in possible differences in cancer-promoting effects of the various types of fat. At very high intakes (40 per cent of dietary energy), polyunsaturated fats are associated with a higher breast cancer tumour yield than saturated fats. A detailed study by Carroll and his colleagues (Hopkins and Carroll 1979) has led to a different and more complex interpretation. Fed at the low level of 3 per cent by weight a polyunsaturated fat was associated with more tumours than seen in animals fed a diet without fat supplements; this is best interpreted as indicating that malignant cells, like normal ones, require essential polyunsaturated fatty acids for growth. At high intakes both polyunsaturated and monounsaturated fatty acids increased the tumour yield. A series of experiments has led to the conclusion that promotion depends on the total intake of fat, probably irrespective of type, and also on the availability of sufficient polyunsaturated fat to prevent the syndrome of essential fatty acid deficiency (Carroll 1981).

The relevance of the experimental and epidemiological findings of a fat–cancer relationship is considerably enhanced by increasing knowledge of mechanisms which could explain these associations on a cause-and-effect basis. The clearest instance is that of colon cancer promotion. Both in the rat (Reddy *et al.* 1977) and in man (Cummings *et al.* 1978) the concentration and excretion of bile acids in faeces may be increased by a high-fat diet but this was not confirmed in a

study on normal man by Brussaard *et al.* (1983). By topical infusion of certain naturally-occurring bile acids into the large intestine of rats (Narisawa *et al.* 1974; Reddy *et al.* 1976), and by biliary diversion experiments (Chomchai *et al.* 1974), strong evidence has been adduced that some bile acids act as promoters in the carcinogen-treated rat. Bile acid concentration is higher in faeces from high-risk populations than in samples from regions of low risk (Hill *et al.* 1971; Hill 1974*a*). Hence there is a rational basis for suggesting that a high intake of fat may be amongst the causes of colon cancer, the effect being mediated by the role of bile acids as promoting agents. A mechanism has also been proposed by which a high intake of fat promotes carcinogenesis in the breast; plasma prolactin levels are increased in rats fed such a diet (Chan and Cohen 1975; Cohen 1981), and there is reasonably consistent data indicating that prolactin has a promoting effect on the induction of experimental breast cancer (Pearson *et al.* 1980). Conclusive evidence has yet to be presented that prolactin secretion is enhanced in women receiving diets high in fat, though one study suggests that this is so (Hill *et al.* 1981).

When food disappearance data are related to colon cancer mortality rates in different countries, the correlation coefficient for dietary cholesterol exceeds that of total fat (Liu *et al.* 1979) A study indicating that dietary cholesterol is a promoter of colon cancer in the treated rat has been reported (Cruse *et al.* 1979), though it is unclear whether it is the cholesterol itself which exerted this effect, or whether the promotion was due to bile acids which are the major end-products (> 80 per cent) of cholesterol metabolism in the rat. Some reservations must be expressed concerning such observations. Food disappearance data provide a highly approximate basis for assessing nutrient intake, due both to wastage and to individual differences in food selection. There is a paucity of food intake data by country, and nutritional assessment is in any case an imprecise undertaking unless formidable efforts are made to reduce the numerous sources of error. Hence small differences in correlation coefficients should, as Liu *et al.* (1979) point out be interpreted with caution. The rat cholesterol-feeding studies are, as mentioned, open to more than one interpretation; in addition they have been criticized on the grounds that the dosage of carcinogen was so high as to limit the power of the experiments to discriminate between dietary promoting effects.

The studies of fat intake and cancer are discussed further below, in relation to their implications for preventive medicine.

Fats and venous thrombosis

During the Second World War the incidence of post-operative venous thrombosis decreased considerably in some west European countries. In Norway the frequency of these complications decreased from about 30 per 1000 operations to 10 per 1000 (Jensen 1952), a decrease reminiscent of that for coronary heart disease mortality. Cross-cultural as well as secular differences have been reported for thrombotic disorders. Post-operative venous thromboses are far less common in some African and Eastern countries than in the UK (Merskey et al. 1960; Hassan et al. 1973). These trends are associated with several differences in behaviour, for example cigarette smoking and physical activity in addition to the great diversity in diet, and are likely to be multifactorial.

A comparison of men from the Moselle and Var regions in France, and from the east and west of Scotland, has show that those from districts in which mean consumption of saturated fat is high had platelets that were more sensitive to aggregating agents than those from men in low-fat-consuming districts (Renaud et al. 1980). The differences in saturated fat intake were relatively small. Cross-over feeding experiments in French volunteers suggested that these differences in platelet function could be reversed by altering saturated fat intake. In another cross-cultural study relationships were shown between saturated fat intake and both platelet function and prostaglandin metabolism in Italian, Finnish, and UK population samples (Iacono et al. 1978).

Experimental findings are concordant with the interpretation that the type and amount of dietary fat are amongst the determinants of the risk of thrombosis events. In animals with extracorporeal vascular shunts, replacement of the habitual low-fat diet with one supplemented with saturated fat and cholesterol promotes thrombosis in the shunt (Mustard et al. 1963; Mathues et al. 1968); and saturated fats without cholesterol enhance venous thrombosis in endotoxin-treated rats (Renaud et al. 1970), due to an effect of such fats on platelet reactivity (Nordöy et al. 1968). Thrombosis is also enhanced in rats fed saturated fat compared with those receiving a polyunsaturated fat containing linoleic acid (Hornstra 1971). In man, too, platelet aggregation in flowing blood occurs more rapidly in subjects receiving a diet rich in dairy fats (a typical Finnish diet) than in those fed a linoleic acid-containing polyunsaturated fat (Hornstra et al. 1973).

Fats and coronary heart disease

The role of diet-induced hypercholesterolaemia as a major component of the aetiology of coronary heart disease is a well-defined model of the triangular relationship that is the subject of this chapter. Possibly no other disease has been the objective of so great a research effort; space permits only a selective (and subjective) review of the relevant nutritional determinants, their metabolic effects, and the consequences of these in terms of cardiovascular pathology. These will be summarized in logical rather than in historical sequence. Some recent reviews are listed (Stamler 1978; Blackburn 1979; Marmot 1979; Lewis 1980, 1981).

Coronary heart disease mortality rates (men 35–74 years, 1977) differ by a factor of ninefold between industrialized countries (NHLBI Working Group 1981) and probably vary far more if developing countries are included in the comparison. If Higginson's and Doll's criteria for evaluating the environmental contribution to cancer causation are adopted for coronary heart disease (Higginson and Muir 1976), it may be inferred that almost 90 per cent of coronary heart disease can be attributed to environmental factors. This is strongly supported by the rapid increase in mortality from this condition when emigration occurs from low- to high-risk countries, for example Yemenites migrating to Israel and, most persuasively, Japanese migrating to the US (Marmot et al. 1975).

Two cross-cultural studies in particular have examined the characteristics of low- and high-risk countries for aetiological clues. The Seven Country Study (Keys 1980) recorded both mortality and incidence of coronary heart disease and identified serum cholesterol level, diet, and blood pressure (and of course age) as correlating with risk, but could not attribute international differences in frequency to smoking habits, obesity, or exercise. Median serum cholesterol was highly correlated with mortality ($r=0.80$) with a linear increase in deaths from 160 to 265 mg/dl (4.1–6.9 mmol/l). Intake of saturated fat was correlated with coronary heart disease mortality ($r=0.84$) and incidence ($r=0.73$). Serum cholesterol was best predicted by a formula incorporating the intakes of saturated and polyunsaturated fats ($r=0.90$). Thus there are strong associations between dietary fats, serum cholesterol, and coronary heart disease rates. The other study, the International Atherosclerosis Project (McGill 1968) avoided the uncertainties of death certification, employing instead the extent of coronary atherosclerosis, as quantitatively assessed in a single laboratory. Again the rank order of frequency of raised atheromatous plaques correlated strongly with saturated fat intake and with serum cholesterol.

Longitudinal studies have established a number of attributes and habits that are predictive of subsequent coronary heart disease risk. Serum cholesterol level is one such risk factor, the association being strong, consistent, independent of other risk factors, close-related, and predictive (that is conforming with Bradford Hill's criteria for causal associations) (Reid et al. 1976; Pooling Project Research Group 1978; Kannel et al. 1979; Keys 1980). However, the relationship is not as linear as in cross-cultural comparisons, and the serum cholesterol–coronary heart disease rate profile differs somewhat in shape in the several prospective studies. In the Seven Countries and the Framingham incidence data the relationship is curvilinear, risk increasing moderately from serum cholesterol 160–179 to 240–259 mg/dl (4.1–4.6 to 6.2–6.7 mmol/l), then steeply with further increments in cholesterol. By contrast the US Pooling Project shows a significant increase with risk in the 3rd, 4th, and 5th quintiles of serum cholesterol compared with the 1st plus 2nd quintiles. In the very large ($n \simeq 320\ 000$) follow up of the Multiple Risk Factor Intervention Trial screenees, risk increased continuously from the lowest to the highest quintile of serum cholesterol (Wentworth, D. and Stamler, I., personal communication).

The level of plasma cholesterol above which coronary heart disease risk begins to increase is of considerable importance, for it has bearing on the definition of 'optimal' cholesterol concentration. The relationship between dietary fats and plasma cholesterol level is one of cause and effect, as amply demonstrated in controlled feeding experiments (for review see Lewis 1976). Saturated fats, especially those rich in palmitic acid (the major saturated fatty acid of butter fat and meats) consistently increase plasma cholesterol; on the other hand mono-unsaturated fats are neutral in this respect and polyunsaturated fats reduce plasma cholesterol in man.

Another important class of longitudinal studies, formidably difficult to perform, has now established that dietary fat intake is predictive of coronary heart disease risk. The ratio of polyunsaturated fatty acids to saturated fatty acids has been measured at baseline; in one such study coronary heart disease incidence in the upper tertile was lower than that in the lower tertile (Morris *et al.* 1977). In the Western Electric Study (Shekelle *et al.* 1981) a diet score was computed for intake of saturated and polyunsaturated fats and cholesterol; lower scores, representing a low ratio of saturated to unsaturated fat and low cholesterol intake, were clearly predictive of low coronary heart disease mortality over a 19-year follow-up. A recent report indicates that the plasma phospholipid fatty acid pattern (probably reflecting dietary fat type) is similarly predictive of a wide range of coronary heart disease risk (Miettinen *et al.* 1982).

These epidemiological findings must be related to other sources of information. Clinical observations have illuminated the population data. Three forms of genetic hyperlipidaemia, in which a single metabolic defect is associated with increased coronary heart disease risk, testify a causal role for lipid transport in the causation of coronary atherosclerosis. In familial hypercholesterolaemia coronary heart disease risk is about ten times commoner in affected men (Slack 1979), and clinical observation suggests a high risk of coronary heart disease also in Type III hyperlipoproteinaemia and in familial combined hyperlipidaemia (Lewis 1976). Furthermore, the rate of progression of atheroma, measured by serial angiography in the human femoral artery, is directly related to plasma levels of low-density lipoprotein, the main form in which plasma cholesterol is transported (Duffield *et al.* 1983).

The significance of animal models of atherosclerosis has been reviewed elsewhere (Wissler and Vesselinovitch 1976; Lewis 1981). Atherosclerosis-like lesions can be induced in a variety of laboratory animals by high fat and/or high cholesterol diets that increase plasma cholesterol, even progressing to myocardial infarction. Correction of the hypercholesterolaemia by other diets or by drugs, leads to slow but striking partial regression of the atherosclerotic lesions in primates and other species (Armstrong and Megan 1972; Wissler and Vesselinovitch 1976) – persuasive evidence for a causal sequence in which the high-fat diet leads in turn to hypercholesterolaemia and to atheroma.

There is also a set of data identifying cellular mechanisms by which this causal sequence is explicable (Lewis 1980). The source of the cholesterol in atheromatous plaques is the cholesterol-transporting lipoproteins of plasma. These lipoproteins transfer into the arterial wall at a rate directly related to their plasma level (Niehaus *et al.* 1977); their uptake and degradation by smooth muscle and macrophages in the intima is the basis of lipid deposition.

Plaque formation is partly due to smooth muscle cell hyperplasia; this may be due to several mitogens, including a subclass of low-density lipoprotein. A further mechanism is related to the effects of dietary fats on platelet function (discussed in an earlier section), and on coagulation factors (Elkeles *et al.* 1980). The thrombotic component of coronary heart disease is thus best conceived as part of a single pathological process rather than as a competing hypothesis of coronary heart disease pathogenesis (Lewis 1981; Steinberg 1983). Another link between lipid and thrombotic mechanisms is the effect of low-density lipoprotein in altering platelet composition, which results in increased sensitivity to aggregating agents (Shastri *et al.* 1980).

The 'bottom line' in assessing these relationships is the controlled clinical trial, by which the lipid hypothesis should be testable and from which the value of dietary modification in preventing coronary heart disease should be measurable. It must be said that trial data are at present the least persuasive component of the body of information on the causes and prevention of coronary heart disease. Only modest benefits have been shown in controlled trials of the treatment of hypertension. The early dietary primary prevention trials (Mann and Marr 1981) were affirmative but mostly imperfect in design and execution. There is little trial data concerning the effects of giving up cigarette smoking; the favourable trend in men who elect to give up cigarettes is encouraging but not comparable to a randomized trial. The Oslo Heart Study was a well-designed trial of dietary and anti-smoking counselling in primary prevention of coronary heart disease (Hjerrman *et al.* 1981). There was a significant and impressive 47 per cent reduction in coronary heart disease events, chiefly attributable on the basis of multivariate analysis to the lipid-lowering diet. No unifactorial trial of diet, of comparable quality, has been performed.

A small trial of a different type has provided some support for a causal role of hyperlipidaemia in atherosclerosis (Duffield *et al.* 1982, 1983). Hyperlipidaemic patients with symptomatic atheroma of the femoral artery were randomized into an intervention group receiving dietary and drug treatment, and a well-matched control group. An extensive reduction of plasma cholesterol was achieved (−25 per cent). By serial quantitative arteriography (the observers being blinded as to treatment status) evidence was obtained that the extent of atheroma progressed about three times less rapidly in the treated group than in the controls. A comparable study of coronary atherosclerosis is under way, employing reduction of plasma cholesterol by diet alone or by diet with cholestyramine (Lewis, B. and Coltart, D.J., unpublished data).

Dietary cholesterol

From the viewpoint of preventive medicine there is little reason to distinguish between dietary cholesterol and saturated fats; the majority of sources of saturated fats (that is dairy and meat products), are also rich in cholesterol. Exceptions are egg yolks and offal with a high content particularly of cholesterol, and certain margarines, rich in saturated fatty acids and, in some, in *trans* fatty acids but not containing cholesterol. Possible associations between dietary cholesterol and colon cancer were discussed in an earlier section. In the control of coronary heart disease two points will suffice. When food disappearance data were related to subsequent mortality from this cause in 20 countries, the simple correlation coefficient for dietary cholesterol and coronary heart disease was slightly higher than that for saturated dietary fat (as g/day or as percentage of energy) and coronary heart disease (Stamler 1979). Secondly, in most people an increase of dietary cholesterol will elevate the plasma cholesterol (Connor *et al.* 1961; Mistry *et al.* 1981), as well as expanding tissue cholesterol pools (Quintao 1971), despite the existence of homeostatic mechanisms.

In many individuals a high intake of cholesterol is partly compensated for by a rise in biliary excretion of cholesterol. Whether this is relevant to the pathogenesis of cholesterol gallstones is unknown. In one migrant study increasing gallstone prevalence was seen in Italian immigrants in Australia, paralleling an increase in dietary cholesterol and fat (Hills 1971).

No such conclusion is yet tenable with regard to colon cancer. Some case-control studies have shown lower vegetable intakes in patients (Modan *et al.* 1975) but this implies differences in several macro- and micro-nutrients as well as fibre. Cross-cultural studies have revealed far stronger positive correlations between both fat and animal protein intake and colon cancer mortality than are evident for fibre (Hill 1974*b*, 1975); an exception is Finland, where a low mortality is associated with a high fat intake but also with a high consumption of fibre (Reddy *et al.* 1978). A high intake of cereal fibre, by increasing faecal bulk reduces the concentration of bile acids and hypothetical carcinogens by dilution, but other forms of fibre increase bile acid concentrations. Shorter transit time could reduce the opportunity for formation of carcinogens by bacterial action, for example nitrosamines, but at present this is speculative. Judgement must be deferred as to the role of fibre in the aetiology of colon cancer, pending much additional information.

Evidence for mutagenic activity in faeces is at present tenuous. Much more information is required as to the promoter effect of faecal bile acids. For example, the measurement of bile acid concentration in faeces is at best a rough index of the exposure of colonic mucosa to these steroids, for bile acids are largely present adsorbed to bacteria, and to some extent to fibre; hence their distribution may be as significant as their overall concentration.

The geographical distribution of coronary heart disease is to some extent inversely related to fibre intake. Recognition of the effects of fruit-and-vegetable-derived fibre in decreasing plasma cholesterol adds credence to the view that fibre deficiency may contribute to the lipid-mediated risk of coronary heart disease. From the point of view of prevention it is relevant that the effects of fibre supplementation are strongly additive with those of fat modification in reducing plasma cholesterol; hence a combination of both these dietary influences has a remarkably potent effect on plasma cholesterol and low-density lipoprotein levels (Lewis *et al.* 1981; Choudhury *et al.* 1983).

Glucose tolerance is improved by diets supplemented with vegetable fibre both in insulin-dependent (IDDM) and non-insulin-dependent (NIDDM) diabetes (Simpson *et al.* 1981). In the latter, postprandial hyperinsulinism is reduced. The findings are becoming accepted as relevant to the treatment of established diabetes; this is not only in the context of reducing mean blood glucose levels, levels of endogenous insulin in NIDDM and dosage of exogenous insulin in IDDM but also in view of the hypolipidaemic effects of vegetable fibre. Since the height of the insulin response to oral glucose is directly and independently related to coronary heart disease risk (Pyörälä 1979), reduction of hyperinsulinism as well as hypercholesterolaemia may prove to be desirable consequences.

Energy balance

Despite extensive research in man and in laboratory animals regrettably little can be said about the aetiology of obesity; hence current approaches to prevention of obesity owe more to 'common sense' than rational understanding. Demonstrable causes (Cushing's syndrome, insulinoma, hypothalamic injury, Willi–Prader syndrome) are rare. The behavioural sciences have provided little in the way of practical bases for prevention. Weight gain reflects an excess of food energy input over expenditure as heat, work, and synthetic processes, on simple thermodynamic grounds; although some obese individuals clearly overeat or obtain excess dietary energy as alcohol, it has proved remarkably difficult to substantiate the hypotheses that high energy intake or subnormal energy expenditure are consistently present as preconditions for the development of obesity. Both lean and obese individuals vary widely in energy expenditure (Warwick *et al.* 1978; Garrow 1981; James 1983) and in metabolic efficiency; that is, in the energy cost of given tasks. The mechanism of obesity (as distinct from its aetiology) can reasonably be regarded as representing an interaction between individual variations in food intake and in energy expenditure such that a positive energy balance is at least intermittently present. Energy expenditure varies widely and overlaps extensively in lean and obese individuals (Ravussin *et al.* 1982). Recently a defect in non-shivering thermogenesis in some obese patients has been postulated to account for low energy expenditure (Jung *et al.* 1979). When adrenaline was infused, the increment in oxygen consumption, that is in metabolic rate, was smaller in subjects with resistant obesity than in lean persons. However, as the basal oxygen consumption was greater in the fat subjects, their overall metabolic rate was no less than in lean controls. This conclusion is supported by direct calorimetry (Blaza and Garrow 1980).

At present the prevention and control of obesity are best directed to controlling energy input (as food and alcohol) and to increasing energy expenditure by aerobic exercise. The prevalence of obesity necessitates a public health approach, obesity becoming a clinical problem when it is pronounced, resistant to self-imposed control, or complicated by medical illness.

The definition of desirable weight has undergone re-examination in recent years, (Bray 1979; Lew and Garfinkel 1979). Earlier use of 'frame size' has been abandoned on the ground that objective assessment is difficult. Present standards allow a slightly higher range of optimal weight than previously, for there is a relatively wide range of weights associated with minimum mortality rate. Weight increase during adult life is clearly associated with an increased incidence of hypertension and of high cholesterol levels (Stamler 1972; Kannel and Sorlie 1974), and is clearly undesirable.

Among the metabolic consequences of obesity are several that further our understanding of the clinical complications to which the fat are prone (Mancini *et al.* 1979). Insulin resistance in adipocytes and perhaps other cells is a part of the derangement characterizing non-insulin dependent diabetes; increased cholesterol turnover and excretion contribute to the risk of cholesterol gallstones. Low adipose tissue lipoprotein lipase activity is at least one of the mechanisms leading to low levels of high-density lipoprotein cholesterol in obesity, conferring an increased risk of coronary heart disease. Increased conversion of endogenous androgenic hormones to oestrogens in adipose tissue may underlie the excess risk of carcinoma of the body of the uterus in obese women.

Evidence that low body weight is associated with excess mortality must be viewed critically. In part this trend may be attributed to the presence of undiagnosed disease (malignancy being currently more important (Rhoads and Kagan 1983) while tuberculosis influenced earlier data). A further cogent reason for the J-shaped curve of mortality may be that some individuals maintain very low weights by smoking, hence that extreme leanness is attained at the price of smoking-related disease.

Protein

In industrialized countries, in peacetime, protein deficiency is usually due to underlying disease, for example, malabsorption, intestinal protein loss, or burns, rather than nutritional deficiency, even at the extremes of age. Occasionally it arises in the infants of parents adhering to extreme cults (Roberts *et al.* 1979). Qualitative aspects of protein nutrition are, however, worthy of mention. Lipid metabolism is influenced by the origin of dietary protein, plasma cholesterol, and/or low-density lipoprotein levels being lower when soybean protein is substituted for mixed proteins (in a typical western diet some two-thirds of protein intake is of animal origin). In some studies the effect is modest (Carroll *et al.* 1978; van Raaij *et al.* 1981), while larger differences have been reported (Sirtori *et al.* 1979). The importance of the protein effect is that it is easier to attain a desirable level of plasma cholesterol by multiple moderate changes in the diet than by extreme changes in one nutrient, for example fat (Lewis *et al.* 1981).

Emphasis on proteins of vegetable origin may be determined by hypersensitivity, for example to milk proteins, and more globally, in the future, as a consequence of cost and availability. Hence it should be said that the notion that all vegetable proteins are nutritionally inferior to animal proteins in the human diet is at best a generalization, and applies to single sources of protein only. Combinations of protein-containing vegetable foods, for example, beans with rice, nuts and wheatgerm, by virtue of their complementary contents of limiting amino-acids, can be nutritionally sound.

Alcohol

The protean effects of alcohol are discussed elsewhere in this textbook (Volume 3, Chapter 23). A few aspects justify inclusion in the present section. In hypertension there is an aetiological role of substantial intakes of alcohol. A remarkably strong positive relationship exists between a stated consumption of six or more drinks per day and mortality from cardiovascular disease (Shaper *et al.* 1981). A similar association has appeared in longitudinal studies (Tibblin *et al.* 1975; Kozararevic *et al.* 1980). The causal nature of these findings is attested by evidence of blood pressure reduction when alcohol is withdrawn in hypertensive patients. The relationship between alcohol intake and coronary heart disease mortality is biphasic, being higher both in abstainers and in heavy drinkers than in moderate drinkers (Marmot *et al.* 1981), with a nadir in the vicinity of 10–30 g alcohol per day. The excess risk in abstainers has been attributed to their lower mean levels of high-density lipoprotein cholesterol. That in heavy drinkers is less readily explained, though hypertension is likely to play a role. It is not due to the association between cigarette use and alcohol consumption.

In addition to the role of alcohol as a cause of primary hepatoma arising in cirrhotic livers, there are well-defined associations between alcohol abuse and oropharyngeal and oesophageal cancers. Concomitant tobacco smoking and alcohol abuse are clearly associated with high risk of cancer in the latter sites (Fraumeni 1975). The molecular basis for this interaction is not clear. A plausible suggestion is that the unbalanced diet of heavy drinkers includes deficient intakes of retinol and perhaps other vitamins with a protective role against carcinogens (Newberne and Rogers 1981).

PHYSICAL EXERCISE

The widespread recent advocacy of, and practice of physical exercise is based on somewhat slender scientific foundations. It is of interest that exercise, unsupported by controlled trials and by no means without hazard (Thompson *et al.* 1982), should have attained a credibility in medical circles not enjoyed by nutritional principles, and a public response seemingly greater than smoking cessation.

In the admirable review by Leon and Blackburn (1977), tallies of affirmative and negative cross-sectional studies are listed including occupational and social groups differing in physical activity: 18 of 30 reports described lower coronary heart disease frequency in active populations. Several prospective studies have indicated a lower coronary heart disease risk in active groups (Kannel 1967; Morris *et al.* 1973; Paffenbarger and Hale 1975), though others detected no protection (Rosenman *et al.* 1977). Even mild activity may be protective (Rose 1969) though most studies refer to vigorous activity (Morris *et al.* 1980). Autopsy findings on active and sedentary groups have been somewhat inconsistent (Leon and Blackburn 1977). Training undoubtedly enhances capacity for sustained physical work in normal subjects and in coronary heart disease patients (Cowan, personal communication 1983), and appears to have other advantageous cardiovascular effects including reduced ventricular premature beats (Blackburn *et al.* 1973). Improved myocardial vascularity is induced by exercise in normal animals (Leon and Bloor 1976), but is not substantiated in man.

The interpretation of studies of subjects who have selected themselves into active and sedentary categories is hampered by coexisting differences in coronary heart disease risk factors. Cigarette use in particular was one-third less in those maintaining high levels of leisure-time activity in a large Irish study (Hickey *et al.* 1975). Also, self-selection may be influenced by effort tolerance, hence in part by pre-existing coronary heart disease.

Cross-cultural studies have shown lower lipoprotein-mediated risk (lower cholesterol, higher high-density lipoprotein cholesterol) in active groups such as marathon runners (Carlson and Mossfeldt 1964; Wood *et al.* 1976) and intervention trials have established that exercise induces such changes (Lopez-S. *et al.* 1974; Ilmarinen and Fardy 1977; Cowan *et al.*, personal communication 1983). It is not clear whether exercise leads to chronically lower blood pressure (Leon and Blackburn 1977).

Evidence from randomized controlled trials has yet to establish that coronary heart disease incidence can be reduced by regular physical activity. There are major problems in conducting such trials. One small primary prevention study failed to demonstrate protection (Ilmarinen and Fardy 1977) while a secondary prevention trial by Wilhelmsen *et al.* (1975) though large and well-matched was characterized by a high number of drop-outs. Treadmill exercise reduced the extent of coronary atherosclerosis in cynomolgus monkeys fed butter and cholesterol, compared with an unexercised control group (Kramsch *et al.* 1981).

Persons involved in leisure-time physical activity are less often obese than those not involved in such activity. Self-selection or overall 'health consciousness' may partly explain such findings. However, exercise has an acute anorectic effect in man and laboratory animals (Mayer *et al.* 1954; Holm *et al.* 1978).

Other beneficial aspects of physical activity are becoming substantiated. That exercise may delay osteoporosis has been suggested on the basis of bone mineral measurements (Aloia *et al.* 1978; Krølner *et al.* 1983), possibly attributable to piezo-electric effects of stresses influencing the crystalline structure of bone mineral. Beneficial effects on the development of osteoarthropathy are often cited. There is good evidence that the frequency of episodes of lower back pain may be reduced by appropriate trunk exercises.

Drugs

Some groups of drugs are used so commonly as to justify inclusion amongst environmental agents with metabolic effects.

Diuretics influence electrolyte, lipid, carbohydrate, and purine metabolism. Benzothiadiazines reduce plasma and in most reports tissue potassium (Hollifield 1980; Morgan and Davidson 1980); frusemide, though a more potent diuretic has a smaller kaliuretic effect (Morgan and Davidson 1980). There is a range of individual susceptibility to hypokalaemia and also to the numerous consequent tachyarrhythmias. Ventricular premature systoles are the commonest of these (Hollifield 1980; Solomon and Cole 1980). Their frequency is greatest in the elderly, in the presence of coexisting coronary heart disease, and in patients receiving cardiac glycosides. Both types of diuretic induce hyperuricaemia and can precipitate gout in predisposed individuals, in those over-indulging in alcohol, and in obese persons on very low calorie diets. Aggravation of pre-existing diabetes mellitus is well recognized. The common side-effect of impotence has yet to be satisfactorily explained. There is an extensive literature on lipoprotein effects of these drugs. Reduction of high-density lipoprotein cholesterol is the most significant, because of its potent inverse relationship to coronary heart disease risk (Ames 1981; Grimm *et al.* 1981). Mild hypertriglyceridaemia is common, but has a controversial relationship to coronary heart disease (Carlson *et al.* 1979; Hulley *et al.* 1980). Elevation of plasma cholesterol is slight with most diuretics, but appears more substantial with chlorthalidone (Ames 1981). Whether the lipoprotein effects of diuretics tend to offset the benefits of their use in treatment of hypertension is uncertain (Robertson 1978). It is clear that treatment of high blood pressure (all trials have included diuretics in the therapeutic programme) has a smaller effect on coronary heart disease risk than on the incidence of stroke (Management Committee 1980; Rosenberg *et al.* 1980) but this is probably due in part to the multiplicity of risk factors for coronary heart disease compared with the pre-eminent relationship between hypertension and stroke. Some beta-blockers, like diuretics, reduce high-density lipoprotein cholesterol.

Possibly related to their effects on lipid metabolism, thiazide use has been found to be associated with an increased risk of cholecystitis (Rosenberg *et al.* 1980).

Oral contraceptive formulations can induce sodium and water retention, aggravate hypertension and diabetes mellitus, and increase plasma triglyceride and (to a smaller extent) cholesterol (Wallace *et al.* 1979); depending on the androgenicity of the progestogen component they may decrease high density lipoprotein cholesterol levels or, if less androgenic, may have no effect (Krauss *et al.* 1977; Bradley *et al.* 1978; Briggs and Briggs 1981). The excess risk of coronary heart disease in women using oestrogen-containing contraceptives appears to be multifactorial. It is especially pronounced when the use of the contraceptive pill coexists with cigarette smoking (Beral and Kay 1977; Vessey *et al.* 1977). Lipoprotein changes and increased blood pressure probably contribute to overall risk. As the pathology of occluded coronary arteries showed a pronounced thrombotic component in three young women dying with myocardial infarction (Spain 1978), oestrogen-induced changes in coagulation factors and platelet function may play an important role.

Oral contraceptives, and also oestrogens increase the risk

of gallstone formation (Boston Collaborative Drug Surveillance Program 1973), due to increased secretion of cholesterol into bile (Bennion *et al.* 1980).

Microsomal enzyme induction is a feature of several drugs in common use (phenytoin, barbiturates, rifampicin) as well as pollutants such as halogenated insecticides. An increase in plasma high-density lipoprotein cholesterol levels is one consequence of exposure to these agents (Nicoll *et al.* 1980). Although there is an inverse relationship between high-density lipoprotein levels and coronary heart disease risk there is at present no evidence that changes in levels of this lipoprotein will alter the frequency of this disease. Other consequences of microsomal enzyme induction are alteration in the metabolism of other drugs, and of steroid hormones. This interaction can impair the efficacy of oral contraceptives (Black and Orme 1977). In experimental models of cancer, the effect of exogenous carcinogens can be considerably reduced by induction of microsomal enzymes, for example by inducers present in natural foodstuffs such as cabbage and other Brassicaceae (Wattenberg 1980).

IMPLICATIONS FOR PREVENTIVE MEDICINE

Many of the foregoing relationships have already influenced the practice of preventive medicine; progress in metabolic research has, by clarifying the mechanisms involved, reinforced the case for interventions already advised on prudent epidemiological grounds. A knowledge of underlying mechanisms is desirable but not essential to health care, as a score of historical examples (Lind, Jenner, Snow, Lister) attests.

The place of efforts to prevent cigarette smoking is a benchmark in translating medical knowledge into practice at the population level. Supported cogently by several sets of epidemiological data and by the demonstration of more than 30 carcinogens in tobacco smoke, but not by the existence of animal models of tobacco-induced lung cancer or coronary heart disease nor by controlled trial evidence, anti-smoking activities are supported with virtual unanimity by the medical profession. The major research need is the development of methods for improving the results of smoking cessation programmes.

Similarly the prevention and treatment of obesity (if defined as a relative body weight exceeding 120 per cent) is advocated by the profession as a whole resting on evidence of association and on a substantial knowledge of pathogenic mechanisms. The poor success rate in treating obesity is common to a wide range of non-invasive therapeutic methods, and may reflect the poverty of understanding of the metabolic and possible psychological bases of the disorder or the refractoriness of these causes to intervention. That a minority of patients do successfully lose weight and maintain a steady state is encouraging. At present the requirements are twofold. First, there is a need for more effective techniques of re-education in eating habits, both quantitative and qualitative. Secondly, basic research is required to establish whether hypometabolism, deficient thermogenesis, or other metabolic lesions contribute to obesity and, if so, their prevalence amongst obese persons. Pending developments in this field

prevention and treatment of obesity continue to depend on manipulation of energy balance. It is fruitful to approach this by dietary restriction (backed by support from the doctor or by formal behaviour modification methods), and simultaneously by a progressive exercise programme appropriate for the subjects' age and cardiorespiratory status.

Reduction in coronary heart disease is a major goal in preventive medicine due to its status as the most important source of mortality and serious illness in western countries. Prevention strategy requires a double approach: that of reduction in the main modifiable risk factors in the community while identifying individuals at particularly high risk by improved case-finding, with a view to specific treatment. The recent statement by a WHO Expert Committee (1982) that 'the major determinants of population rates of coronary heart disease had now been identified' is supported by extensive evidence (Stamler 1978; Blackburn 1979; Marmot 1979; Lewis 1980, 1981). These are diet-related hyperlipidaemia, cigarette smoking, hypertension, and obesity. The case for intervening against hypercholesterolaemia is based on concordant data from epidemiology, clinical observations, animal models, controlled trials, and studies of mechanism; that is, on a wider range of evidence than that accepted to justify cessation of smoking.

Improved case-finding refers particularly to the detection of uncommon severe forms of hyperlipidaemia, and the recognition of hypertension and diabetes (notably NIDDM). The latter are shown by competent clinical examination. The serious but treatable disorder familial hypercholesterolaemia, referred to earlier, has a prevalence of 1 per 400 to 1 per 500 in Britain and the US, and is probably grossly underdiagnosed. Its detection is based on a family history of early-onset coronary heart disease, and/or the presence of xanthomas, for example in the Achilles' tendons or finger extensors. Control of this cause of very premature coronary heart disease will depend on better undergraduate and postgraduate medical education, to ensure recognition of this, one of the commonest inborn errors of metabolism.

Many others among the relationships discussed in this chapter have yet to become entrenched in therapeutic or preventive medical practice. Drug interactions are in large measure a matter for the prescribing doctor; but improved public education is also required if accidents due to tranquillizer–alcohol synergy and oral contraceptive failure due to microsomal enzyme-inducers are to be minimized. There is increasing awareness by practising physicians of the untoward effects of commonly-used antihypertensives; as yet the full potential of non-pharmacological methods of treating mild hypertension has not been sufficiently evaluated.

The possible risks as well as the benefits of these population recommendations require careful scrutiny. This is not a problem in the context of smoking cessation: weight gain is not, as popularly believed, an inevitable consequence, and any risk attendant on moderate increase in weight is outweighed by the benefits of ceasing to smoke.

Some metabolic and other untoward effects of commonly-used antihypertensive drugs were referred to in an earlier section. The recent trials of treatment of mild hypertension (HDFP Cooperative Group 1979; Management Committee

1980), like the earlier moderate hypertension trials, showed clear reductions in the frequency of stroke and hypertensive cardiac failure but only slight downward trends in coronary heart disease. However, recent interest in non-pharmacological control of mild hypertension is justified by these untoward drug effects as well as by cost considerations. Further work is required on the possibility that sodium restriction, reduction of obesity, reduction of heavy alcohol intake, and increase in the ratio of dietary polyunsaturated fatty acids to saturated fatty acids (P:S ratio) have additive effects in hypertension. At present the first three of these interventions are justifiable in clinical and preventive practice.

The concept of optimal plasma cholesterol levels, that is of a distribution associated with minimum risk of disease, has been referred to. Longitudinal and cross-cultural epidemiological findings are one source of such normative data; cell biology, studies of lipoprotein transfer from plasma to the arterial wall, and observations on levels of cholesterol leading to cessation of experimental atherogenesis or its regression have all to be taken into account. A recent WHO report has defined a desirable population mean as <200 mg/dl (5.2 mmol/l) (WHO Expert Committee 1982); the report of a multidisciplinary workshop refers to a mean of 180 mg/dl (4.7 mmol/l) (Blackburn et al. 1979).

Space does not permit an adequate analysis of possible untoward effects of plasma cholesterol reduction. This has been discussed elsewhere (Lewis 1982) and recent epidemiological and metabolic studies have been reassuring (International Collaborative Group 1982; Marenah et al. 1983); the substantive conclusion has been that there is no evidence of a causal link between low plasma cholesterol (in the range attainable by the dietary changes advocated) and non-cardiovascular disease. The dietary recommendations to coronary-heart-disease-prone populations should comprise avoidance or reduction of obesity, reduction of total fat intake to 25–30 per cent of dietary energy, and of saturated fat intake to 8–10 per cent energy (with concurrent reduction of dietary cholesterol to <300 mg/day), an increase in fruit, vegetable, and whole-grain cereal foods, a modest increase in polyunsaturated fat raising the P:S ratio towards, but not exceeding 1.0, reduction in salt consumption and moderation in alcohol intake. This dietary pattern is characteristic of Mediterranean and eastern countries with greater life expectations than exist in Great Britain or the US (Table 16.1).

Existing evidence does not justify nutritional recommendations to reduce cancer risk, an area in which further research is required, including such controlled trials as are feasible. However, the dietary recommendations put forward include several components which would plausibly reduce the risk of common cancers. These include avoidance of obesity (an association between obesity and carcinoma of the uterus has been discussed), reduction in total fat consumption (persuasively linked with breast and colon cancer and associated also with cancers of the ovaries, pancreas, and kidney), increased intake of cereal fibre (linked by limited evidence with colon cancer), and increased intake of retinoids and vitamin C. Inverse relationships between intake of β-carotene and

Table 16.1. *Life expectation in countries with divergent dietary patterns (1970–74 data)*

Mean age (years)	Scotland	England and Wales	US	Italy	Japan
Males					
Birth	67.3	69.0	67.6	68.9	70.9
15	54.3	55.8	54.5	56.6	57.4
35	35.5	36.7	36.3	37.7	38.6
55	18.2	19.1	19.6	20.2	20.9
Females					
Birth	73.8	75.2	75.4	75.2	76.3
15	60.4	61.8	62.0	62.5	62.5
35	40.9	42.3	42.9	43.1	43.1
55	23.1	24.1	25.1	24.6	24.7
Saturated fat intake % energy	18.7	19.4	14.0	9.0	6.0

plasma retinol levels on the one hand, and total cancer mortality, colon cancer, and lung cancer mortality rates are indicated by epidemiological studies (Wald et al. 1980; Shekelle et al. 1981). That these may prove to be causal is suggested by feeding studies in animals and by known actions of these retinoids for example, in inhibiting the activation of carcinogens (Doll and Peto 1981; Newberne and Rogers 1980). A role of vitamin C is less well attested at present. Some geographical studies of gastric cancer mortality rates and of atrophic gastritis and case-control studies have suggested associations of the disease or of its probable precursor with low intake of vegetable thus, *inter alia*, with low availability of vitamin C (Haenzel et al. 1976); mortality rates also show a strong direct cross-cultural relationship with salt consumption (Joosens 1980). The possible relevance of these observations is that vitamin C inhibits the formation of carcinogenic nitrosamines from nitrite and amines (Mirvish 1977) (a reaction postulated to occur in the stomach), and that sodium chloride promotes the effect of carcinogens on the rat stomach (Tatematsu et al. 1975).

In the context of established epidemiological associations, metabolic data has provided strong justifications for certain environmental manipulations in preventive medicine. The interaction between these disciplines is likely to be increasingly fruitful: the recently-coined expression 'metabolic epidemiology' (Weisburger et al. 1977) has earned a place in the medical vocabulary.

REFERENCES

Aloia, J.F., Cohn, S.H., Ostuni, J.A., Cane, R., and Ellis, K. (1978). Prevention of involutional bone loss by exercise. *Ann. Int. Med.* **89**, 356.

Ames. R.P. (1981). Serum lipid and lipoprotein disturbances during antihypertensive therapy. *Hosp. Formulary* **16**, 1476.

Armstrong, M.L. and Megan, B.M. (1972). Lipid depletion in atheromatous coronary arteries in Rhesus monkeys after regression diets. *Circ. Res.* **30**, 675.

Armstrong, B. and Doll, R. (1975). Environmental factors and cancer incidence and mortality in different countries, with special reference to dietary practices. *Int. J. Cancer* **15**, 617.

Back, D.J. and Orme, M.L'E. (1977). Drug interactions with oral contraceptive steroids. *Prescriber's J.* **17**, 137.

Bennion, L.J., Mott, D.M., and Howard, B.V. (1980). Oral contraceptives raise the cholesterol saturation of bile by increasing biliary cholesterol secretion. *Metabolism* **29**, 18.

Beral, V. and Kay, C.R. (1977). Mortality among oral contraceptive users. *Lancet* **ii**, 727.

Blackburn, H. (1979). Diet and mass hyperlipidemia: a public health view. In *Nutrition, lipids and coronary heart disease* (eds. R. Levy, B. Rifkind, B. Dennis, and N. Ernst) p. 309. Raven Press, New York.

Blackburn, H., Lewis, B., and Wissler, R.W. (1979). Conference on the health effects of blood lipids: optimal distributions for populations. *Prev. Med.* **8**, 612.

Blackburn, H., Taylor, H.L., Hamrell, B., Buskirk, E., Nicholas, W.C., and Thorsen, R.D. (1973). Premature ventricular complexes induced by stress testing: their frequency and response to physical conditioning. *Am. J. Cardiol.* **31**, 441.

Blaza, C.E. and Garrow, J.S. (1980). The thermogenic response to comfortable temperature extremes in lean and obese subjects. *Proc. Nutrit. Soc.* **39**, 85A. (Abstr.).

Boston Collaborative Drug Surveillance Program (1973). Oral contraceptives and venous thromboembolic disease, surgically-confirmed gallbladder disease, and breast tumors. *Lancet* **i**, 1399.

Bradley, D.D., Wingerd, J., Petitti, D.B., Krauss, R.M., and Ramcharan, S. (1978). Serum high density lipoprotein cholesterol in women using oral contraceptives, estrogens and progestins. *New Engl. J. Med.* **299**, 17.

Bray, G.A., ed. (1979). *Proceedings of the 2nd Fogarty International Center Conference on Obesity: Obesity in America.* US DHEW Publication No. 79. Washington, DC.

Briggs, M. and Briggs, M. (1981). A randomised study of metabolic effects of four low-estrogen oral contraceptives. *Contraception* **23**, 463.

Brussard, J.H., Katan, M.B., and Hautvast, J.G. (1983). Faecal excretion of bile acids and neutral steroids on diets differing in type and amount of dietary fat in young healthy persons. *Eur. J. Clin. Invest.* **13**, 115.

Bull, A.W., Soullier, B.K., Silson, P.S., Hayden, M.T., and Nigro N.D. (1979). Promotion of azoxymethane-induced intestinal cancer by high-fat diet in rats. *Cancer Res.* **39**, 4956.

Carlson, L.A. and Mossfeldt, F. (1964). Acute effects of prolonged heavy exercise on the concentration of plasma lipids and lipoproteins in man. *Acta Physiol. Scand.* **62**, 51.

Carlson, L.A., Böttiger, L.E., and Ahlfeldt, P.E. (1979). Risk factors for myocardial infarction in the Stockholm Prospective Study. *Acta Med. Scand.* **206**, 301.

Carroll, K.K. (1981). Neutral fats and cancer. *Cancer Res.* **41**, 3695.

Carroll, K.K. (1980). Lipids and carcinogenesis. *J. Environ. Pathol. Toxicol.* **3**, 253.

Carroll, K.K., Giovanetti, P.M., Huff, M.W., Moase, O., Roberts, D.C.K., and Wolfe, B.M. (1978). Hypocholesterolemic effect of substituting soyabean protein for animal protein in the diet of healthy young women. *Am. J. Clin. Nutr.* **31**, 1312.

Chan, P.C. and Cohen, L.A. (1975). Dietary fat and growth promotion of rat mammary tumors. *Cancer Res.* **35**, 3384.

Chomchai, C., Bhadrachari, N., and Nigro, H.D. (1974). The effect of bile on the induction of experimental intestinal tumours in rats. *Dis. Colon. Rectum* **17**, 310.

Choudhury, S., Jackson, P., Katan, M.B., Marenah, C.B., Cortese, C., Miller, N.E., and Lewis, B. (1983). A multifactorial diet in the management of hyperlipidaemia. *Atherosclerosis*, **50**, 93.

Cohen, L.A. (1981). Mechanisms by which dietary fat may stimulate mammary carcinogenesis in experimental animals. *Cancer Res.* **41**, 3808.

Connor, W.E., Hodges, R.E., and Bleiker, R.E. (1961). The serum lipids in men receiving high cholesterol and cholesterol-free diets. *J. Clin. Invest.* **40**, 894.

Cowan, G., and Lewis, B. Unpublished data.

Cruse, P., Lewin, M., and Clark, C.G. (1979). Dietary cholesterol is co-carcinogenic for human colon cancer. *Lancet* **i**, 752.

Cruse, P., Lewin, M., Ferulano, G.P., and Clark, C.G. (1978). Co-carcinogenic effects of dietary cholesterol in experimental colon cancer. *Nature, Lond.* **276**, 822.

Cummings, J.H., Wiggins, H.S., Jenkins, D.J.A. *et al.* (1978). Influence of diets high and low in animal fat on bowel habit, gastrointestinal transit time, fecal microflora, bile acid and fat excretion. *J. Clin. Invest.* **61**, 953.

Doll, R. and Peto, R. (1981). *The causes of cancer.* Oxford University Press, New York.

Doll, R., Payne, P., and Waterhouse, J. (eds.) (1966). *Cancer incidence in five continents.* International Union Against Cancer, Berlin.

Duffield, R.G.M., Miller, N.E., Jamieson, C.W., and Lewis, B. (1982). A controlled trial of plasma lipid reduction in peripheral atherosclerosis – an interim report. *Br. J. Surg.* **69**, 53.

Duffield, R.G.M., Lewis, B., Miller, N.E., Jamieson, C.W., Brunt, J.N.H., and Colchester, A.C.F. (1983). Treatment of hypolipidaemia retards progression of symptomatic femoral atherosclerosis in man. A randomized controlled trial. *Lancet* **ii**, 639.

Elkeles, R.S., Chakrabarti, R., Vickers, M., Stirling, Y., and Meade, T.W. (1980). Effect of treatment of hyperlipidaemia on haemostatic variables. *Br. Med. J.* **281**, 973.

Fraumeni, J.F. (ed.) (1975). *Persons at high risk of cancer: an approach to cancer etiology and control.* Academic Press, New York.

Garrow, J.S. (1981). *Treat obesity seriously: a clinical manual.* Churchill Livingstone, London.

Grimm, R.H., Leon, A.S., Hunninghake, D.B., Lenz, K., Hannan, P. and Blackburn, H. (1981). Effects of thiazide diuretics on plasma lipids and lipoproteins in mildly hypertensive patients. *Ann. Intern. Med.* **94**, 7.

Haenszel, W. and Kurihara, M. (1968). Studies of Japanese migrants. I. Mortality from cancer and other diseases among Japanese in the United States. *J. Natl. Cancer Inst.* **40**, 43.

Haenszel, W., Correa, P., Cuello, C. *et al.* (1976). Gastric cancer in Columbia. II. Case-control epidemiological study of precursor lesions. *J. Natl. Cancer Inst.* **57**, 1021.

Hassan, M.A., Rahman, E.A., and Rhaman, I.A. (1973). Postoperative deep vein thrombosis in Sudanese patients. *Br. Med. J.* **i**, 515.

Hickey, N., Mulcahy, R., Bourke, G.J., Graham, I., and Wilson-Davis, K. (1975). Study of coronary risk factors related to physical activity in 15171 men. *Br. Med. J.* **iii**, 507.

Higginson, J. and Muir, C.S. (1976). The role of epidemiology in elucidating the importance of environmental factors in human cancer. *Cancer Detect. Prev.* **1**, 79.

Hill, M.J. (1974a). Bacteria and the etiology of colonic cancer. *Cancer* **34**, 815.

Hill, M.J. (1974b). Colon cancer: a disease of fibre depletion or of dietary excess? *Digestion* **11**, 289.

Hill, M.J. (1975). The etiology of colon cancer. *CRC Critical Rev. Toxicol.* 31.

Hill, M.J., Drasar, B.S., Hawksworth, G. *et al.* (1971). Bacteria and aetiology of cancer of large bowel. *Lancet* **i**, 95.

Hill, P., Garbaczewski, L., Hellman, P., Walker, A.R.P., Garnes, H., and Wynder, E.L. (1981). Environmental factors and breast and prostatic cancer. *Cancer Res.* **41**, 3817.

Hills, L.L. (1971). Cholelithiasis and immigration. *Med. J. Aust.* **2**, 94.

Hjermann, I., Velve Byre, K., Holme, I., and Leren, P. (1981). Effect of diet and smoking intervention on the incidence of coronary heart disease. *Lancet* **ii**, 1303.

Hollingfield, J.W. (1980). Cardiac arrhythmias associated with diuretic-induced hypokalaemia. *R. Soc. Med. Internal Congress Symposium Series* **44**, 5.

Holm, G., Björntorp, P., and Jagenburg, R. (1978). Effect on carbohydrate, lipid and amino-acid metabolism during the days following submaximal physical exercise in man. *J. Appl. Physiol.* **21**, 118.

Hopkins, G.J. and Carroll, K.K. (1979). Relationship between amount and type of dietary fat in promotion of mammary carcinogenesis induced by 7, 12 dimethylbenz(d)anthracene. *J. Natl. Cancer Inst.* **62**, 1009.

Hornstra, G. (1971). The influence of dietary sunflowerseed oil and hardened coconut fat on intra-arterial occlusive thrombosis in rats. *Nutr. Metab.* **13**, 140.

Hornstra, G., Lewis, B., Chait, A., Turpeinen, O., Karvonen, M.J., and Vergroesen, A.J. (1973). Influence of dietary fat on platelet function in man. *Lancet* **i**, 1155.

Hulley, S.B., Rosenman, R.H., Barvel, R.D., and Brand, R.J. (1980). The association between triglyceride and coronary heart disease. *New Engl. J. Med.* **302**, 1383.

Hypertension Detection and Follow-up Program Cooperative Group (1979). Five-year findings of the hypertension detection and follow-up program. *JAMA* **242**, 2562.

Iacono, J.M., Dougherty, R.M., Paoletti, R. *et al.* (1978). Pilot epidemiological studies in thrombosis. In *The thrombotic process in atherogenesis* (eds. Chandler, Eurenius, McMillan, Nelson, Schwartz, Wessler). Plenum, New York.

Ilmarinen, J. and Fardy, P.S. (1977). Physical activity intervention for males with high risk of coronary heart disease: a three-year follow-up. *Prev. Med.* **6**, 416.

International Collaborative Group (1982). Circulating cholesterol level and risk of death from cancer in men aged 40–69 years. *JAMA* **248**, 2853.

James, W.P.T. (1983). Energy requirements and obesity. *Lancet* **ii**, 386.

Japanese Ministry of Health and Welfare (1982).

Jensen, R.A. (1952). Postoperative thrombosis-emboli. The frequency in the period 1940–1948. *Acta Med. Scand.* **103**, 263.

Joosens, J.V. (1980). Stroke, stomach cancer and salt. In *Epidemiology of arterial blood pressure* (eds. H. Kesteloot, and J.V. Joosens). Nijhoff, The Hague.

Jung, R.T., Shetty, P.S., James, W.P.T., Barraud, M.A., and Callingham, B.A. (1979). Reduced thermogenesis in obesity. *Nature, Lond.* **279**, 322.

Kannel, W.B. (1967). Habitual levels of physical activity and risk of coronary heart disease. The Framingham Study. *Can. Med. Assoc. J.* **96**, 811.

Kannel, W.B. and Sorlie, P. (1974). Hypertension in Framingham. In *Epidemiology and control of hypertension* (ed. O. Paul). Medical Books, Miami.

Kannel, W.B., Castelli, W.P., and Gordon, T. (1979). Cholesterol in the prediction of atherosclerotic disease. *Ann. Intern. Med.* **90**, 85.

Keys, A. (1980). *Seven countries.* Harvard University Press, Cambridge, Mass.

Kozararevic, D., McGee, D., Vojvodic, N. *et al.* (1980). Frequency of alcohol consumption and morbidity and mortality: the Yugoslavian Cardiovascular Disease Study. *Lancet* **i**, 613.

Kramsch, D.M., Aspen, A.J., Abramovits, B.M., Kreimendahl, T., and Hood, W.B. (1981). Reduction of coronary atherosclerosis by moderate conditioning exercise in monkeys on an atherogeneic diet. *New Engl. J. Med.* **305**, 1483.

Krauss, R.M., Lindgren, F.T., Silvers, A., Jutagir, R., and Bradley, D.D. (1977). Changes in serum high density lipoproteins in women on oral contraceptive drugs. *Clin. Chim. Acta* **80**, 465.

Krølner, B., Toft, B., Nielsen, S.P. and Tøndevold, E. (1983). Physical exercise as prophylaxis against involutional vertebral bone loss: a controlled trial. *Clin. Sci.* **64**, 541.

Leon, A.S., and Blackburn, H. (1977). The relationship of physical activity to coronary heart disease and life expectancy. *Ann. NY Acad. Sci.* **301**, 561.

Leon, A.S., and Bloor, C.M. (1976). The effect of complete and partial deconditioning on exercise-induced cardiovascular changes in the rat. *Adv. Cardiol.* **18**, 81.

Lew, E.A. and Garfinkel, L. (1979). Variations in mortality by weight among 750 000 men and women. *J. Chronic Dis.* **32**, 563.

Lewis, B. (1976). *The hyperlipidaemias: clinical and laboratory practice,* Chapter 8. Blackwell Scientific, Oxford.

Lewis, B. (1980). Diet and ischaemic heart disease prevention: a policy for the 80s. *Br. Med. J.* **281**, 177.

Lewis, B. (1981). Ischaemic heart disease: the scientific bases of prevention. *Progress in Cardiology,* **10**, p. 21 (eds. P.N. Yu and J.F. Goodwin).

Lewis, B. (1982). Summary of workshop: hypocholesterolaemia, a risk factor? In *Atherosclerosis VI* (eds. F.G. Schettler and G. Schlierf). Springer, Berlin.

Lewis, B., Hammett, F., Katan, M. *et al.* (1981). Towards an improved lipid-lowering diet: additive effects of changes in nutrient intake. *Lancet* **ii**, 1310.

Liu, K., Stamler, J. Moss, D., Garside, D., Persky, V., and Soltero, I. (1979). Dietary cholesterol, fat, fibre and colon cancer mortality: an analysis of international data. *Lancet* **ii**, 782.

Lopez-S., R., Rial, R., Balart, L., and Arroyave, G. (1974). Effect of exercise and physical fitness on serum lipids and lipoproteins. *Atherosclerosis* **20**, 1.

McGill, H.C.Jr (1968). *The geographic pathology of atherosclerosis.* Williams and Wilkins, Baltimore.

Management Committee (1980). The Australian therapeutic trial in mild hypertension. *Lancet* **i**, 1263.

Mancini, M., Lewis, B., and Contaldo, F. (1979). *Medical complications of obesity.* Academic Press, London.

Mann, J.I. and Marr, J.W. (1981). Coronary heart disease prevention. Trials of diet to control hyperlipidaemia. In *Lipoproteins, atherosclerosis and coronary heart disease* (eds. N.E. Miller and B. Lewis) p. 197. Elsevier-North Holland, Amsterdam.

Marenah, C.B., Lewis, B., Hassall, D., La Ville, A., Cortese, C., Mitchell, W.D., Bruckdorfer, K.R., Slavin, B., Miller, N.E., Turner, P.R., and Meduan, E. (1983). Hypocholesterolaemia and non-cardiovascular disease: metabolic studies on subjects with low plasma cholesterol concentrations. *Br. Med. J.* **286**, 1603.

Marmot, M.G. (1979). Epidemiological basis for the prevention of coronary heart disease. *Bull. WHO* **57**, 331.

Marmot, M.G., Rose, G., Shipley, M.J., and Thomas, B.J. (1981). Alcohol and mortality: a u-shaped curve. *Lancet* **i**, 580.

Marmot, M.G., Syme, S.L., Kagan, A., Kato, H., Cohen, J.B., and Belsky, J. (1975). Epidemiological studies of coronary heart disease and stroke in Japanese men living in Japan, Hawaii and California. *Am. J. Epidemiol.* **102**, 514.

Mathues, J.K., Wolff, C.E., Civallos, W.H., and Holmes, W.L. (1968). Platelet thrombosis and adhesiveness in rabbits on an atherogenic diet. *Med. Exp.* **18**, 121.

Mayer, J., Marshall, N.B., Vitale, J.J., Christensen, J.H., Mashayekki, M.B., and Stare, F.J. (1954). Exercise, food intake and body weight in normal rats and geneticall obese adult mice. *Am. J. Physiol.* **177**, 544.

Merskey, C., Gordon, H., and Lackner, H. (1960). Blood coagulation and fibrinolysis in relation to coronary heart disease; a comparative study of normal white men, white men with overt coronary heart disease, and normal Bantu men. *Br. Med. J.* **i**, 219.

Miettinen, T.A., Naukkarinen, V., Huttunen, J.K., Mattila, S., Kumlin, T. (1982). Fatty-acid composition of serum lipids predicts myocardial infarction. *Br. Med. J.*, **285**, 993.

Miller, A.B. (1977). Role of nutrition in the etiology of breast cancer. *Cancer* **39**, 2704.

Mirvish, S.S. (1977). N-nitroso compounds: their chemical and in-vivo formation and possible importance as environmental carcinogens. *J. Toxicol. Environ. Health* **2**, 1267.

Mistry, P., Miller, N.E., Laker, M., Hazzard, W.R., and Lewis, B. (1981). Indicidual variation in the effects of dietary cholesterol on plasma lipoproteins and cellular cholesterol homeostasis in man. *J. Clin. Invest.* **67**, 493.

Modan, B., Barell, V., Lubin, M., Modan, R., Greenberg, R.A., and Graham, S. (1975). Low fibre intakes as an etiological factor in cancer of the colon. *J. Natl. Cancer Inst.* **55**, 15.

Morgan, D.B. and Davidson, C. (1980). Hypokalaemia and diuretics: an analysis of publications. *Br. Med. J.* **i**, 905.

Morris, J.N., Everitt, M.G., Pollard, R., Chave, S.P.W., and Semmence, A.M. (1980). Vigorous exercise in leisure-time: protection against coronary heart disease. *Lancet* ii, 1207.

Morris, J.N., Chave, S.P.W., Adam, C., Sirey, C., Epstein, L., and Sheehan, D.J. (1973). Vigorous exercise in leisure-time and the incidence of coronary heart disease. *Lancet* i, 333.

Morris, J.N., Marr, J.W., and Clayton, D.G. (1977). Diet and heart: a postscript. *Br. Med. J.* **ii**, 1301.

Morrison, A.S., Lowe, C.R., MacMahon, B. *et al.* (1977). Incidence risk factors survival in breast cancer: report on five years of follow-up observation. *Eur. J. Cancer* **13**, 209.

Mustard, J.F., Rowsell, H.C., Murphy, E.A., and Downie, H.G. (1963). Diet and thrombus formation: quantitative studies using an extracorporeal circulation in pigs. *J. Clin. Invest.* **42**, 1783.

Narisawa, T., Magadid, N.E., Weisburger, J.H., and Wynder, E.L. (1974). Promoting effect of bile acid on colon carcinogenesis after intrarectal instillation of MNNG in rats. *J. Natl. Cancer Inst.* **53**, 1093.

Newberne, P.M. and Rogers, A.E. (1981). Vitamin A, retinoids, and cancer. In *Nutrition and cancer: etiology and treatment* (eds. G.R. Newell and N.M. Ellison). Raven Press, New York.

NHLBI Working Group on Arteriosclerosis (1981). Report Vol. 1. US Public Health Service, National Institutes of Health. US Government Printing Office, Washington, DC.

Nicoll, A., Miller, N.E., and Lewis, B. (1980). High density lipoprotein metabolism. *Adv. Lipid Res.* **17**, 53.

Niehaus, C.E., Nicoll, A., Wootton, R., Williams, B., Lewis, J., Coltart, D.J., and Lewis, B. (1977). Influence of lipid concentrations and age on transfer of plasma lipoprotein into human arterial intima. *Lancet* ii, 469.

Nordöy, A., Hamlin, J.T., Chandler, A.B., and Nuoland, H. (1968). The influence of dietary fats on plasma and platelet lipids and ADP-induced platelet thrombosis in the rat. *Scand. J. Haematol.* **5**, 458.

Paffenbarger, R.S., and Hale, W.E. (1975). Work activity and coronary heart disease mortality. *New Engl. J. Med.* **292**, 545.

Pearson, O.H., Arafah, B., and Manni, A. (1980). Prolactin and mammary cancer. In *Central and peripheral regulation of prolactin function* (eds. R.M. Macleod and U. Scapagnini). Raven Press, New York.

Pooling Project Research Group (1978). Relationship of blood pressure, serum cholesterol, smoking habit, relative weight and ECG abnormalities to incidence of major coronary events. *J. Chronic Dis.* **31**, 201.

Pyörälä, K. (1979). Relationship of glucose tolerance and plasma insulin to the incidence of coronary heart disease: results from two population studies in Finland. *Diabetes Care* **2**, 131.

Quintao, E., Grundy, S.M., and Ahrens, E.H. Jr (1971). Effects of dietary cholesterol on the regulation of total body cholesterol on man. *J. Lipid Res.* **12**, 233.

Ravussin, E., Burnaud, B., Schutz, Y., and Jéquier, E. (1982). Twenty-four-hour energy expenditure and resting metabolic rate in obese, moderately obese, and control subjects. *Am. J. Clin. Nutr.* **35**, 566.

Reddy, B.S., Narisawa, T., Weisburger, J.H., and Wynder, E.L. (1976). Promoting effect of sodium deoxycholate on colon adenocarcinomas in germ-free rats. *J. Natl. Cancer Inst.* **56**, 441.

Reddy, B.S., Naragawa, T., Vukusich, D., Weisburger, J.H., and Wynder, E.L. (1976). Effect of quality and quantity of dietary fat in colon carcinogenesis in rats. *Proc. Soc. Exp. Biol. Med.* **151**, 237.

Reddy, B.S., Mangat, S., Sheinfil, A., Weisburger, J.H., and Wynder, E.L. (1977). Colon carcinogenesis. Effect of type and amount of dietary fat and 1, 2-dimethylhydrazine on biliary bile acids and fecal bile acids and neutral sterols in rats. *Cancer Res.* **37**, 2132.

Rosenberg, L., Shapiro, S., Slone, D., Kaufman, D.W., Miettinen, O.S., and Stolley, P.D. (1980). Thiazides and acute cholecystitis. *New Engl. J. Med.* **303**, 546.

Reddy, B.S., Hedges, A.R., Laakso, K., and Wynder, E.L. (1978). Metabolic epidemiology of large bowel cancer. Fecal bulk and constituents of high-risk North American and low-risk Finnish population. *Cancer* **42**, 2832.

Reid, D.D., Hamilton, P.J.S., McCartney, P., Rose, G., Jarrett, R.J., and Keen, H. (1976). Smoking and other risk factors for coronary heart disease in British civil servants. *Lancet* ii, 979.

Renaud, S., Dumont, E., Godsky, F., Morazain, R., Thevenon, C., and Ortchanian, E. (1980). Dietary fats and platelet function in French and Scottish farmers. *Nutr. Metab.* **24**, 90.

Renaud, S., Kinlough, R.L., and Mustard, J.F. (1970). Relationship between platelet aggregation and thrombotic tendency in rats fed hyperlipemic diets. *Lab. Invest.* **22**, 339.

Rhoads, G. and Kagan, A. (1983). The relation of coronary disease, stroke, and mortality to weight in youth and in middle age. *Lancet* i, 492.

Roberts, I.F., West, R.J., Ogilvie, D., and Dillon, M.J. (1979). Malnutrition in infants receiving cult diets: a form of child abuse. *Br. Med. J.* **i**, 296.

Robertson, J.I.S. (1978). Complications of mild hypertension. *Ann. NY Acad. Sci* **304**, 64.

Rose, G. (1969). Physical activity and coronary heart disease. *Proc. R. Soc. Med.* **62**, 1183.

Rosenman, R.H., Bawol, R.D., and Oscherwitz, M. (1977). A 4-year prosepective study of the relationship of physical activity to risk of ischaemic heart disease in volunteer male Federal employees. *Ann. NY Acad. Sci.* **301**, 627.

Shaper, A.G., Pocock, S.J., Walker, M., Cohen, N.M., Wale, C.J., and Thompson, A.G. (1981). British Regional Heart Study: cardiovascular risk factors in middle-aged men in 24 towns. *Br. Med. J.* **283**, 179.

Shastri, K.M., Carvalho, A.C.A., and Less, R.S. (1980). Platelet function and platelet lipid composition in the dyslipoproteinemias. *J. Lipid Res.* **21**, 467.

Shekelle, R.B., Lepper, M., Liu, S. *et al.* (1981). Dietary vitamin A and risk of cancer in the Western Electric Study. *Lancet* ii, 1185.

Shekelle, R.B., Shryock, A.M., Paul, O. *et al.* (1981). Diet, serum cholesterol and death from coronary heart disease. *New Engl. J. Med.* **304**, 65.

Simpson, H.C.R., Simpson, R.W., Lousley, S. *et al.* (1981). A high carbohydrate liguminous fibre diet improves all aspects of diabetic control. *Lancet* i, 1.

Sirtori, C.R., Gatti, E., Mantero, O. *et al.* (1979). Clinical experience with the soybean protein diet in the treatment of hyper-cholesterolemia. *Am. J. Clin. Nutrit.* **32**, 1645.

Slack, J. (1979). Risks of ischaemic heart disease in familial hyper-liporeoteinaemic states. *Lancet* **ii**, 1380.

Solomon, R. and Cole, A. (1980). Arrhythmias and myocardial infarction: the role of potassium. *R. Soc. Med. International Congress Symposium Series* **44**, 12.

Spain, D.M. (1978). Concerning the pathology of acute coronary heart disease in young women. In *Coronary heart disease in young women.* (ed. M.F. Oliver). p. 61. Churchill Livingstone, Edinburgh.

Spiller, G.A. and Kay, R.M. (1980). *Medical aspects of dietary fiber.* Plenum Medical, New York.

Stamler, J. (1978). Lifestyles, major risk factors, proof and public policy. *Circulation* **58**, 3.

Stamler, J. (1979). Population studies. In *Nutrition, lipids and coronary heart disease* (eds. R.I. Levy, B.M. Rifkind, B.H. Dennis, and M.D. Ernst) p. 25. Raven Press, New York.

Stamler, J. (1972). Prevention in atherosclerosis and hypertension. In *Proceedings of the 60th Meeting of the Medical Section of the American Life Convention,* American Life Convention, Chicago.

Steinberg, D. (1983). Lipoproteins and atherosclerosis. A look back and a look ahead. *Arteriosclerosis* **3**, 283.

Tatematsu, M., Takahashi, M., Fukushima, S., Hanaouchi, M., and Shirai, T. (1975). Effects in rats of sodium chloride on experimental gastric cancers induced by methylnitronitroso-guanidine or nitroquinoline oxide. *J. Natl. Cancer Inst.* **55**, 101.

Tibblin, G., Wilhelmsen, L., and Werkö, L. (1975). Risk factors for myocardial infarction and death due to ischaemic heart disease and other causes. *Am. J. Cardiol.* **35**, 514.

Thompson, P.D., Funk, E.J., Carleton, R.A., and Sturner, W.Q. (1982). Incidence of death during jogging in Rhode Island from 1975 through 1980. *JAMA* **247**, 2535.

Trowell, H.C. and Burkitt, D.P. (1977). Dietary fiber and cardiovascular disease. *Artery* **3**, 107.

van Raaij, J.M.A., Katan, M.B., Hautvast, J.G.A.J., and Hermus, R.J.J. (1981). Effects of casein versus soy protein diets on serum cholesterol and lipoproteins in healthy volunteers. *Am. J. Clin. Nutr.* **34**, 1261.

Vessey, M.P., McPherson, K., and Johnson, B. (1977). Mortality among women participating in the Oxford/Family Planning Association contraceptive study. *Lancet* **ii**, 731.

Wald, N., Idle, M., Boreham, J., and Bailey, A. (1980). Low serum vitamin A and subsequent risk of cancer. *Lancet* **ii**, 813.

Wallace, R.B., Hoover, J., Bassett-Connor, E., Rifkind, B.M., Hunninghake, D., and Heiss, G. (1979). Altered lipid and lipo-protein levels associated with oral contraceptive and oestrogen use. *Lancet* **ii**, 111.

Warwick, P.M., Toft, R., and Garrow, J.S. (1978). Individual variation in energy expenditure. *Int. J. Obes.* **2**, 396.

Wattenberg, L.W. (1980). Inhibitors of chemical carcinogens. *J. Environ. Pathol. Toxicol.* **3**, 35.

Weisburger, J.H., Reddy, B.S., and Wynder, E.L. (1977). Colon cancer: its epidemiology and experimental production. *Cancer* **40**, 2414.

WHO Expert Committee (Chairman G.A. Rose) (1982). *Prevention of coronary heart disease.* WHO, Geneva.

Wilhelmsen, L., Sanne, H., Elmfeldt, D., Grimby, G., Tibblin, G., and Wedel, H. (1975). A controlled trial of physical training after myocardial infarction. *Prev. Med.* **4**, 491.

Wissler, R.W. and Vesselinovitch, D. (1976). Studies of regression of advanced atherosclerosis in experimental animals and man. *Ann. NY Acad. Sci.* **275**, 363.

Wood, P.D., Haskell, W., Klein, H., Lewis, S., Stern, M., and Farquhar, J.W. (1976). The distribution of plasma lipoproteins in middle-aged runners. *Metabolism* **25**, 1249.

Wynder, E.L. and Gori, G.B. (1977). Contribution of the environment to cancer incidence: an epidemiologic exercise. *J. Natl. Cancer Inst.* **58**, 825.

17 Dental public health

John C. Greene and Samuel J. Wycoff

DENTAL DISEASES

Diseases of the teeth and the adjacent oral structures are among the most common maladies affecting human beings. Perhaps because they are so common and seldom life-threatening, they usually do not receive the attention they deserve, either from individuals or from health officials, health planners, or others concerned with improving a population's health status.

The primary function of the dentition is to chew, and healthy teeth permit the ingestion of a nutritious and palatable diet. Untreated dental disease leads to dysfunction and eventual tooth loss. Although dentures can be fabricated to replace lost permanent teeth, no denture can approach the efficiency and comfort of healthy and properly aligned natural teeth.

Speech can be adversely affected by tooth loss or deviations of the oral structure from normal configuration. Disfigurement and pain caused by oral pathology or abnormalities can lead to social maladjustment. Pain and concern about disfigurement and malfunction are the most common consequences of inattention to dental disease and often cause people to seek professional attention.

For most people around the world, oral diseases or their sequelae are a continuum from early childhood to death. In industrialized countries, virtually everyone has personal experience of tooth decay (dental caries) and periodontal disease, the two most common oral health afflictions, at some time during their life. Other significant though less common maladies affecting oral health include malocclusion, craniofacial malformations, and malignancies.

A discussion of each of these diseases and conditions and their epidemiology follows.

Dental caries

Progressive decalcification of dental enamel by organic acids produced by certain bacteria located in dental plaque produces lesions known as tooth decay, or dental caries. For a dental carious lesion to be formed, at least three factors must be present: a susceptible tooth, acid-producing bacteria, and a suitable substrate that is fermentable by the bacteria. The carious lesion cannot form in the absence of any of these three factors.

Most oral bacteria are not cariogenic. *Streptococcus mutans* is particularly adept at colonizing tooth surfaces and is highly virulent. This non-motile, Gram-positive organism is now considered the chief causative agent of caries on the crowns of teeth. Other cariogenic bacteria implicated in various types of dental caries are members of the *Actinomyces* and *Lactobacillus* genera.

Susceptibility of the teeth to dental caries is affected by the incorporation of various trace elements in enamel. For example, the incorporation of fluoride in enamel to form fluorapatite crystals renders the enamel less vulnerable to decalcification by organic acids.

The key to the microorganism's success in causing tooth decay is the availability of fermentable carbohydrates. Cariogenic organisms generate lactic acid as an end product of carbohydrate metabolism. The more frequently suitable carbohydrates are ingested, the more rapidly the caries process advances, as a result of repeated exposure of teeth to an acidic environment.

Relatively rare in ancient times, the prevalence of dental caries has increased with the passage of time until it has become almost ubiquitous in modern man. Its occurrence world-wide is uneven and changing, being still relatively rare in a few parts of the world and rampant in others. For example, an international collaborative study of oral health in five countries yielded a wide divergence in decayed, missing, and filled permanent teeth (DMFT) values for youths 13–14 years of age. Youths examined in Sydney, Australia showed an average DMFT score of 6.7 as compared with 12.6 for youths in Trondelag, Norway. Values in other countries for similarly aged youths included 7.5 in Japan, 8.8 in West Germany, and 10.7 in New Zealand. Major variations in disease attack rates also occur within single countries and populations.

World-wide the prevailing pattern of dental caries has been high prevalence in economically and industrially developed countries and low prevalence in less well developed countries with a lower standard of living. Recent data indicate, however, that the industrialized countries have been experiencing rather striking decreases in caries prevalence. The reductions reported during the last decade range between 10 and 70 per cent, with the greatest reductions in populations exposed to fluoridated drinking water supplies. Recent evidence from the World Health Organization (WHO) suggests that the opposite trend is occurring in developing nations. That is, people in some developing countries are experiencing rapid increases in tooth decay. It is speculated that these sharp increases are the result of growing consumption of refined sugars and other easily fermentable foods characteristic of diets found in industrialized countries.

The onset of coronal caries in susceptible populations is early, usually soon after the eruption of the first deciduous or permanent teeth. Pits and fissures are the most susceptible areas of the tooth, and the first lesions seen in permanent teeth are most often located in the occlusal surface of the lower first molars. The incidence of new lesions remains high through puberty and tapers off rather rapidly afterwards. While the incidence of new carious lesions is highest during early childhood and adolescence, the consequences remain for life. Root caries, on the other hand, typically appears in adults, usually as a result of periodontal disease, when loss of tooth-supporting bone and recession of the gingivae have exposed the cemento-enamel junction to the oral environment.

Females appear to be more susceptible to caries, but this may be explained in large measure by their earlier tooth eruption patterns. Racial differences in caries experience, once thought to be due to intrinsic differences in susceptibility, now appear to be due to environmental and social variables. Thus, certain racial groups in India and Africa, which at one time appeared to be more resistant to dental caries, actually develop a greater propensity for the disease when they move to economically more advanced environments where caries is more prevalent, or when they adopt more 'western' dietary patterns.

A strong association between a high intake of refined sugar and high caries prevalence has been shown in many studies. Variation in the amount of sugar ingested is a major explanation for the diversity of caries experience among different populations. Another explanation is the presence or absence of certain trace elements in water and food. Some researchers have suggested that water with a high mineral content may be associated with reduced tooth decay. It is well known that the ingestion of fluoride in trace amounts during the period of development and maturation of tooth enamel renders the tooth much more resistant to caries. Other trace elements such as lithium, strontium, and boron have also been associated with a lower prevalence of caries, and barium, molybdenum, vanadium, and phosphorus have also been mentioned as possibly beneficial. On the other hand, elements such as selenium and lead have been associated with a higher prevalence.

In summary, the principal epidemiological characteristics of dental caries are: (i) it is common world-wide but variable in intensity; (ii) it tends to be more prevalent in highly industrialized countries and less so in developing countries; (iii) its prevalence rates are falling in highly developed countries and rising in developing countries; (iv) there is a positive relationship between attack rate and the frequency of refined sugar ingestion; (v) carious lesions begin soon after teeth erupt; (vi) the attack rate is highest during childhood and adolescence; and (vii) the caries process is sharply inhibited by the use of fluoride.

Periodontal diseases

For convenience, the periodontal diseases are referred to as a single disease, but there are many. They fall under the general category of periodontal disease primarily because they affect the same tissues. Periodontal disease(s) refers to diseases affecting the hard and soft tissues surrounding and supporting the teeth. The disease usually starts as a mild inflammation of the soft tissue (gingiva) and, if left undisturbed, slowly progresses to involve the deeper structures. As the disease progresses, the bone and the ligaments connecting the teeth to the bony socket become involved and compromised. The attachment apparatus is affected and bone support is lost. If left untreated, the disease usually progresses until the teeth are lost, owing to lack of sufficient support to permit proper function.

While dental caries appears to be a relatively recent significant health problem and was not prevalent in highly developed ancient populations, periodontal disease apparently was common in ancient times and has always been more prevalent and severe in less highly developed populations.

But even in such countries as the US, destructive periodontal disease is the major cause of tooth loss in middle-age and beyond. Whether there is or will be improved periodontal health concomitant with further advancement of developing countries is not known. It can be expected, however, that as highly developed nations extend life expectancy and succeed in reducing tooth loss from caries, periodontal problems will increase because more teeth will be exposed for longer periods of time.

Though the age at onset and the rapidity of progression of the disease vary greatly among population groups, the course of events is essentially the same world-wide. In most cases, the advanced destructive phase of periodontal disease is preceded by inflammatory changes in the gingiva. Gingivitis is common among children, but it is uncommon to find overt evidence of destructive disease in children or teenagers in most population groups.

The prevalence and severity of bone loss increase with each succeeding age group. The rate of increase varies greatly among countries and among people within any given country. In most populations, virtually everyone shows some evidence of loss of supporting bone by middle-age. Unfortunately, because the disease progresses slowly and painlessly, destructive periodontal disease often goes unnoticed by patients until it reaches an advanced stage that imperils the entire dentition.

Descriptive epidemiological studies have shown periodontal disease to be more common in rural areas and to be more prevalent and severe among blacks than whites, among men than women, and among the poor and uneducated, especially those with poor oral hygiene. When persons of equivalent age and oral hygiene status are compared, however, the differences in disease prevalence and severity associated with the other characteristics tend to disappear. No epidemiological factors have been found to be as consistently or closely associated with variations in periodontal health as age and oral cleanliness. The absence of good oral hygiene permits the formation of bacterial plaque. The association with age may not be a reflection of the ageing process *per se*, but more likely reflects the length of time periodontal structures have been exposed to bacterial plaque. The disease is rarely seen in the absence of dental plaque. It has been called a disease of neglect—'neglect of the healthy mouth permits the disease to occur, and neglect of early disease permits it to advance and destroy tooth-supporting bones'.

Clinical studies have demonstrated that, despite large accumulations of plaque, the destructiveness of the disease may vary greatly between individuals and between sites in the same individual. More detailed laboratory studies have found that the bacterial composition of plaque varies greatly, even within the same plaque over time. Microbiologists are currently identifying plaque microflora and further identifying those particular flora associated with the disease processes. The picture is turning out to be very complex.

In short, periodontal disease is more common and severe in males, some racial groups, people of low economic and educational levels, inhabitants of rural areas, older individuals, and persons with inadequate oral hygiene practices. The differences in disease status between various groups tend to disappear when persons of similar age and oral hygiene status are compared. Thus, the single most important factor in the epidemiology of periodontal disease is oral cleanliness. In the absence of good hygiene bacterial plaque forms and the disease process begins, and if left undisturbed it continues to progress.

Craniofacial malformations

Disfiguring and sometimes disabling craniofacial malformations occur all too frequently, but solid information as to just how frequently in the various populations around the world is not available. This is due in large part to the fact that diagnoses, processes for detection, and mechanisms for reporting differ so greatly from one country to another and within countries.

In the US it is estimated that 7 per cent of all infants born alive have mental or physical defects that are evident at birth or later on. Common among the physical defects are cranio-facial malformations, defined as any structural, functional, or biochemical abnormality of the head or face. Topping the list of craniofacial malformations are cleft lip and cleft palate, affecting about one out of every 600 white infants born alive. The incidence is higher among Orientals, native Americans, and Eskimos, and lower among blacks. Other severe craniofacial malformations include deformities of the jaw, dental anomalies, defects in the ossification of facial or cranial bones, too wide or too narrow spacing between the eyes, facial asymmetries such as a disproportionately small half-side of the face, and certain syndromes such as the recently identified fetal alcohol syndrome.

Some craniofacial malformations can be traced to specific genetic or chromosomal disorders. Others may result from potent prenatal environmental factors, such as malnutrition, maternal disease, exposure to radiation, alcohol, or other drugs, and problems in pregnancy and delivery. For the most part, these malformations are viewed as having multifactorial bases. There is fairly firm evidence that both the environment and genetics play a role in cleft lip and cleft palate formation.

Genetic factors obviously contribute to the shaping of the face and oral structures. Environmental factors are known to be significant, too, and operate *in utero* and after birth. Positioning of the embryo can distort facial development. Facial trauma, abnormal breathing patterns, and oral habits such as thumb-sucking can all cause facial deformities and jaw malrelations calling for correction by professional intervention.

Numerous attempts have been made to quantify the prevalence of jaw and teeth malrelations that are severe enough to warrant orthodontic or other professional treatment. The estimates of teenagers needing professional intervention in most populations range between 20 and 30 per cent. When only seriously handicapping conditions are considered, the number drops to 5–10 per cent.

Very little information exists about regional variations in prevalence of jaw and teeth malrelations or about variations in distribution by socio-economic status, sex or race.

Oral malignancies

Oral cancer is more common and more deadly than most people realize. While in most western countries oral malignancies constitute some 5 per cent of all cancers diagnosed, in India the relative frequency of oral cancer is closer to 40 per cent. Even in India the variation in frequency is great in different parts of the country and in different population groups.

Use of tobacco and alcohol are closely associated with the occurrence of oral cancer. The various ways in which tobacco is used – smoked, held in the mouth, chewed – are in turn associated with the location and type of malignancy. Oral cancers develop more frequently in older men, with 70–80 per cent of cases occurring in males and 80 per cent in patients over 50 years of age.

Summary

The public health problems described above have been studied by concerned dental personnel for many years. Although a complete understanding of the causes of malocclusion, craniofacial malformations, and oral cancer has yet to be realized and treatment modalities and epidemiological data still are limited, considerable progress has been made in developing an understanding of the aetiology, pathology, and epidemiology of caries and periodontal disease. It is now clear that the most effective means of controlling these two diseases will be through prevention. Although the need for fundamental research in caries and periodontal disease continues, we already possess the technology to virtually eliminate these two major dental diseases through the use of known preventive methods.

CARIES PREVENTION

Coronal caries can now be prevented. Existing preventive measures using fluoride and adhesive sealants combined with good oral hygiene and wise eating habits can prevent the disease from developing in healthy individuals. Root caries, on the other hand, represents a new and growing challenge to public health. Studies are underway to determine if measures that have proven effective against coronal caries will be effective in the prevention of carious lesions occurring on root surfaces.

The ideal preventive measure for dental caries must not only be effective, it must not be hazardous to life or function. It should take effect immediately upon application, and its potency should be maintained for a substantial time, preferably for the lifetime of the individual. It should be practical, economical in terms of time and cost, easily available to all people in the community, and not dependent on individual action. Some of these requirements are met by timely and competent restorative dental care, but this is treating the consequences of the disease and its cost puts it beyond the reach of many who are in need. Individual efforts by the dental professional or the patient are not sufficient in themselves to attain and maintain optimum oral health because the causes of the disease are so complex. A system which provides for a wide and inexpensive distribution of a preventive agent to the whole community, combined with the individual efforts of dental practitioners and patients, is preferable to any one of these approaches alone.

Fluoride administration

There are two principal methods for administering fluoride: *systemic*, including water fluoridation at school and community levels, fluoride ingestion with salt or milk, prenatal fluoride, and fluoride supplements; and *topical*, which includes the professional or self-application of fluoride rinses, gels, and toothpastes.

Systemic measures

Community water fluoridation

Water fluoridation is the method of choice for administering systemic fluorides on a community level. Once the fluoride content of water is adjusted to an optimal level (about 1 p.p.m.), the consumer need exert almost no effort to receive the anticariogenic benefit of this procedure. As early as the nineteenth century it was known that calcified tissues contain fluoride. Magitot in France and Crichton-Browne in England speculated that fluoride might protect tooth structure. However, the earliest epidemiological studies were concerned with the disfiguring effects on enamel observed in various locations in Italy, Iceland, Argentina, North Africa, and the south-western parts of the US. Later observations indicated a direct relationship between dental fluorosis and reduced dental caries prevalence. Subsequently, the fluoride studies initiated in the early 1930s by Dean and his co-workers (Dean 1938; Dean *et al.* 1942, 1950) confirmed the relationship between naturally occurring fluoride in the water and decreased tooth decay.

Once this relationship was established, four controlled studies were initiated in the US and Canada to test the hypothesis that adding an optimal amount of fluoride to the drinking water would provide beneficial anticaries results equal to those observed in areas where fluoride occurred in the water naturally and without the side-effect of undesirable fluorosis. These studies, initiated between 1944 and 1946, showed clearly that there is an inverse relationship between caries prevalence and fluoride concentration in the drinking water.

There is a considerable body of literature on the anticariogenic benefits of water fluoridation in the UK, USSR, New Zealand, and Australia. These benefits, expressed as reductions in decayed, missing, and filled teeth and surfaces (DMFT–DMFS) and in extraction of first permanent molars, as well as changes in malocclusion status, are positively correlated with community water fluoridation.

Concentrations of 1.0–1.2 p.p.m. of fluoride in drinking water in temperate climates offer significant protection against caries, as compared with communities with less than 0.5 p.p.m. of fluoride in the water. The caries protective effects of fluoride are not limited to young children. Adults who have continually consumed fluoridated water have less tooth loss and fewer decayed, missing, and filled teeth (DMFT) than the corresponding age group living in a low fluoride area. At each age level the DMFT score is approximately 60 per cent lower in communities drinking fluoride-containing water.

Although the overall caries reduction due to fluoridation is between 50 and 60 per cent, a careful examination of the data indicates a selective protection of the proximal and buccolingual surfaces in comparison to the occlusal surfaces. For example, the caries inhibitory effect on gingival carious lesions was 86 per cent, on proximal lesions about 73 per cent, but only about 37 per cent for pit and fissure lesions.

Despite the proven caries-inhibiting benefit and safety of community water fluoridation, it is not practical to institute such a measure in communities without central water systems. Schools in such areas often obtain water from wells, which can be fluoridated readily. Studies have used 2.5–5 p.p.m. fluoride in the water supplies of elementary schools in an attempt to approximate the total fluoride intake of children who drink optimally fluoridated water on a full-time basis. No objectionable dental fluorosis was reported from these studies and the children had 30–40 per cent reductions in dental caries and a 65 per cent reduction in the rate of extraction.

Fluoride ingestion in salt, milk, or tablets

If neither a central nor a school water supply can be fluoridated, fluoride may be administered systematically through regular dietary intake or as a pharmaceutical preparation. The vehicles tested for this purpose include salt, milk, and tablets. Based on the evidence currently available, the addition of fluoride to salt produces some reduction in dental caries, but does not produce optimal effects and has other inherent disadvantages. First, supplementing salt with fluoride makes it difficult to accommodate varying levels of natural fluoride occurring in water over a wide geographic area. Secondly, the inconsistency of advising reduced salt consumption for preventing hypertension while implicitly encouraging its ingestion for prevention of dental caries is bothersome.

Beneficial caries preventive effects of fluoride-supplemented milk have been reported in limited studies. But here too, there are problems with depending on this vehicle as the primary source of fluoride. The amount of milk consumed usually decreases after age two or three, yet fluoride is needed through ages twelve to fourteen in order to produce maximum caries protection. In addition, milk is quite expensive in many countries, and many people avoid it because they are unable to digest it. In spite of these drawbacks, there is continuing interest in some countries in the addition of fluoride to salt and milk.

Although fluoride in the form of tablets is reasonably effective against caries – ranging from 20 to 40 per cent in caries reduction – the problem of patient compliance over the extended period during which fluoride is needed and the necessity of careful supervision are challenging considerations in a public health programme. If community water fluoridation is not feasible, fluoride tablets may be prescribed for home use. The use of fluoride tablets in supervised school programmes has met with considerable success where school authorities and teachers are willing to give such a programme the attention it requires.

Prenatal fluoride and fluoride supplements

For maximum beneficial effect, fluoride should be ingested regularly during the time the crowns of the teeth are calcifying. When this is done, fluoride is incorporated into the enamel, making it more resistant to decalcification. Additional benefits are obtained from topical application of fluoride. Prenatal exposure to fluorides has generally been found to have little, if any, influence on the caries resistance of primary teeth.

In areas of suboptimal water fluoridation, systemic supplements are usually recommended from birth to age 15 years, when enamel formation and eruption of all teeth (except third molars) are essentially complete. Daily systemic doses currently recommended by the American Dental Association are: under two years, 0.25–0.3 mg; two to three years, 0.5 mg; and three years and over, 1.0 mg. These doses are closely approximated by daily water ingestion in communities with public water supplies adjusted to optimum levels as determined by mean annual ambient air temperature. In the temperate zone of the US, this is roughly 1 p.p.m. Systemic fluoride supplements in communities with ample fluoride in the drinking water are not warranted and produce risk of dental fluorosis in children under eight years old.

Topical measures

Topical fluoride treatments are most effective soon after the tooth has erupted. There is evidence, however, that fluoride is continually lost from the outermost enamel layer, where it is most effective in preventing carious lesions. Therefore, in non-fluoridated areas topical applications are indicated in all age groups. Even for persons born and raised in areas with optimum amounts of fluoride in the drinking water, topical applications provide additional benefits and therefore are generally recommended. Children who are caries-prone definitely should be given regular topical applications. If the problem is severe, mouth rinses or gels can be used at home on a daily or weekly basis. Adults with severe xerostomia (dryness of the mouth) or susceptibility to root caries should also receive frequent topical fluoride treatments.

While professional prophylaxis prior to the topical application of fluoride is generally assumed to increase the uptake of fluoride, some studies indicate that such procedures may be unnecessary. Horowitz et al. (1967, 1972, 1974) have shown that a self-applied tooth-brushing was critical to the effectiveness of a self-applied acidulated phosphate fluoride (APF) gel, but made no difference when a less viscous APF solution was used. Self-application of fluoride rinses, gels, toothpastes, and chewable tablets may provide the answer to problems of insufficient professional dental personnel and excessive costs that currently hinder traditional topical fluoride programmes at the public health or school-system level.

Mechanical prophylaxis

Because the bacterial agents causing dental caries thrive in dental plaque, caries is theoretically preventable by regular and careful oral hygiene procedures to remove plaque before decalcification occurs. Caries control by oral hygiene is based on the 'non-specific plaque hypothesis', which implies that all bacteria in plaque are of equal cariogenicity and should therefore be removed. Efforts to relate community-based deplaquing programmes to a lower incidence of caries have been disappointing, but such results are hardly surprising in view of the multifactorial causes of caries and the great difficulty in achieving complete removal of plaque.

A conscientious regimen of proper brushing of the teeth and gums, flossing, and professional removal (scaling) of calculus (one or more times per year, depending on individual need) is helpful in the prevention of both caries and periodontal disease. To be effective, personal measures for primary prevention of caries and periodontal disease, brushing, and flossing should be developed as lifelong daily habits beginning in early childhood. The threat of caries exists from the time the first tooth erupts (at about age six months). Therefore, instruction and help in brushing should begin in infancy.

Dietary modification

The complexities of the human diet and eating habits are such that epidemiological studies are difficult to conduct with the necessary degree of control over extraneous factors, such as can be attained in the laboratory. Even so, the relationship between dental caries and the ingestion of fermentable carbohydrates was well demonstrated before the Second World War by Bunting (1935) and others. Further evidence of the major aetiological role sugar plays in causing caries came from countries that suffered major social disruption during the Second World War. In countries where carbohydrates were greatly reduced, general mortality increased, but caries in the permanent dentition was drastically reduced. By 1949, after food rationing had ended, caries prevalence returned to 1941 levels.

Dietary counselling, then, is a key element in any preventive dentistry programme. Modification of the diet has especially important implications for the control of dental caries.

Numerous researchers have proven that the ingestion of sucrose accelerates plaque accumulation and the production of acid by cariogenic microorganisms. Greater caries activity correlates not so much with absolute sugar intake, but with the length of time sugar and fermentable carbohydrates remain in the oral cavity. Thus, timing of meals, frequency of between-meal snacks, food consistency, and food processing are all important factors in caries development. Beverages with sugar, particularly carbonated beverages, are less cariogenic than solid sugar-starch products. Frequent snacking, especially of fermentable carbohydrates, increases the risk of caries. In contrast, prolonged mastication of fibrous foods stimulates the flow of important buffering salivary fluids (and tends to abrade food debris from tooth surfaces), thus reducing caries activity.

The most significant systemic effects of diet on teeth occur during the developmental stages, not after eruption. Stuart reported that a maternal diet poor in protein or calcium during pregnancy resulted in retarded osseous and dental development in the newborn infant. Because major calcification of bones and primary teeth occurs during the last two months of gestation, the demands of the fetus for calcium and phosphorus necessitate dietary increases of these minerals during the second and third trimesters. Adequate levels of calcium, phosphorus, fluoride, vitamin D, and protein continue to be important throughout childhood and early adolescence to promote the development of caries-resistant teeth.

Pit and fissure sealants

The occlusal surfaces of posterior teeth (first and second molars and bicuspids) have repeatedly been noted to be the most vulnerable locations for dental caries. Fluoride protection is much less effective for surfaces with pits and fissures than for smooth tooth surfaces or interproximal areas. Also, the enamel under deep fissures is thinner—0.2 mm or less, as compared with 1.5–2.0 mm on other tooth surfaces. Fissures generally are tortuous and narrow (0.2 mm), with invaginations and irregularities where bacteria and food are retained. Occlusal sealants, which are plastic-like bonding materials, present a mechanical barrier between these susceptible areas and the cariogenic oral environment. Although some cariogenic bacteria may be sealed within fissures, these bacteria do not produce sufficient acid to initiate carious lesions because they are deprived of an external source of fermentable carbohydrates. There is also evidence that incipient lesions inadvertantly sealed will not progress.

Sealants are indicated for newly erupted teeth with pronounced pits and fissures and for patients with considerable previous occlusal caries experience. They should be applied in suitable cases approximately every 2–3 years until the age of peak caries activity (15–20 years) is past. There is some speculation that caries activity drops off at age 20–25 because there are no remaining caries-susceptible surfaces; normally all have decayed and have been filled. Thus, surfaces protected to the age of 20 years might decay shortly after sealants are discontinued. Sealants have not been in use long enough to confirm or deny such speculations. Nevertheless, even a gain of perhaps 20 caries-free years is of tremendous value when we consider that problems of secondary decay and restoration failure have been avoided for that long.

Use of sealants on a wide-scale public health basis is currently limited by the constraints of professional time and cost. Sufficient clinical data are not available to determine the long-term cost-benefit of sealants. Should sealants be used on all children? Or only on those at high risk of caries? How often must resealing be done? It is to be hoped that clinical trials now in progress will supply answers to these questions.

PERIODONTAL DISEASE PREVENTION

As mentioned previously, both caries and periodontal disease are initiated primarily by microbial colonies in the dental plaque. Thus, current preventive strategies for caries also to some degree prevent periodontal disease, even though the specific causative organisms differ for these diseases. Preventive periodontics encompasses those aspects of dentistry that deal with the establishment of an oral environment conducive to the preservation of sound, healthy supporting structures of the teeth. Its objectives are to promote optimum health of the periodontum so as to maintain a healthy state, to prevent inflammatory changes in the gingivae, and to intercept soft- and hard-tissue lesions already in progress, in order to restore a state of health, and prevent further damage.

Recent advances in the study of periodontal disease have clearly documented that there are many diseases of the periodontium grouped under this title, and that different organisms are associated with different diseases. As the organisms associated with each disease are becoming more specifically identified, antimicrobial therapy is also becoming more specific. Even so, because the pathogens reside in bacterial plaque, proper daily oral hygiene practices are essential both to prevention and treatment.

As mentioned, the association between oral hygiene and periodontal disease is so strong and so consistent in all populations studied world-wide that it overwhelms association with other variables. Numerous investigations have demonstrated that it is possible to prevent and to arrest the progress of most periodontal disease by scrupulous oral hygiene. It is interesting to note that the Swedish study by Bjorn (1974) found little difference in the rate of progress of periodontal disease either by age (25–65 years) or by frequency of visits to the dentist. His conclusion was that simply visiting the dentist regularly without changing oral hygiene habits has little effect on the progression of the disease. Such data emphasize the importance of self-care and home oral hygiene habits as the primary and most effective preventive measures. Studies such as these also emphasize the need for combined home and professional care to make prevention and control a reality. It is evident that neglect is the chief cause of periodontal disease—neglect on the part of the individual patient, the dentist, or both.

Local preventive measures

Plaque removal by the individual patient

Individual self-care and good oral hygiene are the key to prevention of periodontal disease. Individual effort means mechanical plaque removal with the toothbrush and aids such as dental floss, the interproximal brush, and wooden points. Water-pressure devices, while they are no substitute for flossing or brushing, are valuable tools in conjunction with flossing and brushing for retarding the accumulation of plaque and calculus. These devices are especially useful for cleaning around orthodontic appliances and fixed prostheses.

Disclosing tablets, which stain dental plaque, are a valuable aid in helping patients to establish efficient brushing and flossing techniques. Brushing and flossing just to remove obvious food particles do not necessarily remove plaque, the true cause of periodontal disease. A translucent accumulation, plaque must be stained to be seen. Disclosing tablets should be used at least once a week, after brushing and flossing, to reveal areas in which the procedures were ineffectively performed. The elderly, especially those with disabilities affecting joint mobility and co-ordination, may need assistance in brushing and flossing. The latest research indicates that a thorough oral cleansing and plaque removal should be carried out daily as part of a routine that best fits in with a person's daily schedule.

The toothbrush with soft, multitufted bristles is most commonly recommended by dentists. Manual and power driven brushes can be of equal effectiveness, depending on the user. The power driven brush is, of course, more expensive, but is more easily used by older persons who have some manual impairments. A variety of toothbrushing methods are described in the dental literature. Research, however, indicates little real difference among methods in the removal of plaque. The scrub method seems best for most persons, as it is simple and easily learned. There is little research on the difference in effectiveness between types of dental floss. The choice of waxed or unwaxed floss depends on the ease with which a patient can learn to use it.

The faithful practice of regular, thorough plaque removal and oral hygiene depends largely on the interest and motivation of the individual person. Supervised daily tooth-brushing of groups of schoolchildren in Sweden and the US did produce a reduction in gingivitis for the duration of the programme, but the improvement disappeared when the supervision was interrupted by vacation or was ended. The effects of individual instruction by dental health professionals, according to many investigations, have been minor. These examples of the difficulty in motivating people point out that a great deal is yet to be learned about methods of altering individual behaviour. Patients need to be given the facts about periodontal disease and given a clear rationale for the regimens taught. Each patient must be counselled individually, since public health programmes to produce mass improvement in oral hygiene have had limited success. Public health workers should develop better educational methods for improving oral hygiene habits than are available today.

Plaque removal by dental professionals

Most periodontal disease can be successfully prevented and controlled when there is adequate daily attention to oral cleanliness and regular, periodic visits to the dental practitioner for thorough removal of calcified deposits and plaque, and for instruction on necessary improvements in home care. The benefits of professional plaque and calculus removal have been shown in studies of children and adults who were in a state of reasonable periodontal health, as well as in adults who had advanced periodontal disease. In the US, studies of office workers in California by Suomi et al. (1971) showed that professional prophylaxis plus intensive oral hygiene and plaque removal instruction every 2–4 months significantly reduced levels of plaque and gingivitis below those of a control group. These studies also showed that periodontal bone loss was retarded in the experimental group. Axelsson and Lindhe (1974) in Sweden had great success in preventing gingivitis in children by intensive and frequent oral prophylaxis.

Systemic preventive measures

The evidence available today indicates that bacteria in plaque are the major causes of the onset of periodontal disease. However, there is no doubt that systemic factors such as metabolism, nutrition, and hormone balance have an effect on the physiological reactions to the initiating agents. The blood vessel changes in diabetes are an example of these altered reactions. The effects of local agents certainly become exaggerated under the influences of underlying systemic conditions such as diabetes or leukaemia, or of medications such as phenytoin sodium.

A chemical method of plaque prevention or removal or a chemotherapeutic agent that can be used systemically are highly sought-after as panaceas for the prevention of periodontal disease. Antibiotics have been used with some success, but their use on a long-term basis is not practical because of the potential for development of resistant organisms. Metronidazole currently shows some promise. Various enzymes have shown little promise in preventing periodontal disease in humans. Two antiseptic agents, chlorhexidine and alexidine, have received considerable attention during the last decade as potential plaque inhibitors. The early studies conducted by Löe (1973a, b) and others indicated that chlorhexidine rinses inhibited the formation of plaque almost completely. These findings generated great enthusiasm in other researchers about the potential of this agent. However, because the studies were done with periodontally healthy dental students, the applicability of these results to the general public raises some questions. Results of subsequent studies by other researchers using chlorhexidine were less definitive and revealed more side-effects. Staining of teeth and restorations was a persistent problem. Short-term studies with alexidine provided results similar to those found with chlorhexidine. Reductions in plaque and gingivitis were reported, but some were of little significance and staining was also a problem. Results of long-term studies have confirmed reservations about the routine use of these two antiseptics.

The effects of various fluorides on plaque composition and their possible use in the prevention of periodontal disease warrant further investigation. Additional research is needed to identify chemotherapeutic agents that can be effective and safe for use in preventing and controlling periodontal disease.

OROFACIAL MALFORMATIONS AND MALOCCLUSIONS

Orofacial malformations

Orofacial anomalies, especially cleft lip and cleft palate, account for about 13 per cent of all birth defects. Clefts of the lip and palate are two of the most common and dramatic defects noted at birth. These anomalies are caused by genetic factors, by exposure to teratogenic substances, or both. The discussion of this subject in detail is beyond the scope of this chapter. Early diagnosis by an obstetrician or paediatrician soon after birth, with referral and treatment, is the principal measure for preventing and controlling the sequelae of birth defects. The principal measures for prevention are genetic counselling and avoidance of chemical agents and alcohol during the first two trimesters of pregnancy.

Malocclusion

Normal occlusion is the outcome of a smooth, even unfolding of genetic patterns. The orderly unfolding of these patterns can be disturbed by such factors as premature loss of primary teeth, loss of permanent teeth, prolonged retention of primary teeth, abnormal muscular pressures, and destruction of bony growth centres. Early in the development of occlusion, genetic factors seem to dominate. As permanent teeth replace primary teeth, forces generated by chewing and swallowing become the chief factors in the production of malocclusion.

The need for orthodontic treatment in the US can be summarized as follows: among children 6–11 years old, 22 per cent have definite malocclusions for which orthodontic treatment is advised, but elective; nearly 9 per cent have malocclusions for which treatment is highly desirable; and 5.5 per cent have such severe defects that treatment is deemed mandatory. Corresponding figures for youths 12–17 years of age are 25.2 per cent elective, 13 per cent highly desirable, and 16 per cent mandatory. The large jump in the mandatory category is believed to be caused by teeth erupting at or near age 12 years. In Sweden, where orthodontic treatment is routinely provided and is widely available, roughly 45 per cent of all schoolchildren actually undergo orthodontic adjustment.

Water fluoridation, and the resulting reduction in missing teeth, affect the need for orthodontic services in a given population. This is true particularly in the 6–11-year age group. Burt has estimated that 2.5 per cent of all children in non-fluoridated areas would need space maintainers by age 7 years, in comparison to 1 per cent of those in fluoridated areas.

Tooth loss and damage due to trauma is another orthodontic problem prevalent in childhood and adolescence. Burt estimates that of all 12–13-year-olds, 5 per cent will require a one-canal anterior root filling as a result of trauma. The Copenhagen Municipal School Dental Service found that 25–30 per cent of all children and teenagers sustain trauma to anterior teeth before completing school at age 16 years. Their male/female injury ratio was 1.61, with the highest injury rate for both sexes found in the 8–9-year age group.

GERIATRIC DENTISTRY

An area of public health dentistry that is of particular importance and yet suffers from neglect is geriatric dentistry. Chronic dental disease is undeniably more prevalent in older people. In spite of this, the elderly are dentally underserved. As we have seen, the incidence of caries among children has decreased, due in large part to the introduction of fluorides. However, there are no definitive data on the effects of fluoride on the incidence of caries in the elderly, though there is some clinical evidence that they benefit from topical applications of fluoride. As in the general population, periodontal disease continues to be a major problem among the elderly, and oral cancer is more common in this age group.

Current statistics show that by almost every measure, older persons are in greater need of dental services than their younger counterparts in the general population (Wycoff and Epstein 1984). In one 1978 study, almost two-thirds of the subjects between the ages of 65 and 74 years had advanced or destructive periodontal disease, while the prevalence rate in the general population was only 41 per cent. Older persons have an average of 22.5 decayed, missing, or filled teeth—nine more than the average for younger persons. Approximately 50 per cent of Americans have lost some of their teeth by 65 years of age, and over two-thirds are edentulous by age 75 years. Persons 60 years of age and older are more than four times as likely as younger persons to have lost their natural teeth. Epidemiological and clinical evidence demonstrates conclusively that dental disease varies in type, onset, and severity with patient age.

Prevention of dental disease and maintenance of existing

natural dentition must be the primary focus of dental public health for all groups, including the elderly. That tooth loss is a necessary consequence of ageing is an unfortunate myth that remains to be overcome. In point of fact, edentulousness is not inevitable nor should it be accepted as part of the emotional and physical deterioration of the individual.

The field of preventive dentistry is reflecting the youth orientation of our society when its prevention efforts are concentrated chiefly on children and young adults. Although children and adolescents probably benefit most from primary prevention and early detection measures, middle-aged and elderly people also stand to benefit greatly from these measures. If, in a broad sense, preventive dentistry includes any measure to save all or part of a patient's natural dentition, dentists must recognize such needs in people of all ages.

Caries is often characterized as a disease of young people which stabilizes during the mid-twenties and remains dormant until gingival recession or periodontal surgery exposes the cemental surfaces; then, predictably, root caries appears. Although there is a paucity of current data on the attack rate of caries in the older population, some recent information suggests that the prevalence of caries *changes* with age; the problem does not disappear. In a review of the literature on root caries, Banting and Ellen (1976) described three separate studies in which about 60 per cent of the subjects between 50 and 59 years of age exhibited root surface caries. In the group over the age of 60 years, the prevalence rose to 70 per cent. Baum (1979) reported a similar pattern for subjects in the Baltimore longitudinal ageing study. Most root caries lesions are found in molars. About 70 per cent of the cavities are proximal, 20 per cent are facial, and 10 per cent are lingual. Restoration is often extremely difficult, and prevention of both root caries and recurrent proximal caries is an important consideration in caring for older persons.

Presently, no definitive clinical data document the effects of routinely applied fluorides on caries prevention in the elderly. However, it is likely that older persons benefit from using fluoride dentifrices, mouth rinses, and gels. Appropriate fluoride forms should be prescribed according to an individual's anticipated susceptibility to decay and ability to manage the regimen; for example, in cases involving disabled patients, a controlled-release device might be considered. Patients with xerostomia due to irradiation or salivary gland disease, as well as those who use medications that cause reduced salivary flow, run a high risk of caries. Both groups of individuals would benefit from artificial saliva preparations containing fluoride or fluoride gels.

Stamm and Banting (1980) reported that in Canada, the occurrence of root caries in adults who have lived all their lives in areas with fluoridated water was 50 per cent less than in non-fluoridated areas. This is not surprising in view of the high concentrations of fluoride found in gingival crevice fluid and the high uptake of fluoride by cementum and dentin. Experiments *in vitro* show an 80 per cent reduction in acid solubility when acidulated fluorophosphate or stannous fluoride gels are applied to the teeth. Therefore, the daily use of fluorides can prevent caries even in severely compromised adults who have minimal salivary flow owing

to various problems such as irradiation for head and neck cancer.

As for periodontal disease, a number of studies have shown that it progresses at an accelerated rate in elders. For instance, one study showed that gingivitis developed more rapidly in old than in young individuals during an experimental period of abstinence from oral hygiene. Plaque accumulation also was greater for the older subjects than for the younger controls during this period. A second study supported the observation of greater plaque accumulation and also suggested that the microbial composition of plaque is qualitatively different in older persons. In addition, a six-year study by Axelssen and Lindhe (1974) in Malmo, Sweden, showed that the rate of bone loss for subjects over the age of 60 years was much greater than for younger age groups, and that the control subjects aged over 50 years exhibited a greater rate of attachment loss than the younger subjects. These data indicate that plaque control and periodontal health maintenance programmes for elders should be even more vigorous than comparable programmes targeted toward younger patient populations.

Impressive clinical data exist about the efficacy of preventive care for older persons. In dental clinics with limited resources, high-risk patients could be screened and targeted for intensive preventive care. A number of indicators of 'high risk' are currently being examined in various laboratories and clinical centres; however, there is as yet no agreement about reliable determinants.

The increased incidence of oral cancer with age and the tendency for many of the elderly, especially the edentulous, to visit the dentist at infrequent intervals places an extra responsibility, beyond routine examination, on the preventively-oriented public health dentist. Since early detection results in a five-year survival rate well above 50 per cent, a thorough oral examination is a must for all older patients. A preventive programme for oral cancer should include patient education and definitive management of suspicious areas.

The tongue is the most frequent site of oral cancers, of which over 90 per cent are squamous cell carcinomas. Although oral cancer may appear as an ulcer, white patch, red patch, or exophytic growth, the erythroplastic type is the most invasive. Red or white lesions which change size, bleed, ulcerate, or demonstrate induration or fixation should be biopsied for examination. Most oral cancers are painless until they become large, at which time regional metastases are likely to appear.

Patient education programmes should emphasize the following points:

1. The relationship between cancer, cigarette smoking, tobacco chewing, and excessive alcohol consumption.

2. The importance of a balanced diet and adequate intake of all vitamins and minerals.

3. The need for regular dental care to reduce irritation and mechanical injury and to check oral tissues and alveolar bone for primary and metastatic lesions.

4. The importance of watching for the five warning signs in the mouth that may indicate oral cancer: (i) swelling, lumps, or growths; (ii) erythematous or white scaly patches;

(iii) a sore that does not heal; (iv) persistent numbness or pain; and (v) persistent bleeding.

5. The need for those who are exposed to direct sunlight for long periods to use a protective screening lotion on the face and lips. Excessive exposure to the sun is an established factor in lip cancer.

When suspicious lesions are discovered, visual examination should be followed by a biopsy. If the examining dentist is not comfortable performing the biopsy, the patient should be referred to a practitioner who can perform the surgery and the appropriate therapy if a positive diagnosis is made.

The latest studies predict that as a result of routine preventive programmes, older persons in the next decade are likely to retain more of their natural teeth than the current generation of elders. Thus, the emphasis on dental care for older people will probably change direction. Dentists will need to reassess the notion that full dentures are the ultimate resolution of elders' oral health problems and develop and emphasize a more comprehensive approach, including prevention.

CONCLUSION

The beneficial effects of dental public health and preventive dentistry are becoming more obvious than ever before. Yet both dental caries and periodontal disease remain rampant. Dental caries affects more than 95 per cent of the population in the US. Roughly 80 per cent of all middle-aged adults have destructive periodontitis. Nearly 50 per cent of all Americans aged 65 years and over have lost all of their teeth. Indeed, dental disease is the most widespread degenerative disease in the US.

The question is, why? If the two major forms of dental disease are preventable, why are they not being prevented? Pain, altered appearance, loss of function, poor dietary habits, and more serious systemic problems caused by dental disease affect both the health and quality of life of many people world-wide. Can more effective dental educational and preventive programmes be developed?

The solutions to these questions are complex. They are bound up in the attitudes and actions of individuals, the dental profession, and governments. Individuals of all ages are often uninformed about dental disease and the need for effective oral hygiene. Even for those who are informed, knowledge of good dental practice does not always lead to a healthy regimen.

Poor responses to dental health education are generally attributed to misconceptions regarding the likelihood and seriousness of dental disease. Recent surveys show that tooth decay is viewed by the general public as inevitable but not serious. Periodontal disease, on the other hand, is perceived as fairly serious but not very likely. Although most of the survey respondents believed that dental disease could be prevented, there seemed to be little connection in their minds between prevention and regular dental examinations. Only 50 per cent of the total survey sample believed that regular dental visits and early detection were of preventive value. Changing attitudes, however, is not simply the responsibility of individuals; it is the responsibility of the dental profession and of dental public health personnel, since they are the chief channels of information about state-of-the-art for preventive measures.

Comprehensive dental public health outreach programmes are needed that are easily accessible to people at *all* levels of functioning, especially those who are the most underserved. Serious thought should be given as to how geriatric day-treatment centres, senior centres, nutrition projects, and other community programmes could incorporate a continuum of dental services, including screening and preventive education. There is also a need for data about the focus and extent of preventive practices in private dental offices and clinics, as well as the teaching of preventive modalities in dental schools. Multidisciplinary efforts of dental and medical health providers would be a useful strategy to develop comprehensive preventive health services and to press for public policy reform that responds to the health needs of people in all age and socio-economic groups.

FURTHER READING

Alfano, M.C. (1976). Controversies, perspectives, and clinical implications of nutrition in periodontal disease. *Dent. Clin. North Am.* **20**, 519.

American Cancer Society (1982). *Cancer facts and figures, 1981.* ACS, New York.

Andrew, W. (1952). A comparison of age changes in salivary glands of man and of the rat. *J. Gerontol.* **7**, 178.

Arey, L.B., Tremaine, M.J., and Monzingo, F.L. (1935). The numerical and topographical relations of taste buds to circumvallate papillae throughout the life span. *Anat. Rec.* **64**, 9.

Axelsson, P., and Lindhe, J. (1974). The effect of a preventive programme on dental plaque, gingivitis and caries in school children. Results after one and two years. *J. Clin. Periodontol.* **1**, 126.

Azen, E.A. (1978). Salivary peroxidase activity and thiocyanate concentration in human subjects with genetic variants of salivary peroxidase. *Arch. Oral Biol.* **23**, 801.

Banting, D.W., and Ellen, R.P. (1976). Carious lesions on the roots of teeth: a review for the general practitioner. *J. Canad. Dent. Assoc.* **42**, 496.

Bartoshuk, L.M. (1978). The psychophysics of taste. *Am. J. Clin. Nutr.* **31**, 1068.

Baum, B.J. (1979). Aging and oral motor function: response to paper, 'Oral motor behavior and oral prostheses'. In *Oral motor behavior: impact on oral conditions and dental treatment* (eds. P. Bryant, E. Gale, and J. Rugh) p. 244. National Institutes of Health, Publication No. 79-1845, Bethesda, Md.

Baum, B.J. (1984). Evaluation of stimulated parotid saliva flow rate in different age groups. *J. Dent. Res.* in press.

Bertram, U. (1967). Xerostomia. *Acta Odont. Scand.* **25**, Suppl. 49, 1.

Becks, H. (1943). Human saliva, XIV. Total calcium content of resting saliva in 650 individuals. *J. Dent. Res.* **22**, 397.

Bibby, B.G. (1970). Inferences from naturally occurring variations in caries prevalence. *J. Dent. Res.* **49**, 1194.

Bjorn, A. (1974). Dental health in relation to age and dental care. *Odontol. Revy* **25**, Supp. 29, 1.

Blayney, J.R. and Hill, I.N. (1964). Evanston Dental Caries Study XXIV. Prenatal fluorides—value of waterborne fluorides during pregnancy. *J. Am. Dent. Assoc.* **69**, 291.

Bunting, R.W. (1935). Diet and dental caries. *J. Am. Dent. Assoc.* **22**, 114.

Chauncey, H.H., Bell, B., Kapur, K.K., and Feller, R.P. (1975). Parotid fluid composition in a study of healthy aging males. *J. Dent. Res.* **54** (Special Issue A), 57, Abstr. No. 51.

Chauncey, H.H., Kapur, K.K., House, J.E., and Rissin, L. (1978). The incidence of coronal caries in normal aging male adults. *J. Dent. Res.* **57** (Special Issue A), 148, Abstr. No. 296.

Dean, H.T. (1938). Endemic fluorosis and its relation to dental caries. *Public Health Rep.* **43**, 1443.

Dean, H.T., Arnold, F.A. Jr, and Elvove, E. (1942). Domestic water and dental caries. V. Additional studies of the creation of fluoride domestic waters to dental caries experience in 4,425 white children, aged 12 to 14 years, of 13 cities in 4 states. *Public Health Rep.* **57**, 1155.

Dean, H.T., Arnold, F.A. Jr, Jay, P., and Knutson, J.W. (1950). Studies on mass control of dental caries through fluoridation of the public water supply. *Public Health Rep.* **63**, 1403.

DePaola, D.P. and Kuftinec, M.M. (1976). Nutrition in growth and development of oral tissues. *Dent. Clin. North Am.* **20**, 441.

Department of Health and Social Security (1969). *The fluoridation studies in the United Kingdom and the results achieved after eleven years.* p. 33. HMSO, London.

Federation Dentaire Internationale (1977). *Basic fact sheets.* FDI, London.

Feldman, R.S., Kapur, K.K., Alman, J.E., and Chauncey, H.H. (1980). Aging and mastication: changes in performance and in the swallowing threshold with natural dentition. J. Am. Geriatrics Soc. **28**, 97.

Goldman, H.M. and Cohen, D.W. (1980). *Periodontal therapy,* 6th edn. Mosby, St. Louis.

Grad, B. (1954). Diurnal, age, and sex changes in the sodium and potassium concentration of human saliva. *J. Gerontol.* **9**, 276.

Greene, J.C. (1959). Epidemiology and indexing of periodontal disease. *J. Periodontol.* **30**, 133.

Greene, J.C. (1963). Epidemiology of congenital clefts of the lip and palate. *Pub. Health Rep.* **78**, 589.

Greene, J.C. and Suomi, D. (1977). Epidemiology and public health aspects of caries and periodontal disease. *J. Dent. Res.* **56** (Special Issue C), C20.

Grzegorczyk, P.B., Jones, S.W., and Mistretta, C.M. (1979). Age-related differences in salt taste acuity. *J. Gerontol.* **34**, 834.

Gustafsson, B.E., Quensel, C.-E., Lanke, L.S. *et al.* (1954). The Vipeholm dental caries study: the effect of different levels of carbohydrate intake on caries activity in 436 individuals observed for five years. *Acta Odont. Scand.* **11**, 232.

Helfman, P.M. and Price, P.A. (1974). Human parotid α-amylase—a test of the error theory of aging. *Exp. Gerontol.* **9**, 209.

Helöe, B. and Helöe, L.A. Characteristics of a group of patients with temporomandibular joint disorders. *Community Dent. Oral Epidemiol.* **3**, 72.

Horowitz, H.S. and Heifetz, S.B. (1967). Effects of prenatal exposure to fluoridation on dental caries. *Pub. Health Rep.* **82**, 297.

Horowitz, H.S., Heifetz, S.B., and Law, F.E. (1972). Effect of school water fluoridation on dental caries: final results in Elk Lake, Pa., after 12 years. *J. Am. Dent. Assoc.* **84**, 832.

Horowitz, H.S., Heifetz, S.B., McClendon, B.J., Viegas, A.R., Guimaraes, L.O.C., and Lopes, E.S. (1974). Evaluation of self-administered prophylaxis and supervised tooth brushing with acidulated phosphate fluoride. *Caries Res.* **8**, 39.

Institute of Medicine (1980). *Public policy option for better dental health.* National Academy Press, Washington.

Jay, P., Beeuwkes, A.M., and Husbands, J. (1965). *Dietary program for the control of dental caries.* Overbeck, Ann Arbor, Mich.

Jenkins, G.N. (1970). Enamel protective factors in food. *J. Dent. Res.* **49**, 1318.

Jong, A. (1981). *Dental public health and community dentistry.* Mosby, St. Louis.

Jordan, H.V. and Hammond, B.F. (1972). Filamentous bacteria isolated from human root surface caries. *Archs Oral Biol.* **17**, 1333.

Katz, S., Olson, B.L., and Park, K.C. (1975). Factors related to the cariogenic potential of breakfast cereals. *Pharm. Therap. Dent.* **2**, 109.

Kreitzman, S.N. (1976). Nutrition in the process of dental caries. *Dent. Clin. North Am.* **20**, 491.

Loesche, W.J. (1976). Chemotherapy of dental plaque infections. *Oral Sci. Rev.* **9**, 65.

Löe, H. (1973a). Does chlorhexidine have a place in the prophylaxis of dental diseases? *J. Period. Res.* **8**, Suppl. 12, 93.

Löe, H. (1973b). Plaque control in periodontal disease. *J. Am. Dent. Assoc.* **87**, 1034.

Mandel, I.D., and Wotman, S. (1976). The salivary secretions in health and disease. *Oral Sci. Rev.* **8**, 25.

Marthaler, T.M., Mejia, R., Tóth, K., and Viñes, J.J. (1978). Caries-preventive salt fluoridation. *Caries Res.* **12**, Suppl. 1, 15.

Meyer, J. and Necheles, H. (1940). Studies in old age; clinical significance of salivary, gastric, and pancreatic secretion in old age. *JAMA* **115**, 2050.

Meyer, J., Spier, E., and Neuwelt, F. (1940). Basal secretion of digestive enzymes in old age. *Arch. Intern. Med.* **65**, 171.

National Institutes of Health (1979). *Special report on aging: 1979.* NIH Publication No. 80–1907, Washington, DC.

Nedelman, C.I. and Bernick, S. (1978). The significance of age changes in human alveolar mucosa and bone. *J. Prosthet. Dent.* **39**, 495.

Newbrun, E. (1985). *Fluorides and dental caries,* 3rd edn. Thomas, Springfield, Ill. (in press).

Newbrun, E. (1983). *Cariology,* 2nd edn. Williams and Wilkins, Baltimore.

Nikiforuk, G. (1970). Posteruptive effects of nutrition on teeth. *J. Dent. Res.* **49** (6 Part 1), 1252.

Ravn, J. J. (1974). Dental injuries in Copenhagen schoolchildren school years 1967–72. *Community Dent. Oral Epidemiol.* **2**, 231.

Rowe, J.W., Andres, R., Tobin, J.D., Norris, A.H., and Shock, N.W. (1976). The effect of age on creatinine clearance in men: a cross-sectional and longitudinal study. *J. Gerontol.* **31**, 155.

Schiffman, S. (1977). Food recognition by the elderly. *J. Gerontol.* **32**, 586.

Scott, J. (1977). Quantitative age changes in the histological structure of human submandibular salivary glands. *Archs Oral Biol.* **22**, 221.

Shklar, G. (1966). The effects of aging upon oral mucosa. *J. Invest. Derm.* **47**, 115.

Silverman, S. (1958). Geriatrics and tissue changes—problem of the aging denture patient. *J. Prosthet. Dent.* **8**, 734.

Silverman, S. (ed.) (1981). *Oral cancer.* American Cancer Society, New York.

Silverstein, S., Gold, S., Heilbron, D., Nelms, D., and Wycoff, S. (1977). Effects of supervised deplaquing on dental caries, gingivitis, and plaque. *J. Dent. Res.* **56,** (Special Issue A), A85, Abstr. No. 169.

Socransky, S.S. and Manganiello, S.D. (1971). The oral microbiota of man from birth to senility. *J. Periodontol.* **42**, 485.

Stamm, J.W. and Banting, D.W. (1980). Comparison of root caries prevalence in adults with life-long residence in fluoridated and non-fluoridated communities. *J. Dent. Res.* **59** (Special Issue A), 405, Abst. No. 552.

Striffler, D., Young, W.O., and Burt, B.A. (1983). *Dentistry, dental practice, and the community.* Saunders, Philadelphia.

Stuart, H.C. (1945). Findings on examinations of newborn infants and infants during the neo-natal period which appear to have a relationship to the diets of their mothers during pregnancy. *Fedn. Proc. Fedn. Am. Soc. Exp. Biol.* **4**, 271.

Sumney, D.L., Jordan, H.V., and Englander, H.R. (1973). The prevalence of root surface caries in selected populations. *J. Periodontol.* **44**, 500.

Suomi, J.D., Greene, J.C., Vermillion, J.R., Doyle, J., Chang, J.J., and Leatherwood, E.C. (1971). The effect of controlled oral hygiene procedures on the progression of periodontal disease in adults: results after third and final year. *J. Periodontol.* **42**, 152.

Syed, S.A., Loesche, W.J., Pape, H.L. Jr, and Grenier, E. (1975). Predominant cultivable flora isolated from human root surface caries plaque. *Infect. Immun.* **11**, 727.

Thompson, J.R. Sr (1969). Dentofacial growth in the adolescent. *Dent. Clin. North Am.* **13**, 343.

US Department of Health, Education and Welfare (1977). *An assessment of the occlusion of the teeth of youths 12–17 years.* DHEW Publication No. (HRA) 77-1644. Series 11, No. 162. US Government Printing Office, Washington, DC.

Wainwright, W.W. (1943). Human saliva, XV. Inorganic phosphorus content of resting saliva of 650 healthy individuals. *J. Dent. Res.* **22**, 403.

Ward, H. (1978). *A preventive point of view.* Thomas, Springfield, Ill.

Wycoff, S.J. (1975). Current concepts in preventive dentistry. *Am. Coll. Health Assoc. J.* **23**, 356.

Wycoff, S.J. and Epstein, S. (1984). Geriatric dentistry. In *Burket's oral medicine. Diagnosis and treatment,* 8th edn (eds. M.A. Lynch, V.J. Brightman and M.S. Greenberg), p. 560. Lippincott, Philadelphia.

The needs of special client groups

18 Children

Eva Alberman

INTRODUCTION

The care of children of a community is probably the most important, and certainly the most rewarding field in public health. It gives the opportunity of laying the foundations of good adult health in the broadest sense, with the aim of promoting the maximum potential for each individual in terms of physical and mental health and well-being, and the possibility of preventing future handicap and ill health. One of the best accounts of the services required by children in a developed country is the Court Report *'Fit for the future'* (DHSS 1976), in which these functions are discussed.

The field of child health differs in many ways from the health care of adults. First, those concerned with child health must be prepared to care for a constant influx of newborn, their number varying from year to year. Secondly, they are faced with a group of very vulnerable individuals, in successive phases of rapid growth and development.

Most public health services provide some form of health surveillance of new births and young children. This surveillance includes the monitoring of early mortality and morbidity rates and the regular observation of each individual child in order to ascertain as early as possible any important deviation from the normal. The objectives are to detect children at high risk of morbidity or mortality, and to offer primary prevention where possible or, failing this, secondary, or tertiary preventive action. Where necessary the service must also identify and offer special services to children who are already disabled or handicapped.

A special type of primary prevention is to offer immunological protection against infectious diseases wherever possible, usually early in infancy and childhood. It is usually the responsibility of the public health services to oversee or to discharge this function, and to evaluate its effectiveness. Similarly they are responsible for maintaining the surveillance of infectious diseases or other environmental hazards particularly in reference to the health of children.

Lastly, it is in childhood that the basis of adult behaviour becomes established, eating, exercise, and social habits, and the abuse of tobacco, alcohol, or other drugs. It is therefore at this time that health education becomes most important, for it is in infancy and childhood that the foundations of many pathological conditions are laid, predisposing to atheroma, hypertension, and some malignant diseases, as well as psychological disorders.

Child care implies contact with and concern for a whole family unit, and is related to the need for legal safeguards of the rights of children (Deakin 1982) and of parents. Because of the vulnerability of new births most societies expect minimal standards of parental care including the setting of nutritional standards, and in the cases where these are not met it is usually the public health services together with social services who have to be ready to offer alternative sources of care or nutrition.

These functions can only be carried out where the total child population is known to the health authorities, and the services to meet their needs are available. In this chapter I will consider first the effects of variations in numbers of births and some administrative methods available for identifying and regularly surveying all births and the child population, and for providing full preventive cover. The function of public health personnel in laying the foundation of nutritional habits and habits beneficial to long-term health will then be discussed, and finally the role of legislation and the influence and attitude of society to the care of children. The examples will be from the UK, but most are relevant to all developed countries.

DEMOGRAPHIC INFORMATION RELEVANT TO CHILD HEALTH

Vital statistics

Births and deaths

All developed countries now have extensive sets of routinely collected demographic data, much of which is required by local statute. Information available for many countries includes annual reports on population size, its sex and age distribution both on a national and regional scale, number and characteristics of births, and numbers of deaths by place, age, sex, and cause. Tables of such data are published annually by the countries themselves, and by the World Health Organization (*World Health Annual Statistics*). These data are derived from periodic censuses, and from birth and death registrations. The format of the latter is usually based on that recommended by the WHO and the causes of death coded using the International Classification of Diseases (ICD) (WHO 1978*b*), so that there is some degree of comparability between as well as within countries.

There is more variability between the format of birth certificates or notifications used by different countries, or even sometimes in different parts of the same country. Some birth certificates include medical data, as in Sweden. In other countries, as in the UK, medical data are collected from health professionals onto a birth notification which is held by the health authority, while the civil registration is completed by the local Registrar of Births by interview with the parents and sent to the national Office of Population Censuses and Surveys.

Definitions and commonly used rates

In the field of child health particularly there are problems of comparability of definitions used both within and between countries. For instance the definition of legal viability, which distinguishes between a non-registrable abortion and a registrable birth, varies from country to country. Most countries have a lower gestational age limit of viability but this varies from 20 weeks (for example, US) to 28 weeks (UK). Many countries have a lower limit according to crown–heel length (25 cm) or fetal weight (500 or 1000 g). There is not even general agreement on what distinguishes a livebirth from a stillbirth, the UK accepting any signs of life, some countries specifying particular signs of life. Even within a country there may be local customs relating to the distinction between still- and livebirths, or abortions and registrable births, which can make substantial differences to the number of early deaths reported. There is also some difference of opinion about the classification of ages, most counting as the first day of life the first 24 hours, others as the day of birth up to midnight. Guidance on a standard grouping of ages of births and deaths, and the definition of death rates is given by WHO in the ICD manuals.

In the UK the information gathered on mothers and babies has been fragmented, with the demographic characteristics of the mother described on the birth certificate derived from registration and the medical characteristics on the birth notification. Moreover, the death of a liveborn baby is registered on the standard form for deaths at any age and differs from the stillbirth form, the former bearing no information about the mother, or even the maturity of the baby. This fragmentation is gradually being overcome with the increasing use of data linkage, so that data relating to the mother and pregnancy can be brought together with that relating to the birth and subsequent death of a baby. It is this linkage which has made it possible to produce annual reports on the relationship of perinatal, infant, and childhood mortality to personal characteristics of the mothers and babies. It is the function of the public health services to use these data in planning and evaluating child health services.

Changes in birth rates and numbers of births

It is of obvious importance that paediatricians and other child health professionals should be fully aware of current demographic changes in order to forecast future staffing, and long-term training needs, as well as short and long-term hospital provision. It is part of the function of the public health services in many countries to keep paediatricians informed of such trends and to ensure that the planning of childrens' services is swiftly responsive to demographic change.

The absolute number of births per year depends both on the current fertility rate, and on the number of women of childbearing age. Changes in either factor may result in sharp fluctuations in the annual number of births. Over the past century in the UK these have ranged from nearly 1 000 000 births in a year at the turn of the century, to a minimum of 570 000 in 1977. Figure 18.1 illustrates these trends in terms of fertility rate and absolute numbers. Fluctuations of this magnitude have considerable and very variable implications for the paediatric services.

The effect on workload

Their effect on workload depends both on the cumulative trend and the consequent total of children (defined here as under the age of 15 years) and on the year to year variation in births. Table 18.1 shows such variations within the last decade. Between 1971 and 1980 there has been an average fall of over 1 per cent a year in the total number of children of less than 15 years in England and Wales. However, this overall fall conceals sharper annual changes in numbers of births, for example a fall of 7.3 per cent, representing 51 000 births between 1973 and 1974, and a rise of 8.4 per cent representing 48 000 births between 1978 and 1979.

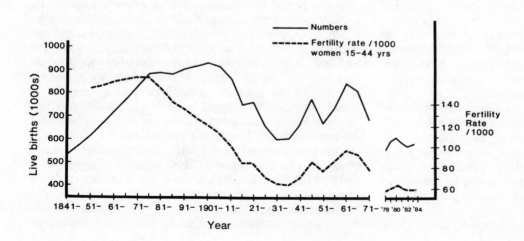

Fig. 18.1. Average of numbers of births and fertility rate, England and Wales: quinquennial 1841–1971, annual 1978–84. (Source: General Registry Office and OPCS Annual Population Statistics.)

Table 18.1. *Population (thousands) under 15 years in England and Wales, 1971–1980*

	<1	1–4	5–9	10–14	All under 15
1971	779	3127	4053	3645	11 604
1972	735	3088	4067	3741	11 631
1973	692	3039	4037	3833	11 601
1974	641	2938	3984	3924	11 487
1975	615	2821	3901	4006	11 343
1976	586	2660	3861	4036	11 143
1977	559	2512	3786	4047	10 904
1978	569	2389	3699	4019	10 676
1979	617	2320	3559	3977	10 473
1980	639	2322	3424	3904	10 289

Source: Office of Population Censuses and Surveys (1981).

The most immediate impact of such changes is on the workload generated by neonates, for instance the needs of low birthweight and sick infants, and on preventive medicine programmes such as screening and immunization. To take some simple examples, the sharp annual changes described will be reflected in the number of neonatal screening tests performed, and the number of doses of vaccine required in a year, as well as in the staff and equipment required for neonatal intensive care.

The demand for hospital admissions in infancy and childhood will also vary with the size of the annual cohort and with the cumulative sum of fifteen consecutive cohorts. For instance, the number of squint and hernia operations carried out in childhood could vary sharply from year to year, as could the number of children with the rare defects which nevertheless generate a great demand for very specialized medical care, such as leukaemia, and other childhood cancers.

This situation does not differ in principle to the problems faced in the planning for the medical care of adults, except that the age span of children is much smaller and far fewer staff and facilities are devoted to their care, so that the opportunity for 'buffering' the effect of short-term changes in population size is reduced. It follows that there must always be a certain amount of 'slack' in the provision for paediatric care, particularly neonatal care, where the impact of change is the greatest.

Other effects of changing age distributions in childhood

There are other, more subtle, effects of variations in the annual number of births. Perhaps the most interesting is the effect on infectious disease transmission of changing the size of the susceptible pool of children from year to year. The possible effect of this has been estimated by the use of mathematical models (Stewart 1972). It will clearly vary from disease to disease, and with the immunity status of the older children.

Other effects may be on behaviour patterns with varying proportions of children of different ages and birth ranks in the community, and this could effect truancy and delinquency rates.

The effects of changing parental demography

The effects of changes in the parental demographic background of births may affect needs for medical care as much, or even more, than changes in absolute numbers.

For instance since 1961 the proportion of births to mothers aged 40–44 years or more has fallen by 34.4 per cent to its present level of less than 1 per cent of all births. The effects of this and other changes in maternal age structure on the incidence of Down's syndrome have been documented (Wynne Griffith 1973) as have the effects of simultaneous changes in maternal age, parity, and social class on perinatal mortality (Hellier 1977). Such changes and others relevant to risk of mortality or morbidity, including illegitimacy, and changes in the distribution of social class or ethnic group of parents must be considered in conjunction with changes in absolute numbers of births in predicting the varying needs for medical care, for depending on their nature they may augment or reduce the needs.

COMMUNITY CHILD-HEALTH SURVEILLANCE

Continuous assessment of the health of children in a community acts as an indicator of standard of living, changes in health care, and of current health priorities. It is particularly valuable if the outcome measures can be compared with other places and other times. Both mortality and morbidity measures can be used for population surveillance, although at present it is easier to compare mortality than morbidity data.

Mortality surveillance

Mortality surveillance is important at several different levels. First national levels of overall early mortality rates are a good indicator of socio-economic, and to some extent, medical facilities, and secondly any study of their causes is helpful in the allocation of health care priorities and resources.

Trends over time and by place and persons

A falling trend in mortality at early ages has been very marked over this century, particularly in the developed countries, and particularly in infants after the first week of life and in childhood, where a large proportion of deaths had been due to diseases now easily preventable – gastroenteritis, respiratory infection, tuberculosis, measles, and so on. Figure 18.2 illustrates some of these changes as they occurred in England and Wales, but other European countries, notably Sweden have achieved even greater falls of mortality over the years. Those changes mean that a rising ratio of early to late neonatal deaths give some measure of the health status of a community, although this reflects the level of sanitation and general nutritional status as much, if not more than the medical care facilities available.

For these reasons infant and childhood mortality rates are always lowest in those countries with the highest standards of living and in the most socially advantaged groups within a given country.

Falls in mortality of groups known to be at very high risk for medical reasons are more likely to reflect specific improvements in medical care. Examples of this are the falls that have occurred in the mortality of the extremely immature

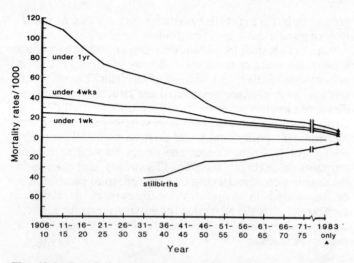

Fig. 18.2. Trends in early mortality rates, England and Wales 1906–83. (Source: General Registry Office and OPCS Annual Statistics.)

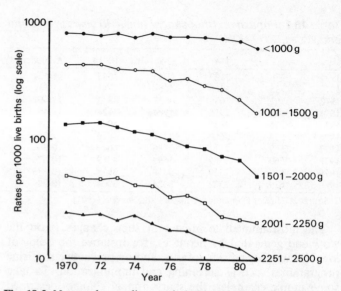

Fig. 18.3. Neonatal mortality rate in babies of birthweight 2500 g or less, England and Wales 1981. (Source: Department of Health and Social Security (1981).)

infant (DHSS 1982) (Fig. 18.3). It is the function of departments of public health, at national and local level, to monitor such trends, in part as an evaluation of the effectiveness of available services, and also as part of the information needed for the planning of future services.

Major causes of mortality

Table 18.2 shows for three developed countries with different standards of living the absolute level of mortality rates for different groups of childhood deaths, and the relative importance of each. In Sweden where the overall levels are consistently low, those deaths most difficult to prevent, namely from congenital malformations and neoplasms, account for more than a third of the deaths in each of the age groups shown. In Chile, where the overall rates are the highest,

deaths from the latter causes account for no more than about one-tenth of all, whereas deaths from infections or parasitic causes are far more important. Between the ages of one to four years accidents are a major cause of death in all countries shown, and after the age of four these consistently become the most important causes, although the level of accidental deaths in childhood in Chile is twice that of Sweden.

As deaths from the more easily preventable causes fall, other types of death, such as those that are sudden and unexpected, become relatively more important. In the UK such deaths now account for about one-third of infant deaths after the neonatal period (OPCS monitor 1982b). Such deaths have also been shown to be most common in disadvantaged families, and it is likely that a proportion even of

Table 18.2. *Major categories of infant and childhood deaths in Sweden, Greece, and Chile—rates per 100 000*

Age (years)	Categories (A-List, ICD-8)									
	Certain causes of perinatal mortality (A 131–135)		Infectious + parasitic diseases (A 1–44)		Neoplasms + congenital malformations (A 45–61 + 126–130)		Remainder		All	
	Rate	% total	Rate	% total	Rate	% total	Rate	% total	Rate	% total
<1										
Sweden (1978)	321	41.4	25	3.2	285	36.7	145	18.7	776	100
Greece (1978)	1090	56.4	145	7.5	450	23.3	248	12.8	1933	100
Chile (1977)	1773	37.3	1017	21.4	392	8.2	1571	33.1	4753	100
	Accidents (E17)		Infectious + parasitic diseases (A1–44)		Neoplasms + congenital malformations (A45–61 + 126–130)		Remainder		All	
1–4										
Sweden (1978)	10.7	29.6	1.5	4.2	16.9	46.8	7.0	19.4	36.1	100
Greece (1978)	21.1	31.4	4.5	6.7	19.4	28.9	22.1	32.9	67.1	100
Chile (1977)	46.1	27.5	26.6	15.9	13.2	7.9	81.8	48.8	167.7	100
5–14										
Sweden (1978)	9.8	40.8	0.9	3.8	8.0	33.3	5.3	22.1	24.0	100
Greece (1978)	11.0	35.0	0.7	2.2	9.9	31.5	9.8	31.2	31.4	100
Chile (1977)	25.1	38.0	6.3	9.5	8.5	12.9	26.2	39.6	66.1	100

Source: WHO, *World Health Statistics Annual* (various years).

these are due to preventable causes (Taylor and Emery 1982).

Demographic characteristics of infant and childhood deaths

Over and above the trends described the risk of early death varies markedly and consistently with other socio-biological characteristics of the mother, such as her age, parity, and whether or not she is supported, as well as with disadvantageous personal habits like smoking or alcohol consumption. However, the patterns of high risk are different at different ages. Primiparity and advanced maternal age are disadvantageous in the perinatal period, but advantages in later infancy (OPCS 1982a) (Fig. 18.4). Low socio-economic status is a high risk factor at all ages, but highest for post-neonatal deaths.

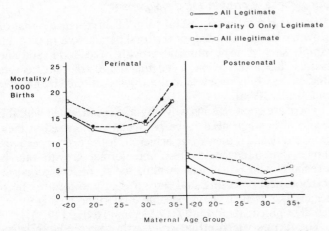
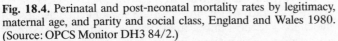

Fig. 18.4. Perinatal and post-neonatal mortality rates by legitimacy, maternal age, and parity and social class, England and Wales 1980. (Source: OPCS Monitor DH3 84/2.)

There are also very marked and important differences in mortality rate with characteristics of the baby itself, particularly its birthweight which itself may reflect the effect of maternal deprivation, and whether it was a singleton or multiple birth (Fig. 18.5). The comparison of rates of multiple and singleton births shows how complex is the relationship between birthweight and mortality; births of different characteristics may have a different 'optimal' birthweight. No comparison of mortality rates in different communities in the perinatal period or infancy can be interpreted without taking into account such differences.

Most countries also have quite marked regional differences in birth and death rates, and the UK is no exception. It is difficult to disentangle the effects of differences of latitude and longitude and the consequent differences in climate and geology, from those of socio-economic or genetic differences in the regional residents. Both throughout the world, and within individual countries, socio-economic advantage tends to be most common where the climate is most moderate and the land the easiest to cultivate. All these factors have a bearing on the health of mothers and children, and this is clearly illustrated in the UK where at all ages, there have been marked and consistent gradients of mortality (and morbidity)

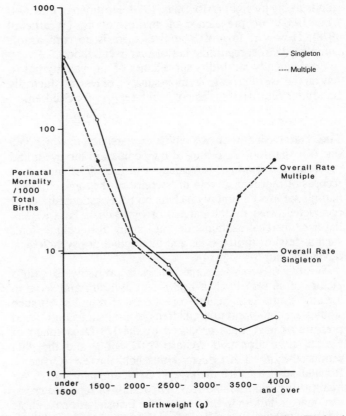

Fig. 18.5. Infant mortality by birthweight and plurality, England and Wales 1983. (Source: OPCS Monitor DH3 85/1.)

falling from north to south, and, to a lesser extent west to east. However, in recent years the gradients have become less, and this may be a sign of increasing social and economic development.

Mortality surveillance, although crude, nevertheless gives an important indication of current priorities to be set for each country, region, or socio-economic group. It also provides an outcome to be used for the evaluation of services offered, and of any innovations in medical technology, although it may be of more limited use than morbidity.

Community morbidity surveillance

Morbidity in childhood covers an extremely wide field for it includes the presence of congenital defects or impairments; deviations from 'normal' physical, mental, or psychological development; signs of malnutrition; the presence of infections, malignant, or metabolic disease; and the effects of accidental or non-accidental injury. Within these are comprised the long-term effects of prenatal, birth, or neonatal damage, and relevant signs or symptoms are an important part of monitoring antenatal, obstetric, and neonatal services.

Since there is no internationally or even nationally agreed system of morbidity reporting, systematic ongoing surveillance is far less easy than for mortality. Birth registration or notification data, where these are standard, and complete have been used for this purpose, particularly in regard to trends in birthweight (Alberman 1974; Hoffman *et al.* 1974; Cole 1981), or prevalence of malformations (Weatherall 1978). However, in most countries there is no comparable complete data set regarding health later in childhood.

Consequently morbidity surveillance of any validity has to rely on the use of repeated sample surveys, or less satisfactorily on routine returns of uptake of health services for children.

Sample surveys

These are basically of two types: *cross-sectional*, which is a one-off 'snapshot' screening of the population surveyed; and repeated, *longitudinal*, screening, with linking of individual records of repeated surveys or 'sweeps' of the same children. Sample surveys commonly include both a questionnaire to be completed often by the parents or by teachers, and a standardized medical examination, and many also include items such as tests of motor skills and intellectual or psychological development.

The use of cross-sectional studies is primarily to gain a picture of current level of health and ill-health and serve to identify immediate health care needs. Examples of such studies are the reports on childrens' dental status and blood pressure as have been produced by the US Department of Health, Education and Welfare (1971, 1973) and the data produced by the UK General Household Surveys (Office of Population Censuses and Surveys, GHS, annual reports). An example is given in Table 18.3. The results of repeated cross-sectional studies, as in the cases of the British national cohort studies (Douglas 1964; Davie *et al.* 1972) makes it possible to compare trends, for instance, in reported levels of disability; observed defects of vision or hearing, and health behaviour and use of medical care. Knowledge of such trends is important for identifying and evaluating effects of social, demographic, and medical care changes.

Table 18.3. *Consultation rates with general practitioners*

Age	Percentage consulting within 14 days of interview		Average number of consultations per person per year	
	Male	Female	Male	Female
0–4	21	17	6.7	5.5
5–14	8	9	2.5	2.7

Source: OPCS. *General Household Survey of Great Britain for the year 1981.*

Longitudinal studies are far more expensive and time consuming. Although they basically consist of repeated linked cross-sectional studies on the same children the linkage of the records and tracing of children who have moved can be very difficult (Fogelman 1976). The success of tracing will depend on whether there is a national population register, or its equivalent, and the constraints of the need for confidentiality of records. Longitudinal data are however unique in providing, for instance, the opportunity to follow through the long-term associations of birth problems, or problems in early childhood, in allowing the measurement of rate and pattern of growth, and relating this to other parameters of development (Davie *et al.* 1972).

In the UK as in other countries efforts are being made to set up a standardized system of pre-school and school surveillance (Walker 1982), which would provide morbidity data on a regional or national scale. These are very ambitious projects, and even where they have been introduced there are problems with quality control, since the data are collected by numerous health staff often without special training to reduce observer variation.

Where these are shown to be complete and valid such data could replace cross-sectional sample surveys, and the linking of the results would provide longitudinal information. Such standardized data collection might in the long run reduce the value of sample surveys, although the former may be found to be the more satisfactory in terms of completeness and quality of data.

Surveillance of growth and development

A special and extremely useful form of surveillance is that of growth whether recorded for the total population, or through sample surveys. The physical growth of children and the factors that affect it has been the subject of innumerable studies, very fully reviewed in the articles collected by Falkner and Tanner (1978).

There are good reasons why physicians concerned with the health of children need to be particularly interested in their growth rate and ultimate size achieved. It has been repeatedly shown that a deviation from the normal growth rate is associated with nutritional, health, social, or intellectual or psychological problems, and since it is easy to measure both height and weight these become important indicators of actual or potential morbidity (Leeder and Holland 1978).

The factors which influence growth do so in close interaction with each other, and with the sex and calendar age of the child. The most important is probably the calorie content and quality of nutritional intake, but other factors, such as the health and psychological well-being of the child are also of considerable importance. Genetic factors also play a role but many apparent ethnic differences in growth rate have been shown to disappear when nutritional and socioeconomic status are improved. Thus studies of Japanese of short stature, who immigrated to the US, have shown that after a single generation their growth rate and final height approximates to that of the indigenous population; similarly in Japan itself when the socio-economic conditions improved the secular trend in growth has shown a rapid increase over the past few decades (Tanner 1978).

Other factors which have been shown to affect growth rate independently are the weight at birth, the number of older and younger siblings, and the maternal age. In a sense these too are a reflection of parental socio-economic or educational status. The overall impression to be gained from studies of infant and childhood growth is the very large part played by environmental and therefore manipulable factors, and the comparatively small part played by genetic factors.

There has been an interesting debate on the best standards to be used from which to judge growth rate, whether it would be best from the point of view of long-term health if the growth of all children approximated to that of the most affluent, white US children, or whether local standards should be used (WHO 1978a). The difficulty is that the fastest growth rate may be an indication of an increased risk for diseases of affluence and may not be the optimum rate to achieve. Nevertheless, evidence of an increasing childhood growth rate in countries where poverty and malnutrition are rife is certainly a sign of improvement in the health of children and conversely a decreasing rate is a danger sign. In many ways the surveillance of childhood growth in a community is one of the best forms of health-care monitoring.

Health care returns

In countries with a national health and social security service it is possible to monitor both the level of use, and the cause for which the services are used. In the UK there are several different data sources which can be used in this way and these are listed in Table 18.4. These data, however, reflect not the need for services, but their use, and must be interpreted with caution. However, comparative rates of childhood hospital admission, or consultations with a general practitioner do provide some insight into levels of perceived ill health. Examples of information from hospital discharge data are given in Table 18.5, and from community services data in Table 18.6.

Table 18.4. *England and Wales – routine statistical returns which provide data relating to ill health or uptake or services*

1. **Records generated by discharge from hospital**
   Hospital In-patient Enquiry (annual)
   Department of Health and Social Security (DHSS)
   Office of Population Censuses and Survey (OPCS)
   Welsh Office

2. **Records generated by visits to general practitioners**
   Morbidity Statistics from General Practice
   (occasional reports)
   Royal College of General Practitioners, DHSS and OPCS

3. **Records generated by community health services**
   Health and Personal Social Services Statistics for England (annual)
   DHSS
   (includes infectious disease notifications)

Table 18.5. *Spells in hospital per 100 of population in age group England and Wales, 1978*

Age (years)	Male	Female
0–4	14.7	10.8
5–14	6.3	4.5

Source: OPCS *et al. Hospital In-patient Enquiry for England and Wales, for the year 1978, 1981.*

Table 18.6. *Percentage acceptance rates of immunization by children in England, 1981*

	Year after end of year of birth	Two years after end of year of birth
Diphtheria	73	84
Tetanus	73	83
Whooping cough	45	45
Poliomyelitis	72	82

Source: Health and Personal Social Services, *Statistics for England, 1982.*

SURVEILLANCE OF THE HEALTH OF INDIVIDUAL CHILDREN

As well as community surveillance, there is a need for health surveillance of individual children, in order to identify as quickly as possible those with impairments, or showing other deviations from the norm, so that preventive or curative action may be instituted before disability or handicap results. Also unique to child health is the requirement to provide health support for the educational service, both in respect to the normal child and very importantly, in respect to children handicapped from birth or early childhood. This function further predicates the need to identify as early as possible any deviation from the normal.

The role of the public health doctor in many developed countries is to set up local standards for different parameters of development, including growth, locomotive, and psychological; of vision, speech, and hearing and to screen for children who are deviating from the norm. It is also to screen for specific impairments where early treatment is of benefit.

Screening in the neonatal period

In the UK routine data available for the neonatal period include the notification of a visible defect within 36 hours of birth, for which there is a voluntary scheme of notification to the Department of Health. Recent years have seen other well organized and well validated schemes for screening for several inborn errors of metabolism particularly phenylketonuria (Bickel *et al.* 1981). It may be that screening for neonatal hypothyroidism will become as important but this is still at an early stage of development. Screening for congenital dislocation of the hips is also commonly carried out in many countries.

Surveillance of individual growth

This is generally carried out by the use of a standard chart appropriate for local use and the height and weight of each individual child from birth, is plotted so that any deviations from the norm may be observed and acted upon. These deviations may take the form of a persistently slow or fast rate of growth, usually indicating longstanding under- or overnutrition, or chronic ill health, or they may represent a sudden departure from a previously normal rate, suggesting an acute event, often physical illness or even a form of child neglect or abuse. In the individual child obesity, in terms of an unduly high body-weight for height, may be as much a sign of a risk of ill health as is an unduly low weight for height. Both are causes for concern for those responsible for the immediate and the long-term health of children. Such recording can be carried out as part of regular pre-school or school health surveillance, and are amongst the most useful screening measures of child health available.

Surveillance of individual psychological and social development

Children who are found to be below their expected chronological developmental quotient or who exhibit clear signs or abnormal behaviour must be observed, and if necessary special education or psychological treatment sought for them. Just as with growth, deviations from normal psychological and social development may be important indicators of social disorder in the child or in its family as well as of a mal-development of a pathological nature. In the UK it is the responsibility of the local (public) health authorities to ascertain children in need of special education and to follow their progress. Unfortunately, screening tests of develop-mental of intelligence level, particularly in young children, do not compare well with measures of stature or weight, as far as their validity is concerned (Clarke and Clarke 1974). Nevertheless there are now numerous age-standardized screening tests for these purposes which if used by well-trained observers, will identify most children at high risk.

The best observers of developmental progress are un-doubtedly the parents, and one of the most important functions of those concerned with the health of children is to be sensitive and alert to parents' concerns and to act upon them swiftly where they are shown to be well-founded.

Surveillance of the special senses

Early, and regular screening for impairments of sight or hearing is essential in the surveillance of the health of young children. The early treatment of squints may save a child from lifelong amblyopia and the early diagnosis of deafness may give an affected child the only opportunity to learn to speak normally.

Many screening methods for visual or hearing impairments have been developed over the past twenty years. They range from tests on very young children which need considerable skill and time to carry out, to tests which make use of instru-ments which reduce much of the testing to a mechanical level and can be carried out by specially trained but less highly qualified observers. Recent articles have been very critical of the validity of some of the commonly used tests of vision and hearing, in part because of the way they are administered (Hall *et al.* 1982; Nietupska and Harding 1982). It should be part of the child health services to constantly evaluate the validity of these tests which form a large part of their work-load in developed countries.

Surveillance of dental health

Dental screening in childhood is of major importance not least because this is a field in which effective preventive action can be offered, but also because the detection of caries, or of missing or filled teeth is a sensitive indicator of the success of health education or nutritional programmes. Intervention in the case of untreated pathology is of course also an essential part of dental health programmes.

Dental inspections are usually carried out in schools, and sometimes child welfare clinics, but the coverage of the population can be checked by reference to the child register. As with other screening programmes there is still a debate about the training and status of those who carry out such

screening. While this may be best performed by fully trained dentists, specially trained dental auxiliaries may prove an acceptable and cheaper alternative.

ORGANIZATION OF CHILD HEALTH SERVICES

The organization of child health services includes the provi-sion of programmes which will allow health surveillance of a community, or individuals and most importantly will ensure that action follows upon the recognition of problems, whether by surveillance, screening, or parental observation. This involves the setting up of programmes of action, their implementation, and the evaluation of their effectiveness, efficiency, and cost–benefit.

Such programmes will vary from country to country, according to need, health policy and culture, and there have been many good accounts of the planning of such services. (Key references include WHO 1966, 1976a,b, 1980a; Scottish Home and Health Department 1973; Department of Health and Social Security 1980.)

A full programme of health surveillance of individual children will require a considerable investment of resources, usually of public health nurses (health visitors) and doctors. Over the years there has been an active debate about the advantages and disadvantages of a uniform programme of surveillance for all children versus positive discrimination in favour of children thought (and registered) as being at higher than average risk. Arguments in favour of the 'risk approach' (WHO 1978c) are largely based on the demonstration that this is a more efficient use of scarce resources. Arguments against it include the disadvantage of 'labelling' a child, the poor predictive value of most factors which commonly place a child into a high-risk group, and consequently the high proportion of children with problems in the low-risk category. Mathematical modelling confirms intuition in showing that the best approach is to give some advantage (for example, more frequent surveillance) to the high-risk group but not to neglect the low-risk group. The advantage of positive discrimination becomes less as resources become more plentiful (Alberman and Goldstein 1970).

In practice child health programmes commonly fall into three classes: first those which comprise the whole of the childhood population; secondly those which concentrate on subgroups thought to be at high risk; and thirdly those for children known to be impaired, disabled, or handicapped. In order to allow such distinctions there need to be 'registers' of children falling into these groups.

Commonly used registers

Child registers

In the UK the notification of a birth, or the movement of a child into the health authority in which the mother is resident, forms the basis of a complete register of children for whom that authority is responsible. This register forms the basis of universal surveillance and immunization programmes, and also offers the opportunity to evaluate the coverage of such programmes.

'At-risk' registers

The registration of infants at high risk for reasons of abnormal maternal, perinatal, or neonatal factors is an essential part of 'risk factor' management and 'risk registers' of neonates were held by most health authorities in the UK for many years. Unfortunately there was no rigorous evaluation of the predictive power of the factors recorded, and indeed the latter varied from place to place. Because of the poor prediction achieved for considerable effort their use fell into disrepute (Oppe 1967). However, well defined high-risk factors, such as very low birthweight, or gestational age, are generally fully recorded on birth notifications, and are important groups to follow-up both because of the relatively high probability that some impairments or disabilities will be present, and as a method of evaluating innovations in obstetric and neonatal care (Chalmers and Mutch 1981).

Handicap registers

The registration of children with existing handicaps is common practice in the UK, for it is mandatory for the health authorities to ascertain at an early age those children who will require special education, and helpful in ensuring that their clinical management is not neglected. The ascertainment of children with handicaps, if these are severe, is usually complete if the handicap is such as to require special educational help or other forms of care. There are, however, considerable difficulties in defining handicaps in any consistent fashion. WHO (1980b) have recently published a suggested coding system for impairments, disabilities, and handicaps which distinguishes between the three.

Impairment: . . . any loss or abnormality of psychological, physiological, or anatomical structure or function.
Disability: . . . any restriction or lack (resulting from an impairment) of ability to perform an activity in the manner or within the range considered normal.
Handicap: . . . a disadvantage for a given individual resulting from an impairment or disability, that limits or prevents the fulfilment of a role that is normal (depending on age, sex and social and cultural factors) for that individual (WHO 1980b).

But a recent review (Balarajan *et al.* 1982) showed that in practice there is still considerable confusion between handicap registers and those listing children with impairments or disabilities of different kinds.

Impairment and disability registers

In contrast to handicap registers, those designed for epidemiological purposes need to include children with impairments and disabilities as well as those with handicaps, for the factors which convert an impairment into a disability or handicap may be purely fortuitous. This introduces the problem of ascertainment of impairments which are of no clinical but only epidemiological importance; an ascertainment which may require population screening to be complete, if indeed the impairment is detectable by non-invasive methods.

Whatever the form, or aim of such registers, they must be based on a geographically, or administratively defined population, so that no children are omitted. This means that they must become the province of the public health authorities rather than of individual clinicians.

Congenital malformation registers

The thalidomide disaster alerted us to the need for a systematic recording of visible congenital malformations, in order to introduce an early warning system of any subsequent disaster of this nature. The UK has introduced a system of voluntary notification of visible congenital malformations on the statutory birth notification (Weatherall 1978). Evaluation of this system has shown that it has worked reasonably well, certainly for the most obvious malformations such as neural-tube defects and cleft lips. The completeness of notification of other malformations varies from place to place and with changes in staff, and with the length of time allowed for late registration of malformations.

International collaboration has stimulated discussion on the resolution of possible ambiguities, such as whether the counts are of children or malformations; and some form of agreement on the definition, nomenclature, and classification of malformations. These are all extremely difficult problems to tackle. Registers which have not been designed to overcome such problems can have little validity, and are probably not worth keeping.

Non-accidental injury registers

Other types of registers kept include those of children at high risk of death, injury, or disease due to social and not purely medical reasons. These include the registration by Social Service Departments of children thought to have received non-accidental injury, so that they and their families may be kept under regular surveillance with the aim of preventing further child abuse. They also include the registration of children who are in local authority care for whatever reason. The role of the child health services in relation to children at social disadvantage varies from place to place, but there can be no doubt of the importance of close observation of the health of such children who are at high risk of most causes of morbidity and mortality. This problem is discussed in a booklet *'Vulnerable families'* (Scottish Home, Health and Education Department 1980a).

Example of a surveillance programme and of the actions that follow

In the UK, and other countries (for example in Scandinavia), child surveillance is largely the responsibility of health visitors (public health nurses). These carry out a programme of health surveillance which, in the UK, starts with a visit to every new birth, usually within days of its discharge from hospital. The first visit includes a simple examination of the baby. It also includes an assessment of home conditions and quality of mothering. Where the baby requires medical attention the health visitor will refer it, usually to the family practitioner; where conditions or mothering standards are inadequate she will embark on measures designed to bring these to an acceptable standard. These may range from directing the parents towards sources of help with housing or financial problems, to advice on feeding. Although the exact content of health visitors' input into family visiting remains ill-defined, some evaluation of their work has suggested that increasing the number of visits to families at high risk reduces the likelihood of sudden infant death (Emery 1981). The usefulness of their visits to families at low risk has not, to the author's knowledge, been formally evaluated.

After the first visit, health visitors' contacts with children for whom they are responsible may be confined to clinic attendances. An increasing proportion of these clinics are held by the children's own general practitioner, usually in his or her own surgery. The majority are in local authority premises. Most local authorities now have a recommended programme of surveillance, including weighing and measuring and tests of vision, hearing, and developmental assessment at specified ages. In some the appointments for testing are computerized, as are some of the clinical results.

Any observed departures from the normal prompt a referral to the family practitioner; or where this has previously been agreed, directly to the appropriate consultant. A method of evaluating the function of such clinics is to record the number of referrals, and to note those later confirmed as abnormal and those regarded as false-positives. Even more important is to record the number of abnormalities missed at routine surveillance and identified later. It would be useful for every clinic to set a target for an acceptable proportion of false-positives, and to make sure that false-negatives are reduced to a minimum.

It is unfortunate that in the field of child health most of the tests which form part of the usual battery for developmental monitoring have not been subjected to rigorous scrutiny in this way (Cochrane and Holland 1971). This means that much of the data we have relating to the prevalence of abnormal signs or symptoms in childhood, derived from routine health surveillance examinations is of questionable value. It is obviously easier to maintain the quality of screening in *ad hoc* sample surveys where there is a small number of workers who can be trained and supervised, than when routine pre-school or school surveillance is carried out, but quality control is just as important in the latter.

Immunization and vaccination

One of the greatest developments in medical care was the ability to protect children and adults against some of the major infectious diseases. Although this remains amongst the most important functions of the public health services, the spread and lethality of many of these infections is considerably curtailed in well-nourished and healthy children, even without immunization. Thus the major protective action against tuberculosis, or whooping cough is a rise in standard of living, although this is not true of polio or rubella. Conversely, it is for the deprived and malnourished that immunological protection is most required, as in the developing world, where, for instance, measles is still a major killer.

However, every health authority with responsibility for child health must have a well-organized programme of immunization as locally appropriate. In this country, as with health surveillance, this function has been partially taken over by family practitioners who are increasing their interest in preventive medicine (Royal College of General Practitioners 1982). It is therefore particularly important for health authorities to record for each child whether immunization and vaccination has been carried out, and if so when, and by whom. This function can be made easier by the use of computerized recall programmes based on the child register and is most successful when combined with a system of paying family practitioners for the immunizations they have carried out.

It behoves the child health services to evaluate the uptake of the immunizations offered, and together with the Public Health Laboratory Service or its equivalent, their safety and effectiveness. Uptake and coverage are certainly affected by the efficiency with which programmes are run, and at least one report has suggested that the number of cases of measles notified was reduced after the introduction of computerized recall systems for immunization and vaccination (Bussey and Harris 1979).

Very much in the province of child health departments is the evaluation of the risk of immunization versus the risk of the natural infection (Department of Health and Social Security 1981). The recent concern about the risks and benefits of whooping cough immunizations has demonstrated the importance of keeping good records of immunizations and adverse reactions.

Handicapped children

It has already been said that the ascertainment of children with handicaps is the responsibility of the child health services, and that this is based on parental observation, neonatal and later screening, and on the more general health-surveillance programmes.

Ascertainment of handicap is not complete until a full assessment of abilities and disabilities has been made by an expert team. In the UK at present this function is usually performed by district handicap teams, which include a paediatrician expert in developmental assessment, often one who is employed by the local authority as a senior clinical medical officer. These teams should be in close contact with all the services necessary for the care and education of the handicapped. This may include the hospital services providing secondary or tertiary preventive care, such as orthopaedic, cardiac, renal, or neurosurgery services. It also includes the provision of education, if necessary special education, appropriate to the needs of each child. In the UK each education authority has appointed to it a medical officer whose responsibility includes that for special education.

Other services available for the handicapped include mobility aids, help with laundry or the provision of disposable sheets or nappies, prostheses where appropriate, hearing or visual aids, and attendance allowances. The parents will need support and guidance, and often genetic counselling and introductions to voluntary services. The final responsibility for the overall care of the handicapped, including plans for care they receive after the age of 18 years, rests with the local health authority.

School health

In the UK, a named doctor in each health authority is responsible for providing health cover to the local schools. It is the policy of the Department (Ministry) of Health of the UK that each school has a named school doctor and school nurse. The doctors may be salaried employees of the health authority (clinical medical officers), or they may be family practitioners paid by the session to provide school medical cover. The nurses are provided by the health authority, and are part of its co-ordinated health visiting service.

Together the school doctor and nurse are responsible for the surveillance of the growth, health, and development of the schoolchildren, and particularly the screening of vision and hearing. A good working relationship between the medical team and the teaching staff offers the best prospects for making sure that each child reaches his or her maximum potential without being handicapped by physical, sensory, or emotional health problems. It also offers the best basis for a good health education programme, including the planning of nutritious and sensible school meals, discouraging in every possible way the habits of smoking, drinking, or drug taking, and providing help and advice to lay the foundations for restrained sexual behaviour, good family planning habits, and preparation for parenthood. An excellent account of a possible organizational framework for school health service is given in a document produced by the Scottish home and Health and Education Department (1980*b*). Much of the debate on child health surveillance has related to the question of where there should be universal or selective medical screening of schoolchildren. This must depend on the age of the children, local circumstances, and resources available. Ways of examining possible options are described clearly in the Scottish document quoted above.

Health advice for local authority children's establishments

All developed countries have some contingency plans for the support and assistance of orphaned, abandoned, or otherwise unsupported children. Whatever the local arrangement there will need to be a liaison between the social services responsible and local authority doctors and nurses who provide the necessary medical support. This may take the form of providing medical cover for residential childrens homes, or for advising on fostering or adoption programmes. A full account of the organization of child care, including medical care, in community homes is given in a report published by the Home Office Advisory Group on Child Care (1970).

Prevention of accidents

One of the most important roles the child health service can play is to offer advice to parents, children, and local building and transport authorities in respect to accident prevention

(Jackson 1977). Accidents are a leading cause of death in childhood. Many could be avoided by relatively simple and inexpensive improvements in building design, road layout and marking, home lighting, and in the education of parents and their children. The marked gradient in mortality risk from accidents between the social classes is a clear indication of the potential for prevention that exists. It should be remembered also that death from accidents is but the tip of the iceberg of morbidity that is caused, much of which may lead to permanent impairment or handicap.

FOUNDATION FOR GOOD ADULT HEALTH

Above all the care of the health of children must include the foundation of good adult physical and mental health. It might be argued that the most important requirement for this is a loving, supportive, and economically secure family; but it includes the development of sensible and well-informed eating and exercise habits, and the avoidance of such adverse behaviour as smoking, drinking, or indiscriminate sexual activity.

This field is comprehensively surveyed in a recent report edited by Falkner (1980), which includes chapters on the prevention in childhood of such problems as obesity, major cardiovascular disease, and oral and mental disease, as well as the influence of malnutrition and childhood infections on adult health.

An indispensable basis for these objectives is a society whose values are such as to support and enhance such aims. Major obstacles are the current political attitudes towards a national food policy, and the lack of a real commitment to reduce smoking and drinking. However, a recent important step towards the prevention of mortality and morbidity in the UK has been the introduction of compulsory seat-belt wearing. The place of public health doctors in promoting legislation conducive to good health is a debatable one, but what is not debatable is their role in promoting good childhood health at local level.

CONCLUSIONS

At the outset of this chapter the Court Report was quoted as giving an excellent account of services required by children in a developed country. In spite of general agreement with its recommendations for a comprehensive and integrated service for children, these have never been fully implemented. It is worth asking why not, and what obstacles stand in the way of such a service, not just in the UK, but in other developed countries.

Sadly, one of the main difficulties in implementing the Court Report proved to be the structure of the medical profession, possibly because the care of child health rather than disease remains a low-prestige occupation, and, certainly in 1976, not acceptable as a sub-specialty either in general practice or in paediatrics.

Another basic and universal problem is that the greatest need for surveillance is in children of impoverished and often unstable families, who rarely stay in any one place for any length of time. An organization that will provide a 'safety net' for the children of such families must be extremely flexible and innovative. Although there have been many local attempts at experimenting with methods to meet the needs of these families these are difficult to write into a national plan.

All over the world the children at highest risk are in these severely disadvantaged mobile families and it is these children, and their offspring who are most likely to get trapped in the 'cycle of deprivation'. Equal opportunity must start with health, and this is the greatest challenge our child health services have to meet.

REFERENCES

Alberman, E.D. (1974). Stillbirths and neonatal mortality in England and Wales by birthweight, 1953–71. *Health Trends* **6**, 14.

Alberman, E. and Goldstein, H. (1970). The 'at risk' register: a statistical evaluation. *Br. J. Prev. Soc. Med.* **24**, 129.

Balarajan, B., Weatherall, J.A.C., Ashley, J.S.A., and Bewley, B.R. (1982). A survey of handicap registers for pre-school children in England and Wales. *Community Med.* **4**, 315.

Bickel, H., Bachmann, C., Beckers, R. *et al.* (1981). Neonatal mass screening for metabolic disorders. Summary of recent sessions of the Committee of Experts to Study Inborn Metabolic Disease, Public Health Committee. Council of Europe. *Eur. J. Pediatr.* **137**, 133.

Bussey, A. and Harris, A.S. 61979). Computers and the effectiveness of the measles vaccination campaign in England and Wales. *Community Med.* **1**, 29.

Chalmers, I. and Mutch, L. (1981). Are current trends in perinatal practice associated with an increase or a decrease in handicapping conditions? (Letter.) *Lancet* i, 1415.

Clarke, A.D.B. and Clarke, A.M. (1974). The changing concept of intelligence: a selective historical review. In *Mental deficiency: the changing outlook* (ed. A.M. Clarke and A.D.B. Clarke), p. 143. Methuen, London.

Cochrane, A.L. and Holland, W.W. (1971). Validation of screening procedures. *Br. Med. Bull.* **27**, 1.

Cole, S.K. (1981). *Birthweight, head circumference and gestational age Scotland 1973–1979.* Information Services Division, Scottish Health Service Common Services Agency, Edinburgh.

Davie, R., Butler, N., and Goldstein, H. (1972). *From birth to seven.* Longman in association with The National Children's Bureau, London.

Deakin, N. (1982). *A voice for all children.* An independent committee of inquiry. Bedford Square Press, NCVO, London.

Department of Health and Social Security (1976). *Fit for the future.* Report of the Committee on Child Health Service. HMSO, London.

Department of Health and Social Security (1980). *Prevention in the child health service.* HMSO, London.

Department of Health and Social Security (1981). The collection of data relating to adverse reactions to pertussis vaccine. In *Whooping cough: Reports from the Committee on Safety of Medicines and the Joint Committee on Vaccination and Immunisation,* p. 27. HMSO, London.

Department of Health and Social Security (1982a). *Report of Birth Notifications 1981.* Form 27/1.

Douglas, J. (1964). *The home and the school.* MacGibbon and Kee, London.

Emery, J.L. (1981). Cot deaths. The current situation and the role of the health visitor today. *Health Visitor* **54**, 318.

Falkner, F. (ed.) (1980). *Prevention in childhood of health problems in adult life.* WHO, Geneva.

Falkner, F. and Tanner, J.M. (1978). *Human growth,* Vols. 1–3. Baillière Tindall, London.

Fogelman, K. (1976). Britain's sixteen-year-olds. Preliminary findings from the third follow-up of the National Child Development Study (1958 cohort). National Children's Bureau Publication, London.

Hall, S.M., Pugh, A.G., and Hall, D.M.S. (1982). Vision screening in the under 5s. *Br. Med. J.* **285**, 1096.

Hellier, J. (1977). Perinatal mortality, 1950 and 1973. *Population Trends* **9**, 13.

Hoffman, H.J., Stark, C.R., Lundin, F.E., and Ashbrook, J.D. (1974). Analysis of birthweight, gestational age, and fetal viability, U.S. births 1968. *Obstet. Gynecol. Survey* **29**, 651.

Home Office Advisory Group on Child Care (1970). *Care and treatment in a planned environment. A report on the Community Homes Project.* HMSO, London.

Jackson, R.H. (1977). *Children, the environment and accidents.* Pitman Medical, London.

Leeder, S.R. and Holland, W.W. (1978). The influence of the environment on disease and growth in children. In *Recent advances in community medicine I* (ed. A.E. Bennet), p. 133. Churchill Livingstone, Edinburgh.

Nietupska, O. and Harding, N. (1982). Auditory screening of school children: fact or fallacy? *Br. Med. J.* **284**, 717.

Office of Population Censuses and Surveys. *The General Household Survey—annual reports.* HMSO, London.

Office of Population Censuses and Surveys (1981). *Population projections 1975–2015. Population Trends No. 26* (Series PP2 No. 7). OPCS, London.

Office of Population Censuses and Surveys (1982a). *Mortality statistics. Perinatal and infant: social and biological factors.* (DH3 No. 7). HMSO, London.

Office of Population Censuses and Surveys (1982b). *Sudden infant death syndrome, 1979 and 1980.* (Monitor DH3 82/1). OPCS, London.

Oppe, T. (1967). Risk registers for babies. *Dev. Med. Child Neurol.* **9**, 13.

Royal College of General Practitioners (1982). Healthier Children – thinking prevention. Report of a Working Party appointed by the Council of the Royal College of General Practitioners, London.

Scottish Home and Health Department (1973). *Towards an integrated child health service.* HMSO, Edinburgh.

Scottish Home and Health Department and Scottish Education Department (1980a). *Vulnerable families.* HMSO, Edinburgh.

Scottish Home and Health Department and Scottish Education Department (1980b). *Towards better health care for school children in Scotland.* HMSO, Edinburgh.

Stewart, G.T. (1972). *Trends in epidemiology,* p. 379. Thomas, Springfield, Ill.

Tanner, J.M. (1978). Foetus into man. *Physical growth from conception to maturity,* p. 150. Open Books Publishing, London.

Taylor, E.M. and Emery, J.L. (1982). Two-year study of the causes of postperinatal deaths classified in terms of preventability. *Arch. Dis. Child.* **57**, 668.

US Department of Health, Education, and Welfare (1971). *Vital and Health Statistics.* Data from the National Health Survey. Decayed, missing and filled teeth among children. Series No. 11, No. 10. US DHEW, Washington, DC.

US Department of Health, Education, and Welfare (1973). *Vital and health statistics. Blood pressure levels of children 6–11 years. Data from the National Health Survey. Relationship to Age, Sex, Race and Socio-economic Status.* Series 11, No. 135. US DHEW, Washington, DC.

Walker, C.H.M. (1982). Child health records and computing. *Br.*

Med. J. **285**, 1671.

Weatherall, J.A.C. (1978). Congenital malformations: surveillance and reporting. *Population Trends* **11**, 27.

World Health Organization (various years). World health statistics annual. WHO, Geneva.

World Health Organization (1966). *Working Group on the early detection and treatment of handicapping defects in young children* WHO, Copenhagen.

World Health Organization (1976a). *New trends and approaches in the delivery of maternal and child care in health service. Sixth Report of the WHO Expert Committee on Maternal and Child Health.* WHO, Geneva.

World Health Organization (1976b). *Immunization programmes for children. Report on a working group with the participation of the international children's centre.* WHO, Copenhagen.

World Health Organization (1978a). *A growth chart for international use in maternal and child health care.* WHO, Geneva.

World Health Organization (1978b). *Manual of the international statistical classification of diseases, injuries and causes of death* (current edition 1978 – ninth revision). WHO, Geneva.

World Health Organization (1978c). *Risk approach for maternal and child health care.* WHO, Geneva.

World Health Organization (1980a). *Towards a better future. Maternal and child health.* WHO, Geneva.

World Health Organization (1980b). *International classification of impairment, disabilities and handicaps.* WHO, Geneva.

Wynne Griffith, G. (1973). The prevention of Down's syndrome (mongolism). *Health Trends* **5**, 59.

19 Adolescents

R.F. Spicer

INTRODUCTION

For the purpose of this chapter adolescence is defined as encompassing the ages of 12 to 22 years. The definition of adolescence, as that age between childhood and adulthood does not offer much information, but if it is seen as a process of movement from a condition of relative dependence upon adults (as parent figures) to one of autonomy, then the characteristics of this group begin to have meaning.

Adolescents suffer to a greater or lesser degree the profound changes taking place within them. The rapid growth in height and changes of body shape, the development of secondary sexual characteristics and onset of the maturation of the sexual organs, and included with this the feelings engendered at this time of sexual fantasies and needs can cause immense emotional upheavals, loss of self value, anxieties, and confusion. The development of intellectual critical faculties, concommitant with the need to throw off parental values, while, at the same time needing to preserve to an extent, a relationship with the parents can cause pain, anger, and anxiety in both parent and child.

The need to accept autonomy and find a way to develop a life-style, career, or job and the uncertainty of self-identification can cause despair and alternating moods of independence and dependency.

The erratic alternation of childhood feelings and those more mature, can be highly disturbing—as though the adolescent longs to put childhood behind yet mourns the loss of this state.

Adolescents lack experience and frequently have a profound distrust of adults and of themselves. They find it difficult to take responsibility for actions, yet fight hard to achieve freedom. Because of lack of experience, they frequently attempt false solutions, and experiment with methods of behaving and living that cause pain to themselves and others. They are, while difficult to live with and work with, at the same time beset by doubts and are, in fact, more susceptible to pressures from without than they would admit. The peer group and the media can, for example, exert great pressure upon them which adolescents frequently find difficult to resist.

The contrariness of adolescents is notorious: they are hypochondriacal yet mistrust doctors; they need support and collaboration from parents and teachers but go out of their way to make this difficult.

Their inadequate understanding of the self, unease in public, and difficulties over making relationships are well known, so too are the aggressive and violent acts that may occur, delinquency, and bad behaviour. Some of the false solutions to their unease are seen in various cults they join and the odd clothes and hair styles they may display. More serious, however, both to them and to society, are the less ordinary ways of attempting solutions. These include the following:

1. The taking of too much alcohol, the use of drugs, and solvent abuse.
2. Delinquency and aggressive behaviour.
3. Running away from home and drifting.
4. Promiscuous sexual behaviour, pregnancy, and venereal disease.
5. Depression or anxiety and inability to work or study.
6. Withdrawal from relationships and loneliness.
7. Risking life by fast driving of motor vehicles.
8. Anorexia and other disorders of feeding.
9. Drug overdose and attempted suicide.

The fact that adolescents are relatively healthy, though often hypochondriacal, does not mean that they do not come to the notice of health authorities. The casualty rate of adolescents on many indices is high. On the other hand, their mistrust of adults may make it difficult for them to seek help unless special provisions are made for them. Their behaviour in hospital and the special facilities that may be needed in the hospital is not a part of this chapter, but the community resources available to them and necessary for them if we are to serve their needs, prevent some of their disorders, and help them through the storms of adolescence, is the theme of this chapter.

Some of the difficulties the young encounter are discussed and ways in which these may be modified are described. The changes of attitudes which have taken place in the last 20 years for making provision for the young are examined, dealing specifically with the following areas:

1. *Educational needs:* the changing role of teachers, school nurses and doctors, sex education in school, special

problems of learning and behaviour, pastoral care, and counselling.

2. *The family:* problems of marital stress and breakdown, results upon adolescents including traffic accidents. Relationship problems with parents.

3. *Special problems of the young:* (a) Delinquency—treatment or punishment? Methods of caring for young offenders. (b) Sexual difficulties—changing attitudes toward sexual experience; problems of sexual identity and behaviour; 'age of consent'; contraception, pregnancy, abortion and single parent families; sexual problems; sexual abuse; venereal disease. (c) Alcohol, drug, and solvent abuse—related to adolescent problems, overdosage, drug addiction. (d) Other problems of adolescents—confusion, loneliness, false solutions to unhappy feelings, unemployment, depression, etc.

4. *Development of special services for young people:* youth clubs, student counselling, 'drop-in' centres, funding, aims and objects, differences in style, the use of volunteers, training of staff, liaison with other organizations, offering of information, advice, and counselling.

5. *Conclusion:* need for variety of services including 'drop-in' centres.

EDUCATIONAL NEEDS

In an 'open' and complex society such as exists now, especially in urban areas, adolescents may present with a number of problems associated with school, ranging from learning problems, behaviour and non-attendance, to depressive feelings, withdrawal, loneliness, drug and alcohol excesses and the like.

Changes in the role of teachers

School staff now accept, in the main, the change that has taken place in their role. Teachers recognize that the child in school is learning not only the facts and information available in the classroom setting, but also social behaviour and attitudes towards relationships. Teachers frequently have to deal with problems as presented by children which though not primarily to do with learning and behaviour yet affect their capacity to study and join in the activities of the school. School populations are now far more mixed than in the past—children having differing ability, social class, ethnic origins, and religious beliefs now attend the same schools. The more old-fashioned methods of assuming, for instance, a Christian background and roughly comparable standards of discipline and behaviour at home, has given way to an acceptance of a mixed society with far more variability of attitudes and ethics. The school, as a part of this mixed society, has had to modify its own methods of teaching to meet the needs of young people. In an open society it becomes more important to develop an understanding of controls in the individual now that external controls of a static and more rigid society have to a great extent disappeared.

Changes in curriculum

Most schools, therefore, both primary and secondary, now include in the curriculum classes which examine society, behaviour, personal relationships, and sexuality. Many schools have classes which also teach child development, health education, and child care, and include the physiology of sex, reproduction, and contraception. The teaching of these subjects is very uneven in Britain (Farrell 1978). In single-sex boys' schools it is very infrequent and in many schools is offered only to the non-academic pupils.

Sex education

There has been a good deal of discussion as to the content of sex education in schools, but most schools accept that there is a need for this subject to be taught. Young people themselves are in no doubt. They are aware of their own ignorance, confusion, and anxiety over their developing sexuality. Parents often find it hard to talk to their children and the adolescent, in any case, may find it hard to confide in parents. Adolescents want to learn and understand far more than the physiology of sex and reproduction. They want to find out about matters that interest and concern them personally. They ask, if given a chance, about masturbation, 'wet dreams', homosexuality, abortion, venereal disease, abnormal pregnancies and child births, and infertility. They also long to discuss attitudes towards sexual behaviour before marriage and the deep and powerful feelings they have about sex, love, and personal relationships, and, particularly, to understand the opposite sex better (Committee on Child Health Services 1977).

Informative lessons can be given in a class-room setting, but the more intimate and personal exchange of feelings can only be done effectively in small groups if young people are to gain an understanding of the self and take responsibility for their own actions. It is essential that the group leader has an understanding of group techniques, because the task is different from that of normal teaching. The teacher has to enable the members of the group to come to their own conclusions, neither force his or her own attitudes nor opinions upon them, nor be dismayed if they differ. Nor must he or she so identify with teenage culture, that the teacher abnegates his or her own values in order to appear to be young and modern. The taking of groups of young people is not, therefore, a task that should be undertaken without experience, understanding, and training. In some schools people are brought in from outside to run these groups, but this is not necessarily a good decision.

Problems in schooling—some solutions

Some children find it quite impossible to make appropriate use of schooling. Apart from the special provisions made for the physically and educationally handicapped young person, the 1981 Education Act now includes, in Special Educational Provision, the use of 'on site' and 'off site' special 'nurture' units for young people who either do not attend school or who are disruptive or unable to study. The schools for maladjusted children still continue (Warnock Committee–Department of Education and Science 1976).

Whilst some adolescents express their difficulties in violent, disruptive behaviour others can, if given the opportunity, share their problems with a member of staff. The organization of pastoral services within schools has changed considerably over the last 10 or 15 years. Many schools now make use of trained counsellors who may also have a teaching commitment. Education Welfare Officers and, in some schools, social workers, may also play a part. There has been discussion concerning the role of the school doctor and school nurse in this respect (Committee on Child Health Services 1977). In some schools either both of these members of the medical team play a part to a greater or lesser extent in dealing with the psychological and social problems of adolescent schoolchildren.The writer believes that school nurses and doctors should receive additional training in the problems of adolescence and should become involved in the organization of pastoral services in schools. There has been a move in some areas for staff to receive greater support and training either by a psychological or some other consultant, to assist them in dealing with the problems that arise in their students. Some young people can talk about their problems to a trusted member of staff, but there are always anxieties of confidentiality, and a school counselling service should be planned and undertaken with the full support and understanding of all staff members.

Special problems

Because adolescents take so much note of peer group behaviour and resist adult norms, and because so much of their time is spent in school, a great number of problems are acted out in school or come to the notice of staff. Apart from noisy and aggressive behaviour and delinquency, adolescents also exhibit the results of solvent abuse and the taking of drugs and alcohol. Outbreaks of this kind of behaviour need to be handled very carefully. There are now several organizations in the UK set up to offer advice on the techniques for coping with group, rather than individual health education (for example, Tacade, Health Education Council).

The school staff team

The primary function of the school is to educate. Any problem that affects a young person's ability to gain from an education is the responsibility of the school. The school itself can offer opportunities for development of potential in young people, and can be sensitive to their needs. If a young person has personality problems expressed in disruptive behaviour which damages the ability of other youngsters to study in peace, then this must be stopped. At the same time, by being sensitive to the confusion which is within some youngsters, the school staff can offer a framework within which this confusion may be ameliorated or, at least, accepted. Teachers, education welfare officers, school doctors and nurses, counsellors, and social workers all have a role in the primary care and education of the students. The link with general practitioner and social services, for instance, must be of trust, while confidentiality is preserved. The organization of the methods of collaboration with parents is an essential part of the school. Adolescents, in their struggle toward adulthood may make the task of collaboration very difficult. They often attempt to split the school from the parent, and can make it hard for either or both, and while confidentiality is important, it is essential that the school and parents work together so long as the adolescent knows what is happening.

However, some adolescents need to talk about problems with someone absolutely separate from family, who is not committed to informing the family as might be the case in school. It is for this reason that there is a need for services outside the school and outside the family doctor's ambience (Committee on Child Health Services 1977).

THE FAMILY

Stress within the family

Adolescents can cause a good deal of anguish and anger at home. The need to gain autonomy can force them into overt or covert battles which are extremely difficult to handle. At the same time, the adolescent may be experiencing severe conflict between parents. A very high proportion of youngsters are brought up in one parent families or are experiencing the tensions of disturbed parental relationships. An unhappy parent can make it extremely difficult for an adolescent to gain independence, almost forcing the adolescent to adopt the parent role. Three-quarters of all divorces involve children under 16 years of age. The after effects of divorce have been studied. The National Children's Bureau (1972) Child Development Study, in the UK, found that children, especially boys, suffer though Douglas (1970) stresses that a good deal of the behaviour problems come from the stormy parental relationship anteceding the divorce. It is important for boys and girls to have access to their fathers. The divorce statistics in Britain show a steep increase since 1969, and so do the statistics for one parent families either by separation or illegitimacy (OPCS monitor). A number of young people do not live in either a complete or a one-parent family. The number of children in care in Britain in 1978–79 was 95 089, of which 56 459 were boys and 38 629 girls. The stresses, therefore, of family life, coupled with the internal and inevitable stress of adolescence combine to make this stage of life a turbulent one. Young people have a healthy capacity to deal with stress and in the main, mature fairly well and cope to a remarkable degree, but there are casualties.

Results of adolescent stress

Almost half of all male deaths between the ages of 15 and 24 years are caused by road accidents and the largest added factor in these casualities is alcohol (Blenerhasset Report –Department of the Environment 1976). At a large specialist hospital for spinal injuries in Stoke Mandeville, England, over half of all accidents involving men 15–24 years of age are road accidents and 25 per cent of the total are motor cycle accidents. Most of these young men are under 20 years, and at least 25 per cent of the total intake to the hospital are between the ages of 16 and 20 years. The intake include, as well as road accidents, sports injuries from diving, rugby football, and horse riding for example. The management of these severely injured young people is very difficult. The aggression and turbulence they show is, of course, partly due to the appalling injuries they have sustained, but it is also observable that many of them had had an accident at a time of particular stress during their adolescence. Young people, and men in particular, have to encounter danger and test their bodies, skills, and courage to the utmost, but some of the casualties could be prevented, perhaps, by paying more heed to the underlying stress that may be present in some of them.

Problems for parents

Some parents find it very difficult to cope with the behaviour of their adolescent children. The attitudes of young people may be very different from those of 20 years ago. Young people can be apparently rebellious, uncaring, lazy, uncooperative, and very bad mannered. They can also exhibit a good deal of unhappiness, anxiety, and withdrawal. Handling adolescents is not easy. Parents discuss the problems of their children with teachers, general practitioners, health visitors, and clergy, they write to various magazines and visit Advice Bureaux. It is therefore more and more necessary for those people in the front line to be trained better to deal with these problems. Gradually school doctors and nurses, family doctors, and health visitors are gaining more understanding of parents' problems. In the discussion document *'Marriage Matters'* (Home Office, 1979), aimed primarily to examine the problems of marriage, it was pointed out that people in trouble knock on many doors, and emphasized the need for training in human relationships and some degree of counselling techniques for those people in the primary health care team and for other professionals to whom troubled people turn.

SPECIAL PROBLEMS OF YOUNG PEOPLE

Delinquency and aggressive behaviour

That there has been a rise in crime is undoubted. The types of crime committed have also changed in that there are more aggressive acts against the person recorded.

Social causes of delinquency

The majority of crimes are committed by young people under 21 years of age of which a very high proportion are boys. A good deal of research has been done in an effort to discover the causes of delinquency and hence to find ways to prevent and to 'cure' it (West 1982). Recognizing that criminal acts are more likely to occur in boys who come from particular groups in society and who attend particular schools, the British Children and Young Persons Act, 1969, made an attempt to treat young criminals not just as offenders, but as children in need. A high preponderance of

delinquents attending Juvenile Court come from large families (five or more), from families with small incomes and from families whose father is either absent by reason of work or a broken marriage, or who is himself delinquent.

Methods of treatment

The educational level of these youngsters is lower than average and they are likely to come from high-density urban areas. They have little sense of right or wrong, little self-esteem, little parental guidance and few opportunities for self expression either verbally or physically. Apart from fining them money, most of the plans made for delinquents are aimed to increase their social competence and to develop internal controls over their own behaviour. Supervision by a social worker of probation officer, may include an intermediate treatment order aimed to offer the young person opportunities to develop these skills. The order might include joining discussion groups, special school facilities, projects involving mountain climbing and canoeing for example, or the driving and maintenance of cars under strict supervision. The aim of the treatment would be to keep young persons in their own environment rather than to take them away from home.

If, however, offences continued, then the court would need to consider a fairly short term in confinement (detention centre), a care order, or, in the last resort, for older boys, particularly where offences against the person were concerned, a Borstal sentence which combines what is, in effect, imprisonment with some degree of training and is, at present, of indeterminate length. There is a good deal of evidence that neither detention centre nor Borstal improves the behaviour of young people, so that on the whole, it can only be seen as a punishment, though many Borstals do offer considerable opportunities for training programmes and for psychological treatment programmes. The care order deprives the parent of his or her rights over the child, authority being placed in the hands of the local authority social services. After assessment, the child is usually placed in a community home, which may provide education, or is fostered with a family especially selected and supported by the social services. The care order is designed to give a child an opportunity to gain, by living with other young people and the residential staff, an opportunity to create a new life and attitudes. A new act came into law in 1983, which has made certain modifications.

Since the 1969 Act, a care order can be made for many reasons, not simply in cases of delinquency. Young children are made subjects of an order if parents for one reason or another are not deemed to be looking after them appropriately. Older children can be given care orders if they are beyond the control of their parent and/or in moral danger. Included in this group would be the children who will not or cannot attend school regularly.

Some children, therefore, are not so much behaving delinquently as showing stress in ways which break a civil law or cause parents to feel helpless to deal with them. There are, among children brought to court for non-attendance at school or for delinquent acts, those who are expressing their difficulties in this way in order to gain help (the neurotic response) though the greater proportion of delinquent acts—taking cars, stealing, snatching handbags, attacks upon others, can be seen as delinquent *per se*. It is a characteristic of adolescents that they find it hard to control emotions and to accept external limits. Some young people in care though needing the regimen of childrens homes, constantly run away or make life so difficult that they are excluded. Occasionally it would seem appropriate to place a person of this kind in a closed unit from which he or she cannot run. The control then passes to the care worker who can prevent the young person from escaping from his or her difficulties and can gradually help him or her to see the need for inner control (Clarke and Cornish 1975).

A growing number of community homes are being established with a therapeutic aim, and with a good deal of decision making being placed with the adolescent, including the selection of new inmates. This would seem a most hopeful step, encouraging young people to take responsibility for the running of the home and for their own decisions.

Community homes include a number of youngsters who have not offended at all but who for various reasons, have no appropriate home to live in. In this way the stigma of the old 'approved school' set up solely to deal with delinquents is now being eradicated.

The residential and day care provisions for disturbed adolescents run as part of the health service provide another source of treatment which serves the general population and are not set up to receive young people in care, but those who, recognizing they have a problem and need help of a certain kind, voluntarily attend. A number of young people in these units may be delinquent, but not necessarily so.

A child who has received very little of the care and affection now recognized as being an essential ingredient for healthy adulthood, may need considerable and long-term treatment. Simply changing his or her environment may not be effective, though it is tempting to assume it could be. The staff of community homes are not yet highly enough considered to have sufficient training and status to do a very difficult job really effectively.

Sexual

The need for sex education in schools was discussed very briefly and it was suggested that young people need far more than education in the facts of reproduction. They need to be able to find a way to understand and handle their own sexuality and to gain some confidence in relating to others.

The impact of developing sexual awareness upon the individual can be very profound. The manner in which a young person copes with sexual drives and moves toward maturity depends upon his or her previous childhood experience and the present situation at home, and in the greater society. The norms of behaviour in society are extremely varied; considerable changes have taken place over the last 50 years. The moral values of parents and grandparents are likely to be at variance with those of the peer group. The confusion in the minds of adults and young

people has made it difficult for parents as well as children. The relaxation from the intensely puritanical attitudes put forward as being the norm in the last century, has given way to a very healthy acceptance of the normality of sexual enjoyment and a reduction in the taboos which frequently caused great unhappiness in marriage and which went some way toward perpetuating the 'dual standard' of men who divided women into the 'good and pure' whom one married and the 'bad and impure' (though pleasure giving) whom one did not. The development of safe contraceptive methods has played a part in the changes in sexual behaviour. However, the increase in sexual relations has also caused considerable use being made in advertising and so on of sexual attractiveness as being a necessary part of successful life and has taken away some of the protections that adolescents may crave for.

Children growing up now have several tasks: they have to throw off attachment to parents and to gain personal autonomy in order to relate successfully. If the child has had very little normal and healthy family life in infancy and childhood, then the development of sexual identity and the capacity to relate to others is diminished. If, at the time of adolescence, the child is placed in a family, either complete or incomplete, where attachment to one or other parent is either over intense, lacking, or violent, then sexual identity is difficult to achieve. The child may respond to the stresses of the situations at home by withdrawal into a state of relative or actual impotence, or into intense sexual activity either in defiance of parental controls or in an unconscious effort to appease or separate from parents. If children are so deprived of affection and love that they cannot find self-esteem, they may seek sexual partners to gain this, or to gain comfort and recognition.

In Britain, the age of consent to intercourse for girls is 16 years. If, as is likely, at least one in eight of girls has first intercourse before this age (Farrell 1978; and also personal findings) then decisions have to be made, first, as to whether to change the law and, secondly, as to society's attitude to the provision of contraception of the young.

The age of consent

This varies in different countries. In Britain as mentioned it is 16 years (which also is the age permitted for marriage with parental consent). There have been many discussions concerning the changing of this law. The Joint Working Party (1979) that produced the document *Pregnant at School* recommended that the law be rescinded and other laws relied upon to protect the young. It based its decision first upon the recognition that one in eight of young people have sex before the age of 16 years and upon the fact that it may be that youngsters do not use contraception partly because of their anxiety over the legal difficulties or that there will be refusal or anger on the part of physicians. It is unlikely that the age of consent will change in the near future, and the Department of Health and Social Security has offered guidelines to physicians in Britain as to how to respond to requests for contraception by girls under 16 years. The Department accepts that it may be in the best interests of the youngster to provide contraception, but stresses the advisability wherever possible, of gaining co-operation from the parents. The guidelines go on to suggest that special facilities should be available to young people where counselling is offered in an atmosphere that is friendly and relaxed (and separate from clinics attended by adults), and that doctors and nurses working with young people should have special knowledge of adolescents.

In spite of sex education in schools and in spite of the availability of contraceptives, young people still get pregnant. There has been a good deal of research both in Britain and America, as to the reasons for this, some of which is quoted in the document *Pregnant at School*. It seems that children brought up in large, perhaps non-caring families, particularly if another child has had an extramarital conception, get pregnant more often. In the writer's experience, deprived youngsters may see pregnancy as a means of obtaining love or status or as an alternative to meaningless schooling. Pregnancy may also occur if the boy–girl relationship is not very open, preventing discussion about contraception, if taboos on sex are high or, sometimes, as a response to stresses at home particularly with the mother.

Of the 12 049 pregnancies in girls of 16 years and under in England and Wales in 1977, more than half were dealt with by medical termination. Far fewer young girls now marry because of pregnancies and far fewer have the child and place it for adoption. The education of pregnant schoolgirls and schoolgirl mothers is often very poor. Many girls who become pregnant have been poor school attenders in any case, but very many never return to schooling. There are many interesting educational projects in America and also in Britain. In these projects girls are helped in childcare and also in general education. The report *Pregnant at school* makes a strong plea for girls to be enabled to return to school after the birth of the baby and points out that the putative fathers are generally in a fairly close relationship with the girls but are given very little say in helping with the problem.

Financially, one-parent families and particularly schoolgirls, are very badly off; housing is poor and opportunities to mix with other people is limited by circumstances. The health of schoolgirl mothers is worse than average, and the morbidity and mortality rates of the babies is higher, partly perhaps, due to poor attendance at antenatal clinics. There would seem to be a clear case for offering special facilities for pregnant girls so that they can receive adequate care separate from adult women. In a survey of schools undertaken by the working party, it became clear that policies vary a good deal throughout Britain. Some schools enable pregnant girls to continue to attend classes and offer counselling to parents and children, others still reject the girls. In some instances, special classes are provided off site for pregnant girls and girls with babies, and opportunities are given to attend antenatal clinics.

After the baby is born, if it is not placed for adoption, a number of young mothers will stay with the grandmother. It is very important for a health visitor to assist both generations to work out a programme that enables the baby's mother to take increasing responsibility for her child.

In those cases where single young parents become homeless, there is priority in housing, but the plight of the young person, thrown into a situation that may be intensely lonely, can cause a number of breakdowns in mother–child relationships and frequently the placing of the baby in care. It is recommended that guidelines should be prepared so that schools can respond to schoolgirl pregnancies in a parallel manner, co-ordinating counselling and parent liaison, schooling programmes, and health care during pregnancies. After the baby is born is it recommended that especial care is given to the young mother to sort out problems of housing and finance, educational needs and, in school leavers, to encourage the development of young mother and baby day centres in order to assist in education in baby care and to prevent the sense of loneliness that many young single-parent families suffer. Health visitors and social workers can combine with doctors in the primary health care team to provide service of this kind.

Contraception and pregnancy counselling

The ability of an adolescent to take responsibility for her sexual life depends, apart from the stability of her personality and the reasons for embarking upon active sex, upon her maturity. It is very difficult for a very young girl to recognize that a sexual encounter may produce a pregnancy, that sex may happen more than once, and that there is a necessity to use effective contraception and use it regularly. Some young people are very ignorant of the biology of reproduction as Farrell (1978) discovered, but many of them, knowing the facts, still risk a pregnancy. It is therefore, essential that young people are educated, not only in the facts of contraception, but also so that they can know where to obtain supplies, can know that they will be given a welcome, and can also be able to discuss fully with a doctor, the implications of their decision.

Young people do not find it easy to use their family doctor, believing, rightly or wrongly, that there will be a lack of confidentiality, or that at the surgery they will meet people who know their parents. Many young people do use the family doctor, but facilities should be available elsewhere as well, set up specifically for the young. At the London Youth Advisory Centre, a young person is given plenty of time to talk about herself, encouraged to bring her boyfriend if she wishes, and seen if it seems appropriate, at least once a month. With the help and guidance of the doctor the young person is encouraged to take increasing responsibility for her behaviour and in moving toward adulthood, to continue to use her contraceptive method properly. The reasons for giving up contraception are frequently very cloudy, there may be a separation from the boyfriend, and perhaps a reuniting later; frequently there is an inadequate reason given, such as that the method is not suiting the patient, or the 'pill' has been lost. Young people take risks because they are young, and attach their failure to use adequate methods to false and inaccurate reasons.

There is no evidence that the oral contraceptive is harmful to young people once regular menstruation is established and most young people prefer the 'pill', though other methods such as the diaphragm are used as is the male condom. Most doctors agree that the intrauterine device is not the method of choice for young people, bringing as it does extra risks of infection, but a girl who has had repeated abortions and seems unable to maintain any other method, may be best suited to the device.

Pregnancy termination

The decision to terminate a pregnancy should rest with the pregnant girl. Parents and to an extent, social workers of a girl in care, may put great emphasis upon the need for termination, but unless a girl is incapable of making a decision by reason of lack of intelligence or gross immaturity, her wishes should be paramount. Termination of pregnancy in proper circumstances is a safe operation. It is not a part of this chapter to discuss in full the medical problems of termination. It is well known that the operation becomes more difficult and therefore more dangerous after the 10th or 12th week of pregnancy. Every encouragement should therefore be given to girls to admit to a pregnancy as early as is possible and the efficacy of pregnancy testing methods has made it very much simpler.

The decision that has to be made is a difficult one. Young people may make decisions at first based upon inappropriate premises, basing them upon what they view as other peoples' wants or upon unreal judgements as to their own situation. Young people may simply say they do want a baby 'as something to love' or that they don't want a baby 'as I want to have a good time'. Either or both statements may be true but what is characteristic is that they rarely, when very young, can accept the ambivalent feelings they have of wanting/not wanting. It is essential, therefore, to counsel these young people very carefully and to help them in a totally non-judgemental way, to understand the complexity of the decision (Cheetham 1977). People 'get over' termination on the whole very well. Some young people do become depressed afterward and grieve considerably or feel guilty. Some of this is expressed as anxiety about possible infertility. If the decision to terminate has been made lightheartedly, as though not very important, then it is possible that the girl may get pregnant a second or third time—seeing termination as a simple birth-control method which is both medically and psychologically unsound. A termination is an important event and pre- and post-abortion counselling is a necessary part of the decision for all age groups but especially for the young.

Sexual problems

Apart from the decisions to be made by adolescents as to whether to embark upon a sexual life and as to how to prevent conception, there are many other fears and fantasies to be dealt with. Young men may worry about potency, or even be impotent, at any rate at first. They may have many anxieties about homosexual feelings, as may girls; at times their anxiety is not expressed consciously, but fear of sexual difficulties may produce many feelings of loneliness and of being different from others. At times their sexual fears are fairly deeply buried and it is characteristic of both sexes to present to a doctor, either because of shame or non-recognition of the problem, with symptoms removed from it. Young

men may present with hypochondriacal fears or anxieties about acne, backache, tiredness, or, more directly, of having a badly shaped or sized penis. Girls may present with similar complaints and talk about bad or irregular periods, weight gain, or the size of breasts. In later adolescence young people will begin to look at the quality of their relationships and at the quality of intercourse. The recognition of the pleasure of sex for both sexes has enabled young people to be far more open than heretofore, and this is seen in the kind of problem presented to doctors, particularly those working in family planning clinics.

Sexual abuse

It is not known how many young people have been involved in incest or other kinds of sexual abuse. The incidence reported by the police in Britain in 1980 of incest was 312 and of unlawful intercourse with girls under the age of 13 years, 3109 (Criminal Statistics 1981). Recent surveys by Beezley Mrazek (1981) put the figure as between a quarter and a third of all children and adolescents as having had at least one sexual experience with an adult, ranging from exhibitionism to sexual intercourse.

Apart from sexually transmitted diseases, a common consequence, there is a risk of congenital malformation in the offspring, and over one-third of children may be psychiatrically disturbed shortly after the incident, which is understandable. Perhaps more important, over one-half exhibited delayed disturbance. Adult women revealed guilt, negative self-image, mistrust of men, and sexual dysfunction (Forward and Buck 1978).

The effect upon family can also, of course be profound. The need for post-abuse treatment is beginning to be recognized both in the US and in Britain, and prevention, necessitating as it does a greater awareness from people in nurturing roles, should include considerably more openess and understanding of the frequency of sexual abuse.

Venereal disease

Because many young people change partners fairly frequently the risk, in adolescence, of VD is high. Although sex education programmes should not overemphasize the danger of VD, young people should be taught about it and should be encouraged in all ways possible to seek help if there is any suspicion of disease. It is easier to consult a doctor in a friendly place in the first instance, but most hospital departments are now more aware of the need to be open and non-judgemental, and to make it easier for young people to attend.

In spite of what is called the sexual revolution, most 16-year-olds (Fogelman 1976) want a permanent commitment in marriage, and describe their relationship with the other sex as important, affectionate, and steady. They believe in faithfulness and sharing of feelings, and see marriage as based upon equality.

Alcohol, drug, and solvent abuse

Because adolescence is a time for experimentation, the testing of adult attitudes, it is likely that many kinds of behaviour will be, if not intrinsically dangerous, yet frowned upon by adults.

Young people experiment with alcohol, and there is evidence that drunkenness has increased a good deal in the last 15 years. Most teenagers level off their consumption and are not going to become alcoholics, though there has been an increase in adolescent alcoholic addiction. Associated with driving it is a dangerous pursuit; over half of all male deaths between the ages of 15 and 24 years (*Blennerhasset Report*—Department of the Environment 1976) are caused by road accidents and alcohol is well established as the largest factor, as it is in many acts of hooliganism and vandalism and, perhaps, unwanted pregnancy.

Solvent abuse is also very much an adolescent activity; practically all young people grow out of it and as in all these activities that provide pleasure and detachment from worries, the more disturbed and unhappy the adolescent, the more likely he or she is to need the drug, and to find it difficult to give it up. The chief lesson to be learnt about teenage activities of this sort, is the need to be very careful when teaching, not to overemphasize the problems, for there is no doubt that the advertising of the problem by adults, increases the uptake (Monitor 1984).

The indiscriminate use of various drugs can, of course, be immediately dangerous if not necessarily addictive and, among those young people experimenting with drugs, there will inevitably be those who, either from genuine confusion or ignorance, or from deeper psychological problems will take an overdose and need hospital care. Laufer (1975) believes that all cases of a drug overdose are a result of a breakdown in the adolescent. I would agree that all such cases should be taken seriously and that the young person should have appropriate counselling or therapy.

Drug addiction

There has been a rise in the number of drug addicts in Britain. Most addicts are young when they first experiment, and nearly all have already taken a variety of other drugs. The death rate is high, partly because of the differing strengths of the drugs available on the 'black market'. Specialist treatment centres are an essential part of modern medicine.

Other problems of adolescence

It is almost normal for adolescents to be, at times, confused, unhappy, emotional, lonely, and unsure of themselves, and at times, very much the reverse. However, the task of adolescence, that of breaking from parents, discovering the self, including the recognition of sexuality, the making of important personal relationships, and the discovering of a mode of life that suits the individual, is not an easy one in a complex society.

Young people are very much in need of help at times and recognize this. The manner in which they get help varies with their maturity, their background, and the nature of the problem.

Some adolescents, as I have suggested, escape their feelings of anxiety, depression, or anger by delinquent or aggressive acts which bring them to the notice of the authorities. Some run away from home and escape to the larger cities, hoping to find freedom and independence but, frequently, only find life even harder. Remaining at home and having it out with parents, while devastating at times, gives some hope of growth, but running away does not.

Some adolescents get pregnant and/or marry. The marital breakdown rate of men and women marrying before the age of 24 years is very high (Home Office 1979). The couples are confused, not only by money problems and by their own immaturity, but, often with the internal difficulties present before the marriage which may have forced them into such precipitate action.

In the last few years, there has been a deteriorating economical situation in most countries. No longer can young people cheerfully leave school and know that they can drift around, earning good wages, working and then relaxing, changing jobs, until finally they settle. Very many young people will not be able to find a job at all. Even those who reach higher education and obtain diplomas or degrees may be out of work for a very long time. If our culture has set so much store on material goods and position in the world as signs of success and value, then young people bereft of money and of jobs, have little to help them gain self-esteem. However, the ability to relate happily to other people is not entirely to do with jobs and money. Young people can be very shy and lonely, and unsure of themselves in any case.

They can also become clinically very depressed and suicidal, or anxious and hysterical. They can, as I have suggested, attempt to solve their problems by false solutions, such as getting pregnant, taking to alcohol or drugs, driving too fast and dangerously, or withdrawing into solitude.

On the whole adolescents get through these crises fairly well, though some do not. Because adolescence is a troublesome time, and because modern living sets particular problems to them, various methods are being employed to try to assist them and to prevent the casualties of adolescence.

THE DEVELOPMENT OF SPECIAL SERVICES FOR YOUNG PEOPLE

I have already briefly mentioned the development within the school of pastoral care and counselling, and of the changing roles of teachers, school nurses, and doctors.

Within the Youth Service changes are also taking place. The *Youth Service Review* (DES 1982), recently published, makes a very strong plea for accepting the needs of young people for advice, information, and counselling, and strongly recommends an increase in counselling centres within and outside the service. The early activities of 'street corner' detached youth workers showed that young, unattached youth could be helped outside the more formal youth clubs. The Youth Service, as will be shown later in this chapter, has made a large contribution toward the development of facilities for the young.

Child guidance clinics have, and will continue to have, a place in the treatment of disturbed youngsters, but adolescents, as I have described, halfway between childhood and adulthood, do not necessarily fit into such clinics. Therefore, separate provision has to be made for them if they are to be helped through some of their difficulties.

Universities and colleges of higher and further education have developed their own medical and counselling services. It has been recognized for some time that students can experience problems in adapting to student life, and in studying, and that it is essential to pay attention to the need of students if they are not to drop out of college or break down. Some industries have accepted that the shift from school to work can be difficult for young people and have enabled factory doctors and personnel to provide added support to new young workers (Court Report—Committee on Child Health Services 1977).

Over the last 20 years or so there has been in addition to this, a very rapid expansion of what are described as 'drop in' centres for the young. The aims and objects, the staffing, and funding of these centres are variable, but what is characteristic of them all is that they are set up specifically to attract young people who can attend without special referral and for a variety of reasons.

The Court Report emphasizes, along with recommendations for caring for schoolchildren, that there should be special provisions for young people who need contraceptive advice and help over psychosexual problems, and also for those with other health, social and psychological problems.

The WHO, in a report of a working group in 1977, has recognized the need for special facilities for the young and examined the various types of services set up for them. The report also emphasizes the need for a common conceptual framework in which local facilities for youth are co-ordinated which requires, of course, the development of strategies to facilitate collaboration and shared training schemes.

In a report written for the British Department of Health and Social Security (Tyler 1978), various types of counselling and advisory services for young people were examined and it was pointed out that, though there is evidence that the services are well used for a number of problems and particularly at times of crisis, yet it would be impossible to provide statistical evidence of their value, nor to know the savings in cost to the State of young people who would otherwise suffer medical, psychiatric, or delinquency problems. Tyler points out also that services cannot be standardized, partly because different areas have different needs.

Bennett (1982) describes the world-wide problems in the delivery of adolescent health care and makes a strong plea for the proper training of health personnel to deal with this very vulnerable group.

The provision of services specifically aimed toward young people is relatively new. In Britain the first services were set up in 1961. The idea of innovating services of this kind took some time to develop, and it was not until 1970 that they became relatively common.

The greater proportion of these services were set up as voluntary organizations though a considerable number were partly, at least, funded by a local authority or the National Health Service. However, most of them have considerable autonomy and it is, perhaps, an advantage in new innovatory projects that this should be so to enable a flexible approach to the work to be made.

Some of the services were set up to provide for specific needs. These would include the provision of contraception and pregnancy and psychosexual counselling; advice and help over drug problems, both legal advice and treatment; help for drifting and homeless young people; information services, career, job, leisure activities, and legal advice. Some would be broader in approach and give a generalized service.

There has been, in addition to actual centres, an increase in the awareness of the media of the needs of adolescents. There is a growing number of magazines aimed specifically at the young, which include articles dealing with various problems and invite correspondence. The number of radio and television programmes aimed at young people has increased and radio 'phone ins' constantly deal with their problems. The London based 'Capital Radio' has specific 'Help Lines' that young people use a good deal and offers help both over the phone and at headquarters upon matters of work, as well as of housing, loneliness, sexual problems, and so on. Specialist organizations also utilize phone lines. There is a specialist phone line for homosexuals for example. The 'Samaritans' who have a network throughout Britain deal with a number of telephone calls from unhappy or frightened young people.

Youth counselling and advisory services now exist though patchily, throughout Britain and throughout Europe (WHO 1977). Apart from the specialist ones already described, the majority attempt to be available to young people and assist them whatever their problem might be or to refer them to specialist organizations.

In Britain, some of these services have been established by the Youth Service sometimes in collaboration with the local authority. In other cases they have been started upon the initiative of the Marriage Guidance Council, or by individuals from a variety of professions, some of whom would come from social services, medicine, and the church, for example. Budgetting has almost always been a problem, as funds and resources have become harder and harder to obtain in a time of recession.

Some of the smaller enterprises failed fairly rapidly. Difficulties over staffing and premises made it impossible to be open for many hours in the week and it is possible that young people did not, therefore, get to know and trust the places sufficiently to use them.

Of the more successful, those that had premises and could be open regularly throughout the week, staffing has varied a good deal. Some services have made good use of volunteers, and by that I mean untrained and frequently unpaid personnel, though all of the units using volunteers have had some kind of support and training scheme for them and have employed at least one trained member of staff. The training of staff varies a good deal. Some of them are social workers, probation officers, and teachers, some are trained counsellors, doctors, nurses, psychotherapists, and analysts. If youth advisory services are to combine the giving of advice and information with counselling, then it is essential that some of the staff be professionally trained.

The National Association of Young People's Counselling and Advisory Services (NAYPCAS) has been established in Britain as a central information resource for counselling centres. Organizations wishing to establish new centres, to receive information on training, or to liaise with other centres, can use the services of NAYPCAS. The British Association of Counselling, also set up fairly recently, as well as offering a forum for people working as counsellors in many different situations has been putting a good deal of thought into establishing a code of good practice for counsellors and standards of training.

There are now a fair number of training courses for counsellors and psychotherapists; some of both these groups will be working with adolescents.

There are no courses specifically designed for doctors or nurses. The specialist training courses in psychiatry do not necessarily offer training in counselling the young. General practitioners can obtain a deeper understanding of the psychological needs of their patients by joining what are often called 'Balint' groups, after the name of the original founder. School doctors, however, have no special training in dealing with the problems of the young. Doctors and nurses working in family planning clinics can obtain a specialist training in dealing with psychosexual problems and health visitors do have some training in handling of the dynamics of family life. Doctors and nurses who wish to work with adolescents have, therefore, to join multidisciplinary training schemes or pick up knowledge as they go along. Very few youth counselling centres employ doctors, though some have doctors attending part-time for contraceptive advice and general counselling.

The London Youth Advisory Centre (LYAC) was started in 1968 by the writer for several reasons. Earlier in 1961, the writer had established what ultimately became the Brook Advisory Centre (BAC) set up to provide contraception to young unmarried girls. But it became clear that sexual difficulties represented only a part of the problems experienced by young people. At least 30 per cent of young people attending the centre had other problems to deal with. Young people given the opportunity can discuss their problems and can gain considerable understanding of them. The development therefore, of a more generalized service seemed a logical next step. And the LYAC therefore, offers a service that includes doctors and counsellors. The doctors have come from various backgrounds and trainings. In order better to understand the problems of young people and to consolidate the staff as a team, LYAC has always had the services of a consultant analyst or psychotherapist, who attends once weekly. This 'in-training', which exists in some places for infant welfare centre staff and some group general practices, has immense advantages particularly in view of the lack of training of most staff and the need to review methods of working in any new venture.

It is essential, as the Court Report points out, for all centres of this kind to establish links with other services. There are regular meetings of the LYAC with social workers, health visitors, and teachers, and it is in contact with hospital staff, general practitioners, and other projects in the area dealing with the young.

The young people themselves can call in without referral and can come for any reason, be it for information about housing, legal rights, or medical problems for instance, or for counselling. The problems as presented by the young include:

1. Sexual—contraceptive advice, problems of suspected venereal disease or pregnancy; sexual problems including homosexuality and deviant sexual behaviour.

2. Family—problems of relationships with parents or desire to leave home; difficulties with separating or divorced parents and step-parents.

3. Housing and legal rights.

4. Job difficulties.

5. Problems of relationships, loneliness, depression, and anxiety.

6. Problems with drugs, alcohol, anorexia, and over-feeding.

7. Medical problems particularly acne, menstrual disorders, and anxieties over sexual characteristics.

Parents also visit the centre in order to discuss the behaviour of their offspring. They present with problems of delinquency, of lack of studying, rudeness, aggressiveness, depression, and drugs for example. In reviewing the symptomatology presented in other centres, there is a common pattern to be found in all. Some centres concentrate more on group information and the running of group activities, others, in addition to counselling the young, have a number of young people attending who though presenting in a crisis situation need quite long-term treatment. Hardly any youth counselling centres offer counselling on more than a once-a-week basis, so that any youngster who needs more than this would need to be referred to a hospital day centre or adolescent unit or for psychotherapy. The liaison, therefore, with psychiatrists offering more formal treatment is an essential part of the service acting, as it does, as a primary health care resource. At times a hospital psychiatrist may, however, wish to refer cases to the centre. Some young people suffering from drug overdose, from mild anorexia, or from the after-effects of abortion for example, will be more able to use a centre set up outside the hospital and not, apparently, too closely associated with the aura of illness and medicine.

Apart from hospital referrals, teachers, social workers, health visitors, and general practitioners, also refer cases who would seem to benefit from the once-weekly consultations offered them.

Young people, as has been said, can also come without referral and more than half of the clients are 'self-referred'. Some come upon the advice of friends or of the media, some have heard about the centre from other people.

A counselling and information service relies heavily upon a network of contacts in a community and can offer, in addition to the main work, that of helping adolescents, a support, information, and teaching resource for other professionals. Experience gained by staff working in youth counselling services can be transmitted to other people. They are in a good position to act as consultants to schools and to organize training programmes and support groups for those who work in other ways with young people.

CONCLUSION

In view of the difficulties young people encounter, particularly in urban societies, special provisions are needed to help prevent some of the casualties of this age group and to assist them in moving forward to adulthood without having made too many mistakes.

Although young people will consult their family doctor in times of illness, they do not find it easy to use him for more private problems. They will, if offered the opportunity, speak to teachers and youth leaders and, upon occasion, school nurses and doctors if available.

The development of counselling in schools and youth clubs is a useful move, but after leaving school young people still encounter problems and even while at school they may not wish to discuss their difficulties in the school environment.

Health visitors are in a good position to assist in health-education programmes and to work with parents, but up till now they have not had much experience with adolescents.

Young people's counselling and advisory services, offering confidentiality and pleasant surroundings, be they specialist, that is for contraception and pregnancy counselling, for loneliness or drugs, for example, or generalist, can attract young people and can fill some of the gaps in the present day health, social, and youth services.

The training schemes now being encouraged for counsellors and the added training just being developed for school nurses and doctors, health visitors, teachers, and youth leaders should be encouraged. Support and 'in training' is recommended for those professionals who meet with the young in order that they can deal more sensitively with their problems, and recognize cases of more serious disability and disturbance which need further treatment.

The development for youth-counselling services may highlight the need for more adolescent units (as described in the Court Report) and, as more research is done into the possible causes and treatment of delinquents more trained personnel will be needed to deal with this group. There is also a need for foster parents, hostels and protected housing for those who, perhaps through no fault of their own, are without homes that can give them the support they need.

Young people often feel disregarded and without a voice of their own. Children in care are gradually being given more opportunity to state what they want. It is important that adolescents know their rights as well as their obligations, and services for this age group should be child centred. The Childrens Legal Advice Centre, divorce conciliation centres, adoption societies such as 'Parents for Children' all have this in mind. As has often been said, but often forgotten, the adolescents of today are the adults of tomorrow.

FURTHER READING

Beezley Mrazek, P. (1981). Sexual abuse of children. An annotation. *J. Chld Psychol. Psychiat.* **21**, 91–5.

Bennett. D.C. (1982). Worldwide problems in the delivery of adolescent health care. *Public Health* **96**, 334–9.

Brown, F. (1968). *Prevention of damaging stress in children.* Churchill, London.

Central Statistical Office (1982). *Social Trends* No. 12. HMSO, London.

Cheetham, J. (1977). *Unwanted pregnancy counselling.* Routledge and Kegan Paul, London.

Clarke, R.V.G. and Cornish, D.B. (1975). *Residential treatment and its effects on delinquency.* Home Office Research Study No. 32. HMSO, London.

Committee on Child Health Services (1977). *Fit for the future* (Court Report). HMSO, London.

Committee on Workings of the Abortion Act (1971). *Report* (Lane Report). HMSO, London.

Criminal Statistics (1981). *England and Wales 1980.* HMSO, London.

Department of Education and Science (1976). *Special educational needs. Report of the Warnock Committee of enquiry into the Education of Handicapped Children and Young People.* HMSO, London.

Department of Education and Science (1982). *Youth service review: experience and participation report.* Cmnd 8686. (Chairman A. Thompson). HMSO, London.

Department of the Environment (1976). *Report of the Committee on Drinking and Driving* (Blennerhasset Report). HMSO, London.

Department of Health and Social Security (Statistics and Research Branch (Annual). *Children in Care.* HMSO, London.

Dominion, J. (1968). *Marital breakdown.* Penguin, Harmondsworth.

Douglas, J.W.P. (1970). Broken families and child behaviour. *J. Ry. Coll. Physicians* **4**, 203.

Education Act (1981). HMSO, London.

Farrell, C. (1978). *My mother said . . . they way young people learned about sex and birth control.* Routledge and Kegan Paul, London.

Fogelman, K. (1976). *Britain's 16 year olds.* National Children's Bureau, London.

Foltz, A.M., Klerman, C.W., and Jekel, J.P. (1972). Pregnancy and special education: who stays in school? *Am. J. Publ. Hlth* **62**, 1612–190.

Forward, S. and Buck, C. (1978). *Betrayal of innocence.* Penguin, Harmondsworth.

Home Office (1979). *Marriage matters. Discussion Document of Working Party.* HMSO, London.

Howard, M. (1971). Pregnant schoolgirls. *US J. School Health,* **4**, 361–4.

Joint Working Party on Pregnant Schoolgirls (1979). *Pregnant at school.* National Council for One Parent Families and Community Development Trust, National Council One Parent Families.

Kempe, R.S. and Kempe, C.H. (1978). *Child abuse.* Fontana, London.

Laufer, M. (1975). *Adolescent disturbance and breakdown.* Penguin, Harmondsworth.

Monitor (1984). *Alcohol education syllabus.* Tacade, Manchester.

National Children's Bureau (1972). *National child development study.* NCB, 8 Wakely Street, London EC1.

Office of Population Censuses and Surveys Monitor (various), St. Catherine's House, 10 Kingsway, London W.C.2.

Pugh, G. (1977). *Fostering children with special needs. Some local authority schemes.* National Children's Bureau, London.

Rutter, M. (1970). Sex differences in children's response to family stress. In *The child and his family* (eds. E.J. Antony and C.M. Koupernick). Wiley, London.

Rutter, M. (1971). Parent-child separation: psychological effects on children. *J. Child Psychol. Psychr.* **12**, 233.

Rutter, M. and Madge, N. (1976). *Cycles of disadvantage*. Heinemann, London.

Tyler, M. (1978). *Advisory and counselling services for young people*. HMSO, London.

Watson, J.M. (1981). Solvent abuse: a retrospective study. *Community Medicine* **1,** 153–6.

West, D.H. (1982). *Delinquency, its roots, careers and prospects*. Heinemann, London.

Westman, J.C., Cline, D.W., Swift, W.J., *et al.* (1970). Role of child psychiatry in divorce. *Arch. Gen. Psychiatry,* **23**, 416.

World Health Organization (1977). *Objectives of youth advisory services*. WHO Regional Office for Europe, Copenhagen.

20 Maternity

Ian A. Baker

INTRODUCTION

Reproduction is seen as a normal activity for most parents. Doctors and midwives are aware that not all women will conceive and not all pregnancies will be normal. Professionals in health services endeavour to prevent abnormal pregnancies and, when these attempts fail, to intervene in different ways to achieve as near normal outcomes as possible. To achieve these ends the understanding and co-operation of parents, with whom the ultimate responsibility for reproduction lies, is sought. Parents most often respect the skills of professionals when the need for assistance is obvious and has proved beneficial by previous experience. But they may less readily appreciate the demands made upon them when risks are not obvious and when compliance with screening, monitoring, or delivery procedures appear to be unrelated to comprehensible need. Maternity needs vary with the acquisition of knowledge by parents and with changing social, economic, cultural, and religious circumstances. With these changing perceptions of maternity, doctors and midwives need to know how far they are able to alter the natural history of pregnancy favourably and how far improvements lie beyond their control before resources are invested into new services and parents and society are offered fresh expectations.

During the years 1950 to the mid-1970s crude birth rates fell in all western European countries and period fertility rates declined. Third- and high-order legitimate births declined markedly from the mid-1960s. The estimated completed fertility of women in the birth cohort of 1940 for western European countries ranges from 1.99 in Germany and 2.49 in France (Van de Kaa 1980). The contribution to total fertility of women under 25 years and over 30 years has diminished with the result that smaller families are born in a shorter interval between maternal ages of 25 and 30 years. In association with more widespread contraception and terminations of unwanted pregnancies the proportion of pregnant brides diminished during the 1970s. At the same time there has been a fall in the number of women of marrying age in western Europe and also a change in the number of marriages per 1000 unmarried women aged 15–49 years. Cohabitation and divorce have become more common and this is reflected in illegitimacy rates in Sweden of 32 per cent in 1975 and an increase in similar rates in England and Wales from 8 per cent in 1967 to 12 per cent in 1980. Further changes occurred in the late 1970s with increases in birth rates especially in non-manual compared with manual social classes and between 1977 and 1980 in England and Wales third-order births increased by 24 per cent and fourth-order by 18 per cent.

Whatever maternity needs are generated by these trends health services should attempt to meet them as effectively and efficiently as possible. The contents of this chapter are necessarily assumptions about many of the needs of maternity and of responses within health services to cope with them.

MATERNAL MORTALITY AND MORBIDITY

Maternal mortality has declined dramatically in all developed countries in the past 30 years (Fig. 20.1). In many countries the risk of maternal mortality is now very low in comparison with the major hazards to life for women in the same age group (Table 20.1). Beral (1979) estimates that deaths associated with the adverse effects of oral contraceptives in 1975 were also greater than those occurring in association with pregnancy, delivery, and the puerperium

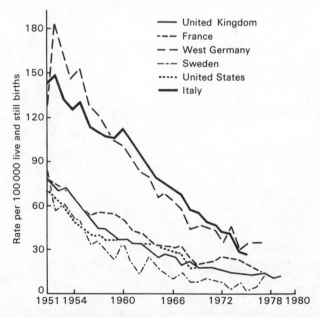

Fig. 20.1. Maternal mortality: international comparison. For 1951 to 1960 inclusive, data relate to Britain only. (Source: Social Trends (1982).)

350

Table 20.1. *Mortality in women aged 15–54 years in England and Wales, 1978 (per million)*

Cause of mortality	Age group (years)			
	15–24	25–34	35–44	45–54
All causes	393	588	1436	4156
Complications of pregnancy, childbirth, and puerperium (ICD 630-678)	6	11	3	1
Motor accidents (ICD 810-819)	103	45	42	53
Accidents. Poisoning–violence (ICD 800-999)	191	156	208	262

combined. She argues that a reproductive mortality rate should be applied to combined maternal deaths from contraception, pregnancy, and abortion. Deaths that do occur in pregnancy and childbirth are subject to confidential enquiry in England and Wales. In the last Report (1976–78), 227 deaths were recorded as directly due to pregnancy and childbirth and 200 deaths were associated with pregnancy of which 97 were indirect obstetric deaths and 103 deaths were fortuitous. The major causes of the true deaths were pulmonary embolism, hypertension, uterine haemorrhage, anaesthesia, ectopic pregnancy, abortion, and sepsis in order of frequency of occurrence. Fifty-eight per cent of the true deaths and 15 per cent of the remainder were associated with 'avoidable' factors according to generally accepted standards of care. The frequency of 'avoidable' factors associated with the true deaths had not changed from the level occurring in the preceding three-year period. Given the variety of causes of death, variable times of occurrence, and the number of avoidable factors, it is difficult to see what policy changes could lead to a significant improvement in mortality rates other than less delegation of care to junior (i.e. trainee-grade) staff. In England in 1980 approximately 70 per cent of doctors engaged in obstetric care were trainees.

Maternal morbidity is less well documented on a population basis. Marked disturbances of mood may occur in around 10 per cent of women postnatally (Kendall *et al.* 1981). These disturbances are associated with a personal or family history of a depressive disorder, a major bereavement in early life, poor mothering in childhood, poor social supports, poor housing, first pregnancy, delivery by caesarean section, a recent concentration of life events, and a high expressed anxiety at the end of pregnancy. These depressive illnesses are usually self-limiting but may damage relationships with the newborn or other members of the family before their course is run. Prevention aims to lessen the secondary impact of the illness on family relations.

SPONTANEOUS ABORTIONS

There is a sizeable number of women who experience a spontaneous abortion following conception. The true rate of conception is difficult to estimate and some women do not realize that a conception and an abortion has taken place. Shapiro *et al.* (1962) estimated the rate of fetal loss to be 142 per 1000 pregnancies with 48 per cent occurring before the 12th week of pregnancy and a further 32 per cent before the 19th week. The overall rate of spontaneous abortion may approach 30 per cent of pregnancies.

The risk of spontaneous abortion appears to increase with age and parity. In the study of Shapiro *et al.* (1962) the risk of spontaneous abortion in primigravida was greatest for those at or over the age of 35 years. Around 5–10 per cent of aborted conceptuses have fetal malformations and it is possible that the factors causing the malformation cause also the abortion (Sentrakul and Potter 1966). Risk of spontaneous abortion has been associated with cigarette smoking (Himmelberger *et al.* 1978) and alcohol consumption (Harlap and Shiono 1980). Women in some occupations as in the chemical industry (Hemminki *et al.* 1980) have a higher risk and paternal exposure to anaesthetic agents (Tomlin 1979) and chemicals like vinyl chloride (Infante *et al.* 1976) also increases the risk for spontaneous abortion. Women who are diabetic have a higher risk for spontaneous abortion (Dekaban and Baird 1955). Infections in the mother like rubella (Sheridan 1964) and toxoplasmosis (Desmonts and Convrens 1974) have been associated with fetal malformation and abortion. Heavy doses of irradiation as that following the nuclear bombing of Japan increased spontaneous abortion rates (Yamazaki *et al.* 1954). Low-dose irradiation to the ovaries before conception has been related to increased spontaneous abortion rates (Alberman *et al.* 1972). The risk of spontaneous abortion is higher in women with previous spontaneous abortions and women who have given birth to malformed babies (Warburton and Fraser 1964). Identification of fetal abnormalities in aborted conceptuses may assist genetic counselling of parents who wish to avoid further pregnancies with risk of fetal malformation. Associations of spontaneous abortions with environmental hazards may indicate preventive possibilities although the timing of the effect of these hazards on the reproductive health of parents may not be clear. Parents who experience spontaneous abortion tend to reproduce more frequently to compensate for the losses of earlier reproduction (Warburton and Fraser 1964).

PERINATAL MORTALITY

Pregnant mothers have expectations for the development and delivery of their babies with minimal disadvantages. Mothers will develop symptoms and anxieties during the course of their pregnancies and be grateful to receive help from midwives and doctors. They will also expect assistance at the time of delivery and with any emergencies that might occur. Midwives and doctors have their own anxieties about the course of pregnancy and delivery in mothers under their care. They seek to minimize adverse developments in the fetus, the rate of stillbirths, preterm delivery, and mortality and morbidity in the newborn and mothers. How far these objectives are achieved depends on the understanding of cause and course of the adverse occurrences in pregnancy and on how far health services and other forms of intervention or education can modify or overcome these factors in mothers who are willing and able to respond to advice. The responses of midwives and doctors have been encompassed in antenatal care services, supervised delivery usually in hospital, emergency services, and postnatal care.

Understanding of the causes of fetal mortality and morbidity is incomplete. Anatomical and physiological defects in the mother, fetus/baby, and placenta may be recognized during life and post-mortem. But the antecedent causes of these defects may remain obscure. Alberman (1974) characterized the registered causes of perinatal deaths in England in 1971 under a number of broad headings so as to indicate the relative contribution of different groups of stillbirths and neonatal deaths (Table 20.2). Around 25 per cent of perinatal deaths are unexplained. Baird *et al.* (1954) analysed perinatal deaths in the population of Aberdeen with a view to prevention through clinical action. They

Table 20.2. *Registered causes of perinatal deaths in England (1971)—percentage distribution of different groups*

Causes	Stillbirths (%)	Neonatal deaths (%)
Congenital malformations	21	18
'Intrapartum events'	30	28
'Antepartum events'	24	
Toxaemia and other maternal complications	22	
'Immaturity'	3	42
'Infection'		6

Source: Alberman (1974).

described three groups: (i) deaths associated with trauma during delivery; (ii) deaths associated with recognized maternal disease; and (iii) unexplained deaths and those associated with physiological factors and hereditary mechanisms in the fetus.

Other workers have sought to explain perinatal mortality by studying the general environmental characteristics of mothers and factors which increase the risk of death for the fetus. Adelstein *et al.* (1978) linked infant death records in England and Wales for the years 1975–77 with birth records to obtain information on the social class of families (by occupational class of the father), parity and ages of mothers, cause of death, and country of birth of mothers. It can be seen in Table 20.3 that stillbirth and perinatal mortality rates for social class V are double that for social class I. Considering as well the influence of parity and maternal age, the lowest rates for stillbirths and perinatal deaths occurred in mothers in their 20s and early 30s having their second child in social classes I and II. The highest rates occurred in mothers of 30 or more years having first or fourth or more pregnancies in social classes IV and V. The difference in the rates of stillbirth and perinatal mortality were around 50 per cent greater in mothers born in the Indian subcontinent. As far as the cause of stillbirth and perinatal death can be determined stillbirths associated with congenital malformations were half as common in social class I compared with social class V. Respiratory causes of perinatal and neonatal mortality were twice as frequent in social class V compared with social class I.

Table 20.3. *Stillbirths and mortality rates in the first year of life for legitimate births 1975–77 by social class*

Rate	All	Social class I	II	IIIN	IIIM	IV	V
Stillbirth*	9.5	7.0	7.7	8.6	10.1	11.1	13.4
Perinatal mortality*	17.3	12.7	14.3	15.2	17.7	19.8	24.7
Neonatal mortality†	9.3	7.0	7.9	8.2	9.3	10.6	13.5
Postneonatal mortality†	4.3	2.8	3.0	3.3	4.1	5.3	8.4
Infant mortality†	13.6	9.8	10.9	11.5	13.3	15.9	21.9

*Per thousand live and stillbirths.
†Per thousand live births.
Source: OPCS (1978).

Cross-sectional analyses of perinatal mortality determine associations between deaths and variables of interest in those fetuses which are born in a particular period of time. Longitudinal studies of pregnancy consider the effect on perinatal mortality of maternal age, parity, and sibling size in cohorts of women who become pregnant. Bakketeig and Hoffman (1979) in a large population based study have shown that perinatal mortality in cohorts of mothers based on attained sibship size decreases as parity increases, but is high for cohorts of large sibships. The effect of parity and sibship on perinatal mortality were related partly to birthweight distributions. The proportion of low-weight births decreases as parity increases within sibships and is higher in large sibships. But birthweight specific perinatal death rates for mothers with two existing children were half those for mothers with more than two children. These mothers were different in that those with more than two children were more likely to have experienced earlier perinatal deaths.

Ashford *et al.* (1973) considered variations in perinatal mortality amongst local authorities in England and Wales. They considered mortality in relation to five performance indicators:

1. Perinatal mortality in babies of birthweight less than 2501 g.
2. Perinatal mortality in babies of birthweight more than 2500 g.
3. Overall perinatal mortality.
4. Percentage of low birthweight babies.
5. Perinatal mortality corrected for birthweight distribution.

Eighty-eight descriptive variables were used to characterize the population of the local authority areas. These included age; changes in the pattern of births and deaths; voting habits; social class; occupations and local industries; death rates for degenerative diseases; education; and geography. The study also recorded two aspects of use of health services in relation to pregnancy—the percentage of low and high birthweight births in institutions and the percentage of low birthweight babies born at home and transferred in the first month of life—as input variables. The results showed that the descriptive variables explained a third of the variation in low birthweight and high birthweight perinatal mortality. Four-fifths of the variation in the low birthweight was attributed to the descriptive variables. The input variables were not closely associated with the performance indicators.

These studies demonstrate that variation in perinatal mortality rates are associated with characteristics of the mother, her history of pregnancies, and the environment in which parents live and reproduce. The studies indicate variables which may be modified in anticipation of lowering perinatal mortality either by preventive action or by treatment responses to fetuses identified as at risk. In spite of limited knowledge of the causes of perinatal mortality, rates have declined persistently in recent decades (Fig. 20.2).

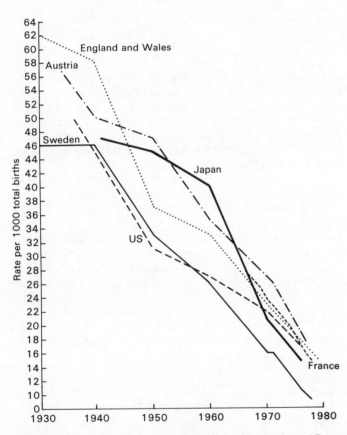

Fig. 20.2. Perinatal mortality per 1000 total births. (Source: Second Report from the Social Services Commiteee (1980).)

This continued decline in perinatal mortality makes the assessment of actions which reduce further these rates in the general population more difficult to achieve. Comparisons need to be made with control populations to determine that benefits to mortality and morbidity outweigh disadvantages. There may be also an irreducible minimum of perinatal deaths which are associated with malformations, very low birthweights, and diseases affecting mothers and fetuses. This minimum may be of the order of 4000 deaths out of the current 9000 perinatal deaths in England and Wales (Social Services Committee 1980).

MEASURES TO IMPROVE PERINATAL HEALTH

Prevention of congenital malformations

Around 2 per cent of live babies have clinically obvious congenital malformations. The percentage of malformed babies increases to nearer 5 per cent as further malformations are revealed during growth (Shapiro *et al.* 1962). The incidence of malformations in all conceptuses is not known as many abort. Of all congenital malformations around a quarter have a genetic component and a further 10 per cent have some known environmental association (Wilson 1973). The majority are subject to continued aetiological studies. When genetic components are identified antenatally, as in thalassaemia, it is possible to offer termination of pregnancy and genetic counselling with regard to further reproduction. Environmental associations with congenital malformations have been established for cigarette smoking (Abel 1980), alcohol consumption (Ouellette *et al.* 1977), certain drugs (McBride 1961; Shapiro *et al.* 1976), and a number of occupational exposures to chemicals (Hemminki *et al.* 1979). The incidence of congenital malformations can be altered if these exposures are avoided or controlled, for example, thalidomide. With the low incidence of most congenital malformations, demonstrating aetiological associations and improvements through prevention can be difficult. Many countries now survey rates of notified congenital malformations and births in order to detect larger than expected variations in the frequency of congenital malformations by type and geographical location. These surveillance programmes have not so far established any positive associations with changes of rates (Heath *et al.* 1975).

It is thought that some congenital malformations may also arise from deficiencies of necessary nutrients. Smithells *et al.* (1980, 1981*a, b*) offered multivitamin–iron supplements to mothers who had one or more infants with neural-tube defects (NTDs) at least one month before conception and up to at least the second missed period. A control group consisted of women who had had one or more NTD infants but were either pregnant or declined to take part in the study after referral. Two cohorts of supplemented and control women have been recruited. The results show that there were three recurrences amongst offspring of 397 fully supplemented mothers and 23 recurrences among 493 offspring of unsupplemented mothers. The result is highly significant statistically. As the mothers involved were not randomly allocated to supplements or no supplements one cannot be certain whether the difference in incidence of NTD at birth is due to differences in mothers and their pregnancies and the supplementation with vitamins and iron or due to the vitamin and iron alone. The rates of spontaneous abortion were similar in the two groups and the recurrence rates in the control group were similar to those quoted for the population at large. Women in the trial were mainly middle class and at low risk. The benefits may not be the same for all women. It is not known if the benefits for some fetuses outweigh possible risks from peri-conceptional and early pregnancy ingestion of multivitamins and minerals.

Table 20.4. *Antenatal screening for fetal malformation and disease*

Disorder	Birth prevalence per 10 000	Primary screening test	Secondary screening test	Primary screening tests	
				Detection rate* (%)	False-positive rate† (%)
Anencephaly	20	Maternal serum	Ultrasound	90	3
Open spina bifida	20	Alpha feto-protein	Ultrasound	75	3
Down's syndrome	15	Maternal age		25	5
Duchenne muscular dystrophy	3	Carrier detection	Creatine kinase assay	35	0.1
Tay–Sachs	0.035	Carrier detection	Hexosaminidase assay	12.5	0.01
Haemophilia	0.4	Carrier detection	Maternal factor VIII assay	70	0.01
Feto-maternal allo-immunization	1	Blood grouping + Coomb's test		95	0.01
Haemolytic disease of newborn	70	Rhesus group and antibodies		85	1
Syphilis	2	VDRL serum test		95	0.5
Congenital herpes simplex	0.3	Inspection of cervix		90	0.1
Rubella syndrome	3	Rubella antibodies		90	10

*Detection rate: proportion of affected individuals with positive primary screening test.

†False-positive rate: proportion of unaffected individuals with positive primary screening test.

Source: Wald (1984).

The possible benefits from multivitamins and minerals in preventing the recurrence of NTD may not be achieved if similar attempts were made to prevent the first occurrence of NTD.

Reduction in the incidence of congenital malformations at birth has been attempted through antenatal screening of fetuses at risk of having malformations and termination of the pregnancy when fetuses are affected. Table 20.4 shows a number of conditions for which antenatal detection of the malformation or disease is possible, the prevalence of the condition, and the detection rates and false-positive rates for the primary screening tests (Wald 1984). As with all screening tests, the benefit for the public health depends very much on the prevalence of the condition, the validity of the screening tests, the characteristics and compliance of the population to be screened. Unless congenital malformations are quickly lethal the cost of care of malformed infants tends to outweigh the cost of screening and termination services.

One example of this approach is screening for neural-tube defects (NTD). Measurement of alpha fetoprotein (AFP) levels in maternal serum above a certain cut-off level in the 16–19 weeks of gestation will detect 80 per cent of fetuses with open spina bifida (UK Collaborative Study 1979). Alpha fetoprotein will also be elevated above the cut-off level in the presence of multiple pregnancies, certain other congenital malformations, and if serum is taken at the wrong gestational age. Hence mothers with raised levels are offered secondary screening by ultrasonography, to exclude multiple pregnancies and the wrong gestational age, and amniocentesis, to measure raised AFP levels in amniotic fluid. Levels obtained at amniocentesis will falsely diagnose as abnormal 0.48 per cent of normal pregnancies and identify 98 per cent of open spina bifida and 98 per cent of anencephaly (Fig. 20.3). The false-positive rate of diagnosis can be caused in part through contamination of amniotic fluid by fetal blood. If bloodstained fluid is obtained amniocentesis can be repeated. In the UK Collaborative Study the

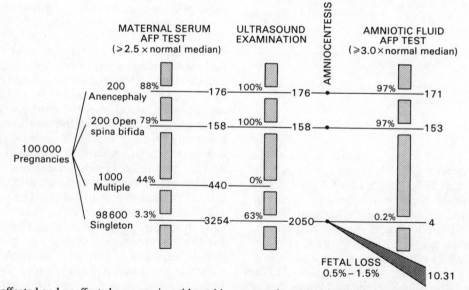

Fig. 20.3. Number of affected and unaffected pregnancies with positive maternal serum—alpha-fetoprotein and amniotic fluid alpha-fetoprotein tests in 100 000 who are screened. (Source: UK Collaborative Study on Alpha-fetoprotein (1979).)

false-positive rate for clear fluids was 0.27 per cent and 0.48 per cent for bloodstained fluids. The false-positive rate can be further reduced by raising the cut-off level for abnormal AFP concentration but such a change would reduce the detection rate for open spina bifida (from 98 to 93 per cent if the cut-off level increased by 0.5 times the median level from the specified level). There is also a loss of unaffected fetuses associated with amniocentesis. The actual loss rate is uncertain, however, if it was 0.5 per cent, the odds ratio of intended fetal loss to unintended fetal loss following termination would be 23:1. If the loss rate was 1.5 per cent, the same odds ratio would be 9:1. No more than 5 per cent of infants with NTD are born to women with previously affected children and 3 per cent or less to women having amniocentesis for other reasons. How are the potential benefits of a screening and termination service to be estimated? Of infants born with open spina bifida only a small number survive for more than five years. The odds ratio of intended fetal loss:unintended fetal loss in relation to infants who might otherwise survive more than five years may then reduce to as low as 1:1. Nevertheless abortion is a more commonly accepted response to pregnancy in society and fertility potential carries different values in different parents. Hence the risk of removing either an affected fetus or an unaffected fetus may be considered by some parents as acceptable when the odds ratio is even, given the consequences of a stillbirth or a malformed liveborn baby.

Although detailed consideration has been given to the validity of the screening tests for NTD the benefits from implementing screening services have not been formally tested. In the US routine screening has not been recommended because of problems of estimating AFP levels, understanding the significance of different elevations of levels, and physician and patients compliance with the necessary procedures. In the UK screening has been offered in many parts of the country since 1976. Amongst declining notification rates for malformations of the central nervous system those that have declined most are those most likely to be detected by AFP screening (Table 20.5). In Northern Ireland, however, Nevin (1981) has demonstrated that the fall in incidence of NTD since 1972 is not accounted for by prenatal diagnosis and termination of pregnancy.

Down's syndrome has a prevalence of around 1 in every 650 newborns. Sex chromosomal aneuploids, like Klinefelter syndrome and Turner syndrome, have a birth prevalence of about 1:400 newborns. These chromosomal malformations can be detected through cultures of fetal cells obtained by amniocentesis and termination of pregnancy considered. One problem in detecting Down's syndrome with amniocentesis concerns which population of mothers to screen. The incidence of Down's syndrome at birth increases markedly in mothers over the age of 35 years from those under 35 years. The number of total births declines with maternal age and the net result of the differences in incidence of Down's syndrome and total number of births by age is that three-quarters of children with Down's syndrome are born to mothers under the age of 35 years. The validity of screening for Down's syndrome according to maternal age has therefore a sensitivity of 25 per cent and a specifity around 95 per cent. Women who are 35 years and over and their medical attendants may or may not wish to comply with the provision of amniocentesis and possible termination of pregnancy. In the South West Health Region of England in 1980, only 25 per cent of 2319 mothers over the age of 35 years had an amniocentesis examination (Baker, unpublished). These 570 examinations revealed 16 cases of Down's syndrome. This number represented 29 per cent of the total identified cases of Down's syndrome recorded in the region in 1960. Another 11 per cent of the total Down's syndrome cases were detected in the 0.4 per cent of women under 35 years who had amniocentesis. In England and Wales, the rate of notifications of Down's syndrome at birth between 1969 and 1980 has shown no change in any age group except mothers over the age of 45 years (Table 20.6). The lack of change in the age groups 35–39 and 40–44 years may reflect an increased true incidence of Down's syndrome or more accurate notification of cases at birth with the effects of screening and termination of pregnancy. It does not seem at present that the provision of amniocentesis, cytogenetic services, and terminations of pregnancy is lowering the burden of care of children with Down's syndrome in society.

Congenital malformations which are caused by infective agents like the rubella virus may be avoided by changing the

Table 20.5. *Babies notified with malformations of the central nervous system: England and Wales, 1974–80*

Malformation	Number							Rate per 10 000 total births						
	1974	1975	1976	1977	1978	1979	1980	1974	1975	1976	1977	1978	1979	1980
Anencephaly only	666	591	500	457	407	369	266	10.3	9.7	8.5	8.0	6.8	5.7	4.0
Hydrocephaly only	222	183	188	192	167	158	166	3.4	3.0	3.2	3.3	2.8	2.5	2.5
Hydrocephaly and spina bifida together	274	252	211	194	222	173	205	4.2	4.1	3.6	3.4	3.7	2.7	3.1
Microcephaly only	32	22	38	28	40	28	44	0.5	0.4	0.6	0.5	0.7	0.4	0.7
Spina bifida only	516	485	379	388	374	419	348	8.0	8.0	6.4	6.8	6.2	6.5	5.3
Spina bifida and talipes together	63	68	49	55	42	47	39	1.0	1.1	0.8	1.0	0.7	0.7	0.6
CNS malformations multiple, or with other malformations	679	626	550	556	505	443	408	10.5	10.3	9.3	9.7	8.4	6.9	6.2
Total babies notified with at least one CNS malformation	2452	2227	1815	1870	1757	1637	1476	37.9	36.5	32.5	32.5	29.2	25.5	22.3

Source: Weatherall (1982).

Table 20.6. *Down's syndrome cases notified at birth analysed by mother's age: England and Wales, 1969–80*

Mother's age	Estimate true incidence in population in 1970*	Rate per 10 000 total births											
		1969	1970	1971	1972	1973	1974	1975	1976	1977	1978	1979	1980
All ages	16.7	6.7	7.3	7.3	7.6	7.6	6.5	7.4	6.8	7.4	7.4	7.2	7.3
<20	9.0	2.9	5.0	3.5	5.5	3.6	3.3	5.0	4.3	5.1	3.9	4.0	5.1
20–24	10.0	3.4	3.8	4.2	4.3	5.3	3.4	3.6	4.2	4.5	4.3	3.1	4.1
25–29	11.0	4.0	4.4	4.4	5.0	5.4	4.0	4.9	4.2	5.5	6.3	5.3	5.6
30–34	20.0	8.4	7.1	8.3	8.5	8.4	9.3	9.5	10.1	8.0	8.2	10.7	8.4
35–39	50.0	17.4	20.9	24.9	21.2	25.3	21.0	29.3	23.7	25.9	24.4	23.6	22.8
40–44	150.0	67.4	88.2	78.1	90.3	67.3	77.9	89.4	60.1	69.1	54.8	63.9	69.6
45 +	300.0	177.7	180.3	153.3	137.9	122.9	193.3	150.5	116.3	149.6	150.1	91.6	46.7

Source: Weatherall (1982); *Griffith (1973).

immune state of mothers through vaccination programmes. Such an approach may avoid also the spontaneous abortions, stillbirths, and growth retardation unassociated with malformations seen with rubella infection. In the UK vaccination against rubella was offered to all girls aged 11–13 years from 1970. More recently the age limit was lowered to girls aged 10 years or more. Current acceptance rates vary in the country but average 70 per cent. In addition, from 1978 screening services have become available for older women to establish their immune state with regard to rubella and to vaccinate those seronegative and not pregnant. Seronegative women who are pregnant are offered vaccination post-partum. The aim of vaccination is to achieve 100 per cent immunity to rubella in women who become pregnant. Gilmore *et al.* (1982) looked for an effect of the rubella vaccination programme for schoolgirls amongst patients aged 12–21 years attending their general practice in a socially deprived part of Glasgow. They found no difference in the proportion of females and males who were susceptible to infection suggesting that there had been no preferential increase in immunity in the female population. Three of 34 women known to have been vaccinated did not have detectable levels of antibody. Weatherall (1982) has studied notifications at birth of malformations associated with rubella infections. Between 1969 and 1980, she found no reduction in the rate of notifications for congenital cardiovascular malformations which can follow rubella infection. An epidemic of rubella occurred in England and Wales in 1978 and the absence of any increase in rates of notifications could suggest that there may have been some control through vaccinations. 'Control' may also occur as infected

fetuses with malformations abort spontaneously or are aborted surgically. Notifications of legal abortions for suspected malformations associated with rubella showed a a marked increase in 1978 and 1979 (Table 20.7). Legal abortions for suspected malformations of any cause in women under the age of 20 years showed less marked changes. Thus it seems that rubella vaccination has not yet achieved demonstrable effects.

Knox (1980) has discussed some of the problems involved in preventing the congenital rubella syndrome through vaccination. Amongst a number of different influences on the effectiveness of vaccination programmes are, the timing of the vaccination; the efficacy or uptake of the programmes; whether vaccinations are offered to girls only or both sexes; the opportunity to repeat vaccinations; variation in the transmission of rubella over time; and the duration of immunity following vaccination. He suggests that a combined programme of vaccination offered to preschool children of both sexes, as in the US, and again to girls only around the age of 14 years may achieve the largest effect although the approach carries the risk of rebound infection amongst a group of women who may miss the earlier vaccination and remain susceptible to the remaining wild virus in the population.

For women who are exposed to rubella during pregnancy it is possible to estimate their state of immunity and to confirm the presence of infection by measuring rubella-specific IgM. Women who are infected and not immune to rubella can be terminated to reduce the risk of birth of a congenitally malformed baby. Some fetuses will be aborted who have not developed malformations. There are problems also

Table 20.7. *Number of legal abortions notified as having been carried out on medical grounds of suspected malformation of the fetus (Ground 4), (a) where rubella (disease, contact or immunization) was given as the reason; (b) in women aged less than 20 years (for all reasons). Residents of England and Wales.*

Condition	Year									
	1971	1972	1973	1974	1975	1976	1977	1978	1979	1980
(a) Rubella	1061	776	839	664	531	253	221	896	731	301
(b) All legal abortions for Ground 4 in women aged less than 20 years	NA	NA	NA	78	76	42	53	87	88	98

NA = not available.
Source: Weatherall (1982).

in confirming the diagnoses of infection very early in pregnancy (Morgan-Capner 1982).

Prevention of fetal or neonatal death not associated with congenital malformations

As has been indicated in Table 20.4, a number of other disease processes occurring in pregnancy which increase the risk of fetal or neonatal death can be the subject of screening and intervention.

Haemolytic disease of the newborn

Rhesus antibodies produced in rhesus-negative mothers to rhesus-positive fetal blood cells can damage the fetus and lead to spontaneous abortions, stillbirths and neonatal death, and kernicterus in the newborn. These consequences of the iso-immunizations can be reduced by immediate diagnosis in and care of affected livebirths; induced delivery of high-risk infants; intrauterine transfusions of the fetus; and the primary prevention of iso-immunization by the use of anti-D gammaglobulin injection following delivery, abortions (spontaneous or therapeutic), and other sensitizing episodes during pregnancy like threatened abortions, antepartum haemorrhages, version, and amniocentesis. Rates of stillbirth and neonatal deaths associated with haemolytic disease of the newborn (HDN) have been decreasing, but, in 1978 in England and Wales, 123 deaths were still recorded. The impact of primary prevention with anti-D gammaglobulin on the incidence of HDN is difficult to determine with changes in the number of pregnancies in rhesus-negative women and improving perinatal care. Tovey *et al.* (1978) surveyed the incidence of rhesus antibodies in pregnant women in Yorkshire between 1970 and 1976 and determined lack of protection by anti-D gammaglobulin due to administrative failures, sensitization of primigravidae, and apparent failure of protection in women who had been given anti-D gammaglobulin. The latter group accounted for about 1 per cent of all rhesus-sensitized women who were given anti-D gammaglobulin. Clarke and Whitfield (1979) noted that there were inaccuracies in recording HDN in death certification but the number of certificates which failed to mention the presence of HDN possibly balanced the number of deaths apparently associated with HDN where the disease could not be substantiated from clinical notes.

As prophylactic measures all Rh(D)-negative women should be given anti-D gammaglobulin within 72 hours of delivery (unless it is established that the baby is rhesus(D)-negative or following abortion or after sensitizing episodes. Anti-D gammaglobulin doses should be repeated until all fetal cells have been eliminated from maternal blood, as determined by the Kleihauer test (Standing Medical Advisory Committee 1981).

Low birthweight

The risk of stillbirth and neonatal death can be described by birthweight. Around two-thirds of all stillbirths and neonatal deaths occur in the small proportion of births (7 per cent in the UK) which have a birthweight of 2500 g or less. Table 20.8, shows the change in risk of early neonatal death by birthweight in Norway, Sweden, and Denmark. Mortality is lowest in the group with birthweight of 3501–5000 g. Knox *et al.* (1980) estimated that 60 per cent of the variation in perinatal mortality rates between 90 Area Health Authorities (AHA) in England in 1974–76 was accounted for by variation in birthweight. The distribution of births by weight in different countries is shown in Table 20.9. It would seem reasonable for public health services to attempt to influence the birthweight distribution towards the right in anticipation that perinatal mortality would be favourably influenced.

A number of factors are associated with the distribution of birthweights. These include: (i) the characteristics of parents; (ii) congenital malformations of the fetus; (iii) infections; and (iv) length of gestation.

The prevention of congenital malformations has been considered above. Infections, such as, of the maternal urinary tract (Kass 1962) or with viruses like the cytomegalovirus (Monif *et al.* 1972), are associated with retarded

Table 20.8. *Early neonatal mortality (%) by birthweight in Norway, Sweden, and Denmark*

Birthweight (g)	Sweden 1973	Denmark 1974	Norway 1975–76
Under 1500	45.8	46.4	55.0
1501–2500	4.6	3.3	3.5
2501–3000	0.47	0.43	0.43
3001–3500	0.18	0.14	0.15
3501–5000	0.11	0.10	0.09*
Over 5000	0.20	–	0.18

*Birthweight interval 3501–4500 g.
Source: Saugstad (1981).

Table 20.9. *Proportion of births by weight and infant mortality rates in certain countries (%)*

Country	Year	≤2500 g	2501–3000 g	3001–3500 g	3501–4000 g	>4000 g	Infant mortality per 1000
Faeroes	1973	3.7	8.3	26.6	38.0	23.4	12.8
Iceland	1972	4.3	8.7	28.2	35.2	23.6	10.1
Norway	1972–4	4.4	11.7	32.9	34.3	16.7	10.4
Sweden	1973	4.6	11.9	34.0	33.7	15.8	8.6
Denmark	1973–4	6.8	17.6	37.1	28.5	10.0	10.7
US	1973	7.6	18.2	38.2	27.0	9.0	17.7
UK	1970	6.8	18.9	39.1	26.8	8.3	16.4

Source: Saugstad (1981).

growth and low birthweights. Active preventive measures are not yet available.

Maternal age, height, parity, social class, smoking and drinking habits, intercurrent illness, and stress have all been associated with variation in the birthweight of babies. Many of these factors are interrelated. Using data from the 1958 British Perinatal Mortality Survey (Butler and Bonham 1963; Butler and Alberman 1969) and the 1970 British Births Survey (Chamberlain et al. 1975, 1978); Peters et al. (1983) have demonstrated that the effect of social class differences on variation in perinatal mortality is marginal when the data are standardized for maternal age, height, parity, smoking, and presence of pre-eclampsia.

In consecutive births to black and white mothers attending the Kansas University Center, Miller et al. (1978) explored the difference of social, economical, and medical factors on the incidence of low birthweight (less than 2500 g). Black and white mothers were divided into poverty and non-poverty groups according to their ability to pay hospital fees and these two groups were further subdivided by occupation. The personal and medical histories of all the mothers were reviewed for seven behavioural components and five medical components thought to be associated with the incidence of low birthweight. These behavioural components were: (i) no prenatal care; (ii) age 35 years; (iii) age 17 years; (iv) underweight for height at conception; (v) low weight gain in pregnancy; (vi) cigarette smoking; and (vii) drug or alcohol addiction. The medical components were: (i) placental complications; (ii) hypertension; (iii) other maternal illnesses; (iv) cervical incompetence; (v) polyhydramnios.

Mothers without any behavioural or medical components in these lists had a low incidence of low birthweight (1–3 per cent) in spite of differing social economic circumstances. The incidence of low birthweights did not vary between socio-economic groupings when mothers were matched for the presence of medical complications and behavioural components. Socio-economic grouping affected the distribution of behavioural components but not medical complications. The behavioural components became more common as socio-economic status declined and were additive in their effect on the incidence of low birthweight.

Birthweight less than 2500 g shows a U-shaped relationship with maternal age and parity. The frequency of births of less than 2500 g is greatest for mothers aged under 18 years, is least for mothers 25–29 years and rises again in mothers over 30 years (Butler and Bonham 1963). Birthweight increases with parity but the greatest increase takes place between parity 1 and 2. Some variation in the mean increase in birthweight by parity between countries is shown in Table 20.10. The frequency of low birthweight increases with diminishing maternal height so that mothers under 146 cm have around three times the risk of a low birthweight baby compared with mothers of 161 cm or more (Butler and Bonham 1963). Smoking is associated with diminishing birthweight and an increase in the frequency of low-birthweight babies. Birthweight differences between babies of smokers and non-smokers is of the order of 150–250 g. The

effect of smoking which increases with the amount smoked is independent of the effect of maternal age and height, parity, and socio-economic status (Butler and Bonham 1963). Meyer et al. (1976) showed an increase in perinatal mortality with smoking a risk that was present even without the influence of low birthweight. Smoking increased the frequency of preterm births and placental complications. Holmes et al. (1977) illustrated how babies of mothers who smoked grew in height along the same low percentile postnatally. Chronic high alcohol consumption has been demonstrated to have associations with growth retardation of the fetus in studies in the US (Harrison et al. 1976) and France (Lemoine et al. 1968). It is not known whether the effect is through ethanol itself and its breakdown products or is associated with secondary malnutrition which may be present in these mothers.

Hence a number of maternal characteristics are associated with the frequency of low birthweight and the characteristics which are unfavourable seem to be influenced in rate of occurrence by diminishing socio-economic status. Preventive efforts can either attempt to modify the individual adverse characteristics or seek to influence factors which determine socio-economic differences.

Longitudinal studies in the UK show that the age of mothers having their first baby in 1970–72 within marriage was 26.3 years in social class 1 and 21.9 years in social class V (Central Statistics Office 1975). The earlier start in social class V is associated with more pregnancies within the fertile period and a greater risk of perinatal death associated with the early start and the greater number of births. Family planning is a mechanism by which upper social classes delay reproduction and although these services need to be available to all adults the motives which defer pregnancies to more mature reproductive ages are not fully understood or universally attractive and applicable. Variation in maternal height is due to genetic and environmental factors acting over a number of generations. Social class differences of mean heights in children have disappeared in communities like Sweden (Lindgren, 1976), but persist unchanged in the UK (Baker et al. 1979; Rona et al. 1979). The social forces that have allowed changes in mating patterns between the tall and short and which have influenced other favourable environmental effects are not specific or clear.

Formal attempts to reduce smoking during pregnancy have not met with much success. A study by Donovan (1977) showed that mothers who were smoking an average of 15 cigarettes a day on entry to a controlled trial reduced this consumption to an average of nine a day with intensive anti-smoking advice. In comparison with the control group of mothers who showed no reduction in the numbers of cigarettes smoked, the birthweight, lengths, and head circumferences of babies born to both groups showed no differences. Whilst the results of a single trial do not undermine too strongly the possible causal relationship between smoking and birthweight, it has to be considered whether the effect of smoking on birthweight, if direct, acts early in pregnancy or even pre-conceptionally. Otherwise smoking may be an indirect indicator of other causal associations like anxiety and stress or of behavioural or constitutional differ-

Table 20.10. *Mean increase in birthweight (g) with parity in selected countries*

Country	Year	Parity 1	Parity 2–3	Parity 3–4	Mean birthweight
Norway	1967	140	40	40	3470
Denmark	1970	150	50	50	3370
England and Wales	1935–46	145	27	–	3257
	1958	140	0	0	3332
UK	1970	138*	–	–	3310
Scotland	1969–73	120	10	20	
US	1966	40	20	10	3300
White births only	1973	50	10	10	3350
New York State					
White births	1959	65	30	30	3372
	1967	50	23	22	3344

*Increase between parity 1 and all later parities.
Source. Saugstad (1981).

ences in mothers. The same considerations may apply to the association of alcohol with low birthweight. In view of the association of smoking with a variety of diseases in adults and the more frequent hospital admissions of children from homes where parents smoke, it may be that the health status of pregnant mothers and their offspring will be better promoted through more general controls and influences on smoking in the community at large.

Some evidence that stress has an effect on birthweight comes from two studies with contrasting approaches. Newton *et al.* (1979) recorded the mean number of major life events, using a modified version of the Life Events Inventory of Cochrane and Robertson (1973), which occurred to mothers having consecutive births in three groups differentiated by length of gestation. There were no differences of maternal age, gravidity, parity, or social class between the groups which had lengths of gestation of 37 weeks or more, 33–36 weeks, or less than 33 weeks. The mean number of life-events increased with decreasing length of gestation. It was possible that the timing of life-events affected the onset of labour. The number of life-events experienced by each mother increased inversely with the length of gestation. The study was retrospective and the occurrence of preterm delivery could have biased the recall of events. Nuckolls *et al.* (1972) in the other study recorded life-events also but in addition attempted to quantify psychosocial assets which were perceived as supports and protection against the stress of adverse life-events. An assessment of psychosocial assets was made at prenatal registration and life events were recalled at the 32nd week of gestation. The sample of mothers were white primigravidae registering before the 24th week of gestation in a military hospital. The authors found no correlation of a number of prenatal, intrapartum, or post-partum complications of pregnancy with the number of life-events or psychosocial assets. Yet they observed that mothers with a high number of life-events and a high number of psychosocial assets had a third of the complication rate of mothers with similar numbers of life-events and low psychosocial assets. Further prospective studies will be required to analyse the effect of stress on pregnancy outcome. But if the balance of stress

and supportive and protective factors rather than stress itself is important then prevention will depend on ways of building up these modifying influences. Newton *et al.* (1979) noted that antenatal attendants were frequently unaware of the life-events experienced by mothers in their care.

Maternal illnesses presenting either before conception or arising during pregnancy, which include hypertension, pre-eclampsia, cardiac disease, renal disease, and anaemia, may affect birthweight and perinatal survival. Anaemia has been associated with low birthweights and increased perinatal mortality but this association is not free of confounding with socio-economic and other nutritional factors (Butler and Alberman 1969). Trials of supplementation with iron and vitamins of the B group have not shown benefits in terms of birthweight and birth outcomes (Hemminki 1982). Although hypertension in pregnancy has been defined in different ways an association is recognized between elevations of blood pressure and intrauterine growth retardation. Mean arterial pressure (taken as the diastolic pressure plus one-third of the pulse pressure) in mid-pregnancy in 15 000 women in the Kaiser Foundation Health Plan in San Francisco (Page and Christianson 1976) showed a U-shaped association with the incidence of small-for-gestational age infants of 37 weeks or more. The incidence in mothers with pressures of 95 mm Hg and above was double that for women with pressures 75–90 mm Hg. The incidence of stillbirths was four times greater in mothers with pressures of 95 mm Hg and above. There was no association with neonatal death rates. Studying a large number of singleton births in Aberdeen between 1948 and 1955 Baird *et al.* (1957) found that mothers who developed severe pre-eclampsia (a diastolic blood pressure rise to 90 mm Hg or more after the 26th week of pregnancy associated with albuminuria of 2 g/l or more daily) had babies with birthweights below the average for all births. Mothers with moderate or mild pre-eclampsia (a similar rise in diastolic blood pressure with albuminuria of less than 2 g/l daily) had babies with birthweights similar to the distribution of birthweight in all the births. Low and Galbraith (1974) following 3428 singleton deliveries found 6.4 per cent of babies with intrauterine growth retardation (IUGR) in mothers with pre-eclampsia. In those mothers who had severe eclampsia (blood pressures of 160/110 mm Hg or more and albuminuria of 5 g/24 h or more) the rate of IUGR was 46 per cent. Redman (1982) estimates that pre-eclampsia contributes to 8 per cent of perinatal deaths. Between the British Perinatal Mortality Survey in 1958 and the British Births Survey in 1970 perinatal mortality rates fell by 51 per cent in mothers with severe pre-eclampsia (a diastolic blood pressure of 110 mm Hg or more or a diastolic blood pressure of 90 mm Hg with proteinuria or evidence of eclampsia) compared with a fall of 24 per cent in unaffected mothers (Chamberlain et al. 1978). In spite of the effect of hypertension and pre-eclampsia on perinatal morbidity and mortality and the risk to mothers of eclampsia there is considerable confusion in diagnosis and assessment of these different conditions Butler and Bonham (1963) for instance found that a quarter of all pregnancies in their surveys had a diastolic blood pressure of 90 mm Hg or more recorded during the antenatal period before labour. The problems of screening for pre-eclampsia are discussed later under the provision of antental services. Assessment of treatment has also been confused by differing definitions of the disease entity. A customary response to pre-eclampsia and hypertension has been hospital admission, bed rest, and sedation. A controlled trial which compared these interventions with mothers randomly allocated to normal activities with and without sedation found no significant differences of outcome between any group (Matthews 1977). Trials of treatment of hypertension with drugs have not clearly established benefits over adverse effects or distinguished mothers with essential hypertension from mothers with pre-eclampsia (Rubin 1981). Elective delivery of a fetus mature enough to survive remains the main form of control of pre-eclampsia.

Interest in the relationship between maternal nutrition and birthweight of babies has been longstanding. During the famine in Holland in the Second World War the birthweight of infants fell by around 300 g (Stein et al. 1975). A number of trials have attempted to demonstrate the effect of dietary supplements for the pregnant mother in increased birthweights of the newborn (Table 20.11). Most trial populations have been chosen with some social and economical disadvantage in order to enhance any beneficial effect of the dietary supplement. Trials which have concentrated on an increase in the proportion of protein in the diet to more than 20 per cent have shown, surprisingly, a decrease in birthweight in babies of mothers receiving the supplement as well as increased premature deliveries and neonatal deaths. Trials which have involved supplements of less than 20 per cent of protein have shown increases in birthweight of between 40 and 90 g for the supplemented group compared with controls.

Protein supplements have shown no significant increase in benefit to birthweight over carbohydrates alone. These findings seem to fit with the observations of Rush et al. (1980) that mothers in the poor urban population in New York involved in their study who weighed less than 140 lb (6350 g) at conception were calorie rather than protein deprived. His treatment groups which received a balanced protein/calorie supplementation showed an increased length of gestation, a reduced proportion of low birthweight infants, and an increase in mean birthweight of 41 g. Rush et al. suggest that a direct relationship may exist between birthweight and nutritional intakes when the latter is especially

Table 20.11. *Controlled trials of dietary supplementation in pregnancy: protein density and birthweight difference between subjects and controls, in rank order by protein density of supplementation*

Study	% of calories as protein	Birthweight difference (g) Subjects vs. Controls	Number Subjects	Number Controls
Marchant and Sheth (1980)	40.0 (high dose)	−17	97	635
	40.0 (lower dose)	−23	136	635
Rush et al. (1980)	34.0	−32	263	272
Adams et al. (1978)	34.0	−45	36	43
Osofsky (1975)	26.0	−113	122	118
Ebbs et al. (1941, 1942)	21.4	−85	90	120
Elwood et al. (1981)	21.2	~55*	510	441
Campbell et al. (1978)	21.2	−54	38	38
			(partway through trial)	
Chow (Herriott et al. 1978)	20.0	51	81	87
(McDonald et al. 1981)	20.0	16	108	105
Mora et al. (1979)	17.9	51	200	207
Qureshi et al. (1973)	16.0	540	39	37
Rush et al. (1980)	7.5	41	263	272
Adams et al. (1978)	7.5	92	36	23
Merchant and Sheth (1980)	6.7 (high dose)	83	122	635
	6.7 (lower dose)	36	157	635
Dieckmann et al. (1944)	Uncertain	45	281	273
Higgins (Rush 1981)	Variable	40	1213	1213

*Controlling (approximately) for disparity in frequency of smoking.
Source: Rush (1982).

low. But when a threshold of intake is passed the amount of nutrition relates to maternal size and only indirectly to birthweight of the newborn. One beneficial effect of the high protein supplement in the study of Rush *et al.* was to nullify the deleterious effect of heavy smoking on birthweight.

Other trials have concentrated on racial groups living in developed countries. Asian immigrants in different parts of the UK have been shown to have clinical and biochemical evidence of vitamin D deficiency (*British Medial Journal* 1979). Pregnant women have low levels of 25-hydroxy vitamin D and produce babies of low birth size compared with caucasians and negroes. Brooke and others (1980) undertook a double-blind trial of vitamin D supplements (argocalciferol 1000 IU/day) compared with placebo during the last trimester in pregnant Asian immigrants. Both experimental and control groups had low levels of serum 25-hydroxy vitamin D on entry to the trial. The groups were similar for maternal age, height, parity, number of vegetarians, countries of origin, sex, and gestation of offspring. Mothers in the experimental group gained weight faster and at term had acceptable plasma 25-hydroxy vitamin D levels, as did their babies. Control mothers and babies had low plasma levels of 25-hydroxy vitamin D. Mean birthweight in the experimental group was 3157 g (SD 61) compared with 3034 g (SD 64) in the control group. Babies in the control group were twice as frequently below the 10th weight percentile for gestational age compared with babies in the experimental group. The differences in mean birthweight and frequency of small babies did not achieve significance statistically. Some babies in the control group had clinical signs of hypocalcaemia and low plasma calcium levels. Vitamin D deficiency in immigrant Asian mothers may be due to inadequate exposure to sunlight, poor diets, or both. There was no evidence of toxicity in the women receiving calciferol. Supplementation of vitamin D can be achieved directly in pregnant women attending for antenatal care or in milk or foodstuff for immigrant Asian populations at large. The findings from the trial although not conclusive suggest that supplementation of the vitamin D intake of Asian mothers may improve fetal size and biochemistry.

Another study (Viegas *et al.* 1982*a*) of dietary supplementation to pregnant Asian women in Birmingham, England compared mean birthweights and birthweights for gestational age in babies of women allocated to receive either a placebo with iron and vitamin C, a carbohydrate energy supplement with iron and vitamin C, or a protein and carbohydrate energy supplement with iron and vitamin C from the 18th to 38th week of pregnancy. There were no differences in birthweights between the groups either in the women overall or in those without complications and who were fully compliant with the trial. A further trial was conducted with pregnant Asian women who had or did not have signs of undernutrition according to change in triceps skinfold thickness between the 18th to 28th week of pregnancy (Viegas *et al.* 1982*b*). Women in these two groups were randomly allocated to receive either multivitamins alone, multivitamins plus energy supplement as carbohydrate, or multivitamins plus energy supplement as milk protein in the third trimester. Protein–energy supplementa-

tion increased mean birthweight and weight for gestational age in the babies of the undernourished mothers. There were no differences in the babies of adequately nourished mothers between the supplemented groups. The experience of Rush and co-workers in New York and the results of these trials on Asian women suggest that protein–energy supplementation may only benefit the growth of the fetus in women who are below a certain threshold in their own nutritional status. In order to improve birthweight of babies by such protein–energy supplementation in developed countries women will have to be screened for their own undernutrition. Triceps skinfold thickness change would seem to be one simple method of screening.

Preterm deliveries, that is, births occurring before the 37th week of pregnancy are associated with lower birthweight distributions and increased perinatal mortality. Compared with term deliveries, of 429 preterm liveborn infants born at the John Radcliffe Hospital in Oxford in 1973 and 1974, 311 (72 per cent) had birthweight of 2500 g or less (Rush *et al.* 1976). Preterm deliveries were responsible for 85 per cent of early neonatal deaths not associated with lethal congenital malformations. Obviously prevention of preterm deliveries may enhance growth of the fetus and reduce perinatal mortality. Amongst the associated causes of preterm delivery are: (i) multiple pregnancies; (ii) fetal abnormalities; (iii) maternal hypertension; (iv) maternal infections; (v) abruptio placentae; (vi) antepartum haemorrhage; and (vii) cervical incompetence. Spontaneous delivery with no apparent reason occurred in 38 per cent of the Oxford cases. Other spontaneous deliveries were associated with fetuses showing growth retardation. The opportunity to prevent preterm delivery would seem to be slight given this list of associations. Prevention or treatment of maternal hypertension, infections, and cervical incompetence may have some small part to play. Attempts to demonstrate that treatment of threatened abortion with oestrogens, progestogens, and betamimetic drugs will avoid preterm delivery and low birthweight have not been successful (Anderson and Turnbull 1982). Instead a number of follow-up studies have indicated an increased prevalence of genital tract abnormalities in the offspring of women treated with oestrogens (Anderson and Turnbull 1982). A case-control study by Herbst *et al.* (1971) showed an increased risk of vaginal adenocarcinoma in the female offspring of mothers treated with stilboestrol).

A WHO study (1979) showed a statistically significant increase in frequency of babies of low birthweight (<2500 g) born to women who had had an induced abortion by dilatation and correctage of their only previous pregnancy compared with babies born to women having had a livebirth in their only previous pregnancy. In a group of cities where vacuum aspiration was the commonest procedure for induced abortion there was no statistically significant difference in the frequency of low-birthweight babies between women in similar groupings although the trend was in the same direction. The frequency of low-birthweight babies born to women who had recorded a spontaneous abortion in their only previous pregnancy was similar to the frequency of low-birthweight babies in the induced abortion groups in their own communities. The differences in frequency of low birthweight were not associated with differences of maternal age, height, or smoking or stage of gestation at booking. Part of the difference in frequency of the low-birthweight babies may be explained by the favourable birth order effect on birthweight reducing the frequency of low birthweight babies in women having their second child. This observational study draws attention towards, but does not establish, induced abortion as a possible mechanism causing low birthweight of similar frequency as spontaneous abortions.

Twenty-eight per cent of the total of preterm deliveries in Oxford were due to deliberate obstetric intervention. These deliveries depend on the calculation that the hazards to the fetus remaining *in utero* (and in some cases hazards for the mother) are greater than the risk of mortality and morbidity subsequent to preterm delivery. The optimal preterm delivery rate depends on the accuracy of diagnosis of the fetal condition and gestational age, the hazards of delivery, and the efficiency of neonatal care. Preterm delivery rates have varied with time and place suggesting that there is limited agreement on the criteria involved. Cartwright (1979) observed that uncertainty over the dates of the last menstrual period varied between 11 per cent in middle social classes to 22 per cent in the unskilled occupational groups. In Norway and Denmark induction rates are currently around 15 per cent. In Britain induction rates rose from 13 per cent in the 1960s to 40 per cent in 1974–75 during which time it has been observed that there was no decline in the number of births weighing 2000–2500 g although there was some fall in births weighing less than 2000 g (Saugstad 1981). In a study of births in Cardiff between 1965–73, Chalmers *et al.* (1976) recorded an increase in rates of induction from 7.5 per cent in 1965 to 26.5 per cent in 1973. During the period mean birthweight of Cardiff babies fell from 3300 to 3240 g with a fall in mean gestational age.

In the US elective deliveries are commonplace. Saugstad (1981) has noticed a less marked mean birthweight gain between first and second babies in the US and UK compared with Norway and Denmark (Table 20.10). In the US there is also lower weight gain of babies in subsequent births than in Norway and Denmark. These differences are ascribed to the higher induction rates of America and the UK and possible restrictions of maternal weight gain in the US through the use of diets and diuretics. Cartwright (1979), observing differences in induction rates between the middle social classes (21 per cent) and the unskilled occupational groups (12 per cent), suggested that the latter mothers may be protected from this form of intervention by their less frequent attendance for antenatal care and admission to hospital during pregnancy—14 per cent compared with up to 25 per cent in other social classes. She accepted also that fetuses of the unskilled group mothers will tend to be smaller and hence less suitable for preterm delivery.

Detection of fetus at risk and avoidance of intrapartum hazards

Toxaemia, placental infarction, and the course of labour may give rise to hypoxia which for some fetuses, already growth retarded or malformed or at other risk, may precipitate intrauterine or neonatal death. Obstetric interest has therefore sought to identify as early as possible indications of these conditions most likely to cause hypoxia, monitor hypoxia itself, and undertake elective delivery for the fetus at risk and compensate for any maladaption of the fetus to the extrauterine environment through intensive neonatal care. The success of this approach depends on the accuracy with which intrauterine events can be measured, the effectiveness of interventions, the compensatory effects of neonatal care, and the compliances of mothers and staff with the service provision, especially those mothers at higher risk.

Intrauterine growth of the fetus can be monitored by ultrasound scanning. Placental function can be monitored by hormone assays and during labour uterine contractions, the fetal electrocardiogram, and pH of the fetal blood can be measured. These techniques can be combined to estimate the viability of the fetus in the uterus and to estimate when elective delivery may enhance its chances of survival. The success of these approaches depends on how far changes in function predict adverse outcomes for the fetus and how far lack of changes predict normal outcomes. A number of studies have indicated that although fetal pH sampling may have acceptable sensitivity and indicate few distressed fetuses as normal the technique more frequently diagnoses fetal distress in babies not showing evidence of distress at birth than it does correctly diagnose intrauterine fetal distress (US Department of Health, Education and Welfare 1979). This lack of validity has been associated with increased caesarean section rates. In three randomized controlled trials where fetal monitoring was compared with conventional auscultation, caesarean section rates were twice as frequent in the monitored group compared with the auscultation group (Renou *et al.* 1976; Kelso *et al.* 1978; Haverkamp *et al.* 1979). Hence the cost of detecting the small percentage of salvageable fetuses at risk from asphyxia is that a larger number of mothers may have anxieties raised and be delivered other than by the normal routine. Even in the absence of this knowledge some women have found fetal monitoring unacceptable and the anxieties aroused by the techniques may themselves contribute to the undesired distress in delivery. Randomized controlled trials which have taken place have not shown clear benefit for the monitored group in terms of decreased mortality, but as the expected benefit is small the trials may not have been large enough to demonstrate any favourable effects. The lack of evidence of effectiveness in compliant populations does not augur well for the effectiveness of the technique when made available to the population at large.

By contrast with the low predictive potential of fetal monitoring by electrocardiogram or pH of fetal blood, a randomized controlled trial of maternal monitoring of fetal movement by Neldam (1980) indicated that women who were taught to monitor fetal movement and who were electively delivered if a decrease or absence of fetal movement was confirmed ultrasonically had no intrauterine deaths compared with eight which occurred in a control group who had received no specific instructions. This result was statistically significant at the 1 per cent level. This simple and low cost approach, applicable in nearly all women, should be tested on additional populations.

PROVISION OF SERVICES

Within the arrangements for health service provision in different countries, maternity care is provided by specialist obstetricians, general practitioners with varying skills or commitment to maternity care, or midwives, or various combinations of these groups of professionals. Delivery in hospital is now commonplace, although this part of maternity care may still be supervised by the general practitioner. In Holland, about one-third of deliveries take place at home but in the UK, as in most other European countries and the US, 95 per cent of deliveries occur in hospital. Antenatal services are either hospital based, general practice based, or shared between both services. For the professionals antenatal clinics are a means of contact with pregnant women giving the opportunity for screening for complications of pregnancy and early intervention. These clinics also offer educative opportunities for preparation for childbirth and motherhood. Doctors and midwives are able to advise on health-promoting behaviour and actions during pregnancy and mothers can seek explanations for their symptoms and counsel for their anxieties. Services will extend to mothers and babies postnatally with home visiting by midwives, community nurses, and general practitioners.

Antenatal care

The sucess of screening and educative activities depends on many well recognized criteria (Wilson and Jungner 1968). Some of these have been discussed already. The response of pregnant women to the provision of antenatal care services is an important determinant of the outcome of the use of valid screening techniques. A survey in Scotland in 1973 showed that the social class distribution of mothers by fathers' occupation influenced the percentage of women who first attended their antenatal clinic before the 20th week of pregnancy (Table 20.12). In France in 1976, 40 per cent of pregnant women attended an antenatal clinic on

Table 20.12. *Late antenatal booking. Percentage of married women in each occupational class making the first antenatal booking after 20 weeks of gestation (Scotland 1971–73)*

Occupational class	1971	1972	1973
I	28.4	27.2	27.0
II	35.3	32.3	29.8
III	36.3	33.4	30.6
IV	39.3	37.8	35.3
V	47.1	44.2	40.5

Source: Brotherston (1976)—data from Scottish Information Services Division.

fewer than five occasions (Rumeau-Rouquette *et al.* 1976). Attendance at antenatal preparation classes was influenced by social class as was the British Births Survey conducted in 1970 (Table 20.13). The effectiveness of some screening tasks as well as educative opportunity may be diminished by this lack of compliance especially in women at greater risk for perinatal mortality according to age, parity and social class.

Butler and Bonham (1963) observed an inverse relationship between the number of antenatal visits and perinatal mortality. This association is probably spurious, however, owing to the greater frequency of attendance by mothers at lower risk according to age and social class and the inevitable decline in the number of antenatal visits occasioned by elective preterm delivery of fetuses with a high risk of dying. In a retrospective study by McKinlay and McKinlay (1979) of women from the Aberdeen population who had three children, it was observed that mothers who experienced premarital conception of their first pregnancy attended antenatal care five weeks later than women conceiving after marriage. There was no evidence that the rate of complications during pregnancy or by outcome was higher in the premaritally conceived babies. When there were no complications with the first of these three pregnancies, the date of attendance for first booking for the second pregnancy was three weeks later, with women in manual social classes being later than those in non-manual classes.

These facts illustrate considerable variation of use of antenatal services by pregnant women according to per-

Table 20.13. *Antenatal preparation and social class—singletons only*

		Social class							
		I	II	III	IV	V	Unsupp.	Rem.	Total
No reported preparation	No.	417	1126	6464	1879	871	1051	429	12 237
	(per cent)	(52.5)	(61.9)	(72.2)	(80.9)	(87.1)	(85.5)	(76.7)	(73.4)
Preparation		377	694	2490	445	129	178	130	4443
No information		6	17	73	14	14	6	5	135
Total		800	1837	9027	2338	1014	1235	564	16 815

*Percentages calculated excluding 'no information'.
Source: Chamberlain *et al.* (1978).

sonal, social, and other characteristics and this variation in uptake will have consequences for the efficiency of screening and health education. In order to assess the use of some aspects of screening in antenatal care, Hall (1982) and others carried out a retrospective audit of the records of 2186 women who were delivered in the city district of Aberdeen in 1975. They noted that 50 per cent of this population first attended antenatal care by the 14th week of gestation; 75 per cent by the 18th week; and 95 per cent by the 30th week. Primigravidae tended to attend earlier than multigravidae and, of those conceiving before marriage or having illegitimate births, 50 per cent first attended after the 20th week of gestation. These investigations concentrated on screening for three asymptomatic complications, IUGR; malpresentation; and pre-eclampsia. For babies with IUGR diagnosed at birth, only 44 per cent were detected during the antenatal period. In addition the condition was diagnosed as present falsely at more than twice its true frequency. The efficiency of detection of IUGR was no greater in parous women where the condition had been recorded in earlier births than in parous women without this complication previously. Malpresentation was studied in terms of breech presentations. Fifty-one out of 58 breech presentations were diagnosed antenatally. In considering the detection of pre-eclampsia it was noted that 30 per cent of women with this condition as defined at the clinic presented with the condition for the first time either in labour or during the puerperium. Before the onset of labour 183 women with pre-eclampsia and 17 with essential hypertension were detected. Another 256 women had hypertensive blood pressures which settled after admission to hospital and did not recur. These women with transient hypertension were considered as false-positives for detection of pre-eclampsia and their offspring had a quarter the rate of perinatal death and around a third of the rate of IUGR than the offspring of mothers with pre-eclampsia or hypertension. Hall and Chng (1982) considered the productivity of total antenatal visits for detection rates for these three complications. For IUGR there was a productivity at best of 0.7 per cent, for breech presentation productivity after 32 weeks gestation was at best 0.9 per cent, and for eclampsia detection exceeded 1 per cent only after the 34th week of gestation in primigravidae and the 40th week for multigravidae. Emergency admissions outnumbered elective admissions resulting from antenatal care throughout pregnancy.

This study from Aberdeen exposes the shortcomings of screening procedures in populations which were compliant to some degree with antenatal care. The shortcomings relate in part to the knowledge of the natural history of the complications, the validity of the screening measures and staff compliance with their use, and the limited interval between detection and natural presentation. Other workers have been concerned with the client rather than the providers of services and have thrown some light on factors which help to explain the utilization of antenatal care. Graham (1977) studied in some depth the perceptions, attitudes, and experiences of a small but randomly selected group of 50 pregnant women in order to avoid the selected biases of

women categorized by marital status or parity. About half of the mothers felt that their pregnancy was 'planned' but this applied to a long-term view of family development rather than any deliberate timing or actions. Becoming pregnant was not seen as a problem but considerable ambivalence was revealed towards pregnancy, childbirth, and motherhood. Those women who appeared more to have 'planned' their pregnancy experienced similar conflicts about their pregnant state. Physiological changes were balanced to some extent with perceived elevations of psychological and social status. Most women, the primiparous and the multiparous, had series of worries which were both personal and directly concerned their pregnancy. These worries concerned their body image, anxieties for possible deformities and handicaps in their babies, and apprehension of childbirth. The latter fears were structured by some knowledge of embryology and of mother–fetus interactions. They concerned also previous experience as to what was done to their bodies in antenatal and intrapartum care and the lack of control over events and eventual outcome. These fears were often not discussed with medical or paramedical staff but were the preserve of close friends. Pregnant women other than the married and primiparae did not feel that they fitted into some aspects of antenatal care. Seeking advice with professionals about the features of pregnancy involved rituals of specific answers for specific questions with little discussion at personal levels.

The tendency for antenatal care to be used by doctors as a search for complications of an anatomical or physiological nature in order to effect some form of intervention is seen as conflicting with the expectations of women seeking counselling for their anxieties and fears of an otherwise normally perceived phase of motherhood. An ambiguous response to the early part of pregnancy may not be conducive with immediate attendance for antenatal care. Reception of antenatal care which ignores women's concern with their babies and their perceived problems and subjects them to ill-understood investigations may further limit their compliance. It is of interest that in the trial undertaken by Neldam (1980) of maternal monitoring of fetal movements the responsibility for screening given to mothers contributed to the eventual benefit in terms of decreased perinatal deaths.

The lack of effectiveness and efficiency of some parts of antenatal care has given rise to proposals for change of its structure and function. Hall *et al.* (1980) suggested that antenatal visits for the normal multiparous women should take place at the 12th, 30th, and 36th weeks of pregnancy and again at term. Primiparous women require more frequent measurement of blood pressure from the 34th week but not necessarily full examinations. Care could be undertaken less frequently by obstetricians when pregnancy is expected to be normal. Midwives and family doctors may comply with the requirements of effective antenatal care more easily than obstetricians or gynaecologists. Ideally, antenatal care should be provided by those best able to make available its qualities. In a project in Edinburgh antenatal care is shared between family doctor, midwife, and visiting obstetrician at a health centre close to the homes of clients (Parboosingh and Kerr 1982). Risk cards are used to record identified risk and to convey the data to the visiting obstetrician. Although comparison is possible only with the historical events of the preceding five years, the number of women visiting before the 16th week of pregnancy has increased by 50 per cent and the number of defaulters from the care programme has diminished from 16 per cent to 1 per cent. There were fewer hospital admissions prenatally and perinatal mortality fell from 25 per 1000 births at the beginning of the project in 1975 to 8 per 1000 in 1980. Increased satisfaction with the changes in care were recorded for clients and staff.

In Glasgow, improvements of antenatal care were sought by relocating hospital care to a peripheral clinic away from the hospital (unpublished communications from the Social Paediatric and Obstetric Research Unit, University of Glasgow). It was thought that this clinic would improve attendance at mothercraft and relaxation classes in a city where attendance for primigravidae had been running at a little over 50 per cent. The peripheral clinic proved to be no more accessible than the hospital clinic for about a third of its clients, the waiting time to see a doctor was as long and the number of doctors seeing women during antenatal care was not reduced. In spite of expectations the care service did not change attitudes or behaviour of hospital staff. Whilst some sharing of care was intended with general practitioners, this involved only the exchange of record cards and little closer co-operation. Shared care increased the number of antenatal visits. Whilst women felt better able to discuss anxieties with general practitioners, when the basis of their fears related to complications of pregnancy the knowledge required was available mainly from obstetricians.

In some countries different aspects of antenatal care are influenced by financial arrangements. In Holland, insurance cover extends to antenatal care by specialists only if approved medical or obstetrical complications occur (Keirse 1982). Until recently, antenatal care by midwives which resulted in referral to an obstetrician resulted in the midwives fee being reduced by two-thirds. This financial penalty may have induced midwives to retain care of pregnant women at risk longer than was perhaps advisable. In France, financial incentives have been available for pregnant women who attend antenatal care early and regularly but, as has been noted, in 1976, 40 per cent of pregnant women attended on fewer than five occasions.

Antenatal care has several components. The contribution of these components to the fulfilment of successful pregnancies varies with the expectations of clients and professional providers and the intrinsic ability of the components and their delivery to alter the outcomes of pregnancy. The relationship of outcomes of various sorts to the process of antenatal care has not been often studied by controlled experimentation.

Hospital maternity services

Women in many countries have become increasingly concerned with the view that hospital obstetric units are the most favourable places for delivery of their children.

Women who see childbirth as a normal physiological process find it difficult to accept the need for standardized and somewhat impersonal care in hospitals where benefit may only accrue to a few mothers and babies and the practising obstetric staff. Determining how necessary hospital delivery is for all mothers is limited by the absence of controlled trials and the limitations of the few observational studies.

Fedrick and Butler (1978) considered the safety of hospital and non-hospital delivery by death rates for stillbirths and neonatal deaths using data from the 1958 Perinatal Mortality Survey. At the time of the survey, 35 per cent of deliveries took place outside hospital obstetric units. Mothers, who were 20–34 years of age and who delivered at term, were considered in three groups, normotensive primiparae, hypertensive primiparae, and normotensive parity 1, 2, or 3 women. Although the death rates were highest in hospital when considered by place of delivery for all three groups, consideration by place of booking for expected delivery showed that death rates in all three groups were highest outside hospital. Analysis of maternal risk factors for perinatal deaths indicated also that mothers in hospital were in fact at highest risk. The conditions that prevailed for both domiciliary and hospital confinements over 20 years ago are not those that prevail today and the distribution of risk between mother by place of booking may have changed also.

Tew (1982) studied the lack of direct association between the size of annual increases of the proportion of births in hospital between 1969 and 1979 in England and Wales and the annual reductions in perinatal mortality rates. The indirect association had a correlation coefficient of -0.74 which was statistically significant. The author argues that if hospital delivery improves perinatal mortality outcome these findings would not have been expected. Equally, however, as the size of the increase in births in hospital fell off the annual decrease in perinatal mortality increased. These associations will vary with the characteristics of the increasing proportion of mothers delivering in hospital. Using the Antenatal Prediction Score for mothers of the British Births survey, Tew determined that if deliveries in hospital and in general practitioner maternity units (GPMU) were standardized by this measure to allow for some maternal characteristics the hospital perinatal mortality rates would decrease and those of the GPMU would increase. The difference, however, remains highly significant. Likewise if deliveries are standardized for low birthweight the perinatal mortality rate in hospitals fall but not to the level of GPMU. Tew concluded that hospital deliveries cannot be safer for all births. The Antenatal Prediction Score is, however, limited and does not include any interpartum complications which contribute to perinatal deaths. Finally, the excess perinatal mortality rates seen in hospital are often associated with the transfer of mothers booked for home confinements who develop complications. But Tew estimates that the perinatal mortality rates of the transferred mothers would not account for the hospital excess over the rates in the GPMU. Therefore hospital deliveries do not bring benefits to all mothers.

Knox *et al.* (1980) have been concerned with how far

health service provision influences perinatal mortality standardized for birthweight. They observed that perinatal mortality rates between the highest and lowest English area health authority varied twofold in the period 1974–76. Birthweight, social, economic, and health service indicators, the latter including obstetric bed usage, special baby care unit beds, GPMUs, and all health professionals except doctors, were recorded by each area. The extent to which variation in perinatal mortality standardized for birthweight was accounted for by these factors was determined. Social variables accounted for most of the variation in perinatal mortality rates. Only two health factors had any association and these were general and not associated with obstetric or neonatal care. Around 18 per cent of the variance was unexplained. Knox *et al.* concluded that any influence that health provision was having on perinatal mortality must have concerned other health determinants and aspects of their use and deployment. The effect of the social variables on the mortality rates did not act through any associated under-provision of health services. The contributions of health care to change in perinatal mortality will be revealed only by controlled trials.

Neonatal intensive care

Obstetric intervention to deliver before term the fetus at risk of intrauterine death has necessitated provision from paediatric services of care for the immature newborn. Such care has been provided to varying proportions of newborns in varying amounts of intensity. Newborns who have experienced birth asphyxia and respiratory distress, infections, and metabolic and drug disturbances are also given intensive care when judged necessary. The benefits of obstetric interventions before term and during labour have then to be assessed in combination with neonatal care. In terms of mortality there is evidence that the combined approach may have succeeded in contributing to the continuing fall in stillbirth and neonatal mortality rates especially in the low-birthweight babies. Pharoah and Alberman (1981) following trends in neonatal deaths in England and Wales from 1953 to 1979 in low-birthweight babies, noted (Fig. 20.4) that day 0 mortality did not begin to improve until the 1960s when neonatal intensive care units became more widespread in the country. In 1981 in England, around 98 per cent of livebirths of 1501–2500 g, 80 per cent of those of birthweight 1001–1500 g, and just under 40 per cent of those of birthweights of 1000 g or less survive the neonatal period (DHSS 1981). More recently MacFarlane (1982) has observed that since 1976 neither late neonatal nor postneonatal mortality rates in England and Wales have shown any decline (Table 20.14). She suggested that this may reflect the postponement of death for some newborn from the early neonatal period due to neonatal intensive care, or the failure of the child to survive when exposed to the environment outside the neonatal care unit.

Whilst there may be some beneficial features of perinatal mortality associated with neonatal intensive care there has been concern with the effect of such care on levels of morbidity in survivors. In Australia (1981), Sweden (1979), and

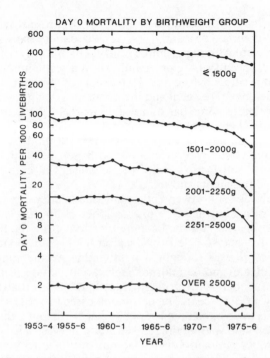

Fig. 20.4. Day 0 mortality according to birthweight group. (Source: Pharoah and Alberman (1981).)

Ireland (1978), it has been observed that rates of cerebral palsy have been rising in communities where neonatal intensive care is employed. In Western Australia, total spastic diplegia rates rose from 0.6 per 1,000 in 1970–75 to 1.3 per 1000 in 1976, and for births under 2500 g the rates were 6.7 and 10.2 for the same periods respectively. Other long-term follow-up data have linked preterm births and care in special baby-care units with increased risks of child abuse (Murphy *et al.* 1981). Neonatal care is expensive and the benefits of obstetric and neonatal interventions for society need to be estimated as further provisions are requested. Benefits and adverse outcomes have to be studied over several years during which time the use and methods of obstetric and neonatal care interventions are changing. Some workers feel that favourable development of liveborn

Table 20.14. *Mortality in the first year of life by year of birth. England and Wales, 1970–79*

| Year of birth | Live births | Deaths per 100 live births | | | |
		Early neonatal	Late neonatal	Post-neonatal	Total (infant)
1970	785 163	10.6	1.7	6.1	18.3
1971	782 602	9.9	1.7	5.5	17.1
1972	725 114	9.9	1.7	5.6	17.2
1973	675 766	9.5	1.6	5.4	16.5
1974	639 699	9.4	1.7	5.0	16.0
1975	603 493	9.1	1.6	4.9	15.6
1976	584 390	8.1	1.5	4.4	14.1
1977	569 068	7.7	1.6	4.6	13.9
1978	596 650	7.1	1.6	4.7	13.4
1979	637 797	6.7	1.5	4.6	12.8

Source: Macfarlane (1982).

neonates weighing 501–1500 g can be achieved without intensive or special care interventions (Steiner *et al.* 1980). The effectiveness and efficiency of neonatal care services can only be fully understood through appropriate randomized controlled trials and estimates then made for future investments and availability (Sinclair *et al.* 1981).

Postnatal care

The end of pregnancy is the beginning of childhood and the investment that has been put into the pregnancy by the mother and her professional attendants needs to be maintained in the postnatal period. For some parents adjustments to the arrival of a new child requires advice and support, especially if hospital stay has been short, and in the case of some single-parent families and for some families facing social and economic difficulties. Cartwright (1979) observed that the majority of mothers found postnatal visits by health visitors to be positive and helpful. For the mothers themselves, postnatal attention was not comprehensively taken up and attendance for postnatal clinics fell with parity and also by social class.

For some parents the outcome of pregnancy may raise the need for genetic or family counselling. It is estimated that around 10 per cent of childhood deaths in hospital are associated with disorders which are largely genetic in cause (Emery 1977). Most genetic disorders can only be avoided in subsequent pregnancies by estimation of risk and subsequent contraception or sterilization, artificial insemination, or adoption. Some disorders, such as Tay–Sachs disease in Ashkenazi Jews and some haemoglobinopathies, can be detected prenatally in the fetus and the pregnancy terminated. Around 20 per cent of cases of autosomal recessive disorders and a similar percentage of X-linked recessive disorders are preventable theoretically through genetic counselling and acceptance of advice to avoid further reproduction. Emery (1977) points out that only a proportion of parents who are at risk especially amongst affected relatives are seen and that many obstetric and paediatric staff and family doctors continue to under-refer for genetic/family counselling advice.

Finally there is consideration for those parents who have experienced stillbirths or neonatal deaths during pregnancy. Newcombe and Rhynas (1962) found that compensation was effective in the first year following stillbirth but that the same families experienced a net reduction in fertility over a four-year period. Similar findings were observed by Vogel and Knox (1975). Women with established fertility compensated well and women with only one or no previous living children compensated less frequently and with fewer subsequent survivors. This differential compensation may be determined by social forces when fertility is established and genetic and physiological forces when it is not. When neonatal deaths occurred, Vogel and Knox observed compensation especially in the second year.

These considerations should be taken into account as obstetric and neonatal services strive to reduce further stillbirth and neonatal mortality.

Acknowledgements

Figures 20.1 and 20.2, and Tables 20.3, 20.5, 20.6 and 20.7, are Crown copyright; reproduced with the permission of the Controller of Her Majesty's Stationery Office.

REFERENCES

Abel, E.L. (1980). Smoking during pregnancy: a review of effects on growth and development of offspring. *Hum. Biol.* **52**, 593.

Adelstein, A.M., MacDonald Davies, I.M., and Weatherall, J.H.C. (1978). *Perinatal and infant mortality: social and biological factors 1975–1977. Studies on medical and population subjects, No. 41.* Office of Populations, Censuses and Surveys. HMSO, London.

Alberman, E. (1974). Factors influencing perinatal wastage. *Clinics in Obstet. Gynaecol.* **1**, 1.

Alberman, E., Polani, P.E., and Fraser Roberts, J. A. (1972). Parental x-irradiation and chromosome constitution in their spontaneously aborted foetuses. *Ann. Hum. Genet.* **36**, 185.

Anderson, A. and Turnbull, A. (1982). Effect of oestrogens, progestogens and betamimetics in pregnancy. In *Effectiveness and satisfaction in antenatal care* (ed. M. Enkin and I. Chalmers) p. 163. Spastics International Medical Publications, London.

Ashford, J.R., Reid, K.L.Q., and Riley, V.C. (1973). An analysis of variations in perinatal mortality amongst local authorities in England and Wales. *Int. J. Epidemiol.* **2**, 31.

Baird, D., Thomson, A.M., and Billewicz, W.Z. (1957). Birthweights and placental weights in pre-eclampsia. *J. Obstet. Gynaecol.* **64**, 370.

Baird, D., Walker, J., and Thomson, A.M. (1954). The causes and prevention of stillbirths and first week deaths. *J. Obstet. Gynaecol.* **61**, 433.

Baker, I.A., Elwood, P.C., and Sweetnam, P.M. (1979). Free school meals and height of Welsh schoolchildren. *Lancet* **ii**, 692.

Bakketeig, L.S. and Hoffman, H.J. (1979). Perinatal mortality by birth order within cohorts based on sibship size. *Br. Med. J.* **ii**, 693.

Beral, V. (1979). Reproductive morality. *Br. Med. J.* **ii**, 632.

British Medical Journal (1979). Rickets in Asian immigrants. (Editorial.) *Br. Med. J.* **i**, 1744.

Brooke, O.G., Brown, I.R.F., Bone, C.D.M. *et al.* (1980). Vitamin D supplements in pregnant Asian women: effects on calcium status and fetal growth. *Br. Med. J.* **i**, 751.

Brotherston, J. (1976). Inequality: is it inevitable? In *Equalities and inequalities in health* (eds. C.O. Carter and J. Peel) p. 73. Academic Press, London.

Butler, N.R. and Alberman, E.D. (1969). *Perinatal problems: the second report of the 1958 British Perinatal Mortality Survey.* Livingstone, Edinburgh.

Butler, N.R. and Bonham, D.G. (1963). *Perinatal mortality: the first report of the 1958 British Perinatal Mortality Survey.* Livingstone, Edinburgh.

Cartwright, A. (1979). *The dignity of labour?: a study of childbearing and induction.* Tavistock Publications, London.

Central Statistics Office (1975). *Social commentary: social class. Social trends*, No. 6, p. 15, HMSO, London.

Chalmers, I., Zlosnik, J.E., Johns, K.A., and Campbell, H. (1976). Obstetric practice and outcome of pregnancy in Cardiff residents. *Br. Med. J.* **i**, 735.

Chamberlain, R., Chamberlain, G., Howlett, B., and Claireaux, A. (1975). *British births 1970. Vol. 1.: the first week of life.* Heinemann, London.

Chamberlain, G., Phillipp, E., Howlett, B.,and Masters, K. (1978). *British births 1970. Vol. 2: Obstetric care.* Heinemann, London.

Clarke, C. and Whitfield, A.G.W. (1979). Deaths from rhesus haemolytic disease in England and Wales in 1977: accuracy of records and assessment of anti-D prophylaxis. *Br. Med. J.* i, *1665*.

Cochrane, R. and Robertson, A. (1973). The life events inventory: a measure of the relative severity of psycho-social stressors. *J. Psychosom. Res.* **17**, 135.

Cooper, L.Z. (1968). Intrauterine infections: birth defects. *Birth Defects Original Article Series* **4**, 21.

Cussen, G.H., Barry, J.E., Moloney, A.M., Buckley, N.M., Crowley, M., and Daly, C. (1978). Cerebral palsy: a regional study (part 1). *J. Irish Med. Assoc.* **71**, 568.

Dekaban, A. and Baird, R. (1955)- The outcome of pregnancy in diabetic women. I. Fetal wastage and morbidity in the offspring of diabetic and control mothers. *J. Pediatr.* **55**, 563.

DHSS (1981). *Annual Report of The Chief Medical Officer. On the state of the public health*, p. 8. HMSO, London.

DHSS (1982). *Report on confidential enquiries into maternal deaths in England and Wales (1976–78). Reports on Health and Social Subjects*, No. 26. HMSO, London

Desmonts, G. and Convreus, J. (1974). Congenital toxoplasmosis: a prospective study of 378 pregnancies. *New Engl. J. Med.* **290**, 1110.

Donovan, J.W. (1977). Randomized controlled trial of anti-smoking advice in pregnancy. *Br. J. Prev. Soc. Med.* **31**, 6.

Emery, A.E.H. (1977). Genetic counselling—its genetic and social implications. In *Equalities and inequalities in family life.* (ed. R. Chester and J. Peel) p. 71. Academic Press, London.

Fedrick, J. and Butler, N.R. (1978). Intended place of delivery and perinatal outcome. *Br. Med. J.* **1**, 763.

Gilmore, D., Robinson, E.T., Harper Gilmer, W., and Urquhart, G.E.D. (1982). Effect of rubella vaccination programme in schools on rubella immunity in a general practice population. *Br. Med. J.* **284**, 628.

Graham, H. (1977). Women's attitudes to conception and pregnancy. In *Equalities and inequalites in family life* (eds. R. Chester and J. Peel) p. 81. Academic Press, London.

Griffith, G.W. (1973). The prevention of Down's syndrome (mongolism). *Health Trends* **5**, 59

Hagberg, B. (1979). Epidemiological and preventive aspects of cerebral palsy and severe mental retardation in Sweden. *Eur. J. Paediatr.* **130**, 71.

Hall, M.H. and Chng, P.K. (1982). Antenatal care in practice. In *Effectiveness and satisfaction in antenatal care* (ed. M. Enkin and I. Chalmers) p. 60. Spastics International and Medical Publications, London.

Hall, M.H., Chng, P.K., and MacGillivray, I. (1980). Is routine antenatal care worth while? *Lancet* ii, 78.

Harlap, S. and Shiono, P.H. (1980). Alcohol, smoking and incidence of spontaneous abortions in the first and second trimester. *Lancet* ii, 173.

Harrison, J.W., Jones, K.L., and Smith, D.W. (1976). Fetal alcohol syndrome. *JAMA* **235**, 1458.

Haverkamp, A.D., Orleans, M., Langendoerfer, S. *et al.* (1979). A controlled trial of the differential effects of intrapartum fetal monitoring. *Am. J. Obstet. Gynaecol.* **134**, 399.

Heath, C.W.Jr., Flynt, J.W., Oakley, G.P.Jr. *et al.*(1975). The role of birth defect surveillance in control of fetal environmental hazards. *Postgrad. Med. J.* **51**, Suppl. 15, 69.

Hemminki, E. (1982). Effect of routine haematinic and vitamin administration in pregnancy. In *Effectiveness and satisfaction in antenatal care* (eds. M. Enkin and I. Chalmers) p. 114. Spastics International Medical Publications, London.

Hemminki, K., Franssila, E., and Vainio, H. (1980). Spontaneous abortions among female chemical workers in Finland. *Int. Arch. Occup. Environ. Health* **45**, 123.

Hemminki, K., Sorsa, M., and Vainio, H. (1979). Genetic risks caused by occupational chemicals. *Scand. J. Work Environ. Health* **5**, 307.

Herbst, A.L., Ulfelder, H., and Poskaner, D.C. (1971). Adenocarcinoma of the vagina. association of maternal stilbestrol therapy with tumour appearance in young women. *New Engl. J. Med.* **284**, 878.

Himmelberger, D.V., Brown, B.W., and Cohen, E.N. (1978). Cigarette smoking during pregnancy and the occurrence of spontaneous abortion and congenital abnormality. *Am. J. Epidemiol.* **108**, 470.

Holmes, G.E., Miller, H.C., Hassanein, K., Lansky, S.B., and Goggin, J.E. (1977). Postnatal somatic growth in babies with atypical fetal growth patterns. *Am. J. Dis. Child.* **131**, 1078.

Infante, P.F., McMichael, A.J., Wagoner, J.K., Waxweiler, R.J., and Falk, H. (1976). Genetic risks of vinyl chloride. *Lancet* i, 734.

Kass, E.H. (1962). Pyelonephritis and bacteriuria. A major problem in preventive medicine. *Ann. Intern. Med.* **56**, 46.

Keirse, M.J.N.C. (1982). Interaction between primary and secondary antenatal care with particular reference to the Netherlands. In *Effectiveness and satisfaction in antenatal care* (eds. M. Enkin and I. Chalmers) p. 222. Spastics International Medical Publications, London.

Kelso, I.M., Parsons, R.J., Lawrence, G.F. *et al.* (1978). An assessment of continuous fetal heart rate monitoring in labor. *Am. J. Obstet. and Gynecol.* **131**, 526.

Kendall, R.E., Rennie, D., Clarke, J.A., and Dean, C. (1981). The social and obstetric correlates of psychiatric admission in the puerperium. *Psychol. Med.* **11**, 341.

Knox, E.G. (1976). Control of haemolytic disease of the newborn. *Br. J. Prev. Soc. Med.* **30**, 163.

Knox, E.G. (1980). Strategy for rubella vaccination. *Int. J. Epidemiol.* **9**, 13.

Knox, E.G., Marshall, T., Kane, S., Green, A., and Mallet, R. (1980). Social and health care determinants of area variations in perinatal mortality. *Community Med.* **2**, 282.

Lemoine, P., Harrousseau, H., and Borteyni, J.P. (1968). Les enfants de parents alcooliques. Anomolies observées. A propos de 127 cas. *Quest Med. France* **59**, 1445.

Lindgren, G. (1976). Height, weight and menarche of Swedish urban-schoolchildren with relative socio-economic and regional factors. *Ann. Hum. Biol.* **3**, 501.

Low, J.A. and Galbraith, R.S. (1974). Pregnancy characteristics of intrauterine growth retardation. *Obstet. Gynecol.* **44**, 122.

McBride, W.G. (1961). Thalidomide and congenital abnormalities. *Lancet* ii, 1358.

MacFarlane, A. (1982). Infant deaths after four weeks. *Lancet* ii, 929.

McKinlay, J.B. and McKinlay, S.M. (1979). The influence of a premarital conception and various obstetric complications on subsequent prenatal health behaviour. *J. Epidemiol. Community Health* **33**, 84.

Matthews, D.D. (1977). A randomised controlled trial of bed rest and sedation or normal activity and non-sedation in the management of non-albuminuric hypertension in late pregnancy. *Br. J. Obstet. Gynaecol.* **84**, 108.

Meyer, M.B., Jones, B.S., and Tonascia, J.A. (1976). Perinatal events associated with maternal smoking during pregnancy. *Am. J. Epidemiol.* **103**, 464.

Miller, H.C., Hassanein, K., and Hensleigh, P.A. (1978). Maternal factors in the incidences of low birthweight infants among black and white mothers. *Paediatr. Res.* **12**, 1016.

Monif, G.R.G., Egan, E.A., Held, B., and Eitzmann, D.V. (1972). The correlation of maternal cytomegalovirus infection during varying stages of gestation with neonatal involvement. *J. Paediatr.* **80**, 17.

Morgan-Capner, P. (1982). Loophole in rubella screening. *Lancet* ii, 1165.

Murphy, J.F., Jenkins, J., Newcombe, R.G., and Sibert, J.R. (1981) Objective birth data and the prediction of child abuse. *Arch. Dis. Child.* **56**, 295.

Neldan, S. (1980). Fetal movements as an indicator of fetal wellbeing. *Lancet* **i**, 1222.

Nevin, N.C. (1981). Neural tube defects. *Lancet* **ii**, 1290.

Newcombe, H.B. and Rhynas, P.O.W. (1962). Child spacing following stillbirths and infant death. *Eugen. Q.* **9**, 25.

Newton, R.W., Webster, P.A.C., Binu, P.S., Maskrey, N., and Phillips, A.B. (1979). Psychosocial stress in pregnancy and its relation to the onset of premature labour. *Br. Med. J.* **ii**, 411.

Nuckolls, K-.B., Cassel, J., and Kaplan, B.H. (1972). Psychosocial assets, life crisis and the prognosis of pregnancy. *Am. J. Epidemiol.* **9**, 431.

Ouellette, E.M., Rossett, H.L., and Rosman, N.P. (1977). Adverse effects on offspring of maternal alcohol abuse during pregnancy. *New Engl. J. Med.* **297**, 628.

Page, E.W. and Christianson, R. (1976). The impact of mean arterial pressure in the middle trimester upon the outcome of pregnancy. *Am. J. Obstet. Gynecol.* **125**, 740.

Parboosingh, J. and Kerr, H. (1982). Innovations in the role of obstetric hospitals in prenatal care. In *Effectiveness and satisfaction in antenatal care* (eds. M. Enkin and I. Chalmers) p. 259. Spastics Intenational Medical Publications, London.

Peters, T.J., Golding, J., Fryer, J.G., Lawrence, C.J., Butler, N.R., and Chamberlain, G.K. (in press). Plus ça change. *Br. J. Obstet. Gynaecol.*

Pharoah, P.O.D. and Alberman, E.D. (1981). Mortality of low birth-weight infants in England and Wales 1953 to 1979. *Arch. Dis. Child.* **56**, 86.

Redman, C. (1982). Screening for pre-eclampsia. in *Effectiveness and satisfaction in antenatal care* (ed. M. Enkin and I. Chalmers) p. 72. Spastics International Medical Publications, London.

Rona, R.J., Chinn, S., and Smith, A.M. (1979). Height of children receiving free school meals. *Lancet* **ii**, 534.

Renou, P., Chang, A., and Anderson, I. (1976). Controlled trial of fetal intensive care. *Am. J. Obstet. Gynecol.* **126**, 470.

Rubin, P.C. (1981). Beta-blockers in pregnancy. *New Engl. J. Med.* **305**, 1323.

Rumeau-Rouquette, C., Breart, G., du Mazaubrun, C., Crost, M., and Rabarison, Y. (1978). Evolution de la pathologie perinatale et de la prevention en France: enquetes nationales INSERM 1972–6. *Gynaecol. Obstet. Biol. Reprod.* **7**, 905.

Rush, D. (1982). Effects of changes in protein and calorie intake during pregnancy on the growth of the human fetus. In *Effectiveness and satisfaction in antenatal care.* (eds. M. Enkin and I. Chalmers) p. 93. Spastics International Medical Publications. London.

Rush, D., Stein, Z. and Susser, M. (1980). A randomized controlled trial of prenatal nutritional supplementation in New York city. *Paediatrics* **65**, 683. Editorial (1978). *Br. Med. J.* **ii**, 1744.

Rush, R.W., Keirse, M.J.N.C., Howat, P., Baum, J.D., and Anderson, A.B.M. (1976). Contribution of preterm delivery to perinatal mortality. *Br. Med. J.* **ii**, 695.

Saugstad, L. F. (1981). Weight of all births and infant mortality. *J. Epidemiol. Community Health* **35**, 185.

Sentrakul, P. and Potter, E.L. (1966). Pathological diagnoses on 2681 abortions at the Chicago Lying-in Hospital, 1957–1965. *Am. J. Public Health* **56**, 2083.

Shapiro, S., Jones, E.W., and Densen, P.M. (1962). A life table of pregnancy terminations and correlates of fetal loss. *Milbank Mem. Fund Q.* **60**, 7.

Shapiro, S., Slone, D., and Hartz, S.C. (1976). Anticonvulsants and parental epilepsy in the development of birth defects. *Lancet* **i**, 272.

Sheridan, M.D. (1964). Final report of a prospective study of children

whose mothers had rubella in early pregnancy. *Br. Med. J.* **ii**, 536.

Sinclair, J.C., Torrance, G.W., Boyle, M.H., Horwood, S.P., Saigal, S., and Sackett, D.L. (1981). Evaluation of neonatal-intensive-care programs. *New Engl. J. Med.* **305**, 489.

Smithells, R.W., Sheppard, S., Sohorah, C.J., *et al.* (1980). Possible prevention of neural-tube defects by periconceptional vitamin supplementation. *Lancet* **i**, 339.

Smithells, R.W., Sheppard, S., Schorah, C.J. *et al.* (1981*a*). Apparent prevention of neural-tube defects by periconceptional vitamin supplementation. *Arch. Dis. Child.* **56**, 911.

Smithells, R.W., Sheppard, S., Schorah, C.J. *et al.* (1981*b*). Vitamin supplementation and neural-tube defects. *Lancet* **ii**, 1425.

Social Services Committee (1980). *Second report. Perinatal and neonatal mortality,* Vol. 1, p. 158. HMSO, London.

Social Trends (1982) No. 12, p. 120. HMSO, London.

Standing Medical Advisory Committee (1981). *Prevention of haemolytic disease of the newborn. Addendum 1981.* DHSS, London.

Stanley, F. and Atkinson, S. (1981). Impact of neonatal intensive care on cerebral palsy in infants of low birthweight. *Lancet* **ii**, 1162.

Stein, Z., Susser, M., Seanger, G., and Marolla, F. (1975). *Famine and human development: the Dutch hunger winter of 1944/45.* Oxford University Press, New York.

Steiner, E.S., Sanders, E.M., Phillips, E.C.K., and Maddock, C.R. (1980). Very low birth weight children at school age: comparison of neonatal management methods. *Br. Med. J.* **ii**, 1237.

Tew, M. (1982). Obstetrics versus midwifery—the verdict of the statistics. *Matern. Child Health* **7**, 198.

Tomlin, P.J. (1979). Health problems of anaesthetists and their families in the West Midlands. *Br. Med. J.* **i**, 779.

Tovey, L.A.D., Murray, J., Stevenson, B.J., and Taverner, J.M. (1978). Prevention of Rh haemolytic disease. *Br. Med. J.* **ii**, 106.

U.K. Collaboration Study on Alpha-fetoprotein in Relation to Neural-tube Defects (1979). Second report. Amniotic-fluid alpha-fetoprotein measurement in antenatal diagnosis of anencephaly and open spina bifida in early pregnancy. *Lancet* **ii**, 654.

US Department of Health, Education and Welfare (1979). *Costs and benefits of electronic fetal monitoring: a review of the literature. Research report Series.* DHEW Publication No. (PHS) 79-3245. Washington DC.

Van de Kaa, D.J. (1980). Recent trends in fertility in Western Europe. In *Demographic patterns in developed societies.* Symposia of the Society for the Study of Human Biology. Vol. 19 (ed. R.W. Hiorns) p. 55. Taylor and Francis, London.

Viegas, O.A.C., Scott, P.H., Cole, T.J., Mansfield, H.N., Wharton, P., and Wharton, B.A. (1982*a*). Dietary protein energy supplementation of pregnant Asian mothers at Sorrento, Birmingham. 1: unselective during second and third trimesters. *Br. Med. J.* **285**, 589.

Viegas, O.A.C., Scott, P.H., Cole, T.J., Eaton, P., Needham, P.G., and Wharton, B.A. (1982*b*). Dietary protein energy supplementation of pregnant Asian mothers at Sorrento, Birmingham. 11: Selective during third trimester only. *Br. Med. J.* **285**, 592.

Vogel, H.P. and Knox, E.G. (1975). Reproductive patterns after stillbirth and early infant death. *J. Biosoc. Sci.* **7**, 103.

Wald, N. (ed.) (1984). *Antenatal and neonatal screening for disease.* Oxford University Press.

Warburton, D. and Fraser, F.C. (1964). Spontaneous abortion risks in man: data from reproductive histories collected in a medical genetics unit. *Hum. Genet.* **16**, 1.

Weatherall, J.A.C. (1982). A review of some effects of recent medical practices in reducing the numbers of children born with congenital abnormalities. *Health Trends* **14**, 85.

Wilson, J.G. (1973). *Environment and birth defects,* p. 48. Academic Press, London.

Wilson, J.M.G. and Jungner, G. (1968). *Principles and practice of screening for disease. Public Health paper* No. 34. WHO, Geneva.

World Health Organization (1970). Spontaneous and induced abortion. *WHO Technical Report Series* **461**, 3.

World Health Organization Task Force (1979). Report of collaborative Study on Sequelae of Abortion. Gestation, birthweight, and spontaneous abortion in pregnancy after induced abortion. *Lancet* **i**, 142.

Yamazaki, J.R., Wright, S.W., and Wright, P.M. (1954). Outcome of pregnancy in women exposed to the atomic bomb in Nagasaki. *Am. J. Dis. Child.* **87**, 448.

21 Workers

J. Froines and Dean Baker

One of them worked in a whitelead factory twelve hours a day. She only expected to get her hands a little paralyzed; but she died.
George Bernard Shaw—1894 (Shaw 1960)

. . . and some of them gets lead poisoned soon, and some of them gets lead poisoned later, and some but not many niver.
Charles Dickens—1869 (Dickens 1958)

Mr. Pearson, our neighbour, died recently at age 65. He just wore out; you know, he had been a working man all his life and it had been hard work. He seemed to age early and grow tired and then he died.
Housewife in California—1982

INTRODUCTION

In a lecture delivered in 1936, Dr Henry E. Sigerist stated: 'The working conditions of a definite period and country represent an important criterion of a given civilization. When we look at the history of civilization from this point of view, we certainly have no reason to be proud of our past' (Marti-Ibanex 1960). The history of work is punctuated with stories of disease, disabling injury, and death in the workplace. Whether it be the chronicles of Agricola (1556), Ramazzini (1713), or more recently Dickens, Shaw, or the profound writing of Alice Hamilton (1943) in the early twentieth century, it is apparent that death, disease, and injury have been an omnipresent fact of life for workers.

It is important to understand that the human toll in the workplace is not only tragic because of the price in human suffering but also because these horrors were and are largely preventable. Thus, the role of the professional in occupational health is similar to that of practitioners of preventive medicine and public health for whom prevention is both the primary goal and strategy. As with certain other public health concerns, many problems of occupational health are ultimately of social, political, and economic origin. The focus of this chapter, however, is not on these socio-political and economic factors influencing occupational health but rather the recognition, evaluation, and control of workplace hazards that are of importance to the public health professional.

SCOPE OF THE OCCUPATIONAL DISEASE PROBLEM

Data on the occupational disease problem in the US can offer some insight into the magnitude of the problem in industrialized countries, while also illustrating the lack of adequate record keeping.

Overall statistics

The goal of the US Occupational Safety and Health Act (OSHA Act) of 1970 was 'to assure so far as possible every working man and woman in the nation safe and healthful working conditions and to preserve our national resources.' In order to effect the purpose of this legislation the US Congress instructed the government to compile statistics on work injuries and illnesses in the US. Prior to the passage of this act, collected statistics essentially were limited to the measurement of work injuries with little attention to occupational illness or disease. Since its passage, there have been increased efforts at estimating the nature and magnitude of workplace-related hazards and illnesses.

The President's report on occupational safety and health (OSHA 1972) estimated that there are 390 000 new illness cases annually and 100 000 deaths per year in the US from occupational diseases. Although these numbers have been criticized, they may be taken as crude estimates which describe the order of magnitude of the problem.

A more recent US Department of Labor report (1980a) assumes that traditional approaches of quantitatively assessing occupational disease underestimate the magnitude of the problem. The report describes an analysis which was based on individual self-reporting of work-related illness and which was limited to disabled individuals between the ages of 20 and 65 years. The data do not include individuals over the age of 65 or those who may have died from occupational diseases. The results of the analysis are described below:

Almost two million workers reported that they were severely or partially disabled from an occupationally-related disease. Approximately 700 000 of these occupational disease victims suffer long-term total disability. The 1.2 million workers partially disabled from an occupational disease were either temporarily out of the labor force because of their disability or limited in the kind and/or amount of work they could perform. These data include chronic cases of totally disabling byssinosis and asbestosis, as well as partially disabling conditions, such as varicose veins, arthritis and ulcers. The major disabling conditions reported by workers as being related to their jobs include: back and spinal conditions (34 per cent); heart and circulatory illnesses (26 per cent); respiratory conditions (13 per cent); mental illnesses (9 per cent); and digestive conditions (8 per cent). In

1978, the lost income for disabling occupational diseases amounted to $11.4 billion.

Causes of underestimation

While the above statistics already indicate a public health problem of large magnitude, it is likely that they substantially underestimate the true extent of the problem. There are many possible sources of underestimation of occupational illness and disease.

A primary cause is the inherent difficulty in establishing cause–effect relationships. Only in rare cases, such as angio-sarcoma of the liver from exposure to vinyl chloride or mesothelioma from asbestos exposure, can a causal relationship between the workplace exposure and the subsequent disease be readily established. The link between disease or illness and occupation is elusive because most occupational diseases are clinically indistinguishable from other chronic diseases of non-occupational origin. For example, lung cancer in an individual due to cigarette smoking is not different clinically or pathologically from that caused by asbestos exposure.

Further, the long latent period or interval which elapses between onset of exposure and the appearance of disease may obscure the causal relationship. For example, few occupational cancers appear immediately or even within 10 or 20 years of first exposure. The affected employee may even have retired, in this case, it is unlikely that he or she would be recorded as having developed a disease of occupational origin.

Lack of awareness among health practitioners contributes to the underestimation of occupational diseases. Neglect in obtaining information on jobs when taking a medical history leads to failure in recognizing occupational diseases. Certain health effects—such as liver disease or damage to the central nervous system—may go undetected throughout a working lifetime. They may be detected only through sophisticated medical testing or in the event of an autopsy. Neither is likely to be done in the absence of specific awareness of occupational problems by the health practitioner. Chronic debilitating, but not overtly disabling conditions are also unlikely to be adequately evaluated as to their occupational origins.

Yet another cause of underestimation is poor data on death certificates which in many countries (and in many states within the US) do not contain accurate information on occupation of the decedent or contain no listing of jobs at all. Lastly, given the potential financial liability associated with finding that a disease has an occupational origin, employers may be resistant to recognizing the workplace origin of a disorder, especially in cases where personal habits (such as smoking) or non-occupational pursuits (such as recreational activities) are possible aetiological factors.

Statistics on occupational cancer

Occupational cancer is an example of the difficulty of estimating the scope of the occupational disease problem. In 1978 scientists from the US Department of Health, Education and Welfare (Bridboard *et al.* 1978) developed a population attributable risk per cent model to estimate the fraction of cancer in the US related to occupational factors. Based on a 'worst case' scenario for six high-volume workplace carcinogens, namely, asbestos, arsenic, benzene, chromium, nickel, and petroleum fractions, they estimated that occupationally-related cancers would account for 20–38 per cent of future cancer mortality. On the other hand, Doll and Peto (1981) subsequently estimated the contribution of occupation to be more of the order of 4 per cent. A US Office of Technology Assessment report (1981) concluded that most estimates of occupationally-related cancer fit in the range of 10 ± 5 per cent.

Debate over these estimates has focused on the relative contribution of life-style (such as smoking and nutrition) as compared to occupational exposure. However, if even 5–10 per cent of all new cancers in the US were related to industrial exposure, this would still result in 20 000 to 40 000 excess cancer deaths per year.

ASSESSMENT OF OCCUPATIONAL HEALTH PROBLEMS

In general, the assessment of health risks due to occupational exposures has been the providence of clinicians, toxicologists, and epidemiologists. Several causes of occupational diseases, such as the relationship between vinyl chloride exposure and angiosarcoma of the liver, were identified through astute clinical observations and case studies of individual patients by clinicians (Creech and Johnson 1974). Unfortunately, these examples are few in number since most clinicians have little training or interest in occupational health problems. Toxicological evaluation of chemicals in bacterial, tissue, and animal systems has contributed substantially to the body of knowledge on the hazards of work. Epidemiology has been used to evaluate the link between occupational exposures and disease. Examples include industry-wide studies such as those of coke oven (Redmond *et al.* 1972), asbestos insulation (Selikoff *et al.* 1973), rubber (Monson and Fine 1978; Monson and Nakano 1976), or textile workers (Merchant *et al.* 1973), as well as cancer registry case-control studies, death certificate surveillance, and cross-sectional medical studies or health hazard evaluations. These approaches are discussed in detail elsewhere and will not be specifically addressed in this chapter (see Hernberg 1980; Monson 1980).

Much less attention has been devoted to assessing risk faced by workers through the quantitative investigation of workplace exposures; by the development of a hazard surveillance system; by the routine use of the occupational health history; and by the implementation of occupational disease surveillance programmes.

Exposure monitoring

Monitoring of worker exposure and monitoring of health effects are equally important in the assessment of occupational disease. Unfortunately less attention has been devoted to exposure monitoring and rarely have the two methods been coupled in a co-ordinated fashion. Certain standards in the US require periodic environmental monitoring, for example, the standards for lead, cotton dust, coke oven emissions, and acrylonitrile, but by and large there is no general requirement for such exposure monitoring. In many European countries, there has been even less attention to industrial hygiene and environmental monitoring.

Environmental monitoring is useful in evaluations to determine exposure levels in the workplace; in medical case studies where the link between a patient's disease and possible workplace exposure is sought; in epidemiological studies when attempting to determine the substances to which workers are—or were—exposed; and in engineering studies where one assesses whether a particular control strategy has reduced levels of a toxic substance. Routine environmental monitoring of employee exposure is an important step in assuring that workers are not placed at risk. Comparison of exposure levels to established guidelines or standards enables the industrial hygienist to determine if a worker is over-exposed and whether control devices are working effectively. Stationary, continuous monitoring devices may be equipped with alarm systems to warn when an over-exposure in a particular work area is occurring.

The measurement of air contaminant levels by an industrial hygienist may assist the physician in establishing a causal relationship between an employee's illness and a particular exposure. For example, a physician may suspect that a disease has an occupational origin, but may not be aware of the worker's exposure. Environmental sampling may be able to detect whether this employee did indeed have significant exposure to the suspected agent.

An important but under-utilized use of monitoring is in epidemiological studies of occupational disease. The epidemiologist requires industrial hygiene data to quantitatively assess risk factors in occupational disease. Dose information on populations under study is vital if the epidemiological findings are to be used to set safe levels of workplace exposure. However, developing dose information is not easy, especially when using retrospective techniques to study a disease with a long latent period, such as cancer. In this situation, current exposure levels and even the substances in use may not be representative of former conditions. Reconstruction of prior conditions may be impossible, resulting in uncertainty in the exposure evaluations. This problem alone justifies routine monitoring, and record collection and maintenance as an aid for future studies.

Hazard-surveillance system

The lack of a national occupational health surveillance system which could provide data on the incidence, demography, secular trends, and mortality related to occupational exposures, has been recognized as a problem for several years. Such a hazard-surveillance system would identify chemicals in use, the industries and occupations where they are used, and worker exposure to them.

The need for a chemical hazard-surveillance system

which includes workers' exposure evaluation is demonstrated by the remarkable growth in chemical production since the Second World War. Production levels of synthetic organic chemicals has doubled every 7–8 years since the 1930s, with total production now over 175 billion pounds per year. Production figures on individual chemicals are often unavailable. Even when they are available, it is difficult to obtain information on actual human exposure; one cannot simply assume that increased production of a particular chemical means increased exposure. A recent review of cancer rates in relation to the production history of industrial carcinogens concluded that it is too soon to reach firm conclusions about the size of the cancer risk, in light of the fact that production and use of many carcinogenic or otherwise hazardous materials have reached high levels only since the early 1960s (Davis et al. 1981).

To assess accurately the risk of a population of a disease associated with occupational exposure, the following parameters need to be determined:

1. Identification of chemicals in use by industry.
2. Description of the industrial process.
3. Assessment of the number of workers exposed to a particular substance.
4. Assessment of the current exposure levels to the agents.
5. Identification of workplace settings in which there is the potential for increased risk owing to the synergistic effects of potential hazards.
6. Assessment of the toxicity of specific agents (animal, human, or short-term test data).
7. Description and assessment of the effectiveness of controls to limit exposure.

These are difficult, but necessary tasks in so far as they represent the only means available to predict the future risks associated with current exposure, especially where agents with long latency periods are an issue.

The only systematic attempt to elicit most of the information described above was carried out by the US National Institute for Occupational Safety and Health (NIOSH) in 1972–74; a second survey is currently under way. The first survey, called the National Occupational Hazard Survey (NOHS) was conducted in a sample of nearly 5000 industrial facilities (NIOSH 1978). More than 9000 different potential health hazards were discovered, with more than 85 000 trade-name products listed. Chemical ingredients for about 60 000 of these trade-name products have been identified by contacting manufacturers. The information from the first NOHS, despite serious limitations in the sample size and the present age of the data, continues to be a major resource used by government, labour and health care providers on the type, extent, and distribution of potential workplace hazards in US workplaces.

Recently, scientists from NIOSH and the Harvard Medical School proposed the use of Sentinel Health Events —SHE(Occupational)—as a basis for public health surveillance and for increasing physician recognition of occupational health problems (Rutstein et al. 1983). A SHE

(Occupational) is a disease, disability, or untimely death which is occupationally related and whose occurrence may (i) provide the impetus for epidemiological or industrial hygiene studies, or (ii) serve as a warning signal that preventive measures to reduce exposures may be required. The proposed list of SHE(Occupational) cross-links 50 diseases (based on the International Classification of Diseases (ICD), 9th Revision) with potential exposures and occupations. This linkage of standard ICD codes to potential occupational exposures should help increase recognition and detection of an occupational disease.

Importance of the occupational health history

The accurate diagnosis of an occupational disease is important for two reasons: (i) determination that an illness or disease has been caused by exposure to a toxic agent will facilitate removal of the patient from exposure, implementation of appropriate exposure-reducing techniques, and treatment of the patient; and (ii) the ascertainment that a disease is of occupational origin will enable preventive steps to be taken to ensure that other workers are not similarly affected.

The occupational health history is an essential element in the diagnosis of workplace disease. Given the general nature of physical examination findings and laboratory tests, the occupational history may be the only means to identify a work-related medical problem. The occupational health history should be obtained in a practical and systematic manner. The extent of detail of the history should depend on the practitioner's level of suspicion that an illness may be work-related. The history should be carefully recorded since there may be legal implications and the information may be used for research purposes.

A systematic approach to history taking and diagnosis of occupational illness developed by Goldman and Peters (1981) is outlined in Fig. 21.1. It proceeds through four steps:

1. Routine screening questions on environmental and occupational origins of illness.

2. Consideration of sources of exposure.

3. Identification of the hazardous materials and their uses.

4. Practical approaches to follow-up, consultation, and resolution of the problems.

Table 21.1, also developed by Goldman and Peters (1981), lists some examples of occupational causes of medical problems which could be identified through use of an occupational history. Patients with health effects outlined in Table 21.1 should be suspected of having an illness of occupational aetiology. Any suspicious exposure would require that the practitioner obtain a complete occupational history. In general, a complete history will contain: (i) description of *all* jobs held; (ii) work exposures, including working conditions; (iii) time course of the patient's symptoms; (iv) significant symptoms or illness among co-workers; and (v) non-work exposures and other factors. Supplementary information may prove useful in the diagnosis. For example,

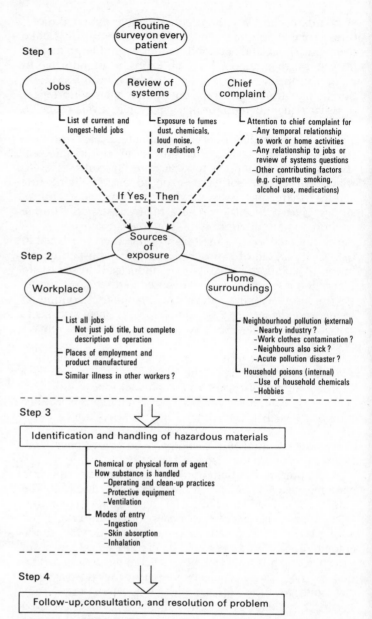

FIG. 21.1. Systematic approach to history taking and diagnosis of occupational or environmental illness. (Source: Goldman and Peters (1981, p. 2832).)

did the patient have preplacement or periodic physical examinations and laboratory examinations at work? Does the patient have any reason to suspect that the symptoms are work-related? Does the patient live near a known hazardous waste site or with someone who brings home toxic substances on work clothes? Above all, while the initial identification of these diseases does not require extensive knowledge of occupational disease and environmental agents, it does require a systematic approach for evaluating hazardous exposures. By combining such a systematic approach to the occupational history with traditional diagnostic techniques, the clinician can play an important role in the detection and prevention of occupational disease.

Table 21.1. *Some occupational causes of medical problems*

Medical problem	Agent	Potential exposures
Immediate or short-term effects		
Dermatoses (allergic or irritant)	Metals (chromium, nickel), fibrous glass, epoxy resins, cutting oils, solvents, caustic alkali, soaps	Electroplating, metal cleaning, plastics, machining, leather tanning, housekeeping
Headache	Carbon monoxide, solvents	Firefighting, automobile exhaust, foundry, wood finishing, dry cleaning
Acute psychoses	Lead (especially organic), mercury, carbon disulphide	Handling gasoline, seed handling, fungicide, wood preserving, viscose rayon industry
Asthma or dry cough	Formaldehyde, toluene diisocyanate, animal dander	Textiles, plastics, polyurethane kits, lacquer use, animal handler
Pulmonary oedema, pneumonitis	Nitrogen oxides, phosgene, halogen gases, cadmium	Welding, farming (' silo filler's disease'), chemical operations, smelting
Cardiac errhythmias	Solvents, fluorocarbons	Metal cleaning, solvents use, refrigerator maintenance
Angina	Carbon Monoxide	Car repair, traffic exhaust, foundry, wood finishing
Abdominal pain	Lead	Battery making, enamelling, smelting, painting, welding, ceramics, plumbing
Hepatitis (may become a long-term effect)	Halogenated hydrocarbons, e.g. carbon tetrachloride virus	Solvent use, lacquer use, hospital workers
Latent or long-term effects		
Chronic dyspnoea, pulmonary fibrosis	Asbestos, silica, beryllium, coal, aluminium	Mining, insulation, pipefitting, sandblasting, quarrying, metal alloy work, aircraft or electrical parts
Chronic bronchitis, emphysema	Cotton dust, cadmium, coal dust, organic solvents, cigarettes	Textile industry, battery production, soldering, mining, solvent use
Lung cancer	Asbestos, arsenic, nickel, uranium, coke-oven emissions	Insulation, pipefitting, smelting, coke ovens, shipyard workers, nickel refining, uranium mining
Bladder cancer	β-Naphthylamine, benzidine dyes	Dye industry, leather, rubber-wokring, chemists
Peripheral neuropathy	Lead, arsenic, n-hexane, methyl butyl ketone, acrylamide	Battery production, plumbing, smelting, painting, shoemaking, solvent use, insecticides
Behavioural changes	Lead, carbon disulphide, solvents, mercury, manganese	Battery makers, smelting, viscose rayon industry, degreasing, manufacturing/repair of scientific instruments, dental amalgam workers
Extrapyramidal syndrome	Carbon disulphide, manganese	Viscose rayon industry, steel production, battery production, foundry
Aplastic anaemia, leukaemia	Benzene, ionizing radiation	Chemists, furniture refinishing, cleaning, degreasing, radiation workers

Source: Goldman and Peters (1981), p. 2833.

It should be noted that merely obtaining the occupational health history is not necessarily sufficient to resolve the problem. At a grand rounds in a Boston hospital some years ago, a physician was describing the importance of taking an occupational history in the diagnosis of a lung cancer. In this particular case the clinician determined by interview that the patient, a non-smoker, had been exposed to bis-chloromethylether (BCME) at work, and concluded that his cancer was an example of a work-related disease. The physician correctly used this case to argue the importance and difficulty of taking an occupational history. On questioning by a Public Health School Faculty member present at the grand rounds, it became apparent that the team of doctors who had provided care for the patient had done nothing further with the information about the work exposure to the carcinogen, BCME. No one had been informed that a workplace exposure had resulted in an employee's developing lung cancer—not the company nor the worker's labour union, not the state health department, federal OSHA or even the worker's family. Thus, while the use of the occupational history had been important in determining the aetiology of the disease, it had been irrelevant in a public health context. If the physician were to play a role in the prevention of future lung cancer cases, he needed to report the occupational hazard and subsequent illness.

Occupational disease surveillance

Occupational disease surveillance by industrial health programmes in the workplace is an important approach to assessing the risk of disease due to occupational exposures (WHO 1975; Zielhuis 1978; Halperin*). Disease surveillance—consisting of biological monitoring and medical screening—uses the health history and physical and laboratory examinations of workers to estimate levels of exposure to specific substances and to assess early effects of exposure. Surveillance of workers is valuable since many occupational standards are based on minimal amounts of human or animal data; thus, it remains unknown whether workers are adequately protected based exclusively on environmental monitoring. Also, individual health effects of workplace

*Halperin *et al.* Medical screening in the workplace: revised principles. Presented at the Society for Epidemiologic Research meeting, June 1982.

exposures may vary depending on the characteristics of the individual worker. For example, the actual amount of dust or vapour in the air that is absorbed varies according to the worker's body size and respiratory rate. Furthermore, individuals in any normal population vary in sensitivity or susceptibility to agents. Thus, surveillance of individual workers is useful to identify and protect workers at increased risk.

Biological monitoring is the systematic collection of biological specimens for the purpose of estimating exposure to environmental agents and hence to determine risk of disease before it occurs. It is therefore a method for primary prevention of occupational disease. Its usefulness depends upon the pharmacokinetics of the specific agent—for example, route of entry and absorption, distribution within the body, target tissue interaction, metabolism, and route of elimination. Knowledge of these parameters allows one to quantitatively estimate exposure based on the amount of excretion of the substance or a metabolite. Biological monitoring techniques are available for a number of toxic substances, the most common being analysis of blood or urine. Other techniques include analysis of the breath, fingernails, hair, and saliva.

Medical screening is the examination of apparently well workers by relatively inexpensive, rapid tests for the purpose of dividing them into groups with a high and low probability of developing or having a given disease. It may represent a form of primary prevention; or secondary prevention—designed to detect workers at an early stage of disease. Examples include the use of pulmonary function testing to detect the early signs of asbestosis—a restrictive lung disease due to asbestos exposure—or anaemia due to exposure to lead or benzene. Criteria for the implementation of medical screening programmes by industrial medicine departments are similar to those for other health screening programmes, namely estimation of the validity, sensitivity, specificity, predictive value, cost-effectiveness, and acceptability of the screening procedure. These criteria are discussed in Volume 3, Chapter 24.

PREVENTION OF OCCUPATIONAL DISEASE

Prevention of disease in the work environment must be accomplished through the reduction of worker exposure to exogenous agents such as chemical, physical, and biological agents, or to other factors such as repetitive motion or stress-producing environments. The reduction of exposure may be accomplished by the variety of techniques listed below in descending order of preference to the public health professional. In considering these measures, one should keep in mind that the three major routes of exposure to toxic agents are inhalation, dermal absorption, and ingestion. The measures are designed to interrupt or reduce the transmission of the agent from the work environment to the body .

Substitution

Substitution of a less hazardous material usually is the most efficacious method of controlling a workplace hazard. In some cases this method also may be the least expensive. Several examples of effective substitution of materials occurred in the late 1970s when outbreaks of neurological disease were documented from exposure to the neurotoxins methyl *n*-butyl ketone (Allen *et al.* 1975), dimethylaminopropionitrile (Feldman *et al.* 1979; Pestronk *et al.* 1979), and Lucel-7 (2.*t*-butylazo-2-hydroxy-5-methyl hexane) (Kurt *et al.* 1980). Recognition of the aetiology of chemically-induced neurological illness resulted from clinical epidemiological studies. In each case the manufacturer discontinued use of the product following identification of the neurotoxic agent, with substitution of a less hazardous product.

Selection of a less hazardous process or equipment also represents a meaningful control strategy. For example, substitution of a continuous process for an intermittent process almost always results in a decrease of exposure. Where an entire process does not need to be changed to reduce hazards, equipment substitution may achieve the desired reduction in exposure. Use of a degreaser with a low-speed hoist to minimize solvent loss to a room as compared to dipping parts by hand, which is faster, is an example of equipment substitution.

Engineering controls

The primary engineering controls used to reduce employee exposure to toxic substances are ventilation and isolation or enclosure. Ventilation is one of the most effective and widely used control measures. Control of hazards by ventilation is usually further subdivided into two categories: local exhaust ventilation and general exhaust or dilution ventilation. An excellent source of information on local exhaust ventilation design is the American Conference of Governmental Hygienists (ACGIH) Industrial Ventilation Manual (1977). The most effective approach for implementing ventilation controls is: (i) to conduct an engineering study to evaluate sources of exposure; (ii) to develop an engineering design; (iii) to install a system based on the design; and (iv) to evaluate the completed system to ensure that the air contaminant has been effectively controlled.

Isolation is the interposing of a barrier between a hazard and workers who might be injured or made ill by the hazard. Isolation may refer to storage of materials, such as flammable liquids; enclosure or removal to another area of equipment (such as noisy generators) ; or isolation of processes or of the workers themselves (e.g. by enclosing a sawmill worker in a soundproof, ventilated booth to protect him from noise and wood dust). The petroleum industry is an example of the use of automated remote processing where the plants are based on centralized control with wide use of computer control of process equipment. Workers are thus largely isolated from the hazards.

Administrative controls

With administrative controls the exposure level of the hazard is not diminished; instead the duration of time that the worker is exposed is reduced. For example, the current air standard for inorganic lead in the US is 50 µg/m³ based on an eight-hour day. A worker could be exposed to 100 µg/m³ for a total of four hours and then rotated to a job without lead exposure as an administrative control. The most common use of administrative controls is to reduce worker noise exposure through rotation. Given the typical demands of production and the potential for misuse, administrative methods of controls are not frequently advised nor employed in most industries.

Work practices

An alteration of work practices can help to reduce exposure to hazards. A common example is wet-sweeping asbestos dust rather than dry-sweeping. Another example would be vacuuming cotton lint off machines rather than cleaning dusty equipment by blowing it off with compressed air, a practice which creates airborne dust particles.

Personal hygiene

Management-instituted programmes for encouraging personal hygiene also can reduce exposure. In some instances, management may encourage or even require showers and a change to clean clothes at the end of the workday. Naturally, management should provide showers, changing facilities, lockers, and work clothes if indicated; in fact, several US OSHA standards now require management to provide such facilities.

A subtle, but potentially important route of exposure is ingestion of toxic agents due to eating or smoking in the workplace. Management should provide separate eating facilities outside of production areas. Workers should be encouraged to wash their hands before eating or smoking.

Use of personal protective equipment

Respirators, gloves, protective clothing, ear plugs, and muffs are all common forms of personal protective equipment in wide use throughout industry. They can play an important protective role provided that carefully designed personal protective equipment programmes are in place. Unfortunately, it is all too often the case that these programmes are ill-defined, poorly maintained, and given inadequate attention.

OVERVIEW OF OCCUPATIONAL DISEASES

Occupational diseases are generally classified according to the agent and/or target organ system. Agents include biological hazards, such as bacteria, viruses, plants, and animals; chemical substances; physical hazards, such as noise, variations in pressure, vibration, and radiation; and social factors, such as work-task organization which results in increased stress. These agents may cause disease through virtually all pathophysiological mechanisms, for example—infection, irritation or inflammation, toxic metabolic effects, trauma, allergy, carcinogenesis, and teratogenesis. Some agents also increase the frequency of stillbirths, spontaneous abortions, reduced fertility, and sterility.

Chemical substances are the largest class of agents in that toxic effects have been reported for nearly 50 000 chemicals which are thought to appear in the workplace—over 2000 (IARC 1972–79) of which are suspected carcinogens based on studies of laboratory animals (NIOSH 1979). Every year, between 500 and 1000 new chemicals are produced in commercial quantities in the US. The health effects of these new chemicals are practically unknown when they are introduced into the workplace, creating an ongoing challenge to the health professional trying to prevent occupational diseases.

All organ systems may be affected by exposures in the workplace, although the lungs and the skin are most often affected since they are the primary organs in direct contact with substances in the work environment. Major lung diseases include infections, cancer, asthma, and the pneumoconioses—the progressively disabling and often fatal lung diseases caused by inhaling inert particulates, such as asbestos fibres, coal dust, cotton dust, silica, and beryllium (Parkes 1982). Because the lung is both a target organ and a portal of entry, the likelihood of toxic exposure is high. For example, an estimated 1.2 million workers each year in the US are exposed to silica dust alone (NIOSH 1974).

Occupational skin diseases are the largest group of reported occupational illnesses (Adams 1983). Most occupational dermatitis is caused by the primary irritant effect of chemicals, although some chemicals also act as allergic sensitizers and photosensitizers. More rarely agents may cause neoplastic and pigmentary changes in the skin. While generally not causing significant mortality, occupational skin diseases are a major source of discomfort and morbidity.

Recently, the US National Institute for Occupational Safety and Health (NIOSH) developed a suggested list of the 10 leading work-related diseases and injuries (NIOSH 1983). Three criteria were used to develop the list: the disease's or injury's frequency of occurrence, its severity in the individual case, and its amenability to prevention. This list—shown in Table 21.2—indicates the major occupational health problems and should assist the health professional in setting priorities for efforts to prevent health problems related to work.

Discussion of each of the major occupational diseases is beyond the scope of this chapter and is covered in texts devoted to this topic (see Zenz 1975; Hunter 1978; Levy and Wegman 1983; Rom 1983). For the purpose of this chapter, it would be constructive to review selected problems which reflect the development and current status of the field of occupational health. This discussion will focus on two classic agents—lead and silica, two organ systems—neurological and reproductive, and two pathogenic mechanisms—carcinogenesis and human factors.

Historical problems which continue today

Lead

The case of lead offers a good opportunity for evaluation. It

Table 21.2. *The ten leading work-related diseases and injuries —United States, 1982. The conditions listed under each category are to be viewed as selected examples, not comprehensive definitions of the category*

1. *Occupational lung diseases:*
   asbestosis, byssinosis, silicosis, coal workers' pneumoconiosis, lung cancer, occupational asthma
2. *Musculoskeletal injuries:*
   disorders of the back, trunk, upper extremity, neck, lower extremity, traumatically induced Raynaud's phenomenon
3. *Occupational cancers (other than lung):*
   leukaemia, mesothelioma, cancers of the bladder, nose, and liver
4. *Amputations, fractures, eye loss, lacerations, and traumatic deaths:*
5. *Cardiovascular diseases:*
   Hypertension, coronary artery disease, acute myocardial infarction
6. *Disorders of reproduction:*
   infertility, spontaneous abortion, teratogenesis
7. *Neurotoxic disorders:*
   peripheral neuropathy, toxic encephalitis, psychoses, extreme personality changes (exposure-related)
8. *Noise-induced loss of hearing*
9. *Dermatological conditions:*
   dermatoses, burns (scaldings), chemical burns, contusions (abrasions)
10. *Psychological disorders:*
    neuroses, personality disorders, alcoholism, drug dependency

Source: NIOSH (1983).

is an old familiar hazard and there has been ample time for society to develop responses to it. Lead was first smelted 6000 years ago and was used for alloying, pigments, and glazes. These uses continue, but now the largest uses are for storage batteries and as a gasoline additive.

The medical effects are well-studied compared to most hazardous substances. Hippocrates described overt symptoms of lead poisoning in 370 BC and in recent years hundreds of papers have appeared documenting much more subtle adverse effects. The signs and symptoms of lead intoxication are well known. They include loss of appetite, metallic taste in the mouth, constipation, nausea, pallor, excessive tiredness, weakness, insomnia, headache, nervousness, irritability, muscle and joint pains, numbness, dizziness and colic. Lead inhibits the synthesis of haeme which results in anaemia, has profound effects on both the central and peripheral nervous systems, and prolonged exposure results in disease of the renal system and affects the reproductive system.

The important question to be asked is given the lengthy history of lead toxicity along with recent research documenting the subtle, subclinical effects of lead exposure, is lead exposure well-controlled and have lead-related disorders disappeared? During the promulgation of the health standard for occupational exposure to lead in 1978, OSHA collected extensive data on air lead and accompanying blood levels in various kinds of industries. These data showed a high percentage of workers in selected lead industries exposed to air lead levels over the OSHA standard in effect from 1970 to 1978 (200 µg of lead per m^3 of air). The majority of workers in the industries studied had blood lead levels over 40 µg/m^3 (US Department of Labor 1978b). Thus, despite the presence of an OSHA limit on air lead

levels from 1970 to 1978, exposures clearly were not fully controlled and the potential for serious lead-related disorders remained high, even with the use of respirators by many workers.

Based on available health effects information and the extent of exposure in 1978, OSHA promulgated a new standard for airborne exposure to lead of 50 µg/m^3 and stated that blood levels should be kept from exceeding 40 µg/m^3 to protect against material impairment of health in adults (US Department of Labor 1978b). No adequate studies have been done to determine if lead exposure for US workers has decreased as a result of implementation of the more stringent 1978 OSHA standard.

The control of lead exposures illustrates the dramatic difference between the public health responses to workplace hazards and to the early infectious diseases. Generally, once the aetiology of the latter was discovered, most infectious diseases were controlled or even eradicated. As with the case of lead exposure, however, there are essentially no examples of eradicating occupational diseases even if harmful effects have been known for hundreds, if not thousands, of years. For workers, the older occupational health hazards have not disappeared and new problems continually arise.

Silica

Occupational lung disease due to silica exposure also has historical roots. Agricola (1556), writing in the sixteenth century, noted that men working in the local mines in the Carpathian mountains died of pulmonary disease at a young age and that women there had as many as seven husbands. The illness of these young miners was later to be related to their exposure to quartz (called silica) and the disease is now termed silicosis. Although the ill-effects of exposure to silica have been known for centuries, the prevalence of disabling silicosis remains high in exposed workers (NIOSH 1974; US Department of Labor 1980a) . In fact, the number of industrial uses and exposed workers has increased despite knowledge of the health effects of silica.

In 1981, NIOSH requested that producers and users of silica flour—a finely milled silica powder—be warned that the risk of developing silicosis may be very high for workers exposed to the flour. A NIOSH study at two silica flour mills had shown that 37 per cent of current and former workers with 1–14 years of exposure to silica dust had radiological evidence of silicosis (NIOSH 1981a). Of particular concern was the evidence of silicosis in workers with short-term silica dust exposures of 2.5–6 years, indicating rapidly developing silicosis. Eighty-five per cent of the air samples collected in these two mills were above the NIOSH recommended level. When NIOSH reviewed the data for 27 flour dust mills employing greater than 1350 workers, 53 per cent of the air samples were in excess of the required standard.

Papers published during the early 1970s documented high rates of silicosis among sandblasters in New Orleans (Samini *et al.* 1974; Jones *et al.* 1975; Ziskind *et al.* 1976). The alarmingly high level of crystalline silica caused silicosis in workers after very brief exposures. Exposure levels of crystalline quartz are still high in US foundries, with 41 per cent of air samples analysed by OSHA in 205 foundries between 1976 and 1981 being non-compliant for silica exposure (Oudiz *et al.* 1983).

In addition to these studies which document continuing high occupational exposure to silica and considerable silicosis in American industry, other research indicates chronic loss of lung function in workers exposed to moderate and even low levels of silica (Theirault 1978). Thus, even well-known toxic agents such as lead and silica continue to be used widely and to cause ill health among a large number of workers.

Discovery of new target organs

As mentioned above, the organ systems most commonly associated with workplace exposures are the lungs and the skin. Research during the past decade has revealed that all organs of the body may be affected. Evaluation of these problems has often required the development of new research techniques. Two pertinent examples are occupational neurological diseases and reproductive hazards.

Neurological diseases

Recently, it has become clear that neurological disease from chemical exposure in the workplace is more common than previously understood (Landrigan *et al.* 1980). During the past decade, several newly introduced chemicals have been identified as causing dramatic outbreaks of overt neurological diseases, such as bladder dysfunction and peripheral neuropathy—chlordecone (Kepone) (Taylor *et al.* 1978), dimethylaminopropionitrile (Feldman *et al.* 1979; Pestronk *et al.* 1979), methyl *n*-butyl ketone (Allen *et al.* 1975), and leptophos (Xinatras *et al.* 1978). These outbreaks were dramatic, but neither unique nor isolated events; they served to increase awareness of the neurotoxicity of chemical substances.

During this same period, awareness increased that while the clinical manifestations of neurological disorders sometimes may be obvious, in other instances the slow, insidious nature of the disease may mask the true nature and origin of the disorders. Subjective symptoms associated with chemically induced central nervous system (CNS) disorders may be so non-specific as to be overlooked or misunderstood. There are numerous examples in which a worker has had his or her work-related neurological illness initially ascribed to psychological disorders.

Overt clinical signs of neurotoxicity may be entirely absent even though extensive damage to the neural tissue has occurred. As a result, new evaluation techniques have had to be developed in this area. Two of the earliest indicators of acute or chronic neurotoxicity are neuro-behavioural and neurophysiological changes. Behaviour is a sensitive indicator of the functions of the CNS and neuro-behavioural testing is thereby useful in detecting preclinical disease from exposures at doses lower than those required for other changes. Similarly, neurophysiological testing elucidates information at the subclinical or preclinical stage of disease.

Johnson and Anger (1983) have recently reviewed the methods used in human behavioural toxicology. These methods include questionnaires, personality tests, performance tests, sensory tests, motor tests, and complex function and memory tests. Thus far, neurobehavioural toxicology has had limited uses in workplace studies. But, while considerable research is necessary to validate these test screens, it is anticipated that these techniques will further elucidate the scope and dimension of occupationally-related neurotoxicity in the future.

Reproductive impairment

During the past few years, there also has developed an increasing awareness of the devastating effects that drugs and chemicals can have on the reproductive systems of those exposed. From both a scientific and social standpoint, our attitudes toward the issue of reproductive failure from chemical exposure in the workplace has been influenced by three particular substances, Thalidomide, lead, and dibromochloropropane.

Thalidomide

While not an occupational exposure, the Thalidomide tragedy—in which thousands of children developed severe limb malformations after their mothers took the drug as a sedative while pregnant—served to alert the scientific community and general population to the potential for teratogenic effects of drugs and chemicals. The drug was withdrawn from the market in 1961.

Scientific research on teratogenesis (generally defined as structural or functional alterations in development) has increased since the Thalidomide episode. Because of the nature of the Thalidomide problem, most early research perhaps incorrectly focused solely on exposure of the pregnant woman to potentially harmful drugs or chemicals.

Lead

The issue of pregnant women's occupational exposure to lead became a focus of attention at the 1977–78 OSHA hearings on its proposed lead standard. It was noted that lead absorbed into the bloodstream of pregnant women crosses the placenta and enters the blood of the fetus. This was, and is, of great concern because excessive exposure to lead during pregnancy may result in neurological damage to the offspring.

The medical questions about health risks took on political overtones and raised questions of discrimination when some witnesses at the hearings suggested that all women of childbearing age should be excluded from work in lead-related industries—on the grounds that the women could become pregnant while being exposed to the substance. After reviewing the scientific evidence, OSHA noted that excessive lead exposure in the workplace could also impair male reproductive function and that the concern about exposed women was too one-sided. OSHA concluded: 'There is no basis in the (hearing) record for preferential hiring of men over women in the lead industry, nor will this final standard create a basis for exclusion from work of any person, male or female, who is capable of procreating' (US Department of Labor 1978*b*, p. 53007).

The issue was again brought to public atention in 1978 when a major American corporation announced a company-wide policy that all fertile women would be removed from exposure to toxic substances that might prove harmful to the fetus, including lead, mercury, benzene, vinyl chloride, acrylamide, carbon disulphide, carbon monoxide, carbon tetrachloride, dimethyl sulphate, and cyanide. Following the announcement of the policy, five women who worked at a lead pigment plant reportedly underwent surgical sterilization to keep their positions (Williams 1981). The need to choose between undergoing an irreversible surgical procedure and keeping one's job presents a major public health policy dilemma. What began as a question of science became both a legal and political issue of major proportion. This has focused attention on the central issue of reproductive impairment for both sexes from exposure to toxic substances, as well as raising the socio-legal issue of job discrimination.

Dibromochloropropane

The fact that male reproduction can be adversely affected by exposure to toxic chemicals is best demonstrated by the case of dibromochloropropane (1,2-dibromo-3-chloropropane, DBCP). This chemical has been used as a fumigant and nematocide in agriculture since 1955. In 1961, Torkelson *et al.* reported that, based on inhalation studies in laboratory animals, DBCP appeared to cause decreased mean weight of the testes, degenerative changes in the seminiferous tubules, a reduction of the number of sperm cells and an increase in the proportion of abnormal sperm cells. These data were virtually ignored until 1977 when a group of workers in California became concerned over their inability to father children. One 30-year-old pesticide production worker had been examined by his physician who noted azoospermia. No connection between the absence of sperm cells and possible chemical exposure was made by the examining physician. This same worker later convinced five co-workers to submit semen samples for analysis. Similar results were obtained. Subsequently Whorton *et al.* (1977) reported the results of tests on 86 workers in the plant which manufactured DBCP. Forty-seven workers had low or zero sperm counts. The suspicion that DBCP was the causative agent was confirmed in subsequent studies. On the basis of these findings, DBCP's use (but not its manufacture) has been suspended by the US Environmental Protection Agency. This episode increased awareness that male reproduction can be impaired by workplace exposures.

Extent of impairment

The extent of reproductive impairment from chemical exposures eludes accurate assessment for several reasons:

1. Toxic chemicals may affect the reproductive process at many developmental stages, and impairment at a particular stage may result in a variety of different adverse outcomes. A partial list of outcomes is shown in Table 21.3.
2. Existing systems for collection of data on reproductive performance are not adequate for surveillance or research

Table 21.3. *List of reproductive outcomes*

1. Sexual dysfunction: loss of libido, potency
2. Sperm abnormalities: affected number, motility, shape
3. Sub-fecundity: abnormal gonads, ducts and external genitalia; abnormal pubertal development: infertility of male or female origin; amenorrhoea; anovulatory cycles
4. Chromosomal abnormalities: polyploidy
5. Spontaneous abortion
6. Perinatal death: intrapartum death, death in the first week
7. Change in gestational age at delivery; prematurity, postmaturity
8. Decreased birthweight
9. Altered sex ratios
10. Multiple births
11. Birth defects: major, minor, mutations
12. Infant death
13. Childhood morbidity
14. Childhood malignancies
15. Age at menopause

Source: Bloom (1981).

purposes. The incidence of reproductive failure in the human population is relatively high with estimates that between 7 and 16 per cent of all newborns have birth defects. The cause of 70 per cent of developmental defects is unknown (Bloom 1981). More than 600 000 lives a year in the US are lost by spontaneous abortion, stillbirths, and infant death; and this number is an underestimate because many early spontaneous abortions go unreported (Wilson 1977). A system is needed to more accurately monitor reproductive outcomes.

3. There are significant methodological problems in the epidemiological investigation of exposure and reproductive outcome because:
- Exposed populations tend to be small in number.
- The exposure is often poorly defined.
- One is often interested in rare events such as specific malformations.
- Publicity relating to the episode under study may produce or accentuate reporting bias (Bloom 1981; Fabro 1983).

4. In the past, reproductive studies have focused almost exclusively on the relationship between maternal exposure to chemical agents during pregnancy and resulting birth defects. Research continues on teratogenicity (Hemminki 1980); but as noted, there has recently been more attention given to the toxic effects on male reproduction (Manson and Simon 1979). Further attention must be devoted to evaluating the full range of reproductive outcomes.

Recent developments in occupational disease mechanisms

Occupational carcinogenesis

As described above, the role of occupational exposure in causing cancer has received considerable attention. If occupation accounts for only 5 per cent of all cancer deaths, there are at least 20 000 preventable deaths a year from occupational cancer in the US alone. Doll and Peto (1981) point out: 'Occupational cancer, moreover, tends to be concentrated in relatively small groups of people among whom the risk of developing the disease may be quite large and such risks can usually be reduced, or even eliminated, once they have been identified. The detection of occupational hazards should therefore have a higher priority in any programme of cancer prevention than their proportional importance might suggest.'

The first recognized occupational cancer, desribed in 1775 by Percival Pott, a surgeon, was scrotal skin cancer among chimney sweeps who were heavily exposed to soot in their work. In the 1800s skin cancer was linked to inorganic arsenic, as well as to tar and paraffin oils, when Japanese scientists succeeded in inducing skin tumours on rabbit ears by daily application of coal tar for a period of six months. In the 1930s bladder cancer was linked with exposure in the dye industry to aromatic amines, such as benzidine and 2-naphthylamine, and the first case report of bronchogenic carcinoma in a patient with asbestosis was published.

More recently, the International Agency for Research on Cancer (IARC) (1972–79) has evaluated the carcinogenic risk of 585 chemical compounds. For only 155 of them (26 per cent) were human data (epidemiological studies, human case reports, or both) available. For 30 of these, the available evidence was sufficient to support a causal relationship with the occurrence of cancer in humans (see Table 21.4). Among these are seven industrial processes for which no direct confirmation has been ascertained of the particular chemical agent responsible for the carcinogenic effect in humans. For 18 of these 30, occupational exposure is the primary source of exposure.

Table 21.5 lists 61 additional compounds which IARC states are probably associated with cancer induction in humans; 33 of these compounds have occupation as their main source of exposure. For the remaining 64 compounds of the 155 for which there are human data, classification as to their human carcinogenicity could not be made because of limitations in the human and/or experimental data or both.

The International Agency for Research on Cancer has also evaluated the possible human cancer risk of exposure to chemicals for which there are only experimental (animal and laboratory) data. The agency has developed criteria to determine which experimental studies demonstrate 'sufficient evidence' of carcinogenicity in test animals to regard the tested chemical as representing a carcinogenic risk to humans. Of the 585 chemicals evaluated by IARC, 147 were shown to have 'sufficient evidence' of carcinogenicity in experimental animals.

To summarize the IARC findings, of 585 compounds and industrial processes studied, 155 had some human evidence of carcinogenicity and 147 had 'sufficient evidence' in experimental animals. Because very few of these compounds and processes are regulated as carcinogens, these data are staggering in their potential health implications.

Evaluation of carcinogenic agents

The most convincing method of establishing a causal relationship between chemical exposure and cancer is

Table 21.4. *Chemicals and industrial processes associated with cancer induction in humans*

Chemicals or industrial process	Main type of exposure	Main route of exposure	Target organ(s)
4-Aminobiphenyl	Occupational	Inhalation Skin p.o.	Bladder
Arsenic compounds	Occupational Medicinal Environmental	Inhalation p.o. Skin	Skin Lung Liver
Asbestos	Occupational Environmental	Inhalation p.o.	Lung Pleural cavity Gastrointestinal tract
Auramine manufacture	Occupational	Inhalation Skin p.o.	Bladder
Benzene	Occupational	Inhalation Skin	Haematopoietic system (leukaemia)
Benzidine	Occupational	Inhalation Skin p.o.	Bladder
N-N-Bis (2-chloro-ethyl)-2-naphthyl-amine	Medicinal	p.o.	Bladder
Bis(chloromethyl) ether	Occupational	Inhalation	Lung
Technical chloro-methyl methyl ether (possibly associated with bis(chloromethyl) ether)	Occupational	Inhalation	Lung
Chromium and certain chromium compounds	Occupational	Inhalation	Lung Nasal cavity
Diethylstilbestrol	Medicinal	p.o. Local, prenatal	Endometrium Vagina, cervix
Haematite mining (? radon)	Occupational	Inhalation	Lung
Manufacture of isopropyl alcohol	Occupational	Inhalation	Nasal cavity Larynx
Melphaian	Medicinal	p.o. i.v.	Haematopoietic system (leukaemia)
Mustard gas	Occupational	Inhalation	Lung Larynx
2-Naphthylamine	Occupational	Inhalation Skin p.o.	Bladder
Nickel-refining	Occupational	Inhalation	Nasal cavity Lung
Soots, tars, and oils	Occupational Environmental	Inhalation Skin p.o.	Lung, skin (scrotum) intestine
Vinyl chloride	Occupational	Inhalation Skin	Liver Brain Lung

*The main types of exposures listed are those in which the association has been demonstrated; exposures other than those listed may occur also.

†The main routes of exposure given may not be the only ones by which the effects could occur.

‡Indicative evidence.

p.o.—oral.   i.v.—intravenous.

Source: Tomatis *et al.* (1982), adapted from IARC Monographs, Vols. 1–20.

Table 21.5. *Compounds which are probably associated with cancer induction in humans*

1. Acrylonitrile	10. Dimethylcarbamoyl chloride
2. Aflatoxins	11. Dimethyl sulphate
3. Amitrole	12. Ethylene oxide
4. Auramine	13. Iron dextran
5. Beryllium and certain beryllium compounds	14. Nickel and certain nickel compounds
6. Cadmium and certain cadmium compounds	15. Oxymetholone
7. Carbon tetrachloride	16. Phenacetin
8. Chlorambucil	17. Polychlorinated biphenyls
9. Cyclophosphamide	18. Thiootepa

These 18 compounds have less sufficient evidence to support a causal relationship with the occurrrence of cancer in humans than do the compounds listed in Table 21.4 according to IARC.
Source: Tomatis *et al.* (1982), adapted from the IARC Monographs.

through the study of human disease. Decoufle (1982) has reviewed the current status of epidemiological findings with respect to occupational origins of cancer. It is apparent from his review that large populations of workers may be at high risk of cancer from such agents as arsenic, asbestos, polycyclic aromatic hydrocarbons, coke oven emissions, radioactive materials, cutting oils, vinyl chloride, acrylonitrile, and metals and also from work in certain occupations, for example, chemists, rubber workers, foundry workers, wood workers, and others. The importance of well-designed epidemiological studies in assessing human risk to chemical carcinogens is apparent from these investigations.

On the other hand, the use of epidemiological studies has several shortcomings (e.g. latency, inadequate records, population size limitations, and inability to assess individual exposures) and should not be the primary means of assuring safety for workers. To maximize the protection of workers exposed to a myriad of unknown chemicals, primary reliance must be on experimental test results.

Although the experimental approach also can be criticized (e.g. because of unusually high exposure levels for the animals tested or because of different routes of administration than in human exposure), one still must rely on it to identify chemicals which present possible carcinogenic risks to humans. With over 50 000 chemicals in common use today, one cannot expect to conduct sufficient numbers of epidemiological studies to pinpoint chemicals which can cause cancer or other adverse health effects.

Tomatis *et al.* (1982) has reviewed the role of experimental studies in the assessment of human risk and has concluded:

1. The majority of chemicals for which there is sufficient evidence of carcinogenicity in humans, and those for which the available evidence indicates probable carcinogenicity in humans, have been shown to be carcinogenic in experimental animals.

2. In several instances, experimental evidence of carcinogenicity preceded human observations.

3. These chemicals may have the same target organs in humans and in experimental animals, but this is by no means an absolute rule.

4. Evidence of carcinogenic effects in experimental animals often is obtained using a route of exposure different from that by which humans may be exposed, or which has been associated with the occurrence of tumours in humans.

Policy aspects of carcinogen evaluation

In 1979, OSHA proposed a general regulation concerning the identification, classification, and control of toxic substances that may pose a carcinogenic risk to US workers (US Department of Labor 1980*b*). This regulation attempts to deal with one of the most important issues OSHA faces, namely the exposure of workers to toxic substances which may be potential carcinogens. Although OSHA recognized that many gaps remain in our understanding of the causes and cures for cancer, the agency decided that it was prudent to develop a workable system to reduce human exposures to those toxic substances for which there is evidence of carcinogenic potential for workers. Such a system should be designed to replace the piecemeal approach to regulating carcinogens on the case-by-case basis which currently is used by OSHA and other US federal agencies.

Four specific categories or classifications were defined of which Class I substances would be those in which carcinogenicity had been demonstrated in man, in two animal species, or in one animal species in which the test was replicated. The standard assumes that no threshold level for cancer exists. This policy is still being challenged, but it is likely that a generic cancer policy will be in use for regulatory purposes in the near future.

Human factors

While ergonomic and stress-related disorders have been recognized for years, only recently has significant attention been devoted to them. Researchers have realized that even if all toxic chemical exposures could be completely controlled, the physical and social organization of work still would affect the health of workers.

The term 'ergonomics' comes from the Greek word *ergon* (work) and *nomos* (law). Ergonomics is an applied science dealing with the relationship between the worker and the work environment. In general, it is concerned with the design of facilities, equipment, tools, jobs, and the work process in a way that is compatible with the anatomical, biochemical, physiological, perceptual, and behavioural characteristics of humans. An example of an ergonomic problem is hand and wrist disorders.

Hand and wrist disorders

Hands and wrists are especially vulnerable to poorly designed tools and equipment because of the confluence of a delicate collection of nerves, tendons, ligaments, bones, and blood vessels. Damage has been demonstrated to occur from a variety of working conditions, including vibrating tools and equipment; repetitive, twisting hand movements; jobs requiring the hands and wrists to exert force in an awkward position; excessive pressure on parts of the hands and wrists; and exertion in combination with any of these conditions.

Disability of the wrist and hand associated with these types of activity generally is caused by repetitive activity over an extended period of time and may be referred to as repetitive trauma or cumulative trauma.

Upholstery stitching, small parts assembly, electronic component assembly, meat cutting, chipping and grinding, and packing are examples of jobs where there is a high risk for hand and wrist disorders such as carpal tunnel syndrome, tendonitis, tenosynovitis, and Raynaud's phenomenon (Wasserman and Badger 1973).

While data on the incidence of these disorders are limited, recent studies suggest the prevalence is greater than generally recognized. A recent study of chippers and grinders, for example, found a high prevalence of Raynaud's phenomenon among workers exposed to hand vibration when using air hammers and grinding tools (NIOSH 1982). The vibration can produce numbness; the disease is sometimes called 'white fingers' or 'dead hand' by workers. A NIOSH survey (1978) indicated that an estimated 1.2 million workers in the US were exposed to occupational hand/arm vibration.

White finger is not a recent phenomenon. In England, reports of an association between Raynaud's phenomenon and the use of chain saws in logging and forestry were noted as early as 1904. In 1970, the British Forestry Commission designed and issued anti-vibrating saws to help reduce the incidence of the condition (Wasserman et al. 1979).

Hand and wrist disorders can result in significant lost time and medical expense. For example, at one upholstery plant during the period from 1971 to 1975 there was an incidence rate of 128 cases of carpal tunnel syndrome per million employee hours worked on certain jobs. The average cost of medical treatment and workers' compensation for each case was over US $3000. Thus, the available evidence suggests a problem of significant proportion, despite the fact that such disorders often go unrecognized as being occupational in origin.

Stress-related disorders

Often it is difficult to separate health effects due to the physical characteristics of the workplace from those due to the social organization of the work itself. An increasing amount of research has indicated that organizational or social characteristics interact with ergonomic factors to produce stress reactions in workers.

The National Institute of Occupational Safety and Health, as well as various European researchers, has conducted research on occupational stress during the past decade (NIOSH 1980a). Major stressors include high work task demands, low utilization of abilities, lack of control or participation in decision making, role ambiguity, machine-pacing, shift work, overtime work, and others (Cooper and Payne 1978). A study of 23 occupational groupings sponsored by NIOSH found that assemblers and relief workers on machine-paced assembly lines have the highest levels of stress and psychological strain among the studied occupations (Caplan et al. 1975). The combination of high work load and time pressures with lack of control, monotony, and repetition is particularly deleterious.

Visual display terminals

Interestingly, one does not generally consider that office work may represent a significant health hazard. On the other hand, it has become clear recently that many of the job characteristics of clerical workers are similar to those described above for assembly line workers. In fact, a recent NIOSH study of visual-display-terminal (VDT) operators found that those operators with regimented, routine, data-entry-type jobs report higher levels of stress that any of the occupations mentioned in the 23 occupations study cited above (NIOSH 1981b). It was concluded that job stress in VDT operators results from both the job content and productivity demands, as well as equipment problems such as surface screen glare and poor ergonomic design of the work station. Most of the research on health impacts from working on VDTs has been carried out in Europe. The focus of this research has been on visual problems of VDT operators, psychological job stress, and strain from posture requirements when working on the terminals. Complaints by operators include monotony, fatigue, stress, headache, dizziness, irritability, and muscular aches and pains. Grandjean (1979) has studied the high frequency of visual complaints among VDT operators. Other scientists have focused their attention on the psychological and physical consequences of VDT work situations (Gunnarsson and Ostberg 1977; Cahin et al. 1978).

Recently, NIOSH proposed guidelines for VDT operation. These include: flexible work stations which allow for operator control of such factors as screen brightness and keyboard height; recommendations on lighting levels; methods of reducing screen glare (such as installation of glare shields and window coverings); mandatory rest-breaks from VDT work (at least 15 minutes every two hours for operators under moderate visual demands); and visual testing of operators (NIOSH 1980b).

The examples of occupational health problems which we have chosen as illustrations—lead, silica, neurological disease, reproductive impairment, cancer, and human factors—are examples of continuing and new problems. We could as easily have chosen other examples, such as noise, radiation, other metals, respiratory disorders, and allergic disorders to illustrate the continuing problem of occupational disease and the need for better means of control and prevention. It suffices to say that the concerns of Sigerist are as relevant today as they were in 1936.

POLICY ISSUES IN OCCUPATIONAL HEALTH

Thus far, this chapter has outlined approaches to the recognition and prevention of occupational disease, as well as discussing some of the major health problems. Another key characteristic of the field of occupational health is the complex relationship between scientific public health issues and the development of public policy. Policy develops through the interaction of workers, management, government, and the scientific public health community. To appreciate the field of occupational health, one should be familiar with some of the major policy issues.

Occupational health standards

Many countries throughout the world rely on US occupational health standards as models or guidance for setting their own countries' standards. For that reason, it is important to discuss some of the main issues involved in occupational health and safety standard-setting in the US.

Prior to passage of the Occupational Safety and Health Act of 1970, a number of voluntary organizations already had developed recommended standards for workplace exposure. Upon passage of the law, OSHA adopted many of the voluntary standards that had been set by organizations such as ANSI (American National Standards Institute), NFPA (National Fire Protection Association) and others. In addition OSHA adopted as 'national consensus standards' a list of over 450 threshold limit values (TLVs) for chemicals and hazardous materials which had been adopted by the ACGIH (American Conference of Governmental Industrial Hygienists). These TLVs are widely used in other countries; they refer to 'airborne concentrations of substances and represent conditions under which it is believed nearly all workers may be exposed day after day without adverse effect.'

The adoption of these TLVs has not been without problem. First, OSHA did not conduct a serious review of the TLVs before adopting them as standards. Secondly, OSHA's definitional base for standards is significantly different from that employed by the ACGIH when it developed the TLVs. Third, the TLVs are simply numerical limits for permissible exposure and are not comprehensive standards requiring medical surveillance, biological, and exposure monitoring, or other special provisions such as personal protective equipment, signs and labels, worker education, and recordkeeping. And finally, there is no mechanism under the OSHA law to update the list of TLVs every year when the ACGIH amends its recommendations. As a result of these problems, many of the OSHA-adopted standards, in reality, do not satisfy the requirements for protection found in the law itself. For example, Section 6(b) (5) of the Act states: 'The Secretary, in promulgating standards dealing with toxic materials or harmful physical agents under this subsection, shall set the standard which most adequately assures, to the extent feasible, on the basis of the best available evidence, that no employee will suffer material impairment of health or functional capacity even if such employee has regular exposure to the hazard dealt with by such standard for the period of his working life. . . . In addition to the attainment of the highest degree of health and safety protection for the employee, other considerations shall be the latest available scientific data in the field, the feasibility of the standards, and experience gained under this and other health and safety laws.'

Since passage of the Act, only 10 new, comprehensive standards for toxic substances have been promulgated by OSHA. Even some of these standards—in particular the regulation set for a group of carcinogens—are severely inadequate. It is apparent that the gap between the number of substances adequately regulated by OSHA and the number of toxic agents is great and growing.

A primary reason for the inadequate number of standards being developed and promulgated is the adversarial nature of the standard-setting process in the US. With only one exception, every new health standard issued by OSHA has met a legal challenge with extended court-room battles.

Substances covered by comprehensive OSHA standards

The 22 toxic substances newly regulated by comprehensive health standards since promulgation of the 1970 OSHA Act (US Department of Labor 1983) are:

- inorganic arsenic
- asbestos
- acrylonitrile
- coke oven emissions
- cotton dust
- DBCP (1,2-dibromo-3-chloropropane)
- lead
- vinyl chloride
- benzene (standard subsequently overturned by US Supreme Court)

and a single standard for the following thirteen carcinogens:

- 4-nitrobiphenyl
- alpha-naphthylamine
- methyl chloromethyl ether
- 3,3-dichlorobenzidine and its salts
- *bis*-chloromethyl ether
- beta-naphthylamine
- benzidine
- 4-aminodiphenyl
- ethyleneimine
- beta-propiolactone
- N-nitrosodimethylamine
- 2-acetylaminofluorene
- 4-dimethylaminoazobenzene

Cost–benefit analysis in standards-setting

The OSHA Act requires that an occupational health standard must be 'feasible', a term whose interpretation is difficult or at least open to controversy. In recent years there has been significant debate in the US and elsewhere as to the use of economic criteria in the setting of occupational health standards, and it is in this context that the debate over the meaning of feasibility has occurred. Should a standard be based only on health criteria and whether controls are technologically feasible? Should cost–benefit or cost–effectiveness analysis be used as a basis for regulatory decision-making?

The costs of controlling exposures to toxic substances may be substantial. For example, in promulgating standards for lead and cotton dust, OSHA estimated that the costs for capital investment to control exposures to the proscribed limits would be US $600 and US $550 million respectively

(US Department of Labor 1978*a,b*). Given these substantial costs, it is reasonable to assume that the role of economic analysis in the promulgation of standards is of great concern. As an analytical tool, cost-benefit analysis can be useful—especially when applied to purely economic issues. However, in promulgating occupational health standards, one is making not only economic decisions but also broad social policy. The fundamental issue is whether cost–benefit analysis should be used to control government decisions in promulgating health standards, or whether it should be used as an analytical tool to facilitate priority setting and decision-making in the regulatory process.

Several problem areas arise in the use of cost–benefit techniques:

1. Costs are easier to quantify than benefits but this makes them no more certain or reliable since estimates generally rely on industry-generated data which may be biased.

2. Estimations of benefits are important but difficult, in part due to poor baseline data on incidence of diseases as well as difficulties in attaching a market value to a human life or to pain and suffering experienced as a result of one's work.

3. The comparison of costs and benefits is beset by serious methodological difficulties (Ashford 1980).

Given the methodological flaws and inequities, cost-benefit techniques would appear to have relatively limited value in a public health context when considering job safety and health regulations.

In its review of the OSHA standard for exposure to cotton dust, the US Supreme Court held that OSHA was not required to conduct cost–benefit analysis of health standards and is in fact precluded from doing so since the OSH Act required analysis of feasibility not cost–benefit analysis.

Access to information: workers 'right to know'

Over the past decade there have been numerous examples of workers themselves playing a direct role in the discovery of occupational health problems. Four examples are the discovery of lung cancer by workers exposed to *bis*-chloromethyl ether, of sterility by workers exposed to dibromochloropropane, of urinary dysfunction by workers exposed to dimethylaminopropionitrile, and of excess brain tumours by workers in the petrochemical industry. These are but a few examples where workers have become aware of previously unrecognized problems and taken steps to obtain further information which ultimately brought these exposures to the attention of the wider occupational health community.

These and other examples lead one to the following important conclusions:

1. Workers have a vital interest in becoming directly and actively involved in occupational health matters at their worksite.

2. If workers and their representatives are to play a meaningful role in the detection, treatment, and prevention of occupational disease they must be able to learn the identity of the chemicals to which they are (or were) exposed, the current and past levels of exposure, and the potential health consequences of these exposures.

3. Employee exposure records, medical records, and results of biological monitoring are critically important to the detection, treatment, and prevention of occupational disease. Workers, their representatives, and their physicians need direct access to this information and to analyses of these records.

These conclusions have been embraced by OSHA which developed a regulation entitled *The access to employee exposure and medical records standard* (US Department of Labor 1980*b*), which attempts to assure that exposure, medical, and biological monitoring records are preserved and that workers, their representatives, and OSHA have right of access to them. Access of the worker to these records is especially important since the worker is ultimately responsible for his or her own health. In addition access by an employee's personal physician will undoubtedly facilitate prompt and accurate diagnosis of occupational illness, thus promoting effective intervention in order to prevent further health impairment. Prompt diagnosis will alert both the union and employer of the need to reduce exposures of other workers.

Employee awareness of health hazards is likely also to result in improved work practices. The control of worker exposure through the use of respirators, protective work clothing, and personal hygiene (showers, washing hands and face before eating, etc.) all rely on employee co-operation.

Lastly, access to exposure and medical records and analyses based on these records should facilitate formal occupational health research. For example, groups of employees or unions can make exposure and medical information (the latter with employee consent) available to researchers in universities and private organizations, or they can press management for joint labour–management research.

While there are obvious benefits from access to information, there are also very complex policy issues which need to be addressed if the proper mix of access and confidentiality is to be achieved. It is beyond the scope of this chapter to discuss all the issues related to access and disclosure of records. These issues are likely to become even more complex and subject to debate as the number of toxic substances used in industrial processes increases and as the work force becomes more aware of the potential hazards.

Labelling

An issue related to record access is labelling, that is the detailed labelling of containers in the workplace with the identity of the hazardous substance. Whether containers, pipes, storage bins, etc. should be labelled has been a topic of considerable debate in the US. The debate has focused on two primary issues, 'trade secrets' and the costs of implementing a labelling system. At this writing there is no provision in the US that requires labelling of containers to facilitate worker awareness of potential hazards, but it is anticipated that there will be federal regulations in the future. Whether national regulations are adopted or not, there is a strong trend in the US for legislation, regulation, or collective bargaining agreements which provide workers with information concerning the identity of, and hazards associated with exposure to, toxic agents encountered in the workplace.

Medical removal protection

An important element of any occupational medical surveillance programme should be medical removal protection (MRP). This is defined as temporary removal from the dangerous jobsite of workers identified through medical surveillance to be at risk of sustaining further health impairment from continued exposure. Temporary medical removal protects the worker's health both by limiting further exposure to toxic agents and by enabling a worker's body to excrete existing toxins and to repair damage.

Participation in medical surveillance programmes may result in temporary removal of workers at risk which, on its face, is a valuable practice. In the absence of some countervailing requirement, however, the temporary medical removal of workers could take the form of a job transfer to a lower paying job, a temporary layoff or possibly even a permanent termination. Thus, without earnings and benefits protection, workers who participate in medical surveillance face a difficult dilemma. Participation could result in loss or reduction in pay, but a decision not to participate could result in a failure to recognize health problems. These considerations led OSHA to adopt an MRP provision in its standard for occupational exposure to lead. This provision mandated that any workers whose blood lead is elevated (greater than 60 µg/100 g of whole blood or at or above 50 µg/100 g averaged over the previous six months) be removed to a work station where the airborne lead concentration is below 30 µg/m³. In addition, during the period of removal the employer must maintain the worker's earnings, seniority, and other employment rights and benefits as though the worker had not been removed. This latter requirement has been named 'rate retention'.

The concept of medical removal protection with earning and benefits protection represents a major innovation in occupational health and was widely praised upon adoption. It also serves as an incentive for firms to reduce levels of exposure. Employers who make good faith efforts to comply with the standard would experience only small numbers of temporary removals, if any, whereas the employer whose lack of controls results in a continuing need for worker removals will be responsible for the associated costs. Medical removal protection, therefore, represents a strong stimulus for employers to protect workers' health and will reward employers who devise better methods of control to protect employee health.

This approach linked to rate retention to maximize the effectiveness of medical surveillance programmes has been adequately applied only to workers exposed to lead. Its applicability to other chemical exposures has yet to be developed, but this novel approach has encouraged the lead industry to develop markedly successful biological monitoring and medical surveillance programmes.

REFERENCES

Adams, R.M. (1983). *Occupational skin disease*. Grune and Stratton, New York.

Agricola, G. (1556). See: *De Re Metallica* (1912) (translated from the first Latin edition). H.C. Hoover and L.H. Hoover, London.

Allen N. *et al.* (1975). Toxic polyneuropathy due to methyl *n*-butyl ketone. *Arch. Neurol.* **32**, 209.

American Conference of Governmental Industrial Hygienists (1977). *Industrial ventilation*, 13th edn. American Conference of Governmental Industrial Hygienists, Cincinnati.

Ashford, N. (1980). *Cost-benefit analysis: wonder tool or mirage*. Testimony before the US House of Representatives, Interstate and Foreign Commerce Committee, Subcommittee on Oversight and Investigation.

Bloom, A.D. (ed.) (1981). *Guidelines for studies of human populations exposed to mutagenic and reproductive hazards*. p. 44. March of Dimes Birth Defect Foundation, New York.

Bridbord, K., Decoufle, P., Fraumeni, J.F. *et al.* (1978). *Estimates of the fraction of cancer in the United States related to occupational factors*. National Cancer Institute, National Institute of Environmental Health Sciences, and National Institute for Occupational Safety and Health, Bethesda, Md.

Cahin, H., Hart, D.J., and Stewart, T.E.M. (1978). *The VDT manual*. Ince-Fiej Research Association, Darmstadt.

Caplan, R.D., Cobb, S., French, J.R.P., *et al.* (1975). *Job demands and worker health*. US Department of Health, Education and Welfare, Washington, D.C.

Cooper, C.L. and Payne, R. (eds.) (1978). *Stress at work*. Wiley, New York.

Creech, J.L. and Johnson, M.N. (1974). Angiosarcoma of liver in the manufacture of polyvinyl chloride. *J. Occup. Med.* **16**, 150.

Davis, D., Bridbord, K., and Schneiderman, M. (1981). Estimating cancer causes: problems in methodology, production and trends. In *Quantification of occupational cancer*. (ed. R. Peto and M. Schneiderman) p. 285. Cold Spring Harbor Laboratory, Cold Spring Harbor, New York.

Decoufle, P. (1982). Occupation. In: *Cancer epidemiology and prevention* (ed. D. Schottenfeld and J.F. Fraumeni), p. 318. Saunders, Philadelphia.

Dickens, C. (1958). *A small star in the east. The uncommercial traveller and reprinted pieces*. Oxford University Press, London.

Doll, R. and Peto, R. (1981). *The causes of cancer*. Oxford University Press, London.

Fabro, S. (1983). Reproductive toxicology: State of the art, 1982. *Am. J. Ind. Med.* **4**, 391.

Feldman, R.G., Siroky, M., Niles, C.A. *et al.* (1979). Neurotoxic dysuria due to dimethylaminoproprionitrile. *Neurology* **29**, 560.

Goldman, R.H. and Peters, J.M. (1981). The occupational and environmental health history. *JAMA* **246**, 2831.

Grandjean, E. (1979). *Ergonomical and medical aspects of cathode ray tube displays*. Federal Institute of Technology, Zurich.

Gunnarsson, E. and Ostberg, O. (1977). *The physical and psychological working environment in a terminal-based computer storage and retrieval system*. National Board of Occupational Safety and Health, Report 35, Stockholm.

Hamilton, A. (1943). *Exploring the dangerous trades; an autobiography*. Little Brown, Boston.

Hemminki, K. (1980). Occupational chemicals tested for teratogenicity. *Int. Arch. Environ. Health* **47**, 191.

Hernberg, S. (1980). Epidemiology in occupational health. In *Developments in occupational medicine* (ed. C. Zenz) p. 3. Year Book Medical, Chicago.

Hunter, D. (1978). *The diseases of occupations*, 6th edn. Hodder and Stoughton, London.

International Agency for Research on Cancer (1972–79). *IARC monographs on the evaluation of the carcinogenic risk of chemicals to man*, Vols. 1–20. International Agency for Research on Cancer, Lyon.

Johnson, B.L. and Anger, W.K. (1983). *Behavioral toxicology in environmental and occupational medicine*. Little Brown, Boston.

Jones, R.N., Weill, H., and Ziskind, M. (1975). Pulmonary function in sandblasters silicosis. *Bull. Physiopathol. Resp.* **11**, 589.

Kurt, T., Webb, C.R. Jr., and Hazard Evaluation and Technical Assistance Branch of NIOSH (1980). Toxic occupational neuropathy—Texas. *MMWR* **29**, 529.

Landrigan, P.J., Kreiss, K., Xintaras, C. *et al.* (1980). Clinical epidemiology of occupational neurotoxic disease. *Neurobehav. Toxicol.* **2**, 43.

Levy, B.S. and Wegman, D.H. (1983). *Occupational health: recognizing and preventing work-related disease*. Little Brown, Boston.

Manson, J. and Simon, R. (1979). Influence of environmental agents on male reproductive failure. In *Work and the health of women* (ed. V. Hunt) p. 155. CRC Press, Boca Raton, Florida.

Marti-Ibanez, F. (ed.) (1960). *Henry E. Sigerist on the history of medicine*. MD Publications, New York.

Merchant, J.A., Lumsden, J.C., Kilburn, K.H. *et al.* (1973). Dose response studies in cotton textile workers. *J. Occup. Med.* **15**, 222.

Monson, R.R. (1980). *Occupational epidemiology*. CRC Press, Boca Raton, Florida.

Monson, R.R. and Fine, L.J. (1978). Cancer mortality among rubber workers. *J. Natl. Cancer Inst.* **61**, 1047.

Monson, R.R. and Nakano, K.K. (1976). Mortality among rubber workers. 1. White male union employees in Akron, Ohio. *Am. J. Epidemiol.* **103**, 284.

NIOSH (1974). Criteria for a recommended standard: occupational exposure to crystalline silica. US Department of Health, education, and Welfare, Washington, DC. (NIOSH Publication No. 75–120.)

NIOSH (1978). *National occupational hazard survey, Vol. III. Survey analysis and supplemental tables*. US Department of Health, Education and Welfare, Washington, DC. (NIOSH Publication No. 78–114.)

NIOSH (1979). *Tumorigenic, teratogenic, and mutagenic citations: subfiles of the registry of toxic effects of chemical substances*. US Department of Health, Education, and Welfare, Washington, DC. (NIOSH Publication No. 80–102.)

NIOSH (1980*a*). *New developments in occupational stress: conference proceedings*. US Department of Health and Human Services, Washington, DC. (NIOSH Publication No. 81–102.)

NIOSH (1980*b*). Working with video display terminals: a preliminary health-risk evaluation. *MMWR* **29**, 307.

NIOSH (1981*a*). *Current intelligence bulletin 36—silica flour: silicosis*. US Department of Health and Human Services, Washington, DC. (NIOSH Publication No. 81–36.)

NIOSH (1981*b*). *Potential health effects of video display terminals*. US Department of Health and Human Services, Washington, DC. (NIOSH Publication No. 81–129.)

NIOSH (1982). *Vibration white finger disease in US workers using pneumatic chipping and grinding tools I: epidemiology*. US Department of Health and Human Services, Washington, DC. (NIOSH Publication No. 82–118.)

NIOSH (1983). Leading work-related diseases and injuries—United States. *MMWR* **32**, 24.

Occupational Safety and Health Administration (OSHA), US Department of Health, Education, and Welfare. Occupational Safety, and Health Review Commission (1972). *The President's report on occupational safety and health*. Government Printing Office, Washington, DC.

Ofice of Technology Assessment, United States Congress (1981). *Assessment of technologies for determining cancer risks from the environment*. US Government Printing Office, Washington, DC. (Pub. OTA-H-128.)

Oudiz, J., Brown, J.W., Ayer, H.E., and Samuels, S. (1983). A report on silica exposure levels in United States foundries. *Am. Ind. Hyg. Assoc. J.* **44**, 374.

Parkes, R. (1982). *Occupational lung disorders*. 2nd edn. Butterworths, London.

pestronk, A., Keogh, J., and Griffin, J.G. (1979). Dimethylaminopropionitrile intoxications: a new industrial neuropathy. *Neurology* **29**, 540.

Ramazzini, R. (1713). *Diseases of workers*. (Translated 1964 by W.C. Wright from *De Morbis Artificum Diatriba*, 1713). Hafner, New York.

Redmond, C.K., Ciocco, A., Lloyd, J.W. *et al.* (1972). Long-term mortality study of steelworkers. VI. Mortality from malignant neoplasms among coke oven workers. *J. Occup. Med.* **14**, 621.

Rom, W.N. (ed.) (1983). *Environmental and occupational medicine*. Little Brown, Boston.

Rutstein, D.D., Mullan, R.J., Frazier, T.M. *et al.* (1983). Sentinal health events (occupational): a basis for physician recognition and public health surveillance. *Am. J. Public Health* **73**, 1054.

Samini, B., Weill, H., and Ziskind, M. (1974). Respirable silica dust exposure of sandblasters and associated workers in steel fabrication yards. *Arch. Environ. Health* **29**, 61.

Selikoff, I.J., Hammond, E.C., and Seidman, H. (1973). Cancer risk of insulation workers in the United States. In *Biological effects of asbestos*, p. 209. International Agency for Research on Cancer, Lyon.

Shaw, G.B. (1960). Mrs Warren's Profession. In *Plays by George Bernard Shaw*, p. 83. New American Library of World Literature, New York.

Taylor, J.R., Selhorst, J.B., Houff, S.A., and Martizez, A.J. (1978). Chlordecone intoxication in man. *Neurology* **28**, 626.

Theriault, G.P., Peters, J.M., and Fine, L.J. (1978). Pulmonary function in granite shed workers of Vermont. *Arch. Environ. Health* **28**, 18.

Tomatis, L., Breslow, N.E., and Bartsch, H. (1982). Experimental studies in the assessment of human risk. In *Cancer epidemiology and prevention* (ed. D. Schottenfeld and J.F. Fraumeni) p. 46. Saunders, Philadelphia.

Torkelson, T.R., Sadek, S.E., Rowe, V.K. *et al.* (1961). Toxicologic investigations of 1,2-dibromo-3-chloropropane. *Toxicol. Appl. Pharmacol.* **3**, 545.

US Department of Labor (1978*a*). *Standard for exposure to inorganic lead*, 43(122) Federal Register. pp. 27369–79.

US Department of Labor (1978*b*). *Standard for exposure to inorganic lead*, 43(225) Federal Register. pp. 54453–6.

US Department of Labor (1980*a*). An interim report to congress on occupational diseases. Washington, DC.

US Department of Labor (1980*b*). *Access to employee exposure and medical records*. 45 Federal Register (29 CFR 1910.20).

US Department of Labor, Occupational Safety and Health Administration (1983). OSHA safety and health standards (29 CFR 1910).

Wasserman, D.E. and Badger, D.W. (1973). Vibration and the worker's health and safety. National Institute for Occupational Safety and Health, Cincinnati, Ohio. (NIOSH Technical Report No. 77.)

Wasserman, D.E., Asburry, W., and Doyle, T.B. (1979). Whole-body vibration of heavy equipment operators. *Shock Vibration Bull.* **49**, 47.

Whorton, D.M., Krauss, R.M., Marshall, S. *et al.* (1977). Infertility in male pesticide workers. *Lancet* **ii**, 1259.

Williams, W. (981). Firing the woman to protect the fetus: the reconciliation of fetal protection with equal employment opportunity goals under Title VII. *Georgetown Law J.* **69**, 641.

Wilson, J. (1977). Current states of teratology—general principles and mechanism derived from animal studies. In *Handbook of teratology* (ed. J. Wilson and F. Fraser) p. 47. Plenum, New York.

World Health Organization (1975). *Early detection of health impairment in occupational exposures to health hazards.* (Technical Report Series No. 571). World Health Organization, Geneva.

Xintaras, C., Burg, J.R., Tanaka, S. *et al.* (1978). Occupational exposure to leptophos and other chemicals. Department of Health, Education, and Welfare, Washington, DC. (NIOSH Publication No. 78–136.)

Zenz, C. (ed.) (1975). *Occupational medicine: principles and practice.* Year Book Medical Publishers, Chicago.

Zielhuis, R.L. (1978). Biological monitoring. *Scan, J. Work Environ. health.* **4**, 1.

Ziskind, M., Jones, R.N., and Weill, H. (1976). Silicosis. *Am. Rev. Resp. Dis.* **113**, 643.

22 The health needs of disadvantaged client groups

Raymond Illsley and Ken Mullen

INTRODUCTION

The welfare state is based upon the recognition that social inequity exists and will continue to exist. Social services are provided and organized to identify individuals and groups whose resources are inadequate to meet the normal needs of daily living, to compensate them partially for these inadequacies, and to minimize the consequences for their health and welfare (Beveridge 1942). Some services are clearly intended to redistribute income from richer to poorer groups (progressive taxation, supplementary benefits, and rent and rate rebates); some, whilst still having a redistributive intention are also designed to protect socially vulnerable groups (child allowances and old age pensions); some compensate for temporary social misfortunes (unemployment pay) and, physical or mental disabilities or sickness (mobility and attendant allowances or sickness pay); and others, covered by the personal social services, are intended to assist individuals with a wide variety of problems of daily living they cannot personally and financially cope with. All, however, make the assumption that the operation of the social and economic structure will produce inequalities in both needs and resources whose consequences, without collective intervention, would be unacceptable to public morality.

The National Health Service, an integral component of the welfare state in the UK, shared only a part of these assumptions and objectives. It recognized that the incidence of illness would fall unevenly upon individuals and that without collective provision, access to medical care would reflect ability to pay rather than the intrinsic treatment needs created by illness. It therefore established a service designed to provide equality of access, irrespective of the individual's ability to pay, and created a structure of treatment services. The underlying assumption was that social groups, because of inequalities in wealth and income, would otherwise receive inequality of treatment. Certain services were targetted upon particular population groups, such as mothers and children, and indirectly this provided special protection for some social groups. Essentially, however, this was a service as accessible and freely available to the rich as to the poor. No structural features were built into the service to acknowledge either that health itself was unequally distributed between social categories or that social categories known to have poor health should receive 'compensation' by way of targetted services or of disproportionate attention to their health needs (Royal Commission on the National Health Service 1979).

The ensuing years have brought changes in both thought and practice. The Health Departments have formulated priorities which in some instances would, if applied, entail positive discrimination in favour of socially, rather than medically defined categories of the population. (The Scottish Home and Health Department (1976), for example, recommended priority for multiply-deprived families.) A formula for the reallocation of resources between geographical areas has been applied which tends to reduce disparity between prosperous and poor areas of the UK (DHSS 1976; Berthoud et al. 1981). Across the country many schemes have been evolved which redirect resources to particularly vulnerable localities or social groups (Windass 1982). The most important questions, however, remain unsolved. Certain groups of the population, defined in social or economic terms, for example, the low-paid, the unskilled, or the unemployed, are known to have exceptionally high rates of morbidity and mortality (DHSS 1980; Carter and Peel 1976). Their health problems are the result of social experience and their position in the social structure. They cause disproportionate costs to both the health and social services (partly as a result of their ill-health) (Le Grand 1982). Should the health services allocate disproportionate effort to these groups? Should the health services be used to correct or mitigate the consequences of activity in other sectors of society and the economy? In any case, can health services effectively and efficiently correct social evils? What would be the implication for the structure of services and the activities of health personnel? To a very large extent the answers to these questions depend on who 'the disadvantaged' are and how they have become disadvantaged.

WHO ARE THE DISADVANTAGED?

The terms poverty, deprivation, and disadvantage are sometimes used interchangeably, but often they denote different segments of a larger group. Poverty may have been an adequate generic title at a time when a larger section of the population existed at standards of living barely sufficient to maintain life or to provide the basic ingredients of welfare—food, shelter, heat, and clothing. In his study of poverty in York in 1899, Joseph Rowntree felt able to calculate, in terms of food, rent, and a few household sundries, the 'minimum necessary expenditure for the maintenance of merely physical health' and to estimate that 28 per cent of the population of York lived below that minimum poverty level (Rowntree 1901). When he repeated this study in 1936 he still used an approach based on 'minimum necessary expenditure', but based his criteria on current conventions of necessity rather than upon 'the maintenance of merely physical health' (Rowntree 1941). He had thus introduced a concept of relative poverty, based on notions of disadvantage or inequality. With rising general standards of living, the borderline between poverty and normality is inevitably subject to constant change and two main approaches have subsequently been used by investigators. The first merely adopts the official poverty line calculated by Government to indicate levels of supplementary benefit (Berthoud *et al.* 1981). In one sense this means nothing more than the level a government feels able to pay and to defend politically. The second measure was evolved by Townsend following his empirical observation that participation in a sample of conventional behaviours, which did not vary much across most economic groups, fell sharply below a certain level of income (Townsend 1979). Both these measures are different in kind from the original 'minimum necessary' approach and Townsend's differs qualitatively in its overt acknowledgement of the human need to participate in social activity.

'Deprivation' and 'disadvantage' remain as concepts without any established criteria and thus can be, and are, used more loosely. Deprivation places an emphasis upon the absence of necessary components of living and the presumed material and psychological states which occur in consequence. Disadvantage places the emphasis upon social and economic status compared with average or just-below-average experience and thus has a stronger connotation of inequity (Brown and Madge 1982).

The identity of the groups which fall into the category of relative poverty or of disadvantage and the contribution which they each made to the total volume of poverty at any one time necessarily changes historically with economic, social, and demographic change. Large families, which constituted a sizeable proportion of Rowntree's poverty group are becoming infrequent and even the idea of what constitutes a large family has changed. On the other hand, the elderly constitute a much larger proportion of today's population—as do ethnic minorities, which barely existed in York in 1899 (Fiegehen *et al.* 1977). Perhaps of equal importance are the welfare measures, sickness and unemployment pay, retirement pensions, child allowances, and housing subsidies, for they affect not merely the number of the disadvantaged but the subgroups of which they are composed.

A commonsense approach based upon popular know-ledge and values would probably today characterize the following groups as disadvantaged: low-paid workers, unskilled workers, the unemployed and the underemployed, multichild families, one-parent families, elderly persons, ethnic minorities, the chronic sick, and the mentally or physically handicapped. Such an approach, useful as a first approximation, suffers from several conceptual and statistical problems. First, until checked against empirical evidence, it remains a hunch subject to the known deficiencies of partial knowledge and of personal and social values. Other groups, for example, the institutionalized, could be added according to the viewpoint of the observer; some might be contested on the ground that they were not blameless for their condition, for example, one-parent families, or that they were privileged to be in this country (e.g. ethnic minorities). Second, it is clear that some of these categories contain many individuals who are not poor and many who are rich and privileged.

The numerical approach used by Townsend (1979) has certain advantages. It specifies a single dimension—namely, a criterion of poverty empirically based upon inability, through lack of resources, to participate in normal social activities. The level at which this is placed is subject to change over time, it may weight the index towards particular groups, and must be subject to some degree of debate. It also requires for its application rather detailed knowledge of a sensitive kind.

A simplified version of results obtained by Townsend in his 1970 survey are given in Table 22.1. Seven per cent of Townsend's sample (123 households) were found to be under the state's poverty line based on rates paid by the Supplementary Benefit Commission. Townsend's own deprivation line puts the figure at 25 per cent. The percentage of households in poverty within each disadvantaged group varies from 5 per cent of those born in Eire to 26 per cent of those with a disabled or handicapped child. Using Townsend's classification, poverty is most common among the elderly incapacitated, though the unemployed appear less disadvantaged. The percentage of households in poverty who are not members of any disadvantaged group is also high at 22 per cent. The large amount of overlap among the disadvantaged categories should be noted with 857 households having one or more characteristic of disadvantage.

The diversity of the major groups falling into the low-income category draws attention to the variety of ways in which people become disadvantaged and to the equally varied ways in which services may have to be organized in order to meet both their social and their health needs. First, however, it is necessary to give an account of the known health and disease experience of these groups.

THE HEALTH STATUS OF THE DISADVANTAGED: ITS SOCIAL AETIOLOGY

For most of this century death rates for the UK can be calculated by 'social classes' by combining data collected on birth and death certificates with occupational data collected at the Decennial Census (OPCS 1978). Examples are given in

Table 22.1. *Percentages of households belonging to certain social minorities with relatively low incomes*

Household characteristic	Percentage with income below the state's standard*	Percentage with income last year below the deprivation standard†	Total numbers‡
One-parent family	17	32	54
Woman and adult dependants	0	25	14
Large family (four or more children)	17	53	69
Unemployed eight weeks or more (under 65 years)	8	20	74
Sick or injured eight weeks or more (under 65 years)	6	33	144
Disabled adult (under 65 years)	7	39	177
Borderline disabled (under 65 years)	7	22	328
Disabled or handicapped child	26	(44)	19
Elderly incapacitated (over 65 years)	14	68	129
Low-paid women (under £8 per week)	11	29	64
Low-paid men (under £14 per week)	12	46	81
Non-white	6	32	33
Born in Eire	5	25	41
At least one characteristic	9	29	857
None of above characteristics	5	22	911
All	7	25	1768

*The state's standard is based on the rates paid by the Supplementary Benefits Commission.
†Townsend's own deprivation standard, a standard of income below which people experience deprivation disproportionately to income.
‡These numbers apply to the first column but are slightly lower (totalling 1634) for the second column.
Source: Townsend (1979).

Table 22.2 and in Figs. 22.1 and 22.2. Both reproductive and adult mortality death rates increase regularly and often sharply with falling social class and this disparity has existed to almost the same degree for many decades. Explanation would, of course, be relatively simple if such class differentials applied only to a few major causes of death and even simpler if it were possible to identify a linkage between cause of death and risks arising in the working conditions of particular occupations. Class differentials, however, exist, although to varying degrees, in each of the 14 major cause-of-death categories used in the International Classification of Diseases (ICD). Moreover, when married women are classified according to their husband's occupation, similar if lesser differentials also appear, even though few women are subjected to the same occupational hazards as their husbands.

Reliable data on the distribution of morbidity across occupational groups are scarce. The best available data, on a national basis, are derived from the General Household Survey (OPCS 1982). Responses to questions about long-standing illness, restrictions upon activity, and recent episodes of illness make it possible to identify chronic illness, chronic handicapping illness, and recent acute illness. In all three categories the rate of self-reported illness rises sharply with social class for adult males—the evidence is more erratic for children, women, and elderly persons (Table 22.3). Data from other sources less dependent upon self-reporting tend to confirm these findings. In general the evidence suggests that disparities in illness, and especially chronic illness, are at least as wide as disparities in death.

These facts are not challenged; controversy lies in their interpretation and in the implication of different interpretations for policies of preventive or corrective action (DHSS 1980).

Social class is a general measure obtained by combining occupational groups roughly equivalent in skill and 'general standing in the community' to form occupational classes; conventionally five occupational groups, in a hierarchy of skill, are known as 'social classes' (Leete and Fox 1977). Occupational groups can justifiably be regarded as social classes in that occupational skill is an indirect indicator of education, income, standards of living, environmental, and

Table 22.2. *Changes in mortality by social class, England and Wales*

Occupational class	Ratios of actual to expected deaths of infants			Male mortality 15–64 years (SMR's)		
	1930–32	1970–72	Percentage change	1930–32	1970–72	Percentage change
I Professional	53	66	+26	90	77	−14
II Managerial	73	77	+5	94	81	−14
III Skilled manual and non-manual	94	94	+0	97	104	+7
IV Partly skilled	108	111	+3	102	114	+12
V Unskilled	125	175	+40	111	137	+23

Source: Registrar General's Decennial Supplement and Occupational Mortality Tables.

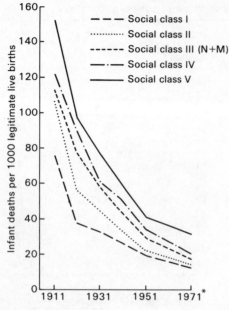

Fig. 22.1. Trends in infant mortality by social class. England and Wales, 1911–71 (deaths per 1000 live births). (Source: OPCS (1978).) *Deaths per 1000 live births.

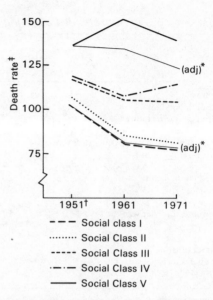

Fig. 22.2. Recent trends in death rates by social class for men aged 15–64 years, England and Wales, 1951–71. *1961 and 1971 rates for social class I and V were adjusted to the 1950 classification. †1951 rates were adjusted for errors to company directors and changes to social class IV. ‡Direct age-standardized death rates per 100 000 living at ages 15–64 years using all men in 1970–72 as the standard. (Source: OPCS (1978).)

working conditions, and through these of social milieu and broad life-style. The data presented above show that the application of the classification and the ranking do produce a hierarchy of death rates.

Various theories have been advanced to account for the existence of class differentials and for their persistence over time. Some require only brief attention. When it became evident shortly after the introduction of the NHS that class differentials persisted despite equal access to treatment a hypothesis of *cultural lag* was invoked which suggested that time was required before the long-term effects of past disadvantage disappeared. Time has not eroded the differentials and indeed they are still wider in the younger than in the older adults whose upbringing pre-dated the NHS. One part of the hypothesis, however, remains correct, that preventive health behaviour is more slowly established in the lower social groups. This point is discussed more fully below. A further hypothesis, that both social position and

health are genetically determined and that inequalities are the result of *natural selection* has never been substantiated.

Most evidence and discussion centre around a combination of structural and behavioural explanations. The structural explanation accepts that our social structure is characterized by permanent social and economic inequality which exposes individuals to different probabilities of ill-health and injury. Stated briefly, and therefore more starkly than its sophisticated exponents would accept, the argument is that combined social and health inequality begin when babies of the lower social classes are born to mothers of poorer physique and health, evidenced by lower birth weights and higher perinatal death rates. The effects of the intrauterine environment are reinforced by the social, economic, and cultural environment of the home, the social

Table 22.3. *Morbidity in Great Britain by socio-economic group*

Socio-economic group	Chronic sickness		Acute sickness
	Percentage reporting long-standing illness	Percentage reporting limiting long-standing illness	Percentage reporting acute sickness
Professional	20.2	10.0	10.3
Employers and managers	26.0	14.5	10.5
Intermediate and junior non-manual	27.6	15.8	12.2
Skilled manual and own account non-professional	28.5	16.5	11.5
Semi-skilled manual and personal service	34.2	22.2	13.1
Unskilled manual	39.2	25.5	14.6
All persons	29.0	17.5	12.0

Source: General Household Survey (1981).

group, and the locality such that children from the lower social classes simultaneously receive poorer food and health care, less stimulation, and an inferior formal education resulting in diminished physical and intellectual education. With this background they have a lower probability of occupational success, move into an unskilled job and, through the probabilities of assortative mating, marry someone with a similar history. In their working life they are more subject to physical stress, low income, and unemployment (Illsley 1955; 1980).

The accompanying behavioural explanation suggests that low socio-economic status, low pay, and insecurity produces inadequacies in diet and dietary values, lack of knowledge and of long-term goals giving lesser possibilities of making maximum use of health and other services and of taking preventive health measures.

For each of these steps in a life-history, there is ample empirical evidence in the sense of group probabilities, that is, children of poor socio-economic backgrounds are shorter in stature, do achieve less well in school, and are more likely to move into less skilled jobs (Blaxter 1981). The process, however, is infinitely more complex and less deterministic than the stark history sketched above, partly because it is built up of probabilities at each stage. The evidence from studies of social mobility show a constant and heavy stream of movement between classes of origin and classes in adult life. Whilst the children of semi-skilled or unskilled workers are less likely than those of skilled workers to move into upper class positions, nevertheless approximately two-thirds do move into classes higher than those of their fathers. And conversely, approximately 60 per cent of clases I to III had their origins in lower social classes (Goldthorpe 1980). The process is more complex because histories are influenced by a multiplicity of factors such as family size, position in family, housing conditions, unevenness in educational facilities, religious and ideological beliefs, movements in local and national job markets, parental personality, genetic endowment, and illness, disability, and accident.

The structural explanation provides a framework within which these multiple influences operate. It suggests linkages between social origins, life-events, and health based on the protective effect of advantage and the reinforcement of disadvantage. Societies in the western industrial world have experienced a century or more of economic growth, of increases in living standards, and of health but at all stages there have been groups high or low in income, education, and security, and the structural explanation attempts to show how and why health is constantly associated with social advantage and disadvantage. In so doing it emphasizes the point that both social and health inequalities are socially created manifestations of social structure rather than the innate attributes of individuals. It does not explain why differentials have persisted to the same degree over many decades. That argument is more controversial. For some, relative disparities in health have remained unchanged because relative disparates in wealth have also remained unchanged.

An alternative argument holds that the picture of persist-ence is an artefact of the methods of measurement (Illsley 1980). A combination of social improvement and the application of medical knowledge has brought down the death rates in all social groups over the last century. Social and economic changes have also led to the progressive reduction in size of those occupational classes with the highest risks of mortality and morbidity caused by poverty and social conditions. The lowest death rates therefore now apply to a larger segment of the population and the highest rates to a smaller segment. The net result of this process is shown in Table 22.4 which gives the fall in infant mortality in England and Wales between 1930–32 and 1978–80. Using death rates as the measurement of change the familiar picture

Table 22.4. *Changes in infant mortality between 1930–32 and 1978–80, England and Wales*

Indicator	Levels in 1978–80 as a percentage of 1930–32				
	I	II	III	IV	V
Rates of death	29	22	19	21	22
Number of deaths	111	42	17	16	6

Sources: General Register Office, Decennial Supplement England and Wales 1931 Part IIa Occupational Mortality, HMSO (1938); OPCS Monitor, DH1 80/2, Infant and Perinatal Mortality, June 1980.

emerges of an almost equal fall in each social class. Using the number of deaths as the indicator, however, deaths in the highest class have actually increased, whereas deaths in class V stand at only 6 per cent of their level in 1930–32.

The artefactual argument makes the further point that occupational class is an inefficient indicator of need. The fact that more than half of today's classes IV and V were reared in classes I, II, and III suggests that occupational classes are very heterogeneous in their living conditions. A more effective and efficient policy would attempt to identify the actual conditions—in family, work, and community life—which affect life-chances and health risks.

The use of occupational class is, however, only one way of subdividing the population according to social characteristics and its widespread use in vital statistics probably owes as much to its historical availability as an index and to its ease of collection as to its intrinsic aetiological significance. As other measures of socio-economic status have become available it has become more obvious that occupational class owes its predictive effectiveness to its close correlation with other aspects of social life. Fox and Goldblatt (1982) analysed the death over the next five years of persons enumerated in the 1971 census using, as well as occupation, other characteristics recorded at the census. They found that for many purposes a threefold measure of housing tenure (owner occupation, and rented tenancy of private and local authority housing) discriminated as efficiently as social class. Other measures such as car-ownership, educational qualifications, migration status, and certain types of household structure also showed good discrimination in some situations. These are not causes of death but component characteristics of life-histories, life-styles, and of living and working conditions which may have a more direct impact upon health. Membership of social class IV and V is not in itself a sufficient cause of premature death, but like membership of other relatively disadvantaged groups, is indicative of the presence in disproportionate numbers of persons who have been subjected to unhealthy experiences.

The heterogeneity of these disadvantaged groups is well illustrated by Townsend (1979) who listed major social groups according to the percentage living in poverty (based on the state poverty standard). Those groups containing 15 per cent more in poverty included: the non-white, those unemployed for 10 weeks or more, those with appreciable or severe disability, unskilled manual workers, members of one-patient and/or fatherless families, those with less than nine years' education, persons of pensionable age (especially those living alone or over 80 years old), and households of four or more children. The process by which they reached a state of poverty clearly differs from group to group. For many of those with disability, their poverty is a consequence of their ill health and is already indicative of higher mortality risks; for others such as the unemployed or one-parent families it may be a temporary state; for some of the elderly poverty may have been a lifelong state, for it is the final point of a long and healthy life.

This argument suggests that, to understand aetiology and thus to evolve preventive or corrective policies it is necessary to disaggregate large general categories of disadvantage and to examine the subgroups of which they are composed.

THE DISAGGREGATION OF DISADVANTAGE

Social disadvantage takes many forms; the processes which produce it are varied; the consequences for health differ between forms; and policies to prevent its occurrence or to mitigate its effects may need to be adapted to the different forms, processes, and consequences. There are, however, dangers in disaggregation which should be borne in mind as each component is isolated and treated separately. Disadvantages overlap and the presence of multiple disadvantages is most likely to be indicative of ill-consequences and least likely to offer opportunities for corrective action. To be elderly is part of normal existence in an affluent society; to be 80, poor, and living alone is to live in a state of extreme vulnerability. To be non-white is only a disadvantage in a society which stigmatizes colour; in Britain to be non-white carries a series of simultaneous disadvantages. In a comment on Townsend's survey of poverty Blaxter (1981) points out that 43 per cent of households with one or more non-white members were in social classes IV and V compared with 26 per cent of the sample as a whole: 14 per cent were in or on the margins of poverty compared with 9 per cent; and 42 per cent were defined as 'deprived' by Townsend's index compared with 16 per cent. In a study of multiply deprived households in Scotland (Scottish Office 1980) it emerged that whilst the head of household was unemployed in 5 per cent of Scottish households, the comparable figure in severely deprived local authority housing areas was 17 per cent and that in these latter households 31

per cent contained four or more dependant children, 47 per cent were living in 1–3 rooms, and in 64 per cent the unemployed head had previously worked in a low-paid job. Mortality and morbidity statistics have not been designed to identify these combinations of disadvantage.

Table 22.1 lists specific categories of the population and their ranking in terms of three indices of poverty. Using another data source (the official Family Expenditure Survey of 1971) and adopting the more stringent criteria of the Supplementary Benefit Commission, Fiegehen and his colleagues (1977) attempted to estimate the comparative contribution of two broad causes of poverty and to identify their distribution between categories of the population. They distinguished between economic disadvantage, stemming from position in the labour market (unemployment and low pay for employed persons) and demographic disadvantage arising out of imbalance between income and the need for resources associated with particular phases of the life-cycle. Their summary of the situation (in 1977) is reproduced as Table 22.5. They stress the approximate nature of their judgements because, as indicated above, disadvantages are often multiple; the poverty of old people may reflect their low wages or unemployment prior to retiral; that of single parents may reflect employment in part-time or low-paid jobs or unequal opportunities to work; several categories will contain a proportion of chronically sick heads of household either unable to work, or able to work only part-time or in a low-paid job.

What emerged from their analysis was the predominance of life-cycle factors as the major cause of contemporary poverty. They concluded that old age was the main systematic cause of poverty whilst at younger ages the predominant factors were single parenthood and employment problems caused by being a woman or being sick. Economic causes were directly responsible for only 27 per cent of poverty. Apart from the authors' own reservations about the arbitrariness of separating the two categories, several further caveats are required; unemployment or low

Table 22.5. *Demographic and economic causes of poverty (percentage)**

Characteristics of head of household	Causes Mainly demographic	Mainly economic
Employment hindered by		
Retirement and/or old age	48	—
Being a single parent	10	—
Being female (not retired)	5	—
Other reasons (unoccupied)	7	—
Available for employment but		
Unemployed	—	10
Employed, 4–6 children	3	—
Low income from :		
Self-employment	—	10†
Employment	—	7†
All poor individuals	73	27

*Proportions of poor individuals in specified categories of households.
†Estimated as residual categories.
Source: Fiegehen *et al.* (1977).

earnings because of chronic sickness and disablement are not identified separately; the general rate of unemployment was very low in 1971 compared with all subsequent periods and particularly with the years from 1979 onwards; the proportion of single-parent households has also increased greatly since 1971; no separate mention is made of non-white populations with their history of high unemployment rates. Nevertheless the results show that 'most poverty arises where there exists a specific identifiable risk, but there is still a need for a comprehensive policy to meet the essential symptoms of poverty—low income'. Some of the specific identifiable groups are discussed in more detail below.

Disadvantages stemming from labour market status

Disadvantage in the labour market is characterized by low pay, job insecurity, underemployment and unemployment, and poor working conditions. To assess the impact of these conditions upon health it would be necessary to distinguish between the underlying health and behaviour of the occupants of low status jobs and the specific contribution of the conditions themselves. In most instances available data have not been adequate for such a complicated task.

No routine data exist, for example, on the health of *low-paid workers*. Berthoud and Brown (1981) state 'Industries which pay low wages are frequently characterised by poor working conditions and high labour turnover. Low-paid workers are highly vulnerable to unemployment, have less access to fringe benefits and receive less benefit from official schemes where they are related to pay, length of service, and contribution record.' Unskilled work has usually been used as a proxy indicator for low-paid work on the grounds that it is closely correlated with low pay, job insecurity, and heavy manual work. Its major deficiency as a proxy is that it underestimates the number of female workers who are paid low rates for skilled and semi-skilled work. The health status of unskilled workers and the selective nature of recruitment into the category have been discussed above but specific health effects of low pay cannot be disentangled.

Unemployed workers are normally drawn disproportionately from semi-skilled and unskilled workers and from Northern Ireland and the heavy-industry areas of Wales, the North of England, and Scotland. 'In 1979 . . . while approximately 53 per cent of the labour force were manual workers they constituted 72 per cent of the unemployed. A Manpower Services Commission survey of the long-term unemployed in 1979 found that almost three-quarters of their sample had previously been manual workers, the majority of whom had done semi-skilled or unskilled jobs' (Berthoud and Brown 1981). In times of economic depression other categories are disproportionately affected—especially those aged under 25 or over 55 years, ethnic minorities, and disabled persons—and the traditional composition and the health status of the category will be altered by the entry of skilled and white-collar workers previously unaffected.

Studies of the effects of unemployment on physical health have produced inconclusive results—mainly because it is difficult to separate pre-existing ill health from the effects of unemployment itself in a population heavily biassed towards low economic status and poor health. The association clearly exists; death rates rise in times of economic depression (Brenner 1979); the unemployed have higher death rates than the employed (McMichael 1976); and death rates rise with increasing duration of unemployment (Colledge and Bartholomew 1980). Perhaps the most reliable British results derive from Fox and Goldblatt's (1982) longitudinal study of deaths to persons identified in the 1971 census. Death rates in the following five years for men unemployed in 1971 but still seeking work were 30 per cent higher than the national average (but 20 per cent lower for women). Inspection of the cause of death suggests strongly that part of this excess (e.g. high death rates from malignant neoplasms) could not be attributed to unemployment. On the other hand deaths from accidents, violence, and circulatory and respiratory disease were also excessive—but the intrinsic effect of unemployment cannot be determined. Whilst the scientific status of many studies is questionable, the volume of evidence supports the hypothesis of damaging consequences (Brenner and Mooney 1983). The small amount of data on the children of the unemployed suggests retardation of growth (Rona *et al.* 1978).

Jahoda and Rush (1980) argue that employment is one of several categories of experience relevant to psychological well-being. They consider that a job has certain latent functions for the worker, additional to income. It provides (i) a measure of enforced activity which (ii) establishes social contacts outside the family in (iii) the pursuit of collective purposes which go beyond personal immediate goals and with (iv) a time structure governing the execution of the activity and (v) a social status in terms of both a role and a reward for contribution to society's welfare. Testing these hypotheses on samples of employed and unemployed men, Miles (1983) found strikingly higher levels of symptomatology and lower levels of reported well-being and life-satisfaction in the unemployed, even after controlling for background variables. These results support earlier findings by Warr and his colleagues (Warr 1978; Hartley 1980; Hepworth 1980; Stafford *et al.* 1980) based partially on controlled before-and-after measurement. Their findings show that the impact of unemployment on measures of psychological well-being varies with the degree of work involvement, with age, and with prior occupational status. Whilst stress measurements reach levels normally regarded clinically as depression, the effects of short-term unemployment seem quickly reversible. On the other hand at least one major study of the American depression of the 1930s reports measureable effects 40 years later.

The political and economic forces which impel international migration bring many separate streams of migration to Britain. Some are temporary migrants pursuing education and careers before returning to their homeland and their low death rates reflect their higher socio-economic status and selectivity for youth and health. Concern in Britain centres around the larger and more permanent streams of migration of *non-white ethnic minorities* from the New Commonwealth countries of Asia, Africa, and the West Indies. Because most migrating populations are young and because the peak flow of migration from these countries is relatively recent, their adult mortality rates are low. Even after standardization for both age and social class, their low rates persist (OPCS 1978) suggesting that they were either formally or informally selected for their health and fitness. Their major source of disadvantage stems from their low market status, resulting partly from language and cultural factors, but principally from discrimination against non-whites in the economy. Unemployment rates are exceptionally high and there is evidence that they occupy in this country jobs of lower status than their qualifications would permit (Runnymede Trust 1980). Whilst a high proportion, particularly of Asian immigrants, are owner-occupiers, the concentration of non-white populations in inner cities, itself influenced by discriminatory pressures, in effect means a lower standard of both housing and public amenities.

Resistance to census questions about colour or ethnic origin means that very little information exists about the British-born descendants of non-white immigrants. On the other hand perinatal and infant deaths to non-white immigrants are substantially higher than those to other migrant groups or to the native British population—a phenomenon in sharp contrast to the low death rates of the original male migrants (Adelstein *et al.* 1980). Those born to Pakistani immigrants have a significantly higher rate of post-neonatal deaths, the indicator normally most sensitive to environmental poverty. The Community Relations Commission (1977) drew attention to the frequently reported excess of low-birthweight babies among non-white birds and to cultural factors leading to under-utilization of antenatal and postnatal services.

Certain diseases are known to occur more commonly in particular migrant groups—thalassaemia in Cypriots, sickle-cell anaemia in Africans and West Indians, and rickets and osteomalacia in Asians. The latter condition is attributed to a combination of dietary habits and low exposure to sunlight in Asian women in Britain and experiments in Glasgow (Dunningan *et al.* 1981; Robertson *et al.* 1982; Henderson and Dunnigan 1983) suggest that it may be susceptible to vitamin B_{12} supplementation. There is, however, evidence that the dietary intake of the children of immigrants is deficient in other components.

Non-white immigrants have entered Britain at different phases, responding to many different pressures, coming from different cultures and having varied adaptibility to British conditions, life-styles and institutions. They cannot therefore be regarded as a homogeneous group experiencing identical conditions merely because of their skin colour.

Disadvantages related to phases of the life-cycle

It is convenient for purposes of both explanation and of service provision to separate life-cycle disadvantages from each other and from problems of market-status. For other purposes, and particularly for the understanding of how disadvantage arises and accumulates, they should not be separated. Townsend calculated from his data on social minorities with low incomes (see Table 22.1 above) that 24

per cent of his households belonged simultaneously to two disadvantaged groups and 9 per cent to three or more. Disadvantage from certain life-cycle characteristics frequently means economic disadvantage through its impact on the ability to work and on the level of earnings.

This is evident in the circumstances of *one-parent families,* the fastest-growing disadvantaged group in contemporary Britain. Leete (1978) calculates that the number of one-parent families rose from 570 000 in 1971 to 750 000 in 1976 (an increase of 32 per cent). Since about half of lone parents had two or more dependant children, more than 1.25 million dependant children were living in one-parent families in 1976. Most of the increase came from the rise in broken marriages and, to a lesser extent, from a rise in the number of unmarried mothers with children. Given the fluidity of relationships, lone parenthood may often be a temporary state, but the frequency of change cannot be calculated from existing sources of data.

One-parent families differ in relation to the number of children and the marital status of the parent (single, widowed, separated, or divorced), most of whom are women. Layard *et al.* (1978) estimate from re-analysis of the 1975 General Household Survey that 30 per cent of one-parent families, compared with 4 per cent in two-parent families, were living below the supplementary benefit standard, the worst off being single women (58 per cent), divorced women (51 per cent), and separated women (43 per cent). Whilst many women, particularly never-married women, lived with their mother, 32 per cent of all one-parent families were below the supplementary benefit level, even allowing for total household income. Their poverty is due to two main factors—their inability to work at all or to work full-time because of family responsibilities and the operation of the social security regulations which reduce supplementary benefit so sharply with any increase in earnings that recipients are deterred from taking work.

High stillbirth and infant death rates in unmarried mothers have been recorded since the beginning of birth and death registration and were mainly attributable to the poor background and development of the mother (Illsley and Gill 1968; Illsley 1980). The single-parent family, as described above, is, however, a more recent phenomenon, distributed more widely across educational and social class groups. Depression in young mothers in working-class families lacking adequate material and emotional support has been found by Brown and Harris (1978). In the absense of well-documented studies of the contemporary single-parent family, the health status of both mothers and children can be only inferred.

Large families, the classical source of life-cycle disadvantage, are becoming uncommon. Births to mothers with three or more previous liveborn children constituted only 7.3 per cent of births in 1980 compared with 15 per cent 20 years earlier. The risk of poverty to couples with four or more children is still high, despite children's allowances, compared with all family sizes (13 per cent below the supplementary benefit level against 4 per cent according to Layard *et al.* (1978)). It is still appreciably lower than that of single-parent families, by whom they are now outrumbered in the population. Various studies have shown that both physical and intellectual development is impeded in the large families of working-class parents (Davie *et al.* 1972; Rona *et al.* 1978; Blaxter 1981).

One-half of all people living at or below the supplementary benefit level are *elderly* (Layard *et al.* 1978). They thus constitute the largest single group of disadvantaged people in Britain. The proportion of the elderly who are poor increases with age and is higher for spinsters and widows than for married couples and lone men. What takes elderly people above the poverty line are earnings for those who work, occupational pensions, home ownership, and unearned income. Those at or below the poverty line receive almost the whole of their income from the state pension or supplementary benefit. Since the ability to continue work, and particularly at rates of pay which compensate them for deductions from their pensions, tend to come from the higher socio-economic groups, the state of poverty in old age is heavily dependent upon their ability to accumulate resources during their working life.

The extent and severity of poverty in elderly people might be expected to show very strong associations between health status and levels of disadvantage. And indeed there is such evidence ranging from longstanding illness or severe disablement (Townsend 1979; OPCS 1982) through nutritional deficiencies (DHSS 1972; Lonergan *et al.* 1975; Exton-Smith 1980) to hypothermia (Supplementary Benefits Commission 1977; Wicks 1978). Inequalities in death rates persist into old age but are less marked than at earlier ages. Nevertheless, considering the consensus on the poverty and vulnerability of the elderly, data of good epidemiological quality on their health and disease status are remarkably scarce.

The application of the concept of disadvantage to the elderly brings out overtly an aspect of disadvantage which is implied for other groups such as single-parent famlies but which is rarely quantified. The problems specific to old age are the increasing frequency of illness, increasing fragility and expectation of fragility, lack of mobility, and greater difficulty in social participation. Resources to meet these problems include, as well as economic security, personal coping skills, advice and practical help from relatives, friends and professional agencies, and the ability to contribute positively in social relationships so as to diminish the feeling of one-way dependency. It is arguable that confronted with these needs, the comparative importance of relative poverty is diminished. This possibility emerges from a longitudinal study of elderly people conducted in Aberdeen by Taylor and Ford (1983). They assessed the status of 11 risk-groups along six major dimensions—health, psychological functioning, activity, confidence, support, and material resources. Those living below the supplementary benefit level score significantly lower than the sample mean on all their four measures of health and they were also lower on three out of four measures of psychological functioning and all three measures of confidence. On the other hand they were not lonely and they received more visits from family members than the sample as a whole. The investigators were primarily concerned to establish efficient

methods of case-finding for general practitioners and health visitors and they therefore compared the poor with other categories of high vulnerability. Taking as their measure of vulnerability the number of deviations below the mean for each of their six dimensions, they assessed those at greatest risk as those who had recently moved, those recently discharged from hospital, the divorced or separated and the very old. Their second set of at-risk groups, characterized by deviations above and below the mean were the recently widowed, those living alone, the poor, and those from social class V. Those minimally at risk were the isolated, the never-married, and the childless whose disadvantages on a specific dimension did not spill over into other dimensions of well-being. These results raise questions about what counts as vulnerability in old age and how far resources in one area of functioning compensate for deficiencies in others.

Disabled persons fit uneasily between the two categories of economic and life-cycle disadvantage. Persons born with a disabling impairment, because of its impact upon their lifelong earning capacity may always be low-paid; others affected in mid-life by a newly acquired disability join the low paid; the majority of disabled persons become disabled when they have retired from paid work but their disability may create the need for additional resources. Disadvantage in the form of limited participation may be present at all ages.

Estimates of the number of disabled persons vary wildly. A government survey (Harris 1971) produced a British estimate of three million impaired persons living in private households compared with figures nearer to six or seven million disabled persons in the General Household Survey and in Townsend's (1979) survey. Between these extremes lie a host of differing definitions and questionnaires and interview techniques. Opinion is now crystallizing around a WHO definition (WHO 1976) in which impairment refers to a biological condition, disability to a functional condition, and handicap to the effect of impairment and disability on reduced social and economic activity. This still leaves room for substantial variations caused by data-collection methods, levels of severity, and the use of either self-reported or externally assessed perceptions. Additional problems arise concerning the definition of chronic illness (particularly mental illness) and its relationship to disability and handicap. Whilst the Harris figure seems to underestimate both impairment and handicap, the 'true' figure is conjectural.

Disability increases with age, and the rise is particularly sharp after the age of 50 years, with the corollary that, because of the preponderance of elderly females in the population, any crude estimate will show more disabled women than men. The prevalence of disability also increases with falling occupational class, but how far this results from occupation and/or class position or from the occupational downgrading of disabled persons is problematic. Disadvantage in the labour market is of course the primary cause of poverty in disabled and chronically sick persons, partly because of their functional limitations and partly because of the ambivalent attitudes of employers and of the public to many categories of disablement. Once they become unemployed, disabled persons have great difficulty in getting employment, and are frequently forced to accept work which is low-paid and insecure—research findings on this point antedate the high unemployment rates of 1979 onwards and its seems likely that the employment problems of disabled people will have increased disproportionately. Social security regulations create complex problems for many categories of disabled and chronically sick persons, partly because of uncertainties about diagnosis, partly because past employment histories had reduced entitlements to benefit and partly because administrative regulations pressure people into sharply defined categories of well/not well, fit for work/incapacitated, seeking work/retired, which do not fit their perceptions of their status (Blaxter 1976).

The net result of multiple disability, unemployment, and social security problems (see Table 22.1) is that very high proportions of the disabled groups fall below the statutory poverty level.

More than other groups described in this chapter, disabled persons are the clear responsibility of the health system because they enter the category of disadvantage on account of their health and not their social status. Both the Tunbridge Committee (DHSS 1972) and the Royal Commission on the NHS (1975, 1979) reported unfavourably on the failure of medical education and medical practice to appreciate the importance of effective rehabilitation, to liaise both within the system and with related systems to minimize the social and economic consequences of disability.

THE PREVENTION AND MITIGATION OF DISADVANTAGE

Disadvantage emerges from this review as a convenient concept for describing the condition of many populations whose command over resources threatens both their social well-being and their health. They reach their disadvantaged condition by many different routes, by birth and upbringing in deprived environments; by inability to compete successfully in a competitive labour market; by either personal or culturally determined behaviour which reduces their earning power or creates excessive demands upon attainable resources; by ill health, injury, and disablement; by the breakdown of supportive environments; and, most commonly, by a combination of reinforcing events and influences over a lifetime. For children and young people and for non-white immigrant populations the initial disadvantage may determine the course of their lives, for others it may be a temporary state, for yet others it may be the inescapable end-point of a life-history. The multiplicity of routes to disadvantage and the variety of its manifestations implies multiple causation which, in turn, suggests that single-factor solutions are likely to be inappropriate and ineffective. Nevertheless, the picture is not one of random activities of individuals, but of whole groups of people sharing common features which are integral parts of contemporary social structure. Low pay may be a salient characteristic of an individual but the existence of a large low-paid population is a characteristic of society itself.

Single parenthood may frequently be a regrettable and avoidable condition of an individual, but the emergence in the last decade of a substantial body of one-parent families is a feature of our society. It is therefore necessary to go beyond the individual in the search for causes and for measures by which disadvantage may be minimized in its coverage and consequences. The following generalizations appear appropriate.

1. The main component of disadvantage lies in the impact of demographic and life-cycle events upon single parent families, large families and the elderly, and upon disabled and chronically sick persons. The redistributive action of welfare policy is not sufficient to offset the loss of income and the need of extra resources imposed by these life-cycle factors. Some action by health and social services might be effective in avoiding the incidence of such factors and reducing their impact upon health and well-being.

2. A second, but still substantial component stems from the existence of low pay and unemployment. These are consequences of economic structure and economic and social policy and are not remediable by individual action or by the activities of health and social service agencies.

3. Disadvantage from a particular cause is rarely a discrete factor separate from other stresses and events. Whilst the stereotype of populations born into poverty, transmitting the culture of poverty and remaining problem families over the generations is overdrawn, the longitudinal studies of children show how multiple factors, operating through poor physical, mental, and educational growth and development, determine the future course of life-chances. And conversely the situation of people in old age appears as the cumulative result of previous work, income, and physical and social environment upon the resources available to cope with the demands of ageing. This does at least raise the possibility of turning points.

If far-reaching improvements are to be achieved in the prevention of disadvantage and the mitigation of its effects, the most effective intervention must come from changes in economic and social policy. The continuous production of cohorts of the disadvantaged is a structural problem susceptible only to structural (political and economic) remedies. The persistent gap in death rates between the poor and the affluent, between the south of England and the north of Britain, between outer suburbs and inner cities, is not remediable by individual effort or by the operation of treatment agencies.

A second level of intervention, largely mitigating rather than preventive, can best be achieved through changes in social policy, social security, and the social services. Already many measures—unemployment and sick pay, old age pensions, allowances for the disabled, housing provision and subsidy, children's allowances, supplementary benefit, and a number of specific allowances, subsidies, and aids—exist for this purpose. Their impact on the structure of inequality through transfers of real income is slight (Le Grand 1982) and although they reduce hardship and keep many above the poverty line their effect is still so small that, as many soundly-documented studies have shown, approximately 7 per cent of households still fall below the bare minimum state poverty level and a quarter fall below the Townsend deprivation standard.

Three major strategies are available through which social policy might reduce the proportion of the total population living below the poverty line. The first stems from the fact that about half of the 'poor' eligible for social security benefits do not take up their full entitlement. Whilst the reasons are complex, involving for example feelings of pride and independence, simplification of the procedures and the provision of positive assistance by the social security system and by social workers would considerably increase the take-up of entitlement. This would have greatest impact upon the old. The second strategy would be revision of the benefit scales above the bare minimum of supplementary benefits to approximate more closely to the standards required by a social-participation criterion. This would require a deliberate change in previous social policy from that pursued since 1945 because it would represent a transfer of incomes between major sections of the population. The third, and more mitigating than preventive, strategy would involve an increase in public service provision directed towards assistance in kind (home-helps, assistance with major expenses, etc.) or towards helping individuals to work or to work longer hours (e.g. creches for single parents).

THE ROLE OF THE HEALTH SERVICE

Since the reduction of poverty is primarily an issue for political and social action, does this mean that the health system and the health professions are not, need not, and should not be involved? Medicine, in particular, has historically adopted an apolitical stance arguing that its responsibility lay with the impartial treatment of the sick and that its involvement in political action could diminish its influence and its power to relieve suffering. Political action, however, is difficult to define unambiguously and particularly so when, as now, health systems are concerned with populations as well as with individuals, and when the NHS is funded by public taxation to maintain the nation's health. It is therefore worth considering what options, short of direct political action, are available to the health service and its component organizations and professions to prevent or reduce the impact of disadvantage upon the population's health.

Research and information

Policy decisions on priorities and resource allocation by governments and other health authorities are taken partly on the basis of knowledge about health needs, the costs associated with types of provision to meet needs, and the effectiveness of particular strategies in both meeting needs and preventing costs. Research over many years has amply demonstrated the impact of disadvantage on mortality rates. Premature mortality on the scale demonstrated is clearly undesirable on almost all definitions of social equity. Debate has centred around mortality because it is most easily measured but behind mortality lie levels of acute and chronic sickness, of physical and mental malfunctioning, and of pain and discomfort which have hitherto defied precise and comprehensive measurement. Policy cannot easily respond to unsubstantiated truths. Severe gaps remain of which the following are the most important.

1. *The production of data, on a routine basis, relating to the health status of disadvantaged client groups.* The continued use of social class as the major indicator of social position and welfare can no longer be justified in the light of the knowledge, summarized in Table 22.1, about specific disadvantaged groups and the indication that contemporary poverty derives less from the traditional categories of low social class and low pay than from life-cycle factors. Data on the health of these specific categories, culled from disparate sources and *ad hoc* studies, often of small scale, is inadequate and can only be improved by the conscious collection and analysis of data focused directly upon them.

2. *The development of more sensitive and accurate indicators of health, disease, sickness, and functioning* capable of demonstrating what lies behind the gross figures of mortality. Such indicators would, of course, be valuable for all groups of the population and are a necessary feature of good accounting. Their special relevance to the disadvantaged is the probability that the volume of sub-lethal problems is especially high.

3. *Knowledge of the natural history of the health consequences of disadvantage.* Longitudinal studies of children have provided a unique source of information on how early life-experiences are translated into health and development. Virtually no equivalent data exist for adult populations so that the severity, duration, and reversibility of problems encountered at particular phases of the life-cycle exist. Whilst, for example, the phenomenon of single-parent families is now a large and established feature of our society, and whilst such families constitute an increasing proportion of the disadvantaged, the implications for parents and for children over the next phases of their lives in incalculable.

4. *Knowledge about the use of health services by disadvantaged groups.* Broad indicators (Brotherston 1976; DHSS 1980) suggest that disadvantaged populations use more health resources than other groups. Such broad indicators cannot identify particular populations, but above all they are unable to assess the relationship between use and different definitions of need. They suggest only a small excess in use by the lower social groups. Whether this is sufficient depends upon the nature and timing of that use for prevention, treatment, and rehabilitation for specific symptoms and conditions. It also depends upon the effectiveness of health services in preventing, mitigating, or reversing the consequences of disadvantage. Answers to this question involve knowledge of the effectiveness of particular techniques but also knowledge about how sensitive services and professionals are in adapting to specific needs.

The absence of such essential knowledge is itself a commentary upon the priorities and practices embodied in our systems of professional education and of prevention and treatment. Improvement in our understanding of these issues would provide a necessary input to debates and decisions about economic and social policy, but would be of direct value in informing policy and practice within the health system itself.

Directions and priorities in health policy and practice

It is certainly arguable, and probably correct, that a deliberate concentration of resources upon the improvement of the health of disadvantaged groups, apart from ethical considerations, would ultimately reduce the cost of health services. The cost argument is most convincing when applied to children and young persons for whom poor early development may result in enhanced service costs across their lifetime. Baird (1952) demonstrated, decades ago, that poor physical growth in the children of the disadvantaged resulted in higher levels of morbidity and mortality in their adult child-bearing histories, and although no similarly definitive evidence has been produced, it seems very probable that such early influences lead to impaired functioning and increased morbidity in other domains of adult health. The general economic argument for concentrating more resources upon the disadvantaged elderly is perhaps less forcible than the 'quality of life' argument, and given the vastly different costs of caring for the elderly in the community, in residential homes, or in hospital (Mooney 1981), the economic case for redirecting resources towards community care is still powerful.

Changes in policy and priorities inevitably mean reallocation of resources of both money and manpower. And reallocation to groups based on social criteria raises problems of equity not foreseen in the principles upon which the NHS was originally based. The relevant principle would not be equality of access, but equality in relation to either need or outcome. The original principle has already been breached in, for example, the differential allocation of resources between regions (DHSS 1976) and it was implicit in the first major DHSS policy statement (DHSS 1972) advocating priority to the elderly, the handicapped, and the chronic sick, all of whom, as groups, fall within the definition of relative poverty.

Whereas regional reallocation of resources can be implemented directly from the top, policies for priority to particular groups need, for their implementation, co-operation through every decision-making body of the NHS, the professions, and the unions, and their acceptance as part of their clinical behaviour by health personnel. As the Royal Commission on the NHS remarked (1979) there is a difference between stating priorities and making them stick. Many factors are involved—the history of medicine, medical education, the existing structure of services, professions and jobs, the activities of contrary pressure groups, and scarcity of the funds required for a radical re-structuring of effort. Against these pressures, the demands of groups which are, by definition, poor and powerless, tend to be ineffective.

A change in priorities, apart from the issues of principle mentioned above, would involve earmarking resources for preventive medicine, health education, community services, and rehabilitation, and require close co-operation with non-health agencies—none of which is a popular or rewarding activity in traditional medicine, where the greatest prestige has attached to curative techniques.

An effective policy would require that the health system should promote preventive policies (in addition to the primary prevention of poverty) aimed at the regulation of domestic, road, and industrial accidents, the controlled use of harmful substances (alcohol and drugs), the promotion of healthy foods, the improvement of working conditions, and the reduction of environmental pollution (see McKeown 1979). Whilst these are universal dangers, the causes of death show that their impact falls heavily upon disadvantaged groups. Such policies would need to be accompanied by health education measures across a wide range of behaviours at least as intensive as those currently devoted to tobacco abuse, and involving not merely public advertisements and information but direct counselling by health personnel. Health education appears to have had limited effects, but it has also had limited resources, contradictory messages from government (and particularly the Treasury), and weak participation by health personnel. More active targeting of services upon vulnerable populations is also essential through specialized services encouraging access to prevention, treatment, and care either through service location in appropriate areas, communication techniques adopted to particular groups, school and domiciliary screening for at-risk individuals and families, and the provision of supportive services. Populations with increasing social and economic opportunities tend to adapt their own behaviour, in a favourable service climate, to reach their widening objectives; this is the lesson provided by the fall in family size in the 1960s and 1970s. Populations without such increasing expectations need active communication, contact, and support. Such positive 'therapy' demands a reorientation of medical practice away from institutions to community, the reduction of the barrier between institutions and individuals, an active recruitment of at-risk patients, and the use of innovative techniques of practice based on understanding of the patient's motivations, pressures, and language. In terms of personnel and resources it means the upgrading of community services and closer links with social services.

This chapter has been concerned with socially disadvantaged groups. It is however important to emphasize that disadvantage is a heterogeneous category consisting of many and different sets of individuals whose health problems are more specific to their situation, for example, single-parents, disabled adults, infirm elderly, etc. In some, ill health results from poverty, in some poverty results from ill health. Their needs for counselling, support, treatment, rehabilitation, and care are equally diverse. Policies and practice appropriate to each subgroup are beyond the scope of this single chapter but some needs common to all disadvantaged groups have implications for service organization and practice. The needs stem from a mixture of powerlessness in the face of officialdom, inertia caused by pressure on their daily lives, and lack of knowledge or limited expectations about the availability or efficiency of preventive action. These characteristics imply the need for positive and selective identification of vulnerable individuals and families, information and counselling on available benefits and services, community or domiciliary based services, and active policies of collaboration with social service and voluntary agencies. This entails a modification of medicine's traditional orientation towards the individual and the evolution of services and practice based upon the social origins of ill health.

The health system and health personnel cannot prevent the existence of socially-caused poverty and have only a limited ability to prevent its health consequences (Blaxter 1983). They do however have the obligation to know and to make known the extent of its impact upon the health of the nation and the groups of which it is composed. They have the further responsibility, by adapting their policies and practice, to the problems of populations, as well as individuals, to prevent and limit available repercussions on health.

REFERENCES

Adelstein, A.M., Macdonald Davies, I.M., and Weatherall, A.C. (1980). *Perinatal and infant mortality: social and biological factors 1975-77.* Studies on medical and population subjects No. 41. HMSO, London.

Baird, D. (1952). Preventive medicine in obstetrics. *New Engl. J. Med.* **246,** 56.

Berthoud, R., Brown, J.C., and Cooper, S. (1981). *Poverty and the development of anti-poverty policy in the UK.* p. 206. Heinemann, London.

Beveridge, W. (1942). *Social insurance and allied services.* Cmnd. 6404, HMSO, London.

Blaxter, M. (1976). *The meaning of disability.* Heinemann, London.

Blaxter, M. (1981). *The health of the children.* Heinemann, London.

Blaxter, M. (1983). Health services as a defence against the consequences of poverty in industrial societies. *Soc. Sci. Med.* **17,** 1139.

Brenner, M.H. (1979). Mortality and the national economy: a review and the experience of England and Wales, 1936-76. *Lancet* ii, 568.

Brenner, M.H. and Mooney, A. (1983). Unemployment and health in the context of economic change. *Soc. Sci. Med.* **17,** 1125.

Brotherston, J. (1976). The Galton Lecture, 1975: Inequality, is it inevitable? In *Equalities and inequalities in health* (eds. C.O. Carter and J. Peel) p. 73. Academic Press, London.

Brown, G.W. and Harris, T. (1978). *Social origins of depression: a study of psychiatric disorder in women.* Tavistock, London.

Brown, M. and Madge, N. (1982). *Despite the welfare state.* Heinemann, London.

Carter, C.O. and Peel, J. (eds.) (1976). *Equalities and inequalities in health.* Academic Press, London.

Colledge, M. and Bartholemew, R. (1980). The long-term unemployed: some new evidence. *Department of Employment Gazette,* January.

Community Relations Commission (1977). *Evidence to the Royal Commission on the National Health Service.* Community Relations Commission, London.

Davie, R., Butler, N., and Goldstein, H. (1972). *From birth to seven: the second report of the National Child Development Study (1958 cohort).* Longman, London.

Department of Health and Social Security (1972). *Report on Health and Social Subjects,* No. 3. HMSO, London.

Department of Health and Social Security, Central Health Service Council (1972). *Rehabilitation: report of a sub-committee of the Standing Medical Advisory Committee.* (Tunbridge Report.) HMSO, London.

Department of Health and Social Security (1976). *Sharing resources for health in England, Report of the Resource Allocation Working Party.* HMSO, London.

Department of Health and Social Security (1980). *Inequalities in health: Report of a research working group.* (The Black Report.) HMSO, London.

Dunnigan, M.G., McIntosh, W.B., Sutherland, G.R., *et al.* (1981). A policy for the prevention of Asian rickets in Britain: an assessment of the Glasgow rickets campaign. *Br. Med. J.* **282,** 357.

Exton-Smith, A.N. (1980). *Feeding the elderly: food and health.* British Nutritional Foundation, London.

Fiegehen, G.C., Lansley, P.S., and Smith, A.D. (1977). *Poverty and progress in Britain 1953-1973.* Cambridge University Press.

Fox, A.J. and Goldblatt, P.O. (1982). *Longitudinal study: socio-demographic mortality differentials.* Office of Population Censuses and Surveys, Series LL, No. 1. HMSO, London.

Goldthorpe, J.H. (1980). *Social mobility and class structure in modern Britain.* Clarendon Press, Oxford.

Harris, A.I. (1971). *Handicapped and impaired in Great Britain.* HMSO, London.

Hartley, J.F. (1980). The impact of unemployment upon the self-esteem of managers. *J. Occup. Psychol.* **53,** 147.

Henderson, J.B. and Dunnigan, M.G. (1983). Asian rickets and osteomalacia: lessons for the aetiology and prevention of nutritional vitamin D deficiency. *Human Nutr.* in press.

Hepworth, S.J. (1980). Moderating factors of the psychological impact of unemployment. *J. Occup. Psychol.* **53,** 139.

Illsley, R. (1955). Social class selection and class differences in relation to stillbirths. *Br. Med. J.* **ii,** 1520.

Illsley, R. (1980). *Professional or public health? Sociology in health and medicine.* Rock Carling Fellowship 1980. The Nuffield Provincial Hospitals Trust, London.

Illsley, R. and Gill, D.G. (1968). Changing trends in illegitimacy. *Soc. Sci. Med.* **2,** 415.

Jahoda, M. and Rush, H. (1980). *Work, employment and unemployment: an overview of ideas and research results in the social science literature.* Science Policy Research Unit, Occasional Paper Series, No. 12. University of Sussex.

Layard, R., Piachaud, D., and Stewart, M. (1978). *The causes of poverty.* Royal Commission on the Distribution of Income and Wealth. Background Paper No. 5. HMSO, London.

Le Grand, J. (1982). *The strategy of inequality: redistribution and the social services.* Allen and Unwin, London.

Leete, R. (1978). *One parent families: numbers and characteristics.* Population Trends 13. HMSO, London.

Leete, R. and Fox, A.J. (1977). *Social class: the origins and use of the classification.* Population Trends, 8. HMSO, London.

Lonergan, M., Milne, J.S., Maule, M.M., and Williamson, J. (1975). A dietary survey of older people in Edinburgh. *Br. J. Nutr.* **34,** 517.

McKeown, T. (1979). *The role of medicine.* Blackwell, Oxford.

McMichael, A.J. (1976). Standardised mortality ratios and the healthy worker effect: scratching beneath the surface. *J. Occup. Med.* **18,** 3.

Miles, I. (1983). *Adaptation to unemployment?* Science Policy Research Unit, Occasional Paper Series, No. 20, University of Sussex.

Mooney, G.H. (1981). Marginal analysis in planning for the care of the elderly. In *The provision of care for the elderly* (eds. J. Kinnaird, Sir J. Brotherston, and J. Williamson) p. 98. Churchill Livingstone, London.

Office of Population Censuses and Surveys (1978). *Occupational Mortality 1970-72 Decennial Supplement.* HMSO, London.

Office of Population Censuses and Surveys (1982). *The General Household Survey.* HMSO, London.

Robertson, I., Glekin, B.M., Henderson, J.B., McIntosh, W.B., Lakhani, A., and Dunnigan, M.G. (1982). Nutritional deficiencies among ethnic minorities in the United Kingdom. *Proc. Nutr. Soc.* **41**, 243.

Rona, R.J., Swan, A.V., and Altman, D.G. (1978). Social factors and height of primary schoolchildren in England and Scotland. *J. Epidemiol. Community Health* **32**, 147.

Rowntree, S. (1901). *Poverty: a study of town life.* Macmillan, London.

Rowntree, S. (1941). *Poverty and progress.* Longman, London.

Royal Commission on the National Health Service (1975). *Care of disabled people in Britain.* HMSO, London.

Royal Commission on the National Health Service (1979). *Report.* Cmnd. 7615. HMSO, London.

Runnymede Trust and the Radical Statistics Race Group (1980). *Britain's black population.* Heinemann, London.

Scottish Home and Health Department (1976). *The health service in Scotland: the way ahead.* HMSO, Edinburgh.

Scottish Office (1980). *A study of multiply deprived households in Scotland.* Central Research Unit, Edinburgh.

Stafford, E.M., Jackson, P.R., and Banks, M.H. (1980). Employment, work involvement and mental health in less qualified young people. *J. Occup. Psychol.* **53**, 291.

Supplementary Benefits Commission (1977). *Annual report 1976.* HMSO, London.

Taylor, R. and Ford, G. (1983). Inequalities in old age: an examination of age, sex and class differences in a sample of community elderly. *Ageing Soc.* **3**, 2.

Townsend, P. (1979). *Poverty in the United Kingdom.* Penguin, Harmondsworth.

Warr, P.B. (1978). A study of psychological well-being. *Br. J. Psychol.* **69**, 111.

Wicks, M. (1978). *Old and cold: hypothermia and social policy.* Heinemann, London.

Windlass, S. (1982). *Local initiatives in Great Britain,* Vol. I. II, and III. New Foundations for Local Initiative Support, Banbury.

World Health Organization (1976). *International classification of impairments, disabilities and handicaps.* WHO, Geneva.

23 Acute emergencies

Bryan Jennett and John S. Bryden

INTRODUCTION

Emergencies comprise an increasing proportion of admissions to acute hospitals in westernized countries, because the investigation and treatment of many other conditions are shifting to the out-patient clinic or to the community. The siting, size, and staffing of hospitals, and also the level of provision of certain specialized services, should therefore take account of the number and distribution of patients in a defined population that are likely to be injured or to become suddenly ill. Some of the issues involved in dealing with this problem in general will be illustrated by reference to head injury. This common condition is potentially life-threatening, presents in considerable numbers at the emergency departments of hospitals, and also makes substantial demands both on the wards of general hospitals and on tertiary regional centres. Moreover there is enough epidemiological data (largely generated through the initiative of neurosurgeons) to make comparisons between practice in Britain, in North America, and in Australia.

WHAT IS AN EMERGENCY?

A situation that is perceived by the victim of sudden illness or accident, or to those with him or her, as requiring immediate medical attention may reasonably be regarded as an acute emergency. Once seen by a doctor, either at hospital or elsewhere, the patient may be deemed not to require further medical care. It is tempting then to conclude that such patients did not 'need' to see a doctor at all, or at least did not have to see one urgently. That is to overlook the contribution made to the well-being not only of the patient but of the onlookers by authoritative reassurance that nothing serious has in fact happened. Neither such reassurance, nor the carrying out of certain urgent procedures, need be the prerogative of doctors. Several formal studies in the UK have shown that in some urgent situations nurses are acceptable in place of primary care physicians as the point of initial contact with health care services (Barber *et al.* 1976). Only a proportion of calls answered by these nurses result in onward referral to a doctor. Other personnel, specifically trained for the purpose, are used in many countries as the first stage in the triage of patients whose condition does not necessarily demand medical care; or to deal with serious situations in the interim before a doctor can reach the patient, as in the use of emergency medical technicians or paramedics at accident scenes (*Journal of the American Medical Association* 1980). The training of members of the general public in cardiorespiratory resuscitation for use on victims of cardiac arrest in public places, or of respiratory obstruction in unconscious accident victims, has been successful in places (Vincent 1982).

It can be assumed that for every mildly affected patient who reaches a doctor there must be some similarly afflicted who do not. Several factors determine whether medical aid is sought. *Where* the emergency occurs is an important influence, and who else is there. In some circumstances (for example, at work or at sporting events) there may be staff specifically trained to deal with minor medical problems. Distance from the nearest doctor enforces its own triage. If the crisis is a recurring one, such as attacks of epilepsy or asthma, then the presence of relatives may defuse the situation and obviate the need for referral to hospital. On the other hand, certain circumstances may have the opposite effect, leading the patient to hospital for other than pressing medical reasons. Legal considerations may result in quite minor accidents on the road or at work being referred to hospital. Other social situations that may encourage not only referral but also admission to hospital include the elderly living alone or children from a deprived environment.

There can therefore be no satisfactory definition of an acute emergency. Rather than seeking to count the uncountable it seems reasonable to limit the definition to those who present at hospital—accepting that there will be many other cases that have been disposed of by primary care physicians, or by non-medical personnel. The present account will therefore begin in the hospital emergency room and then consider the minority of attenders that are admitted to hospital; and the even smaller subset of these that are referred on to specialist services. Emergencies that occur to patients already in hospital are different, in that the question of access to medical services does not arise; many such incidents are predictable and lend themselves to forward planning, for example, cardiac arrest or obstetric crises. They will be referred to here only when discussing outcome and audit, when comparison between such events occurring in the community with those that happen in hospital indicates the importance of early access to medical care.

Degrees of severity

The administrative hierarchy of disposal within the health care system that has been described may seem to provide a simple severity scale—according to whether the patient only attends hospital, or is admitted, or is referred to a specialist. Several factors other than the biological severity of the condition influence attendance at hospital, and to a lesser extent whether this results in admission; in addition to those already mentioned, there is the level of provision of health care facilities. The importance of taking account of severity when assembling statistics about emergencies is well illustrated by considering the causes of head injury. The distribution of causes varies considerably acccording to severity; for example, road accidents account for only a small minority of cases that are disposed of in the accident department but make up more than half of severe or fatal cases (Table 23.1).

Particularly after accidents, administrative classifications can be misleading; thus accidents on the road or at work are categorized in the UK as *serious* if the patient is admitted to hospital—even though many such patients are discharged the next day. Further confusion arises from publication of statistics which aggregate 'fatal and serious' accidents. In an attempt to clarify the definition of severity, a number of scales have been introduced for different conditions; examples are the abbreviated injury scale (Petrucelli *et al.* 1981), the Glasgow Coma Scale for head injury (Teasdale and Jennett 1974), and the acute physiology score for intensive care units (Knaus *et al.* 1980). These are descriptive, using agreed definitions. They have prognostic value, and this in turn makes them useful for several purposes. Deciding what management is needed, whether a matter of triage or choosing which of alternative methods is appropriate, usually depends eventually on 'severity'. When assessing the relationship between treatment and outcome, particularly when comparing different methods, it is essential to have groups of patients whose condition is similarly severe.

Degree of urgency

While the condition of some patients presenting as emergencies raises doubts as to whether they need medical care at all, there are others in definite need of attention but who do not necessarily require it immediately. Sometimes the crisis is over, and what is needed in due time is investigation as to whether the incident that happened bespeaks underlying disease (for example, a single epileptic fit). In others a slowly developing condition has been ignored by the patient or his doctors, until a crisis has gradually developed. In others again, non-acute conditions may present for social or other reasons, and such cases make up a sizeable proportion of self-referrals to emergency departments of hospitals in large conurbations.

ACCIDENT AND EMERGENCY DEPARTMENTS

It is surprisingly difficult to obtain reliable data for the incidence even of well-defined diagnostic subgroups of acute emergencies, even in Britain where almost all such cases are treated within a single hospital system. No national patient-based records are kept of accident and emergency attenders, only a small proportion of whom are admitted. However, the emergence of accident and emergency consultants in the UK (emergency physicians in the US) is leading to systematic accumulation of data about the case loads in some hospitals; from these the scale and scope of some acute medical problems that present in the country as a whole can be estimated. In spite of the supposed universal provision of primary medical care on demand from general practitioners, about half the emergencies presenting in accident and emergency departments in the UK are self-referred, particularly in the centres of large cities; the same problem occurs in the US (Lee and Gibson 1982). Many of these do not qualify as emergencies, and many are not in need of hospital referral at all. Trauma accounts for only 15 per cent of emergencies presenting at hospitals in the UK and US, hence the renaming of casualty departments as accident *and* emergency departments, and the appointment in some places of physicians rather than surgeons to take charge.

Variations in the case mix between different hospitals are considerable; the more common causes for these should be considered before drawing conclusions about the incidence of emergencies in the community as a whole. Whatever lines the planners put on maps, geographical considerations combined with the vagaries of local transportation may distort the zoned catchment area from which a hospital supposedly draws its patients. For example, casualties from

Table 23.1. *Frequency distribution of causes in head injuries of varying severity*

Frequency of each cause	Severity of injuries				
	A/E sent home*	PSW admission*	NSU admission*	Severe injuries†	Deaths‡
Total number	2735	1181	424	1000	476
Road Accidents	13%	34%	38%	58%	56%
Adults (>15 years)					
Assaults	23%	20%	11%	7%	7%
Alcoholic falls	7%	12%	19%	16%	29%
Work (not road)	12%	7%	9%	7%	4%

A/E=accident and emergency; PSW=primary surgical ward; NSU=neurosurgical unit.
Source: *Jennett *et al.* (1977*a*); †Jennett *et al.* (1977*b*); ‡Registrar General for Scotland (1975).

an accident on the north-bound carriageway of a motorway might more readily reach a certain hospital than those occurring on the other side of the central divide. The presence of specialized hospitals (for example, for children or ones happening to house regional specialist units), may also result in preferential primary distribution of cases, especially of trauma, either by design or by the initiative of ambulance crews. Valid samples of all emergencies will therefore more likely be found outside of large conurbations, in places where there is only one general hospital available. Such a hospital may also have a lower proportion of trivial and self-referred cases than are found in a metropolis.

Different methods for completing returns for accident and emergency departments may also affect the mix of cases—in particular, whether or not referred admissions from general practitioners are included (for example, acute abdomens, strokes, and heart attacks). Only the most frequent and obvious confounding factors have been mentioned, as a caution against too facile an interpretation of statistics quoted about accident and emergency practice—especially as those available at present depend on locally collected data.

Head injuries in accident and emergency departments

When the epidemiology of a given type of acute emergency is considered the accident and emergency department seems always to be the missing link. Recent reviews of head injuries in the US as a whole (Kalsbeck *et al.* 1980), in Southern California (Marshall *et al.* 1979), in Virginia (Rimel *et al.* 1981), and in Olmsted County (Annegers *et al.* 1980) all dealt with admissions, but with some reference to deaths that had occurred before hospital; so did recent surveys in New South Wales and South Australia (Simpson *et al.* 1981). By contrast the Scottish Head Injury Management Study (Jennett *et al.* 1977*a*) included data from accident and emergency departments, based on a stratified sample of records from all acute hospitals in Scotland (Strang *et al.* 1978). To these 3558 emergency room patients was added a series of 716 attenders similarly collected in one English area (Jennett and MacMillan 1981), and a prospective consecutive series of 784 adults from one Glasgow hospital (Swann *et al.* 1982). The data from these separate emergency room sources proved to be remarkably similar, and from them age-specific rates of incidence have been calculated for head injuries that reach accident and emergency departments in Britain (Jennett and McMillan 1981). Of the 1500 attenders each year with head injury per 100 000 population, only one in four or five is admitted. As the characteristics of patients admitted are different from those sent home (or those dying before reaching hospital), analyses that are limited to admissions can be misleading. Only when surveys include accident and emergency rooms can they provide data of value to those planning not only the location of emergency facilities, but also how the staff should be deployed to ensure adequacy at time of peak demand. For example, although head injuries were found to

show little variation throughout the year more than half arrive on Friday and Saturday evenings.

Emergency admissions to hospital

Data about admissions are readily available at the hospital level in many places, but Britain is fortunate in having had statistics on discharges from NHS hospitals over many years—based in Scotland on all cases (SHHD 1975) and in England and Wales on a 10 per cent sample (DHSS *et al.* 1974). As well as age, sex, duration of stay, and whether admission was as an emergency or not, all cases are disease classified, using the 'N' code of the International Classification of Diseases (ICD). It is therefore possible, for a number of clearly defined conditions, to study secular trends as well as regional differences. Examples of the value of such a national data base are reports on the geographical variations in admission rates for acute appendicitis, for fractured neck of femur (Rees 1982), and for head injury (Field 1976).

It has been said that one of the undeniable achievements of the NHS in Britain has been the provision of urgent care for acute illness, and this the British public now takes for granted. Indeed for many patients and their general practitioners, emergency care seems often to be synonymous with admission to hospital, and on occasions both patients and doctors seem to consider such admission as a right. Nevertheless, changes in the practice of medicine are now making admission less often necessary, at least for medical reasons. Avoiding admission is also an important contribution of cost containment in the hospital sector. Whether or not admission is appropriate depends to some extent on local circumstances, in particular on what alternatives there are. It is therefore not possible to make statements that will be generally applicable. What is useful, however, is to analyse the objectives which admission aims to meet—and then to consider how these might best be met in different situations.

The four main reasons for admission are for diagnosis, observation, or therapy, or to solve a social problem. When series of cases are reported, neatly segregated into diagnostic categories, it is easy to forget that it is only cases of trauma that can usually be categorized on clinical grounds almost instantly—for example, as fractured neck of femur, broken ribs with pneumothorax, or facial injury. Most other emergencies present as diagnostic problems—coma, collapse, chest pain, haematemesis, abdominal pain, acute headache.

Diagnosis is nowadays often achieved by limited but well-selected laboratory tests, radiological examination, or endoscopy. Admission may still be necessary for these to be done, but such investigations can often be made available in association with short-stay beds so that many fewer emergency patients need to come into 'ordinary' wards—where they often disrupt the management of planned cases. For example, a daily gastroscopy or cystoscopy session may enable cases of haematemesis or haematuria to be sorted out rapidly into those needing further in-patient care and those who do not.

Observation may be a legitimate reason for admission, when recurrence of a critical situation is likely and will call for urgent action (for example, myocardial infarction, haematemesis from certain conditions, and subarachnoid haemorrhage); and when rapidly developing complications are a risk (for example, intracranial haematoma after recent head injury). However, careful analysis of the outcome of large numbers of different kinds of case now makes it possible to calculate the risk factors for patients in these kinds of situation. This enables selection for continued observation of the minority of high-risk cases, and may also indicate the time scale of the risk, making early discharge possible once the probability of recurrence or of complications is acceptably low.

Treatment of a kind that can only be done in hospital provides the most obvious reason for admission. Examples are open reduction of a fracture, continuing support such as mechanical ventilation, parenteral feeding or dialysis, or the provision of intensive nursing care.

Social reasons for admission are sometimes inevitable, especially in inner urban areas where there is deprivation. This applies particularly to the elderly, less often to children. By the same token if a patient has a caring family and a good family doctor it may be possible to entrust to them the observation and nursing of patients that might traditionally have been regarded as 'hospital cases'. One example is stroke (Brocklehurst 1977) and another is the widely reported claim that some patients with myocardial infarction fare as well under family doctor care in Britain as in hospital. However, unrecognized selection factors may readily bias such comparisons (Hill *et al.* 1978).

Admission after recent head injury

This is an interesting condition to study because it accounts for a considerable proportion of emergency admissions to surgical wards, and because evidence is emerging that many of these admissions could be avoided. Moreover it is a condition where recent technology is changing attitudes to the relative risks associated with alternative methods of management in the acute stage. Furthermore there are interesting contrasts in how this condition is dealt with in different countries.

Admission rates after head injury for England and Wales from 1963 to 1972 were analysed in a Department of Health Report (Field 1976); this report also considered deaths in hospital and those occurring before admission was possible. The analysis was based on routinely collected hospital data (DHSS *et al.* 1974) and registered deaths (OPCS 1976). A similar analysis of Scottish statistics was supplemented by a survey of admissions to Scottish hospitals in 1974 (MacMillan *et al.* 1979; Jennett and MacMillan 1981); because of this and the completeness of the Scottish sample there were more details about the Scottish cases, including their distribution between different types of hospital. The admission rate for England and Wales for head injury was 270 per 100 000 population, ranging from 210 to 360 in different regions; in Scotland it was 313, ranging from 306 to 404. The death rate was similar in the

two countries, at 9 per 100 000 including those not reaching hospital alive.

In both countries the standardized mortality ratios for head injury have been falling and so have admission rates for more severe injuries (as judged by ICD codes, and by more prolonged stay in hospital) (DHSS *et al.* 1974; SHHD 1975). Yet the total admissions for head injury have been increasing due to larger numbers of mild injuries being admitted. Reports from the US and Australia reveal death rates more than twice those in the UK, but admission rates that are proportionally much lower (Table 23.2). These findings suggest that in the US, in spite of the litigious

Table 23.2. *Head injuries in different countries (per 10^5 population per year)*

	Deaths	Admissions
England and Wales	9	270
Scotland	9	313
San Diego	22	245
Charlottesville	25	216
New South Wales	28	376

framework within which medicine is practised, fewer of the mild head injuries are admitted. There is direct evidence of this in the higher proportion of admissions that are in coma in San Diego (10 per cent) and in Charlottesville (20 per cent), compared with Scotland (5 per cent).

Detailed studies of admissions to Scottish hospitals indicate that mild injuries do indeed comprise a significant proportion of admissions, but because they stay only briefly they contribute proportionally less to occupied bed days attributed to head injury (Table 23.3). Another category of admissions after mild injury are those with major extracranial injury, and this may also account for more prolonged stay in hospital (MacMillan *et al.* 1979). The main reason why so many mildly injured patients are admitted briefly to hospital is because of the known risk that a very few will develop serious complications, in particular intracranial haematomas. It has for long been believed that a brief period of amnesia is a significant risk factor, but recent studies suggest that this alone is not a useful discriminator (Mendelow *et al.* 1982). Of more importance are the occurrence of marked headache or vomiting, the persistence of mild mental confusion, or the presence of a linear fracture of the skull vault.

There has been considerable controversy about the significance of finding a skull fracture, particularly in a patient who appears to have recovered from a recent injury. Radiologists on both sides of the Atlantic have conducted a campaign in recent years deploring the supposedly wasteful over-use of skull radiography in accident departments (Jennett 1980). However, the data published by the Royal College of Radiologists together with that from other sources can be shown to support the view that a skull fracture is an important risk factor, *vis-à-vis* intracranial

Table 23.3. *Length of stay: median in days*

Severity of head injury	Total number	Extracranial injury (median stay in days)			
		None	Minor	Major	Major/Minor
Number	1165	714	269	182	451
No brain damage	421	1.3	2.2	7.2	3.0
History of altered consciousness	516	1.3	1.5	6.3	2.3
Signs or symptoms	228	1.7	1.8	6.0	2.7
No skull fracture	1087	1.3	1.9	6.7	2.5
With skull fracture	78	3.8	4.8	7.5	5.3
All cases (% discharged 2 days)	1165 (67%)	1.3 (78%)	1.9 (62%)	6.8 (30%)	2.6 (49%)

haematoma (Table 23.4) (Galbraith *et al.* 1981; Mendelow *et al.* 1983). Far from being a needless expense, if fractures could be excluded by skull radiography many fewer patients would need to be admitted. Because even overnight admission is much more expensive than a skull X-ray, the savings could be considerable (Table 23.5).

SPECIALIST SERVICES FOR ACUTE EMERGENCIES

Many specialist services are available in only a limited number of hospitals, because significant economies derive from concentration of both staff and equipment. These units can then provide a service for a catchment area that includes many other hospitals, but this can pose a problem for acute emergencies needing these specialists. For a minority of emergencies there is the added problem that the services of more than one specialist is required (for example, multiple trauma, or organ failure affecting more than one system).

Table 23.4. *Relative risk of haematoma for adult patients in accident and emergency departments (A/E)*

Feature	Frequency of feature		Relative risk in A/E
	in haematoma cases	in all A/E attenders	
No skull fracture			
Orientated	5.3%	91.6%	×1
Not orientated	19.1%	6.6%	×50
Skull fracture			
Orientated	10.1%	0.9%	×190
Not orientated	65.5%	0.8%	×1400

Table 23.5. *Some cost landmarks in the UK emergency care of the head injured per million population per annum*

20 000 attenders at the emergency room		
10 000 or more skull radiographs	£130 000	$200 000
3500 admitted for observation @ 6 days		
@ £70 per day	£1 470 000	$2 249 100
190 transferred to neurosurgical care at		
10.5 days @ £90 per day	£179 500	$274 711

1=$1.53.

These latter problems may be dealt with by the designation of certain intensive care units to which various specialists provide a service.

Much more common, and therefore perhaps more important, are the many less threatening conditions which none the less stand to benefit significantly from management by a particular specialist. Examples include head injury, haematemesis, acute retention of urine, and peripheral nerve injuries. In most such instances the need for specialist intervention is short-lived, because the situation rapidly resolves—often after a single crucial specialized investigation or therapeutic intervention. To make such specialized skills rapidly available usually involves the patient having to be moved to the specialist centre. But if such referred patients were then all to become the continuing responsibility of the specialist regional centre, provision for other less-urgent cases requiring specialist care would soon suffer. This commonly happens where traumatic and elective orthopaedic services share the same facilities. The queue of patients waiting for a hip replacement tends to grow longer unless the orthopaedic service has firm arrangements for the early transfer of old ladies with fractured femurs to non-acute, and preferably non-surgical, wards.

Neurosurgeons face a similar dilemma in deploying their special facilities between different kinds of case. Unless they can send head injuries back to the primary surgical wards as soon as the patient no longer needs the special facilities of the neurosurgical unit, then that unit will neither be able to deal expeditiously with the next head injury nor to fulfil its commitment to non-traumatic patients. The same applies to patients with subarachnoid haemorrhage or malignant brain tumours; for them to remain long in specialized units is an inappropriate use of expensive resources, and it reduces the capacity to deal effectively with emergencies. The dilemma of allocating functions between general and specialized units in the face of changing technology is vividly demonstrated by controversies about the role of neurosurgeons in the care of head injuries, which have been heightened by the development of computer-assisted tomography (CAT 'scanning').

Role of neurosurgery in the care of acute head injuries

There are interesting differences in the management of head injuries in the US and in Britain. It has already been noted that severe head injuries are more than twice as frequent in the US as in the UK, but that fewer trivial injuries are admitted to hospital. Another difference stems from the fact that neurosurgeons in the US are about seven times more numerous than in Britain or most of Europe. Almost all large acute hospitals in the US have neurosurgeons on their staff, and even small community hospitals often have one who visits regularly. The consequence is that more patients admitted to hospital in America after head injury either come to the neurosurgical service or have an early neurosurgical consultation as a routine. In hospitals with a training programme for neurosurgical residents, these trainees are commonly called to the emergency room to advise about whether admission is necessary, and their greater confidence in discharging patients home may account in part for the lower admission rate of minor injuries.

In the UK by contrast, all neurosurgeons are concentrated in some 30 regional units; most of these serve a population of about two million, taking patients by secondary referral from 15–20 general hospitals. Only about 5 per cent of head injuries admitted to primary surgical wards of general hospitals reach one of these specialized units. There are considerable regional variations, however; a very few neurosurgeons have arrangements similar to the American pattern whilst in other regions little more than 1 per cent of admitted head injuries are seen by a neurosurgeon.

North American neurosurgeons have been critical of the British system for caring for head injuries (Drake 1978). Recently, neurosurgeons in the UK have themselves begun to question whether the policy of leaving so many patients in other hands is acceptable, especially now that neurosurgical units have new technology to offer (e.g. CAT scan, intracranial pressure monitoring). Prior to these developments neurosurgeons in Britain defended their practice of selective transfer of very few cases on the three main grounds that: (i) only about 1 per cent of hospitalized head injuries required neurosurgical operative intervention; (ii) the well-trained general surgeon could be relied on to make an emergency burr hole when necessary; and (iii) beds in regional neurosurgical units were so restricted that if admission of head injuries was not strictly controlled then neurosurgical provision for other conditions would be jeopardized.

Before the introduction of CAT scanning, neurosurgeons and neuropathologists in Glasgow had begun to review the outcome of head injuries transferred by the traditional, selective policy. Their investigations revealed that avoidable factors contributed to more than half the deaths after transfer to the neurosurgical unit, and also to morbidity in survivors (Jennett and Carlin 1978). A subsequent study in an English region confirmed these findings (Jeffreys and Jones 1981). The commonest avoidable factor was delayed diagnosis and treatment of an intracranial haematoma. CAT scanning has proved to be a reliable way of diagnosing intracranial haematoma and it has shown that this complication is more common than had been realized. It also transpires that the clinical features traditionally associated with this complication, which used to be the basis of selection for transfer to neurosurgical units, frequently do not develop until deterioration is so advanced that treatment cannot be effective.

One solution to this problem would be to transfer more patients to regional neurosurgical units, in order to be scanned and to have surgery if indicated; also that attempts should be made to get them there sooner than happened previously. A contrary view is that scanners should be set up in general hospitals in order to screen cases of recent head injury, and thus to avoid the unnecessary transfer of patients without surgical lesions, as well as identifying those who need neurosurgical care (Bartlett et al 1978). The admission of 1000 head injuries a year to a large district general hospital might seem a plausible basis for installing a scanner. However, our detailed surveys indicate that this would yield no more than two cases a week justifying a scan. Not only would such a throughput be uneconomical but it would be insufficient to develop and maintain skills in securing and interpreting scans. This dilution of experience by the duplication of facilities is an important reason for questioning the benefits to be derived from significantly increasing the number of scanners or of neurosurgical units.

For this reason, attention has been focused on moving patients to specialist facilities and back again. Although there are undoubted hazards associated with transporting patients in coma (Gentleman and Jennett 1981), these dangers are limited in number, predictable, and largely preventable by adequate foresight. Rather than seeking to reduce the number of patients moved to specialist facilities, attention should be focused on means of increasing the speed and safety of their transfer. This problem applies also to the transfer of other seriously ill patients between different parts of the hospital system, which is increasingly often required as more specialist services are established.

This should not be confused with arrangements for the primary transfer of patients from the scene of an accident to the first hospital—where the requirements are rather different. This latter problem has been subjected to considerable research on both sides of the Atlantic, with the development of a variety of schemes, including those that use trained paramedical technicians (Baskett 1982). There is some argument about the effectiveness of such schemes (Irvine 1982).

In Glasgow in 1978 the criteria for transfer of head injury patients to the regional neurosurgical unit were deliberately changed, so as to encourage more cases to come and to be transferred sooner. The effect of this was to double the annual number of cases transferred and there was an improvement in the outcome of patients with intracranial haematoma (Teasdale et al. 1983). Moreover, many more cases were detected than had previously been realized to occur. The effect of this deliberate policy change on the use of neurosurgical resources has been analysed, and estimates made of the implication of adopting such a policy on a national scale (Bryden and Jennett 1983).

OUTCOME AND AUDIT OF EMERGENCIES

Assessment of outcome depends both on the particular measures used, which properly vary according to the type of emergency under consideration, and on the population reviewed. Most reports relate to cases that satisfied certain diagnostic definitions—whether that is a first-order diagnosis (such as haematemesis or subarachnoid haemorrhage) or a more definite pathological lesion (for example, oesophageal varices or ruptured aneurysm). Other reports deal with administrative definitions—such as admission to an acute receiving ward, or to an intensive care unit. In either event outcome measures are almost worthless unless there are adequate details of the admission and/or transfer policies in operation at different places, or at different time periods—if comparison is being made between changes in a given centre. The mix of a series of emergency cases is particularly sensitive to selection criteria, which may not always be known or acknowledged by the clinicians concerned. For them interest begins when the patients arrive in a particular unit, and they can be impatient of enquiries about the larger population from which these have been selected. Published reports seldom provide enough information for such influences to be inferred, and it is even rarer for explicit data to be given about this aspect of a clinical series.

Unfortunately the same often applies to assessment of outcome, the clinician being primarily concerned with the patient's state when he or she leaves the acute service. Even with as crude a measure as mortality, the result will depend on whether it is based only on deaths in the acute unit, or within a given time span, or it includes deaths over a longer period. When morbidity in survivors is concerned it is even more important to know how long was the follow-up period. There is no ideal duration for this—it must vary with the condition. When trauma affects a young person, follow-up should be long enough for a stable final state to have been reached. With recurring crises in progressive disease, such as cardiorespiratory disease or renal failure, it is rescue from a particular episode that is usually reported; long-term survival may indeed not be particularly relevant. With malignant disease the situation is somewhere in between. For these reasons comparisons of crude mortality rates or survival times are of limited value and may be misleading. In survivors, the quality of life is increasingly recognized as important, but assessment of disability is seldom easy for the emergency doctor to discover, unless he or she makes a determined effort to find out. This may mean encouraging other professionals to carry out a late assessment and to report back.

Indeed this may be a more valid way of assessing outcome than relying on the judgement of the therapeutic team who were involved in the emergency stage. Outcome is essentially a comparison, and for the patient and the family the standard is how the patient was *before* the emergency. By contrast the emergency team inevitably make their comparison, and therefore their assessment of outcome, with the patient's state on admission—in life-threatening collapse, in coma, or in acute pain. Even very incomplete recovery may then seem to be satisfactory, but this may result in an overly optimistic assessment of the ultimate outcome. What is needed is a simple scale of outcomes, each of which is strictly defined. Such a scale has been used for the outcome of coma, whether due to trauma or non-traumatic brain damage (Jennett and Bond 1975; Jennett *et al.* 1981).

Avoidable factors

It is not sensible to presume that all deaths at the scene or in general units would have been averted if the patients had been more rapidly conveyed to hospital, or to a specialist unit respectively. It is, however, useful to review the cause of death in order to discover whether avoidable factors have contributed to death. A confidential enquiry into maternal mortality has been established for many years in the UK, and is held to have contributed signficantly to reducing avoidable deaths. A similar approach to the problem of head injury revealed that between a half and two-thirds of deaths in patients transferred to regional neurosurgical units are attributable to avoidable factors (Jennett and Carlin 1978; Jeffreys and Jones 1981).

Autopsy has an important role to play in reaching a conclusion about the cause of death, and in deciding the importance of avoidable factors. Although this might seem self-evident, there is abundant evidence that autopsy rates are much lower than they used to be, even in teaching hospitals. Deaths from conditions that present as emergencies, whether due to trauma or not, seldom excite academic interest whereas they often attract the attention of Coroners and medical examiners. Autopsies done for legal purposes seldom provide the opportunity for detailed examination that the academic pathologist and clinician would wish. There is a need for special efforts if such matters as avoidable factors contributing to death are to be discovered.

Assessing effectiveness of management

Comparisons between different series of emergencies that are concerned with assessing the relative effectiveness of alternative regimens of management are often rendered invalid by failure to match cases sufficiently carefully. With emergencies, organizational or geographical factors are particularly liable to influence the patterns of referral or admission of cases to different units (West *et al.* 1979). Another source of bias is the exclusion of cases deemed moribund by one centre but not by another (Cayten and Evans 1979). Moreover, there are very few emergencies that occur with sufficient frequency to allow for alternative methods to be assessed in sufficient numbers of cases by any one centre to satisfy statisticians. It is therefore essential to consider how multicentre studies can be successfully mounted. These require careful standardization of data collection and the development of systems of assessing severity of the initial condition, and of the different outcomes. There have been such data banks for severe head injury (Jennett *et al.* 1979; 1980) and for intensive care admissions (Knaus *et al.* 1982) that show the feasibility of this approach.

CONCLUSION

Medical emergencies form an important part of the burden on health care facilities in development countries. Unless their frequency and distribution are systematically stated, and their needs carefully considered, then it is all too easy to make arrangements in advance that may be inadequate or too elaborate or wrongly placed geographically. Unless outcomes are assessed within a community (rather than a hospital) there may be a failure to adjust arrangements to make them more appropriate. But it is much more difficult to apply the principles of epidemiology and audit to emergency conditions than to those that develop more slowly.

REFERENCES

Annegers, J.F., Grabow, J.D., Kurland, L.T., Laws, P.H., and Laws, E.R. (1980). Incidence, causes and secular trends of head trauma in Olmsted County, Minnesota 1935–1974. *Neurology* **30**, 912.

Barber, J.H., Moore, M.F., Robinson, E.T., and Taylor, T.R. (1976). Urgency and risk in first-contact decisions in general practice. *Health Bull.* **34**, 21.

Bartlett, J.R., Neil-Dwyer, G., Banham, J.M.M., and Cruickshank, D.G. (1978). Evaluating cost effectiveness of diagnostic equipment: the brain scanner case. *Br. Med. J.* **ii**, 815.

Baskett, P.S.F. (1982). The need to disseminate knowledge of resuscitation into the community. *Anaesthesia* **37**, 74.

Brocklehurst, J.C. (1977). Alternatives to geriatric care. In *Clinical practice and economics* (eds. C.I. Phillips and J.N. Wolfe) p. 81. Pitman Medical, London.

Bryden, J. and Jennett, B. (1983). Neurosurgical resources and transfer policies for head injuries. *Br. Med. J.* **286**, 1191.

Cayten, R.G. and Evans, W. (1979). Severity indices and their implications for emergency medical services. Research and evaluation. *J. Trauma* **79**, 98.

Department of Health and Social Security OPCS Welsh Office (1974). *Hospital in-patient enquiry for England and Wales.* HMSO, London.

Drake, C.G. (1978). Neurosurgery: considerations for strength and quality: the 1978 AANS Presidential Address. *J. Neurosurg.* **49**, 483.

Field, J.H. (1976). *Epidemiology of head injuries in England and Wales, 1976.* HMSO, London.

Galbraith, S., Mendelow, D., and Jennett, B. (1981). Skull x-rays. (Letter.) *Lancet* **ii**, 1350.

Gentleman, D. and Jennett, B. (1981). Hazards of inter-hospital transfer of comatose head injured patients. *Lancet* **ii**, 853.

Hill, J.D., Hampton, J.R., and Mitchell, J.R.A. (1978). A randomised trial of home versus hospital management for patients with suspected myocardial infarction. *Lancet* **ii**, 147.

Irvine, M. (1982). Care of the acutely ill and injured. In *Care of the acutely ill and injured* (eds. D.H. Wilson and A.K. Marsden). Wiley, Chichester.

Jeffreys, R.V. and Jones, R.R. (1981). Avoidable factors cotributing to death of head injury patients in general hospitals in the Mersey region. *Lancet* **ii**, 459.

Jennett, B. (1980). Skull x-rays after recent head injury. *Clin. Radiol.* **31**, 463.

Jennett, B. and Bond, M. (1975). Assessment of outcome after severe brain damage. *Lancet* **i**, 480.

Jennett, B. and Carlin, J. (1978). Preventable mortality and morbidity after head injury. *Injury* **10**, 31.

Jennett, B. and MacMillan, R. (1981). Epidemiology of head injury. *Br. Med. J.* **282**, 101.

Jennett, B., Snoek, J., Bond, M.R., and Brooks, N. (1981). Disability after severe head injury: observations on the use of the Glasgow Outcome Scale. *J. Neurol. Neurosurg. Psychiatry* **44**, 285.

Jennett, B., Murray, A., MacMillan, R., Macfarlane, J., Bentley, C., and Hawthorne, V. (1977a). Head injuries in Scottish Hospitals. *Lancet* **ii**, 696.

Jennett, B., Teasdale, G., Braakman, R., Minderhoud, J., Heiden, J., and Kurze, T. (1979). Prognosis of patients with severe head injury. *Neurosurgery* **4**, 283.

Jennett, B., Teasdale, G., Fry, J. *et al.* (1980). Treatment for severe head injury. *J. Neurol. Neurosurg. Psychiatry* **43**, 289.

Jennett, B., Teasdale, G., Galbraith, S. *et al.* (1977b). Severe head injuries in three countries. *J. Neurol. Neurosurg. Psychiatry* **43**, 289.

Journal of the American Medical Association (1980). Standards and guidelines for cardiopulmonary resuscitation and emergency cardiac care. *JAMA* **244**, 453.

Kalsbeek, W.D., McLaurin, R.L., Harris, B.J.H., and Miller, J.D. (1980). The National Head and Spinal Injury Study—major findings. *J. Neurosurg.* **53**, 519.

Knaus, W.A., Zimmerman, J.E., Wagner, D.P., Draper, E.A., and Lawrence, D.E. (1980). 'APACHE'—acute physiology and chronic health evaluation: a physiologically based classification system. *Crit. Care Med.* **9**, 591.

Knaus, W.A., Wagner, D.P., Loirat, P. *et al.* (1982). A comparison for intensive care in USA and France. *Lancet* **ii**, 642.

Lee, K. and Gibson, G. (1982). Emergency departments: an across the Atlantic comparison. In *Care of the acutely ill and injured* (eds. D.H. Wilson and A.K. Marsden) p. 17. Wiley, Chichester.

MacMillan, R., Strang, I., and Jennett, B. (1979). Head injuries in primary surgical wards in Scottish hospitals. *Health Bull.* **37**, 75.

Marshall, L.F., Smith, R.W., and Shapiro, H.M. (1979). The outcome with aggressive treatment in severe head injuries. Part I: The significance of intracranial pressure monitoring. *J. Neurosurg.* **50**, 20.

Mendelow, A.D., Teasdale, G., Jennett, B., Bryden, J., Hessett, C., and Murray, G. (1983). Risks of intracranial haematoma in head injured adults. *Br. Med. J.* **287**, 1173.

Mendelow, A.D., Campbell, D.A., Jeffrey, R.R. *et al.* (1982). Admission after mild head injury: benefits and costs. *Br. Med. J.* **285**, 1530.

Officer of Population Censuses and Surveys (1976). *Review of the Registrar General on deaths in England and Wales, 1976.* HMSO, London.

Petrucelli, E., States, J.D., and Hames, L.W. (1981). The Abbreviated Injury Scale: evolution, usage and future adaptability. *Accid. Anal. Prev.* **13**, 29.

Rees, J.L. (1982). Accuracy of hospital activity analysis data in estimating the incidence of proximal femoral fracture. *Br. Med. J.* **284**, 1856.

Registrar General for Scotland (1975). *Annual report, 1975.* HMSO, Edinburgh.

Rimel, R.W., Giordani, B., Barth, S.T., Boll, J.B., and Jane, J.A. (1981). Disability caused by minor head injury. *Neurosurgery* **9**, 222.

Scottish Home and Health Department (1975). *Scottish hospital in-patients statistics, 1974.* Information Services Division of Common Services Agency, Edinburgh.

Simpson, D., Antonio, J.D., North, J.B. *et al.* (1981). Fatal injuries of the head and spine. Epidemiological studies in New South Wales and South Australia. *Med. J. Aust.* **2**, 660.

Strang, I., MacMillan, R., and Jennett, B. (1978). Head injuries in accident and emergency departments in Scottish hospitals. *Injury* **10**, 154.

Swann, I.J., MacMillan, R., and Strang, I. (1982). Head injuries at an inner city accident and emergency department. *Injury* **12,** 274.

Teasdale, G. and Jennett, B. (1974). Assessment of coma and impaired consciousness: a practical scale. *Lancet* **ii,** 81.

Teasdale, G., Galbraith, S., Murray, G., Ward, P., Gentleman, D., and McKean, M. (1983). Management of traumatic intracranial haematoma. *Br. Med. J.* **285,** 1695.

Vincent, R. (1982). Resuscitation by volunteers. In *Care of the acutely ill and injured* (eds. D.H. Wilson and E.A.K. Marsden). Wiley, Chichester.

West, J.G., Trunkey, D.D., and Lim, R.C. (1979). Systems of trauma care. *Arch. Surg.* **114,** 455.

24 Physical disabilities resulting in handicap

John A.D. Anderson

Note

The legislative and social provisions described in this chapter are based on the British pattern. However, both statutory and voluntary services for the handicapped vary between countries depending not only on national customs but also on legal systems and such variations lead to differences in emphasis and implementation. Thus, in Britain health services are based mainly on national funding with social services being delegated to local government authorities, while services in *the private sector, including voluntary agencies, tend to be used to plug gaps. In the US and many other countries, greater reliance is placed on the contribution of the private sector both in terms of insurance and the provision of care. In addition to international variations there are also differences between states or provinces within the US, Canada, and Australia and, indeed, to a lesser extent between England, Scotland, Wales, and Ireland within Britain itself.*

INTRODUCTION

'At present a paralysis or deformity is too often accepted by patients and even by medical men as permanent and incurable. This is due to want of knowledge of the parents and those responsible for care of what can be done ... as a consequence, such children have been sent to a busy general hospital where owing to pressure of beds it has not been possible to keep patients long enough; further there has been no after care organisation and the whole treatment has been nullified by the inevitable tendency to relapse.'

Many of those concerned with the care of the physically disabled might be excused from thinking that the above quotation could have formed part of the introduction to the *International Classification of Impairments, Disabilities and Handicaps* (WHO 1980) or the report by Knight and Warren on physically disabled people living at home (DHSS 1978). In fact it was quoted from a paper relating to handicapped children by Jones and Girdlestone written in 1919. The same concepts were discussed in relation to long-term illness among adults in the Piercy Report (Ministry of Labour and National Service 1956). *Plus ça change, plus c'est la même chose.*

Changes in morbidity patterns and greater acceptance of the need for rehabilitation as distinct from cure have meant that the care of the chronic sick and handicapped is thought of in different terms today than was the case at the end of the First World War. However, surveys, reports, and even supportive legislation are insufficient on their own unless they are accompanied by changes in the attitudes adopted by the members of the caring professions and, indeed, by the changes in the expectations of those who have handicaps, or their parents; their expectations are likely to be influenced in turn by the doctors, nurses, and others responsible for care. Indeed one of the points made in the Tunbridge Report

(DHSS and Welsh Office 1972) was that earlier recommendations had not been implemented because medical schools had not taken the problem seriously.

Hopes were raised that things might have been changing for the better by the establishment in the 1970s of the European Chair of Rehabilitation at Southampton and a similar development by the University of Edinburgh. However, the Southampton chair remained unfilled long after the retirement of the first incumbent and the economic climate of the 1980s is not such as to encourage expansion of academic facilities. This is hardly surprising when the division of the financial cake in university terms is made mainly on the recommendations of professors of such entrenched subjects as medicine, surgery, pathology, anatomy, and physiology whose visions for new developments are blurred by the threat of compensatory contractions in their own spheres of influence. It is important, therefore, that those concerned with all branches of medicine in both academic and clinical fields should ensure that a reasonable proportion of resources are available to support the chronically sick and disabled for whom there is no complete cure and who at the same time can be expected to live for many years with their handicap.

Changes in thinking which have occurred in the last 50 years can be epitomized by the changes of policy and legislation in the UK during this period. Initially the main thrust of government activity was along three broad lines: education, employment, and community care. These in turn had stemmed from ideas developed during the late nineteenth and early twentieth centuries and which were indeed implemented by statute or on a voluntary basis in a fragmented way during this era of Victorian prosperity.

Special schools for the educational needs of disabled groups were confirmed in the Education Act (Great Britain

1944*a*). However, in recent years these have tended to concentrate on children with intellectual or emotional problems and to be less concerned with those of a physical nature—particularly as handicaps arising from such infectious diseases as poliomyelitis and tuberculosis have diminished.

The second set of legislative procedures which has had a bearing on those with physical problems are the Disabled Persons Employment Acts (Great Britain 1944*b* and 1958). Under the terms of these Acts employers are required to accept a proportion of the workforce from among those registered as disabled from any cause. This requirement extended to all sections of the British workforce the idea of ensuring employment for the disabled which had originally been limited to the designation of selected occupations such as car-park attendants and lift operators for war wounded. Government-sponsored sheltered workshops (Remploy) for those with more serious handicaps helped to produce a wide range of opportunities to meet occupational needs.

Legislative changes

In relation to community care as a whole there has been increasing emphasis on legislation. This is exemplified by the National Health Service Act (Great Britain 1946) and the National Assistance Act (Great Britain 1948). Part III of the former act dealt with services provided by local government authorities and in particular Section 22 (dealing with care and after care in the community setting) empowered these authorities to provide services for the continuing care of those not in hospital. Similarly, the National Assistance Act ensured the availability of sheltered housing and hostel accommodation for those unable to care for themselves in normal living conditions.

Each of the above activities still has its place in meeting the needs of those who have physical disabilities causing handicap. However, circumstances have altered substantially and in particular the domination of the relevant services by the medical profession with its systematized concepts. The view held by some medical practitioners in the past, particularly those responsible for public health, was that they alone had the capacity to assess needs of disabled people, plan services to meet those needs and evaluate their outcome. This led to the establishment in some local government authorities of joint departments of health and welfare. Well intentioned though such moves were, they led to resentment among those with clinical responsibility for patients suffering from handicapping disabilities, such as general practitioners, rheumatologists, neurologists, and orthopaedic surgeons. Such attitudes also led to resentment among social workers anxious to obtain recognition of their independent professional status and the contribution they could and should make in their own right to the care of those with handicaps. Such views were expressed first in Britain in the Younghusband Report (Ministry of Health and Scottish Department of Health 1959) and later in the Seebohm Report (Great Britain 1968); Similar opinions were also expressed elsewhere (Boh 1979; Ritenour *et al.* 1978).

These views were reflected in the passing of the Chronically Sick and Disabled Persons Act (Great Britain 1970) and the combined legislation in relation to Health and Social Services which was implemented in 1974 (Great Britain 1972 and 1973). The intention of this legislative package was to bring about greater integration of hospital and community based *health* services while establishing departments based on local authorities with responsibilities for *social* services including the care of the disabled.

Other counties have gone through similar changes of attitude in relation to handicap (see prefix to this chapter). Those in North America (Katz *et al.* 1963) and Scandinavia (Swedish Board of Health and Welfare 1978) are well developed but other reports (Thangavelu 1980; Weiss 1980; Renker *et al.* 1981; Cardenal 1981) though differing in detail suggest that many others are approaching a similar state of mind. The culmination of these efforts in the international field was the declaration by the United Nations (UN) that 1981 should be designated the International Year for Disabled Persons (UN 1976). This produced an incentive for member nations to take a fresh look at the problems of those with handicap encouraged by such international bodies as WHO and UNICEF.

WHO CLASSIFICATION

One outcome was the publication of the International Classification of Impairments, Disabilities and Handicaps (WHO 1980). Prior to this there had seldom been any attempt at standardization of terminology—even between countries supposedly using a common language. Hopefully the report reflects that a consensus has been achieved and that there may be less confusion in the future.

It is not unnatural that different authorities in a developing field should have put different interpretations on some of the terms used, particularly as these tend to be changed in the light of experience and as a result of discussion with others. A brief summary of the relevant terms, their meanings, and limitations, culminating in the definitions recommended by WHO, may help to avoid confusion in the rest of this chapter.

Impairments

An abnormality is any deviation from the norm and in physical terms this could mean a gross mutilation such as the absence of a limb either congenitally or from trauma. However, the term could also be applied to the presence of an extra nipple or having one brown eye and one blue. The important thing from the point of view of the affected person is not so much the existence of the abnormality but whether or not there is any interference with normal function.

To imply from this that malfunction is necessarily a more advanced stage than abnormality in the overall concept of disablement is an over-simplification since some disorders of function impose little or no restriction on those affected, at least in their early stages, for example, glucose metabolism; such disorders may only come to light as a result of a screening test or other investigation carried out by a clinical observer. It is for these reasons that WHO recommends the term impairment should be used to include both abnormalities and malfunctions (including malfunctions of intellect or emotion which are not the immediate concern of this chapter).

The definition recommended by WHO is: 'In the context of health experience, an *impairment* is any loss or abnormality of psychological, physiological or anatomical structure or function'. The explanatory notes (WHO 1980) stress that an impairment is either present or absent and that the concept of a latent impairment is therefore unjustified. Furthermore it can often happen that the affected individuals are unaware that they have impairments which are essentially perceived by observers though, of course, their presence may be pointed out to the affected individuals.

Disability

When an *impairment* results in a reduction in what would be regarded as normal activity for the affected individual then the term disability may be appropriately used. The WHO suggested definition is: 'In the context of health experience, a *disability* is any restriction or lack (resulting from an impairment) of ability to perform an activity in the manner or within the range considered normal for a human being'.

Handicap

A person with a *disability* cannot perform as well as his or her peer group and there is an awareness of this situation by the affected person, relatives, or both. However, such a loss of activity may cause little or no embarrassment to the individual. It is only when the limitation impinges directly on an activity which the individual wants to perform for social,

recreational, or occupational advancement that it imposes a *handicap*, for which the suggested definition is: 'In the context of health experience, a *handicap* is a disadvantage for a given individual, resulting from an *impairment* or a *disability* that limits or prevents the fulfillment of a role that is normal (depending on age, sex, and social and cultural factors) for that individual'.

Problems in practice

Table 24.1 lists the rubrics given under the general headings of impairment, disability, and handicap together with some explanatory notes. Thus a child with strabismus because of focusing difficulty has an ocular impairment (1.5). If untreated, this will lead to ambliopia with disability in relation to particular skills (2.8) where appreciation of parallax is necessary. The extent to which this constitutes a handicap will depend on circumstances. Many children will be self-conscious of the strabismus and experience social integration handicap (3.5); in later life an ambition to work as an airline pilot would lead to an occupational handicap (3.4) in that ambliopia will totally exclude the affected person from his desired activity.

It is, therefore, somewhat artificial to differentiate between handicap arising from physical causes and that arising from emotional or intellectual causes. Even though disability may stem from what appears to be a purely physical impairment it is axiomatic that there will be concurrent intellectual, emotional, and social effects on the disabled person. it is the interaction of all these components in relation to the requirement for that individual to perform one or more routine activities that constitutes a handicap.

Classifications of this kind tend to be based on a series of compromises drawn from conflicting views and the WHO classification of impairments, disabilities, and handicaps is

Table 24.1. *Classification of impairments, disabilities and handicaps (with abridged explanatory notes)*

1. Impairments	2. Disabilities	3. Handicap
1. Intellectual	1. Behaviour	1. Orientation
2. Other psychological	2. Communication	2. Physical independence
3. Language	3. Personal care	3. Mobility
4. Aural	4. Locomotor	4. Occupation
5. Ocular	5. Body disposition	5. Social integration
6. Visceral	6. Dexterity	6. Economic self-sufficiency
7. Skeletal	7. Situational	7. Other
8. Disfiguring	8. Particular skill	
9. Generalized, sensory, and other	9. Other activity restrictions	
Impairment is characterized by losses or abnormalities that may be temporary or permanent, and that include the existence or occurrence of an anomaly, defect, or loss in a limb, organ, tissue, or other structure of the body, including the systems of mental function. Impairment represents exteriorization of a pathological state, and in principle it reflects disturbances at the level of the organ	Disability is characterized by excesses or deficiencies of customarily expected activity performance and behaviour, and these may be temporary or permanent, reversible or irreversible, and progressive or regressive. Disabilities may arise as a direct consequence of impairment or as a response by the individual, particularly psychologically, to a physical, sensory, or other impairment. Disability represents objectification of an impairment, and as such it reflects disturbances at the level of the person	Handicap is concerned with the value attached to an individual's situation or experience when it departs from the norm. It is characterized by a discordance between the individual's performance or status and the expectations of the individual himself or of the particular group of which he is a member. Handicap thus represents socialization of an impairment or disability, and as such it reflects the consequences for the individual—cultural, social, economic, and environmental—that stem from the presence of impairment and disability

Source: WHO (1980).

no exception. Wood and Badley (1978) recognized four aspects of disablement (impairment, functional limitation, activity restriction, and handicap) and they suggested the fusion of functional limitation and activity restriction under the heading of disability to give three working categories. Subsequently the recommendations of WHO (1980) were based on the same terminology but as explained above functional limitation was merged with impairment while the term disability was reserved for activity restriction.

Time will tell whether or not the definitions suggested by WHO and the classification into these broad groups will prove workable. There are obvious initial difficulties because legislation in different countries already uses such terms as disabled and handicapped in ways which do not conform to those suggested by WHO. Thus in Britain the Register of Disabled Persons and the Register of Persons Substantially or Permanently Handicapped have statutory meanings in relation to the Disabled Persons Employment Act and the National Assistance Act respectively; these and similar differences of interpretation not only in relation to legislative measures but also in common usage among different nationalities may well lead to confusion.

PUBLIC HEALTH ISSUES

In spite of the above reservations on the suggested WHO classification it is still desirable in public health terms to indentify the needs of affected individuals, estimate the size of the problem thus created, and consider the services available to meet those needs including some evaluation of their effectiveness. In this context it is often convenient to distinguish those disabilities which are predominately of physical origin from those arising primarily from intellectual or emotional causes; the latter are considered in a separate chapter.

Assessment of needs

In the final analysis the needs of an individual with a physical disability depend on the extent to which that disability causes handicap. As discussed above, this means putting the physical disability into a social context. This entails assessing the extent to which the reduced activity of a disabled person intereferes with such social aspiration as normal daily living, recreational activity, and occupational status.

It may be possible to judge the extent of handicap by inference from disabilities or even the impairments which cause those disabilities if those affected are included in some form of register. Thus most children with cerebral palsy will be known to both hospitals and education authorities. The majority are likely to have one or more disabilities as defined by WHO and a substantial number will have handicaps. Other conditions commonly associated with disability are the arthritides, asthma, cerebrovascular accidents, chronic bronchitis, coronary heart disease, epilepsy, and multiple sclerosis. In addition, some serious injuries such as fractured femur, pelvis, or spine and head injuries are likely to lead to disability.

Medical records

Table 24.2 shows annual consultation rates with general practitioners for the potentially disabling conditions described above. Because of the system in Britain by which patients register with general practitioners it is possible to express these as persons consulting per 1000 registered patients. Such information may have some epidemiological merit in terms of objectivity and standardization but it gives

Table 24.2. *Disabling conditions. Consultation rates in general practice (persons per 100 registered: n=292 265)*

Diagnoses (ICD)	Persons consulting per 1000 per annum
Arthritides (712,3)	30.3
Asthma (493)	10.2
Cerebrovascular disease (430–438)	5.3
Chronic bronchitis (491)	11.5
Coronary disease (410–414)	11.7
Epilepsy (345)	3.0
Multiple sclerosis (340)	0.7
Head injury and fractures of spine, pelvis and femur (N800, 1, 2, 3, 5, 6, 8, 20, 21, 50–54)	2.2

Source: OPCS (1974*a*).

no indication of the extent to which the patients with these conditions experience interference with everyday activities except in so far as they were obliged to consult their doctors.

Demands of patients

Another method of assessing need, which is in marked contrast with the first in that the information is highly subjective, is by obtaining information from the handicapped themselves or where appropriate their supporting relatives. In effect this usually amounts to a record of demands for assistance and replies to such enquiries inevitably depend on the personalities of the responders and their attitudes towards their disabilities. Thus, the demands recorded by masochists, stoics, and those with strong religious views on the immortal benefits of physical deprivation may be less than expected. By contrast, those who accept the philosophy that health is complete physical, mental, and social well-being and that it is the right of every human being are likely to list extreme demands; that is even more likely if the responder believes that it is the duty of the government or some other agency to supply everything requested to achieve that goal. An additional factor likely to affect the answers is that demands will be coloured by the availability of services and the knowledge of the responder about that availability.

Independent assessment

A third approach is to leave the measurement of need and the services required to meet them to an independent assessor. Here again the philosophical, political, or other views of the assessors can be expected to cause differences in emphasis.

Simple assessments by observers have been made for a number of years at pre-employment medical examinations.

In broad terms, these identify potential employees whose handicaps are such as to make them suitable or unsuitable for certain tasks. A more sophisticated formula in relation to industrial rehabilitation grades the disabilities of workers on their capacity to perform such tasks of stooping, lifting, climbing ladders, and working outdoors.

A more numerical approach has been used for many years in the assessment of employability of individuals (and by implication their disabilities) in relation to the armed forces. The so-called PULHEEMS classification grades individuals in respect of **P**hysique, functional capacity of **U**pper limbs and **L**ower limbs, **H**earing, visual acuity of right and left **E**yes, **M**ental capacity and emotional **S**tability. A notional scale of 1 to 8 is applied to each factor with high numbers implying reduced ability though in practice the number of available options for certain factors is limited. When a recruit is graded below the normally acceptable standard for P, U, L, or S then the examining doctor indicates the impairment which led to that decision. This system, though intended to assist the processes of enlistment and posting within the services, can also give an indication of likely handicap to a doctor trained in its use.

Social input

Several other classifications have been evolved which are more appropriate for use in people with severe handicap. Many of these have little medical orientation as several professional groups who contribute to the support of those with handicap are not themselves medically qualified. These classifications tend to be based on such factors as dependency on others, ability to perform **A**ctivities in relation to Daily Living (ADL), mobility, or combinations of these; there is also considerable variation in their complexity depending on the group being studied. Unfortunately there has been little opportunity so far to make cross comparisons as those working in this field have tended to develop their own definitions and standards(Duckworth 1980).

Some classifications are more useful than others; one in particular is widely quoted and was used by Harris, Cox, and Smith (OPCS 1971). They used a numerical scale for assessing handicap among those aged 16 years and over in an extensive study of 250 000 British households. Eight categories were used with that relating to the least handicapped being subdivided into two. These are listed in Table 24.3 and in the explanatory notes it is pointed out that the categories are not discrete but are at different levels of a continuum. Also shown in Table 24.3 are the grouped headings suggested by the authors and the distribution of handicap levels in the population by age in each group.

The three broad gradings of handicap suggested by Harris and her co-workers may be compared with a comparatively simple grading used by Anderson and Southwood (1974) for assessing handicap in children in a study of how specialized health visitors support the families concerned. This classification, depicted in Table 24.4, was based on an adaptation of dependency grades described by Lowther (1973). However, in addition, the three-point scale of handicap was combined with a mobility score and an assessment of ADL (minor, medium, or high) in relation to dressing, feeding, toilet, and washing. Table 24.5 shows the gradings as described by the parents of 129 children with severe handicaps who volunteered to take part in the study. it was

Table 24.3. *Categories and degrees of handicap*

Category and definition	Percentage in age group					
	16–	30–	50–	65–	75+	All ages
Very severe						
1. Contains people who need help going to or using the WC practically every night. In addition, most of those in this group need to be fed and dressed or, if they can feed and/or dress themselves, they need a lot of help during the day with washing and WC or are incontinent						
2. Contains people who need help with the WC during the night but not quite so much help with feeding, washing, dressing, or while not needing night-time help with the WC need a great deal of day-time help with feeding and/or washing and the WC						
3. Contains those who are permanently bedfast or confined to a chair and need help to get in or out, or are senile or mentally impaired, or are not able to care for themselves as far as normal everyday functions are concerned, but who do not need as much help as categories 1 and 2	5.5	3.4	3.2	4.0	9.4	5.3
Severe						
4. Contains people who either have difficulty doing everything, or find most things difficult and some impossible						
5. Contains people who find most things difficult, or three or four items difficult and some impossible						
6. Contains people who can do a fair amount for themselves but have difficulty with some items, or have to have help with one or two minor items						
7. Contains people who can do everything themselves, but have difficulty with one or two items	4.7	8.2	11.3	11.1	14.4	11.6
Appreciable						
8. Contains people to whom physical impairment presents no difficulty in taking care of themselves, but whose main impairment is mental, endocrinal, sensory, etc.	11.6	15.0	19.4	23.2	20.0	16
Minor or nil						
9. Contains people to whom impairment presents no difficulty in taking care of themselves	78.2	73.4	66.1	61.7	56.0	63.1
Total number	344	1418	3294	3679	3527	12 262

Source: OPCS (1971).

Table 24.4. *Grades of handicap (based on mobility and dependency assessments)*

Grade	Mobility	Special Senses	Dependency	
Mild	No buses	One of:		Occasional incontinence. Assistance with dressing, feeding, toilet, ablution, in/out bed
A				
Moderate	Housebound No stairs	Blind or	Two of:	
B	Supported movement	deaf		
Severe	Bedridden Chairbound	Blind and	Three of:	
C	Immobile	deaf		Also Regular incontinence

Source: Lowther (1973).

clear from the comments of the parents that from their point of view children with difficulty in the use of toilet facilities posed the greatest problems. This is in keeping with the findings of Harris *et al.* and confirms the generally accepted view that regular incontinence is one of the main causes of handicap, not least because of the social isolation that ensues.

Size of the problem

This obviously varies with which of the factors discussed in the last section are used as a basis for the head-count and the emphasis they receive. At the same time the completeness of the information will depend on the mechanism used for its collection.

Routine statistics

Early censuses in Britain obtained information about the numbers of blind and deaf persons in each household. Such material backed as it was by a statutory requirement to complete the census truthfully was probably reasonably accurate, but the relevant questions have not been included since 1911.

Thereafter the only source of information with anything approaching a comprehensive background was in relation to educational requirements. Parents were obliged to let their children be assessed by officers of their education authority to ensure that each child was educated in an environment best suited to what was described as the age, ability, and aptitude of that child.

Until recently there has been considerable reluctance on the part of those affected, or their parents in the case of children, to admit to being abnormal from any cause, and terms such as 'delicate', though intended to be less abrasive to patients or relatives, soon came to assume sinister undertones of inadequacy. This natural reluctance to admit publicly to a handicap was enhanced by tales of extermination of such people during the Second World War. Though these stories were probably exaggerated for propaganda purposes there seems little doubt that such practices occurred and the development of a body of opinion strongly opposed to any form of registration of people with disabilities was a natural consequence.

Nevertheless financial constraints tend to be coercive in this respect. Thus the Register of Disabled Persons was introduced for the purpose of ensuring protected or sheltered employment for those with disabilities (Great Britain 1944*b* and 1958). Similarly, the Register of Persons Substantially and Permanently Handicapped (Great Britain 1948), aimed at meeting the financial needs of those unable to work and ineligible for national insurance benefits. Both these registers were voluntary but they form a possible basis for estimating the size of the problem.

In theory, statistics from these sources could indicate the proportion of the available work force who have registered disabilities; similarly those registered under Section 29 of the National Assistance Act as being substantially or permanently handicapped could be expressed as being a percentage of the population aged 15 to 65 years. However, for the reasons discussed such figures are unlikely to be accurate though they might provide a rough guide to trends over a period of time.

Comparative indicators can also be obtained by consideration of the structure of the population in terms of age and other social indices. Thus a town such as Brighton with 9 per cent of its population over 75 years can be expected to have a higher proportion of disabled people for that reason alone than, say, a new town such as Harlow where the population over 75 years is 3 per cent (OPCS 1982). On the other hand the social class distribution of the population in

Table 24.5. *Dependency gradings. Parents descriptions of 128 severely handicapped children*

Grade	Description	Activity (%) Mobility	Dressing*	Feeding	Toilet*	Ablution*
0	Completely independent	31.3	24.4	71.8	41.5	27.6
1	Needs occasional help for difficult aspects	20.3	21.1	14.1	19.5	11.4
2	Needs help most of the time but makes a contribution	31.3	46.3	9.4	8.1	47.2
3	Totally dependent on others	17.2	8.1	4.7	30.9	13.8

*Children under three years excluded: $n=123$.
Source: Anderson and Southwood (1974).

Brighton (22 per cent social classes IV and V) may insulate the population against the handicapping effect of disability more than would be the case in a conurbation such as Liverpool with 35 per cent in social classes IV and V (OPCS 1974b) particularly if there is also a high unemployment rate. However, it is important to remember when calculating the size of the problem from such factors that social disadvantage has a significant effect on life-expectancy and also tends to influence the way people use available services as discussed in the Black report (DHSS 1980).

Other social factors such as a high proportion of first generation immigrants with communication difficulties or cultural differences may also be relevant. Thus the supportive attitude of some cultures where the family is expected to care for those of its own community affected by disability might effectively reduce the number of those with handicap or at least the severity of their problems. By contrast other cultures where there is a feeling of disgrace about having a member of the family with an impairment leading to obvious disability tend to aggravate handicaps by isolation of the affected person and attempted concealment.

It follows that broad-based morbidity studies conducted for other purposes and a knowledge of the social structure of population, while sometimes helpful in giving an approximate indication, can never provide the level of accuracy needed to plan services. Attempts to provide such information are on the whole based on one of two approaches. The first stems from epidemiological studies of clinical syndromes; the second from more specifically orientated enquiries about handicap as a whole.

Special surveys

Sample surveys by those with special interest in syndromes can provide useful information on the handicapping effects of disabilities arising from the disease or group of diseases under study. Initially those conducting such surveys drew up their own criteria in relation to such symptoms as angina or calf pain on effort for circulatory disorders (Rose 1962), respiratory symptoms for chronic pulmonary diseases (Fletcher 1978), and musculoskeletal pain for those with rheumatic diseases (Anderson 1971). Even when, after several such ad hoc definitions have been used, there emerges a consensus among epidemiologists in respect of the criteria of handicap from one disease or a related group (for example, chronic obstructive airways disease), it does not necessarily follow that these are comparable in terms of disability let alone handicap with the criteria agreed by epidemiologists with another special interest (for example, the arthritides).

It was because of such shortcomings that there developed increasing pressure to establish a broader base on which to assess problems. This tendency was particularly strong among social scientists (Jeffreys et al. 1969; Townsend 1973) but was also acknowledged and supported by epidemiologists (Warren 1977; Wood and Badley 1978), general practitioners (Taylor and Fairrie 1968; McMullen 1971), and geriatricians (Williamson 1964; Brocklehurst 1972). Psychiatrists have also expressed concern about the restrictions of medical diagnoses in relation to handicaps

though the latter naturally tended to be more interested in emotional and intellectual impairments rather than physical (Wing and Bailey 1972; Rutter et al. 1973).

It was against this background that formal legislation was introduced such as the Chronically Sick and Disabled Persons Act (Great Britain 1970). Many of the provisions of this Act might be described more properly as focusing on the reduction of handicap as well as the correction of disability as defined by WHO. However, the Act preceded the suggested classification of impairments, disabilities and handicaps by some 10 years and so differences in nomenclature are inevitable. One requirement of the Act is particularly relevant in the context of assessing the size of the problem in that it contains the following directive:

It shall be the duty of every local authority having functions under Section 29 of the National Assistance Act 1948 to inform themselves of the number of persons to whom that Section applies within their area and of the need for the making by the authority of arrangements under that Section for such persons.

Inevitably some local government authorities responded more rapidly and effectively to the requirements of the legislation than others. Furthermore, since each local government authority had to assess the size of its own problem it was necessary for each to do its own survey and there were no statutory criteria of what constituted handicap even though explicit suggestions were made by the Secretary of State of the day that categories 1–6 described by Harris et al. would cover most of those with physical handicaps likely to qualify for services.

The survey by Knight and Warren (DHSS 1978) was carried out three years after the implementation of the Act and they reported that 82 out of 157 local government authorities in England had conducted surveys and prepared reports. From them it was estimated that between 40 and 70 per 1000 of the population had physical impairments and that one third to one half of them were experiencing significant disadvantage in one way or another (i.e. had a handicap). Just 1 per cent of the population surveyed had what the authors described as very severe or severe handicaps which corresponded to the categories designated by Harris et al. (OPCS 1971) as special care and very severe handicap respectively. The prevalence of these two major categories varied with age ranging from around 3 per cent among those aged 15 years or less to over 7 per cent for those over 75 years.

Even if these rates are accepted as the best possible estimate of prevalence in England, there remains the difficulty of assessing what services are required to meet the needs of those deemed to be handicapped. This is exemplified by the fact that Knight and Warren showed that there was considerable variation even in what they describe as the mid-range of those needing services (see Table 24.6). As the authors rightly pointed out, the more those with disability leading to mild or negligible handicap are included in such surveys the lower will be the percentage of those deemed to require services.

It should be clear from the foregoing résumé that even on a national basis and with the stimulus of legislation which

Table 24.6. *Support at home. Mid-range proportions of persons needing or wanting services, aids, or adaptations*

Service or aid requested	Mid-range* needing service		
	Percentage of those interviewed	Per 1000 of population	Per 1000 of population aged 65+
Home-help	6– 9	2.4–4.1	18–31
Meals	2– 4	0.7–1.8	5–12
Voluntary help:			
Window cleaning	10–17	3.6–7.2	24–57
Gardening	8–15	2.6–5.9	25–43
Mobile library	9–12	3.5–4.5	28–33
Chiropody			
Domiciliary	15–23	4.5–8.9	36–67
Clinic	5	1.9–2.4	13–18
Telephone	20–37	6.5–13.5	53–98
Aids:			
Bath rails	11–19	4.1–7.1	33–35
Bath seats	8–11	3.0–4.5	23–34
Showers	4– 8	1.6–3.2	12–23
Raised WC seat †	2– 3	0.5–1.0	4–10
Hoists or bars	3– 5	1.1–1.8	9–15
Shoe/stocking aid‡	4– 7	1.5–2.3	13–18
Adaptations:			
Ramp	3– 5	0.9–1.4	6–10
Stair rail	5– 7	1.2–2.5	10–19
Kitchen aid‡	5– 7	1.8–2.4	14–18

*Mid-range: an approximation to the interquartile range comprising approximately half of the surveys.

†In some instances includes people needing rails.

‡In some instances includes people who only need advice.

Source: DHSS (1978).

made it mandatory for those with handicap to be identified there were marked discrepancies in the estimates from such surveys. It follows therefore that in international terms there will be an even wider range of interpretation even if it is assumed that there is to be general acceptance of the WHO criteria which is by no means certain. Cultural, economical, and other social constraints prevailing in different countries will affect not only decisions about who should be deemed to have handicaps and the severity of gradings but to an even greater extent there will be variation in the measures which are felt to be necessary in order to reduce such handicaps.

Services available

Cultural, political, and other differences mean that the organizational deployment of resources varies from country to country as does the extent to which statutory and voluntary services are involved. However, there is general agreement about the types of service required to cope with handicaps—assuming needs are known—even though the best method of deploying the different resources remains a matter of debate or even controversy.

The complexity of the British system is no worse than those found in other countries comprising as it does hospital services, primary care services, and community health services which are in effect funded from Exchequer sources as part of the National Health Service. These are comple-

mented by social services which are the responsibility of local government. Also under control of local government authorities are education, housing, and environmental aspects of health, all of which are relevant to the support of those with handicaps arising from physical disabilities. Apart from these statutory services there are voluntary agencies designed to fill or bridge gaps and many of these are of particular value to those with handicaps.

Several attempts have been made both by co-operative effort and by legislation to rationalize and integrate the health and social services in Britain. In fact such reorganizations, intended to improve matters, have been disruptive and the separate components in the caring system have often remained fragmented. Furthermore, the situation has sometimes been aggravated by those who should be concerned with the care and support of those with handicaps being swept up in a maelstrom of bureaucracy and demarcation disputes. This can be particularly unfortunate for those who need the services as such people are among the most vulnerable in the community and are least able to make their feelings known or exert political pressure.

Hospital-based services

In spite of such organizational difficulties certain features emerge. Thus in combating handicap a key component of any service, however it is organized or funded, is the specialist medical service associated with the treatment of underlying impairments and, so far as it is possible, the limitation of disabilities. In most health-care systems this is based on hospitals which provide residential care for those who need intensive nursing and such other remedial services which require costly equipment such as designing and fitting prostheses and certain aspects of physiotherapy. There is also a requirement for supportive investigatory services including laboratories to help assess the extent of disabilities and how best to minimize their effects so that hospitals form a useful centre for both in-patient and out-patient evaluative and therapeutic services.

However, few people concerned with handicap today would accept that services should be confined to passing patients through a gadget-ridden annexe of an orthopaedic hospital. Certainly the technological advances which have been made, for instance in limb replacement, have been substantial in the last 30 years. These have included devices for moving arms and hands in particular which are highly complex and which have been achieved by judicious interplay of electronics, compressed air, and lightweight alloys. These have revolutionized the prognosis of those deprived of the use of one or more limbs either from birth or in later life.

Community-based services

The requirement for complementary services based in the community is appreciated by most hospital specialists. Thus few in-patient units caring for such characteristically disabling conditions in terms of mobility as the arthritides, multiple sclerosis, strokes, and traumatic surgery, as well as those concerned with the care of the blind and deaf, are prepared to let patients be discharged from hospital without preparatory training under the supervision of occupational and other remedial therapists. Home visits by such therapists or others concerned with domiciliary care are undertaken commonly if not routinely in advance of discharge.

The Tunbridge Report (DHSS and Welsh Office 1972) devoted one of its longer chapters to the topic of community health in relation to the disabled while the Court report on the care of children (Great Britain 1976) also had a chapter on handicap. These developments are hardly surprising as the number of affected individuals is so large that any attempt to provide a comprehensive service would be futile unless it includes general practitioners, health visitors, and others in the primary care team, as well as those from other community-based services such as the local government authority and the employment and voluntary agencies.

VULNERABLE GROUPS

Such services or their equivalents are to be found in most developed countries and given that these services exist then it should be possible to meet the needs of those with handicaps provided that they are deployed with this in mind. However, needs are known to vary between different subgroups in the community and in particular with the age of the individual. Accordingly services will be considered in relation to the following client groups: pre-school children and schoolchildren, adults seeking employment, housewives, and the elderly.

Each of the groups listed presents special problems with special solutions and it is convenient to emphasize them under the appropriate headings of the section which follows. However, certain services (e.,g. the need for holidays or special transport) though highly relevant to particular groups are also applicable to others.

Pre-school children

Most infants and children up to school age are cared for by their parents. Where this is not the case then residential care or day supervision in nurseries is necessary regardless of whether the child has a disability or not. The difference in the case of those with disabilities is that such arrangements may increase the resulting educational handicap unless care is taken to place these children with parent substitutes who have special awareness of their needs and special training in how to meet those needs.

Many such children require specialist medical supervision to cope with the underlying cause of their disabilities or when appropriate to provide prostheses and give training in their use. In such cases it is obviously essential to establish and maintain close rapport between the specialist unit and the parents or substitute. General practitioners and home nurses contributing to the care programme may act as useful links with the hospital but it is unwise to rely entirely on these services because both doctors and nurses in the community tend to have heavy case loads and may be unable to devote more than a limited amount of time to recognizing and assisting with the reduction of handicaps.

Some specialist units achieve liaison with families by employing special home visitors based on the hospitals or by ensuring that the community visitor responsible for family health (e.g. health visitor) has access to a hospital and can discuss medical problems with consultants, nursing staff, remedial therapists, and others. The question of whether a generic health visitor with a normal client load should retain responsibility for families where there is a seriously disabled child or whether they should hand over their care to specialist colleagues remains an open one. The comparative rarity of many disabling conditions and the changing attitudes of therapists towards their care are arguments of favour in specialization. So too is the need for adequate time to be allocated to interpreting the comments of specialists and discussing problems with parents as well as allaying spoken and unspoken fears. On the other hand the advantage of treating the family as normally as possible could be an argument in favour of retaining contact with a health visitor who is not dealing exclusively with children with handicaps and who has responsibility for the health and supervision of normal families in the neighbourhood.

Parent groups

Also a matter for debate is the vexed question of parents' clubs or groups at which the special problems relevant to the underlying impairment can be discussed openly and ideas for coping with the handicapping effects of disabilities exchanged. One possible danger of such organizations is that they may become introspective, highlighting how the affected children and their parents are different from others rather than encouraging the view that they should aim to be as normal as possible and think of themselves in that light.

Schoolchildren

In this age-group it is of paramount importance that the educational potential of those with disabilities should be encouraged so that handicap is minimized in terms of career prospects. The Warnock Committee, looking at the special educational needs of children with handicaps (Great Britain 1975), estimated that one-sixth of the schoolchildren population need special provision at any one time with one-fifth requiring such provision at some time during their period of schooling. One of the important recommendations of the committee was that the statutory categorization of children should be abandoned.

For some children, for example, those with congenital deafness, special schools are essential since both staff and teaching programmes have to be orientated to the needs posed by such handicapping conditions in a way that would make it impossible to integrate into a normal teaching schedule. Other factors such as frailty may put affected children at risk of ridicule or danger if exposed to the hurly-burly of normal schooling. The same considerations as well as those of distance from a suitable school will have a bearing on the need for special transport.

It is important that the assessment of educational need is made well before the normal time for starting school as special preparation in the pre-school period may be necessary. It is also important to explain the problem to both child and parents and to ensure that they understand the situation. Both may require time to atune themselves to the prospect of special schooling and having their fears allayed. This is particularly so if the population density is such that the special school indicated is far away from home; either the family has to move, possibly jeopardizing the job of the wage-earning parent, or the child may have to board.

Even if as in Britain the local government authority for education has statutory responsibility for assessment and the administration of educational arrangements it is important to strive for continuity of care from the pre-school phase. Thus it may be unwise for a stranger from the Education Department to appear at the home and start laying down the law about how the child should be educated. The health visitor who normally sees the family should be used either to introduce or perhaps act on behalf of the agent from the education authority. Health visitors—particularly those with special training—may also continue to act as long-term links between authorities and the families. It is perhaps regrettable in this context that health visitors who were formerly employed under the terms of the British National Health Service by local government authorities were transferred to specially appointed exchequer funded health authorities in 1972. Whatever advantages were achieved in terms of closer liaison with hospitals and general practitioners tended to be counterbalanced by greater separation from local government authority services —not only social services but also education and housing.

Residential schools

If residential education is deemed necessary then it is important to try and arrange for children to return home each weekend. If this is not feasible then there must be long enough breaks at half-term to enable the child to re-integrate with home and family. Holidays are also important in this connection both from the point of view of the disabled children themselves but also for the sake of their supporting relatives. Ideally the aim should be to have a family holiday in suitable accommodation provided either through statutory services or, as frequently occurs, through voluntary agencies. Some special holiday arrangements enable the child with a handicap to go with one parent while the other copes with the remaining children at home. If no arrangements can be made to have a holiday with the rest of the family then it is important to bear in mind that both parents and siblings will tend to become resentful of children with handicaps if they are seen to be the stumbling block to the sort of family holidays enjoyed by others in similar social circumstances.

Finally, it is important to ensure that by concentrating the attention of parents on a child with a handicap one does not alienate the siblings or upset them psychologically. All too often, lack of attention to this point results in truancy, encopresis, and other behavioural disturbances among siblings and preventive action by anticipation is likely to be much less costly in time and effort as well as being much less trau-

matic to the family than attempting to repair the damage after it has occurred.

Occupational rehabilitation

Normal work or modification of working routines to suit the limitations of those with occupational handicap are often more difficult to achieve than might at first appear. Obviously every encouragement should be given to follow a normal working pattern but for most people with occupational handicap this is not possible. Ensuring that school leavers have adequate training is axiomatic. Those at special schools can stay on for an extra year; in the main this is intended to make up for lost time either because of bouts of sickness absence or because educational training has to be given at a slower pace. However, it also enables older pupils to adapt more gradually to the prospect of occupational activity.

For those whose handicap arises later in life, perhaps as a result of injury or illness, it is important to ensure that rehabilitative measures are initiated sooner rather than later and that employment prospects should be discussed as soon as it is safe to do so. This may need close liaison between the employing authority and the hospital where the patient is receiving acute medical services. Close liaison is also necessary in the case of those whose handicaps stem from chronic progressive disease. For such individuals the general maxim that they should be encouraged to accept posts which make demands at the upper limit of their functional capacity may need to be weighed against the possibility that the handicap may increase as the disease progresses., Repeated moves into less-demanding posts may prove demoralizing to the affected person and relatives as well as being unsatisfactory from the point of view of the employer.

Some large employing organizations go to considerable lengths to re-absorb former employees who are smitten with illness or injury to the extent that they are unable to hold down their former jobs. Indeed some run their own rehabilitation units in which it is possible to return to less strenuous work or that requiring reduced output earlier than might otherwise be possible. The majority of such units also have scope for incorporating remedial exercises where these are appropriate as an integral part of the tasks allotted.

Even though there is a continuing tendency for employers to become more enlightened and more understanding about chronic illness it is by no means universal. Some react adversely on hearing that a member of staff has developed a handicap. Others perhaps from mistaken good intentions or through fear of Trades Union pressures and litigation prevail on those with handicaps to accept lighter work with consequent loss of earnings and prestige when there is no real need for such drastic action.

For these and other reason every attempt should be made to achieve close links between specialists and general practitioners in the health service and their counterparts in the occupational health service, financed by employers. Liaison is also desirable with doctors in the government sponsored Employment Medical Advisory Service. The fact that the latter is funded through the Department of Employment rather than the DHSS is an added complication which is believed by some to result in a greater likelihood of poor communication.

Disablement resettlement service

In view of the uncertainties as far as employment is concerned, not only for school leavers with handicaps from the outset but also for those who develop them later in life, it is advisable to ensure that those affected have the help of any statutory agencies set up for this purpose. The Manpower Services Commission (MSC) established in Britain in 1974 is the most recent of a series of such developments. The Commission has responsibility through its Employment Service Division (ESD) and Training Services Division (TSD) for job placement and training respectively. Both

Divisions have special responsibility for those with handicaps as a result of injury, chronic disease, or congenital impairment from any cause. Figure 24.1 together with the explanatory notes gives an outline of the help available. A key figure is the Disablement Resettlement Officer (DRO) of the ESD and contact can be made through the nearest job centre though a few hospitals have such an officer seconded to work on the premises.

Those with handicaps can be *registered* with the ESD but unfortunately some regard this as branding and resist registration. Indeed the system may be discontinued in the near future; however, there are some advantages to such a register which include:

1. Obligation by larger firms to include a percentage of *registered* people in their workforce.

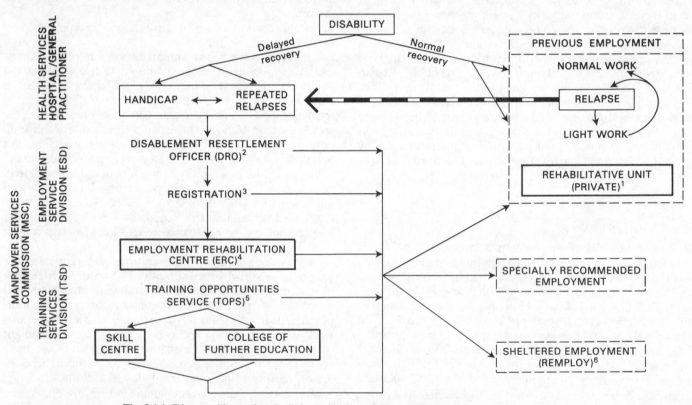

Fig. 24.1. Diagram illustrating the help available to those with handicap in relation to work.

1. Rehabilitation unit (private): administered by a firm for its own employees though occasionally a number of firms share such a resource as part of a privately financed occupational health service.

2. Disablement resettlement officer (DRO): special officers of the ESD with local knowledge of the job opportunities for those with handicap; also providing a range of services for employers prepared to accept handicapped staff.

3. Provides protection for those whose handicaps prevent them from performing certain tasks or who have prolonged and/or repeated periods of sickness absence.

4. Employment rehabilitation centre (ERC): used to assess the potential of those requiring a change of job; has both clerical and industrial sections. Also helpful in reacclimatizing those with erratic work attendance, emphasis on rhythm in working routine by setting standards within functional capacity, and insistence on compliance.

Doctor and gymnasium available so remedial programmes started elsewhere can be continued. NB: (i) limited number of centres may pose travelling problems or necessitate temporary absence from home; (ii) if the proportion of depressed patients among attending clientele is unduly high this may be detrimental to those with physical disabilities.

5. Training opportunities scheme (TOPS): courses arranged by TSD held at either a *skill centre* or a College of Further Education. Not exclusively for handicapped but those officially recognized as being handicapped stand a good chance of acceptance particularly if previously assessed at an ERC.

6. Sheltered workshops (REMPLOY): government maintained to provide employment for severely handicapped, particularly those with below average production speeds. Limited number of able-bodied supervisors may also carry out complicated/hazardous tasks.

2. Insurance companies generally include *registered* persons in the employers liability policy on the same terms as the able-bodied since the inference is that account has been taken of disability when allocating tasks.

3. Help may be given with fares or transport to and from work to selected persons on the *register.*

4. Special equipment to obtain or maintain employment may be provided (on loan) from public funds.

In the past registration has tended to make it easier to obtain placement at an Employment Rehabilitation Centre (ERC) particularly for those in need of re-adjustment to the working situation following disabilities arising in later life. Such people are also more likely to obtain a place in a retraining scheme (at a skill centre or college of further education) offered under the training opportunities scheme (TOPS) of the TSD.

Apart from the job itself, some provision must be made to transport those with mobility handicap to and from their place of work. Individual invalid carriages or other conspicuous transporting devices are much less acceptable than production models—not least because the latter can be used to transport other members of the family. Government funding is available and most local authorities who have responsibility for areas of high traffic congestion give special dispensation to enable those with mobility handicap to park their cars.

Housewives

Housewives are often forgotten when planning services to combat handicap. However, Harris *et al.* (OPCS 1971) devoted a special section of their report to the problems of this group including those of the small number of affected males in the community who effectively act as housewives either because they are single, widowed, or divorced or because they have had to assume this role through even greater handicap in their wives. For a few men there is a reversal of role because of inability to work with the result that the female partner has to become the effective wage earner.

The special poblem areas for housewives of either sex are household chores, shopping, and child care. However, those of holidays and transport mentioned earlier in connection with schoolchildren and occupational rehabilitation are also relevant to housewives.

Some of the tasks generally performed by housewives may be undertaken in a nuclear family by the spouse or older school children when they return home or at the weekends. For others there is a need to provide home-helps or meals-on-wheels both of which come under the auspices of the social service departments of local government authorities. Recommendation for these services may originate from health service staff either in hospital or in the community but such a recommendation is not a statutory prerequisite for the provision of such services.

Local government authority services

It is also necessary to bear in mind that when, as in Britain, responsibility for these services rests with the director of social services or his nominee then the decision to provide is not primarily a medical one. Thus although medical factors may and often do determine the degree of priority it cannot be assumed that merely because there is a medical recommendation that the service will be forthcoming. Obviously the question of whether or not a service is to be available may well influence the medical decision as to when a patient can be discharged from the shelter of a hospital environment.

The same arguments also apply to the exchange of housing so that a person with locomotor handicap may be spared having to climb stairs while the provision of a ramp for front door access or rails for the bath and lavatory may help to meet the needs of those with physical independence handicap.

Alterations to furniture and fittings as well as layout of kitchens may be of great benefit in reducing handicap in the domiciliary setting. Some such adaptations reported by housewives in the study by Harris *et al.* (OPCS 1971) are shown in Table 24.7. However, the extent to which the cost of these is met from public funds is likely to depend on policy of the local government authority concerned and the income of the family unit affected by the handicap.

Table 24.7. *Home alterations to reduce handicap. Alterations or additions made to the furniture, fittings, or layout of the kitchen reported by women housewives doing at least a little cooking*

Alteration/fitting	%
Shelves moved to a more convenient height	41
Sink unit adapted	17
Cooker/refrigerator/washing-machine moved	13
Ordinary appliances installed	7
Appliances changed for others easier to handle	6
Cooker specially adapted	5
Other alterations	27
Number on which % based	414

Source: OPCS (1971).

Those with handicaps may have difficulty in visualizing how such devices can be of benefit. For this reason a few centres have been established at which appliances may be on display and where those affected or their relatives can have a chance to handle them and try them out. Ideally such centres should be provided on the basis of at least one per 250 000 population and it is obviously essential that adequate parking arrangements are available.

The elderly

The services required to help elderly people who are also housewives naturally include those already listed above. However, there may be additional factors in relation to old people in that they are more likely to be living alone because of the death of a spouse. Also the fact that their children may have established homes of their own at some distance could accentuate the problems of isolation and dependency. Even if an elderly person has a surviving spouse it is quite possible that both partners will be suffering from handicaps. Furthermore the probability is that infirmity will increase as time passes and this can be further aggravated by progressive blurring of vision, hearing, and thought processes so that constant review and reassessment are necessary.

Problems of mobility and personal care feature largely and parallel studies in three industrial societies (Shanas *et al.* 1968) confirmed the international nature of these difficulties among the elderly. A scoring system was used based on six activities: mobility both within the house and outdoors, stair-climbing, washing, dressing, and cutting toenails. Zero was scored for unaided performance, one for partially aided, and two if help was always needed. Table 24.8 summarizes the findings on an effective scale of 1–12 and shows close similarities in the three countries.

Outdoor mobility can be enhanced by the use of a motor car for those who are still able to drive. However, the confidence of older people in this respect is not always mirrored either by their insurance companies or by statutory requirements. Nevertheless the introduction of automatic transmision and power-assisted steering and brakes as standard fittings on many cars and other adaptations can help to prolong the driving life of older people.

Another way of ensuring some degree of mobility among old people in the community which also helps to keep them reasonably alert is to provide day centres for recreation or occupational therapy. Such centres, run either by local government authorities or voluntary agencies, may also act as lunch clubs and thereby ensure that at least some hot meals are consumed. An additional provision in some centres is a simple medical assessment from time to time to get early indications of physical deterioration at a stage when remedial care may still be possible. Indeed the absence of a regular attender at such a centre may itself act as a stimulus for social workers, health visitors, or other suitable persons to check up on how things stand with the absentee.

Within the home itself aids such as rails, ramps, and appliances may be used to assist the elderly and maintain normal living standards. In addition there is the problem of stairs which may have presented little or no difficulty at a younger age but which become increasing impediments as time passes. If the apartments have a lift which is operational then the problem may be lessened but rehousing is often desirable; this may be difficult as single people and childless old couples get low priority and medical reasons for rehousing are somewhat imprecise.

Sheltered housing

Graduated relocation may be necessary from normal housing to ground floor dwellings (or apartments at higher levels with adequate lifts) through so-called sheltered housing to special homes for the elderly. Sheltered housing usually has a warden living on the estate and preferably some form of alarm system. Unfortunately these may be over-used by some residents and so bring the system into disrepute. For those without such devices the provision of a telephone not only reduces the sense of isolation but gives a feeling of security in case of emergency.

Homes for the elderly always require staff in attendance and unlike sheltered housing provide regular meals for the residents. It is not essential to have a registered nurse in residence but many homes do have such a qualified person in attendance. This is necessary if anything other than very trivial illness is to be treated in the home. It is clearly undesirable that a home should seek to emulate the intensity of care available in a hospital; never the less, confusion and anxiety will be diminished if a certain amount of care can be given in familiar surroundings. As pressure for places increases with the ageing of populations so too does the need for hospital beds for the elderly. These combined pressures often lead to difficulty in transferring sick people from homes to hospitals and vice versa; a situation made worse if, as in Britain, the home is run as part of the social services by local government authorities and the hospital is part of the health service funded by central government.

PLANNING AND EVALUATION OF SERVICES

It is possible to make predictions of probable need and to draw up plans for meeting these needs in accordance with generally recognized formulae of staffing, equipment, and premises (Wood and Lennox Holt 1980). However, even if such proposals are accepted and implemented—and if there is a climate of economic stringency this is by no means certain—it is likely to be many years before it will be possible to make an effective evaluation.

Much routinely collected data such as hospital activity analysis reflects services provided (process) or what administrators regard as *output* rather than *outcome* in terms of

Table 24.8. *Incapacity gradings (excluding bedfast responders). Percentage of elderly population in three countries*

Index score*	Denmark			Britain			United States		
	Men	Women	All	Men	Women	All	Men	Women	All
0	58	48	53	65	48	55	68	58	63
1–2	26	27	26	22	25	24	21	23	22
3–4	7	13	10	7	12	10	6	9	7
5–6	5	6	6	3	7	5	4	3	4
7 or more	4	6	5	3	8	6	1	6	4
Total	100	100	100	100	100	100	100	100	100
n	1130	1286	2416	985	1462	2447	1080	1352	2432

*Score/=no problem; 1=some difficulty; 2=total inability for each of: mobility indoors: washing/bathing; Mobility outdoors; dressing (including shoes); stair climbing; cutting toenails.
Source: Shanas *et al.* (1968).

benefit to the patient; it is obviously the latter which is important in the evaluation of services to alleviate handicap. Ideally this means conducting specially designed intervention studies using two different approaches to care and assessing outcome in terms of the nearest approximation to normal living achieved by those with handicaps who are subjected to the respective regimens.

Since assessment of need, discussed earlier in this chapter, remains a matter of controversy it follows that deciding on outcome goals must also be a matter for debate. Furthermore the difficulties are likely to be even greater in respect of measuring outcome than assessing need. The latter can be made in most cases on the basis of a point prevalence study but outcome has to be considered over a period of time probably extending until the death of those affected. The achievement of short-term goals does not necessarily mean long-term improvement in the quality of life nor of increased life-expectancy. Indeed an improvement in one may even be counter-productive in terms of the other.

It is also important to bear in mind that able-bodied assessors may not necessarily be the best judges of what criteria would be acceptable as an indication of success as far as those with handicaps are concerned. As with the able-bodied, some of those with handicaps deriving from physical disability may prefer to risk a shorter survival time with maximum enjoyment and participation while others may prefer to 'enjoy' their handicap to a ripe old age.

REFERENCES

Anderson, J.A.D. (1971). Rheumatism in industry: a review. *Br. J. Ind. Med.* **28,** 103.

Anderson, J.A.D. and Southwood, V. (1974). *The specialised health visitor for the handicapped baby, young child and schoolchild.* Disabled Living Foundation, London.

Boh, K. (1979). Intervention strategies and health outcome measures: family and community support policies. *Soc. Sci. Med.* **13A,** 563.

Brocklehurst, J.C. (1972). Welfare of the aged. *Community Health* **4,** 87.

Cardenal, F. (1981). Recent features of the WHO programme for disability prevention in the Agrican region. *Int. Rehabil. Med.* **3,** 210.

Department of Health and Social Security (1978). *Report on health and social subjects 13. Physically disabled people living at home: a study of numbers and needs.* HMSO, London.

Department of Health and Social Security (1980). *Inequalities in health. Report of a research working group* (Chairman D. Black) DHSS. London.

Department of Health and Social Security and Welsh Office: Central Health Services Council (1972). *Rehabilitation. Report of a sub-committee of the Standing Medical Advisory Committee* (Chairman R. Tunbridge). HMSO, London.

Duckworth, D. (1980). *The measurement of disabilities by means of summed ADL indices. Int. Rehabil. Med.* **2,** 194.

Fletcher, C.M. (1978). Terminology in chronic obstructive lung diseases. *J. Epidemiol. Community Health* **32,** 282.

Great Britain (1944a). *Education act.* HMSO, London.

Great Britain (1944b). *Disabled persons (employment) act.* HMSO, London.

Great Britain (1946). *National health service act.* HMSO, London.

Great Britain (1948). *National assistance act.* HMSO, London.

Great Britain (1958). *Disabled persons (employment) act.* HMSO, London.

Great Britain (1968). *Report of the committee on local authority and allied personal social services.* (Chairman F. Seebohm). HMSO, London.

Great Britain (1970). *Chronically sick and disabled persons act.* HMSO, London.

Great Britain (1972). *Local government act.* HMSO, London.

Great Britain (1973). *National health service reorganisation act.* HMSO, London.

Great Britain (1976). *Report of the committee on child health services.* (Chairman S.D.M. Court). HMSO, London.

Great Britain (1978). *Report of the committee of enquiry into the education of handicapped children and young people.* (Chairman H.M. Warnock). HMSO, London.

Grimby, A. and Hook, O. (1979). Rehabilitation in Sweden—education and research. *Int. Rehabil. Med.* **1,** 213.

Hook, O. (1979). Rehabilitation in Sweden—organisational concepts. *Int. Rehabil. Med.* **1,** 208.

Jefferys, M., Millard, J.B., and Hyman, M. (1969). Measurement of disability. *J. Chronic. Dis.* **22,** 303.

Jones, R.J. and Girdlestone, G.R. (1919). The cure of crippled children—proposed national scheme. *Br. Med. J.* **ii,** 457.

Katz, S., Ford, A.B., Moskowitz, R.W., Jackson, B.A., and Jaffe, M.W. (1963). The index of ADL. *JAMA* **185,** 914.

Lowther, C.P. (1973). *Studies in disabilities in Exeter and Edinburgh.* University of Exeter.

McMullan, J.J. (1971). Assessment of ability. challenge or handicap. *J. R. Coll. Gen. Pract.* **21,** 65.

Ministry of Health and Scottish Department of Health (1959). *Report of the working party on social workers in the local authority health and welfare services.* (Chairman E. L. Younghusband). HMSO, London.

Ministry of Labour and National Service (1956). *Report of the committee of enquiry on the rehabilitation training and resettlement of disabled persons.* (Chairman W.J. Piercy). HMSO, London.

Office of Population Censuses and Surveys (1971). *Handicapped and impaired in Britain, Part I.* HMSO, London.

Office of Population Censuses and Surveys (1974a). *Morbidity statistics from general practice: second national study 1970–71.* HMSO, London.

Office of Population Censuses and Surveys (1974b). *Report on 1971 census: employment status.* HMSO, London.

Office of Population Censuses and Surveys (1982). *Report on 1981 census: county reports of East Sussex and Essex.* HMSO, London.

Renker, K., Renker, U., and Presber, W. (1981). Disability in the family in the German Democratic Republic. *Int. Rehabil. Med.* **3,** 44.

Ritenour, R.A., Mazzi, E., and Gutberlet, R. L. (1978). The Maryland State intensive care neonatal program part V. The role of the department of medical social work. *Md. State Med. J.* **27**(3), 55.

Rose, G.A. (1962). The diagnosis of ischaemic heart pain and intermittent claudication in field surveys. *Bull. WHO* **27,** 645.

Rutter, M., Shaffer, D., and Shepherd, M. (1973). An evaluation of the proposal for a multi-axial classification of child psychiatric disorders. *Psychol. Med.* **3,** 244.

Shanas, E., Townsend, P., Wedderburn, D., Friish Milhoj, P., and Stehovwer, J. (1968). *Old people in three industrial societies.* Routledge and Kegan Paul, London.

Swedish Board of Health and Welfare (1978). *Principle program for rehabilitation medicine.* Stockholm.

Taylor, P.J. and Fairrie, A.J. (1968). Chronic disability in men of middle age. *Br. J. Prev. Soc. Med.* **22,** 183.

Thangavelu, M. (1980). Programme for disability prevention and medical rehabilitation in countries in South-East Asia. *Int. Rehabil. Med.* **2,** 153.

Townsend, P. (1973). Old people alone. *Proc. R. Soc. Med.* **66**, 885.

United Nations (1976). *Resolution of General Assembly 21/123*. UN, New York.

Warren, M.D. (1977). Disability and rehabilitation research programme of the health services research unit, University of Kent. *Rheumatol. Rehabil.* **16**, 248.

Weiss, M. (1980). Rehabilitation in Poland. *Int. Rehabil. Med.* **2**, 194.

Williamson, J., Stokoe, I.H., and Gray, S. (1964). Old people at home: their unreported needs. *Lancet* **i**, 1117.

Wing, J.K. and Hailey, A.M. (eds.) (1972). *Evaluating a community psychiatric service*. Oxford University Press. Nuffield Provincial Hospitals Trust.

Wood, P.H.N. and Badley, E.M. (1978). Setting disablement in perspective. *Int. Rehabil. Med.* **1**, 32.

Wood, P.H.N. and Lennox Holt, P.J. (1980). The development of strategic guidelines for regional planning of rehabilitation. *Int. Rehabil. Med.* **2**, 143.

World Health Organization (1980). *International classification of impairments, disabilities and handicaps*. WHO, Geneva.

25 Handicap due to intellectual impairment

Tom Fryers

INTRODUCTION

The public health tradition arose from the need to protect 'the public' from the spread of communicable disease. This required thorough study of epidemiology, a preventive approach which included early diagnosis and prompt treatment, and a community overview of service provision. These three features characterize public health involvement in the field of intellectual impairment. There is little of contagion, perhaps, but persons living in a community are interdependent, and serious disadvantage or handicap, in some, affects all members in a broader commonality of health, disease, and disorder. A humane and compassionate society acknowledges this, and our common responsibility wherever possible to prevent, treat, ameliorate, and care for those who are most damaged and most disadvantaged, and ultimately to share the burden that falls upon them. In the field of intellectual impairment, the burden falls not only on affected individuals, but also on their immediate families to a disproportionate degree, and sharing this burden is the most obvious need in the wider community.

The three principal elements of public health concern are, therefore, the epidemiological elucidation of the nature and the size of the problem, the promotion of prevention, and the provision of community-based programmes of habilitation and care. Epidemiology will include a search for causes, studies of incidence and prevalence in different communities and, at different times, the classification and distribution of specific disabilities, and service evaluation. Preventive programmes will include primary prevention through mass screening or control of the physical environment, early assessment and monitored programmes of habilitation to minimize secondary disabilities, and the prevention of handicap by professional support of the family, ameliorating individual social conditions and challenging stigmatizing attitudes in the social environment. Community-based habilitation requires a thorough understanding of the nature of community as well as the nature of intellectual impairment and its associated problems, and will be characterized by problems of co-ordination and integration of the interests of a wide variety of agencies and personnel.

Attitudes have changed very rapidly in the last 20 years. Our inherited systems of care, usually based on large residential institutions, medically dominated and capital intensive, are essentially alien to the basic philosophy of normalization and integration which lies at the heart of modern public health work for the disabled, elderly, or chronic sick, and which is necessarily multidisciplinary and personnel intensive. Changes on the scale required cannot be brought about without commitment, conflict, and cost. They bring problems of a high order for the public health physician and his colleagues and are amongst the most challenging in the current public health scene.

CONCEPTS, CLASSIFICATIONS, NAMES, AND LABELS

The field is beset by serious problems of conceptualization, classification, and terminology. Moves towards normalization of life-style has led some to question classification *per se*, which identifies children with types of disorder or problem, and carries inherent dangers of 'labelling'. This concern is entirely proper, but no epidemiology and little planning can take place without categories of some sort, and accurate scientific measurement is dependent upon clarity of definition and logic of classification. Moreover, however desirable the integration of disabled people into ordinary society, if they disappear from view they are likely to be ignored in the provision of the special help they need. They do have special needs, by definition. They cannot compete on equal terms with their fellows and are unlikely, without the effort of others, to escape the stigma and low status that have always been their lot. Epidemiological work creates visibility: normalization must not excuse invisibility and ignorance, leaving the burden of care entirely to the disabled person and his or her immediate family. Clear thinking about disabled people and their needs is required, to argue for positive discrimination of assistance and special allocation of resources.

Concepts have generally changed over the last century from the idea of a fixed and immutable biological characteristic, present at birth and largely inherited, to the current general concensus of maladaptation and development resulting from a wide range of interacting biological and social determinants. Concepts and definitions of phenomena cannot be divorced from the means employed to measure them. Different professions tend, therefore, towards different views or emphases, and interprofessional conflict is inevitable. An inherent difficulty lies in trying to measure aspects of development in childhood which predict 'ultimate incapacity' in adult life. We can only compare indicators of physical, intellectual, and social development in particular children, with recognized age-related norms of function and behaviour, but these are not readily susceptible to precise measurement and classification and are variably culture specific. There are also difficulties of degree, since milder forms of intellectual impairment raise essentially different issues, and merge into the 'normal' range, but divisions are arbitrary. The basic concept of people at the very bottom of the scale of human competence, who do not have the potential to live independently, who cannot adequately care for themselves, and cannot compete in any aspect of life with their more adequate peers, may be ambiguous but acceptable for those with severe intellectual impairment, but is clearly inapplicable to the less impaired for whom any component of such a description may be only partially true or not true at all. A satisfactory concept must also accommodate dynamic change; environmental factors affect behaviour, performance, and their measurement to varying degrees, and classifications should always be viewed as 'current' rather than 'permanent', useful 'constructs' rather than fixed 'truth'.

Over the last decade a growing convention (now enshrined in the WHO International Classification of Impairments, Disabilities and Handicaps 1980) has helped to clarify concepts and terms by distinguishing between impairment, disability, and handicap. Generally speaking, *impairment* is conceived as the basic biological fault in a tissue or organ, *disability* as the limitation of function consequent upon impairment, and *handicap* the resulting personal and social disadvantage. The WHO definition of impairment refers to function as well as structure and has, therefore, two potentially distinct components. The definitions are as follows: 'Impairment: in the context of health experience an impairment is any loss or abnormality of psychological, physiological or anatomical structure or function. Disability: . . . any restriction or lack (resulting from an impairment) of ability to perform an activity in the manner or within the range considered normal for a human being. Handicap: . . . a disadvantage for an individual, resulting from an impairment or disability, that limits or prevents the fulfilment of a role that is normal (depending on age, sex and social and cultural factors) for that individual'.

This is a very useful classification, especially if we separate impairment of structure and function of an organ, tissue, or biochemical system. The latter is usually consequent upon the former, and often results in disability defined in terms of personal activity. Aetiological diagnosis is largely concerned with specific pathology or patterns of structural impairment and their causal processes, whilst a neurological diagnosis will include impairments of both structure and function. 'Disability assessments' are usually concerned with functional impairments and activity disabilities in WHO terms. Psychological measures of intelligence are concerned with impairment of intellectual function or learning capacity, implying no particular theory of structure and function of the 'mind'. Handicap is necessarily situation specific as well as individual specific and can generally be classified or compared only in broad descriptive terms.

Terminology should ideally reflect current underlying concepts, but terms we inherit in law, convention, or common use are not easy to change. Acceptability to parents is equally important but does not necessarily follow the same logic. 'Mental deficiency' has largely gone from daily use, and 'subnormality' appears to be going. Neither reflects current concepts and both tend to be offensive. 'Mental handicap' is currently accepted in many countries, though 'mental' is not really liked. It is often used perjoratively and reinforces an inappropriate medical image which promotes the common and damaging confusion with mental illness. Moreover, 'handicap' raises conceptual difficulties which 'retardation', in common use in North America, avoids. These traditional terms are being challenged by 'developmental disability', and 'intellectual disability' or 'intellectual impairment', which are rather more accurate and acceptable. Of the WHO categories, 'impairment' is clearly the most appropriate and precise term, and impairment of intellect is obviously at the root of current concepts.

To use 'handicap' to describe a group of people characterized by intellectual impairment does mischief to its technical meaning, but it may properly be used to describe the field of interest, for it is the full spectrum of personal and social disadvantage, that is, handicap, associated with intellectual impairment, with which we are concerned.

There have been many criteria used for classification. Intellectual criteria have depended largely upon intelligence quotients (IQ). Most classifications have used IQ equivalents with a division at IQ 50, and there is little else to substitute as a global indicator of intellectual ability and learning potential. For practical use, tests should be professionally administered, repeated several times, and include sub-scores. They provide guidelines only, and many mildly impaired children show increments in IQ as they grow older, probably 'recovering' from early deprivation. Measured intelligence is undoubtedly influenced by both nature and nurture, and there are major problems of standardized measurement and predictive value. This is even more true for 'development tests' in very young children, though they remain useful for monitoring development.

Clinical criteria have traditionally merely added weight to other criteria. A diagnosis of Down's syndrome has usually led to classification as severely intellectually impaired though this is not entirely consistent with intellectual or social criteria. Until recently, aetiological diagnosis has been possible for only a minority even of the severely impaired, but in recent years paediatritions have been able to provide a diagnosis with aetiological implications for 80 to 90 per cent of children. Paediatric data of such thoroughness are not available everywhere, and do not imply complete knowledge of ultimate causes. They offer clearly distinguished aetiological categories for epidemiological work and planning for prevention, but barely relate to specific disabilities or need for care.

Neurological diagnosis bears more upon needs. Virtually all severely intellectually impaired people by IQ definition (<50 equivalent) have demonstrable disorders of the central nervous system at autopsy, but in recent years paediatric neurologists have been able clinically to detect minimal abnormalities even in many mildly impaired people. Neurological diagnosis is important in itself, but does not tie in with intellectual criteria for classification.

Quite different criteria have been gaining ground in the last decade with the development of disability assessment schedules. These vary from simple records of continence, mobility, speech, and behaviour to detailed epidemiological instruments attempting to discriminate distinct syndromes of disability and to describe their distribution. These offer hope of classifications of need to guide service planning and individual programme monitoring. They are mutable with age and therapeutic or educational intervention, but may eventually discriminate relatively discrete syndromes after the manner of autism.

Disability assessment is likely to overlap with measurement of social skills and the American Association of Mental Deficiency Adaptive Behaviour Scales incorporate both. On the basis of 'standards of personal independence and social responsibility expected of his age and cultural group', four categories of 'behavioural age' are defined, which are not necessarily consistent with intelligence 'grades' and are dependent on environmental influences susceptible to change. For this reason criteria of social incompetance have had little success in spite of long use. They have characterized descriptive definitions in the past, usually in terms of self-care, self-protection and task performance, but their ambiguity and inconsistency and their capricious application have generally been useless or harmful. The Vineland Social Maturity Scale has been standardized for certain North American populations and can be useful elsewhere if applied with care.

In summary, most systems have relied on IQ equivalents to define degrees of intellectual impairment. Under IQ 70 has usually been accepted for 'mild' impairment; for 'severe' impairment <IQ 55 has a mathematical logic (three standard deviations below the mean for test of SD 15) but <IQ 50 has proved more useful empirically, and has currency in the epidemiological literature. 'Profound' impairment is commonly applied to <IQ 20 or 25. No set of definitions and classifications is wholly satisfactory. Research workers need to be exceptionally wary and clear-thinking and service planners should try to understand the conceptual problems before applying simple criteria. It is very important that no classification system, however elegant to the epidemiologist or convenient to the administrator, should be allowed to determine the lifetime services for an individual. Classification systems are generally applicable only to groups: individuals require thorough, multidisciplinary professional assessment, constantly monitored and up-dated, and involving the client and his or her family. This should help to avoid the dangers of labelling, administrative determinism, institutional batch management and inflexible service structures, and ensures the best practical attention to changing individual needs.

FREQUENCY IN SPACE AND TIME: PREVALENCE

Variation in concepts, definitions, and terminology affect the accuracy, validity, and comparability of epidemiological studies as do problems of identification and demographic denominators. Even greater difficulties lie in the subtle, intricate, and usually unknown interrelationship between aetiology, ascertainment and mortality. A multiplicity of causative factors operate at various times before conception, throughout fetal life and the birth process, and in early childhood. Their effects become evident progressively, and ascertainment is often prolonged, while high mortality operates throughout. Children at any particular age are merely known survivors for whom ascertainment has been completed (Fig. 25.1). 'True' incidence is necessarily difficult to establish; in Down's syndrome it must take account of aborted conceptuses and this is not easy to estimate. In perinatal aetiologies it must relate to all similar processes whether or not the result is intellectual impairment. The incidence of affected births is dependent upon the population birth rate, so that prevalence at birth (the number of cases in a standard continuous series of births in a given population), is generally far more useful. Even this is extremely difficult to establish except for well-defined syndromes susceptible to diagnosis soon after birth.

Severe intellectual impairment

Point prevalence studies understandably dominate the literature but many are not reliable, comparable, or useful. Prevalence studies count only survivors at a point in calendar time, and different age groups represent different cohorts of births. To be useful, prevalence ratios must apply to small age groups; five years is usually the best compromise. The youngest age-group (birth to five years) can never be satisfactory (except possibly for Down's syndrome) as it excludes those not yet ascertained. In most countries with universal primary education, ascertainment should now be reasonably complete by five years, and the two 'school-age' groups, 5–9 and 10–14 years provide the most satisfactory basis for comparison. In older cohorts it may be even more difficult to discriminate between prevalence at birth and the effects of mortality, but data may provide evidence of temporal change. Age groups will vary in prevalence, but all are equally important for planning.

Many authors appear to assume consistency in the prevalence of severe intellectual impairment, independent of time, place, and culture, variations being ascribed to differential ascertainment or methods of data collection. The known plethora of factors affecting aetiology and survival, including maternal age distributions, extent of birth control, effectiveness of antenatal care, immune status of the population, medical fashions in obstetrics, access to antibiotics, efficiency of screening programmes, and so on, should lead us to *expect* considerable variations in prevalence at particular ages between different communities and at different times. This is what is found.

Table 25.1 gives apparently reliable age-specific prevalence ratios for severe impairment from published studies since 1960. The variation is from 1.62 per 1000 population in the 5–9-year age group in Salford in 1960 to 7.34 per

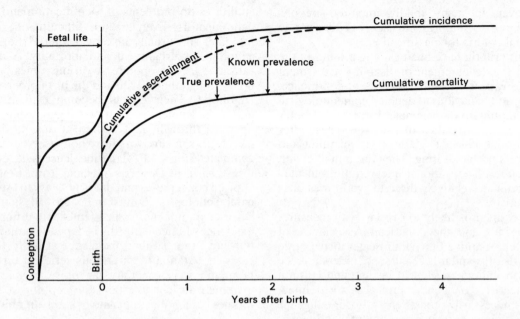

Fig. 25.1. Schematic diagram of the relationship between aetiology, mortality, and ascertainment in severe intellectual impairment.

The two vertical lines represent conception and birth respectively. The upper curve represents the cumulative incidence of disorders associated with severe intellectual impairment in a notional cohort of conceptuses. At conception, many individuals are already impaired, more arise early in fetal life, fewer later on. The perinatal period results in a relatively large increase in numbers, but incidence thereafter progressively diminishes.

The lower curve represents the cumulative mortality of affected individuals within the cohort. Many impaired fetuses die early in fetal life, fewer later on. The perinatal period carries higher risks but after birth mortality progressively diminishes.

The vertical distance between the two curves represents the 'true prevalence' at any given age. Not all those impaired at birth are recognized at that time; ascertainment is progressively achieved, as represented by the dotted curve. The 'known prevalence' at any given age is represented by the vertical distance between the ascertainment curve and the mortality curve.

1000 in 13-year-olds in Amsterdam in 1970. Methodologies appear comparable but there is no obvious pattern of distribution. Comparisons of prevalence in different populations over a 20-year period are obviously confounded by any temporal variations. The few populations subject to more than one prevalence study give evidence of considerable changes over time, confirmed by recent analyses of data for the same population for 20 years, from the Salford Case Register (Fryers 1984b).

In comparing prevalence ratios it is possible to discriminate between secular and temporal variations by relating the age-specific ratios in small age groups, to the years of birth of each cohort. In Fig. 25.2, for severe intellectual impairment, brackets describe each cohort from a particular study, whilst annual data from Salford are plotted as points.

There is considerable variation between different communities at any one time, but also consistent general trends in prevalence of severe intellectual impairment over 20 years, from both geographically dispersed studies and the

Salford data. Prevalence roughly doubled in cohorts born between the early 1950s and the mid-1960s, diminishing since then. The range changed from approximately 1.5 per 1000 to 4.0 per 1000, to approximately 3.3 per 1000 to 5.5 per 1000 with later figures lower again and the Salford figures followed this rather more dramatically. It must be remembered that the prevalence in each case applies to a specific age group between 5 and 14 years, and this analysis cannot in itself discriminate between changes in incidence between cohorts, and changes in mortality. There is no evidence for a significant increase in incidence at that time, and it is impossible that any one type of aetiology, even Down's syndrome, should influence the total to this degree. The increase in prevalence at school ages is most likely due primarily to increased survival consequent upon improved care of neonates, infants, and young children in the early 1960s common to most developed communities. More precise evidence of increased survival is difficult to establish except for Down's syndrome, but this is demonstrated by the com-

Table 25.1. *Prevalence of severe intellectual impairment in children born 1946–76*

Study/place	Year of study	Age group	Years of birth	Ratio/1000 population
1. Salford	1960	5–9	1951–55	1.62
		10–14	1946–50	2.54
2. Middlesex	1960	5–9	1951–55	3.02
		10–14	1946–50	3.61
London	1960	5–9	1951–55	1.86
		10–14	1946–50	2.81
3. Aberdeen	1962	8–10	1952–54	3.70
4. Aarhus	1962	5–9	1953–57	2.81
		10–14	1948–52	3.69
5. Wessex	1963	5–9	1954–58	2.41
		10–14	1949–53	2.57
6. N. Ireland	1964	5–9	1955–59	3.40
		10–14	1950–54	3.60
7. United Kingdom	1964	7	1958 (1 week)	2.60
		Birth	1958 (1 week)	3.40
8. Newcastle	1965–67	5	1960–62	4.90
9. Salford	1965	5–9	1956–60	2.97
		10–14	1951–55	2.16
	1970	5–9	1961–65	4.59
		10–14	1956–60	3.28
	1975	5–9	1966–70	4.90
		10–14	1961–65	4.52
	1980	5–9	1971–75	3.62
		10–14	1966–70	5.24
10. N.E. Scotland	1966	5–9	1957–61	3.50
		10–14	1952–56	2.30
11. Quebec	1966–69	8–12	1958	3.84
12. Camberwell	1967	5–9	1958–62	4.09
		10–14	1953–57	3.91
	1973	5–9	1964–68	4.92
		10–14	1959–63	6.15
	1977	5–9	1968–72	4.90
		10–14	1963–67	5.45
	1981	5–9	1972–76	4.00
		10–14	1967–71	5.65
13. Sheffield	1968	5–9	1959–63	3.70
		10–14	1954–58	3.66
14. Amsterdam	1970	10	1960	7.25
		13	1957	7.34
15. Aarhus	1970	5–9	1961–65	3.45
		10–14	1956–60	4.50
16. Eire	1974	5–9	1965–69	5.19
		10–14	1960–64	5.45
	1981	5–9	1972–76	3.95
		10–14	1967–71	4.70
17. Mannheim	1974	7–11	1963–67	4.34
		12–16	1958–62	4.20
18. Sheffield	1975	5–9	1966–70	3.61
		10–14	1961–65	4.24
	1982	5–9	1973–77	3.06
		10–14	1968–72	3.21
19. Northern Ireland	1975	5–9	1966–70	3.30
		10–14	1961–65	4.16
20. Uppsala	1975	1	1959–64	3.30
		1	1965–70	2.54
21. Vasterbotten	1976	1	1959–62	5.32
		1	1963–66	3.40
		1	1967–70	3.10
22. Manchester	1977	5–9	1968–72	3.33
		10–14	1963–67	4.13
23. Bristol	1977	5–9	1968–72	3.10
		10–14	1963–67	4.70
	1980	5–9	1971–75	3.20
		10–14	1966–70	4.00
24. Lanarkshire	1978	5–6	1972–73	2.30
		7–9	1969–71	2.60
		10–14	1964–68	3.60

Table 25.1.—*continued*

Study/place	Year of study	Age group	Years of birth	Ratio/1000 population
25. Dumfries and Galloway	1979	5–9	1970–74	2.60
		10–14	1965–69	3.60
26. Cornwall	1979	5–9	1970–74	3.30
		10–14	1965–69	3.67
27. Manchester	1981	5–9	1972–76	3.00
		10–14	1967–71	3.80

Sources:
1. Kushlick, A. (1961). Subnormality in Salford. In *A report on the mental health services of the city of Salford for the year 1960* (eds. M.W. Susser and A. Kushchik). Health Department, Salford.
2. Goodman, N. and Tizard, J. (1962). Prevalence of imbecility and idiocy among children. *Br. Med. J.* i, 216.
3. Birch, H.C., Richardson, S.A., Baird, D., Horobin, G., and Illsley, R. (1970). *Mental subnormality in the community*. Williams and Wilkins, Baltimore.
4. Brask, B.H. (1972). Prevalence of mental retardation among children in the county of Aarhus, Denmark. *Acta Psychiatr. Scand.* **48**, 480.
5. Kushlick, A. and Cox, G. (1973). The epidemiology of mental handicap. *Dev. Med. Child. Neurol.* **15**, 748.
6. Scally, B.G. and Mackay, D.N. (1964). Mental subnormality and its prevalence in Northern Ireland. *Acta Psychiatr. Scand.* **40**, 203.
7. Davie, R., Butler, N., and Goldstein, H. (1972). *From birth to seven*. Longmans, London.
8. Neligan, G., Prudham, D., and Steiner, H. (1974). *The formative years*. Oxford University Press for the Nuffield Provincial Hospitals Trust, London.
9. Fryers, T. (1984). *The epidemiology of severe intellectual impairment: the dynamics of prevalence*. Academic Press, London.
10. Innes, G., Kidd, C., and Ross, H.S. (1968). Mental subnormality in north east scotland. *Br. J. Psychiatry* **114**, 35.
11. McDonald, A.D. (1973). Severely retarded children in Quebec: prevalence, causes and care. *Am. J. Ment. Def.* **78**, 205.
12. Wing, L. (1971). Severely retarded children in a London area: prevalence and provision of services. *Psychol. Med.* **1**, 405.
    Der, G. (1983). Data from Camberwell Register. Personal Communication.
13. Bayley, M.J. (1973). *Mental handicap and community care*. Routledge and Kegan Paul, London.
14. Sorel, F.M. (1974). *Prevalence of mental retardation*. Tilburg University Press, Netherlands.
15. Bernsen, A.H. (1976). Severe mental retardation among children in the county of Aarhus, Denmark. *Acta Psychiatr. Scand.* **54**, 43.
16. Mulcahy, M., O'Connor, S., and Reynolds, A. (1983). *Census of the mentally handicapped in the Republic of Ireland, 1981*. Medico-Social Research Board, Dublin.
17. Cooper, B. (1983). Personal communication.
18. Martindale, A. (1977). *Trends in the prevalence of mental handicap in Sheffield since the Register was set up in 1975*. Report of the Sheffield Case Register, Ryegate Centre, Sheffield.
19. Macdonald, G. and Mackay, D.N. (1978). Mental subnormality in Northern Ireland. *J. Ment. Def. Res.* **22**, 83.
20. Gustavson, K.H., Hagberg, B., Hagberg, G., and Sars, K. (1977a). Severe mental retardation in a Swedish county. I. Epidemiology etc. *Acta Paediatr. Scand.* **66**, 373.
21. Gustavson, K.H., Holmgren, G., Jonsell, R. and Son Blomquist, H.K. (1977b). Severe mental retardation in children in a northern Swedish county. *J. Ment. Def. Res.* **21**, 161.
22. Thomas, A. (1978). *A population study of children with severe mental handicap*. Unpublished thesis, University of Manchester.
23. Russell, O. and Hall, V. (1980). *Mental handicap and functional disability*. Mental Handicap Studies Research Report 6. Department of Mental Health, Bristol University, UK.
24. Stewart, G.H. (1979). *A survey of severe mental handicap in children under 16 years of age in Lanarkshire*. Unpublished submission for MFCM part II. Faculty of Community Medicine of the Royal Colleges London.
25. Cunningham, M.A. (1981). *A survey of mental handicap in Dumfries and Galloway: a study of needs*. Dumfries and Galloway Health Board, Scotland.
26. Lindsay, M.P. and Russell, C.M. (1981). Mental handicap in the county of Cornwall: prevalence and the use of services. *J. Ment. Def. Res.* **25**, 77.
27. Akinsola, H.A. (1983). *Patterns of disability in severely mentally retarded children*. Unpublished M.Sc. dissertation. Department of Community Medicine, University of Manchester.

parison of life tables shown in Table 25.2. Similar improvement in survival might be expected in other aetiological groups.

Survival has no doubt continued to improve, so recent lower prevalence ratios at school ages must reflect lower prevalence at birth. Several factors are implicated. Demographic changes reduced Down's syndrome, and perhaps others, by the reduction in maternal age during the 1970s in most developed countries. With increasingly easy contraception, births to older women have fallen dramatically. In some communities amniocentesis and abortion may also have played a part. Screening programmes for inherited disorders of metabolism and hypothyroidism are now common, and further improvements in perinatal care have probably reduced the numbers of children surviving with brain damage. A few children may have moved out of the 'severe' category with early stimulation and education. However, these do not seem to offer a complete explanation of the recent fall in prevalence ratios.

To summarize, there can be no single common prevalence ratio for severe intellectual impairment. Such statistics only have meaning when related to specified small age groups, particular times, and particular places. There is secular variation and a pattern of temporal variation reflecting cohort differences which may help us to predict future numbers in broad terms. Generally, age-specific prevalence ratios of 5 per 1000 are *currently* not uncommon for older children and young adults, but lower ratios are to be expected for younger children.

Mild intellectual impairment

The problems of sensibly describing the prevalence of mild intellectual impairment are almost insuperable. The range of ability equivalent to IQ 50–69 (assuming normal distribution of IQ, SD 15) would include 25 per 1000 of the

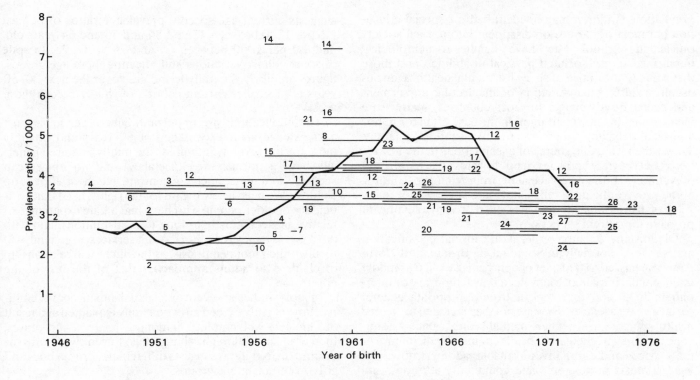

Fig. 25.2. Severe intellectual impairment (IQ50) in Salford CB and from published studies. Age-specific prevalence ratios in school-age children related to years of birth, 1946–77. (Reference key see Table 25.1; continuous line—Salford.)

Table 25.2. *Down's syndrome: international life table comparison of survival rates*

Period of births	Birmingham 1942–52 (a) $n = 252$	London 1944–55 (attending) (b) $n = 698$	Victoria 1948–57 (c) $n = 729$	Glasgow 1953–58 (d) $n = 117$	Massachusetts 1950–66 (e) $n = 2421$	British Columbia 1952–71 (f) $n = 927$	Northern Ireland 1960–69 (g) $n = 101$	Salford 1961–80 (h) $n = 59$	Japan 1966–75 (i) $n = 1052$	Western Australia 1966–76 (j) $n = 231$
Birth	100	100	100	100	100	100	100	100	100	100
1 month	68.8	70.0	—	88.9	92.8 (28 days)	—	—	89.8	—	97.0
1 year	49.9	46.9	68.9	76.1	76.4	89.4	64.4	81.4	93.6	83.5
2 years	47.4	43.3	57.9	70.9	72.6	87.3	—	81.0	90.4	77.7
3 years	45.6	42.1	54.0	—	70.5	85.8	—	79.2	89.0	75.4
4 years	45.2	40.5	51.4	—	69.2	85.2	—	77.3	88.1	74.8
5 years	44.1	39.7	49.4	—	68.5	84.9	—	77.2	87.1	—
10 years	—	36-8	46-2	—	64.5	82.1	—	70.7 (1961–70)	86.0	—

Sources:
(a) Record, R.G. and Smith, A. (1955). Incidence, mortality and sex distribution of mongoloid defectives. *Br. J. Prev. Soc. Med.* **9**, 1.
(b) Carter, C.D. (1958). A life table for mongols with causes of death. *J. Ment. Def. Res.* **2**, 64.
(c) Collman, R.D. and Stoller, A. (1963). A life table for mongols in Victoria. *Aust. J. Ment. Def. Res.* **7**, 1.
(d) Lunn, J.E. (1959). A survey of mongol children in Glasgow. *Scot. Med. J.* **4**, 368.
(e) Fabia, A. and Drolette, M. (1970). Life tables up to age 10 for mongols with and without congenital heart defect. *J. Ment. Defic. Res.* **14**, 235.
(f) Gallagher, R.P. and Lowry, R.B. (1975). Longevity in Down's syndrome in British Columbia. *J. Ment. Def. Res.* **19**, 157.
(g) Elwood, J.H. and Darragh, P.M. (1981). Prevalence of mongolism in Northern Ireland. *J. Ment. Def. Res.* **25**, 157.
(h) Fryers, T. (1984). *The epidemiology of severe intellectual impairment: the dynamics of prevalence.* Academic Press, London.
(i) Masaki, M., Higurashi, M., Iijima, K. *et al.* (1981). Mortality and survival for Down's syndrome in Japan. *Am. J. Hum. Genet.* **33**, 629.
(j) Mulachy. M.T. (1979). Down's syndrome in Western Australia: mortality and survival. *Clin. Genet.* **16**, 103.

population. Children may be identified for special education but most of these soon disappear into normal society on leaving school. Few have significant neurological impairments, or associated physical disabilities, and those that come to the notice of specialist 'mental health' agencies usually exhibit a combination of intellectual impairment and social disadvantage. In most countries, many were incarcerated in large institutions in the past, often for minor antisocial behaviour in the absence of a supportive family. They were a valuable source of cheap labour in the institutions but current policies tend towards discharge and prevention of their replacement from younger cohorts. Some prove difficult to rehabilitate into society after many years of institutional life, and they still represent a significant problem for current services.

Diminishing reliance on legal and formal classification and services especially in Scandinavia, Britain, and North America, has led to far fewer people being labelled as mildly intellectually impaired. Many need only temporary or intermittent help, and may seek it from appropriate general social welfare agencies. They are not then included in 'mental health' statistics. Even where mental health agencies dominate, numbers of clients will be determined by the nature of the services and alternatives available, administrative and legal contexts professional and community attitudes, and social conditions such as unemployment. Administrative statistics are never likely to be comparable.

Satisfactory epidemiological studies of mild intellectual impairment are few and mostly focus on the predominance amongst lower socio-economic classes and associated phenomena. Some at the lower end of this IQ range have similar syndromes to the severely impaired and should be offered the same services: dividing lines are arbitrary and should be recognized as such. General prevalence figures are not useful: for local planning, the mildly impaired within the services need to be counted and estimates made of their likely replacement in the light of the future social, professional, and administrative conditions. It should also be recognized that, for themselves, their families and social agencies, they represent in general a very different set of problems and needs from the severely impaired and possibly should not be planned for in common.

Age and sex distribution

Cohort variations necessarily produce age variations in any point prevalence study, but these are also affected by progressive mortality. In many communities, as we have seen, cohorts born in the 1960s tend to be large, probably because these were the first to benefit from dramatically reduced early mortality. They will benefit from reduced mortality at all ages and will continue to exceed cohorts on either side as they move through successive ages. Currently they are mostly young adults and impose a severe strain on the services. Earlier cohorts have also experienced lower mortality, and older age groups are steadily increasing in most developed communities, so that among the *severely* impaired, there are more adults aged over 45 years than there are children aged under 15 years. In Britain, evidence

suggests current age-specific prevalence ratios of at least 2.0 per 1000 between 45 and 54 and 55 and 64 years old, and 1.0 per 1000 between 65 and 74 years old. In spite of some cohort variations still affecting these age groups, figures are likely generally to increase over the next 30–50 years until smaller current cohorts of children reach these ages.

The implications are important. School curricula must acknowledge a life-expectancy of 60 years and possibly more for the severely impaired (the mildly impaired generally have a normal life-expectancy) and no longer can agencies and personnel concentrate all their efforts on children. We need a new regard for the rights, needs, and difficulties of older people who have had a long experience of relative neglect, mostly in long-term institutions, and with no effective family remaining. Adult services, in general, will require much more emphasis, as the numerical relationship of children to adults approaches that of the rest of the population.

In most studies of severe intellectual impairment in children, boys slightly exceed girls, generally explained as a result of greater vulnerability amongst male conceptuses. Increased survival might change this. Recent work on syndromes of disabilities suggests different patterns in boys and girls, in certain ethnic groups.

Social class distribution

It has generally been taught that there is an equal distribution of severe intellectual impairment in all social classes, whilst mild impairment shows a clear social class gradient greatly emphasizing lower socio-economic groups. There is little doubt about the latter, and the interaction of poor intellectual ability with poor education, poor social environment, and emotional deprivation seems readily to account for this phenomenon. An even social class distribution for severe intellectual impairment is surprising, however, in the light of the social class distribution of most measures of morbidity and mortality.

Since many causes of severe impairment involve environmental factors, one would expect a social class gradient, though less pronounced than that for mild impairment because of genetic aetiologies. But one would also expect a similar gradient for early mortality in these vulnerable children, and it seems likely that these have previously balanced each other out in prevalence studies during later childhood. Increased survival would therefore reveal the previously hidden social class gradient in severe intellectual impairment. This is supported by some recent studies in West Germany and Britain, though not conclusively.

IMPAIRMENT: AETIOLOGICAL DIAGNOSIS AND PREVENTION

It is characteristic of the intellectually impaired that they encompass a wide variety of different aetiological processes, often complex and not fully understood and in which heredity and environment both play their part in the final picture of impairment, disability, and handicap. Until recently, only a quarter to a third of the severely impaired could be given an aetiological diagnosis, mostly Down's syndrome, but this is no longer so. Where paediatric assessment facilities are of the highest quality, between 80 and 90 per cent can be given a diagnosis with aetiological implications with reasonable confidence. This is not to claim that the ultimate cause is known but that important factors in the aetiological process are clearly understood, the type of cause and the period of development are identified, and there are useful implications for preventive action.

Most causes result in a range of severe and mild intellectual impairment. Many also produce physical impairments not exclusively associated with intellectual impairment. Although the aetiological diagnosis has little relevance to needs for care, it has immense relevance to prevention. Since there is little potential for cure, preventive programmes and relevant research should have the highest priority. It may influence care in helping parents to understand and accept the reality of impairment and to work positively with their child, especially where they know the full potential of modern science has been exercised in understanding the nature and cause of the child's impairment, and where a clear explanation can be offered. The intellectually impaired have the same rights to careful investigation, assessment, and diagnosis as anyone else.

The assessment of associated physical disabilities is also important. First, they complicate the measurement of intelligence and a child's potential for development. Secondly, they represent additional burdens and fewer opportunities which must be accommodated in treatment, training, or care. Thirdly, their presence does not in itself indicate intellectual impairment. Many children with deafness, or motor impairments such as those of cerebral palsy, have been wrongly judged 'retarded' in the past and spend a lifetime in institutions. Careful and comprehensive assessment of intellectual, neurological, and sensory impairments is essential to good paediatric practice.

Table 25.3 orders clinical syndromes by the period of development of the principal aetiological factors. It provides a brief description of the syndrome and its aetiology, estimates of current incidence or prevalence at birth, and current possibilities of prevention. There are difficulties in estimating the frequency of particular disorders. For many, there is little confirmed information and, with the exception of Down's syndrome, each disorder is rare and service populations may be too small to reveal them. Figures may not be applicable everywhere or consistent over time. Studies giving only proportions of particular syndromes amongst the intellectually impaired have little beyond local value. They cannot usefully be compared, since the proportion of each group is affected by the incidence of all other groups. It is therefore, worth discussing the factors affecting the balance of causes in particular populations.

Down's syndrome is prominent in most populations, and changes in prevalence at birth are likely significantly to affect the total. It is especially sensitive to the number of births to older women: thus Down's syndrome is particularly common in Eire where there are traditions of late marriage and large families and policies restricting contraception. In most parts of Britain, northern Europe, and North America, low birth rates recently amongst older women have resulted in few Down's syndrome children. Traditional patterns of consanguineous marriage may produce larger numbers of congenital abnormalities, as in some communities in India, some Jewish communities, and remote rural communities in Sweden. Local customs and conditions may increase environmental causes, such as high rates of alcoholism in North American Indians causing fetal alcohol syndrome.

Environments will also vary. The status of communicable diseases such as measles and pertussis will affect the numbers of intellectually impaired children due to encephalitis or encephalopathy. Hazards in the physical environment such as the presence of lead or the frequency of accidents will also vary in their effects.

The availability and quality of medical care is also an important variable, especially with regard to low birthweight and perinatal causes, which feature prominently in most studies. Health care policies regarding amniocentesis and abortion, or surgical intervention for spina bifida in the presence of significant brain damage, also vary. Finally the expertise and attention given to the elucidation of causes will significantly affect the numbers identified in particular groups.

Since most developed countries share many social changes but not entirely 'in phase', many factors affecting the secular distribution of aetiologies and the balance of causes, will also produce temporal variations. It seems likely that all communities will eventually experience reduced prevalence at birth of Down's syndrome as maternal age distribution changes, though this could be reversed in the most 'advanced' communities. In such communities, Down's syndrome is currently a far smaller proportion of intellectually impaired children under 10 years old than in older groups, where diminishing mortality increased the numbers with Down's syndrome compared to still older cohorts. Similarly, most Down's syndrome children are now born to young mothers. A concurrent reduction in paternal age may also have contributed to the smaller numbers.

There is some evidence of changes in the incidence of perinatal causes over the past 20 years. Though not conclusive, it seems likely that obstetric and neonatal care in the early 1960s saved the lives of many low birthweight babies, but left them damaged, and in some cases severely impaired intellectually. Further improvements in care and a better understanding of early nutritional requirements seem, since then, to have diminished perinatal causes.

Preventive programmes have reduced some specific causes almost to nothing in some communities and others will follow, but these trends are variably offset by increased survival at all ages, so that the distribution of causes will vary between cohorts and, therefore, between different age groups in the current population.

The effect of these changes on the school-age population is considerable. Children with Down's syndrome are relatively easy to teach, pleasant and rewarding, but have become relatively rare. Many brain-damaged children are profoundly impaired. have multiple disabilities including

Table 25.3. *Intellectual impairments: aetiologies, frequencies, and prevention*

(This chart provides a systematic structure for aetiologies contributing to severe intellectual impairment. Frequency data are very difficult to obtain and necessarily vary in time and space: none can be universally or permanently applicable. Data included are drawn from as authoritative sources or recent reviews as possible, but are inevitably particular and provisional. Nevertheless, they give some guidance as to the probable order of frequencies, and readers may update the chart, or localize it to accommodate more reliable or more precise information. References are listed at the end of the chart.)

Disorder		Frequency in population		Relationship to intellectual impairment	Possibility of prevention
(A) Primary disorders (chromosome aberrations; present at conception)					
(1) Down's syndrome	(i, ii)	Maternal Age	Prevalence at Birth/1000		
(a) Trisomy 21 ≃ 94%		20–24	0.67	Probably all intellectually impaired mostly severely	Fundamental cause unknown: Avoidance of high-risk pregnancy in older women. Amniocentesis can detect affected fetus to offer abortion
		25–29	0.89		
		30–34	1.40		
		35–39	4.56		
		40–44	16.01		
		45–49	56.52		
(b) Trisomy Mosaics ≃ 3%			0.03	Very variable	As above
(c) Translocation ≃ 3%			0.03	Probably all intellectually impaired, mostly severely	(Familial) genetic counselling
(2) Other autosomal anomalies (inc. Patau syndrome (Tri. 13) Edward syndrome (Tri. 17 or 18) *Cri-du-chat* syndrome (anom. 5)	(iii)	Prevalence at birth 2.0/1000		Occasionally severe or mild intellectual impairment	None at present
(3) Sex chromosome disorders (mostly Klinefelter syndrome)	(iii)	Prevalence at birth 3/1000		Occasionally severe or mild intellectual impairment	None at present
(4) Non-specific disorders leading to intellectual impairment					
(a) recessive	(iv)	Prevalence at birth Possibly 0.5/1000		By definition all intellectually impaired	None at present
(b) X-linked	(iv, v)	Prevalence at birth 0.1–1.0/1000		By definition all intellectually impaired	None at present
(5) Mechanism not clear—probably primary					
(a) De Lange syndrome		No adequate data		Always intellectually impaired	None at present
(b) Severe hypercalcaemia syndrome		No adequate data		Usually intellectually impaired later in childhood	None at present
(B) Primary disorders with secondary neurological damage (genetic; metabolic or other impairment present at conception; intellectual impairment arises later as a secondary effect)					
(1) Defects of protein metabolism					
(a) Phenylketonuria (PKU)	(iv)	Prevalance at birth 0.05–0.2/1000		Serious intellectual impairment if not treated	Screening programme after birth Special diet required from early infancy: available for PKU and some others
(b) Others	(iv)	Prevalence at birth 0.1/1000		Serious intellectual impairment if not treated	
(2) Defects of carbohydrate metabolism Galactosaemia	(iv)	Prevalence at birth 0.02/1000		Serious intellectual impairment and early death if not treated very early	Screening propgramme after birth Diet available
(3) Defects of lipid metabolism					
(a) Tay–Sach disease	(iv)	Prevalence at birth 0.04/1000 (almost limited to Ashkenazi Jewish communities)		All intellectually impaired: death in early childhood	No treatment available Genetic counselling possible
(b) Batten disease		No adequate data		All intellectually impaired: death in later childhood	No treatment available Genetic counselling possible
(4) Defects of mucopolysaccharide metabolism (mostly Hurler syndrome)	(iv)	Prevalence at birth 0.03/1000		All severely intellectually impaired	No treatment available
(5) Defects of hormone system Congenital hypothyroidism	(vi)	Prevalence at birth 0.1–1.59/1000 (overt) Prevalence at birth 0.25–0.3/1000 (biochem. UK)		Severe intellectual impairment unless treated	Screening programme after birth Treatment with thyroxin from infancy avoids intellectual impairment

Table 25.3.—*continued*

Disorder	Frequency in population	Relationship to intellectual impairment	Possibility of prevention
(6) Mechanism not clear			
(a) Epiloia (tuberous sclerosis) (iv)	Prevalence at birth 0.01/1000	Many severely intellectually impaired	No treatment available
(b) Microcephaly (some)	Very variable in different communities	Very variable	No treatment available

(C) Secondary disorders (normal zygotes at conception affected by environmental insults resulting in neurological damage)

Disorder	Frequency in population	Relationship to intellectual impairment	Possibility of prevention
(1) Antenatal factors			
(a) Neural-tube defects (ix, viii, vii)	Prevalence at birth 1–8/1000 with considerable variation in space and time	Spina bifida and hydrocephalus have very variable effects: possible 10 per cent show severe intellectual impairment Anencephalics will die soon after birth	Dietary supplement before conception may be preventive Early intervention in hydrocephalus may limit damage
(b) Rhesus incompatibility (xviii)	No adequate data Very rare now if pregnancies properly managed	Some show intellectual impairment of various degrees	Immunization during pregnancy
(c) Communicable disease:			
Rubella (x, xi)	Congenital infection 0.03–0.1/1000 births (possibly 80 per cent of surviving pregnancies affected before 13 weeks)	Possibly up to 40 per cent show physical defects: severe intellectual impairments uncommon	Immunization in girls before childbearing age
Cytomegalovirus (xii, xiii)	Congenital infection 2–23/1000 births	0.04–0.4/1000 births	No safe or effective vaccine available
Toxoplasmosis (xiv)	Congenital infection 0.2–1.0/1000	Uncommon	Hygiene in pregnancy may reduce risk
Syphilis	Congenital infection now rare in developed communities	Now very rare in developed communities	Screening and treatment for syphilis in pregnancy
(d) Other agents:			
Fetal alcohol syndrome (FAS) (xv)	Up to 1.7/1000 reported: culturally variable	High proportion of full FAS show serious intellectual impairment	Avoidance of agent during pregnancy
Drugs, Irradiation, etc. (xvi)	Variable: no data	Rare: variable	Avoidance
(2) Perinatal Factors (including gross trauma; hypoxia; hypoglycaemia and cerebral thrombosis)	Prevalence at birth of such factors are virtually unmeasurable except where effects are gross	Some show intellectual impairment of varying degrees Often also show physical impairments	High-quality antenatal and perinatal care. Early feeding of premature babies to avoid hypoglycaemia
Cerebral palsy, of varied aetiology, mostly perinatal (xvii)	Prevalence in school-age children: 2–24/1000: variable diagnostic criteria	$\simeq$ 25 per cent severe intellectual impairment $\simeq$ 20 per cent mild intellectual impairment	As above
(3) Postnatal factors			
(a) Physical trauma; accidents	Incidence is very variable in different communities and at different times	Very variable	General preventive programmes
(b) Communicable disease			
Encephalitis (TB and others)	No data available, but very variable	Very variable	Immunization and treatment programmes
Encephalopathy (pertussis, measles and mumps)	No data available, but very variable	Very variable	Immunization programmes
(c) Chemical agents (especially lead)	Incidence is very variable in space and time	Still in doubt	Remove lead from paint and motor fuel. Replace lead water pipes
(d) Nutritional (especially high-solute feeds with fever)	No adequate data	Very variable	Breast-feeding; Low-solute feeds only

Sources:
(i)   Hook, E.B. (1980). Down syndrome: its frequency in human populations and some factors pertinent to variation in rates. In *Trisomy 21* (Down's syndrome) (eds. F. De la Cruz and P.S. Gerald). MTP, Lancaster.
(ii) Weatherall, J.A.C. (1982). A review of some effects of recent medical practices in reducing the numbers of children born with congenital abnormalities. *Health Trends* **14**, 85.
(iii) Evans, H.J. (1977). Chromosome anomalies among live-births. *J. Med. Gen.* **14**, 309.

(iv)   Carter, C.O. (1977). Monogenic disorders. *J. Med. Gen.* **14**, 316.

(v)   Crawfurd, M. d'A. (1982). Severe mental handicap: pathogenesis, treatment and prevention. *Br. Med. J.* **285**, 762.

(vi)   Chamberlain, J., Graham, R., and Stewart, M.J. (1980). *Screening for congenital mental and physical handicap.* S.W. Thames Regional Health Authority, London.

(vii)   Barron, S.L. and Thomson, A.M. (eds.) (1983). *Obstetrical epidemiology.* Academic Press, London.

(viii)   Leck, I. (1983a). Epidemiological clues to the causation of neural tube defects. In *Prevention of spina bifida and other neural tube defects* (ed. J. Dobbing). Academic Press, London.

(ix)   Leck, I. (1983b). Foetal malformations. In *Obstetrical epidemiology* (eds. S.L. Barron and A.M. Thomson). Academic Press, London.

(x)   Miller, E., Cradock-Wilson, J.E., and Pollock, T.M. (1982). Consequences of confirmed maternal rubella at successive stages of pregnancy. *Lancet* ii, 781.

(xi)   Smithells, R.W. and Sheppard, S. (1982). National congenital rubella surveillance programme, 1971–81. *Br. Med. J.* **285**, 1363.

(xii)   *Lancet* (1983b). Congenital cytomegalovirus infection. *Lancet* i, 801.

(xiii)   Peckham, C.S. *et al.* (1983). Cytomegalovirus infection in pregnancy: preliminary findings from a prospective study. *Lancet* i, 1352.

(xiv)   *Lancet* (1980). Congenital toxoplasmosis. *Lancet* i, 578.

(xv)   *Lancet* (1983a). Alcohol and the foetus—is zero the only option? *Lancet* i, 682

(xvi)   Ashton, H. (1983). Teratogenic drugs. *Adverse Drug Reaction Bull.* **101**, 372.

(xvii)   Alberman, E. (1978). Main causes of major mental handicap: prevalence and epidemiology. In *Major mental handicap: methods and costs of prevention.* CIBA Foundation Symposium. 59 (new series) Elsevier.

(xviii) Zipursky, A. (1977). Rhesus haemolytic disease of the newborn—the disease eradicated by immunology. *Clin. Obstet. Gynaecol.* **20**, 759.

poor communication, and are extremely demanding; these children now feature far more prominently in the classroom and this alters the nature of teaching, and the training and resources required. Similar effects will be seen later in older age groups, but the future differential survival of these aetiological groups cannot be predicted.

Preventive programmes

It is worth summarizing the potential for prevention in terms of community programmes which may affect different aetiologies for convenience of organization. Preventive activity can be described in five levels of application: health promotion; specific protection; early treatment; disability limitation; rehabilitation. The first two are essentially primary prevention of specific impairments; the third is secondary prevention by limiting the length, severity, and complications of disease; and the last two are varieties of tertiary prevention of long-term sequelae.

For many familial disorders, some of which cause intellectual impairment, it is only possible to prevent subsequent births in families with one affected child. Genetic registers allow monitoring and assist genetic counselling. Screening programmes using amniocentesis are now common, though are not properly preventive since they merely allow fetuses with Down's syndrome to be identified for abortion. There are risks to normal fetuses in the procedure and there are problems of false-negatives and positives. It has generally been offered to women aged over 35 years because higher risks in older mothers are seen to justify the costs, but recent changes in maternal age have seriously reduced its effectiveness as the number of older mothers has fallen. Detection of fetal cells in maternal blood samples may become a safer and cheaper screening test in the future.

Neonatal screening programmes to detect inborn errors of metabolism are also common. In Britain there is a nationwide programme that allows early and effective intervention with special diets for affected children. There is some evidence of behaviour problems in treated children, but no severe intellectual impairment. Phenylketonuria has been the main focus of intervention but screening programmes can easily include other metabolic disorders though effective intervention is not yet available for all. A blood sample is taken by heel prick about one week after birth. Cost-benefit studies have proved positive, and a recently developed blood spot test for hypothyroidism can be added to the same programme at little extra cost. Cretinism should now be a thing of the past.

Immunization programmes are relevant to the prevention of intellectual impairment. Though the recent debate about pertussis has concluded that there is no evidence of risk of encephalopathy due to immunization, there are undoubted risks due to infection with the wild virus. Ethical problems in relating individual risks and benefits, and communal risks and benefits, and problems of decision making in government departments and professional bodies compounded the difficulties and confounded the debate (DHSS 1981). Measles immunization of infants and rubella immunization of infants or teenage girls do not share these problems and should be promoted comprehensively. Immunization against sensitization to rhesus positive cells in rhesus-negative women is now effectively preventing kernicteric brain damage. Early diagnosis and more effective treatment of syphilis and tuberculosis have largely prevented congenital syphilis and tubercular meningitis.

Reducing lead in the environment also raises problems of political decision-making and industrial pressure groups. Many countries insist on minimal lead in petrol though this has not been fully accepted in Britain. Paint can also be made lead-free, but lead water pipes in old dwellings are not so easily changed. Control of industrial wastes usually requires legislation and organized monitoring to reduce mercury and radiation hazards. The control of accidents is far more complex and is rarely tackled comprehensively.

Programmes of prevention which aim at behavioural change have had limited success. Personal behaviour is closely interwoven with cultural attitudes, traditions, and pressures. In clearly defined groups, high rates of alcoholism amongst pregnant women may be tackled to prevent fetal alcohol syndrome. Family planning programmes will continue to influence maternal age distribution, and the number of Down's syndrome children conceived, though different emphases will be needed in predominantly Roman Catholic communities. Changing patterns of consanguinity is likely to be difficult where social isolation limits marital choice, or where religious or racial factors predominate. Programmes to prevent Tay–Sachs disease in Ashkenazi Jewish communities in the US were successful but attempts to reproduce this in London failed.

General programmes to improve nutrition, general health, and health care of mothers and children will contribute to the reduction of perinatal causes, and prevention of intellectual impairments, whilst health education has a part to play in promoting any preventive work.

Early diagnosis, including neurological, psychological, and social development assessment, has improved with the establishment of multidisciplinary child assessment centres in many countries. They have focused attention on the limitation of disabilities and the positive habilitation of children with intellectual impairment.

DISABILITY: INDIVIDUAL NEEDS AND CARE

Measurement of disability has only recently been given the attention it deserves, and poses formidable epidemiological problems of standardization of instruments and classification of discrete syndromes of disability. Instruments in use generally provide individual profiles, to help individual programme planning, and monitoring. They use standardized descriptions of type and degree of physical impairment and disability, and often include aspects of social behaviour. The American Association on Mental Deficiency Adaptive Behaviour Scales record coping behaviour in many specific areas of development and maladaptation, while the Gunzberg Progress Assessment Chart identifies inadequacies in self-help skills, communication socialization, and occupation. The Vineland Social Maturity Scale gives a 'social age' score from a wide range of behaviour and skills. Wing's HBS Schedule (Handicap, Behaviour, and Skills) has been used successfully as a research instrument in Britain, Denmark, and Germany and has given rise to a short Disability Assessment Schedule suitable for careful service use. The great demand in recent years for pragmatic disability assessments to guide planning of individual programmes and group facilities has led, in Britain, to official national recommendation of a simple schedule based on Kushlick's pioneering work, recording continence, ambulation, and 'behaviour problems', with some aspects of self-help skills and communication. These records can be translated into four empirical NDG (National Development Group) categories relating to behaviour, skills, and 'need for care'. The danger here is of gross oversimplification of 'needs' in terms of current service provisions.

Beyond individual profiles, storage and analysis of these data is not easy. Discrimination of definable syndromes requires much more sophistication and rigour but has specific relevance and great importance for care, unlike aetiological diagnosis. Syndromes of disability and behaviour (like neurological diagnoses), may relate to several aetiological processes. The clearest example of this, and of its importance, is the emergence of autism as a definable syndrome of disabilities. Its discrimination as a separate entity does not imply any one aetiological process, and indeed, it may result from many, but it has permitted concentrated attention to be given to the special needs of special children with some success. Other syndromes may follow.

Epidemiological investigation of disabilities may also raise causal hypotheses. Work with the HBS schedule is accumulating evidence of different patterns of disability and behaviour in severely intellectually impaired children of different ethnic origins, from different communities and in different sexes. This suggests variations in neurological impairments, perhaps as variations in response to similar environmental insults. More work is needed to explore further this field.

In guiding service planners and care personnel, the best general indicators of need for care seem to be mobility and degree of social interaction, predicting behaviour better than IQ. Mobile, socially impaired children are particularly difficult to manage at home, in school, or in any other setting. Prevalence ratios in British populations are likely to be 0.25–0.5/1000, about 75 per cent of these being severely intellectually impaired, and a small number of normal intelligence.

Many surveys have recorded large numbers of other impairments associated with intellectual impairment, generally increasing with lower IQ. Congenital abnormalities tend to cluster and many aetiological processes produce motor or sensory disorders as well as impairment of intellect, but none are exclusively associated with it. They are described usually as clinical syndromes, or problems of clinical management but are generally ill-defined, and survey results are not readily compared. Because they relate to some aetiologies more than others, these associated disabilities must also vary, especially as survey populations include varying proportions of mild intellectual impairment.

Figures for proportions can therefore, give only crude expectations: they are no substitute for careful description of observed impairments and disabilities. Epilepsy is very common, reported between 20 and 50 per cent of severely intellectually impaired children, many controlled by drugs. Cerebral palsy is reported between 15 and 40 per cent depending on definition and thoroughness of investigation. Significant visual disability is reported in 10 to 30 per cent and hearing defects in up to 5 per cent. Serious speech disorders are extremely common, reported between 60 and 85 per cent. Behaviour problems are very difficult to define: relatively minor ones are extremely common, but gross disturbances which require very specialized provision may be 5 to 10 per cent. The HBS schedule's 'mobile non-sociable' category gives hope of more precision in definition and measurement, and therefore in provision of care. Frank mental illness may have an increased frequency, especially in the mildly impaired, but observation of classical symptoms and signs in the severely impaired is difficult, and the range of clinical syndromes accepted by psychiatrists is very variable.

The first important implication for care is the need for careful and thorough clinical investigation and assessment of impairments, disabilities, and abilities, in standardized form where possible. This will promote clear thinking and encourage programmes of education, habilitation, treatment, and care tailored to individual need and able to be precisely and professionally monitored. It should also clarify the variation in behaviour and function in different environments: assessments in institutional settings or in deprived homes may exaggerate disabilities and problems, and underestimate potential for independence.

The second important implication is that 'good care' means carefully planned positive habilitation or rehabilitation, with clear objectives and professional techniques. It is essential to accept that every impaired person can develop and learn new skills and many can contribute to the community. Early stimulation, even for profoundly impaired children, may be particularly important.

With such a range of disorders it is inevitable that multidisciplinary care is required. Medical treatment needs to be thorough when indicated; behaviour modification programmes should be professionally designed; teaching and nursing needs special skills, and social work requires special experience if the various disabilities of intellectually impaired people are to be minimized and their lives enhanced. Many others may be involved and there is a danger of in-coordination, lack of focus and inefficiency. It is possible for the family to be neglected as the most important source of care, and in their own needs, and for the client himself to be lost to view! In co-ordinating the delivery of care, the 'key worker' concept is valuable especially in the context of community based teams. There are important implications also for staff training in new attitudes, knowledge, and skills relating to the assessment of need and delivery of care.

HANDICAP: COMMUNITY NEED AND SERVICES

Since the latter part of the nineteenth century intellectual impairment has gradually emerged as a distinct and significant problem in developed communities. Severe 'mental deficiency' was at first discriminated from serious mental illness and the extension of primary education revealed lesser degrees of learning difficulty. Associations with poverty and social deprivation fed false eugenic assumptions and fears of progressive degradation of the population if such people were allowed freely to reproduce. Legislative measures were rapidly taken to provide special institutions, usually remote, custodial in character, and housing anything from 50 to 5000 inmates. They were generally under-funded and attracted poor quality and ill-trained staff, yet constituted the bulk of the service for the intellectually impaired, effectively hiding them from public view and promoting stigma and pessimism. Most countries have been struggling in the last 20 years to overcome this tragic inheritance and build a humane, individualized, and professional community based service complex. Most of the current dilemmas in service provision reflect this radical change.

As scientists have engaged major problems in this field,

professionals have focused on individual needs, and parents have demanded their voice to be heard, so have ignorance, fear, stigma, and prejudice been effectively challenged, and optimism, enthusiasm, imagination, and compassion allowed to inform the development of care. Inevitably, progress has varied greatly. For some communities, and some professionals, little has changed: for others practical progress has constantly outstripped plans, and demonstrations of 'good practice' forced revision of expectations, as we relearn that we tend always to underestimate the positive capacities and potential of the intellectually impaired when provided with optimal circumstances, opportunities, and care.

By association with 'mental asylums', institutions developed medical models of care under the domination of doctors within the psychiatric specialty. The word 'mental' remains a source of confusion, though intellectual impairment and mental illness *per se* have relatively little in common, representing different concepts, populations, problems, and solutions. There is, of course, some overlap, where an intellectually impaired child also exhibits bizarre behaviour, or where organic psychiatric disease has sequellae not unlike 'intellectual impairment'. With proliferation of services, the field is now characterized by many professional interests including psychology and education, medicine and nursing, social work, administration, and law. Agencies of care have also multiplied in statutory, voluntary, and private sectors. Medical dominance has largely disappeared in many countries, except in developmental paediatrics, and each professional and specialist group can claim a legitimate contribution. The plethora of personnel, professions, and agencies has raised immense problems of co-ordination and control, with serious risks of confusion, ineffectiveness, and inefficiency. A disorganized service may be adequately resourced and contain all desirable elements, yet fail to provide for individual and family need as and when required.

Comprehensive, community-based services

This overwhelming need places intellectual impairment firmly in the public health domain. Comprehensive, community-based, integrated services are required, with a degree of co-ordination which ensures joint planning, monitoring, and evaluation, a management structure accepted by all agencies, and interdisciplinary team work. There are many examples of partial realization of these principles, and many are moving in this direction.

In the US and Australia, there is great variety of service provision at state level and below. East Nebraska has pioneered a community service of great imagination and committment but many people remain in their large institutions. Western Australia has achieved a service without any large institution for residential care largely based on ordinary-type homes. Queensland is following suit with a rapid shift of philosophy and policy towards non-health-dominated community-based services. In Canada this process has gone further and more generally, with 'cost-sharing' encouragement at federal level. In Denmark and Sweden recent decentralization has been associated with policies of integration into 'normal' services, together with provision for professional advocacy. Norway has been developing interdisciplinary teams.

Israel has a strong element of 'community treatment networks' but they exclude larger residential care establishments, and are controlled nationally. New Zealand has been moving strongly towards comprehensive community-based services since 1974, through a creative partnership between state and voluntary bodies. In Eire, voluntary church bodies, but state funded, provide most care under national 'health' planning, and progress is not easy. It is harder still in the Netherlands, where independent voluntary bodies lack co-ordination though quality of care through a multiplicity of overlapping agencies may be very high. In West Germany, rigidities of service structure make it difficult for the parents and concerned professionals to develop community-based care.

In Britain too there have been strong moves towards comprehensive community—based services, seriously inhibited by the division of responsibility and variation in funding, between local government and NHS district authorities. The principle recommendation from the Sheffield Evaluation Study has resulted in Joint Management proposals with responsibilities shared and delegated from parent authorities (Heron and Myers 1983). Newcastle on Tyne has developed similar policies. In many of these examples, the key issues relate to co-ordinating management from traditionally separate authority structures, and merging funds from several sources.

Professional rigidities also pose problems. It can be argued that medical, and specifically psychiatric domination has generally damaged the interests of intellectually impaired people and their families, in spite of much committed, compassionate, and imaginative work by some individual doctors. It is not that other professional groups should 'take over'—we might expect no better—but that general de-professionalizing of the field might facilitate development of home-based care, rights to 'ordinary' services, and flexible team work.

Normalization and integration

A comprehensive and efficient service, however, does not guarantee high quality unless it is firmly underlain by a strong philosophy emphasizing humane values. Most recent developments have used the principle of 'normalization' (including 'integration') arising from similar values to the 1971 UN Declaration on the Rights of Mentally Retarded People. The principle does not provide a set of rules and is not always easy to apply, but provides a philosophical guide to those who plan or mediate care and a reminder of the essence of client-centred professional work.

Normalization states that people with intellectual impairment have the same human value as others and the same human rights. They are developing human beings, with their own abilities, preferences, and needs, should be involved in decisions affecting their own lives as far as possible, and should not normally be segregated from the rest of the community. They should normally expect to live with their own families or foster parents, and participate in those aspects of community life which give value in their own cultures. Whatever their needs for professional services, the general resources available to other members of the community should be used wherever possible and in similar ways, encouraging maximum independence, and normal social networks. Where special services are required, goals should as far as possible encompass normal valued life-styles and behaviour appropriate to their age and culture.

These are much more difficult to achieve with profound or multiple impairment, where the parent is both the 'key worker' and the 'client' and needs to be involved in all decision making. Services to parents and families and to the intellectually impaired themselves are complementary but their interests are not necessarily the same. If conflicts are to be sensitively resolved, services must be local and accessible, with no barriers of status or stigma, and mediated personally.

A highly personal service is also likely to comply with certain other principles. 'Advocacy' tries to guarantee legal and civil rights, and protection from exploitation, abuse, or degrading treatment. Rights to welfare benefits sometimes require legal or political action; the establishment of voting rights has made little headway yet. Guardianship arrangements are more commonly found. Parents' rights to information are frequently resisted by doctors or social workers and parents frequently complain of the way they were told, or not told, of their child's impairment. Relief of suffering and guilt, and the realization of their potential to help their child are more likely to be achieved if parents are early informed and drawn into the care team. Parent groups and societies have had a key role in stimulating, demanding, and developing services, often in creative partnership with professionals.

The practical application of these principles requires a cadre of domiciliary workers in teams serving small areas. In most developed countries conflicts may arise between social workers, public health nurses or health visitors, 'mental handicap' nurses extending their roles outside institutions, and volunteers or members of parent groups. Roles including practical aid and advice, emotional support and counselling, mediating welfare benefits, parental training, co-ordination and supervision of local residential care, and referral to specialists, are difficult to combine in one person, and current professionals tend to reflect the emphases of their own training and traditions.

Increasing professionalization has characterized both social work and nursing over the past two decades and is prominent in mental-handicap nursing. Relative independence from doctors and their own hierarchy makes domiciliary work attractive, but rarely has training kept pace. They remain, usually, the most numerous care workers committed to the field of intellectual impairment and represent the main resources of personnel for at least the next decade. The challenge is to ensure appropriate re-training for all care workers and to help establish new roles, professional objectives and attitudes and, probably, a new name, to escape from the inappropriate connotations of 'nurse' and the taint of institutional traditions. Common elements of basic training for relevant professions would be useful, but common in-service training built into the structure of the service and properly resourced, is essential.

Priorities for care

Domiciliary care assumes greater importance as more intellectually impaired people live at home with their families or in similar substitute accommodation. The first priority in most services is the avoidance of new admissions to the large institutions. In Britain, admission of children to mental handicap hospitals has virtually ceased and adult admissions are small. More difficult is the rehabilitation of people who suffer additional disabilities from years of institutionalization, with little personal stimulus or responsibility. Many no longer 'belong' to any communities other than those of the hospitals, most of which require dramatic upgrading and improvement if they are to retain even a residual acceptable role. Radically different patterns of residential care cannot be constructed overnight, which raises the dilemma of funding new developments whilst not neglecting the improvement of existing facilities. This should not be allowed to inhibit starting to run down the hospitals and rehabilitate intellectually impaired people in the community.

It generally appears that, where there is an atmosphere of professional optimism and a willingness to support, most parents of intellectually impaired children wish to keep their child at home. They require practical help and support to do this without destruction of their personal or family life. Short-term residential care for week-ends, holidays, or emergencies is important, and need not subject children to the rigours of institutional life, where hostels, houses, or fostering are provided to which parents and children can become familiar before admission. Some are experimenting with a group of substitute 'aunts' and 'uncles' to create something akin to the extended family network seldom available to families in urban industrialized societies. Where medical or surgical treatment requires admission, this should be in a general or paediatric hospital.

As yet there is little provision for young people to leave home when they reach adult life as others do. Few services plan for this but it should not be assumed that intellectually impaired young people, or their parents or siblings, will wish to continue living together for ever. Where the parental home has broken down, or parents have died or become too frail, a wide variety of supervised housing options is required, dispersed throughout the community. Homes, not hospitals, are required. Many hostels for 10–20 people have been built in the last 20 years but are often unsatisfactory. Staff and residents may be isolated and institutional features readily arise, whilst offering a very limited range of relationships and activities. It is possible to break these down into small 'family' groups. Some less-impaired people may live independently, or in twos and threes with varying degrees of assistance. Self-contained flats may be provided alongside non-handicapped people or with a paid warden. Fostering and adoption arrangements are increasing for children and adults, but some require a staffed small-group home. Such arrangements need cost no more than *satisfactory* institutional care, and are likely to offer a much more acceptable quality of life, less stigmatizing, and far more responsive to individual needs. Dwellings can often be provided by voluntary groups, housing associations, or local authorities at no cost to social welfare or health authorities.

An alternative model favoured by some, is the 'village community' where the intellectually impaired may experience freedom of movement, self-care, and personal decision making as much as possible, and a range of relationships and activities within a protected community setting. This is not integrated into the rest of the community, but offers many other elements of normalization which may provide the happiest life-style compromise for some adults.

There are many different examples of 'good practice', but one typical service pattern has emerged with a community team of two or more care professionals supervising 25–30 people in a 'cluster' of about 10 alternative home arrangements in an area of about 20 000 population. At least one home is staffed and forms a focus for communication and domiciliary support within the area. A 'key worker' or 'named person' is the principal worker for any given family or home. Several clusters form a district service providing specialist personnel, facilities, or agencies on referral.

Day services raise different problems. In most developed countries education for the intellectually impaired has made immense progress in the last two decades and frequently shares similar standards of resources, staffing, and organization as for other children. Special schools or special classes are common, but many individuals can be integrated successfully into ordinary classes. However, severely impaired children compete so unfavourably that some are likely to remain best served by special facilities. Early stimulation is of great benefit and this may be given in school, or at home, with parents trained in educational techniques. The 'Portage Project' and its many adaptations have demonstrated the potential of home based programmes (Shearer and Shearer 1972). Parent workshops have also proved of great value.

Leaving school for many intellectually impaired children is a stressful time. Many mildly impaired young adults obtain work, sheltered or not, though in times of economic recession and high unemployment they are likely to be the least-favoured employees. The severely impaired will not generally work in conventional jobs but need the dignity of work, satisfying occupation, and continuing education for their personal and social development. Education is increasingly provided in ordinary Further Education Colleges or the like. Small groups may work in industrial 'enclaves' under supervision, or in semi-commercial sheltered employment, but most countries provide day centres which are generally inadequate in concept, practice, and extent, finding it difficult to reconcile work, occupation, training, and education objectives. Many adults reject them, especially older people, who may remain largely at home with their ageing parents or be admitted to institutional care as the only alternative. The help and companionship which they give should not be undervalued, and the crisis of bereavement and loss of home needs to be anticipated, prepared for, and thoroughly worked through. There is a need everywhere for imaginative provision of day care for older intellectually impaired people to enrich their lives and provide continuity through crises. There is a special challenge posed by profoundly or multiply impaired people, who increasingly are being integrated in 'special needs' units attached to day centres. For clients, families, and professionals, increasing life-expectancy has altered the perspective of education, training, and care.

Evaluation

There is also a need to build evaluation procedures into new forms of service organization and styles of care. The epidemiologist and public health physician must accept much of the responsibility for the paucity of studies or even satisfactory measures. Heron's thorough, though largely descriptive evaluation of the Sheffield development project is one of very few examples of previous experience (Heron and Myers 1983). The PASS evaluation package (Program Analysis of Service Systems—Wolfensberger and Glenn 1975) has proved a useful means of measuring local services against a normalization ideal. The proliferation of District Mental Handicap Registers in recent years as information systems to support and monitor the development of community-based services for intellectually-impaired people, also offers hope for quantitative evaluation of some aspects of care.

CONCLUSIONS

Intellectual impairment is the result of many different aetiologies, some of which we can now prevent. In the last 10 years the prevalence at birth has diminished but survival has greatly increased. A very large cohort is currently found in most developed countries in the young adult age group, and increasing numbers are expected to reach old age. Already there are generally more severely impaired people over 45 than under 15 years of age.

Their needs are individual and varied, and thorough assessment of the full range of disabilities can be standardized and individual programmes monitored. Services should be guided by the general principles of normalization and integration, which accord intellectually impaired individuals as far as possible the same rights, privileges and responsibilities as other people, to live according to common expectations of life-style in their own culture, neither isolated nor alienated from their peers and neighbours. They should not be made invisible, however, to planners of services and providers of resources, for they necessarily need positive discrimination.

There is much to overcome from the past. Although intellectually impaired people have not offended, they have been put in custodial care; although they pose no threat to the community, their lives have been removed to distant institutions; although they are not sick, they have been dominated by doctors. This is all changing. Increasingly, need for medical care, education, substitute home, and so on, are being

judged on similar criteria to the rest of the population, and provided by the same agencies and personnel. They and their families are people first and foremost, with a wide range of common cultural expectations which are not easy to fulfil for the severely intellectually impaired.

Care in the community and by the community is probably no more expensive than institution-based care, but it is more demanding, if potentially more satisfying, for personnel. It is difficult to maintain the necessary commitment, imagination, zest, and sensitivity without full support of senior personnel and service managers, and satisfactory pay and conditions of service. The public health challenge is to facilitate clients themselves, their families, and the full range of general social services providing conditions for satisfactory lives for intellectually impaired people and their personal care-providers, in a comprehensive, community-based service, sensitively supplemented where necessary with specialist assistance. Designing new management structures, making them work, and undertaking vigorous evaluation are part of the challenge which makes intellectual impairment one of the most exciting current fields of activity.

BIBILIOGRAPHY

General

Bicknell, J. (1981). *Mental handicap in the eighties.* National Society for Mentally Handicapped Children and Adults, London.

Clarke, A.D.B. and Mittler, P. (eds.) (1980). *Mental retardation: prevention, amelioration and service delivery. Joint Commission on International Aspects of Mental Retardation. A Report Commissioned by the World Health Organization.* International League of Societies for People with Mental Handicap, Brussels.

Clarke, A.M. and Clarke, A.D.B. (eds.) (1985). *Mental deficiency: the changing outlook.* 4th edn. Methuen, London.

Cooper, B. (ed.) (1981). *Assessing the handicaps and needs of mentally retarded children.* Academic Press, London.

Fryers, T. (1984*a*) Current issues in intellectual impairment. In *Recent advances in community medicine.* 3rd edn (ed. A. Smith). Oxford.

Greer, J.G., Anderson, R.M., and Odle, S.J. (1982). *Strategies for helping severely and multiply handicapped citizens.* UPP, Baltimore and MTP, Lancaster.

Matson, J.L. (1981). *Philosophy and care of the mentally retarded: a worldwide status report.* Pergamon, Oxford.

Mittler, P. (ed.) (1977). *Research to practice in mental retardation, Vol. 1. Care and intervention. Vol. 2. Education and training. Vol. 3. Biomedical aspects.* UPP, Baltimore.

Mittler, P. (1979). *People not patients. Problems and policies in mental handicap.* Methuen, London.

Mittler, P. (ed.) (1981). *Frontiers of knowledge in mental retardation, Vol. 1. Social education and behavioural aspects. Vol. 2. Biomedical aspects.* UPP, Baltimore and MTP, Lancaster.

Mittler, P. and McConachie, H. (1983). *Parents, professionals and mentally handicapped people. Approaches to partnership.* Croom Helm, Beckenham.

Ryan, J. and Thomas, F. (1980). *The politics of mental handicap.* Penguin, Harmondsworth.

Shearer, A. (1981*a*). *Disability: whose handicap?* Blackwell, Oxford.

Williams, P. and Shoultz, B. (1982). *We can speak for ourselves. Self advocacy by mentally handicapped people.* Souvenir, London.

Epidemiology

Belmont, L. (ed.) (1981). Severe mental retardation across the world: epidemiological studies. *Int. J. Mental Health* **10**(1).

Birch, H.G., Richardson, S.A., Baird, D., Horobin, G., and Illsley, R. (1970). *Mental subnormality in the community—a clinical and epidemiological study.* Williams and Wilkins, Baltimore.

Elwood, J.M. and Elwood, J.H. (1980). *Epidemiology of anencephalus and spina bifida.* Oxford University Press.

Fryers, T. (1984b). *Epidemiology of severe intellectual impairment. The dynamics of prevalence.* Academic Press, London.

Grossman, H.J. (1983). *Classification in mental retardation.* American Association on Mental Deficiency, Washington, DC.

Innes, G., Johnson, A.W. and Millar, W.M. (1978). *Mental subnormality in north-east Scotland. A multi disciplinary study of total population.* Scottish Health Service Studies No. 38. Scottish Home and Health Department, Edinburgh.

Richardson, S. (1985). Epidemiology. In *Mental deficiency: the changing outlook.* 4th edn (eds. A.M. Clarke and A.D.B. Clarke). Methuen, London.

Schmidt, M.H. and Remschmidt, H. (eds.) (1983). *Epidemiological approaches in child psychiatry, II. International symposium, Mannheim 1981.* Georg Thieme Verlag, Stuttgart and Thieme-Stratton, New York.

World Health Organization (1978). *Mental disorders: glossary and guide to their classification in accordance with the ninth revision of the international classification of diseases.* WHO, Geneva.

World Health Organization (1980). *International classification of impairments, disabilities, and handicaps: a manual of classification relating to the consequences of disease.* WHO, Geneva.

Impairment, disability, and prevention

Anastasiow, N.J. *et al.* (1982). *Identifying the developmentally delayed child.* Edward Arnold, London.

Barron, S.L. and Thomson, A.M. (eds.) (1983). *Obstetrical epidemiology.* Academic Press, London.

Brent, R.L. and Harris, M.I. (1979). *Prevention of embryonic, fetal and perinatal disease.* Castle House Publications, Tunbridge Wells.

Bricker, D.D. (ed.) (1982). *Intervention with at-risk and handicapped infants.* Edward Arnold, London.

Carter, C.H. (1979). *Handbook of mental retardation syndromes,* 3rd edn. Thomas, Springfield, Illinois.

Cleland, C.C. (1979). *The profoundly mentally retarded.* Prentice-Hall, London.

Cockburn, F. (1982). *Inborn errors of metabolism in humans* (Proceedings of the International Symposium, Interlaken, Switzerland). MTP, Lancaster.

Davies, J.A. and Dobbing, J. (eds.) (1981). *Scientific foundations of pediatrics,* 2nd edn. Heinemann, London.

De La Cruz, F. and Gerald, P.S. (eds.) (1980). *Trisomy 21 (Down's syndrome).* MTP, Lancaster.

DHSS (1981). *Whooping cough: reports from the Committee on Safety of Medicines and the Joint Committee on Vaccination and Immunisation.* HMSO, London.

Dobbing, J. (ed.) (1983). *Prevention of spina bifida and other neural tube defects.* Academic Press, London.

Illingworth, R.S. (1982). *Basic developmental screening 0–4 years,* 3rd edn. Blackwell, London.

Lewis, M. and Taft, L.T. (eds.) (1982). *Developmental disabilities: theory assessment and intervention.* MTP, Lancaster.

McCormack, M.K. (ed.) (1980). *Prevention of mental retardation and other developmental disabilities.* Pediatric häbilitation series, Vol. 1. Marcel Dekker, Switzerland.

Matson, J.L. and Barrett, R.P. (1982). *Psychopathology in the mentally retarded.* Grune and Stratton, New York.

Thompson, R.J. and O'Quinn, A.N. (1979). *Developmental disabilities: etiologies, manifestations and treatments.* Oxford University Press, New York.

United Nations Educational, Scientific and Cultural Organization (1982). *Handicapped children: early detection, intervention and education. Selected case studies from: Argentina, Canada, Denmark, Jamaica, Jordan, Nigeria, Sri Lanka, Thailand and the United Kingdom.* UNESCO, Paris.

Valletutti, P.J. (1979). *Preventing physical and mental disabilities: multidisciplinary approaches.* UPP, Baltimore.

Wing, L. (1980). *Autistic children,* 2nd edn. Constable, London.

Wing, L. and Gould, J. (1979). Severe impairments of social interaction and associated abnormalities in children: epidemiology and classification. *J. Autism Devel. Disorders* **9**, 11.

World Health Organization (1980). *Early detection of handicap in children.* WHO, Geneva.

Community service overview: law, planning, evaluation

Boswell, D.M. and Wingrove, J.M. (eds.) (1975). *The handicapped person in the community: a reader and sourcebook.* Tavistock, London and Open University Press, Milton Keynes.

Brown, J. (1980). *Hospital and community: the integration of services.* National Society for Mentally Handicapped Children and Adults, London.

Burgdorf, R.L. (ed.) (1980). *The legal rights of handicapped persons: cases, materials, and text.* Paul H. Brookes, Baltimore.

Flynn, R.J. and Nitsch, K.E. (eds.) (1981). *Normalisation, social integration and community services.* UPP, Baltimore.

Gladstone, D. (1982). Community, co-ordination and collaboration: some themes in policy for the mentally handicapped. In *The year book of social policy in Britain 1980–81* (ed. C. Jones and J. Stevenson). Routledge and Kegan Paul, London.

Gostin, L. (1983). *A practical guide to mental health law.* MIND, London.

Hayes, S.C. and Hayes, R. (1982). *Mental retardation law, policy and administration.* The Law Book, Sydney.

Heron, A. (1982). *Better services for the mentally handicapped? Lessons from the Sheffield Evaluation Studies.* King's Fund Project Paper No. 34. King's Fund Centre, London.

Heron, A. and Myers, M. (1983). *Intellectual impairment. The battle against handicap.* Academic Press, London.

Independent Development Council (1982). *Elements of a comprehensive local service for people with mental handicap.* Independent Development Council for People with Mental Handicap, London.

Jones, K. (1960). *Mental health and social policy 1845–1959.* Routledge and Kegan Paul, London.

Kahn, J. and Kamerman, S.B. (1976). *Child-care program in nine countries: a report from the Cross-National Studies of Social Services Systems,* Columbia University School of Social Work. US Department of Health, Education and Welfare, Office of Child Development, Research, and Evaluation Division, Washington, DC.

King's Fund (1982). *An ordinary life. Comprehensive locally-based residential services for mentally handicapped people.* King's Fund Project Paper No. 24. King's Fund Centre, London.

Kuh, D. (1978). *Review of the technique 'Program Analysis of Service Systems' (PASS).* Institute of Biometry and Community Medicine, The University, Exeter.

Mittler, P. (1980). *Mental handicap: progress, problems and priorities. A review of mental handicap services in England since the 1971 White Paper.* DHSS, London.

Mittler, P. and Serpell, R. (1985). Services: an international perspective. In *Mental deficiency: the changing outlook*, 4th edn (eds. A.M. Clarke and A.D.B. Clarke). Methuen, London.

National Development Group for the Mentally Handicapped (1980). *Improving the quality of services for mentally handicapped people. A checklist of standards.* DHSS, London.

North Western Regional Health Authority (1982). *Services for people who are mentally handicapped: a model district service.* NWRHA, Manchester.

Raynes, N.V., Pratt, M.W., and Roses, S. (1979). *Organisational structure and the care of the mentally retarded.* Croom Helm, London.

Roos, P. *et al.* (1980). *Shaping the future: comunity-based residential services and facilities for mentally retarded people.* UPP, Baltimore.

Snowden, L.R. (ed.) (1982). *Reaching the underserved. Mental health needs of neglected populations*, Vol. 3. Sage Annual Reviews of Community Mental Health. Sage, London.

Sterner, R. (1976). *Social and economic conditions of the mentally retarded in selected countries.* International League of Societies for People with Mental Handicap, Brussels.

Susser, M. (1968). *Community psychiatry: epidemiologic and social themes.* Randon House, New York.

Wagenfield, M.O., Lemkau, P.V., and Justice, B. (eds.) (1982). *Public mental health; perspectives and prospects*, Vol. 5. Sage Studies in Community Mental Health. Sage, London.

Welsh Office (1978). *NIMROD: report of a joint working party on the provision of a community-based mental handicap service in South Glamorgan.* Welsh Office, Cardiff.

Welsh Office (1983). *All Wales strategy for the development of services for mentally handicapped people.* Welsh Office, Cardiff.

Wood, G.E. (1983). *Care of the mentally handicapped. Past and present.* Wright, Bristol.

World Health Organization (1978). *Care of the mentally retarded in the community.* WHO, Copenhagen.

Wolfensberger, W. and Glenn, L. (1975). *Program analysis of service systems.* National Institute for Mental Retardation, Toronto.

Elements of care

Barber, J.H. and Kratz, C.R. (eds.) (1980). *Towards team care.* Churchill Livingstone, Edinburgh.

Bellamy, G.T., Horner, R.H., and Inman, D.P. (1979). *Vocational habilitation of severely retarded adults.* UPP, Baltimore.

Bradley, V.J. (1978). *Deinstitutionalization of developmentally disabled persons: a conceptual analysis and guide.* UPP, Baltimore.

Darnbrough, A. and Kinrade, D. (1979). *Directory for the disabled: a handbook of information and opportunities for disabled and handicapped people.* Woodhead-Faulkner for the Royal Association for Disability and Rehabilitation, Cambridge.

DHSS (1979). *Report of the Committee of Enquiry into Mental Handicap Nursing and Care.* Commd. 7468-1. HMSO, London.

Dybwad, R.F. (ed.) (1979). *International directory of mental retardation resources.* US Department of Health, Education and Welfare, President's Committee on Mental Retardation, Washington.

Fryers, T. (1983). *Standardisation of district mental handicap registers.* APMH, London.

Gathercole, C.E. (1981). *Residential alternatives for adults who are mentally handicapped*, 1–4. British Institute of Mental Handicap, Kidderminster.

Hofmann, T. (ed.) (1983). *Altwerden von Menschen mit geistiger Behinderung. Vortrage, Berichte und erganzende Beitrage zum Internationalen Workshop 1981.* Marburg/Lahn.

King's Fund (1982). *The portage model of home learning services.* King's Fund Centre, London.

King's Fund (1983). *Long term and community care.* Report KFC 83/79. King's Fund Centre, London.

National Development Group for the Mentally Handicapped (1977). *Pamphlets 1–5.* National Development Group, London.

National Development Group for the Mentally Handicapped (1978). *Helping mentally handicapped people in hospital. A report to the Secretary of State for Social Services.* DHSS, London.

Oswin, M. (1978). *Children living in long stay hospitals.* Spastics International Medical Publications and Heinemann, London.

Plank, M. (1982). *Teams for mentally handicapped people. A report of an enquiry into the development of multidisciplinary teams.* Enquiry Paper 10. Campaign for Mentally Handicapped Publications, Gamlingay, Bedfordshire.

Plog, S.C. and Santamour, M.B. (eds.) (1980). *The year 2000 and mental retardation.* Plenum, London.

Roos, P., McCann, B.M., and Addison, M.R. (eds.) (1980). *Shaping the future: community-based residential services and facilities for mentally retarded people.* UPP, Baltimore.

Russell, O. and Ward, L. (1983). *Houses or homes? Evaluating ordinary housing schemes for people with mental handicap.* Centre on Environment for the Handicapped, London.

Shearer, A. (1983). *Living independently.* King's Fund/CEH, London.

Sweeney, D.P. and Wilson, T.Y. (eds.) (1979). *Double jeopardy. The plight of aging and aged developmentally disabled persons in mid-America. A research monograph.* University of Michigan.

Ward, L. (1982). *People first: developing services in the community for people with mental handicap: a review of recent literature.* King's Fund Centre, London.

Wilkin, D. (1979). *Caring for the mentally handicapped child.* Croom Helm, London.

Many important publications on services for intellectually impaired people are available from:

The Campaign for Mentally Handicapped People (CMH), London, UK.

The King's Fund, London, UK.

The Association of Professionals for People with Mental Handicap (APMH), London, UK.

The British Institute of Mental Handicap (BIMH), Kidderminster, UK.

Royal MENCAP, London, UK.

The President's Committee on Mental Retardation (PCMR), Washington, DC.

The National Institute for Mental Retardation (NIMR), Toronto, Canada.

The American Association for Mental Deficiency (AAMD), Washington, DC.

The International League of Societies for People with Mental Handicap (ILSMH), Brussels.

Other national associations.

26 Special needs of the elderly

Robert L. Kane

INTRODUCTION

This chapter looks at the special needs of the elderly, an area conspicuous for its lack of clarity. Not only do such discussions raise moral questions, the very terms employed are imprecise. Much of the collected data relate to a population aged 65 years and older, as though such a boundary created a homogeneous subgroup; it does not.

The demographic facts are closely linked with epidemiological puzzles. While mortality is declining, the changes in morbidity are less clear. The numbers of the elderly are growing, but their status is uncertain. The absolute growth in disabled persons has obvious implications for services, but the most effective configuration of services is not often established.

The chapter attempts to link demography and policy questions through the common ground of programmes needed and available to meet the demands of the elderly. Despite the anachronistic nature of the definition, we will retain the age 65 years as the threshold (this designation goes back at least a century to the era of Bismarck's social insurance programme and surely deserves reconsideration in modern light), but will attend more closely to the differences inherent in this enforced collectivity.

One indication of technological development is the proportion of elderly in a population. One measure of how civilized we are is how we treat those elderly. From the perspective of species survival, the old offer no great benefit once they have passed the reproductive years. In an era of technological explosion, the traditional role of the elderly as the repository of wisdom is less applicable. Economists are likely to see the elderly as consumers of services rather than producers; they tend to be classified in the numerator of dependency ratios.

Several factors outline the special needs and the special circumstances of the elderly in the 'developed' countries. They are:

- the fastest-growing segment of the population
- disproportionately heavy users of medical services
- less likely than other subgroups to have natural social support groups.
- vulnerable to a variety of insults: physical, psychological, economical, and social

Any examination of the circumstances of the elderly must recognize the need to deal with multiple facets of the problem simultaneously. Programmes developed to sustain the elderly must recognize this interrelationship. The elderly maintain a tenuous equilibrium; a disruption in one sector can often lead to disorganization in the entire system. Because of this tendency toward a final common pathway, discussions about the care of the elderly too often become embroiled in non-production arguments about the relative advantages of a social or medical model when, in fact, both perspectives must be harnessed.

Discussions about the needs of the elderly must first recognize the danger of over simplification. The ecological fallacy is as prevalent here as elsewhere. The elderly are a very heterogeneous group. Simply being old does not imply a great deal about one's health status except often as eligibility for various public (and sometimes private) programmes.

Science has not yet identified the basis of ageing, nor has it been very successful in separating so-called 'normal ageing' from the results of accumulating chronic diseases. One of the great epidemiological challenges lies in establishing this distinction. We are still at the stage of trying to construct cohort data from cross-sectional sources. As more longitudinal information becomes available, we are even beginning to question the few things we thought we knew. For example, the studies done by Shock and his colleagues suggested a general pattern of declining organ function at a rate of about 1 per cent per year beginning in young adulthood (Shock 1977). Old age was then marked as that period when this decline crossed a clinical threshold and became symptomatic, at least in times of stress. But much of these data were based on cross-sectional data of different age groups. More recent data, based on longitudinal studies (Schaie 1970) and inter-cohort comparisons (Svanborg *et al.* 1982), have suggested that the rate of decline for an individual may have been over-emphasized. The decline may begin much later or may not begin at all.

At this point, we face more confusion than clarity. Careful epidemiological and clinical work is needed, but such longitudinal research is slow and difficult to maintain. The results, however, will have major implications for health planning.

DEMOGRAPHY

The basic demographic trends seem more certain. The proportion of elderly persons is growing. This is already apparent in the developed world and a similar pattern can

Table 26.1. *Population estimates—1980–2020*

Item	Total population (millions)	% ≥60 years	% ≥65 years	% ≥70 years	% ≥80 years
1960					
World	3037.2	8	5	3	1
More developed regions*	944.9	13	8	5	1
Less developed regions†	2092.3	6	4	2	0.4
1980					
World	4432.1	8	6	4	1
More developed regions	1131.3	15	11	7	2
Less developed regions	3300.8	6	4	2	0.4
2000					
World	6118.9	10	7	4	1
More developed regions	1272.2	18	13	9	2
Less developed regions	4846.7	7	5	3	1
2020					
World	7813.0	12	8	5	1
More developed regions	1360.2	22	16	10	3
Less developed regions	6452.8	11	7	4	1

*More developed regions include North America, Japan, Europe, Australia, New Zealand, and USSR.
†Less developed regions include Africa, Latin America, China, East Asia (excluding Japan), South Asia, Melenesia, and Micronesia-Polynesia.
Source: UN data cited by Siegel (1982).

be predicted for the less developed countries over the next half-century. Table 26.1 describes the United Nations' demographic forecasts of world population through to the year 2020. The proportion of persons aged 65 years and older will almost double over the 60-year span. Less clear in the table, by 1980, there were more elderly persons in the less-developed nations than in the more developed regions of the world. By 2020, two out of every three persons 65 years and older will live in the less developed regions.

Although demographic forecasts about the aged are usually made with confidence because all the people described have alread been born, the more current projections have been called into question as underestimates. Predictions about the elderly are a product of two basic components: births and deaths. The numbers of elderly in the US are expected to swell through the early part of the next century as the post-Second World War baby boom ages, but even those with large numbers may be increased as a result of reduced mortality rates among the elderly (Fig. 26.1). If the current reduction in death rate attributable to cardiovascular disease (which accounts for two-thirds of the deaths of those reaching age 65 years) persists, there may be far more elderly in the US by the turn of the century. Between 1970 and 1978, the death rate for diseases of the heart among those 65 years and older fell by 10 per cent (Brody and Brock, in press).

The expected additional years of life for the elderly have increased in the last 25 years (Table 26.2). The average 65-year-old man in the US can now expect to live another 14 years, and a woman, over 18 years. Programmes based on serving the elderly, such as retirement benefits, must contend with the economic impact of this achievement.

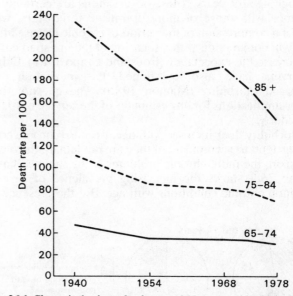

Fig. 26.1. Change in death rate for those aged 65 years or older, United States 1940–78. (Source: Brody and Brock (in press).)

Table 26.2. *Expected years of life remaining at age 65 years, United States*

Population	1940	1968	1978
White male	12.1	12.8	14.0
Non-white male	12.2	12.1	14.1
White female	13.6	16.4	18.4
Non-white female	13.9	15.1	18.0

Source: Brody and Brock (in press).

The differential life-expectancy between the sexes, which is greater than the differences between whites and non-whites, has produced a nation of widows. Not only are women more likely than men to be widowed, they are more likely to survive widowhood (Helsing *et al.* 1981). As a result of this asynchrony, the living arrangements for older men and women differ substantially. As shown in Fig. 26.2, women are much more likely to live alone. This lack of social support may render them more susceptible to institutionalization as disabilities develop.

The reductions in mortality can produce increases in the prevalence of morbidity. Unfortunately, data on morbidity are much less abundant and less precise than those for mortality. Recent US data support the contention that persons with chronic illnesses are surviving and consequently increasing the prevalence of chronic disease morbidity. Using published reports from the National Center for Health Statistics' National Health Interview Survey, Colvez and Blanchet (1981) described an increase in disability rates for various age groups, including those age 65 years and older, over the ten years from 1966 to 1976. Unfortunately, they had to rely on only published data and could not disaggregate the rates for the elderly subgroups. Feldman (1982) has shown a similar increase in work disability rates over the decades 1970–80 for five-year age groups through age 69 years. These observations are certainly at variance with those of more optimistic forecasters, who expect a compression of the period of chronic disease morbidity in conjunction with a squaring of the life-span curve to increase life-expectancy (Fries and Crapo 1981). Other observers have also questioned the inevitability of increased morbidity (Manton 1980). The question has major implications for any estimates of the service needs of the elderly.

Morbidity does increase with age. Because chronic conditions tend to accumulate (if they are not lethal), the older a person, the more chronic problems he or she may have. Figure 26.3 shows the increasing prevalence of several common chronic conditions with age. But the presence of

chronic disease is not tantamount to disability. Figure 26.4 shows a similar pattern of progressive disability with age. Here the measure of disability is reflected in limitations on an individual's ability to perform his or her major activity. Such a measure is clearly sensitive to varying definition with age and social role. None the less, even among those 85 years and over, 40 per cent report no limitation, and only a third are unable to carry on their major activity.

As the measure of disability becomes more discrete, the proportion of disabled changes. Assessment of mobility limitations indicates that less than 10 per cent of the very old are confined to bed and less than 20 per cent are confined to their home (Fig. 26.5). Figure 26.6 looks at basic

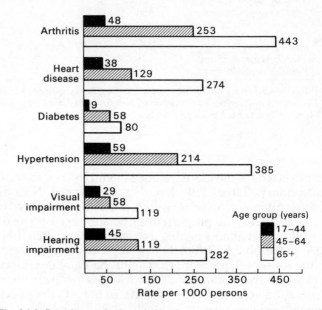

Fig. 26.3. Prevalence of selected chronic conditions, United States, 1979. (Source: Allen and Brotman (1981).)

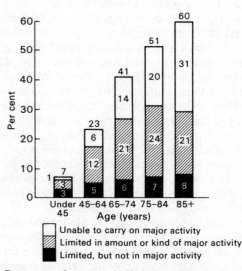

Fig. 26.4. Percentage of persons with limitation of activity due to a chronic condition, by age group and type of limitation, United States, 1979. Elderly in institutions are excluded. (Source: Allan and Brotman (1981).)

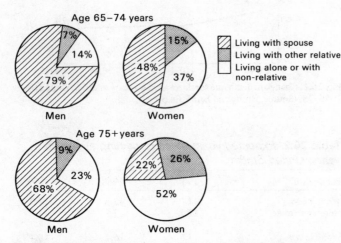

Fig. 26.2. Living arrangements of non-institutionalized men and women aged 65 years and older by age, United States 1979. (Source: Allen and Brotman (1981).)

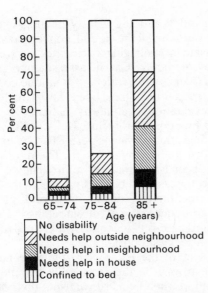

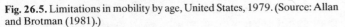

Fig. 26.5. Limitations in mobility by age, United States, 1979. (Source: Allan and Brotman (1981).)

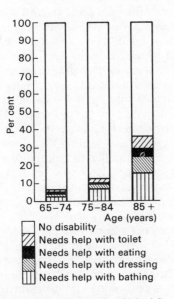

Fig. 26.6. Limitations in self-care activities, United States, 1979. (Source. Allan and Brotman (1981).)

self-care activities often referred to as activities of daily living (ADL). Both these figures address only the community-dwelling elderly; both demonstrate a pattern of increasing disability with age, with the inflection point after age 75 years.

Thus, regardless of whether there is a true inter-cohort change in morbidity rates, the ageing of the population—especially the rapid growth among the very oldest groups—will mean an overall increase in morbidity among the elderly.

UTILIZATION OF HEALTH CARE SERVICES

The increasing morbidity rates in the absence of access barriers to care should result in proportionately greater use of health care services among the elderly. The basic patterns confirm this trend, but the specific uses made of services vary according to the type of care system available. In the US, elderly persons seem to use more hospital and institutional services and fewer ambulatory services than would be predicted from the age-specific disability rates (Kane *et al.* 1981). The discrepancies correspond to the incentives under the several health payment programmes for the elderly. Table 26.3 summarizes some of the differences in utilization rates for various health care services with age.

Table 26.3. *Health service utilization by various age groups in the United States*

Health service utilization	Age group (years)		
	45–64	65–74	75+
Mean number of physician contacts per year	5.7	6.9	6.8
Mean number of dental visits per year	1.8	1.3	0.8
Percentage seeing a physician in past year	76*	80	81
Percentage seeing a dentist in past year	58.8	34.7	22.7
Nursing-home residents per 1000 persons	3.7	12	97.3†
Non-federal hospital days per non-institutionalized person	1.75	3.28	5.86
Operations per 1000 persons	124.6	165.9‡	

*Rate for ages 50–64 years.
†Rate for ages 75–84 is 58.9 and for 85+ is 236.6.
‡Rate for ages 65+.
Sources: Composite data from the Health Interview Survey, US DHEW National Center for Health Statistics, Series 10; and special analyses of NHIS data by Rand.

The pattern of disproportionately high utilization among the elderly and concomitantly high costs of health care has been the subject of much concern. Rice and Feldman (1982) summarize the concern of American health-care officials for the future. At present in the US, the 11 per cent of the population aged 65 years and over accounts for almost 30 per cent of personal health care expenditures. By the year 2040, the proportion of elderly in the country will have doubled, and it is projected that they will use nearly half the nation's personal health-care resources (Fig. 26.7).

Each advance in medical technology hangs like a two-edged sword. As mortality is postponed, high-cost care is clustered around the terminal years of life, now moved into the ninth decade. As Brody and Brock (in press) note, 30 per cent of all deaths now occur in the small group of persons aged over 80 years. These deaths are often expensive (Schroeder *et al.* 1979). In the US, the Health Care Financing Administration has repeatedly noted that a disproportionate amount of an individual's lifetime health expenditures are clustered in the last year of life. As economic pressures grow, increasing attention it being focused on the elderly, especially the dependent elderly.

The concern is based in part on the actual pattern of expenditures, but it is also based on societal values. There

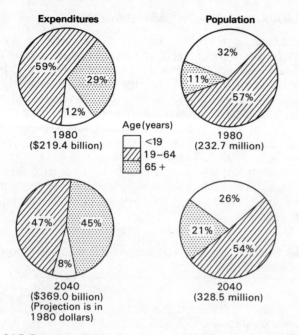

Fig. 26.7. Percentage distribution of personal health care expenditures and population by age-group and year. (Source: Rice and Feldman (1982).)

remains a bias toward the young. Whether we cite economic arguments of potential social contribution or a belief that an older person has 'had a full life' but a child is an innocent victim, or a sense that there is nothing one can do in the face of inevitable deterioration, the older person is at a great disadvantage in the competition for scarce resources. We are all familiar with examples of this prejudice, which Butler (1975) has termed 'agism'. As economic conditions decline, the elderly may become even more of a scapegoat (Binstock 1978; Hudson 1978).

The prejudice against the elderly carries over also into areas of care. Perhaps one of the most difficult challenges in medicine is the distinction between changes characteristic of normal ageing and those that represent pathology. Intellectually, the distinction is complicated because a hallmark of ageing is the accumulation of chronic diseases and their sequelae. To talk about pure ageing changes, we must move into the laboratory. Plans for population-based longitudinal studies that exclude those with chronic illness represent very biased samples. It is equivalent to using germ-free animals to study infection.

The elderly present difficult diagnostic challenges because of our inability to identify readily those changes that are natural concomitants of biological ageing from those attributable to chronic illness and those associated with the other processes that accompany ageing (for example, bereavement and retirement). It is not at all clear when the answers are more likely to be found in traditional medical responses and when the best response involves a change in environment to support the older person's performance and encourage autonomy.

What is clear is the need for careful assessment to unravel

the problem and its aetiology. Hasty labelling may impose a tremendous burden. All the careful, concerned support will not compensate for managing a demented person who does not really have dementia. Careful assessment of patients has been shown to uncover a variety of treatable conditions. In some areas, special units have been established to conduct systematic evaluations of elderly patients to seek both medical and functional problems (Rubenstein *et al.* 1982). In other settings, this service is performed by existing geriatric units (Brocklehurst *et al.* 1978). The traditional battle between the social and medical approaches is irrelevant. The elderly often need both. The first task of the health care system is to treat the remediable. Its second is to avoid the iatrogenic consequences of mislabelling. The equally important third task, is to recognize the critical role of environmental and social support.

The problem of the elderly are multifaceted. Often a single problem may be the result of a complex chain of decompensation whereby a critical event disrupts the individual's delicate equilibrium. Because the elderly person may suffer from a number of simultaneous conditions, an important adjunct of the traditional diagnostic nomenclature is the use of functional assessment—measures that express the individual's ability to carry out a variety of tasks necessary for daily life (Kane and Kane 1981). Such assessments must recognize that an individual's functional state is the result of both his or her basic state of health and the environment in which he or she lives. The same individual can be functional in one setting and dysfunctional in another. This important distinction underlies the World Health Organiation's International Classification of Impairments, Disabilities and Handicaps (WHO 1980).

The common presenting problems of elderly persons can be conveniently listed as a series of 'Is': immobility; instability; incontinence; intellectual impairment; infection; impairment of vision and hearing (eyes and ears); isolation (depression); inanition (malnutrition); impecunity; iatrogenesis; insomnia; immune deficiency; and impotence (sexual dysfunction).

A problem may occur for a variety of diverse reasons. For example, an individual may be immobilized by a broken hip, by severe angina, or by arthritis. But he may also be immobilized by fear. The elderly patient with a successfully repaired hip fracture may be unwilling to walk again for fear of falling and sustaining another fracture. Or an elderly person living in a deteriorated neighbourhood may be confined to his or her home, not because of physical limitations, but because he or she fears being molested. Such an individual may decide to enter a long-term care institution to seek a safer environment. In each instance, the physician and co-workers must obtain a sufficient history to understand the true aetiology of the problem if they are to develop a successful approach to remedying the condition.

At a somewhat more subtle level, physicians must be aware of the forces that foster dependency among caregivers. Patients may be immobile because of the care they get. One important factor is risk-aversion. Nursing personnel may be reluctant to mobilize a patient for fear he or she will fall and sustain an injury. Staff need to be assured that they will not be penalized for appropriately activating patients. Nor is risk-aversion confined to professionals. Families may be equally protective, insisting on limiting an older relative's activities or moving him or her to a more closely supervised situation. Such fears are often infused with guilt and may be manifested as anger. Families can be helped to see the dangers of such restricted activity.

Another factor in generating dependency is cost. It is often much easier and cheaper to do things *for* people with limitations of function than to invest the effort needed to encourage them to do for themselves. Unfortunately, such savings are short-ranged; they will increase the level of dependency and ultimately the amount of care needed.

The list of Is includes iatrogenesis. The least-desirable outcome of medical care is to decrease the patient's health as a result of his or her contact with the care system. In some cases, there is a real risk that untoward consequences of treatment may worsen a patient's health. The risk–benefit calculation as a basis for urging intervention must be performed carefully for each elderly patient in the context of his or her condition. Many risks are within the ordinary bounds of medicine.

We are concerned here with those events that result from indifferent or superficial care. The physician who casually adds another drug to the patient's polypharmacy portfolio is playing with a living chemistry set. The reduced rate of drug metabolism and excretion in many elderly exacerbates the problem of drug interactions. Even more dangerous is the careless, overhasty application of clinical labels. The patient who becomes confused and disoriented in the hospital may not be suffering from dementia. The individual who has an occasional urinary accident is not necessarily incontinent. Labelling patients as demented or incontinent is too often the first step toward their entering the nursing home, a setting that can make such labels self-fulfilling prophecies. We must exercise great caution in applying such potent labels. They should be reserved for patients who have been carefully evaluated, lest we unnecessarily condemn such persons to a lifetime of institutionalization.

Ironically, the elderly receive relatively less attention from the medical profession. Although the elderly use substantial numbers of services, the quality of the encounters may not be adequate. A study of physician–patient encounters in the US indicates an inverse relationship between patient contact time and patient age. regardless of the site of care (office or hospital) or the specialty of the doctor, the older the patient, the less time he or she spends with the doctor (Keeler *et al.* 1982). Similar data are not available for other countries where primary care is more organized and where geriatrics is a more established medical specialty.

There are, however, some hopeful signs. Spurred by the demographic pressures (and perhaps even more by the rather dramatic recognition of these gradual demographic trends), programmes have been implemented to focus more attention on the special needs of the geriatric population. These efforts have been longest under way in Europe, where the proportion of elderly is higher. The form of the response varies from country to country, but the elements include a cadre of physicians with special training in the care of the elderly and special resources devoted to that care (Williamson 1979; Kane *et al.* 1981).

PREVENTION

Prevention has been a popular idea among health-care planners for some time (Breslow and Somers 1977). Some have argued that the best way to attack the problems of chronic disease is for each individual to undertake major behavioural change to revise unhealthful habits (LaLonde 1974). Others have suggested that prevention can lead too easily to blaming the victim (Knowles 1977), a special problem for the elderly.

The paradigms already developed in this chapter have special implications for prevention. The emphasis on function recognizes two principal components to action. The first is addressed to the innate capacity of the client or patient and is the usual focus of medical attention. Here prevention may include such activities as increasing resistance to disease through vaccination and exercise to early detection and treatment (for example, of high blood pressure or breast cancer). The number of such medically oriented preventive activities designed especially for the elderly is small. Most are extensions of tasks performed for younger people (Medical Practice Committee 1981), but the cost-effectiveness can be higher with the old than the young (Willems *et al.* 1980). Perhaps the most important geriatric preventive step is the avoidance of iatrogenic disease already noted.

The other half of the function formula holds more promise for prevention in the elderly. Once an individual has been assisted to achieve his best ability, his functioning depends on his environment. Much can be done to prevent environmentally imposed dysfunction in both the physical and the social environment. Architecture, engineering, and psychology have much to offer in maintaining an elderly person at the highest level of functioning possible.

LONG-TERM CARE

The pattern of resources available to support the elderly varies from country to country, but the general content is similar. The elderly are the primary users of long-term care services. The very term is imprecise. What is 'short-term' care? None the less, it implies a response to a sustained period of dependency. The response may be professionally delivered or family-supplied. It may emphasize medical care or social supports.

Although the emphasis on institutional care over community-based care differs from place to place, its forms are widely in evidence. The most common form of institutional care is the nursing home, a term connoting chronic care at a less intensive level than that provided in the acute hospital. Such care is provided by nursing personnel under the formal direction of one or more physicians. In some societies, most notably in the UK and Canada, this mode of care spills over into a more social model built around sheltered housing or homes for the aged. (In the UK, the most prevalent model is sponsored by local authorities and referred to as Part III Accommodation).

In the US, the nursing-home dominates the care of the dependent elderly. There are more nursing-home beds than acute hospital beds in this country. The nursing home has been a source of continuous concern and occasional scandal (Vladeck 1980). Funded primarily through a welfare programme operated jointly by each state and the federal government, there is great variation from state to state.

Overall we frequently see a US figure of around 5 per cent of those aged 65 years and older in nursing homes at any given time. This statistic is generally comparable to rates of institutionalization in other developed societies (with a range of 3–10 per cent), although the types of institutions vary. But the single number hides a great deal of variation. The most dramatic variable is age. Only about 1 per cent of those aged 65–69 years are in nursing homes, but over 20 per cent of those aged 85 years and older are institutionalized. The few longitudinal studies available suggest that a person aged 65 years has a probability of between 0.25 and 0.40 of spending some time in a nursing home before death (Vincente *et al.* 1979). When nursing-home residents are compared to the elderly living in the community, the former are more likely to be older, female, white, and widowed.

The latter characteristic points to the importance of social support. Persons with comparable physical disabilities may remain in the community and be institutionalized depending on the support available. Estimates based on national surveys suggest that, for every person in a nursing home, there is at least one equally disabled person living in the community (Willging and Neuschler 1982).

The nursing home is generally believed to be over-utilized in the US, although it is preferred by neither patients nor providers. A government report (US Comptroller General 1979*b*) identified several reasons for this excessive use:

1. A lack of information about non-institutional long-term care options.

2. The difficulties involved in locating and obtaining the appropriate mix of health and social services from the fragmented and confusing array of public and private service providers.

3. The inability to obtain all the essential community services because the individual cannot meet the eligibility criteria for each service and cannot afford to purchase this care.

4. The unavailability of the non-institutional long-term care services and housing options required to permit an individual to remain in the community.

5. The inability of their families to continue bearing the emotional, physical, and financial strain of providing care in the absence of any support from public programmes.

6. The tendency of the professionals (physicians, social

Table 26.4. *Examples of case management programmes*

Project	Description	Results

Triage (Quinn *et al.* 1982)	Quasi-experimental design:
	    307 clients from community
	    195 controls from another community
	Services authorized by Triage under Medicare waivers
		Utilization of services and costs higher for Triage
		Mental status outcome better for Triage
		Physical and social outcomes not different

ACCESS (Eggert *et al.* 1980)	Descriptive report with comparisons to other counties in New York Pre-admission screening of patients referred for institutional care Implemented and monitored service under Medicaid waiver; now Medicare, too	1979: of patients from hospital, 57 per cent of Medicaid and 20 per cent of self-pay went home; of patients from community, 96 per cent and 89 per cent, respectively, stayed home Costs less than equivalent institutional care, but no real control group
Wisconsin Community Care Care Organization (Applebaum *et al.* 1980)	Experimental design attempted: 71 of 263 experimentals excluded Used Medicaid waivers to serve clients from hospital and community	Experimentals cost less Rate of admission to hospital and nursing home no different but total days less

Georgia Alternative Health Services Project (Skellie *et al.* 1982)	Experimental design:
	    572 experimentals
	    172 controls
	    one-year follow-up
	Services included alternative living arrangements, day care, and home care
		Experimentals had lower mortality rate and higher costs, but fewer nursing-home days

Multipurpose Senior Services Project	Eight sites in California Clients from community, hospital, and nursing home Medicaid waivers used to purchase needed services after extensive assessment Comparison group identified separately	None available yet
Long-term Care Chanelling Demonstration	Sites in 10 states Two levels of programme: 1. case management only and with additional funds 2. authorisation controls Random allocation possible in most places	None available yet

workers, hospital discharge planners) assisting the elderly to recommend nursing-home placement because they lack the time or the expertise to plan, arrange, and co-ordinate the community services needed to enable the elderly individual to remain in the community.

The critical role of community supports has been ever more appreciated as the costs of institutional care has grown. Attention has been focused on two major strategies to avert or delay institutionalization of the elderly. Programmes to redirect nursing-home-bound clients generally involve some form of case management whereby the individual's needs are assessed and a package of services developed to meet those needs. Emphasis is placed on maintaining the person in the community whenever it is economically and practically feasible.

In the US, experience with case management has been largely limited to demonstration projects (Table 26.4) (US Comptroller General 1979*b*). The results have been mixed. In several experiments, active case management has led to improved survival (Applebaum *et al.* 1980; Skellie *et al.*

1982). Such a benefit, while of value in itself, complicates the interpretation of other programme effects by introducing a selection bias into the treatment group. This survival differential means that the treatment group will contain more disabled persons who are likely to use more resources, thus underestimating the benefit of the intervention. Other projects that used comparison groups showed substantial aggregate savings (Eggert *et al.* 1980).

The success of case management depends heavily on the community resources available. Organized community-based long-term care is much less developed in the US than in western Europe. Organized programmes to provide home nursing and homemaking are much further advanced in those countries (Trager 1980). Reviewing the data from the various demonstration programmes, the US General Accounting Office (1982) acknowledged that more available home health services might increase the health and happiness of the disabled elderly, but at a cost: such services tended to be additions to, rather than substitutes for, nursing-home care.

Table 26.5. *Examples of long-term care alternative programmes*

Project	Description	Results
Housing		
Community Housing for the Elderly (Brody 1978)	Experimental design Clients aged 62+, not functionally impaired 24 clients offered and accepted purpose-built community housing Of 63 control group members, 22 moved on their own Three-year follow-up	Mortality lower and satisfaction higher among experimental group Movers did better than non-movers among control group members
Highland Heights (Sherwood *et al.* 1981)	228 elderly physically impaired experimental group members admitted to special housing unit Matched to 228 control group members Five-year follow-up	Experimental group had lower mortality and lower nursing-home entry Generally fewer hospital and nursing-home days 59 clients admitted from nursing home (i.e. deinstitutionalized)
Support services		
Lifeline (Ruchlin and Morris 1981)	Emergency alarm system linked to emergency response station Matched pairs of experimental and control-group members drawn from public housing —35 severely functionally impaired and socially isolated (I) —46 severely functionally impaired and not socially isolated (II) —58 socially isolated and moderately functionally impaired or medically vulnerable (III)	30 per cent refused the service Fewer experimental group members entered hospital or nursiung home Benefit–cost ratio highest for group II
Kent Community Care Project (Davies and Challis 1980)	Management team of social workers and community nurse Paid and unpaid community workers used to meet specific client needs Disabled clients living in community; 35 experimental group members and 35 control group members Quasi-experimental	Fewer experimental group members entered residential care
Capitation		
Social Health Maintenance Organization (Diamond and Berman 1980)	Four demonstration projects now under way Single rate covers case management, physician care, home care, hospital, and limited nursing-home care plus social services Method of calculating capitation rates not yet fixed Marketing not established	Not yet available

Services can also be provided in other settings. Day-care centres, day hospitals, congregate meals, and meals-on-wheels can provide important services to keep elderly persons out of nursing homes (Brocklehurst and Tucker 1980; O'Brien 1982). Table 26.5 indicates some of the innovative approaches tried in the US. Such programmes require their own support systems to provide necessary client transportation. Although not necessarily cheaper, the services are often preferred by clients, most of whom are eager to avoid institutionalization.

Even the most advanced programmes cannot rely entirely on paid services. The backbone of community care of the elderly remains the social support system provided by family and friends. In many European countries, family members can be paid for some of the services they provide, thus blurring the distinction. The relative contribution of informal support as opposed to formal services varies depending on the generosity of the latter. In fact, a major policy concern now is the fear that overgenerous coverage of paid services will discourage informal support.

The crucial role of the informal network is illustrated by data from a Government Accounting Office study in Cleveland, Ohio, which followed a large sample of community elders. Figure 26.8 shows that by far the largest proportion of care in each service category was provided by unpaid persons (US Comptroller General 1979a).

The critical question in pursuing comunity care as a primary option to institutional care is how to target services, especially when those services are publicly provided. Clearly the further removed is an individual from imminent admission to a nursing home, the less certainly one can predict that an intervention will avert institutionalization. If the estimates of lifetime risk of institutionalization are correct, then the average 65-year-old has one chance in four of admission some time before death. Any programme that is to be cost-effective must target very accurately to avoid

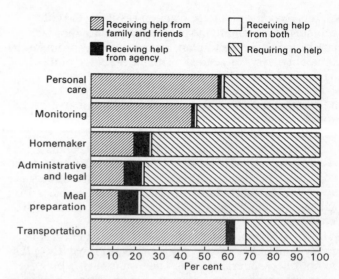

Fig. 26.8. Persons aged 65 years and older receiving selected home services provided by family members and agencies. (Source: Allan and Brotman (1981).)

treating those three persons who would not be institutionalized in any event.

Data to facilitate targeting are not yet precise. Beyond the comparisons of nursing home patients to community elders already noted, the studies paint a rather hazy picture. Table 26.6 summarizes the findings to date. Even those studies that have demonstrated statistically significant associations between variables and admission to a nursing home have been able to explain only a small proportion of the variance (Branch and Jette 1982). Clinical judgment seems to be the most useful guide at this stage and patient factors identified by clinicians are summarized in Table 26.7.

Because long-term care is so amorphous a concept

Table 26.6. *Research-generated risk factors for nursing-home admission*

Source	Sample	Risk factors
National Center for Health Statistics (1981)	Survey of nursing home residents in 1977 (compared to those age 65+ years living in the community)	Age, female, white, unmarried
Vicente *et al.* (1979)	Nine-year follow-up of residents age 55+ years in Alameda County, California	Age, poverty, white, lack of social supports
Palmore (1976)	Twenty-year follow-up of residents age 60+ years in Piedmont North Carolina area	Unmarried, white
Weissert *et al.* (1980*a*)	One-year study of day-care receipients and controls in six sites	Primary diagnostic conditions, impairment prognosis, hospital out-patient, or other ambulatory use
Weissert *et al.* (1980*b*)	One-year study of homemaker recipients and controls in four sites; patients were hospitalized for at least three days during the two weeks prior to the study	Primary diagnostic conditions, activities of daily prognosis, bed disability prognosis, hospital out-patient, or other ambulatory use
McCoy and Edwards (1981)	National sample of welfare recipients age 65+ years	Age, functional impairment, white, living alone or with non-relatives, lack of social supports
Branch and Jette (1982)	Six-year follow-up of community sample aged 65+ years in Massachusetts	Age, living alone, use of ambulation aid, mental deterioration, use of assistance in instrumental activities of daily living

Table 26.7. *Clinically identified factors associated with nursing-home admission*

Characteristics of the individual
    Age, sex, race
    Marital status
    Living arrangements
    Degree of mobility
    Activities of daily living
    Urinary continence
    Behaviour problems
    Mental status
    Memory impairment
    Mood disturbance
    Vertigo and falls
    Ability to manage medication
    Clinical prognosis
    Income
    Payment eligibility
    Need for special services

Characteristics of support systems
    Family capability
        For married respondents, age of spouse
        Presence of responsible relative (usually adult child)
        Employment status of responsible relative
    Physician availability
    Amount of care currently received from family and others

Community resources
    Formal community resources
    Informal support systems
    Presence of long-term care institutions
    Characteristics of long-term care institutions

whereby it is difficult to prove how a given action can lead to a clearly superior result, there is ample reason to argue for flexibility. Different approaches may work better in different situations. At the same time, programmes require accountability. We are most familiar with using professional training for that purpose; a licensed practitioner is expected to deliver good care. Sometimes we look directly at the care on the assumption that doing the right things will produce good results. This belief is essentially a reaffirmation of professional orthodoxy.

In the case of the elderly, with the emphasis placed on the functioning of persons suffering multiple simultaneous problems, the approach to accountability may better lie in outcomes. If appropriate outcomes can be defined and measured and if the probabilities of a client's reaching these can be predicted, we have a method to reward systems whose clients achieve or exceed reasonable expectations. Work on such predictors is just beginning (Kane *et al.* 1983).

The outcome approach offers a way to provide incentives while retaining flexibility. Because it emphasizes outcomes in lieu of process, comparisons across modalities of care are feasible. Carried to its full potential, the attainment of achievable functional goals can be linked to a reward system to provide direct incentives for better care.

PRIORITIES

Some societies have chosen to view community care not as an alternative to nursing-home placement but as a primary

end in itself. Care in the community is preferred by the large majority of dependent elderly persons. It seems more appropriate then to view the nursing home as an alternative to community care rather than the other way around.

This difference in socio-political philosophy underlies an important aspect of any care system for the elderly, or any other dependent population, for that matter. The system tends to reflect societal values. Although those value preferences are rarely explicated, they can be readily appreciated in the form of care made available, the constraints imposed, and the payment exacted. Thus one can observe substantial differences across nations. Some like the US retain a private enterprise approach relegating support for long-term care to a welfare system in which poverty is a prerequisite. Other countries (like the Scandinavian countries, the UK, and several Canadian provinces) have held such care to be a basic entitlement of residents and have either provided it directly from government sources or subsidized it under universal entitlement insurance schemes.

Whatever the philosophy of the country, the common theme is a growing appreciation that resources are finite. As the potential of health care expands, so too does the capacity to expend funds with decreasing marginal return. The elderly are a vulnerable target for such challenges. Because they suffer more chronic disease and have greater rates of resultant disability, they are disproportionately heavy consumers of medical services. In an unrestricted setting, those charged with the responsibility for tending to their needs will be tempted to wield the full force of modern technology on their behalf.

With an appreciation of limited resources comes rationing in one form or another. When budgets are presented in terms of the constituencies they serve, different services may find themselves in competition. Is it better to build housing for the elderly than to provide more sophisticated hospital care? Such questions involve both values and knowledge. One must be in a position to estimate the effects of such investments on pertinent parameters and then to find means to compare parameters drawn from different dimensions. Despite the proliferation of cost–effectiveness and cost–benefit techniques, few societies have yet used these methods to make policy. Much of our decision-making with regard to services for the elderly is based on past behaviour and advocacy.

The competition is not limited to the various services directed toward the elderly. As resources are constricted, especially in times of economic depression, different groups within the society will vie for the support available. In the US, one hears frequent references to the 'greying' of the federal budget (Binstock 1978; Hudson 1978). The Social Security system is projected into fiscal peril; every gain in life-expectancy achieved by improved social conditions represents a growing demand on intergenerational transfer payments.

Ironically, the elderly are one of the groups most responsive to treatment. From both the medical and social perspective, small investments may reap large dividends. Careful assessment can reveal remediable conditions (Williams *et al.* 1973; Brocklehurst *et al.* 1978; Rubenstein *et al.* 1981). Institutionalized persons respond dramatically to small environmental changes, which permit them greater control (Mercer and Kane 1979). Sometimes doing less is better than doing more, as in the case of drug therapy.

To realize these potential benefits, the elderly will need a cadre of skilled professionals, trained to provide appropriate care, concerned about both immediate and longer-term impacts of treatment and willing to serve as conscious advocates for their constituents. If demography can be believed, the future will be increasingly defined by the elderly. Whether that future will be bleak and sterile depends on the interest of today's professionals in preparing themselves to meet such a challenge.

REFERENCES

Allan, C. and Brotman, H. (compl.) (1981). *Chartbook on aging in America.* The 1981 White House Conference on Aging, Washington, DC.

Applebaum, R., Seidl, F.W., and Austin, C.D. (1980). The Wisconsin Community Care Organization: preliminary findings from the Milwaukee experiment. *Gerontologist* **20**, 350.

Binstock, R.H. (1978). Federal policy toward the aging. *Nat. J.* **10**, 1838.

Branch, L.G. and Jette, A.M. (1982). A prospective study of long-term care institutionalization among the aged. *Am. J. Public Health* **72**, 1373.

Breslow, L. and Somers, A.R. (1977). The lifetime health-monitoring program: a practical approach to preventative medicine. *New Engl. J. Med.* **296**, 601.

Brocklehurst, J.C. and Rucker, J.F. (1980). *Progress in geriatric day care.* King Edward Hospital Fund, London.

Brocklehurst, J.C., Carty, M.H., Leeming, J.T., and Robinson, J.M. (1978). Medical screening of old people accepted for residential care. *Lancet* **ii**, 141.

Brody, E.M. Community housing for the elderly: the program, the people, the decision-making process, and the research. *Gerontologist* **18**, 121.

Brody, J.A. and Brock, D.B. (in press). Epidemiologic and statistical characteristics of the United States elderly population. In *Handbook of aging and social sciences,* 2nd edn (eds. R.H. Binstock and E. Shanas). Van Nostrand Reinhold, New York.

Butler, R. (1975). *Why survive: being old in America.* Harper and Row, New York.

Colvez, A. and Blanchet, M. (1981). Disability trends in the United States population 1966–76: analysis of reported causes. *Am. J. Public Health* **71**, 464.

Davies, B. and Challis, D. (1980). Experimenting with new roles in domiciliary service: the Kent Community Care Project. *Gerontologist* **20**, 288.

Diamond, L. and Berman, D. (1980). The social/health maintenance organization: a single entry, prepaid long-term care delivery system. In *Reforming the long-term care system: financial and organizational options* (eds. J.J. Callahan, Jr. and S. Wallack). Lexington Press, Lexington, Mass.

Eggert, G.M., Bowlyow, J.E., and Nichols, C.W. (1980). Gaining control of the long-term care systems: first returns from the ACCESS experiment. *Gerontologist* **20**, 356.

Feldman, J.J. Work ability of the aged under conditions of improving mortality. Statement before the National Commission on Social Security Reform, 21 June 1982.

Fries, J.S. and Crapo, L.M. (1981). *Vitality and aging.* Freeman, San Francisco.

Helsing, K.J., Szklo, M., and Comstock, G.W. (1981). Factors associated with mortality after widowhood. *Am. J. Public Health* **71**, 802.

Hudson, R.B. (1978). Political and budgetary consequences of an aging population. *Nat. J.* **10**, 1699.

Kane, R.A. and Kane, R.L. (1981). *Assessing the elderly: a practical guide to measurement.* Heath, Lexington, MA.

Kane, R.L., Bell, R., Riegler, S., Wilson, A., and Keeler, E. (1983). Predicting the outcomes of nursing-home patients. *Gerontologist* **23**, 200.

Kane, R.L., Solomon, D.H., Beck, J.C., Keeler, E., and Kane, R.A. (1981). *Geriatrics in the United States: manpower projections and training considerations.* Heath, Lexington, Mass.

Keeler, E.B., Solomon, D.H., Beck, J.C., Mendenhall, R.C., and Kane, R.L. (1982). Effect of patient age on duration of medical encounters with physicians. *Med. Care* **20**, 1101.

Knowles, J. (ed.) (1977). *Doing better and feeling worse: health in the United States.* Norton, New York.

LaLonde, M. (1974). *A new perspective on health of Canadians.* Department of National Health and Welfare, Ottawa.

McCoy, J.L. and Edwards, B.E. (1980). Contextual and socio-demographic antecedents of institutionalization among aged welfare recipients. *Med. Care* **19**, 907.

Manton, K. (1980). Changing concepts of morbidity and mortality in the elderly population. *Health Soc.* **60**, 183.

Medical Practice Committee (1981). Periodic health examination: a guide for designing individualized preventive health care in the asymptomatic patient. *Ann. Intern. Med.* **95**, 729.

Mercer, S. and Kane, R.A. (1979). Helplessness and hopelessness in the institutionalized elderly. *Health Soc. Work* **4**, 90.

National Center for Statistics (1981).

O'Brien, C.L. (1982). *Adult day care: a practical guide.* Wadsworth Health Sciences Press, Monterey, Calif.

Palmore, E. (1976). Total chance of institutionalization. *Gerontologist* **16**, 504.

Quinn, J., Segal, J., Maisz, H., and Johnson, C. (eds.) (1982). *Coordinating community services for the elderly.* Springer, New York.

Rice, D.R. and Feldman, J.J. (1982). Tables and charts for demographic changes and the health needs of the elderly. Handout for Institute of Medicine Annual Meeting *Aging and health: new perspectives in science and policy,* Washington, DC. October 20.

Rubenstein, L.Z., Abrass, I.B., and Kane, R.L. (1981). Improved care for patients on a new geriatric evaluation unit. *J. Am. Geriat. Soc.* **29**, 531.

Rubenstein, L.Z., Rhee, L., and Kane, R.L. (1982). The role of geriatric assessment units in caring for the elderly: an analytic review. *J. Gerontol.* **37**, 513.

Ruchlin, H.S., and Morris, J.N. (1981). Cost-benefit analysis of an emergency alarm and response system: a case study of a long-term care program. *Health Serv. Res.* **16**, 65.

Schaie, K.W. (1970). A reinterpretation of age related changes in cognitive structure and functioning. In *Life-span developmental psychology: research and theory* (eds. L.R. Goulet and P.B. Baltes). Academic Press, New York.

Schroeder, S.A., Showstack, J.A., and Roberts, H.E. (1979). Frequency and clinical description of high-cost patients in 17 acute-care hospitals. *New Engl. J. Med.* **300**, 1306.

Sherwood, S., Greer, D.S., Morris, J.N., and Mor, V. (1981). *An alternative to institutionalization: the Highland Heights Experiment.* Ballinger, Cambridge, Mass.

Shock, N.W. (1977). System integration. In *Handbook of the biology of aging* (eds. C.E. Finch and L. Hayflick). Van Nostrand Reinhold, New York.

Siegel, J.S. (1982). Demographic aspects of the health of the elderly to the year 2000 and beyond. World Health Organization, Geneva (mimeo).

Skellie, P.A., Mobley, G.M., and Coan, R.E. (1982). Cost-effectiveness of community-based long-term care: current findings of Georgia's alternative health services project. *Am. Public Health* **72**, 353.

Svanborg, A., Bergstrom, G., and Mellstrom, D. (1982). *Epidemiological studies on social and medical conditions of the elderly.* WHO Regional Office for Europe, Copenhagen.

Trager, B. (1980). *Home health care and national health policy* (Special issue of *Home Health Care Serv. Qtly.* Haworth Press, New York.

US Comptroller General (1979*a*). *Conditions of older people: national information system needed* (HRD 79-95). Government Printing Office, Washington, DC.

US Comptroller General (1979*b*). *Entering a nursing home—costly implications for Medicaid and the elderly* (PAD 80-12). Government Printing Office, Washington, DC.

US DHSS, NCHS (1981). *Characteristics of nursing home residents, health status and care received: national nursing home survey, United States, May–December 1977* (PHS 81-1712), Vital and Health Statistics, Series 13 #51 NCHS, Hyattsville, MD.

US General Accounting Office (1982). *The elderly should benefit from expanded home health care but increasing these servies will not insure cost reductions.* General Accounting Office, Washington, DC.

Vicente, L., Wiley, J.A., and Carrington, R.A. (1979). The risk of institutionalization before death. *Gerontologist* **19**, 361.

Vladeck, B.G. (1982). *Unloving care: the nursing home tragedy.* Basic Books, New York.

Weissert, W., Wan, T.T.H., Livieratos, B., and Katz, S. (1980*a*). Effects and costs of day-care services for the chronically ill: a randomized experiment. *Med. Care* **18**, 567.

Weissert, W.G., Wan, T.T.H., Livieratos, B., and Pellegrino, J. (1980*b*). Cost-effectiveness of homemaker services for the chronically ill. *Inquiry* **17**, 230.

Willems, J.S., Sanders, C.R., Riddiough, M.A., and Bell, J.C. (1980). Cost effectiveness of vaccination against pneumococcal pneumonia. *New Engl. J. Med.* **303**, 553.

Willging, P.R. and Neuschler, E. (1982). Debate continues on future of federal financing of long-term care. *Hospitals,* July, 61.

Williamson, J. (1979), Geriatric medicine: whose speciality? *Ann. Intern. Med.* **91**, 774.

Williams, T.F., Hill, J.G., Fairbank, M.E., and Knox, K.G. (1973). Appropriate placement of the chronically ill and aged. *JAMA* **226**, 1332.

World Health Organization (1980). *International classification of impairment, disabilities and handicaps: a manual of classification relating to the consequences of diseases.* World Health Organization, Geneva.

Index